- "If you're writing because you can't help it, because you have a story to tell and you have the drive to pursue your work, if you are serious about the refining and rewriting process, the likelihood is that you will achieve some measure of success. Continue to trust in your ability. Don't keep that manuscript in your drawer. Send it out and be active in pursuing your goal."
  —Emilie Buchwald, CEO of Milkweed Editions, page 419

- "Write the best novel you can possibly write. Keep shaping and polishing, and never send an editor or an agent anything that might be considered a first draft."
  —Sara Ann Freed, executive editor of Mysterious Press, page 475

- "Religious fiction is 'growing up.' It's becoming more sophisticated and we'll be looking for better story-tellers. . . . If you want to preach, become a preacher. If you want to write novels, become a storyteller."
  —Leonard Goss, vice president of Crossway Books, page 458

- "The writers I most enjoy working with are those who write because they have stories to tell, stories that will in some way make a difference, large or small, in my life. They are people who recognize that we are not in an adversarial relationship and that I am as concerned with their success as they are."
  Michael Seidman, senior editor at Walker and Company, page 21

1997
NOVEL &
SHORT STORY
WRITER'S MARKET

1 9 9 7
NOVEL &
SHORT STORY
WRITER'S
MARKET

WHERE & HOW TO SELL YOUR FICTION

EDITED BY

BARBARA KUROFF

SMILEY MEMORIAL LIBRARY
411 Central Methodist Square
Fayette, MO 65248-1198

WRITER'S DIGEST BOOKS
CINCINNATI, OHIO

If you are a publisher of fiction and would like to be considered for a listing in the next edition of *Novel & Short Story Writer's Market*, send a SASE (or SAE and IRC) with your request for a questionnaire to *Novel & Short Story Writer's Market*—QR, 1507 Dana Ave., Cincinnati OH 45207. Questionnaires received after July 15, 1997, will be held for the 1999 edition.

Managing Editor, Market Books Department:
Constance J. Achabal
Supervisory Editor: Mark Garvey
Production Editor: Megan Lane.

International Standard Serial Number ISSN 0897-9812
International Standard Book Number 0-89879-764-0

Cover illustration: Brenda Grannan

Attention Booksellers: This is an annual directory of F&W Publications. Return deadline for this edition is April 30, 1998.

Contents

1 **From the Editor**

3 **How to Use This Book to Publish Your Fiction**

Writing Techniques
Writing and Publishing

9 **The Business of Fiction Writing**
All the fiction business basics, from manuscript preparation to rights.

17 **Book Publishers' Roundtable, by Robin Gee**
Top book editors—Joanna Cagan (Leisure/Love Spell); Laura Anne Gilman (Roc); and Michael Seidman (Walker and Company)—discuss the market for novel-length fiction, including what they look for when reviewing novel manuscripts.

24 **Approaching Agents and Editors: Tools and Tactics, by Blythe Camenson and Marshall J. Cook**
Inside tips on ways to get your novel through the doors of publishers and agents, including how to write a query letter and synopsis that will make them ask for the entire manuscript.

29 **Key to a $1,000 Market**
Brooke Comer, fiction editor of Woman's World, identifies, step-by-step, the elements that make her happy to pay $1,000 for an 1,800-word romantic short story.

34 **Fiction Report, by Barbara Kuroff**
The editor takes a look at the current marketplace for all types of fiction.

Craft and Technique

41 **Writing from the Inside Out: Letting Your Characters Tell Their Stories, by Colleen Mariah Rae**
Rae shares her workshop techniques on how to slip into characters' minds and bodies to write powerful stories that are rich with detail.

45 **Fiction's Connecting Link: Emotion, by Kathy Jacobson**
Novelist Jacobson shows how to bridge the distance between writer and reader and write fiction that editors will publish and readers can't put down.

51 **Where's the Story?, by Tim Parrish**
Parrish addresses one of the most common complaints from editors today as he gives valuable tips and techniques for writing fiction that really does tell a story.

55 **How to Set Up (and Stick to) a Writing Schedule, by Jack M. Bickham**
Successful author Bickham gives tips on how to plan and maintain a writing schedule that works for you—and your fiction.

Personal Views

60 **David Guterson: On Writing an Award-Winning Novel, by Jack Heffron**
Guterson, whose first novel Snow Falling on Cedars won the 1995 Pen Faulkner Award and the 1996 American Booksellers Association ABBY, talks about writing this "literary" novel that became Vintage's fastest-selling novel ever.

68 **Bobbie Ann Mason: Crafting Extraordinary Stories About Ordinary People, by Mary Jennings**
One of today's top short story writers and novelists, Mason encourages writers to "write what you know" and shares her positive experience with rejection that ultimately brought her success.

72 **An Interview with Scott Turow, by Anne Bowling**
Author of the blockbuster novels The Burden of Proof, Presumed Innocent *and* The Laws of our Fathers, *Turow talks about his writing experience and gives helpful advice for writing novels that captivate editors and readers.*

79 **First Bylines, by Chantelle M. Bentley**
Five fiction writers share their experiences of being published for the first time.

The Markets

89 **Literary Magazines**

Insider Reports:
109 **Doug Lawson**, The Blue Moon Review
Online magazines offer instant feedback from a worldwide audience

151 **David Hamilton**, The Iowa Review
Committed to publishing new voices

189 **Daniel Kunitz**, The Paris Review
No substitute for exceptional prose and a well-told story

254 **Small Circulation Magazines**

Insider Reports:
259 **Marion Zimmer Bradley**, Marion Zimmer Bradley's Fantasy Magazine
Writing well and following guidelines are no fantasy

297 **Dorman Nelson**, Western Tales
Forget "Slim" and "Trigger" when writing today's westerns

304 **Zines**

Insider Reports:
317 **Ariel Gore**, hip Mama
Zines offer writers artistic freedom and niche audiences

327 **Seth Friedman**, FactSheet Five
Zines: a great way to "get your words out there"

337 **Commercial Periodicals**

Insider Reports:
344 **C. Michael Curtis**, The Atlantic Monthly
Precise language, flawless mechanics and a story: vital elements for Atlantic *fiction*

383 **Brooke Comer**, Woman's World
Women's magazines: a golden market for skillful writers

389 **Small Press**

Insider Reports:
419 **Emilie Buchwald**, *Milkweed Editions*
Looking for literature that can change the world

434 **Daniel Simon**, *Seven Stories Press*
A home for new voices

448 **Commercial Book Publishers**

Insider Reports:
453 **Marcia Markland**, *Avalon Books*
Always looking for good writing

458 **Leonard Goss**, *Crossway Books*
Religious fiction: growing up with "salt and light"

465 **Gary Jennings**, *Author*
Writing "the other half" of history

475 **Sarah Ann Freed**, *Mysterious Press*
Looking for "something new" from mystery writers

487 **Contests and Awards**

Insider Report:
505 **Sarah Heekin Redfield**, *The Heekin Group Foundation*
Three sisters supporting writers

Resources

532 **Conferences and Workshops**

566 **Retreats and Colonies**

575 **Organizations and Resources**

584 **Publications of Interest to Fiction Writers**

588 **Websites of Interest**

590 **Canadian Writers Take Note**

591 **Printing and Production Terms Defined**

593 **Glossary**

597 **Category Index**

621 **Markets Index**

From the Editor

"I think I always knew I wanted to write [fiction]."

Bobbie Ann Mason, page 68

"I had written some fiction very young, as early as 11 or 12. By the time I went to college, I had decided that I was going to be a novelist."

Scott Turow, page 72

"[Until my junior year of college], I had never considered writing—as a hobby or a career or anything."

David Guterson, page 60

When did you first realize that you wanted to write fiction? For me, it was at age seven, sitting at our kitchen table, using a chubby #2 pencil and wide-ruled writing pad. Over the years, the pencil and paper have given way to a manual typewriter (used), then a new electric typewriter (with memory), and, finally, miracle of miracles for my chronic urge to revise, the luminous screen and easy touch of a personal computer. But, regardless of the medium, that early desire to create fiction has remained with me.

No matter when you started writing fiction, or whether you are a beginner looking for your first byline, or already published and looking for more outlets for your fiction, we've prepared this edition of *Novel & Short Story Writer's Market* with your needs in mind. The bulk of this book contains markets for your fiction, including two new market sections: Small Circulation Magazines and Zines. Each of the nearly 2,000 magazine and book publishers listed here represents an opportunity to get your short story or novel off your desk and into print. Over 300 markets appear here for the first time, and all listings have been updated to reflect what editors are looking for in 1997.

Literary Magazines, our largest market section, lists independent and university-affiliated literary journals. These publications pride themselves on publishing fine writing by new writers beside that of well-known authors. David Hamilton, editor of the *Iowa Review*, is committed to publishing new voices (page 151). Daniel Kunitz, managing editor of *The Paris Review* says, "[Last year], we took almost twice as many previously unpublished writers as we have before (page 189)." And, literary has gone electronic, too. Doug Lawson, editor of *The Blue Moon Review*, an online literary magazine that's been on the World Wide Web since 1994, says online magazines can offer a writer instant feedback from a worldwide audience (page 109).

Our new Small Circulation Magazines section features magazines devoted to almost every topic, every level of writing and every type of writer. Also new to this edition, our Zines section lists small publications that offer the big benefits of self-expression, artistic freedom and niche audiences. Zines are also the markets most open to publishing beginning writers. Ariel Gore, founder of the popular parenting zine *hip Mama*, says zines are the perfect place to start your writing career (page 319). Beginning on page 327, Seth Friedman, editor of *Factsheet Five*, the "bible" of the zine community, offers his insider's overview of today's zine marketplace.

The Commercial Periodicals section lists the fiction needs of many top-paying magazines. C. Michael Curtis, senior fiction editor at *The Atlantic Monthly*, talks about writing fine fiction in general and about writing for the high-paying *Atlantic* in particular (page 344). Brooke Comer, fiction editor of *Woman's World*, which pays $1,000 for an 1,800-word romantic short story, gives helpful inside tips on writing for that lucrative market (page 383). And, as a special "gift," Comer shares her Key to a $1,000 Market beginning on page 29.

If you write novel-length fiction, you'll be glad to hear that many publishers listed in our Small Press section are open to new talent. Daniel Simon, founder of Seven Stories Press, says, "The more the big publishers shy away from developing writers, the more room there is for independent publishers to find those voices" (page 434).

Many of the editors in the Commercial Book Publishers section also find great satisfaction in publishing a writer's first novel. Marcia Markland, vice president and publisher of Avalon Books, says, "I'm always, always, always looking for good writing" (page 453). And Sara Ann Freed, executive editor at Mysterious Press, says a new writer with a good manuscript and no track record is often viewed more favorably than a published writer with a bad sales history (page 475).

In the Writing and Publishing section, you'll get information on everything from business basics to an overview of today's fiction marketplace. In our Book Publishers' Roundtable (page 17), three top book editors discuss the market for novels, including what they look for when reviewing manuscripts. For more tips on how to get your manuscript read, see Approaching Agents and Editors: Tools and Tactics (page 24).

The articles in our Craft and Technique section contain a wealth of advice for making your fiction better. In Writing from the Inside Out (page 41), Colleen Rae shows how to let characters tell their own stories. In Fiction's Connecting Link: Emotion (page 45), novelist Kathy Jacobson presents techniques for writing fiction that readers can connect with. Where's the Story? (page 51) addresses one of the most common complaints I hear from editors as Tim Parrish gives tips on how to write fiction that *really does tell a story.* And Jack Bickham draws from experience as a successful, productive author to show you How to Set Up (and Stick to) a Writing Schedule (page 55).

Our Personal Views section features interviews with David Guterson, whose first novel, *Snow Falling on Cedars*, won the 1995 Pen Faulkner Award and the 1996 American Booksellers Association ABBY; Bobbie Ann Mason, author of *Shiloh and Other Stories* and *Feather Crowns*; and Scott Turow, author of the legal thrillers *Presumed Innocent* and *The Laws of Our Fathers*. And, in First Bylines, five fiction writers share their experiences of being published for the first time.

Since writing fiction can be lonely, we've included a section of resources to help you stay connected with the writing world. This section includes listings for Conferences and Workshops (where I hope to meet some of you during 1997); Retreats and Colonies; Publications of Interest to Fiction Writers; and this year for the first time, a list of Websites of Interest to writers.

As I begin work on the *1998 Novel & Short Story Writer's Market*, I'll be thinking of you, sitting at your computer or typewriter or with pen in hand, writing your short stories and novels. And I welcome your comments about this edition of *Novel & Short Story Writer's Market* as well as suggestions for making our next edition even better. Best wishes for a creative and productive year writing—and marketing—your fiction.

Barbara Kuroff

Editor
wdigest@aol.com

How to Use This Book to Publish Your Fiction

Like most of the people who use *Novel & Short Story Writer's Market*, chances are you've already put a great deal of time and effort into your writing. Many of you write regularly and are well-read, especially in the area in which you write. Some of you are formally studying writing while some are receiving feedback on your work by sharing it with a writers' group. You've been spending lots of time on writing and rewriting your work, making it the best it can be, and now you feel it's time to share your work with others.

If we could open this book with just one piece of advice it would be this: Take as much care searching for potential markets for your work as you have in crafting it. With this in mind, this book is designed as a tool to help you in your search, and we hope you will use it as a starting place for your overall marketing plan. The temptation when using any book like this is to go straight to the listings and start sending out your work. Perhaps this is the fastest, but it's not the most efficient route to publication.

While we do offer listings of nearly 2,000 markets and other opportunities for fiction writers, the listings contain only a portion of the information available to you in *Novel & Short Story Writer's Market*. In addition to the listings, we offer interviews with published authors and editors and a wide range of articles on the craft of writing, and information on all aspects of marketing and publishing your work. Reading the material covered here, as well as other books on writing and publishing, will help you make informed decisions that will further your writing career.

WHAT YOU'LL FIND HERE

Novel & Short Story Writer's Market is divided into three parts, each presenting a different type of information. The first part is Writing Techniques. Here we provide informational pieces on the business of publishing, articles on the craft of writing, and in-depth interviews with established authors. This is where you will find the Business of Fiction Writing and the annual fiction report, in addition to other articles on writing and publishing fiction.

Following Writing Techniques is The Markets, the heart of our book. This part is divided into seven sections. The Literary Magazines section includes literary journals of all sizes. Next comes the Small Circulation Magazines section, featuring publications (most paying) with circulations of under 10,000. Our new Zines section follows and includes a number of exciting formats that welcome the voices of new writers. The Commercial Periodicals section features popular magazines with circulations of more than 10,000. After this is the Small Press section, which includes small presses and some larger independent presses. Commercial Book Publishers, the next section, features listings of major publishers of commercial hardcover, trade paperback and mass market books. Finally, the Contests and Awards section offers listings for contests, awards and grants available to fiction writers.

Within the four magazine and two book publisher sections, you will find a main section of markets from North America [Canadian markets are noted with a maple leaf symbol (✦)]. The Literary Magazines, Small Circulation Magazines, Small Press and

Commercial Book Publishers sections are each followed by a list of international markets. Many of these markets are open to writers of English from all over the world. The contest section also includes international markets, but these are not listed separately.

Throughout The Markets, you'll find features called Insider Reports. These are short interviews with editors, publishers and writers designed to give you an inside look at specific writing areas and a behind-the-scenes look at particular publications or publishers. These pieces offer valuable tips on breaking into markets in their areas of expertise.

Resources, the last section of the book, is included for the support and information those listed there provide to writers, including places to make contact with other writers. Here you will find Conferences and Workshops, Retreats and Colonies, Organizations and Resources, Publications of Interest to Fiction Writers and Websites of Interest.

DEVELOPING YOUR MARKETING PLAN

After reading the articles and interviews that interest you, the next step in developing your marketing plan is to use the book to come up with a preliminary list of potential markets. If you are not sure what categories your work falls into or if you just want to explore the possibilities, start by reading the section introductions and browsing through the sections to find markets that interest you. This approach will familiarize you with the many different types of markets for your writing and may lead you to a market you haven't thought of before.

To help you with your market search, we include a Category Index, beginning on page 597. The Category Index is divided into sections corresponding to the four magazine and two book publisher sections in The Markets. Under each section in the index, you'll find fiction types such as romance, mystery, religious, regional, etc. Subject headings are then followed by the names of listings expressing an interest in that specific type of fiction.

You may notice that not all the listings in the magazine and book publisher sections appear in the Category Index. Some said they were only interested in very specific topics such as fiction about hiking or hot air ballooning or about the Civil War. Whether your writing subjects are general or specific, we recommend a combination of the browsing method and the Category Index method.

To further help you narrow your list of potential markets, we include ranking codes that identify the level of openness of each listing. These codes, Roman numerals I through V, appear just after each listing's name. In the magazine and book sections, codes indicate whether editors are open to work from writers on all levels, are only open to work by established writers, only accept work by writers from a certain region or who write on a specific subject, or are closed to unsolicited submissions. In the Contest section, ranking codes let you know if entries should be published or unpublished or should be work from certain groups of writers or about certain regions. The ranking codes and explanations for each are given after each section introduction.

You will also notice symbols at the start of some listings. Listings new to our book this year are indicated by a double dagger symbol (‡). Many are newly established markets, and often these are most open to the work of new writers. Some are not new, but have decided to list with us because they have increased their fiction needs.

READING THE LISTINGS

Once you've come up with a list of potential markets, read each listing carefully. You will find you can further streamline your list based on the market's editorial statement, advice, specific needs, terms, payment and reputation.

While different sections contain slightly different listings, there are some things all listings have in common:

After the name and contact information for each listing, you'll find a brief description of the market's publishing philosophy and intended audience. Following this is often a physical description of the magazine or books published. Physical descriptions can tell you a lot about the market's budget and give you hints about its quality and prestige. There is a brief explanation of printing terms to help you get a better picture of the publications as they are described in the listings. This information is included in Printing and Production Terms Defined on page 591. Also check the establishment date, circulation or number of books published.

In some listings, following the profile, we've added our own editorial comment, set off by a bullet. This feature allows us to pass on additional information we've learned about the listing. Included here is information about the market's honors or awards or its treatment of writers.

For example, here is the editorial comment for *Ploughshares*:

● Work published in *Ploughshares* continues to be selected for inclusion in the *Best American Short Stories* and *O. Henry Prize* anthologies. In fact the magazine has the honor of having the most stories selected from a single issue (three) to be included in *B.A.S.S.* Recent guest editors have included Richard Ford, Tim O'Brien and Ann Beattie.

Next comes the **Needs** section of the listing. In addition to a list or description of the type of work the market is seeking, you'll also find how much work the market receives from writers in a given time, how much it publishes and what percentage of its writing is acquired through agents. This will help you determine your competition. Also included are specifics on length and other requirements.

The **Needs** section of *Ellery Queen's Mystery Magazine* offers the following information:

Needs: "We accept only mystery, crime, suspense and detective fiction." Receives approximately 400 unsolicited fiction mss each month. Accepts 10-15 mss/issue. Publishes ms 6-12 months after acceptance. Agented fiction 50%. Recently published work by Peter Lovesey, Anne Perry, Marcia Muller and Ruth Rendell. Published new writers within the last year. Length: up to 7,000 words, occasionally longer. Publishes 1-2 short novels of up to 17,000 words/year by established authors; minute mysteries of 250 words; short, humorous mystery verse. Critiques rejected mss "only when a story might be a possibility for us if revised." Sometimes recommends other markets.

After **Needs** comes **How to Contact**, where you'll find out how to approach a market and what material to include with your submission. We suggest you follow the requirements for submission carefully. You will notice that some markets have told us they accept disk or e-mail submissions. Although some listings have included e-mail and fax numbers, it is always best to *get permission before submitting a manuscript to a publisher by fax or e-mail*. For more information on submission, presentation and cover letters, see The Business of Fiction Writing on page 9.

Here is how the contact information for a magazine might look:

How to Contact: Send complete ms with a cover letter or send ms in electronic form (disk or e-mail). Include estimated word count, short bio and list of publications. Reports in 3 weeks on queries; 2 months on mss. Send SASE for reply, return of ms or send disposable copy of ms. Simultaneous, reprint and electronic submissions OK. Sample copy for SAE and 5 first-class stamps. Fiction guidelines for 8½ × 11 SAE.

A book publisher might require the following:

How to Contact: Accepts unsolicited mss. Query with outline/synopsis and 3 sample chapters. Include short bio and list of publishing credits. SASE. Reports in 2 weeks on queries; 3-4 months on mss. Simultaneous submissions OK.

Next is the **Payment/Terms** section. When possible, we've provided a range of payment, but note that many publications in the Literary and Zine sections pay only in copies or subscriptions. We also indicate when you will be paid and for what rights. For more on rights and what to look for concerning terms, see the Business of Fiction Writing.

The **Payment/Terms** information for *Asimov's Science Fiction* magazine is:

Payment/Terms: Pays 6-8¢/word for stories up to 7,500 words; 5¢/word for stories over 12,500; $450 for stories between those limits. Pays on acceptance for first North American serial rights plus specified foreign rights, as explained in contract. Very rarely buys reprints. Sends galleys to author.

When an editor provides additional information that might be of benefit, we include that in the **Advice** section at the end of listings. Editor C. Michael Curtis tells writers the following in the **Advice** section of *The Atlantic Monthly*:

Advice: When making first contact, "cover letters are sometimes helpful, particularly if they cite prior publications or involvement in writing programs. Common mistakes: melodrama, inconclusiveness, lack of development, unpersuasive characters and/or dialogue."

Your marketing research should begin with a careful study of the listings, but it should not end there. Whenever possible obtain a sample copy or catalog. Editors and successful writers agree there is no substitution for reading copies of magazines that interest you. Likewise, you should familiarize yourself with the books of publishers to whom you'd like to submit.

To find out more about a potential market, send a self-addressed, stamped envelope for submission guidelines. Most magazines have sample copies available for a modest price. For book publishers, check *Books in Print* at the library to find the publishers of books you admire or feel are similar to the one you are writing. The library also has publishing industry magazines such as *Publishers Weekly* as well as magazines for writers. Some of these magazines are listed in Publications of Interest to Fiction Writers beginning on page 584. These can help you keep informed of new publishers and changes in the field.

THE FOLLOW THROUGH

After careful study and narrowing your list of potential markets to those who represent the most suitable places for your work, the next step, of course, is to mail out your work. If you have any questions on how to present your work, see the Business of Fiction Writing. When in doubt, remember to make it as easy as possible for editors to read and respond to your work. They're a busy lot and will not waste time with submissions that are messy and difficult to read. It may be good writing, but the editor may never read a poorly presented manuscript to find that out. If you show you care about your work, the editor will too.

Also keep accurate records. We've asked our listings to indicate how long it will take them to report on a submission, but at times throughout the year the market may get behind. Note that with small magazines and literary journals (especially those published by universities) response time tends to be slower in the summer months. Keeping track of when you sent your manuscript will help you decide when it is time to check on the status of your submission.

ABOUT OUR POLICIES

We occasionally receive letters asking why a certain magazine, publisher or contest is not in the book. Sometimes when we contact a listing, the editor does not want to be listed because they: do not use very much fiction; are overwhelmed with submissions; are having financial difficulty or have been recently sold; use only solicited material; accept work from a select group of writers only; do not have the staff or time for the many unsolicited submissions a listing may bring.

Some of the listings do not appear because we have chosen not to list them. We investigate complaints of unprofessional conduct in editors' dealings with writers and misrepresentation of information provided to us by editors and publishers. If we find these reports to be true, after a thorough investigation, we will delete the listing from future editions. See Important Listing Information on page 88 for more about our listing policies.

If a listing appeared in our book last year but is no longer listed, we list it in the Markets Index, beginning on page 621, with a code explaining why it is not listed. The key to those codes is given in the introduction to the Markets Index. Sometimes the listing does not appear because the editor did not respond in time for our press deadline, or it may not appear for any of the reasons previously mentioned above.

If you feel you have not been treated fairly by a market listed in our book, we advise you to take the following steps:
• First, try to contact the listing. Sometimes a phone call or letter can quickly clear up the matter.
• Be sure to document all your correspondence with the listing. When you write to us with a complaint, we will ask for the name of your manuscript, the date of your submission and the dates and nature of your subsequent correspondence.
• We will write to the publisher or editor and ask him to resolve the problem. Then, we will enter your letter into our files.
• The number, frequency and severity of unresolved complaints will be considered in our decision to delete a listing from the book.

Listings appearing in *Novel & Short Story Writer's Market* are compiled from detailed questionnaires, phone interviews and information provided by editors, publishers and awards directors. The publishing industry is volatile and changes of address, editor, policies and needs happen frequently. To keep up with the changes between editions of the book, we suggest you check the monthly Markets column in *Writer's Digest* magazine.

Club newsletters and small magazines devoted to helping writers also list market information. For those writers with access to online services, several offer writers' bulletin boards, message centers and chat lines with up-to-the-minute changes and happenings in the writing community. Some of these resources are listed in our Websites of Interest (page 588).

We rely on our readers as well, for new markets and information about market conditions. Write us if you have any new information or if you have suggestions on how to improve our listings to better suit your writing needs.

Writing
Techniques

Writing and Publishing 9

Craft and Technique......................... 41

Personal Views 60

The Business of Fiction Writing

It's true there are no substitutes for talent and hard work. A writer's first concern must always be attention to craft. No matter how well presented, a poorly written story or novel has little chance of being published. On the other hand, a well-written piece may be equally hard to sell in today's competitive publishing market. Talent alone is just not enough.

To be successful, writers need to study the field and pay careful attention to finding the right market. While the hours spent perfecting your writing are usually hours spent alone, you're not alone when it comes to developing your marketing plan. *Novel & Short Story Writer's Market* provides you with detailed listings containing the essential information you'll need to locate and contact the markets most suitable for your work.

Yet once you've determined where to send your work, you must turn your attention to presentation. We can help here, too. We've included the basics of manuscript preparation here, along with a compilation of information on submission procedures and approaching markets. In addition we provide information on setting up and giving readings. We also include tips on promoting your work. No matter where you are from or what level of experience you have, you'll find useful information here on everything from presentation to mailing to selling rights to promoting your work—the "business" of fiction.

Approaching magazine markets: While it is essential for nonfiction markets, a query letter by itself is usually not needed by most magazine fiction editors. If you are approaching a magazine to find out if fiction is accepted, a query is fine, but editors looking for short fiction want to see *how* you write. A cover letter, however, can be useful as a letter of introduction, but it must be accompanied by the actual piece. Include basic information in your cover letter—name, address, a brief list of previous publications—if you have any—and two or three sentences about the piece (why you are sending it to *this* magazine or how your experience influenced your story). Keep it to one page and remember to include a self-addressed, stamped envelope (SASE) for reply. See the winning letter from our Short Story Cover Letter Contest on page 15.

Agents: Agents are not usually needed for short fiction and most do not handle it unless they already have a working relationship with you. For novels, you may want to consider working with an agent, especially if marketing to publishers who do not look at unsolicited submissions. For more on approaching agents see *The Guide to Literary Agents* (Writer's Digest Books).

Approaching book publishers: Some book publishers do ask for queries first, but most want a query plus sample chapters or an outline or, occasionally, the complete manuscript. Again, make your letter brief. Include the essentials about yourself—name, address, phone number and publishing experience. Include only the personal information related to your story. Show that you have researched the market with a few sentences about why you chose this publisher.

Book proposals: A book proposal is a package sent to a publisher that includes a cover letter and one or more of the following: sample chapters, outline, synopsis, author bio, publications list. When asked to send sample chapters, send up to three *consecutive* chapters. An outline covers the highlights of your book chapter by chapter. Be sure to include details on main characters, the plot and subplots. Outlines can run up to 30 pages, depending on the length of your novel. The object is to tell what happens in a concise, but clear, manner. A synopsis is a very brief description of what happens in the story. Keep it to two or three pages. The terms synopsis and outline are sometimes used interchangeably, so be sure to find out exactly what each publisher wants. (For more on writing the outline and synopsis and on dealing with book publishers and agents, see Approaching Agents and Editors: Tools and Tactics, beginning on page 24, and Book Publishers' Roundtable, beginning on page 17.)

Manuscript mechanics: A professionally presented manuscript will not guarantee publication. But a sloppy, hard-to-read manuscript will not be read—publishers simply do not have the time. Here's a list of suggested submission techniques for polished manuscript presentation:

• Use white, $8\frac{1}{2} \times 11$ bond paper, preferably 16 or 20 lb. weight. The paper should be heavy enough so that it will not show pages underneath it and strong enough to take handling by several people.

• Type your manuscript on a computer using a laser or ink jet printer, or on a typewriter using a new ribbon.

• Proofread carefully. An occasional white-out is okay, but don't send a marked up manuscript with many typos. Keep a dictionary, thesaurus and stylebook handy and use the spellcheck function of your computer.

• Always double space and leave a $1\frac{1}{4}$ inch margin on all sides of the page. For a short story manuscript, your first page should include your name, address and phone number (single-spaced) in the upper left corner. In the upper right, indicate an approximate word count. Center the name of your story about one-third of the way down, skip two or three lines and center your byline (byline is optional). Skip three lines and begin your story.

• On subsequent pages, put last name and page number in the upper right hand corner.

• For book manuscripts, use a separate cover sheet. Put your name, address and phone number in the upper left corner and word count in the upper right. Some writers list their agent's name and address in the upper right (word count is then placed at the bottom of the page). Center your title and byline about halfway down the page. Start your first chapter on the next page. Center the chapter number and title (if there is one) one-third of the way down the page. Include your last name and page number in the upper right of this page and each page to follow. Start each chapter with a new page.

• If you work on a computer, chances are your word processing program can give you a word count. If you are using a typewriter, there are a number of ways to count the number of words in your piece. One way is to count the words in five lines and divide that number by five to find an average. Then count the number of lines and multiply to find the total words. For long pieces, you may want to count the words in the first three pages, divide by three and multiply by the number of pages you have.

• Always keep a copy. Manuscripts do get lost. To avoid expensive mailing costs, send only what is required. If you are including artwork or photos, but you are not positive they will be used, send photocopies. Artwork is hard to replace.

• Most publishers do not expect you to provide artwork and some insist on selecting their own illustrators, but if you have suggestions, please let them know. Magazine publishers work in a very visual field and are usually open to ideas.

• If you want a reply or if you want your manuscript returned, enclose a self-addressed, stamped envelope (SASE). For most letters, a business-size (#10) envelope will do. Avoid using any envelope too small for an $8\frac{1}{2} \times 11$ sheet of paper. For manuscripts, be sure to include enough postage and an envelope large enough to contain it. You might also consider sending a disposable manuscript that saves editors time and saves you money. If you are requesting a sample copy of a magazine or a book publisher's catalog, send an envelope big enough to fit.

• When sending electronic (disk or modem) submissions, *contact the publisher first for specific information and follow the directions carefully.* Always include a printed copy with any disk submission. *Fax or e-mail your submissions only with prior approval of the publisher.*

• Keep accurate records. This can be done in a number of ways, but be sure to keep track of where your stories are and how long they have been "out." Write down submission dates. If you do not hear about your submission for a long time—about three weeks to one month longer than the reporting time stated in the listing—you may want to contact the publisher. When you do, you will need an accurate record for reference.

Some mailing tips: Manuscripts under five pages long can be folded into thirds and sent in a business-size (#10) envelope. For submissions of five pages or more, however, mail it flat in a 9×12 or 10×13 envelope. Your manuscript will look best if it is mailed in an envelope only slightly larger. For the return envelope, fold it in half, address it to yourself and add a stamp (or clip IRCs to it with a paper clip). Computer disks may be sent in official mailers or mid-size envelopes with stiffening for 78¢.

Mark both of your envelopes in all caps, FIRST CLASS MAIL or SPECIAL FOURTH CLASS MANUSCRIPT RATE. The second method is cheaper, but it is handled the same as Parcel Post (Third Class). First Class mailing assures fastest delivery and better handling.

Book manuscripts should be mailed in a sturdy box (a ream-size typing paper box works well). Tape the box shut and tape corners to reinforce them. To ensure your manuscript's safe return, enclose a self-addressed and stamped insulated bag mailer. You may want to check with the United Parcel Service (UPS) or other mailing services for rates.

If you use an office or personal postage meter, do not date the return envelope—it could cause problems if the manuscript is held too long before being returned. First Class mail is forwarded or returned automatically. Mark Third or Fourth Class return envelopes with "Return Postage Guaranteed" to have them returned.

It is not necessary to insure or certify your submission. In fact, many publishers do not appreciate receiving unsolicited manuscripts in this manner. Your best insurance is to always keep a copy of all submissions and letters.

Approaching markets outside your own country: When sending return postage to another country, do not send stamps. You must purchase International Reply Coupons (IRCs). The publisher can use the IRCs to buy stamps from his/her own country. In the US, IRCs cost $1.05 cents each and can be purchased at the main branch of your local post office. If you live in Canada, see Canadian Writers Take Note on page 590.

Main branches of local banks will cash foreign checks, but keep in mind payment quoted in our listings by publishers in other countries is usually payment in their currency. Also note reporting time is longer in most overseas markets. To save time and money, you may want to include a return postcard (and IRC) with your submission and forgo asking for a manuscript to be returned.

Rights: Know what rights you are selling. The Copyright Law states that writers are selling one-time rights (in almost all cases) unless they and the publisher have agreed otherwise. A list of various rights follows. Be sure you know exactly what rights you are selling before you agree to the sale.

• Copyright is the legal right to exclusive publication, sale or distribution of a literary work. This right is that of the writer or creator of the piece and you need simply to include your name, date and the copyright symbol © on your piece in order to copyright it. You can also register your copyright with the Copyright Office for additional protection. Request information and forms from the Copyright Office, Library of Congress, Washington DC 20559. To get specific answers to questions about copyright (but not legal advice) you can call the Copyright Public Information Office at (202)707-3000 weekdays between 8:30 a.m. and 5 p.m. EST. Publications listed in *Novel & Short Story Writer's Market* are copyrighted *unless* otherwise stated. In the case of magazines that are not copyrighted, be sure to keep a copy of your manuscript with your notice printed on it. For more information on copyrighting your work see *The Copyright Handbook: How to Protect and Use Written Works* by Stephen Fishman (Nolo Press, 1992).

• First Serial Rights—This means the writer offers a newspaper or magazine the right to publish the article, story or poem for the first time in any periodical. All other rights to the material remain with the writer. The qualifier "North American" is often added to this phrase to specify a geographical limit to the license.

When material is excerpted from a book scheduled to be published and it appears in a magazine or newspaper prior to book publication, this is also called first serial rights.

• One-time Rights—A periodical that licenses one-time rights to a work (also known as simultaneous rights) buys the *nonexclusive* right to publish the work once. That is, there is nothing to stop the author from selling the work to other publications at the same time. Simultaneous sales would typically be to periodicals without overlapping audiences.

• Second Serial (Reprint) Rights—This gives a newspaper or magazine the opportunity to print an article, poem or story after it has already appeared in another newspaper or magazine. Second serial rights are nonexclusive—that is, they can be licensed to more than one market.

• All Rights—This is just what it sounds like. All Rights means a publisher may use the manuscript anywhere and in any form, including movie and book club sales, without further payment to the writer (although such a transfer, or *assignment*, of rights will terminate after 35 years). If you think you'll want to use the material later, you must avoid submitting to such markets or refuse payment and withdraw your material. Ask the editor whether he is willing to buy first rights instead of all rights before you agree to an assignment or sale. Some editors will reassign rights to a writer after a given period, such as one year. It's worth an inquiry in writing.

• Subsidiary Rights—These are the rights, other than book publication rights, that should be covered in a book contract. These may include various serial rights; movie, television, audiotape and other electronic rights; translation rights, etc. The book contract should specify who controls these rights (author or publisher) and what percentage of sales from the licensing of these sub rights goes to the author. For more information, see Selling Subsidiary Rights.

• Dramatic, Television and Motion Picture Rights—This means the writer is selling his material for use on the stage, in television or in the movies. Often a one-year option to buy such rights is offered (generally for 10% of the total price). The interested party then tries to sell the idea to other people—actors, directors, studios or television networks, etc. Some properties are optioned over and over again, but most fail to become dramatic productions. In such cases, the writer can sell his rights again and again—as long as there is interest in the material. Though dramatic, TV and motion picture rights are more important to the fiction writer than the nonfiction writer, producers today are increasingly interested in nonfiction material; many biographies, topical books and true stories are being dramatized.

Selling Subsidiary Rights: The primary right in the world of book publishing is the right to publish the book itself. All other rights (such as movie rights, audio rights, book club rights, electronic rights and foreign rights) are considered secondary, or subsidiary, to the right to print publication. In contract negotiations, authors and their agents traditionally try to avoid granting the publisher subsidiary rights that they feel capable of marketing themselves. Publishers, on the other hand, typically hope to obtain control over as many of the sub rights as they can. Philosophically speaking, subsidiary rights will be best served by being left in the hands of the person or organization most capable of—and interested in—exploiting them profitably. Sometimes that will be the author and her agent, and sometimes that will be the publisher.

Larger agencies have experience selling foreign rights, movie rights and the like, and many authors represented by such agents prefer to retain those rights and let their agents do the selling. Book publishers, on the other hand, have subsidiary rights departments, which are responsible for exploiting all sub rights the publisher was able to retain during the contract negotiation. That job might begin with a push to sell foreign rights, which normally bring in advance money which is divided among author, agent and publisher.

Further efforts then might be made to sell the right to publish the book as a paperback (although many book contracts now call for hard/soft deals, in which the original hardcover publisher buys the right to also publish the paperback version). Any other rights which the publisher controls will also be pursued. Publishers, however, usually don't control movie rights to a work, as those are most often retained by author and agent.

The marketing of electronic rights to a work, in this era of rapidly expanding capabilities and markets for electronic material, can be tricky. With the proliferation of electronic and multimedia formats, publishers, agents and authors are going to great pains these days to make sure contracts specify exactly *which* electronic rights are being conveyed (or retained).

Readings: Attending public readings of poetry and fiction has become very popular in many cities. The general public seems to be just now catching on to something writers and avid readers have known for years: Readings offer a unique opportunity for those who love literature to experience it together.

If you are comfortable in front of a crowd and you'd like to share your work with others, try giving a reading. Not only does a reading allow you the opportunity to gauge reaction to your unpublished work, it's also an invaluable tool for promoting published short story collections and novels.

While there are some very prestigious reading series such as the "Main Reading Series" sponsored by The Unterberg Poetry Center of the 92nd Street Y in New York City, many readings are local events sponsored by area writers' clubs. You can start small, if you like, with one of the open-mike readings held in most cities in neighborhood coffee houses and taverns or, if you are published, look for bookstores that offer readings by authors whose books they sell.

Other reading outlets include libraries, churches, hospitals, radio stations and public-access cable television stations. Some series are well-established, while in other cases, you may have to approach a location and suggest a reading. It all depends on the amount of time and effort you'd like to invest.

If you decide to create your own reading opportunity, you may have to supply publicity and refreshments as well as a location. Established authors sometimes charge fees to sponsoring organizations, but newer writers usually feel the exposure is enough. If you have published work, however, you may want to bring copies to sell or arrange with your local bookstore to set up a table to sell your books. If you want to join an established series, keep in mind it can be competitive. You may be asked to submit work for consideration and a formal application.

For more information on readings, see *The Writer's Book of Checklists* by Scott Edelstein (Writer's Digest Books).

Promotion tips: Everyone agrees writing is hard work whether you are published or not. Yet, once you arrive at the published side of the equation the work changes. Most published authors will tell you the work is still hard but it is different. Now, not only do you continue working on your next project, you must also concern yourself with getting your book into the hands of readers. It becomes time to switch hats from artist to salesperson.

While even bestselling authors whose publishers have committed big bucks to promotion are asked to help in promoting their books, new authors may have to take it upon themselves to plan and initiate some of their own promotion, sometimes dipping into their own pockets. While this does not mean that every author is expected to go on tour, sometimes at their own expense, it does mean authors should be prepared to offer suggestions for promoting their books.

Depending on the time, money and the personal preferences of the author and publisher, a promotional campaign could mean anything from mailing out press releases to setting up book signings to hitting the talk-show circuit. Most writers can contribute to their own promotion by providing contact names—reviewers, home-town newspapers, civic groups, organizations—that might have a special interest in the book or the writer.

Above all, when it comes to promotion, be creative. What is your book about? Try to capitalize on it. For example, if you've written a mystery whose protagonist is a wine connoisseur, you might give a reading at a local wine-tasting or try to set something up at one of the national wine events. For more suggestions on promoting your work see *The Writer's Guide to Promotion & Publicity*, by Elane Feldman (Writer's Digest Books).

The sample cover letter: A successful cover letter is no more than one page (20 lb. bond paper), single spaced with a double space between paragraphs, proofread carefully, and neatly typed in a standard typeface (not script or italic). The writer's name, address and phone number appear at the top, and it is addressed, ideally, to a specific editor. (If the editor's name is unavailable, address to "Fiction Editor.")

The body of a successful cover letter contains the name and word count of the story, the reason you are submitting to this particular publication, a short overview of the story, and some brief biographical information, especially when relevant to your story. Mention that you have enclosed a self-addressed, stamped envelope or post card for reply. Also let the editor know if you are sending a disposable manuscript that doesn't need to be returned. (More and more editors prefer disposable manuscripts that save them time and save you postage.) When sending a computer disk, identify the program you are using. Remember, however, that even editors who appreciate receiving your story on a disk usually also want a printed copy. Finally, don't forget to thank the editor for considering your story.

Sample cover letter contest winner: There were several impressive entries in this, our third *Novel & Short Story Writer's Market* Short Story Cover Letter Contest. When making our final decision, however, one entry was clearly the winner. That cover letter (on page 15) was written by Bette Anne Rieth and originally accompanied her submission of "One Good Turn" to *Highlights for Children*.

Rieth's letter incorporates all the basic elements of a good cover letter. She has placed her name, address and phone number at the top right of the page and addressed it to a specific editor, Rich Wallace, coordinating editor of *Highlights for Children*. In the first paragraph, she gives the name and word count of her short story, "One Good Turn," and states why she is submitting this particular story to them.

SAMPLE COVER LETTER

Name
Address
Phone

September 22, 1995

Rich Wallace, Coordinating Editor
Highlights For Children
803 Church Street
Honesdale PA 18431

Dear Mr. Wallace,

Enclosed for your consideration is my manuscript, "One Good Turn," a short story, 900 words in length. After reading your call for sports fiction in the October, 1995, edition of *Writer's Digest*, I felt "One Good Turn" might work for you. I hope you agree.

Like the central character of "One Good Turn," my daughter also swims competitively. Volunteering as a timer at her meets, I've witnessed the concerns of young swimmers as they climb the starting block, and their triumphs and disappointments when the race is done. Based on this experience, I created Jen, and the challenges she faces in "One Good Turn."

Along with being a "swim Mom" in the last three years, I've also been busy writing. My poetry and short stories have appeared in magazines such as *Byline*, *Just A Moment* and *St. Joseph Messenger*. My story, "Christmas Stollen," has been accepted by Augsberg Fortress Publishers for the 1996 edition of *CHRISTMAS: An Annual Treasury*.

I have enclosed a SASE for your convenience. Thank you for your consideration.

Sincerely,

Bette Anne Rieth

Bette Anne Rieth *is a fiction writer, a mother of two teenagers, and a part-time bookkeeper. "I love to write," she says, and is currently working on her first long project, a romance novel.*

In paragraph two, Rieth mentions that she is the mother of a daughter who swims competitively. This piece of biographical information and Rieth's well-crafted paragraph establish her credibility for writing a story about the fictional character Jen. Rieth adds to her credentials as a writer by listing her publication credits in paragraph three.

In her closing paragraph, Rieth mentions that she has enclosed a SASE and, very importantly, she thanks the editor for considering her submission.

For more on cover letters and formats, see *The Writer's Digest Guide to Manuscript Formats*, by Dian Dincin Buchman and Seli Groves. If you feel you have a successful cover letter, we hope you will consider entering our 1998 Short Story Cover Letter Contest. The winning letter will be published in the next edition. Our criteria is simple: We're looking for a letter that helped lead to the *acceptance* of a short story between May 1996 and May 1997. Keep in mind the letter must include the elements of a good cover letter as outlined. The deadline is May 15, 1997. Send the letter with your address and phone number and proof of acceptance (a copy of the letter of acceptance will do) to Cover Letter, *Novel & Short Story Writer's Market*, 1507 Dana Ave., Cincinnati OH 45207.

In addition to publication in the 1998 edition of *Novel & Short Story Writer's Market*, the writer will receive a small cash payment for publication of the letter, a copy of the book and the opportunity to select two titles from our Writer's Digest Books catalog.

Book Publishers' Roundtable

BY ROBIN GEE

Unless you can buttonhole an editor, agent or book publisher at a convention or social event, it's hard to find someone with the time and experience to answer all your questions about the publishing process. New writers have many basic questions about how to approach publishers and agents, but even established authors welcome an opportunity to pick their editors' brains to find out exactly what they want from writers and how it all works on the other side of the publishing fence.

The following roundtable discussion offers us the opportunity to ask a successful group of editors some of the questions writers ask most. We asked Joanna Cagan, editor at Leisure Books who handles both the Leisure and Love Spell imprints; Laura Anne Gilman, executive editor of ROC, the science fiction division of Dutton Signet; and Michael Seidman, writer, lecturer and senior editor at Walker Books, specializing in mysteries. These editors' answers were sometimes surprising, often candid and very informative for new and established authors alike.

What advice do you give people who tell you they have written a novel or short story collection? Is there something you wish every writer knew?
Joanna Cagan: I tell them they should know their market. They need to find out who we are and what our house does. That can't be over emphasized. I *wish* I could tell them getting published is a long shot. It takes a lot of work. I wish I could relay to writers that rejection is 90 percent of what this business is. I really hate to see new writers discouraged by something that is par for the course in publishing.

Laura Anne Gilman: The first thing I tell people is that they've just finished the easy part. From here on in, it's not a solo work, but a collaboration, and the writer isn't always going to be the senior collaborator.

Michael Seidman: When I'm approached, I know that what they want to hear from me is an invitation to submit. Or, almost as often, they want me to ask about the work, to express interest in what they've done. My days are filled with people who've just written something, my desk groans under the evidence of the obsession.

My first comment is to ask, "What's the book about?" The usual answer is a description of the plot, so I ask the question again and again, as often as necessary until I elicit the response I'm looking for—the theme, the reason for the book. Then I ask, why should someone read your book, rather than the one next to it on a book rack? Inevitably, that's a question I have to answer if I'm going to attempt to acquire publication rights, and I want to know if the author has any idea of how the work in question fits into the scheme of things. Finally, I try to discover if there's a story worth telling in the book. I won't necessarily agree with the author that the story is worth telling, but if I come to accept that the author does, that's sufficient for my purposes.

ROBIN GEE, *former editor of* Novel & Short Story Writer's Market, *now lives in Madison, Wisconsin, where she is a freelance writer and frequent contributor to* Writer's Digest Books.

I'll respond to any specific requests for information or direction and offer whatever insights I can. A lot depends on my mood, though; just as with doctors and lawyers, people seem to think they can request anything of an editor in terms of career guidance, and there are times when I resent it.

There are also times when, being told that someone wrote something, I'll ask, "Why?" The answer I look for, the one that will pique my interest is, "Because I have something to say, something that has to be said." That answer is applicable to the most basic and formulaic genre novel as it is to the more esoteric literary efforts.

What advice do you wish someone had given you when you first became an editor and started working with writers?

Cagan: I got a pretty good education about what fragile egos writers have. Yet there are certain things about the writer's world I didn't know until I was a part of that world. Writers have explained to me that the waiting while a manuscript is being considered is a lot harder than the actual rejection. I think in the beginning I would have restructured my time if I'd known how hard it was for them. Now, when I think about people checking their mailboxes everyday it speeds me up a bit, but I still get bogged down.

Gilman: I also got very good advice when I starting out, thankfully. Part of that was the reminder that the editor has to walk a fine line between being the author's advocate inhouse, and being the company's advocate to the author. It's a narrow line, with a very sharp edge.

Seidman: A large part of my career has been spent in the developing and nurturing of new writers and watching them jump ship at the first opportunity. It's rather disappointing. I wish I'd been told that writers have little idea of the real economics of the industry, that they don't think they have to understand my side of the business in order to participate in it.

Many publishers only accept submissions through agents. Do you have any advice on finding an agent? What should an agent be able/willing to do for a writer? What makes a good agent?

Cagan: The best way to find an agent is by talking to other writers. By joining a local writers' group or a local chapter of the Writers Guild, you can learn about agents by word of mouth—at least you can learn who to avoid. Books on agents and other research can also help. Knowing about agents is as important as knowing about publishers. As with publishers, you don't want to send your work to the wrong place. You don't want to send your mystery to an agent who does not handle mystery.

A good agent is interested in career-building, not just selling individual books, but thinking long term. Most writers want to be regularly published, so it's best for their agent to have a sense of long-term goals and plan with the writer's career in mind. It's also really important they know the market and are honest with writers about how the market works.

Gilman: I'm going to pass on this one, except to say that a good agent is one that the writer feels comfortable with, and trusts with his or her career. A great agent is one who delivers on that trust.

Seidman: My first comment about agents is that it only takes a post office box and a business card to become an agent, so caution is the watchword. I don't think a listing in *Literary Marketplace* or any of the other guides to agents is sufficient information.

Networking, either through writers' conferences or other gatherings of that sort, is probably best, along with the personal recommendations from other authors or editors willing to suggest people. Interview as many agents as possible, either at a conference or by visiting them. I'd also suggest getting in touch with the Association of Authors Representatives. It will supply lists of members and a copy of its Code of Ethics, which offers lots of insights into how the business relationship should be run. You will have the satisfaction of knowing that a member agency should adhere to those rules, offering you some protection from the people who might be less than honest and open in their dealings with writers. And I would never pay a fee. Period. The agency should be deriving its income from the placing of various controlled rights to your work.

Depending on your needs, a good agent should offer reasonable career guidance, have solid contacts at as many publishing houses as possible, and provide the time needed to look after your interests. A good agent should keep you up to date in terms of submissions, rejections and offers, and should be willing and able to intercede for you if the editorial relationship sours. You and the agent must be able to trust each other, implicitly and explicitly.

Do you prefer to see an entire manuscript or a query with chapters? There is some confusion over the terms "synopsis," "summary" and "outline." What do these terms mean to you and which do you like to see?

Cagan: I prefer a query with the first three chapters. In our house, a synopsis is a description of the completed work. It should be pretty detailed, but ideally between four and eight pages long. I love to get them at about five pages. I don't want a scene by scene description which is what I would call an outline. To me an outline is more mechanical than a synopsis needs to be. In a synopsis, I look for flow, emotional development, progression of plot and resolution of conflict. Myself and the other editors here are not looking for dazzling writing in the synopsis. We always read the first three chapters first. If we like the writing, then we will go to the synopsis. It's not the main selling point for the book.

Gilman: To me, a synopsis is a brief description of the entire plot line, usually a page or two in length. A summary is a "quick hit" description of the book, usually a paragraph in length. An outline is a chapter-by-chapter depiction of the action, including the main plot and any subplots. I usually suggest a paragraph per chapter. I want to see the first three chapters of the book, a synopsis and an outline of the rest of the book (beyond the first three chapters).

Seidman: I prefer a query with chapters—I've got enough paper in my office as it is. I don't need 300 pages when five are more than enough for me to know whether I want to read more. I use outline, synopsis and summary interchangeably and don't have the time or inclination to bother with the semantics of it all. As long as you're telling me what the rest of the book is about (and don't think you can get away with saying that I have to read it to learn the ending; I don't and won't), I don't care what you call it.

What makes a submission stand out? What do you look for in a manuscript?

Cagan: It's hard to say. At a bare minimum I'm looking for a cleanly presented submission, free of typos, etc. You have to at least pass minimum standards to get an editor to look at your submission. But in terms of standing out, it's tricky. I look for crisp prose, shoulders above the rest, but that's so subjective. There are a lot of good, adequate writers, but a very small number have this indescribable quality. There's a spark in the character, plot, writing that makes a manuscript stand out.

Gilman: I look for good writing in clean presentation.

Seidman: The thing I look for in a manuscript is the quality of the writing—that's what makes one stand out about the other. I have pet bugaboos. I dislike adjectives telling me how dialogue is delivered. If the text itself doesn't provide that information, it has to be changed; saying "he said, angrily" doesn't make it so. I don't like having the action stop for three paragraphs of description. When someone walks into a room or meets someone, they rarely "see" everything at once, yet too many writers insist on offering description that way.

I look for writers who understand that there is a rhythm to our language, a meter, and that it can and should be used to good effect. They are not tools solely of poets. Every writer should make use of every tool at his disposal to make a written piece stand out and be memorable. It's not just age that causes me to forget what I've read. It's the fact that there is no reason to remember it any more than I will remember a cotton candy eaten at the state fair.

I also look for characters who are fully rounded and who evolve during the course of the story. If they are the same people at the end as they were at the beginning, then nothing has happened in the tale and if nothing has happened, what's the point?

And I want a story worth telling. I want surprises. I want expectations rattled in their cages. I realize that what makes genre work, what allows publishers to create specific guidelines, is that readers want the comfort of familiarity. I find that cold comfort. I want originality, a work that doesn't jump on the bandwagon but creates it.

If you work with series books, do you want a new author to mention series possibilities when submitting a book proposal?

Cagan: It doesn't affect me, because I don't work with series books. But I don't think it hurts to mention series possibilities. It wouldn't detract from submission. Yet, a manuscript still has to stand on its own.

Gilman: If the author intends the book to be a series, it should be mentioned in the cover letter, and additional book ideas should be included at the end of the first manuscript.

Seidman: Sure, if you're doing a series, let me know that you've got ideas for subsequent titles. Don't send me all the outlines (summaries or synopses)—just let me know. Though, after all these years, if I can't tell what you have in mind simply by reading the first few chapters of book one, I shouldn't be doing this job.

What "traits" would you say identify "professional" authors—those you enjoy working with and would want to work with again?

Cagan: I really enjoy working with authors in general, but the ones I like working with most are those respectful of deadlines and who enjoy the give and take between writer and editor. I also respect those who feel strongly about their work and who are enthusiastic about the process of turning a manuscript into a book.

Gilman: Being on time for deadlines and upfront about possible problems are the surest signs I know of a professional.

Seidman: The person who asks what I'm looking for and then says that's what they will write isn't a professional. Why is it that so many people consider a writer who can and will do anything a professional, but expect a doctor or lawyer to just do the one thing? When it comes to writing . . . there is very little crossover. A successful horror writer cannot necessarily become a romance author with the same level of success. Sure, there are exceptions, but we know them because of the exception, because of the rarity. A professional is someone who does some *thing* and leaves other things to those who can do them better.

The writers I most enjoy working with are those who write because they have stories to tell, stories that will in some way make a difference, large or small, in my life. They are people who recognize that we are not in an adversarial relationship and that I am as concerned with their success as they are; after all, their success is reflected in my professional success. I want to work with authors who are continuing to learn. If I have to make the same editorial changes in the successive books, I begin to lose interest.

Professional writers are those who recognize and acknowledge the fact that publishing is not pro bono and that any given writing is only one product for a company that manufactures many. While their careers are important to us, more important is the performance of the entire list, its balance, shape and form.

There's been a lot of talk in the press about the "blockbuster" syndrome— big advances and large publicity campaigns for select authors at the expense of new and midlist authors. What are your thoughts on this and do you see any changes on the horizon?

Cagan: It's really complicated and there are so many components or factors contributing to it. The biggest one has been changes in the wholesale marketplace. As the number of wholesale buyers out there is consolidated, the buyer's decision is becoming more important. One order can be thousands of copies, so publishers want to go with a sure thing. It's frustrating for me as an editor to know that writing a good book is not enough. I can understand writers' frustrations when they see reissues of [blockbuster] writers instead of new books. Yet they really sell. With that in mind, it's harder to convince a publisher to devote more time to the unknown.

At Leisure, we've been focusing on packaging our midlist better to get wholesalers' attention. That has spurred some creativity on the publisher's part. The one good thing from all this is, because it is terribly competitive, the overall quality of the mass market is up.

Gilman: That "blockbuster syndrome" has always existed; it's just more noticeable in today's pared-down market. Like any feeding frenzy, eventually it will die down.

Seidman: Yes, "blockbuster syndrome" is not new, like everything else in publishing, it is cyclical. Many publishers, especially the bigger ones, need to do it regularly in order to support the midlist and other efforts. If a blockbuster pulls someone into a bookstore, there is a possibility, no matter how remote, that the customer will buy something else.

I've spent my career working at niche houses, publishers who are satisfied to fill a particular need in the marketplace. They aren't quite as blockbuster oriented (though we wouldn't mind having one), nor are they usually in a financial position to play in that game. All publishing is a risk. I've often described my job as spending an evening at the poker table, drawing to an inside straight on each hand. The blockbuster risk can bring a jackpot, but the smaller games can be rewarding as well and I prefer to stay in them.

Remember though, that without the blockbuster success, many new writers would have no chance at all. No one tries to make every book on a list a blockbuster, so there is always room for something that some editor believes in.

What are some ways authors can help the sales of their books? Any tips for keeping momentum going after a first book?

Cagan: That's a tough question. There are no easy answers to what helps sales figures. I'm alarmed that some authors are being pushed to spend too much time and money, especially when we don't always know what works in promoting a career. Book signing can work, but that usually just affects regional sales. Ads sometimes work, but timing is critical. If authors have an eagerness to work on promotion, they should let their editors know. I really sympathize with authors who, when we're getting dismal figures, call up and say "what can I do?" With so many unknowns, we don't always know. I would rather writers get busy writing a great second book. In mass market especially the important step in a career is to produce more than one quality book.

Gilman: Self-promote! I can't say that enough. It may not save dying sales, but every little bit the author does to get his or her name in front of the readers is a help. Some authors make up t-shirts with their titles listed. Others have home pages linked to on-line bookstores. The possibilities are endless, and most of them are reasonably priced, although renting a skywriter probably isn't cost-effective.

Seidman: In the best of all possible worlds, a question about what the author can do to help the sales of a book would be answered briefly—follow your publisher's directions. This, however, isn't that world. There's still a short answer—whatever one can do should be done. After that, we might have to go on forever with all the variations on that theme. Any local exposure the author can create should be created. Talk shows, signings, getting stories into the local papers—*if* you can do it. If you need help, call your editor and discuss what can be done.

Certain organizations, most notably Sisters in Crime, have been working with their members to offer information about self-promotion. If there's a group that might be right for you, join. Become involved with peer groups: Mystery Writers of America, Science Fiction and Fantasy Writers of America, Romance Writers of America, etc. They often have useful ideas. If another local author has just published a book, see if you can work together, sharing expenses for a short tour.

As far as keeping momentum going, the best advice is to complete the second novel on time, so a good publishing schedule may be established and kept. Learn from your reviews, fan letters, etc.. Know what your readers want and expect and try to fill those needs. When you are out and about, promoting yourself, keep in mind that you're not the only author out there, nor are you the first to have a book published, so try not to antagonize booksellers, reviewers or anyone else who may have some kind of power over the way your book will be seen. There are writers who have been banned literally from certain bookstores.

And make sure your next book is better. In every way. Always.

Do you see any trends in the industry that may affect fiction authors in the near future?

Cagan: I don't think there is anything earth shattering on the horizon. Authors are getting more savvy about their careers. The market is getting tighter, more frustrating. To do well, keep an ear to the ground, note what's hot but on the other hand, write from your heart. Sometimes you must buck the trend and write what fascinates you. The idea of knowing your market and what's out there is not contradictory with that advice, because the starting point has to be with what inspires you no matter what experts say trends are.

Gilman: The loss of the many outlets in the wholesale market has hit genre fiction pretty hard. I'm encouraged by the growth of on-line bookstores, but it's not enough to offset the loss of those "extension" markets.

I'm also worried about the fact that science fiction isn't picking up the readers it did in the past. Kids used to pick up science fiction or fantasy when they were done with "kiddie" books, but weren't interested in anything else yet. Now, with the proliferation of R.L. Stine and all the related books, it's tougher to catch that reader's attention. And it's a shame, because science fiction is one of those fields where kids and adults can read the same books, and find a common meeting ground.

Seidman: I don't spend much time looking at trends; I'm too busy looking at manuscripts. Fads come and go, good books remain a staple. Don't worry about trends; worry about your writing, your storytelling. Write it one word at a time and begin again on the next book or story or article.

I'm not certain about what's going to happen because of or on the Internet. I've seen a lot of material "published" on-line and seen very little that impressed me. Maybe I've looked in the wrong places, but maybe everyone shouldn't have access to a "printing press." My own semi-Luddite feelings notwithstanding, something *is* going to happen because so many have the ability to share their work. Hindsight will establish just what those changes are going to be. I do think any form of written communication that resorts to "emoticons," those cyberspace glyphs to indicate humor, sarcasm and most other subtleties, is lacking in power, but I'm old, tired, conservative and curmudgeonly.

What should one write next? That seems to be the point of the question as it is usually presented to me and the answer I give is always this: Write what you want to write and what you write well. I wish that were more of a trend.

Approaching Agents and Editors: Tools and Tactics

BY BLYTHE CAMENSON AND MARSHALL J. COOK

One of the nicest moments a writer gets to experience is typing the words "The End" on the last page. But for the beginning novelist, the sense of accomplishment can often be short-lived. The manuscript is done, but now what?

Market-savvy writers know that a polished, saleable manuscript is not the only step in making a good impression with prospective agents or editors; the tools and tactics you use to approach these publishing professionals can be as important as stellar writing.

THE TOOLS

Our philosophy is give 'em what they want. Many agents and editors list their preferences in the various Writer's Digest market books. Most also provide free guidelines in exchange for a SASE. Many insist on being queried first, before they'll look at sample chapters, let alone your complete manuscript. Even if their market book listings suggest you send in the entire manuscript, we think querying first is the wisest route. The query is a quick and easy way for agents and editors to see if your project interests them—and if it doesn't, it saves you unnecessary photocopying and postage expenses.

The Query

The most effective query is a straightforward, polished one-pager designed to hook the reader's attention. It describes your novel's plot and main characters, focusing on the elements that are most intriguing or compelling; it lists your relevant credentials and publishing credits, if any; and, if you've hit the mark, it entices the editor to ask for more.

There are two formats you can use for your query. Some writers start with a formal approach, mentioning that they are seeking representation or publication for their book and giving some of its vital statistics—word count, genre, title—up front. Others jump right into the plot's action, starting with a good, attention-grabbing sentence. The first two or three paragraphs provide a mini-synopsis of the novel's plot. The next section highlights credentials.

BLYTHE CAMENSON *is a fulltime writer with more than 20 books and 100 articles to her credit. She is director of Fiction Writer's Connection, a membership organization for new writers and is editor of its newsletter,* Fiction Writer's Guideline. *She also teaches a course on America Online called "How to Approach Editors and Agents." Her novel* Widow *is currently under option for a TV movie, and she has just completed another, called* Parker's Angel.

MARSHALL J. COOK *teaches writing workshops for the University of Wisconsin-Madison and is a frequent speaker at conferences nationwide. He has written six books, including* Freeing Your Creativity (*Writer's Digest Books*) *and hundreds of articles (for* Writer's Digest *magazine and other publications) as well as short stories. He edits* Creativity Connection, *a newsletter for writers and independent publishers.*

Credentials?

You bet. If you're a lawyer working on a legal thriller, tell them. Been coaching Little League for 30 years? Tell them that, too, but *only* if your novel concerns Little League. If you have any nonfiction publication credits, say so. If you don't have prior credits, don't apologize or even mention it. That's a surefire way of pointing out your amateur status. You want to convey confidence and knowledge of your subject matter. But don't worry if you lack a string of credits. Your writing will speak for itself.

What do agents and editors look for in a query letter?

Elisa Wares, senior editor at Ballantine, says: "A well-written query letter is really the unsolicited writer's best foot in the door. You want to sell yourself as well as the idea of your book. A long, involved description of the work to follow is not necessary. The letter should be entertaining, intriguing and informative. You want the editor to read on, not stop with the initial letter. I must admit that if an author bores me in the letter, I will not read that submission. It sounds unfair, but writers have no idea how many queries and manuscripts editors get every day. An author has just a few minutes to catch somebody's attention."

Says literary agent Evan Marshall, "I like a professional-sounding letter that describes the book in objective terms (its genre, if any, its word count, etc.), gives a brief plot synopsis, and provides pertinent author credentials. What I (and I think most agents) hate is a hyped-up, selling query. These are amateurish and self-serving. It's the work that matters—obviously the author would think it's great!"

Michael Seidman, mystery editor at Walker and Company agrees. "In query letters I look for calm professionalism. I want to know what the book is, who you are (if that's pertinent), the length, and that's about it. Hype is beside the point; telling me my business is beside the point; telling me of the award you won from a contest is beside the point. (I've judged too many contests to take them that seriously as validation.)" He also advises writers to keep it to one page.

Agent Cherry Weiner says other turnoffs include addressing a female agent as "Mr." or "Sir" or saying you write like a particular bestselling writer. You should just say you write in the same genre as the author.

Most agents and editors also warn against talking about how many people have read and loved your book. The opinion of your Aunt Mary and Uncle Fred won't help build your case. The agents and editors would prefer to decide for themselves.

All suggest you avoid using self-glorifying adjectives (save those for the book reviewers) or predicting your book's climb up the bestseller lists (*no one* can predict that).

Only propose one project in a single query. If you are writing a series, say so, but your query should propose Book One. Sending out a query for Book Two before Book One has been accepted tells agents and editors that the first book didn't fly. And never put yourself down in a query letter. Don't say it's your first book or you hope they'll like it. Of course, you hope they like it. Close your query letter by saying simply, "May I send you the completed manuscript?" (You shouldn't be querying if your manuscript isn't complete.)

Writing a good query letter can often be a revealing exercise. If it's proving to be overly troublesome—you can't seem to find the hook or identify your main character's conflict, for example—the problem might be a flawed plot. The hook or conflict just isn't there to identify. This is a hard—but incredibly valuable—lesson to learn. It means putting the query letter aside and going back to the plotting board.

Pitchline Protocol

You may be able to skip the querying step altogether by meeting face-to-face with the agent or editor. This doesn't mean you can just drop into their office uninvited, though. Agents and editors often attend writers conferences around the country as a way to share information and meet new writers. The benefits to you are obvious. But be prepared for the encounter. Have your pitchline ready.

The pitch is a one-line (yes—one line!) summation that gives the essence of your novel. It must hook the listener—and go right for the *oooh* factor: make them say, "*Oooh*, I want to read that book." What is the essence of your novel? Conflict! Your pitch should show the main problem your hero or heroine will face.

Here's an example of a pitchline. Recognize the book? "Recent law school grad is offered a job that seems too good to be true—and it is." You got it. That's a one-line summation of John Grisham's *The Firm*.

You may also use a pitchline to begin your query letter. "In your letter state in one sentence what the book is about," advises literary agent Susan Zeckendorf. "You have to catch the agent's eye right away."

Here's the pitchline Blythe Camenson used to start her query for her new book, *Parker's Angel*. "Unlucky in love, Parker wouldn't recognize an angel if she pulled one down from heaven with her—which is exactly what happens." And landing a new agent with that query letter is what happened for Blythe.

Just as with your query letter, developing a good pitchline to use with an agent or editor will also help you to define the focus of your book for yourself. If you have trouble with your pitchline, it may indicate a basic problem with your plot. And you need to have that all sorted out before you begin the next step.

The Synopsis

If all goes well with the querying or pitching process, the agent or editor will ask to see more. In addition to sample chapters or your complete manuscript, "more" usually means a synopsis. There's no need to be put off by the idea of trying to summarize your novel in a few pages—or less. You've mastered the pitchline and the query—a synopsis just expands on what you've already begun. But if you are put off, you're not alone. Even top-selling novelists don't relish the task. Dean Koontz frankly admits, "I hate writing a synopsis."

Koontz is one of the lucky ones, though. He and scores of other bestselling authors don't have to write them anymore. Says Stephen King, "I send 'em the book; they publish it. It's a great deal. And give me credit for this: I'm smart enough to be grateful."

But until you reach that level, the synopsis is an essential tool for selling your novel. So, what is a synopsis? It's a summary with feeling. It's a good read with strong narrative writing in the present tense, an opening hook, quick sketches of the main characters woven into your narrative, the core conflict, plot high points and the conclusion.

Agents or editors may use the terms "outline" and "synopsis" interchangeably. Don't be confused here. Nobody wants a formal outline, with the letters of the alphabet and Roman numerals. Some may want a synopsis *and* a chapter outline, which in this case would be an expanded version of the synopsis, summarizing each chapter in a paragraph.

Author Marilyn Campbell (*Pretty Maids in a Row, See How They Run*) offers these words of advice for your synopsis: "Open with a hook, just as you would in a novel. Detail the beginning and ending scenes and one or two in the middle that give an indication of the kind of emotional intensity or type of action to be expected. If your story contains explicitly graphic sex or violence, that should be obvious in the synopsis. Summarize the rest in short, tight paragraphs, using strong action verbs whenever possible and descriptive adjectives and adverbs sparingly. The characters' physical descriptions are not vital, but their motivations are. Use dialogue only for occasional emphasis. Make sure every loose thread is tied up and never leave an editor guessing about anything."

Neither the query nor the synopsis is the place for promotional-style book jacket copy, a medley of adjectives and adverbs, or every possible scene and background detail. It should be the tightest writing you've ever produced, not an exercise in "synopsis-speak." Stick with the same writing style you've used in your novel. Dark, brooding novel—dark, brooding synopsis. Chatty upbeat novel—chatty upbeat synopsis. If your synopsis is flat and stilted, the agent or editor will assume that your manuscript is, too.

And, finally, a synopsis is not a quiz or puzzle. Don't close with a cliffhanger. Revealing the ending to your novel will not spoil the story for them. It will show that you know how to successfully conclude your plot. Literary agent Pesha Rubenstein stresses: "The synopsis *must* include the novel's ending. I cannot stand teasers saying, 'Well, you'll just have to read the manuscript to find out what the end is.' I need to know the whole story in order to see if it makes sense."

How long should your synopsis be? That varies depending upon who asked for it and why. If it's part of your initial contact with an agent or editor, a one-pager is often the best bet. It's a chance to show how tight your writing is, it won't put them to sleep, and the shorter the synopsis, the easier it is to refrain from getting long-winded and making mistakes.

"I recently heard a great description of a synopsis," says editor Michael Seidman. "Make it read as if you were explaining a movie to a ten-year-old—or vice versa. The more complex you make it, the more holes will open."

There might be occasions, however, when a one-pager just won't do the job. For example, your agent would prefer a longer, more detailed synopsis or outline. Elmore Leonard took 15 pages for the treatment for an original screenplay he titled *Legends*. The screenplay didn't sell, but Leonard's agent submitted the treatment as a novel synopsis, and Signet published the book as *Gunsights*.

Cover Letter Etiquette

You've queried or pitched your idea, you've completed your synopsis, labeled your SASE, and your submission packet is almost ready for a trip to the post office. But there's one more item you need to include—your cover letter. This accompanies (literally covers) your proposal package. It states simply what you have enclosed and serves as a reminder. "It was a pleasure meeting you at the State Conference. Here's the synopsis for the novel we discussed . . . ." Or, "As I mentioned in my query, my good friend Mary Higgins Clark suggested I contact you . . ." (Obviously, we claim such contacts only if they're TRUE.)

Just as with the other selling tools, your cover letter must be professional, typo-free, and well-written. Invest in letterhead stationery or design your own. Be sure to include your phone number with your address. You'll be surprised how many agents or editors will pick up the phone if they get excited about a submission that crosses their desk.

That submission could be yours. Just to make sure, read on.

TACTICS

You now know about the tools you'll use to get your novel considered—but what about the tactics? We want you to feel reassured to know you don't need to do anything clever—or devious—to be noticed. As we said at the top—give 'em what they want. And don't give them a reason to turn you down.

If an editor prefers to see sample chapters and a query letter, don't send a full manuscript. And if you're sending sample chapters, make sure you send the *right* chapters. "Send the *first* few consecutive chapters, approximately 50 pages," says Anne Savarese, an editor at St. Martin's Press.

But what if chapter one is weak? Rewrite it until it's strong. You won't sell a book with a weak first chapter.

If you've enclosed the first three chapters in your submission packet, don't begin your synopsis at chapter four. Let the agent or editor get an accurate sense of your story from the beginning.

Double space, with clear black ink on only one side of white paper, and use a legible typeface. Fancy packages will not impress anyone. What? No red ink on green paper for your Christmas story? No Gothic type for your historical romance?

No. None of that.

This is a business letter. You'll catch positive attention with good writing and a good plot, not with special effects and gimmicks.

"I get things on pink paper, with perfume sprinkled over them and wrapped with ribbons," says agent Evan Marshall. "I get things single-spaced and printed on both sides of the page. I get things packed so tight it's like breaking into a Brink's truck."

He even gets proposals with a hero named "Evan." "I picture all these writers sitting at their computers," he says, "changing the main characters' names depending upon the agent to whom they are submitting."

He gets them. And then he rejects them.

Elisa Wares agrees. "Something that will cause me to reject a manuscript immediately is the 'sneaky trick' factor. Writers will stick together pages of the manuscript with paste, or flip pages upside down, so they can tell if an editor has read that far. I cannot tell you how unprofessional that practice is." Although she doesn't expect perfection, Wares also notes that she doesn't care much for spelling and glaring grammatical errors.

Finally, don't forget your self-addressed, stamped envelope for the return of your material. If your manuscript is disposable, say so, but include a #10 SASE for a reply.

Of course, you're hoping your material won't be returned or discarded—but even if you do everything just right in approaching an agent or editor, you still face the possibility of rejection. When rejection comes (and it most likely will—the only writers who never get rejected are the ones who never send anything out), don't take it too hard, and don't over-analyze it. "No" just means "no," on this proposal, for this agent or editor, right now. Pick yourself up, dust yourself off, and get that proposal out again.

Bestselling novelist Barbara Kingsolver puts it this way: "This manuscript of yours that has just come back from another editor is a precious package. Don't consider it rejected. Consider that you've addressed it 'to the editor who can appreciate my work' and it has simply come back stamped 'Not at this address.' Just keep looking for the right address."

Key to a $1,000 Market

Woman's World fiction editor Brooke Comer sends the following "breakdown of a successful story" to writers whose submissions are close to, but not quite, what she looks for in a romantic short story. The guideline includes "Something Precious," written by Carin T. Ford, and Comer's accompanying key to what makes Ford's story worthy of the $1,000 which *Woman's World* pays for 52 such stories each year. To use the key (continued on page 33), match the comments in Comer's letter with the corresponding sections of Ford's story. (For more information on this lucrative market, see the Insider Report with Brooke Comer on page 383 of the Commercial Periodicals section in this book.)

Hi [writer's name],
   Here's a breakdown of a successful story to show you how we like the pace to move.

a   Author opens with lively dialogue for a brisk start.

b   A *brief* paragraph sets the scene behind the voices.

c   Another *brief* paragraph of description tells us all we need to know: that Tracy is soon to be divorced, that angry words caused the breakup.
   Also, Tracy's quarrelsome tone with her son tells us she's none too happy with the way things worked out. The author has created a subtext which tells us that Tracy is lonely, anxious, and might not be adverse to an olive branch.
   A less experienced writer might spend several lengthy paragraphs saying just that, but Carin—this writer—knows how to cut to the chase.

d   Ted calls! With only 1,900 words, you can't waste a beat. This writer gets Tracy in contact with her ex immediately. Note her use of question as in ". . . would Ted's voice always hit me like a punch in the stomach?" A lesser writer might say "Ted's voice hit her like a punch in the stomach." But we get more intimacy from Tracy asking herself. Though she could also ask a sister or friend, Carin's keeping her story lean and mean by avoiding excess characters.
   Again, Carin uses the phone conversation with Ted to "open up" the story of what went wrong between Ted and Tracy. Notice how her dialogue propels the story, intermixed with description. As Tracy's boys talk to their dad, she wonders what went wrong.

e   Now we learn what went wrong. It may seem like a long way down but it's perfectly timed. Carin has built up a convincing, believable scene, and we read it like we're watching a TV movie: Now it's time for the explanation. And we get it.
   Notice Carin uses dialogue from the past to briskly cover old ground (i.e., why Ted wouldn't turn down the promotion and moved on while she stayed behind).

f   Here comes the crisis line. Little Danny wants to go camping for his birthday, like they did last year. But what was a fun family trip could now become a very uncomfortable weekend for his estranged parents.
   Carin brings in dialogue from the past to bring her "flashback" to life. A less experienced writer might use the past tense which would drag down the pace and bore us.

ROMANTIC SHORT STORY

When the trouble between Tracy and Ted escalated into nonstop fighting, they almost lost sight of why they'd fallen in love in the first place—<u>almost</u>, but not quite . . .

Something Precious

BY CARIN T. FORD

a

"Stop fighting or I'm going to send both of you to your rooms!"

b

The boys were in the living room but I could hear the shouting from up in my bedroom. I left the clean laundry on the bed and headed downstairs.

"Danny and Michael, what did I tell you?" I frowned as they continued squabbling.

"He started it!" Danny shouted back.

"I don't care who started it. I want it to end." A wry smile crossed my face. So often lately, my sons made me think of my husband and me. My

c

soon-to-be ex-husband, I silently corrected myself.

How many times had Ted and I fought with angry words and bitter accusations, like the boys were now? And whose fault had it been?

It didn't really matter now because we had ended it. Ted had walked out the door, taking the fighting and the shouting and our marriage with him.

As I began picking up the toys that littered the living room, the telephone rang and I absently reached for it.

"Hi there, Tracy." It was Ted. "How are you doing?" he asked.

d

Was it because I'd been thinking about him, or would Ted's voice always hit me like a punch in the stomach?

"I'm fine," I answered. "And you?"

"Everything is okay."

Our conversations were so polite, so . . . civilized. Yet our behavior for much of the past year had been anything but.

"Good," I said, not sure that I meant it. "Hold on."

I called for Danny and Michael. As they took turns speaking to their father, I couldn't help wondering for the ten-thousandth time where we'd gone wrong. We'd started out like all married couples, seeing a straight road ahead full of love and laughter, children and dreams. But somewhere there'd been a curve in the road, and now Ted lived 1,000 miles away.

But no, it wasn't fair to say Ted had moved because our marriage broke up. It was really the other way around.

I remembered the conversation as clearly as if it had happened yesterday.

e

"They're offering me a promotion, Tracy," Ted had said. "I can't say no to it."

SOMETHING PRECIOUS, *continued*

"Can't or *won't*?"

It had been a typical fight, like the ones we'd been having for months. Yet this time we didn't try to make up; we didn't try to ignore the anger. Ted took the job while the boys and I stayed behind.

"Can I, Mom?"

I realized that Danny was asking me something.

"Can you what, sweetheart?" I asked.

f "Can I have the same kind of birthday I had last year? Dad said to ask you."

I took a deep breath before speaking into the phone. "What did you tell him, Ted."

"I told him we'd have to discuss it."

There was silence on the line while Ted and I both traveled back to Danny's fifth birthday. Ted had bought a tent and camping equipment and we'd driven to the mountains where we'd spent the day hiking and the night sleeping under the stars.

I've never been an outdoors kind of person, and I wasn't thrilled when Ted suggested his plan.

"But it was a good idea, wasn't it?" Ted had whispered to me that night as we lay side by side in our sleeping bags with the boys resting near us.

"Don't gloat," I'd said with a chuckle.

"Gloating wasn't what I had in mind." Ted reached for me and I'd moved into his arms . . .

"It might be . . . uncomfortable," I finally said.

"Maybe we could put aside our differences for one day," Ted said.

Could we? A sudden shiver crept up my spine—but whether it was from dread or anticipation, I wasn't sure . . .

g "Can we go look for snakes now, Dad?" Danny grabbed his father's hand just as Ted finished setting up the tent.

"I don't see why not," Ted smiled and reached for Michael with his free hand. "You coming, Tracy?"

I gazed at the boys standing with their father, all of them smiling at me and looking so much alike. Ever since we'd arrived at our mountain site, I'd found myself forgetting that Ted and I no longer lived together.

"No, I think I'll just stay here and get supper ready."

Was that disappointment flashing across Ted's face—or was I merely hoping it was?

I busied myself preparing our meal and it wasn't until a half hour later that I heard voices and laughter. As Ted and our sons came into view, I experienced a sharp ache.

Maybe I couldn't forget our disagreements, but I also couldn't forget how much I loved watching Ted's eyes crinkle at the corners when he laughed or the way he always ran his fingers through his hair, making it stand on end. These were little unimportant things. But maybe, I wondered for the first

SOMETHING PRECIOUS, *continued*

time, so were our disagreements.

After dinner, we lit six candles for Danny's birthday, and as they burned against the darkening sky, I closed my eyes and inhaled the scent of pine.

"Tracy, are you all right?"

I jumped at Ted's voice.

What if I told him the truth? What if I said, "I thought I was all right until this weekend. But being around you again has confused me." But this was happening too fast, and I wasn't sure I could trust my feelings.

That night, I lay in my sleeping bag between the boys while Ted slept along one side of the tent. It was silly of me, but I suddenly felt awkward around the man I'd known for 10 years. Without looking Ted in the eyes, I positioned my bag between the boys and waited for sleep to come. But it didn't. Hours passed and I still couldn't sleep.

h
Finally, I crept out of my sleeping bag and walked out into the starry night. Wrapping my arms around myself for warmth, I stared up at the sky. I never even heard Ted approach. "Why aren't you sleeping?" said a soft voice behind me.

I whirled around and saw Ted in the darkness, a blanket draped over his shoulders. I laughed with relief.

"I could ask you the same thing, you know."

He sat down on a large rock and held out his arm to me, and I hesitated.

"You'll freeze out there, Tracy. Come on, it's warm under the blanket." I walked over to Ted, allowing him to wrap the blanket around both of us. "It's hard to believe that Danny is six," he said.

I smiled in the darkness. "I remember the day he was born as if it were just yesterday."

"Who could forget it? When his heartbeat dropped and they thought . . ." Ted couldn't finish the sentence.

We had almost lost Danny, and then suddenly, like a miracle, he had recovered—and now he was six. Without thinking, I reached under the blanket for Ted's hand.

"We almost lost something precious," I said softly.

Ted looked at me intently, our faces only inches apart. "Are we willing to risk it again?"

i
I frowned in confusion and Ted continued. "These past months we've been apart I've felt empty and I tried to tell myself it was the boys. But seeing you this weekend . . ."

He reached up to take my face in his hands. "I know how hurtful this past year has been. I was so wrapped up in work."

"We were both wrapped up in ourselves," I interrupted. "We didn't discuss anything; we took opposite sides and fought as if we were playing on two different teams."

Ted gently traced a pattern around my mouth with his finger. "I want to play on the same team, Tracy. But can we put it all behind us?"

"I'd like to try."

SOMETHING PRECIOUS, *continued*

j   Ted kissed me firmly and I wrapped my arms around his waist.

The children were quiet in the car the next day as we drove along the highway. Ted and I still had a lot to work out—what should we do now? Where should we live?

And then the answer came so easily and unexpectedly. "How long until we're home?" Danny asked sleepily from the back seat.

I was about to answer and then stopped. Because suddenly, home wasn't the house where I'd been living so many years. Without Ted, it was just a building. I glanced at my husband's strong hands on the steering wheel and at his familiar profile. Home isn't a place, I realized. Home is being with the people you love.

I reached across the seat and took Ted's hand in mine. "We *are* home," I said quietly.

---

g   Carin doesn't waste a minute loading up the station wagon or worrying about the choice of hot dogs versus hamburgers. She gets her family right there, to the campsite. She doesn't need to elaborate on the green trees or sparkling lake. There isn't a lot of time for such detail and besides these stories concentrate on interior detail, which Carin gives us. She shows us Tracy's ambiguity about the breakup, and suggests regret. Note again Carin's use of dialogue to make the trip come to life. She has not gone overboard, but keeps it brisk, light and real.

h   The Moment of Truth: Tracy can't sleep, gets up; Ted finds her, they are alone in the moonlight. They reminisce about how Danny was almost not born, or not born alive, without any extra detail or needless description. There was a crisis, Danny's heartbeat dropped, but the crisis is over and now he's a healthy child. Note how Carin's mini-story within the story parallels what's going on with her adult characters: Their heartbeats, figuratively, are slowing. Can they survive and save "something precious?"

i   Tracy has her say: Now she and Ted have a chance to reveal their feelings. They admit they were selfish. Can this marriage be saved? Again, note use of light dialogue supplemented with active description like "Ted gently traced a pattern around my mouth with a finger. . . ."

j   Home Stretch: Ted kisses Tracy. Carin gets us out of the woods literally and figuratively without excess fuss and no mosquito bites. We're driving home when little Danny—what a convenient child!—asks how long till they're home. This gives Carin her Golden Moment, when Tracy realizes "Home isn't a place. Home is being with the people you love."

The ending is perfect; it's a physical manifestation of that philosophy.

Fiction Report

BY BARBARA KUROFF

Even though the publishing industry is admittedly in a slump, 1996 was an eventful and exciting year for fiction. Here are just a few interesting—and heartening—things that happened in 1996:

• Major publishers of fiction were optimistic going into 1997, with fall releases of novels by blockbuster authors, including Mary Higgins Clark, John le Carré, Michael Crichton, Barbara Taylor Bradford, Laura Esquivel and Scott Turow (see our interview with Turow on page 72).

• David Guterson's award-winning first novel, *Snow Falling on Cedars*, became Vintage's fastest-selling novel ever, with nearly two million copies in print (see our interview with Guterson on page 60).

• The serial novel returned. All six parts of Stephen King's *The Green Mile* serial from Signet appeared at the same time on *The New York Times* paperback bestsellers list. Ballantine Publishing Group President Linda Grey is quoted as saying King's success "has whet the appetites of readers for serialized novels." At the same time, Grey announced the serialization of John Saul's *The Blackstone Chronicles*. The first installment of Saul's six-part novel was released by Fawcett in February 1997, with five more volumes following monthly through July.

• The "twin novel" was born. Stephen King's *Desperation* was released by Viking while *The Regulators*, written by Richard Bachman (King's pseudonym), appeared as a Dutton title on the same day. The respective protagonists of these books, although polar opposites, are twins.

• When bestselling mystery author Patricia Cornwell left Scribner for Putnam, Scribner signed a previously unpublished author, Dr. Kathleen J. Reichs, to a 1.2 million two-book contract. Reichs, a forensic anthropologist and professor at the University of North Carolina, submitted her unsolicited manuscript, *Déjà Dead*, to a Scribner assistant editor who circulated it to the top Scribner and Pocket Books editors within a week. Reichs's book will be published as a Scribner hardcover in October 1997 and a Pocket Books mass market title in 1998.

• Nicholas Evans received an unprecedented $3 million from Robert Redford for film rights to *The Horse Whisperer*, Evans's first novel.

• Oprah Winfrey initiated a reading group on national television.

• Booksellers—chains and independents—continued to be havens for writers as well as readers by providing space for writers' and readers' groups, sponsoring readings by local as well as nationally-known writers, and allowing patrons to browse through their shelves that provide a wealth of information on what's being published and by whom.

Among the things negatively impacting publishing houses this year were large returns of unsold books from retailers. The September/October 1996 issue of *Small Press* gives the example of one bookseller who placed a $188,000 order from a small publisher and returned all but $36,000 worth of the books. Some larger publishers with even greater returns have been forced to temporarily dedicate portions of their warehouses to receiving returns and hire additional employees to process those returns. On a lighter and very ingenious note, one fiction writer who heard that signed copies were considered "defaced" and could not be returned, signed shelf copies to ensure fewer of his titles went back to the publisher.

The displacement of many small independent distributors by less than a handful of huge distributing companies has also contributed to the publishing industry's woes. Where small independent distributors once worked their territories supplying outlets, small and large, with titles, many smaller retail book outlets are no longer serviced by the huge distributors looking for big orders. This problem literally hit home recently for one popular Southern romance writer. Upon visiting her local bookstore to sign her newest title as she always had, she was surprised to find it was not available. The store's owner told her that the old independent distributor had been bought by a new, large distributor and her new book had not been among the titles offered.

Although all the editors and publishers I spoke with while preparing this report acknowledged that times were not that good and possibly as bad as they could remember, all were hopeful that this time would pass and the industry would be stronger than ever. Some even predict that this period of fierce competition will produce a marked improvement in all areas of the industry, including in the quality of fiction. In the editorial in the October/November 1996 *Small Press*, Executive Editor Mardi Link says, "If you're good at what you do, be it publishing books or magazines or supporting those who do through offering conferences or running a trade association, you won't be threatened by competition, but rather energized by it."

Now, here's a closer look at some specific fiction categories:

CHILDREN'S AND YOUNG ADULT FICTION

The children's book market, particularly paperbacks, is strong and continues to grow. Sales of children's paperback books were up 23.1% during the first seven months of 1996. According to a recent Communications Industry Forecast by the investment banking firm Veronis, Suhler & Associates, sales of children's books will continue to enjoy healthy growth at least through the year 2000. Credited for this highly optimistic forecast are the success of movie and TV tie-ins, the cheaper price of paperbacks, and the broader acceptance of paperbacks in bookstores, schools and libraries. As another indication of how important children's books are in today's popular culture, R.L. Stine appeared on the 1996 *Entertainment Weekly* "100 Most Powerful People" list.

Scholastic's Goosebumps series has also been a major reason for increased children's paperback sales (more than 32 million Goosebumps titles were sold in 1995 alone). In fact, Scholastic had record revenues and a 60% increase in sales in fiscal 1996. According to Alice P. Buening, editor of *Children's Writer's & Illustrator's Market*, series packagers remain increasingly important. The Babysitter's Club, Sweet Valley High, and Sweet Valley University series have each provided opportunities for writers. Buening also says most editors continue to be open to middle grade (ages 8-12) fiction which is the core audience of the children's market. However, says Buening, this core audience continues to be ill-defined: since these readers seem to keep getting younger, even bookstores often have difficulty deciding where to shelve titles.

Emily Easton, editor of young adult titles at Walker and Company, says she is seeing too many submissions of problem novels for her age group. Although she says there is still a place for the problem novel, she also says, "I would like more submissions that are about just ordinary kids in ordinary situations."

Easton emphasizes the importance that reviews and awards play in the success of a young adult novel, especially hardcover titles. "In this market, things that do not receive stars or awards are a really hard sell. And in this market, there's no middle ground— either a book sells or it doesn't." However, the need for stars, reviews and awards can actually be an advantage for unpublished authors, says Easton: "Often new authors are received better than people who've had three or four books behind them that didn't do well. We're always looking for fresh, new voices"

HORROR

"There continues to be a trend to not label horror as horror," says Lawrence Watt-Evans, president of the Horror Writer's Association. "If you can't find some other way to repackage it as suspense or dark romance or dark fantasy, it's very hard to break into this market today." Watt-Evans notes that Zebra Books canceled their horror line in fall 1996 because titles categorized as horror were not selling well enough. But he says, "Horror has always run on a boom and bust cycle. We had the biggest boom ever in the 80s and now we're at the worst bust ever, but I think if you hang in there it will turn upward again, the way it always has. I think we've hit bottom and are starting back up."

The big names in horror—Stephen King, Anne Rice, Dean Koontz and John Saul—continue to do well. Stephen King's successful six-part serialization of *The Green Mile* and Fawcett's publication of *The Blackstone Chronicles*, a six-part serialized novel by John Saul, are proof that there is still a huge market for horror.

Horror mixed with romance and vampires remains popular. The November 1996 issue of *Romantic Times Magazine* features Anne Rice on the cover with the caption "Anne Rice Embraces Romance." In that same issue, Maggie Shayne, successful author of "dark paranormal romances" (notice they're not called horror) talks about "exploring the dark side of romance" in her novels: "I think we who read a lot of the really dark romances, those books with undertones of horror lurking in their hearts, understand their appeal. I've been in love with horror since I was old enough to shiver."

MYSTERY

The mystery genre remains strong according to Priscilla Ridgeway, executive director of Mystery Writers of America who says, "Consumer interest in mystery is still there and growing. *Small Press* magazine noted in its July/August 1996 issue devoted to the mystery genre that of the 1,500 mystery titles published annually, 850 to 900 are new titles. Also in that issue, Barbara Peters, owner of the Poisoned Pen Bookstore in Scottsdale, Arizona, says her business has grown about 30 percent a year for the past five years. Peters says first mysteries by new authors sell well for her "because they are the most collectible or potentially collectible books." Regional mysteries and historical mysteries are also big sellers in Peters's thriving shop.

Marcia Markland, vice president and publisher at Avalon Books, says she is seeing many more three-dimensional, well-developed characters than three years ago. Markland says plots, too, are not as straightforward as before, but are more complex and deal with a variety of issues. Although Avalon makes it a policy not to publish books with sex and violence because their books are distributed to libraries, Markland is noticing less sex and violence in a number of new titles by other publishers. She points out that even Hollywood is turning to the classics and writers like Jane Austin for movie story lines that contain little graphic sex and violence.

Michael Seidman, mystery editor at Walker and Company, says the trend toward female protagonists that was so popular five years ago is leveling off. The female private investigator is still there, but there continue to be more mysteries involving a soft- to medium-boiled male detective. He also says series continue to be strong as do amateur detectives in various forms.

Seidman, who strongly favors character-driven rather than plot-driven novels, says, "Start with some people and see what happens." He also discourages writers from being influenced by fads. Instead, they should read a lot of mysteries and "figure out what makes the mystery work." Writers should also "understand an audience's need for justice, not for law." He points out that today's readers don't want mysteries based on the headlines. "They get too much of that in the newspaper and on TV." What today's mystery readers want, says Seidman, is "the puzzle. Readers don't want to solve the crime early on. They want to be fooled. If your readers solve the case consistently before your detective, you are going to lose those readers."

Last, but certainly not least, the thriller novel is as strong as ever. With new releases by Tom Clancy, John Grisham and Scott Turow, 1996 was an especially fruitful year for super-selling thrillers with blockbuster movie potential (movie rights to Turow's *The Laws of Our Fathers* sold in six hours).

ROMANCE

The romance genre continues to enjoy its acceptance as a valid, enjoyable and saleable form. Romance authors, whose titles appear on the paperback and hardback bestseller lists, are as celebrated as their mainstream counterparts. For instance, stories featuring bestselling romance authors Julie Garwood and Sandra Brown dominated the July 22, 1996, edition of *Publishers Weekly*. Garwood's fourteenth book, *The Wedding*, was number ten on bestseller lists within the first week of release. And, says Isabel Swift, editorial director at Silhouette, once a category romance author makes the mainstream bestseller lists, it's not unusual for that author's category romances to be repackaged and reissued. An example of this successful repackaging would be the one-volume trade size collection of Nora Roberts's four-book Calhoun Women series, released by Silhouette in December 1996.

Janice Reams Hudson, president of the Romance Writers of America, says, "sales of the genre overall are strong and there are more authors and more titles than ever." But, she says, "because of the increase in the number of authors and titles, there are fewer numbers of each book selling. A book that would have sold well two years ago, publishers won't even buy today. It can't just be a good book today—it has to be a great book. It's a buyer's market for the editors because there are so many manuscripts out there."

Hudson also notes that Penquin Books has dropped their dark fantasy line and Fawcett is no longer looking for Regencies. Also, Pearson, the British holding company that owns Penguin, has bought Putnam. Since Putnam owns Berkley, publisher of several genres of fiction including historicals, Hudson says this could seriously affect the market for writers.

Although a tight marketplace is not necessarily great for the individual writers, Hudson says, "it is the best thing that could happen to the genre. It brings in new ideas—these new authors are always testing the boundaries and pushing them out. We welcome new members into RWA, including those who haven't sold yet. It gets tougher for them to sell because the market gets tight, but it also makes the books better. Keeping the new writers coming in makes all of us stay on our toes."

Swift credits the variety within the genre as another reason the romance field remains strong and keeps getting stronger. "In the romance genre, we write science fiction romances, we write mystery romances, western romances—there are virtually no limits to what somebody can write in the romance genre." And Hudson adds that, along with historicals, ghost stories and vampire tales, "inspirational romances from Christian publishers have really boomed in the last year or so." Swift says "the classic plots are popular and remain popular—cowboys, babies, marriages of convenience, twins, amnesia." The trick, she says, is to "take that classic element and tell it in a fresh way, tell it in a modern way, tell it in a believable way to explore the inherent emotional aspect of those plots."

When submitting to Silhouette, Harlequin or other romance line, the best advice is still to read those books to learn exactly what each line publishes. Swift says readers have specific expectations when they pick up a novel of a particular romance line. Those expectations are part of a "trust," she says, that is established with readers. "This readers' trust is also why we get to publish so many new authors—readers will buy a romance book in a particular line, regardless of the author's name. The reader trusts us. This is a phenomenal advantage for writers in comparison to mainstream publishing—it's like having an unbelievable magic wand." And Swift notes that "between Harlequin and Silhouette, we most likely publish more never-before-published authors than any other publisher."

Hudson advises those thinking about writing romance, "If you don't love it, don't try it. The mistake people make is hearing someone say, 'Romances are really selling. You ought to write one and make a lot of money.' A new romance writer can't make a lot of money, and, if you don't love the books, it will show in your writing. Write what you love to read. Find out what type of romance you want to write and study those kinds of romance novels and find out what houses are buying them. And join RWA."

SCIENCE FICTION & FANTASY

Peter Pautz, executive secretary of Science Fiction & Fantasy Writers of America, says, "The genre is perfectly poised to take advantage of the Internet explosion. I think with the explosion of multimedia, particularly the Internet, we are going to see a lot more ancillary and secondary markets for science fiction and fantasy writers during the coming year. We're already seeing electronic science fiction and fantasy magazines on the Internet. Of course what that may mean about quality, for a while at least, remains to be seen." There are also more female science fiction writers, a trend, Pautz says, that has been going on for the last decade, if not the last two, and shows no sign of abating.

Susan Allison, editor-in-chief at Berkley/Ace Books, says, "Things are not easy for publishing in general right now, especially in paperback. And science fiction is traditionally a paperback-based genre, so that means times are tough. On the other hand, I would say that the number of readers who are willing to take a chance on a story line that once would have been thought of as a purely science fiction, back-of-the-bookstore kind of storyline seems to have grown a lot during the last couple of years. I think that's a trend that will continue. People are prepared now to read about cloning and aliens and time travel—not just people who would normally buy a stack of science fiction books, but people who buy all kinds of fiction are prepared for those topics. So I think there's a chance for us in the science fiction field to reach out to that group of readers and to expand our readership that way."

Allison says there seems to be a lot of boundary crossing among the genres. "There are books on the bestseller lists that are romances, but with time travel, for instance. It's interesting how people are prepared to accept more than they once did outside the boundaries of the traditional genre."

Allison is particularly optimistic about the literary end of the science fiction market. "We've done some literary-type science fiction books that get put on the front tables of the booksellers, right up with the Vintage trade paperback fiction. I think readers of a slightly less commercial, more literary novel have become accustomed to the trade paperback form, and are willing to try a book that is interestingly packaged. Some of our trade paperback science fiction first novels have been done that way with success."

Agents, according to Allison, are more important than ever in helping writers get published. "Because publishers must be 'lean and mean' these days, everybody is more understaffed and overworked than they used to be. The agent's role has become much more important because most of us are not doing as good a job of reading the unsolicited manuscripts as we used to. Agents, not publishers, are now often the ones reading slush piles. So I think authors need to spend a lot of time working on getting an agent. It's more important now than it ever has been, at least in the science fiction market which was one in which you traditionally didn't particularly need an agent to get started."

Series remain popular, but Allison says to "make sure each book stands alone and it's a satisfying reading experience by itself. We cannot guarantee by any means that someone has read book one when book two comes out."

WESTERN

"Western fiction has its mountains and valleys—it's always going up and then down and back up," says James Crutchfield, executive secretary of the Western Writers of America. "Right now, the publishing houses are tightening their belts and it's not as lucrative as it once was. But this has happened before and it's going to happen again."

Crutchfield says today's Western readers are more sophisticated than they once were. "There will always be a market for the shoot-em-ups, but, on the other hand, I think overall the Western market is getting more sophisticated than that. Editors are looking for more in-depth story lines and stories built around historical events, stories that are more believable than the same old soup served over again."

Today's Western writers must also be good researchers, says Crutchfield, because today's readers of Westerns are more knowledgeable about the country's history than many of their predecessors. "Readers are quick to point out inaccuracies in fiction. They want to see authentic wear, authentic jargon and authentic weapons. They can pick up on the fact, for instance, that you're writing about the Mexican War but you have a character using a revolver that didn't come out until the Civil War."

Crutchfield says today's Western fiction is often centered around contemporary themes. By contemporary, he means "it's Western in that it occurs or has some setting in the West, but it might be a 1916 Pancho Villa story or a novel set during the building of Boulder Dam, something much different than the shoot-em-ups that used to be the traditional Westerns." Some other areas Crutchfield says Western writers are exploring and should explore more are: "Eastern Westerns," set east of the Mississippi in the 1700s when pioneers were coming across the Alleghenies and Appalachians and settling Tennessee, Kentucky, Ohio and Indiana; the Florida cowboys (a large cattle business developed in Florida in the 1800s); the Mountain Men Era; the work of the army engineers in the West; and the Gold Rush.

OTHER AREAS OF GROWTH

The online possibilities for writers continue to grow and every day seems to bring something new. Kensington Publishing, for instance, has set up a website that features chat rooms, a weekly interactive chat, and a summary of guidelines for submission. (See our Websites of Interest on page 588.)

Religious publishers continue to successfully compete for shelf space with mainstream fiction in a wide variety of genres—including mystery, romance, thriller and horror. Leading the wave of religious-oriented genre fiction are the increasingly popular thrillers of author Frank Peretti.

Social fiction, defined as fiction dedicated to social change, is also gaining recognition and awards. At the 1996 American Booksellers Association annual meeting, Curbstone Press, started in 1975 by Alexander "Sandy" Taylor and his wife Judith Doyle in reaction to human rights violations in Chile, won its fourth award in eight months.

(For more on fiction intended to transform society, see the Insider Report with Emilie Buchwald, Milkweed Editions, on page 419.)

Ethnic fiction is also gaining momentum. In a June 24, 1996, *New York Times* article titled "An Emerging Prominence for Blacks in Publishing," Doreen Carvajal notes that, although black readers buy 160 million books a year, only 3.4 percent of the managers, editors and professionals who choose the nation's popular literature are black. In an effort to help black publishers, author Walter Mosley waived his usual six-figure advance in favor of taking his unpublished manuscript, *Gone Fishin'*, to the independent Black Classic Press who released it in January 1997.

KEEPING AN EYE ON THE MARKET

Every year as we update *Novel & Short Story Writer's Market*, we ask each publisher who lists here to comment on how they are being affected by industry trends. What we keep hearing from editors and publishers, however, is that most pay little attention to trends. By the time a trend in an industry is reported, they say, it's over and something new has taken its place. With that in mind, here are some suggestions for keeping your eyes on the fiction marketplace, while realizing that it is constantly changing.

There are numerous ways to keep an eye on the fiction market. Get to know your local booksellers. These are the people on the front lines of the publishing industry. Not only are they painfully aware of what is not selling well or what seems to be flooding the market, they are also keen observers of what is becoming popular with readers. It's their business to know.

Networking is an excellent way to keep tabs on what's happening in the publishing industry. In addition to local writers' groups, organizations such as the Romance Writers of America, Horror Writers Association, Science Fiction and Fantasy Writers of America, Western Writers of America, Mystery Writers of America and the Society of Children's Book Writers and Illustrators offer support, encouragement and a wealth of "insider" information through newsletters, meetings and conferences. (You'll find information on most of these groups in our Organizations and Resources section.)

Writers' conferences offer other opportunities to learn about what's happening in the industry. These are great places to meet editors and agents as well as other writers. Most include trend topics in their programs. Conferences are held across North America and around the world. See the Conferences and Workshops section of this book for listings organized by regions, or pick up a copy of *Writer's Digest* magazine's conference issue published each May.

Writers' magazines and trade journals can also help you keep up with the market. In addition to *Writer's Digest*, which includes a monthly markets column, you'll find a wealth of market information in such publications as *Locus*, *Scavenger's Newsletter* and *The Writers' Nook News*. Industry journals such as *Publishers Weekly*, *Small Press* and *Quill & Quire* provide up-to-date news on publishing and bookselling.

If you have a computer and a modem, you also have access to the most current information available on the various online services and bulletin boards. America Online, GEnie, Compuserve and eWorld all include writers' areas, and there are several internet e-mail groups catering to specific genres. Also see Websites of Interest on page 588 for a list of websites for writers.

It pays to know your market and your competition, but this trend-watching can only go so far. Every year, as we gather information for this report, we are reminded by writers, editors and agents that quality goes a long way no matter what you are writing. If you believe in what you've written and have taken the time to carefully craft your prose, by all means send it out. Regardless of any trend, there's always room for well-done fiction.

Writing from the Inside Out: Letting Your Characters Tell Their Stories

BY COLLEEN MARIAH RAE

One of the biggest mistakes we writers make is thinking we have to write our own stories. What I call "writing from the outside" often leads to wooden pieces with no emotional pulse. But when you write from the inside out and let your characters tell their stories, it can produce such powerful work that it will leave you reeling.

Writing from the inside out has two components: one is entering the emotion and the other is entering the body of the character. I'll talk about both in turn.

EXPERIENCING YOUR CHARACTER'S EMOTIONS

Imagine right now that you're standing in the middle of a frozen snow field. There is no sound. Fog wisps around you so that no matter where you look, you can't see more than a few feet ahead. Everything is white, white, white. In your panic, you suck deep breaths through your nose, but with each breath your nostrils contract against the dry bite of air. You tuck back deeper into your parka so that its furry edging circles your face. In that steamy space, you taste your fear. Where to go? You came from the north, you know. But where's north? There? You take one step, and your boot crashes through the crust of ice. The edges grab at your knee, a bear-trap claw against bone. You ease down to your belly, hoping the surface will hold your weight as you snake your way forward, pulling your leg from the hole. Just as you do, you hear, faint in the distance, someone calling your name.

If you were imaging this up as you read, not only would you have heard and smelled and tasted and touched and seen the world I described, but you might also have felt a sense of relief at the end when your name was called.

There's a reason for this: It's absolutely impossible to have an image in our mind's eye without having a concomitant emotional response. I call this the image-emotion coin, and it's the basis for my techniques that I describe at length in my book, *Movies in the Mind: How to Build a Short Story*. For the sake of this article, though, the important element is this: If you imagined the passage above as a movie in the mind, your body participated.

Now isn't that the key to writing fiction? We want to pull readers in as participants. We do that through well-chosen details, of course. But the trick to getting the right details is to have the movies in the mind so vivid that all you have to do is simply record what you smell, hear, touch, taste, see, and feel in your mind's eye.

COLLEEN MARIAH RAE *is the author of two novels,* Perchance to Dream *and* Warrior at the Edge of the World *and founding editor and publisher of the* Santa Fe Literary Review. *Also author of* Movies in the Mind: How to Build a Short Story, *Rae has taught her innovative writing technique at workshops and writers' conferences around the country.*

ENTERING YOUR CHARACTER'S BODY

The easiest way to do that is by entering our characters' bodies. With each of them, we have to do more than walk a mile in their moccasins. We have to stand in their skin, smelling and tasting and touching and seeing and hearing the world as they do—from the inside out. Then and only then can their stories really be told.

I call our ability to slip into our characters' bodies, our *Seventh Sense*. It's our capacity for empathy, which *Webster's Third* defines as "the capacity for participating in or a vicarious experiencing of another's feelings, volitions, or ideas and sometimes another's movements to the point of executing bodily movements resembling his."

FACE TO FACE WITH YOUR CHARACTER

Right now, I want you to take a moment and do an exercise that should illustrate what I'm talking about. First of all, I want you to imagine that you're looking at yourself in a mirror. Study your reflection closely. Now imagine that the light is on a dimmer switch. Slowly turn the light up, watching what happens to your face. Where do the shadows fall? What part of your face catches the light? What does the brightening light do to your skin coloring?

Now slowly dim the light, and as you do so, watch what happens to your reflection. Where do the shadows fall? How does the coloring change? And what is the last part of your face you see before the light goes to black?

Turn the light back up so it's at a comfortable level. Now I want you to imagine that one of your characters walks into the room and that you can see him or her walking toward you as a reflection in the mirror. Your character then comes and stands next to you so that you can see both of your reflections clearly. Watch your character studying you. Now study your character. Notice the details. What color hair, shape of face, size of nose? How tall is your character? What's he or she wearing? Try the dimmer switch and see what you see.

INSIDE YOUR CHARACTER'S SKIN

After both you and your character have had a chance to check each other out, I'd like you to go one step further. As though you're putting your hand into a glove, I want you to slip into your character's body.

What does it feel like in there? Is it a tight squeeze or roomy?

Now I want you to look through your *character's* eyes at your *character's* reflection in the mirror. Remember: You are your character looking through his or her eyes.

When I have students do this, they almost invariably express surprise because their character's reflection takes on a whole new aspect. When they're looking through their character's eyes, they see as we all see when we look at ourselves—details stand out vividly; flaws take on an importance that would surprise an outside observer. Emotions also rear their heads.

One of my female students climbed into a male character's body only to discover that she felt as though she were in a large, dark, hollow space. And when she looked through his eyes, rather than seeing a face reflected in the mirror, she heard his thoughts: "I'm just a goddamned failure. They need too much from me. All the family needs too much. I can't give them what they crave. I don't have the earning power. I'll never make enough. I'll never achieve enough."

With these words came a feeling of wanting to flee because everything felt so impossibly overwhelming. This came as a revelation to my student because this character was based on her father who, from the outside had always seemed so strong and assured. She said, "It was as if, when he was over 60 years of age, I was learning about him and his point of view for the first time." Only by getting into her character's body and seeing him through his eyes, could she really come to know his inner life, which is, of course, his motivation.

EXPERIENCING YOUR CHARACTER

When you're inside your character, it's not just a matter of seeing a reflection. We are able to feel our character's feelings and get a sense of what it's like to be him or her. We can do more as well. From inside your character, touch "your" skin in your mind's eye. (Remember: When you're inside, you are always the character, not yourself.) What does "your" skin feel like? Is it rough or silky? And what do you smell like?

Imagine now that your character is eating his or her favorite food. What is the experience like for your character? Where does the taste touch the tongue? How does it feel to the body? Is there a warm satisfaction or a "yes!" of triumph? And here's a real stretch for you—a way to know if you're really in your character's body and not just "thinking it": Imagine that your character is eating something you detest. For me that would be frozen mixed vegetables; it makes me gag to think of them; it reminds me of hiding them under the rim of my dinner plate as a child, of sticking them in my pocket—anything to avoid eating them. Now, variations of taste being what they are, it would be truly astounding to have a character who had the same visceral reaction to frozen veggies. Try it with your least favorite food and see. And try it with your favorite food and see the difference in your character's response. I've been doing this technique with students for a long time, and the most constant reaction is the sense of awe when a character responds differently than we ourselves would. And characters do respond differently. I don't know how it is that we can do this—actually enter the body of our character—but I've never known a person who couldn't do it to some extent.

BECOMING YOUR CHARACTER

There are many things you can do from inside your character. For instance, you can let your character speak through you to have a conversation with someone else. When I'm working with students, I'll ask them questions when they're inside the body of the character (with a frequent admonition to, say, a student named Ted of "This isn't Ted speaking here; this is Susan. Susan, get the author out of the way. What do *you*, Susan, feel?") At first this may seem odd, but very quickly you'll come to see that in fact the character can speak through your mouth. Equally, you can do this alone with a pen and paper or with a computer keyboard. Record both the questions asked and the answers given by your character. Clearly, though, if you can find someone to ask you the questions while you're "in character," it can be a lot more fun.

In writing from the inside out, we don't just stay in our characters' bodies. We have to see them from other angles as well. But it's still writing from the inside out because we're letting them tell us their stories. We can do that by observing them.

COMMUNING WITH YOUR CHARACTER

One day I was working with a student on his character named Hillary while he and I sat at his picnic table in his yard. I said to him, "Do you see Hillary over there by the arroyo?" Yes, he said he could. "What's she wearing?" I asked. He described her outfit in great detail so that I began to see her too—sandals, a gathered skirt and "a beige shell." And then he added with a bemused expression: "What's a shell?" It was an interesting moment when you know there's real communion with a character. Probably not many men know the word, but my student's character who lives in the 70s would comfortably use it to describe the sleeveless simple blouse she wore.

I then asked him to have Hillary come toward us and had him describe for me how she walked. He said her stride was confident and graceful, but, more than that, what struck him was how alive and sensitive she was—and how aware she was of him. "Who are you?" she asked him. "What are you doing here?" Her inquisitiveness struck him because he had thought he was the one who would be asking the questions.

The most powerful moment for my student, however, was when his character came close and he smelled her: "It was not a manufactured scent; it didn't come out of a bottle. It was her scent, and it was no scent. It was clean mud and wet grass. Where there's grass, people lie in it and the next thing they know they're wanting to eat it because it's such an inviting scent. But it's not a scent, it's that you sense something. This scent of hers—it was not a familiar scent; it was *her* scent."

It was this scent that most of all made him a believer in writing from the inside out. Hillary's smell caused a physical sensation inside of him, and that was all he needed to know her reality as a character separate from himself.

I should add that this student has been publishing fiction since the late 50s. At first, he was very resistant to working with me, saying to himself as he told me later, "What have I got to learn from her? I'm down the road and way ahead, so why am I looking back at what she's going to be telling me?" But finally he did come to work with me because he felt himself incapable of writing from a woman's point of view, something his story wanted him to do. Not only did he discover he was more than equal to the task, but he found that he had a remarkable capacity for getting out of his own way and letting his characters tell the story—and what a story it was! Nothing he ever could have thought of by himself.

INSIDE VERSUS OUTSIDE

And so writing from the inside out involves getting into your characters' bodies or observing your characters as they move in their worlds or feeling their emotions and then writing from those emotions. When something is written from the outside, we write as observers detailing up the scene. When it's written from the inside out, the emotion colors the things observed.

Here's an example of a passage that was written from the outside:

> The obligatory reception was held in the big house where Savannah had grown up. Looking around at the heavy furniture and antimacassars, Lacey had difficulty picturing her brash, wild-child friend in such stifling surroundings. No wonder her mother was nuts, Lacey thought. She was living amid centuries of someone else's musty stuff.

Not bad, but it lacks the power of this that my student later wrote from the inside out:

> She looked over at Savannah where she had sunk into one of the huge carved chairs. Even now in this profound grief, Savannah was breathtakingly beautiful and so alive. It was like a candle burned inside her, illuminating her from the inside out.

There's a power in those words, a pulse of life that draws the reader in. This is writing from the inside out. You become your character, and you let your character tell his or her story. It's one that may surprise you; often you'll find that it certainly isn't the one you thought you were going to tell, but because it's truly your character's story, it will be a much richer tale.

Fiction's Connecting Link: Emotion

BY KATHY JACOBSON

Without emotion, fiction becomes flat and boring. With it, you hook your readers, pull them in, hold them to the end, *and* make them eager for your next story or novel. So let's look at how you can enrich your writing by increasing the emotional level.

First of all, consider emotion as a triangle. One side represents the emotion of the author (your enthusiasm for the story); the second represents the emotions of the characters (how they interpret and respond to the events of the story); and the third represents the emotion of the readers (how closely they will identify with the characters). Your challenge is to make each side of the triangle strong enough to ensure the book doesn't collapse on itself (fail to interest an editor).

YOUR ENTHUSIASM

Do you love the genre you've picked? Are you an avid fan? You must have passion for the *type* of novel or story you plan to write or your work will lack excitement. The subject matter must fill you with enthusiasm, or the task of putting words on paper will soon become drudgery.

Love your work, love your story, love your characters, love the challenge of creating a book. Even when things don't go well, or you get a rejection, or your critique group discovers holes in your plot, remember that you write for the joy of it.

Also, don't be afraid of your own emotions. In the course of living, you've experienced hate, love, joy, anger, success, disappointment, fulfillment and heartache. Strip away any inhibitors and screens you've developed to protect yourself from those who don't understand you, and let your feelings pour out on the page.

THE CHARACTER'S EMOTIONS

Stories are about people. They tell the stories of the characters that fill them. They describe who the characters are, where they go, what they do, who they encounter. But most important, stories portray *why* characters behave in certain ways, and *why* always arises from emotion.

Suppose your character gets shoved while walking down the sidewalk. Will he beg pardon, swear but hurry on, shove back, or pull a knife? His reaction will come from his unique emotional state, whether he's frightened, harassed, or angry, whether he views himself as a victim or a fighter. Obviously, the better you know your characters the more surely you'll give them the right emotional reaction.

Unlike real life, where human beings often act irrationally, story people must behave with a certain consistency. You can't have your young heroine be naive one moment

KATHY JACOBSON *has three novels in print, two under pseudonyms:* Blue Skies and Promises, *by Kate Logan, and* Home Ties, *by Kara Larkin. She is currently working on another book for* Silhouette *and has taught novel writing since 1991.*

and seductive the next. If she's shy and innocent, she'll be horrified by violence and profanity. On the other hand, if she's street-wise and cynical, she won't be looking at the world through rose-colored glasses. Her behavior will be believable because it will match her emotional reactions.

READER IDENTIFICATION

Readers like books to carry them into the unknown. They like characters who are unusual, who open new arenas for them, who introduce them to situations they might never personally experience. This means as writers we have unlimited opportunities to explore new worlds. But we must also give readers something they can relate to, something that will form a bridge between the familiar and the unknown. Emotion will *always* create such a bridge.

WHEN THE TRIANGLE DOESN'T WORK

Okay, so you're passionate about your story, your character's emotions are well-motivated, and you believe any reader who picks up your book will be entranced by it. Then you give your manuscript to a friend (or your spouse or your mother) who returns it with an enthusiastic, "What a nice little story." Or worse, "Well, you know I don't really like romances, but this one seemed okay." Or more obtuse, "You really made me see the setting." Or you might be lucky enough to have a reader with guts enough to say, "You've got some good stuff here, but something's missing. I just don't know what it is."

When this happens, it is most often the second part of the triangle—the character's emotional response—that you'll need to shore up. So let's see how you can build your character's emotions into a strong connecting link between you, the writer, and your reader.

CONVEYING THE CHARACTER'S EMOTIONS

Your first challenge is deciding what the character feels. If you were to identify the character's primary driving emotion, what word would you use? Is he angry, eager, curious, hurt, happy, depressed? Try to find *one* adjective that best fits his emotional state, then identify how that one emotion defines his character.

If he's angry, how does he express that anger? Does he wear it like armor to deflect all attackers (real or imaginary)? Does he keep it locked tightly inside, like a bomb ready to explode? Or does he use it as a weapon, coldly and with firm purpose to get what he wants.

If he's eager, does this make him confident, aggressive, responsive to others, indifferent to roadblocks?

If he's hurt, does he keep a running total of insults and slights, letting them become the entire focus of his life? Or is he hunting for a cure, moving from psychiatrists to self-help books, to love relationships, to drugs, always hoping for something outside himself to solve his problem?

As you can see, the primary driving emotion gives you a cornerstone, and developing an emotional profile becomes your foundation. Once you have this foundation firmly in your mind, build the emotional framework by considering the following:

1. Identify your character's worst fault.

To help you pinpoint the characteristic that will serve you best in looking for such a weakness, look to the end of your story. What insecurity, blind spot, failing, or fear will propel your character into the final crisis or black moment? He'll need to be working from some expectation or agenda that keeps him from resolving his problem until circumstances force him into it. What inner failing drives that expectation or agenda? What keeps him from making the choices that would have prevented the crisis?

Depending on the type of story you're writing, you may have to present the worst fault in a way that keeps the character likeable. For instance, in a romance, you can't allow your heroine to come across as a whiner or have your hero still needing to prove himself to his father. But don't short-change your characters by choosing tepid weaknesses. Remember, the harder the struggle, the more emotion you can build.

2. Recognize your character's greatest strength.

What sets your character apart from the crowd? What inner emotional resource does your hero have that he can call on or discover to help him conquer in the end? Again, look to the final crisis of the story and consider what it will take for him to win. Just as you've given your character a fault to propel him into the black moment, give him a positive trait that will provide him with the power to overcome both his opponent and his own weaknesses.

3. Give your characters specific, urgent goals.

What the characters want must be strong enough to drive them to get it against all complications, all adversity, any danger and often in spite of their better judgment. Does your character want anything that intensely?

Don't skimp. Make the goals important. Make them believeable, and make sure they'll have emotional impact for the reader. If the character's long-range goal is to find happiness or inner peace, you'll have to give him a dramatic, difficult history that will infuse the goal with power through contrast.

No matter how important the goal is, it has to be urgent in order to have emotional force. Put pressure on the character's ability to achieve the goal. Make it a race—against time, an enemy, his own mental stability, financial security, danger, another's choices, etc.—to keep the tension high.

4. Consider how your character will react in various situations.

Is he likely to become insecure or belligerent when threatened? How does he react to generosity? When he's angry, does he erupt or hold it in? How can you tell if he's bored? Excited? Frustrated? Annoyed? What mannerisms does he adopt? What physical manifestations will his body exhibit?

Make sure his reactions are consistent. The reader will believe a character who trembles with anger, fidgets when bored and cries for victims *if* you've shown that he wears his emotions on his sleeve. If he's built an emotional shell around himself so his eyes never fill with tears and he never raises his voice, we can believe he'd kill the man who raped his daughter *if* you show that by holding his emotions in, they've reached fever pitch.

5. Give the character an inner conflict.

Why is the character insecure, unhappy, angry, afraid or frustrated? What motivates him to act? Will he fight or flee? Why? Can you force him into a situation (the conflict of your story) in which he must act against his true nature? If he's a fighter, what would it take to make him run? If he'd normally take flight, what circumstances would make him stand his ground?

6. Integrate your character well.

Since good fiction depends on good conflict, you want to build conflict wherever possible. But even when your fighter must flee, you have to make him self-consistent. You have to motivate the conflicts within your character as well as without, so make sure his goals reflect his personality and his strengths don't preclude his weaknesses. Make him as complex as you want, but be sure his personality reflects his background and motivations.

CONNECTING WITH THE READER

Once you know how the character will react, you have to present the emotions behind the reactions in a way that makes the reader *feel* what the character feels. You can do this in a number of ways, and showing is better than telling.

Some verbs always tell and never show—especially any form of *to be* or *to feel*. For example, if you write, *Mark was bitter*, or *Mark felt bitter*, you're telling. If you write, *Mark crumpled the letter from his father, vowing never to return home again*, you've given him two specific actions that *show* his emotion and help the reader *feel* Mark's bitterness.

Use verbs that connote emotion rather than merely describe action. For instance, strode, paced, ambled, marched, strolled, and tromped are all better than walked. In order, they convey purpose, anxiety, contentment, anger, leisure, and duty, while walked only shows movement.

Use adjectives that indicate the character's emotional interpretation. A room can be dingy, sterile, homey, oppressive, crowded, busy, inviting, silent, tacky, impressive, or intimidating, depending on who's looking at it. Be sure to choose adjectives that reflect the character's view and not your own, since the emotional bridge you want to build is between the *character* and the reader.

WATCH YOUR POINT OF VIEW

Recognize that the character is a stronger narrator than the author. Any time you start describing the action rather than letting the character experience it, you're distancing the character from the reader. This will cost you both immediacy and emotion. Look at this example in which an omniscient narrator describes Mark's situation:

> Mark's father had always ordered him around, and this letter was just another good example. Mark read it again and again, and bitterness grew acrid inside him. The daughter of one of his dad's old cronies would be visiting next week, and Mark was instructed to come home and meet her. Crumpling the letter, he decided the time had come to make a break.

Now look at it from Mark's point of view:

> Mark crumpled his father's letter and lobbed it into the garbage can. After two years, the old man still didn't get it. Mark made his own decisions now. He chose his own girlfriends. He sure as hell didn't rush home to meet the daughter of one of his dad's old cronies.

Can you see the difference in these two examples? Although both are well written, one pulls the reader tighter into the character's point of view and therefore his emotional state. Where the first describes the emotion, the second lets the character experience it.

APPLY THE EMOTIONAL FILTER

Everything in your story will have greater impact if you have your character interpret it emotionally. Involve the five senses to give your writing strong sensory texture, then make sure you convey your character's emotional assessment of what she experiences.

For example, on assignment for the Star System Regulatory Agency, Lily lands on a planet she's never visited before. She's going to notice the color of the sky, the bleakness of the landscape, the odor of the air, and the flavor of the water, but her impressions are going to be more important than the details in drawing your reader into the scene. Let's see a simple description first:

> Lily stepped through the Theta Gate and took in the scene before her. Humanoids from a dozen planets mingled with multi-pods, avians, and the local Zerips. Pink clouds floated across the red sky. The air had a distinctly chlorine odor, and a few leafless trees lined the main route into the city.

Now let's run the scene through Lily's emotional filter and see how much richer it becomes:

> Lily stepped through the Theta Gate and wrinkled her nose in distaste. Humanoids from a dozen planets mingled with multi-pods, avians and the local Zerips, but only the Zerips looked at home under the hideous red sky. She tried to filter enough oxygen out of chlorine-heavy air to satisfy her lungs, but gave up after a few breaths. The air mix wouldn't kill her, although it didn't seem to do much for the few leafless trees that lined the main route into the city.

As a rule of thumb, if your character doesn't care enough about what she sees, hears, tastes, touches and smells to give some emotional assessment to it, the reader won't care either. And this applies to everything—action, dialogue, description and other characters. Here's an example of an exchange between two characters:

> Angie watched Hugh stride between the rows of computer terminals. He didn't glance at any of the data operators, but kept his eyes fixed on her. When he reached her desk, he smiled.
> "We brought Williams in last night," he said.
> She pressed her palms flat against her thighs. "Did he confess?"
> "Not in so many words." Hugh lifted his hand and examined his nails. When he spoke again, his eyes were serious. "He said Charlotte Mason was having an affair with Johnny Keno."
> Angie let the information sink in.

We have dialogue and action, but no emotion. We don't know Angie's opinion of Hugh, or his of her. We have no hint of whether she's glad or sorry to hear the news about Williams, or what effect the information about Charlotte has on her. To give your work more potency, run it through your focal character's emotional filter. Keep the reader constantly connected to the character by giving the character opinions and judgments. Let's look at the previous exchange again, this time with Angie's emotion filter in place.

> With her heart beating double time, Angie watched Hugh stride between the rows of computer terminals. Until yesterday, just being in his presence had sent her heart racing. Today, she feared what he would tell her.
> He didn't glance at any of the data operators, but kept his eyes fixed on her. When he reached her desk, he smiled. "We brought Williams in last night."
> Max Williams knew everything, but how much would he tell? Angie cleared

her throat, hoping no trace of her fear would show in her voice. "Did he confess?"

"Not in so many words." Hugh lifted his hand to examine his nails and let the suspense build.

Suddenly she saw his hand in the whole sordid affair. He'd seduced her for what he could get from her, and now he toyed with her like a cat who'd cornered a mouse. She pressed her palms flat on her thighs to keep from wringing her hands together.

When Hugh spoke again, his eyes were hard. "He said Charlotte Mason was having an affair with Johnny Keno."

The words flowed through Angie's mind and pooled near her heart like congealing tar. So Charlotte had been in on it all along.

Notice in the second version that Angie interprets her own reactions for the reader *and* conveys hints on Hugh's agenda. Since you don't want to go into Hugh's mind while in Angie's point of view, she has to transmit his behavior. Since she can't know what's going on in his head, she has to interpret it based on her own assumptions, which means we see him through her emotional filter.

OPINIONS AND JUDGMENTS

The emotional filter is always subjective. It presents your focal character's view of your story world, the situation, the other characters and the conflicts. By attaching his opinions to his observations and having him make judgments on everyone else's behavior, he not only becomes a stronger character, but your reader will form a stronger emotional bond with him.

Every once in a while you may find yourself writing a scene through the eyes of your villain or some other unsympathetic character. Be sure to make his filter true to him. Present his warped view in the living color of his hang ups and destructive agenda. If you do this well, the reader will love reading about him because he will be so compellingly *un*likeable.

If you find it difficult to include the subtleties of an emotional filter while writing your first draft, don't self-edit during the creative process. Write your dialogue or your action and add opinions and judgments on the second—or third—time through. Invest heavily where you have the most control (your own effort and emotion), and reap the benefits when the reader connects emotionally to your characters and loves your story.

Where's the Story?

BY TIM PARRISH

Good question. Wish I had an easy answer. Maybe the best place to start is to talk about *what* story is. The idea of story that I'm interested in grows from a reader who says, "Okay, the piece is well-written, but where's the story?" This reader is most likely referring to what Michael Curtis, fiction editor of the *Atlantic Monthly*, has called "narrative purpose."

In its most basic sense, story or narrative purpose means that the writing has a beginning, a middle and an end. The writer sets events in motion through the agent of conflict, these events complicate (or, as I say, "complexify"), the events reach a climax or crisis, then they are resolved. Easy to say. Harder to do.

Several models (such as Freitag's Pyramid and the inverted check mark) describe this notion of story and include the element of tension that rises until it reaches a point at which there must be a release. A simple example: A man gets lost in the Arctic and needs to build a fire to survive. He has only one match. He struggles to find the necessary kindling and firewood. Finally, wood prepared, he strikes the match. Snow falls from the tree above him and extinguishes the match. Story ends. Man is doomed.

You might recognize this as a bastardized version of Jack London's "To Build a Fire." In my overly-simplified version, the external conflict is that the man is freezing to death. His internal conflict is the stress that this possibility causes. The tension rises as conditions grow worse and the man weakens as he searches for firewood. Tension reaches a crisis point when he strikes the match and snow falls on it. The story is resolved because we know that the man will die. There is no need to show anything more. The writing has story because all events are related to the man's central conflict and because that central conflict is resolved. I offer this example not as a model to follow, but as one to illustrate story in its basic form.

Here's a somewhat more complex example culled from one of my stories (like London's story, mine is ironic, but I'm not going to deal with that aspect). The river is rising. The narrator's marriage is in a rut. The river keeps rising. The narrator and his wife develop a morbid fascination with the river. The river threatens to change course. The narrator and his wife start having better sex. The river is definitely going to change course. The narrator and his wife have great sex. The river changes course while the narrator and his wife watch, their excitement and connection to one another at a peak. The river leaves their town on a stinky lake, a serious let-down, but at least the narrator and his wife have the memory of the excitement to sustain them.

This example contains both an external conflict (river rising) and an internal conflict (emotional doldrums) which are related because of the narrator's perception of, and reaction to, what's happening around him. These conflicts complicate when the possibility of the river changing course becomes real, and the narrator begins to search for meaning in the relationship between what's happening to the river and to his marriage.

TIM PARRISH'S *fiction has appeared numerous places, including* Shenandoah, Black Warrior Review *and in the anthology* Walking on Water. *He is writing a novel titled* Scabs, *set in south Louisiana. He teaches at Southern Connecticut State University.*

The conflicts climax both literally and figuratively when the river breaks free from its previous course. The conflicts are resolved through the narrator's attempt to come to terms with the aftermath. This narrative might be said to have story because all of the elements (character, plot, setting, style/voice, point of view) combine to create a discovery for both the reader and the characters. Furthermore, the external world connects with the characters' internal world. Everything that happens in the story functions to reveal character and to resolve conflict.

Story, then, might be defined as a series of casually-related events (plot) that propel characters through some conflict or disconnection and that also lead the characters to an emotional/psychological resolution, or ironic irresolution. Events in a story must have significance, meaning an incident (or series of incidents) which does not reveal character or create and resolve tension is not a story; it is simply an incident.

GIVE YOUR CHARACTER A PROBLEM

So, then, how do you do it? Make story? A simple way is to give a character a problem, preferably an internal conflict that can be manifested, or mirrored, externally. Let's examine a first story from an introduction-to-fiction-writing student of mine at Southern Connecticut State University and see what he does. In this story the narrator is a young, mildly-retarded man named Charlie who works in a drug store as a janitor. Already the story has tension in that the young man's perception of events will probably be less acute than the reader's (this, however, also holds the pitfall that the story could be sentimental, cute and/or condescending). The situation entails internal conflict because the young man is very aware that he is not in the mainstream of adult society, an awareness intensified by his attraction to a woman named Angela, who comes in with her thuggish, smart-aleck boyfriend to have her prescription filled and who flirts with Charlie in a manner which we see to be condescending but which only intensifies Charlie's fascination with her. All of this is established on the first page, where Angela enters the store while Charlie is sweeping. Charlie's description of events (what he perceives), the other characters' actions (what they say and do) and Charlie's own actions and reactions reveal these conflicts.

LET EXTERNAL EVENTS COMPLICATE THE PROBLEM

The first external conflict occurs when Charlie discovers Angela's dropped lipstick and slips it into his pocket. His decision to keep the lipstick in his pocket and not tell Angela that he has it is a lie of omission and a complication which promises consequences and significance. External action (the dropping of the lipstick) has intensified Charlie's internal conflict (he has a tangible connection to his object of desire) and offers a means by which to further reveal Charlie.

At home, Charlie obsesses over the lipstick, which has a strand of hair stuck to it and which holds the imprint of Angela's lips (Whoo whoo!). He imagines Angela's beauty and tells his little sister that the lipstick is a "magic stick." And, yes, Charlie does put the lipstick on his own lips. Charlie is revealed as a man with adult desires, an active imagination and, in his dealings with his little sister, as a person with a kind, non-threatening heart (he is generous and playful with her).

The following week Angela arrives at the store, looking haggard and tense and not as pretty to Charlie as before. She pays no attention to Charlie as she hurries to fill her prescription. Charlie hears her voice raised and eases closer to find that her prescription has been cancelled (we, unlike Charlie, understand that Angela's scrip is a forgery; i.e. dramatic irony). When Angela storms out of the store, Charlie follows her. Angela sees him and calls him over to her car to tell him that if he'll get the pills she needs from behind the counter, he can come to her house and "do whatever he wants." Complication and plot. Charlie tells her he can't steal the pills because he might lose his job, but seeing that she looks worse for wear than before, he pulls the lipstick from his pocket and offers it to her. She accuses him of having stolen it, clearly gaining leverage over him. A major complication. She tells him that if he doesn't steal the pills, then she will tell his boss that he is a thief. Charlie reluctantly agrees to get the pills, reluctantly because of practical reasons (he wants to keep his job) not ethical ones (it doesn't worry him that he was going to keep the lipstick). He believes that Angela's earlier offer to come to her house still stands. Charlie is seen to be not an innocent, but rather a man driven by fear and desire, a man who wants to both keep his job and make real the fantasy that he has been cultivating.

Charlie steals the pills for her, and she tells him that she will be back soon for more. As the story ends, Charlie believes that he is strong in that he has kept his job and will perhaps be able to go to Angela's house. The ending implies further action (most likely two huge disappointments for Charlie), but the story is resolved because all of the major character elements and the main plot points have come to fruition. (Plot points: Charlie likes Angela; Charlie pockets lipstick; Charlie puts on lipstick; Angela is refused drugs she needs; Angela bribes Charlie for drugs; Charlie produces lipstick; Angela blackmails Charlie; Charlie steals pills.) Character leads to conflict, action and psychology lead to plot and further complication results in resolution. External actions reveal and resolve internal conflicts. Every element that is established pays off. This narrative has story. This narrative *is* a story.

ONLY INCLUDE ELEMENTS THAT CONTRIBUTE TO "STORY"

Let's suppose, though, that the narrative ended when Charlie pocketed the lipstick. Would *this* be a story? Would it *have* story? Charlie's attraction to Angela is probably what causes him to keep the lipstick, so we get a glimpse into Charlie's desire. Charlie's retardation causes Angela's idiotic boyfriend to verbally abuse Charlie, so we see that Charlie is somewhat defenseless in a sometimes uncaring world. Still, these things are mostly incidental because Charlie remains under-developed, the plot never really begins and nothing is complicated. In other words, let's ask what purpose certain elements have in this truncated version of the narrative.

First, why set the shorter story in a drugstore? Angela can drop her lipstick anywhere because her need for drugs is no longer part of the plot. And wouldn't it be more informative in our one-scene story if Charlie *placed* himself somewhere to watch her everyday, hoping that she would drop something, and thereby revealing his alienation and obsession. Why a hoodlum boyfriend? We don't need to know that Angela herself is a tough woman who comes in regularly for drugs because there is no plot necessity to make her a character whose need would lead her to lies and coercion. Why a lipstick? In the shorter story, Charlie simply finds it and puts it in his pocket. There's no need for it to be an object which has intimately touched Angela and which Charlie can likewise intimately touch. Why not an ATM deposit slip? Charlie could get a glimpse into Angela's bank account and find out if he, as a poorly paid drugstore worker, has a chance to move in on Angela. Okay, I'm being ridiculous, but you see my point. In the first scene of the longer story, the writer is setting up character traits that will be developed as well as providing a setting that will further plot. That said, the argument can be made, as I did earlier, that the first scene (or shorter version) does comprise a story, just not a very rich or complex or revealing one. In good stories everything counts.

MAKE EACH SENTENCE PROVIDE SOMETHING NEW

Another way to describe story might be as narrative movement in which all elements come to fruition or "add up." Movement is also a type of tension but not necessarily dynamic in a physical sense. Movement means that each sentence must provide something new. The writer must create in the reader a need to discover, to further understand, to desire what comes next. Stasis does not produce story (Andy Warhol's *Empire* makes this point).

A photograph might be said to tell a story, but you'll probably find that the story a photograph is telling you is the story you're creating by extrapolating from the details of a single moment. Of course, there are stories in which nothing physical happens, no characters change and/or no external action takes place (Sandra Cisnero's short short "A House of My Own" taken in isolation covers all three of these), but even in those, there is movement in that each sentence builds on the one before to reveal character and engage the reader.

Ideally, the whole leads to something greater than the parts. This result seems to be one of those you'll-know-it-when-you-see-it kinds of things, and I daresay every reader has experienced it, a moment in which you set down a book, shake your head and say, "Wow." All elements of story should create an organic whole. Words should build to more than paragraphs and pages; they should build to insight and meaning.

FINDING *YOUR* "STORY"

So, where's the story? The other way of looking at this question is, "Where's *my* story, the story *I* have to tell, the story *I* need to tell?" My answer is wherever you find it. It could be in one of those "elements of fiction"—point of view, tone, plot—or in an event you've witnessed or experienced, in a voice you've heard or used, in a feeling, or more likely, in some combination of these.

For me, story derives mostly from character and place, in particular from middle and working-class people from the hard-edged yet surreal industrial landscape of southeastern Louisiana, characters struggling to survive vocationally and morally in a racially and culturally charged setting.

For you, story might come from the mystery genre that sends you to your dreams each night, or from the moment you first saw your mother as a separate person. Maybe you'll discover your story only after you've written for 20 years and then, unexpectedly, you'll write a sentence that points to a vision that you could never have pre-conceived or mechanically created through the methods I've provided above. Fiction writing, although mosty hard work, still contains some element of the mysterious and, yeah, the mystical. At least something beyond the conscious.

Finally, let's face it, after a certain level of competence and even vision, what story is comes down to personal esthetic. And if you're interested in publishing, you have to suit certain expectations of the editor you're trying to win over. Disheartening? Ultimately no. You might not make the big money you dream of making, but perhaps you'll be writing a story that only you are qualified to write and that only a particular editor and audience are suited to appreciate. Yes, it's true, the house of fiction has many rooms. If yours happens to be a small one in the attic, well, it's better than living in the yard.

How to Set Up (and Stick to) a Writing Schedule

BY JACK M. BICKHAM

Some writers seem to have little or no trouble setting up a realistic schedule for writing, or for sticking to it on a regular, productive basis. If you're young and compulsive, as many of us were when we started, you may have no difficulty. If you're established and selling your work at a great rate, then confidence and the expectation of another paycheck may keep you going steadily, too.

But many writers with great talent are neither young and driven, nor yet earning enough money with their work to make a regular writing schedule easy. If you happen to be one of these, how do you get yourself set up so you produce more work, and seldom if ever look up with horror to realize a week—or longer—has passed with no new pages produced?

ATTITUDE

There are a few tricks that can help. But more important than any specific work habit or technique is the bedrock attitude necessary for maintaining steady, reliable work over long periods of time. That attitude is one of confidence and expectation. As a teacher of writing as well as a practicing novelist, I have seen this proven time and again.

Once not long ago I was working in a class with a woman of great creative talent. She wrote beautifully, her characters and plots were excellent, and every page she turned in was a gem. That was the good news. The bad news was that many weeks she came in with no pages at all.

"I just couldn't get going this week," she would sigh. Or: "I couldn't find time." Or: "Nothing would come to me."

We talked about it and tried different "get started" techniques. Nothing seemed to work.

Then one night she came to class with about 40 pages of wonderful new copy. I asked how she had managed to maintain such a work schedule all week long.

"In last week's Wednesday night class," she told me, "you said something—I'm not even sure I remember exactly what it was—that made things click for me. Suddenly I felt I really understood how to put a story together.

"I drove all the way home—more than 40 miles—banging my fist on the steering wheel and saying over and over again, 'I can *do* this! I can *do* this!' And the next morning I got up early and just started my schedule filled with happiness and certainty."

She had found *confidence* that the work she was doing was good—or could be revised and made good. She had at the same time been filled with *expectation* that her

JACK M. BICKHAM'S *novels include thrillers, mysteries and westerns. He is also the author of* Writing and Selling Your Novel, Scene & Structure, The 38 Most Common Fiction Writing Mistakes (And How to Avoid Them), Setting *and* Writing the Short Story. *He lives in Norman, Oklahoma.*

work would be accepted and pay off for her. Gone were self-doubts, second-guessing, worry about mistakes, fear of rejection, memory of past failures, and everything else of a negative nature. She had learned to plunge in and *do the work*, sure at last that everything else would take care of itself if she would just allow it to happen.

A ZEN KIND OF THING

Zen devotees in sports, for example, never say they "shoot the arrow" or "aim for the hoop." They speak of finding some kind of interior mental zone in which the arrow shoots itself, or the ball seems to launch itself toward the basket. They have practiced, they have found the kind of internal serenity that can only come from *trust in the process*, and so they grow and work regularly, on schedule, productively, without fear or other negatives that can bind up the very soul and make good work impossible no matter how hard one tries.

So it is that the first step toward setting up a regular work schedule, and then following it, is the development of a positive, trusting, even serene attitude that says, "The past is behind me, the future will be; today I will believe and do the work." This attitude is absolutely essential.

EXERCISES

A few simple mental exercises will help in developing a positive, productive attitude. Every day, several times:

1. Find a few quiet moments, close your eyes, and imagine the success your current writing project is going to be: how well-worded, how clear and moving, how well-received. Concentrate on the feeling of bliss you will experience when this success has taken place, how confident you will be.

2. Close your eyes, breathe slowly, and see yourself at your word processor, fully concentrated on your task, typing without hesitation or concern, joyful in the job itself and how well it is going.

3. With your eyes closed, relax and think back to the best paragraph or the best page you ever wrote, and how wonderful you felt. Remember that you can have many more such experiences in the future—and you will.

4. Think of tomorrow with glad anticipation. Be thankful you will have time to work, and you will work because it's a gift of God, being allowed to do work like this that you love.

5. Every time a negative thought, a fear, a self-criticism, or some bad experience from your past writing occurs to you, jot it down on a slip of paper in as few words as possible—*very* few. Then crumple the piece of paper and throw it in the trash, or even burn it in the fireplace, because now that past bad element has been banished forever.

6. At least once a day, close your eyes and whisper to yourself, "I can do this. I am doing this. It will be all right."

Within an amazingly short time—a day or two, perhaps, or a week at the most—you will find your entire attitude toward your work schedule changing. You will find yourself eager to work, and happy.

Continue the mental exercises, and develop others of your own. Be alert for other patterns of thinking or activities that help maintain a confident, productive work schedule. Many find a morning or evening walk is a tremendous stimulus to the kind of relaxed, idle thinking that lets the unconscious mind play—and provide new ideas. Others find similar inspiration in regularly watching the sunset, or in listening to quiet music alone, or in traditional prayer. Remember that development and maintenance of a calm, accepting, trusting attitude toward your work is a lifelong job, and one never to be taken for granted.

GET INTO A ROUTINE

In addition to this bedrock approach to maintaining an attitude that will help you set up and stay on schedule, here are some general observations about the work routine that successful writers never forget.

1. Set a realistic daily production quota.

This quota should be in desired number of words or pages aimed at as the regular daily goal. For one writer it might be ten or more pages of printed-out copy—3,000 words or more. For another who works at a slower pace, 1,000 words might be more sensible. The goal should be chosen with realism in mind: This is a wordage total the writer will force herself to produce day after day, at least five days every week. It does no good to set a goal impossibly high, then get discouraged and fall back to writing nothing again. Neither does it do much good to set a goal of, say, 75 words a day when that total can be ripped off inside 15 minutes. Taking into account available time, fatigue factors, personal writing speed and likely regular interruptions, the goal should be set, tried for a few days, readjusted if necessary, and then given the highest priority in the writer's life.

It should be noted, too, that this is a *production* goal, not a time period. It's far too easy to say you'll write three hours a day, then find yourself day-dreaming those three hours away and finding nothing in the "out" box. The writer with a production quota works. The writer with a time quota too often stares at the wall. (Knowing you have to produce, say, six pages before you let yourself get out of the chair in front of the computer is a powerful incentive to *work*!)

2. Any words produced on paper are better than none at all.

It's easy to promise to meet a daily production goal, but sometimes even easier to get hung up trying to find the right word or phrase, second-guessing some previous day's writing decision, or worrying if today's work is really quite "good enough." Professionals realize that good work is not merely written but re-written, often more than once. They further realize that some revision is inevitable no matter how grand this first draft may be. Therefore, they seldom allow themselves to get hung up on minor technicalities; they *produce their pages.* Errors can always be fixed later. Once something is printed out, the writer has something with which to work; until first-draft pages are in the box, the writer has nothing but expectations.

Some days a writer will produce her quota of pages and feel she has done wonderful work. Other days the production may be drudgery, and the pages may feel flat and insipid. But if she is a professional, she will produce the pages regardless. If the "bad day pages" really are bad, she will find a way to fix them later. Chances are, however, that a month from now she'll look back at her mounting stack of pages and be unable to figure out which pages were supposed to be so bad. That's because every writer writes up to a certain general level of ability, and the "good" days and "bad" days are more a reflection of the writer's subjective feelings about life in general on a given day, or on her generalized mood, than they are on the actual quality of what she may be typing at the moment.

3. The carrot and stick method helps.

A daily quota should be set, as noted above, for five days a week. The writer who sets a daily quota of four pages a day, for example, obviously will have a *weekly* quota of 20 pages. If a day comes along when the quota is missed, then the writer should strive for the discipline to work either Saturday or Sunday—or both—to make up for lost pages during the scheduled five-day work week.

Some who begin such a disciplined schedule find themselves working a lot on weekends at first because they failed to make their quota one or more weekdays. But it doesn't take long for the self-imposed carrot-and-stick methodology to kick in: "If I get my pages done Monday through Friday," the writer suddenly realizes, "I get the weekend off." Amazingly, this kind of disciplined self-motivation works.

4. A small daily quota is preferable to a larger sporadic one.

Here's what is meant: The writer's imagination thrives on continuing contact with the project at hand. It's far better to do two pages a day, five days a week, than to schedule *no* work during the week, then a 15-page orgy over the weekend.

Why? Because the imagination and the unconscious mind don't know regular working hours. If the writer pounds away on a regular schedule, day after day, the imagination and unconscious will tend to become preoccupied with the work even during times when the writer is thinking consciously about something else entirely, or even while she is sleeping. But the sporadic writer—one who tries to "turn it on" and then "turn it off" again once a week or so—is not devoting enough continuous attention to the project; the imagination and unconscious do not become preoccupied, and will not cooperate so well with fresh, unexpected ideas or new enthusiasm.

This is a point nonwriters find very difficult to understand, but professionals understand instantly. A writer working diligently and very regularly on a project will find that ordinary events in the nonworking day often begin to *assume relevance to the project* in surprising ways: A chance encounter on the street may suggest a nuance of character to a writer who is struggling daily with a character in a story, whereas the weekend writer might not even notice the real person; or a chance remark made by someone may kick off an entirely new line of story- or article-thinking to the writer deeply involved on a daily basis. Nothing aids the imagination and creativity like sustained daily effort on the project.

5. The writing of even a single page every day will produce the first draft of a novel in one year's time.

Thinking about the book, worrying about lack of time, or postponing the work until tomorrow will produce—nothing.

TRICKS AND TECHNIQUES

A few other homespun tricks and techniques can help a writer set up and maintain a solid, functional working schedule. Some of these sound so simple that new writers might ignore or forget them. Yet, as basic as these aspects may be, in their totality they can make regular, sustained production of saleable copy more satisfying and surefire. It's worthwhile to consider each of them and do a bit of self-examination—whether each production-enhancer is being used to the maximum degree.

I. Have a regular writing place.

Among my acquaintances are writers who work at the office of their regular employer early in the morning or late at night, after company hours; another writes on a notebook in a café during lunch hour; another has a sacrosanct private office away from home; still others work in a private office room in the home. Every writer's chosen spot will be dictated to some degree by other circumstances in his life. But such a spot should be chosen and used as much as possible. Somehow, walking into a particular room and sitting down in a particular chair help signal the imagination that "work time" is now at hand. The physical act of entering a familiar room, the place where the schedule is regularly met, facilitates getting started right away on that work.

2. Have a regular starting time for daily work.

Some writers do their best very early in the morning, others very late at night, others in the middle of the day. There is no pattern that's best for everyone. But as with a special place to work, having a usual, habitual starting time for work is helpful in maintaining creativity and momentum.

Life situations may change, and a writer's available starting time may have to change with it. The attorney with a usual 8-to-5 day at the office may have established a writing time of 10 p.m. to midnight, for example.

But if a big case suddenly requires her to work nights for several weeks or months, there is no reason why she can't readjust her writing time to start at a very early hour, instead of late at night when other duties intrude.

The point here is that the regular work period shoud *not* be allowed to jump around every day for no reason. But if life changes require readjustments, that's not a disaster as long as a new, regular time is chosen.

It should be noted, too, that the term "starting time" was used in defining a work schedule. If the writer is adhering stringently to a production quota, there's no sure way to predict the *duration* of a given work session: Some days it may be an hour or two, other days it might be twice as long.

3. Work in the way that's most comfortable.

Your precise writing methodology doesn't matter. Most writers today compose at the keyboard of a computer. But there are plenty still out there who labor at a typewriter, and a few who compose first drafts in longhand. Production is the key, not fancy equipment. No one ever miraculously improved her production just by getting a fancy new machine or posture chair.

4. Demand respect for your dedication.

It may be difficult at times, but family and friends can be taught to respect your working time. That routine household or office question can be held until you're through the day's quota; if there's no one else to answer the telephone, the answering machine can get it, or it can just ring unanswered, or a friend can be told, "I'm sorry, I really want to talk with you, but right now I'm at work." Good friends—and good family—can be taught to understand this, and will admire you for your commitment.

5. When you're not at work, be good to yourself.

Healthy exercise makes the hours at the keyboard seem less laborious. Reading a good book, listening to music, working in the garden or simple meditation can be refreshing too. Having a professional writing schedule—and sticking to it—does not mean becoming a dour drudge.

It seems so simple, doesn't it? And it can be. For, if you tried to summarize these observations and tips about how professional writers set up and maintain a regular writing schedule, you might come up with a few words, very old ones, that apply in other phases of life, too. They are: faith, serenity, determination, discipline and tenacity. With these, everything else will follow.

David Guterson: On Writing an Award-Winning Novel

BY JACK HEFFRON

Bestselling first novels are supposed to bring fame, fortune and a fast-lane lifestyle to their young authors. In true Fitzgeraldian style, said author sips buckets of champagne, snags a trendy place on the Upper West Side, and tosses glib *bon mots* at an adoring and envious public. David Guterson, author of the wildly successful *Snow Falling on Cedars*, doesn't act much like the stereotype. He has the movie deal, the chubby royalty checks and the adoring public, but purposely avoids the glamour.

He still lives on tiny, somewhat primitive Bainbridge Island in Puget Sound, off the coast of Washington, where he has lived for the past 15 years. During this interview, thanks to a squall blowing through the Sound, the phone went dead three times. Between thoughtful responses and frequent disconnections, he made lasagna for his children, and like many a parent, had a heck of a time getting them to come downstairs to eat.

Born and raised in Seattle, Guterson moved to the island in the early 1980s and took a job teaching English at the high school. He wrote and published a number of short stories, and began a novel, which he wrote, on and off, for nearly a decade before submitting it to publishers. Set in the mid-1950s on an island in the Pacific Northwest, *Snow Falling on Cedars* concerns a murder trial in which a Japanese fisherman is accused of killing a popular Anglo fisherman. The wounds opened on both sides by World War II have yet to heal, so the island community must confront larger issues of forgiveness, human responsibility, and racial prejudice. The novel explores its themes with depth and candor, and yet it's also a page-turner—a combination that accounts for its astonishing success.

Since its publication in 1994, *Snow Falling on Cedars*, and its young author, have won numerous prizes and honors: the PEN/Faulkner, the ABBY, the Pacific Northwest Booksellers Award, and the Barnes & Noble Discover Great New Writers Award, to mention only the larger ones. Guterson also was chosen as one of *Granta* magazine's 20 best young writers in America. Heady stuff for a writer who had previously published only a collection of short stories (*The Country Ahead of Us, the Country Behind*), which did not sell well, and a nonfiction book titled *Family Matters: Why Home Schooling Makes Sense*.

Even as *Snow Falling on Cedars* remains on the bestseller lists, Guterson is anxious to settle back into his old quiet life. The success of the novel has allowed him to quit teaching and write fulltime, but otherwise the life of the rising young author is the same as before.

How did you get started in writing?

I was a college junior and I had never even considered writing—as a hobby or a career or anything. I didn't have any idea what I wanted to do. I was just randomly taking

JACK HEFFRON *is acquiring editor of Writer's Digest Books, Betterway Books and senior editor of Story Press. His short stories have appeared in literary magazines, including* Beloit Fiction Journal, The Chariton Review, North American Review *and* TriQuarterly.

Photo by Jill Sabella

college classes. And I took a beginning short story writing class, and almost from the first day I knew this was something that I was very interested in. And within two weeks I had become completely serious about it.

Were any writers especially influential?

In Jack Brenner's class [at the University of Washington] and in subsequent classes, we read the conventional anthologies, and I took that seriously and read beyond the anthologies, tried to read collections by all the standards who were offered at the time— Katherine Mansfield, Katherine Ann Porter, Chekhov, du Maupassant, Cheever, Eudora Welty. I read them all and read them extensively. They were all influential.

I read somewhere that Charles Johnson compares you to Raymond Carver. Certainly there's the Northwest connection, but did Carver have any special influence on you?

I went through a stage early on, like a lot of American writers of my era, when I couldn't help being in the shadow of Carver. I became temporarily imitative and derivative of Carver, but I ultimately emerged out of that. I have enormous respect for Carver, but I don't think I have a particular affinity for him stylistically. I think we do share something temperamentally. . . .

In interviews surrounding *Snow Falling on Cedars*, you have mentioned the influence of *To Kill a Mockingbird*.

I taught high school for ten years and read *To Kill a Mockingbird* probably once or twice a year. There were a number of other books that I was reading in the same way, but these books went stale or wore thin, but that book didn't. It continued to absorb me. It grew richer and more complex. I found that my students were always touched by it emotionally and intellectually. I found that their characters were shaped by this book, that it was memorable for them. In that regard, I became cognizant of the potential influence of a well-told story on people's lives. I did consciously aspire in writing *Snow Falling on Cedars* to have that kind of impact.

How much did you write before being published?

I sort of cut my teeth writing short stories, and I guess I wrote them for two or three years before I thought about sending them out. And then I sent them to small literary reviews, and I published something in the University of Washington newspaper and then something in the *Seattle Review*, which was the literary periodical put out by the University of Washington. I just kept writing stories and sending them out in a relentless way. I even kept a chart. So I always had stories going out, and I always had stories coming back. I got everything from form rejections to the phone call to let's make some changes and everything in between.

What gave you the confidence to continue despite all the rejections?

I built confidence in myself through the success I was having on campus. And I had enough positive feedback from places like *Prairie Schooner* and *Iowa Review* that I felt it was worthwhile to keep going. But even if I hadn't had that feedback I would have kept going because I loved doing it. I had enough faith in myself that the letters of rejection seemed to have nothing to do with it. I took such great pleasure in the act itself that I was going to keep doing it no matter what.

I read where you were happy that the story collection was being republished, and, probably much to the consternation of your publicist, you described the stories as "flawed but interesting."

I see all those stories as suggestive of a young writer who was searching for a style and a voice and trying a lot of different things and imitating a lot of different people.

But what flaws specifically were you working hard to overcome?

Most writers are privately insecure and are awestruck that other people take them seriously. I see all kinds of problems with my work all the time. I'm never satisfied. I'm surprised that anybody reads it.

I think you can divide writers into two categories. You've got writers who are very logical, rational, analytical, and they bring those skills to what they do. They write very well-ordered, plotted, and tightly scripted books. And then you've got writers who are very impulsive and creative. They can just gush on to the page. I'm the analytical type. And the other side of it, which is vey important, is more difficult for me. I have to exert myself to make that happen. I think most writers recognize in themselves an affinity for one side or the other, and they have to exert themselves to deal with their weakness. The most accomplished writers, the real geniuses, have a natural gift at both ways. And most of us don't.

You say that in the first collection you were imitating a lot of other writers. Was there a moment or some point at which you recognized your own voice as a writer?

Nothing very dramatic. It's something that happens with maturity. As you emerge out of your twenties and into your thirties, you settle into your identity as an adult, and as that process unfurled, the same thing happened in my writing. It's just a natural development, and I think it coincided with the early drafts of *Snow Falling on Cedars*. In working through and establishing the voice of that book, which was a long struggle over the course of two or three years, I came to a sense of my own manner as a writer.

Any advice on how best to handle one's apprenticeship years?

A lot of people believe that there's some secret inside politics to publishing, and I don't believe that. Worry about the quality of your manuscript and nothing else. Work on the story. Forget about believing you have to know somebody or you have to have an agent or have the right stationery or have to know how to write the proper cover letter. All that stuff is irrelevant. It's the story. The editor on the other end is going to read that first paragraph and either be drawn in or not. And the only thing that really counts is the story you've written.

In *Snow Falling on Cedars* you handle a variety of subjects with great authority. Fishing, growing strawberries, World War II, the Japanese internment. How much research did you do for the book?

The quality of authority that permeates certain novels does come from in-depth knowledge of the subject matter. If you aren't confident that you know your material you can't bring any authority to it. So you do have to do research, and I do a substantial amount of it, partly because I enjoy it and partly because I recognize its necessity. I do a lot of hands-on, experiential research and I do archival research as well.

So you go to strawberry farmers and ask them. . . .

I go pick strawberries. If I need to find out about autopsies, I'll go and watch one, and talk to the coroner and take notes. Whatever it takes.

And those details add such texture to your work. They give it depth. I hear editors complain that too often writers are in such a hurry to get published and to declare a work finished that they don't do those extra revisions that add those extra layers. The work lacks depth and texture.

That sense of being in a hurry is just fatal. It just destroys so many people who are trying to write. There's absolutely no point in putting something out in the world that isn't ready. You're just setting yourself up for failure. I see these people at conferences. They're just desperate to be famous or successful or something, I don't know what it is. They just need it and they need it now. And that's all they want to know. They don't want to know how to write and they're not interested in craft. They're interested in knowing some secret magic trick that will get them famous tomorrow. And it's ridiculous. You're much better off spending ten years on a book instead of two, making sure that the book is right, then take it from there.

How long did you spend writing the novel?

After a few years of living on the island, I started wondering if there was a possibility of a story here. Then I started working on it, and I went through a couple of drafts. The first one was over 200 pages and the other was over a hundred pages. But I reached a dead-end on both. Then I got into a couple hundred pages of a third draft, then stopped altogether and wrote the home-schooling book and got back to it and wrote a couple hundred more pages. And while all of this was going on I was teaching and doing a lot of journalism. It wasn't that all I did was work on the novel for eight or nine years. But it took a long time.

Let's talk about how you write, your work habits and such.

For a long time there was a pretty definable pattern. When I was in college, I would write at night for as long as I could. Two hours, four hours, six hours. When I started teaching, I'd write in the morning before class and on weekends and during the summer.

I'd begin by reading the most recent material from the last few days of writing. I'd try to revise it to where I'd left off and try to add a couple more pages. Then I'd read it all again and revise it, then come back the next day and do it all again. I spend two-thirds of my time revising. Some days all I do is revise.

And you're comfortable with that approach? You don't try to quantify your time, pushing yourself to write a certain number of pages per day?

I don't have a particular number of pages in mind, but I can definitely feel when I'm intellectually exhausted and it's pointless to go on. I just can't stay focused and the work isn't as good.

When you sent out *Snow Falling on Cedars*, you were an unknown. It was a first novel, a literary novel, and it must have been over 600 pages in manuscript. What made you think it would ever be published?

I never thought about that. I'm worried about writing. I don't worry what happens when I get finished. I couldn't think about, "Is it going to get published" or "Is anyone going to want to read it" or "How big of an advance am I going to get?" It's all irrelevant. None of that stuff happens unless it's a good book.

Certainly you must have recognized that it had greater commercial potential than the collection of stories.

That thought never came into my head. I think about the story itself. I don't think is it more commercial or less commercial, is it more artistic, will the critics like it, will the public like it, are my readers going to be college students? It's just ridiculous. What's important is the writing.

To get back to the writing then, *Snow Falling on Cedars* has been praised for its vivid characters. Are they based on people that you know or composites of people you know?

No. Everybody in the book is imagined. A couple of the minor characters have elements of people I know, but certainly the major characters are people I conjured up from my imagination.

And has this always been true in your writing?

Yeah, I'm not very autobiographical. I don't write out of the well of my own experience.

Writers sometimes debate the artistic efficacy of writing from experience, whether it's less artistic. Is this then a philosophical choice that you make?

I don't find myself making a philosophical choice so much as being condemned to whatever I have. It's not so much a choice as accepting whatever limits have been placed on me artistically by fate.

The characters have a Dickensian richness about them. In fact, there's a 19th-century quality to the novel as a whole. Was that a conscious choice?

Not really. My reading is primarily from the past. For some reason I don't get that interested in what's being written right now. I don't know why. When I open a book, I just go by if I like the first page then I go to the second. And that seems to happen more with books from the past. The other thing is, I personally, as a human being, I am not that contemporary. The things that are going on right now, and the way people think, I'm not too lined up with it. Maybe I have a 19th-century sensibility.

Part of what makes your characters so strong is your wonderful ear for dialogue. In *Snow Falling on Cedars*, so much of the action occurs at the trial, and you have to get through a certain amount of dry business—courtroom Q&A—and still keep the dialogue interesting. Was that an especially daunting challenge for you?

It's funny. A minute ago you brought up characterization and now you're bringing up dialogue. These are two areas where I feel insecure. I feel like I'm lousy at dialogue. But to answer the particular question, to make courtroom dialogue work, you've got to think like the people in the courtroom. You have to be the defense attorney and say "If I were him and it was my job to defend my client, what would I say next?" Or the prosecutor, or the judge. You've got to be those people.

Do you always use that strategy in writing dialogue?

Yes. You have to become the person and think about the moment they're in.

But you see yourself as a much more descriptive, atmospheric writer than a dramatist with gifts for dialogue?

I don't see myself as atmospheric. I try to be as strong as I can in every area of my craft. Whatever it is. I view them all with dispassionate equality. I wouldn't want to favor one over the other.

Okay, then to switch to a different element, in *Snow Falling on Cedars* you use an omniscient point of view, moving into the minds of a lot of characters. And by the end, this stance plays a thematic role as well as a structural one. Was that something you had in mind from the start?

That's something I had in mind from the start. I'm what I would call a thematic writer. The most important guiding principle for me is a clear understanding of what my theme is. Once I know the area of human experience that I'm addressing and exploring, then all the craft choices are made on the basis of that. Including the choices about point of view. And this is a great way to work because it supplies so much cohesion. Everything has a purpose. Every decision you make is relevant to your aspiration. You're not just searching in the dark. You have a logical premise behind all your choices.

That's very interesting, because writers so often dismiss the notion of "theme" as a creative element, sensing in it, I guess, the whiff of the chalkboard, that themes are more the realm of college professors than writers.

Yeah, but it's like I said earlier about some writers being more analytical. I guess I'm one of them.

So do you write it down, try to capture the theme in a paragraph that you can refer to?

No, I know it because I live it every day. You don't have to write it down. It's just there.

But to use theme as a guide while writing, can you articulate it? Can you say, I'm writing a novel about XYZ?

Yes, absolutely. With *Snow Falling on Cedars*, I said to myself, "I've got this question in front of me, which is 'How to live?' " I see all around me, people my age making choices. Some of them are becoming materialists. They think the important thing is to acquire. And others are becoming sensualists. They want to have experiences, feel good, go places. And other people are becoming more despairing. They're becoming nihilists. They don't know how to respond except to be cynical. That's the guiding question: how to live. Who do you want to be?

So if theme, rather than plot, was your guiding principle, did you know from the start how it would end?

There was no question in my mind.

We're talking about this book as a novel of themes and ideas. But I think the main reason for its success is that it's such a page-turner.

I'm a huge believer in that. You want the reader to turn the page to find out what happens next. That's the basic principle of storytelling. If you want people to stay at the campfire and listen to your voice, you'd better draw them in and make them wonder what's going to happen next. Your artistic and literary aspirations *can* be achieved, but only in the context of keeping people turning the pages.

There have been many articles about this novel in publishing trade magazines, analyzing why this book has been so successful. Do you have any sense of why it captured so large an audience?

I've heard all kinds of explanations and I'm amused by a lot of them, because everyone takes credit. Everyone believes it had to do with publicity or promotion or marketing or timing or strategy. It's all crazy. The truth of the matter is, there's something very human in the response. People are looking always, desperately, for stories that are mythic, that address their deepest needs as human beings, that speak to their hearts. That's it. It's that simple. It's always been that way and always will be.

Does the sudden fame—the book tours and interviews and all that—cut into your writing time?

Yes. I've been on a two-year jag of being an author. Not a writer, an author. And I'm really tired of it. I'm about to call it quits and put *Snow Falling on Cedars* behind me. It's just an intrusion. If you think that the book has some value to people, something important to say, or that it's worth bringing it to people's attention, then there's some value in talking about it, promoting it and giving readings. But at a certain point it becomes ridiculous. You could go on forever. Everyday there are faxes and phone calls and letters asking me to come here and do this or that and I've sort of had it.

You don't seem like someone who would enjoy all the attention.

The part of it I like is the actual reading and the questions and interviews like this one. They're fine. What I don't like is signing books and shaking hands and making small talk and everyone being your friend for ten minutes. That part I really can't stand. Suddenly you've got a thousand new best friends. It's just ridiculous. But a serious discussion of the book and writing, I can do that without any misgivings.

How has all of this success and attention changed you as a writer?

The actual act of writing is no easier than it was. You can have all the awards and sales and reviews you want, it doesn't get any easier the next day. On the other hand, I feel a deeper confidence in myself. It doesn't come from *Snow Falling on Cedars*. It comes from the years going by. I feel more confident because I've practiced more. The more you do this, the better you're going to get.

You're working on a new novel?

Sort of. But, as I said, I've been so busy being an author instead of a writer that I haven't been able to work on it as much as I'd like.

Given the success of the first novel, do you feel any pressure in undertaking this new one?

No. The pressure has always been huge. The first day I decided to write, I felt the enormity of the task. It's a hugely serious and beautiful thing. But it can't possibly get any more serious or beautiful as a result of things that happen to you. It is, by definition, that. So I have no more trepidation than I ever did, but I've always had enormous trepidation.

Bobbie Ann Mason: Crafting Extraordinary Stories About Ordinary People

BY MARY JENNINGS

"I think I always knew I wanted to write," says short story writer and novelist Bobbie Ann Mason. I always loved language and reading. But it wasn't clear to me for a long, long time that one could actually be a writer, and certainly not that I could do it for a living. So I had to go to many other things before gravitating toward what I wanted to do all along."

At age 39, Mason decided to make more of a commitment to her lifelong passion of writing. So, she packaged up a short story and sent it off to *The New Yorker*. It came back and she tried again. A total of 20 short stories and 19 tries later, the magazine published "Offerings," a story which explores a woman's relationship with her mother and grandmother and her country home.

The nerve to send out her work was a coming of age of sorts, Mason says. She had earned her doctorate in English several years earlier and was teaching journalism at Mansfield State College in Pennsylvania. "I guess it was that mid-life urgency, because I knew when I was 12 that I wanted to write and somehow I hadn't done it. I had written two novels during the 70s, just kind of dabbling and doing little bits at a time, and not getting too much satisfaction or encouragement. But I had steadily tried. Then I just gave myself a big push."

Early in her career, Mason received encouragement from other writers she met at workshops. "I think one thing that spurred me on and gave me a lot of direction and energy at that point, was that I went to a couple of summer writers' conferences. They stimulated me a great deal and gave me lots of focus. Writers were leading the workshops, and for a week everyone was writing and talking about writing." Meeting other writers like herself who were struggling with their craft helped Mason cement plans to pursue writing as a career.

Now, with two published short story collections and three novels on her resume, Mason looks back on her early experience with *The New Yorker* as a part of her development. "I think it just came together better, and I learned a lot in that little apprenticeship of writing 20 stories. I worked very hard on the stories, and seemed to learn more with each one."

Mason also credits her *New Yorker* experience with giving her the confidence to keep writing. Referring to the letters in which Roger Angell, senior fiction editor, encouraged her to keep trying, Mason says, "This was encouragement of the highest order. He picked me out of the slush pile. I don't think I expected to publish a story in *The New Yorker*. It was just gratifying that they were interested."

MARY JENNINGS, *formerly a journalist for 12 years, is a freelance writer living in Cincinnati, Ohio.*

Photo by Marion Ettinger

Once "Offerings" was published in 1978, Mason's writing career took off. Her stories have since been published in such magazines as *The Paris Review, Atlantic Monthly, Redbook* and *Washington Post Magazine*. Her reputation as a writer received an additional boost after her first collection, *Shiloh and Other Stories* published in 1985, won the Ernest Hemingway Foundation Award for first fiction from PEN American Center.

In Country, Mason's first novel, was published in 1985 and received an award from the Vietnam Veterans of America for its contribution to the arts. The book, which explores the effects the Vietnam War has on a family, sold more than 150,000 copies and was made into a motion picture. Her novel *Spence + Lila* was published in 1988, and a second short story collection, *Love Life*, came out in 1989. Her third novel, *Feather Crowns* was released in 1993 and won the Southern Book Critic's Circle Award for Fiction in 1994.

Mason says she worked hardest on her book *Feather Crowns* and finds writing novels very rewarding. "The novel is longer and more challenging [than the short story]. It's more commitment of time and energy. But you feel like you've actually accomplished something when you have finished a novel and made it work. A short story has more instant gratification, because it takes so much less time and space. And it's more intense. To expand a short story into a novel at that rate of intensity would be impossible."

While novels require hard work, it is nonfiction Mason struggles with most. "I have a much harder time with nonfiction because you have to stick with the facts. That means organizing and keeping track of details and putting all those things first before you can put your imagination into them. I always found term papers very intimidating. I could never work up the courage to write them without some effort. I'm trying to write some nonfiction now, and I'm finding it as hard as ever." Nevertheless, Mason's considerable nonfiction credits include *The Girl Sleuth*, first published in the 70s and again by University Press of Georgia in 1995, "Talk of the Town" pieces for *The New Yorker*, humor, travel writing and a personal history she is currently working on.

FAMILIAR PLACES AS SETTINGS

The stories and novels Mason writes are based on what she knows—Western Kentucky. She draws many of her ideas from Graves County, the farming region where she was born and raised. Her parents ran a 54-acre dairy farm there; her job growing up was cleaning out the milk cans and rounding up the cows in the afternoon. "It's an inescapable formative place. It's home. And I think for whatever reason, Southerners feel very much attached to their place of origin. I grew up on a farm, and those ties are very strong."

ORDINARY PEOPLE AS CHARACTERS

Mason's characters are ordinary people, with everyday problems. She weaves their stories with simple yet engaging descriptions that leave a lasting impression on her readers. In her short story "Piano Fingers" in the *Love Life* collection, the character Dean struggles with his dreams of doing better. He translates those dreams into his love for his children. *Spence + Lila* spins a touching love story about an older farm couple facing mortality and illness for the first time.

Often, Mason's ideas for characters are spawned by actual events and people. In Mason's home town, a woman had quintuplets in 1896, the first recorded set. "That's where I got the notion for *Feather Crowns*," Mason says. "There hadn't been much written about it, so I just made up the rest." In Mason's book about the event, the babies, born in an age of mysticism, bring profound changes to the lives of the main character Christianna Wheeler and her family.

CHARACTERS WITH A LIFE ALL THEIR OWN

The directions her characters take sometimes surprise even Mason. "They take on a life of their own. I have to kind of follow them." In *Feather Crowns*, for example, Mason says, "I didn't have it all mapped out. I did have a loose notion of the structure of it, not exactly the plot but the situation. I knew the general direction it would take. But I didn't know who the characters were. So I had to invent this entire huge family, and all these complicated relationships."

PLOTS THAT TAKE THEIR OWN PATHS

Mason's plots, too, can take off along their own paths. She doesn't always know how they'll end up or sometimes how they start out. "Usually I back into a story. I don't know what's going to happen, and I don't know what it's about. With *Feather Crowns*, I had a pretty clear guideline of what was necessary for the story. But with *In Country*, I didn't at all. I just wandered around for a long time before I discovered it was about Vietnam. Most of my stories are like that. I fool around until I find something that clicks."

With all the hard work it entails, Mason enjoys the self-indulgent aspects of the writer's work. "I think writers want to be their own bosses, to create something that's outside themselves and yet still theirs. I love to play with words and sounds, and have stories emerge from them." When a story isn't working, however, Mason is not afraid to bury it in her bottom desk drawer. "If it's there, I've put it aside because it didn't work. Or it wasn't good enough. Then I kind of lose interest and go on to something new."

Like many writers, the hardest part of writing for Mason is simply getting started. "It's a constant problem. Once I'm into something, I don't have any trouble." Penning those first few words takes discipline she says. "And coffee." And the one other requirement Mason says she finds absolutely vital to her work "is that you have a cat sitting on your desk." Her feline companion and "personal assistant" in the otherwise solitary writer's life is named Kiko.

PROCESS FIRST, MARKETS LATER

Mason recommends literary and little magazines as good markets for writers. Her advice, however, is to enjoy the process of writing, rather than writing with a market in mind. "The kind of writing I do doesn't work if you start with a commercial motivation. It only works if you really want to write it, and write it well and do the best you can. Being too concerned with where you're going to sell your work is counterproductive. I try to write something that's not bounded by that concern, which may or may not be any good, or may not reach an audience. But, first, I work to produce something I can be proud of. Then I think about an outlet for it."

"KEEP SENDING IT OUT"

If your story is rejected by a publisher, Mason gives the same advice she used when sending those 20 stories to *The New Yorker* in the 70s: "Just keep sending it out. Or write another." Writers, she says, shouldn't get discouraged by a turndown. It often can be viewed as encouragement. And, when they get a note from an editor, writers ought to take that as encouragement, not as rejection.

An Interview with Scott Turow

BY ANNE BOWLING

If a novelist approached a publisher with Scott Turow's personal story as his plot, he might find the manuscript sent back for major revisions. It's too much of a stretch, the editor might say, to ask readers to believe an unpublished author could meet with that kind of success—that a first novel would draw a record-setting $200,000 advance; that the book would then go on to $3 million in paperback sales, another first for a first novel; that a paperback publisher would choose the book for its first prime time television promotion; and that Hollywood would then pay $1 million for the film rights. Make your protagonist a success, the editor might say, but scale it back a bit to make it believable.

But Scott Turow's story is more evidence to support the axiom that truth is stranger than fiction. Turow went from a complete unknown to the pages of *Time* magazine and *The New York Times* with publication of *Presumed Innocent* (Farrar, Strauss & Giroux, 1987), the legal thriller featuring prosecutor Rusty Sabich, who finds himself being tried for the murder of a colleague with whom he had an affair. The novel opened the door on an explosion in popularity of legal thrillers. But *Presumed Innocent* was only the beginning of Turow's success story.

Turow's second novel, *The Burden of Proof* (1990), features the *Presumed Innocent* character Alejandro Stern who, while investigating his wife's suicide, uncovers a web of corruption in the commodities market. *Pleading Guilty* (1993) departs from Turow's earlier characters with Mack Malloy, who must find a colleague who disappears. Enter Turow's current title, *The Laws of Our Fathers* (1996), the story of two generations of characters linked together by a murder trial. *The Laws of Our Fathers* will match the success of its predecessors if most readers agree with *Publishers Weekly*, which dubbed the book "a rich, complex and ultimately profoundly moving tale that, like all Turow's work, is quarried from the mysteries of human character rather than simply from the sometimes too-easy drama of the courtroom."

Even more unusual than the immediate and sustained success of his fiction writing is that through it all, Turow has continued his law practice as a partner with Sonnenschein, Nath & Rosenthal in Chicago. Bouyed by the success of *Presumed Innocent*, Turow cut his practice in half and, since 1988, has managed the dual careers of fiction writer and lawyer.

In the telling of Turow's success story, however, not much attention is paid to the years of study and struggle that came before the blockbuster sales and magazine features. In the 70s, he studied fiction writing with writers-in-residence at Amherst College before moving on to a teaching fellowship at Stanford University, where he spent five years polishing his craft. His first novel, *The Way Things Are*, written while he taught at Stanford, remains unpublished. His first break in publishing—*One L* (Putnam Books, 1977), a nonfiction account of his freshman year at Harvard Law School—was an

---

ANNE BOWLING *is a Cincinnati-based freelance writer, and frequent contributor to Writer's Digest Books.*

Photo by Sigrid Estrada

accident, coming right on the heels of his decision to pursue law as a career. Turow spent eight years working on *Presumed Innocent*—written largely on a commuter train as he went to and from his position as a public prosecutor—in the days before he could afford a computer.

Here Scott Turow discusses his fiction writing career, and the hard work and persistence that made his success story happen.

I read that you knew from a very young age that you wanted to be a novelist. What influence did your family have on this decision?

My mother always wanted to be a novelist. She wrote children's stories and some adult fiction. She was like many writers in the sense that she had a household to run and she had a hard time getting down to writing. She did write a few things that she shared during my childhood, and it was always very exciting when she would read what she had written to my sister and me. I had written some fiction very young, as early as 11 or 12. My grandfather's advice to me was "what kind of life is that, locked up in a room all day with a pencil?" He couldn't comprehend it. But by the time I went to college, I had decided that I was going to be a novelist. I don't know if that was a ridiculous declaration or not, but I had made it.

Were there writers or particular works of fiction that influenced you as you got older?

When I was at Amherst College, a poet gave me some very worthwhile advice—he said "I don't know anything about writing novels, but if I wanted to be a novelist I would stuff myself with novels." That was great advice. And that's what I tried to do—stuff myself with novels and short fiction throughout my college career.

As a college freshman, I remember reading *The Alexandria Quartet* (by Lawrence Durrell), and being just enthralled by that high-flown prose. When I told one of my professors I was reading it, he looked at me askance and asked "don't you feel like you're sticking your fingers in jelly?" And now of course, 30 years later, I understand exactly what he meant. The fact of the matter is *The Alexandria Quartet* may have been written with a sort of adolescent excess, but since I was on the lee side of adolescence it worked for me. *The Hall of Mirrors* (by Robert Stone) was a different case. It had this exceptional voice. What I liked best about *Hall of Mirrors* was that this was clearly a book in which every sentence was wrought with enormous intelligence, and it was obviously a serious, reflective novel, but it had a story to tell.

Did you follow a writing program in college, or teach yourself to write?

There wasn't much available at Amherst, because they ascribed to the notion that creative writing wasn't worth teaching. They now have a writing program, but 30 years ago you couldn't persuade anybody that there was something to teach students about writing literature that they couldn't learn by trying to write it. Because there wasn't any classroom instruction, I had to sort of lobby to bring certain writers to Amherst, and I studied in tutorial with some writers in residence. They read my stuff and talked to me about books, and I continued my project of stuffing myself with novels . . . I think all writers are self-taught in certain ways. No one can do it for you. No one can guide your hand on the page.

Would you advise aspiring novelists to study fiction writing formally?

There are two general pieces of advice I have. One is that poet's advice to me—"stuff yourself with novels." It's clearly correct. You will not understand what strategies work in literature without reading a lot and saying to yourself, "Gee that really works for me, how did he or she do that?" You do not know the traditions; you do not know the conventions; you don't know anything without reading.

The second thing is, write. Generally speaking, it is much harder to write in isolation. I think what the classroom gives you is a community of other people who are interested in literature and a professor who, if he or she is good, can give you reasonable criticism. And if nothing else, taking a class forces you to make the time to write. Yes, I would encourage classroom study. I would note that in my generation—American novelists who are 55 and under—an enormous number of us are products of creative writing programs. If you look at the biographies of contemporary American writers, especially those who are born after World War II, you will find most of them passed some time in writing programs.

How did you find an agent to represent the first novel you wrote, *The Way Things Are*?

This is a funny story. My senior year at Amherst I wrote a novella, and a series of short stories. The stories were pretty good, and a couple of them were published—one in the *Transatlantic Review*. An editor at Viking saw the story and asked to see the book. So of course I was thrilled and sent the novella and stories to that editor. Time began to pass. I went off to Stanford as a writing fellow—it was then October and I'd delivered the stories in May—and I'd written a few letters saying "where's my manuscript, what do you think?" No answer.

Finally, it was November and I had written saying "return my manuscript," because at that time I didn't have the temerity to make simultaneous submissions. I read an article in *Newsweek* about Lynn Nesbit, who was just starting the apogee of her renown as a literary agent, and out of desperation I called her. I don't know by what miracle she decided to come to the phone, but I will always be grateful to her. She got my work back, and gave the stories to an agent at International Creative Management.

In the meantime, I wrote *The Way Things Are* and sent it to the agent, but she didn't want to represent it. Meanwhile a friend of mine had written a book and sent it to his agent, and she didn't like it. So somehow he and I arranged a swap—I would introduce him to my agent if he would introduce me to his. I would say my friend got the better end of the deal in that his book was sold and mine wasn't, although, looking back on it now, what my friend had written was a hell of a lot better.

Did you retain the same agent for *One L*?

Yes, and she sold the book accidentally. I had written her a letter telling her I was going to law school, and she had made such heavy efforts trying to sell *The Way Things Are* I felt like I owed her, and I did. So I said "by the way, do you know any good writers of nonfiction?" I was thinking a nonfiction account of law school would be a great book for someone to write, so I explained the idea and suggested she pass it along. She read the letter quickly I guess, and didn't realize that I was not saying I wanted to write this book. She presented the letter to an editor who said "oh, that's a wonderful idea. I'll buy that."

So I got a book contract back in the mail. Surprised? It was one of the most astonishing moments of my life. Maybe the most. I just opened this envelope—I had gotten dozens of rejections—and here was a book contract. And I had gotten it by deciding to go to law school without totally abandoning the writer's life and at least trying to maintain some kind of contact with the writing world. It was amazing. Then I had to decide whether I was actually going to write the book, because I hadn't the remotest idea of how I was going to do it. But that didn't take much persuasion.

Was the positive reception of *One L* the success you needed to continue writing?

I think it proved to be an incredibly successful opening wedge in my career, and I think in retrospect it helped create this market (for legal fiction). But in spite of *One L*'s success, I was smitten enough with the law and intuitively much more sure that law was right for me as a career that I didn't give a thought to not practicing. But, because of that pledge I had made when I started college, I was also determined to continue to write. And so, I went through my years as an assistant United States attorney knowing secretly that I was really a writer. It was pretty much a secret, since I wrote on the commuter train in the mornings, but I had a wife at home who continued to believe that I was a writer. Her joke was that she married a writer and ended up with a lawyer.

To what do you attribute your ability to excel in so many areas of fiction writing—plot, dialogue and characterization?
Those five years at Stanford represented a course of scrutiny and study of just what goes into good dialogue and characterization. I've been a lifelong beneficiary of that and of having that much time to think relentlessly about those kinds of questions and to practice writing.

Plotting, ironically, is in some ways the easiest element. I came of age during the death of the novel. There is a lot of writing now about how plot, almost dead and gone around 1970, has returned to the novel. I had always been attracted to plots. As I said, one of the things I liked about *Hall of Mirrors* was that it had a good plot. But it was very hard to be a serious writer and write with plot—indeed plot was passe, and even kind of lowbrow. So most of what I learned about plotting I sort of absorbed accidentally from sources as varied as television shows and Charles Dickens.

Do you outline your novels and sketch your characters before you begin writing, or do you let the story unfold as you create it?
There are virtually no rules about the way I work. I have a theory about writing, at least my own writing. Once I have a general idea of what I'm writing about, I do best when I write from inspiration and passion. For example, once I know the characters, ideas come to me, usually in the form of scenes, snatches of dialogue, impressions of a character, particular events that I think are neat, and moments of realization I think a character might have. When I write those passages down, they imply a constellation of events around them. I've been thinking about a passage I wrote really early on. Sonny (from *The Burden of Proof* and *The Laws of Our Fathers*) is thinking—she's been to bed with her old boyfriend from graduate school who has returned to the scene. This is a tremendous point of arrival for Sonny and it basically implied a book. There had to be a romance and there had to be a lot of reluctance about it. All the implied events were built in.

After I've sort of piled things up that way—this happens over about six months— then I start asking myself, how are you going to pull all this together? Why is she reluctant; what would make her reluctant? Well, if she shouldn't be seeing this guy for professional reasons, why would she not see him for professional reasons? It would compromise her impartiality? How would it compromise her impartiality? Well, because she's a judge.

I know that sounds like I write backwards, but the major elements of *The Laws of Our Fathers* literally sprang from that passage. You say, "oh yeah, that passage is good, I really want to write a book where Sonny comes to that moment."

The character Alejandro "Sandy" Stern originated in *Presumed Innocent*, and returned to center stage as the main character in *The Burden of Proof*. The Sonny Klonsky character first appeared in *Burden of Proof*, and is back for a major role in *The Laws of Our Fathers*. Do some characters' voices become so strong and clear to you that they end up with their own books?
Exactly. If things are going well for me, there's a character who runs away with the novel. In 1989 as I was coming to the end of *The Burden of Proof*, (Sonny's voice

began coming through), and an editor said "I really like this writing, but it starts halfway through the novel. This book seems to belong to Sandy Stern. You really can't do that. If you want her to have a book, you're going to have to write another book." And that immediately hit a chord with me because I had always had this longing to write about the 60s. Sonny is my age, maybe a year older, and I immediately said "okay, she's going to be in my 60s book" which came to be *The Laws of Our Fathers*.

As soon as I put down *The Burden of Proof*, I started writing *The Laws of Our Fathers*. I'd gotten through this mental process I just described . . . but I really hit the rocks because I figured I really had two stories to tell. What I basically wanted to write about was the 60s, but it didn't work, because (Sonny's) story didn't connect with the 60s. I write in this sort of intuitive way, so I don't ask myself at first what the hell things have to do with each other. When I finally began to do that in a conscientious way, I couldn't figure out the answer.

Norman Mailer once wrote that the greatest disaster that can befall a novelist is realizing you made a big mistake about 50 pages back. And that's what I did. I had wasted about 18 months at that point. So I put it aside. Having done that once before, with *Presumed Innocent*, I had confidence that I could get back to the book. And if I didn't get back to it, it wasn't worth writing.

You hit an impasse in the plot with *Presumed Innocent*?

Yes. I put the book down because I (ran into problems with) the plot. I got to the precise moment where Raymond Horgan reaches into his drawer and hands Rusty Sabich the B file. I was writing sequentially at that point, sort of following it along. I had my prosecutor who was investigating the death of this woman, but at that point I had no idea what was in that file—I had no idea who killed this woman. I took two years away from it and came back to it later.

Are there specific methods you use to give your characters the complexity that makes them so believable?

Every writer talks about how characters develop on their own outside the author, and I think that's mystifying to a lot of people. And yet it is from writers having this sense—that fictional characters have an existence apart from their creators—that the most telling stuff comes. It's very hard to instruct somebody in how to do that, because I think it is in many ways mysterious for writers as well.

One common pitfall for me is that I have never been able to really make a character get up off the page when I'm writing from a one-to-one correspondence with somebody. And for that reason I probably have shunned that practice. I do not try to write about people I know. I understand that this works for some other writers, so I can't criticize it, but for me it doesn't. I just find I get into that process of mimicking someone I know. For me, what is much more successful is, if something is striking about somebody I know, I'll go with that. Then I'll choose another attribute from somebody else. Pretty soon, I will have staked out about three or four characteristics and the face of the fictional character begins to take shape.

What finally happened with that manuscript of *The Way Things Are*?

Right at the moment it's about two feet from me. Depending on my mood it sits under my computer monitor. That's what I use to prop it up. Every now and then I'm sort of embarrassed by the heavy-handed symbolism of doing that and I put it back on the shelf.

But my wife says "you've been writing *The Laws of Our Fathers* for 25 years," and that *The Way Things Are* is really, on an emotional level, a first draft of this book.

Many of the same themes and a few passages in *The Laws of Our Fathers* were taken from this *The Way Things Are*.

In all candor, *The Ways Things Are* was not so flawed that it could not have been published, but it was not so great that it demanded to be published. It was a book about the 60s that I was trying to have published in the 70s. Americans were pretty fed up with the excesses of the 60s and there was no market for it. Among "hey man" novels there weren't any great successes this side of Richard Brautigan. People didn't want to read about it. Now, 25 years later, film rights to *The Laws of Our Fathers*—which is heavily rooted in the 60s—took only six hours to sell. So times change.

After having spent eight years working on *Presumed Innocent*, you've begun finishing novels in about three years. Has the process become faster for you?

I have more time to write. It seems like every three years I end up with a novel. I'm interested to see how long it takes me to write the next one, because in this case I absolutely know the plot and the setting and the characters. So how long will it take me to write this next book? A betting person would say it'll still take me three years.

How do you balance the demands of your legal work, novel writing and family?

Since 1989, I've been a part-time lawyer, and that works well for me. People are always sort of amazed, like "how can you do this?" The answer is that it's just who I am. It's no different than my wife being able to be a painter and a mother, and switch back and forth.

Do you have any general advice you'd like to offer in closing to writers aspiring to publish legal fiction?

I'll tell you one thing, there are a hell of a lot of lawyers out there writing books. I do not think that you need to be a lawyer to write these kinds of novels, although having legal credentials does give you a certificate of authenticity with publishers. It does not look to me like this market is dying away. It seems to be a very steady portion of the drugstore rack bestsellers . . . so my one steady bit of advice to aspiring writers is like the Nike ad: just do it.

First Bylines

BY CHANTELLE M. BENTLEY

The pursuit of publication is a worthy, albeit, consuming task. And many writers spend their entire lifetimes trying to find that one gimmick that will capture a publisher's attention and turn them into bestselling authors.

The truth lies in the writing, however. And as the following five authors will attest, to be a writer all you must do is write. To experience the dream of publication, you must dedicate and devote yourself to exploring the writer within.

SCOTT BLACKWOOD
"Riverfest," *Whetstone*

Although he was an avid reader and wrote poetry in high school, "really bad poetry that I would burn if I knew where it was now," Scott Blackwood's interest in writing did not sprout until he was already enrolled at the University of Texas as a psychology major. "I was really set on becoming a clinical psychologist. But by the time I was a junior, I had already decided against it and was more interested in English and reading and writing."

Blackwood's desire to write was encouraged by a professor who complimented and challenged him. "He would say, 'You have talent. You need to come in here and we need to work on this.' It was a complete surprise to me. He saw something and was pushing me." As a result, Blackwood spent more time reading and discussing books with friends. "I read Hemingway's short story collection *In Our Time* and that really impressed me. I started writing really bad short stories that were very imitative. Then I took a creative writing class and realized I didn't know what I was doing at all."

But Blackwood endured and, in the end, he graduated with a psychology degree, the equivalent of a degree in English and also received a teaching certificate in secondary education. His first teaching position was at a school for pregnant teenage girls. "I taught there a year and it had a profound affect on me. The first good story I wrote came out of that experience." The school lost its grant, however, and Blackwood moved on to teach one year at the elementary level and then two more years of high school.

In 1991, Blackwood purchased a copy of *Novel & Short Story Writer's Market* and began submitting his work. Usually sending the same story, he submitted to magazines indicating an openness to new writers. "On some level I thought [about the magazines], I don't really belong here but I'll try. So I sent them out and they came back; however, some came back with notes on them," he says. "I received one rejection from the *Black*

CHANTELLE BENTLEY, *is the editor of* Poet's Market *and former production editor of* Novel & Short Story Writer's Market.

Warrior Review with some really nice compliments and advice which was helpful. I revised the story and kept sending it out and I think I was getting a little bit better."

Then, in 1992, Blackwood was accepted into the MFA program at Southwest Texas State University, but was only in the program a short time before having to quit due to financial pressures. A year later a friend and teacher at Southwest informed Blackwood of an assistanceship that was available. He applied, got the position and started back into the MFA program. "It was one of those proverbial 'never be the same again' moments and, at the time, I was pretty discouraged about writing. It just seemed like I would never be able to balance everything. But after I got the assistanceship things changed and I really started writing. It was like living two different lives."

After taking a few months to settle into his new position, Blackwood returned to writing and finished the rough draft of a story by the summer of his first year at Southwest Texas State. But the story, entitled "Riverfest," wasn't ready to send out until the following November. "I actually revised the story three times and then sent it out in two batches," says Blackwood. "I don't believe in sending one submission at a time. Most editors don't like simultaneous submissions but the odds are just so long that it seems silly." Blackwood still used *NSSWM* to locate markets, but felt he knew a lot more about the different magazines to which he submitted than he did when he first began. "When you are in an MFA program, there is a lot of talk about the market. I even took a class on literary journals and what kind of work was being published. We talked about the styles of stories different editors were looking for and their biases. And it was all very helpful, but after that it's just a crap shoot."

While still in the process of choosing markets for his story, Blackwood came across the literary journal *Whetstone* quite by chance. "A copy of the journal had been passed around by the director of the MFA program. He thought a lot of the editors and the work they published. I read some of the journal and was really impressed with the writing." So Blackwood simultaneously submitted "Riverfest" to *Whetstone* and five other magazines including the *Atlantic Monthly*. "You feel like you've neglected something if you don't have a rejection from them," he says.

About four or five months after sending out his submissions, Blackwood received a call from Julie Fleenor, one of *Whetstone*'s editors, saying they wanted the story. However, the acceptance came with a few suggested revisions. "I was under the impression that once a story was taken you might have to change some punctuation, maybe a few words. They literally sent me three single-spaced pages of suggestions. And my first reaction was 'What! I am not going to change a damn thing.' Then my idea of myself as a genius wore off and I started looking at the suggestions closely and, in general, they were good suggestions." Blackwood reworked about 50 percent of the suggestions and then sent a three-page letter rebutting the other 50 percent. "I don't know how it typically works but there was an interesting dialogue going on between us. They were very careful readers and I found some things I could tighten in the story by reading it even closer than I had. The experience was educational, even though at first it was a little ego bruising." After returning the revised story, *Whetstone* sent Blackwood a contract and the story was published in December of 1996.

"I guess what I came out of that experience with was to stand pretty firm on the essential aspects of the story and the essential language. I had to go back and reevaluate all that stuff, and then I came up with fairly concise arguments for each thing I wouldn't change. I even broke down the structure of the story into sections, then matched my arguments with each section. I showed why each piece was essential to that section of the story and, if you can do that, the editors will respect you more."

KATHLEEN CAMBOR
The Book of Mercy, Farrar, Straus and Giroux

"I try to write before I do very much else in the morning and I often read poetry before I write," says Kathleen Cambor. "I find that if I read even the newspaper, my prose begins to sound like what I am reading. Where poetry is so much about the particulars of language, it helps me to let my ordinary life fall away and fall into a world of language again."

A Pittsburgh native who has lived in Houston since the early 1970s, Cambor returned to her childhood love of writing—she wrote a novel of the Nancy Drew variety at the age of eight—after beginning a career as a psychiatric nurse. "I became a nurse at my parent's insistence and, in many ways, it was the best thing that happened to me. It gave me an opportunity to understand and know things about the way people live in their hearts that I think I wouldn't have learned under any other circumstance." But with the birth of her second child came Cambor's increased desire to see if writing was a viable possibility.

After testing the waters in an undergraduate writing class, Cambor enrolled in the University of Houston's Graduate Writing Program in 1981. She then began to write *The Book of Mercy* as her master's thesis. By the time she received her degree, the manuscript was 600 pages long and she and her adviser, Donald Barthelme, were in the process of revising. However, when Barthelme died in 1989, Cambor lost the will to finish the revisions and put the manuscript away for about a year. She then turned her interest to writing short stories.

And, fortunately for Cambor, it was the publication of one of those short stories in a literary journal that got the attention of a New York agent. "She got in touch with me, told me how much she liked the story and wondered if I needed representation. I said I didn't think I was ready at that point, but she suggested we keep in touch." Cambor then contacted the agent when she felt *The Book of Mercy* was ready and asked if she wanted to see it. She did and the manuscript was sold in 3½ months to Farrar, Straus and Giroux. "When my agent originally agreed to represent the book, she thought it might take a year because it is a literary novel and that market had become more, not less, difficult. It was all very fortunate."

Published in June of 1996, *The Book of Mercy* was very well received by reviewers and chosen by both Borders and Barnes & Noble for their special promotional programs—giving the book prominent display in all their stores nationwide. Cambor promoted the book by appearing at author signings in Houston, Austin, Dallas/Ft. Worth and Pittsburgh. The brisk sales required a second printing and hinted at the possibility of the need for a third. Also, the paperback rights were sold and it will appear in that format around the middle of 1997.

Now, with her foot in the door of a successful writing career and a new novel underway, Cambor's only regret is her lack of aggression when submitting earlier work. "I work hard; I care very deeply about what I am working on, but I probably did not submit things as much as I might have. I think it is very important to just keep your work out there to give people a chance to see it, even if you're being rejected. I would encourage other writers to write a lot and send it out and not be frightened by rejection."

And as an author who also does a lot a community-based teaching, Cambor does not hesitate to encourage others into a market that is already tight or worry about sharing her piece of success. "There is a lot of thinking right now that there is this tub of success and if you allow anyone to get to the trough there is going to be less for you. But I have always believed that good work finds its place, and when I teach I am always very happy to help students in any way I can—suggest markets, give them names of editors and publishers, photocopy pages, loan them books, even suggest how to go about finding an agent.

"And I really do believe that good work finds its place in the world, if you are persistent, thoughtful and careful. I'm not saying that every student should be told they are Thomas Hardy. But I think one never knows how far a student can progress and finding ways to be supportive and encouraging, especially when people are beginning to write, is extremely important. Writing is a question of practicing and getting better. There are so many stories of writers who were rejected over and over again who clearly made themselves writers by being persistent. You never know what can happen."

JOYCE DOLAN
"Flowers and Clouds," *St. Anthony Messenger*

After spending many years dreaming about writing and becoming a writer, Joyce Dolan decided it was time to make her dream come true. The first step was to force herself to begin writing on a regular basis. "It's hard to make yourself sit down and write, especially when it is not the focus of your work life and you are doing all kinds of other things. In fact, I have only been writing for the last five years or so. I just decided that writing was a goal I had to reach."

But after Dolan had been earnestly writing for a while, she realized that her writing needed some help. "I knew I needed help; I knew that what I was doing just wasn't polished. But I didn't want to give up my evenings to take a class at a university because that's the only time I have to write." Then she heard about a correspondence writing program offered through a division of Writer's Digest. The goal of the program is to complete one short story in a period of about two years with the help of a professional writer. "You complete a profile and on the profile they ask you all kinds of questions about your favorite authors, what kind of writing you like and your background. Then they use the profile to match you up with one of their instructors."

During the time she was in the program, Dolan worked with instructor Marian Blue and, together, they revised the very first short story Dolan had written. "This story, which is based on a true occurrence between myself and my grandmother, is what actually made me sit down and start writing. I wanted to somehow get the incident and a description of my grandma down, to express it some way in writing."

Dolan completed the reworking of the story and the program in a year's time and was very pleased with the attention, advice and criticism she received from Blue. "Right from the beginning, when the story was just a dumb essay, Marian was very encouraging. Although she would be critical and give me suggestions, she would also tell me 'These are beautiful phrases' or 'This is nice.' So, it all validated my writing and what I was doing." Blue also suggested that she try submitting her story to *St. Anthony Messenger*, a Catholic magazine located in Dolan's home region of southwest Ohio.

So, on her teacher's advice, Dolan submitted her short story to *St. Anthony Messenger* (*SAM*). She then received her first rejection from *SAM*. "They sent the manuscript back to me with this very nice rejection letter saying, 'Our staff really enjoyed your story, but we have some problems.' " The rejection letter went on to list the concerns the editors of *SAM* had with the story—some were very minor, but a couple of the concerns Dolan figured were nearly impossible to address. "I was just sick. I had worked so hard on this story and I had already done so many revisions. It had gone through the writing program with these problems and no one had noticed them. I just couldn't think of it anymore." So she put the manuscript away.

After a couple of weeks Dolan realized that if she wanted to publish the story she would have to address the concerns raised by the editors at *SAM*. "When I finally got the manuscript back out, I thought to myself, 'I am this close, I have to do something.' And I just got to it and fixed it. It wasn't that hard to do." And although *SAM* had not asked her to resubmit the story upon completing the changes, Dolan sent the revised manuscript along with a thank you letter. "I had wanted to send them a thank you letter anyway since they had taken so much time and gave me such helpful comments and took the time to write a letter.

"So, in my letter, I thanked them and then added as an aside, 'Oh, by the way, I attached the revised manuscript if you want to read it again.' But, I didn't make that the main focus of the letter. And, I would have never not sent them a thank you letter, I just think that is common courtesy, especially when somebody takes the time to try to help you." The aside worked, however, and *SAM* accepted Dolan's story for publication in their March or April 1997 issue. "When I got the acceptance letter, I surprised myself by how happy I was—I screamed and jumped right up in the air."

Currently, Dolan is enrolled in the advanced short story writing program of the Writer's Digest school and is trying to refrain from browbeating herself for not starting her writing career sooner. "I tell myself to not regret starting when I did because I just had to take care of business as things went along. This was the time for it."

JEAN HEGLAND
Into the Forest, Calyx Books

Even though Jean Hegland's first experience with the submission process left her with nearly 50 rejections for her creative nonfiction work (entitled *The Life Within: Celebration of a Pregnancy*) before it found a home at Humana Press in 1991, she has managed to maintain a realistic view of the process and to continue sending out her work. "Since then my essays and poems have been rejected by many journals and magazines, and accepted by a few. I try to think of submitting as a game of chance similar to playing the lottery. It's exciting to play and—who knows—I might win, but it's not wise to stake much on it."

With a similarly realistic attitude toward the writing process, this part-time creative writing teacher and full-time mother of three manages to squeeze her writing in during the baby's naps and after all the kids are in bed. "Of course, there are a million things that can threaten an ideal schedule, but, even so, I seem to be single-minded enough to manage ten to fifteen writing hours a week. It's not nearly as much time as I'd like, but it does add up." However, writing is not the only activity contained in this schedule and time must also be made for revision and marketing.

But Hegland begins her process with the basics—getting the word on the page. "I write wildly chaotic first drafts, allowing myself the freedom to write whichever parts of the story I've got in mind that seem most interesting, and I try not to worry about how those parts will be hooked together. I write notes to myself about what seem like significant insights about characters or plot or point of view, I leave blanks on the page when I can't immediately supply the right word or detail." Hegland continues working on a particular piece of the story until she loses her momentum or loses the "energy of discovery."

After getting all her ideas down, she then begins what most consider the tedious task of revising. But for Hegland, revising is the enabling factor for her writing. "If I couldn't revise, I don't believe I could ever write anything worth reading. Over the years I've come to rely more and more heavily on the opportunities offered by revision." Upon completing a first draft, Hegland then spends her time cutting, pasting, reshuffling current scenes and adding new ones. "Finally, once the characters seem clear and the structure sturdy, I get to do what I've been longing to do since I began— polish language, resort to the thesaurus, and try to make each sentence as perfect as possible." But Hegland realizes that perfection is an unattainable goal. "Someone once said that no piece of writing is ever completed—it's just finally abandoned. I know something of mine is to the abandoning point when I seem to have reached the limits of my ability to improve it."

Hegland's novel *Into the Forest* took five years to write and went through at least 25 revisions before it was ready to be "abandoned." She then spent quite a bit of time looking for an agent willing to represent her and the book. "Although a number of agents flirted with me, no one ultimately proposed. Finally, I turned to the literary market guides and culled from them a list of presses I thought might be interested in *Into the Forest* and with whom I felt I'd like to work." So, Hegland sent a query letter, synopsis and sample of the novel to several dozen of the most promising presses. Calyx Books was the first to contact Hegland and express interest. "I'd just read an article about Calyx in *Poets and Writers*, so my concerns about whether or not it was the right press for my book were not as large as they might otherwise have been."

But by the time her manuscript was accepted, Hegland had already decided it was in need of further revision and, ultimately, Calyx agreed. So, she spent another six months working on the manuscript before sending Calyx the final draft. "That draft was edited by a team of marvelous editors who gave me many invaluable suggestions for yet a further series of revisions." *Into the Forest* was finally published in June of 1996, two years after being accepted for publication by Calyx.

When contemplating the sale of her first work of fiction, Hegland has no regrets. "I don't think I could possibly be more pleased with the enthusiasm and attention Calyx has given my novel. The editors I worked with were superb; the book design and cover art are gorgeous; and Calyx has proven to be very committed to promoting the book as aggressively as possible." In fact, the biggest challenge Hegland has had to face with the publication of her work is the need to divide her time between promoting her current novel and working on her next. "I'd like to think that the publication of *Into the Forest* will make the publication of my next novel easier, especially since the book seems to be doing well both critically and commercially, but, of course, that remains to be seen."

Even with the success of her first novel, Hegland tries to keep an unclouded view of what being published ultimately means. "Publication is a wonderful way of validating what it is you do at your desk day after day. Being published helps you feel less crazy when you find you have to admit to the person sitting next to you that you are a writer, and being published can help you to feel more justified when you sneak away from all the rest of your obligations to write.

"But publication is also fluky and ephemeral. Manuscripts get rejected or accepted for a cluster of reasons, only some of which have to do with the ultimate worth of the writing. Books go out of print, and the remaining copies are subject to the normal ravages of time. Therefore, I think that it's important for all writers to remember that it's those hours spent at the desk, when we're engaged in the work and play of understanding what it means to be a human on earth, awash in language and images and ideas and emotions, that is really what writing is all about. If writing itself isn't soul-satisfying, then publication will ultimately feel hollow; but if it is soul-satisfying, then publication will only be the icing on an already very rich cake."

GEORGE RABASA
Glass Houses, Coffee House Press

With 35 years of writing behind him, George Rabasa's idea of what defines a writer hasn't changed since the first time he put words to a page. "I have always considered myself a writer. And I think the reward of writing is in the writing—that's the battle, that's what defines a writer." But now, with the recent publication of his first short story collection, Rabasa can also be considered a writer by the general public. "That's the nice thing about publishing the collection and really all I expected after coming out with a book—besides the inner satisfaction of having pulled it off."

Photo by Curtis Johnson

To get to this point in his writing career, however, Rabasa decided to give up the career that had defined his life for so many years and devote his time to writing. "Until about five years ago I was a creative director here [in Minneapolis] at a pretty big direct marketing firm. Then I realized I was spending all my time supervising people rather than doing creative work." So Rabasa quit his job, kept his 11-year-old car and started doing freelance work to help make ends meet.

For most of the first three years after quitting his job, Rabasa worked on his stories. During this time, however, he was contacted by a writer he'd recently met who had read one of his stories in an anthology of local writers. The writer asked to see more of his work and, upon reading the stories, suggested he try turning them into a book. "After that I began submitting, mainly to small presses. I guess I am realistic enough to realize agents don't generally want to deal with short stories unless you have a lot of glamorous publication credits like the *The New Yorker* and *Harper's*."

Rabasa also submitted his collection to a lot of literary contests, including the Writer's Voice Capricorn Award for Excellence in Fiction which he won in late 1993. Rabasa received a $1,000 prize and was asked to read his work in New York the following year. "Winning the Capricorn Award proved really quite good and helped in gaining credibility." In fact, Rabasa used the award to impress a Minneapolis press that already had the manuscript under consideration. "The collection had been at Coffee House Press over a year when I won the award. So, I basically pulled the old manuscript out and said 'If you haven't made a decision, here is the new version [which won the Capricorn Award] for you to consider.' " The impetus worked and, one year and eight months after receiving the manuscript, editor Allan Kornblum of Coffee House called Rabasa with an offer.

After accepting the collection, Kornblum gave Rabasa another year to "noodle" around with the manuscript. "When Allan accepted the collection [in 1994], he told me the book was going to be released in the fall of 1996. So, he gave me a year to keep noodling it. I don't know if that was by design, but in that year I did a lot of revising stories, pulling stories and adding new ones. It was wonderful because the pressure was off."

When the revised manuscript was turned in a year later, very few further revisions were required by Kornblum. "Allan is a wonderful editor and he, at least in my case, allows the writer to take full responsibility for his writing; he allows the writer to have the say he needs. I think that shows respect for what the writer is trying to do. If Allan accepts a writer's book, it is because he accepts what the writer is doing. I have had friends who have published with major houses and they've been run ragged with revisions, reshaping and reconcepting of what the book ought to be rather than what it is. I think that would be very painful."

And, in addition to being pleased with their thoughtful editing, Rabasa is delighted with Coffee House Press as a whole. "I think my book found the perfect publisher. I like the books they put out and working with them has been a joy. They took me into account on cover design, on the overall look of the book and even on such small things as the back jacket bio. And to see four or five people working hard on your book is a rewarding thing."

Of course, Rabasa had no way of knowing how Coffee House operated when he submitted his manuscript. Initially, he chose the press because of the books it had published in the past. "I chose Coffee House because it is a quality press that has done unusual books. It doesn't do a lot of safe books. It has done some slightly wacky stuff, so I figured an editor there might want to take a chance on what I am doing." Coffee House's openness to take a chance has not only led to the publication of Rabasa's short story collection *Glass Houses* (published in October of 1996), it has also led to the acceptance of a novel which he finished while revising the collection (the novel is tentatively scheduled for publication in the fall of 1997).

But how does Rabasa really view publication and all this recent success? "At my ripe age, if I say I'm a writer, the first question is 'Where is your work?' So now when people ask me what I do for a living, I can say, 'I have a book out.' And even though what qualifies me as a writer is that I write, the rest of the world doesn't really believe unless you have something substantial to point to. And now I do."

The Markets

Literary Magazines.. 89

International Literary Magazines 246

Small Circulation Magazines 254

International Small Circulation Magazines....................... 300

Zines.. 304

Commercial Periodicals........................... 337

International Commercial Periodicals 387

Small Press... 389

International Small Press 446

Commercial Book Publishers................. 448

International Commercial Book Publishers 484

Contests and Awards............................ 487

IMPORTANT LISTING INFORMATION

- Listings are not advertisements. Although the information here is as accurate as possible, the listings are not endorsed or guaranteed by the editor of *Novel & Short Story Writer's Market*.
- *Novel & Short Story Writer's Market* reserves the right to exclude any listing that does not meet its requirements.

KEY TO SYMBOLS AND ABBREVIATIONS

‡ New listing in all sections
● Comment by editor of *Novel & Short Story Writer's Market*
♣ Canadian listing
ms—manuscript; **mss**-manuscripts
b&w—black and white
SASE—self-addressed, stamped envelope
SAE—self-addressed envelope
IRC—International Reply Coupon, for use on reply mail from other countries

(See Glossary for definitions of words and expressions used in writing and publishing.)

The Markets

Literary Magazines

Formerly Literary and Small Circulation Magazines, the Literary Magazines section contains over 530 markets for your literary short fiction. (Small circulation magazines looking for types of fiction other than literary can now be found in their own new section which follows this one.) Nearly 100 of these markets are new to this edition, and all listings which appeared in last year's edition have been updated to reflect editors' current needs. While many are university-affiliated and some independently owned, the editors at each have told us they are actively seeking fiction for their respective publications.

Although definitions of what constitutes "literary" writing vary, editors of literary journals agree they want to publish the "best" fiction available today. Qualities they look for in stories include creativity, style, flawless mechanics, and careful attention to detail in content and manuscript preparation. Most of the authors writing such fiction are well-read and well-educated, and many are students and graduates of university creative writing programs. In this marketplace, however, fine writing will always take precedence over formal training. In the Insider Report with David Hamilton, long-time editor of the prestigious *Iowa Review*, Hamilton prides himself on reaching beyond academia for fresh, new voices: "Most of the writers who send work to us are either in or have been in creative writing programs, and that means middle-class, college-educated America. . . . I'm not against an academic story, but I certainly don't want an issue full of them."

STEPPING STONES TO RECOGNITION

Some well-established literary journals pay several hundred dollars for a short story. Those paying more include *Story* which pays $1,000 per story and $750 per short short story. Most, though, can only pay with contributor's copies or a subscription to their publication. However, being published in literary journals offers the important benefits of experience, exposure and prestige. Editors of these publications pride themselves on finding "new voices," and the work of beginners is often published beside that of well-known, established writers. Agents and major book publishers read literary magazines in search of new writers. Work from among these journals is also selected for inclusion in annual prize anthologies such as *The Best American Short Stories, Prize Stories: The O. Henry Awards, Pushcart Prize: Best of the Small Presses*, and *New Stories from the South: The Year's Best*.

You'll find most of the well-known prestigious literary journals listed here. Many, including *Carolina Quarterly* and *Ploughshares*, are associated with universities, while others such as *The Quarterly* and *The Paris Review* are independently published. *Story*, published by the publisher of *Novel & Short Story Writer's Market*, won the coveted National Magazine Award for fiction in 1992 and 1995 and was a finalist for that award in 1994 and 1996.

Among the new listings in this section is *The Blue Moon Review*, an electronic literary magazine attracting 1,500 to 2,000 on-line readers each month. In the Insider Report with Doug Lawson, editor of *The Blue Moon Review*, Lawson says, "There's the potential to have millions of people reading your work worldwide." With rising paper and printing costs and with funding always a problem for many hard copy journals, it could be that more literary publications will make the decision to go on-line in the future.

SELECTING THE RIGHT LITERARY JOURNAL

Once you have browsed through this section and have a list of journals you might like to submit to, read those listings again, carefully. Remember that this is information editors present to help you in submitting work that fits their needs. How to Use This Book to Publish Your Fiction, starting on page 3, describes in detail the listing information common to all markets in our book, including information that pertains especially to literary publications.

This is the only section in which you will find magazines that do not read submissions all year long. Whether limited reading periods are tied to a university schedule or meant to accommodate the capabilities of a very small staff, those periods are noted within listings. The staffs of university journals are usually made up of student editors and a managing editor who is also a faculty member. These staffs often change every year. Whenever possible, we indicate this in listings and give the name of the current editor and the length of that editor's term. Also be aware that the schedule of a university journal usually coincides with that university's academic year, meaning that the editors of most university publications are difficult or impossible to reach during the summer.

FURTHERING YOUR SEARCH

It cannot be stressed enough that reading the listing is only the first part of developing your marketing plan. The second part, equally important, is to obtain fiction guidelines and read the actual magazine. Reading copies of a magazine helps you determine the fine points of the magazine's publishing style and philosophy. There is no substitute for this type of hands-on research.

Unlike commercial periodicals available at most newsstands and bookstores, it requires a little more effort to obtain some of the magazines listed here. The new super chain bookstores are doing a better job these days of stocking literaries and you can find some in independent and college bookstores, especially those published in your area. You may, however, need to send for a sample copy. We include sample copy prices in the listings whenever possible.

Another way to find out more about literary magazines is to check out the various prize anthologies and take note of journals whose fiction is being selected for publication there. Studying prize anthologies not only lets you know which magazines are publishing award-winning work, but it also provides a valuable overview of what is considered to be the best fiction published today.

Award-winning publications, as well as other information we feel will help you determine if a listing is the right market for you, are noted in editorial comments identified with a bullet (●). The comments section also allows us to explain more about the special interests or requirements of a publication and any information we've learned from our readers that we feel will help you choose potential markets wisely.

Among the awards and honors we note are inclusion of work in:

• *Best American Short Stories*, published by Houghton Mifflin, 222 Berkeley St., Boston MA 02116.

• *New Stories from the South: The Year's Best*, published by Algonquin Books of Chapel Hill, P.O. Box 2225, Chapel Hill NC 27515.

- *Prize Stories: The O. Henry Awards*, published by Doubleday/Anchor, 1540 Broadway, New York NY 10036.
- *Pushcart Prize: Best of the Small Presses*, published by Pushcart Press, Box 380, Wainscott NY 11975.

The well-respected *Poet* magazine (published by Cooper House Publishing Inc., P.O. Box 54947, Oklahoma City OK 73154) annually honors the best literary magazines (those publishing both fiction and poetry). The program is titled The American Literary Magazine Awards and most recipients of editorial content awards have listings in this section. To find out more about the awards, see the *Poet*'s fall issue.

FOR MORE INFORMATION

See The Business of Fiction Writing for the specific mechanics of manuscript submission. Above all, editors appreciate a professional presentation. Include a brief cover letter and send a self-addressed envelope for a reply or a self-addressed envelope in a size large enough to accommodate your manuscript, if you would like it returned. Be sure to include enough stamps or International Reply Coupons (for replies from countries other than your own) to cover your manuscript's return.

North American publications are listed in the following main section of listings; it is followed by listings for other English-speaking markets around the world. To make it easier to find Canadian markets, we include a maple leaf symbol (✹) at the start of those listings.

If you're interested in learning more about literary and small magazines, you may want to look at *The International Directory of Little Magazines and Small Presses* (Dustbooks, Box 100, Paradise CA 95967); the *Directory of Literary Magazines*, published by the Council of Literary Magazines and Presses (3-C, 154 Christopher St., New York NY 10014-2839); or *The Association of American University Presses Directory* (584 Broadway, New York NY 10012).

The following is the ranking system we have used to categorize the listings in this section.

I   **Publication encourages beginning or unpublished writers to submit work for consideration and publishes new writers regularly.**

II **Publication accepts outstanding work by beginning and established writers.**

III **Publication does not encourage beginning writers; prints mostly writers with previous publication credits; very few new writers.**

IV **Special-interest or regional publication, open only to writers in certain genres or on certain subjects or from certain geographical areas.**

V   **Closed to unsolicited submissions.**

ACM, (ANOTHER CHICAGO MAGAZINE), (II), Left Field Press, 3709 N. Kenmore, Chicago IL 60613. Editor: Barry Silesky. Fiction Editor: Sharon Solwitz. Magazine: 5½ × 8½; 200-220 pages; "art folio each issue." Estab. 1977.
  ● *ACM* is best known for experimental work or work with political slants, clear narrative voices. The editor looks for "engaged and unusual writing."
Needs: Contemporary, literary, experimental, feminist, gay/lesbian, ethnic, prose poem, translations and political/socio-historical. Receives 200 unsolicited fiction mss each month. Recently published work by Robin Hemley, Maxine Chernoff, Josip Novakovich and Chris Mazza. Published new writers in the last year. Also publishes literary essays.
How to Contact: Unsolicited mss acceptable with SASE. "Send only one story (unless you work short, less than ten pgs.) then we'll read two. We encourage cover letters." Publishes ms 6-12 months after acceptance. Sample copies are available for $8 ppd. Reports in 2-5 months. Receives small press collections.

Payment/Terms: Pays small honorarium plus contributor's copy. Acquires first North American serial rights.

Advice: "Get used to rejection slips, and don't get discouraged. Keep introductory letters short. Make sure ms has name and address on every page, and that it is clean, neat and proofread. We are looking for stories with freshness and originality in subject angle and style, and work that encounters the world and is not stuck in its own navel."

‡THE ACORN, a journal of the Western Sierra, (IV), Hot Pepper Press, P.O. Box 1266, El Dorado CA 95623. E-mail: jalapep@spider.lloyd.com. Editor: Judy Graham and committee. Fiction Editor: Verma Goodwin. Magazine: 8½×5½; 44 pages. *The Acorn* publishes work about the "western slope of Sierra Nevada and rural lifestyle." Quarterly. Estab. 1993. Circ. 200.

Needs: Adventure, literary, mainstream/contemporary, regional, senior citizen/retirement. "No porn or erotica." Receives 2-3 unsolicited mss/month. Accepts 5-6 mss/issue; 24 mss/year. Publishes ms 1 month after acceptance. Recently published work by Kirk Colvin, Judith T. Graham, Dianne Chapman McCleery and Verma Goodwin. Length: 1,500 words maximum. Publishes short shorts. Also publishes literary essays and poetry. Often critiques or comments on rejected mss. Sponsors contest; send SASE for information.

How to Contact: Send complete ms with a cover letter. Include 1-paragraph bio and list of publications. Reports in 4 months on mss. Send SASE for reply, return of ms or send a disposable copy of ms. No simultaneous submissions, reprints and electronic submissions OK. Sample copy for $4. Fiction guidelines for #10 SAE.

Payment/Terms: Pays 2 contributor's copy on publication; additional copies for $3.75. Acquires one-time rights. Sometimes sends galleys to author.

Advice: Looks for "memorable work that captures the flavor of our region—its history, landforms and wildlife and rural lifestyle. Good writing helps too."

ACORN WHISTLE, (II), 907 Brewster Ave., Beloit WI 53511. Editor: Fred Burwell. Magazine: 8½×11; 75-100 pages; uncoated paper; light card cover; illustrations; photos. "*Acorn Whistle* seeks accessible and personal writing, art and photography that appeals to readers on both emotional and intellectual levels. Our intended audience is the educated non-academic." Semiannually. Estab. 1995. Circ. 500.

● Editor Fred Burwell is also editor of *Beloit Fiction Journal*.

Needs: Ethnic/multicultural, feminist, historical (general), humor/satire, literary, mainstream/contemporary, regional. No erotica, experimental, fantasy, horror, religious or science fiction. Accepts 5-7 mss/issue; 10-15 mss/year. Publishes ms within a year after acceptance. Recently published work by Tessa Dratt, K.B. DeLong and Scott Landers. Length: open. Publishes short shorts. Also publishes memoir and poetry. Often critiques or comments on rejected ms.

How to Contact: Send complete ms with a cover letter. Should include bio. Reports in 2 weeks on queries; 1-8 weeks on mss. Send SASE for reply, return of ms or send a disposable copy of ms. Simultaneous submissions OK. Sample copy for $5. Fiction guidelines for #10 SASE.

Payment/Terms: Pays 2 contributor's copies. Acquires first North American serial rights. Features expanded contributor's notes with personal comments from each author.

Advice: "We prefer realistic story telling, strong characterization, a vivid presentation. Writing that moves both heart and mind has an excellent chance here. We encourage a friendly working relationship between editors and writers. We seek fiction that communicates and illuminates shared human experience. Don't let a rejection discourage you from trying us again."

ADRIFT, Writing: Irish, Irish American and . . . , (II), 46 E. First St. #4D, New York NY 10003. Editor: Thomas McGonigle. Magazine: 8×11; 32 pages; 60 lb. paper stock; 65 lb. cover stock; illustrations; photos. "Irish-Irish American as a basis—though we are interested in advanced writing from anywhere." Semiannually. Estab. 1983. Circ. 1,000.

Needs: Contemporary, erotica, ethnic, experimental, feminist, gay, lesbian, literary, translations. Receives 40 unsolicited mss/month. Accepts 3 mss/issue. Published work by Francis Stuart; published new writers within the last year. Length: open. Also publishes literary criticism. Sometimes critiques rejected mss.

MARKET CATEGORIES: (I) Open to new writers; (II) Open to both new and established writers; (III) Interested mostly in established writers; (IV) Open to writers whose work is specialized; (V) Closed to unsolicited submissions.

How to Contact: Send complete ms. Reports as soon as possible. SASE for return of ms. Sample copy for $5. Reviews novels or short story collections.
Payment/Terms: Pays $7.50-300 on publication for first rights.
Advice: "The writing should argue with, among others, James Joyce, Flann O'Brien, Juan Goytisolo, Ingeborg Bachmann, E.M. Cioran, Max Stirner, Patrick Kavanagh."

‡**ADVENTURES OF SWORD & SORCERY, (I, II)**, Double Star Press, P.O. Box 285, Xenia OH 45385. E-mail: dspress@erinet.com. Website: http://www.erinet.com/dspress/. Editor: Randy Dannenfelser. Magazine: 8½×11; 80 pages; slick cover stock; illustrations. "We publish sword and sorcery, heroic and high fantasy fiction." Quarterly. Estab. 1995. Circ. 7,000.
Needs: Fantasy (sword and sorcery). "We want fiction with an emphasis on action and adventure, but still cognizant of the struggles within as they play against the struggles without. Include sexual content only as required by the story, but not excessive/porn." Receives approximately 250 unsolicited mss/month. Accepts 9 mss/issue; 36 mss/year. Publishes ms 1 year after acceptance. Agented fiction 5%. Recently published work by Mike Resnick, Stephen Baxter and Darrell Schweitzer. Length: 5,000 words average; 1,000 words minimum; 20,000 words maximum. Also publishes literary criticism and book reviews (only solicited). Always critiques or comments on rejected mss.
How to Contact: Send complete ms with a cover letter. Include estimated word count, Social Security number, list of publications, phone number and e-mail address. Reports in 1 month on queries; 2 months on mss. Send SASE for reply, return of ms. No simultaneous submissions. Electronic submissions (disk or modem) OK. Sample copy $5.50. Fiction guidelines for #10 SASE. Reviews novels and short story collections.
Payment/Terms: Pays 3-6¢/word on acceptance and 3 contributor's copies; additional copies 40% discount plus shipping. Acquires first North American serial rights. Sends galleys to author.
Advice: "Recently we are looking for more adventuresome work with settings other than generic medieval Europe. Think about the audience we are targeted at, and send us appropriate stories."

AETHLON, (I,II,IV), East Tennessee State University, Johnson City TN 37614-1000. (423)929-5671. Editor-in-Chief: Don Johnson. Magazine: 6×9; 180-240 pages; illustrations and photographs. "Theme: Literary treatment of sport. We publish articles on that theme, critical studies of author's treatment of sport and original fiction and poetry with sport themes. Most of our audience are academics." Semiannually. Estab. 1983. Circ. 800.
Needs: Sport. "Stories must have a sport-related theme and subject; otherwise, we're wide open." Receives 15-20 fiction mss/month. Accepts 6-10 fiction mss/issue; 12-20 fiction mss/year. Publishes ms "about 1 year" after acceptance. Length: 2,500-5,000 words average; 500 words minimum; 7,500 words maximum. Also publishes literary essays, literary criticism, poetry. Sometimes critiques rejected mss.
How to Contact: Send complete ms and brief cover letter with 1-2 lines for a contributor's note. Reports in 6-12 months. SASE in size to fit ms. No simultaneous submissions. Electronic disk submissions OK. Final copy must be submitted on disk (WordPerfect). Sample copy for $12.50. Reviews novels and short story collections. Send books to Prof. Joe Dewey, Dept. of English, University of Pittsburgh-Johnstown, Johnstown PA 15601.
Payment/Terms: Pays 1 contributor's copy and 5 offprints.
Advice: "We are looking for well-written, insightful stories. Don't be afraid to be experimental. Take more care with your manuscript. Please send a legible manuscript free of grammatical errors. Be willing to revise."

AFRICAN AMERICAN REVIEW, (II), Indiana State University, Department of English, Root Hall A218, Terre Haute IN 47809. (812)237-2968. Fax: (812)237-3156. E-mail address: aschoal@amber.ind state.edu. Editor: Joe Weixlmann. Fiction Editor: Reginald McKnight. Magazine: 7×10; 176 pages; 60#, acid-free paper; 100# skid stock cover; illustrations and photos. "*African American Review* publishes stories and poetry by African American writers, and essays about African American literature and culture." Quarterly. Estab. 1967. Circ. 3,764.
● *African American Review* is the official publication of the Division of Black American Literature and Culture of the Modern Language Association. The magazine received American Literary Magazine Awards in 1994 and 1995.
Needs: Ethnic/Multicultural: experimental, feminist, gay, lesbian, literary, mainstream/contemporary. "No children's/juvenile/young adult/teen." Receives 10 unsolicited mss/month. Accepts 6-8 mss/year. Publishes ms 1 year after acceptance. Agented fiction 10%. Published work by Clarence Major, Ann Allen Shockley, Alden Reimoneng. Length: 3,000 words average. Also publishes literary essays, literary criticism, poetry. Sometimes critiques or comments on rejected mss.
How to Contact: Send complete ms with a cover letter. Reports in 2 weeks on queries; 3 months on mss. Send SASE for reply, return of ms or send a disposable copy of ms. Sample copy for $6. Fiction guidelines for #10 SASE. Reviews novels and short story collections. Send books to Keneth Kinnamon, Dept. of English, Univ. of Arkansas, Fayetteville, AR 72701.

Payment/Terms: Pays $50-100 and 10 contributor's copies on publication for first North American serial rights. Sends galleys to author.

AGNI, (III), Creative Writing Program, Boston University, 236 Bay State Rd., Boston MA 02215. (617)353-5389. Fax: (617)353-7136. Editor-in-Chief: Askold Melnyczuk. Magazine: 5½×8½; 320 pages; 55 lb. booktext paper; recycled cover stock; occasional art portfolios. "Eclectic literary magazine publishing first-rate poems and stories." Semiannually. Estab. 1972.
• Work from *Agni* has been selected regularly for inclusion in both *Pushcart Prize* and *Best American Short Stories* anthologies. "We tend to be backlogged with fiction."
Needs: Stories, excerpted novels, prose poems and translations. Receives 250 unsolicited fiction mss/month. Accepts 4-7 mss/issue, 8-12 mss/year. Reading period October 1 to April 30 only. Recently published work by Joyce Carol Oates, Madison Smartt Bell, Alice Adams, Ha Jin. Rarely critiques rejected mss.
How to Contact: Send complete ms with SASE and cover letter listing previous publications. Simultaneous and electronic (disk) submissions OK. Reports in 1-4 months. Sample copy for $6.
Payment/Terms: Pays $10/page up to $150; 2 contributor's copies; one-year subscription. Pays on publication for first North American serial rights. Sends galleys to author. Copyright reverts to author upon publication.
Advice: "Read *Agni* carefully to understand the kinds of stories we publish. Read—everything, classics, literary journals, bestsellers."

THE AGUILAR EXPRESSION, (II), 1329 Gilmore Ave., Donora PA 15033. Editor: Xavier F. Aguilar. Magazine: 8½×11; 10-16 pages; 20 lb. bond paper; illustrations. "We are open to all writers of a general theme—something that may appeal to everyone." Semiannually. Estab. 1989. Circ. 150.
• The editor is particularly interested in stories about the homeless in the U.S. but publishes fiction on other topics as well.
Needs: Adventure, ethnic/multicultural, experimental, horror, mainstream/contemporary, mystery/suspense (romantic suspense), romance (contemporary). No religious or first-person stories. Will publish annual special fiction issue or anthology in the future. Receives 10 unsolicited mss/month. Accepts 1-2 mss/issue; 2-4 mss/year. Publishes ms 1 month to 1 year after acceptance. Recently published work by Michael D. Cohen, R.G. Cantalupo and Kent Braithwaite. Length: 1,000 words average; 750 words minimum; 1,500 words maximum. Also publishes poetry.
How to Contact: Send complete ms with cover letter. Reports on queries in 1 week; mss in 1 month. Send SASE for reply to a query or send a disposable copy of ms. No simultaneous submissions. Sample copy for $6. Fiction guidelines for #10 SASE.
Payment/Terms: Pays 1 contributor's copy; additional copies at a reduced rate of $3. Acquires one-time rights. Not copyrighted. Write to publication for details on contests, awards or grants.

ALABAMA LITERARY REVIEW, (II), Smith 253, Troy State University, Troy AL 36082. (334)670-3286, ext. 3307. Fax: (334)670-3519. Editor: Theron Montgomery. Magazine: 7×10; approximately 100 pages; top paper quality; light card cover; some illustrations. "National magazine for a broad range of the best contemporary fiction, poetry, essays and drama that we can find." Annually. Estab. 1987.
Needs: Contemporary, experimental, humor/satire, literary, prose poem, science fiction, serialized/excerpted novel, translations. "Serious writing." Receives 50 unsolicited fiction mss/month. Accepts 5 fiction mss/issue. Publishes ms 5-6 months after acceptance. Recently published work by Reina McKeithew, Patricia Cronin, Jay Prefontaine, Barry Bradford and Richard Wirick. Published new writers within the last year. Length: 2,000-3,500 words average. Publishes short shorts of 1,000 words. Also publishes literary essays, literary criticism, poetry and drama. Sometimes comments on rejected mss.
How to Contact: Send complete ms with cover letter or submit through agent. Reports on queries in 2 weeks; on mss in 2 months (except in summer). SASE. Simultaneous submissions OK. Sample copy for $4 plus postage. Reviews novels or short story collections. Send to Steve Cooper.
Payment/Terms: Pays in contributor's copies and honorarium when available. First rights returned to author upon publication. Work published in *ALR* may be read on state-wide (nonprofit) public radio program.
Advice: "Read our publication first. Avoid negative qualities pertaining to gimmickry and a self-centered point of view. We are interested in any kind of writing if it is *serious* and *honest* in the sense of 'the human heart in conflict with itself.' "

ALASKA QUARTERLY REVIEW, (II), University of Alaska—Anchorage, 3211 Providence Dr., Anchorage AK 99508. (907)786-4775. Fiction Editor: Ronald Spatz. Magazine: 6×9; 200 pages; 60 lb. Glatfelter paper; 10 pt. C15 black ink varnish cover stock; photos on cover only. *AQR* "publishes fiction, poetry, literary nonfiction and short plays in traditional and experimental styles." Semiannually. Estab. 1982. Circ. 1,500.

• Work appearing in the *Alaska Quarterly Review* has been selected for the *Pushcart Prize*, *Best American Essays*, *Best American Poetry* and *Best American Short Stories* anthologies.

Needs: Contemporary, experimental, literary, prose poem and translations. Receives 200 unsolicited fiction mss/month. Accepts 7-13 mss/issue, 15-24 mss/year. Does not read mss May 15 through August 15. Length: not exceeding 50 pages. Recently published work by Patricia Hampl, Stuart Dischell and Hayden Carruth. Published new writers within the last year. Publishes short shorts.

How to Contact: Send complete mss with SASE. Simultaneous submissions "undesirable, but will accept if indicated." Reports in 2-3 months "but during peak periods a reply may take up to 5 months." Publishes ms 6 months to 1 year after acceptance. Sample copy for $5.

Payment/Terms: Pays 1 contributor's copy and a year's subscription. Pays $50-200 honorarium when grant funding permits. Acquires first rights.

Advice: "We have made a significant investment in fiction. The reason is quality; serious fiction *needs* a market. Try to have everything build to a singleness of effect."

ALLEGHENY REVIEW, (IV), Box 32, Allegheny College, Meadville PA 16335. (814)332-6553. Senior Editor: Brooke Balta. Editors: Amy Augustyn, Jason Ramsey. Magazine: 8×5; 82 pages; white paper; illustrations and photos. "The *Allegheny Review* publishes short fiction, poetry and short nonfiction; our intended audience is other college students, professors and interested readers. Annually. Estab. 1980. Circ. 500.

Needs: Adventure, ethnic/multicultural, experimental, fantasy, feminist, gay, historical (general), horror, humor/satire, lesbian, literary, mainstream/contemporary, mystery/suspense, psychic/supernatural/occult, regional, religious/inspirational, science fiction (soft/sociological), westerns. Receives 40 unsolicited mss/month. Buys 7 mss/issue; 7 mss/year. Does not read mss May-August. Publishes ms 2 months after deadline. Length: 2,000 words average; 3,000 words maximum. Publishes short shorts. Also publishes literary essays, poetry.

How to Contact: *Open to work by undergraduate writers only.* Sometimes critiques or comments on rejected ms. Send complete ms with a cover letter. Should include 1 page bio. SASE for reply. Sample copy for $5.

Payment/Terms: Pays free subscription and 1 contributor's copy; additional copies for $4.

Advice: Looking for "interesting plot, mature style and good technique. Proofread! Avoid clichés."

ALPHA BEAT PRESS, (I, IV), 31 A Waterloo St., New Hope PA 18938. Editor: Dave Christy. Magazine: 7½×9; 95-125 pages; illustrations. "Beat and modern literature—prose, reviews and poetry." Semiannually. Estab. 1987. Circ. 600.

• Work from *Alpha Beat Press* has appeared in *Pushcart Prize* anthologies. Alpha Beat Press also publishes poetry chapbooks and supplements. The magazine is known for writings associated with modern and beat culture.

Needs: Erotica, experimental, literary and prose poem. Recently published work by Elliott, Jan Kerouac, Chris Diamant, Ken Kesey and Charles Plymell. Published new writers within the last year. Length: 600 words minimum; 1,000 words maximum. Also publishes literary essays, literary criticism, poetry.

How to Contact: Query first. Reports on queries within 2 weeks. SASE. Simultaneous and reprint submissions OK. Sample copy for $10. Reviews novels and short story collections.

Payment/Terms: Pays in contributor's copies. Rights remain with author.

Advice: "*ABP* is the finest journal of its kind available today, having, with 17 issues, published the widest range of published and unpublished writers you'll find in the small press scene."

AMELIA, (II), 329 E St., Bakersfield CA 93304. (805)323-4064. Editor-in-Chief: Frederick A. Raborg, Jr. Magazine: 5½×8½; 124-136 pages; perfect-bound; 60 lb. high-quality moistrite matte paper; kromekote cover; four-color covers; original illustrations; b&w photos. "A general review using fine fiction, poetry, criticism, belles lettres, one-act plays, fine pen-and-ink sketches and line drawings, sophisticated cartoons, book reviews and translations of both fiction and poetry for general readers with eclectic tastes for quality writing." Quarterly. Plans special fiction issue each July. Estab. 1984. Circ. 1,750.

• *Amelia* sponsors a long list of fiction awards.

---

‡ **THE DOUBLE DAGGER** before a listing indicates that the listing is new in this edition. New markets are often the most receptive to submissions by new writers.

Needs: Adventure, contemporary, erotica, ethnic, experimental, fantasy, feminist, gay, historical, humor/satire, lesbian, literary, mainstream, mystery/suspense, prose poem, regional, science fiction, senior citizen/retirement, sports, translations, western. Nothing "obviously pornographic or patently religious." Receives 160-180 unsolicited mss/month. Accepts up to 9 mss/issue; 25-36 mss/year. Recently published work by Michael Bugeja, Jack Curtis, Thomas F. Wilson, Maxine Kumin, Eugene Dubnov, Matt Mulhern and Merrill Joan Gerber. Published new writers within the last year. Length: 3,000 words average; 1,000 words minimum; 5,000 words maximum. Usually critiques rejected mss.

How to Contact: Send complete ms with cover letter with previous credits if applicable to *Amelia* and perhaps a brief personal comment to show personality and experience. Reports in 1 week on queries; 2 weeks to 3 months on mss. SASE. Sample copy for $8.95. Fiction guidelines for #10 SASE. Sends galleys to author "when deadline permits."

Payment/Terms: Pays $35-50 on acceptance for first North American serial rights plus 2 contributor's copies; extras with 20% discount.

Advice: "Write carefully and well, but have a strong story to relate. I look for depth of plot and uniqueness, and strong characterization. Study manuscript mechanics and submission procedures. Neatness does count. There is a sameness—a cloning process—among most magazines today that tends to dull the senses. Magazines like *Amelia* will awaken those senses while offering stories and poems of lasting value."

AMERICAN LITERARY REVIEW, A National Journal of Poems and Stories, (II), University of North Texas, P.O. Box 13827, Denton TX 76203-6827. (817)565-2127. Editor: Barb Rodman. Magazine: 7×10; 128 pages; 70 lb. Mohawk paper; 67 lb. Wausau Vellum cover. "Publishes quality, contemporary poems and stories." Semiannually. Estab. 1990. Circ. 800.

Needs: Mainstream and literary only. No genre works. Receives 50-75 unsolicited fiction mss/month. Accepts 7-10 mss/issue; 14-20 mss/year. Publishes ms within 2 years after acceptance. Published work by Gordon Weaver, Gerald Haslam and William Miller. Length: less than 10,000 words. Critiques or comments on rejected mss when possible. Also accepts poetry and essays.

How to Contact: Send complete ms with cover letter. Reports in 2-3 months. SASE. Simultaneous submissions OK. Sample copy for $8. Fiction guidelines free.

Payment/Terms: Pays in contributor's copies. Acquires one-time rights.

Advice: "Give us distinctive styles, original approaches, stories that are willing to take a chance. We respond to character first, those that have a past and future beyond the page." Looks for "literary quality and careful preparation. There is a sameness to most of the stories that we receive—somebody dies or a relationship ends. We would love to see stories beyond those topics that grab us immediately and keep us interested throughout."

AMERICAN SHORT FICTION, (II), English Dept., Parlin 108, University of Texas at Austin, Austin TX 78712-1164. (512)471-1772. Editor: Joseph Kruppa. Magazine: $5\frac{3}{4} \times 9\frac{1}{4}$; 128 pages; 60 lb. natural paper; 8015 karma white cover. "*American Short Fiction* publishes fiction *only*, of all lengths, from short short to novella." Quarterly. Estab. 1990. Circ. 1,200.

Needs: Literary. "No romance, science fiction, erotica, mystery/suspense and religious." Receives 500 unsolicited mss/month. Acquires 6 mss/issue; 25-30 mss/year. Accepts mss September 1 through May 31. Publishes ms up to 1 year after acceptance. Agented fiction 20%. Recently published work by Michael Guista, Alyce Miller, Steve Lattimore and Natasha Waxman. Length: open. Sponsors contest. Send SASE for details.

How to Contact: Send complete ms with cover letter. Reports in 3-4 months on mss. Send SASE for reply, return of ms or send disposable copy of the ms. Simultaneous submissions OK if informed. Sample copy for $9.95. Fiction guidelines for #10 SASE.

Payment/Terms: Pays $400/story for first rights. Sends galleys to author.

Advice: "We pick work for *American Short Fiction* along simple lines: Do we love it? Is this a story we will be happy reading four or five times? We comment only *rarely* on submissions because of the volume of work we receive."

‡AMERICAN WRITING; A Magazine, (I, II), Nierika Editions, 4343 Menayunk Ave., Philadelphia PA 19128. (215)483-7051. Editor: Alexandra Grilikhes. Magazine: $8\frac{1}{2} \times 5\frac{1}{2}$; 80-88 pages; matte paper and cover stock; photos. "We publish new writing that takes risks. We are interested in the voice of the loner, the artist as shaman, the powers of intuition, exceptional work of all kinds." Semiannually. Estab. 1990. Circ. 2,500.

Needs: Contemporary, excerpted novel, ethnic/multicultural, experimental, feminist, gay, lesbian, literary, translations. No mainstream. Receives 100-200 unsolicited mss/month. Accepts 4-5 mss/issue; 10-11 mss/year. Does not read mss June, December, January. Publishes ms 6-12 months after acceptance. Agented fiction less than 1%. Recently published work by Karen Backstrom, Samantha Gillison, Stephen Poleskie, Chris Semansky, Kirkly Tittle, Sally Borden, Sallie Bingham and Alvaro Cardona-Hine. Length: 3,500 words average; 5,000 words maximum. Publishes short shorts. Also publishes literary essays, literary criticism and poetry. Critiques or comments on rejected mss "when there is time."

How to Contact: Send complete ms with a cover letter. Include brief bio and list of publications if applicable. Reports in 1 month on queries; 6-8 weeks on mss. Send SASE for reply, return of ms or send a disposable copy of ms. Simultaneous submissions OK. Sample copy for $6; fiction guidelines for #10 SASE.

Payment/Terms: Pays 2 contributor's copies; additional copies at half price. Acquires first rights or one-time rights.

Advice: "We look for intensity, vision, imaginative use of language, freshness, craft, sophistication; stories that delve. Read one or two issues of the magazine *carefully.*"

THE AMERICAS REVIEW, A Review of Hispanic Literature and Art of the USA, (II, IV), Arte Publico Press, 4800 Calhoun, University of Houston, Houston TX 77204-2090. (713)743-2841. Fax: (713)743-2847. Editors: Lauro Flores and Evangelina Vigil-Pinon. Magazine: 5½×8½; 128 pages; illustrations and photographs. *"The Americas Review* publishes contemporary fiction written by U.S. Hispanics—Mexican Americans, Puerto Ricans, Cuban Americans, etc." Triannually. Estab. 1972.

Needs: Contemporary, ethnic, literary, women's, hispanic literature. No novels. Receives 12-15 fiction mss/month. Accepts 2-3 mss/issue; 8-12 mss/year. Publishes mss 6 months to 1 year after acceptance. Recently published work by Nash Candelaria, Roberto Fernández, Sheila Ortiz Taylor, Omar Castañeda, Kathleen Alcala and Daniel Orozco. Length: 3,000-4,500 average number of words; 1,500 words minimum; 6,000 words maximum (30 pages maximum, double-spaced). Publishes short shorts. Sometimes critiques rejected mss.

How to Contact: *"You must subscribe upon submitting materials."* Send complete ms. Reports in 3-4 months. SASE. No simultaneous submissions. Accepts electronic submissions via IBM compatible disk. Sample copy for $5; $10 double issue.

Payment/Terms: Pays $50-200; 2 contributor's copies on acceptance for first rights, and rights to 40% of fees if story is reprinted. Sponsors award for fiction writers.

Advice: "There has been a noticeable increase in quality in U.S. Hispanic literature."

‡♣**THE AMETHYST REVIEW, (I, II)**, Marcasite Press, 23 Riverside Ave., Truro, Nova Scotia B2N 4G2 Canada. (902)895-1345. Editors: Penny Ferguson and Lenora Steele. Magazine: 8¼×6¾; 84 pages; book weight paper; card stock cover; illustrations. "We publish quality contemporary fiction and poetry of interest to the literary reader." Semiannually. Estab. 1993. Circ. 150.

Needs: Literary. List of upcoming themes available for SASE. Receives 10 unsolicited mss/month. Accepts 2-3 mss/issue; 4-6 mss/year. Publishes ms maximum 6 months after acceptance, "usually much sooner." Recently published work by Rick Wenman, Brenda Mier, Patience Wheatley, Ruth Latta, Theresa Wallace, Steve Vernon and Lor Pelton. Length: 5,000 words maximum. Publishes short shorts. Also publishes poetry. Sponsors contest; send SASE for information. Always critiques or comments on rejected mss.

How to Contact: Send complete ms with cover letter. Include estimated word count, a 50-word bio and list of publications. Reports in 2-28 weeks on mss. Send SASE or SAE and IRCs for reply, return of mss or send a disposable copy of ms. Sample copy for $6 (current) or $4 (back issues). Fiction guidelines for SASE or SAE and IRCs. Reviews novels and short story collections "only by people we have published."

Payment/Terms: Pays 1 contributor's copy; additional copies $4. Pays on publication. Acquires first North American serial rights.

Advice: "Quality is our criterion. Don't try to shock us. Try to delight us with originality and craft. Send for guidelines and sample. We don't look for a specific type of story. We publish the *best* of what we receive."

ANTIETAM REVIEW, (I, II, IV), Washington County Arts Council, 7 W. Franklin St., Hagerstown MD 21740. (301)791-3132. Editor: Susanne Kass. Fiction Editors: Susanne Kass and Ann Knox. Magazine: 8½×11; 54-68 pages; glossy paper; light card cover; photos. A literary journal of short fiction, poetry and black-and-white photographs. Annually. Estab. 1982. Circ. 1,800.
  ● *Antietam Review* has received several awards including First-runner Up (1993-94) for Editorial Content from the American Literary Magazine Awards. Work published in the magazine has been included in the *Pushcart Prize* anthology and *Best American Short Stories.*

Needs: Condensed/excerpted novel, contemporary, ethnic, experimental, feminist, literary and prose poem. "We read manuscripts from our region—Delaware, Maryland, Pennsylvania, Virginia, West Virginia and Washington D.C. only. We read from September 1 to February 1." Receives about 100 unsolicited mss/month. Buys 8-10 stories/year. Publishes ms 2-3 months after acceptance. Recently published work by Stephen Dixon, Jonathan Bowen, Joan Connor and Roberta Murphy. Published new writers within the last year. Length: 3,000 words average. Also publishes poetry.

How to Contact: "Send ms and SASE with a cover letter. Let us know if you have published before and where." Include estimated word count, 1-paragraph bio and list of publications. Reports in 2-4 months. "If we hold a story, we let the writer know. Occasionally we critique returned ms or ask for rewrites." Sample copy for $5.25. Back issue $3.15. Guidelines for legal SAE.

Payment/Terms: "We believe it is a matter of dignity that writers and poets be paid. We have been able to give $50-100 a story and $25 a poem, but this depends on funding. Also 2 copies." Buys first North American serial rights. Sends galleys to author if requested.

Advice: "We look for well-crafted work that shows attention to clarity and precision of language. We like relevant detail but want to see significant emotional movement within the course of the story—something happening to the central character. This journal was started in response to the absence of fiction markets for emerging writers. Its purpose is to give exposure to fiction writers, poets and photographers of high artistic quality who might otherwise have difficulty placing their work."

✤THE ANTIGONISH REVIEW, (I, II), St. Francis Xavier University, P.O. Box 5000, Antigonish, Nova Scotia B2G 2W5 Canada. (902)867-3962. Fax: (902)867-2389. E-mail: tar@stfx.ca. Editor: George Sanderson. Literary magazine for educated and creative readers. Quarterly. Estab. 1970. Circ. 800.

Needs: Literary, contemporary, prose poem and translations. No erotic or political material. Accepts 6 mss/issue. Receives 50 unsolicited fiction mss each month. Published work by Arnold Bloch, Richard Butts and Helen Barolini. Published new writers within the last year. Length: 3,000-5,000 words. Sometimes comments briefly on rejected mss.

How to Contact: Send complete ms with cover letter. SASE ("U.S. postage not acceptable"). No simultaneous submissions. Electronic (disk compatible with WordPerfect/IBM and Windows or e-mail) submissions OK. Prefers hard copy with disk submission. Reports in 6 months. Publishes ms 3 months to 1 year after acceptance.

Payment/Terms: Pays 2 contributor's copies. Authors retain copyright.

Advice: "Learn the fundamentals and do not deluge an editor."

ANTIOCH REVIEW, (II), Box 148, Yellow Springs OH 45387. (513)767-6389. Editor: Robert S. Fogarty. Associate Editor: Nolan Miller. Magazine: 6×9; 128 pages; 50 lb. book offset paper; coated cover stock; illustrations "seldom." "Literary and cultural review of contemporary issues in politics, American and international studies, and literature for general readership." Quarterly. Published special fiction issue last year; plans another. Estab. 1941. Circ. 4,500.

Needs: Literary, contemporary, experimental and translations. No children's, science fiction or popular market. Accepts 5-6 mss/issue, 20-24 mss/year. Receives approximately 275 unsolicited fiction mss each month. Approximately 1-2% of fiction agented. Length: any length the story justifies.

How to Contact: Send complete ms with SASE, preferably mailed flat. Reports in 2 months. Publishes ms 6-9 months after acceptance. Sample copy for $6. Guidelines for SASE.

Payment/Terms: Pays $10/page; 2 contributor's copies. $3.30 for extras. Pays on publication for first and one-time rights (rights returned to author on request).

Advice: "Our best advice, always, is to *read* the *Antioch Review* to see what type of material we publish. Quality fiction requires an engagement of the reader's intellectual interest supported by mature emotional relevance, written in a style that is rich and rewarding without being freaky. The great number of stories submitted to us indicates that fiction still has great appeal. We assume that if so many are writing fiction, many must be reading it."

APHRODITE GONE BERSERK, (IV), A journal of erotic art, Red Wine Press, 233 Guyon Ave., Staten Island NY 10306. Editors: C. Esposito, E Eccleston. Magazine: 8½×11; 50 pages; illustrations and photos. "*AGB* publishes fiction, poetry, essays, photography, etc. that deal with the erotic or sexuality in all styles and from any perspective or orientation." Semiannually. Estab. 1996.

Needs: Erotica: condensed/excerpted novel, experimental, feminist, gay, lesbian, literary, translations. Upcoming theme: "Public Exposure" (winter 1997). List of upcoming themes available for SASE. Receives 10 unsolicited mss/month. Accepts 3 mss/issue; 6 mss/year. Publishes ms 6-12 months after acceptance. Publishes short shorts. Also publishes literary essays, literary criticism, poetry.

How to Contact: Send complete ms with a cover letter. Reports in 2 weeks on queries; 1 month on mss. Send SASE for reply, return of ms or send a disposable copy of ms. Simultaneous and reprint submissions OK. Reviews novels or short story collections.

Payment/Terms: Pays 1 contributor's copy. Acquires one-time rights.

Advice: "Stay away from the cliché and tired, and write honestly from the heart. We do not allow industry trends to affect the type of fiction we accept for publication."

APPALACHIAN HERITAGE, (I, II), Hutchins Library, Berea College, Berea KY 40403. (606)986-9341. Fax: (606)986-9494. E-mail: sidney~a.farr@berea.edu. Editor: Sidney Saylor Farr. Magazine: 6×9; 80 pages; 60 lb. stock; 10 pt. Warrenflo cover; drawings and b&w photos. "*Appalachian Heritage* is a southern Appalachian literary magazine. We try to keep a balance of fiction, poetry, essays, scholarly works, etc., for a general audience and/or those interested in the Appalachian mountains." Quarterly. Estab. 1973. Circ. approximately 600.

Needs: Regional, literary, historical. "We do not want to see fiction that has no ties to Southern Appalachia." Receives 6-8 unsolicited mss/month. Accepts 2-3 mss/issue; 12-15 mss/year. Publishes ms 1-2 years after acceptance. Recently published work by Garry Barker, James Still and Rhonda Strickland. Published new writers within the last year. Length: 3,000 words maximum. Publishes short shorts. Length: 500 words. Occasionally critiques rejected mss.

How to Contact: Send complete ms with cover letter. Include estimated word count, 2-3-sentence bio and list of publications. Reports in 3-4 weeks on queries; 4-6 weeks on mss. Send SASE for reply, return of ms or send a disposable copy of ms. Simultaneous and electronic submissions OK. Sample copy for $6. Guidelines free.

Payment/Terms: Pays 3 contributor's copies; $6 charge for extras. Acquires first North American serial rights.

Advice: "Get acquainted with *Appalachian Heritage*, as you should with any publication before submitting your work."

ARARAT QUARTERLY, (IV), Ararat Press, AGBU., 585 Saddle River Rd., Saddle Brook NJ 07662. (212)765-8260. Editor: Dr. Leo Hamalian. Magazine: 8½×11; 72 pages; illustrations and b&w photographs. "*Ararat* is a forum for the literary and historical works of Armenian intellectuals or non-Armenian writers writing about Armenian subjects."

Needs: Condensed/excerpted novel, contemporary, historical, humor/satire, literary, religious/inspirational, translations. Publishes special fiction issue. Receives 25 unsolicited mss/month. Accepts 5 mss/issue; 20 mss/year. Length: 1,000 words average. Publishes short shorts. Length: 500 words. Also publishes literary essays, literary criticism, poetry. Sometimes critiques rejected mss and recommends other markets.

How to Contact: Send complete ms with cover letter. Reports in 1 month on queries; 3 weeks on mss. SASE. Simultaneous and reprint submissions OK. Sample copy for $7 and $1 postage. Free fiction guidelines. Reviews novels and short story collections.

Payment/Terms: Pays $40-75 plus 2 contributor's copies on publication for one-time rights. Sends galleys to author.

ARK/ANGEL REVIEW, (II), NYU Creative Writing Program, 19 University Place, 2nd Floor, New York NY 10003. (212)998-8816. Fax: (212)995-4019. Editor: Helen Ellis. Fiction Editor: Hannah Tinti. Editors change each year. Magazine: 5½× 8½; 120 pages. Semiannually. Estab. 1987. Circ. 1,000.

Needs: Literary. Accepts 6-8 mss/issue; 12-14 mss/year. Does not read mss April 1-August 15. Publishes ms 6 months after acceptance. Agented fiction 50%. Recently published work by Wesley Brown, Pagan Kennedy, Jonathan Dee. Length: 5,000 words maximum. Publishes short shorts. Also publishes poetry. Sometimes critiques or comments on rejected ms.

How to Contact: Send complete ms with a short cover letter. Reports in 4 months on mss. SASE for return of ms. Simultaneous submissions OK. Sample copy for $5.

Payment/Terms: Pays 3 contributor's copies. Acquires first North American serial rights.

Advice: "Please send polished, proofread manuscripts only."

ARNAZELLA, (II, IV), English Department, Bellevue Community College, 3000 Landerholm Circle SE, Bellevue WA 98007. (206)641-6032. Advisor: Woody West. Editors change each year; contact advisor. Magazine: 10×9; 104 pages, 70 lb. paper; heavy coated cover; illustrations and photos. "For those interested in quality fiction." Annually. Estab. 1976. Circ. 500.

Needs: Adventure, contemporary, ethnic, experimental, fantasy, feminist, gay, historical, humor/satire, lesbian, literary, mainstream, mystery/suspense, regional. Submit Sept. 1-Dec. 31 for issue published in spring. Recently published work by Judith Skillman, Linda Elegant, Blaine Hammond, Duncan Z. Saffir and Christy Soto. Published new writers within the last year. Publishes short shorts. Also publishes literary essays and poetry. *Northwest contributors only, including British Columbia.*

How to Contact: Send complete ms with cover letter. "We accept submissions September through December only." Reports on mss in spring. SASE. No simultaneous submissions. Sample copy for $5. Guidelines for SASE.

Payment/Terms: Pays in contributor's copies. Acquires first rights.

Advice: "Read this and similar magazines, reading critically and analytically. Since *Arnazella* does not edit for anything other than very minor problems, we need pieces that are technically sound."

ARTFUL DODGE, (II), Dept. of English, College of Wooster, Wooster OH 44691. (216)263-2000. Editor-in-Chief: Daniel Bourne. Magazine: 150-200 pages; illustrations; photos. "There is no theme in this magazine, except literary power. We also have an ongoing interest in translations from Eastern Europe and elsewhere." Annually. Estab. 1979. Circ. 1,000.

Needs: Experimental, literary, prose poem, translations. "We judge by literary quality, not by genre. We are especially interested in fine English translations of significant contemporary prose writers. Translations should be submitted with original texts." Receives 40 unsolicited fiction mss/month. Accepts 5 mss/year. Recently published fiction by Edward Kleinschmidt, Terese Svoboda, David Surface, Greg Boyd and Zbigniew Herbert; and interviews with Tim O'Brien, Lee Smith, Michael Dorris and Stuart Dybek. Published 1 new writer within the last year. Length: 10,000 words maximum; 2,500 words average. Also publishes literary essays, literary criticism, poetry. Occasionally critiques rejected mss.
How to Contact: Send complete ms with SASE. Do not send more than 30 pages at a time. Reports in 1 week to 6 months. No simultaneous or reprint submissions. Sample copies of older, single issues are $2.75 or five issues for $5; recent issues are double issues, available for $5.75. Fiction guidelines for #10 SASE.
Payment/Terms: Pays 2 contributor's copies and honorarium. Acquires first North American serial rights.
Advice: "If we take time to offer criticism, do not subsequently flood us with other stories no better than the first. If starting out, get as many *good* readers as possible. Above all, read contemporary fiction and the magazine you are trying to publish in."

ARTISAN, a journal of craft, (I, II), P.O. Box 157, Wilmette IL 60091. (847)673-7246. E-mail: artisanjnl@aol. Editor: Joan Daugherty. Tabloid: 8½×11; 20-28 pages; colored bond paper; illustrations. "The philosophy behind *artisan* is that anyone who strives to express themselves through their craft is an artist and artists of all genres can learn from each other." For artists and the general public. Estab. 1995. Circ. 200.
Needs: Adventure, condensed/excerpted novel, erotica (mild), ethnic/multicultural, experimental, fantasy (science fantasy, sword and sorcery), feminist, horror, humor/satire, literary, mainstream/contemporary, mystery/suspense, psychic/supernatural/occult, science fiction, sports, westerns. "No pornography, or anything too sweet or saccharine." Receives 25 unsolicited mss/month. Accepts 6-8 mss/issue; 40 mss/year. Publishes ms 4-8 months after acceptance. Recently published work by Crissa-Jean Chappell, Eric Spitznagel, Ruth McLaughlin and Ben Ohmart. Length: 2,000 words average; 4,000 words maximum. Publishes short shorts. Also publishes literary essays, literary criticism, poetry. Sometimes critiques or comments on rejected mss.
How to Contact: Send complete ms with cover letter. Include estimated word count. Reports in 1 month on queries; 3 months on mss. SASE for reply and send a disposable copy of ms. Simultaneous and electronic submissions (e-mail or ASCII) OK. Sample copy for $2.50. Fiction guidelines for #10 SASE. Guidelines also posted on the Internet at http://members.aol.com/artisanjnl. Will sponsor a short fiction competition for 1997: $200 1st prize; $100 2nd prize. Send SASE for guidelines.
Payment/Terms: Pays 3 contributor's copies; additional copies $2. Acquires first rights.
Advice: "Innovative phrasing and subject matter stand out. Strive to use fresh language and situations, but don't disregard the basics of good writing and storytelling."

‡ASCENT, (II), Dept. 9 English, Concordia College, Moorhead MN 56562. Editor: W. Scott Olsen. E-mail: ascent@cord.edu. Magazine: 6×9; 50-70 pages. Triannually. Estab. 1976. Circ. 1,000.
● *Ascent* has received grants from the Illinois Arts Council. Work published in the magazine has been selected for *Pushcart* Awards and inclusion in the *Best American Short Story Anthology*.
Needs: Literary. Receives 40-50 unsolicited mss/month. Accepts 4-5 mss/issue; 12-15 mss/year. Publishes ms 3-6 months after acceptance. Recently published work by Alvin Greenberg, K.C. Frederick and Erin McGraw. Length: 3,000 words average. Also publishes poetry and essays. Sometimes critiques or comments on rejected mss.
How to Contact: Send complete ms. Reports in 2 weeks on queries; 2-8 weeks on mss. Send SASE for reply, return of ms or send a disposable copy of ms. Simultaneous submissions OK. Sample copy for $4. Fiction guidelines for SASE.
Payment/Terms: Pays 3 contributor's copies.
Terms: Acquires first rights. Sends galleys to author.

ASIAN PACIFIC AMERICAN JOURNAL, (I, II, IV), The Asian American Writers' Workshop, 37 St. Marks Place, New York NY 10003-7801. (212)228-6718. Fax: (212)228-7718. E-mail: aaww@panix.com. Editors: Eric Gamalinda, Eileen Tabios. Magazine: 5½×8½; 150 pages; illustrations. "We are interested in publishing works by writers from all segments of the Asian Pacific American community. The journal appeals to all interested in Asian-American literature and culture." Semiannually. Estab. 1992. Circ. 1,500.
● *Asian Pacific American Journal* received a NEA grant in 1995.
Needs: Adventure, condensed/excerpted novel, erotica, ethnic/multicultural, experimental, feminist, gay, historical (general), humor/satire, lesbian, literary, mainstream/contemporary, regional, serialized novel, translations, Asian-American themes. "We are interested in anything related to the Asian American community." Upcoming guest editors: Garrett Hongo (fiction), Chitra Divakaruni (poetry), Spring/

Summer 1997. Publishes annual special fiction issue or anthology. Receives 75 unsolicited mss/month. Accepts 15 mss/issue; 30 mss/year. Does not read September-October, March-April. Publishes ms 3-4 months after acceptance. Agented fiction 5%. Recently published work by Shawn Wong, Arthur Sze, Yusef Komunyakaa. Length: 3,000 words average; 1,500 words minimum; 5,000 words maximum. Publishes short shorts. Also publishes literary essays, poetry. Sometimes critiques or comments on rejected ms.

How to Contact: Query first. Send SASE for guidelines. Should include estimated word count, 3-5 sentence bio, list of publications. Reports in 1 month on queries; 4 months on mss. SASE for reply or send a disposable copy of ms. Simultaneous, reprint, electronic (disk, Macintosh or IBM, preferably Microsoft Word 5 for Mac) submissions OK. Sample copy for $12. Fiction guidelines for SASE. Reviews novels and short story collections.

Payment/Terms: Pays 2 contributor's copies; additional copies at 40% discount. Acquires one-time rights. Sends galleys to author. Sponsors contests, awards or grants for fiction writers. "Send query with SASE."

‡ASSPANTS, (I, II), Asspants Publications, 856 Baker St., San Francisco CA 94115. (415)440-2665. E-mail: asspants@sirius.com. Editors: Michael Barnett and Chad Lange. Magazine: 8½×8½; 67 pages; illustrations and photos. "We value quality above and beyond any other factor. In addition to fiction, we also publish poetry and black-and-white artwork. Our intention is to show talented writers/artists that publishing *is* possible." Quarterly. Estab. 1996. Circ. 150 (in Bay Area).

Needs: "We consider any material as long as it is intelligent and well-written. We do not like to limit topics." Receives approximately 10 unsolicited mss/month. Accepts 2-3 mss/issue. Publishes ms 4-5 months after acceptance. Recently published work by Brian Weaver, Constance Bowell Mastores, Chad Lange and Michael Barnett. Length: 10-15 pages maximum.

How to Contact: Send complete ms with a cover letter. Include bio. Send SASE for return of ms or send a disposable copy of ms. Simultaneous and electronic (disk or modem) submissions OK. Sample copy for $7 and 8½×11 SAE. Fiction guidelines for legal-size SASE.

Payment/Terms: Pays 1 contributor's copy; additional copies for $7. Acquires one-time rights; rights revert to author. Not copyrighted.

Advice: "*Asspants* seeks well-written fiction on slightly off-beat, often morbid topics. While we do not adhere to a set style, the editors can tell immediately if manuscript will fit in with the overall feeling of the publication."

ATHENA INCOGNITO MAGAZINE, (II), 1442 Judah St., San Francisco CA 94122. (415)665-0219. Editor: Ronn Rosen. Magazine: 8½×11; approximately 30-40 pages; illustrations; photocopied photos. "Open-format magazine with emphasis on experimental, avante-garde works only. Emphasis on poetry and experimental artwork especially." Quarterly. Estab. 1980. Circ. 100.

● Work included in *Athena Incognito* tends to be Dada, surrealistic, stream-of-consciousness material.

Needs: Any subjects OK. Receives 15 unsolicited mss/month. Publishes ms usually 6-8 months after acceptance. *Requires magazine subscription "to cover postage and expense of publication" of $5 (for 1 issue) before reading ms.* Published new writers within the last year. Publishes short shorts. No long pieces over 2 pages. Sometimes critiques rejected mss.

How to Contact: *Magazine requires copy purchase before consideration.* Send complete ms with cover letter. Reports in 2 weeks to 1 month. SASE. Simultaneous and reprint submissions OK. Sample copy for $5; fiction guidelines for SASE.

Payment/Terms: Pays in contributor's copies. Acquires all rights. Publication not copyrighted.

Advice: "Experiment and practice eclecticism of all kinds! Discover! Pioneer! Dada lives!"

ATOM MIND, (II), Mother Road Publications, P.O. Box 22068, Albuquerque NM 87154. Editor: Gregory Smith. Magazine: 8½×11; 128 pages; 60 lb. paper; 80 lb. cover; illustrations and photos. "*Atom Mind* reflects the spirit of the 1960s; it is dedicated to the memory of Steinbeck, Hemingway, Kerouac, Bukowski et al." Quarterly. Estab. 1992. Circ. 1,000.

Needs: Condensed/excerpted novel, erotica, ethnic/multicultural, experimental, humor/satire, literary, mainstream/contemporary, serialized novel and translations. No juvenile, romance, science fiction or young adult/teen. Receives 200-300 unsolicited mss/month. Accepts 5-6 mss/issue; 20 mss/year. Publishes ms 1-2 years after acceptance. Recently published work by Michael Phillips, Al Masarik, Rick Kempa and Jerry Kamstra. Length: 1,000 words minimum; 6,000 words maximum. Also publishes literary essays, literary criticism and poetry. Sometimes critiques or comments on rejected mss.

How to Contact: Send complete ms with a cover letter. Include estimated word count. Reports in 2 weeks on queries; 1-2 months on mss. Send SASE for reply, return of ms or send a disposable copy of ms. Simultaneous and reprint submissions OK. Sample copy $5. Fiction guidelines free.

Payment/Terms: Pays in contributor's copies. Some cash payments in certain cases. Acquires first North American serial rights.

Advice: "*Atom Mind* is very much a one-man operation and therefore subject to the whims and personal biases of the editor. I would like to see more satirical short fiction. Read at least one issue of any magazine you intend to submit to. Writers can save an immense amount of time and money by sending their work ONLY to those journals for which it is suitable—study the markets!"

AURA LITERARY/ARTS REVIEW, (II), University of Alabama at Birmingham, Box 76, Hill University Center, Birmingham AL 35294. (205)934-3354. Fax: (205)934-8050. Editor: Michael Mc-Cracken. Editors change each year. Magazine: 6×9; 140 pages; 70 lb. Moistrite matte paper; 80 lb. matte cover; b&w illustrations and photos. "*Aura* is a quality literary and arts review magazine focused on poetry, short fiction and photography." Semiannually. Estab. 1974. Circ. 3,000.
Needs: Adventure, contemporary, ethnic, experimental, fantasy, feminist, gay, historical, horror, humor, lesbian, literary, mystery/suspense, regional, religious/inspirational, romance, senior citizen, science fiction, sports and westerns. Acquires 5-6 mss/issue. Receives 30-40 unsolicited fiction mss each month. Recently published works by William John Watkins, Vivian Shipley and Holly Day. Published new writers within the last year. Length: up to 5,000 words. Publishes short shorts. Length: 300 words. Also publishes poetry. Critiques rejected mss when there is time.
How to Contact: Send complete ms with SASE. Include estimated word count and 20- to 40-word bio. Simultaneous and electronic (disk) submissions OK. Reports in 3 months. Sample copy for $2.50. "Occasionally" reviews novels and short story collections.
Payment/Terms: Pays 2 contributor's copies. Acquires first rights.
Advice: Looks for "strong verbs, connection and movement."

THE AZOREAN EXPRESS, (I, IV), Seven Buffaloes Press, Box 249, Big Timber MT 59011. Editor: Art Cuelho. Magazine: 6¾×8¼; 32 pages; 60 lb. book paper; 3-6 illustrations/issue; photos rarely. "My overall theme is rural; I also focus on working people (the sweating professions); the American Indian and Hobo; the Dustbowl era; and I am also trying to expand with non-rural material. For rural and library and professor/student, blue collar workers, etc." Semiannually. Estab. 1985. Circ. 600.
Needs: Contemporary, ethnic, experimental, humor/satire, literary, regional, western, rural, working people. Receives 10-20 unsolicited mss/month. Accepts 2-3 mss/issue; 4-6 mss/year. Publishes ms 1-6 months after acceptance. Length: 1,000-3,000 words. Also publishes short shorts, 500-1,000 words. "I take what I like; length sometimes does not matter, even when longer than usual. I'm flexible."
How to Contact: "Send cover letter with ms; general information, but it can be personal, more in line with the submitted story. Not long rambling letters." Reports in 1-4 weeks. SASE. Sample copy for $6.75. Fiction guidelines for SASE.
Payment/Terms: Pays in contributor's copies. "Depends on the amount of support author gives my press." Acquires first North American serial rights. "If I decide to use material in anthology form later, I have that right." Sends galleys to the author upon request.
Advice: "There would not be magazines like mine if I was not optimistic. But literary optimism is a two-way street. Without young fiction writers supporting fiction magazines the future is bleak, because the commercial magazines allow only formula or name writers within their pages. My own publications receive no grants. Sole support is from writers, libraries and individuals."

✦B&A: NEW FICTION, (I, II), (formerly *Blood & Aphorisms*), P.O. Box 702, Station P, Toronto, Ontario M5S 2Y4 Canada. E-mail: blood@io.org. Website: www.io.org:80~blood. Publisher: Tim Paleczny. Fiction Editor: Dennis Bock. Managing Editor: Mark Hickmott. Magazine: 8½×11; 48 pages; bond paper; illustrations. "We publish new and emerging writers whose work is fresh and revealing, and impacts on a literary readership." Quarterly. Estab. 1990. Circ. 2,500.
Needs: Experimental, humor/satire, literary. No gratuitous violence or exploitive fiction. Publishes anthology every 2 years. Receives 50 unsolicited mss/month. Accepts 12-15 mss/issue; 45-55 mss/year. Publishes ms 3-6 months after acceptance. Length: 2,500-4,000 words average; 150 words minimum; 5,500 words maximum. Publishes short shorts. Often critiques rejected mss. Sponsors fiction contest: $5,000 in prizes; up to 2,500 words; $18 entry fee includes subscription. SASE for information. Deadline March 11, 1997.
How to Contact: Send complete ms with a cover letter. Should include estimated word count, short bio, list of publications with submission. Reports in 2 weeks on queries; 2 months on mss. SASE for reply to a query or return of ms. Simultaneous (please advise) and electronic (disk with hard copy) submissions OK. Sample copy for $6. Fiction guidelines for SASE. Reviews novels and short story collections.
Payment/Terms: Pays subscription to the magazine plus $20/printed page. Additional copies $6. Acquires first North American serial rights, electronic distribution for current issue sampling on Home Page, and the right to use work in anthology.
Advice: "Be honest, take chances, find the strength in your own voice, show us your best and keep an open mind—we're ready for anything. Know the magazine you're sending to."

‡**BARBARIC YAWP, (I,II)**, Bone World Publishing, 3706 County Rt. 24, Russell NY 13684. (315)347-2609. Editor: John Berbrich. Fiction Editor: Nancy Berbrich. Magazine: digest-size; 40-50 pages; 24 lb. paper; matte cover stock. "We are not preachers of any particular poetic or literary school. We publish any type of quality material appropriate for our intelligent and wide-awake audience." Semiannually. Estab. 1997. Circ. 100.

Needs: Adventure, experimental, fantasy (science, sword and sorcery), historical, horror, humor/satire, literary, mainstream/contemporary, psychic/supernatural/occult, regional, religious/inspirational, science fiction (hard, soft/sociological). "We don't want any pornography, gratuitous violence or whining." Receives 8-10 unsolicited mss/month. Accepts 5 mss/issue; 10 mss/year. Publishes ms within 6 months after acceptance. Length: 600 words average; 1,000 words maximum. Publishes short shorts. Also publishes literary essays, literary criticism and poetry. Often critiques or comments on rejected mss.

How to Contact: Send complete ms with a cover letter. Include estimated word count, brief bio and list of publications. Reports in 2 weeks on queries; 1-2 months on mss. Send SASE for reply, return of ms or send a disposable copy of ms. Simultaneous submissions and reprints OK. Sample copy for $3. Fiction guidelines for #10 SASE.

Payment and Terms: Pays 1 contributor's copy; additional copies $3. Acquires one-time rights.

Advice: "We are primarily concerned with work that means something to the author, but which is able to transcend the personal into the larger world. Send whatever is important to you. We will use Yin and Yang. Work must hold my interest and be well-crafted. Read, read, read; write, write, write— then send us your best. Don't get discouraged. Believe in yourself. Take risks."

THE BELLETRIST REVIEW, (I, II), Marmarc Publications, P.O. Box 596, Plainville CT 06062-0596. Editor: Marlene Dube. Fiction Editor: Marc Saegaert. Magazine: 8½ × 11; 80 pages. "We are interested in compelling, well-crafted short fiction in a variety of genres. Our title *Belletrist*, means 'lover of literature.' This magazine will appeal to an educated, adult audience that appreciates quality fiction." Semiannually.

● The editors would like to see more "light" and humorous fiction.

Needs: Adventure, contemporary, erotica, horror (psychological), humor/satire, literary, mainstream, mystery/suspense, regional. No poetry, fantasy, juvenile, westerns, or overblown horror or confessional pieces. Accepts 10-12 mss/issue; approximately 25 mss/year. Publishes ms within 1 year after acceptance. Recently published work by William John Watkins, Daniel Quinn and Mary Overton. Length: 2,500-5,000 words preferred; 1,000 words minimum; 5,000 words maximum. Comments on or critiques rejected mss when time permits. Special fiction contest in September (deadline: July 15). The award is $200. Send SASE for contest rules.

How to Contact: Send complete ms with cover letter including brief biographical note and any previous publications. Reports in 1 month on queries; 2 months on mss. SASE. Simultaneous submissions OK.

Payment/Terms: Pays contributor's copies. Acquires one-time rights.

Advice: "Please submit only one story at a time, double-spaced and unstapled. Don't tell us in your cover letter how great the story is or what it's about. In our roles as editors, we commonly find ourselves saying the following when preparing a rejection: 'It was well-written and professionally presented, but we didn't care at all about the characters or what happened to them.' Another frequent cause for rejection: stories that resolve everything on the first page, or don't really get started until the middle. We also tend to reject stories which appear to be written for the shock value, or which seem to be thinly-disguised accounts of the writer's own experiences and read like a diary entry. While there's no such thing as an original plot, take a fresh angle and a creative approach in developing your characters."

THE BELLINGHAM REVIEW, (II), Western Washington University, MS9053, Bellingham WA 98225. Editor: Robin Henley. Magazine: 5½ × 8; 120 pages; 60 lb. white paper; varied cover stock. "A literary magazine featuring original short stories, novel excerpts, essays, short plays and poetry of palpable quality." Semiannually. Estab. 1977. Circ. 700.

● *The Bellingham Review* has increased its page count from 64 pages to 120 pages and, also, is accepting submissions of up to 10,000 words.

Needs: All genres/subjects considered. Accepts 1-2 mss/issue. Publishes short shorts. Published new writers within the last year. Length: 10,000 words or less. Also publishes poetry.

● **A BULLET INTRODUCES COMMENTS** by the editor of *Novel & Short Story Writer's Market* indicating special information about the listing.

How to Contact: Send complete ms. Reports in 2 weeks to 3 months. Publishes ms an average of 1 year after acceptance. Sample copy for $5. Reviews novels and short story collections.

Payment/Terms: Pays 1 contributor's copy plus 2-issue subscription. Charges $2.50 for extras. Acquires first North American serial and one-time rights.

Advice: "We look for work that is ambitious, vital, and challenging both to the spirit and the intellect. We hope to publish important works from around the world, works by older, neglected writers, and works by unheralded but talented new writers."

BELLOWING ARK, A Literary Tabloid, (II), P.O. Box 45637, Seattle WA 98145. (206)545-8302. Editor: R.R. Ward. Tabloid: 11½×16; 32 pages; electro-brite paper and cover stock; illustrations; photos. "We publish material which we feel addresses the human situation in an affirmative way. We do not publish academic fiction." Bimonthly. Estab. 1984. Circ. 500.

● Work from *Bellowing Ark* appeared in the *Pushcart Prize* anthology. The editor says he's using much more short fiction and prefers positive, life-affirming work. Remember he likes a traditional, narrative approach and "abhors" minimalist and post-modern work.

Needs: Contemporary, literary, mainstream, serialized/excerpted novel. "Anything we publish will be true." Receives 600-800 unsolicited fiction mss/year. Accepts 2-3 mss/issue; 12-18 mss/year. Time varies, but publishes ms not longer than 6 months after acceptance. Published work by Diane Trzcinski, Shelly Uva, Dorothy Worfolk, Jim Bernhard, Lucas Doolin and David Ross. Published new writers within the last year. Length: 3,000-5,000 words average ("but no length restriction"). Publishes short shorts. Also publishes literary essays, literary criticism, poetry. Sometimes critiques rejected mss.

How to Contact: No queries. Send complete ms with cover letter and short bio. "Prefer cover letters that tell something about the writer. Listing credits doesn't help." No simultaneous submissions. Reports in 6 weeks on mss. SASE. Sample copy for $3, 9×12 SAE and $1.24 postage.

Payment/Terms: Pays in contributor's copies. Acquires all rights, reverts on request.

Advice: "*Bellowing Ark* began as (and remains) an alternative to the despair and negativity of the Workshop/Academic literary scene; we believe that life has meaning and is worth living—the work we publish reflects that belief. Learn how to tell a story before submitting. Avoid 'trick' endings—they have all been done before and better. *Bellowing Ark* is interested in publishing writers who will develop with the magazine, as in an extended community. We find *good* writers and stick with them. This is why the magazine has grown from 12 to 32 pages."

BELOIT FICTION JOURNAL, (II), Box 11, Beloit College WI 53511. (608)363-2028. Editor: Fred Burwell. Magazine: 6×9; 150 pages; 60 lb. paper; 10 pt. C1S cover stock; illustrations and photos on cover. "We are interested in publishing the best contemporary fiction and are open to all themes except those involving pornographic, religiously dogmatic or politically propagandistic representations. Our magazine is for general readership, though most of our readers will probably have a specific interest in literary magazines." Semiannually. Estab. 1985.

● Work first appearing in *Beloit Fiction Journal* has been reprinted in award-winning collections, including the *Flannery O'Connor* and the *Milkweed Fiction Prize* collections.

Needs: Contemporary, literary, mainstream, prose poem, spiritual and sports. No pornography, religious dogma, political propaganda. Receives 400 unsolicited fiction mss/month. Accepts 8-10 mss/issue; 16-20 mss/year. Replies take longer in summer. Publishes ms within 9 months after acceptance. Recently published work by Nance Van Winckel, Dinty W. Moore, David Milofsky and Debbie Lee Wesselmann. Length: 5,000 words average; 250 words minimum; 10,000 words maximum. Sometimes critiques rejected mss and recommends other markets.

How to Contact: Send complete ms with cover letter. Reports in 1 week on queries; 2-8 weeks on mss. SASE for ms. Simultaneous submissions OK if identified as such. Sample copy for $6. Fiction guidelines for #10 SASE.

Advice: "Many of our contributors are writers whose work we have previously rejected. Don't let one rejection slip turn you away from our—or any—magazine."

✤BENEATH THE SURFACE, (II), McMaster University Society of English, Dept. of English, Chester New Hall, McMaster University, Hamilton, Ontario L8S 4S8 Canada. E-mail: ~9217332@mus s.cis.mcmaster.ca. Contact: Editor. Editors change every four months. Magazine: 21cm × 13.5cm; 25-55 pages; illustrations and photos. "Primarily, university audience intended. Also targets general reading public." Semiannually. Estab. 1984. Circ. varies.

Needs: Ethnic/multicultural, experimental, fantasy (non-formula), feminist, gay, historical (general), horror, humor/satire, lesbian, literary, mystery/suspense (non-formula), psychic/supernatural/occult, science fiction (non-formula). Accepts 15 mss/issue; 30 mss/year. Does not read mss during summer months. Publishes ms 1-4 months after acceptance. Recently published work by William Lantry, Sean Brendan-Brown and Gene Shannon. Length: 3,000 words maximum. Publishes short stories. Also publishes literary essays and poetry.

How to Contact: Send complete ms with a cover letter. Should include short bio and list of publications. Reports in 6 months on mss. Send a disposable copy of ms. Electronic submissions (disk or modem) OK. Sample copy for $4.
Payment/Terms: Pays contributor's copies. Not copyrighted; copyrights belong to authors.
Advice: Avoid formula fiction. For experimental writers: we are looking for *your* experimentation, not someone else's."

BERKELEY FICTION REVIEW, (II), 703 Eshleman Hall, University of California, Berkeley CA 94720. (510)642-4005. Editors change yearly. Magazine: 5½×8½; 160 pages; perfect-bound; glossy cover; some b&w art; photographs. "We publish a wide variety of contemporary short fiction for a literary audience." Annually. Estab. 1981. Circ. 1,000.
Needs: Contemporary/mainstream, literary, experimental. "Quality, inventive short fiction. No poetry or formula fiction." Receives 60 unsolicited mss/month. Accepts 10-20 mss/issue. Recently published work by Michael Propsom, Sarah Odishoo, Doug Rennie and Josh Stevens. Published work by new writers in the last year. Also publishes short shorts. Occasionally comments on rejected mss.
How to Contact: Send complete ms to "Editor" with very brief cover letter and SASE. Simultaneous submission OK. Usually reports in 2-3 months, longer in summer. Sample copy for $8. Guidelines for SASE.
Payment/Terms: Pays 1 contributor's copy. Acquires first rights. Sponsors short story contest with $100 first prize. Entry fee: $5. Send SASE for guidelines.
Advice: "Read the magazine you are submitting to! Know your market. Although we publish many new and promising writers, our criteria is still fiction that resonates; stories that stick with the reader long after the last page has been read. Be brief in your cover letter and do not summarize the story. Let the work speak for itself."

BILINGUAL REVIEW, (II, IV), Hispanic Research Center, Arizona State University, Box 872702, Tempe AZ 85287-2702. (602)965-3867. Editor-in-Chief: Gary D. Keller. Scholarly/literary journal of US Hispanic life: poetry, short stories, other prose and short theater. Magazine: 7×10; 96 pages; 55 lb. acid-free paper; coated cover stock. Published 3 times/year. Estab. 1974. Circ. 2,000.
Needs: US Hispanic creative literature. "We accept material in English or Spanish. We publish original work only—no translations." US Hispanic themes only. Receives 50 unsolicited fiction mss/month. Accepts 3 mss/issue; 9 mss/year. Publishes ms an average of 1 year after acceptance. Published work by Ernestina N. Eger, Leo Romero, Connie Porter and Nash Candelaria. Published work of new writers within the last year. Also publishes literary criticism on US Hispanic themes and poetry. Often critiques rejected mss.
How to Contact: Send 2 copies of complete ms with SAE and loose stamps. Reports in 1-2 months. Simultaneous and high-quality photocopied submissions OK. Sample copy for $6. Reviews novels and short story collections.
Payment/Terms: Pays 2 contributor's copies. 30% discount for extras. Acquires all rights (50% of reprint permission fee given to author as matter of policy).
Advice: "We do not publish literature about tourists in Latin America and their perceptions of the 'native culture.' We do not publish fiction about Latin America unless there is a clear tie to the United States (characters, theme, etc.)."

THE BLACK HAMMOCK REVIEW, A Literary Quarterly, (I, II, IV), P.O. Box 621031, Oviedo FL 32762-1031. (407)365-5798. Editor: Edward A. Nagel. Magazine: 8½×11; 40 pages; 20 lb. paper; illustrations and photos. "*The Black Hammock Review* is published by Quantum Press, a Florida non-profit cooperative. It was established to publish works which reflect rural motifs, for example, such settings as Oviedo, Geneva, Chuluota and the Black Hammock area in east-central Florida; however, other 'motifs' will be considered." Quarterly. Estab. 1992.
  ● Note that *The Black Hammock Review* is published co-operatively with memberships required and members share publishing costs. Editor Edward A. Nagel has published a book, *No Entry,* with Four Walls Eight Windows. The magazine has a new address this year.
Needs: Ethnic/multicultural, experimental, fantasy (artistic), humor/satire, literary, contemporary, psychic/supernatural, regional, "bucolic themes." Receives 10 unsolicited mss/month. Accepts 4 mss/issue; 16 mss/year. Publishes ms 3 months after acceptance. Recently published work by Tito Perdue, Andy Rusnak, Elizabeth Ramadorai and Jack Pulaski. Length: 2,500 words preferred; 1,500 words minimum; 3,500 words maximum. Also publishes literary essays, literary criticism and poetry. Always critiques or comments on returned mss.
How to Contact: Send complete ms with a cover letter. Should include bio (short), list of publications and brief statement of writer's artistic "goals." Reports in 2 weeks. Send SASE for reply, return of ms or a disposable copy of the ms. No simultaneous submissions. Sample copy for $4 and 8½×11 SAE.
Payment/Terms: *Charges membership fee: $25 for individual; $50 for 3 writers.* Fee waivers available for first-rate, first-time writers. Each member of the cooperative is assured publication of at least

one carefully edited piece each year, subject to editorial approval. Pays $50-75 *for selected works of established authors* on publication for one-time rights. Pays 6 contributor's copies (or membership contribution); additional copies for $2.

Advice: Looks for "work that evokes in the reader's mind a vivid and continuous dream, vivid in that it has density, enough detail and the right detail, fresh with the author, and shows concern for the characters and the eternal verities. And continuous in that there are no distractions such as poor grammar, purple prose, diction shifts, or change in point of view. Short fiction that has a beginning, middle and end, organically speaking. Immerse yourself in the requested genre, format; work the piece over and over until it is 'right' for you, does what you want it to do; read the masters in your genre on a stylistic and technical level. Transmute your emotions into the work—write about what fascinates you, how people think and act; suspend moral and ethical judgment; 'see' as artist and 'write short.' "

THE BLACK HOLE LITERARY REVIEW, (I), 333 Shoshone Ct., Cincinnati OH 45215. (513)821-6670 or (513)821-6671. E-mail: sysop@holer.org. Editor: Wm. E. Allendorf. Electronic Bulletin Board. "This is an attempt to revolutionize publishing—no paper, no rejection slips, no deadlines. For any person with access to a home computer and a modem." Estab. 1989. Circ. 8,000.

Needs: "Any or all fiction and nonfiction categories are acceptable. Any size, topic, or inherent bias is acceptable. The only limitation is that the writer will not mind having his piece read, and an honest critique given directly by his readership. In the past two years, our regular contributors have moved out of the realm of normal prose and concentrated on participatory fiction. Making full use of the electronic medium available at BHLR, they have concentrated on performing collaborative works with interweaving plots. We currently have several of these works in progress—the longest has survived over 2 years with over a dozen writers collaborating and the plot and characters remain fresh and entertaining." Plans future hardcopy anthology. Publishes ms 1-2 days after acceptance. Length: 2,000-10,000 words. Publishes short shorts, poetry, essays and novels. "Critique given if not by editor, then by readers through e-mail."

How to Contact: Upload as e-mail to the editor. Cover letter should include "titles, description (abstract), copyright notice." Reports in 1-2 days. Simultaneous submissions OK.

Payment/Terms: Pays in royalties, *but charges fee for initial inputting. Charges $5 minimum subscription.* Royalties are accrued each time the piece is read. Contact editor for details. Acquires one-time rights.

Advice: "If the concept of the electronic magazine goes over with the public, then the market for fiction is limitless. Any piece that an author has taken the trouble to set to print is worth publishing. However, *The Hole* is looking for writers that want to be read—not ones that just want to write. The electronic magazine is an interactive medium, and pieces are judged on their ability to inspire a person to read them." Writers interested in submitting should: "Do it. You would be the first to be rejected by *The Hole*, if we did not use your piece; to make matters easier for all concerned, submit your piece as a ASCII text file via the modem. If you do not have access to a home computer with a modem, buy one, borrow one, steal one. This is the wave of the future for writers."

‡BLACK ICE, (I, II, IV), Campus Box 494, Boulder CO 80309-0494. (303)492-8947. Publisher: Ronald Sukenick. Magazine: 5½×8½; 100 pages; glossy cover; photography on cover. "Publishes the most experimental innovative writing being written today for writers, critics, sophisticated readers." Published 3 times/year. Estab. 1984. Circ. 700.

Needs: Experimental, literary, translations. Does not want to see "anything that's not ground-breaking." Receives 50-75 unsolicited mss/month. Accepts approximately 12-15 mss/issue; approximately 40 mss/year. Publishes ms 2-4 months after acceptance. Published work by Ursula Molinaro, Eurudice, Ricardo Cruz, Diane Glancy. Sometimes critiques rejected mss and recommends other markets.

How to Contact: Send complete manuscript with cover letter. Reports in 3-6 months on queries; 3-6 months on mss. SASE. Simultaneous submissions OK. Sample copy for $7. Fiction guidelines for #10 SAE and 1 first-class stamp.

Payment/Terms: Pays in contributor's copies. Acquires first rights.

Advice: "Expand your 'institutionalized' sense of what a story should be so that you include (open yourself up to) language play, innovative spatial composition, plots that die trying, de-characterizations whipped up in the food processor, themes barely capable of maintaining equilibrium in the midst of end-of-the-century energy crisis/chaos, etc."

BLACK JACK, (IV), Seven Buffaloes Press, Box 249, Big Timber MT 59011. Editor: Art Cuelho. "Main theme: Rural. Publishes material on the American Indian, farm and ranch, American hobo, the common working man, folklore, the Southwest, Okies, Montana, humor, Central California, etc. for people who make their living off the land. The writers write about their roots, experiences and values they receive from the American soil." Annually. Estab. 1973. Circ. 750.

Needs: Literary, contemporary, western, adventure, humor, American Indian, American hobo, and parts of novels and long short stories. "Anything that strikes me as being amateurish, without depth, without craft, I refuse. Actually, I'm not opposed to any kind of writing if the author is genuine and has spent his lifetime dedicated to the written word." Receives approximately 10-15 unsolicited fiction mss/month. Accepts 5-10 mss/year. Length: 3,500-5,000 words (there can be exceptions).

How to Contact: Query for current theme with SASE. Reports in 1 week on queries; 2 weeks on mss. Sample copy for $6.75.

Payment/Terms: Pays 1-2 contributor's copies. Acquires first North American serial rights and reserves the right to reprint material in an anthology or future *Black Jack* publications. Rights revert to author after publication.

Advice: "Enthusiasm should be matched with skill as a craftsman. That's not saying that we don't continue to learn, but every writer must have enough command of the language to compete with other proven writers. Save postage by writing first to find out the editor's needs. A small press magazine always has specific needs at any given time. I sometimes accept material from writers that aren't that good at punctuation and grammar but make up for it with life's experience. This is not a highbrow publication; it belongs to the salt-of-the-earth people."

BLACK LACE, (I, IV), BLK Publishing Co., P.O. Box 83912, Los Angeles CA 90083. (310)410-0808. Fax: (310)410-9250. E-mail: newsroom@blk.com. Editor: Alycee Lane. Magazine: 8⅛ × 10⅞; 48 pages; electrabrite paper; color glossy cover; illustrations and photographs. Quarterly. Estab. 1991.

Needs: Ethnic/multicultural, lesbian. Accepts 4 mss/year. Recently published work by Danielle Fox, Claudia Washington, Letitia Howard and Donna Rose. Publishes short shorts. Also publishes literary essays, literary criticism and poetry.

How to Contact: Query first with clips of published work or send complete ms with a cover letter. Should include bio (3 sentences). Send a disposable copy of ms. No simultaneous submissions. Electronic submissions OK. Sample copy for $7. Fiction guidelines free.

Payment/Terms: Pays free subscription, 5 contributor's copies. Acquires first North American serial rights and right to anthologize.

BLACK RIVER REVIEW, (II), 855 Mildred Ave., Lorain OH 44052. (216)244-9654. E-mail: brr@freenet.lorain.oberlin.edu. Editors: Deborah Glaefke Gilbert and Kaye Coller. Fiction Editor: Jack Smith. Magazine: 8½ × 11; 60 pages; glossy cover stock; b&w drawings. "Contemporary writing and contemporary American culture; poetry, book reviews, essays on contemporary literature, short stories." Annually. Estab. 1985. Circ. 400.

Needs: Contemporary, experimental, humor/satire and literary. No "erotica for its own sake, stories directed toward a juvenile audience." Accepts up to 5 mss/year. Does not read mss May 1 through December 31. Publishes ms no later than July of current year. Published work by David Shields, Jeanne M. Leiby and Louis Gallo. Length: up to 3,500 words but will consider up to 4,000 maximum. Publishes short shorts. Also publishes literary essays, literary criticism, poetry. Sometimes critiques rejected mss.

How to Contact: Reports on mss no later than August. SASE. "Will consider simultaneous submissions, but submissions may not be withdrawn after May 1." Sample copy for $3.50 plus $1.50 shipping and handling for back issue; $4 plus $1.50 for current issue. Fiction guidelines for #10 SASE. Reviews novels and short story collections.

Payment/Terms: Pays in contributor's copies. Acquires one-time rights.

Advice: "Since it is so difficult to break in, much of the new writer's creative effort is spent trying to match trends in popular fiction, in the case of the slicks, or adapting to narrow themes ('Gay and Lesbian,' 'Vietnam War,' 'Women's Issues,' etc.) of little and literary journals. An unfortunate result, from the reader's standpoint, is that each story within a given category comes out sounding like all the rest. Among positive developments of the proliferation of small presses is the opportunity for writers to decide what to write and how to write it. My advice is to support a little magazine that is both open to new writers and prints fiction you like. 'Support' doesn't necessarily mean 'buy all the back issues,' but, rather, direct involvement between contributor, magazine and reader needed to rebuild the sort of audience that was there for writers like Fitzgerald and Hemingway."

BLACK WARRIOR REVIEW, (I, II), Box 862936, Tuscaloosa AL 35486-0027. (205)348-4518. Editor-in-Chief: Mindy Wilson. Fiction Editor: Jim Hilgartner. Magazine: 6 × 9; 170 pages; illustrations and photos occasionally. "We publish contemporary fiction, poetry, reviews, essays and interviews for a literary audience." Semiannually. Estab. 1974. Circ. 2,000.

● Work that appeared in the *Black Warrior Review* has been included in the *Pushcart Prize* anthology, *Best American Short Stories*, *Best American Poetry* and in *New Short Stories from the South*.

Needs: Contemporary, literary, short and short-short fiction. No genre fiction please. Receives 200 unsolicited fiction mss/month. Accepts 5 mss/issue, 10 mss/year. Approximately 15% of fiction is agented. Recently published work by A. Manette Ansay, Alison Baker and Robert Olmstead. Published new writers within the last year. Length: 7,500 words maximum; 3,000-5,000 words average. Also publishes essays, poetry. Occasionally critiques rejected mss. Unsolicited novel excerpts are not considered unless the novel is already contracted for publication.

How to Contact: Send complete ms with SASE (1 story per submission). Simultaneous submissions OK. Reports in 1-4 months. Publishes ms 2-5 months after acceptance. Sample copy for $6. Fiction guidelines for SASE. Reviews novels and short story collections.

Payment/Terms: Pays up to $100 per story and 2 contributor's copies. Pays on publication.

Advice: "Become familiar with the magazine prior to submission. "We're increasingly interested in considering good experimental writing and, especially, in reading short-short fiction." Regular submission deadlines are June 1 for the fall issue and November 31 for the spring issue."

‡**BLACK WRITER MAGAZINE, (II)**, Terrell Associates, Box 1030, Chicago IL 60690. (312)924-3818. Editor: Mable Terrell. Fiction Editor: Herman Gilbert. Magazine: 8½×11; 40 pages; glossy paper; glossy cover; illustrations. "To assist writers in publishing their work." For "all audiences, with a special emphasis on black writers." Quarterly. Estab. 1972.

Needs: Ethnic, historical, literary, religious/inspirational, prose poem. Plans annual anthology. Receives 20 unsolicited mss/month. Accepts 15 mss/issue. Publishes ms on average of 6 months after acceptance. Length: 3,000 words preferred; 2,500 words average; 1,500 words minimum. Also publishes literary essays. Sometimes critiques rejected mss and recommends other markets. Sponsors awards for fiction writers. Contest deadline: May 30

How to Contact: Send complete ms with cover letter, which should include "writer's opinion of the work, and rights offered." Reports in 3 weeks. SASE. Simultaneous submissions OK. Sample copy for 8½×11 SAE and 70¢ postage. Fiction guidelines for SASE. Reviews novels and short story collections. Send books to the editor.

Payment/Terms: Pays subscription to magazine. Acquires one-time rights.

Advice: "Write the organization and ask for assistance."

THE BLACKSTONE CIRCULAR, (II), 26 James St., Suite B-8, Toms River NJ 08753. Editor: Linda Rogers. Magazine: 8½×11; 12-20 pages; copy paper; corner stapled. "Fiction and nonfiction for all interested readers; including gay and lesbian." Monthly. Estab. 1995.

Needs: No juvenile, young adult, psychic/supernatural/occult, erotica. Publishes yearly anthology. Accepts up to 10 mss/issue. Recently published work by Clara Nipper, Michael DeWitt and C.E. Lindstrom. Length: 10 words minimum; 3,000 words maximum. Publishes short shorts. Also publishes literary essays and poetry. Often comments on rejected ms.

How to Contact: Send complete ms with a cover letter. Reports on mss in 2 months. Simultaneous, reprint submissions OK. Sample copy for $2. Make check payable to Linda Rogers.

Payment/Terms: Pays 1 contributor's copy. Acquires one-time rights.

Advice: "Strive for universality."

BLACKWATER REVIEW, (II), Tidewater Community College, 1700 College Crescent, Virginia Beach VA 23464. (804)427-7272. Editor: Robert P. Arthur. Fiction Editor: Juliet Crichton. Magazine: 6×9; 150 pages; illustrations and photos. Annually. Estab. 1995. Circ. 1,000.

Needs: Adventure, experimental, feminist, historical (general), horror, humor/satire, literary, regional, science fiction (soft/sociological). Accepts 6-8 mss/issue. Publishes ms September after acceptance. Length: 8,000 words maximum. Publishes short shorts. Also publishes literary essays, literary criticism, poetry. Often critiques or comments on rejected mss.

How to Contact Send complete ms with a cover letter. Should include 3-5 line bio. Reports in 3 weeks on ms. Simultaneous, reprint, electronic submissions OK. Sample copy for $6, 8×11 SAE and $3 postage. Fiction guidelines for 8×11 SAE. Reviews novels and short story collections.

Payment/Terms: Pays 2 contributor's copies; additional copies $6. Acquires one-time rights. Sponsors contests, awards or grants for fiction writers.

Advice: "We prefer experimental fiction but will print any high-quality work. Writers should avoid sending work that is commonplace or experimental work lacking clarity."

BLUE MESA REVIEW, (I, IV), Creative Writing Program, University of New Mexico, Dept. of English, Albuquerque NM 87131. (505)277-6347. Fax: (505)277-5573. E-mail: psprott@unm.edu. Managing Editor: Patricia Lynn Sprott. Magazine: 6×9; 200 pages; 55 lb. paper; 10 pt CS1; photos. "*Blue Mesa Review* publishes the best/most current creative writing on the market." Annually. Estab. 1989. Circ. 1,200.

Needs: Adventure, ethnic/multicultural, feminist, gay, historical, humor/satire, lesbian, literary, mainstream/contemporary, regional, westerns. Contact for list of upcoming themes. Receives 60-120 unsolicited mss/year. Accepts 10 mss/year. Accepts mss May-October; reads mss November-December; responds in January. Publishes ms 5-6 months after acceptance. Published work by Kathleen Spivack, Roberta Swann and Tony Mares. Publishes short shorts. Also publishes literary essays, poetry.

How to Contact: Send complete ms with a cover letter. Should include 1 paragraph bio. Send SASE for reply, return of ms or send a disposable copy of ms. Electronic submissions (disk or e-mail) OK. Sample copy for $12. Reviews novels and short story collections.

INSIDER REPORT

Online magazines offer instant feedback from a worldwide audience

A few clicks of a mouse provide readers instant access to *The Blue Moon Review*, an online literary magazine that's been making its home on the World Wide Web since 1994. As an online magazine, it offers writers a chance to have their work seen by an unlimited number of readers. Editor Doug Lawson sees that as being *The Blue Moon*'s greatest advantage. "There's the potential to have millions of people reading your work worldwide," he says. Realistically, *The Blue Moon* attracts between 1,500 and 2,000 readers per month. But the neat thing is that they can be anywhere. "We have readers in New Zealand, England and Australia, and a wide variety of places that, if we were doing a print magazine, it would be incredibly difficult to get to."

Doug Lawson

Photo by Giselle Gautreau

Aside from the fact that *The Blue Moon Review* offers unlimited access to readers throughout the world, Lawson sees his magazine as no different from any other quality literary publication. "Essentially it's a change in distribution, not a change in content," he says. "We can include work with experimental mixes of video, collages and words, things that you can't do in print. But other than that I don't think that we're any different from a normal literary magazine."

The goal of *The Blue Moon Review* is to offer creative new works, without overwhelming its audience with eye-popping graphics and screaming sound bites. "I like to see what we can do creatively online," says Lawson. "I'm not necessarily concerned with having whistles and bells. You see a lot of that in online publications. In a lot of ways *The Blue Moon* may be a conservative online publication. We're looking for literary caliber and decent work, and we want to have a layout that adds to that work but doesn't detract from it. I don't want to be slick or overly hyped. I don't think literary readers necessarily want that."

Even so, *The Blue Moon Review* provides more information than many literary magazines are able to offer within their printed pages. Along with special touches like color graphics that move to make the magazine more visually interesting, *The Blue Moon* offers discussion groups, ways for writers to win cash awards, and the chance for readers to deliver instant feedback to writers regarding their work. "A lot of writers have found that they've drawn comments from the work they publish in *The Blue Moon*, and when they publish in a normal literary magazine they don't hear a thing," Lawson says. With an online magazine, "you have direct access to that interactivity. If writers want us to, we can incorporate their e-mail addresses into the publication. If someone reads a story and really likes it or hates it, they can click on the name of the writer, a menu box pops up and they can send a message to the writer. A lot of writers enjoy that—regardless of whether it's good feedback or bad feedback. The fact that someone's reading and responding means something. It can even help offset that loneliness that comes from being part of the writing profession.''

Another interactive component of *The Blue Moon Review* is the Cafe Blue, which Lawson describes as "an online discussion group for writers, readers and editors. Anyone can participate and start a topic of discussion through e-mail, which is sent out to all other members of the list. It's a good place for ideological battles.''

Since *The Blue Moon* is not able to provide financial compensation to writers, it offers quarterly awards for the best story and poem in each issue. But these awards have a twist—they're chosen by *Blue Moon* readers. "Through commercial sponsorships,'' Lawson explains, "we've been able to offer awards for writers who publish with *The Blue Moon*. We offer a $100 prize for fiction and a $50 prize for poetry, and leave it up to the readers to decide who wins. Since you can be interactive online, why not let people who are reading the magazine decide what they like, and let the writers benefit? Because the production costs for an online magazine are so low, sponsorship money can go directly to the writers.''

This interactivity between readers and writers is what makes online magazines unique, and Lawson sees their ranks growing as acceptance of them increases. But with this increased acceptance comes increased competition. "At this point, you can publish anything you want to online, whether you do it yourself or you do it in a magazine,'' Lawson says. "The more crowded the Internet gets, the harder it's going to be for readers to find your work. Writers who are looking for visibility through publishing online are best served by going through one of the established online magazines.''

Lawson sees the recent increase in online literary journals as a direct result of the fact that there are no printing costs involved in producing an online magazine. "To a certain extent, I see online publishing replacing a good deal of publishing. But I don't subscribe to the idea that online publishing is going to put *all* publishing out of business. I don't see it replacing novel publishing—it's horrible to read a novel online and I don't think people want to. I think you're going to see more and more publications that do two things, that have a print version and an online version. Then, in the online version you can include editors' and writers' thoughts that never made it into the printed version. That lets you into the authors' process. And smaller literary magazines, through smaller universities, may move to being exclusively online if funding becomes a problem.''

The only disadvantage Lawson sees in publishing online is that "you can't stick it up on the shelf next to the *Paris Review*. And that certain tangibleness is something a lot of writers really like. You can make great full-color reproductions of anything online, but it's not the same. Online publishing is definitely ahead of the game in terms of distribution, but it's behind the game in that physical experience. That's important to a lot of writers, and writers who are looking at

INSIDER REPORT, *Lawson*

online publications need to keep that in mind."

The fact that *The Blue Moon Review* is online makes no difference when it comes to the quality of the work Lawson chooses for publication, however. When reading fiction submissions, Lawson says a story must stand on its own terms. Experimental or realistic, stories should have a goal in mind, and then fulfill the promise of that goal. "We look for a story that speaks to us and tells us something we haven't seen or heard before, one that depicts a character in a very interesting or unique way, or just mystifies us all." But Lawson realizes that no matter how good a story may be, it can come down to the taste of a particular editor. "Everything is really a subjective experience," he says, "and work that I turn away may be accepted by another editor and do very well. It's important for writers to understand that."

Lawson would like to see more submissions in the experimental vein. "A good experimental piece is rare these days." Beginning writers tend to look towards traditional, realistic stories and are less willing to take risks. I like a great realistic story and I think you can go places within that realm that experimental pieces don't. But writers who are taking the leap to define their own reality and pulling it off are very rare."

Lawson's advice to writers, writing for online publications or printed ones, is simple. "Follow your inclinations, and follow them for a very long time. And practice, practice, practice. Spend a lot of time writing. In the end it's the butt-in-the-chair thing, that you have to sit there and write, and keep working and keep rewriting, and eventually something comes out of it or something doesn't. I really think there's no replacement for the sweat and the effort that you have to put into developing your craft."

—Cindy Laufenberg

Payment/Terms: Pays 2 contributor's copies for one-time rights.
Advice: "Get to the point—fast. A short story does not allow for lengthy intros and descriptions. Take a class and get the teacher to edit you! Now that we are using themes, we would like to see theme-related stories. Avoid thought pieces on 'vacations to our enchanting state.' "

THE BLUE MOON REVIEW, (II), P.O. Box 48, Ivy VA 22945-0045. E-mail: dlawson@ebbs.englis h.vt.edu. Website: http://ebbs.english.vt.edu/olp/bpq/front-page.html. Editor: Doug Lawson. Electronic magazine: Illustrations and photos. Quarterly. Estab. 1994. Circ. 3,000-7,000.
● The editors advise writers to contact them through e-mail because the magazine's address may change.
Needs: Experimental, feminist, gay, lesbian, literary, mainstream/contemporary, regional, translations. No genre fiction. Receives 40-70 unsolicited mss/month. Accepts 7-10 mss/issue; 28-40 mss/year. Publishes ms up to 9 months after acceptance. Published work by Edward Falco, Deborah Eisenberg, Robert Sward and Eva Shaderowfsky. Length: open. Publishes short shorts. Also publishes literary essays, literary criticism and poetry. Sometimes critiques or comments on rejected mss.
How to Contact: Send complete ms with a cover letter. Include a brief bio, list of publications and e-mail address if available. Reports in 1-3 months on mss. Send SASE for reply, return of ms or send a disposable copy of ms. Send e-mail address for reply if available. Simultaneous and electronic submissions OK. Sample copy and fiction guidelines available at above website. Reviews novels and short story collections.
Payment/Terms: Offers prizes for fiction and poetry. Acquires first electronic rights. Rights revert to author upon request.
Advice: "We look for strong use of language or strong characterization. Manuscripts stand out by their ability to engage a reader on an intellectual or emotional level. Present characters with depth

regardless of age and introduce intelligent concepts that have resonance and relevance. We recommend our writers be electronically connected to the Internet."

BLUELINE, (II, IV), English Dept., SUNY, Potsdam NY 13676. (315)267-2000. E-mail: tylerau@pot sdam.edu. Editor: Tony Tyler. Magazine: 6×9; 112 pages; 70 lb. white stock paper; 65 lb. smooth cover stock; illustrations; photos. "*Blueline* is interested in quality writing about the Adirondacks or other places similar in geography and spirit. We publish fiction, poetry, personal essays, book reviews and oral history for those interested in the Adirondacks, nature in general, and well-crafted writing." Annually. Estab. 1979. Circ. 400.

Needs: Adventure, contemporary, humor/satire, literary, prose poem, regional, reminiscences, oral history and nature/outdoors. Receives 8-10 unsolicited fiction mss/month. Accepts 6-8 mss/issue. Does not read January through August. Publishes ms 3-6 months after acceptance. Published fiction by Jeffrey Clapp. Published new writers within the last year. Length: 500 words minimum; 3,000 words maximum; 2,500 words average. Also publishes literary essays, poetry. Occasionally critiques rejected mss.

How to Contact: Send complete ms with SASE, word count and brief bio. Submit mss August through November 30. Reports in 2-10 weeks. Sample copy for $3.50. Fiction guidelines for 5×10 SASE.

Payment/Terms: Pays 1 contributor's copy for first rights. Charges $3 each for 3 or more extra copies.

Advice: "We look for concise, clear, concrete prose that tells a story and touches upon a universal theme or situation. We prefer realism to romanticism but will consider nostalgia if well done. Pay attention to grammar and syntax. Avoid murky language, sentimentality, cuteness or folksiness. We would like to see more good fiction related to the Adirondacks. If manuscript has potential, we work with author to improve and reconsider for publication. Our readers prefer fiction to poetry (in general) or reviews. Write from your own experience, be specific and factual (within the bounds of your story) and if you write about universal features such as love, death, change, etc., write about them in a fresh way. Triteness and mediocracy are the hallmarks of the majority of stories seen today."

BOGG, A Magazine of British & North American Writing, (II), Bogg Publications, 422 N. Cleveland St., Arlington VA 22201. (703)243-6019. U.S. Editor: John Elsberg. Magazine: 6×9; 64-68 pages; 70 lb. white paper; 70 lb. cover stock; line illustrations. "American and British poetry, prose poems, experimental short 'fictions,' reviews, and essays on small press." Published triannually. Estab. 1968. Circ. 850.

● The editors at *Bogg* are most interested in short, wry or semi-surreal fiction.

Needs: Very short experimental and prose poems. "We are always looking for work with British/Commonwealth themes and/or references." Receives 25 unsolicited fiction mss/month. Accepts 1-2 mss/issue; 3-6 mss/year. Publishes ms 3-18 months after acceptance. Recently published work by Nigel Hinshelwood. Published 50% new writers within the last year. Length: 300 words maximum. Also publishes literary essays, literary criticism, poetry. Occasionally critiques rejected mss.

How to Contact: Query first or send ms (2-6 pieces) with SASE. Reports in 1 week on queries; 2 weeks on mss. Sample copy for $3.50 or $4.50 (current issue). Reviews novels and short story collections.

Payment/Terms: Pays 2 contributor's copies; reduced charge for extras. Acquires one-time rights.

Advice: "Read magazine first. We are most interested in prose work of experimental or wry nature to supplement poetry, and are always looking for innovative/imaginative uses of British themes and references."

‡BONE & FLESH, (II), Bone & Flesh Publications, P.O. Box 728, Concord NH 03302-0728. (603)225-0521. Fiction Editors: Amy Shea, Frederick Moe, Lester Hirsh. Magazine: 8×11; 50 pages; quality paper and cover stock; illustrations. "*Bone & Flesh* publishes diverse prose, poetry and art for an independent, progressive literate audience. We are the longest-lived literary magazine in northern New England." Semiannually. Estab. 1988. Circ. 500. Member CLMP.

Needs: Experimental, literary. Receives 20 unsolicited mss/month. Accepts 4-6 mss/issue; 6-10 mss/year. Does not read mss June through January. Publishes mss up to one year after acceptance. Recently published work by Rebecca Rule, Albert Russo and Susan Bartlett. Length: 2,100 words average; 50 words minimum; 2,600 words maximum. Publishes short shorts. Also publishes literary essays, literary criticism, poetry.

How to Contact: Often critiques or comments on rejected mss. Send complete ms with a cover letter. Include estimated word count and bio with submission. Reports in 3 months on mss. SASE for reply. Reprint submissions OK. Sample copy for $7. Fiction guidelines free.

Payment/Terms: Pays free subscription to the magazine and 2 contributor's copies; additional copies 50% off cover price. Acquires first North American serial rights.

Advice: "Excellent use of language is our only criteria. Read a sample copy and follow guidelines closely."

BOOKLOVERS, (I, II), Jammer Publications, P.O. Box 93485, Milwaukee WI 53203-0485. (414)541-7510. E-mail: rjammer@omnifest.uwm.edu. Editor: Jill Lindberg. Magazine: 8½×11; 32 pages; high-grade newsprint paper; photos. *"BookLovers* is a literary magazine aimed at avid readers and writers. Includes book reviews, author interviews, book lists, features on unique book stores and profiles of book discussion groups." Quarterly. Estab. 1992. Circ. 800.
Needs: Adventure, ethnic/multicultural, fantasy (children's), historical, humor/satire, literary, mainstream/contemporary, mystery/suspense (amateursleuth, cozy, police procedural), regional, romance (gothic, historical), serialized novel, sports, young adult/teen (adventure, mystery, science fiction). List of upcoming themes available for SASE. Receives 10 unsolicited mss/month. Buys 3-4 mss/issue; 10-12 mss/year. Publishes ms 6 months after acceptance. Recently published work by Shirley Mudrick, Lois Schmidt and Jane Farrell. Length: 800-1,000 words average; 500 words minimum; 1,500 words maximum. Publishes short shorts. Length: 300 words. Also publishes literary essays, literary criticism, poetry.
How to Contact: Send complete ms with a cover letter. Should include estimated word count and bio (200 words maximum). Reports in 2-3 months. Send SASE for reply, return of ms or send a disposable copy of ms. Simultaneous, reprint, electronic (Macintosh only) submissions OK. Sample copy for 9×12 SAE and 5 first-class stamps. Fiction guidelines for #10 SASE.
Payment/Terms: Pays 2-5 contributor's copies. Acquires one-time rights.
Advice: Looking for "unique story line, good grammar, syntax (very important), interesting literature-related articles and book reviews, articles written in succinct manner."

‡BOSTON LITERARY REVIEW (BLUR), (I, II), P.O. Box 357, West Somerville MA 02144. (617)666-3080. Editor: Gloria Mindock. Magazine: 24-30 pages. Semiannually. Estab. 1985. Circ. 500.
Needs: Condensed/excerpted novel, experimental, literary, mainstream/contemporary, translations. "We are open to all styles of fiction but especially interested in work that is experimental or takes risks." Receives 100 unsolicited mss/month. Accepts 2 mss/issue; 4 mss/year. Publishes ms 1 year after acceptance. Length: 1,500 words average; 2,000 words maximum. Publishes short shorts. Also publishes poetry. Often critiques or comments on rejected mss.
How to Contact: Send complete ms with a cover letter. Include estimated word count, paragraph bio and list of publications. Reports in 1 month on queries; 6 weeks on mss. Send SASE for reply, return of ms or send a disposable copy of ms. Sample copy for $4.
Payment/Terms: Pays 2 contributor's copies. Acquires all rights. Sends galleys to author.
Advice: Looking for "neatness and fiction that takes risks. Send your work out and don't let any rejections stop you."

BOTTOMFISH MAGAZINE, (II), De Anza College, 21250 Stevens Creek Blvd., Cupertino CA 95014. (408)864-8623. Editor-in-Chief: David Denny. Magazine: 7×8½; 80-100 pages; White Bristol vellum cover; b&w high contrast illustrations and photos. "Contemporary poetry, fiction, b&w graphics and photos." Annually. Estab. 1976. Circ. 500.
Needs: "Literary excellence is our only criteria. We will consider all subjects." Receives 50-100 unsolicited fiction mss/month. Accepts 5-6 mss/issue. Recently published work by Keith Dawson, Steven Carter, and Sarah Hendon. Length: 500 words minimum; 5,000 words maximum; 2,500 words average.
How to Contact: Reads mss September to February. Submission deadline: February 1; publication date: end of March. Submit 1 short story or up to 3 short shorts with cover letter, brief bio and SASE. No reprints. Reports in 3-4 months. Publishes mss an average of 6 months to 1 year after acceptance. Sample copy for $5.
Payment/Terms: Pays 2 contributor's copies. Acquires one-time rights.
Advice: "Strive for originality and high level of craft; avoid clichéd or stereotyped characters and plots."

BOUILLABAISSE, (I, IV), Alpha Beat Press, 31 Waterloo St., New Hope PA 18938. (215)862-0299. Editor: Dave Christy. Magazine: 11×17; 120 pages; bond paper; illustrations and photos. Semiannually. Estab. 1986. Circ. 600.
● Work included in *Bouillabaisse* has been selected for inclusion in the *Pushcart Prize* anthology.
Needs: Beat generation and modern sub-cultures: adventure, condensed/excerpted novel, erotica, literary. Receives 15 unsolicited mss/month. Accepts 2 mss/issue; 4 mss/year. Publishes ms 6 months after acceptance. Recently published work by Ken Kesey, Ted Joans, Charles Plymell and Daniel Crocker. Length: no limit. Publishes short shorts. Also publishes literary essays, literary criticism and poetry. Sometimes critiques or comments on rejected mss.
How to Contact: Query first. Include bio with submission. Reports in 1 week. Send SASE for reply or return of ms. Simultaneous submissions OK. Sample copy for $10. Reviews novels and short story collections.

Payment/Terms: Pays 1 contributor's copy.

BOULEVARD, (II), Opojaz Inc., P.O. Box 30386, Philadelphia PA 19103-8386. (215)568-7062. Editor: Richard Burgin. Magazine: 5½ × 8½; 150-225 pages; excellent paper; high-quality cover stock; illustrations; photos. "*Boulevard* aspires to publish the best contemporary fiction, poetry and essays we can print." Published 3 times/year. Estab. 1986. Circ. about 3,000.

● A story originally printed in *Boulevard* was included in *Prize Stories 1995: The O. Henry Awards.*

Needs: Contemporary, experimental, literary. Does not want to see "anything whose first purpose is not literary." Receives over 400 mss/month. Accepts about 8 mss/issue. Does not accept manuscripts between May 1 and October 1. Publishes ms less than 1 year after acceptance. Agented fiction ⅓-¼. Length: 5,000 words average; 8,000 words maximum. Publishes short shorts. Recently published work by Stephen Dixon, Madison Smartt Bell, Joan Silber, Gordon Lish, Joyce Carol Oates and Jonathan Baumbach. Also publishes literary essays, literary criticism, poetry. Sometimes critiques rejected mss and recommends other markets.

How to Contact: Send complete ms with cover letter. Reports in 2 weeks on queries; 3 months on mss. SASE for reply. Simultaneous submissions OK. Sample copy for $7 and SAE with 5 first-class stamps.

Payment/Terms: Pays $50-150; contributor's copies; charges for extras. Acquires first North American serial rights. Does not send galleys to author unless requested.

Advice: "We are open to different styles of imaginative and critical work and are mindful of Nabokov's dictum 'There is only one school, the school of talent.' Above all, when we consider the very diverse manuscripts submitted to us for publication, we value original sensibility, writing that causes the reader to experience a part of life in a new way. Originality, to us, has little to do with a writer intently trying to make each line or sentence odd, bizarre, or eccentric, merely for the sake of being 'different.' Rather, originality is the result of the character or vision of the writer; the writer's singular outlook and voice as it shines through in the totality of his or her work."

(the) BRAVE NEW TICK, (I, IV), Graftographic Press, P.O. Box 24, S. Grafton MA 01560. (508)799-3769. E-mail: tick@ultranet.com. Editor: Paul Normal Dion-Deitch. Newsletter: 8½ × 11; 10 pages; standard paper; b&w illustrations. "Civil rights for all, focus on gay rights, activisim. Would very much like to publish gay fiction—no porn." Monthly. Estab. 1993. Circ. 75-100.

Needs: Mild erotica (gay), gay, lesbian short stories; general poetry, art, political commentary. Receives 1-2 unsolicited mss/month. Length: 1 or 2 typed pages maximum. Publishes short shorts. Also publishes literary essays, literary criticism and poetry.

How to Contact: Open to any method of submission. Include bio. Send SASE for return of ms. Simultaneous, reprint and electronic submissions OK (IBM compatible, ASCII files accepted and preferred). Sample copy for #10 SAE and 2-3 loose first-class stamps.

Payment/Terms: Pays contributor's copies. "Rights remain with contributor."

Advice: Looks for fiction "related to gay rights, growing up gay, living in a straight world, gay culture, gay pride that is well written, thought provoking, visually interesting. Hard core porn is not what I'm looking for."

THE BRIAR CLIFF REVIEW, (II), Briar Cliff College, 3303 Rebecca St., Sioux City IA 51104-2100. (712)279-1651 or 279-5321. Fax: (712) 279-5410. Editors: Tricia Currans-Sheehan and Jeanne Emmons. Magazine: 8½ × 11; 64 pages; 70 lb matte paper; 10 Pt CIS cover stock; illustrations and photos. "*The Briar Cliff Review* is an eclectic literary and cultural magazine focusing on (but not limited to) Siouxland writers and subjects. We are happy to proclaim ourselves a regional publication. It doesn't diminish us; it enhances us." Annually. Estab. 1989. Circ. 500.

● *The Briar Cliff Review* has received The Gold Crown and Silver Crown awards from the Columbia Scholastic Prize Association and the Pacemaker Award from the Associated Collegiate Press.

Needs: Ethnic/multicultural, feminist, historical, horror, humor/satire, literary, mainstream/contemporary, regional. Accepts 5 mss/year. Reads mss only between August 1 and November 1. Publishes ms 3-4 months after acceptance. Published work by Robley Wilson, Mary Helen Stefaniak, Bill Franzen, Brian Bedard and Carol Bly. Length: 3,000 words average; 2,500 words minimum; 3,500 words maximum. Also publishes literary essays, literary criticism and poetry. Sometimes critiques or comments on rejected mss.

How to Contact: Send complete ms with a cover letter. Include estimated word count, bio and list of publications. Reports in 3-4 months on mss. Send a SASE for return of ms. Electronic submissions (disk) OK. No simultaneous submissions. Sample copy for $5 and 9 × 12 SAE. Fiction guidelines free for #10 SASE. Reviews novels and short story collections.

Payment/Terms: Pays 2 contributor's copies for first rights; additional copies available for $2.

Advice: "Send us your best."

THE BROWNSTONE REVIEW, (II), 331 16th St., #2, Brooklyn NY 11215. Fiction Editor: Laura Dawson. Magazine: 5½×8½; 60 pages. Semiannually. Estab. 1995. Circ. 250.
Needs: Adventure, erotica, ethnic/multicultural, experimental, feminist, gay, historical, horror, humor/satire, lesbian, literary, mainstream/contemporary, mystery/suspense, regional, science fiction, senior citizen/retirement, sports, westerns. No romance, religious, children's stories or occult/gothic horror. Planning future special fiction issue or anthology. Receives 50 unsolicited mss/month. Accepts 3-6 mss/issue; 6-12 mss/year. Publishes ms 6-9 months after acceptance. Length: 1,000-2,000 words average; 250 words minimum; 10,000 words maximum. Publishes short shorts. Also publishes poetry. Sometimes critiques or comments on rejected ms.
How to Contact: Send complete ms with a cover letter. Should include list of publications. Reports in 3 months. Send SASE for reply, return of ms or send a disposable copy of ms. Simultaneous submissions OK.
Payment/Terms: Pays 2 contributor's copies. Acquires first North American serial rights.
Advice: "Revise, revise, revise . . . "

BRÚJULA/COMPASS, (I, II, IV), Latin American Writers Institute, % Hostos Community College, 500 Grand Concourse, Bronx NY 10451. (718)518-4195. Fax: (718)518-4294. Editor: Isaac Goldemberg. Tabloid: 10×14; 40 pages; 50 lb. bond paper; illustrations and photos. "*Brújula/Compass* is devoted exclusively to Latino writers living in the U.S. and writing in English and/or Spanish." Quarterly. Estab. 1988. Circ. 10,000.
Needs: Ethnic/multicultural, feminist, gay, humor/satire, lesbian, mainstream/contemporary, translations. Publishes annual special fiction issue or anthology. Receives 25 unsolicited mss/month. Accepts 3 mss/issue; 10-12 mss/year. Publishes ms 3 months after acceptance. Agented fiction 20%. Published work by Oscar Hijuelos, Julia Alvarez, Ariel Dorfman. Length: 3,000 words average. Publishes short shorts. Also publishes literary essays, literary criticism, poetry.
How to Contact: Send complete ms with a cover letter. Send SASE for reply, return of ms or send a disposable copy of ms. Simultaneous, reprint, electronic submissions OK. Sample copy free. Reviews novels and short story collections.
Payment/Terms: Pays 10 contributor's copies, free subscription of magazine. Acquires one-time rights.

BURNT ALUMINUM, (II), P.O. Box 3561, Mankato MN 56001. Editors: Jim Redmond and Brian Batt. Magazine: 8½×7; 60 pages. "*Burnt Aluminum* is a mainstream fiction magazine. We prefer realistic themes." Semiannually. Estab. 1995. Circ. 150.
Needs: Condensed/excerpted novel, literary, mainstream/contemporary. No horror, mystery or science fiction. Receives 10 unsolicited mss/month. Accepts 6-8 mss/issue; 12-16 mss/year. Publishes ms 6 months after acceptance. Recently published work by Mike Magnuson and R.J. Bledsoe. No preferred length.
How to Contact: Send complete ms with a cover letter. Include one-paragraph bio and list of publications with submission. Send SASE for reply, return of ms or send a disposable copy of ms. Simultaneous submissions OK. Sample copy for $4 and $1.50 postage.
Payment/Terms: Pays 2 contributor's copies. Acquires first North American serial rights.
Advice: "We prefer stories with strong characters and strong character development. Plot is secondary. We also prefer realistic fiction—like Ray Carver's or Richard Ford's—stories representative of life in today's world. We do not like anything related to fantasy or horror, or trivial writing."

‡BUTTON, New England's Tiniest Magazine of Poetry, Fiction & Gracious Living, (II), P.O. Box 26, Lunenburg MA 01462. E-mail: symboline@juno.com. Editor: S. Cragin. Fiction Editor: Adena Dawes. Magazine: 4×5; 34 pages; bond paper; color cardstock cover; illustrations; photos. Estab. 1993. Circ. 1,500.
Needs: Literary. No genre fiction. Receives 20-40 unsolicited mss/month. Accepts 1-2 mss/issue; 3-5 mss/year. Publishes ms 3-9 months after acceptance. Recently published work by Sven Birkerts, Stephen McCauley, Wayne Wilson, Romayne Dawney and Lawrence Millman. Length: 500-2,500 words. Also publishes literary essays and poetry. Sometimes critiques or comments on rejected mss "if it shows promise."
How to Contact: Request guidelines. Send ms with bio, list of publications and advise how you found magazine. Reports in 1 month on queries; 2-4 months on mss. SASE. Sample copy for $1. Fiction guidelines for SASE. Reviews novels and short story collections. Send book to editor.
Payment/Terms: Pays multiple free subscriptions to the magazine on publication. Acquires first North American serial rights. Sends galleys to author if there are editorial changes.
Advice: "I started *Button* so that a century from now when people read it in landfills or, preferably, libraries, they'll say, 'Gee what a wonderful time to have lived—wish I'd lived back then.' "

BY THE WAYSIDE, (I), 5 West St., Wilmington MA 01887. Editor: Stephen Brown. Tabloid: 6 pages; plain bond. "*By the Wayside* is intended for those who enjoy P.G. Wodehouse, Robert Benchley and the Marx Brothers." Triannually. Estab. 1995. Circ. 100.
Needs: Humor/satire. Receives 15 unsolicited mss/month. Accepts 3 mss/issue; 10 mss/year. Publishes ms 3 months after acceptance. Published work by Boko Fittleworth and Louis Saccocea. Length: 800 words average; 100 words minimum; 1,100 words maximum. Publishes short shorts. Length: 800 words. Sometimes critiques or comments on rejected ms.
How to Contact: Send complete ms with a cover letter. Reports in 1-2 months. Send SASE for reply, return of ms or send a disposable copy of ms. Simultaneous submissions OK. Sample copy for $3, 7×10 or 8×11 SAE and 2 first-class stamps.
Payment/Terms: Pays 5 contributor's copies. Acquires one-time rights. Not copyrighted.
Advice: "I want to provide humor writers, particularly new ones, with an outlet for their work. Attitude is more important than ideas. Get a sample copy before submitting."

BYLINE, (I, II), Box 130596, Edmond OK 73013. (405)348-5591. Website: http://www.bylinemag.c om. Editor-in-Chief: Marcia Preston. Managing Editor: Kathryn Fanning. Monthly magazine "aimed at encouraging and motivating all writers toward success, with special information to help new writers." Estab. 1981.
Needs: Literary, genre and general fiction. Receives 100-200 unsolicited fiction mss/month. Accepts 1 ms/issue, 11 mss/year. Published work by Susan McKeague Karnes and Michael Bugeja. Published many new writers within the last year. Length: 4,000 words maximum; 2,000 words minimum. Also publishes poetry.
How to Contact: Send complete ms with SASE. Simultaneous submissions OK, "if notified. For us, no cover letter is needed." Reports in 6-12 weeks. Publishes ms an average of 3 months after acceptance. Sample copy, guidelines and contest list for $4.
Payment/Terms: Pays $100 on acceptance and 2 contributor's copies for first North American rights.
Advice: "We're very open to new writers. Submit a well-written, professionally prepared ms with SASE. No erotica or senseless violence; otherwise, we'll consider most any theme. We also sponsor short story and poetry contests."

CALLALOO, A Journal of African-American and African Arts and Letters, (I, II, IV), Dept. of English, 322 Bryan Hall, University of Virginia, Charlottesville VA 22903. (804)924-6637. E-mail: callaloo@virginia.edu. Editor: Charles H. Rowell. Magazine: 7×10; 250 pages. Scholarly magazine. Quarterly. Plans special fiction issue in future. Estab. 1976. Circ. 1,500.
● One of the leading voices in African-American literature, *Callaloo* has received NEA literature grants. Work published in *Callaloo* received a 1994 *Pushcart Prize* anthology nomination and inclusion in *Best American Short Stories*.
Needs: Contemporary, ethnic (black culture), feminist, historical, humor/satire, literary, prose poem, regional, science fiction, serialized/excerpted novel, translations. Also publishes poetry and drama. Themes for 1996: Australian Aboriginal Literature; Dominican Arts and Letters. Accepts 3-5 mss/ issue; 10-20 mss/year. Length: no restrictions. Published work by Chinua Achebe, Rita Dove, Reginald McKnight, Caryl Philips and John Edgar Wideman.
How to Contact: Submit complete ms in triplicate and cover letter with name, mailing address, e-mail address if possible and SASE. Reports on queries in 2 weeks; 3-4 months on mss. Previously published work accepted "occasionally." Sample copy for $8.
Payment/Terms: Pays in contributor's copies. Acquires all rights. Sends galleys to author.
Advice: "We strongly recommend looking at the journal before submitting."

CALLIOPE, (V), Creative Writing Program, Roger Williams University, Bristol RI 02809. (401)254-3217. Coordinating Editor: Martha Christina. Magazine: 5½×8½; 40-56 pages; 50 lb. offset paper; vellum or 60 lb. cover stock; occasional illustrations and photos. "We are an eclectic little magazine publishing contemporary poetry, fiction, and occasionally interviews." Semiannually. Estab. 1977. Circ. 400.
Needs: Literary, contemporary, experimental/innovative. "We try to include at least 2 pieces of fiction in each issue." Receives approximately 10-20 unsolicited fiction mss each month. Does not read mss

---

✦ **THE MAPLE LEAF** symbol before a listing indicates a Canadian publisher, magazine, conference or contest.

mid-March to mid-August. Published new writers within the last year. Length: open. Publishes short shorts under 20 pages. Critiques rejected mss when there is time.

How to Contact: *"Until further notice we will not be accepting fiction submissions."* Sample copy for $2.

Payment/Terms: Pays 2 contributor's copies and one year's subscription beginning with following issue. Rights revert to author on publication.

Advice: "We are not interested in reading anyone's very first story. If the piece is good, it will be given careful consideration. Reading a sample copy of *Calliope* is recommended. Let the characters of the story tell their own story; we're very often (painfully) aware of the writer's presence. Episodic is fine; story need not (for our publication) have traditional beginning, middle and end."

CALYX, A Journal of Art & Literature by Women, (II), Calyx, Inc., P.O. Box B, Corvallis OR 97339. (541)753-9384. Fax: (541)753-0515. E-mail: calyx@proaxis.com. Managing Editor: Margarita Donnelly. Editorial Coordinator: Beverly McFarland. Editors: Teri Mae Rutledge, Linda Varsell Smith, Micki Reaman, Lois Cranston, Dorothy Mack and Yolanda Calvillo. Magazine: 7×8; 128 pages per single issue, 250 per double; 60 lb. coated matte stock paper; 10 pt. chrome coat cover; original art. Publishes prose, poetry, art, essays, interviews and critical and review articles. "*Calyx* editors are seeking innovative and literary works of exceptional quality." Biannually. Estab. 1976. Circ. 6,000.

● *Calyx* received an Honorable Mention for editorial content and First Place for cover design in 1995 from the American Literary Magazine Awards and the Oregon Governor's Arts Award in 1996.

Needs: Receives approximately 300 unsolicited fiction mss each month. Accepts 4-8 prose mss/issue, 9-15 mss/year. Reads mss October 1-November 15; submit only during these periods. Recently published work by M. Evelina Galang, Basha Faber, Carolyn Barbier, Lynne Hugo de Courcy and Melissa Kwasny. Published new writers within the last year. Length: 5,000 words maximum. Also publishes literary essays, literary criticism, poetry.

How to Contact: Send ms with SASE and bio. Simultaneous submissions OK. Reports in up to 8 months on mss. Publishes ms an average of 8 months after acceptance. Sample copy for $9 plus $1.50 postage. Guidelines available for SASE. Reviews novels, short story collections, poetry and essays.

Payment/Terms: "Combination of payment, free issues and 1 volume subscription."

Advice: Most mss are rejected because "the writers are not familiar with *Calyx*—writers should read *Calyx* and be familiar with the publication."

✵CANADIAN AUTHOR, (IV), Canadian Author Association, 27 Doxsee Ave. N, Campbellford, Ontario K0L 1L0 Canada. (705)653-0323. Fax: (705)653-0593. E-mail: canauth@redden.on.ca. Editor: Welwyn Wilton Katz. Fiction Editor: Bill Valgardson. Magazine: 8¼×10¾; 32 pages; glossy paper; illustrations and photos. "Features in-depth profiles and interviews with the people who influence Canadian literature, as well as articles on the craft and business of writing." Quarterly. Estab. 1919. Circ. 4,000.

Needs: Ethnic/multicultural, experimental, feminist, historical, humor/satire, literary, mainstream/contemporary, regional, senior citizen/retirement. *Must be by a Canadian author only.* Receives 50 unsolicited mss/month. Accepts 1 mss/issue; 4 mss/year. Publishes ms 6-9 months after acceptance. Length: 3,000 words average; 2,000 words minimum; 3,000 words maximum. Also publishes literary essays and poetry.

How to Contact: Send complete ms with a cover letter. Include estimated word count, short bio and list of publication. Reports in 3-5 months. Send SASE for reply, return of ms or send a disposable copy of ms. Simultaneous and reprint submissions OK. Sample copy for $6.50 (Canadian) and 9×12 SAE with 88¢ postage.

Payment/Terms: Pays $125 on publication for first rights. Usually sends galleys to author.

Advice: "We look for quality fiction. Read our magazine. Better yet, subscribe."

✵CAPERS AWEIGH MAGAZINE, (I, II, IV), Cape Breton Poetry & Fiction, Capers Aweigh Small Press, P.O. Box 96, Sydney, Nova Scotia B1P 6G9 Canada. (902)567-1449. Editor: John Mac-Neil. Magazine: 5×8; 80 pages; bond paper; Cornwall-coated cover. "*Capers Aweigh* publishes poetry and fiction of, by and for Cape Bretoners." Publication frequency varies. Estab. 1992. Circ. 500.

Needs: Adventure, ethnic/multicultural, fantasy, feminist, historical, humor/satire, literary, mainstream, contemporary, mystery/suspense, psychic/supernatural/occult, regional, science fiction. List of upcoming themes available for SASE. Receives 2 unsolicited mss/month. Accepts 30 mss/issue. Publishes ms 9 months after acceptance. Published work by C. Fairn Kennedy and Shirley Kiju Kawi. Length: 2,500 words. Publishes short shorts. Also publishes literary criticism and poetry. Sponsors contests only to Cape Bretoners fiction writers.

How to Contact: Query first. Send SASE for reply or send a disposable copy of ms. Electronic submissions OK (IBM). Sample copy for $3 and 6×10 SAE.

Payment/Terms: Pays free subscription to the magazine and 1 contributor's copy; additional copies for $3. Acquires first North American serial rights. Sends galleys to author.

‡❦**THE CAPILANO REVIEW, (II)**, 2055 Purcell Way, North Vancouver, British Columbia V7J 3H5 Canada. (604)984-1712. Fax: (604)983-7520. E-mail: erains@capcollege.bc.ca. Editor: Robert Sherrin. Magazine: 6×9; 90-120 pages; book paper; glossy cover; perfect-bound; b&w illustrations and photos. Magazine of "fresh, innovative art and literature for literary/artistic audience." Triannually. Estab. 1972. Circ. 900.

Needs: Experimental, literary and drama. Receives 80 unsolicited mss/month. Accepts 3-4 mss/issue; 10 mss/year. Recently published works by Philip Russell, Natalee Caple and K.D. Miller. Published new writers within the last year. Length: 4,000 words average. Publishes short shorts. Also publishes literary essays and poetry. Occasionally recommends other markets.

How to Contact: Send complete ms with cover letter and SASE. Include 2- to 3-sentence bio and brief list of publications. Reports on mss in 2-4 months. Send SAE with IRCs for return of ms. Simultaneous submissions OK. Sample copy for $9 (Canadian).

Payment/Terms: Pays $50-200, 2 contributor's copies and one year subscription. Pays on publication. Acquires first North American serial rights.

Advice: "We are looking for exceptional, original style; strong thematic content. Read several issues before submitting and make sure your work is technically perfect."

CAROLINA QUARTERLY, (II), Greenlaw Hall CB #3520, University of North Carolina, Chapel Hill NC 27599-3520. Editor-in-Chief: John R. Black. Fiction Editor: Shannon Wooden. Literary journal: 70-90 pages; illustrations. Triannually. Estab. 1948. Circ. 1,400.

● Work published in *Carolina Quarterly* has been selected for inclusion in *Best American Short Stories* and in *Short Stories from the South: The Year's Best*.

Needs: Literary. Receives 150-200 unsolicited fiction mss/month. Accepts 5-7 mss/issue; 15-20 mss/year. Publishes ms an average of 4 months after acceptance. Published work by Barry Hannah, Nanci Kincaid and Doris Betts. Published new writers within the last year. Length: 7,000 words maximum; no minimum. Also publishes short shorts, literary essays, poetry. Occasionally critiques rejected mss.

How to Contact: Send complete ms with cover letter and SASE to fiction editor. No simultaneous submissions. Reports in 2-4 months. Sample copy for $5; writer's guidelines for SASE.

Payment/Terms: Pays in contributor's copies for first rights.

CAYO, A Chronicle of Life in the Keys, (II, IV), 116 Avenue D, Key West FL 33040. (305)296-4286. Editor: Alyson Simmons. Magazine: 8½×11; 40-48 pages; glossy paper; 70 lb. cover stock; illustrations and photos. Magazine on Keys-related topics or by Keys authors. Quarterly. Estab. 1993. Circ. 500.

Needs: Condensed/excerpted novel, experimental, literary, regional. Receives 4-5 unsolicited mss/month. Accepts 2-3 mss/issue; 8-12 mss/year. Recently published work by Alma Bond, Robin Shanley and Lawrence Ferlinghetti. Length: 3,000 words average; 800 words minimum; 3,000 words maximum. Publishes short shorts. Also publishes literary essays and poetry. Often critiques or comments on rejected mss.

How to Contact: Send complete ms with a cover letter. Include bio and list of publications with submission. Reports in 6 weeks on queries; 3 months on mss. Send SASE for reply, return of ms or send a disposable copy of ms. Simultaneous, reprint and electronic (ASCII text on disk) submissions OK. Sample copy for $4. Fiction guidelines for #10 SASE.

Payment/Terms: Pays in contributor's copies. Acquires one-time rights.

Advice: "The story has to stand on its own and move the reader."

CHAMINADE LITERARY REVIEW, (II, IV), Chaminade Press, 3140 Waialae Ave., Honolulu HI 96816. (808)735-4723. Editor: Loretta Petrie. Magazine: 6×9; 200 pages; 50 lb. white paper; 10 pt. C1S cover; photographs. "Multicultural, particularly Hawaii—poetry, fiction, artwork, criticism, photos, translations for all English-speaking internationals, but primarily Hawaii." Annually. Estab. 1987. Circ. 350.

Needs: Excerpted novel, ethnic, experimental, humor/satire, literary, religious/inspirational, translations. "We have published a variety including translations of Japanese writers, a fishing story set in Hawaii, fantasy set along the Amazon, but the major point is they are all 'literary.' " Receives 8 unsolicited mss/month. Accepts 5-8 mss/issue. Publishes ms 3-6 months after acceptance. "We haven't published short shorts yet, but would depending on quality." Sometimes critiques rejected ms.

How to Contact: Send complete ms with cover letter. Include short contributor's note. Reporting time depends on how long before deadlines of May 15 and December 15. SASE. Reprint submissions OK. Sample copy for $5.

Payment/Terms: Pays subscription to magazine. Acquires one-time rights.

Advice: "We look for good writing; appeal for Hawaii audience and writers everywhere. *CLR* was founded to give added exposure to Hawaii's writers, both here and on the mainland, and to juxtapose Hawaii writing with mainland and international work."

THE CHARITON REVIEW, (II), Truman State University, Kirksville MO 63552. (816)785-4499. Fax: (816)785-7486. Editor: Jim Barnes. Magazine: 6×9; approximately 100 pages; 60 lb. paper; 65 lb. cover stock; photographs on cover. "We demand only excellence in fiction and fiction translation for a general and college readership." Semiannually. Estab. 1975. Circ. 700.
Needs: Literary, contemporary, experimental and translations. Accepts 3-5 mss/issue; 6-10 mss/year. Recently published work by Ann Townsend, Glenn DelGrosso, Dennis Trudell and X.J. Kennedy. Published new writers within the last year. Length: 3,000-6,000 words. Also publishes literary essays, poetry. Critiques rejected mss when there is time.
How to Contact: Send complete ms with SASE. No book-length mss. No simultaneous submissions. Reports in less than 1 month on mss. Publishes ms an average of 6 months after acceptance. Sample copy for $5 with SASE. Reviews novels and short story collections.
Payment/Terms: Pays $5/page up to $50 maximum and contributor's copy on publication; additional copies for $5.50. Buys first North American serial rights; rights returned on request.
Advice: "Do not ask us for guidelines: the only guidelines are excellence in all matters. Write well and study the publication you are submitting to. We are interested only in the very best fiction and fiction translation. We are not interested in slick material. We do not read photocopies, dot-matrix, or carbon copies. Know the simple mechanics of submission—SASE, no paper clips, no odd-sized SASE, etc. Know the genre (short story, novella, etc.). Know the unwritten laws. There is too much manufactured fiction; assembly-lined, ego-centered personal essays offered as fiction."

THE CHATTAHOOCHEE REVIEW, (I, II), DeKalb College, 2101 Womack Rd., Dunwoody GA 30338. (770)551-3166. Editor: Lamar York. Magazine: 6×9; 150 pages; 70 lb. paper; 80 lb. cover stock; illustrations; photographs. Quarterly. Estab. 1980. Circ. 1,250.
● Fiction from *The Chattahoochee Review* has been included in *Best New Stories of the South*.
Needs: Literary, mainstream. No juvenile, romance, science fiction. Receives 500 unsolicited mss/ month. Accepts 5 mss/issue. Published work by Leon Rooke, R.T. Smith; published new writers within the last year. Length: 2,500 words average. Also publishes literary essays, literary criticism, poetry. Sometimes critiques rejected mss.
How to Contact: Send complete ms with cover letter, which should include sufficient bio for notes on contributors' page. Reports in 2 months. SASE. May consider simultaneous submission "reluctantly." Sample copy for $5. Fiction and poetry guidelines available on request. Reviews novels and short story collections.
Payment/Terms: Contact Managing Editor for rates. Acquires first rights.
Advice: "Arrange to read magazine before you submit to it." Known for publishing Southern regional fiction.

CHELSEA, (II), Chelsea Associates, Inc., Box 773, Cooper Station, New York NY 10276. Editor: Richard Foerster. Magazine: 6×9; 185-235 pages; 60 lb. white paper; glossy, full-color cover; artwork; occasional photos. "We have no consistent theme except for single special issues. Otherwise, we use general material of an eclectic nature: poetry, prose, artwork, etc., for a sophisticated, literate audience interested in avant-garde literature and current writing, both national and international." Annually. Estab. 1958. Circ. 1,400.
● *Chelsea* sponsors the Chelsea Awards. Entries to that contest will also be considered for the magazine, but writers may submit directly to the magazine as well. Fiction originally appearing in *Chelsea* was selected for inclusion in the *1995 O. Henry Prize Stories* and the magazine was the recipient of a New York State Council for the Arts grant in 1995-96.
Needs: Literary, contemporary short fiction, poetry and translations. "No romance, divorce, racist, sexist material or I-hate-my-mother stories. We look for serious, sophisticated literature from writers willing to take risks with language and narrative structure." Receives approximately 100 unsolicited fiction mss each month. Approximately 1% of fiction is agented. Recently published work by Gladys Swan, Rush Rankin, Cary Holladay, K. Margaret Grossman, Kim Addonizio and Steven Huff. Length: not over 25 printed pages. Publishes short shorts of 6 pages. Sponsors annual Chelsea Award, $750 (send SASE for guidelines).
How to Contact: Send complete ms with SASE and succinct cover letter with previous credits. No simultaneous submissions. Reports in 3 months on mss. Publishes ms within a year after acceptance. Sample copy for $7.
Payment/Terms: Pays contributor's copies and $15 per printed page for first North American serial rights plus one-time non-exclusive reprint rights.
Advice: "Familiarize yourself with issues of the magazine for character of contributions. Manuscripts should be legible, clearly typed, with minimal number of typographical errors and cross-outs, sufficient return postage. Most mss are rejected because they are conventional in theme and/or style, uninspired, contrived, etc. We see far too much of the amateurish love story or romance. Writers should say something that has never been said before or at least say something in a unique way. There is too much focus on instant fame and not enough attention to craft. Our audience is sophisticated, international, and eclectic and expects freshness and originality."

CHICAGO REVIEW, (II), 5801 S. Kenwood Ave., Chicago IL 60637. Fax: (312)702-0887. Fiction Editors: Leigh Anne Duck, Lisa McNair and John Roberts. Magazine for a highly literate general audience: 6×9; 128 pages; offset white 60 lb. paper; illustrations; photos. Quarterly. Estab. 1946. Circ. 2,600.
Needs: Literary, contemporary and experimental. Accepts up to 5 mss/issue; 20 mss/year. Receives 80-100 unsolicited fiction mss each week. Recently published work by Greg Johnson, Maxine Chernoff and S.L. Wisenberg. No preferred length, except will not accept book-length mss. Also publishes literary essays, literary criticism, poetry. Sometimes recommends other markets.
How to Contact: Send complete ms with cover letter. SASE. No simultaneous submissions. Reports in 4-5 months on mss. Sample copy for $6. Guidelines with SASE. Reviews novels and short story collections. Send books to Book Review Editor.
Payment/Terms: Pays 3 contributor's copies and subscription.
Advice: "We look with interest at fiction that addresses subjects inventively, work that steers clear of clichéd treatments of themes. We're always eager to read writing that experiments with language, whether it be with characters' viewpoints, tone or style. However, we have been receiving more submissions and are becoming more selective."

CHIRICÚ, (II, IV), Ballantine Hall 849, Indiana University, Bloomington IN 47405. Editorial Assistant: B. Santos. "We publish essays, translations, poetry, fiction, reviews, interviews and artwork (illustrations and photos) that are either by or about Latinos. We have no barriers on style, content or ideology, but would like to see well-written material. We accept manuscripts written in English, Spanish or Portuguese." Annually. Estab. 1976. Circ. 500.
Needs: Contemporary, ethnic, experimental, fantasy, feminist, humor/satire, literary, mainstream, prose poem, science fiction, serialized/excerpted novel, translations. Published new writers within the last year. Length: 7,000 words maximum; 3,000 words average. Occasionally critiques rejected mss.
How to Contact: Send complete ms with cover letter. "Include some personal information along with information about your story." SASE. No simultaneous submissions. Reports in 5 weeks. Publishes ms 6-12 months after acceptance. Sample copy for $5. Guidelines for #10 SASE.
Advice: "Realize that we are a Latino literary journal so, if you are not Latino, your work must reflect an interest in Latino issues or have a Latino focus." Mss rejected "because beginning writers force their language instead of writing from genuine sentiment, because of multiple grammatical errors."

CHIRON REVIEW, (I, II), 522 E. South Ave., St. John KS 67576-2212. (316)549-3933. Editor: Michael Hathaway. Tabloid: 10×13; minimum 24 pages; newsprint; illustrations; photos. Publishes "all types of material, no particular theme; traditional and off-beat, no taboos." Quarterly. Estab. 1982. Circ. 1,200.
● *Chiron Review* is known for publishing experimental and "sudden" fiction.
Needs: Contemporary, experimental, humor/satire, literary. Receives 20 mss/month. Accepts 1-3 ms/issue; 4-12 mss/year. Publishes ms within 6-18 months of acceptance. Recently published work by Albert Huffstickler, James Mechem, Ray Sepeda, Christian Gholson and D.S. Lliteras. Length: 3,500 words preferred. Publishes short shorts. Sometimes recommends other markets to writers of rejected mss.
How to Contact: Query. Reports in 6-8 weeks. SASE. No simultaneous or reprint submissions. Deadlines: November 1 (Winter), February 1 (Spring), May 1 (Summer), August 1 (Autumn). Sample copy for $4 ($8 overseas). Fiction guidelines for #10 SASE.
Payment/Terms: Pays 1 contributor's copy; extra copies at 50% discount. Acquires first rights.

‡CHRISTIANITY AND THE ARTS, (II), 1100 N. Lakeshore, #33-A, P.O. Box 118088, Chicago IL 60611. (312)642-8606. Fax: (312)266-7719. E-mail: chrnarts@aol.com. Editor: Marci Whitney-Schenck. Magazine: 8½×11; 52 pages; 60 lb. gloss paper; illustrations and photos. Publishes work on "Christian expression—visual arts, dance, music, literature, film. We reach Protestant, Catholic, and Orthodox readers throughout the United States and Canada. Our readers tend to be upscale and well-educated, with an interest in several disciplines, such as music and the visual arts." Quarterly. Estab. 1994. Circ. 4,000.
● *Christianity and the Arts* received an award from Associated Church Press in 1995 and 1996.
Needs: Mainstream/contemporary, religious/inspirational. No erotica. "We generally treat two themes in each issue." Upcoming themes: Paradise (May 1997); arts based on the Lutheran tradition (August 1997). Receives 3-4 unsolicited mss/month. "We hope to publish one fiction manuscript per issue." Publishes ms 6 months after acceptance. Length: 3,000 words maximum. Publishes short shorts. Also publishes literary essays. Sometimes critiques or comments on rejected mss.
How to Contact: Send complete ms with a cover letter. Include bio, estimated word count and list of publications. SASE for reply. Simultaneous submissions OK. Sample copy for $6. Reviews novels and short story collections.
Payment/Terms: No payment. Sends galleys to author.

CHRYSALIS READER, Journal of the Swedenborg Foundation, (II), The Swedenborg Foundation, P.O. Box 549, West Chester PA 19381-0549. (610)430-3222. Send mss to: Rt. 1, Box 184, Dillwyn VA 23936. (804)983-3021. Editor: Carol S. Lawson. Book series: 7½×10; 160 pages; archival paper; coated cover stock; illustrations; photos. "A literary magazine centered around one theme per issue. Publishes fiction, essays and poetry for intellectually curious readers interested in spiritual topics." Biannually. Estab. 1985. Circ. 3,000.
Needs: Adventure (leading to insight), contemporary, experimental, historical, literary, mainstream, mystery/suspense, science fiction, spiritual, sports. No religious, juvenile, preschool. Upcoming themes: "Choice" (September 1997); "Education" (January 1998). Receives 60 mss/month. Accepts 6-7 mss/issue; 12-14 mss/year. Publishes ms within 2 years of acceptance. Published work by Robert Bly, Larry Dossey, John Hitchcock, Betty Bone Schiess and Barbara Marx Hubbard. Length: 2,000 words minimum; 3,500 words maximum. Also publishes literary essays, literary criticism, chapters of novels, poetry. Sometimes critiques rejected mss and recommends other markets.
How to Contact: Query first and send SASE for guidelines. Reports in 2 months. SASE. No simultaneous, reprinted or in-press material. Sample copy for $10. Fiction guidelines for #10 SASE.
Payment/Terms: Pays $75-250 and 5 contributor's copies on publication for one-time rights. Sends galleys to author.
Advice: Looking for "1. *Quality*; 2. appeal for our audience; 3. relevance to/illumination of an issue's theme."

CICADA, (II, IV), 329 "E" St., Bakersfield CA 93304. (805)323-4064. Editor: Frederick A. Raborg, Jr. Magazine: 5½×8¼; 24 pages; matte cover stock; illustrations and photos. "Oriental poetry and fiction related to the Orient for general readership and haiku enthusiasts." Quarterly. Estab. 1985. Circ. 600.
Needs: *All with Oriental slant*: Adventure, contemporary, erotica, ethnic, experimental, fantasy, feminist, historical (general), horror, humor/satire, lesbian, literary, mainstream, mystery/suspense, psychic/supernatural/occult, regional, contemporary romance, historical romance, young adult romance, science fiction, senior citizen/retirement and translations. "We look for strong fiction with Oriental (especially Japanese) content or flavor. Stories need not have 'happy' endings, and we are open to the experimental and/or avant-garde. Erotica is fine; pornography, no." Receives 30 unsolicited mss/month. Accepts 1 ms/issue; 4 mss/year. Publishes ms 6 months to 1 year after acceptance. Agented fiction 5%. Published work by Gilbert Garand, Frank Holland and Jim Mastro. Length: 2,000 words average; 500 words minimum; 3,000 words maximum. Critiques rejected ms when appropriate. Also publishes poetry.
How to Contact: Send complete ms with cover letter. Include Social Security number and appropriate information about the writer in relationship to the Orient. Reports in 2 weeks on queries; 3 months on mss (if seriously considered). SASE. Sample copy for $4.95. Fiction guidelines for #10 SASE.
Payment/Terms: Pays $10-25 and contributor's copies on publication for first North American serial rights; charges for additional copies. $5 kill fee.
Advice: Looks for "excellence and appropriate storyline. Strong characterization and knowledge of the Orient are musts. Neatness counts high on my list for first impressions. A writer should demonstrate a high degree of professionalism."

CIMARRON REVIEW, (II), Oklahoma State University, 205 Morrill, Stillwater OK 74078-0135. (405)744-9476. Editor: Edward P. Walkiewicz. Magazine: 6×9; 100 pages. "Poetry and fiction on contemporary themes; personal essay on contemporary issues that cope with life in the 20th century, for educated literary readers. We work hard to reflect quality." Quarterly. Estab. 1967. Circ. 500.
Needs: Literary and contemporary. No collegiate reminiscences or juvenilia. Accepts 6-7 mss/issue, 24-28 mss/year. Published works by Peter Makuck, Mary Lee Settle, W. D. Wetherell, John Timmerman. Published new writers within the last year. Also publishes literary essays, literary criticism, poetry.
How to Contact: Send complete ms with SASE. "Short cover letters are appropriate but not essential, except for providing *CR* with the most recent mailing address available." No simultaneous submissions. Reports in 3 months on mss. Publishes ms within 1 year after acceptance. Sample copy with SASE and $3. Reviews novels, short story collections, and poetry collections.
Payment/Terms: Pays one-year subscription to author, plus $50 for each prose piece. Acquires all rights on publication. "Permission to reprint granted freely."
Advice: "Short fiction is a genre uniquely suited to the modern world. *CR* seeks an individual, innovative style that focuses on contemporary themes."

✱**THE CLAREMONT REVIEW, The Contemporary Magazine of Young Adult Writers, (I, IV)**, The Claremont Review Publishers, 4980 Wesley Rd., Victoria, British Columbia V8Y 1Y9 Canada. (604)658-5221. Fax: (604)658-5387. E-mail: aurora@islandnet.com. Editors: Terence Young and Bill Stenson. Magazine: 6×9; 110-120 pages; book paper; soft gloss cover; b&w illustrations. "We are dedicated to publishing emerging young writers aged 13-19 from anywhere in the English-speaking world, but primarily Canada and the U.S." Biannually. Estab. 1992. Circ. 350.

Needs: Young adult/teen ("their writing, not writing for them"). Plans special fiction issue or anthology. Receives 10-12 unsolicited mss/month. Accepts 10-12 mss/issue; 20-24 mss/year. Publishes ms 3 months after acceptance. Recently published work by Lisa Ellingson, Heath Johns, Kyra Haver and Shannon Horlor. Length: 1,500-3,000 words preferred; 5,000 words maximum. Publishes short shorts. Also publishes prose poetry. Always comments on rejected mss.

How to Contact: Send complete ms with cover letter. Include 2-line bio, list of publications and SASE. Reports in 6 weeks-3 months. Simultaneous and electronic (disk or modem) submissions OK. Sample copy for $6 with 6×9 SAE and $2 Canadian postage. Guidelines free with SAE.

Payment/Terms: Pays 1 contributor's copy on publication for first North American and one-time rights. Additional copies for $6.

Advice: Looking for "good concrete narratives with credible dialogue and solid use of original detail. It must be unique, honest and a glimpse of some truth. Send an error-free final draft with a short covering letter and bio; please, read us first to see what we publish."

THE CLIMBING ART, (I, II, IV), 6390 E. Floyd Dr., Denver CO 80222-7638. (303)757-0541. E-mail: clang@iastate.edu. Editor: Ron Morrow. Fiction Editor: Christiana Langenberg. Magazine: 5½×8½; 150 pages; illustrations and photos. "*The Climbing Art* publishes literature, poetry and art for and about the spirit of climbing." Semiannually. Estab. 1986. Circ. 1,200.

Needs: Adventure, condensed/excerpted novel, ethnic/multicultural, experimental, fantasy, historical, literary, mainstream/contemporary, mystery/suspense, regional, science fiction, sports, translations. "No religious, rhyming, or non-climbing related." Receives 50 unsolicited mss/month. Accepts 4-6 mss/issue; 10-15 mss/year. Publishes ms up to 1 year after acceptance. Agented fiction 10%. Length: 500 words minimum; 10,000 words maximum. Publishes short shorts. Also publishes literary essays, literary criticism and poetry. Sometimes critiques or comments on rejected mss. Sometimes sponsors contests.

How to Contact: Send compelete ms with a cover letter. Include estimated word count, 1-paragraph bio and list of publications. Reports in 2 weeks on queries; 2-8 weeks on mss. SASE. Simultaneous and electronic submissions OK. Sample copy $7. Reviews novels and short story collections.

Payment/Terms: Pays free subscription and 2 contributor's copies; additional copies for $4. Acquires one-time rights.

Advice: "Read several issues first and make certain the material is related to climbing and the spirit of climbing. We have not seen enough literary excellence."

CLOCKWATCH REVIEW, A Journal of the Arts, (II), Dept. of English, Illinois Wesleyan University, Bloomington IL 61702. (309)556-3352. Editor: James Plath. Magazine: 5½×8½; 64-80 pages; glossy cover stock; illustrations; photos. "We publish stories which are *literary* as well as alive, colorful, enjoyable—stories which linger like shadows," for a general audience. Semiannually. Estab. 1983. Circ. 1,500.

- *Clockwatch Review* is planning a western issue and would like to see more high-quality genre fiction that breaks the mold.

Needs: Contemporary, experimental, humor/satire, literary, mainstream, prose poem and regional. Receives 50-60 unsolicited mss/month. Accepts 2 mss/issue; 4 mss/year. Published work by Ellen Hunnicutt, Beth Brandt, Charlotte Mandel; published new writers within the last year. Length: 2,500 words average; 1,200 words minimum; 4,000 words maximum. Occasionally critiques rejected mss if requested.

How to Contact: Send complete ms. Reports in 6-12 months. SASE. Publishes ms 3-12 months after acceptance. Sample copy for $4.

Payment/Terms: Pays 3 contributor's copies and small cash stipend (currently $50, but may vary) for first serial rights.

Advice: "*Clockwatch* has always tried to expand the audience for quality contemporary poetry and fiction by publishing a highly visual magazine that is thin enough to invite reading. We've included interviews with popular musicians and artists in order to further interest a general, as well as academic, public and show the interrelationship of the arts. We're looking for high-quality literary fiction that brings something fresh to the page—whether in imagery, language, voice or character. Give us characters with meat on their bones, colorful but not clichéd; give us natural plots, not contrived or melodramatic. Above all, give us your *best* work."

COLLAGES AND BRICOLAGES, The Journal of International Writing, (II), P.O. Box 86, Clarion PA 16214. (814)226-5799. E-mail: fortis@vaxa.clarion.edu. Editor: Marie-José Fortis. Magazine: 8½×11; 100-150 pages; illustrations. "The magazine includes essays, short stories, occasional interviews, short plays, poems that show innovative promise. It is often focus or issue oriented—themes can either be literary or socio-political." Annually. Estab. 1987.

Needs: Contemporary, ethnic, experimental, feminist, humor/satire, literary, philosophical works. "Also symbolist, surrealist b&w designs/illustrations are welcome." Receives about 60 unsolicited fiction mss/month. Publishes ms 6-9 months after acceptance. Recently published work by Catherine

Scherer, Keith Laing, Stephen-Paul Martin, Jo Santiago and Kenneth Bernard. Published new writers within the last year. Publishes short shorts. Also publishes literary essays, literary criticism, poetry. Critiques rejected ms "when great potential is manifest."
How to Contact: Send complete ms with cover letter that includes a short bio. Reports in 1-3 months. SASE. Sample copy for $8.50. Reviews novels and short story collections. "How often and how many per issue depends on reviewers available."
Payment/Terms: Pays 2 contributor's copies. Acquires first rights. Rights revert to author after publication.
Advice: "Avoid following 'industry trends.' Do what you must do. Write what you must write. Write as if words were your bread, your water, a great vintage wine, salt, oxygen. Also, very few of us have a cornucopia budget, but it is a good idea to look at a publication before submitting."

‡COLORADO REVIEW, (II), English Department, Colorado State University, Fort Collins CO 80523. (970)491-5449. Editor: David Milofsky. Literary journal: 160 pages; 70 lb. book weight paper. Semiannually. Estab. as *Colorado State Review* 1966. Circ. 2,000.
   ● *Colorado Review*'s circulation has increased from 500 to 2,000.
Needs: Contemporary, ethnic, experimental, literary, mainstream, translations. Receives 300 unsolicited fiction mss/month. Accepts 3-4 mss/issue. Published work by Stanley Elkin, T. Alan Broughton, Gladys Swan; published new writers within the last year. Length: under 6,000 words. Does not read mss May through August. Also publishes literary essays, book reviews, poetry. Occasionally critiques rejected mss.
How to Contact: Send complete ms with SASE (or IRC) and brief bio with previous publications. Reports in 3 months. Publishes ms 6-12 months after acceptance. Sample copy for $5. Reviews novels or short story collections.
Payment/Terms: Pays $5/printed page for fiction; 2 contributor's copies; extras for $5. Pays on publication for first North American serial rights. "We assign copyright to author on request." Sends galleys to author.
Advice: "We are interested in manuscripts which show craft, imagination and a convincing voice. If a story has reached a level of technical competence, we are receptive to the fiction working on its own terms. The oldest advice is still the best: persistence. Approach every aspect of the writing process with pride, conscientiousness—from word choice to manuscript appearance."

COLUMBIA: A JOURNAL OF LITERATURE & ART, (II), 404 Dodge Hall, Columbia University, New York NY 10027. (212)854-4391. Editors: Lori Soderlind and Gregory Cowles. Fiction Editor: Elizabeth Hickey. Editors change each year. Magazine: 5¼ × 8¼; approximately 200 pages; coated cover stock; illustrations, photos. "We accept short stories, novel excerpts, translations, interviews, nonfiction and poetry." Biannually.
Needs: Literary and translations. Accepts 3-10 mss/issue. Receives approximately 125 unsolicited fiction mss each month. Does not read mss May 1 to August 31. Recently published work by Stewart O'Nan, Sherman Alexie, Diane Lefer, Elizabeth Graver and Jan Meisner. Published 5-8 unpublished writers within the year. Length: 20 pages maximum. Publishes short shorts.
How to Contact: Send complete ms with SASE. Accepts computer printout submissions. Reports in 1-2 months. Sample copy for $5.
Payment/Terms: Offers yearly contest with guest editors and cash awards. Send SASE for guidelines.
Advice: "We always look for story—too often, talented writers send nice prose filled with good observations but forget to tell a story. We like writing which is lively, honest, thoughtful, and entertaining. Because our staff changes each year, our specific tastes also change, so our best advice is to write what you want to write."

✳COMPENIONS, The Quarterly Publication of the Stratford Writer's Workshop, (I), P.O. Box 2511, St. Marys, Ontario N4X1A3 Canada. (519)284-1675. Contact: Marco Balestrin. Magazine: 8½ × 11; 12-20 pages; bond paper; card stock cover; computer graphics illustrations. "We have expanded the mandate of our magazine to include the work of outside writers. We would like to see serious beginning writers who give original twists to the old forms." Quarterly. Estab. 1983. Circ. 25 issues to members and contributors.
Needs: Adventure, ethnic/multicultural, experimental, fantasy (science), feminist, historical, horror, humor/satire, literary, mainstream/contemporary, mystery/suspense (amateur sleuth, private eye/hard-boiled, romantic suspense), psychic/supernatural/occult, regional, romance (contemporary, gothic), science fiction (hard science, soft/sociological), translations, westerns (frontier, traditional). "No pornography, ultra-religious or 'cutesy' stuff." Upcoming themes: "Work" (deadline February 1, 1997); "Play" (deadline May 1, 1997); "Rest" (deadline August 1, 1997); "Motion" (deadline November 1, 1997). Receives 3 unsolicited mss/month. Accepts 5 mss/issue; 15-20 mss/year. Publishes ms 3 months after acceptance. Recently published work by Ken Sieben and Anderson Council. Length: 800-1,000 words preferred; 100 words minimum; 3,000 words maximum. Publishes short shorts. Length:

300-400 words preferred. Also publishes literary essays and poetry. Often critiques or comments on rejected mss.

How to Contact: *Charges $4.50 reading fee per manuscript* (up to 3,000 words). Send complete ms with a cover letter and reading fee. Include estimated word count, 1-page bio and "anything unusual that may be of interest." Reports in 2 months on queries; 3 months on mss. Send SASE for reply, return of ms or send a disposable copy of ms. Simultaneous, reprint and electronic submissions OK. Sample copy for $4, 9×12 SAE and 2 IRCs (if outside Canada). Make checks payable to "Stratford Writer's Workshop."

Payment/Terms: Pays 2 contributor's copies; additional copies for $4 and 2 IRCs. Acquires one-time rights.

Advice: "A manuscript must be compelling. We will forgive rawness if it exposes us to a new slant on an old theme."

CONCHO RIVER REVIEW, (I, II, IV), Fort Concho Museum Press, 630 S. Oakes, San Angelo TX 76903. Fax: (915)942-2155. E-mail: me.hartje@mailserv.angelo.edu. Magazine: 6½×9; 100-125 pages; 60 lb. Ardor offset paper; Classic Laid Color cover stock; b&w drawings. "We publish any fiction of high quality—no thematic specialties—*contributors must be residents of Texas or the Southwest generally.*" Semiannually. Estab. 1987. Circ. 300.

 • The magazine is considering featuring "guest editors" with each issue, but manuscripts should still be sent to the editor, Mary Ellen Hartje.

Needs: Contemporary, ethnic, historical, humor/satire, literary, regional and western. No erotica; no science fiction. Receives 10-15 unsolicited mss/month. Accepts 3-6 mss/issue; 8-10 mss/year. Publishes ms 4 months after acceptance. Recently published work by Gordon Alexander, Riley Froh, Gretchen Geralds and Kimberly Willis Holt. Length: 3,500 words average; 1,500 words minimum; 5,000 words maximum. Also publishes literary essays, poetry. Sometimes critiques rejected mss and recommends other markets.

How to Contact: *Send submissions to Mary Ellen Hartje, English Dept., Angelo State University, San Angelo, TX 76909.* Send complete ms with SASE; cover letter optional. Reports in 3 weeks on queries; 3-6 months on mss. SASE for ms. Simultaneous submissions OK (if noted). Sample copy for $4. Fiction guidelines for #10 SASE. Reviews novels and short story collections. Books to be reviewed should be sent to Dr. James Moore.

Payment/Terms: Pays in contributor's copies; $4 charge for extras. Acquires first rights.

Advice: "We prefer a clear sense of conflict, strong characterization and effective dialogue."

CONDUIT, (II), Conduit, Inc., 510 Eighth Ave. NE, Minneapolis MN 55413. (612)362-0995. E-mail: conduit@bitstream.net. Editor: William Waltz. Fiction Editor: Brett Astor. Magazine: 4¼×11; 60 pages; letterpress cover; illustrations and photos. "*Conduit* is primarily a poetry magazine, but we're eager to include lively fiction verbally speaking and otherwise. *Conduit* publishes work that is intelligent, serious, irreverent and daring." Triquarterly. Estab. 1993. Circ. 700.

Needs: Experimental, literary, translations. Upcoming theme: "Is Rebellion Possible?" Receives 25 unsolicited mss/month. Accepts 4 mss/issue; 12 mss/year. Publishes ms 3-6 months after acceptance. Length: 1,500-2,000 words maximum. Publishes short shorts. Also publishes poetry. Sometimes critiques or comments on rejected ms.

How to Contact: Send complete ms with a cover letter. Reports in 2 months. Send SASE for reply, return of ms or send a disposable copy of ms. Electronic submissions OK. Sample copy for $4, 4¾×11 SAE and 92¢ postage. Fiction guidelines free for SASE. Reviews novels or short story collections.

Payment/Terms: Pays 3 contributor's copies. Acquires first North American serial rights.

Advice: "Write and send work that feels like it is absolutely essential, but avoid the leg-hold traps of self-importance and affectation."

CONFLUENCE, (II), Sponsored by Ohio Valley Literary Group & Marietta College, Box 336, Belpre OH 45714. (304)422-3112. E-mail: bornd@mcnet.marietta.edu. Fiction Editor: Daniel Born. Editors change each year. Magazine: 6½×8; 112-120 pages; acid-free paper; illustrations. Annually. Estab. 1989. Circ. 500.

 • *Confluence* sponsors an annual short story contest. Guidelines are available January 1 to March 1 each year.

Needs: Condensed/excerpted novel, ethnic/multicultural, feminist, humor/satire, literary, mainstream/contemporary, mystery/suspense, regional, science fiction, translations. "No romance, homophobia." Receives 75-150 mss/reading period. Accepts 7-15 mss/issue. Does not read mss March 2 through December 30. Publishes ms 3-5 months after acceptance. Published work by Mitch Levenberg, Thea Caplan, Frank Tota. Length: 4,500 words maximum. Publishes short shorts. Also publishes literary essays and poetry. Always critiques or comments on rejected mss.

How to Contact: Send complete ms with a cover letter. Include estimated word count and 2-4 sentence bio. Reports in 1-2 weeks on queries; 1-2 months on mss. Send SASE for reply, return of ms or send a disposable copy of ms. Simultaneous submissions OK if indicated by author; occasionally

considers reprints; electronic submissions OK (disk or e-mail). Sample copy for $3 and 6×9 SAE.
Payment/Terms: Pays 1 contributor's copy. Acquires one-time rights.
Advice: "We like stories grounded in lived detail, regardless of whether they're traditional or experimental narratives."

CONFRONTATION, (I), English Dept., C.W. Post of Long Island University, Brookville NY 11548. (516)299-2391. Fax: (516)299-2735. Editor: Martin Tucker. Magazine: 6×9; 190-250 pages; 70 lb. paper; 80 lb. cover; illustrations; photos. "We like to have a 'range' of subjects, form and style in each issue and are open to all forms. Quality is our major concern. Our audience is made up of literate, thinking people; formally or self-educated." Semiannually. Estab. 1968. Circ. 2,000.
  • *Confrontation* has garnered a long list of awards and honors, including the Editor's Award for Distinguished Achievement from CCLM (now the Council of Literary Magazines and Presses) and NEA grants. Work from the magazine has appeared in numerous anthologies including the *Pushcart Prize, Best Short Stories* and *O. Henry Prize Stories*.
Needs: Literary, contemporary, prose poem, regional and translations. No "proseletyzing" literature. Accepts 30 mss/issue; 60 mss/year. Receives 400 unsolicited fiction mss each month. Does not read June through September. Approximately 10-15% of fiction is agented. Recently published work by Irving Feldman, David Ray, Lynn Freed and William Styron. Published many new writers within the last year. Length: 500-4,000 words. Publishes short shorts. Also publishes literary essays and poetry. Critiques rejected mss when there is time. Sometimes recommends other markets.
How to Contact: Send complete ms with SASE. "Cover letters acceptable, not necessary. We accept simultaneous submissions but do not prefer it." Accepts diskettes if accompanied by computer printout submissions. Reports in 6-8 weeks on mss. Publishes ms 6-12 months after acceptance. Sample copy for $3. Reviews novels, short story collections, poetry and literary criticism.
Payment/Terms: Pays $20-250 on publication for all rights "with transfer on request to author"; 1 contributor's copy; half price for extras.
Advice: "Keep trying."

CONTEXT SOUTH, (II), Box 4504, Kerrville TX 78028. E-mail: drpoetry@hilconet.com. Editor: David Breeden. Fiction Editor: Craig Taylor. Magazine: digest sized; 65 pages; illustrations and photos. Annually. Estab. 1988. Circ. 500.
Needs: Experimental, feminist, literary. List of upcoming themes available for SASE. Receives 10-15 unsolicited mss/month. Does not read in summer. Publishes ms up to 1 year after acceptance. Agented fiction 10%. Recently published work by Thea Caplan and David Vigoda. Length: 500 words minimum; 3,000 words maximum. Publishes short shorts. Also publishes literary essays, literary criticism, poetry. Sometimes critiques or comments on rejected mss.
How to Contact: Send complete ms with a cover letter. Include short bio. Reports in 2 weeks on queries; 3 months on mss. SASE for return of ms. Simultaneous and electronic (disk) submissions OK. Sample copy for $5. Reviews novels and short story collections.
Payment/Terms: Pays 2 contributor's copies. Acquires one-time rights. Sends galleys to author.
Advice: "Read a good deal of fiction, current and past. Avoid sending the trite and that which depends merely on shock."

CORONA, Marking the Edges of Many Circles, (II), Dept. of History and Philosophy, Montana State University, Bozeman MT 59717. (406)994-5200. Co-Editors: Lynda Sexson, Michael Sexson. Managing Editor: Sarah Merrill. Magazine: 7×10; 130 pages; 60 lb. "mountre matte" paper; 65 lb. Hammermill cover stock; illustrations; photos. "Interdisciplinary magazine—essays, poetry, fiction, imagery, science, history, recipes, humor, etc., for those educated, curious, with a profound interest in the arts and contemporary thought." Published occasionally. Estab. 1980. Circ. 2,000.
Needs: Comics, contemporary, experimental, fantasy, feminist, humor/satire, literary, prose poem. "Our fiction ranges from the traditional Talmudic tale to fiction engendered by speculative science, from the extended joke to regional reflection—if it isn't accessible and original, please don't send it." Receives varying number of unsolicited fiction mss/month. Accepts 6 mss/issue. Published work by Rhoda Lerman and Stephen Dixon; published new writers within the last year. Publishes short shorts. Also publishes literary essays and poetry. Occasionally critiques rejected mss.

CHECK THE CATEGORY INDEXES, located at the back of the book, for publishers interested in specific fiction subjects.

How to Contact: Query. Reports in 6 months on mss. Sample copy for $7.
Payment/Terms: Pays minimal honorarium; 2 free contributor's copies; discounted charge for extras. Acquires first rights. Sends galleys to author upon request.
Advice: "Be knowledgeable of contents other than fiction in *Corona*; one must know the journal."

‡**CRAB CREEK REVIEW, (V)**, 4462 Whitman Ave. N., Seattle WA 98103. (206)633-1090. Editor: Linda Clifton. Fiction Editor: Carol Orlock. Magazine: 6×9 paperbound; 160 pgs., line drawings. "Magazine publishing poetry, short stories, art and essays for adult, college-educated audience interested in literary, visual and dramatic arts and in politics." Published irregularly. Estab. 1983. Circ. 450.
● Note *Crab Creek Review* is not reading unsolicited manuscripts until further notice.
Needs: Contemporary, humor/satire, literary and translations. No confession, erotica, horror, juvenile, preschool, religious/inspirational, romance or young adult. Receives 20-30 unsolicited mss/month. Recently published work by Rebecca Wells, Joan Fiset, Perle Besserman and Yehuda Amichai. Published new writers within the last year. Length: 3,000 words average; 1,200 words minimum; 4,000 words maximum. Publishes short shorts.
How to Contact: *Not reading unsolicited mss until further notice. Query first.* Send complete ms with short list of credits. Reports in 3 months. SASE. No simultaneous submissions. Sample copy for $3. *Anniversary Anthology* $10, *Bread for This Hunger* (1996 anthology) $8.
Payment/Terms: Pays 2 contributor's copies; $2 charge for extras. Acquires first rights. Rarely buys reprints.
Advice: "We appreciate 'sudden fictions.' Type name and address on each piece. Enclose SASE. Send no more than one story in a packet (except for short shorts—no more than three, ten pages total)."

CRAZYQUILT, (II), P.O. Box 632729, San Diego CA 92163-2729. (619)688-1023. Fax: (619)688-1753. Editor-in-Chief: Jim Kitchen. Fiction and Drama Editor: Marsh Cassady. Magazine: 5½×8½; 92 pages; illustrations and photos. "We publish short fiction, poems, nonfiction about writing and writers, one-act plays and b&w illustrations and photos." Quarterly. Estab. 1986. Circ. 175.
Needs: Contemporary, ethnic, excerpted novel, fantasy, gay, historical, humor/satire, literary, mainstream, mystery/suspense, science fiction. "Shorter pieces are preferred." Receives 85-100 unsolicited mss/quarter. Accepts 6-8 mss/issue; 25-35 mss/year. Publishes 1 year after acceptance. Recently published work by Arthur Winfield Knight and Charlotte Peters; published new writers within the last year. Length: 500 words minimum; 4,000 words maximum. Also publishes literary essays, literary criticism, poetry. Occasionally critiques rejected mss.
How to Contact: Send complete ms with cover letter and SASE. Reports in 2 weeks on mss. Simultaneous and electronic (disk) submissions OK. Sample copy for $9 (all issues are now double issues), $6 for back issue. Fiction guidelines for SASE.
Payment/Terms: Pays 2 contributor's copies. Acquires first North American serial rights or one-time rights.
Advice: "Write a story that is well constructed, develops characters and maintains interest."

THE CREAM CITY REVIEW, (I, II), University of Wisconsin-Milwaukee, Box 413, Milwaukee WI 53201. (414)229-4708. Website: http://www.uwm.edu/Dept/English. Editor-In-Chief: Staci Leigh O'Brien. Contact: Fiction Editor. Editors rotate. Magazine: 5½×8½; 200-300 pages; 70 lb. offset/perfect-bound paper; 80 lb. cover stock; illustrations; photos. "General literary publication—an eclectic and electric selection of the best we receive." Semiannually. Estab. 1975. Circ. 2,000.
Needs: Ethnic, experimental, humor/satire, literary, prose poem, regional and translations. Receives approximately 300 unsolicited fiction mss each month. Accepts 6-10 mss/issue. Does not read fiction or poetry May 1 through August 31. Recently published work by Stephen Dixon, Heather McKey, Carmen Elizaga and Gordon Lish. Published new writers within the last year. Length: 1,000-10,000 words. Publishes short shorts. Also publishes literary essays, literary criticism, poetry.
How to Contact: Send complete ms with SASE. Simultaneous submissions OK. Reports in 6 months. Sample copy for $5 (back issue); $7 (current issue). Reviews novels and short story collections.
Payment/Terms: Pays 1 year subscription or in copies.
Terms: Acquires first rights. Sends galleys to author. Rights revert to author after publication.
Advice: "Read as much as you write so that you can examine your own work in relation to where fiction has been and where fiction is going. We are looking for strong, consistent voices and fresh voices."

THE CRESCENT REVIEW, (II), The Crescent Review, Inc., P.O. Box 15069, Chevy Chase MD 20825. (301)986-8788. Editor: J.T. Holland. Magazine: 6×9; 160 pages. Triannually. Estab. 1982.
● Work appearing in *The Crescent Review* has been included in *O. Henry Prize Stories*, *Best American Short Stories*, *Pushcart Prize* and *Black Southern Writers* anthologies and in the *New Stories from the South*.

Needs: "Well-crafted stories" Does not read submissions May-June and November-December.
How to Contact: Reports in 1-4 months. SASE. Sample issue for $9.40.
Payment/Terms: Pays 2 contributor's copies; discount for contributors. Acquires first North American serial rights.

‡**CRIPES!, (I, II)**, 514½ E. University Ave., Lafayette LA 70503. (318)261-0997. E-mail: kes7524@usl.edu. Fiction Editor: Kelly Stern. Poetry Editor: James Tolan. Magazine: 5½×8½; 52 pages; card cover stock; illustrations; photos. "We look for poetry, prose, art, cartoons and many things in between—as long as it maintains a strong balance between passion (impulse) and craft. Our audience is made up largely of the 18-50 age group, many of whom are associated with the university and/or the community art 'scene'." Estab. 1994. Circ. 200.
Needs: Condensed/excerpted novel, experimental, humor/satire, literary, mainstream/contemporary. Especially looking for short short fiction. No religious or westerns. Receives 6-8 unsolicited mss/month. Accepts 3-5 mss/issue; 6-10 mss/year. Publishes ms within 6 months after acceptance. Recently published work by Tom Whalen, Charlie Riley, Matthew Firth, Kendall Delacambre, Gerald Sierveld, P.S. Hanlon, Daniel Glisson and Adrienne Goering. Length: 2,500-3,000 words maximum. Publishes short shorts. Also publishes poetry. Always critiques or comments on rejected mss.
How to Contact: Send complete ms with a cover letter. Include a 1-paragraph bio and "tell us how you learned about us." Send SASE for reply, return of ms or send 2 disposable copies of ms. Simultaneous submissions and reprints OK. Sample copy for $3 and 6×9 SAE with 3 first-class stamps. Fiction guidelines free.
Payment/Terms: Pays 2 contributor's copies on publication; addtional copies for $3. Acquires one-time rights.
Advice: Looks for "originality, unpredictability, fresh language, a carefully prepared manuscript, focus and playfullness. Look at *Cripes!* to see what we publish."

CRUCIBLE, (I, II), English Dept., Barton College, College Station, Wilson NC 27893. (919)399-6456. Editor: Terrence L. Grimes. Magazine of fiction and poetry for a general, literary audience. Annually. Estab. 1964. Circ. 500.
Needs: Contemporary, ethnic, experimental, feminist, gay, lesbian, literary, regional. Receives 20 unsolicited mss/month. Accepts 5-6 mss/year. Publishes ms 4-5 months after acceptance. Does not normally read mss from April 30 to December 1. Published work by William Hutchins and Guy Nancekeville. Length: 8,000 words maximum. Publishes short shorts.
How to Contact: Send 3 complete copies of ms unsigned with cover letter which should include a brief biography, "in case we publish." Reports in 1 month on queries; 3-4 months on mss (by June 15). SASE. Sample copy for $6. Fiction guidelines free.
Payment/Terms: Pays contributor's copies. Acquires first rights.
Advice: "Write about what you know. Experimentation is fine as long as the experiences portrayed come across as authentic, that is to say, plausible."

❖**THE DALHOUSIE REVIEW, (II)**, Room 314, Dunn Building, Dalhousie University, Halifax, Nova Scotia B3H 3J5 Canada. Editor: Dr. Alan Andrews. Magazine: 15cm×23cm; approximately 140 pages; photographs sometimes. Publishes articles, book reviews, short stories and poetry. Published 3 times a year. Circ. 600.
Needs: Literary. Length: 5,000 words maximum. Also publishes essays on history, philosophy, etc., and poetry.
How to Contact: Send complete ms with cover letter. SASE (Canadian stamps). Prefers submissions on computer disk (WordPerfect). Sample copy for $8.50 (Canadian) plus postage. Occasionally reviews novels and short story collections.

DAN RIVER ANTHOLOGY, (I), P.O. Box 298, S. Thomaston ME 04861. (207)354-0998. Fax: (207)354-8953. E-mail: olrob@midcoast.com. Editor: R. S. Danbury III. Book: 5½×8½; 156 pages; 60 lb. paper; gloss 65 lb. full-color cover; b&w illustrations. For general/adult audience. Annually. Estab. 1984. Circ. 800.
Needs: Adventure, contemporary, ethnic, experimental, fantasy, historical, horror, humor/satire, literary, mainstream, prose poem, psychic/supernatural/occult, regional, romance (contemporary and historical), science fiction, senior citizen/retirement, suspense/mystery and western. No "evangelical Christian, pornography or sentimentality." Receives 150 unsolicited fiction mss each submission period (January 1 through March 31). "We generally publish 12-15 pieces of fiction." Reads "mostly in April." Length: 2,000-2,400 words average; 800 words minimum; 2,500 words maximum. Also publishes poetry.
How to Contact: *Charges reading fee: $1 for poetry; $3 for prose* (cash only, no checks). Send complete ms with SASE. Reports by May 15 each year. No simultaneous submissions. Sample copy for $12.95 paperback, $19.95 cloth, plus $2.75 shipping. Fiction guidelines for #10 SASE.

Payment/Terms: Pays $5/page, minimum *cash advance on acceptance* against royalties of 10% of all sales attributable to writer's influence: readings, mailings, autograph parties, etc., plus up to 50% discount on copies, plus other discounts to make total as high as 73%. Acquires first rights.
Advice: "Know your market. Don't submit without reading guidelines."

DAVIDS' PLACE JOURNAL, An AIDS Experience Journal, (I, II, IV), P.O. Box 632759, San Diego CA 92103. (619)294-5775. Fax: (619)683-9230. Website: http://www.davidsplace.com. Editor: R. Osborne. Magazine: 8½×7; 125 pages; illustrations and photos. The philosophy of *Davids' Place Journal* is "to communicate the HIV/AIDS experience, to reach the whole community. Submissions may be popular or scholarly." Quarterly. Estab. 1994. Circ. 500.
  • *Davids' Place Journal* was named for a not-for-profit cafe in San Diego supportive of people with HIV/AIDS and their friends.
Needs: HIV/AIDS experience. "No erotica." Upcoming theme: Humor. Receives 15 unsolicited mss/month. Accepts 10-15 mss/issue; 40-60 mss/year. Publishes ms 3-6 months after acceptance. Published work by Jameison Currior, Crystal Bacon, Gary Eldon Peter. Length: 5,000 words maximum. Publishes short shorts. Also publishes literary essays, poetry. Sometimes critiques or comments on rejected mss.
How to Contact: Send complete ms with a cover letter. Include 1-paragraph bio with submission. Send SASE for reply. Simultaneous and electronic (modem) submissions, reprints OK. Sample copy $4.
Payment/Terms: Pays 2 contributor's copies. Acquires one-time rights.
Advice: Looking for "authentic experience or artistic relevance to the AIDS experience."

DENVER QUARTERLY, (II, III), University of Denver, Denver CO 80208. (303)871-2892. Editor: Bin Ramke. Magazine: 6×9; 144-160 pages; occasional illustrations. "We publish fiction, articles and poetry for a generally well-educated audience, primarily interested in literature and the literary experience. They read *DQ* to find something a little different from a strictly academic quarterly or a creative writing outlet." Quarterly. Estab. 1966. Circ. 1,000.
  • *Denver Quarterly* received an Honorable Mention for Content from the American Literary Magazine Awards.
Needs: "We are now interested in experimental fiction (minimalism, magic realism, etc.) as well as in realistic fiction and in writing about fiction." Recently published work by Lucie Broch-Broido, Judith E. Johnson, Stephen Alter and Josh Russell. Published new writers within the last year. Also publishes poetry.
How to Contact: Send complete ms and brief cover letter with SASE. Does not read mss May-September 15. Do not query. Reports in 3 months on mss. Publishes ms within a year after acceptance. Electronic submissions (disk, Windows 6.0) OK. No simultaneous submissions. Sample copy for $7 (anniversary issue), $6 (all other issues) with SASE.
Payment/Terms: Pays $5/page for fiction and poetry and 2 contributor's copies for first North American serial rights.
Advice: "We look for serious, realistic and experimental fiction; stories which appeal to intelligent, demanding readers who are not themselves fiction writers. Nothing so quickly disqualifies a manuscript as sloppy proofreading and mechanics. Read the magazine before submitting to it. We try to remain eclectic, but the odds for beginners are bound to be small considering the fact that we receive nearly 8,000 mss per year and publish only about ten short stories."

DJINNI, (II), 29 Front St., #2, Marblehead MA 01945. Fax: (617)631-8595. E-mail: kaloclarke@aol.com. Editors: Kim A. Pederson and Kalo Clarke. Magazine: digest-sized; 60-100 pages; perfect-bound; matte card cover. "An international magazine, *Djinni* publishes contemporary poetry, short fiction (including novel excerpts), short drama, essays, and drawings by well-knowns and new talent. The annual issue is published when sufficient quality material has been selected—usually late fall or early winter." Annually. Estab. 1990.
Needs: "The editors are especially interested in short work (1,200-3,000 words) that explores new directions."
How to Contact: Send ms including brief bio (and/or comment on the work). Open submissions are read May through November. Reports in 1-3 months on mss. SASE. Simultaneous submissions OK. Accepts hard copy by mail or fax; prefers e-mail attachment or disk (word for PC). Sample copy for $5.
Payment/Terms: Pays 1 contributor's copy. Acquires first North American serial rights.
Advice: Looks for "intensity, originality, striking use of language in dealing with contemporary issues."

DODOBOBO, A New Fiction Magazine of Washington D.C., (I), Dodobobo Publications, P.O. Box 57214, Washington DC 20037. Editor: Brian Greene. Magazine: 5½×8½; 20-35 pages; illustrations and photos. "We're a literary fiction magazine which intends to give voice to writers the more well-known literary magazines would not be open to." Quarterly. Estab. 1994. Circ. 500.

Needs: Experimental, feminist, gay, historical, humor/satire, lesbian, literary, mystery/suspense, psychic/supernatural/occult, regional, science fiction and serialized novel. Receives 20 unsolicited mss/month. Accepts 2-4 mss/issue; 8-16 mss/year. Publishes ms 1-12 months after acceptance. Published work by Dean Richard, Henry Skinpole and Carlton Jolly. Length: 3,000 words maximum. Sometimes critiques or comments on rejected ms.

How to Contact: "Send complete ms, with or without cover letter." Reports in 2 months on mss. Send SASE for reply, return of ms or send a disposable copy of ms. Simultaneous and reprint submissions OK. Sample copy for $2 (including postage). Fiction guidelines for SASE.

Payment/Terms: Pays 2 contributor's copies. Acquires one-time rights. Sends galleys to author if requested.

Advice: "We like stories which illustrate the reality of the human experience—people's existential crises, their experiences with other people, with their own psyches. Get a copy or two of the magazine and read the stories we've printed."

DOGWOOD TALES MAGAZINE, For the Fiction Lover in All of Us, (I, II), Two Sisters Publications, P.O. Box 172068, Memphis TN 38187. E-mail: write2me@aol.com. Editor: Linda Ditty. Fiction Editor: Peggy Carman. Magazine: 5½ × 8½; 52 pages; 20 lb. paper; 60 lb. cover stock; illustrations. "Interesting fiction that would appeal to all groups of people. Each issue will have a Special Feature Story about a Southern person, place or theme." Bimonthly. Estab. 1993.

• *Dogwood Tales* was rated #19 in the *Writer's Digest* "Top 50 Best Short Story Markets."

Needs: Adventure, mainstream/contemporary, mystery/suspense, romance. No erotica, children and westerns. Strong offensive language or subject matter will be automatic rejection. Accepts 7-9 mss/issue; 42-54 mss/year. Publishes ms within 1 year after acceptance. Recently published work by Nancy Gotter Gates, Anne Weatherford, Marjorie Krog and Dave Lopardo. Length: 1,350 words preferred; 200 words minimum; 4,500 words maximum. Publishes short shorts. Length: 200-500 words. Sometimes critiques or comments on rejected mss.

How to Contact: Send complete ms with a cover letter. Should include estimated word count and list of publications. Reports within 10 weeks on mss. Send SASE for reply, return of ms or send a disposable copy of ms. Simultaneous and electronic submissions (disk, ASCII only, or modem) OK. Sample copy for $3.25. Fiction guidelines for #10 SASE.

Payment/Terms: Pays ¼¢ to ½¢ per word on acceptance plus 1 contributor copy; additional copies at reduced rate. Acquires first serial rights and reprint rights.

Advice: "We like fresh and action moving stories with a strong ending. Must be tightly written and reach out and grab the reader. Revise and send your best. Don't be afraid to submit. Don't be discouraged by rejections."

DOWNSTATE STORY, (II, IV), 1825 Maple Ridge, Peoria IL 61614. (309)688-1409. E-mail: ehopkins@prairienet.org. Website: http://www.wiu. bqu.edu/users/mfgeh/dss. Editor: Elaine Hopkins. Magazine: illustrations. "Short fiction—some connection with Illinois or the Midwest." Annually. Estab. 1992. Circ. 500.

Needs: Adventure, ethnic/multicultural, experimental, historical, horror, humor/satire, literary, mainstream/contemporary, mystery/suspense, psychic/supernatural/occult, regional, romance, science fiction, westerns. Accepts 10 mss/issue. Publishes ms up to 1 year after acceptance. Length: 300 words minimum; 2,000 words maximum. Publishes short shorts. Also publishes literary essays.

How to Contact: Send complete ms with a cover letter. Reports "ASAP." SASE for return of ms. Simultaneous submissions OK. Sample copy for $8. Fiction guidelines for SASE.

Payment/Terms: Pays $50 maximum on acceptance for first rights.

‡DROP FORGE, Literature for the Lost, (I, II), Jade Moon Publications, P.O. Box 7237, Reno NV 89510. E-mail: dropforge@jonestown.reno.nv.us. Editor: Sean Winchester. Magazine: 7 × 8½; 32 pages; illustrations. "*Drop Forge* focuses on experimental and surreal material. There is a strong emphasis on language and syntax experimentalism. *Drop Forge* wants to know how you communicate with infinity." Published irregularly. Estab. 1993. Circ. 500.

Needs: Experimental and surreal: Erotica, gay, lesbian, literary, non-stereotypical, philosophical, science fiction (bio surreal), translations. "No material conforming to established-genre standards. We are not 'standard.' " Receives 10-15 unsolicited mss/month. Accepts 5-10 mss/issue. Publishes ms 2-8 months after acceptance. Length: 5 words minimum; 3,000 maximum. Publishes short shorts. Length: shorter than 500 words. Also publishes literary essays and poetry. Often critiques or comments on rejected mss.

How to Contact: Send complete ms with a cover letter. Include bio. "Send me a letter that lets me know there's a human on the other side." Reports in 4-5 weeks on queries; 3 months on mss. Send SASE for reply, return of ms or send a disposable copy of ms. No simultaneous submissions. Electronic submissions OK. Sample copy for $2.50. Fiction guidelines for #10 SASE. Reviews novels or short story collections. "Please note: I review only very small press releases, and only those coinciding with the interests of *Drop Forge*."

Payment/Terms: Pays 1 contributor's copy; additional copies available for postage. Acquires one-time rights.

Advice: "I'm interested in works that transcend themselves and the limitations of ordinary type. Take it further than it is willing to go. Don't send imitations. Don't send amusing moral anecdotes."

EAGLE'S FLIGHT, A Literary Magazine, (I, II), P.O. Box 832, Granite OK 73547. Editor: Shyamkant Kulkarni. Fiction Editor: Rekha Kulkarni. Tabloid: 8½×11; 4-8 pages; bond paper; broad sheet cover. Publication includes "fiction and poetry for a general audience." Quarterly.

Needs: Literary, mainstream, mystery/suspense, romance. Plans to publish special fiction issue in future. Accepts 2-4 mss/year. Does not read mss June-December. Recently published work by Jack Creek, Shyamkant Kulkarni, Mike Cluff and Linda Healy. Length: 1,500 words preferred; 1,000 words minimum; 2,000 words maximum. Publishes short shorts. Also publishes literary criticism, poetry.

How to Contact: Query first. Reports in 6 weeks on queries; 3-4 months on mss. SASE. Sample copy or fiction guidelines for $1.25 and #10 SASE. Reviews novels and short story collections.

Payment/Terms: Pays $5-20 on publication for first North American serial rights or one-time rights or subscription to magazine, contributor's copies; charge for additional copies.

Advice: "We look for form, substance and quality. Read and study what you want to write and work at it. Our Annual Best Story Award is given in March/April for the best short story published during the previous year."

ECHOES, (I, II), Echoes Magazine, P.O. Box 3622, Allentown PA 18106. Fax: (610)776-1634. E-mail: echoesmag@aol.com. Website: http://users.aol.com/echoesmag/. Editor: Peter Crownfield. Magazine: 6×9; 64 pages.; 60 lb. offset paper; 65-80 lb. cover; illustrations and photos. "*Echoes* publishes stories, poetry, and drawings from people in all walks of life—beginners and professionals, students and teachers. We look for writing that is creative and thought-provoking—writing that speaks to the ideas and feelings that connect us all." Bimonthly. Estab. 1994.

Needs: "*Echoes* will consider any genre as long as the work is thought-provoking and interesting to readers." The following categories are of special interest: ethnic/multicultural, fantasy, humor/satire, literary, mainstream/contemporary, regional, senior citizen/retirement, young adult/teen. "We will not print any work containing gratuitous profanity, sex, or violence." Annual Memorial Day issue "features work about veterans and people in the military. Should have personal appeal—no strident pro- or anti-war themes." Deadline February 15. Publishes annual special fiction issue or anthology. Receives 50-70 unsolicited mss/month. Accepts 5 mss/issue; 30 mss/year. Publishes ms 6 weeks-8 months after acceptance. Recently published work by Carole Bellacera, Susan Dugan, Gene Moser, Doug Rennie and Barbara Schnell. Length: 3,000 words average; 200 words minimum; 7,500 words maximum. Publishes short shorts. Also publishes poetry and drawings. Usually critiques or comments on rejected mss.

How to Contact: Send complete ms with a cover letter. Include estimated word count and 50-word bio. Reports in 6-12 weeks. Send SASE for return of ms and/or comments. Reprints and electronic submissions (disk or e-mail) OK. Sample copy $5. Fiction guidelines for SASE or at *Echoes*' Homepage.

Payment/Terms: Pays 6 contributor's copies; additional copies for $4 plus postage. Sponsors contests. Send SASE for guidelines.

Advice: "We appreciate stories with a personal viewpoint, well-developed characters and a clear story line—writing that makes us care what happens to the characters. Make your story clear and complete, and make sure it has a point that others will understand. Avoid rambling personal reminiscences."

8, Dancing With Mr. D, (II), Screaming Toad Press/Dancing With Mr. D Publications, 809 W. Broad St., #221, Falls Church VA 22046. Editor: Llori Steinberg. Magazine: 5×7; illustrations and photos. Monthly. Estab. 1994. Circ. 200.

Needs: Adventure, erotica, experimental, fantasy (children's, science), horror, humor/satire, literary, mystery/suspense (amateur sleuth, police procedural, private eye/hardboiled. romantic), psychic/supernatural/occult. List of upcoming themes available for SASE. Receives 100 unsolicited mss/month. Accepts 2-5 mss/issue; 6-9 mss/year. Published work by Steven Conan, Regent Kyler and Tom Head. Length: 5,000 words minimum; 8,000 words maximum. Publishes short shorts. Also publishes literary essays, literary criticism, poetry. Sometimes critiques or comments on rejected mss.

How to Contact: Query with clips of published work and SASE with proper postage. Include bio with list of publications. Reports in 5 weeks on queries; 6-8 weeks on mss. Send SASE for reply. Simultaneous submissions and electronic (Windows only) submissions OK. Sample copy for $6 and 6×9 SAE with 5 first-class stamps. Fiction guidelines free for #10 SAE with 2 first-class stamps.

Payment/Terms: None. Sponsors contests; guidelines for SASE.

Advice: "Be original—don't try to prove a thing other than your honest self. Just send 'talk' to me—tell me your goals and 'loves.' " Does not want to see "Gothic vampire horror. There's already too much of it."

1812, A Literary Arts Magazine, (I, II), P.O. Box 1812, Amherst NY 14226-7812. E-mail: newwriting@aol.com or thebookdoc@aol.com. Fiction Editor: Richard Lynch. Magazine: 5½ × 8½; 150 pages; coated cover stock; illustrations and photographs. "We want to publish work that has some *bang*." Annually. Estab. 1994.

● Work published in *1812* has been described as "experimental, surreal, bizarre."

Needs: Experimental, humor/satire, literary, mainstream/contemporary, translations. Does not want to see "stories about writers, stories about cancer, stories containing hospitals or stories that sound like they've been told before." Also publishes literary essays, literary criticism and poetry. Often critiques or comments on rejected mss.

How to Contact: Send complete ms with a cover letter. Include brief list of publications. Reports in 2 months. SASE for return of ms. Simultaneous, reprint and electronic submissions OK. Reviews novels and short story collections.

Payment/Terms: Payment is "arranged." Acquires one-time rights.

Advice: "Our philosophy can be summed up in the following quote from Beckett: 'I speak of an art turning from it in disgust, weary of its puny exploits, weary of pretending to be able, of being able, of doing a little better the same old thing, of going a little further along a dreary road.' Too many writers copy. We want to see writing by those who aren't on the 'dreary road.' "

ELF: ECLECTIC LITERARY FORUM, (I, II), P.O. Box 392, Tonawanda NY 14150. Phone/fax: (716)693-7006. E-mail: elf@econet.net. Website: http://www.cais.net/aesir/fiction/elforum. Editor: C.K. Erbes. Magazine: 8½ × 11; 56 pages; 60 lb. offset paper; coated cover; 2-3 illustrations; 2-3 photographs. "Well-crafted short stories, poetry, literary essays for a sophisticated audience." Quarterly. Estab. 1991. Circ. 5,000.

Needs: Adventure, contemporary, ethnic, fantasy, feminism, historical, humor/satire, literary, mainstream, mystery/suspense (private eye), prose poem, regional, science fiction (hard science, soft/sociological), sports, western. No violence and obscenity (horror/erotica). Accepts 4-6 mss/issue; 16-24 mss/year. Publishes ms up to 1 year after acceptance. Recently published work by W. Edwin Verbecke, Sarah Zale, John Dickson, Gary Earl Ross, Dean Monti. Length: 3,500 words average. Publishes short shorts. Length: 500 words. Sometimes critiques rejected mss.

How to Contact: Send complete ms with optional cover letter. Reports in 4-6 weeks on mss. SASE. Simultaneous submissions OK (if so indicated). Sample copy for $5.50 ($8 foreign). Fiction guidelines for #10 SASE.

Payment/Terms: Pays contributor's copies. Acquires first North American serial rights.

Advice: "Short stories stand out when dialogue, plot, character, point of view and language usage work together to create a unified whole on a significant theme, one relevant to most of our readers. We also look for writers whose works demonstrate a knowledge of grammar and how to manipulate it effectively in a story. Each story is read by an Editorial Board comprised of English professors who teach creative writing and are published authors."

EMRYS JOURNAL, (II), The Emrys Foundation, P.O. Box 8813, Greenville SC 29604. Editor: Jeanine Halva-Neubauer. Catalog: 9 × 9¾; 80 pages; 80 lb. paper (glossy). "We publish short fiction, poetry, and essays. We are particularly interested in hearing from women and other minorities. We are mindful of the southeast but not limited to it." Annually. Estab. 1984. Circ. 400.

Needs: Contemporary, feminist, literary, mainstream and regional. "Since 1997-98 is a theme issue for us, we will be a joint publication with the Greenville County Museum of Art titled "Women, Women, Women! Contemporary American Art By and About the Superior Sex" in conjunction with a major exhibition. Short fiction in keeping with this theme would be welcome. Reading period: May 1-September 1, 1997." Accepts 10 mss/issue. Publishes mss in February. Length: 3,500 words average; 2,500 words minimum; 6,000 words maximum. Publishes short shorts. Recently published work by Gil Allen, Carole Chipps Carlson, Patricia Cumbie, Arlene McKanic and Tracy Burns. Length: 1,600 words.

How To Contact: Send complete ms with cover letter. Reports in 6 weeks. SASE. Sample copy for $15 and 7 × 10 SAE with 4 first-class stamps. Fiction guidelines for #10 SASE.

Payment/Terms: Pays in contributor's copies. Acquires first rights. "Send to managing editor for guidelines."

Advice: Looks for "fiction by women and minorities, especially but not exclusively southeastern."

FOR INFORMATION ON ENTERING the *Novel & Short Story Writer's Market* Cover Letter Contest, see page 16.

EPOCH MAGAZINE, (II), 251 Goldwin Smith Hall, Cornell University, Ithaca NY 14853. (607)255-3385. Editor: Michael Koch. Submissions should be sent to Michael Koch. Magazine: 6×9; 128 pages; good quality paper; good cover stock. "Top level fiction and poetry for people who are interested in good literature." Published 3 times a year. Estab. 1947. Circ. 1,000.

• Work originally appearing in this quality literary journal has appeared in numerous anthologies including *Best American Short Stories*, *Best American Poetry*, *Pushcart Prize*, *The O. Henry Prize Stories*, *Best of the West* and *New Stories from the South*.

Needs: Literary, contemporary and ethnic. Accepts 15-20 mss/issue. Receives 400 unsolicited fiction mss each month. Does not read in summer (April 15-September 15). Published work by Denis Johnson, Harriet Doerr, Lee K. Abbott; published new writers in the last year. Length: no limit. Also publishes literary essays, poetry. Critiques rejected mss when there is time. Sometimes recommends other markets.

How to Contact: Send complete ms with SASE. No simultaneous submissions. Reports in 3-4 weeks on mss. Publishes ms an average of 6 months after acceptance. Sample copy for $5.

Payment/Terms: Pays $5-10/printed page on publication for first North American serial rights.

Advice: "Read the journals you're sending work to."

EUREKA LITERARY MAGAZINE, (I, II), P.O. Box 280, Eureka College, Eureka IL 61530. (309)467-6336. Editor: Loren Logsdon. Fiction Editor: Nancy Perkins. Magazine: 6×9; 100 pages; 70 lb. white offset paper; 80 lb. gloss cover; photographs (occasionally). "No particular theme or philosophy—general audience." Semiannually. Estab. 1992. Circ. 400.

Needs: Adventure, ethnic/multicultural, experimental, fantasy (science), feminist, historical, humor/satire, literary, mainstream/contemporary, mystery/suspense (private eye/hardboiled, romantic), psychic/supernatural/occult, regional, romance (historical), science fiction (soft/sociological), translations. "We try to achieve a balance between the traditional and the experimental. We do favor the traditional, though." Receives 25 unsolicited mss/month. Accepts 4 mss/issue; 8-9 mss/year. Does not read mss mainly in late summer (August). Publishes ms usually within the year after acceptance. Recently published work by Samuel Floyd Cross, Leslie Schenk, Catherine Ryan Hyde, John M. Floyd and Joann Azen Bloom. Length: 4,500 words average; 7,000-8,000 words maximum. Publishes short shorts. Also publishes poetry.

How to Contact: Send complete ms with a cover letter. Should include estimated word count and bio (short paragraph). Reports in 1 week on queries; 4 months on mss. Send SASE for reply, return of ms or send a disposable copy of ms. Simultaneous submissions OK. Sample copy for $5.

Payment/Terms: Pays free subscription to the magazine and 2 contributor's copies. Acquires first rights or one-time rights.

Advice: "Does the writer tell a good story—one that would interest a general reader? Is the story provocative? Is its subject important? Does the story contain good insight into life or the human condition? We don't want anything so abstract that it seems unrelated to anything human. We appreciate humor and effective use of language, stories that have powerful, effective endings."

❧EVENT, (II), Douglas College, Box 2503, New Westminster, British Columbia V3L 5B2 Canada. Fax: (604)527-5095. Editor: Calvin Wharton. Fiction Editor: Christine Dewar. Assistant Editor: Bonnie Bauder. Magazine: 6×9; 144 pages; quality paper and cover stock; illustrations; photos. "Primarily a literary magazine, publishing poetry, fiction, reviews; for creative writers, artists, anyone interested in contemporary literature." Triannually. Estab. 1971. Circ. 1,000.

Needs: Literary, contemporary, feminist, humor, regional. "No technically poor or unoriginal pieces." Receives approximately 100 unsolicited fiction mss/month. Accepts 6-8 mss/issue. Recently published work by David Bergen, Elisabeth Harvor and André Alexis. Published new writers within the last year. Length: 5,000 words maximum. Also publishes poetry. Critiques rejected mss "when there is time."

How to Contact: Send complete ms, bio and SAE with Canadian postage or IRC. Reports in 1-4 months on mss. Publishes ms 6-12 months after acceptance. Sample copy for $5.

Payment/Terms: Pays $22/page and 2 contributor's copies on publication for first North American serial rights.

Advice: "A good narrative arc is hard to find."

THE EVERGREEN CHRONICLES, A Journal of Gay, Lesbian, Bisexual & Transgendered Arts & Cultures, (II), P.O. Box 8939, Minneapolis MN 55408. E-mail: evergreen@freenet.msp.mn. us. Contact: Managing Editor. Magazine: 7×8½; 90-100 pages; linen bond paper; b&w line drawings and photos. "We look for work that addresses the complexities and diversities of gay, lesbian, bisexual and transgendered experiences." Triannually. Estab. 1985. Circ. 1,000.

• The magazine sponsors an annual novella contest; deadline September 30. Send SASE for guidelines.

Needs: Gay or lesbian: adventure, confession, contemporary, ethnic, experimental, fantasy, feminist, humor/satire, literary, romance (contemporary), science fiction, serialized/excerpted novel, suspense/mystery. "We are interested in works by artists in a wide variety of genres. The subject matter need not be specifically lesbian, gay, bisexual or transgender-themed, but we do look for a deep sensitivity to that experience." Accepts 10-12 mss/issue; 30-36 mss/year. Publishes ms approximately 2 months after acceptance. Published work by Terri Jewel, Lev Raphael and Ruthann Robson. Published new writers in the last year. Length: 3,500-4,500 words average; no minimum; 5,200 words maximum. 25 pages double-spaced maximum on prose. Publishes short shorts. Sometimes comments on rejected mss.

How to Contact: Send 4 copies of complete ms with cover letter. "It helps to have some biographical information included." Submission deadlines: January 1 and July 1. Reports on queries in 3 weeks; on mss in 3-4 months. SASE. Sample copy for $8 and $1 postage. Fiction guidelines for #10 SASE.

Payment/Terms: Pays honorarium for one-time rights.

EVERY SO OFTEN . . . , (I), Brand New Publications, 13 Cuttermill Rd., #154, Great Neck NY 11021. E-mail: adamfcohen@aol.com. Editor: Adam F. Cohen. Magazine on World Wide Web. 8½ × 11; 20-50 pages, 20 lb. paper; 20 lb. cover; illustrations and photos. "*Every So Often* strives for work that is thought provoking. No genre is taboo, save for overly 'lovey-dovey' poetry. Audience is composed of authors, teachers and literate, intelligent people." Bimonthly. Estab. 1993. Circ. 200.

Needs: Adventure, children's/juvenile (1-4 years, 5-9 years), condensed/excerpted novel, erotica, ethnic/multicultural, experimental, fantasy, feminist, gay, historical, horror, humor/satire, lesbian, literary, mainstream/contemporary, mystery/suspense, psychic/supernatural/occult, regional, religious/inspirational, romance (contemporary), science fiction (soft/sociological), young adult/teen. Upcoming themes: "Winter Blue(s)" (December/January—erotica); "Poetry in Motion" (June/July—poetry). Plans special fiction issue or anthology. Receives 20 unsolicited mss/month. Buys 2 mss/issue; 26 mss/year. Publishes ms 1-2 months after acceptance. Recently published Mark Louis Feinson and Kathleen McDonald. Length: 8,500 words average; 8,500 words maximum. Publishes short shorts. Also publishes literary essays, literary criticism, poetry. Often critiques or comments on rejected ms.

How to Contact: Send complete ms with a cover letter. Should include 100-word bio and list of publications. Reports in 1 month on queries; 6 weeks on mss. Send SASE for reply to query or return of ms. Simultaneous, reprint and electronic submissions OK. Fiction guidelines free for #10 SASE.

Payment/Terms: Pays free subscription to the magazine and 2 contributor's copies. Acquires one-time rights. Not copyrighted.

Advice: "Pieces should have a pulse, mood or ideas within them. Nothing banal or overly wordy. Our writers have evolved with the publication. We like to see material and writers develop in their own time. Send material because you want to and believe in it, not because you want it printed. Be gutsy. Avoid 'I love my wife and girlfriend' slush at all costs. I want to see at least two pieces at once to get an idea of what interests and provokes a writer."

EXCURSUS, Literary Arts Journal, (III), P.O. Box 1056 Knickerbocker Station, New York NY 10002. Publisher: Giancarlo Malchiodi. Magazine: 8½ × 11; 100 pages; 28 lb. paper; glossy card cover; illustrations and photographs. "Eclectic, takes creative risks without lapsing into absurdity. The reader should 'travel' through the narrative with interest." Annually. Estab. 1995. Circ. 1,000.

● Publisher Giancarlo Malchiodi has been involved in small press publishing through his work with *The New Press* where he served as associate publisher, essay editor and co-poetry editor. Fiction is selected for *Excursus* by an editorial collective.

Needs: Condensed/excerpted novel, ethnic/multicultural, experimental, feminist, humor/satire, literary, mainstream/contemporary. No romance, religious ("unless atypical in thought and non-soapbox"). Receives 60-70 unsolicited mss/month. Accepts 4-7 mss/year. Does not read mss July 1-September 30 (returned unread during this time). Publishes ms up to a year after acceptance. Recently published work by Amanda Gardner, Robert Wexler, Linda Vanessa Hewitt, Adam Berlin and Scott Bresinger. Length: 2,500 words average; 1,700 words minimum; 4,500 words maximum. Also publishes literary essays, literary criticism and poetry. Sometimes critiques or comments on rejected mss.

How to Contact: Send complete ms (2 short stories maximum) with a cover letter. Include estimated word count and an informational and friendly cover letter. Reports in 3-4 months on mss. Send SASE for return of ms. Simultaneous submissions OK. Sample copy for $7.50. Fiction guidelines for #10 SASE.

Payment/Terms: Pays 1 contributor's copy. Additional copies for $5. Acquires one-time rights. Sends galleys to author for proofing.

Advice: Looks for "insight, positive or negative, into the human condition. New twists on 'old' themes. No pablum! Nothing trite or overly sentimental. No gratuitous violence. Want to see work that tackles, in any way subtle or obvious, issues affecting society. Take risks in content and form, but try to 'work the balance' between convention and avant-garde. Seek power through your characters, their interplay, and their setting. No first drafts."

EXPLORATIONS '97, (I, II), University of Alaska Southeast, 11120 Glacier Highway, Juneau AK 99801. (907)465-6418. Fax: (907)465-6406. E-mail: jnamp@acadl.alaska.edu. Editor: Art Petersen. Magazine: 5½ × 8¼; approximately 44 pages; heavy cover stock; b&w illustrations and photographs.

"Poetry, prose and art—we strive for artistic excellence." Annually. Estab. 1980. Circ. 750.

Needs: Experimental, humor/satire, traditional quality fiction, poetry, and art. Receives about 1,000 mss/year. Recently published work by Jamison Koehler, Nicchia P. Leamer, Grace Toll and Robert G. Berger.

How to Contact: *Reading/entry fee $5/story required.* Send name, address and short bio on *back* of first page of each submission. All submissions entered in contest. Submission postmark deadline is March 21. Reports in 2-3 months. Mss cannot be returned. Simultaneous and reprint submissions OK. Sample copy for $5.

Payment/Terms: Pays 2 contributor's copies. Acquires one-time rights (rights remain with the author). Also awards 4 annual prizes of $500 for prose, $500 for poetry and $125 for art ($100, $50 and $25—UAS students only).

Advice: "It is best to send for full guidelines. Concerning poetry and prose, standard form as well as innovation are encouraged; appropriate and fresh *imagery* (allusions, metaphors, similes, symbols . . .) as well as standard or experimental form draw editorial attention. 'Language really spoken by men' and women and authentically rendered experience are encouraged. Unfortunately, requests for criticism usually cannot be met. The prizes for 1997 will be awarded by the poet and critic John Haines."

EXPLORER MAGAZINE, (I), Flory Publishing Co., Box 210, Notre Dame IN 46556. Editor: Raymond Flory. Magazine: 5½×8½; approximately 32 pages; 20 lb. paper; 60 lb. or stock cover; illustrations. Magazine with "basically an inspirational theme including love stories in good taste." Christian writing audience. Semiannually. Estab. 1960. Circ. 300.

• The magazine sponsors The Joseph Flory Memorial Award and the Angel Light Award. Awards are $10 and a plaque.

Needs: Literary, mainstream, prose poem, religious/inspirational, romance (contemporary, historical, young adult) and science fiction. No pornography. Accepts 2-3 mss/issue; 5 mss/year. Recently published work by Roger Lee Kenvin, James M. Lane, L.J. Cardin and Terry Peterson. Length: 600 words average; 300 words minimum; 700 words maximum. Also publishes literary essays. Occasionally critiques rejected mss.

How to Contact: Send complete ms with SASE. Reports in 1 week. Publishes ms up to 3 years after acceptance. Simultaneous submissions OK. Sample copy for $3. Fiction guidelines for SASE.

Payment/Terms: Cash prizes of $25, $20, $15 and $10 based on subscribers' votes. The first prize winner also receives a plaque.

Advice: "I need short material, preferably no longer than 700 words—the shorter the better. I always like 'slice of life' with a message, without being preachy. Look for fiction with a 'message' in all styles that are written with feeling and flair. Just keep it short, 'camera-ready' and always in good taste."

EXPRESSIONS, Literature and Art by People with Disabilities and Ongoing Health Problems, (IV), Serendipity Press, P.O. Box 16294, St. Paul MN 55116-0294. (612)552-1209. Fax: (612)552-1209. Editor: Sefra Kobrin Pitzele. Magazine: 5½×8½; 84-124 pages; 60 lb. biodegradable paper; 80 lb. semigloss cover; illustrations and photographs. "*Expressions* provides a quality journal in which to be published when health, mobility, access or illness make multiple submissions both unreachable and unaffordable." Semiannually. Estab. 1993. Circ. 750.

Needs: *Material from writers with disabilities or ongoing health problems only.* Adventure, ethnic/multicultural, experimental, fantasy, feminist, gay, historical, horror, humor/satire, lesbian, literary, mainstream/contemporary, mystery/suspense, psychic/supernatural/occult, regional, religious/inspirational, romance, science fiction, senior citizen/retirement, sports and westerns. "We have no young readers, so all fiction should be intended for adult readers." Does not read mss from December 15 to February 1. Publishes ms 3-5 months after acceptance. Length: 1,500-2,000 words average. Publishes short shorts. Also publishes literary essays, literary criticism and poetry. Sometimes critiques or comments on rejected mss. Sponsors a fiction contest. Send #10 SASE for more information. "Eight to ten reader/scorers from across the nation help me rank each submission on its own merit." Awards are $50 (first place), $25 (second place) and a year's subscription (third place).

How to Contact: *Requires $5 reading fee.* Write for fiction guidelines; include SASE. Submission deadlines: May 15 and November 15. Reports in 2-6 weeks on queries; 2-4 months on mss. SASE for reply to query or return of ms. Simultaneous, reprint and electronic submissions OK. Sample copy for $6, 6×9 SAE and 5 first-class stamps.

Payment/Terms: Pays 2 contributor's copies. Acquires one-time rights.

THE FARMER'S MARKET, (II), Midwestern Farmer's Market, Inc., Elgin Community College, 1700 Spartan Dr., Elgin IL 60123-7193. Fiction Editor: Rachael Tecza. Poetry Editor: Joanne Lowery. Magazine: 5½×8½; 100-200 pages; 60 lb. offset paper; 65 lb. cover; b&w illustrations and photos. Magazine publishing "quality fiction, poetry, nonfiction, author interviews, etc., in the Midwestern tradition for an adult, literate audience." Semiannually. Estab. 1982. Circ. 500.

• *The Farmer's Market* has received numerous honors including Illinois Arts Council Literary

Awards and grants. Work published in the magazine has been selected for the *O. Henry Prize* anthology.

Needs: Contemporary, feminist, humor/satire, literary, regional and excerpted novel. "We prefer material of clarity, depth and strength with strong plots and good character development." No "romance, juvenile, teen." Reading periods: March-May, September-November. Accepts 10-20 mss/year. Recently published work by Beth Lordan, Curt Dawkins, Don Kurtz, Jean C. Lee, Philip Brown and Jeffrey Ihlenfeldt. Published new writers within the last year. Also publishes literary essays, poetry. Occasionally critiques rejected mss or recommends other markets.

How to Contact: Send complete ms with SASE. Reports in 1-3 months. No simultaneous submissions. Publishes ms 4-8 months after acceptance. Sample copy for $5.50 and $1 postage and handling.

Payment/Terms: Pays 2 contributor's copies plus one-year subscription. (Other payment dependent upon grants). Authors retain rights.

Advice: "We're always interested in regional fiction but that doesn't mean cows and chickens and home-baked apple pie, please. We are publishing more fiction and we are looking for exceptional manuscripts. Read the magazine before submitting. If you don't want to buy it, ask your library. We receive numerous mss that are clearly unsuitable. We're not sweet; we're not cute and we're not 'precious!' "

FAT TUESDAY, (I, II), 560 Manada Gap Rd., Grantville PA 17028. Editor-in-Chief: F.M. Cotolo. Editors: B. Lyle Tabor and Thom Savion. Associate Editors: Lionel Stevroid and Kristen vonOehrke. Journal: 8½×11 or 5×8; 27-36 pages; bond paper; heavy cover stock; saddle-stitched; b&w illustrations; photos. "Generally, we are an eclectic journal of fiction, poetry and visual treats. Our issues to date have featured artists like Patrick Kelly, Charles Bukowski, Joi Cook, Chuck Taylor and many more who have focused on an individualistic nature with fiery elements. We are a literary mardi gras— as the title indicates—and irreverancy is as acceptable to us as profundity as long as there is fire! Our audience is anyone who can praise literature and condemn it at the same time. Anyone too serious about it on either level will not like *Fat Tuesday*." Annually. Estab. 1981. Circ. 700.

● *Fat Tuesday* is best known for first-person "auto fiction."

Needs: Comics, erotica, experimental, humor/satire, literary, prose poem, psychic/supernatural/occult, serialized/excerpted novel and dada. "Although we list categories, we are open to feeling out various fields if they are delivered with the mark of an individual and not just in the format of the particular field." Receives 20 unsolicited fiction mss/month. Accepts 4-5 mss/issue. Published new writers within the last year. Length: 1,000 words maximum. Publishes short shorts. Occasionally critiques rejected mss and usually responds with a personal note or letter.

How to Contact: Send complete ms with SASE. "No previously published material considered." No simultaneous submissions. Reports in 1 month. Publishes ms 3-10 months after acceptance. Sample copy for $5.

Payment/Terms: Pays 1 contributor's copy. Acquires one-time rights.

Advice: "As *Fat Tuesday* crawls through its second decade, we find publishing small press editions more difficult than ever. Money remains a problem, mostly because small press seems to play to the very people who wish to be published in it. In other words, the cast is the audience, and more people want to be in *Fat Tuesday* than want to buy it. It is through sales that our magazine supports itself. This is why we emphasize buying a sample issue ($5) before submitting. As far as what we want to publish—send us shorter works that are 'crystals of thought and emotion which reflect your individual experiences—dig into your guts and pull out pieces of yourself. Your work is your signature; like time itself, it should emerge from the penetralia of your being and recede into the infinite region of the cosmos,' to coin a phrase, and remember *Fat Tuesday* is mardi gras—so fill up before you fast. Bon soir."

FAULT LINES, Dedicated to the Image and the Idea, (I, II), Club Mad Publishing, 107 Demoss Rd., #2, Nashville TN 37209. (615)356-6591. E-mail: rextasy@aol.com. Editors: Rex McCulloch, Mark Roberts. Fiction Editor: Rex McCulloch. Magazine: 5½×8½; 32 pages; 20 lb. white bond paper; 60 lb. cover; illustrations. Semiannually. Estab. 1994. Circ. 300.

Needs: Ethnic/multicultural, experimental, humor/satire, literary, translations. "We feel that film is one of the most powerful artistic mediums available today and are always interested in fiction and nonfiction with a film theme." Receives 10-20 unsolicited mss/month. Accepts 4-5 mss/issue; 10 mss/ year. Publishes ms 1 month after acceptance. Length: 2,500 words maximum. Publishes short shorts. Also publishes literary essays, poetry. Sometimes critiques or comments on rejected ms.

How to Contact: Send complete ms with a cover letter. Should include estimated word count and brief bio with list or partial list of previous publications. Reports in 2-3 months on mss. Simultaneous, reprint, electronic (Macintosh compatible) submissions OK. Sample copy for $2. Fiction guidelines for #10 SASE. Reviews novels and short story collections. Send books to Rex McCulloch, 915 Ewing Blvd., B11, Murfreesboro TN 37130.

Payment/Terms: Pays 1 contributor's copy. Acquires one-time rights.

Advice: "It's better to write interesting fiction about an unassuming subject than to try to fake an exciting story. Neatness and careful editing always make a good impression. In any genre, the elements of good fiction are always the same: idea, character development, and above all, the ability to make the reader care."

FEMINIST STUDIES, (II, IV), Department of Women's Studies, University of Maryland, College Park MD 20742. (301)405-7415. Fax: (301)314-9190. E-mail: femstud@umail.umd.edu. Editor: Claire G. Moses. Fiction Editor: Alicia Ostriker. Magazine: journal-sized; about 200 pages; photographs. "Scholarly manuscripts, fiction, book review essays for professors, graduate/doctoral students; scholarly interdisciplinary feminist journal." Triannually. Estab. 1974. Circ. 7,500.

Needs: Contemporary, ethnic, feminist, gay, lesbian. Receives about 15 poetry and short story mss/month. Accepts 2-3 mss/issue. "We review fiction twice a year. Deadline dates are May 1 and December 1. Authors will receive notice of the board's decision by June 30 and January 30, respectively." Recently published work by Barbara Wilson, Su Fidler Cowling, Frances Webb and Lisa Chewning. Sometimes comments on rejected mss.

How to Contact: Send complete ms with cover letter. No simultaneous submissions. Sample copy for $12. Fiction guidelines free.

Payment/Terms: Pays 2 contributor's copies and 10 tearsheets. Sends galleys to authors.

FICTION, (II), % Dept. of English, City College, 138th St. & Convent Ave., New York NY 10031. (212)650-6319/650-6317. Editor: Mark J. Mirsky. Managing Editor: Francesca A. Pennisi. Magazine: 6×9; 150-250 pages; illustrations and occasionally photos. "As the name implies, we publish *only* fiction; we are looking for the best new writing available, leaning toward the unconventional. *Fiction* has traditionally attempted to make accessible the unaccessible, to bring the experimental to a broader audience." Biannually. Estab. 1972. Circ. 4,500.

● Stories first published in *Fiction* have been selected for inclusion in the *Pushcart Prize* and *Best of the Small Presses* anthologies.

Needs: Contemporary, experimental, humor/satire, literary and translations. No romance, science-fiction, etc. Receives 200 unsolicited mss/month. Accepts 12-20 mss/issue; 24-40 mss/year. Does not read mss May-October. Publishes ms 1-12 months after acceptance. Agented fiction 10-20%. Published work by Harold Brodkey, Joyce Carol Oates, Peter Handke, Max Frisch, Susan Minot and Adolfo Bioy-Casares. Length: 6,000 words maximum. Publishes short shorts. Sometimes critiques rejected mss and recommends other markets.

How to Contact: Send complete ms with cover letter. Reports in approximately 3 months on mss. SASE. Simultaneous submissions OK, but please advise. Sample copy for $5. Fiction guidelines for SASE.

Payment/Terms: Pays in contributor's copies. Acquires first rights.

Advice: "The guiding principle of *Fiction* has always been to go to terra incognita in the writing of the imagination and to ask that modern fiction set itself serious questions, if often in absurd and comic voices, interrogating the nature of the real and the fantastic. It represents no particular school of fiction, except the innovative. Its pages have often been a harbor for writers at odds with each other. As a result of its willingness to publish the difficult, experimental, unusual, while not excluding the well known, *Fiction* has a unique reputation in the U.S. and abroad as a journal of future directions."

FICTION INTERNATIONAL, (II), English Dept., San Diego State University, 5500 Campanile Dr., San Diego CA 92182-8131. (619)594-5469. Editor: Harold Jaffe. "Serious literary magazine of fiction, extended reviews, essays." Magazine: 200 pages; illustrations; photos. "Our twin biases are progressive politics and post-modernism." Annually. Estab. 1973. Circ. 1,000.

Needs: Literary, political and innovative forms. Receives approximately 300 unsolicited fiction mss each month. Unsolicited mss will be considered only from September 1 through December 15 of each year. Published new writers within the last year. No length limitations but rarely use manuscripts over 25 pages. Portions of novels acceptable if self-contained enough for independent publication.

How to Contact: Send complete ms with SASE. Reports in 1-3 months on mss. Sample copy for $9: query Sheila Dollente, Circulation Manager, (619)357-5536.

Payment/Terms: Pays in contributor's copies.

Advice: "Study the magazine. We're highly selective. A difficult market for unsophisticated writers."

FISH DRUM MAGAZINE, (II), Murray Hill Station, P.O. Box 966, New York NY 10156. Editor: Suzi Winson. Magazine: 5½×8½; 40-odd pages; glossy cover; illustrations and photographs. "Lively, emotional vernacular modern fiction, art and poetry." Annually. Estab. 1988 by Robert Winson (1959-1995). Suzi says, "It is my intention to complete Robert's work and to honor his memory by continuing to publish *Fish Drum*." Circ. 500.

Needs: Contemporary, erotica, ethnic, experimental, fantasy, gay, lesbian, literary, prose poem, regional, science fiction. "Most of the fiction we've published is in the form of short, heightened prose-pieces." Receives 6-10 unsolicited mss/month. Accepts 1-2 mss/issue. Also publishes literary essays, literary criticism, poetry.

How to Contact: Send complete manuscript. No simultaneous submissions. Reports on mss in 2-3 months. SASE. Reviews novels and short story collections.

Payment/Terms: Pays in contributor's copies. Charges for extras. Acquires first North American serial rights. Sends galleys to author.

FISH STORIES, Collective II, (II), WorkShirts Writing Center, 5412 N. Clark St., South Suite, Chicago IL 60640. Editor: Amy G. Davis. Magazine: 5⅜ × 8½; 224 pages; 60 lb. white paper; 4-color C1S cover. "We are seeking vivid stories that stand up to a second reading, but don't require it. While our fiction is literary, we have readers outside that audience. *Fish Stories* strives for a diverse collection of work." Annually. Estab. 1995. Circ. 1,200.

Needs: Ethnic/multicutural, experimental, feminist, gay, lesbian, literary, regional. No mainstream, science fiction or any other genre fiction. "We seek experimental or traditional literary work." Receives 65 unsolicited mss/month. Accepts 15-20 mss/issue. Does not read February through July. Publishes ms 2-8 months after acceptance. Recently published work by Tobias Wolff, Yusef Komunyakaa, Li-Young Lee, Maxine Chernoff and 5 previously unpublished writers and poets. Length: 3,000-5,000 words average; 10,000 words maximum. Publishes short shorts. Also publishes poetry. Sometimes critiques or comments on rejected mss.

How to Contact: Send for guidelines. "Read a sample copy first, then send mss." Include estimated word count, brief bio, Social Security number, list of publications. Reports in 6 months on mss. Send SASE for reply, return of ms or send a disposable copy of ms. Simultaneous and reprint submissions OK. Sample copy for $10.95. Fiction guidelines free for #10 SASE.

Payment/Terms: Pays 2 contributor's copies; additional copies half-price. Acquires one-time rights.

Advice: Looks for "a strong introduction that is followed through by the rest of the story. The manuscripts that stand out are polished with careful attention to the holistic use of language, point of view, etc."

FLIPSIDE, (I, II), Professional Writing Program, Dixon 109, California University, California PA 15419. (412)938-4082. Editor: Joseph Szejk. Tabloid: 11½ × 17; 45-60 pages; illustrations; photos. "We publish highly descriptive fiction with characters who 'do something' and are set in scenes which the reader can see." Semiannually. Estab. 1987. Circ. 5,000.

• *Flipside* received an American Scholastic Press Association Award for the Most Outstanding College Magazine for 1995.

Needs: Contemporary, experimental, literary. No genre fiction. Receives 5-6 unsolicited mss/month. Accepts 2-3 mss/issue; 6-8 mss/year. Publishes ms 1-6 months after acceptance. Length: 1,000-5,000 words average; 8,000 words maximum. Also publishes literary essays, literary criticism, some poetry.

How to Contact: Send complete ms with cover letter. Reports in 2-4 weeks on queries; 1-2 months on mss. SASE. Simultaneous submissions OK. Sample copy and fiction guidelines for 9 × 12 SAE and $2 postage.

Payment/Terms: Pays 3 contributor's copies. Acquires first North American serial rights.

Advice: "We *do* want heavy description, strong metaphors, highly visible and memorable characters as well as scenes. We do not waste our time with bogus ramblings in a narrator's head in situations or places the reader cannot visualize."

THE FLORIDA REVIEW, (II), Dept. of English, University of Central Florida, Orlando FL 32816. (407)823-2038. Contact: Russell Kesler. Magazine: 5½ × 8½; 120 pages; semigloss full-color cover; perfect-bound. Semiannually. Estab. 1972. Circ. 1,000.

Needs: Contemporary, experimental and literary. "We welcome experimental fiction, so long as it doesn't make us feel lost or stupid. We aren't especially interested in genre fiction (science fiction, romance, adventure, etc.), though a good story can transcend any genre." Receives 200 mss/month. Accepts 8-10 mss/issue; 16-20 mss/year. Publishes ms within 3-6 months of acceptance. Recently published work by Alyce Miller, Michael W. Cox and Kathleen Coskran. Publishes short shorts. Also publishes literary criticism, poetry and essays.

How to Contact: Send complete ms with cover letter. Reports in 2-4 months. SASE required. Simultaneous submissions OK. Sample copy for $4.50; fiction guidelines for SASE. Reviews novels and short story collections.

Payment/Terms: Pays in contributor's copies. Small honorarium occasionally available. "Copyright held by U.C.F.; reverts to author after publication. (In cases of reprints, we ask that a credit line indicate that the work first appeared in the *F.R.*)"

Advice: "We publish fiction of high 'literary' quality—stories that delight, instruct, and aren't afraid to take risks."

‡FLYING HORSE, P.O. Box 445, Marblehead MA 01945. Editor: Dennis Must. Associate Editor: David Wagner. Magazine: 6 × 9; 100 pages; 50 lb. Finch Opaque paper; 70 lb. cover stock; illustrations;

photographs. "*Flying Horse* is an alternative literary journal. Although we welcome contributions from all talented artists, we particularly hope to give voice to those often excluded from the dominant media. For example, we actively encourage submissions from inner city learning centers, community and public colleges, prisons, homeless shelters, social service agencies, unions, the military, hospitals, clinics or group homes, Indian reservations and minority studies programs." Semiannually. Estab. 1996. Circ. 1,000.

Needs: Condensed/excerpted novel, ethnic/multicultural, experimental, literary, mainstream/contemporary, translations. Receives 75-100 unsolicited mss/month. Accepts 20 mss/issue; 40 mss/year. Publishes ms generally in the next issue. Recently published work by Robert Kelsey, P.R. Smith, Phyllis Burton, Daniel Lazar, Scott Antworth, David Wagner and Salim Sadiki. Length: 2,500-5,000 words average; 7,500 words maximum. Publishes short shorts. Also publishes literary essays, literary criticism and poetry. Often critiques or comments on rejected mss.

How to Contact: Send complete ms with a cover letter. Include estimated word count and short bio with submission. Reports in 3 months on mss. Send SASE for reply, return of ms or send a disposable copy of ms. Simultaneous submissions OK. Sample copy for $4. Fiction guidelines for #10 SASE.

Payment/Terms: Pays $10-25 and 2 contributor's copies on publication for one-time rights. Sends galleys to author.

Advice: "*Flying Horse* seeks heterogeneity of voice. Circumstance, class, and formal education are not weighed. Nor do we count writing credits. What moves us to say *yes* is the authority of a submitted work, its conviction and originality of expression. The reader will encounter authors from starkly diverse corners of our society in our journal. What unites us, our common fuel, is the *written word*, and our firmly held conviction in its powers of transformation."

THE FLYING ISLAND, (II, IV), Writers' Center of Indianapolis, P.O. Box 88386, Indianapolis IN 46208. (317)929-0625. Editor: Jerome Donahue. Tabloid: 24 pages; illustrations and photos. "A magazine of fiction, essays, reviews and poetry by Indiana-connected writers." Semiannually. Estab. 1979. Circ. 700.

Needs: Ethnic/multicultural, experimental, fantasy, feminist, gay, lesbian, literary, mainstream/contemporary, mystery/suspense, psychic/supernatural/occult, science fiction. Receives 1,000 unsolicited mss/year. Accepts 4-5 mss/issue; 8-10 mss/year. Does not read mss March-May and September-November. Publishes ms 2 months after acceptance. Length: 4,000 words average. Publishes short shorts. Also publishes literary essays, literary criticism and poetry.

How to Contact: Send two copies of complete ms with a cover letter. Should include short bio explaining Indiana connection. Write for guidelines. Reports in 3-5 months on mss. SASE for return of ms. Simultaneous submissions OK. Fiction guidelines for #10 SASE. Reviews novels and short story collections "if story or author has some connection to Indiana."

Payment/Terms: Pays 2 contributor's copies plus honorarium. Pays on publication.

Advice: "We have published work by high school and college students as well as work by 1994 Pulitzer Prize winner Yusef Komunyakaa and Edgar nominee Terence Faherty. Our readers enjoy a wide variety of settings and situations. We're looking for quality and we tend to overlook gimmicky and sentimental writing."

FOLIO: A LITERARY JOURNAL, (II), Department of Literature, American University, Washington DC 20016. (202)885-2990. Editor changes yearly. Send mss to attention: Editor. Magazine: 6×9; 64 pages. "Fiction is published if it is well written. We look for language control, skilled plot and character development." For a scholarly audience. Semiannually. Estab. 1984.

Needs: Contemporary, literary, mainstream, prose poem, translations, essay, b&w art or photography. No pornography. Occasional theme-based issues. See guidelines for info. Receives 150 unsolicited mss/month. Accepts 3-5 mss/issue; 6-40 mss/year. Does not read mss during May-August. Published work by Henry Taylor, Kermit Moyer, Linda Pastan; publishes new writers. Length: 2,500 words average; 4,500 words maximum. Publishes short shorts. Occasionally critiques rejected mss.

How to Contact: Send complete ms with cover letter. Include a brief bio. Reports in 1-2 weeks on queries; 1-2 months on mss. SASE. Simultaneous and reprint submissions OK (if noted). Sample copy for $5. Guidelines for #10 SASE.

Payment/Terms: Pays in contributor's copies. Acquires first North American rights. "$75 award for best fiction and poetry. Query for guidelines."

FOOTWORK, The Paterson Literary Review, (II), Passaic County Community College, One College Blvd., Paterson NJ 07505. (201)684-6555. Editor: Maria Mazziotti Gillan. Magazine: 8½×11; 300 pages; 60 lb. paper; 70 lb. cover; illustrations; photos. Annually.

● *Footwork* was chosen by *Library Journal* as one of the ten best literary magazines in the U.S.

Needs: Contemporary, ethnic, literary. "We are interested in quality short stories, with no taboos on subject matter." Receives about 60 unsolicited mss/month. Publishes ms about 6 months to 1 year after acceptance. Published new writers within the last year. Length: 2,000-3,000 words. Also publishes literary essays, literary criticism, poetry.

How to Contact: Submit no more than 1 story at a time. Submission deadline: March 1. Send SASE for reply or return of ms. "Indicate whether you want story returned." Simultaneous submissions OK. Sample copy for $12. Reviews novels and short story collections.
Payment/Terms: Pays in contributor's copies. Acquires first North American rights.
Advice: Looks for "clear, moving and specific work."

‡**FOURTEEN HILLS: The SFSU Review, (II)**, Dept. of Creative Writing, San Francisco State University, 1600 Holloway Ave., San Francisco CA 94132. (415)338-3083. E-mail: hills@sfsu.edu. Editors change each year. Magazine: 6×9; 160 pages; 60 lb. paper; 10 point C15 cover. "*Fourteen Hills* publishes the highest quality innovative fiction and poetry for a literary audience." Semiannually. Estab. 1994. Circ. 700.
Needs: Ethnic/multicultural, gay, humor/satire, lesbian, literary, mainstream/contemporary, translations. "No sexist or racist work, and no stories in which the plot has been chosen for its shock value. No genre fiction, please." Receives 100 unsolicited mss/month. Accepts 8-10 mss/issue; 16-20 mss/year. Does not usually read mss during the summer. Publishes ms 2-4 months after acceptance. Recently published work by Mary Gaitskill, Alice Notley and Nobel Prize nominee Josef Skvorecky. Length: 7,000 words maximum. Publishes short shorts. Also publishes literary essays, poetry. Sometimes critiques or comments on rejected mss.
How to Contact: Send complete ms with a cover letter. Include brief bio and list of publications. Reports in 3-5 months on mss. SASE for return of ms. Simultaneous submissions OK. Sample copy for $5. Fiction guidelines for #10 SASE.
Payment/Terms: Pays 2 contributor's copies on publication. Acquires one-time rights. Sends galleys to author.
Advice: "Please read an issue of *Fourteen Hills* before submitting."

‡**FRONTIERS, (II), A Journal of Women Studies**, Washington State University, Frontiers W St. Wilson 10, Pullman WA 99164-4007. E-mail: frontier@wsu.edu. Editor: Sue Armitage. Magazine: 6×9; 200 pages; photos. "Women studies; academic articles in all disciplines; criticism, book and film reviews; exceptional creative work (art, short fiction, photography, poetry)."
Needs: Feminist, lesbian. Upcoming themes: Women and War; Ecofeminism. Receives 15 unsolicited mss/month. Accepts 7-12 mss/issue. Publishes ms 6-12 months after acceptance. Sometimes critiques rejected mss.
How to Contact: Send 3 copies of complete ms with cover letter. Reports in 1 month on queries; 3-6 months on mss. SASE. Fiction guidelines for #10 SASE. Sample copy for $8.
Payment/Terms: Pays 2 contributor's copies. Acquires first North American serial rights.
Advice: "We are a *feminist* journal. *Frontiers* aims to make scholarship in women studies, and *exceptional* creative work, accessible to a cross-disciplinary audience inside and outside the university. Read short fiction in *Frontiers* before submitting."

FUGUE, Literary Digest of the University of Idaho, (I), English Dept., Rm. 200, Brink Hall, University of Idaho, Moscow ID 83844-1102. (208)885-6156. Website: http://www.uidaho.edu/LS/Eng/Fugue.Executive Editor: Eric Isaacson. Editors change each year. Send to Executive Editor. Magazine: 5½×8½; 60-100 pages; 20 lb. stock paper. "We are interested in all classifications of fiction—we are not interested in pretentious 'literary' stylizations. We expect stories to be written in a manner engaging for anyone, not just academics and the pro-literatae crowd." Semiannually. Estab. 1990. Circ. 500.
Needs: Adventure, ethnic/multicultural, experimental, fantasy, historical, horror, humor/satire, literary, mainstream/contemporary, mystery/suspense, regional, romance, science fiction, sports, westerns. Receives 50 unsolicited mss/month. Accepts 4-8 mss/issue; 8-16 mss/year. Does not read May-September. Publishes ms 3-8 months after acceptance. Recently published work by Brenda Hillman, Michael Arnzen, Mary Clearman Blew and an interview with Samuel R. Delaney. Length: 3,000 words average; 50 words minimum; 7,000 words maximum. Publishes short shorts. Also publishes literary essays and poetry. Sometimes critiques or comments on rejected mss.
How to Contact: Send complete ms with cover letter. "Obtain guidelines first." Include estimated word count, Social Security number and list of publications. Report in 2 weeks on queries; 2-3 months on mss. SASE for a reply to a query or return of ms. No simultaneous submissions. Sample copy for $5. Fiction guidelines for #10 SASE.
Payment/Terms: Pays $5-20 on publication for first North American serial rights. All contributors receive a copy; extra copies available at a discount.
Advice: Looks for "innovative and somewhat experimental fiction, competent writing, clarity and consideration for the reader above stylism. Do not send us the traditional themes considered to be 'literary.' Be original and inventive. Don't rely on the traditional approaches to fiction or poetry. Take chances, but present your work as a professional. Professionalism is a must. Proper manuscript format is essential."

THE G.W. REVIEW, (I, II), The George Washington University, Box 20B, The Marvin Center, 800 21st St., N.W., Washington, DC 20052. (202)994-7288. Editor-in-Chief: Jane Roh. Magazine: 6×9; 64 pages; 60 lb. white offset paper; 65 lb. Patina cover; cover illustration. *"The G.W. Review* publishes poetry, short fiction and essays for the Washington DC metropolitan area and national subscribers." Semiannually. Estab. 1980. Circ. 4,000 (annually).
Needs: Condensed/excerpted novel, contemporary, experimental, humor/satire, literary, mainstream, prose poem, translations. *"The G.W. Review* does not accept previously published material. No pornography or proselytizing religious manuscripts." Does not read mss May 15 through August 15. Publishes ms up to 6 months after acceptance. Recently published work by Kermit Moyer and Beth Kephart Sulit. Length: 2,500 words average; 6,000 words maximum. Sometimes critiques rejected mss.
How to Contact: Send complete ms with cover letter. Include biographical information, places previously published, previous books, etc. Reports in 3-6 weeks on queries; 4-10 weeks on mss. SASE. Simultaneous submissions OK. Sample copy for $3. Fiction guidelines for SASE.
Payment/Terms: Pays in contributor's copies. Acquires one-time rights.
Advice: *"The G.W. Review* seeks to publish the best contemporary writing from outside the Washington, DC literary community as well as the best from within. Initially intended for distribution to the surrounding Washington, DC metropolitan area, *The G.W. Review* has since attained a more widespread national distribution and readership."

A GATHERING OF THE TRIBES, (II), A Gathering of the Tribes, Inc., P.O. Box 20693, Tompkins Square Station, New York NY 10009. (212)674-3778. Fax: (212)674-5576. E-mail: tribes@pop.interport. Editor: Steve Cannon. Fiction Editors: Renée McManus and Adnan Ashraf. Magazine: 8×10; 100-200 pages; glossy paper and cover; illustrations and photos. A "multicultural and multigenerational publication." Estab. 1992. Circ. 2,000-3,000.
  ● *A Gathering of the Tribes* received a 1995 American Literary Award for editorial content.
Needs: Erotica, ethnic/multicultural, experimental, fantasy (science), feminist, gay, historical, horror, humor/satire, lesbian, literary, mainstream/contemporary, romance (futuristic/time travel, gothic), science fiction (soft/sociological), senior citizen/retirement, translations. "We are open to all; just no poor writing/grammar/syntax." List of upcoming themes available for SASE. Receives 100 unsolicited mss/ month. Publishes ms 3-6 months after acceptance. Recently published work of Carl Watson, Alice Notely and Victor Cruz. Length: 500 words average; 200 words minimum; no maximum. Publishes short shorts. Also publishes literary essays, literary criticism and poetry.
How to Contact: Send complete ms with a cover letter. Include estimated word count, half-page bio, list of publications, phone and fax numbers and address with submission. Send SASE for reply, return of ms or send a disposable copy of ms. Simultaneous, reprint and electronic submissions OK. Sample copy for $10. Reviews novels and short story collections.
Payment/Terms: Pays 1 contributor's copy; additional copies $5. Sponsors contests, awards or grants for fiction writers. "Watch for ads in *Poets & Writers* and *American Poetry Review.*"
Advice: Looks for "unique tone and style, offbeat plots and characters, and ethnic and regional work. Type manuscript well: readable font (serif) and no typos. Make characters and their dialogue interesting. Experiment with style, and don't be conventional. Do not send dragged-out, self-indulgent philosophizing of life and the universe. Get specific. Make your characters soar!"

GEORGETOWN REVIEW, (II), G & R Publications, P.O. Box 6309, Southern Station, Hattiesburg MS 39406-6309. Phone/fax: (601)583-6940. E-mail: jsfulmer@whale.st.usm.edu. Editor: John Fulmer. Fiction Editor: Victoria Lancelotta. Magazine: 5½×8½; 100-150 pages; smooth offset paper; 10 pt. CS1 cover. "We want to publish quality fiction and poetry." Published twice a year. Estab. 1993. Circ. 600.
Needs: Condensed/excerpted novel, ethnic/multicultural, experimental, feminist, gay, humor/satire, lesbian, literary, science fiction. No romance, juvenile, fantasy. Receives 150 mss/month. Does not read mss May through August. Agented fiction 10%. Recently published work by Walter Cummins, Frederick Barthleme and Francois Camion. Length: 3,000 words average; 300 words minimum; 6,500 words maximum. Publishes short shorts. Length: 300 words. Also publishes poetry.
How to Contact: Send complete ms with a cover letter. Reports in 2-4 months on mss. SASE. Simultaneous and electronic submissions OK. Sample copy for $5. Guidelines free for SAE and 1 first-class stamp.
Payment/Terms: Pays 2 contributor's copies. Acquires first rights. Sends galleys to author.
Advice: "We simply look for quality work, no matter what the subject or style."

THE GEORGIA REVIEW, (I, II), The University of Georgia, Athens GA 30602-9009. (706)542-3481. Editor-in-Chief: Stanley W. Lindberg. Associate Editor: Stephen Corey. Assistant Editor: Janet Wondra. Journal: 7×10; 208 pages (average); 50 lb. woven old-style paper; 80 lb. cover stock; illustrations; photos. *"The Georgia Review* is a journal of arts and letters, featuring a blend of the best in contemporary thought and literature—essays, fiction, poetry, visual art and book reviews for the intelligent nonspecialist as well as the specialist reader. We seek material that appeals across disciplinary

lines by drawing from a wide range of interests." Quarterly. Estab. 1947. Circ. 6,000.
- This magazine has an excellent reputation for publishing high-quality fiction.

Needs: Experimental and literary. "We're looking for the highest quality fiction—work that is capable of sustaining subsequent readings, not throw-away pulp magazine entertainment. Nothing that fits too easily into a 'category.' " Receives about 400 unsolicited fiction mss/month. Accepts 3-4 mss/issue; 12-15 mss/year. Does not read unsolicited mss in June, July or August. Would prefer *not* to see novel excerpts. Published work by Louise Erdrich, Frederick Busch, Kelly Cherry. Published new writers within the last year. Length: Open. Also publishes literary essays, literary criticism, poetry. Occasionally critiques rejected mss.

How to Contact: Send complete ms (one story) with SASE. No multiple submissions. Usually reports in 2-3 months. Sample copy for $6; guidelines for #10 SASE. Reviews short story collections.

Payment/Terms: Pays minimum $35/printed page on publication for first North American serial rights, 1 year complimentary subscription and 1 contributor's copy; reduced charge for additional copies. Sends galleys to author.

THE GETTYSBURG REVIEW, (II), Gettysburg College, Gettysburg PA 17325. (717)337-6770. Editor: Peter Stitt. Assistant Editor: Jeff Mock. Magazine: 6¾ × 10; 170 pages; acid free paper; full color illustrations. "Quality of writing is our only criterion; we publish fiction, poetry, and essays." Quarterly. Estab. 1988. Circ. 4,500.
- Work appearing in *The Gettysburg Review* has also been included in *Prize Stories: The O. Henry Awards*, the *Pushcart Prize* anthology, *Best American Poetry*, *New Stories from the South*, *Harper's*, and elsewhere. It is also the recipient of a Lila-Wallace Reader's Digest grant and a NEA grant.

Needs: Contemporary, experimental, historical, humor/satire, literary, mainstream, regional and serialized novel. "We require that fiction be intelligent, and aesthetically written." Receives 160 mss/month. Accepts 4-6 mss/issue; 16-24 mss/year. Publishes ms within 1 year of acceptance. Recently published work by Robert Olen Butler, Joyce Carol Oates, Naeem Murr, Tom Perrotta, Jacoba Hood and Tom House. Length: 3,000 words average; 1,000 words minimum; 20,000 words maximum. Occasionally publishes short shorts. Also publishes literary essays, some literary criticism, poetry. Sometimes critiques rejected mss.

How to Contact: Send complete ms with cover letter. Reports in 3-6 months. SASE. No simultaneous submissions. Sample copy for $7 (postage paid). Does not review books per se. "We do essay-reviews, treating several books around a central theme." Send review copies to editor.

Payment/Terms: Pays $25/printed page, subscription to magazine and contributor's copy on publication for first North American serial rights. Charge for extra copies.

Advice: "Reporting time can take more than three months. It is helpful to look at a sample copy of *The Gettysburg Review* to see what kinds of fiction we publish before submitting."

THE GLASS CHERRY, A poetry magazine, (II), The Glass Cherry Press, 901 Europe Bay Rd., Ellison Bay WI 54210-9643. (414)854-9042. Editor: Judith Hirschmiller. Magazine: 5 × 7; 60 pages; high-tech laser paper; cover stock varies; illustrations and photos. "Our goal is to combine diversity with quality to promote good literature by a variety of writers. New writers are encouraged to submit." Quarterly. Estab. 1994. Circ. 500.

Needs: Condensed/excerpted novel, gay, historical, horror, lesbian, literary, mainstream/contemporary, science fiction, serialized novel, translations. "No pornography." Publishes special fiction issues or anthologies. Receives 6-12 unsolicited mss/month. Accepts 1-2 mss/issue; 4-8 mss/year. Does not read books May-December; reads fiction for magazine all year. Publishes ms 1 year after acceptance. Recently published work by Charles Chaim Wax and Richard Peabody. Length: 1,000 words maximum. Publishes short shorts. Also publishes literary essays, literary criticism and poetry. Critiques or comments on rejected ms "only if requested to do so by author."

How to Contact: Query first. Include short bio and list of publications with submission. Reports in 3 weeks on queries; 3 months on mss. SASE for reply. No simultaneous submissions. Sample copy for $5; back issue, $6. Fiction guidelines for #10 SASE. Reviews novels and short story collections.

Payment/Terms: Pays 1 contributor's copy. Acquires one-time rights.

Advice: "The ordinary, familiar experiences of life are your richest source for writing. Comments without opinions are appreciated and much more interesting. We would like more translations, book reviews, plays and short fiction of personal glimpses (individual, unusual events of a personal nature)."

SENDING TO A COUNTRY other than your own? Be sure to send International Reply Coupons instead of stamps for replies or return of your manuscript.

GLIMMER TRAIN STORIES, (II), Glimmer Train Press, 710 SW Madison St., Suite 504, Portland OR 97205. Fax: (503)221-0836. Editors: Susan Burmeister and Linda Davies. Magazine: 6¾×9¼; 160 pages; recycled, acid-free paper; 20 illustrations; 12 photographs. Quarterly. Estab. 1991. Circ. 21,000.

● The magazine also sponsors an annual short story contest for new writers.

Needs: Literary. Plans to publish special fiction issue or anthology. Receives 3,000 unsolicited mss/ month. Accepts 10 mss/issue; 40 mss/year. Reads in January, April, July, October. Publishes ms 4-9 months after acceptance. Agented fiction 20%. Recently published work by Evan Connell, Ellen Gilchrist, Tess Gallagher, Abigail Thomas, David Huddle and George Clark. Length: 1,200 words minimum; 8,000 words maximum.

How to Contact: Send complete ms with a cover letter. Include estimated word count and list of publications. Reports in 3 months. Send SASE for return or send a disposable copy of ms (with stamped postcard or envelope for notification). Simultaneous submissions OK. Sample copy for $9. Fiction guidelines for #10 SASE.

Payment/Terms: Pays $500 and 10 contributor's copies on acceptance for first rights.

Advice: "If you're excited about a story you've written, send it to us! If you're not very excited about it, wait and send one that you are excited about."

✤**GRAIN, (II)**, Saskatchewan Writers' Guild, Box 1154, Regina, Saskatchewan S4P 3B4 Canada. Fax: (306)244-0255. E-mail: grain.mag@sk.sympatico.ca. Editor: J. Jill Robinson. Literary magazine: 6×9; 144 pages; Chinook offset printing; chrome-coated stock; illustrations; some photos. "Fiction and poetry for people who enjoy high quality writing." Quarterly. Estab. 1973. Circ. 1,800-2,000.

● *Grain* received the National Magazine Award-Gold Award for Fiction-1996.

Needs: Contemporary, experimental, literary, mainstream and prose poem. "No propaganda—only artistic/literary writing." No mss "that stay *within* the limits of conventions such as women's magazine type stories, science fiction; none that push a message." Receives 80 unsolicited fiction mss/month. Accepts 8-12 mss/issue; 32-48 mss/year. Length: "No more than 30 pages." Also publishes poetry and creative nonfiction. Occasionally critiques rejected mss.

How to Contact: Send complete ms with SASE (or IRC) and brief letter. No simultaneous submissions. Reports within 4 months on mss. Publishes ms an average of 4 months after acceptance. Sample copy for $6.95 plus postage.

Payment/Terms: Pays $30-100 and 2 contributor's copies on publication for first Canadian serial rights. "We expect acknowledgment if the piece is republished elsewhere."

Advice: "Submit a story to us that will deepen the imaginative experience of our readers. *Grain* has established itself as a first-class magazine of serious fiction. We receive submissions from around the world. If Canada is a foreign country to you, we ask that you *do not* use U.S. postage stamps on your return envelope. If you live outside Canada and neglect the International Reply Coupons, we *will not* read or reply to your submission."

GRAND STREET, (V), 131 Varick St., #906, New York NY 10013. (212)807-6548. Fax (212)807-6544. Editor: Jean Stein. Managing Editor: Deborah Treisman. Magazine: 7×9; 240-270 pages; illustrations; art portfolios. "We publish new fiction and nonfiction of all types." Quarterly. Estab. 1981. Circ. 7,000.

● Work published in *Grand Street* has been included in the *Best American Short Stories*.

Needs: Fiction, poetry, essays, translations. Receives 400 unsolicited mss/month. Accepts 12 mss/ issue; 48 mss/year. Time between acceptance of the ms and publication varies. Agented fiction 90%. Published work by David Foster Wallace, Stephen Millhauser, Dennis Hopper, Paul Auster, John Ashbery, Duong Thu Huong, William T. Vollmann. Length: 4,000 words average; 9,000 words maximum.

How to Contact: *Not accepting unsolicited fiction mss.* Sample copy for $15; $18 overseas and Canada.

Payment/Terms: Pays $250-1,000 and 2 contributor's copies on publication for first North American serial rights. Sends galleys to author.

✳ **GRASSLANDS REVIEW, (I, II)**, P.O. Box 626, Berea OH 44017. E-mail: lkennelly@aol.com. Editor: Laura B. Kennelly. Magazine: 6×9; 80 pages. *Grasslands Review* prints creative writing of all types; poetry, fiction, essays for a general audience. Semiannually. Estab. 1989. Circ. 300.

Needs: Contemporary, ethnic, experimental, fantasy, horror, humor/satire, literary, mystery/suspense, prose poem, regional, science fiction and western. Nothing pornographic or overtly political or religious. Accepts 5-8 mss/issue. Reads only in October and March. Publishes ms 6 months after acceptance. Recently published work by Paddy Reid, Mary Ann Taylor, Dawn A. Baldwin and Seth Kaplan. Length: 100-3,500 words; 1,500 words average. Publishes short shorts (100-150 words). Also publishes poetry. Sometimes critiques rejected mss and recommends other markets.

How to Contact: Send complete ms in October or March *only* with cover letter. No simultaneous submissions. Reports on mss in 3 months. SASE. Sample copy for $3. May review novels or short story collections.

Payment/Terms: Pays in contributor's copies. Acquires one-time rights. Publication not copyrighted.

Advice: "We are looking for fiction which leaves the reader with a strong feeling or impression—or a new perspective on life. The *Review* began as an in-class exercise to allow experienced creative writing students to learn how a little magazine is produced. It now serves as an independent publication, attracting authors from as far away as the Ivory Coast, but its primary mission is to give unknown writers a start."

THE GREEN HILLS LITERARY LANTERN, (I, II), Published by North Central Missouri College and The North Central Missouri Writer's Guild, P.O. Box 375, Trenton MO 64683. (816)359-3948, ext. 324. E-mail: jsmith@ncmc.cc.mo.les. Editors: Jack Smith and Ken Reger. Fiction Editor: Sara King. Magazine: 5½×8½; 150-160 pages; 60 lb. natural opaque paper with vellum finish; 80 lb. text cover. "We are interested in writers whose voices make the reader listen, who offer no definite solutions—but who state the problem well. We want fiction that makes readers look more closely at their own lives." Annually. Estab. 1990.
● *The Green Hills Literary Lantern* received a Missouri Arts Council grant in 1996.

Needs: Ethnic/multicultural, experimental, feminist, humor/satire, literary, mainstream/contemporary and regional. "Fairly traditional short stories but we are open to experimental. Our main requirement is literary merit." Receives 15-20 unsolicited mss/month. Accepts 6-7 mss/issue. Publishes ms 6-12 months after acceptance. Recently published work by Geoffrey Clark, Doug Rennie, Joseph Boyden and Leslie Pietrzyk. Length: 3,000 words average; 5,000 words maximum. Publishes short shorts. Also publishes poetry. Sometimes critiques or comments on rejected mss.

How to Contact: Send complete ms with a cover letter. Include bio (50-100 words) with list of publications. Reports in 3 months on mss. SASE for return of ms. No simultaneous submissions. Sample copy for $5.95 (includes envelope and postage).

Payment/Terms: Pays two contributor's copies. Acquires one-time rights. Sends galleys to author.

Advice: "Send stories with all the subtleties of ordinary life. Make sure the language is striking. Don't tell the story. Let the story tell itself. We look for fiction which speaks to the heart, the mind, the soul—fiction which is as complex, as dense, as layered as the most simple of human existences and as subtle and as provocative as the best of literary art."

GREEN MOUNTAINS REVIEW, (II), Johnson State College, Box A-58, Johnson VT 05656. (802)635-2356, ext. 350. Editor: Neil Shepard. Fiction Editor: Tony Whedon. Magazine: digest-sized; 125-175 pages. Semiannually. Estab. 1975 (new series, 1987). Circ. 1,500.

Needs: Adventure, contemporary, experimental, humor/satire, literary, mainstream, serialized/excerpted novel, translations. Receives 80 unsolicited mss/month. Accepts 6 mss/issue; 12 mss/year. Publishes ms 6-12 months after acceptance. Reads mss September 1 through May 1. Recently published work by Lynne Sharon Schwartz, Carol Emshwiller, Ian MacMillan, Toni Graham and Ntozake Shange. Length: 25 pages maximum. Publishes short shorts. Also publishes literary criticism, poetry. Sometimes critiques rejected mss.

How to Contact: Send complete ms with cover letter. Reports in 1 month on queries; 3-6 months on mss. SASE. Simultaneous submissions OK (if advised). Sample copy for $5.

Payment/Terms: Pays contributor's copies, 1-year subscription and small honorarium, depending on grants. Acquires first North American serial rights. Rights revert to author upon request. Sends galleys to author upon request.

Advice: "The editors are open to a wide spectrum of styles and subject matter as is apparent from a look at the list of fiction writers who have published in its pages. One issue was devoted to Vermont fiction, and another issue filled with new writing from the People's Republic of China. The Spring/Summer 1994 issue was composed entirely of women's fiction."

✣GREEN'S MAGAZINE, Fiction for the Family, (I, II), Green's Educational Publications, Box 3236, Regina, Saskatchewan S4P 3H1 Canada. Editor: David Green. Magazine: 5¼×8; 100 pages; 20 lb. bond paper; matte cover stock; line illustrations. Publishes "solid short fiction suitable for family reading." Quarterly. Estab. 1972.

Needs: Adventure, fantasy, humor/satire, literary, mainstream, mystery/suspense and science fiction. No erotic or sexually explicit fiction. Receives 20-30 mss/month. Accepts 10-12 mss/issue; 40-50 mss/year. Publishes ms within 3-6 months of acceptance. Agented fiction 2%. Recently published work by David Galef, Beatrice Fines and Gerald Standley. Length: 2,500 words preferred; 1,500 words minimum; 4,000 words maximum. Also publishes poetry. Sometimes critiques rejected mss.

How to Contact: Send complete ms. "Cover letters welcome but not necessary." Reports in 2 months. SASE (or IRC). No simultaneous submissions. Sample copy for $4. Fiction guidelines for #10 SASE. Reviews novels and short story collections.

Payment/Terms: Pays in contributor's copies. Acquires first North American serial rights.

GREENSBORO REVIEW, (I, II), University of North Carolina at Greensboro, Dept. of English, Greensboro NC 27412. (910)334-5459. Fax: (910)334-3281. E-mail: clarkj@fagan.uncg.edu. Editor: Jim Clark. Fiction Editor: Steve Almond. Fiction editor changes each year. Send mss to the editor. Magazine: 6×9; approximately 136 pages; 60 lb. paper; 65 lb. cover. Literary magazine featuring fiction and poetry for readers interested in contemporary literature. Semiannually. Circ. 600.
Needs: Contemporary and experimental. Accepts 6-8 mss/issue, 12-16 mss/year. Recently published work by Steven Hayward, John Biguenet, George Singleton, Robert Olmstead, Ron McFarland, Lan Samantha Chang and Jeanne M. Leiby. Published new writers within the last year. Length: 7,500 words maximum.
How to Contact: Send complete ms with SASE. No simultaneous submissions. Unsolicited manuscripts must arrive by September 15 to be considered for the winter issue and by February 15 to be considered for the summer issue. Manuscripts arriving after those dates may be held for the next consideration. Reports in 2 months. Sample copy for $4.
Payment/Terms: Pays in contributor's copies. Acquires first North American serial rights.
Advice: "We want to see the best being written regardless of theme, subject or style. Recent stories from *The Greensboro Review* have been included in *The Best American Short Stories, Prize Stories: The O. Henry Awards, New Stories from the South* and *Best of the West*, anthologies recognizing the finest short stories being published."

GULF COAST, A Journal of Literature & Fine Arts, (II), Dept. of English, University of Houston, Houston TX 77204-3012. (713)743-3013. Contact: Fiction Editors. Editors change each year. Magazine: 6×9; 144 pages; stock paper, gloss cover; illustrations and photographs. "Innovative fiction for the literary-minded." Estab. 1984. Circ. 1,500.
● Work published in *Gulf Coast* has been selected for inclusion in the *Pushcart Prize* anthology.
Needs: Contemporary, ethnic, experimental, literary, regional, translations. No children's, religious/ inspirational. Receives 150 unsolicited mss/month. Accepts 8-10 mss/issue; 16-20 mss/year. Publishes ms 6 months-1 year after acceptance. Agented fiction 5%. Recently published work by Madison Smartt Bell, Lee K. Abbott and Tracy Daugherty. Length: no limit. Publishes short shorts. Sometimes critiques rejected mss.
How to Contact: Send complete ms with brief cover letter. "List previous publications; please notify us if the submission is being considered elsewhere." Reports in 3-6 months. Simultaneous submissions OK. Back issue for $6, 7×10 SAE and 4 first-class stamps. Fiction guidelines for #10 SASE.
Payment/Terms: Pays contributor's copies and *small* honorariam for one-time rights.
Advice: "Rotating editorship, so please be patient with replies. As always, please send one story at a time."

GULF STREAM MAGAZINE, (II), Florida International University, English Dept., North Miami Campus, N. Miami FL 33181. (305)940-5599. Editor: Lynne Barrett. Editors change every 1-2 years. Magazine: 5½×8½; 96 pages; recycled paper; 80 lb. glossy cover; cover illustrations. "We publish *good quality*—fiction, nonfiction and poetry for a predominately literary market." Semiannually. Estab. 1989. Circ. 500.
Needs: Contemporary, literary, mainstream. Nothing "radically experimental." Plans special issues. Receives 100 unsolicited mss/month. Accepts 5 mss/issue; 10 mss/year. Does not read mss during the summer. Publishes ms 3-6 months after acceptance. Published work by Alan Cheuse, Ann Hood and David Kranes. Length: 5,000 words average; 7,500 words maximum. Publishes short shorts. Also publishes poetry. Sometimes critiques rejected mss.
How to Contact: Send complete manuscript with cover letter including list of previous publications and a short bio. Reports in 3 months. SASE. Simultaneous submissions OK "if noted." Sample copy for $4. Free fiction guidelines.
Payment/Terms: Pays in gift subscriptions and contributor's copies. Acquires first North American serial rights.
Advice: "Looks for good concise writing—well plotted with interesting characters."

HALF TONES TO JUBILEE, (II), English Dept., Pensacola Junior College, 1000 College Blvd., Pensacola FL 32504. (904)484-1416. Editor: Walter Spara. Magazine: 6×9; approx. 100 pages; 70 lb. laid stock; 80 lb. cover. "No theme, all types published." Annually. Estab. 1985. Circ. 500.
Needs: Open. Accepts approx. 6 mss/issue. "We publish in September." Recently published work by Mark Spencer. Length: 1,500 words average. Publishes short shorts. Also publishes poetry. Sometimes critiques rejected mss and recommends other markets.
How to Contact: Send complete ms with cover letter. SASE. Sample copy for $4. Free fiction guidelines.
Payment/Terms: Pays 2 contributor's copies. Acquires one-time rights.
Advice: We are moving away from linear development; we are noted for innovation in style."

HAPPY, (I, II), The Happy Organization, 240 E. 35th St., 11A, New York NY 10016. (212)689-3142. E-mail: bayardx@aol.com. Editor: Bayard. Magazine: 5½×8; 68-84 pages; 60 lb. text paper; 100 lb. cover; perfect-bound; illustrations and photos. Quarterly. Estab. 1995. Circ. 500.
Needs: Erotica, ethnic/multicultural, experimental, fantasy, feminist, gay, horror, humor/satire, lesbian, literary, psychic/supernatural/occult, science fiction. Receives 300-500 unsolicited mss/month. Accepts 20 mss/issue; 80-100 mss/year. Publishes ms 6-12 months after acceptance. Length: 1,000-3,500 words average; 6,000 words maximum. Publishes short shorts. Often critiques or comments on rejected mss.
How to Contact: Send complete ms with a cover letter. Include estimated word count. Reports in 1 months on mss. Send SASE for reply, return of ms or send a disposable copy of ms. Simultaneous submissions OK. Sample copy for $7.
Payment/Terms: Pays 5¢/word, minimum $5 on publication and 1 contributor's copy for one-time rights.
Advice: "If your work is like TV—stay home and watch it."

HAYDEN'S FERRY REVIEW, (II), Box 871502, Arizona State University, Tempe AZ 85287-1502. (602)965-1243. Fax: (602)965-6704. E-mail: hfr@asuvm.inre.asu.edu. Website: http://news.vpsa.asu.edu/HFR/HFR.html. Managing Editor: Salima Keegan. Editors change every 1-2 years. Magazine: 6×9; 128 pages; fine paper; illustrations and photographs. "Contemporary material by new and established writers for a varied audience." Semiannually. Estab. 1986. Circ. 1,200.
• Work from *Hayden's Ferry Review* was selected for inclusion in the *Pushcart Prize* anthology.
Needs: Contemporary, ethnic, experimental, fantasy, feminist, gay, historical, humor/satire, literary, mainstream, prose poem, psychic/supernatural/occult, regional, romance (contemporary), science fiction, senior citizen/retirement. Possible special fiction issue. Receives 150 unsolicited mss/month. Accepts 5 mss/issue; 10 mss/year. Publishes mss 3-4 months after acceptance. Published work by T.C. Boyle, Raymond Carver, Ken Kesey, Rita Dove, Chuck Rosenthal and Rick Bass. Length: No preference. Publishes short shorts. Also publishes literary essays.
How to Contact: Send complete ms with cover letter. No simultaneous submissions. Reports in 3-5 months from deadline on mss. SASE. Sample copy for $6. Fiction guidelines for SAE.
Payment/Terms: Pays 2 contributor's copies. Acquires first North American serial rights. Sends page proofs to author.

THE HEARTLANDS TODAY, (II, IV), The Firelands Writing Center, Firelands College of BGSU, Huron OH 44839. (419)433-5560. Editors: Larry Smith and Nancy Dunham. Magazine: 6×9; 160 pages; b&w illustrations; 25-30 photographs. *Material must be set in the Midwest.* "We prefer material that reveals life in the Midwest today for a general, literate audience." Annually. Estab. 1991.
Needs: Ethnic, humor, literary, mainstream, regional (Midwest). Receives 15 unsolicited mss/month. Accepts 6 mss/issue. Does not read mss August-December. "We edit between January 1 and June 5. Submit then." Publishes ms 6 months after acceptance. Published work of Wendell Mayo, Tony Tomassi, Gloria Bowman. Length: 4,500 words maximum. Also publishes literary essays, poetry. Sometimes critiques rejected mss.
How to Contact: Send complete ms with cover letter. Reports in 2 months on mss. Send SASE for ms, not needed for query. Simultaneous submissions OK, if noted. Sample copy for $5.
Payment/Terms: Pays $20-25 on publication and 2 contributor's copies for first rights.
Advice: "We look for writing that connects on a human level, that moves us with its truth and opens our vision of the world. If writing is a great escape for you, don't bother with us. We're in it for the joy, beauty or truth of the art. We look for a straight, honest voice dealing with human experiences. We do not define the Midwest, we hope to be a document of the Midwest. If you feel you are writing from the Midwest, send your work to us. We look first at the quality of the writing."

HEAVEN BONE, (II, IV), Heaven Bone Press, Box 486, Chester NY 10918. (914)469-9018. Editors: Steven Hirsch and Kirpal Gordon. Magazine: 8½×11; 49-78 pages; 60 lb. recycled offset paper; full color cover; computer clip art, graphics, line art, cartoons, halftones and photos scanned in tiff format. "New consciousness, expansive, fine surrealist and experimental literary, earth and nature, spiritual path. We use current reviews, essays on spiritual and esoteric topics, creative stories and fantasy. Also: reviews of current poetry releases and expansive literature." Readers are "scholars, surrealists, poets, artists, musicians, students." Semiannually. Estab. 1987. Circ. 2,500.
Needs: Esoteric/scholarly, experimental, fantasy, psychic/supernatural/occult, regional, religious/inspirational, spiritual. "No violent, thoughtless or exploitive fiction." Receives 45-110 unsolicited mss/month. Accepts 5-15 mss/issue; 12-30 mss/year. Publishes ms 2 weeks-10 months after acceptance. Published work by Fielding Dawson, Janine Pommy Vega, Charles Bukowski and Marge Piercy. Published new writers within the last year. Length: 3,500 words average; 1,200 words minimum; 5,000 words maximum. Publishes short shorts. Also publishes literary essays, literary criticism, poetry. Sometimes critiques rejected mss.

How to Contact: Query first; send complete ms with cover letter. Include short bio of recent activities. Reports in 3 weeks on queries; 3 weeks-6 months on mss. Send SASE for reply or return of ms. Reprint submissions OK. Accepts electronic submissions via "Apple Mac versions of Macwrite, Microsoft Word 5.1 or Writenow 3.0." Sample copy for $6. Fiction guidelines free. Reviews novels and short story collections.

Payment/Terms: Pays in contributor's copies; charges for extras. Acquires first North American serial rights. Sends galleys to author, if requested.

Advice: "Read a sample issue first. Our fiction needs are temperamental, so please query first before submitting. We prefer shorter fiction. Do not send first drafts to test them on us. Please refine and polish your work before sending. Always include SASE. We are looking for the unique, unusual and excellent."

HIGH PLAINS LITERARY REVIEW, (II), 180 Adams St., Suite 250, Denver CO 80206. (303)320-6828. Editor-in-Chief: Robert O. Greer, Jr. Magazine: 6×9; 135 pages; 70 lb. paper; heavy cover stock. "The *High Plains Literary Review* publishes poetry, fiction, essays, book reviews and interviews. The publication is designed to bridge the gap between high-caliber academic quarterlies and successful commercial reviews." Triannually. Estab. 1986. Circ. 1,100.

Needs: Most pressing need: outstanding essays, serious fiction, contemporary, humor/satire, literary, mainstream, regional. No true confessions, romance, pornographic, excessive violence. Receives approximately 400 unsolicited mss/month. Accepts 4-6 mss/issue; 12-18 mss/year. Publishes ms usually 6 months after acceptance. Published work by Richard Currey, Joyce Carol Oates, Nancy Lord and Rita Dove. Published new writers within the last year. Length: 4,200 words average; 1,500 words minimum; 8,000 words maximum; prefers 3,000-6,000 words. Also publishes literary essays, literary criticism, poetry. Occasionally critiques rejected mss.

How to Contact: Send complete ms with cover letter. Include brief publishing history. Reports in 4 months. Send SASE for reply or return of ms. Simultaneous submissions OK. Sample copy for $4.

Payment/Terms: Pays $5/page for prose and 2 contributor's copies on publication for first North American serial rights. "Copyright reverts to author upon publication." Sends copy-edited proofs to the author.

Advice: "*HPLR* publishes *quality* writing. Send us your very best material. We will read it carefully and either accept it promptly, recommend changes or return it promptly. Do not start submitting your work until you learn the basic tenets of the game including some general knowledge about how to develop characters and plot and how to submit a manuscript. I think the most important thing for any new writer interested in the short story form is to have a voracious appetite for short fiction, to see who and what is being published, and to develop a personal style."

HILL AND HOLLER: Southern Appalachian Mountains, (II, IV), Seven Buffaloes Press, P.O. Box 249, Big Timber MT 59011. Editor: Art Cuelho. Magazine: 5½×8½; 80 pages; 70 lb. offset paper; 80 lb. cover stock; illustrations; photos rarely. "I use mostly rural Appalachian material: poems and stories, and some folklore and humor. I am interested in heritage, especially in connection with the farm." Annually. Published special fiction issue. Estab. 1983. Circ. 750.

Needs: Contemporary, ethnic, humor/satire, literary, regional, rural America farm. "I don't have any prejudices in style, but I don't like sentimental slant. Deep feelings in literature are fine, but they should be portrayed with tact and skill." Receives 10 unsolicited mss/month. Accepts 4-6 mss/issue. Publishes ms 6 months-1 year after acceptance. Length: 2,000-3,000 words average. Also publishes short shorts of 500-1,000 words.

How to Contact: Query first. Reports in 2 weeks on queries. SASE. Sample copy for $6.75.

Payment/Terms: Pays in contributor's copies. Acquires first North American serial rights "and permission to reprint if my press publishes a special anthology." Sometimes sends galleys to author.

Advice: "In this Southern Appalachian rural series I can be optimistic about fiction. Appalachians are very responsive to their region's literature. I have taken work by beginners that had not been previously published. Be sure to send a double-spaced clean manuscript and SASE. I have the only rural press in North America; maybe even in the world. So perhaps we have a bond in common if your roots are rural."

HOME PLANET NEWS, (II), Home Planet Publications, P. O. Box 415, New York NY 10009. (718)769-2854. Tabloid: 11½×16; 24 pages; newsprint; illustrations; photos. "*Home Planet News*

● **A BULLET INTRODUCES COMMENTS** by the editor of *Novel & Short Story Writer's Market* indicating special information about the listing.

publishes mainly poetry along with some fiction, as well as reviews (books, theater and art), and articles of literary interest. We see *HPN* as a quality literary journal in an eminently readable format and with content that is urban, urbane and politically aware." Triannually. Estab. 1979. Circ. 1,000.

● *HPN* has received a small grant from the Puffin Foundation for its focus on AIDS issues.

Needs: Ethnic/multicultural, experimental, feminist, gay, historical, lesbian, literary, mainstream/contemporary, science fiction (soft/sociological). No "children's or genre stories (except rarely some science fiction)." Upcoming themes: "AIDS." Publishes special fiction issue or anthology. Receives 12 mss/month. Accepts 1 ms/issue; 3 mss/year. Reads fiction mss only from February to May. Publishes 1 year after acceptance. Published work by Maureen McNeil, Eugene Stein, B.Z. Niditch and Layle Silbert. Length: 2,500 words average; 500 words minimum; 3,000 words maximum. Publishes short shorts. Also publishes literary criticism, poetry.

How to Contact: Send complete ms with a cover letter. Reports in 3-6 months on mss. Send SASE for reply, return of ms or send a disposable copy of the ms. Sample copy for $3. Fiction guidelines for SASE.

Payment/Terms: Pays 3 contributor's copies; additional copies $1. Acquires one-time rights.

Advice: "We use very little fiction, and a story we accept just has to grab us. We need short pieces of some complexity, stories about complex people facing situations which resist simple resolutions."

THE HOPEWELL REVIEW 1996: New Work by Indiana's Best Writers, (II, IV), 409 Tyrone Dr., Muncie IN 47304. (317)284-9456. Editor: Joseph F. Trimmer. Magazine: 5½×8½; 128 pages; perfect bound. "*The Hopewell Review* is an annual anthology of fiction, poetry and essays. The primary criterion for selection is high literary quality." Annually. Estab. 1989.

Needs: Condensed/excerpted novel, contemporary, experimental, humor/satire, literary, prose poem, regional, translations. "Writers must currently live in Indiana or have an extraordinary tie." Receives 1,200 unsolicited mss/year. Accepts 4-6 mss/issue. Publishes annually (September). Recently published work by Scott Russell Sanders, Susan Neville, Barbara Shoup and Julie Herrick White.. Length: 4,000 words maximum. Sometimes critiques rejected mss.

How to Contact: Send complete ms with cover letter. Include brief biography. Annual deadline: March 1. Notification: June. SASE. Simultaneous submissions OK with notification. Sample copy for $6.95 and $2.50 postage. Fiction guidelines for SASE.

Payment/Terms: Pays $125-625 ($500 award of excellence) and 2 contributor's copies on publication for first rights and one-time rights; charges for additional copies.

Advice: "Fresh perspectives and use of the English language make a manuscript stand out."

THE HUNTED NEWS, (I, II), The Subourban Press, P.O. Box 9101, Warwick RI 02889. (401)739-2279 or (401)826-7307. Editor: Mike Wood. Magazine: 8½×11; 30-35 pages; photocopied paper. "I am looking for good writers in the hope that I can help their voices be heard. Like most in the small press scene, I just wanted to create another option for writers who otherwise might not be heard." Annually. Estab. 1991. Circ. 200.

Needs: Experimental, historical, horror, literary, mainstream/contemporary, regional, religious/inspirational, translations. "No self-impressed work, shock or experimentation for its own sake." Receives 50-60 unsolicited mss/month. Acquires 3 mss/issue. Publishes ms within 3-4 months after acceptance. Published work by Janet Daily, Darryl Smyers and Charles Bukowski. Length: 700 words maximum. Publishes short shorts. Also publishes literary essays, literary criticism and poetry. Often critiques or comments on rejected mss.

How to Contact: Send complete ms with cover letter. Reports in 1 month. Send SASE for return of ms. Simultaneous and reprint submissions OK. Sample copy for 8½×11 SAE and 3 first-class stamps. Fiction guidelines free. Reviews novels or short story collections.

Payment/Terms: Pays 3-5 contributor's copies. Acquires one-time rights.

Advice: "I look for an obvious love of language and a sense that there is something at stake in the story, a story that somehow needs to be told. Write what you need to write, say what you think you need to say, no matter the subject, and send it to me. A writer will always find an audience if the work is true."

‡HYPHEN MAGAZINE, (II), P.O. Box 10481, Chicago IL 60610. (312)465-5985. E-mail: ingebret @interaccess.com. Editor/Publisher: Mark Ingebretsen. Fiction Editor: Serafina Chamberlin. Magazine: 8½×11; 80 pages; white bond paper; glossy cover; illustrations and photos. Purpose is "to present art and writing and ideas that have an impact: work that makes you think, makes you laugh, breaks your heart or takes your breath away. *Hyphen* seeks to demystify art by building bridges and exploring common ground between the arts. Recent interviews have included writer Mark Amerika and performance artist Ron Athey. Multicultural, multidisiplinary, eclectic and unorthodox in outlook and tastes." Triannually. Estab. 1991. Circ. 1,500.

Needs: Well-written fiction, reviews, interviews. Receives about 30 unsolicited mss/month. Accepts 4 mss/issue; 12 mss/year. Publishes ms 2-6 months after acceptance. Recently published work by Evangeline Blanco and Meg Satterthwaite. Length: 2,500 words average; 6,000 words maximum.

Publishes short shorts. Length: 100-400 words. Also publishes poetry, art, photography, interviews, essays. Comments on rejected mss if requested.

How To Contact: Send complete ms with cover letter. Include a 1-paragraph bio with submission. Reports in 1 month on queries; 4-5 months on mss. Send SASE for reply, return of ms or send disposable copy of ms. Simultaneous submissions OK. Sample copy for $6. Guidelines for #10 SASE. Reviews novels and short story collections.

Payment/Terms: Pays 2 contributor's copies, subscription. Additional copies for $3. Acquires first North American serial rights or one-time rights.

Advice: Looks for "committed and vigorous writing. Never send a first draft, but never forget your first impulse. If the story doesn't move you, it will not move anyone else."

i.e. magazine: A Journal of Literature and the Arts, (II), P.O. Box 73403, Houston TX 77273-3403. E-mail: yoly@flex.net. Managing Editor: Yolande Gottlieb. Fiction Editor: Augusta Griffith. Nonfiction Editor: John Gorman. Nonprofit magazine: digest-sized; 48-50 pages; 70 lb. glossy paper; 80 lb. glossy cover; illustrations and photos. "*i.e. magazine* is open to different themes. We want quality, innovative, imaginative stories for a literary audience." Quarterly. Estab. 1990. Circ. 200.

Needs: Adventure, experimental, fantasy, historical, humor/satire, literary, mainstream/contemporary, mystery/suspense, romance, science fiction, translations, play reviews (with photos; "large metropolitan area theaters only"), visual arts. Receives 50 unsolicited mss/month. Accepts 4-5 mss/issue; 46-48 mss/year. Publishes ms 3-6 months after acceptance. Recently published work by Lee Nelson and Eric Muirhead. Publishes short shorts. Also publishes literary essays, literary criticism, poetry. Sometimes critiques or comments on rejected mss.

How to Contact: Send complete ms with a cover letter. Include estimated word count, bio (maximum ½ page), Social Security number, list of publications and 2×2 photo to include with bio when story is printed. Reports in 3-4 weeks on queries; 2-4 months on mss. Send SASE for reply, return of ms or send a disposable copy of ms. No simultaneous submissions. Sample copy for $6 postpaid. Guidelines for #10 SAE and 2 first-class stamps.

Payment/Terms: Pays 1-2 contributor's copies on publication; additional copies available. Acquires one-time rights. Sponsors contests: fiction, nonfiction, poetry, poetry chapbooks and visual arts. Send SASE for contest guidelines.

Advice: "We suggest contributors familiarize themselves with our editorial preferences."

THE ICONOCLAST, (II), 1675 Amazon Rd., Mohegan Lake NY 10547. Editor: Phil Wagner. Journal. 8½×5½; 28-32 pages; 20 lb. white paper; 20 lb. cover stock; illustrations. "*The Iconoclast* is a self-supporting, independent, unaffiliated general interest magazine with an appreciation of the profound, absurd and joyful in life. Material is limited only by *its* quality and *our* space. We want readers and writers who are open-minded, unafraid to think, and actively engaged with the world." Published 8 times/year. Estab. 1992. Circ. 500.

● *The Iconoclast* has grown from a 16-page newsletter to a 28-32-page journal and is, subsequently, buying more fiction.

Needs: Adventure, ethnic/multicultural, humor/satire, literary, mainstream/contemporary, science fiction. "Nothing militant, solipsistic, or silly." Receives 50 unsolicited mss/month. Accepts 3-4 mss/issue; 15-20 mss/year. Publishes ms 6-9 months after acceptance. Recently published work by Ben Pastor, Robert C. Smith and Barbara Westwood Diehl. Length: 2,000-2,500 words preferred; 100 words minimum; occasionally longer. Publishes short shorts. Also publishes essays, criticism and poetry. Often critiques or comments on rejected mss.

How to Contact: Send complete ms. Reports in 1 month. Send SASE for reply, return of ms or send a disposable copy of the ms. Simultaneous and reprint submissions OK, when noted. Sample copy for $1.75. Reviews novels and short story collections.

Payment/Terms: Pays 1-2 contributor's copies; additional copies $1.05 (40% discount). Acquires one-time rights.

Advice: "We like fiction that has something to say (and not about its author). We hope for work that is observant, intense and multi-leveled. Follow Pound's advice—'make it new.' Write what you want in whatever style you want without being gross, sensational, or needlessly explicit—then pray there's someone who can appreciate your sensibility."

‡THE IDIOT, (II), Anarchaos Press, 40 Edgelea Dr, Chambersburg PA 17201, (216)257-3321. Editor: Sam Hayes. Magazine: 5½×8½; 48 pages; 20 lb. white paper; glossy cardboard cover; illustrations. "For people who enjoy TV shows such as 'The Simpsons' and 'Mystery Science Theater 3000' as well as those who like Woody Allen and S.J. Perelman. I've had letters from engineers to teenagers saying they loved it, so you have to be both funny and weird and sophisticated all at once." Semiannually. Estab. 1993. Circ. 250.

Needs: Humor/satire. Publishes ms 4-8 months after acceptance. Recently published work by Freud Pachenko, Harry Huffenhoffer and Joe Deasy. Length: 1,500 words average; 2,500 words maximum. Publishes short shorts. Also publishes poetry. Sometimes critiques or comments on rejected mss.

How to Contact: Send complete ms with a cover letter. Include estimated word count and bio (30-50 words). Reports in 1 month on queries; 3 months on mss. Send SASE for reply, return of ms or send a disposable copy of ms. Simultaneous, reprint and electronic submissions OK. Sample copy for $5.

Payment/Terms: Pays 1-2 contributor's copies. Acquires one-time rights. Sometimes sends galleys to author.

Advice: "Do not send anything if it isn't hilarious. If I don't laugh out loud by the second page I stop reading. It must be consistently funny—most submissions are merely 'cute.' Also, read the magazine to see what we're doing."

‡**IMAGE, A Journal of the Arts & Religion, (II)**, Hillsdale Review Inc., 323 S. Broad St., P.O. Box 674, Kennett Square PA 19348. Phone/fax: (610)444-8065. E-mail: 73424.1024@compuserve.c om. Editor: Greg Wolfe. Magazine: 7×10; 140 pages; glossy cover stock; illustrations and photos. "*Image* is a showcase for the encounter between religious faith and world-class contemporary art. Each issue features fiction, poetry, essays, memoirs, an in-depth interview and articles about visual artists, film, music, etc. and glossy 4-color plates of contemporary visual art." Quarterly. Estab. 1989. Circ. 4,200. Member CLMP.

- Two essays from *Image* were included as honorable mentions in *Best American Essays*, 1995.

Needs: Humor/satire, literary, regional, religious/inspirational, translations. Receives 40 unsolicited mss/month. Accepts 2 mss/issue; 8 mss/year. Publishes ms within 1 year after acceptance. Agented fiction 5%. Recently published work by Madison Smartt Bell, Tim Winton, Wally Lamb, Jon Hassler, Ron Hansen and Lawrence Dorr. Length: 5,000 words average; 2,000 words minimum; 8,000 words maximum. Also publishes literary essays and poetry.

How to Contact: Send complete ms with a cover letter. Include bio. Reports in 1 month on queries; 3 months on mss. Send SASE for reply, return of ms or send a disposable copy of ms. Electronic (disk or modem) submissions OK. Sample copy for $10. Reviews novels and short story collections.

Payment/Terms: Pays $100 maximum and 4 contributor's copies on publication; additional copies for $5. Sends galleys to author.

Advice: "Fiction must have a religious aspect to it."

‡**IMPLOSION, A Journal of the Bizarre and Eccentric, (II)**, P.O. Box 533653, Orlando FL 32853. (407)645-3924. E-mail: smudge21@aol.com. Editor: Cynthia Conlin. Magazine: $8\frac{1}{2} \times 11$; 60 pages; 50 lb. glossy paper; 80 lb. glossy cover stock; illustrations and photos. "*Implosion* explores the odd and bizarre side of human existence. It seeks out all things highly unusual." Quarterly. Estab. 1995. Circ. 12,000.

Needs: Adventure, experimental (science fantasy), horror, psychic/supernatural/occult, science fiction (hard science, soft/sociological). Especially interested in "material with weird and bizarre themes and overtones." Receives 100 mss/month. Accepts 5-7 mss/issue; 25-30 mss/year. Publishes ms 4-7 months after acceptance. Recently published work by J. Spencer Dreischarf, Bert Benmeyer, D.F. Lewis and Rick Reed. Length: 2,000 words average; 12,000 words maximum. Publishes short shorts. Also publishes literary criticism and poetry. Sometimes critiques or comments on rejected mss.

How to Contact: Send complete ms with cover letter. Include estimated word count and list of publications. Reports in 2-3 months on mss. Send SASE for reply, return of ms or send a disposable copy of ms. Simultaneous, reprint and electronic (e-mail) submissions OK. Sample copy for $5. Guidelines for SASE. Reviews novels and short story collections. Send books to editor.

Payment/Terms: Pays 1-2¢/word on acceptance and 2 contributor's copies; additional copies for $3. Acquires first or one-time rights. Sends galleys to author.

Advice: "We want new ideas and concepts, not clichéd rehashes of 'Twilight Zone' plots. A bit of humor doesn't hurt, either. Remember that 'bizarre' doesn't mean silly or pointless. Check your work for grammatical errors and the like—there's no greater turnoff than poorly constructed manuscripts."

‡**IN THE SPIRIT OF THE BUFFALO, A Literary Magazine (I)**, In the Spirit of the Buffalo, 3430 S. 40th St., Lincoln NE 68506. (402)488-0333. Fax: (402)464-1604. E-mail: buffalo369@aol.c om. Editor: Mark A. Reece. Newsletter: 11×14; 4 pages; newsprint; illustrations and photos. "*ITSOTB* showcases the human condition and our ability to survive. We publish poetry, short fiction, essays, cartoons, puzzles and artwork targeted toward adults who enjoy self-expression." Quarterly. Estab. 1996. Circ. 1,000.

Needs: Adventure, fantasy, historical, horror, humor/satire, literary, regional, science fiction (soft/ sociological), westerns. "No erotica or sword and sorcery." Receives 4-5 unsolicited mss/month. Accepts 1 ms/issue; 4 mss/year. Publishes ms within 4 months after acceptance. Recently published work by Brad Duncan. Length: 800 words average; 500 words minimum; 1,200 words maximum. Publishes short shorts. Also publishes literary essays and poetry. Sometimes critiques or comments on rejected mss.

How to Contact: Send complete ms with a cover letter or send e-mail. Include ½-page bio. Reports in 3 months on mss. SASE for return of ms. No simultaneous submissions. Reprints and electronic submissions (e-mail) OK. Sample copy and fiction guidelines for #10 SASE.

Payment/Terms: Pays 5 contributor's copies on publication; additional copies for 50¢. Acquires one-time rights.

Advice: "I like good dialogue between characters, characters people can relate to and a subtle lesson or moral that makes the story worth reading. Keep the work under 1,200 words, proofread and use dialogue. The story should have a purpose. I haven't seen enough short shorts with impact and development."

INDIANA REVIEW, (I, II), 465 Ballantine, Bloomington IN 47405. (812)855-3439. Editor: Geoffrey Pollock. Editors change every 2 years. Magazine: 6×9; 200 pages; 50 lb. paper; Glatfelter cover stock. *Indiana Review* is a "magazine of contemporary fiction and poetry in which there is a zest for language, a relationship between form and content, and awareness of the world. For fiction writers/readers, followers of lively contemporary prose." Semiannually. Estab. 1976. Circ. 3,000.

● Work published in *Indiana Review* was selected for inclusion in the *O. Henry Prize Stories* anthology.

Needs: Ethnic, literary, regional, translations. Also considers novel excerpts. Receives 300 unsolicited mss each month. Accepts 7-9 prose mss/issue. Recently published work by Lisa Glait, Danit Braun and Wendell Mays. Length: 1-35 magazine pages. Also publishes literary essays, poetry.

How to Contact: Send complete ms with cover letter. "Cover letters need to be concise and to the point. Encapsulating a piece's theme or content is unacceptable." SASE. Simultaneous submissions OK (if notified *immediately* of other publication). Reports in 3 months. Publishes ms an average of 2-4 months after acceptance. Sample copy for $7.

Payment/Terms: Pays $5/page and 2 contributor's copies for North American serial rights.

Advice: "We look for prose that is well-crafted, socially relevant. We are interested in innovation, unity and social context. All genres that meet some of these criteria are welcome."

‡INTERIM, (II), Dept. of English, University of Nevada, Las Vegas NV 89154. (702)739-3172. Editor and Founder: A. Wilber Stevens. Magazine: 6×9; 48-64 pages; heavy paper; semigloss cover with illustration. Publishes "poetry and short fiction for a serious, educated audience." However, they focus more on poetry than fiction. Semiannually. Estab. 1944; revived 1986. Circ. 600-800.

Needs: Contemporary, experimental, literary. Accepts 1-2 mss/issue. Publishes ms 6 months to 1 year of acceptance. Recently published work by G.K. Wvori and Evelyn Livingston. Length: 4,000 words preferred; 7,500 words maximum.

How to Contact: Send complete ms with cover letter. Reports on mss in 4-6 weeks. SASE. Sample copy for $5.

Payment/Terms: Pays in contributor's copies and two-year subscription to magazine.

Advice: Looks for "strong characters, engaging story lines and solid, meaningful endings."

INTERNATIONAL QUARTERLY, Essays, Fiction, Drama, Poetry, Art, Reviews, (II), P.O. Box 10521, Tallahassee FL 32302-0521. (904)224-5078. Fax: (904)224-5127. Editor: Van K. Brock. Magazine: 7½×10; 176 pages; 50 lb. text paper; 60 lb. gloss cover; fine art illustrations. "*International Quarterly* seeks to bridge boundaries between national, ethnic and cultural identities, and among creative disciplines, by providing a venue for dialogue between exceptional writers and artists and discriminating readers. We look for work that reveals character and place from within." Quarterly. Estab. 1993.

Needs: Ethnic/multicultural, experimental, humor/satire, literary, mainstream/contemporary, regional, translations. "We would consider work in any of the genres that transcends the genre through quality of language, characterization and development. Our sympathies are strongly feminist. Many of the genre categories imply simplistic and limited literary purposes. Any genre can transcend its limits." No issue is limited to work on its regional or thematic focus." Accepts 5 mss/issue; 20 mss/year. "We read all year, but fewer readers are active in July and August." Publishes ms 3-9 months after acceptance. Published work by Edmund Keeley, Iván Mándy, Gary Corgeri, S.P. Elledge. Publishes short shorts. Also publishes literary essays, literary criticism (for general readers), poetry. Sometimes critiques or comments on rejected mss.

How to Contact: Query first or send complete ms with a cover letter. Include estimated word count, bio, list of publications. Include rights available. "We prefer first rights for all original English texts." Reports in 1-2 weeks on queries; 2-4 months on mss. Send SASE for reply, return of ms or send a disposable copy of ms. Simultaneous, reprint (please specify) and electronic submissions OK. Sample copy for $6 (a reduced rate) and 4 first-class stamps. Fiction guidelines for #10 SASE. Reviews novels and short story collections. Send books to Book Review Editor.

Payment/Terms: Pays free subscription to magazine and 1 contributor's copy. Acquires first North American serial rights. Sends galleys to author.

Advice: "We would like to see more fiction break out of conventional thinking and set fictional modes without straining or trying to shock and fiction that presents the world of its characters from inside the skin of the culture, rather than those outside of the culture, tourists or short-termers, as it were,

INSIDER REPORT

The Iowa Review: committed to publishing new voices

"Work hard at what you want to write," advises David Hamilton, now in his twentieth year as editor of *The Iowa Review.* "Don't try to outguess magazines and their editors—don't snoop around and try to figure out what we want." According to Hamilton, new writers need most to write what they are committed to and feel passionate about.

Such a philosophy reflects the spirit with which *The Iowa Review* has evolved over the years since its inaugural issue in 1970. Although the magazine began as a typical small university review that featured contemporary critical essays as the dominant genre, Hamilton has allowed fiction and poetry to take precedence over the essay. It only follows that the prominence assigned to these genres has opened

David Hamilton

the door to new fiction writers and poets. Hamilton points out that writers like T.C. Boyle and Mona Simpson who now publish in high-paying commercial magazines got started in literary journals like *The Iowa Review.*

Since assuming editorship in 1977, Hamilton has remained committed to giving new writers exposure in *The Iowa Review*: "We do like to be open to new writers—that's one of the things we pride ourselves on." While he admits the advantages to publishing in a literary journal "certainly aren't financial," there decidedly are advantages. "Smaller magazines serve as a proving ground for new writers. You get exposure, recognition. People see you; some work gets selected for prize volumes. Sometimes agents notice the work and write letters that say, 'How can we get in touch with so-and-so?' and sometimes books come from that." As Hamilton reasons, exposure in a high-quality literary magazine helps a writer build up a record of publishing, which may attract editors at major publishing houses.

Of particular importance to Hamilton is publishing fresh voices outside the academic community, from whom a significant proportion of the offerings in *The Iowa Review* come. Despite the obvious advantage of being tied to a university with modest financial support and dependable editorial assistance, *The Iowa Review*'s association with the academic world also has its drawbacks. "We are more or less locked into a university community, so we see less of life in other circumstances," Hamilton says. "Most of the writers who send work to us are either in or have been in creative writing programs, and that means middle-class, college-educated America is the locus of most of this work. I'm not against an academic story, but I certainly don't want an issue full of them."

In reaching out for new voices, part of *The Iowa Review*'s mission is to better represent America's diversity by including more minorities and other marginalized voices. But this isn't always easy. "The fact is we get fewer offerings from minorities," says Hamilton. In some cases, he says a particular effort has been made to ensure these voices find their way onto the pages of *The Iowa Review*. The all-poetry issue of fall 1996, for instance, featured a guest editor with connections to a number of Black writers, which resulted in an issue with more minority participation than usual. Still, says Hamilton, minority work doesn't come in the proportions they'd like.

While the magazine is looking for ways to attract a variety of new voices, Hamilton admits, "We run the risk of seeming hypocritical because we're going to turn a lot of submissions down. But we turn a lot of everything down." Hamilton estimates that the magazine must reject about 95-98% of what comes in. This may seem high, but with the exception of three recent genre-specific issues (all poetry, all fiction, all essay), most issues include 98% unsolicited work as selected by the editorial staff. So while only a small percentage of submissions actually make it onto the pages of *The Iowa Review*, a large portion of the work in the regular issues comes from relatively unknown writers. In keeping with its mission, the staff tries to present as wide a variety of American voices as possible in these issues.

Hamilton credits his long-time assistant Mary Hussmann and a team of graduate students with ensuring each of these voices is considered for publication. "In many ways, Mary's the secret editor of the magazine," says Hamilton. Although editing *The Iowa Review* has increasingly become his major role at the university, Hamilton still teaches one or two classes a semester, usually in modern or contemporary poetry, which is a little "closer to the life of the magazine" than the Shakespeare and Chaucer he taught for years. "Without the good help of the graduate students and Mary, I don't see how I could also be a professor." And with hundreds of submissions each week, there's plenty to do. "During the school year when we're most active, there are always manuscripts coming in, there are always manuscripts being returned, and there's always some effort to isolate six or seven stories that we can look at more closely . . . and you make some choices." Admittedly, says Hamilton, these are sometimes hard choices to make.

Still, his advice remains: "Work hard at what *you* want to write." In many ways, the evolution of *The Iowa Review* from a typical small university critical review to a journal of fiction and poetry on the lookout for new voices is testament to Hamilton's own commitment to the work he has felt passionate about for 20 years. His formula has remained a simple one: "Ours seemed to me a nice way to run a magazine, so that's the way we did it."

—*Carla Thomas*

commenting on the world of a story's subjects from outside, lamenting that it has fallen into our consumerist ways, etc., lamentable as that may be. Works we publish do not have to be foreign, they may arise out of a profound understanding of any culture or locale, as long as they provide the reader with an authentic experience of that locale, whatever the origin of the author. We have no taboos, but we want writing that understands and creates understanding, writers who want to go beyond cultural givens."

THE IOWA REVIEW, (II), University of Iowa, 308 EPB, Iowa City IA 52242. (319)335-0462. Editor: David Hamilton. Associate Editor: Mary Hussmann. Magazine: 6×9; 200 pages; first-grade offset paper; Carolina CS1 10-pt. cover stock. "Stories, essays, poems for a general readership interested in contemporary literature." Triannually. Estab. 1970. Circ. 1,200.
● Work published in *Iowa Review* regularly has been selected for inclusion in the *Pushcart Prize* and *Best American Short Stories* anthologies. The editors are especially interested in work from minority writers or those whose "voices have been marginalized."
Needs: Literary, ethnic. Receives 150-200 unsolicited fiction mss/month. Agented fiction less than 10%. Accepts 4-5 mss/issue, 12-16 mss/year. Does not read mss April-August. Published work by Curtis White, Kathy Acker, and Sherley Anne Williams. Published new writers within the last year. Also publishes literary essays, literary criticism, poetry.
How to Contact: Send complete ms with SASE. "Don't bother with queries." Simultaneous submissions OK. Reports in 2-4 months on mss. Publishes ms an average of 4-12 months after acceptance. Sample copy for $5. Reviews novels and short story collections (3-6 books/year).
Payment/Terms: Pays $10/page on publication and 2 contributor's copies; additional copies 30% off cover price. Acquires first North American serial rights.

IOWA WOMAN, (II), P.O. Box 680, Iowa City IA 52244-0680. Contact: Editorial Collective. Nonprofit magazine "dedicated to encouraging and publishing women writers and artists internationally." Quarterly. Estab. 1979. Circ. 2,000.
● *Iowa Woman* has received numerous awards and honors including Iowa Community Cultural Grant Awards. The magazine has also had essays and fiction included in the *Best American Essays* and *Best American Short Stories*. In 1995 the magazine celebrated its 15th anniversary with a retrospective anthology "The Best of Iowa Woman."
Needs: Historical, literary, regional, women's. Receives 200 unsolicited mss/month. Accepts 3 mss/ issue; 12 mss/year. Length: 6,500 words maximum. Also publishes literary essays, book reviews, and sponsors annual contest.
How to Contact: Send complete ms. Reports in 3 months. SASE. Sample copy for $6.95. Fiction or contest guidelines for SASE. Reviews novels and short story collections. Send books to Kristen Gandrow, Books Editor.
Payment/Terms: Pays $5/published page when funds are available and 2 contributor's copies; additional copies $4. Acquires first serial rights. Offers advertising discounts to writers and artists published in *Iowa Woman*.
Advice: "Our editorial collective often responds with rejections. We want strong character-driven stories with women or women's experience as the center."

IRIS: A Journal About Women, (II, IV), Box 323 HSC, University of Virginia, Charlottesville VA 22908. (804)924-4500. Fiction Editor: Kristen Staby Rembold. Managing Editor: Susan Brady. Magazine: 8½×11; 72 pages; glossy paper; heavy cover; illustrations and photographs. "Material of particular interest to women. For a feminist audience, college educated and above." Semiannually. Estab. 1980. Circ. 3,500.
Needs: Experimental, feminist, lesbian, literary, mainstream. "I don't think what we're looking for particularly falls into the 'mainstream' category—we're just looking for well-written stories of interest to women (particularly feminist women)." Receives 300 unsolicited mss/year. Accepts 5 mss/year. Publishes ms within 1 year after acceptance. Length: 4,000 words average. Sometimes critiques rejected mss.
How to Contact: Send complete ms with cover letter. Include "previous publications, vocation, other points that pertain. Make it brief!" Reports in 3 months on mss. SASE. Simultaneous submissions OK. Accepts electronic submissions via disk or modem. Sample copy for $5. Fiction guidelines for #10 SASE.
Payment/Terms: Pays in contributor's copies and 1 year subscription. Acquires one-time rights.
Advice: "I select mss which are lively imagistically as well as in the here-and-now; I select for writing which challenges the reader. My major complaint is with stories that don't elevate the language above the bland sameness we hear on the television and everyday. Read the work of the outstanding women writers, such as Alice Munroe and Louise Erdrich."

JANUS, A JOURNAL OF LITERATURE, (III), Janus, P.O. Box 376, Collingswood NJ 08108. Editors: David Livewell and Scott Jermyn. Magazine: 5½×8½; 30 pages. "We are interested in the well-crafted fiction of new and established writers and offer a forum where the two can coexist in an exciting way." Biannually. Circ. 500.

Needs: Literary, mainstream/contemporary. "We do not accept pornography, autobiography, or nonsense fiction in the guise of 'stream of consciousness' prose." Receives 20 unsolicited mss/month. Accepts 2 mss/issue. Publishes ms in next available issue. Recently published work by Fred Chappell and Cary Holladay. Length: 10-15 typed pages. Also publishes literary essays, literary criticism and poetry. Often critiques or comments on rejected mss.

How to Contact: Send complete ms with a cover letter. Include 1-paragraph bio and list of publications. Reports in 2 weeks on queries; 2 months on mss. SASE for reply. No simultaneous submissions.

Payment/Terms: Pays in contributor's copies. Acquires first North American serial rights.

Advice: "We like to see that a great deal of time and attention went into a story, that all elements—characterization, plot, imagery, rhetorical devices—are fittingly assembled in order to create a moving story."

JAPANOPHILE, (I, II, IV), Box 223, Okemos MI 48864. (517)669-2109. E-mail: japanlove@aol.com. Editor-in-Chief: Earl Snodgrass. Magazine: 5¼×8½; 58 pages; illustrations; photos. Magazine of "articles, photos, poetry, humor, short stories about Japanese culture, not necessarily set in Japan, for an adult audience, most with a college background and who like to travel." Quarterly. Estab. 1974. Circ. 800.

● Most of the work included in *Japanophile* is set in recent times, but the magazine will accept material set back as far as pre-WWII.

Needs: Adventure, historical, humor/satire, literary, mainstream, and mystery/suspense. Published special fiction issue last year; plans another. Receives 40-100 unsolicited fiction mss/month. Accepts 12 ms/issue, 20-30 mss/year. Recently published work by Barbara Fuller, Mary Waters and Forrest Johnson. Published new writers within the last year. Length: 4,000 words average; 2,000 words minimum; 6,000 words maximum. Also publishes essays, book reviews, literary criticism and poetry.

How to Contact: Send complete ms with SASE, cover letter, bio and information about story. Simultaneous and reprint submissions OK. Reports in 3 months on mss. Sample copy for $4; guidelines for #10 SASE.

Payment/Terms: Pays $20 on publication for all rights, first North American serial rights or one-time rights (depends on situation). Stories submitted to the magazine may be entered in the annual contest. *A $5 entry fee must accompany each submission* to enter contest. Prizes include $100 plus publication for the best short story. Deadline: December 31.

Advice: "Short stories usually involve Japanese and 'foreign' (non-Japanese) characters in a way that contributes to understanding of Japanese culture and the Japanese people. However, a *good* story dealing with Japan or Japanese cultural aspects anywhere in the world will be considered, even if it does not involve this encounter or meeting of Japanese and foreign characters. Some stories may also be published in an anthology with approval of the author and additional payment."

JEOPARDY, Literary Arts Magazine, (II), CH 132, Western Washington University, Bellingham WA 98225. (360)650-3118. Editor: James Houle. Editors change every year. Magazine: 6×9; 192 pages; 70 lb. paper; glossy cover stock; illustrations and photographs. "*Jeopardy Magazine*'s intended audience is an intelligent readership which enjoys risks, surprises and subtlety. Our philosophy is that reputation is nothing and words/images are everything." Annually. Estab. 1965. Circ. 1,000.

Needs: Adventure, contemporary, erotica, ethnic, experimental, feminist, gay, historical, humor/satire, lesbian, literary. No long stories. Receives 50-100 unsolicited mss/month. Accepts 4-8 mss/year. Does not read mss January 15-September 1. Publishes mss 3 months after acceptance. Length: 1,500 words average; 250 words minimum; 5,000 words maximum. Also publishes literary essays, poetry.

How to Contact: Send complete ms with cover letter and 50-word bio. SASE and disposable copy of the ms. Does not return mss. Simultaneous submissions OK. Reports in 1-6 months. Sample copy for $5. Fiction guidelines for #10 SASE.

Payment/Terms: Pays 1 contributor's copy. Acquires one-time rights.

Advice: "A clear, insightful voice and style are major considerations. Things that will get your manuscript recycled: tired representations of sex and/or death and/or angst. We like writers who take risks! Know your characters thoroughly—know why someone else would want to read about what they think or do. Then, submit your work and don't give up at initial failures. Don't send us stories

---

READ THE BUSINESS OF FICTION WRITING section to learn the correct way to prepare and submit a manuscript.

about being a writer/artist and/or a college student/professor. We would like to see more fiction pieces which involve unique or unexpected situations and characters."

THE JOURNAL, (II), Dept of English, Ohio State University, 164 W. 17th St., Columbus OH 43210. (614)292-4076. Editors: Kathy Fagan (poetry); Michelle Herman (fiction). Magazine: 6×9; 100 pages. "We are open to all forms of quality fiction." For an educated, general adult audience. Semiannually. Estab. 1973. Circ. 1,300.
Needs: "Interested in all literary forms." No romance or religious/devotional. Accepts 2 mss/issue. Receives approximately 100 unsolicited fiction mss/month. "Usually" publishes ms within 1 year of acceptance. Agented fiction 10%. Recently published work by Nell Beram, Kay Sloan, Mark Jacobs and Duncan Greenlaw. Published new writers within the last year. Length: Open. Also accepts poetry. Critiques rejected mss when there is time.
How to Contact: Send complete ms with cover letter. Reports "as soon as possible," usually 3 months. SASE. Sample copy for $5.50; fiction guidelines for SASE.
Payment/Terms: Pays $25 stipend when funds are available; contributor's copies; $5.50 charge for extras.
Terms: Acquires First North American serial rights. Sends galleys to author.
Advice: Mss are rejected because of "lack of understanding of the short story form, shallow plots, undeveloped characters. Cure: read as much well-written fiction as possible. Our readers prefer 'psychological' fiction rather than stories with intricate plots. Take care to present a clean, well-typed submission."

THE JOURNAL, (I, II), Poetry Forum, 5713 Larchmont Dr., Erie PA 16509. Phone/fax: (814)866-2543. (Faxing hours: 8-10 a.m. and 5-8 p.m.) E-mail: 75562.670@compuserve.com. Editor: Gunvor Skogsholm. Journal: 5½×8½; 18-20 pages; light card cover. Looks for "good writing—for late teens to full adulthood." Quarterly. Estab. 1989. Circ. 200.
  ● *The Journal* is edited by Gunvor Skogsholm, the editor of *Poetry Forum Short Stories* and *Short Stories Bimonthly*. This magazine is not strictly a pay-for-publication, "subscribers come first.'
Needs: Mainstream. Plans annual special fiction issue. Receives 25-30 unsolicited mss/month. Accepts 1 ms/issue; 7-10 mss/year. Publishes mss 2 weeks to 7 months after acceptance. Agented fiction 1%. Length: 500 words preferred; 300 words average; 150 words minimum. Publishes short shorts. Length: 400 words. Sponsors contest. Send SASE for details.
How to Contact: Send complete ms. Reports in 2 weeks to 7 months on mss. SASE. Simultaneous submissions OK. Accepts electronic disk submissions. Sample copy for $3. Fiction guidelines for SASE.
Payment/Terms: No payment. Acquires one-time rights. Not copyrighted.
Advice: "Subscribers come first!" Looks for "a good lead stating a theme, support of the theme throughout and an ending that rounds out the story or article. Make it believable, please don't preach, avoid propaganda, and don't say, 'This is a story about a retarded person'; instead, prove it by your writing. Show, don't tell."

JUST WRITE, (I, II), Write Away Literary, 101 N. Main St., Suite 13, Crystal Lake IL 60014. (815)455-6404. Fax: (815)455-6484. Editor: Gloria J. Urch. Fiction Editor: E.J. Shumak. Magazine: 8½×11; 36 pages; 60 lb. paper; glossy stock cover; illustrations and photos. "The focus of the magazine is instruction and motivation for writers. We use short fiction and novel excerpts in each issue." Quarterly. Estab. 1993. Circ. 500.
  ● *Just Write* is affiliated with McHenry County College.
Needs: Adventure, condensed/excerpted novel, ethnic/multicultural, experimental, fantasy, feminist, historical, horror, humor/satire, literary, mainstream/contemporary, mystery/suspense "No extreme violence, profanity, bigotry, war, satanic." Publishes special fiction issue or anthology. Receives 5-10 unsolicited mss/month. Accepts 2-3 mss/issue; 25-36 mss/year. Publishes ms 3-4 months after acceptance. Recently published work by Carla Fortier, Tom Gardner, Thomas Canfield. Length: 400-1,500 words average; 400 words minimum; 2,000 words maximum. Publishes short shorts. Also publishes literary essays; literary criticism and poetry. Always critiques or comments on rejected ms. The magazine sponsors a contest. Send SASE for guidelines.
How to Contact: Send complete ms with a cover letter. Should include estimated word count, ¼-page bio, Social Security number, list of publications and b&w glossy photo to run with work. Reports in 8-10 weeks on queries; 4-8 weeks on mss. Send SASE for reply, return of ms or send a disposable copy of ms. Simultaneous, reprint and electronic submissions (call first for modem) OK. Sample copy for $4. Reviews novels and short story collections.
Payment/Terms: Pays $5-35 on publication and 1 contributor's copy for first North American serial rights. Occasionally sends galleys to author.
Advice: "We like dialogue, strong characterization, tight writing. Get to the story quickly. Cut the flowery language and give us the guts of the story. We would like to see more contemporary or

mainstream fiction." No horror or science fiction "unless it is strongly character-based."

KALEIDOSCOPE: International Magazine of Literature, Fine Arts, and Disability, (II, IV), 326 Locust St., Akron OH 44302. Phone/fax: (330)762-9755. Editor-in-Chief: Darshan Perusek, Ph.D. Senior Editor: Gail Willmott. Magazine: 8½ × 11; 56-64 pages; non-coated paper; coated cover stock; illustrations (all media); photos. "*Kaleidoscope* creatively explores the experiences of disability through fiction, essays, poetry, and visual arts. Challenges and transcends stereotypical and patronizing attitudes about disability." Semiannually. Estab. 1979. Circ. 1,000.

● *Kaleidoscope* has received awards from the Great Lakes Awards Competition and Ohio Public Images. The editors are looking for more fiction .

Needs: Personal experience, drama, fiction, essay, artwork. Upcoming theme: "Disability: The Lighter Side" (deadline March 1997). Receives 20-25 unsolicited fiction mss/month. Accepts 10 mss/year. Approximately 1% of fiction is agented. Recently published work by John Hockenberry and Nancy Mairs. Published new writers within the last year. Length: 5,000 words maximum. Also publishes poetry.

How to Contact: Query first or send complete ms and cover letter. Include author's educational and writing background and if author has a disability, how it has influenced the writing. Simultaneous submissions OK. Reports in 1 month on queries; 6 months on mss. Sample copy for $4. Guidelines for #10 SASE.

Payment/Terms: Pays $10-125 and 2 contributor's copies on publication; additional copies $4. Acquires first rights. Reprints permitted with credit given to original publication.

Advice: "Read the magazine and get submission guidelines. We prefer that writers with a disability offer original perspectives about their experiences; writers without disabilities should limit themselves to our focus in order to solidify a connection to our magazine's purpose. Do not use stereotypical, patronizing and sentimental attitudes about disability."

KALLIOPE, A Journal of Women's Art, (II), Florida Community College at Jacksonville, 3939 Roosevelt Blvd., Jacksonville FL 32205. (904)381-3511. Editor: Mary Sue Koeppel. Magazine: 7¼ × 8¼; 76-88 pages; 70 lb. coated matte paper; Bristol cover; 16-18 halftones per issue. "A literary and visual arts journal for women, *Kalliope* celebrates women in the arts by publishing their work and by providing a forum for their ideas and opinions." Short stories, poems, plays, essays, reviews and visual art. Triannually. Estab. 1978. Circ. 1,250.

● Kalliope has received the Frances Buck Sherman Award from the local branch of the National League of Pen Women. The magazine has also received awards and grants for its poetry, grants from the Florida Department of Cultural Affairs and the Jacksonville Club Gallery of Superb Printing Award.

Needs: "Quality short fiction by women writers." Accepts 2-4 mss/issue. Receives approximately 100 unsolicited fiction mss each month. Published work by Layle Silbert, Robin Merle, Claudia Brinson Smith and Colette. Published new writers within the last year. Preferred length: 750-2,500 words, but occasionally publishes longer (and shorter) pieces. Also publishes poetry. Critiques rejected mss "when there is time and if requested."

How to Contact: Send complete ms with SASE and short contributor's note. No simultaneous submissions. Reports in 2-3 months on ms. Publishes ms an average of 1-3 months after acceptance. Sample copy: $7 for current issue; $4 for issues from '78-'88. Reviews short story collections.

Payment/Terms: Pays 3 contributor's copies or 1-years subscription for first rights. $7 charge for extras, discount for 4 or more. "We accept only unpublished work. Copyright returned to author upon request."

Advice: "Read our magazine. The work we consider for publication will be well written and the characters and dialogue will be convincing. We like a fresh approach and are interested in new or unusual forms. Make us believe your characters; give readers an insight which they might not have had if they had not read you. We would like to publish more work by minority writers." Manuscripts are rejected because "1) nothing *happens*!, 2) it is thinly disguised autobiography (richly disguised autobiography is OK), and 3) ending is either too pat or else just trails off."

‡KANSAS QUARTERLY/ARKANSAS REVIEW, (II), Department of Engineering and Philosophy, P.O. Box 1890, Arkansas State University, State University AR 72467. (501)972-3043. Fax: (501)972-2795. Editor: Norman Lavers. Magazine: 8¼ × 10¾; 84-92 pages; coated, matte paper; matte, 4-color cover stock; illustrations and photos. "We aspire to be a first-rate international journal publishing mainly fiction (stories and novel excerpts) and creative nonfiction. We have no restrictions on length or subject or style, high quality being the only criterion. If you can delight us, and an intelligent sophisticated audience, we'll take it." Triannually. Estab. 1996. Circ. 900.

Needs: Excerpted novel, mainstream/contemporary, translations. "No genre fiction." Receives 65 unsolicited mss/month. Accepts 9-14 mss/issue; 35 mss/year. Publishes ms 6-12 months after acceptance. Agented fiction 1%. Recently published work by Donald Harington, John Bensko, Carole Glickfeld, George Chambers and Raymond Federman. Also publishes literary essays and poetry. Sometimes critiques or comments on rejected mss.

How to Contact: Send complete ms with cover letter. Include a brief list of major publications. Reports in 2 weeks on queries; 2 months on mss. Send SASE for reply, return of ms or send a disposable copy of ms. Simultaneous submissions OK. Sample copy for $6. Fiction guidelines free for #10 SASE.

Payment/Terms: Pays $10-25/page on publication and 2 contributor's copies; additional copies for $6. Acquires first North American serial rights.

Advice: "We publish new writers in every issue. We look for distinguished, mature writing, surprises, a perfect ending and a story that means more than merely what went on in it. We don't like recognizable imitations of currently fashionable writers. Writers with a Kansas connection who are accepted for publication are automatically in the running for the $1,000 Seaton award for best work by a Kansas-connected author (born there, lived there, went to school there). No application. Upon having your work accepted, state your Kansas connection."

KELSEY REVIEW, (I, II, IV), Mercer County College, P.O. Box B, Trenton NJ 08690. (609)586-4800. E-mail: kelsey.review@mccc.edu. Editor: Robin Schore. Magazine: 7×14; 80 pages; glossy paper; soft cover. "Must live or work in Mercer County, NJ." Annually. Estab. 1988. Circ. 2,000.

Needs: Open. Regional (Mercer County only). Receives 120 unsolicited mss/year. Accepts 24 mss/issue. Reads mss only in May. Publishes ms 1-2 months after acceptance. Length: 2,000 words maximum. Publishes short shorts. Also publishes literary essays, literary criticism and poetry. Always critiques or comments on rejected mss.

How to Contact: Send complete ms with cover letter. SASE for return of ms. No simultaneous submissions. Reports in 1-2 months. Sample copy free. Reviews "anything."

Payment/Terms: Pays 5 contributor's copies. Rights revert to author on publication.

Advice: Looks for "quality, intellect, grace and guts. Avoid sentimentality, overwriting and self-indulgence. Work on clarity, depth and originality."

KENNESAW REVIEW, (II), Kennesaw State University, Dept of English, 1000 Chastain Rd., Kennesaw GA 30144-5591. (770)423-6346. Editor: Dr. Robert W. Hill. Magazine. "Just good fiction, all themes, for a general audience." Semiannually. Estab. 1987.

Needs: Excerpted novel, contemporary, ethnic, experimental, feminist, gay, humor/satire, literary, mainstream, regional. No romance. Receives 25-60 mss/month. Accepts 2-4 mss/issue. Publishes ms 12-18 months after acceptance. Published work by Julie Brown, Stephen Dixon, Robert Morgan, Carolyn Thorman. Length: 9-30 pages. Length: 500 words. Rarely comments on or critiques rejected mss.

How to Contact: Send complete ms with cover letter. Include previous publications. Reports 2 months on mss. SASE. Simultaneous submissions OK. Sample copy and fiction guidelines free.

Payment/Terms: Pays in contributor's copies. Acquires first publication rights only. Acknowledgment required for subsequent publication.

Advice: "Use the language well and tell an interesting story. Send it on. Be open to suggestions."

THE KENYON REVIEW, (II), Kenyon College, Gambier OH 43022. (614)427-5208. Fax: (614)427-5417. E-mail: kenyonreview@kenyon.edu. Editor: David H. Lynn. "Fiction, poetry, essays, book reviews." Triannually. Estab. 1939. Circ.5,000.

● Work published in the *Kenyon Review* has been selected for inclusion in *Pushcart Prize* anthologies.

Needs: Condensed/excerpted novel, contemporary, ethnic, experimental, feminist, gay, historical, humor/satire, lesbian, literary, mainstream, translations. Receives 400 unsolicited fiction mss/month. Does not read mss April through August. Publishes ms 12-18 months after acceptance. Recently published work by Joyce Carol Oates, Lewis Hyde, Pamela Painter and Dabney Stuart. Length: 3-15 typeset pages preferred.

How to Contact: Send complete ms with cover letter. Reports on mss in 2-3 months. SASE. No simultaneous submissions. Sample copy for $8.

Payment/Terms: Pays $10/page on publication for first-time rights. Sends copyedited version to author for approval.

MARKET CONDITIONS are constantly changing! If you're still using this book and it is 1998 or later, buy the newest edition of *Novel & Short Story Writer's Market* at your favorite bookstore or order from Writer's Digest Books.

Advice: "Read several issues of our publication. We remain invested in encouraging/reading/publishing work by writers of color, writers expanding the boundaries of their genre, and writers with unpredictable voices and points of view."

KEREM, Creative Explorations in Judaism, (IV), Jewish Study Center Press, Inc., 3035 Porter St. NW, Washington DC 20008. Fax: (202)364-3806. Editors: Sara Horowitz and Gilah Langner. Magazine: 6×9; 128 pages; 60 lb. offset paper; glossy cover; illustrations and photos. "*Kerem* publishes Jewish religious, creative, literary material—short stories, poetry, personal reflections, text study, prayers, rituals, etc." Annually. Estab. 1992. Circ. 2,000.
Needs: Jewish: ethnic/multicultural, feminist, humor/satire, literary, religious/inspirational. Receives 1-2 unsolicited mss/month. Accepts 1-2 mss/issue. Publishes ms 2-10 months after acceptance. Recently published work by Mark Mirsky. Length: 6,000 words maximum. Publishes short short stories. Also publishes literary essays, poetry.
How to Contact: Send complete ms with a cover letter. Should include 1-2 line bio. Reports in 2 months on queries; 4-5 months on mss. Send SASE for reply, return of ms or send a disposable copy of ms. Simultaneous submissions OK. Sample copy for $8.50.
Payment/Terms: Pays free subscription and 2-10 contributor's copies. Acquires one-time rights.
Advice: "We want to be moved by reading the manuscript!"

KESTREL, A Journal of Literature and Art in the New World, (II), Division of Language and Literature, Fairmont State College, 1201 Locust Ave., Fairmont WV 26554-2470. (304)367-4778. Editors: Martin Lammon, Valerie Nieman, Mary Stewart, John King. Magazine: 6×9; 100 pages; 60 lb. paper; glossy cover; photographs. "An eclectic journal publishing the best fiction, poetry, creative nonfiction and artwork for a literate audience. We strive to present contributors' work in depth." Semiannually. Estab. 1993. Circ. 500.
  ● *Kestrel* has received funding grants from the NEA and the West Virginia Commission of the Arts.
Needs: Condensed/excerpted novel, literary, translations. "No pornography, children's literature, romance fiction, pulp science fiction—formula fiction in general." Receives 10-20 unsolicited mss/month. Acquires 2-3 mss/issue; 4-6 mss/year. Publishes ms 3-12 months after acceptance. Recently published work by Colleen Anderson, Ethel Morgan, John Sullivan and Maria Beig (German author translated by Jaimy Gordon and Peter Blickel). Length: 1,500 words minimum; 6,000 words maximum. Publishes short shorts. Also publishes literary essays and poetry. Sometimes critiques or comments on rejected mss.
How To Contact: Send complete ms with "short but specific" cover letter. Include list of publications. Reports in 3 months on mss. SASE for return of ms or disposable copy of ms. No simultaneous submissions. Electronic (disk) submissions OK. Sample copy for $5.
Payment/Terms: Pays 2 contributor's copies. Rights revert to contributor on publication.
Advice: Looks for "maturity, grace and verve . . . whether you're 21 or 81 years old. Live with a story for a year or more before you send it anywhere, not just *Kestrel*."

KINESIS, The Literary Magazine For The Rest of Us, (I, II), P.O. Box 4007, Whitefish MT 59937. (406)756-1193. E-mail: kinesis@netrix.net. Editor: Leif Peterson. Magazine: 8½×11; 56 pages; Mondo Supreme paper; Mondo cover; illustrations and photographs. "Our magazine is wide open. We publish fiction, poetry, essays and reviews as well as several regular columnists. Our audience is anyone with a heartbeat." Monthly. Estab. 1992. Circ. 5,000.
  ● *Kinesis* is a member of the Council for Literary Magazines & Presses (CLMP).
Needs: Experimental, humor/satire, literary, mainstream/contemporary and regional. Receives 50 unsolicited submissions/month. Accepts 4 mss/issue; 48 mss/year. Publishes ms 1 month after acceptance. Recently published work by Mark Wisniewski, Christine Japely, H.E. Francis and S.A. Flygare. Length: 5,000 words average; 1,000 words minimum; 7,000 words maximum. Publishes short shorts. Also publishes literary essays, literary criticism and poetry. Sponsors contest; Send SASE for details.
How to Contact: Send complete ms with a cover letter. Include estimated word count, short bio and list of publications. Reports in 1 month. Send SASE for reply, return of ms or send a disposable copy of ms. Simultaneous, reprint and electronic (disk) submissions OK. Sample copy for $3, 10×13 SAE and $1 postage. Fiction guidelines for #10 SASE. Reviews novels and short story collections. Send books to Books Editor.
Payment/Terms: Pays free subscription and 5 contributor's copies. Acquires one-time rights.
Advice: "We're looking for writing that moves—on the page and in our souls."

KIOSK, (II), English Department, S.U.N.Y. at Buffalo, 306 Clemens Hall, Buffalo NY 14260. Editor: Tracee Howell. Fiction Editor: Jonathan Pitts. Magazine: 5½×8½; 150 pages; 80 lb. cover; illustrations. "We seek innovative, non-formula fiction and poetry." Annually (may soon be Biannually). Estab. 1986. Circ. 750.

Needs: Literary. "While we subscribe to no particular orthodoxy, our fiction editors are most hospitable to stories with a strong sense of voice, narrative direction and craftsmanship." Receives 50 mss/month. Accepts 10-20 mss/issue. Publishes ms within 6 months of acceptance. Recently published work by Ray Federman, Lance Olsen and Mark Jacobs. Published new writers within the last year. Length: 3,000 words preferred; 7,500 words maximum. Publishes short shorts, "the shorter the better." Also publishes poetry. Sometimes critiques rejected mss.

How to Contact: Send complete mss with cover letter. Does not read from June through August. Reports in 3-4 months on mss. SASE. Simultaneous and reprint submissions OK. Sample copy for $5. Guidelines for SASE.

Payment/Terms: Pays in contributor's copies. Acquires one-time rights.

Advice: "First and foremost *Kiosk* is interested in sharp writing. There's no need to be dogmatic in terms of pushing a particular style or form, and we aren't. At the same time, we get tired of reading the same old story, the same old poem. Make it new, but also make it worth the reader's effort. Our last issue, 'RUST BELT,' focused upon a pretty specific theme. Because we are anticipating changes in our editorial staff, it would be a good idea to send a self-addressed stamped envelope for the most recent writer's guidelines."

LACTUCA, (I, II), % Mike Selender, 159 Jewett Ave., Jersey City NJ 07304-2003. E-mail: lactuca@aol.com. Editor: Mike Selender. Magazine: Folded 8½×14; 72 pages; 24 lb. bond; soft cover; saddle-stapled; illustrations. Publishes "poetry, short fiction and b&w art, for a general literary audience." Published annually. Estab. 1986. Circ. 700.

Needs: Adventure, condensed/excerpted novel, confession, contemporary, erotica, literary, mainstream, prose poem and regional. No "self-indulgent writing or fiction about writing fiction." Receives 30 or more mss/month. Accepts 3-4 mss/issue; 10-12 mss/year. Publishes ms within 3-12 months of acceptance. Published work by Douglas Mendini, Tom Gidwitz and Ruthann Robson; published new writers within the last year. Length: around 12-14 typewritten double-spaced pages. Publishes short shorts. Often critiques rejected mss and recommends other markets.

How to Contact: "Query first to see if we're reading before sending manuscripts. We are backlogged and probably won't resume accepting work until mid-1997 or later." Cover letter should include "just a few brief notes about yourself. Please no long 'literary' résumés or bios. The work will speak for itself." Reports in 6 weeks-3 months. SASE. No simultaneous or previously published work. Accepts electronic submissions via "MS DOS formatted disk. We can convert most word-processing formats." Sample copy for $4. Fiction guidelines for #10 SASE.

Payment/Terms: Pays 2-5 contributor's copies, depending on the length of the work published. Acquires first North American serial rights. Sends galleys to author. Copyrights revert to authors.

Advice: "We want fiction coming from a strong sense of place and/or experience. Work with an honest emotional depth. We steer clear of self-indulgent material. We particularly like work that tackles complex issues and the impact of such on people's lives. We are open to work that is dark and/or disturbing."

THE LAMPLIGHT, (II), Beggar's Press, 8110 N. 38 St., Omaha NE 68112. (402)455-2615. Editor: Richard R. Carey. Fiction Editor: Sandy Johnsen. Magazine: 8½×11; 60 pages; 20 lb. bond paper; 65 lb. stock cover; some illustrations; a few photographs. "Our purpose is to establish a new literature drawn from the past. We relish foreign settings in the 19th century when human passions transcended computers and fax machines. We are literary but appeal to the common intellect and the mass soul of humanity." Semiannually.

Needs: Historical (general), humor/satire, literary, mystery/suspense (literary), romance (gothic, historical). "Settings in the past. Psychological stories." Plans special fiction issue or anthology in the future. Receives 60-70 unsolicited mss/month. Accepts 2 mss/issue; 4 mss/year. Publishes ms 4-12 months after acceptance. Published work by Fredrick Zydek, John J. McKernan. Length: 2,000 words preferred; 500 words minimum; 3,500 words maximum. Publishes short shorts. Length: 300 words. Also publishes literary criticism and poetry. Critiques or comments on rejected mss.

How to Contact: Send complete ms with cover letter. Include estimated word count, bio (a paragraph or two) and list of publications. Reports in 1 month on queries; 2½ months on mss. SASE. Simultaneous and reprint submission OK. Sample copy for $10.95, 9×12 SAE. Fiction guidelines for #10 SASE. Reviews novels and short story collections.

Payment/Terms: Pays 2 contributor's copies. Acquires first North American serial rights.

Advice: "We deal in classical masterpieces. Every piece must be timeless. It must live for five centuries or more. We judge on this basis. These are not easy to come by. But we want to stretch authors to their fullest capacity. They will have to dig deeper for us, and develop a style that is different from what is commonly read in today's market."

THE LAMP-POST, of the Southern California C.S. Lewis Society, (II, IV), 29562 Westmont Ct., San Juan Capistrano CA 92675. E-mail: lamppost@ix.netcom.com. Senior Editor: James Prothero.

Magazine: 5½×8½; 34 pages; 7 lb. paper; 8 lb. cover; illustrations. "We are a literary review focused on C.S. Lewis and like writers." Quarterly. Estab. 1977. Circ. 200.

● C.S. Lewis was an English novelist and essayist known for his science fiction and fantasy featuring Christian themes. He is especially well-known for his children's fantasy, *The Chronicles of Narnia*. So far, the magazine has found little fiction suitable to its focus, although they remain open.

Needs: "Literary fantasy and science fiction for children to adults." Publishes ms 9 months after acceptance. Recently published work by Lydia Priest. Length: 2,500 words average; 1,000 words minimum; 5,000 words maximum. Also publishes literary essays, literary criticism and poetry. Sometimes critiques or comments on rejected mss.

How to Contact: Query first or send complete ms with a cover letter. Include 50-word bio. Reports in 6-8 weeks. Send SASE for reply, return of ms or send a disposable copy of ms. No simultaneous submissions. Reprints and electronic (disk) submissions OK. Sample copy for $3. Fiction guidelines for #10 SASE. Reviews fiction or criticism having to do with Lewis or in his vein. Send books to: M.J. Logsdon, Editor, The Lamp-Post, 119 Washington Dr., Salinas CA 93905.

Payment/Terms: Pays 3 contributor's copies; additional copies $3. Acquires first North American serial rights or one-time rights.

Advice: "We look for fiction with the supernatural, mythic feel of the fiction of C.S. Lewis and Charles Williams. Our slant is Christian but we want work of literary quality. No inspirational. Is it the sort of thing Lewis, Tolkien and Williams would like—subtle, crafted fiction? If so, send it. Don't be too obvious or facile. Our readers aren't stupid."

THE LAUREL REVIEW, (III), Northwest Missouri State University, Dept. of English, Maryville MO 64468. (816)562-1265. Co-editors: William Trowbridge, David Slater and Beth Richards. Associate Editors: Nancy Vieira Couto, Randall R. Freisinger, Steve Heller. Magazine: 6×9; 124-128 pages; good quality paper. "We publish poetry and fiction of high quality, from the traditional to the avant-garde. We are eclectic, open and flexible. Good writing is all we seek." Biannually. Estab. 1960. Circ. 900.

● A story published in *The Laurel Review* in 1996 was selected for inclusion in the annual *Pushcart Prize* anthology.

Needs: Literary and contemporary. Accepts 3-5 mss/issue, 6-10 mss/year. Receives approximately 120 unsolicited fiction mss each month. Approximately 1% of fiction is agented. Recently published work by Jonis Agee, James B. Lee and Tim Bridgford. Length: 2,000-10,000 words. Sometimes publishes literary essays; also publishes poetry. Reads September to May.

How to Contact: Send complete ms with SASE. No simultaneous submissions. Reports in 1-4 months on mss. Publishes ms an average of 1-12 months after acceptance. Sample copy for $3.50.

Payment/Terms: Pays 2 contributor's copies and 1 year subscription. Acquires first rights. Copyright reverts to author upon request.

Advice: Send $3.50 for a back copy of the magazine.

LIBIDO, The Journal of Sex and Sensibility, (I, II, IV), Libido, Inc., P.O. Box 146721, Chicago IL 60614. (312)281-5839. Editors: Jack Hafferkamp and Marianna Beck. Magazine: 6½×9¼; 88 pages; 70 lb. non-coated; b&w illustrations and photographs. "Erotica is the focus. Fiction, poetry, essays, reviews for literate adults." Quarterly. Estab. 1988. Circ. 9,000.

● Specializing in "literary" erotica, this journal has attracted a number of top-name writers.

Needs: Condensed/excerpted novel, confession, erotica, gay, lesbian. No "dirty words for their own sake, violence or sexual exploitation." Receives 25-50 unsolicited mss/month. Accepts about 5 mss/issue; about 20 mss/year. Publishes ms up to 1 year after acceptance. Recently published work by Larry Tritten, Catherine O'Sullivan and Sophie du Chien. Length: 1,000-3,000 words; 300 words minimum; 5,000 words maximum. Also publishes literary essays, literary criticism. Sometimes critiques rejected mss and recommends other markets.

How to Contact: Send complete ms with cover letter including Social Security number and brief bio for contributor's page. Reports in 6 months on mss. SASE. No simultaneous submissions. Reprint submissions OK. Sample copy for $8. Free fiction guidelines. Reviews novels and short story collections.

Payment/Terms: Pays $15-50 and 2 contributor's copies on publication for one-time or anthology rights.

Advice: "Humor is a strong plus. There must be a strong erotic element, and it should celebrate the joy of sex. Also, stories should be well written, insightful and arousing. Bonus points given for accuracy of characterization and style."

‡THE LICKING RIVER REVIEW, (II), University Center, Northern Kentucky University, Highland Heights KY 41076. (606)572-5416. Editor: Charles Wheatley. Fiction Editor: Renee Riegler. Magazine: 7×11; 104 pages; photos. Annually. Estab. 1991. Circ. 1,500.

Needs: Experimental, literary, mainstream/contemporary. Receives 40 unsolicited mss/month. Accepts 7-9 mss/year. Does not read mss February through July. Publishes ms 6 months after acceptance. Recently published work by Charles Koppelman, Cheryl Rogers, Carl Morris, Toni Herzog, John Aber and Anne Jupiter. Length: 5,000 words maximum. Publishes short shorts. Also publishes poetry.

How to Contact: Send complete ms with a cover letter. Include list of publications. Reports in 3-6 months on mss. SASE for return of manuscript or send disposable copy of ms. No simultaneous submissions. Sample copy for $5.

Payment/Terms: Pays 2 contributor's copies on publication.

Advice: Looks for "good writing and an interesting and well-told story. Read a sample copy first."

LIGHT QUARTERLY, (II), P.O. Box 7500, Chicago IL 60680. Editor: John Mella. Magazine: 8½×11; 32 pages; Finch opaque (60 lb.) paper; 65 lb. color cover; illustrations. "Light and satiric verse and prose, witty but not sentimental. Audience: intelligent, educated, usually 'professional.' " Quarterly. Estab. 1992. Circ. 1,000.

Needs: Humor/satire, literary. Upcoming theme: Ogden Nash parody issue. Receives 10-40 unsolicited fiction mss/month. Accepts 2-4 mss/issue. Publishes ms 6-24 months after acceptance. Published work by X.J. Kennedy, J.F. Nims and John Updike. Length: 1,200 words preferred; 600 words minimum; 2,000 words maximum. Publishes short shorts. Also publishes literary essays, literary criticism and poetry. Sometimes critiques or comments on rejected mss.

How to Contact: Query first. Include estimated word count and list of publications. Reports in 1 month on queries; 2-4 months on mss. Send SASE for reply, return of ms or send a disposable copy of ms. No simultaneous submissions. Electronic submissions (disk only) OK. Sample copy for $4. Fiction guidelines for #10 SASE. Reviews novels and short story collections. Send review copies to review editor.

Payment/Terms: Pays contributor's copies (2 for domestic; 1 for foreign). Acquires first North American serial rights. Sends galleys of longer pieces to author.

Advice: Looks for "high literary quality; wit, allusiveness, a distinct (and distinctive) style. Read guidelines first."

LIMESTONE: A LITERARY JOURNAL, (II), University of Kentucky, Dept. of English, 1215 Patterson Office Tower, Lexington KY 40506-0027. (606)257-7008. Editor-in-Chief: Jennifer Stimson. Magazine: 6×9; 50-75 pages; standard text paper and cover; illustrations; photos. "We publish a variety of styles and attitudes, and we're looking to expand our offering." Annually. Estab. 1981. Circ. 1,000.

Needs: "Quality poetry and short fiction, literary, mainstream, thoughtful. No fantasy or science fiction. No previously published work." Receives 200 mss/year. Accepts 15 mss/issue. Does not read mss May through September. Publishes ms an average of 6 months after acceptance. Publishes new writers every year. Length: 3,000-5,000 words preferred; 5,000 words maximum. Publishes short shorts.

How to Contact: Send complete ms with cover letter. Include publishing record and brief bio. Reports in 1 month on queries; 7 months or longer on mss. SASE. Simultaneous submissions OK. Sample copy for $2.

Payment/Terms: Pays 2 contributor's copies. Rights revert to author.

LINES IN THE SAND, (I, II), LeSand Publications, 890 Southgate Ave., Daly City CA 94015. (415)992-4770. Editor: Nina Z. Sanders. Fiction Editors: Nina Z. Sanders and Barbara J. Less. Magazine: 5½×8½; 32 pages; 20 lb. bond; King James cost-coated cover. "Stories should be well-written, entertaining and suitable for all ages. Our readers range in age from 7 to 90. No particular slant or philosophy." Bimonthly. Estab. 1992. Circ. 100.

- *Lines In The Sand* is known for quirky fiction with surprise endings. Humorous and slice-of-life fiction has a good chance here.

Needs: Adventure, experimental, fantasy, horror, humor/satire, literary, mainstream/contemporary, mystery/suspense (private eye/hard-boiled, amateur sleuth, cozy, romantic), science fiction (soft/sociological), senior citizen/retirement, westerns (traditional, frontier, young adult), young adult/teen (10-18 years). "No erotica, pornography." Receives 70-80 unsolicited mss/month. Accepts 8-10 mss/issue; 50-60 mss/year. Publishes ms 2-4 months after acceptance. Recently published work by Norbert Petsch, Tim Watts, Steve Burt and Leslie A. Duncan. Length: 1,200 words preferred; 250 words minimum; 2,000 words maximum. Publishes short shorts. Length: 250 words. Also publishes poetry. Often critiques or comments on rejected mss. Sponsors contests. To enter contest submit 2 copies of story, 2,000 words maximum, double-spaced, typed and $5 reading fee for each story submitted.

How to Contact: Send complete ms with cover letter containing estimated word count and bio (3-4 sentences). Reports in 2-6 months on mss. Send SASE for reply, return of ms or send disposable copy of themes. Simultaneous and reprint submissions OK. Sample copy for $3.50. Fiction guidelines for #10 SASE.

Payment/Terms: Pays one contributor's copy. Acquires first North American serial rights.
Advice: "Use fresh, original approach; 'show, don't tell'; use dialogue to move story along; and be grammatically correct. Stories should have some type of conflict. Read a sample copy (or two). Follow guidelines carefully. Use plain language; avoid flowery, 'big' words unless appropriate in dialogue."

LITERAL LATTÉ, A Journal of Prose, Poetry & Art, (II), 61 E. Eighth St., Suite 240, New York NY 10003. (212)260-5532. #E-mail: litlatte@aol.com. Accepts outstanding work by beginning and established writers. Editor: Jenine Gordon Bockman. Fiction Editor: Jeffrey Michael Gordon Bockman. Tabloid: 11 × 17; 24 pages; 35 lb. Jet paper; 50 lb. cover; illustrations and photos. "*LL* is a high-quality journal of prose, poetry and art distributed free in cafés and bookstores in New York and by subscription ($15/year)." Bimonthly. Estab. 1994. Circ. 20,000.
  • *Literal Latté* recently received a *Pushcart Prize.*
Needs: Experimental, fantasy (science), humor/satire, literary, science fiction. Receives 2,500 mss/year. Accepts 30-60 mss/year. Publishes ms within 1 year after acceptance. Recently published work by Ray Bradbury, Stephen Dixon and Robert Olen Butler. Length: 6,000 words maximum. Publishes short shorts. Also publishes literary essays, poetry. Sometimes critiques or comments on rejected mss.
How to Contact: Send complete ms with a cover letter. Include estimated word count, bio, list of publications. Reports in 2-3 months on mss. SASE for reply. Simultaneous submissions OK. Sample copy for $5. Fiction guidelines for #10 SASE.
Payment/Terms: Pays free subscription and 5 contributor's copies. Acquires first rights. Sponsors contests, awards or grants for fiction writers; send #10 SASE marked "Fiction Contest" or "Poetry Contest."
Advice: "Reading our paper is the best way to determine our preferences. We judge work on quality alone and accept a broad range of extraordinary stories, personal essays, poems and graphics. Include a SASE large enough to house our comments (if any), and news on contests, readings or revised guidelines. Don't send a postcard. Include a phone number, in case we have questions like 'Is this still available?' "

LITERARY FRAGMENTS, (I, II, IV), Cedar Bay Press, L.L.C., P.O. Box 751, Beaverton OR 97075. E-mail: editor@cedarbay.com. Website: http://www.teleport.com/~cedarbay/lf.html. Editor: Susan Roberts. Monthly electronic magazine and periodic pulp magazine. "*Literary Fragments* accepts unpublished writers and is distributed worldwide through Internet. New, unpublished writers are the mainstay of our magazine." Estab. 1980.
Needs: Open. Periodically publishes pulp fiction issue or anthology. Length: 300-10,000 words. Publishes short shorts. Also publishes novellas, poetry.
How to Contact: Send complete ms with cover letter with ASCII text on diskette or e-mail. Sample issue (pulp) and guidelines for $6. Fiction guidelines for $2 and #10 SASE or free via e-mail request.
Payment/Terms: Payment depends on grant/award money available or copy when pulp issue is available. Acquires one-time rights for both electronic and pulp issues.
Advice: "Read a current copy of either our electronic or pulp edition to get the flavor of our eclectic style."

THE LITERARY REVIEW, An International Journal of Contemporary Writing, (II), Fairleigh Dickinson University, 285 Madison Ave., Madison NJ 07940. (201)593-8564. Fax: (201)443-8564. E-mail: tlr@fdu.edu. Website: http://www.cais.net/aesir/fiction/tlr/. Editor-in-Chief: Walter Cummins. Magazine: 6 × 9; 450 pages; professionally printed on textpaper; semigloss card cover; perfect-bound. "Literary magazine specializing in fiction, poetry, and essays with an international focus." Quarterly. Estab. 1957. Circ. 2,500.
  • This magazine has received grants from a wide variety of international sources including the Spanish Consulate General in New York, the Program for Cultural Cooperation between Spain's Ministry of Culture and U.S. Universities, Pro Helvetia, the Swiss Center Foundation, The Luso-American Foundation, Japan-U.S. Friendship Commission. Work published in *The Literary Review* has been included in *Editor's Choice*, *Best American Short Stories* and *Pushcart Prize* anthologies.
Needs: Works of high literary quality only. Upcoming themes: "Dutch and Flemish Writing" (Winter 1997) and "Irish Writing" (Summer 1997). Receives 50-60 unsolicited fiction mss/month. Approximately 1-2% of fiction is agented. Recently published work by Irvin Faust, Ivan Stavans, Peter La Salle, Robert Wexelblatt. Published new writers within the last year. Acquires 10-12 mss/year. Also publishes literary essays, literary criticism, poetry. Occasionally critiques rejected mss.
How to Contact: Send complete ms with SASE. "Cover letter should include publication credits." Reports in 3 months on mss. Publishes ms an average of 1-1½ years after acceptance. Sample copy for $5; guidelines for SASE. Reviews novels and short story collections.
Payment/Terms: Pays 2 contributor's copies; 25% discount for extras. Acquires first rights.
Advice: "We want original dramatic situations with complex moral and intellectual resonance and vivid prose. We don't want versions of familiar plots and relationships. Too much of what we are

seeing today is openly derivative in subject, plot and prose style. We pride ourselves on spotting new writers with fresh insight and approach."

LITERARY ROCKET, (I, II), (formerly *Rocket Press*), P.O. Box 672, Water Mill NY 11976. (516)287-4233. E-mail: rocketusa@delphi.com. Editor: Darren Johnson. Magazine: 4¼×11; 24-40 pages; white 24 lb. paper; color 67 lb. cover. "A Rocket is a transcendental, celestial traveler—innovative and intelligent fiction and poetry aimed at opening minds—even into the next century." Biannually. Estab. 1993. Circ. 300-500.
 • This editor prefers to be contacted via e-mail rather than phone. Although the circulation has been around 500, Johnson has published a 2,000 circulation issue.
Needs: Erotica, experimental, humor/satire, literary, special interests (prose poetry). "No genre, auto-biographical fiction, writing without a story, anything derivative in the least." Publishes annual special fiction issue or anthology. Receives 20 unsolicited mss/month. Accepts 2-4 mss/issue; 8-16 mss/year. Recently published work by Chris Woods, Brandon Freels and Toni Herzog. Length: 1,000 words average; 500 words minimum; 1,500 words maximum. Publishes short shorts. Length: 400 words. Also publishes poetry. Sometimes critiques or comments on rejected mss.
How to Contact: Send complete ms with a cover letter. Include estimated word count and bio (100 words) with submission. Reports in 2 weeks on queries; 1 month on mss. Send SASE for reply, return of ms or send a disposable copy of ms. Simultaneous submissions OK. "Subscribers are allowed to submit via e-mail which saves postage." Sample copy for $1.50. Make checks to D. Johnson, please.
Payment/Terms: Pays 1 copy or free subscription to the magazine; additional copies for $1. Acquires one-time rights.
Advice: "Very few people who submit to me seem to understand the small, basement press. Slick form cover letters and even slicker prose have driven me to chop off one of my ears (the left, if you must know). I urge all writers to subscribe to a few idiosyncratic, low-budget litmags, like *Rocket*. They're cheap—and what they lack in gloss, they make up for in integrity and sincerity."

‡THE LONG STORY, (II), 18 Eaton St., Lawrence MA 01843. (508)686-7638. E-mail: rpbtls@aol.com. Editor: R.P. Burnham. Magazine: 5½×8½; 150-200 pages; 60 lb. paper; 65 lb. cover stock; illustrations (b&w graphics). For serious, educated, literary people. No science fiction, adventure, romance, etc. "We publish high literary quality of any kind, but especially look for stories that have difficulty getting published elsewhere—committed fiction, working class settings, left-wing themes, etc." Annually. Estab. 1983. Circ. 1,000.
Needs: Contemporary, ethnic, feminist and literary. Receives 30-40 unsolicited mss/month. Accepts 6-7 mss/issue. Length: 8,000 words minimum; 20,000 words maximum.
How to Contact: Send complete ms with a brief cover letter. Reports in 2 months. Publishes ms an average of 3 months to 1 year after acceptance. SASE. May accept simultaneous submissions ("but not wild about it"). Sample copy for $5.
Payment/Terms: Pays 2 contributor's copies; $4 charge for extras. Acquires first rights.
Advice: "Read us first and make sure submitted material is the kind we're interested in. Send clear, legible manuscripts. We're not interested in commercial success; rather we want to provide a place for long stories, the most difficult literary form to publish in our country."

LOONFEATHER, (II), P.O. Box 1212, Bemidji MN 56619. (218)751-4869. Editor: Betty Rossi. Magazine: 6×9; 48 pages; 60 lb. Hammermill Cream woven paper; 65 lb. vellum cover stock; illustrations; occasional photos. A literary journal of short prose, poetry and graphics. Mostly a market for Northern Minnesota, Minnesota and Midwest writers. Semiannually. Estab. 1979. Circ. 300.
Needs: Literary, contemporary, prose and regional. Accepts 2-3 mss/issue, 4-6 mss/year. Published new writers within the last year. Length: 600-1,500 words (prefers 1,500). Not accepting novel length fiction submissions in the 1997 book year.
How to Contact: Send complete ms with SASE, and short autobiographical sketch. Reports within 4 months of submission deadlines (January 31 and July 31). Sample copy for $2 back issue; $5 current issue.

‡ **THE DOUBLE DAGGER** before a listing indicates that the listing is new in this edition. New markets are often the most receptive to submissions by new writers.

Payment/Terms: Free author's copies. Acquires one-time rights.
Advice: "Send carefully crafted and literary fiction. The writer should familiarize himself/herself with the type of fiction published in literary magazines as opposed to family magazines, religious magazines, etc."

LOST AND FOUND TIMES, (II, IV), Luna Bisonte Prods, 137 Leland Ave., Columbus OH 43214. (614)846-4126. Editor: John M. Bennett. Magazine: 5½×8½; 56 pages; good quality paper; good cover stock; illustrations; photos. Theme: experimental, avant-garde and folk literature, art. Published irregularly (twice yearly). Estab. 1975. Circ. 375.
Needs: Contemporary, experimental, literary, prose poem. Prefers short pieces. Also publishes poetry. Accepts approximately 2 mss/issue. Published work by Spryszak, Steve McComas, Willie Smith, Rupert Wondolowski, Al Ackerman. Published new writers within the last year.
How to Contact: Query with clips of published work. SASE. No simultaneous submissions. Reports in 1 week on queries, 2 weeks on mss. Sample copy for $6.
Payment/Terms: Pays 1 contributor's copy. Rights revert to authors.

LOUISIANA LITERATURE, A Review of Literature and Humanities, (I, II, IV), Southeastern Louisiana University, SLU 792, Hammond LA 70402. (504)549-5022. Editor: David Hanson. Magazine: 6¾×9¾; 100 pages; 70 lb. paper; card cover; illustrations. "Essays should be about Louisiana material; preference is given to fiction and poetry with Louisiana and Southern themes, but creative work can be set anywhere." Semiannually. Estab. 1984. Circ. 400 paid; 500-700 printed.
Needs: Literary, mainstream, regional. "No sloppy, ungrammatical manuscripts." Upcoming themes: Louisiana nature writing, detective fiction and Tennessee Williams (planned for Spring 1997, Fall 1997 and Spring 1998). Receives 100 unsolicited fiction mss/month. Accepts mss related to special topics issues. May not read mss June through July. Publishes ms 6-12 months maximum after acceptance. Recently published work by Robert Olen Butler, Patty Friedmann and Robin Beeman. Published new writers within the last year. Length: 3,500 words preferred; 1,000 words minimum; 6,000 words maximum. Also publishes literary essays (Louisiana themes), literary criticism, poetry. Sometimes comments on rejected mss.
How to Contact: Send complete ms. Reports in 1-3 months on mss. SASE. Sample copy for $5. Reviews novels and short story collections (mainly those by Louisiana authors).
Payment/Terms: Pays usually in contributor's copies. Acquires one-time rights.
Advice: "Cut out everything that is not a functioning part of the story. Make sure your manuscript is professionally presented. Use relevant specific detail in every scene."

THE LOUISVILLE REVIEW, (II), Department of English, University of Louisville, Louisville KY 40292. (502)852-6801. Editor: Sena Jeter Naslund. Managing Editor: Karen J. Mann. Magazine: 6×8¾; 100 pages; Warren's Old Style paper; cover photographs. Semiannually. Estab. 1976. Circ. 750.
Needs: Contemporary, experimental, literary, prose poem. Receives 30-40 unsolicited mss/month. Acquires 6-10 mss/issue; 12-20 mss/year. Publishes ms 2-3 months after acceptance. Published work by Maura Stanton, Patricia Goedicke and Michael Cadnum. Length: 50 pages maximum. Publishes short shorts. Sponsors contest. SASE for information.
How to Contact: Send complete ms with cover letter. Reports on queries in 2-3 weeks; 2-3 months on mss. SASE. Sample copy for $4. Fiction guidelines for #10 SASE.
Payment/Terms: Pays in contributor's copies. Acquires first North American serial rights.
Advice: Looks for "integrity and vividness in the language."

‡LULLWATER REVIEW, (II), Emory University, P.O. Box 22036, Atlanta GA 30322. Editor: Hannah McLaughlin. Fiction Editors: Becky Brooks and Eric Brignac. Magazine: 6×9; 100 pages; 60 lb. paper; photos. "We look for fiction that reflects the issues and lifestyles of today, in whatever form it might arrive, whether as a story, short story or a novel excerpt. We hope to reach the average person, someone who might not ordinarily read a publication like ours, but might be attracted by our philosophy." Semiannually. Circ. 2,000. Member of the Council of Literary Magazines and Presses.
Needs: Condensed/excerpted novel, ethnic/multicultural, experimental, feminist, gay, humor/satire, lesbian, literary, mainstream/contemporary, regional. "No science fiction, fantasy or romance, please." Receives 12-14 unsolicited mss/month. Accepts 3-4 mss/issue; 6-7 mss/year. "Response time is slower in the summer, but we are always reading." Publishes ms within 2 months after acceptance. Recently published work by Lynne Burris Butler, Meghan Keith-Hynes and Patricia Flinn. Length: 10 pages average; 30 pages maximum. Publishes short shorts. Length: 300-500 words. Also publishes poetry. Sometimes critiques or comments on rejected mss. Sponsors contest; send SASE for information in early fall.
How to Contact: Send complete ms with cover letter. Include bio and list of publications. Reports in 1-2 weeks on queries; 2-3 months on mss. Send SASE for reply, return of ms or send a disposable copy of ms. Simultaneous submissions OK. Sample copy for $5. Fiction guidelines for SASE.

Payment/Terms: Pays 3 contributor's copies; additional copies for $5. Acquires first North American serial rights.

Advice: "We at the *Lullwater Review* look for clear cogent writing, strong character development and an engaging approach to the story in our fiction submissions. Stories with particularly strong voices and well-developed central themes are especially encouraged. Be sure that your manuscript is ready before mailing it off to us. Revise, revise, revise!"

LUNA NEGRA, (II), S.P.P.C., Kent State University, Box 26, Student Activities, Kent OH 44242. (330)672-2676. Editor: Teresa Metcalfe. Magazine: 6×9; 50 pages; b&w illustrations and photographs. "The *Luna Negra* is a poetry, short story, photography and art biannual." Biannually. Estab. 1956. Circ. up to 2,000.

Needs: Receives 3-4 unsolicited mss/month. Does not read mss in summer months. Publishes short shorts. Sometimes comments on rejected mss.

How to Contact: Send complete ms with cover letter. SASE. Simultaneous, photocopied and reprint submissions OK. Accepts computer printout submissions. Free sample copy. Fiction guidelines for #10 SAE.

Payment/Terms: Pays in contributor's copies. Acquires one-time rights. Rights revert to author after 60 days.

LYNX EYE, (I, II), ScribbleFest Literary Group, 1880 Hill Dr., Los Angeles CA 90041. Editors: Pam McCully and Kathryn Morrison. Magazine: 5½×8½; 120 pages; 60 lb. book paper; varied cover stock. "*Lynx Eye* is dedicated to showcasing visionary writers and artists, particularly new voices." Quarterly. Estab. 1994. Circ. 300.

Needs: Adventure, condensed/excerpted novel, erotica, ethnic/multicultural, experimental, fantasy (science), feminist, gay, historical, horror, humor/satire, lesbian, literary, mainstream/contemporary, mystery/suspense, romance, science fiction, serialized novel, translations, westerns. Receives 200 unsolicited mss/month. Accepts 30 mss/issue; 120 mss/year. Publishes ms approximately 3 months after acceptance (contract guarantees publication within 12 months or rights revert and payment is kept by author). Recently published work by Bayard, Ben Miller and Sarah Odishoo. Length: 2,500 words average; 500 words minimum; 5,000 words maximum. Also publishes artwork, literary essays, poetry. Often critiques or comments on rejected mss.

How to Contact: Send complete ms with a cover letter. Include name and address on page one; name on *all* other pages. Reports in 2-3 months. Send SASE for reply, return of ms or send a disposable copy of ms. Simultaneous submissions OK. Sample copy for $5. Fiction guidelines for #10 SASE.

Payment/Terms: Pays $10 on acceptance and 3 contributor's copies for first North American serial rights; additional copies $3.75.

Advice: "We consider any well-written manuscript. Characters who speak naturally and who act or are acted upon are greatly appreciated. Your high school English teacher was correct. Basics matter. Imaginative, interesting ideas are sabotaged by lack of good grammar, spelling and punctuation skills. Most submissions are contemporary/mainstream. We could use some variety. Please do not confuse confessional autobiographies with fiction."

THE MACGUFFIN, (II), Schoolcraft College, Department of English, 18600 Haggerty Rd., Livonia MI 48152. (313)462-4400, ext. 5292 or 5327. Fax: (313)462-4558. E-mail: alindenb@schoolcraft.cc.m i.us. Editor: Arthur J. Lindenberg. Fiction Editor: Gary Erwin. Magazine: 6×9; 144 pages; 60 lb. paper; 110 lb. cover; b&w illustrations and photos. "*The MacGuffin* is a literary magazine which publishes a range of material including poetry, nonfiction and fiction. Material ranges from traditional to experimental. We hope our periodical attracts a variety of people with many different interests." Triannual. Quality fiction a special need. Estab. 1984. Circ. 600.

Needs: Adventure, contemporary, ethnic, experimental, fantasy, historical (general), humor/satire, literary, mainstream, prose poem, psychic/supernatural/occult, science fiction, translations. No religious, inspirational, confession, romance, horror, pornography. Upcoming theme: "American Athletics" (June 1997). Receives 25-40 unsolicited mss/month. Accepts 5-10 mss/issue; 10-30 mss/year. Does not read mss between July 1 and August 15. Publishes 6 months to 2 years after acceptance. Agented fiction: 10-15%. Recently published work by Arlene McKanic, Joe Schall, Beverly Olevin, Mark Safranko and Joseph Benevento. Published new writers within the last year. Length: 2,000-2,500 words average; 400 words minimum; 4,000 words maximum. Publishes short shorts. Length: 400 words. Also publishes literary essays. Occasionally critiques rejected mss and recommends other markets.

How to Contact: Send complete ms with cover letter, which should include: "1. *brief* biographical information; 2. note that this *is not* a simultaneous submission." Reports in 2-3 months. SASE. Reprint and electronic (disk) submissions OK. Sample copy for $4; current issue for $4.50. Fiction guidelines free.

Payment/Terms: Pays 2 contributor's copies. Acquires one-time rights.
Advice: "Be persistent. If a story is rejected, try to send it somewhere else. When we reject a story, we may accept the next one you send us. When we make suggestions for a rewrite, we may accept the revision. There seems to be a great number of good authors of fiction, but there are far too few places for publication. However, I think this is changing. Make your characters come to life. Even the most ordinary people become fascinating if they live for your readers."

‡**THE MADISON REVIEW, (II),** Department of English, Helen C. White Hall, 600 N. Park St., University of Wisconsin, Madison WI 53706. (608)263-0566. Rotating Editors. Current Fiction Editor: Joley Wood. Magazine: 6×9; 180 pages. "Magazine of fiction and poetry with special emphasis on literary stories and some emphasis on Midwestern writers." Semiannually. Estab. 1978. Circ. 1,000.
Needs: Experimental and literary stories, prose poems, novel excerpts and stories in translation. Receives 10-50 unsolicited fiction mss/month. Acquires approximately 6 mss/issue. Does not read mss May through September. Recently published work by Leslie Pietrzyk, Stephen Shugart and Ira Gold. Published new writers within the last year. Length: 4,000 words average. Also publishes poetry.
How to Contact: Send complete ms with cover letter and SASE. Include estimated word count, 1-page bio and list of publications. "The letters should give one or two sentences of relevant information about the writer—just enough to provide a context for the work." Reports in 6 months on mss. Publishes ms an average of 4 months after acceptance. Sample copy for $2.50.
Payment/Terms: Pays 3 contributor's copies; $2.50 charge for extras.
Terms: Acquires first North American serial rights.

MAGIC REALISM, (II, III, IV), Pyx Press, P.O. Box 922648, Sylmar CA 91392-2648. Editor and Publisher: C. Darren Butler. Editor: Julie Thomas. Associate Publisher: Lisa S.Laurencot. Magazine: 5½×8½; 80 pages; 20 lb. paper; card stock or bond cover; b&w illustrations. "Magic realism, exaggerated realism, some genre fantasy/dark fantasy, literary fantasy, occasionally glib fantasy of the sort found in folk, fairy tales and myths; for a general, literate audience." Quarterly. Estab. 1990. Circ. 600.
• *Magic Realism* was selected for inclusion in the 1996 *Writer's Digest* "Fiction 50" list of top fiction markets. The magazine also sponsors a new contest, *The Magic Realism* Short-Fiction Award.
Needs: Condensed novel excerpts, experimental, fantasy, literary, magic realism, serialized novel, translations. "No sorcery/wizardry, witches, sleight-of-hand magicians, or occult." Receives 300 unsolicited mss/month. Accepts 15-25 mss/issue; about 70 mss/year. Publishes ms 4-24 months after acceptance. Recently published work by Brian Evenson, Daniel Quinn, Edith Pearlman and Batya Weinbaum. Length: 4,000 words preferred; 100 words minimum; 8,000 words maximum. "Fiction is considered at any length, but query for more than 8,000 words. Short shorts and microfictions are always needed." Rarely critiques rejected mss and recommends other markets.
How to Contact: Send complete ms with cover letter. Include bio, list of credits. "Response time is generally within 3-6 months." SASE. Simultaneous submissions OK. Back issue: $4.95; current issue: $5.95. Fiction guidelines for SASE.
Payment/Terms: Pays ¼¢/word and 3 contributor's copies for first North American serial rights or one-time rights and nonexclusive reprint rights "in case we want to use the work in an anthology." Sends galleys to author.
Advice: "I like finely controlled feats of association; works wherein the human imagination defines reality. Magic realism subverts reality by shaping it into a human mold, bringing it closer to the imagination and to the subconscious. For example, people used to believe that swans migrated to the moon in autumn or that high-speed vehicles would be useless because human bodies would break apart at high speeds. We are especially interested in encouraging new writers working in this difficult genre, and try to feature at least one unpublished writer in every issue."

❖**MALAHAT REVIEW,** University of Victoria, P.O. Box 1700, Victoria, British Columbia V8W 2Y2 Canada. Editor: Derk Wynand. Quarterly. Circ. 2,000.
Needs: "General fiction and poetry, book reviews." Publishes 3-4 stories/issue. Length: 10,000 words maximum.
How to Contact: "Enclose proper postage on the SASE." Sample copy: $7 available through the mail; guidelines available upon request.
Payment/Terms: Pays $25/page and contributor's copies.

MANGROVE, Fiction, Interviews and Poetry from Around the World, (I, II), University of Miami, English Dept., Box 248145, Miami FL 33124-4632. (305)284-2182. Editors change each year. Magazine: 120 pages. *Mangrove* is "a literary magazine publishing short fiction, poetry, memoirs and interviews." Semiannually. Estab. 1994. Circ. 500.
Needs: Literary, ethnic/multicultural, mainstream/contemporary, regional, translations. Receives 60-100 unsolicited mss/month. Accepts 6-8 mss/issue; 12-15 mss/year. Publishes ms 4-6 months after

acceptance. Published work by Robert Olen Butler, Maxine Kumin and Catherine Bowman. Length: 5,000 words maximum. Publishes short shorts. Also publishes poetry. Sometimes critiques or comments on rejected ms.

How to Contact: Send complete ms with a cover letter. Include estimated word count, one-paragraph bio and list of publications with submission. SASE for reply. Simultaneous submissions OK. Sample copy for $5, SAE. Fiction guidelines for SASE.

Payment/Terms: Pays 1 contributor's copy. Acquires one-time rights.

Advice: "We look for stories with a distinct voice that make us look at the world in a different way. Send only one story at a time and send us your best work."

manna, The Literary-Professional Quarterly of manna forty, inc., (I, IV), manna forty, inc., Route 1, Box 548, Sharon OK 73857-9761. (405)254-2660 (evenings). Fax: (405)256-5777. Editor: Richard D. Kahoe. Newsletter: 8½ × 11; 8 pages; 72 lb. recycled paper and cover; illustrations. "*manna* is interested only in nature/religion/psychology, and especially in interfaces of two or three of these subjects." Quarterly. Estab. 1987. Circ. 300-350.

Needs: Ethnic/multicultural, feminist, religious/inspirational, senior citizen/retirement. "We have room for only short-short fiction: parables, personal experience, etc." List of upcoming themes available for SASE. Receives 1 unsolicited mss/month. Accepts 1 mss/issue; 4-8 mss/year. Publishes ms 1-11 months after acceptance. Published work by Jo Anna Peard. Length: 500 words average; 150 words minimum; 750 words maximum. Also publishes literary essays, poetry. Always critiques or comments on rejected ms.

How to Contact: Send complete ms with a cover letter. Include cover letter "telling who you are." estimated word count and 100-word bio. Reports in 1 month on mss. SASE for return of ms or send a disposable copy of the ms. Simultaneous and reprint submissions OK. Sample copy for SASE.

Payment/Terms: Pays 2 contributor's copies; additional copies for 25¢ plus postage. Acquires one-time rights.

Advice: Looking for "human interest, touching on two or more of our subject areas (nature, religion, psychology) and presuming good literary quality, grammar, word selection, etc. Don't send anything that is not relevant to at least one of our basic subjects."

MANOA, A Pacific Journal of International Writing, (II), English Dept., University of Hawaii, Honolulu HI 96822. (808)956-3070. Fax: (808)956-3083. Editor: Frank Stewart. Fiction Editor: Ian MacMillan. Magazine: 7 × 10; 240 pages. "An American literary magazine, emphasis on top US fiction and poetry, but each issue has a major guest-edited translated feature of recent writings from an Asian/Pacific country." Semiannually. Estab. 1989.

● *Manoa* has received numerous awards, and work published in the magazine has been selected for prize anthologies.

Needs: Contemporary, excerpted novel, literary, mainstream and translation (from US and nations in or bordering on the Pacific). "Part of our purpose is to present top U.S. fiction from throughout the US, not only to US readers, but to readers in Asian and Pacific countries. Thus we are not limited to stories related to or set in the Pacific—in fact, we do not want exotic or adventure stories set in the Pacific, but good US literary fiction of any locale." Accepts 8-10 mss/issue; 16-20/year. Publishes ms 6 months-2 years after acceptance. Agented fiction 10%. Recently published work by Robert Olen Butler, Monica Wood, Sussy Chalcó, Andrew Lam, H.E. Francis and Barry Lopez. Publishes short fiction. Also publishes essays, book reviews, poetry.

How to Contact: Send complete ms with cover letter or through agent. Reports in 4-6 months. SASE. Simultaneous and electronic submissions OK; query before sending e-mail. Sample copy for $10. Reviews novels and short story collections. Send books or reviews to Reviews Editor.

Payment/Terms: Pays "highly competitive rates so far," plus contributor's copies for first North American serial rights and one-time reprint rights. Sends galleys to author.

Advice: "*Manoa*'s readership is (and is intended to be) mostly national, not local. It also wants to represent top US writing to a new international market, in Asia and the Pacific. Altogether we hope our view is a fresh one; that is, not facing east toward Europe but west toward 'the other half of the world.' "

MANY MOUNTAINS MOVING, (II), a literary journal of diverse contemporary voices, 420 22nd St., Boulder CO 80302. (303)545-9942. Fax: (303)444-6510. Editors: Naomi Horii and Marilyn Krysl. Fiction Editor: May-lee Chai. Magazine: 6 × 9; 192 pages; acid-free paper; color/heavy cover; illustrations and photos. "We publish fiction, poetry, general-interest essays and art. We try to seek contributors from all cultures to promote appreciation of diverse cultures." Triannually. Estab. 1994. Circ. 2,000.

Needs: Ethnic/multicultural, experimental, feminist, gay, historical, humor/satire, lesbian, literary, mainstream/contemporary, translations. "No science fiction or horror, please." Plans special fiction issue or anthology. Receives 300 unsolicited mss/month. Accepts 4-6 mss/issue; 12-18 mss/year. Publishes ms 2-8 months after acceptance. Agented fiction 5%. Recently published work by W.D. Wether-

ell, Sherman Alexie, Alyce Miller and May-lee Chai. Length: 3,000-5,000 words average. Publishes short shorts. Also publishes literary essays, poetry. Sometimes critiques or comments on rejected mss.
How to Contact: Send complete ms with a cover letter. Include estimated word count, list of publications. Reports in 2 weeks on queries; 4-8 weeks on mss. Send SASE for reply, return of ms or send a disposable copy of ms. Simultaneous submissions OK. Sample copy for $6.50 and enough IRCs for 1 pound of airmail/printed matter. Fiction guidelines free for #10 SASE.
Payment/Terms: Pays 3 contributor's copies; additional copies for $3. Acquires first North American serial rights. Sends galleys to author "if requested." Sponsors a contest. Send SASE for guidelines. Deadline: December 31.
Advice: "We look for top-quality fiction with fresh voices and verve. Read at least one issue of our journal to get a feel for what kind of fiction we generally publish."

MARK, A Journal of Scholarship, Opinion, and Literature, (II), University of Toledo, 2801 W. Bancroft SU2514, Toledo OH 43606. (419)530-2072. Editors: Mike Donnelly and Jennifer Kohout. Magazine: 6×9; 72 pages; acid-free paper; some illustrations; photographs. Annually. Estab. 1967. Circ. 3,500.
Needs: Contemporary, ethnic, humor/satire, literary, regional and science fiction. Also accepts pen and ink drawings and b&w photos. "We do not have the staff to do rewrites or heavy copyediting—send clean, legible mss only. We're presently interested in socially and politically engaged and responsible working. Nothing racist, sexist or heterosexist." Receives 20-25 unsolicited fiction mss/month. Accepts 7-10 mss/year. Does not read June to September. Publishes ms 6 months after acceptance. Publishes short shorts.
How to Contact: Send complete ms with cover letter, name, address and phone number. SASE. Reports in January each year. Sample copy for $3 plus 7x10 SAE with 72¢ postage.
Payment/Terms: Pays 2 contributor's copies. Acquires one-time rights.

MARYLAND REVIEW, (I, II), Department of English and Modern Languages, University of Maryland Eastern Shore, Princess Anne MD 21853. (410)651-6552. E-mail: mandersn@umes_bird.umd.edu. Editor: Mignon H. Anderson. Literary journal: 6×9; 100-150 pages; quality paper stock; heavy cover; illustrations; "possibly" photos. "We have a special interest in black literature, but we welcome all sorts of submissions. Our audience is literary, educated, well-read." Annually. Estab. 1986. Circ. 500.
Needs: Contemporary, humor/satire, literary, mainstream, black literature. No genre stories; no religious, political or juvenile material. Accepts approximately 12-15 mss/issue. Publishes ms "within 1 year" after acceptance. Recently published work by Errol Miller, Mary Beth Malooly and Shannon Locke. Published new writers within the last year. Publishes short shorts. "Length is open, but we do like to include some pieces 1,500 words and under." Also publishes poetry.
How to Contact: Send complete ms with cover letter. Include a brief autobiography of approximately 75 words. Reports "as soon as possible." SASE, *but does not return mss*. No simultaneous submissions. "No fax copies, please. No submissions by e-mail." Sample copy for $6.
Payment/Terms: Pays in contributor's copies. Acquires first serial rights only.
Advice: "Think primarily about your *characters* in fiction, about their beliefs and how they may change. Create characters and situations that are utterly new. We will give your material a careful and considerate reading. Any fiction that is flawed by grammatical errors, misspellings, etc. will not have a chance. We're seeing a lot of fine fiction these days, and we approach each story with fresh and eager eyes. Ezra Pound's battle-cry about poetry refers to fiction as well: 'Make it New!' "

THE MASSACHUSETTS REVIEW, (II), Memorial Hall, University of Massachusetts, Amherst MA 01003. (413)545-2689. Editors: Mary Heath, Jules Chametzky, Paul Jenkins. Magazine: 6×9; 172 pages; 52 lb. paper; 65 lb. vellum cover; illustrations and photos. Quarterly.
Needs: Short stories. Does not read fiction mss June 1-October 1. Published new writers within the last year. Approximately 5% of fiction is agented. Critiques rejected mss when time permits.
How to Contact: Send complete ms. No ms returned without SASE. Simultaneous submissions OK, if noted. Reports in 2 months. Publishes ms an average of 9-12 months after acceptance. Sample copy for $6.50. Guidelines available for SASE.
Payment/Terms: Pays $50 maximum on publication for first North American serial rights.
Advice: "Shorter rather than longer stories preferred (up to 28-30 pages)."

MATRIARCH'S WAY; JOURNAL OF FEMALE SUPREMACY, (I, II), Artemis Creations, 3395 Nostrand Ave., 2J, Brooklyn NY 11229-4053. Phone/fax: (718)648-8215. E-mail: nohel@aol.com. Editor: Shirley Oliveira. Magazine: 5½×8½; illustrations and photos. *Matriarch's Way* is a "matriarchal feminist" publication. Quarterly. Estab. 1996.
Needs: Condensed/excerpted novel, erotica (quality), ethnic/multicultural, experimental, fantasy (science, sword and sorcery), feminist (radical), horror, humor/satire, literary, psychic/supernatural/occult, religious/inspirational, romance (futuristic/time travel, gothic, historical), science fiction (soft/socio-

logical), serialized novel. Receives 4 unsolicited mss/month. Often critiques or comments on rejected mss.

How to Contact: Query first, query with clips of published work or query with synopsis plus 1-3 chapters of novel. Include estimated word count, bio and list of publications with submission. Reports in 1 week on queries; 6 weeks on mss. SASE for reply or send a disposable copy of ms. Simultaneous, reprint and electronic submissions (3.5 ASCII, DOS) OK. Sample copy for $4. Reviews novels and short story collections and excerpts "We need book reviewers desperately, original or reprints. We supply books."

Payment/Terms: Contributors, $4.50/issue or free tearsheet with request. Acquires one-time rights. Sends galleys to author.

Advice: Looks for "a knowledge of subject, originality and good writing style."

THE MAVERICK PRESS, (II), Box 4915, Rt. 2, Eagle Pass TX 78852. Phone/fax: (210)773-1836. Editor: Carol Cullar. Magazine: 8½×5½; 76-80 pages; recycled paper; hand-printed, block print cover; illustrations. Semiannually. Estab. 1992. Circ. 200.

Needs: Experimental, literary, mainstream/contemporary, sudden fiction (1-5 pages). "No children's/ juvenile, gothic, horror, religious diatribe, young adult/teen." November issue is always thematic; write with SASE for guidelines. Receives 15-20 mss/month. Accepts 6-8 mss/issue; 12-16 mss/year. Reads mss every 2 months. Publishes ms 6 months-1 year after acceptance. Recently published work by Robert Perchan, Rebecca Davis, Arthur W. Knight, Don Stockard, C.B. Thatcher and Mike Lipstock. Length: 1,500 words maximum. Publishes short shorts. Also publishes poetry. Sometimes critiques or comments on rejected mss.

How to Contact: Send complete ms with a cover letter. Include estimated word count, half-page bio and list of publications with submission. Reports immediately on queries; 2 months on mss. Send SASE for reply, return of ms or send a disposable copy of ms. Simultaneous and electronic submissions (IBM formatted disks) OK. Sample copy for $7.50. Fiction guidelines for #10 SASE.

Payment/Terms: Pays 1 contributor's copy. Acquires one-time rights. Occasionally sends galleys to author.

Advice: "We publish sudden or short fiction with little expository writing; *in media res*, bare-bones with prose poem feel to it. Figurative language always attracts this editor. Avoid cliches, pedestrian adjectives or hackneyed adverbs. In fact, avoid adverbs that qualify, weaken or cripple your verbs; use a stronger verb or an original metaphor instead. I see too many stories written from a child's point of view or about children or teens."

MERLYN'S PEN: The National Magazines of Student Writing, Grades 6-12, (I, II, IV), Box 1058, East Greenwich RI 02818. (401)885-5175. Fax: (401)885-5222. E-mail: merlynspen@aol.com. Editor: R. Jim Stahl. Managing Editor: Christine Lord. Magazines: 8⅛×10⅞; 32 pages; 50 lb. paper; 70 lb. gloss cover stock; illustrations; photos. Two editions: Middle School (6-9) and Senior (9-12). Student writing only (grades 6 through 12) for libraries, homes and English classrooms. Bimonthly (September-April). Estab. 1985. Circ. 35,000 (combined).
- Winner of the Paul A. Witty Short Story Award and Selection on the New York Public Library's Book List of Recommended Reading.

Needs: Adventure, fantasy, historical, horror, humor/satire, literary, mainstream, mystery/suspense, romance, science fiction, western, young adult/teen. Also publishes editorial reviews, puzzles, word games, poetry. Must be written by students in grades 6-12. Receives 1,200 unsolicited fiction mss/ month. Accepts 25 mss/issue; 100 mss/year. Publishes ms 3 months to 1 year after acceptance. Length: 1,500 words average; 25 words minimum; 4,000 words maximum. Publishes short shorts. Responds to rejected mss.

How to Contact: Send for cover-sheet template. *Charges submission fee: $5/3 titles; $2 to subscribers.* Reports in 10-12 weeks. Electronic (fax or e-mail) submissions OK, "but no response letter or feedback critique will be sent to these submissions." Sample copy for $5.

Payment/Terms: Pays $10 for works of 1 magazine page or more; $5 for works shorter than 1 magazine page and 3 contributor's copies, charge for additional copies. Published works become the property of Merlyn's Pen, Inc.

Advice: "Write what you *know*; write where you are. We look for the authentic voice and experience of young adults."

MICHIGAN QUARTERLY REVIEW, University of Michigan, 3032 Rackham, Ann Arbor MI 48109-1070. (313)764-9265. Editor: Laurence Goldstein. "An interdisciplinary journal which publishes mainly essays and reviews, with some high-quality fiction and poetry, for an intellectual, widely read audience." Quarterly. Estab. 1962. Circ. 1,800.
- Stories from *Michigan Quarterly Review* were selected for inclusion in the past two issues of *The Best American Short Stories*.

Needs: Literary. No "genre" fiction written for a "market." Upcoming themes: Special issue on disabilities (Spring 1998); deadline: September 1, 1997. Receives 200 unsolicited fiction mss/month.

Accepts 2 mss/issue; 8 mss/year. Recently published work by Alice Adams, Alyce Miller and Jim Shepard. Published new writers within the last year. Length: 1,500 words minimum; 7,000 words maximum; 5,000 words average. Also publishes poetry, literary essays.

How to Contact: Send complete ms with cover letter. "I like to know if a writer is at the beginning, or further along, in his or her career. Don't offer plot summaries of the story, though a background comment is welcome." Reports in 6-8 weeks. SASE. No simultaneous submissions. Sample copy for $2.50 and 2 first-class stamps.

Payment/Terms: Pays $8-10/printed page on publication for first rights. Awards the Lawrence Foundation Prize of $1,000 for best story in *MQR* previous year.

Advice: "Read back issues to get a sense of tone; level of writing. *MQR* is very selective; only send the very finest, best-plotted, most-revised fiction."

MID-AMERICAN REVIEW, (II), Department of English, Bowling Green State University, Bowling Green OH 43403. (419)372-2725. Fiction Editor: Rebecca Meacham. Magazine: 5½ × 8½; 100-150 pages; 60 lb. bond paper; coated cover stock. "We publish serious fiction and poetry, as well as critical studies in contemporary literature, translations and book reviews." Biannually. Estab. 1981.

● A story published in the magazine was reprinted in *Best Short Stories of 1996*.

Needs: Experimental, literary, memoir, prose poem, traditional and translations. Receives about 120 unsolicited fiction mss/month. Accepts 5-6 mss/issue. Does not read June-August. Approximately 5% of fiction is agented. Recently published work by Robert Hildt, Jean Thompson, Lucy Hochman, Ron Wiginton, Tenaya Darlington and Rita Welty Bourke. Published new writers within the last year. Also publishes literary essays, literary criticism, poetry. Occasionally critiques rejected mss. Sponsors the Sherwood Anderson Short Fiction Prize.

How to Contact: Send complete ms with SASE. No simultaneous submissions. Reports in about 3 months. Publishes ms an average of 6 months after acceptance. Sample copy for $5. Reviews novels and short story collections. Send books to editor-in-chief.

Payment/Terms: Payment offered pending funding; usually pays $10-50 on publication and 2 contributor's copies for one-time rights; charges for additional copies.

Advice: "We just want *quality* work of whatever vision and/or style. The old adage is true: interesting people are interested; writers need to be interested in their subjects, their characters, their stories. This interest—whether it's a fascination with a person, curiosity about a situation, or simply taking pleasure in the details of a place—should infuse the work, from its language to its point-of-view to its structure. We'd like to see stories that take risks with characters and with the telling of their stories; we want to be interested by what interests the writer. Engage our senses and sensibilities."

MIDLAND REVIEW, (II), Oklahoma State University, English Dept., Morrill Hall, Room 205, Stillwater OK 74078. (405)744-9474. Editors change every year. Send to "Editor." Magazine: 6½ × 9½; 128 pages; 80 lb. paper; perfect bond cover stock; illustrations; photos. "A mixed bag of quality work." For "anyone who likes to read and for those that want news that folks in Oklahoma are alive. Publishes 25-30% OSU student material." Annually. Estab. 1983. Circ. 300.

Needs: Eclectic, ethnic, experimental, feminist, historical (general), literary, prose poem, regional, translations. Receives 15 unsolicited fiction mss/month. Accepts 4 mss/issue. Publishes ms 6-10 months after acceptance. Does not read in May, June or July. Published work by Brian Evenson, Jene Friedemann, Steffie Corcoran, Bruce Michael Gans. Published new writers within the last year. Length: 4-10 pages double-spaced, typed. Publishes short shorts of 2-4 pages. Also publishes literary essays, literary criticism, poetry.

How to Contact: Send complete ms with cover letter. Reports in 8-10 weeks on queries. SASE for ms. Simultaneous submissions OK. Sample copy for $5 plus 90¢ postage and 9 × 12 SAE. Fiction guidelines for #10 SASE.

Payment/Terms: Pays 1 contributor's copy. Copyright reverts to author.

Advice: "We want to encourage good student stories by giving them an audience with more established writers."

MINAS TIRITH EVENING-STAR, (IV), W.W. Publications, Box 373, Highland MI 48357-0373. (813)585-0985. Editor: Philip Helms. Magazine: 8½ × 11; 40 pages; typewriter paper; black ink illustrations; photos. Magazine of J.R.R. Tolkien and fantasy—fiction, poetry, reviews, etc. for general audience. Quarterly. Published special fiction issue; plans another. Estab. 1967. Circ. 500.

Needs: "Fantasy and Tolkien." Receives 5 unsolicited mss/month. Accepts 1 ms/issue; 5 mss/year. Published new writers within the last year. Length: 1,000-1,200 words preferred; 5,000 words maximum. Publishes short shorts. Also publishes literary essays, literary criticism, poetry. Occasionally critiques rejected mss.

How to Contact: Send complete ms and bio. Reports in 1-2 months. SASE. No simultaneous submissions. Reprint submissions OK. Sample copy for $1. Reviews novels and short story collections.

Terms: Acquires first rights.
Advice: Goal is "to expand knowledge and enjoyment of J.R.R. Tolkien's and his son Christopher Tolkien's works and their worlds."

MIND IN MOTION, A Magazine of Poetry and Short Prose, (II), Box 7070, Big Bear Lake CA 92315. Editor: Céleste Goyer. Magazine: 5½×8½; 64 pages; 20 lb. paper; 50 lb. cover. "We prefer to publish works of substantial brilliance that engage and encourage the reader's mind." Quarterly. Estab. 1985. Circ. 350.
● This magazine is known for surrealism and poetic language.
Needs: Experimental, fantasy, humor/satire, literary, prose poem, science fiction. No "mainstream, romance, nostalgia, un-poetic prose; anything with a slow pace or that won't stand up to re-reading." Receives 50 unsolicited mss/month. Acquires 10 mss/issue; 40 mss/year. Reads mss October through July. Publishes ms 2-12 weeks after acceptance. Recently published work by William Jackson, Tom Whalen, Patricia Flinn and Charles Chaim Wax. Length: 2,000 words preferred; 250 words minimum; 3,500 words maximum. Also publishes poetry. Sometimes critiques rejected mss.
How to Contact: Send complete ms. "Cover letter or bio not necessary." SASE. Simultaneous (if notified) submissions OK. Sample copy for $3.50. Fiction guidelines for #10 SASE.
Payment/Terms: Pays 1 contributor's copy; charge for additional copies. Acquires first North American serial rights.
Advice: "We're now taking more stories per issue, and they may be a bit longer, due to a format modification. *Mind in Motion* is noted for introspective, philosophical fiction with a great deal of energy and originality."

MIND MATTERS REVIEW, (I,II), Box 234, 2040 Polk St., San Francisco CA 94109. (415)775-4545. Editor: Carrie Drake. Magazine: 8 1/2×11; 30-64 pages; illustrations and photos. "*MMR* is basically a philosophical publication. We have published two short stories that were written in the form of parables." Audience is "conservative intellectually, but liberal fiscally." Quarterly. Estab. 1988. Circ. 1,000.
Needs: Historical (general), literary, prose poem. No "utopian" fiction. Accepts 1 ms/issue; 4 mss/year. Publishes ms 6-12 months after acceptance. Published work by Manuel Dominguez and Charles Corry. Length: 800 words preferred; 400 words minimum; 2,000 words maximum.
How to Contact: Query first. Reports in 3 weeks. SASE. Simultaneous and reprint submissions OK. Sample copy for $3.50. Fiction guidelines for SASE.
Payment/Terms: Pays contributor's copies. Acquires one-time rights. Sends galleys to author.
Advice: "A beginning fiction writer for *MMR* should first be familiar with the overall frame of reference of *MMR* and its range of flexibility and limitations. We seek writers who are able to tap moral principles as a source of imagination and inspiration. The moral principle can be atheistic or Christian or Buddhist—whatever—as long as there is a logical structure. Characters and plots do not have to be complex or have strong emotional appeal as long as they draw attention to life experiences that give the reader something to think about."

THE MINNESOTA REVIEW, A Journal of Committed Writing, (I, II), Dept. of English, East Carolina University, Greenville NC 27858. (919)328-6388. Fax: (919)328-4889. Editor: Jeffrey Williams. Magazine: 5¼×7½; approximately 200 pages; some illustrations; occasional photos. "We emphasize socially and politically engaged work." Semiannually. Estab. 1960. Circ. 1,500.
Needs: Experimental, feminist, gay, historical, lesbian, literary. Receives 50-75 mss/month. Accepts 3-4 mss/issue; 6-8 mss/year. Publishes ms within 6 months-1 year after acceptance. Recently published work by Laura Nixon Dawson, Jameson Currier, Jiqi Kajane and Stephen Guiterrez. Length: 1,500-6,000 words preferred. Publishes short shorts. Also publishes literary essays, literary criticism, poetry. Occasionally critiques rejected mss and recommends other markets.
How to Contact: Send complete ms with optional cover letter. Reports in 2-3 weeks on queries; 2-3 months on mss. SASE. Simultaneous submissions OK. Reviews novels and short story collections. Send books to book review editor.
Payment/Terms: Pays in contributor's copies. Charge for additional copies. Acquires first rights.
Advice: "We look for socially and politically engaged work, particularly short, striking work that stretches boundaries."

‡MISSISSIPPI MUD, (I, II), 1505 Drake Ave., Austin TX 78704. (512)444-5459. Editor: Joel Weinstein. Magazine: 7¾×10; 96 pages; coated and uncoated paper; coated cover; illustrations; photographs. "*Mississippi Mud* publishes fiction, poetry and artworks reflecting life in America at the end of the 20th century. Good writing is its focus, but it is not for the timid or humorless." Published irregularly. Estab. 1973. Circ. 1,600.
Needs: Excerpted novel, erotica, ethnic/multicultural, experimental, humor/satire, literary, mainstream/contemporary, translations. "No religious or romance." Receives 5-10 unsolicited mss/month. Accepts 8-10 mss/year. Publishes ms 8-18 months after acceptance. Recently published work by Ursula

K. Leguin, Robert Gregory, Blake Nelson and Jana Harris. Length: 5,000 words average; 100 words minimum; 25,000 words maximum. Publishes short shorts. Also publishes poetry. Sometimes critiques or comments on rejected mss.

How to Contact: Send complete ms with a cover letter. Include list of publications. Reports in 6-8 weeks on queries; 4-6 months on mss. Send SASE for reply, return of ms or send a disposable copy of ms. Simultaneous and electronic (disk) submissions OK. Sample copy for $6.

Payment/Terms: $50-100 and 2 contributor's copies on publication for first North American serial rights.

MISSISSIPPI REVIEW, (III), University of Southern Mississippi, Box 5144, Hattiesburg MS 39406-5144. (601)266-4321. E-mail: sushi.st.usm.edu/~barthelm/index.html. Editor: Frederick Barthelme. "Literary publication for those interested in contemporary literature—writers, editors who read to be in touch with current modes." Semiannually. Estab. 1972. Circ. 1,500.

● *Mississippi Review* has been devoting entire issues to single authors and may not be accepting manuscripts. Check with them before submitting.

Needs: Literary, contemporary, fantasy, humor, translations, experimental, avant-garde and "art" fiction. No juvenile. Buys varied amount of mss/issue. Does not read mss in summer. Recently published work by Jason Brown, Mervyn Morris, Terese Svoboda, Brenda Williams and Ian McDonald. Length: 100 pages maximum.

How to Contact: *See editor's note above.* Send complete ms with SASE including a short cover letter. Sample copy for $8.

Payment/Terms: Pays in contributor's copies. Acquires first North American serial rights.

THE MISSOURI REVIEW, (II), 1507 Hillcrest Hall, University of Missouri—Columbia, Columbia MO 65211. (573)882-4474. Fax: (573)884-4671. Editor: Speer Morgan. Magazine: 6×9; 212 pages. Theme: fiction, poetry, essays, reviews, interviews, cartoons, "all with a distinctly contemporary orientation. For writers, and the general reader with broad literary interests. We present nonestablished as well as established writers of excellence. The *Review* frequently runs feature sections or special issues dedicated to particular topics frequently related to fiction." Published 3 times/academic year. Estab. 1977. Circ. 6,800.

Needs: Condensed/excerpted novel, ethnic/multicultural, humor/satire, literary, contemporary. "No genre or flash fictions; no children's." Receives approximately 400 unsolicited fiction mss each month. Accepts 5-6 mss/issue; 15-20 mss/year. Recently published work by Robert Olen Butler, Mary Bush, Paula Huston and Gerald Shapiro. Published new writers within the last year. No preferred length. Also publishes personal essays, poetry. Often critiques rejected mss.

How to Contact: Send complete ms with SASE. Include brief bio and list of publications. Reports in 10 weeks. Send SASE for reply, return of ms or send disposable copy of ms. Sample copy for $7.

Payment/Terms: Pays $20/page minimum on signed contract for all rights.

Advice: Awards William Peden Prize in fiction; $1,000 to best story published in *Missouri Review* in a given year. Also sponsors Editors' Prize Contest with a prize of $1,500 for fiction, $1,000 for essays and $750 for poetry; and the Tom McAfee Discovery Prize in poetry for poets who have not yet published a book.

MOBIUS, The Journal of Social Change, (II), 1250 E. Dayton #3, Madison WI 53703. (608)255-4224. E-mail: smfred@aol.com. Editor: Fred Schepartz. Magazine: $8\frac{1}{2} \times 11$; 32-64 pages; 60 lb. paper; 60 lb. cover. "Looking for fiction which uses social change as either a primary or secondary theme. This is broader than most people think. Need social relevance in one way or another. For an artistically and politically aware and curious audience." Quarterly. Estab. 1989. Circ. 1,500.

Needs: Contemporary, ethnic, experimental, fantasy, feminist, gay, historical, horror, humor/satire, lesbian, literary, mainstream, prose poem, science fiction. "No porn, no racist, sexist or any other kind of ist. No Christian or spiritually proselytizing fiction." Receives 15 unsolicited mss/month. Accepts 3-5 mss/issue. Publishes ms 3-9 months after acceptance. Recently published work by JoAnn Yolanda Hernández, Patricia Stevens and Rochelle Schwab. Length: 3,500 words preferred; 500 words minimum; 5,000 words maximum. Publishes short shorts. Length: 500 words. Always critiques rejected mss.

How to Contact: Send complete ms with cover letter. Reports in 2-4 months. SASE. Simultaneous and reprint submissions OK. Sample copy for $2, 9×12 SAE and 3 first-class stamps. Fiction guidelines for 9×12 SAE and 4-5 first-class stamps.

Payment/Terms: Pays contributor's copies. Acquires one-time rights and electronic rights for www version.

Advice: "We like high impact, we like plot and character-driven stories that function like theater of the mind." Looks for "first and foremost, good writing. Prose must be crisp and polished; the story must pique my interest and make me care due to a certain intellectual, emotional aspect. Second, *Mobius* is about social change. We want stories that make some statement about the society we live in, either on a macro or micro level. Not that your story needs to preach from a soapbox (actually, we prefer that it doesn't), but your story needs to have *something* to say."

‡**modern words, a thoroughly queer literary journal, (II, IV)**, Garland Richard Kyle, 350 Bay St., #100, Box 325, San Francisco CA 94133. Editor: Garland Richard Kyle. Magazine: 4×7½; 264 pages; Simpson paper; Karma cover stock; photos. *modern words* Publishes "gay and lesbian, very eclectic work." Annually. Member of Council of Literary Magazines & Small Presses.
Needs: Condensed/excerpted novel, erotica, ethnic/multicultural, experimental, feminist, gay, lesbian, literary, serialized novel, translations. Receives 24 unsolicited mss/month. Accepts 12-14 mss/year. Recently published work by Roberto Friedman, Karl Soehnlein, J.L. Schneider, Alex Jeffers, Terry Wolverton, Gregg Shapiro, William Sterling Walker, Guy Wolf, Elise D'Haene, Gene-Michael Higney and Mark D. Jordan. Publishes short shorts. Also publishes literary essays and poetry.
How to Contact: Send complete ms with cover letter including phone number. Reports promptly on queries and mss. Send SASE for reply, return of ms or send a disposable copy of ms. Simultaneous submissions OK.
Payment/Terms: Pays 2 contributor's copies. Acquires first rights. Sends galleys to author.
Advice: "Read an issue prior to submitting work."

‡**THE MOODY STREET REVIEW, (I, II)**, 205 E. 78th St., #19L, New York NY 10021. Editor: David Gibson. Magazine: 8½×11; glue and tape binding; illustrations and photographs. "This is a literary magazine plain and simple. I make no pretenses about offering *alternative* or *quality* writing. It's just what I like, that's it. Send the work, not queries." Estab. 1988. Circ. 500-1,000.
Needs: "I don't like using categories. Human experience is not a library, it's a continuum. There is no exact order. I like writing that comes from the gut and brain alike. I like all sorts of perspectives, of descriptiveness, of emotionality. Now, I don't mean histrionics masquerading as literary endeavour. I do mean serious fiction, poetry, essays, etc. Some of my favorite fiction writers are Andre Dubus, Padgett Powell and Walter Mosley." Receives "a couple hundred mss per year, and usually accepts 10% of them." Reads mss all year long, but responses may be on the slow side during summer months. Recently published work by Rod Kessler, Catherine Gammon, Janice Levy and Jim Morgan. Length: 1,000-3,000 words.
How to Contact: Electronic submissions (Word for Windows, WordPerfect 5.1, DOS, 3.25 only). Sample copy $6, cash or check, payable in the editor's name. Reports in 3 months on mss. "After that, I rescind consideration; fairer to you, the writer."
Payment/Terms: Pays 2 contributor's copies; more at a discount, with postage prepaid. Not copyrighted.
Advice: "Although I like serious literary writing, it doesn't mean I expect everyone's work to rise to the same standard as established writers. Don't be afraid to be yourself on paper. Even if that self is a complete beginner. I'll do what I can to help."

THE MUSING PLACE, The Literary & Arts Magazine of Chicago's Mental Health Community, (IV), The Thresholds, 4101 N. Ravenswood, Chicago IL 60613. (773)281-3800, ext. 2465. Fax: (773)281-8790. Editor: Linda Krinsky. Magazine: 8½×11; 36 pages; 60 lb. paper; glossy cover; illustrations. "All material is composed by mental health consumers. The only requirement for consideration of publication is having a history of mental illness." Semiannually. Estab. 1986. Circ. 1,000.
Needs: Adventure, condensed/excerpted novel, ethnic/multicultural, experimental, fantasy (science fantasy, sword and sorcery), feminist, gay, historical (general), horror, humor/satire, lesbian, literary, mainstream/contemporary, mystery/suspense, regional, romance, science fiction and serialized novel. Publishes ms up to 6 months after acceptance. Published work by Allen McNair, Donna Willey and Mark Gonciarz. Length: 500 words average; 700 words maximum. Publishes short shorts. Length: 500 words. Also publishes poetry. Sometimes critiques and comments on rejected mss.
How to Contact: Send complete ms with a cover letter. Include bio (paragraph) and statement of having a history of mental illness. Reports in 6 months. Send a disposable copy of ms. Simultaneous and reprint submissions OK. Sample copy free.
Payment/Terms: Pays contributor's copies. Acquires one-time rights.

THE MYTHIC CIRCLE, (I), The Mythopoeic Society, Box 6707, Altadena CA 91001. Co-Editors: Tina Cooper and Christine Lowentrout. Magazine: 8½×11; 50 pages; high quality photocopy paper; illustrations. "A triannual fantasy-fiction magazine. We function as a 'writer's forum,' depending heavily on letters of comment from readers. We have a very occasional section called 'Mythopoeic Youth' in which we publish stories written by writers still in high school/junior high school, but we are not primarily oriented to young writers. We give subscribers' submissions preference." Triannually. Estab. 1987. Circ. 150.
Needs: Short fantasy. "No erotica, no graphic horror, no 'hard' science fiction." Receives 25 unsolicited ms/month. Accepts 19-20 mss/issue. Publishes ms 1-2 years after acceptance. Published work by Charles de Lint, Gwyneth Hood and Angelee Sailer Anderson. Published new writers within the last

year. Length: 3,000 words average. Publishes short shorts. Length: 8,000 words maximum. Always critiques rejected mss.

How to Contact: Send complete ms with cover letter. "We give each ms a personal response. We get many letters that try to impress us with other places they've appeared in print—that doesn't matter much to us." Reports in 6 months. SASE. No simultaneous submissions. Sample copy for $6.50; fiction guidelines for #10 SASE.

Payment/Terms: Pays in contributor's copies; charges for extras. Acquires one-time rights.

Advice: "There are very few places a fantasy writer can send to these days. *Mythic Circle* was started because of this; also, the writers were not getting any kind of feedback when (after nine or ten months) their mss were rejected. We give the writers personalized attention—critiques, suggestions—and we rely on our readers to send us letters of comment on the stories we publish, so that the writers can see a response. Don't be discouraged by rejections, especially if personal comments/suggestions are offered."

NASSAU REVIEW, (II), Nassau Community College, State University of New York, Stewart Ave., Garden City NY 11530-6793. (516)572-7792. Editor: Paul A. Doyle. Magazine: 5½×8½; 80-120 pages; heavy stock paper; b&w illustrations and photographs. For "college teachers, libraries, educated college-level readers." Annually. Estab. 1964.

Needs: Contemporary, fantasy, historical (general), literary, mainstream, serialized novel. Receives 600-800 unsolicited mss/year. Accepts 15 mss/issue. Does not read mss August through November. Publishes ms 6 months after acceptance. Published work by Dick Wimmer, Louis Phillips and Norbert Petsch. Length: 800-1,500 words preferred; 1,000 words minimum; 1,500 words maximum. Publishes short shorts "occasionally."

How to Contact: Send complete ms with cover letter. Include basic publication data. Reports in 1 month on queries; 8 months on mss. SASE. No simultaneous submissions. Sample copy for 9×12 SAE.

Payment/Terms: No payment. Acquires first rights or one-time rights.

Advice: Looks for "imaginative, concrete writing on interesting characters and scenes. Avoid the bizarre." Send story ms before March 1, $150 prize to best story published each year.

NEBO, A Literary Journal, (II), Arkansas Tech University, Dept. of English, Russellville AR 72801. (501)968-0256. Editors change each year. Contact Editor or Advisor: Dr. Michael Karl Ritchie. Literary, fiction and poetry magazine: 5×8; 50-60 pages. For a general, academic audience. Annually. Estab. 1983. Circ. 500.

Needs: Literary, mainstream, reviews. Upcoming theme: pop icon fiction and poetry (fiction and poetry that plays with the roles of pop icons). Receives 20-30 unsolicited fiction mss/month. Accepts 2 mss/issue; 6-10 mss/year. Does not read mss May 1-September 1. Recently published work by Steven Sherrill, J.B. Bernstein, Jameson Currier, Tricia Lande and Joseph Nicholson. Published new writers within the last year. Length: 3,000 words maximum. Also publishes literary essays, literary criticism, poetry. Occasionally critiques rejected mss.

How to Contact: Send complete ms with SASE and cover letter with bio. No simultaneous submissions. Reports in 3 months on mss. Publishes ms an average of 6 months after acceptance. Sample copy for $5. "Submission deadlines for all work are November 15 and January 15 of each year." Reviews novels and short story collections.

Payment/Terms: Pays 1 contributor's copy. Acquires one-time rights.

Advice: "A writer should carefully edit his short story before submitting it. Write from the heart and put everything on the line. Don't write from a phony or fake perspective. Frankly, many of the manuscripts we receive should be publishable with a little polishing. Manuscripts should *never* be submitted with misspelled words or on 'onion skin' or colored paper."

THE NEBRASKA REVIEW, (II), University of Nebraska at Omaha, Omaha NE 68182-0324. (402)554-2771. Fiction Editor: James Reed. Magazine: 5½×8½; 72 pages; 60 lb. text paper; chrome coat cover stock. "*TNR* attempts to publish the finest available contemporary fiction and poetry for college and literary audiences." Publishes 2 issues/year. Estab. 1973. Circ. 1,000.

• *The Nebraska Review* has published a number of award-winning writers.

Needs: Contemporary, humor/satire, literary and mainstream. Receives 40 unsolicited fiction mss/month. Accepts 4-5 mss/issue, 8-10 mss/year. Reads for the *Nebraska Review* Awards in Fiction and Poetry September 1-November 30; Open to submissions January 1-April 30; does not read May 1-August 31. Recently published work by Cris Mazza, Joseph Geha, Stewart O'Nan, Leslie Pietrzyk and Stephen Pett. Published new writers within the last year. Length: 5,000-6,000 words average. Also publishes poetry.

How to Contact: Send complete ms with SASE. Reports in 1-4 months. Publishes ms an average of 6-12 months after acceptance. Sample copy for $2.50.

Payment/Terms: Pays 2 contributor's copies plus 1 year subscription; $2 charge for extras. Acquires first North American serial rights.

Advice: "Write stories in which the lives of your characters are the primary reason for writing and techniques of craft serve to illuminate, not overshadow, the textures of those lives. Sponsors a $500 award/year—write for rules."

‡**NEOLOGISMS, A Journal of the Written Word, (I, II)**, Big Snapper Publishing, 1102 Pleasant St., P.O. Box 869, Worcester MA 01602. Editor: Jim Fay. Magazine: 8½×11; 70-90 pages; 60 lb. paper; 80 lb. cover stock; illustrations and photos. "*Neologisms* is dedicated to the written word in all forms and shapes." Quarterly. Estab. 1996. Circ. 125.

Needs: "No overly erotic, gay/lesbian, or children-oriented work." Upcoming themes: #5, education (Fall 1997, deadline May 1997); #7, music (Winter 1998, deadline November 1997). List of upcoming themes available for SASE. Receives 10 unsolicited mss/month. Accepts 5-8 mss/issue; 20-40 mss/year. Recently published work by Robert Ready, Jenny Curtis and Greg St. Thomasino. Length: 1,100 words average; 50 words minimum; 5,000 words maximum. Publishes short shorts. Also publishes literary essays, literary criticism and poetry.

How to Contact: Send complete ms with a cover letter. Include estimated word count, bio and list of publications. Reports in 2 weeks on queries; 1 month on mss. Send SASE for reply, return of ms or send a disposble copy of ms. Simultaneous and reprint submissions OK. Sample copy for $4. Free fiction guidelines. Reviews novels and short story collections.

Payment/Terms: Pays 1 contributor's copy; additional copies for $4. Acquires first rights "and option to use a second time if I ever do a 'Best of' issue." Sends galleys to author only if requested. Not copyrighted.

Advice: "Fiction must have originality and be able to catch my eye."

NERVE, (I, II), P.O. Box 124578, San Diego CA 92112-4578. Fax: (619)699-6308. E-mail: ptarmigan @gnn.com. Website: http://members.gnn.com/ptarmigan/nerve.htm. Editor: Geoffrey N. T. Young. Magazine: 5½×8½; 32-40 pages; 60 lb. cover stock; illustrations. "We are eager to work with un- or underpublished writers. We publish pieces that have something to say and that say it well." Triannually. Estab. 1994. Circ. 300.

Needs: Adventure, erotica, ethnic/multicultural, experimental, feminist, gay, historical (general), humor/satire, lesbian, literary, mainstream/contemporary, regional, sports. "No pornography. Nothing that insults the reader's intelligence." Receives 10-15 unsolicited mss/month. Accepts 1-3 mss/issue; 3-9 mss/year. Publishes ms 1-4 months after acceptance. Recently published work by Anjali Banerjee, Richard Kostelanetz and Mark Salfi. Length: 1,500 words average; 2,500 words maximum. Publishes short shorts. Also publishes literary essays and poetry. Rarely critiques or comments on rejected mss.

How to Contact: Send complete ms with a cover letter. Include estimated word count and 2-5 line bio. Reports in 2-4 months. Send SASE for reply, return of ms or send a disposable copy of ms. No simultaneous submissions. Sample copy for $3 (checks to Geoffrey N. T. Young). Reviews novels and short story collections. "We also publish *nerve online*, a monthly literary magazine on the Internet. Send stories to our e-mail address."

Payment/Terms: Pays 3 contributor's copies. Sends galleys to author upon request. Copyright reverts to author upon publication.

Advice: "Strong characters, good use of dialogue make a manuscript stand out. We want to see dialogue that advances the story. We see a lot of stories without dialogue, or with dialogue that merely chatters. Show us an exciting new topic, a fresh angle on an old topic. Take risks. Practice your craft. We receive too many submissions from authors with wonderful ideas, but who have not yet found their voice. And, of course, once you have a product, research the markets diligently. We encourage submissions of short shorts."

NEW ENGLAND REVIEW, (II), Middlebury College, Middlebury VT 05753. (802)443-5075. E-mail: nereview@mail.middlebury.edu. Editor: Stephen Donadio. Magazine: 6×9; 180 pages; 70 lb paper; coated cover stock; illustrations; photos. A literary quarterly publishing fiction, poetry and essays with special emphasis on contemporary cultural issues, both in the limited states and abroad. For general readers and professional writers. Quarterly. Estab. 1977. Circ. 2,000.

● *New England Review* has long been associated with Breadloaf Writer's Conference, held at Middlebury College.

Needs: Literary. Receives 250 unsolicited fiction mss/month. Accepts 5 mss/issue; 20 mss/year. Does not read ms June-August. Published work by Robert Olen Butler, Grace Paley, Charles Baxter, Joyce Carol Oates and Marge Piercy. Published new writers within the last year. Publishes ms 3-9 months after acceptance. Agented fiction: less than 5%. Publishes short shorts. Sometimes critiques rejected mss.

How to Contact: Send complete ms with cover letter. "Cover letters that demonstrate that the writer knows the magazine are the ones we want to read. We don't want hype, or hard-sell, or summaries of the author's intentions. Will consider simultaneous submissions, but must be stated as such." Reports in 10-12 weeks on mss. SASE.

Payment/Terms: Pays $10/page, $20 minimum and 2 contributor's copies on publication; charge for extras. Acquires first rights and reprint rights. Sends galleys to author.
Advice: "It's best to send one story at a time, and wait until you hear back from us to try again."

NEW LAUREL REVIEW, (II), New Orleans Poetry Forum/New Laurel Review, P.O. Box 770257, New Orleans LA 70112. (504)947-6001. Editor: Lee Meitzen Grue. Magazine: 6½ × 8; 125 pages; 60 lb. white paper; illustrations and photos. Journal of poetry, fiction, critical articles and reviews. "We have published such internationally known writers as James Nolan, Tomris Uyar and Yevgeny Yevtushenko." Readership: "Literate, adult audiences as well as anyone interested in writing with significance, human interest, vitality, subtlety, etc." Published irregularly. Estab. 1970. Circ. 500. Member of Council of Editors of Learned Journals.
Needs: Literary, ethnic/multicultural, excerpted novel, translations, "cutting edge." No "dogmatic, excessively inspirational or political" material. Acquires 1-2 fiction mss/issue. Receives approximately 25 unsolicited fiction mss each month. Does not read mss during summer months and December. Agented fiction 10%. Length: about 10 printed pages. Publishes short shorts. Also publishes literary essays and poetry. Critiques rejected mss when there is time.
How to Contact: Send complete ms with a cover letter. Include bio and list of publications. Reports in 3 months. Send SASE for reply or return of ms. No simultaneous submissions. Sample copy for $7. "Authors need to look at sample copy before submitting."
Payment/Terms: Pays 1 contributor's copy; additional copies $7, discounted. Acquires first rights.
Advice: "We are interested in fresh, original work that keeps a reader reading. Send a finished manuscript: clean."

NEW LETTERS MAGAZINE, (I, II), University of Missouri-Kansas City, 5100 Rockhill Rd., Kansas City MO 64110. (816)235-1168. Fax: (816)235-2611. Editor: James McKinley. Magazine: 14 lb. cream paper; illustrations. Quarterly. Estab. 1971 (continuation of *University Review*, founded 1935). Circ. 2,500.
Needs: Contemporary, ethnic, experimental, humor/satire, literary, mainstream, translations. No "bad fiction in any genre." Published work by Tess Gallagher, Jimmy Carter and Amiri Baraka; published work by new writers within the last year. Agented fiction: 10%. Also publishes short shorts. Rarely critiques rejected mss.
How to Contact: Send complete ms with cover letter. Does not read mss May 15-October 15. Reports in 3 weeks on queries; 2-3 months on mss. SASE for ms. No simultaneous or multiple submissions. Sample copy: $8.50 for issues older than 5 years; $5.50 for 5 years or less.
Payment/Terms: Pays honorarium—depends on grant/award money; 2 contributor's copies. Sends galleys to author.
Advice: "Seek publication of representative chapters in high-quality magazines as a way to the book contract. Try literary magazines first."

NEW ORLEANS REVIEW, (I, II), Box 195, Loyola University, New Orleans LA 70118. (504)865-2295. Fax: (504)865-2294. E-mail: noreview@beta.loyno.edu. Editor: Ralph Adamo. Magazine: 8½ × 11; 160 pages; 60 lb. Scott offset paper; 12 + King James C1S cover stock; photos. "Publishes poetry, fiction, translations, photographs, nonfiction on literature and film. Readership: those interested in current culture, literature." Quarterly. Estab. 1968. Circ. 1,300.
Needs: "Storytelling between traditional and experimental." Recently published work by Gordon Lish, Steven March, Norman Germain, Michelle Fredette, Alfred Schwaid, C. Semansky, Trudy Lewis and Ellen Gandt.
How to Contact: Send complete ms with SASE. Does not accept simultaneous submissions. Accepts disk submissions; inquire about system compatibility. Prefers hard copy with disk submission. Reports in 2-12 weeks. Sample copy for $9.
Payment/Terms: "Inquire." Most payment in copies. Pays on publication for first North American serial rights.

THE NEW PRESS LITERARY QUARTERLY, (II), 63-44 Saunders St., Suite 3, Rego Park NY 11374. (718)459-6807. Fax: (718)275-1646. Editor: Joe Sullivan. Magazine: 8½ × 11; 40 pages; medium bond paper and thick cover stock; b&w illustrations and photographs. "Poems, short stories,

---

FOR INFORMATION ON ENTERING the *Novel & Short Story Writer's Market* Cover Letter Contest, see page 16.

commentary, personal journalism. Original, informative and entertaining." Quarterly. Estab. 1984. Circ. 2,000.

Needs: Experimental, humor/satire, mainstream, mystery/suspense. No gratuitous violence. Receives 25 unsolicited mss/month. Accepts 5 mss/issue; 20 mss/year. Publishes ms 12 months after acceptance. Recently published work by Sol Rubin, Les Haber and Mark Blickley. Published new writers within the last year. Length: 22 double-spaced pages. Also publishes literary essays, literary criticism and poetry.

How to Contact: *Charges reading fee for nonsubscribers. $5/short story (22-double-spaced pages maximum).* Send complete ms with cover letter. Reports in 6 months. SASE. Simultaneous submissions OK. Sample copy for $5.50; fiction guidelines for SASE. $15 for one-year (4 issues) subscription, add $5 for foreign subscription.

Payment/Terms: Pays 2 contributor's copies plus $15 maximum for each prose piece over 500 words ($10 for prose 500 words or less) for first rights.

Advice: "Our approach is eclectic. We want to bring literary participation to as many people as possible. We accept works by established writers and by literary newcomers. Our works appeal to a broad spectrum because they are sensitive to human relationships without prejudice or hatred."

the new renaissance, (II), 9 Heath Rd., Arlington MA 02174. Fiction Editors: Louise T. Reynolds, Michal Anne Kuchauki and Patricia Michaud. Magazine: 6×9; 144-182 pages; 70 lb. paper; laminated cover stock; artwork; photos. "An international magazine of ideas and opinions, emphasizing literature and the arts, *tnr* takes a classicist position in literature and the arts. Publishes a variety of very diverse, quality fiction, always well crafted, occasionally experimental. *tnr* is unique among literary magazines for its marriage of the literary and visual arts with political/sociological articles and essays. We publish the beginning as well as the emerging and established writer." Biannually. Estab. 1968. Circ. 1,500.

● Work published in *the new renaissance* has been chosen for inclusion in *Editor's Choice III, Editor's Choice IV* and *Sudden Fiction*.

Needs: Serious, quality literary, humorous, off-beat fiction. Accepts 4-5 mss/issue, 6-10 mss/year. Receives approximately 80-140 unsolicited fiction mss each month. Reads only from January 2 through June 1 and from September 1 through October 31. Agented fiction approx. 5-8%. Recently published work by Marvin Mandell, Richard Lynch, G.P. Vimal, Mitch Evich and Nicholas Emmett. Length of fiction: 3-36 pages. Also publishes articles, essays, literary criticism, poetry translations. Comments on rejected mss "if we feel we might be helpful. If writers prefer not to have their mss very briefly commented on, we ask that they let us know at the time they submit."

How to Contact: *"Entry fee of $15 required for nonsubscribers," $10 for subscribers.* All fiction mss received without the entry fee are returned unread. Send complete ms with SASE or IRC of sufficient size for return. "Inform us if multiple submission. If you query, enclose SASE, IRC or stamped post card." Reluctantly accepts simultaneous submissions but "we ask that you notify us if the ms has been accepted elsewhere. If we haven't yet read your story, we will accept a substitution either at the time of such notification or within 2 months thereafter." Reports in 5-9 months on mss. Publishes ms an average of 12-18 months after acceptance. Reviews novels and short story collections, also biography, poetry collections, etc.

Payment/Terms: Pays $42-85 after publication; 1 contributor's copy. "We offer contributors' discounts for 3 or more copies. All fiction and poetry submissions are now tied into our awards program for the best fiction and poetry published in a three-issue volume of *tnr*. Subscribers: $10 entry fee, non-subscribers: $15 entry fee; writers will receive 2 back issues or a recent issue." Acquires all rights in case of a later *tnr* book collection; otherwise, rights return to the writer.

Advice: "This may be preaching to the converted—but we strongly recommend that writers consult current market directories for guidelines on submitting AND that they read them carefully. This past year, for example, we've had to return more than 350 manuscripts (fiction) UNREAD because they didn't pay attention to our entry fee and awards programs. Also, when writers receive an issue of *tnr* or any other litmag that they are considering submitting to, they should read the fiction very carefully and closely, not just scan it. We continue to receive fiction from subscribers and others who have seen at least one or two issues of *tnr* which is absolutely wrong (most frequently in tone or statement but sometimes also in style) for us. Had they read our fiction those manuscripts would never have ended up at *tnr*. We have a wide range but we're not 'anything goes.' We favor writing that is personal, compelling, something that is layered so that on successive readings, the story continues to offer revelations on our common human condition, All of our fiction is not like that, of course, but we continue to look for fiction that can hold up to repeated readings regardless of the statement. We don't want to see well-done, technically proficient 'So what' stories. Learn to edit your own work so that it does not seem self-indulgent to the reader/stranger. And read—read contemporary fiction, modern fiction, and fiction that is not of our time. A wonderful thing about fiction is that it can take us into other cultures, other ages, other sensibilities; at *tnr*, we're looking for a lens, not a mirror."

‡NEW WRITING, A Literary Magazine for New Writers, (I), P.O. Box 1812, Amherst NY 14226-7812. E-mail: newwriting@aol.com. Editor: Sam Meade. Electronic magazine: 150 pages;

coated cover stock; illustrations and photographs. "We publish work that is deserving." Annually. Estab. 1994.

Needs: Work by new writers: action, experimental, horror, humor/satire, literary, mainstream/contemporary, romance, translations, westerns. Length: open. Publishes short shorts. Often critiques or comments on rejected mss. Sponsors an annual award.

How to Contact: Send complete ms with a cover letter. Include *brief* list of publications and *short* cover letter. Reports in 1-2 months. Send SASE for return of ms. Simultaneous submissions OK. Reviews novels and short story collections.

Payment/Terms: Pays 2 contributor's copies. Acquires one-time rights.

Advice: "Don't send first copies of *any* story. Always read over, and rewrite!" Avoid "stories with characters who are writers, and death and dying stories—we get too many of them."

✤NeWEST REVIEW, (II, IV), Box 394, R.P.O. University, Saskatoon, Saskatchewan S7N 4J8 Canada. Fax: (306)343-8579. E-mail: verne.clemence@sk.sympatico.ca. Editor: Verne Clemence. Magazine: 40 pages; book stock; illustrations; photos. Magazine devoted to western Canada regional issues; "fiction, reviews, poetry for middle- to high-brow audience." Bimonthly (6 issues per year). Estab. 1975. Circ. 1,000.

Needs: "We want fiction of high literary quality, whatever its form and content. But we do have a heavy regional emphasis." Receives 15-20 unsolicited mss/month. Accepts 1 ms/issue; 10 mss/year. Recently published work by Betty Jane Hegerat, Dave Margoshes, Shelley A. Leedahl and Helen Mourre. Length: 2,500 words average; 1,500 words minimum; 5,000 words maximum. Sometimes recommends other markets.

How to Contact: "We like *brief* cover letters." Reports very promptly in a short letter. SAE, IRCs or Canadian postage. No multiple submissions. Electronic submissions (disk or e-mail) OK. Sample copy for $5.

Payment/Terms: Pays $100 maximum on publication for one-time rights.

Advice: "We don't want unpolished, careless submissions. We do want to be intrigued, entertained and stimulated. Polish your writing. Develop your story line. Give your characters presence. If we, the readers, are to care about the people you create, you too must take them seriously."

NIGHTSUN, (II), Department of English, Frostburg State University, Frostburg MD 21532. Editor: Douglas DeMars. Magazine: 6×9; 64 pages; recycled paper. "Although *Nightsun* is primarily a journal of poetry and interviews, we are looking for excellent short-short fiction (5 pgs. maximum)." Annually. Estab. 1981. Circ. 300-500.

How to Contact: Send inquiry with SASE. No simultaneous submissions. Reports within 2-3 months. Sample copy for $6.50.

Payment/Terms: Pays 2 contributor's copies. Acquires one-time rights (rights revert to author after publication).

NIMROD, International Journal of Prose and Poetry, (II), University of Tulsa, 600 S. College Ave., Tulsa OK 74104. (918)631-3080. Editor-in-Chief: Francine Ringold. Magazine: 6×9; 160 pages; 60 lb. white paper; illustrations; photos. "We publish one thematic issue and one awards issue each year. A recent theme was "The City," a compilation of poetry and prose from all over the world." We seek vigorous, imaginative, quality writing." Semiannually. Estab. 1956. Circ. 3,000.

● *Nimrod* received an Honorable Mention from the 1995 American Literary Magazine Awards.

Needs: "We accept contemporary poetry and/or prose. May submit adventure, ethnic, experimental, prose poem, science fiction or translations." Upcoming theme: "From time to time" (1997). Receives 120 unsolicited fiction mss/month. Published work by Janette Turner Hospital, Josephine Jacobson, Alice Walker, Francois Camoin and Gish Jen; published 15 new writers within the last year. Length: 7,500 words maximum. Also publishes poetry.

How to Contact: Reports in 3-5 months. Sample copy: "to see what *Nimrod* is all about, send $6 for a back issue. To receive a recent awards issue, send $8 (includes postage).

Payment/Terms: Pays 2 contributor's copies, plus $5/page up to $25 total per author per issue for one-time rights.

Advice: "We have not changed our fiction needs: quality, vigor, distinctive voice. We have, however, increased the number of stories we print. See current issues. We look for fiction that is fresh, vigorous, distinctive, serious and humorous, seriously-humorous, unflinchingly serious, ironic—whatever. Just so it is quality. Strongly encourage writers to send #10 SASE for brochure for annual literary contest with prizes of $1,000 and $2,000."

96 Inc., (I, II), P.O. Box 15559, Boston MA 02215. (617)267-0543. Fiction Editors: Julie Anderson and Nancy Mehegan. Magazine: 8½×11; 50 pages; 20 lb. paper; matte cover; illustrations and photos. "*96 Inc.* promotes the process; integrates beginning/young with established writers; reaches out to audiences of all ages and backgrounds." Semiannually. Estab. 1992. Circ. 3,000.

Needs: Gay, historical (general), humor/satire, lesbian, literary and translations. Receives 200 unsolicited mss/month. Accepts 12-15 mss/issue; 30 mss/year. Agented fiction 10%. Recently published work by Gordon Lish, Mark Goldstein, Mary Hazzard, Frances Wosmek, Syd Gold and Carl Vigeland. Length: 1,000 words minimum; 7,000 words maximum. Publishes short shorts. Also publishes literary essays, literary criticism and poetry. Sometimes critiques or comments on rejected mss.
How to Contact: Query first. Include estimated word count, bio (100 words) and list of publications. Reports in 3 weeks on queries; 6-12 months on mss. Send SASE for reply, return of ms or send a disposable copy of ms. Simultaneous and electronic submissions OK. Sample copy for $5.50. Fiction guidelines for #10 SASE. Reviews novels and short story collections.
Payment/Terms: Pays $20-100 (if funds are available, not depending on length or merit), free subscription and 4 contributor's copies on publication for one-time rights.
Advice: Looks for "good writing in any style. Pays attention to the process. Read at least one issue. Be patient—It takes a very long time for readers to go through the thousands of manuscripts."

NITE-WRITER'S INTERNATIONAL LITERARY ARTS JOURNAL, (I, II), Nite Owl Press, 3101 Schieck St., Suite 100, Pittsburgh PA 15227-4151. (412)882-2259. Editor: John A. Thompson, Sr. Magazine: 8½×11; 30-50 pages; bond paper; illustrations. "*Nite-Writer's International Literary Arts Journal* is dedicated to the emotional intellectual with a creative perception of life." Quarterly. Estab. 1993. Circ. 100.
Needs: Adventure, erotica, historical, humor/satire, literary, mainstream/contemporary, religious/inspirational, romance, senior citizen/retirement, sports, young adult/teen (adventure). Plans special fiction issue or anthology. Receives 3-5 unsolicited mss/month. Accepts 1-2 mss/issue; 5-8 mss/year. Publishes ms within 1 year after acceptance. Recently published work by Julia Klatt Singer, Jean Oscarson Schoell, Lawrence Keough and S. Anthony Smith. Length: 150 words average; 150 words minimum; 250 words maximum. Publishes short shorts. Also publishes literary essays, literary criticism, poetry. Often critiques or comments on rejected mss.
How to Contact: Send complete ms with a cover letter. Include estimated word count, 1-page bio, list of publications. Reports in 4-6 weeks. SASE for return of ms. Simultaneous submissions OK. Sample copy for $6, 9×13 SAE and 6 first-class stamps. Fiction guidelines for legal size SASE.
Payment/Terms: Does not pay. Acquires first North American serial rights. Sponsors contests.
Advice: "Read a lot of what you write, study the market; don't fear rejection, but use it as a learning tool to strengthen your work before resubmitting. Express what the heart feels."

THE NORTH AMERICAN REVIEW, University of Northern Iowa, Cedar Falls IA 50614. (319)273-6455. Editor: Robley Wilson. Publishes quality fiction. Bimonthly. Estab. 1815. Circ. 4,500.
Needs: Open (literary). Reads mss from January 1 to April 1 only.
How to Contact: Send complete ms with SASE. Sample copy for $5.
Payment/Terms: Pays approximately $20/printed page; 2 contributor's copies on publication for first North American serial rights. $3.50 charge for extras.
Advice: "We stress literary excellence and read 3,000 manuscripts a year to find an average of 35 stories that we publish. Please *read* the magazine first."

NORTH DAKOTA QUARTERLY, (II), University of North Dakota, Box 7209, University Station, Grand Forks ND 58202. (701)777-3321. Editor: Robert W. Lewis. Fiction Editor: William Borden. Poetry Editor: Jay Meek. Magazine: 6×9; 200 pages; bond paper; illustrations; photos. Magazine publishing "essays in humanities; some short stories; some poetry." University audience. Quarterly. Estab. 1910. Circ. 800.
● Work published in *North Dakota Quarterly* was selected for inclusion in *The O. Henry Awards* anthology. The editors are especially interested in work by Native American writers.
Needs: Contemporary, ethnic, experimental, feminist, historical, humor/satire and literary. Receives 20-30 unsolicited mss/month. Accepts 4 mss/issue; 16 mss/year. Published work by Naguib Mahfouz, Jerry Bumpus, Carol Shields, Rilla Askew and Chris Mazza. Published new writers within the last year. Length: 3,000-4,000 words average. Also publishes literary essays, literary criticism, poetry.
How to Contact: Send complete ms with cover letter. "But it need not be much more than hello; please read this story; I've published (if so, best examples) . . ." SASE. Reports in 3 months. Publishes ms an average of 1 year after acceptance. Sample copy for $5. Reviews novels and short story collections.
Payment/Terms: Pays 3 contributor's copies; 30% discount for extras; year's subscription. Acquires one-time rights.

NORTHEAST ARTS MAGAZINE, (II), Boston Arts Organization, Inc., P.O. Box 94, Kittery ME 03904. Editor: Mr. Leigh Donaldson. Magazine: 6½×9½; 32-40 pages; matte finish paper; card stock cover; illustrations and photographs. Bimonthly. Estab. 1990. Circ. 750.
Needs: Ethnic, gay, historical, literary, mystery/suspense (private eye), prose poem (under 2,000 words). No obscenity, racism, sexism, etc. Receives 50 unsolicited mss/month. Accepts 1-2 mss/issue;

5-7 mss/year. Publishes ms 2-4 months after acceptance. Agented fiction 20%. Length: 750 words preferred. Publishes short shorts. Sometimes critiques rejected mss.

How to Contact: Send complete ms with cover letter. Include short bio. Reports in 1 month on queries; 2-4 months on mss. SASE. Simultaneous submissions OK. Sample copy for $4.50, SAE and 75¢ postage. Fiction guidelines free.

Payment/Terms: Pays 2 contributor's copies. Acquires first North American serial rights. Sometimes sends galleys to author.

Advice: Looks for "creative/innovative use of language and style. Unusual themes and topics."

NORTHEAST CORRIDOR, (II), Beaver College, 450 S. Easton Rd., Glenside PA 19038. (215)572-2963. Editor: Susan Balée. Fiction Editor: Peggy Finn. Magazine: 6¾ × 10; 120-180 pages; 60 lb. white paper; glossy, perfect-bound cover; illustrations and photos. "Interested in writers and themes treating the Northeast Corridor region of America. Literary fiction, poetry, drama, essays." Semiannually. Estab. 1993. Circ. 1,000.

● *Northeast Corridor* has received grants from the Daphne Foundation, the Ruth and Robert Satter Foundation, the Cottonwood Foundation and the Nicholas Roerich Museum.

Needs: Literary: excerpted novel, ethnic/multicultural, feminist, humor/satire, literary, regional, translations. No religious, western, young adult, science fiction, juvenile, horror. List of upcoming themes available for SASE. Planning future special fiction issue or anthology. Receives 100 unsolicited mss/ month. Accepts 2-6 mss/issue; 4-12 mss/year. Reads mss infrequently during June, July and August. Publishes ms 6 months after acceptance. Recently published work by Glen Weldon, Eleanor Wilner, Dana Gioia, Rita Ciresi and Stephen Dobyns. Length: 2,500 words average; 1,000 words minimum; 4,500 words maximum. Publishes literary essays, interviews and poetry. Often critiques or comments on rejected mss.

How to Contact: Send complete ms with a cover letter. Include word count, 1-2 line bio and publications list. Reports in 2-4 months on mss. SASE for reply, return of ms or send a disposable copy of ms. Simultaneous submissions OK if indicated. Sample copy for $5, 9 × 12 SAE and $1.21 postage. Fiction guidelines for #10 SASE.

Payment/Terms: Pays $10-100 and 2 contributor's copies on publication for first North American serial rights; additional copies for $3.50/copy.

Advice: "In selecting fiction we look for love of language, developed characters, believable conflict, metaphorical prose, satisfying resolution. Read everything from Chekov to Alice Munro and write at least 10-20 stories before you start trying to send them out. We would like to see more humor. Writers should avoid sending work that is 'therapy' rather than 'art.' "

NORTHWEST REVIEW, (II), 369 PLC, University of Oregon, Eugene OR 97403. (503)346-3957. Editor: John Witte. Fiction Editor: Janice MacCrae. Magazine: 6 × 9; 140-160 pages; high quality cover stock; illustrations; photos. "A general literary review featuring poems, stories, essays and reviews, circulated nationally and internationally. For a literate audience in avant-garde as well as traditional literary forms; interested in the important writers who have not yet achieved their readership." Triannually. Estab. 1957. Circ. 1,200.

● *Northwest Review* has received the Oregon Governor's Award for the Arts. The work included in *Northwest Review* tends to be literary, heavy on character and theme.

Needs: Contemporary, experimental, feminist, literary and translations. Accepts 4-5 mss/issue, 12-15 mss/year. Receives approximately 100 unsolicited fiction mss each month. Published work by Diana Abu-Jaber, Madison Smartt Bell, Maria Flook and Charles Marvin. Published new writers within the last year. Length: "Mss longer than 40 pages are at a disadvantage." Also publishes literary essays, literary criticism, poetry. Critiques rejected mss when there is time. Sometimes recommends other markets.

How to Contact: Send complete ms with SASE. "No simultaneous submissions are considered." Reports in 3-4 months. Sample copy for $4. Reviews novels and short story collections. Send books to John Witte.

Payment/Terms: Pays 3 contributor's copies and one-year subscription; 40% discount on extras. Acquires first rights.

NORTHWOODS JOURNAL, A Magazine for Writers, (I, II), Conservatory of American Letters, P.O. Box 298, Thomaston ME 04861. (207)354-0998. Fax: (207)354-8953. E-mail: olrob@-midcoast.com. Editor: R.W. Olmsted. Fiction Editor: Ken Sieben. Magazine: 5½ × 8½; 32-64 pages; white paper; 65 lb. card cover; some illustrations and photographs. "No theme, no philosophy—for people who read for entertainment." Quarterly. Estab. 1993. Circ. 500.

Needs: Adventure, erotica, experimental, fantasy (science fantasy, sword and sorcery), literary, mainstream/contemporary, mystery/suspense (amateur sleuth, police procedural, private eye/hard-boiled, romantic suspense), psychic/supernatural/occult, regional, romance (gothic, historical), science fiction (hard science, soft/sociological), sports, westerns (frontier, traditional). Publishes special fiction issue or anthology. Receives 50 unsolicited mss/month. Accepts 12-15 mss/year. Recently published work by Harold Hahn, Bert Benmegee, Anne H. Bahr and Colquitt James. Length: 2,500 words maximum. Also publishes literary essays, literary criticism and poetry.

How to Contact: Read guidelines *before* submitting. Send complete ms with a cover letter. Include word count and list of publications. Reports in 1-2 days on queries; by next deadline plus 5 days on mss. Send SASE for reply, return of ms or send a disposable copy of ms. No simultaneous submissions. Sample copies: $5 next issue, $7.75 current issue, $10 back issue (if available), all postage paid. Fiction guidelines for #10 SASE. Reviews novels, short story collections and poetry.

Payment/Terms: Varies, "minimum $5/published page on acceptance for first North American serial rights."

Advice: "Read guidelines, read the things we've published. Know your market."

‡**NYX OBSCURA MAGAZINE, Delicate Decadence & Ethereal Music, (II)**, P.O. Box 5554, Atlanta GA 31107. (404)373-1132. E-mail: obscura@mindspring.com. Editor: Diana McCrary. Magazine: 6×9; 40 pages; 30 lb. paper; 80 lb. cover stock; illustrations and photos. Annually. Estab. 1994. Circ. 1,500.

Needs: Erotica, fantasy, psychic/supernatural/occult. "Nothing set in the 20th century." Publishes special fiction issues or anthologies. Receives 50-100 unsolicited mss/month. Accepts 2-3 mss/issue; 2-5 mss/year. Publishes ms 6 months after acceptance. Recently published work by Patricia Russo, A.D. Ian and D.F. Lewis. Publishes short shorts. Often critiques or comments on rejected mss.

How to Contact: Query with clips of published work. Reports in 3 weeks on queries; 8 months on mss. Send SASE for reply, return of ms or send 2 disposable copies of ms. Simultaneous and electronic submissions OK. Sample copy for $5. Fiction guidelines for #10 SASE. Reviews novels and short story collections.

Payment/Terms: Pays 1 contributor's copy on publication; additional copies for $2. Acquires one-time rights and rights to reprint on web page.

Advice: Looks for "unusual or archaic themes—fresh, skillful, elegant writing. Scour your manuscript for clichés and eliminate them. Read your manuscript aloud."

OASIS, A Literary Magazine, (I, II), P.O. Box 626, Largo FL 33779-0626. (813)449-2186. Editor: Neal Storrs. Magazine: 70 pages. "Literary magazine first, last and always—looking for styles that delight and amaze, that are polished and poised. Next to that, content considerations relatively unimportant—open to all." Quarterly. Estab. 1992. Circ. 500.

Needs: High-quality writing. Receives 150 unsolicited mss/month. Accepts 6 mss/issue; 24 mss/year. Publishes ms 4-6 months after acceptance. Recently published work by George R. Clay, Al Masarik, Mark Wisniewski and James Sallis. Length: no minimum or maximum. Also publishes literary essays and poetry. Often critiques or comments on rejected mss.

How to Contact: Send complete ms with or without a cover letter. Usually reports same day. Send SASE for reply, return of ms or send a disposable copy of ms. Simultaneous and reprint submissions OK. Sample copy for $6.50. Fiction guidelines for #10 SASE.

Payment/Terms: Pays $15-50 and 1 contributor's copy on publication for first rights.

Advice: "Revise till your fingers bleed. If you want to write good stories, read good stories. Cultivate the critical ability to recognize what makes a story original and true to itself."

‡**OATMEAL & POETRY, Wholesome Nutrition From The Heart, (I, II)**, Voyager Publishing, P.O. Box 2215, Stillwater MN 55082. (612)578-9589. E-mail (inquiries only): daflanagan@admin.stkat e.edu. Editor: Demitra Flanagan. Magazine: 8½×11; 40 pages; bond paper; parchment cover stock; illustrations and photos. *Oatmeal & Poetry* is a forum for new and growing writers. We publish short stories, articles and poetry that are tasteful, well written and entertaining. Our philosophy is stated in our subtitle 'wholesome nutrition—from the heart.' Our intended audience includes all persons who appreciate well-crafted and well-written stories, shorts, articles, editorials and poetry that deal with both the dark and light side of life while maintaining integrity." Quarterly. Estab. 1994. Circ. 500. "A nominal fee of $2/story or article and $1/poem is charged to offset costs of cash awards granted in each issue."

Needs: Adventure (10-12 years), condensed/excerpted novel, ethnic/multicultural, fantasy (children's, science), historical, humor/satire, literary, mainstream/contemporary, mystery/suspense (amateur sleuth, cozy, police procedural, private eye/hardboiled, romantic suspense), psychic/supernatural/occult, regional, religious/inspirational, romance (contemporary, futuristic/time travel, gothic, historical), science fiction, senior citizen/retirement, westerns (frontier, traditional), young adult/teen (adventure, mystery, romance). "No gay/lesbian plots, explicit sex, erotica, pornography or excessive violence. This is a family magazine. Our magazine generally focuses on the changing seasons, the holidays and how we live through them all." List of upcoming themes available for SASE. Publishes annual special fiction issue or anthology. Receives 15-20 unsolicited mss/month. Accepts 4-6 mss/issue; 24 mss/year. Publishes ms 3-6 months after acceptance. Recently published work by Don Porter, Robert Trudel, William Cain, William Parsons, Carol Veitenheimer and Carrie Johanne. Length: 1,200-1,500 words average; 500 words minimum; 2,000 words maximum. Publishes short shorts. Also publishes literary essays, literary criticism and poetry. Often critiques or comments on rejected mss.

How to Contact: "First, obtain our complete guidelines, then submit accordingly." Include estimated word count, half-page bio and social security number. Reports in 1-2 weeks on queries. Send SASE for reply, return of ms or send a disposable copy of ms. No simultaneous submissions. Reprints OK.Query for sample copy price. Fiction guidelines for #10 SASE.

Payment/Terms: Writers who contribute literary articles receive free subscription. Pays contributor's copies on publication; additional copies for $4.50. Acquires first rights or one-time rights. Sends galleys to author. Sponsors contests. Send #10 SAE for guidelines and information on cash prizes for short story and article contests (also poetry and anthology).

Advice: "The opening must grab the reader, follow through with a story that flows, present strong characters and be visual. Stories *must have* a strong ending! The storyteller must know how to *show* me what he/she is saying. Write, take healthy criticism and rewrite, and rewrite and rewrite. Never let rejection stop you. Writers learn from rejection (or at least the successful ones do)."

OBSIDIAN II: BLACK LITERATURE IN REVIEW, (II, IV), Dept. of English, North Carolina State University, Raleigh NC 27695-8105. (919)515-4153. Editor: Gerald Barrax. Fiction Editor: Susie R. Powell. Magazine: 6×9; 130 pages. "Creative works in English by black writers, scholarly critical studies by all writers on black literature in English." Published 2 times/year (spring/summer, fall/winter). Estab. 1975. Circ. 500.

Needs: Ethnic (pan-African), feminist. No poetry, fiction or drama mss not written by black writers. Accepts 7-9 mss/year. Published new writers within the last year. Length: 1,500-10,000 words.

How to Contact: Send complete ms in duplicate with SASE. Reports in 3 months. Publishes ms an average of 4-6 months after acceptance. Sample copy for $6.

Payment/Terms: Pays in contributor's copies. Acquires one-time rights. Sponsors contests occasionally; guidelines published in magazine.

THE OHIO REVIEW, (II), 209C Ellis Hall, Ohio University, Athens OH 45701-2979. (614)593-1900. Editor: Wayne Dodd. Assistant Editor: Robert Kinsley. Magazine: 6×9; 200 pages; illustrations on cover. "We attempt to publish the best poetry and fiction written today. For a mainly literary audience." Semiannually. Estab. 1971. Circ. 3,000.

Needs: Contemporary, experimental, literary. "We lean toward contemporary on all subjects." Receives 150-200 unsolicited fiction mss/month. Accepts 5 mss/issue. Does not read mss June 1-September 15. Publishes ms 6 months after acceptance. Also publishes poetry. Sometimes critiques rejected mss and/or recommends other markets.

How to Contact: Query first or send complete ms with cover letter. Reports in 6 weeks. SASE. Sample copy for $6. Fiction guidelines for #10 SASE.

Payment/Terms: Pays $5/page, free subscription to magazine and 2 contributor's copies on publication for first North American serial rights. Sends galleys to author.

Advice: "We feel the short story is an important part of the contemporary writing field and value it highly. Read a copy of our publication to see if your fiction is of the same quality. So often people send us work that simply doesn't fit our needs."

OLD CROW REVIEW, (I, II), FKB Press, P.O.Box 662, Amherst MA 01004-0662. Editor: John Gibney. Magazine: 5½×8½; 100 pages; 20 lb. paper; 90 lb. cover stock; illustrations and photos. Semiannually. Estab. 1991. Circ. 500.

Needs: Erotica, experimental, literary, mainstream/contemporary, psychic/supernatural/occult, regional, translations. Receives 20-40 unsolicited mss/month. Accepts 3-5 mss/issue; 6-10 mss/year. Publishes ms 1-3 months after acceptance. Agented fiction 25%. Recently published work by William Monahan, Michael Ventura and Elizabeth Haliwell-Borden. Length: 3,000 words average; 6,000 words maximum. Publishes short shorts. Also publishes literary essays, literary criticism and poetry.

How to Contact: Send complete ms with a cover letter. Should include estimated word count, bio (2-5 sentences) and list of publications. Reports in 1 month on queries; 2 months on mss. Send SASE for reply, return of ms or send a disposable copy of ms. Simultaneous and reprint submissions OK. Sample copy for $5; make check payable to John Gibney. Fiction guidelines for #10 SASE.

Payment/Terms: Pays 1 contributor's copy; additional copies for $5.

Advice: "A piece must seem true to us. If it strikes us as a truth we never even suspected, we build an issue around it. Visions, or fragments of visions, of a new myth emerging at the millennial end are welcome. We haven't seen enough writers taking risks with their stories. Avoid sending pieces which sound just like somebody else's."

THE OLD RED KIMONO, (I, II), Floyd College, Box 1864, Rome GA 30162. (706)295-6363. Editors: Jeff Mack and Jonathan Hershey. Magazine: 8×11; 65-70 pages; white offset paper; 10 pt. board cover stock. Annually. Estab. 1972. Circ. 1,500.

Needs: Literary. "We will consider good fiction regardless of category." No children's fiction. Receives 200 mss/month. Accepts 3-5 mss/issue. Does not read mss March 1 through September 30.

"Issue out in May every year." Recently published work by Ruth Moon Kempher, David Huddle, Adam Stanley and Peter Huggins. Length: 2,500 words maximum. Publishes short shorts. Also publishes poetry.

How to Contact: Send complete ms with cover letter. Reports in 2 weeks on queries; 2-3 months on mss. SASE. Simultaneous submissions OK, but "we would like to be told." Sample copy for $3. Fiction guidelines for #10 SASE.

Payment/Terms: Pays 2 contributor's copies. Acquires first rights.

ONIONHEAD, (II), Literary Quarterly, Arts on the Park, Inc., 115 N. Kentucky Ave., Lakeland FL 33801. (941)680-2787. Co-Editors: Susan Crawford, Dot D. Davis, K.C. Jarrett, Brenda J. Patterson. Magazine: digest-sized; 40 pages; 20 lb. bond; glossy card cover. "Provocative political, social and cultural observations and hypotheses for a literary audience—an open-minded audience." Estab. 1989. Circ. 250.

Needs: Contemporary, ethnic, experimental, feminist, gay, humor/satire, lesbian, literary, prose poem, regional. "*Onionhead* focuses on provocative political, social and cultural observations and hypotheses. Must have a universal point (international)." Publishes short fiction in each issue. Receives 100-150 unsolicited mss/month. Acquires approximately 28 mss/issue; 100 mss (these numbers include poetry, short prose and essays)/year. Publishes ms within 18 months of acceptance. Recently published work by Gregory Kane, Kristy Athens and Vickie Nelson. Length: 2,500 words average; 3,000 words maximum. Publishes short shorts. Also publishes poetry.

How to Contact: Send complete ms with cover letter that includes brief bio and SASE. Reports in 3 weeks on queries; 6 months on mss. No simultaneous submissions. Sample copy for $3 postpaid. Fiction guidelines for #10 SASE.

Payment/Terms: Pays in contributor's copy. Charge for extras. Acquires first North American serial rights.

Advice: "Review a sample copy of *Onionhead* and remember *literary quality* is the prime criterion. Avoid heavy-handed approaches to social commentary—be subtle, not didactic."

ORACLE STORY, (I, II), Rising Star Publishers, 2105 Amherst Rd., Hyattsville MD 20783. (301)422-2665. Fax: (301)422-2720. Editor: Obi H. Ekwonna. Magazine: 5½ × 8½; 38 pages; white bond paper; 60 lb. Ibs cover. "Didactic well-made stories; basically adults and general public (mass market)." Quarterly. Estab. 1993. Circ. 500.

  • *Oracle Story* is a member of the Association of African Writers. The editors are interested in all genres of fiction but with an African-cultural slant.

Needs: Condensed/excerpted novel, ethnic/multicultural, folklore (African), historical, horror, humor/satire, literary, mainstream/contemporary, mystery/suspense (romantic suspense), serialized novel, young adult/teen (horror and mystery). "No gay or lesbian writings." List of upcoming themes available for SASE. Publishes annual special fiction issue or anthology. Receives 60 unsolicited mss/month. Accepts 8 mss/issue; 26 mss/year. Publishes ms 6-12 months after acceptance. Recently published work by Chris Haley, Denise Johnson, Mary Winters, Cynthia F. Hatten, Stanley R. Thomas, Lorenzo Jones, Carol J.W. Randolph, W.A. Byrd, Kainoa Koeninger and Terry W. McKinnon. Length: "not more than 20 typewritten pages." Publishes short shorts. Also publishes literary essays, literary criticism and poetry. Sometimes critiques or comments on rejected mss.

How to Contact: Send complete ms with a cover letter. Include bio with SASE. Reports in 4-6 weeks. SASE for reply or return of ms. No simultaneous submissions. Electronic submissions OK (disks in WordPerfect 5.1, IBM readable format). Sample copy for $5 plus $1.50 postage. Fiction guidelines for SASE. Reviews novels and short story collections.

Payment/Terms: Pays contributor's copy. Acquires first North American seial rights.

Advice: Looks for work that is "well made, well written, and has good language." Especially interested in African folklore.

OTHER VOICES, (I, II), The University of Illinois at Chicago, Dept. of English (M/C 162), 601 S. Morgan St., Chicago IL 60607. (312)413-2209. Editors: Sharon Fiffer and Lois Hauselman. Magazine: 5⅞ × 9; 168-205 pages; 60 lb. paper; coated cover stock; occasional photos. "Original, fresh, diverse stories and novel excerpts" for literate adults. Semiannually. Estab. 1985. Circ. 1,500.

  • *Other Voices* received an Illinois Arts Council Award for the 1994/95 year.

Needs: Contemporary, excerpted novel, experimental, humor/satire and literary. No taboos, except ineptitude and murkiness. No fantasy, horror, juvenile, psychic/occult. Receives 300 unsolicited fiction mss/month. Accepts 20-23 mss/issue. Recently published work by Cris Mazza, Jim Sloan and G.K. Wvori. Published new writers within the last year. Length: 4,000 words average; 5,000 words maximum.

How to Contact: Send ms with SASE or submit through agent October 1 to April 1 only. Mss received during non-reading period are returned unread. Cover letters "should be brief and list previous publications. Also, list title of submission. Most beginners' letters try to 'explain' the story—a big mistake." Simultaneous submissions OK. Reports in 10-12 weeks on mss. Sample copy for $7 (includes postage). Fiction guidelines for #10 SASE.

Payment/Terms: Pays in contributor's copies and modest cash gratuity (when possible). Acquires one-time rights.

Advice: "There are so *few* markets for *quality* fiction! We—by publishing 40-45 stories a year—provide new and established writers a forum for their work. Send us your best voice, your best work, your best best."

‡**OUT OF THE CRADLE, An Uncommon Reader, (I, II)**, P.O. Box 129, South Paris ME 04281-0129. (207)743-6738. Editor: Jeanette Baldridge. Magazine: 8½×11; 48-56 pages; 60 lb. paper; heavy cover stock; illustrations; photos. "*OOTC* has two goals. One is to provide exposure for new writers. Each issue features at least one previously unpublished writer, balancing the stronger work of experienced writers. The second purpose is to provide an uncommon reader for a diverse audience." Quarterly. Estab. 1995. Circ. 700. Member Maine Writers and Publishers Association (MWPA).

Needs: Adventure, ethnic/multicultural, feminist, gay, historical, lesbian, literary, mainstream/contemporary. "No pornography, violence, political propaganda, religious dogma, science fiction or fantasy." Publishes special fiction issues or anthologies. Receives 50-100 unsolicited mss/month. Accepts 5-6 mss/issue; 20-22 mss/year. Publishes ms 1 year after acceptance. Recently published work by Willa Doppmann, Dianne Benedict, Beverly Sheresh, Irving Greenfield, Eric Pinder and Jack Barnes. Length: 2,500-3,000 words average; 1,000 words minimum; 5,000 words maximum. Publishes short shorts. Also publishes poetry and creative nonfiction in the form of personal narratives. Often critiques or comments on rejected mss.

How to Contact: Send complete ms with a cover letter. "I like a cover letter that tells me about the writer, not the story which must stand on its own." Include estimated word count, 1-paragraph bio and list of publications. Reports in 2-3 months on mss. Send SASE for reply, return of ms or send a disposable copy of ms. Simultaneous submissions and reprints OK. Sample copy for $6. Fiction guidelines for #10 SASE.

Payment/Terms: Pays $5-25 and 2 contributor's copies; additional copies for $3. Pays on publication. Acquires one-time rights. Sends galleys to author "if I've made significant changes." Sponsors contests; see notification in magazine.

Advice: "Good writing is a necessity, but not enough in itself. I like stories that keep me interested. The ending doesn't have to be happy, but I do want closure, to feel satisfied and changed (more aware or enlightened) by having read the story. I'm bored with pointlessness and stories that leave the reader hanging. I want well-crafted, high-quality stories that are original in approach and written in a believable voice. Generally I am looking for stories that are an honest portrayal of the human condition. I would like to see more stories that expose prejudice and injustice and show how various people cope with these situations. Aspiring writers should not try to be trendy. Learn to develop your own voice. Pay attention to your craft and strive constantly to develop it by reading and studying other writers, and by getting feedback on your work."

OUTERBRIDGE, (II), English 25-28, The College of Staten Island (CUNY), 2800 Victory Blvd., Staten Island NY 10314. (718)982-3651. Editor: Charlotte Alexander. Magazine: 5½×8½; approximately 110 pages; 60 lb. white offset paper; 65 lb. cover stock. "We are a national literary magazine publishing mostly fiction and poetry. To date, we have had several special focus issues (the 'urban' and the 'rural' experience, 'Southern,' 'childhood,' 'nature and the environment,' 'animals'). For anyone with enough interest in literature to look for writing of quality and writers on the contemporary scene who deserve attention. There probably is a growing circuit of writers, some academics, reading us by recommendations." Annually. Estab. 1975. Circ. 500-700.

Needs: Literary. "No *Reader's Digest* style; that is, very popularly oriented. We like to do interdisciplinary features, e.g., literature and music, literature and science and literature and the natural world." Accepts 8-10 mss/year. Does not read in July or August. Published work by William Davey, Ron Berube, Patricia Ver Ellen. Published new writers within the last year. Length: 10-25 pages. Also publishes poetry. Sometimes recommends other markets.

How to Contact: Query. Send complete ms with cover letter. "Don't talk too much, 'explain' the work, or act apologetic or arrogant. If published, tell where, with a brief bio." SASE (or IRC). Reports in 8-10 weeks on queries and mss. No multiple submissions. Sample copy for $6 for annual issue.

Payment/Terms: Pays 2 contributor's copies. Charges ½ price of current issue for extras to its authors. Acquires one-time rights. Requests credits for further publication of material used by *OB*.

Advice: "Read our publication first. Don't send out blindly; get some idea of what the magazine might want. A *short* personal note with biography is appreciated. Competition is keen. Read an eclectic mix of classic and contemporary. Beware of untransformed autobiography, but *everything* in one's experience contributes."

OXFORD MAGAZINE, (II), Bachelor Hall, Miami University, Oxford OH 45056. (513)529-1954 or 529-5221. Editor: Elizabeth Glass. Editors change every year. Send submissions to "Fiction Editor."

Magazine: 6×9; 85-100 pages; illustrations. Biannually. Estab. 1985. Circ. 500-1,000.

- *Oxford* has been awarded two Pushcart Prizes.

Needs: Literary, ethnic, experimental, humor/satire, feminist, gay/lesbian, translations. Receives 50-60 unsolicited mss/month. May not read mss May 1 through Sepetember 4. Published work by Tony Earley and Ann Harleman. Published new writers within the last year. Length: 2,000-4,000 words average. "We will accept long fiction (over 6,000 words) only in cases of exceptional quality." Publishes short shorts. Also publishes literary essays, literary criticism, poetry.

How to Contact: Send complete ms with cover letter, which should include a short bio or interesting information. Simultaneous submissions OK, if notified. Reports in 3-5 months, depending upon time of submissions; mss received after January 1 will be held over for following year's issue. SASE. Sample copy for $5.

Payment/Terms: Pays in contributor's copies. Acquires one-time rights.

Advice: "*Oxford Magazine* is looking for humbly vivid fiction; that is to say, fiction that illuminates, which creates and inhabits an honest, carefully rendered reality populated by believable, three-dimensional characters. We see far too many glib, sitcom-ish stories, too many saccharine hospital tales, too many brand-name-laden records of GenX angst, too many stories which are really overeager European travelogues. Send us stories that are unique; we want fiction no one else but you could possibly have written."

OXYGEN, A Spirited Literary Magazine, (II), 535 Geary St., #1010, San Francisco CA 94102. (415)776-9681. Editor/Publisher: Richard Hack. Magazine: 8½×11; 64 pages; 60 lb. vellum paper; glossy cover, perfect-bound. "We are an eclectic, community-spirited magazine looking for vivid, meaningful writing. We welcome fiction and poetry in modes realistic, surreal, expressionist, devotional, erotic, satiric, and invective. We stand for inclusive, democratic values and social equality." Publishes 3-4 issues/year. Estab. 1991. Circ. 400.

Needs: Very general and diverse, including translations (especially from Spanish; bilingual contributions preferred). "Nothing overly commercial, insincere, or mocking, though we enjoy hard satire." Receives 100 unsolicited mss/month. Accepts 3-4 mss/issue; 12-16 mss/year. Publishes ms up to 3 or 4 months after acceptance. Recently published work by Mia Stageberg, Eugene Wildman, David Fisher and Patrick Reid. Length: 500-7,500 words. Publishes short shorts. Also publishes poetry, occasional essays and reviews.

How to Contact: Send complete ms with a cover letter. Include bio (1-2 paragraphs), list of publications (not necessary). Reports in 2-8 weeks. Send SASE for reply or return of ms. Simultaneous, reprint and electronic submissions (ASCII, WordPerfect 5.1 or lower) OK. Sample copy for $4; send to their distributor: B. DeBeer, 113 E. Centre St., Nutley NJ 07110. Fiction guidelines for #10 SASE.

Payment/Terms: Pays 2-4 contributor's copies. All rights revert to contributors.

Advice: "We want vivid, efficient, honest fiction. It can be a short story, tale, fragment, experimental piece, or an excerpt from a novel. We like meaningful writing that is community-spirited, hopefully rich and suggestive writing, or a style with a nice feel to it. Does it believe in something, does it love life? Does it satirize injustice and abuse? What kind of personal quality does it demonstrate?"

PACIFIC COAST JOURNAL, (I, II), French Bread Publications, P.O. Box 355, Campbell CA 95009-0355. E-mail: paccoastj@aol.com. Editor: Stillson Graham. Fiction Editor: Stephanie Kylkis. Magazine: 5½×8½; 56 pages; 20 lb. paper; 67 lb. cover; illustrations; photos. "We just want quality material. Slight focus toward Western US/Pacific Rim." Quarterly (or "whenever we have enough money"). Estab. 1992. Circ. 200.

Needs: Ethnic/multicultural, experimental, feminist, historical, humor/satire, literary, science fiction (soft/sociological, magical realism). Receives 30-40 unsolicited mss/month. Accepts 3-4 mss/issue; 10-12 mss/year. Publishes ms 6-18 months after acceptance. Recently published work by Hugh Fox, Cris Mazza and Rita Welty Bourke. Length: 2,500 words preferred; 4,000 words maximum. Publishes short shorts. Also publishes literary essays and poetry. Sometimes critiques or comments on rejected mss. Sponsors contest. Send SASE for details.

How to Contact: Send complete ms with a cover letter. Include bio (less than 50 words) and list of publications. Reports in 2-4 months. Send SASE for reply, return of ms or send a disposable copy of ms. Simultaneous, reprint and electronic submissions OK (Mac or IBM disks or e-mail). Sample copy for $2.50, 6×9 SASE. Reviews novels and short story collections.

Payment/Terms: Pays 1 contributor's copy. Acquires one-time rights.

Advice: "We tend to comment more on a story not accepted for publication when an e-mail address is provided as the SASE."

PACIFIC REVIEW, (II), Dept. of English and Comparative Lit., San Diego State University, San Diego CA 92182-0295. (619)594-5443. Contact: Garrick Davis, editor. Magazine: 6×9; 75-100 pages; book stock paper; paper back, extra heavy cover stock; illustrations, photos. "There is no designated theme. We publish high-quality fiction, poetry, and familiar essays: we accept one in a hundred stories and never print more than three stories in one issue, so fiction is not used as filler." Biannual. Estab. 1973. Circ. 1,000.

Needs: "We do not restrict or limit our fiction in any way other than quality. We are interested in all fiction, from the very traditional to the highly experimental. Acceptance is determined by the quality of submissions." Upcoming themes: "We are accepting essays, pseudo-essays, fiction, and poetry concerning any aspect of the Unabomber, his manifesto, or the media's role in the melee." Does not read June-August. Recently published work by Jay Atkinson and Harold Jaffe. Published new writers within the last year. Length: 4,000 words max. Publishes short shorts.

How to Contact: Send original ms with SASE. No unsolicited submissions. Reports in 3-5 months on mss. Sample copy for $3.

Payment/Terms: 1 contributor's copy. "First serial rights are *Pacific Review*'s. All other rights revert to author."

Advice: "We accept work that has clearly been composed in the late twentieth century. That is, the author is aware of the differences between this particular era and every other. In an age radically altered by science, most of the stories we receive look like antiques or unconvincing evasions."

PAINTED BRIDE QUARTERLY, (II), Painted Bride Art Center, 230 Vine St., Philadelphia PA 19106. (215)925-9914. Website: http://www.libertynet.org/pbq~/. Fiction Editor: Kathy Volk-Miller. Literary magazine: 6×9; 96-100 pages; illustrations; photos. Quarterly. Estab. 1973. Circ. 1,000.

Needs: Contemporary, ethnic, experimental, feminist, gay, lesbian, literary, prose poem and translations. Recently published work by Lisa Borders, Jeannie Tietja, Kevin Miller, Mark LaMonda and Jennifer Moses. Published new writers within the last year. Length: 3,000 words average; 5,000 words maximum. Publishes short shorts. Also publishes literary essays, literary criticism, poetry. Occasionally critiques rejected mss.

How to Contact: Send complete ms. Reports in 6 months. SASE. Sample copy for $6. Reviews novels and short story collections. Send books to editor.

Payment/Terms: Pays $5/accepted piece and 1 contributor's copy, 1 year free subscription, 50% off additional copies. Acquires first North American serial rights.

Advice: Looks for "freshness of idea incorporated with high-quality writing. We receive an awful lot of nicely written work with worn-out plots. We want quality in whatever—we hold experimental work to as strict standards as anything else. Many of our readers write fiction; most of them enjoy a good reading. We hope to be an outlet for quality. A good story gives, first, enjoyment to the reader. We've seen a good many of them lately, and we've published the best of them."

†PALACE CORBIE, (I, II, IV), Merrimack Books, P.O. Box 83514, Lincoln NE 68501-3514. Editor: Wayne Edwards. Perfect-bound trade paperback: 5½×8½; 180-300 pages; 60 lb. offset paper; illustrations. Annually. Estab. 1989. Circ. 1,000.

Needs: Fantasy (dark), horror, psychic/supernatural/occult, science fiction. Publishes ms up to 1 year after acceptance. Agented fiction 5%. Recently published work by Steve Rasnic Tein, Elizabeth Eugstrom, Douglas Clegg and Yvonne Navarro. Length: 2,000 words minimum; 8,000 words maximum.

How to Contact: Send complete ms. Include estimated word count. Reports in 1 week. Send SASE for reply or send a disposable copy of ms. No simultaneous submissions. Sample copy for $10.95. Fiction guidelines for #10 SAE and 1 first-class stamp.

Payment/Terms: Variable. Pays contributor's copy only for unsolicited submissions. Sends galleys to author.

Advice: Looks for "psychologically disturbing stories with high emotional impact."

PALO ALTO REVIEW, A Journal of Ideas, (I, II), Palo Alto College, 1400 W. Villaret, San Antonio TX 78224. (210)921-5255 (or 921-5017). Fax: (210)921-5008. E-mail: eshull@accdum.aced. edu or brichmon@accdum.accd.edu. Editors: Bob Richmond and Ellen Shull. Magazine: 8½×11; 60 pages; 60 lb. natural white paper (50% recycled); illustrations and photographs. "Not too experimental nor excessively avant-garde, just good stories (for fiction). Ideas are what we are after. We are interested in connecting the college and the community. We would hope that those who attempt these connections will choose startling topics and interesting angles with which to investigate the length and breadth of the teaching/learning spectrum." Semiannually (spring and fall). Estab. 1992. Circ. 500-600.

Needs: Adventure, ethnic/multicultural, experimental, fantasy, feminist, historical, humor/satire, literary, mainstream/contemporary, mystery/suspense, regional, romance, science fiction, translations, westerns. Upcoming themes available for SASE. Receives 100-150 unsolicited mss/month. Accepts 2-4 mss/issue; 4-8 mss/year. Does not read mss March-April and October-November when putting out each issue. Publishes ms 2-15 months after acceptance. Recently published work by Gayle Silbert, Naomi Chase, Kenneth Emberly, C.J. Hannah, Tom Juvik, Kassie Fleisher and Paul Perry. Length: 5,000 words maximum. Publishes short shorts. Also publishes articles, interviews, literary essays, literary criticism, poetry. Always critiques or comments on rejected mss.

How to Contact: Send complete ms with a cover letter. "Request sample copy and guidelines." Include brief bio and brief list of publications. Reports in 3-4 months. Send SASE for reply, return of ms or send a disposable copy of ms. Simultaneous and electronic (Macintosh disk) submissions OK. Sample copy for $5. Fiction guidelines for #10 SASE.

Payment/Terms: Pays 2 contributor's copies; additional copies for $5. Acquires first North American serial rights.

Advice: "Good short stories have interesting characters confronted by a dilemma working toward a solution. So often what we get is 'a moment in time,' not a story. Generally, the characters are interesting because the readers can identify with them and know much about them. Edit judiciously. Cut out extraneous verbage. Set up a choice that has to be made. Then create tension—who wants what and why they can't have it."

PANGOLIN PAPERS, (II), Turtle Press, P.O. Box 241, Nordland WA 98358. (360)385-3626. Editor: Pat Britt. Magazine: 5½ × 8½; 120 pages; 24 lb. paper; 80 lb. cover. "Best quality literary fiction for an informed audience." Triannually. Estab. 1994. Circ. 500.

Needs: Condensed/excerpted novel, experimental, humor/satire, literary, translations. No "genre such as romance or science fiction." Plans to publish special fiction issues or anthologies in the future. Receives 20 unsolicited mss/issue. Accepts 7-10 mss/issue; 20-30 mss/year. Does not read mss in July and August. Publishes ms 4-12 months after acceptance. Agented fiction 10%. Recently published work by Jack Nisbet, Donald Kern and Cullen Gerst. Length: 3,500 words average; 100 words minimum; 7,000 words maximum. Publishes short shorts. Length: 400 words. Also publishes literary essays. Sometimes critiques or comments on rejected mss.

How to Contact: Send complete ms with a cover letter. Include estimated word count and short bio. Reports in 2 weeks on queries; 2 months on mss. Send SASE for reply, return of ms or send a disposable copy of ms. No simultaneous submissions. Electronic and reprint submissions OK. Sample copy for $5.95 and $1 postage. Fiction guidelines for #10 SAE.

Payment/Terms: Pays 2 contributor's copies. Offers annual $200 prize for best story. Acquires first North American serial rights. Sometimes sends galleys to author.

Advice: "We are looking for original voices. Follow the rules and be honest in your work."

‡PAPER RADIO, (I,II), P.O. Box 425, Brementon WA 98337. Editor: N.S. Kvern. Magazine: 48-64 pages; photocopied and/or offset paper and cover; illustrations; b&w photographs. "We're open to anything, but it has to be short—usually less than 2,500 words." Readers are "mostly people who are interested in avant garde, political, bizarre, surrealism, cyberpunk, literary/experimental writing and computers." Published 12 times/year. Estab. 1986. Circ. 2,000.

Needs: Erotica, experimental, fantasy, literary, prose poem, science fiction. Receives 50 unsolicited fiction mss/month. Accepts 4-5 mss/issue; 50 mss/year. Publishes ms an average of 6 months after acceptance. Length: 2,000 words average; 3,500 words maximum. Publishes short shorts. Sometimes critiques rejected mss. Will have a submission fee for unsolicited ms beginning in March 1996. Send SASE for guidelines.

How to Contact: Send complete ms with cover letter. "Some autobiographical information is helpful—one or two paragraphs—and I like to know where they heard about our magazine." Reports in 2 months. SASE (or IRC). Simultaneous submissions OK. Sample copy for $4.50.

Payment/Terms: Pays contributor's copies.

Terms: Acquires first rights.

Advice: "We are devoted to the cause of experimentation and literature and we like a wide variety of fiction. Best to see a sample copy. Our publication is orderly in its chaos, wild and untameable in its order."

‡✹PAPERPLATES, a magazine for fifty readers," (II), Perkolator kommunikation, 19 Kenwood Ave., Toronto, Ontario M6C 2R8 Canada. (416)651-2551. Fax: (416)651-2910. E-mail: paperplates@p erkolator.com. Editor: Bernard Kelly. Magazine: 8½ × 11; 48 pages; recycled paper; illustrations and photos. Published 2-3 times/year. Estab. 1990. Circ. 350. Member of Toronto Small Press Group and Canadian Magazine Publishing Association.

Needs: Condensed/excerpted novel, ethnic/multicultural, feminist, gay, lesbian, literary, mainstream/ contemporary, translations. "No science fiction, fantasy or horror." Receives 2-3 unsolicited mss/ month. Accepts 2-3 mss/issue; 6-9 mss/year. Publishes ms 6-8 months after acceptance. Recently

---

✹ **THE MAPLE LEAF** symbol before a listing indicates a Canadian publisher, magazine, conference or contest.

published work by Celia Lottridge, C.J. Lockett, Deirdre Kessler and Marvyne Jenoff. Length: 5,000 words average; 1,500 words minimum; 15,000 words maximum. Publishes short shorts. Also publishes literary essays, literary criticism and poetry.

How to Contact: Send complete ms with a cover letter. Reports in 6 weeks on queries; 3 months on mss. Send SASE for reply, return of ms or send a disposable copy of ms. Simultaneous submissions and electronic submissions OK. Sample copy for $5. Fiction guidelines for #10 SASE.

Payment/Terms: Pays 2 contributor's copies on publication; additional copies for $5. Acquires first North American serial rights.

PARAMOUR MAGAZINE, Literary and Artistic Erotica, (IV), P.O. Box 949, Cambridge MA 02140-0008. (617)499-0069. E-mail: paramour@paramour.com. Website: http://www.paramour.com/. Publisher/Editor: Amelia Copeland. Senior Editor: Marti Hohmann. Magazine: 9 × 12; 36 pages; matte coated stock; illustrations and photos. "*Paramour* is a quarterly journal of literary and artistic erotica that showcases work by emerging writers and artists. Our goal is to provoke thought, laughter, curiosity and especially, arousal." Quarterly. Estab. 1993. Circ. 12,000.

● Work published in *Paramour* has been selected for inclusion in *Best American Erotica*.

Needs: Erotica. Receives 50 unsolicited mss/month. Accepts 3-5 mss/issue; 12-20 mss/year. Length: 2,000 words average; 1 word minimum; 4,000 words maximum. Publishes short shorts. Also publishes literary essays, literary criticism and poetry.

How to Contact: Request guidelines prior to submissions: call, write or e-mail. Send complete ms with a cover letter. Include estimated word count, name, address and phone number. Reports in 3 weeks on queries; 4 months on mss. SASE for return of ms and send disposable copy of ms. No simultaneous submissions. Sample copy for $4.95. Fiction guidelines for #10 SAE and 1 first-class stamp. Reviews novels and short story collections.

Payment/Terms: Pays free subscription to the magazine plus contributor's copies. Acquires first rights.

Advice: "We look for erotic stories which are well-constructed, original, exciting and dynamic. Clarity, attention to form and image, and heat make a ms stand out. Seek striking and authentic images and make the genre work for you. We see too many derivative rehashes of generic sexual fantasies. We love to see fresh representations that we know will excite readers."

THE PARIS REVIEW, (II), 45-39 171 Place, Flushing NY 11358 (*business office only, send mss to address below*). Editor: George A. Plimpton. Managing Editor: Daniel Kunitz. Magazine: 5¼ × 8½; about 260 pages; illustrations and photographs (unsolicited artwork not accepted). "Fiction and poetry of superlative quality, whatever the genre, style or mode. Our contributors include prominent, as well as less well-known and previously unpublished writers. *The Art of Fiction, Art of Poetry, Art of Criticism* and *Art of Theater* interview series include important contemporary writers discussing their own work and the craft of writing." Quarterly.

Needs: Literary. Receives about 1,000 unsolicited fiction mss each month. Published work by Raymond Carver, Elizabeth Tallent, Rick Bass, John Koethe, Sharon Olds, Derek Walcott, Carolyn Kizer, Tess Gallagher, Peter Handke, Denis Johnson, Bobbie Ann Mason, Harold Brodkey, Joseph Brodsky, John Updike, Andre Dubus, Galway Kinnell, E.L. Doctorow and Philip Levine. Published new writers within the last year. No preferred length. Also publishes literary essays, poetry.

How to Contact: *Send complete ms with SASE to Fiction Editor, 541 E. 72nd St., New York NY 10021.* Reports in 2 months. Simultaneous submissions OK. Sample copy for $11.50.

Payment/Terms: Pays for material. Pays on publication for first North American serial rights. Sends galleys to author.

PARTING GIFTS, (II), 3413 Wilshire, Greensboro NC 27408. Editor: Robert Bixby. Magazine: 5 × 7; 60 pages. "High-quality insightful fiction, very brief and on any theme." Semiannually. Estab. 1988.

Needs: "Brevity is the second most important criterion behind literary quality." Publishes ms within one year of acceptance. Recently published work by David Chorlton, Ben Miller, Deborah Bayer, Brad Field, Mary Rohrer-Dann, Peter Markus and Ray Miller. Length: 250 words minimum; 1,000 words maximum. Also publishes poetry. Sometimes critiques rejected mss.

How to Contact: Send complete ms with cover letter. Simultaneous submissions OK. Reports in 1 day on queries; 1-7 days on mss. SASE.

Payment/Terms: Pays in contributor's copies. Acquires one-time rights.

Advice: "Read the works of Amy Hempel, Jim Harrison, Kelly Cherry, C.K. Williams and Janet Kauffman, all excellent writers who epitomize the writing *Parting Gifts* strives to promote. I need more than ever for my authors to be better read. I sense that many unaccepted writers have not put in the hours reading."

PARTISAN REVIEW, (II), 236 Bay State Rd., Boston MA 02215. (617)353-4260. Editor-in-Chief: William Phillips. Editor: Edith Kurzweil. Magazine: 6 × 9; 160 pages; 40 lb. paper; 60 lb. cover stock.

INSIDER REPORT

No substitute for exceptional prose and a well-told story

Conventional wisdom says that publishing literary fiction is becoming harder and harder. Daniel Kunitz begs to differ. "I personally don't buy it. Tons of good literary fiction is being published. I don't know of that many people who are deserving who can't get published, although it may be difficult. More books are being published all the time." And, he adds, "it's certainly not worse for us. We're doing as well as ever."

"We" is *The Paris Review*, one of the most prestigious independent literary journals in the English-speaking world, where Kunitz serves as managing editor. The magazine was founded in 1953 by a circle of writers, poets and artists that included George Plimpton and Peter Matthiessen, who continue at the *Review*, along with others such as Donald Hall and Maxine Groffsky. Kunitz came to the *Review* in 1991 as an intern, then took six months off as a freelance copyeditor in and around New York. On returning to Columbia University for an MFA in poetry he began working part-time at the magazine again, first as assistant editor and then associate editor. After graduation he landed a fulltime job as senior editor, and eventually became managing editor.

From the beginning, the philosophy of the *Review* has been to discover as many new writers as possible and publish them alongside better-known names, many of whom themselves were discovered by the *Review* editors: Writers such as William Styron and Philip Roth were published first here. This past year produced a bumper crop of exciting new writers, so much so that Kunitz devoted an entire issue to them. "We took almost twice as many previously unpublished writers as we have before. We usually publish 16 stories, and this past year we did eight from unpublished writers."

Bear in mind, however, that's 16 stories published out of the 1,000 fiction submissions he receives each month. Being so well known is both an advantage and disadvantage, Kunitz says, in that the magazine does receive such a large number of submissions. "Most fiction is unsolicited. The vast majority is unagented. And they're all read. We have a group of people who help us read those thousands of manuscripts. Ones that we like, we pass around the office. If more than a couple of people like a story, we put it aside in a special group to be more seriously considered by the top editors—George, myself, James Linville, Anne Fullenwider and Brigid Hughes. We all make comments on those stories and then choose from them. We have a very high standard to uphold, and that means working harder, looking at things more closely, searching more widely for better stories."

While he doesn't look for any particular style or subject, what Kunitz does

INSIDER REPORT, *continued*

insist upon is outstanding writing. "The only way people write exceptional prose is if they read an enormous amount. I would guess that if you've never read the magazine and you submit to it, you don't have a chance, because you won't have a sense of what we're about, what we're doing, the kind of stories we're interested in publishing and the level of stories we present. We're always looking for solid writing, a fresh style and a well-told story. There's nothing other than writing extremely well that's going to attract my attention."

Kunitz encounters several very prominent mistakes in the stories he reads. "I find that people take too long to get into the story they're trying to tell. They lead up to it, they describe, they do anything but tell the story. The second thing that happens is that no story gets told. You have slices of life, you have character studies, you have all sorts of things, but you don't have a narrative arc, an actual story. Another that is very common is a poor command of the English language. Also, many writers don't read their work over carefully and it's full of errors, both grammatical and spelling. If you're asking others to read your story and you obviously haven't read it closely yourself, they are not going to be that interested, and why should they be?"

While the "corporatization" of publishing houses has definitely hurt the prospects of literary fiction in the short run, in the longer run Kunitz sees some positive things beginning to happen in literary publishing. "Smaller presses are coming in and picking up some of the slack, challenging the bigger houses to start publishing more literary stuff. Random House, for instance, is opening up a more literary fiction imprint.

"From the standpoint of literary magazines, the lack of government funding doesn't help, and the smaller the magazine the more it hurts. It's obviously the small, unfunded, underrepresented people who have the most difficulty publishing a literary magazine. *The Paris Review* isn't going to go under because the NEA won't give us a grant, but a lot of deserving, small magazines will. So, in that sense I think it's bad.

"On the other hand, the fact that in most affluent suburbs there are Borders Books, Barnes & Nobles and other large bookstores is actually very good for literary publishing because they are opening up a huge audience. I don't think that's begun to be felt back in the publishing area. There is a lot of scepticism among book publishers. Those who want to see literary fiction published are not pushing the case enough. Those who do are quite successful. Many books get launched, and many books, even short fiction, are getting large advances. If you're somewhat savvy and market yourself, and can convince companies to market you, then these books will sell."

In terms of learning to market yourself, Kunitz thinks it really depends on the individual and what they are willing to do. There aren't any rules to follow for that. "The best advice comes back to writing really well. Reading and writing. It's very easy to tell the difference between a writer who reads a lot and a writer who doesn't. We look for people who love English prose and write it very well. Nothing is going to substitute for that. It's just the most important thing. And it will always win through. I believe that."

—*Kirsten Holm*

"Theme is of world literature and contemporary culture: fiction, essays and poetry with emphasis on the arts and political and social commentary, for the general intellectual public and scholars." Quarterly. Estab. 1934. Circ. 8,000.

Needs: Contemporary, experimental, literary, prose poem, regional and translations. Receives 100 unsolicited fiction mss/month. Buys 2 mss/issue; 8 mss/year. Published work by José Donoso, Isaac Bashevis Singer, Doris Lessing. Published new writers within the last year. Length: open.

How to Contact: Send complete ms with SASE and cover letter listing past credits. No simultaneous submissions. Reports in 4 months on mss. Sample copy for $6 and $1.50 postage.

Payment/Terms: Pays $25-200 and 1 contributor's copy. Pays on publication for first rights.

Advice: "Please, research the type of fiction we publish. Often we receive manuscripts which are entirely inappropriate for our journal. Sample copies are available for sale and this is a good way to determine audience."

PASSAGER, A Journal of Remembrance and Discovery, (I, II, IV), University of Baltimore, 1420 N. Charles St., Baltimore MD 21201-5779. Editors: Kendra Kopelke and Mary Azrael. Magazine: 8¼ square; 32 pages; 70 lb. paper; 80 lb. cover; photographs. "We publish stories and novel excerpts, poems, interviews with featured authors. One of our missions is to provide exposure for new older writers; another is to function as a literary community for writers across the country who are not connected to academic institutions or other organized groups." Quarterly. Estab. 1990. Circ. 750.

Needs: "Special interest in discovering new older writers, but publishes all ages." Receives 200 unsolicited mss/month. Accepts 2-3 prose mss/issue; 8-12/year. Does not read mss June through August. Publishes ms up to 1 year after acceptance. Published work by Thomas Fitzsimmons, Will Inman, Wayne Karlin, Hilda Morley, Ruth Daigon. Length: 250 words minimum; 4,000 words maximum. Publishes short shorts. Also publishes poetry.

How to Contact: Send complete ms with cover letter. Reports in 3 months on mss. SASE. Simultaneous submissions OK, if noted. Sample copy for $4. Fiction guidelines for #10 SASE.

Payment/Terms: Pays subscription to magazine and 2 contributor's copies. Acquires first North American serial rights. Sometimes sends galleys to author.

Advice: "*Get a copy* so you can see the quality of the work we use. We seek powerful images of remembrance and discovery from writers of all ages. No stereotyped images of older people—we are interested in promoting complex images of aging that reveal the imagination and character of this stage of life."

‡PASSAGES NORTH, (I, II), Northern Michigan University, 1401 Presque Isle Ave., Marquette MI 49855. (906)227-2715. Fax: (906)227-1096. Editor: Anne Ohman Youngs. Fiction Editor: Jennifer Ward. Magazine: 8×5½; 110-130 pages; 80 lb. paper. "*Passages North* publishes quality fiction, poetry and creative nonfiction by emerging and established writers." Readership: General and literary. Semiannually. Estab. 1979. Circ. 300.

Needs: Ethnic/multicultural, literary, mainstream/contemporary, regional. Receives 100-200 mss/ month. Accepts 8-12 mss/year. Does not read May through August. Recently published works by Michael Chitwood, Bill Meissner and Kirsten Backstrom. Published new writers within the last year. Length: 5,000 words maximum. Critiques returned mss when there is time.

How to Contact: Send complete ms with SASE and estimated word count. Reports in 3-6 months. No simultaneous submissions. Sample copy for $6. Fiction guidelines free.

Payment/Terms: Pays 1 contributor's copy. Rights revert to author on request.

‡PAVLOV NERUDA/MANUSLAVE PRESS, (II, III), 3451 Randolph St., Jacksonville FL 32207. Editor: Karin Murphy. Fiction Editor: Robert Murphy. Magazine: 40 pages; acid-free or recycled paper; recycled coverstock; illustrations. "We are a nonprofit publication." Annually sometimes biannually. Estab. 1987. Circ. 500.

Needs: Erotica, ethnic/multicultural, experimental, feminist, gay, horror, humor/satire, lesbian, literary, mystery/suspense (police procedural), psychic/supernatural/occult, religious/inspirational, romance (futuristic/time travel), science fiction, senior citizen/retirement, translations, westerns, poetic fiction and shorter fiction. "We are eclectic." Publishes special fiction issues and anthologies. Receives 500 unsolicited mss/month. Accepts 3 mss/year. Publishes mss "as funds allow." Recently published work by Matt Jasper, Marina Gipps, James Williams, Andrew McCarter and Jason Anthony. Also publishes poetry.

How to Contact: Send complete ms with a cover letter. Length: 5-6 pages maximum; shorter works preferred. Reports in 1 year on queries. SASE for return of ms or send a disposable copy of ms. Simultaneous and reprint submissions OK. Sample copy for $4.

Payment/Terms: Pays 2 contributor's copies.

Advice: Looks for "an original voice, style, story, lyrical fiction—something that takes risk without being obnoxious (French, Russian, South American etc.). We do not consider *beginning* writers, but conciseness, clarity, imagery help. Also, we do *discourage* plot-oriented fiction. A strong voice carries our interest. *Nothing message-oriented.*. If you send a romance, it had better *not* be pulp. Be subversive."

PEARL, A Literary Magazine, (II, IV), Pearl, 3030 E. Second St., Long Beach CA 90803. (310)434-4523. Editors: Joan Jobe Smith, Marilyn Johnson and Barbara Hauk. Magazine: 5½×8½; 96 pages; 60 lb. recycled, acid-free paper; perfect-bound; coated cover; b&w drawings and graphics. "We are primarily a poetry magazine, but we do publish some *very short* fiction and nonfiction. We are interested in lively, readable prose that speaks to *real* people in direct, living language; for a general literary audience." Triannually. Estab. 1974 ("folded" after 3 issues but began publishing again in 1987). Circ. 600.
Needs: Contemporary, humor/satire, literary, mainstream, prose poem. "We will only consider short-short stories up to 1,200 words. Longer stories (up to 4,000 words) may only be submitted to our short story contest. All contest entries are considered for publication. Although we have no taboos stylistically or subject-wise, obscure, predictable, sentimental, or cliché-ridden stories are a turn-off." Publishes an all fiction issue each year. Receives 10-20 unsolicited mss/month. Accepts 1-10 mss/issue; 12-15 mss/year. Submissions accepted September-May *only*. Publishes ms 6 months to 1 year after acceptance. Published work by MacDonald Harris, Josephine Marshall, Gerald Locklin, Lisa Glatt and Richard Farrell. Length: 1,000 words average; 500 words minimum; 1,200 words maximum. Also publishes poetry. Sponsors an annual short story contest. Send SASE for complete guidelines.
How to Contact: Send complete ms with cover letter including publishing credits and brief bio. Simultaneous submissions OK. Reports in 6-8 weeks on mss. SASE. Sample copy for $6 (postpaid). Fiction guidelines for #10 SASE.
Payment/Terms: Pays 2 contributor's copies. Acquires first North American serial rights. Sends galleys to author.
Advice: "We look for vivid, *dramatized* situations and characters, stories written in an original 'voice,' that make sense and follow a clear narrative line. What makes a manuscript stand out is more elusive, though—more to do with feeling and imagination than anything else . . ."

THE PEGASUS REVIEW, (I, IV), P.O. Box 88, Henderson MD 21640-0088. (201)927-0749. Editor: Art Bounds. Magazine: 5½×8½; 6-8 pages; illustrations. "Our magazine is a bimonthly, entirely in calligraphy, illustrated. Each issue is based on specific themes." Estab. 1980. Circ. 250.
　● Because *The Pegasus Review* is done in calligraphy, submissions must be very short. Two pages, says the editor, are the ideal length.
Needs: Humor/satire, literary, prose poem and religious/inspirational. Upcoming themes: "Laughter" (January/February); "Earth" (March/April); "Home" (May/June); "Patriotism" (July/August); "Books" (September/October); "Holidays" (November/December). "Themes may be approached by humor, satire, inspirational, autobiographical, prose. Nothing like a new slant on an old theme." Receives 35 unsolicited mss/month. Accepts "about" 60 mss/year. Published work by new writers within the last year. Publishes short shorts of 2-3 pages; 500 words. Themes are subject to change, so query if in doubt. "Occasional critiques."
How to Contact: Send complete ms. SASE "a must." Brief cover letter with author's background, name and prior credits, if any. Simultaneous submissions acceptable, if so advised. Reports in 1-2 months. Sample copy for $2.50. Fiction guidelines for SAE. Subscription: $10/year.
Payment/Terms: Pays 2 contributor's copies. Occasional book awards. Acquires one-time rights.
Advice: "Read and write; write and read. Above all, make time—even if only for one hour—to write on a daily basis. Get involved with a local writers' group and pay heed to any critiquing."

PEMBROKE MAGAZINE, (I, II), Box 60, Pembroke State University, Pembroke NC 28372. (910)521-6000. Editor: Shelby Stephenson. Fiction Editor: Stephen Smith. Magazine: 6×9; approximately 200 pages; illustrations; photos. Magazine of poems and stories plus literary essays. Annually. Estab. 1969. Circ. 500.
Needs: Open. Receives 120 unsolicited mss/month. Publishes short shorts. Published work by Fred Chappell, Robert Morgan. Published new writers within the last year. Length: open. Occasionally critiques rejected mss and recommends other markets.
How to Contact: Send complete ms. No simultaneous submissions. Reports in up to 3 months. SASE. Sample copy for $5 and 9×10 SAE.
Payment/Terms: Pays 1 contributor's copy.
Advice: "Write with an end for *writing*, not publication."

PENNSYLVANIA ENGLISH, (I), English Department, Penn State University—Erie, Humanities Division, Erie PA 16563. (814)898-6205. Fax: (814)898-6032. Editor: Gregory Morris. Magazine: 7×8½; 100 pages; 20 lb. bond paper; 65 lb. matte cover. For "teachers of English in Pennsylvania at the high school and college level." Semiannually. Estab. 1985. Circ. 300.
Needs: Literary, contemporary mainstream. Does not read mss from May to August. Publishes ms an average of 6 months after acceptance. Recently published work by Deborah Scott-Spera and William

Snyder, Jr. Length: 5,000 words maximum. Publishes short shorts. Also publishes literary essays, literary criticism, poetry. Sometimes critiques rejected mss.

How to Contact: Send complete ms with cover letter. Reports in 2 months. SASE. Simultaneous submissions OK.

Payment/Terms: Pays in contributor's copies. Acquires first North American serial rights.

Advice: Looks for "stories that tend to be realistic in nature; stories that are shorter rather than longer (because of space limitations.)"

PEREGRINE, The Journal of Amherst Writers and Artists, (II), Amherst Writers and Artists Press, Box 1076, Amherst MA 01004. (413)253-7764. Editor: Pat Schneider. Fiction Editor: Rebekah Boyd. Magazine: 5×7; 90 pages; sturdy matte white paper; heavier cover stock. "Poetry and prose— short stories, short short stories, short prose fantasies, essays or reflections. Publishes two pages in each issue of work in translation." Annually.

● *Peregrine* was awarded a Graphic Design Honorable Mention from the 1995 American Literary Magazine Awards.

Needs: "No specific 'category' requirements; we publish what we love." Accepts 2-4 mss/issue. Publishes ms an average of 6 months after acceptance. Published work by Anna Kirwan Vogel, Jane Yolen and Barbara VanNoord. Published new writers within the last year. Length: under 4,500 words preferred. Publishes short shorts. "Short pieces have a better chance of publication. Prefer ten pages or less."

How to Contact: Send complete ms with cover letter, include 40-word biographical note. "May take one year to report." SASE. Simultaneous submissions are encouraged. Sample copy for $4. Reviews books.

Payment/Terms: Pays contributor's copies. All rights return to writer upon publication.

Advice: "We look for heart and soul as well as technical expertise. Shorter is better than longer; you stand your best chance under 4,500 words. Every manuscript is read by three or more readers. We publish what we love most—and it has varied widely."

PHANTASM, (I, II), Iniquities Publishing, 235 E. Colorado Blvd., Suite 1346, Pasadena CA 91101. E-mail: phantasmjg@aol.com. Editor: J.F. Gonzalez. Magazine: 8½×11; 48-52 pages; b&w gloss cover; illustrations and photographs. "Horror fiction (see guidelines) for anybody who has an interest in horror (books, film, etc.)." Quarterly. Estab. 1990. Circ. 1,000.

● Work published in *Phantasm* has been included in the *Year's Best Fantasy and Horror*.

Needs: Horror, mystery/suspense and science fiction (soft sociological). No sword and sorcery, romance, confessional, pornography. Receives 250 unsolicited mss/month. Buys 6-8 mss/issue; 30-35 mss/year. Publishes ms 6 months-1½ years after acceptance. Recently published work by William F. Nolan, Douglas Cleggy, A.R. Murlan, Mick Garris, S.K. Epperson and Ramsey Campbell. Length: 4,000-6,000 words preferred; 10,000 words maximum. Publishes short shorts. Sometimes critiques rejected mss and recommends other markets.

How to Contact: Send complete ms with cover letter. Include "credits, if any, name, address and phone number. I don't want the writer to tell me about the story in the cover letter." Reports in 1-3 weeks on queries; 6 months on mss. SASE. "We are currently backlogged 9-12 months with submissions." Simultaneous and reprint submissions OK. "No e-mail submissions!" Sample copy for $4 plus $1 p&h (payable to *Iniquities Publishing*). Fiction guidelines for #10 SASE.

Payment/Terms: Pays 1¢/word on publication for first North American serial rights. Sends galleys to author.

Advice: Looks for "believable characters and original ideas. Good writing. Fantastic writing. Make the words flow and count for the story. If the story keeps us turning the pages with bated breath, it has a great chance. If we get through the first two pages and it's sloppy, displays weak or uninteresting characters or a contrived plot, we won't even finish it. Chances are the reader won't either. Know the genre and what's been done. *Invest in a sample copy.* While we are open to different styles of horror, we have high expectations for the fiction we publish. The only way a beginner will know what we expect is to buy the magazine and read what we've published."

PHOEBE, An Interdisciplinary Journal of Feminist Scholarship, (II, IV), Theory and Aesthetics, Women's Studies Program, State University of New York, College at Oneonta, Oneonta NY 13820. (607)436-2014. Fax: (607)436-2656. E-mail: phoebe@oneonta.edu. Editor: Kathleen O'Mara. Journal:

FOR INFORMATION ON ENTERING the *Novel & Short Story Writer's Market* Cover Letter Contest, see page 16.

7×9; 140 pages; 80 lb. paper; illustrations and photos. "Feminist material for feminist scholars and readers." Semiannually. Estab. 1989. Circ. 400.

Needs: Feminist: ethnic, experimental, gay, humor/satire, lesbian, literary, translations. Receives 25 unsolicited mss/month. "One-third to one-half of each issue is short fiction and poetry." Does not read mss in summer. Publishes ms 3-4 months after acceptance. Recently published work by Kristan Ruona, Sylvia Van Nooten, Maxine Hartman and Lyn Lifshin. Length: 1,500-2,500 words preferred. Publishes short shorts. Sometimes critiques rejected mss and recommends other markets.

How to Contact: Send complete ms with cover letter. Reports in 1 month on queries; 15 weeks on mss. Electronic (WordPerfect/Microsoft Word disk) submissions OK. Sample copy for $7.50. Fiction guidelines free.

Payment/Terms: Pays in contributor's copies. Acquires one-time rights.

Advice: "We look for writing with a feminist perspective. *Phoebe* was founded to provide a forum for cross-cultural feminist analysis, debate and exchange. The editors are committed to providing space for all disciplines and new areas of research, criticism and theory in feminist scholarship and aesthetics. *Phoebe* is not committed to any one conception of feminism. All work that is not sexist, racist, homophobic, or otherwise discriminary, will be welcome. *Phoebe* is particularly committed to publishing work informed by a theoretical perspective which will enrich critical thinking."

PHOEBE, A Journal of Literary Arts, (II), George Mason University, 4400 University Dr., Fairfax VA 22030. (703)993-2915. Contact: Fiction Editor. Editors change each year. Magazine: 6×9; 116 pages; 80 lb. paper; 0-5 illustrations; 0-10 photographs. "We publish fiction, poetry, photographs, illustrations and some reviews." Published 2 times/year. Estab. 1972. Circ. 3,000.

Needs: "Looking for a broad range of poetry, fiction and essays. Encourage writers and poets to experiment, to stretch the boundaries of genre." No romance, western, juvenile, erotica. Receives 20 mss/month. Accepts 3-5 mss/issue. Does not read mss in summer. Publishes ms 3-6 months after acceptance. Length: no more than 35 pages. Also publishes literary essays, literary criticism, poetry.

How to Contact: Send complete ms with cover letter. Include "name, address, phone. Brief bio." SASE. Simultaneous submissions OK. Sample copy for $6.

Payment/Terms: Pays 2 contributor's copies. Acquires one-time rights. All rights revert to author.

Advice: "We are interested in a variety of fiction, poetry and nonfiction. We suggest potential contributors study previous issues. Each year *Phoebe* sponsors poetry and fiction contests, with $500 awarded to the winning poem and short story. The deadline for the Greg Grummer Award in Poetry is December 15; the deadline for the Phoebe Fiction Prize is March 15. Those interested in entering should write for full contest guidelines."

PIG IRON, (II), Box 237, Youngstown OH 44501. (330)747-6932. Fax: (330)747-0599. Editor: Jim Villani. Annual series: 8½×11; 128 pages; 60 lb. offset paper; 85 pt. coated cover stock; b&w illustrations; b&w 120 line photographs. "Contemporary literature by new and experimental writers." Annually. Estab. 1975. Circ. 1,000.

Needs: Literary and thematic. No mainstream. Upcoming themes: "Years of Rage: 1960s" (December 1997) and "Religion in Modernity" (December 1998). Accepts 10-20 mss/issue. Receives approximately 75-100 unsolicited mss/month. Published work by John Druska, Joel Climenhaga, Larry Smith, Wayne Hogan and Andrena Zawinski. Length: 8,000 words maximum. Also publishes literary nonfiction, poetry. Sponsors contest. Send SASE for details.

How to Contact: Send complete ms with SASE. No simultaneous submissions. Reports in 4 months. Sample copy for $4.

Payment/Terms: Pays $5/printed page and 2 contributor's copies on publication for first North American serial rights; $5 charge for extras.

Advice: "Looking for works psychological, new critical, aggressive, poised for a new century unfolding, unveiling." Rejects manuscripts "lacking modern style, experimental style. Editors look for stylistic innovation."

PIKEVILLE REVIEW, (I), Pikeville College, Sycamore St., Pikeville KY 41501. (606)432-9387. Editor: James Alan Riley. Magazine: 8½×6; 120 pages; illustrations and photos. "Literate audience interested in well-crafted poetry, fiction, essays and reviews." Annually. Estab. 1987. Circ. 500.

Needs: Ethnic/multicultural, experimental, feminist, humor/satire, literary, mainstream/contemporary, regional, translations. Receives 25 unsolicited mss/month. Accepts 3-4 mss/issue. Does not read mss in the summer. Publishes ms 6-8 months after acceptance. Length: 5,000 words average; 15,000 words maximum. Publishes short shorts. Also publishes literary essays and poetry. Often critiques rejected mss. Sponsors occasional fiction award: $50.

How to Contact: Send complete ms with cover letter. Include estimated word count. Send SASE for reply, return of ms or send a disposable copy of ms. Simultaneous submissions OK. Sample copy for $3. Reviews novels and short story collections.

Payment/Terms: Pays 5 contributor's copies; additional copies for $3. Acquires first rights.

Advice: "Send a clean manuscript with well-developed characters."

THE PINK CHAMELEON, (I, II, IV), 170 Park Ave., Hicksville NY 11801. Editor: Dorothy (Paula) Freda. Magazine: 5½ × 8½; 100 pages; 20 lb. bond paper; laminated card stock cover; illustrations and photographs. *The Pink Chameleon* is an "upbeat, family-oriented magazine that publishes any genre as long as the material submitted is in good taste and gives hope for the future, even in sadness." Annually. Estab. 1985.

Needs: Adventure, condensed/excerpted novel, ethnic/multicultural, experimental, fantasy, historical, humor/satire, literary, mainstream/contemporary, mystery/suspense (amateur sleuth, cozy, romantic), religious/inspirational, romance (contemporary, futuristic/time travel, gothic, historical), science fiction (soft/sociological), senior citizen/retirement, sports, westerns (frontier, traditional), young adult/teen (adventure, mystery, romance, science fiction, western), children's/juvenile (1-12 years). "No pornography or graphic language." Accepts 12 mss/year. Publishes ms 18-24 months after acceptance. Recently published work by Karen Blicker, Al Manachino and Jené. Length: 3,500 words maximum. Publishes short shorts. Also publishes literary essays and poetry. Often critiques or comments on rejected mss.

How to Contact: *Subscribers only* should send complete ms with a cover letter. Subscription $10; make check payable to Dorothy P. Freda. Send SASE for reply, return of ms or send a disposable copy of ms. Reprint submissions OK. Fiction guidelines free.

Payment/Terms: Pays $10 and 1 contributor's copy. Acquires one-time rights.

Advice: "Avoid wordiness; use simple, evocative language, and remember that *The Pink Chameleon* is a family-oriented magazine."

A PLACE TO ENTER, Contemporary Fiction by Emerging Writers of African Descent, (I, II, IV), Drayton-Iton Communications, Inc. (DICOM), 1328 Broadway, Suite 1054, New York NY 10001. (212)714-7032. Editor: Brian Iton. Magazine: 8½ × 11; 40 pages; 45 lb. Arbor paper; 80 lb. enamel cover; saddle stitch binding. "*A Place to Enter* is the largest, noninstitutional, literary magazine in the African-American community. We publish short fiction (short stories and novel excerpts) by writers of African descent, and reviews of new releases by black writers." Estab. 1994. Circ. 5,000. Distributed nationally through bookstores in more than 30 states and Canada. Nominated for the 1996 *Writer's Digest* Fiction 50.

Needs: All fiction genres. Adventure, condensed/excerpted novel, ethnic/multicultural, humor/satire, literary, mainstream/contemporary, mystery/suspense, religious/inspirational, romance, science fiction. Receives 25-30 unsolicited mss/month. Accepts 1-2 mss/issue; 4-8 mss/year. Publishes up to 6 months after acceptance. Agented fiction 0-10%. Recently published work by Yusef Salaam, Loni Johnson, Jackie Joice, David Haynes and Clarence Major. Length: 5,000 words average; 1,000 words minimum; 10,000 words maximum. Sometimes critiques or comments on rejected ms.

How to Contact: Send complete ms with a cover letter. Include estimated word count, 1-page bio. Reports in 3-4 months on mss. Send SASE for return of ms. Fiction guidelines for #9 SASE. Single copy/bookstore price $2.95. Back issue/sample copy price $4; 1-year subscription (4 quarterly issues): individual rate $11; institutional rate $19.

Payment/Terms: Pays $100 90 days after publication for first North American serial rights. One contributor's copy sent on publication.

Advice: "Before sending us a manuscript get a copy of our writer's guidelines, or better yet a sample issue. This will give you a sense of our energies and focus, and should help guide your decision of which of your stories to submit. Remember that we *want* to publish your story, so make it as easy as possible for us to make that decision: Tighten your writing as much as possible; please spell-check and proofread your work. We are distributed through all the major black bookselling outlets in the country—that's bookstores in more than 50 major cities—so give us your best work."

‡PLEIADES, (II), Department of English & Philosophy, Central Missouri State University, Martin 336, Warrensburg MO 64093. (816)543-4425. Fax: (816)543-8006. Executive Editor: R.M. Kinder. Magazine: 5½ × 8½; 120 pages; 60 lb. paper; perfect-bound; 8 pt. C1S cover. "*Pleiades* emphasizes cultural diversity, publishes poetry, fiction, literary criticism, belles lettres (occasionally) and reviews for a general educated audience." Semiannually. Estab. 1939. Circ. 300.

Needs: Ethnic/multicultural, experimental, feminist, gay, humor/satire, lesbian, literary, mainstream/contemporary, regional, translations. "No westerns, romance, mystery, etc. Nothing pretentious, didactic or overly sentimental." Plans special fiction issue or anthology. Receives 20 unsolicited mss/month. Accepts 4-8 mss/issue; 8-16 mss/year. "We're slower at reading manuscripts in the summer." Publishes ms 3-8 months after acceptance. Recently published work by Edward Hower, Marianne Luban, Natalia Singer and L. Peat O'Neil. Length: 3,000-6,000 words average; 800 words minimum; 8,000 words maximum. Also publishes literary essays, literary criticism and poetry. Sometimes critiques or comments on rejected mss.

How to Contact: Send complete ms with a cover letter. Include 75-100 bio, Social Security number and list of publications. Reports in 3 weeks on queries; 4 months on mss. Send SASE for reply, return of ms or send a disposable copy of ms. Simultaneous submissions OK. Sample copy (including guidelines) for $5.

Payment/Terms: Pays $10 and 1 contributor's copy on publication. Acquires first North American serial rights. Plans a contest for 1998.

Advice: Looks for "a blend of language and subject matter that entices from beginning to end. Send us your best work. Don't send us formula stories. While we appreciate and publish well-crafted traditional pieces, we constantly seek the story that risks, that breaks form and expectations and wins us over anyhow."

PLOUGHSHARES, (II), Emerson College, 100 Beacon St., Boston MA 02116. (617)824-8753. Editor: Don Lee. "Our mission is to present dynamic, contrasting views on what is valid and important in contemporary literature, and to discover and advance significant literary talent. Each issue is guest-edited by a different writer. We no longer structure issues around preconceived themes." Triquarterly. Estab. 1971. Circ. 6,000.

 • Work published in *Ploughshares* has been selected continuously for inclusion in the *Best American Short Stories* and *O. Henry Prize* anthologies. In fact the magazine has the honor as having the most stories selected from a single issue (three) to be included in *B.A.S.S.* Recent guest editors have included Richard Ford, Tim O'Brien and Ann Beattie.

Needs: Literary. "No genre (science fiction, detective, gothic, adventure, etc.), popular formula or commercial fiction whose purpose is to entertain rather than to illuminate." Buys 25 mss/year. Receives 400-600 unsolicited fiction mss each month. Published work by Rick Bass, Joy Williams and Andre Dubus. Published new writers within the last year. Length: 300-6,000 words.

How to Contact: Reading period: postmarked August 1 to March 31. Cover letter should include "previous pubs." SASE. Reports in 3-5 months on mss. Sample copy for $6. (Please specify fiction issue sample.) Current issue for $8.95. Fiction guidelines for #10 SASE.

Payment/Terms: Pays $25/page, $50 minimum per title; $250 maximum, plus copies and a subscription on publication for first North American serial rights. Offers 50% kill fee for assigned ms not published.

Advice: "Be familiar with our fiction issues, fiction by our writers and by our various editors (e.g., Sue Miller, Tobias Wolff, Rosellen Brown, Jay Neugeboren, Jayne Anne Phillips, James Alan McPherson) and more generally acquaint yourself with the best short fiction currently appearing in the literary quarterlies, and the annual prize anthologies (*Pushcart Prize, O. Henry Awards, Best American Short Stories*). Also realistically consider whether the work you are submitting is as good as or better than—in your own opinion—the work appearing in the magazine you're sending to. What is the level of competition? And what is its volume? (In our case, we accept about one ms in 200.) Never send 'blindly' to a magazine, or without carefully weighing your prospect there against those elsewhere. Always keep a log and a copy of the work you submit."

❦THE PLOWMAN, (I, II), Box 414, Whitby, Ontario L1N 5S4 Canada. Editor: Tony Scavetta. Tabloid: 56 pages; illustrations and photos. Monthly. Estab. 1988. Circ. 15,000.

Needs: "An international journal publishing all holocaust, relition, didactic, ethnic, eclectic, love and other stories." Recently published work by Lolita T. Levrone, Percy Harrison, Dan Leach, Jasmen Tucker, Alice Donatelli, Eric F.J. Marten, Jennifer Kurera, Michael Cross and James Pullega, Jr.

How to Contact: Send complete ms with cover letter. Reports in 1 week. Simultaneous and reprint submissions OK. Sample copy and fiction guidelines for SAE.

Payment/Terms: Pays in contributor's copies; charges for extras. Acquires one-time rights. Sends galleys to author.

Advice: "No satanic or rude language."

‡POETIC SPACE, A Magazine of Poetry & Fiction, (I, II), Poetic Space Press, P.O. Box 11157, Eugene OR 97440. E-mail: poeticspac@aol.com. Editor: Don Hildenbrand. Fiction Editor: Thomas Strand. Magazine: 8½ × 11; 32 pages; bond paper; heavy cover; b&w art. "Social, political, avant-garde, erotic, environmental material for a literary audience." Biannually (summer and winter). Estab. 1983. Circ. 600.

Needs: Erotica, ethnic, experimental, feminist, gay, lesbian, literary. No sentimental, romance, mainstream. Receives about 20 unsolicited mss/month. Accepts 3-4 mss/issue; 8-10 mss/year. Publishes ms 6 months after acceptance. Recently published work by David Scott Martin, Bruce Holland Rogers, Robert Weaver and Laton Carter. Length: 10 double-spaced pages. Publishes short shorts. Also pub-

---

MARKET CATEGORIES: (I) Open to new writers; (II) Open to both new and established writers; (III) Interested mostly in established writers; (IV) Open to writers whose work is specialized; (V) Closed to unsolicited submissions.

lishes literary essays, literary criticism, poetry. Often critiques rejected mss and recommends other markets.

How to Contact: Send complete ms with cover letter that includes estimated word count, short bio and list of publications. Reports in 1 week on queries; 2 months on mss. SASE. Simultaneous, reprint and electronic submissions OK. Sample copy for $3, 4×9 SAE and 45¢ postage. Fiction guidelines for #10 SAE and 1 first-class stamp (or IRC). Reviews novels and short story collections. Send books to Don Hildenbrand.

Payment/Terms: Pays 1 contributor's copy. Acquires one-time rights or "reserves anthology rights."

POETRY FORUM SHORT STORIES, (I, II), Poetry Forum, 5713 Larchmont Dr., Erie PA 16509. (814)866-2543. Fax: (814)866-2543 (fax hours 8-10 a.m., 5-8 p.m.). E-mail: 75562.670@compuserve.com. Editor: Gunver Skogsholm. Newspaper: 7×8½; 34 pages; card cover; illustrations. "Human interest themes (no sexually explicit or racially biased or blasphemous material) for the general public—from the grassroot to the intellectual." Quarterly. Estab. 1989. Circ. 400.

Needs: Confession, contemporary, ethnic, experimental, fantasy, feminist, historical, literary, mainstream, mystery/suspense, prose poem, religious/inspirational, romance, science fiction, senior citizen/retirement, young adult/teen. "No blasphemous, sexually explicit material." Publishes annual special fiction issue. Receives 50 unsolicited mss/month. Accepts 12 mss/issue; 40 mss/year. Publishes ms 6 months after acceptance. Agented fiction less than 1%. Length: 2,000 words average; 500 words minimum; 5,000 words maximum. Also publishes literary essays, literary criticism, poetry.

How to Contact: *This magazine charges a "professional members" fee of $36 and prefers to work with subscribers.* The fee entitles you to publication of a maximum of 3,000 words. Send complete ms with cover letter. Reports in 3 weeks to 2 months on mss. SASE. Simultaneous and reprint submissions OK. "Accepts electronic submissions via disk gladly." Sample copy for $3. Fiction guidelines for SASE. Reviews novels and short story collections.

Payment/Terms: Preference given to submissions by subscribers. Acquires one-time rights.

Advice: "Tell your story with no padding as if telling it to a person standing with one hand on the door ready to run out to a meeting."

‡POETRY IN MOTION MAGAZINE, (II), National Poet's Association, P.O. Box 173, Bayport MN 55003-0173. (612)779-6952. E-mail: poem@wwcoinc.com. Editor: Nadia Giordana. Magazine: 8½×11; 64 pages; 35 lb. web paper; full color, glossy cover stock; illustrations; photos. "We include numerous local advertising to fund circulation. We publish a wide variety of subjects in each issue. We have national subscribers across the country and very heavy distribution throughout Minnesota and Wisconsin—those are our readers. Our contributors are from all over the country." Quarterly. Estab. 1994. Circ. 5,000.

Needs: Adventure, experimental, fantasy (science, sword and sorcery), mainstream/contemporary, mystery/suspense (amateur sleuth, private eye/hardboiled), psychic/supernatural/occult, regional, science fiction, westerns (frontier, traditional). Receives 3-5 unsolicited mss/month. Accepts 3-6 mss/issue; 12-24 mss/year. Publishes ms 1-3 months after acceptance. Recently published work by Robert Mariani, Marian Ford Park, Lain McNeill and Ken Cook. Length: 1,500 words average; 250 words minimum; 2,000 words maximum. Publishes short shorts. Also publishes literary essays and poetry.

How to Contact: Send complete ms with a cover letter. Include estimated word count, short bio and list of publications. Reports in 2-4 months on mss. Send SASE for reply, return of ms or send a disposable copy of ms. Reprints and electronic submissions OK. Sample copy for $5. Fiction guidelines for #10 SASE.

Payment/Terms: Pays 1 contributor's copy on publication; additional copies for $5. Acquires one-time rights and one-time electronic rights.

Advice: "An interesting twist at the end rather than a predictable ending will put a manuscript at the top of the stack. Avoid clichés. Be patient; my response time can take 2-4 months."

✦POETRY WLU, (I), Wilfrid Laurier University, Wilfrid Laurier University, Waterloo, Ontario N2L 3C5 Canada. (519)884-1970. Managing Editor: Ed Jewinski. Editors change each year. Magazine: 8½×7; 50-60 pages; standard bond paper; illustrations. "*Poetry WLU* is a place for the new, young, unknown and talented." Annually. Estab. 1981. Circ. 250.

Needs: Literary. Receives 5-10 unsolicited mss/month. Accepts 2-3 mss/issue. "All reading and assessing is done between January and March." Publishes ms 2 months after acceptance. Length: 100 words minimum; 1,500 words maximum. Publishes short shorts. Also publishes poetry.

How to Contact: Send complete ms with a cover letter and SASE. Reports in 2 months. SASE for reply or return of ms. Sample copy for $2.

Payment/Terms: Pays 1 contributor's copy; additional copies for $2. Sponsors contests, awards or grants for fiction writers. "The applicant must be a registered Wilfrid Laurier University student."

POET'S FANTASY, (I), 227 Hatten Ave., Rice Lake WI 54868-2030. (715)234-7472. Editor: Gloria Stoeckel. Magazine: 8½×4½; 40 pages; 20 lb. paper; colored stock cover; illustrations. *Poet's Fantasy* is a magazine of "fantasy, but not conclusive." Bimonthly. Estab. 1992. Circ. about 250.

Needs: Fantasy (science), literary. Receives 2-3 unsolicited mss/month. Accepts 6 mss/year. Recently published work by Douglas Johnson, Elton Warrick and Jim Mesnard. Length: 1,000 words average; 500 words minimum; 1,500 words maximum. Publishes short shorts. Also publishes literary essays and poetry. Sometimes critiques or comments on rejected mss.

How to Contact: Send complete ms with a cover letter. Include estimated word count and list of publications. Reports in 3 weeks. Send SASE for reply or return of ms. Simultaneous submissions OK. Sample copy for $3. Fiction guidelines free.

Payment/Terms: Pays $3 coupon on publication toward purchase of subscription for first North American serial rights.

Advice: Wants fiction with "tight writing, action and ending twist. Edit and re-edit before sending."

THE POINTED CIRCLE, (II), Portland Community College-Cascade, 705 N. Killingsworth St., Portland OR 97217. (503)978-5230. E-mail: rstevens@pcc.edu. Editors: Student Editorial Staff. Magazine: 80 pages; b&w illustrations and photographs. "Anything of interest to educationally/culturally mixed audience." Annually. Estab. 1980.

Needs: Contemporary, ethnic, literary, prose poem, regional. "We will read whatever is sent, but encourage writers to remember we are a quality literary/arts magazine intended to promote the arts in the community." Acquires 3-7 mss/year. Accepts submissions only December 1-February 15, for October 1 issue. Recently published work by Joyful Freeman, Michael Dembrow and William Feustle. Length: 3,000 words maximum.

How to Contact: Send complete ms with cover letter and brief bio. SASE. Sample copy for $4.50. Fiction guidelines for #10 SASE.

Payment/Terms: Pays in contributor's copies. Acquires one-time rights.

Advice: "Looks for quality—topicality—nothing trite. The author cares about language and acts responsibly toward the reader, honors the reader's investment of time and piques the reader's interest."

‡PORCUPINE LITERARY ARTS MAGAZINE, (II), P.O. Box 259, Cedarburg WI 53012-0259. (414)377-3962. Editor: W.A. Reed. Fiction Editor: Barb Joosse. Magazine: 5×8½; 100 pages; glossy color cover stock; illustrations and photos. Publishes "primarily poetry and short fiction. Novel excerpts are acceptable if self-contained. No restrictions as to theme or style." Semiannually. Estab. 1996. Circ. 1,500.

Needs: Condensed/excerpted novel, ethnic/multicultural, literary, mainstream/contemporary. Receives 10 unsolicited mss/month. Accepts 3 mss/issue; 6 mss/year. Publishes ms within 6 months of acceptance. Recently published work by Carol Lynn Schowalter and Christine Tachick. Length: 3,500 words average; 2,000 words minimum; 7,500 words maximum. Publishes literary essays and poetry. Sometimes critiques or comments on rejected mss.

How to Contact: Send complete ms with a cover letter. Include estimated word count, 5-line bio and list of publications. Reports in 2 weeks on queries; 2 months on mss. Send SASE for reply, return of ms or send a disposable copy of ms. No simultaneous submissions. Sample copy for $5. Fiction guidelines for #10 SASE.

Payment/Terms: Pays 1 contributor's copy on publication; additional copies for $7.95. Acquires one-time rights.

Advice: Looks for "believable dialogue and a narrator I can see and hear and smell. Form or join a writers' group. Read aloud. Rewrite extensively."

PORTLAND REVIEW, (I, II), Portland State University, Box 347, Portland OR 97207-0347. (503)725-4533. Fax: (503)725-5860. E-mail: review@vanguard.vg.edu. Editor: Amber Black. Magazine: 9×6; 200 pages; linen stock paper; heavy linen cover stock; b&w drawings and photos. "We seek to publish fiction in which content takes precedence over style." Quarterly. Estab. 1955. Circ. 1,500.

● The editors say they are looking for experimental work "with darker, harsher, more introspective tones."

Needs: Adventure, erotica, ethnic/multicultural, experimental, fantasy (science), feminist, gay, historical, humor/satire, lesbian, literary, mainstream/contemporary, mystery/suspense, regional, science fiction (hard sf), serialized novel, translation. "We could do without all the vampire submissions." Receives about 100 mss each month. Accepts 4-6 mss/issue; 25-30 mss/year. Publishes 1 month after acceptance. Also publishes critical essays, poetry, drama, interviews and reviews.

How to Contact: Submit complete ms with short bio. SASE. Simultaneous and electronic submissions OK (if noted). Reports in 1 month. Sample copy for $5 plus $1 postage. Fiction guidelines free.

Payment/Terms: Pays contributor's copies. Acquires one-time rights.

Advice: "Our editors, and thus our tastes/biases change annually, so keep trying us."

POTATO EYES, (II), Nightshade, P.O. Box 76, Troy ME 04987-0076. (207)948-3427. Fax: (207)948-5088. E-mail: potatoeyes@uninet.net. Editors: Carolyn Page and Roy Zarucchi. Magazine:

5½ × 8½; 120 pages; 60 lb. text paper; 80 lb. Curtis flannel cover. "We tend to showcase Appalachian talent from Alabama to Quebec, and in doing so, we hope to dispel hackneyed stereotypes and political borders. However, we don't limit ourselves to this area, publishing always the best that we receive." Estab. 1988. Circ. 800.

Needs: Contemporary, humor/satire, literary, mainstream, regional, feminist and ecological themes. A *Nightshade Nightstand Short Story Reader* with forward by Fred Chappell was published in 1995. Receives 200 unsolicited mss/month. Accepts 5 mss/issue; 10 mss/year. Publishes ms 2 months-2 years after acceptance. Recently published work by Richard Abrons, Rachel Piceione, Judy Darke Delogue, Marcus Parr and Matt Roberson. Length: 3,000 words maximum; 2,000 average. Publishes short shorts. Length: 450 words. Also publishes poetry (looking for English/French translations of Franco poems) plus 1 or 2 novels. Sometimes critiques rejected mss.

How to Contact: Send complete ms with cover letter. Reports in 1-2 months on mss. SASE. Sample copy for $5, including postage. Fiction guidelines for #10 SAE.

Payment/Terms: Pays in contributor's copies. Acquires first North American serial rights.

Advice: "We care about the larger issues, including pollution, ecology, bio-regionalism, uncontrolled progress and 'condominia,' and women's issues, as well as the rights of the individual. We care about television, the great sewer pipe of America, and what it is doing to America's youth. We are exploring these issues with writers who have originality, a reordered perspective, and who submit to us generous sprinklings of humor and satire. Although we do occasionally comment on valid fiction, we have walked away unscathed from the world of academia and refuse to correct manuscripts. We respect our contributors and treat them as professionals, however, and write personal responses to every submission if given a SASE. We expect the same treatment—clean copy without multi folds or coffee stains or corrections. We like brief non-Narcissistic cover letters containing the straight scoop. We suggest that beginning fiction writers spend the money they have set aside for creative writing courses or conferences and spend it instead on subscriptions to good little literary magazines."

POTOMAC REVIEW, The Quarterly with a Conscience, (I, II), Potomac Review, Inc., P.O. Box 354, Port Tobacco MD 20677. (301)934-1412. Editor: Eli Flam. Magazine: 5½ × 8½; 88 pages; 50 lb. paper; 65 lb. cover; illustrations. "*Potomac Review* is a mainstream literary quarterly with a challenging diversity." Estab. 1994. Circ. 1,500.

Needs: Excerpted novel—"stories with a vivid, individual quality that get at 'the concealed side' of life. Regionally rooted, with an area or theme focus each isse (e.g., 'Baltimore: A Writer's City," winter 1996-97); we also keep an eye on the wider world." Upcoming themes (subject to change): Spring: "The Middle Kingdom"—Frederick/Shepherdstown; Summer: "Upriver"—Cumberland to Frostburg"; Fall: "The Patuxent Revisited"; Winter: "Baltimore Now." Receives 100 unsolicited mss/month. Accepts 20-30 mss/issue of all sorts; 80-120 mss/year. Publishes ms 2-4 months after acceptance as a rule. Agented fiction 10%. Recently published work by Thomas E. Kennedy, Helen Chappell, Elisavietta Ritchie and Mark Blickley. Length: 2,000 words average; 100 words minimum; 3,000 words maximum. Publishes short shorts. Length: 250 words. Also publishes poetry, essays and cogent, issue-oriented nonfiction. Humor is welcome.

How to Contact: Send complete ms with a cover letter. Include estimated word count, 2-3 sentence bio, list of publications and SASE. Reports in 2 weeks on queries; 2-3 months on mss. Send SASE for reply, return of ms or send a disposable copy of ms. Simultaneous and reprint submissions OK. Sample copy for $5. Submission guidelines for #10 SASE. Reviews novels, short story collections, other books.

Payment/Terms: Pays 1 contributor's copy; additional copies for $4.

Advice: "Send your best work—though our nonprofit quarterly is regionally rooted in the Potomac River basin, which reaches from Virginia and West Virginia up through Maryland into Pennsylvania, with Washington, DC, and Baltimore two polar sites—we are open to good writing from all points."

POTPOURRI, (II), P.O. Box 8278, Prairie Village KS 66208. (913)642-1503. Fax: (913)642-3128. Senior Editor: Polly W. Swafford. Magazine: 8 × 11; 64 pages; glossy cover. "Literary magazine: short stories, verse, essays, travel, prose poetry for a general adult audience." Quarterly. Estab. 1989. Circ. 4,500.

Needs: Adventure, contemporary, ethnic, experimental, fantasy, historical (general), humor/satire, literary, mainstream, suspense, prose poem, romance (contemporary, historical, romantic suspense), science fiction (soft/sociological), western (frontier stories). "*Potpourri* accepts a broad genre; hence its name. Guidelines specify no religious, confessional, racial, political, erotic, abusive or sexual preference materials unless fictional and necessary to plot." Receives 75 unsolicited fiction mss/month. Accepts 10-12 fiction mss/issue; 60-80 prose mss/year. Publishes ms 6-15 months after acceptance. Agented fiction 1%. Recently published work by Thomas E. Kennedy, David Ray, Walter Cummins, F.D. Reeve, Judith Felsenfeld, Deborah Shouse, John Sokol and Arthur Winfield Knight. Length: 3,500 words maximum. Also publishes poetry and literary essays. Sometimes critiques rejected mss. *Potpourri* offers annual awards (of $100 each) in fiction and poetry, more depending on grants received, and sponsors the Annual Council on National Literatures Award of $100 each for poetry and fiction on alternating years. "Manuscripts must celebrate our multicultural and/or historic background." 1997 poetry entry deadline: August 31, 1997. Reading fee: $3. Send SASE for guidelines.

How to Contact: Send complete ms with cover letter. Include "complete name, address, phone number, brief summary statement about submission, short author bio." Reports in 2-4 months. SASE. Simultaneous submissions OK. Sample copy for $4.95 with 9×12 envelope. Fiction guidelines for #10 SASE.

Payment/Terms: Pays contributor's copies. Acquires first rights.

Advice: "We look for well-crafted stories of literary value and stories with reader appeal. First, does the manuscript spark immediate interest and the introduction create the effect that will dominate? Second, does the action in dialogue or narration tell the story? Third, does the conclusion leave something with the reader to be long remembered? We look for the story with an original idea and an unusual twist."

❧**THE POTTERSFIELD PORTFOLIO, (I, II)**, The Gatsby Press, 5280 Green St., P.O. Box 27094, Halifax, Nova Scotia B3H 4M8 Canada. Phone/fax: (902)443-9178. E-mail: icolford@is.dal.ca. Editor: Ian Colford. Fiction Editor: Karen Smythe. Magazine: 6×9; 100 pages; recycled acid-free paper and cover; illustrations. "Literary magazine interested in well-written fiction and poetry. No specific thematic interests or biases." Triannually. Estab. 1979. Circ. 500.

Needs: Receives 30-40 fiction mss/month. Buys 4-8 fiction mss/issue. Recently published work by Alan R. Wilson, Carol Bruneau and Joan Givner. Length: 3,500 words average; 500 words minimum; 5,000 words maximum. Publishes short shorts. Sometimes comments on rejected mss.

How to Contact: Send complete ms with cover letter. Include estimated word count and 50-word bio. No simultaneous submissions. Reports in 3 months. SASE. Sample copy for $7 (US), 10½×7½ SAE and 4 first-class stamps.

Payment/Terms: Pays contributor's copy on publication for first Canadian serial rights.

Advice: "Provide us with a clean, proofread copy of your story. Include a brief cover letter with biographical note, but don't try to sell the story to us. *Always* include a SASE with sufficient *Canadian* postage, or IRCs, for return of the manuscript or a reply from the editors."

PRAIRIE DOG, A Quarterly for the Somewhat Eccentric, (II, III), P.O. Box 470757, Aurora CO 80047-0757. (303)696-0490. Fax: (303)671-6742. Editor-in-Chief: John Hart. Magazine: 8½×11; 40 pages; bond paper; parchment cover; illustrations and photos. Biannual. Estab. 1988 as *Infinity Limited*. Circ. 1,000.

Needs: Adventure, contemporary, erotica, ethnic, experimental, fantasy, historical, humor/satire, literary, prose poem, regional, science fiction, translations. "No space opera, gratuitous violence, or pornography." Receives approximately 50 unsolicited mss/month. Acquires 5-7 mss/issue; 20-28 mss/year. Publishes ms 2-12 months after acceptance. Recently published work by Hugh Fox, Terry Thomas and Michael Estabrook. Length: 10,000 words maximum. Publishes short shorts, poetry, essays and occasional book reviews. Sometimes critiques rejected mss.

How to Contact: Send complete ms with cover letter. Include brief bio and $2 reading fee per story, essay or ten poems. Reports in 3-5 months on mss. SASE. Simultaneous (if noted in cover letter) and electronic (disk) submissions OK. Sample copy for $5.95 plus $1 p&h and 9×12 SAE. Fiction guidelines for #10 SASE.

Payment/Terms: Pays 2 contributor's copies. Acquires one-time and reprint rights.

Advice: "We read everything and will respond if you provide an SASE. We accept double-sided and photocopied manuscripts (save the trees) but will not read faint dot matrix and single-spaced manuscripts. Don't summarize your plot in your cover letter. We would like to feature one 'youthful new voice' (under 25, just beginning to be published) per issue, but our standards are high. Mass submissions based on class assignments are sure to be rejected."

❧**PRAIRIE FIRE, (II)**, Prairie Fire Press Inc., 100 Arthur St., Room 423, Winnipeg, Manitoba R3B 1H3 Canada. (204)943-9066. Fax: (204)942-1555. Managing Editor: Andris Taskans. Magazine: 6×9; 128 pages; offset bond paper; sturdy cover stock; illustrations; photos. "Essays, critical reviews, short fiction and poetry. For writers and readers interested in Canadian literature." Published 4 times/year. Estab. 1978. Circ. 1,500.

● *Prairie Fire* recently received two Silver National Magazine Awards for poetry and personal journalism and was nominated for six Western Magazine Awards (Canada).

Needs: Literary, contemporary, experimental, prose poem, reviews. "We will consider work on any topic of artistic merit, including short chapters from novels-in-progress. We wish to avoid gothic, confession, religious, romance and pornography." Buys 3-6 mss/issue, 12-24 mss/year. Does not read mss in summer. Recently published work by Carol Shields, Robert Kroetsch, Greg Hollingshead and Lorna Crozier. Published new writers within the last year. Receives 70-80 unsolicited fiction mss each month. Publishes short shorts. Length: 5,000 words maximum; 2,500 words average. Also publishes literary essays, literary criticism, poetry. Critiques rejected mss "if requested and when there is time."

How to Contact: Send complete ms with IRC w/envelope and short bio. No simultaneous submissions. Reports in 4-5 months. Sample copy for $10 (Canadian). Reviews novels and short story collections. Send books to Andris Taskans.

Payment/Terms: Pays $40 for the first page, $35 for each additional page; 1 contributor copy; 60% of cover price for extras. Pays on publication for first North American serial rights. Rights revert to author on publication.

Advice: "We are publishing more fiction, and we are commissioning illustrations. Read our publication before submitting. We prefer Canadian material. Most mss are not ready for publication. Be neat, double space, and put your name and address on everything! Be the best writer you can be."

✤**THE PRAIRIE JOURNAL OF CANADIAN LITERATURE, (I, II)**, Prairie Journal Press, Box 61203, Brentwood Postal Services, Calgary, Alberta T2L 2K6 Canada. Editor: A.E. Burke. Journal: $7 \times 8\frac{1}{2}$; 50-60 pages; white bond paper; Cadillac cover stock; cover illustrations. Journal of creative writing and scholarly essays, reviews for literary audience. Semiannually. Published special fiction issue last year. Estab. 1983.

Needs: Contemporary, literary, prose poem, regional, excerpted novel, novella, double-spaced. Canadian authors given preference. Publishes "a variety of types of fiction—fantasy, psychological, character-driven, feminist, etc. We publish authors at all stages of their careers from well-known to first publication." No romance, erotica, pulp. Publishes anthology series open to submissions: *Prairie Journal Poetry II* and *Prairie Journal Fiction III*. Receives 20-40 unsolicited mss each month. Accepts 10-15 mss/issue; 20-30 mss/year. Suggests sample issue before submitting ms. Published work by Nancy Ellen Russell, Carla Mobley, Patrick Quinn. Published many new writers within the last year. Length: 2,500 words average; 100 words minimum; 3,000 words maximum. Deadlines: April 1 for spring/summer issue; October 1 for fall/winter. Also publishes literary essays, literary criticism, poetry. Sometimes critiques rejected mss and recommends other markets.

How to Contact: Send complete ms. Reports in 1 month. SASE. Sample copy for $6 (Canadian) and SAE with $1.10 for postage or IRC. Include cover letter of past credits, if any. Reply to queries for SAE with 52¢ for postage or IRC. No American stamps. Reviews novels and short story collections.

Payment/Terms: Pays contributor's copies and modest honoraria. Acquires first North American serial rights. In Canada author retains copyright.

Advice: Interested in "innovational work of quality. Beginning writers welcome. There is no point in simply republishing known authors or conventional, predictable plots. Of the genres we receive fiction is most often of the highest calibre. It is a very competitive field. Be proud of what you send. You're worth it."

PRAIRIE SCHOONER, (II), University of Nebraska, English Department, 201 Andrews Hall, Lincoln NE 68588-0334. (402)472-0911. Editor: Hilda Raz. Magazine: 6×9; 200 pages; good stock paper; heavy cover stock. "A fine literary quarterly of stories, poems, essays and reviews for a general audience that reads for pleasure." Quarterly. Estab. 1926. Circ. 3,200.

● *Prairie Schooner*, one of the oldest publications in this book, has garnered several awards and honors over the years. Work appearing in the magazine has been selected for various anthologies.

Needs: Good fiction (literary). Accepts 4-5 mss/issue. Receives approximately 200 unsolicited fiction mss each month. Mss are read September through May only. Published work by Julia Alvarez, Reynolds Price, Maxine Kumin and Robley Wilson. Published new writers within the last year. Length: varies. Also publishes poetry. Offers annual prize of $1,500 for best fiction, $500 for best new writer (poetry or fiction), two $500 awards for best poetry.

How to Contact: Send complete ms with SASE and cover letter listing previous publications—where, when. Reports in 3-4 months. Sample copy for $5. Reviews novels and short story collections.

Payment/Terms: Pays in contributor's copies and prize money awarded. Acquires all rights. Will reassign rights upon request after publication.

Advice: "*Prairie Schooner* is eager to see fiction from beginning and established writers. Be tenacious. Accept rejection as a temporary setback and send out rejected stories to other magazines. *Prairie Schooner* is not a magazine with a program. We look for good fiction in traditional narrative modes as well as experimental, meta-fiction or any other form or fashion a writer might try."

‡**PRESS, (III)**, Daniel Roberts Inc., 2124 Broadway, Suite 323, New York NY 10023. (212)579-0873. Fax: (212)579-0776. E-mail: pressltd@aol.com. Editor: Daniel Roberts. Magazine: $6\frac{3}{4} \times 10$; 160 pages; cougap-opaque paper; loe cream cover. Features fiction, poetry and "articles about writing and writers; features that humanize literature, celebrate talent and beauty, and expose fraudulence and pomposity. *Press* will stand not only as the most absolute record of contemporary, American, literary talent, but as a means by which the public can commune with literature." Quarterly. Estab. 1996. Circ. 15,000.

Needs: Receives 800 unsolicited mss/month. Accepts 10 mss/issue; 40 mss/year. Publishes ms 6-10 weeks after acceptance. Agented fiction 10%. Recently published work by Joyce Carol Oates, Anthony

Hecht, Philip Levine, William J. Cobb, James Gallant, Gordon Lish and Harry Mathews. Also publishes poetry. Sometimes comments on or critiques rejected mss. Sponsors annual writing contest for New York City public high school students.

How to Contact: Send complete ms with a cover letter. Include a short bio and list of publications. Reports in 2 months on queries; 4 months on mss. Send SASE for reply, return of ms or send a disposable copy of ms. Sample copy for $8. Fiction guidelines free.

Payment/Terms: Pays $100 minimum and 1 contributor's copy; additional copies for $6. Pays on acceptance for first rights, first North American serial rights or one-time rights. Sends galleys to the author.

Advice: "While almost all forms are acceptable, prose poems and more experimental writing (stories that don't actually tell a story) are discouraged. We are looking for a strong and specific plot (where 'something' actually happens); one that makes a reader want to turn the page. We want stories where the author's style does not interfere with the plot, but strengthens the expression of that plot."

PRIMAVERA, (II, IV), Box 37-7547, Chicago IL 60637. (312)324-5920. Editorial Board. Magazine: 5½ × 8½; 128 pages; 60 lb. paper; glossy cover; illustrations; photos. Literature and graphics reflecting the experiences of women: poetry, short stories, photos, drawings. Readership: "an audience interested in women's ideas and experiences." Annually. Estab. 1975. Circ. 1,000.
- *Primavera* has won grants from the Illinois Arts Council, the Puffin Foundation and from Chicago Women in Publishing.

Needs: Literary, contemporary, fantasy, feminist, gay/lesbian, humor and science fiction. "We dislike slick stories packaged for more traditional women's magazines. We publish only work reflecting the experiences of women, but also publish manuscripts by men." Accepts 6-10 mss/issue. Receives approximately 40 unsolicited fiction mss each month. Recently published work by Carol A. Turner, Jessica Roeder, Beth Kephart Sulit and Sheila Mulligan-Webb. Published new writers within the last year. Length: 25 pages maximum. Also publishes poetry. Critiques rejected mss when there is time. Often gives suggestions for revisions and invites re-submission of revised ms. Occasionally recommends other markets.

How to Contact: Send complete ms with SASE. No post cards. Cover letter not necessary. No simultaneous submissions. Reports in 1-6 months on mss. Publishes ms up to 1 year after acceptance. Sample copy for $5; $10 for recent issues. Guidelines for SASE.

Payment/Terms: Pays 2 contributor's copies. Acquires first rights.

Advice: "We're looking for artistry and deftness of untrendy, unhackneyed themes. An original slant on a well-known theme, an original use of language, and the highest literary quality we can find."

✿PRISM INTERNATIONAL, (I, II), E462-1866 Main Mall, University of British Columbia, Vancouver, British Columbia V6T 1Z1 Canada. (604)822-2514. E-mail: prism@unixg.ubc.ca. Website: http://www.arts.ubc.ca/crwr/prism/prism.html. Executive Editor: Tim Mitchell. Editor: Sara O'Leary. Magazine: 6 × 9; 72-80 pages; Zephyr book paper; Cornwall, coated one side cover; photos on cover. "A journal of contemporary writing—fiction, poetry, drama, creative nonfiction and translation. *Prism*'s audience is world-wide, as are our contributors." Readership: "public and university libraries, individual subscriptions, bookstores—an audience concerned with the contemporary in literature." Quarterly. Estab. 1959. Circ. 1,200.
- *Prism International* received a Journey Prize Award and work published in the magazine has been selected for inclusion in the 1995 *Journey Prize Anthology* and nominated for the 1996 *Journey Prize Anthology.*

Needs: Literary, contemporary, prose poem or translations. "Most any category as long as it is *fresh.* No overtly religious, overtly theme-heavy material or anything more message- or category-oriented than self-contained." Buys approximately 70 mss/year. Receives 50-100 unsolicited fiction mss each month. Recently published work by Gail Anderson-Dargatz, Elise Levine, Mark Jarman, Paul Rawlins and Donald Anderson. Published new writers within the last year. Length: 5,000 words maximum "though flexible for outstanding work." Publishes short shorts. Also publishes poetry. Critiques rejected mss when there is time. Sponsors annual short fiction contest. Contest issue comes out in April. Grand prize is $2,000 (Canadian). Send SASE for details.

How to Contact: Send complete ms with SASE or SAE, IRC and cover letter with bio, information and publications list. "Keep it simple. U.S. contributors take note: U.S. stamps are not valid in Canada and your ms will not likely be returned if it contains U.S. stamps. Send International Reply Coupons instead." Reports in 4 months. Electronic submissions OK (e-mail, web). Sample copy for $5 (U.S./ Canadian).

Payment/Terms: Pays $20 (Canadian)/printed page, 1 year's subscription on publication for first North American serial rights. Selected authors are paid an additional $10/page for digital rights.

Advice: "Too many derivative, self-indulgent pieces; sloppy construction and imprecise word usage. There's not enough attention to voice and not enough invention. We are committed to publishing outstanding literary work in all genres. We are on the lookout for strong, believable characters; real 'voices'; interesting ideas/plots. We *do not* want 'genre' fiction (i.e., romance, horror) . . . which does not mean genres should be avoided . . . rather, they should be integrated."

PROVINCETOWN ARTS, (II), Provincetown Arts, Inc., 650 Commercial St., P.O. Box 35, Provincetown MA 02657. (508)487-3167. Editor: Christopher Busa. Magazine: 9 × 12; 184 pages; 60 lb. coated paper; 12 pcs. cover; illustrations and photographs. "*PA* focuses broadly on the artists, writers and theater of America's oldest continuous art colony." Annually. Estab. 1985. Circ. 8,000.
 • *Provincetown Arts* won First Place for Editorial Content and Cover Design from the American Literary Magazine Awards in 1992, 1993 and 1994, and is a recipient of a CLMP seed grant. Provincetown Arts Press has an award-winning poetry series.
Needs: Plans special fiction issue. Receives 300 unsolicited mss/year. Buys 5 mss/issue. Publishes ms 3 months after acceptance. Published work by Carole Maso and Hilary Masters. Length: 3,000 words average; 1,500 words minimum; 8,000 words maximum. Publishes short shorts. Length: 1,500-8,000 words. Also publishes literary essays, literary criticism, poetry. Sometimes critiques rejected mss and recommends other markets.
How to Contact: Send complete ms with cover letter including previous publications. No simultaneous submissions. Reports in 2 weeks on queries; 3 months on mss. SASE. Sample copy for $7.50. Reviews novels and short story collections.
Payment/Terms: Pays $75-300 on publication for first rights. Sends galleys to author.

PUCK, The Unofficial Journal of the Irrepressible, (II), Permeable Press, 47 Noe St., #4, San Francisco CA 94114-1017. E-mail: bcclark@igc.apc.org. Editor: Brian Clark. Magazine: 8½ × 11; 96 pages; recycled uncoated paper; coated cover; illustrations and photos. "Our audience does not accept mainstream media as presenting anything even vaguely resembling reality. We publish poetry, prose and dozens of reviews in our humble attempt to counteract the hogwash of *Time, Paris Review,* et al." Triannually. Estab. 1984. Circ. 8,000.
Needs: Condensed novel, erotica, ethnic/multicultural, experimental, fantasy (science fantasy), feminist, gay, historical, horror, humor/satire, lesbian, literary, psychic/supernatural/occult, regional, religious/inspirational, science fiction (cyberpunk, hard science, soft/sociological), translations. List of upcoming themes available for SASE. Receives 300 unsolicited mss/month. Buys 20 mss/issue; 100 mss/year. Publishes ms within 6 months after acceptance. Agented fiction 10%. Published work by Stan Henry, Hugh Fox and Paul di Filippo. Publishes short shorts. Also publishes literary essays, literary criticism, poetry. Sometimes critiques or comments on rejected mss.
How to Contact: Send complete ms with cover letter. Include bio (under 50 words), list of publications. Reports in 2 months. Send SASE for reply or return of ms. No simultaneous submissions. Accepts reprints and electronic (disk or modem) submissions. Sample copy for $6.50. Fiction guidelines for #10 SAE and 2 first-class stamps. Reviews novels and short story collections. Send review copies to Attn: Reviews Editor at above address.
Payment/Terms: Pays 2 or more contributor's copies plus honorarium (40%) on publication. Buys first North American serial rights.
Advice: Looks for "a certain 'je ne sais quois'—as if the work has been channeled or written in a fit of brilliant rage. Keep trying to pull your head out of this ocean of bogus media we're being drowned in. Subscribe."

PUCKERBRUSH REVIEW, (I, II), Puckerbrush Press, 76 Main St., Orono ME 04473. (207)866-4868/581-3832. Editor: Constance Hunting. Magazine: 9 × 12; 80-100 pages; illustrations. "We publish mostly new Maine writers; interviews, fiction, reviews, poetry for a literary audience." Semiannually. Estab. 1979. Circ. approx. 500.
Needs: Belles-lettres, experimental, gay (occasionally), literary. "Nothing cliché." Receives 30 unsolicited mss/month. Accepts 6 mss/issue; 12 mss/year. Publishes ms 1 year after acceptance. Recently published work by Carolyn Cooke, David Fickett and Margaret Bryant. Sometimes publishes short shorts. Also publishes literary essays, literary criticism, poetry. Sometimes critiques rejected mss.
How to Contact: Send complete ms with cover letter. Reports in 2 months. SASE. Simultaneous submissions OK. Sample copy for $2. Fiction guidelines for SASE. Sometimes reviews novels and short story collections.
Payment/Terms: Pays in contributor's copies.
Advice: "I don't want to see tired plots or treatments. I want to see respect for language—the right words."

PUERTO DEL SOL, (I), New Mexico State University, Box 3E, Las Cruces NM 88003. (505)646-3931. Editors: Antonya Nelson and Kevin McIlvoy. Magazine: 6 × 9; 200 pages; 60 lb. paper; 70 lb. cover stock; photos sometimes. "We publish quality material from anyone. Poetry, fiction, art, photos, interviews, reviews, parts-of-novels, long poems." Semiannually. Estab. 1961. Circ. 1,500.
Needs: Contemporary, ethnic, experimental, literary, mainstream, prose poem, excerpted novel and translations. Receives varied number of unsolicited fiction mss/month. Acquires 8-10 mss/issue; 12-15 mss/year. Does not read mss March through August. Published work by Ricardo Augilar Melantzon,

Steven Schwartz and Judith Ortiz Cofer. Published new writers within the last year. Also publishes poetry. Occasionally critiques rejected mss.
How to Contact: Send complete ms with SASE. Simultaneous submissions OK. Reports in 3 months. Sample copy for $7.
Payment/Terms: Pays 2 contributor's copies. Acquires one-time rights (rights revert to author).
Advice: "We are open to all forms of fiction, from the conventional to the wildly experimental, as long as they have integrity and are well written. Too often we receive very impressively 'polished' mss that will dazzle readers with their sheen but offer no character/reader experience of lasting value."

QUANTA, (II), 1509 R St. NW, #3, Washington DC 20009. E-mail: quanta@quanta.org. Editor: Daniel K. Appelquist. Electronic magazine; hard copy version: $8\frac{1}{2} \times 11$; 35-40 pages; illustrations; photos. "*Quanta* is primarily an electronic publication, distributed across computer networks to an international audience. It is dedicated to bringing the works of new and amateur authors to a wide readership." Bimonthly. Estab. 1989. Circ. 3,500.
Needs: Fantasy (science fantasy), psychic/supernatural/occult, science fiction (hard science, soft/sociological). Plans special fiction issue or anthology. Receives 20 mss/month. Accepts 5 mss/issue; 20 mss/year. Publishes 1-2 months after acceptance. Published work by J. Palmer Hall, Michael C. Berch, Jason Suell and Phillip Nolte. Publishes short shorts. Also publishes literary essays, literary criticism, poetry. Always critiques rejected manuscripts.
How to Contact: Send complete ms with a cover letter; send ms in electronic form (disk or e-mail). Include estimated word count, short bio and list of publications. Reports in 3 weeks on queries; 2 months on mss. Send SASE for reply, return of ms or send disposable copy of ms. Simultaneous, reprint and electronic submissions OK. Sample copy for SAE and 5 first-class stamps. Fiction guidelines for $8\frac{1}{2} \times 11$ SAE.
Payment/Terms: Pays 1 contributor's copy. Acquires one-time rights.
Advice: "Interesting or novel narratorial style or good content. I shy away from 'formula' pieces (e.g., hack 'n' slash fantasy). Send electronic manuscript if possible."

THE QUARTERLY, The Magazine of New Writing, (I, II), 650 Madison Ave., Suite 2600, New York NY 10022. E-mail: shiyate@alias.com. Editor: Gordon Lish. Managing Editors: Dana Spiotta and Jodi Davis. Magazine: 6×9; 246 pages; matte cover; illustrations. Quarterly. Estab. 1987. Circ. 8,000.
  ● *The Quarterly* received the George Andrew Memorial Award.
Needs: Literary. Receives 1,200 mss/month. Accepts 40-80 mss/issue; 160-340 mss/year. Publishes ms usually within 6 months. Published work by Thomas Glynn, Ben Marcus and Barry Hannah. Publishes short fiction and poetry. Sometimes critiques and comments on rejected mss.
How to Contact: Send complete ms. Reports in 5 days on receipt of ms. SASE for return of ms. Simultaneous and electronic submissions OK. Sample copy for $10.
Payment/Terms: Pays in contributor's copies. Acquires one-time and anthology rights.

QUARTERLY WEST, (II), University of Utah, 317 Olpin Union, Salt Lake City UT 84112. (801)581-3938. Editors: Lawrence Coates and Margot Schilpp. Fiction Editors: Wendy Mai Rawlings and Heather Hirschi. Editors change every 2 years. Magazine: 6×9; 200 pages; 60 lb. paper; 5-color cover stock; illustrations and photographs rarely. "We try to publish a variety of fiction and poetry from all over the country based not so much on the submitting author's reputation but on the merit of each piece. Our publication is aimed primarily at an educated audience interested in contemporary literature and criticism." Semiannually. "We sponsor a biennial novella competition." (Next competition held in 1998). Estab. 1976. Circ. 1,800.
  ● *Quarterly West* is a past recipient of a grant from the NEA and was awarded Third Place for
  Editorial Content from the American Literary Magazine Awards. Work published in the maga-
  zine has been selected for inclusion in the *Pushcart Prize* anthology and *The Best American
  Short Stories* anthology.
Needs: Literary, contemporary, experimental translations. Accepts 6-10 mss/issue, 12-20 mss/year. Receives 100 unsolicited fiction mss each month. Recently published work by Fred Chappell, Thomas Russell, Rita Ciresi and Jane Smiley; published new writers within the last year. No preferred length; interested in longer, "fuller" short stories, as well as short shorts. Critiques rejected mss when there is time.
How to Contact: Send complete ms. Brief cover letters welcome. Send SASE for reply or return of ms. Simultaneous submissions OK with acknowledgement. Reports in 2-3 months; "sooner, if possible." Sample copy for $6.50.
Payment/Terms: Pays $15-500 and 2 contributor's copies on publication for all rights (negotiable).
Advice: "We publish a special section or short shorts every issue, and we also sponsor a biennial novella contest. We are open to experimental work—potential contributors should read the magazine! We solicit quite frequently, but tend more toward the surprises—unsolicited. Don't send more than one story per submission, but submit as often as you like."

RAG MAG, (II), Box 12, Goodhue MN 55027. (612)923-4590. Publisher/Editor: Beverly Voldseth. Magazine: 6×9; 60-112 pages; varied paper quality; illustrations; photos. "We are eager to print poetry, prose and art work. We are open to all styles." Semiannually. Estab. 1982. Circ. 300.

Needs: Adventure, comics, contemporary, erotica, ethnic, experimental, fantasy, feminist, literary, mainstream, prose poem, regional. "Anything well written is a possibility. It has to be a good adult story, tight, with plot and zip. I also like strange but well done. No extremely violent or pornographic writing." Upcoming theme: "Families," October issue, accepting April through June 1997. Receives 100 unsolicited mss/month. Accepts 4 mss/issue. Recently published work by Marilyn J. Boe, May Summerville, Irl Mowery and Joan Doll. Published new writers within the last year. Length: 1,000 words average; 2,200 words maximum. Occasionally critiques rejected mss. Sometimes recommends other markets.

How to Contact: Send 3-6 pages, brief bio and brief cover letter. SASE. Reports in 3-4 weeks. Simultaneous and previously published submissions OK. Single copy for $6.

Payment/Terms: Pays 1 contributor's copy; $4.50 charge for extras. Acquires one-time rights.

Advice: "Submit clean copy on regular typing paper (no tissue-thin stuff). We want fresh images, sparse language, words that will lift us out of our chairs. I like the short story form. I think it's powerful and has a definite place in the literary magazine."

RAMBUNCTIOUS REVIEW, (I, II), Rambunctious Press, Inc., 1221 W. Pratt Blvd., Chicago IL 60626. Editor: Mary Alberts. Fiction Editor: Nancy Lennon. Magazine: 10×7; 48 pages; illustrations and photos. Annually. Estab. 1983. Circ. 300.

Needs: Experimental, feminist, humor/satire, literary, mainstream/contemporary. List of upcoming themes available for SASE. Receives 30 unsolicited mss/month. Accepts 4-5 mss/issue. Does not read mss May through August. Publishes ms 5-6 months after acceptance. Recently published work by Sharon Sloan Fiffer, Hugh Fox, Lyn Lifshin and Stephen Schroder. Length: 12 double-spaced pages. Publishes short shorts. Also publishes poetry. Sometimes critiques or comments on rejected ms. Sponsors contest. Send SASE for details.

How to Contact: Send complete ms with a cover letter. Include estimated word count. Reports in 9 months. Send SASE for reply, return of ms or send a disposable copy of ms. Simultaneous submissions OK. Sample copy for $4.

Payment/Terms: Pays 2 contributor's copies. Acquires one-time rights.

✦RAW FICTION, (II), Oppidan Publications, Box 4065, Edmonton, Alberta T6E 4S8 Canada. (403)431-0771. Editor: Timothy Campbell. Magazine: 8½×11; 36 pages; 60 lb. paper; 100 lb. cover stock. *Raw Fiction* publishes "stories with an edge, about life without artifice and pretension." Bimonthly. Estab. 1995. Circ. 500.

Needs: Erotica, experimental, literary, mainstream/contemporary. No stories "with a mandate." Plans special fiction issues or anthologies. Accepts 8-10 mss/issue. Publishes ms 4 months after acceptance. Recently published work by Beth Goobie, R.N. Friedland, Alex Keegan and Leon Jones. Length: 500 words minimum; 4,000 words maximum. Publishes short shorts. Sometimes critiques or comments on rejected ms. Sponsors contests; guidelines advertised in *Raw Fiction* and elsewhere.

How to Contact: Send complete ms with a cover letter. Include quarter-page bio and list of publications with submission. Reports in 3 months. Send SASE for reply, return of ms or send a disposable copy of ms. Reprint submissions OK. Sample copy for $6. Fiction guidelines for #10 SASE.

Payment/Terms: Pays $75 per story. Acquires anthology rights.

Advice: "We enjoy stories that are written well, that reflect the writer's conscienciousness towards the art. We also like writers willing to take on controversial issues with an understanding of several viewpoints, not a single-minded mandate. We have published stories which are controversial in nature, and are becoming recognized as a publication that is writing to publish what other magazines might be afraid to touch."

‡READER'S BREAK, (I), Pine Grove Press, P.O. Box 40, Jamesville NY 13078. (315)423-9268. Editor: Gertrude S. Eiler. Annual anthology with an "emphasis on short stories written with style and ability. Our aim has always been to publish work of quality by authors with talent, whether previously published or not."

Needs: "We welcome stories about relationships, tales of action, adventure, science fiction and fantasy, romance, suspense and mystery. Themes and plots may be historical , contemporary or futuristic. No "pornography, sexual perversion, incest or stories for children." Length: 3,500 words maximum. Also publishes "poems to 75 lines in any style or form and on any subject with the above exceptions."

How to Contact: Accepts unsolicited mss. Include SASE. Reports in 3-5 months "since the stories are considered by a number of editorial readers."

Terms: Pays 1 contributor's copy for one-time rights; additional copies at 20% discount.

Advice: "We prefer fiction with a well-constructed plot and well-defined characters of any age or socio-economic group. Upbeat endings are not required. Please check the sequence of events, their cause-and-effect relationship, the motivation of your characters, and the resolution of plot."

RE:AL, The Journal of Liberal Arts, Stephen F. Austin State University, P.O. Box 13007, Nacogdoches TX 75925. (409)468-2059. Fax: (409)468-2614. E-mail: real@titan.sfasu.edu. Editor: W. Dale Hearell. Academic journal: 6×10; perfect-bound; 120-150 pages; "top" stock. Editorial content: 30% fiction, 30% poetry, 30% scholarly essays and criticism; an occasional play, book reviews (assigned after query) and interviews. Work is reviewed based on the intrinsic merit of the scholarship and creative work and its appeal to a sophisticated international readership (U.S., Canada, Great Britain, Ireland, Brazil, Puerto Rico, Italy)." Semiannually. Estab. 1968. Circ. 400.
Needs: Adventure, contemporary, genre, feminist, science fiction, historical, experimental, regional. Receives 1,400-1,600 unsolicited mss/2 issues. Accepts 2-5 fiction mss/issue. Publishes 1-6 months after acceptance; one year for special issues. Published work by Joe R. Lansdale, Lewis Shiner, Walter McDonald, Peter Mattheisson. Length: 1,000-7,000 words. Occasionally critiques rejected mss and conditionally accepts on basis of critiques and changes.
How to Contact: Send complete ms with cover letter. No simultaneous submissions. Reports in 2 weeks on queries; 3-4 weeks on mss. SASE. Sample copy and writer's guidelines for $6.50. Guidelines for SASE.
Payment/Terms: Pays 2 contributor's copies; charges for extras. Rights revert to author.
Advice: "Please study an issue. Have your work checked by a well-published writer—who is not a good friend. Also proofread for grammatical and typographical errors."

RED CEDAR REVIEW, (II), Dept. of English, 17C Morrill Hall, Michigan State University, East Lansing MI 48824. (517)355-9656. Editors change. Fiction Editor: David Sheridan. Magazine: 5½×8½; 100 pages. Theme: "literary—poetry and short fiction." Biannual. Estab. 1963. Circ. 400.
Needs: Literary. "Good stories with character, plot and style, any genre, but with a real tilt toward literary fiction." Accepts 3-4 mss/issue, 6-10 mss/year. Published work by Diane Wakoski, Tom Paine and Mark Jacobs. Length: Open. Also publishes poetry, 4 poems per submission.
How to Contact: Query with unpublished ms with SASE. No simultaneous submissions. Reports in 2-3 months on mss. Publishes ms up to 4 months after acceptance. Sample copy for $5.
Payment/Terms: Pays 2 contributor's copies. $5 charge for extras. Acquires first rights.
Advice: "It would be nice to see more stories that self-confidently further our literary tradition in some way, stories that 'marry artistic vision with moral insight.' What does your story discover about the human condition? What have you done with words and sentences that's new? Hundreds of journals get hundreds of manuscripts in the mail each month. Why does yours need to get printed? I don't want to learn yet again that innocent people suffer, that life is hollow, that the universe is meaningless. Nor do I want to be told that a warm kitten can save one from the abyss. I want an honest, well crafted exploration of where and what we are. Something after which I can no longer see the world in the same way."

‡REED MAGAZINE, (I, II), % English Dept., San Jose State University, 1 Washington Square, San Jose CA 95192. (408)924-4425. Fax: (408)924-4580. Contact: Fiction Editor. Editors change each year. Magazine: 5×8; 120 pages; matte paper; glossy cover; illustrations; photos. "We publish the highest quality material we can find, with some California and Bay Area slant." Annually. Estab. 1946. Circ. 500.
Needs: Experimental, humor/satire, literary, regional. "All quality work is considered." Receives 7-10 unsolicited mss/month. Accepts 6-7 mss/issues. Does not read mss November through July. Publishes ms 3-4 months after acceptance. Recently published work by Philip Krayra and Flossie Lewis. Length: 3,000 words average. Publishes short shorts. Also publishes literary essays and poetry.
How to Contact: Send complete ms with a cover letter. Include estimated word count and list of publications. Reports in 6 weeks on queries; 3 months on mss. Send SASE for reply, return of ms or send a disposable copy of ms. Electronic submissions OK; include hard copy. Sample copy for $4.95 and 6×9 SASE with 3 first-class stamps. Fiction guidelines given in the magazine.
Payment/Terms: Pays 1 contributor's copy. Author retains all rights.
Advice: Looks for "quality and originality. Most of all, we're looking for a distinctive voice. Read the best magazines and make yourself an expert in what makes a story work. We'd like to see more lovingly obsessive attention to detail. We don't want to see generic and undetailed five-page stories."

MARKET CONDITIONS are constantly changing! If you're still using this book and it is 1998 or later, buy the newest edition of *Novel & Short Story Writer's Market* at your favorite bookstore or order from Writer's Digest Books.

REFLECT, (II, IV), 3306 Argonne Ave., Norfolk VA 23509. (804)857-1097). Editor: W.S. Kennedy. Magazine: 5½ × 8½; 48 pages; pen & ink illustrations. "Spiral Mode fiction and poetry for writers and poets—professional and amateur." Quarterly. Estab. 1979.
Needs: Spiral fiction. "The four rules to the Spiral Mode fiction form are: (1) The story a situation or condition. (2) The outlining of the situation in the opening paragraphs. The story being told at once, the author is not overly-involved with dialogue and plot development, may concentrate on *sound*, *style*, *color*—the superior elements in art. (3) The use of a concise style with euphonic wording. Good poets may have the advantage here. (4) The involvement of Spiral Fiction themes—as opposed to Spiral Poetry themes—with love, and presented with the mystical overtones of the Mode." No "smut, bad taste, socialist. . . ." Accepts 2-6 mss/issue; 8-24 mss/year. Publishes ms 3 months after acceptance. Recently published work by Ruth Wildes Schuler, Greg Smith and Gurattan Khalsa. Length: 1,500 words average; 2,500 words maximum. Publishes short shorts. Sometimes critiques rejected mss.
How to Contact: Send complete ms with cover letter. Reports in 2 months on mss. SASE. No simultaneous submissions. Sample copy for $2. (Make checks payable to W.S. Kennedy.) Fiction guidelines in each issue of *Reflect*.
Payment/Terms: Pays contributor's copies. Acquires one-time rights. Publication not copyrighted.
Advice: "Subject matter usually is not relevant to the successful writing of Spiral Fiction, as long as there is some element or type of *love* in the story, and provided that there are mystical references. (Though a dream-like style may qualify as 'mystical.')"

‡**the review, Fort Wayne's Weekly Alternative Paper, (I, II)**, JGS Communications, P.O. Box 5276, Fort Wayne IN 46895-5276. Phone/fax: (219)422-2253. Co-editors: Glenn Berggoetz and Jeff McBride. Magazine: 8½ × 11; 16 pages; newsprint; illustrations and photos. "*the review* publishes editorials, essays, fiction and poetry for a literate, free-thinking audience." Weekly. Estab. 1996. Circ. 5,000.
Needs: Erotica, ethnic/multicultural, experimental, feminist, gay, historical, horror, humor/satire, lesbian, literary, mainstream/contemporary, psychic/supernatural/occult, regional. Especially interested in "environmental fiction, a la Edward Abbey. No children's, young adult, westerns, romance, sports, religious, sci-fi, fantasy or mystery." Accepts 52 mss/year. Publishes ms 1-2 months after acceptance. Length: 1,500 words average; 500 words minimum; 2,500 words maximum. Publishes short shorts. Also publishes literary essays and poetry. Sometimes critiques or comments on rejected mss.
How to Contact: Send complete ms; "cover letter is optional." Include estimated word count. Reports in 1 month on queries; 6-8 weeks on mss. Send SASE for reply, return of ms or send a disposable copy of ms. Simultaneous submissions and reprints OK. Sample copy for 9 × 12 SAE and 55¢ or 2 IRCs. Fiction guidelines for #10 SASE. Reviews novels and short story collections.
Payment/Terms: Pays 3 contributor's copies on publication; additional copies for $1. Acquires one-time rights; all rights revert back to author upon publication.
Advice: "We're looking for writing that makes us angry, that makes us laugh, that makes us re-evaluate who we are and what we believe. Write to change the world, not to make money or be famous. We're looking for writing that makes people think and changes people's lives. Challenge yourself and your readers. We're especially partial to experimental writing (fiction and prose poetry) and essays."

REVIEW: LATIN AMERICAN LITERATURE AND ARTS, 680 Park Ave., New York NY 10021. (212)249-8950, ext. 366. Editor: Alfred MacAdam. Managing Editor: Daniel Shapiro. "Magazine of Latin American fiction, poetry and essays in translation for academic, corporate and general audience." Biannual.
Needs: Literary. No political or sociological mss. Receives 5 unsolicited mss/month. Accepts 20 mss/ year. Length: 1,500-2,000 words average. Occasionally critiques rejected mss.
How to Contact: Query first. Reports in 3 months. Previously published submissions OK if original was published in Spanish. Simultaneous submissions OK, if notified of acceptance elsewhere. Sample copy free. Reviews novels and short story collections. Send books to Daniel Shapiro, Managing Editor.
Payment/Terms: Pays $50-200 and 2-3 contributor's copies on publication.
Advice: "We are always looking for good translators."

RIVER STYX, (I, II), Big River Association, 3207 Washington Ave., St. Louis MO 63103-1218. Editor: Richard Newman. Magazine: 6 × 9; 90 pages; color card cover; perfect-bound; b&w visual art. "No theme restrictions; only high quality, intelligent work." Triannual. Estab. 1975.
Needs: Excerpted novel chapter, contemporary, ethnic, experimental, feminist, gay, satire, lesbian, literary, mainstream, prose poem, translations. "Avoid 'and then I woke up' stories." Receives 15 unsolicited mss/month. Accepts 1-3 mss/issue; 3-8 mss/year. Reads only May through November. Recently published work by Margaret Atwood, Ha Jin, Stuart Dybek and Constance Urdang. Length: no more than 20-30 manuscript pages. Publishes short shorts. Also publishes poetry. Sometimes critiques rejected mss and recommends other markets.
How to Contact: Send complete ms with name and address on every page. SASE required. Reports in 3-5 months on mss. Simultaneous submissions OK, "if a note is enclosed with your work and if

we are notified immediately upon acceptance elsewhere." Sample copy for $7. Fiction guidelines for #10 SASE.

Payment/Terms: Pays 2 contributor's copies, 1-year subscription and $8/page "if funds available." Acquires first North American serial rights.

Advice: "We want high-powered stories with well-developed characters. Strong plots with at least three memorable scenes. No thin, flimsy fiction."

RIVERSEDGE, A Journal of Art & Literature, (II), CAS 266, UT-PA, 1201 W. University Dr., Edinburg TX 78539-2999. (210)381-3638. Fax: (210)381-2177. Editor: Dorey Schmidt. Magazine: 100 pages; b&w illustrations and photos. "As a 'Third Coast' publication, *RiverSedge* prints regional and national creative voices whose origin or content speaks specifically to the unique multicultural reality of the Southwest, while retaining a commitment to the universality of quality art and literature." Semiannually. Estab. 1972. Circ. 300.

Needs: Ethnic/multicultural, experimental, feminist, historical, literary, mainstream/contemporary, regional, translations. Upcoming themes: "Youth/Age" (April '97) and "International" (November '97). List of upcoming themes available for SASE. Plans annual special fiction issue or anthology in the future. Receives 10-12 unsolicited mss/month. Accepts 6-8 mss/issue; 12-16 mss/year. Does not read mss in summer. Publishes ms 4-6 weeks after acceptance. Recently published work by Jan Epton Seale, Greg Garrett, Amy Hatfield, Stephen Porter and Jeffrey DeLotto. Length: 1,600 words preferred; 100 words minimum; 2,500 words maximum. Also publishes literary essays and poetry. Sometimes critiques or comments on rejected mss.

How to Contact: Send complete ms with a cover letter and bio (not over 200 words). Submission deadlines: April 15 and November 15. Reports in 4 months on mss. Send SASE for reply, return of ms or send a disposable copy of ms. Simultaneous (if noted) and electronic (Mac disk) submissions OK. Sample copy for SASE.

Payment/Terms: Pays 2 contributor's copies; additional copies for $6. Acquires one-time rights.

Advice: Looks for "general literariness—a sense of language as link, not lectern. Characters who look and act and speak in believable ways. Stories which are not simply outpourings of human angst, but which acknowledge life. Find some positive aspects of life to write about. Read several issues of the publication first!" Would like to see more "stories which do not depend on excessive profanity, violence, pain and sexist attitudes. If everyone is screaming at a high pitch, no one hears anything. How about just a few quiet helpful whispers?"

RIVERWIND, (I, II), General Studies/Hocking College, 3301 Hocking Pkwy., Nelsonville OH 45764. (614)753-3591 (ext. 2375). Editors: Deni Naffziger and Jane Ann Devol-Fuller. Fiction Editor: Robert Clark Young. Magazine: 7 × 7; 60 lb. paper; cover illustrations; "College press, small literary magazine." Annually. Estab. 1975.

 • In addition to receiving funding from the Ohio Arts Council since 1985, *Riverwind* has won the Septa Award and a Sepan Award.

Needs: Contemporary, ethnic, feminist, historical, humor/satire, literary, mainstream, prose poem, spiritual, sports, regional, translations. No juvenile/teen fiction. Receives 30 mss/month. Does not read during the summer. Published work by Roy Bentley and Greg Anderson; published new writers within the last year. Sometimes critiques rejected mss.

How to Contact: Send complete ms with a cover letter. No simultaneous submissions. Reports on mss in 1-4 months. SASE. Sample back issue: $1.

Payment/Terms: Pays in contributor's copies.

Advice: "Your work must be strong, entertaining. It helps if you are an Ohio/West Virginia writer. We hope to print more fiction. We now publish mainly regional writers (Ohio, West Virginia, Kentucky)."

ROANOKE REVIEW, (II), English Department, Roanoke College, Salem VA 24153. (703)375-2500. Editor: Robert R. Walter. Magazine: 6 × 9; 40-60 pages. Semiannually. Estab. 1967. Circ. 300.

Needs: Receives 50-60 unsolicited mss/month. Accepts 2-3 mss/issue; 4-6 mss/year. Publishes ms 6 months after acceptance. Length: 2,500 words minimum; 7,500 words maximum. Publishes short shorts. Occasionally critiques rejected mss.

How to Contact: Send complete ms with a cover letter. Reports in 1-2 weeks on queries; 10-12 weeks on mss. SASE for query. Sample copy for $3.

Payment/Terms: Pays in contributor's copies.

‡ROCK SPRINGS REVIEW, (I, II), P.O. Box 30772, Columbia MO 65205-3772. Editor: Daren Dean. Magazine: 5½ × 8½; 20-50 pages; 20 lb. bond ivory/cream paper; 65 lb. bond cover. "*Rock Springs Review* is a literary magazine featuring short stories, poetry, essays and interviews." Quarterly. Estab. 1996. Circ. 50.

Needs: Contemporary, ethnic/multicultural, historical, humor/satire, literary, mainstream, religious. Receives 1-5 unsolicited mss/month. Accepts 6-9 mss/issue; 20-30 mss/year. Publishes mss "sometimes up to one year" after acceptance. Recently published work by Flannery Bateman, Elizabeth

Moore and LeeAnne Ogletree. Length: 1,500-3,000 words preferred; 3,000 words maximum. Also publishes essays, interviews with artists and writers, and poetry. Often critiques or comments on rejected mss.

How to Contact: Send complete ms with a cover letter. Include estimated word count and 25- to 50-word bio. Encourages hard copy and disk submissions (ASCII). Reports in 4-6 weeks on ms (depends on editor's work load). Send SASE for reply, return of ms or send a disposable copy of ms. Simultaneous and reprint submissions OK for essays (with proper credits). Sample copy for $3.50 and 9½×11 SASE. (Make checks payable to Daren Dean.) Fiction guidelines for #10 SASE.

Payment/Terms: Pays 1 contributor's copy. Acquires one-time rights.

Advice: "This magazine has a vision for developing new and talented writers. We prefer fiction which has strong characters and themes. We have a commitment to publishing only the highest quality! Read the great American writers, especially Southern writers. We would like to see writers tackle more serious subjects."

THE ROCKFORD REVIEW, (I, II), The Rockford Writers Guild, Box 858, Rockford IL 61105. Editor-in-Chief: David Ross. Magazine: 5⅜×8½; 50 pages; b&w illustrations; b&w photos. "We look for prose and poetry with a fresh approach to old themes or new insights into the human condition." Triquarterly. Estab. 1971. Circ. 750.

Needs: Ethnic, experimental, fantasy, humor/satire, literary, regional, science fiction (hard science, soft/sociological). Recently published work by Valerie Ann Leff, Tom Deiker, William Gorman and Melanie Coronetz. Length: Up to 1,300 words. Also publishes one-acts and essays.

How to Contact: Send complete ms. "Include a short biographical note—no more than four sentences." Simultaneous submissions OK. Reports in 6-8 weeks on mss. SASE. Sample copy for $5. Fiction guidelines for SASE.

Payment/Terms: Pays contributor's copies. "Two $25 editor's choice cash prizes per issue." Acquires first North American serial rights.

Advice: "Any subject or theme goes as long as it enhances our understanding of our humanity." Wants more "satire and humor, good dialogue."

‡SALOME, (II, IV), Telling Moment Productions, 2211 NE Halsey #3, Portland OR 97232. E-mail: griot@mail.well.com. Editor: Bill Olver. Magazine: 8½×7; 60 pages; 20 lb. white paper; card cover stock; 5-10 photographs/illustrations per issue. "*Salome* publishes work by, for and about queers. Defining 'queer' is up to the contributor. We specifically want nongenre literary work. Experimental work is encouraged, but should follow a narrative structure. Narrative poetry is preferred, but non-narrative considered." Bimonthly. Estab. 1996. Circ. 300.

Needs: Gay, lesbian, bisexual, transgender, queer, feminist, ethnic/multicultural literary work. No specific themes, but seriously considers holiday material for December issue and erotica/romance for February issue. Accepts 2-4 mss/issue; 8-16 mss/year. Publishes ms 1-3 months after acceptance. Length: 3,000 words preferred. Publishes short shorts. Also publishes literary essays, poetry, photography, artwork and comics/cartoons. Sometimes critiques or comments on rejected mss.

How to Contact: Send complete ms with a cover letter. Include estimated word count, 50-word bio and list of publications. Reports in 1 month on queries; 3 months of mss. Send a disposable copy of ms. Electronic submissions in Macintosh format strongly encouraged; e-mail submissions OK. Photocopies OK. Sample copy for $5. Fiction guidelines for #10 SAE and 2 first-class stamps.

Payment/Terms: Pays 2 contributor copies. Acquires one-time rights.

Advice: "The Biblical Salome had a mind for politics and a body for sin, and used both to decapitate an important Christian. Keep that in mind: tell a good story; entertain us; don't be afraid to gut a sacred cow for personal gain. We value work that examines and critiques social, political and cultural standards from an individual's standpoint. Don't be timid in your beliefs, but don't be pigheaded, either. Tell your truths without disrespecting others' lives. Reject political correctness in favor of cultural justice. Above all, have fun. If you're not having fun, it's just not worth it."

SALT LICK PRESS, (II), Salt Lick Foundation, Salt Lick Press/Lucky Heart Books, 1900 West Hwy. 6, B205, Waco TX 76712. Editor: James Haining. Magazine: 8½×11; 100 pages; 70 lb. offset stock; 65 lb. cover; illustrations and photos. Irregularly. Estab. 1969.

Needs: Contemporary, erotica, ethnic, experimental, feminist, gay, lesbian, literary. Receives 25 unsolicited mss each month. Accepts 4 mss/issue. Length: open. Occasionally critiques rejected mss.

How to Contact: Send complete ms with cover letter. Reports in 2 weeks on queries; 1 month on mss. SASE. Simultaneous and reprint submissions OK. Sample copy for $6, 9×12 SAE and 3 first-class stamps.

Payment/Terms: Pays in contributor's copies. Acquires first North American serial rights. Sends galleys to author.

SANSKRIT, Literary Arts Publication of UNC Charlotte, (II), University of North Carolina at Charlotte, Highway 49, Charlotte NC 28223. (704)547-2326. Contact: Literary Editor. Magazine:

9 × 12, 60-90 pages. "We are a general lit/art mag open to all genres, if well written, for college students, alumni, writers and artists across the country." Annually. Estab. 1968.

• *Sanskrit* has received the Pacemaker Award, Associated College Press, Gold Crown Award and Columbia Scholastic Press Award.

Needs: Contemporary, erotica, ethnic, experimental, feminist, gay, humor/satire, lesbian, mainstream, prose poem, regional, translations. No formula, western, romance. Receives 6-10 unsolicited mss/month. Acquires 3-6 mss/issue. Publishes in late March. Deadline: November 15. Recently published work by Chaim Bertman, Kat Meads and Kerry Madden-Lunsford. Length: 250 words minimum; 5,000 words maximum. Publishes short shorts. Also publishes poetry. Sometimes critiques rejected mss.

How to Contact: Send complete manuscript with cover letter. SASE. Simultaneous submissions OK. Sample copy for $6. Fiction guidelines for #10 SAE.

Payment/Terms: Pays contributor's copies. Acquires one-time rights. Publication not copyrighted.

Advice: "We have actually been noted for our poetry. Fiction tends to be '*New Yorker*'-esque, but we are encouraging more provocative styles. We ask that you be original and creative, but not so avant-garde that we'd need a team of linguists to decipher your work."

SANTA BARBARA REVIEW, Literary Arts Journal, (II), 104 La Vereda Lane, Santa Barbara CA 93108. (805)969-0861. Fax: (805)965-3049. Editor: Patricia Stockton Leddy. Fiction Editor: Diane de Avalle-Arce. Magazine: 6 × 9; 184 pages, 60 lb. opaque paper; 10 pt. CS1; illustrations and photos. "The goal of *The Santa Barbara Review* is to find stories that entertain, surprise, and shed light on the vast human condition." Triannually. Estab. 1993.

• *Santa Barbara Review* is a member of the Council of Literary Magazines and Presses.

Needs: Literary. "No children's fiction. We try to avoid topics for their news value or political correctness." Receives 50-100 unsolicited fiction mss/month. Accepts 6-8 mss/issue; 24 mss/year. Publishes ms 1 year after acceptance. Recently published work by Hugh Fox. Length: 3,500-4,000 words average. Occasionally publishes short shorts. Length: 500 words. Also publishes literary essays and poetry. Often critiques or comments on rejected mss. Sponsors annual contest. First place: $350. Send SASE for details.

How to Contact: Send complete ms with a cover letter. Include 2-3 line bio and list of publications. "Always send a disk upon acceptance, Macintosh or IBM." Reports in 2 weeks on queries; 6 months on mss. Send SASE for reply, return of ms or send a disposable copy of ms. Electronic (disk) submissions OK. Sample copy for $5 and $2.40 postage. Reviews novels and short story collections.

Payment/Terms: Pays 2 contributor's copies; additional copies for standard bookrate. Acquires one-time rights.

Advice: "First thing we look for is voice. Make every word count. We want to see immediate involvement, convincing dialogue, memorable characters. Show us connection between things we had previously thought disparate. The self-indulgent, feel sorry for yourself polemic we really don't like. We are very fond of humor that is not mean spirited and wish to see more."

‡SATIRE, (I, II), C&K Publications, P.O. Box 340, Hancock MD 21750-0340. (301)678-6999. E-mail: satire@intrepid.net. Editor: Larry Logan. Magazine: 5½ × 8½; 100 pages; bond paper; illustrations. "We hope that our quarterly provides a home for contemporary literary satire that might make you laugh . . . make you squirm . . . and make you think." Quarterly. Estab. 1994. Circ. 500.

Needs: Humor/satire, literary. "We will consider all categories as long as a satiric treatment is incorporated." Receives 60-80 unsolicited mss/month. Accepts 20 mss/issue; 80 mss/year. Publishes ms within 6 months after acceptance. Recently published work by Mark Cohen, James Miller, Rob Kocur, Harold Huber, Katherine Brooks, Dick Lancaster, Len Messineo, Madeline Begun Kane and William F. Lantry. Length: 6,000 words maximum. Publishes short shorts. Also publishes literary essays, condensed/excerpted novel, poetry and 3-6 cartoons/issue. Sometimes critiques or comments on rejected mss.

How to Contact: Send complete ms with cover letter. Include estimated word count, a short bio and list of publications. Reports in 3 months on mss. Send SASE for reply, return of ms or send a disposable copy of ms. Simultaneous, reprint and electronic submissions OK. Sample copy for $5 and #10 SASE. Fiction guidelines free.

Payment/Terms: Pays 2 contributor's copies for works over 1 page; additional 5 copies at cost to authors. Acquires one-time rights. Sends galleys to author.

Advice: "Think and write with quality, and be sure that a 'well-read' audience can identify the satiric target(s). Clever humor and wit is prized within a well-developed story. Study an issue or two before you submit."

SCREAMING TOAD PRESS, Dancing with Mr. D. Publications, (II), 809 W. Broad St. #221, Falls Church VA 22046. Editor: Llori Steinberg. Magazine: 6 × 9; 20-30 pages; 60 lb. cover; illustrations and photos. "Fiction/nonfiction—usually warped, mind ripping gore or truelife experience." Quarterly. Estab. 1993. Circ. 500.

Needs: Erotica (horror), experimental, fantasy (children's fantasy, science fantasy), horror, humor/satire, mystery/suspense (amateur sleuth). No religion/Christian. List of upcoming themes available for SASE. Receives 100-350 unsolicited mss/month. Accepts 2 mss/issue; 2-8 mss/year. Published work by Gregory Bryant and Keith Cummings. Length: 1,000 words average; 300-500 words minimum; 1,000 words maximum. Publishes short shorts. Also publishes literary essays and literary criticism. Sometimes critiques or comments on rejected mss.

How to Contact: Send complete ms. Include bio (any length). Reports in 2-6 weeks on queries; 6-12 weeks on mss. Send SASE for reply, return of ms or send a disposable copy of ms. Simultaneous and reprints submissions OK. Sample copy for $5 (payable to Llori Steinberg), #10 SAE and 2 first-class stamps. Fiction guidelines for #10 SAE and 2 first-class stamps.

Payment/Terms: No payment. Copies $5. All rights revert to author.

Advice: "I got to enjoy it—it's gotta be you!"

‡SE LA VIE WRITER'S JOURNAL, (I), Rio Grande Press, P.O. Box 71745, Las Vegas NV 89170. Phone/fax: (702)436-6312. Editor: Rosalie Avara. Magazine: 8½×5½; 68-74 pages; bond paper; illustrations. *SLVWJ* accepts work through its short short story contests. "Manuscripts should reflect the 'that's life' (Se La Vie) theme, intended for young adult to adult readers. We also publish *The Story Shop*, an annual anthology of short stories. For *The Story Shop*, we accept any type of wholesome stories (no porn or erotica)." Quarterly. Estab. 1987. Circ. 150.

Needs: Adventure, ethnic/multicultural, humor/satire, literary, mystery/suspense (amateur sleuth, private eye/hardboiled, romantic suspense), regional. "No science fiction, porn or erotica; nothing political or feminist; no alternate lifestyles; no extreme religious (although some spiritual)." Receives 8-10 unsolicited mss/month. Accepts 2 mss/issue for *SLVWJ*; 12-15 mss/issue for *The Story Shop*. Publishes ms 3 months after acceptance; 1 year after acceptance for *The Story Shop*. Recently published work by Marian Ford Park, Edgar H. Thompson and Michael R. Drury. Length: 500 words average; 300 words minimum; 500 words maximum. Length (for *The Story Shop*): 1,500 words average; 1,000 words minimum; 1,500 words maximum. Publishes short shorts. Length: 400 words. Also publishes literary essays and poetry. Sometimes critiques or comments on rejected mss.

How to Contact: Send SASE first for guidelines, then send complete ms with cover letter. Include estimated word count. Reports in 2 weeks on queries and mss. Send SASE for reply, return of ms or send a disposable copy of ms. Sample copy for $2. Contest and fiction guidelines for #10 SASE. Reviews novels and short story collections.

Payment/Terms: Pays $5-25 to contest winners; copies of *The Story Shop* available for $6.95 each. Pays on publication. Acquires first North American serial rights.

Advice: *Se La Vie* looks for stories with surprise endings. *The Story Shop* looks for "any story that can hold my interest for the first three pages." For both publications, "believable characters, good dialogue, good description, good plot, etc."

SENSATIONS MAGAZINE, (I, II), 2 Radio Ave., A5, Secaucus NJ 07094. Founder: David Messineo. Magazine: 8½×11; 100 pages; 20 lb. paper; full color cover; color photography. "We publish short stories and poetry, no specific theme." Magazine also includes the Rediscovering America in Poetry research series. Semiannually. Estab. 1987.

● *Sensations Magazine* received an Honorable Mention for Editorial Comment in the 1995 American Literary Magazine Awards. This is one of the few markets accepting longer work.

Needs: Fantasy, gay, historical, horror, humor/satire, lesbian, literary, mystery/suspense (private eye), science fiction, western (traditional). "We're not into gratuitous profanity, pornography, or violence. Sometimes these are needed to properly tell the tale. We'll read anything unusual, providing it is submitted in accordance with our submission policies. No abstract works only the writer can understand." Accepts 2-4 mss/issue. Publishes ms 2 months after acceptance. Recently published work by Diana Lee Goldman and Eliot Sekuler. Length: 35 pages maximum.

How to Contact: Send SASE for guidelines. Simultaneous submissions OK. Accepts electronic submissions (Macintosh only). *Must first make $12 advance payment.* Check payable to David Messineo. *"Do not submit material before reading submission guidelines."* Next deadline: April 1, 1997.

Payment/Terms: Pays $25-75 per story on acceptance for one-time rights.

Advice: "Each story must have a strong beginning that grabs the reader's attention in the first two sentences. Characters have to be realistic and well-described. Readers must like, hate, or have some

---

‡   **THE DOUBLE DAGGER** before a listing indicates that the listing is new in this edition. New markets are often the most receptive to submissions by new writers.

emotional response to your characters. Setting, plot, construction, attention to detail—all are important. We work with writers to help them improve in these areas, but the better the stories are written before they come to us, the greater the chance for publication. Purchase sample copy first and read the stories."

SHADOW, Between Parallels, (I, II), Shadow Publications, P.O. Box 5464, Santa Rosa CA 95402. Phone/fax: (707)542-7114. E-mail: brianwts@aol.com. Editor-in-Chief: Brian Murphy. Submissions Editor: Lisa Boone. Magazine: 8½×5½; 36 pages; standard white paper; card stock cover. "*Shadow* is aimed at teen readers. Our goal is to provide well-written fiction for young adults. We also support teen writers and make a special point to respond to their work." Quarterly. Estab. 1995.
Needs: Young adult/teen. Receives 20-45 unsolicited mss/month. Accepts 5-7 mss/issue; 25-30 mss/year. Publishes ms 3 months after acceptance. Agented fiction 6%. Recently published work by Susan Sanchez, Guilford Barton and John Downing. Length: 3,000 words average; 750 words minimum; 10,000 words maximum. Also publishes literary essays and literary criticism. Often critiques or comments on rejected mss.
How to Contact: Send complete ms. Include estimated word count, bio (1 page or less), Social Security number and list of publications. Reports in 3 weeks on queries; 6-8 weeks on mss. Send SASE for reply. Simultaneous, reprint and electronic submissions OK. Sample copy for $2 and 2 first-class stamps. Fiction guidelines for #10 SASE.
Payment/Terms: Pays 2-3 contributor's copies; additional copies for a reduced price. Acquires one-time rights. Sponsors contest. Send SASE for details.
Advice: "We want fiction that has depth to it and that will make our readers stop and think. Work that leaves a lasting impression. New writers should make sure their work is polished before submitting. We still make a point to comment often on work from new writers."

SHATTERED WIG REVIEW, (I, II), Shattered Wig Productions, 425 E. 31st, Baltimore MD 21218. (410)243-6888. Editor: Collective. Magazine: 8½×8½; 70 pages; "average" paper; cardstock cover; illustrations and photos. "Open forum for the discussion of the absurdo-miserablist aspects of everyday life. Fiction, poetry, graphics, essays, photos." Semiannually. Estab. 1988. Circ. 500.
Needs: Confession, contemporary, erotica, ethnic, experimental, feminist, gay, humor/satire, lesbian, literary, prose poem, psychic/supernatural/occult, regional. Does not want "anything by Ann Beattie or John Irving." Receives 15-20 unsolicited mss/month. Publishes ms 2-4 months after acceptance. Recently published work by Al Ackerman, Kim Harrison and Mok Hossfeld; published new writers within the last year. Publishes short shorts. Also publishes literary criticism, poetry. Sometimes critiques rejected mss and recommends other markets.
How to Contact: Send complete ms with cover letter. Reports in 2 months. Send SASE for return of ms. Simultaneous and reprint submissions OK. Sample copy for $4.
Payment/Terms: Pays in contributor's copies. Acquires one-time rights.
Advice: "The arts have been reduced to imploding pus with the only material rewards reserved for vapid stylists and collegiate pod suckers. The only writing that counts has no barriers between imagination and reality, thought and action. Send us at least three pieces so we have a choice."

‡SHENANDOAH, The Washington and Lee Review, (II), 2nd Floor, Troubadour Theater, Lexington VA 24450. (540)463-8765. Editor: R.T. Smith. Magazine: 6×9; 124 pages. "We are a literary journal devoted to excellence." Quarterly. Estab. 1950. Circ. 2,000.
Needs: Literary. Receives 400-500 unsolicited fiction mss/month. Accepts 4 mss/issue; 16 mss/year. Does not read mss during summer. Publishes ms 6 months to 1 year after acceptance. Recently published work by Kent Nelson, Barry Gifford, Nicholas Delbanco and Reynolds Price. Publishes short shorts. Also publishes literary essays, literary criticism and poetry.
How to Contact: Send complete ms with cover letter. Include a 3-sentence bio and list of publications ("just the highlights"). Reports in 10 weeks on mss. Send a disposable copy of ms. Sample copy for $3. Fiction guidelines for #10 SASE. Reviews novels and short story collections.
Payment/Terms: Pays $25/page and free subscription to the magazine on publication. Acquires first North American serial rights. Sends galleys to author. Sponsors contest; all published mss eligible.
Advice: Looks for "thrift, precision, originality. As Frank O'Connor said, 'Get black on white.' "

‡SHOCKWAVES, New Fiction, (I, III), Permeable Press, 2336 Market St., #14, San Francisco CA 94114. (415)255-9765. Fax: (415)431-1456. E-mail: bcclark@igc.org. Editor: Brian Clark. Fiction Editor: Quark Bosch. Magazine: 5×7; approximately 50 pages; recycled book paper; recycled cover stock, uncoated; illustrations and photos. "*ShockWaves* has been described as publishing 'the literature of convulsive beauty.' We publish avant-garde material with a pop culture twist; short, previously unpublished fiction for adventurous readers." Semiannually. Estab. 1996. Circ. 500 (available by subscription only).
Needs: Condensed/excerpted novel, erotica, ethnic/multicultural, experimental, fantasy (science fantasy), feminist, gay, historical (general), horror, humor/satire, lesbian, literary, mainstream/contempo-

rary, psychic/supernatural/occult, science fiction (hard science, soft/sociological, experimental). "No genre, no cliches, no minimalist 'contemporary.' Break out!" List of upcoming themes available for SASE. Receives hundreds of unsolicited mss/month. Accepts 3 or more/issue; approximately 40 mss/year (includes anthology). "We read for very limited periods; query with SASE first." Publishes ms 3-6 months after acceptance. Recently published work by Lance Olsen, Sarah Hafner, Paul Di Filippo, Thom Metzger and Eugene Stein. Length: open/varies; 1,000 words minimum; 10,000 words maximum. Publishes short shorts; length varies. Also publishes literary essays and literary criticism. Sometimes critiques or comments on rejected mss.

How to Contact: Query first with SASE. Include estimated word count, bio (25-50 words). Reports in 2 weeks on queries; 2 months on mss. SASE for reply or return of ms. "No 'disposable' manuscripts!" Reprint submissions OK. Sample copy for $5. Fiction guidelines for #10 SAE with 2 first-class stamps. Reviews novels and short story collections. Send books to Reviews Editor.

Payment/Terms: Pays $10 minimum, ½¢/word maximum and 5 contributor's copies on publication; additional copies 55% discount. Acquires first North American serial rights. Sends galleys to author. Sponsors contests; send SASE for current calendar.

Advice: "The work must be fully alive—no dead metaphors or self-indulgent postmodernisms. Check out our web site to read what we've published over the years, or buy a sample copy. Get to know our work and the work of other independent publishers."

SHORT STORIES BIMONTHLY, (I, II), Poetry Forum, 5713 Larchmont Dr., Erie PA 16509. Phone/fax: (814)866-2543. E-mail: 75562.670@compuserve.com. Editor: Gunvor Skogsholm. Newsletter: 11×17; 14 pages; 20 lb. paper; illustrations. Estab. 1992. Circ. 400.

Needs: Literary, mainstream. Receives 30 unsolicited mss/month. Accepts 8-10 mss/issue; 48-60 mss/year. Publishes ms 1-9 months after acceptance. Recently published work by Chris Jopher Essex, Vincent Zandri, Katherine Cress and John Morgan. Length: 1,800 words average; 600 words minimum; 4,000 words maximum. Publishes short shorts. Length: 600 words. Also publishes literary essays and literary criticism.

How to Contact: Send complete ms with a cover letter. Include estimated word count. Reports in 3 weeks to 6 months on mss. Send SASE for reply, return of ms or send a disposable copy of ms. Simultaneous and electronic submissions OK. Sample copy for $3. Fiction guidelines free. Favors submissions from subscribers. "We exist by subscriptions and advertising." Reviews novels and short story collections.

Payment/Terms: Acquires one-time rights. Sponsors contests, awards or grants for fiction writers. Send SASE.

Advice: "Be original, be honest. Write from your deepest sincerity—don't play games with the readers. Meaning: we don't want the last paragraph to tell us we have been fooled."

SHORT STUFF MAGAZINE FOR GROWN-UPS, (I, II), Bowman Publications, P.O. Box 7057, Loveland CO 80537. (970)669-9139. Editor: Donna Bowman. Magazine: $8½ \times 11$; 40 pages; bond paper; enamel cover; b&w illustrations and photographs. "Nonfiction is regional—Colorado and adjacent states. Fiction and humor must be tasteful, but can be any genre, any subject. We are designed to be a 'Reader's Digest' of fiction. We are found in professional waiting rooms, etc." Publishes 10 issues/year; "we combine July/August and January/February."

Needs: Adventure, contemporary, historical, humor/satire, mainstream, mystery/suspense (amateur sleuth, English cozy, police procedural, private eye, romantic suspense), regional, romance (contemporary, gothic, historical), western (frontier). No erotica. "We use holiday themes." Receives 150 unsolicited mss/month. Accepts 9-12 mss/issue; 76 mss/year. Publishes accepted work immediately. Recently published work by Susanne Shaphren, William Hallstead, Eleanor Sherman, Sam Cushing, Birdie Etcheson, Guy Belleranti and Jane McBride Choate. Length: 1,000 words average; 1,800 words maximum.

How to Contact: Send complete ms with cover letter. SASE. Reports in 3-6 months. Sample copies for $1.50 and 9×12 SAE with $1.50 postage. Fiction guidelines for SASE.

Payment/Terms: Pays $10-50 and subscription to magazine on publication for first North American serial rights. $1-5 for fillers (less than 500 words). "We do not pay for single jokes or poetry, but do give free subscription if published."

Advice: "We seek a potpourri of subjects each issue. A new slant, a different approach, fresh viewpoints—all of these excite us. We don't like gore, salacious humor or perverted tales. Prefer third person. Be sure it is a story with a beginning, middle and end. It must have dialogue. Many beginners do not know an essay from a short story. Essays frequently used if *humorous*. We'd like to see more young (25 and over) humor; 'clean' humor is hard to come by."

SIDE SHOW, Short Story Annual, (II), Somersault Press, P.O. Box 1428, El Cerrito CA 94530-1428. (510)215-2207. Editor: Shelley Anderson, Kathe Stolz and Marjorie K. Jacobs. Book (paperback): $5½ \times 8½$; 300 pages; 50 lb. paper; semigloss card cover with color illustration; perfect-bound. "Quality short stories for a general, literary audience." Annually. Estab. 1991. Circ. 3,000.

• Work published in *Side Show* has been selected for inclusion in the *Pushcart Prize* anthology.

Needs: Contemporary, ethnic, feminist, gay, humor/satire, lesbian, literary, mainstream. Nothing genre, religious, pornographic. Receives 50-60 unsolicited mss/month. Accepts 25-30 mss/issue. Publishes ms up to 9 months after acceptance. Recently published work by Dorothy Bryant, Susan Welch, Tim Schell, Marianne Rogoff and Miguel Rios. Length: Open. Critiques rejected mss, if requested.

How to Contact: All submissions entered in contest. *$10 entry fee* (includes subscription to next *Side Show*). Deadline: June 30. No guidelines. Send complete ms with cover letter and entry fee. Reports in 3-4 weeks on mss. SASE. Simultaneous submissions OK. Multiple submissions "in same envelope" encouraged. Sample copy for $10 and $2 postage and handling ($.83 sales tax CA residents).

Payment/Terms: Pays $10/printed page on publication for first North American serial rights. Sends galleys to author. All submissions entered in our contest for cash prizes of $500 (1st), $200 (2nd) and $100 (3rd).

Advice: Looks for "readability, vividness of characterization, coherence, inspiration, interesting subject matter, point of view, originality, plausibility. If your fiction isn't inspired, you probably won't be published by us (i.e., style and craft alone won't do it)."

SIDEWALKS, (II), P.O. Box 321, Champlin MN 55316. (612)421-3512. Editor: Tom Heie. Magazine: 5½ × 8½; 60-75 pages; 60 lb. paper; textured recycled cover. "*Sidewalks* . . . place of discovery, of myth, power, incantation . . . places we continue to meet people, preoccupied, on our way somewhere . . . tense, dark, empty places . . . place we meet friends and strangers, neighborhood sidewalks, place full of memory, paths that bring us home." Semiannually. Estab. 1991. Circ. 500.

Needs: Experimental, humor/satire, literary, mainstream/contemporary, regional. No violent, pornographic kinky material. Accepts 6-8 mss/issue; 12-16 mss/year. Work is accepted for 2 annual deadlines: May 31 and December 31. Publishes ms 10 weeks after deadline. Published work by Jonathan Gillman and Jean Ervin. Length: 2,500 words preferred; 3,000 words maximum. Publishes short shorts. Also publishes poetry.

How to Contact: Send complete ms with cover letter. Include estimated word count, very brief bio, list of publications. Reports in 1 week on queries; 1 month after deadline on mss. Send SASE for reply, return of ms or send a disposable copy of ms. No simultaneous submissions. Accepts electronic submissions. Sample copy for $5.

Payment/Terms: Pays 1 contributor's copy; additional copies $5. Acquires one-time rights.

Advice: "We look for a story with broad appeal, one that is well-crafted and has strong narrative voice, a story that leaves the reader thinking after the reading is over."

SIERRA NEVADA COLLEGE REVIEW, (I, II), Sierra Nevada College, P.O. Box 4269, Incline Village NV 89450. (702)831-1314. Editor: June Sylvester. Magazine: 5½ × 8½; 50-100 pages; coated paper; card cover; saddle-stitched. "We are open to many kinds of work but avoid what we consider trite, sentimental, contrived. . . ." Annually. Estab. 1990. Circ. 200-250 (mostly college libraries).

• The majority of work published in this review is poetry.

Needs: Experimental, literary, mainstream/contemporary, regional. Receives about 50 unsolicited mss/month. Accepts 2-3 mss/year. Does not read mss April 1 through September 1. Work is published by next issue (published in May, annually). Recently published work by Jamie Andree and James Braziel. Length: 500 words average; 1,000 words maximum. Publishes short shorts. Also publishes literary essays, literary criticism and poetry. Sometimes critiques or comments on rejected mss.

How to Contact: Send complete ms with a cover letter. Include estimated word count and bio. Send SASE for reply, return of ms or send a disposable copy of ms. Simultaneous submissions OK. Sample copy for $2.50.

Payment/Terms: Pays 2 contributor's copies. Acquires one-time rights.

Advice: Looks for "memorable characters, close attention to detail which makes the story vivid. We are interested in flash fiction. Also regional work that catches the flavor of place and time—like strong characters. No moralizing, inspirational work. No science fiction. No children's stories. Tired of trite love stories—cynicism bores us."

THE SILVER WEB, A Magazine of the Surreal, (II), Buzzcity Press, Box 38190, Tallahassee FL 32315. E-mail: annkl9@mail.idt.net. Editor: Ann Kennedy. Magazine: 8½ × 11; 64 pages; 20 lb. paper; glossy cover; b&w illustrations and photographs. "Looking for unique character-based stories that are off-beat, off-center and strange, but not inaccessible." Semiannually. Estab. 1989. Circ. 1,000.

• Work published in *The Silver Web* has appeared in *The Year's Best Fantasy and Horror* (DAW Books) and *The Year's Best Fantastic Fiction*.

Needs: Experimental, horror, science fiction (soft/sociological). No "traditional storylines, monsters, vampires, werewolves, etc." *The Silver Web* publishes surrealistic fiction and poetry. Work too bizarre for mainstream, but perhaps too literary for genre. This is not a straight horror/sci-fi magazine. No typical storylines." Receives 500 unsolicited mss/month. Accepts 8-10 mss/issue; 16-20 mss/year. Does not read mss October through December. Publishes ms 6-12 months after acceptance. Recently published work by Jeffrey Thomas, Sue Storm and Tom Precirilli. Length: 6,000 words average; 100

words minimum; 8,000 words maximum. Publishes short shorts. Also publishes poetry. Sometimes critiques rejected ms.

How to Contact: Send complete ms with a cover letter. Include estimated word count. Reports in 1 week on queries; 6-8 weeks on mss. Send SASE for reply, return of ms or send a disposable copy of ms plus SASE for reply. Simultaneous and reprint submissions OK. Sample copy for $5.95. Fiction guidelines for #10 SASE. Reviews novels and short story collections.

Payment/Terms: Pays 2-3¢/word and 2 contributor's copies; additional copies for $3.50. Acquires first North American serial rights, reprint rights or one-time rights.

Advice: "I have a reputation for publishing excellent fiction from newcomers next to talented, established writers, and for publishing cross-genre fiction. No traditional, standard storylines. I'm looking for beautiful writing with plots that are character-based. Tell a good story; tell it with beautiful words. I see too many writers writing for the marketplace and this fiction just doesn't ring true. I'd rather read fiction that comes straight from the heart of the writer." Read a copy of the magazine, at least get the writer's guidelines.

SILVERFISH REVIEW, (II), Box 3541, Eugene OR 97403. (503)344-5060. Editor: Rodger Moody. High quality literary material for a general audience. Published in June and December. Estab. 1979. Circ. 1,000.

Needs: Literary. Accepts 1-2 mss/issue. Recently published work by Sherrie Flick, Lidia Yuknavitch and Dennis Duhamel. Also publishes literary essays, poetry, interview, translations.

How to Contact: Send complete ms with SASE. No simultaneous submissions. Reports in 2-3 months on mss. Sample copy for $4 and $1.50 postage.

Payment/Terms: Pays 3 contributor's copies and one year subscription; $5/page when funding permits. Rights revert to author.

Advice: "We publish primarily poetry. We will, however, publish good quality fiction. *SR* is mainly interested in the short short story (one-minute and three-minute)."

SING HEAVENLY MUSE!, Women's Poetry and Prose, (I, II, IV), Box 13320, Minneapolis MN 55411. Contact: Editorial Circle. Magazine: 6×9; 100 pages; 55 lb. acid-free paper; 10 pt. glossy cover stock; illustrations; photos. "We foster the work of women poets, prose writers and artists and work that shows an awareness of women's consciousness." Annually. Estab. 1977. Circ. 300.

Needs: Literary, feminist, prose poem and ethnic/minority. List of upcoming themes and reading periods available for SASE. Receives approximately 30 unsolicited fiction mss each month. Accepts 3-6 mss/issue. Recently published work by Patricia Dubrava, Jana Zvibloman and Alison Townsend. Length: 10,000 words maximum. Publishes short shorts. Also publishes literary essays, poetry. Sometimes critiques or comments on rejected mss.

How to Contact: Query for information on theme issues, reading periods or variations in schedule. Include cover letter with "brief writing background and publications." No simultaneous submissions. Reports in 1-2 months on queries; 3-9 months on mss. Publishes ms an average of 1 year after acceptance. Sample copy for $4. Fiction guidelines for #10 SASE.

Payment/Terms: Pays 2 contributor's copies and honorarium, depending on funding. Acquires one-time rights. Sends galleys to author.

SKYLARK, (II), Purdue University Calumet, 2200 169th St., Hammond IN 46323. (219)989-2262. Fax: (219)989-2581. Editor-in-Chief: Pamela Hunter. Magazine: 8½×11; 100 pages; illustrations; photos. Fine arts magazine—short stories, poems and graphics for adults. Annually. Estab. 1971. Circ. 600-1,000.

Needs: Contemporary, ethnic, experimental, fantasy, feminist, humor/satire, literary, mainstream, mystery/suspense (English cozy), prose poem, regional, romance (gothic), science fiction, serialized/excerpted novel, spiritual, sports and western (frontier stories). Upcoming theme: "Home" (submit by April 1997). Receives 20 mss/month. Accepts 8 mss/issue. Recently published work by Michael Beres, Tom Ewart, Martha Vertreace and Joanne Zimmerman; published new writers within the last year. Length: 4,000 words maximum. Also publishes essays and poetry.

How to Contact: Send complete ms. Send SASE for return of ms. Reports in 4 months. No simultaneous submissions. Sample copy for $7; back issue for $5.

Payment/Terms: Pays 1 contributor's copy. Acquires first rights. Copyright reverts to author.

Advice: "The goal of *Skylark* is to encourage *creativity* and give beginning and published authors showcase for their work. "We seek fiction that presents effective imagery, strong plot, and well-developed characterization. Graphic passages concerning sex or violence are unacceptable. We're looking for dramatic, closely-edited short stories. We receive too many stories from writers who do not know how to copyedit. Manuscripts *must* be carefully prepared and proofread."

SLIPSTREAM, (II, IV), Box 2071, New Market Station, Niagara Falls NY 14301. (716)282-2616. Editor: Dan Sicoli. Fiction Editors: R. Borgatti, D. Sicoli and Livio Farallo. Magazine: 7×8½; 80-

100 pages; high quality paper; card cover; illustrations; photos. "We use poetry and short fiction with a contemporary urban feel." Estab. 1981. Circ. 500.

Needs: Contemporary, erotica, ethnic, experimental, humor/satire, literary, mainstream and prose poem. No religious, juvenile, young adult or romance. Occasionally publishes theme issues; query for information. Receives over 75 unsolicited mss/month. Accepts 2-4 mss/issue; 6 mss/year. Recently published work by E.R. Baxter III, Katherine Katsens, B.D. Love and Robert Perchan. Length: under 15 pages. Publishes short shorts. Rarely critiques rejected mss. Sometimes recommends other markets.

How to Contact: "Query before submitting." Reports within 2 months. Send SASE for reply or return of ms. Sample copy for $5. Fiction guidelines for #10 SASE.

Payment/Terms: Pays 2 contributor's copies. Acquires one-time rights.

Advice: "Writing should be honest, fresh; develop your own style. Check out a sample issue first. Don't write for the sake of writing, write from the gut as if it were a biological need. Write from experience and mean what you say, but say it in the fewest number of words."

THE SMALL POND MAGAZINE, (II), Box 664, Stratford CT 06497. (203)378-4066. Editor: Napoleon St. Cyr. Magazine: 5½ × 8½; 42 pages; 60 lb. offset paper; 65 lb. cover stock; illustrations (art). "Features contemporary poetry, the salt of the earth, peppered with short prose pieces of various kinds. The college educated and erudite read it for good poetry, prose and pleasure." Triannually. Estab. 1964. Circ. 300.

Needs: "Rarely use science fiction or the formula stories you'd find in *Cosmo, Redbook, Ladies Home Journal*, etc." Accepts 10-12 mss/year. Longer response time in July and August. Receives approximately 40 unsolicited fiction mss each month. Recently published work by Gary Whitehead, Michael Scott and Heidi Cloeren. Length: 200-2,500 words. Critiques rejected mss when there is time. Sometimes recommends other markets.

How to Contact: Send complete ms with SASE and short vita. Reports in 2 weeks to 3 months. Publishes ms an average of 2-18 months after acceptance. Sample copy for $3; $2.50 for back issues.

Payment/Terms: Pays 2 contributor's copies for all rights; $2.50/copy charge for extras.

Advice: "Send for a sample copy first. All mss must be typed. Name and address and story title on front page, name of story on succeeding pages and paginated." Mss are rejected because of "tired plots and poor grammar; also over-long—2,500 words maximum. Don't send any writing conference ms unless it got an A or better."

SNOWY EGRET, (II), The Fair Press, P.O. Box 9, Bowling Green IN 47833. (812)829-1910. E-mail: 00pcrepp@bsu.edu. Publisher: Karl Barnebey. Editor: Philip Repp. Magazine: 8½ × 11; 50 pages; text paper; heavier cover; illustrations. "Literary exploration of the abundance and beauty of nature and the ways human beings interact with it." Semiannually. Estab. 1922. Circ. 500.

Needs: Nature writing, including 'true' stories, eye-witness accounts, descriptive sketches and traditional fiction. "We are particularly interested in fiction that celebrates abundance and beauty of nature, encourages a love and respect for the natural world, and affirms the human connection to the environment. No works written for popular genres: horror, science fiction, romance, detective, western, etc." Receives 25 unsolicited mss/month. Accepts up to 6 mss/issue; up to 12 mss/year. Publishes ms 6 months to 1 year after acceptance. Recently published works by Jane Candia Coleman, Tama Janowitz, David Abrams and Eva LaSalle Caram. Length: 1,000-3,000 words preferred; 500 words minimum; 10,000 words maximum. Publishes short shorts. Length: 400-500 words. Sometimes critiques rejected mss.

How to Contact: Send complete ms with cover letter. "Cover letter optional: do not query." Reports in 2 months. SASE. Simultaneous (if noted) and electronic (Mac, ASCII) submissions OK. Sample back issues for $8 and 9 × 12 SAE. Send #10 SASE for writer's guidelines.

Payment/Terms: Pays $2/page and 2 contributor's copies on publication; charge for extras. Acquires first North American serial rights and reprint rights. Sends galleys to author.

Advice: Looks for "honest, freshly detailed pieces with plenty of description and/or dialogue which will allow the reader to identify with the characters and step into the setting. Characters who relate strongly to nature, either positively or negatively, and who, during the course of the story, grow in their understanding of themselves and the world around them."

SO TO SPEAK, A Feminist Journal of Language and Art, (II, IV), George Mason University, Sub1, Room 254A, 4400 University Dr., Fairfax VA 22030. (703)993-3625. Editor: Wendi Kaufman. Editors change every 2 years. Magazine: 7 × 10; approximately 70 pages. "We are a feminist journal of high-quality material geared toward an academic/cultured audience." Semiannually. Estab. 1988. Circ. 1,300.

Needs: Ethnic/multicultural, experimental, feminist, lesbian, literary, mainstream/contemporary, regional, translations. "No science fiction, mystery, genre romance, porn (lesbian or straight)." Receives 100 unsolicited mss/month. Accepts 2-3 mss/issue; 6 mss/year. Publishes ms 6 months after acceptance. Recently published work by Rita Ciresi, Leslie Johnson, Julianna Baggott and Jessica Jordan Nudel. Length: 4,000 words average; 6,000 words maximum. Publishes short shorts. Also publishes literary

essays, literary criticism, book reviews and poetry. Sometimes critiques or comments on rejected mss.
How to Contact: Send complete ms with a cover letter. Include bio (50 words maximum) and SASE.
Reports in 6 months on mss. SASE for return of ms or send a disposable copy of ms. Simultaneous
submissions OK. Sample copy for $5. Fiction guidelines for #10 SASE.
Payment/Terms: Pays contributor's copies for first North American serial rights.
Advice: "We look for skill with language, feeling behind the words. All our fiction should mean
something. Make sure it is polished and pertinent to women's lives."

THE SOFT DOOR, (I, II), 202 S. Church St., Bowling Green OH 43402. E-mail: terria@bgnet.bgsu.
edu. Editor: T. Williams. Magazine: 8½×11; 30-60 pages; bond paper; heavy cover; illustrations and
photos. "We publish works that explore human relationships and our relationship to the world."
Irregularly.
Needs: Literary, mainstream/contemporary. Upcoming theme: "Custer And The Indians" (October
'97). Receives 25 mss/month. Accepts 5 mss/year. Does not read mss November through December.
Publishes ms up to 1 year after acceptance. Recently published work by Mark Sa Franko, Simon Peter
Buehrer, E.S. Griggs, Jennifer Casteen and Jim Feltz. Length: 5,000 words average; 10,000 words
maximum. Publishes short shorts. Also publishes poetry. Sometimes critiques or comments on rejected
mss.
How to Contact: Send complete ms with a cover letter. Include "short statement about who you
are and why you write, along with any successes you have had. Please write to me like I am a human
being." Send SASE for reply, return of ms or send a disposable copy of ms. "Please include SASE
with all correspondence. Do not send postcards." Simultaneous submissions OK.
Payment/Terms: Pays 1 contributor's copy. Acquires one-time rights.
Advice: "Read as much contemporary fiction and poetry as you can get your hands on. Write about
your deepest concerns. What you write can, and does, change lives. Always interested in works by
Native American writers."

SOUTH CAROLINA REVIEW, (I, II), Clemson University, Clemson SC 29634-1503. (803)656-
3151. Editors: Frank Day and Carol Johnston. Magazine: 6×9; 200 pages; 60 lb. cream white vellum
paper; 65 lb. cream white vellum cover stock; illustrations and photos rarely. Semiannually. Estab.
1967. Circ. 700.
Needs: Literary and contemporary fiction, poetry, essays, reviews. Receives 50-60 unsolicited fiction
mss each month. Does not read mss June through August or December. Published work by Joyce Carol
Oates, Rosanne Coggeshall, Stephen Dixon; published new writers within the last year. Rarely critiques
rejected mss.
How to Contact: Send complete ms with SASE. Reports in 6-9 months on mss. Sample copy for
$5.
Payment/Terms: Pays in contributor's copies.
Advice: Mss are rejected because of "poorly structured stories, or stories without vividness or intensity. The most celebrated function of a little magazine is to take a chance on writers not yet able to
get into the larger magazines—the little magazine can encourage promising writers at a time when
encouragement is vitally needed. (We also publish 'name' writers, like Joyce Carol Oates, Stephen
Dixon, George Garrett.) Read the masters extensively. Write and write more, with a *schedule*. Listen
to editorial advice when offered. Don't get discouraged with rejections. Read what writers say about
writing (e.g. *The Paris Review* interviews with George Plimpton; Welty's *One Writer's Beginnings*,
etc). Take courses in writing and listen to, even if you do not follow, the advice."

SOUTH DAKOTA REVIEW, (II), University of South Dakota, Box 111, University Exchange,
Vermillion SD 57069. (605)677-5966. Editor: Brian Bedard. Editorial Assistant: Geraldine Sanford.
Magazine: 6×9; 180 pages; book paper; glossy cover stock; illustrations sometimes; photos on cover.
"Literary magazine for university and college audiences and their equivalent. Emphasis is often on
the West and its writers, but will accept mss from anywhere. Issues are generally essay, fiction, and
poetry with some literary essays." Quarterly. Estab. 1963. Circ. 500.
● A story by Richard Plant, published in *SDR* was selected for inclusion in the *Sudden Fiction*
anthology published in Spring 1996, and *SDR* was selected for inclusion in the *Writer's Digest*
"Fiction 50" list of top fiction markets.
Needs: Literary, contemporary, ethnic, experimental, excerpted novel, regional. "We like very well-
written, thematically ambitious, character-centered short fiction. Contemporary western American setting appeals, but not necessary. No formula stories, horror or adolescent 'I' narrator." Receives 40
unsolicited fiction mss/month. Accepts about 40 mss/year. Assistant editor accepts mss in June through
July, sometimes August. Agented fiction 5%. Publishes short shorts of 5 pages double-spaced typescript. Recently published work by Dan O'Brien, Clay Reynolds, Margaret Kingery and Alan Davis.
Published several new writers within the last year. Length: 1,000-1,300 words minimum; 6,000 words
maximum. (Has made exceptions, up to novella length.) Sometimes recommends other markets.

How to Contact: Send complete ms with SASE. "We like cover letters that are not boastful and do not attempt to sell the stories but rather provide some personal information about the writer." No multiple submissions. Reports in 5-7 weeks. Publishes ms an average of 1-6 months after acceptance. Sample copy for $5.

Payment/Terms: Pays 1-year subscription, plus 2-4 contributor's copies, depending on length of ms; $3 charge for extras. Acquires first and reprint rights.

Advice: Rejects mss because of "careless writing; often careless typing; stories too personal ('I' confessional), adolescent; working manuscript, not polished; subject matter that editor finds clichéd, sensationalized, pretentious or trivial. We are trying to use more fiction and more variety."

SOUTHERN CALIFORNIA ANTHOLOGY, (III), Master of Professional Writing Program—USC, MPW-WPH 404 USC, Los Angeles CA 90089-4034. (213)740-3252. Fax: (213)740-5775. Contact: Editor. Magazine: 5½×8½; 142 pages; semigloss cover stock. "The *Southern California Anthology* is a literary review that is an eclectic collection of previously unpublished quality contemporary fiction, poetry and interviews with established literary people, published for adults of all professions; of particular interest to those interested in serious contemporary literature." Annually. Estab. 1983. Circ. 1,500.

Needs: Contemporary, ethnic, experimental, feminist, historical, humor/satire, literary, mainstream, regional, serialized/excerpted novel. No juvenile, religious, confession, romance, science fiction or pornography. Receives 40 unsolicited fiction mss each month. Accepts 10-12 mss/issue. Does not read February through September. Publishes ms 4 months after acceptance. Recently published work by Susan Fromberg Schaeffer, Stuart Dybek, Robley Wilson and Ross Talarico. Length: 10-15 pages average; 2 pages minimum; 25 pages maximum. Publishes short shorts.

How to Contact: Send complete ms with cover letter or submit through agent. Cover letter should include list of previous publications. Reports on queries in 1 month; on mss in 4 months. Send SASE for reply or return of ms. Sample copy for $4. Fiction guidelines for #10 SASE.

Payment/Terms: Pays in contributor's copies. Acquires first rights.

Advice: "The *Anthology* pays particular attention to craft and style in its selection of narrative writing."

SOUTHERN HUMANITIES REVIEW, (II, IV), Auburn University, 9088 Haley Center, Auburn University AL 36849. Co-editors: Dan R. Latimer and Virginia M. Kouidis. Magazine: 6×9; 100 pages; 60 lb. neutral pH, natural paper; 65 lb. neutral pH med. coated cover stock; occasional illustrations and photos. "We publish essays, poetry, fiction and reviews. Our fiction has ranged from very traditional in form and content to very experimental. Literate, college-educated audience. We hope they read our journal for both enlightenment and pleasure." Quarterly. Estab. 1967. Circ. 800.

Needs: Serious fiction, fantasy, feminist, humor and regional. Receives approximately 25 unsolicited fiction mss each month. Accepts 1-2 mss/issue, 4-6 mss/year. Slower reading time in summer. Published work by Anne Brashler, Heimito von Doderer and Ivo Andric; published new writers within the last year. Length: 3,500-15,000 words. Also publishes literary essays, literary criticism, poetry. Critiques rejected mss when there is time. Sometimes recommends other markets.

How to Contact: Send complete ms (one at a time) with SASE and cover letter with an explanation of topic chosen—"special, certain book, etc., a little about author if he/she has never submitted." Reports in 3 months. Sample copy for $5. Reviews novel and short story collections.

Payment/Terms: Pays 2 contributor's copies; $5 charge for extras. Rights revert to author upon publication. Sends galleys to author.

Advice: "Send us the ms with SASE. If we like it, we'll take it or we'll recommend changes. If we don't like it, we'll send it back as promptly as possible. Read the journal. Send typewritten, clean copy carefully proofread. We also award annually the Hoepfner Prize of $100 for the best published essay or short story of the year. Let someone whose opinion you respect read your story and give you an honest appraisal. Rewrite, if necessary, to get the most from your story."

THE SOUTHERN REVIEW, (II), Louisiana State University, 43 Allen Hall, Baton Rouge LA 70803. (504)388-5108. Fax: (504)388-5098. Editors: James Olney and Dave Smith. Magazine: 6¾×10; 240 pages; 50 lb. Glatfelter paper; 65 lb. #1 grade cover stock. "A literary quarterly publishing critical essays, poetry and fiction for a highly intellectual audience." Quarterly. Estab. 1935. Circ. 3,100.

Needs: Literary. "We emphasize style and substantial content. No mystery, fantasy or religious mss." Accepts 4-5 mss/issue. Receives approximately 300 unsolicited fiction mss each month. Does not read mss June through August. Publishes ms 6-9 months after acceptance. Agented fiction 1%. Recently published work by Joyce Carol Oates, Steve Yarbrough, Bobbie Ann Mason and Ellen Douglas. Published new writers within the last year. Length: 2,000-10,000 words. Also publishes literary essays, literary criticism, poetry. Sponsors annual contest for best first collection of short stories published during the calendar year.

How to Contact: Send complete ms with cover letter and SASE. "Prefer brief letters giving information on author concerning where he/she has been published before, biographical info and what he/she is doing now." Reports in 2 months on mss. Sample copy for $6. Fiction guidelines free for SAE. Reviews novels and short story collections.
Payment/Terms: Pays $12/printed page; 2 contributor's copies on publication for first North American serial rights. Sends galleys to author.
Advice: "Develop a careful, clear style."

SOUTHWEST REVIEW, (II), Box 374, 307 Fondren Library West, Southern Methodist University, Dallas TX 75275. (214)768-1037. Editor: Willard Spiegelman. Magazine: 6×9; 144 pages. "The majority of our readers are college-educated adults who wish to stay abreast of the latest and best in contemporary fiction, poetry, literary criticism and books in all but the most specialized disciplines." Quarterly. Estab. 1915. Circ. 1,600.
Needs: "High literary quality; no specific requirements as to subject matter, but cannot use sentimental, religious, western, poor science fiction, pornographic, true confession, mystery, juvenile or serialized or condensed novels." Receives approximately 200 unsolicited fiction mss each month. Recently published work by Brad Barkley, E. Shaskan Bumas, Hilary Steinitz, Richard Stern and Wakeko Yamauchi. Length: prefers 3,000-5,000 words. Also publishes literary essays and poetry. Occasionally critiques rejected mss.
How to Contact: Send complete ms with SASE. Reports in 6 months on mss. Publishes ms 6-12 months after acceptance. Sample copy for $5. Guidelines for SASE.
Payment/Terms: Payment varies; writers receive 3 contributor's copies. Pays on publication for first North American serial rights. Sends galleys to author.
Advice: "We have become less regional. A lot of time would be saved for us and for the writer if he or she looked at a copy of the *Southwest Review* before submitting. We like to receive a cover letter because it is some reassurance that the author has taken the time to check a current directory for the editor's name. When there isn't a cover letter, we wonder whether the same story is on 20 other desks around the country."

SOU'WESTER, (II), Southern Illinois University—Edwardsville, Edwardsville IL 62026-1438. (618)692-3190. Managing Editor: Fred W. Robbins. Magazine: 6×9; 120 pages; Warren's Olde Style paper; 60 lb. cover. General magazine of poetry and fiction. Biannually. Estab. 1960. Circ. 300.
● The *Sou'wester* is known for publishing traditional, well-developed and carefully crafted short stories. Work published here has received an Illinois Arts Council Literary Award for "Best Illinois Fiction" and the Daniel Curley Award.
Needs: Receives 50-100 unsolicited fiction mss/month. Accepts 6 mss/issue; 12 mss/year. Recently published work by Robert Wexelblatt, Julie Simon, John Pesta, Samuel Atlee and Patrick Bennett; published new writers within the last year. Length: 10,000 words maximum. Also publishes poetry. Occasionally critiques rejected mss.
How to Contact: Send complete ms with SASE. Simultaneous submissions OK. Reports in 6-8 months. Publishes ms an average of 6 months after acceptance. Sample copy for $5.
Payment/Terms: Pays 2 contributor's copies; $5 charge for extras. Acquires first serial rights.

‡A SPARE ROOM, (II), 2221 Carver, Simi Valley CA 93063-2616. Nonfiction Editor: Roma Donovan. Fiction Editor: Kristine Hawes. Poetry Editor: Victoria Giannecchini. Magazine: 5½×8; 30-40 pages; glossy card cover. "*A Spare Room* is a small literary magazine dedicated to bringing new thought to old culture. We are looking for topics of leading edge interest, works which crack open paradigms and create new cultural norms (especially in the areas of metaphysics, health of mind and body, and human technologies, such as lucid dreaming). Poetry, fiction, nonfiction and personal essays are welcome." Semiannually. Estab. 1997.
Needs: Ethnic/multicultural, experimental, literary, mainstream/contemporary, "New Age," spiritual. Accepts 2-3 mss/issue; 4-6 mss/year. Publishes ms 2-4 months after acceptance. Length: 2,000 words average; 250 words minimum; 2,500 words maximum. Publishes short shorts. Length: 400 words. Also publishes literary essays. Sometimes critiques or comments on rejected mss.
How to Contact: Send complete ms with a cover letter. Include bio. Reports in 4 months on mss. Send a disposable copy of ms. Simultaneous and reprint submissions OK. Sample copy for $4. Fiction guidelines for #10 SASE.
Payment/Terms: Pays 2 contributor's copies. Acquires first North American serial rights.
Advice: "Tightly written, evocative pieces are our favorites. Edit keenly, take out unnecessary words and write from the heart."

‡SPELUNKER FLOPHOUSE, (II), P.O. Box 617742, Chicago IL 60661. E-mail: spelunkerf@aol.com. Editors: Chris Kubica and Wendy Morgan. Magazine: 8½×7; 80-96 pages; offset print; perfect-bound; 4-color matte card cover. "We offer the best poetry, fiction and artwork we can in an inventive, original format. We cooperate regularly with other literary magazines." Quarterly. Estab. 1996. Press run: 1,000.

Needs: Ethnic/multicultural, experimental, feminist, humor/satire, literary, translations. "We are especially interested in fiction and poetry exploring small details of everyday life." Receives 30 unsolicited mss/month. Accepts 5-10 mss/issue; 20-40 mss/year. Publishes ms 4 months after acceptance. Agented fiction: 5%. Length: 100 words minimum; 5,000 words maximum. Publishes short shorts. Also publishes poetry. Often critiques or comments on rejected mss. Sponsors contest. Look for guidelines in the magazine.

How to Contact: Send complete ms with a cover letter. Include bio, list of publications if available and any brief interesting information about yourself. Reports in 4-10 weeks on mss. Send SASE for return of the ms or send a disposable copy of the ms. Simultaneous submissions OK, if noted. Sample copy for $6.95 postpaid. Fiction guidelines free with #10 SASE. Occasionally reviews fiction or poetry in book form.

Payment/Terms: Pays "depending on current cash flow and 2 contributor's copies. Pays on publication. Acquires first North American serial rights. Sends galleys to author.

Advice: "We are interested in stories that have a strong sense of character, technique, language, realistic dialogue, unique style/voice, and (if possible) a plot. No restrictions on length or subject matter except no genre work or 'statements.' Nothing patently cute. Support this necessary forum for the arts by purchasing copies of literary magazines, reading them, and increasing local awareness of magazines/forums such as ours whenever you possibly can. Study the market; then submit. And keep in touch. We love to hear from members/supporters of the literary community."

SPINDRIFT, (II), Shoreline Community College, 16101 Greenwood Ave. North, Seattle WA 98133. (206)546-4785. Editor: Carol Orlock, adviser. Magazine: 140 pages; quality paper; photographs; b&w artwork. "We look for fresh, original work that is not forced or 'straining' to be literary." Annually. Estab. around 1967. Circ. 500.

● *Spindrift* has received awards for "Best Literary Magazine" from the Community College Humanities Association both locally and nationally and awards from the Pacific Printing Industries.

Needs: Contemporary, ethnic, experimental, historical (general), prose poem, regional, science fiction, serialized/excerpted novel, translations. No romance, religious/inspirational. Receives up to 150 mss/year. Accepts up to 20 mss/issue. Does not read during spring/summer. Publishes ms 3-4 months after acceptance. Published work by David Halpern and Jana Harris; published new writers within the last year. Length: 250 words minimum; 3,500-4,500 words maximum. Publishes short shorts.

How to Contact: Send complete ms, and "bio, name, address, phone and list of titles submitted." Reports in 2 weeks on queries; juries after February 1 and responds by March 15 with SASE. Sample copy for $6, 8×10 SAE and $1 postage.

Payment/Terms: Pays in contributor's copies; charge for extras. Acquires first rights. Publication not copyrighted.

Advice: "The tighter the story the better. The more lyric values in the narrative the better. Read the magazine, keep working on craft. Submit by February 1."

SPITBALL, (I), 5560 Fox Rd., Cincinnati OH 45239. (513)385-2268. Editor: Mike Shannon. Magazine: 5½×8½; 96 pages; 55 lb. Glatfelter Natural, neutral pH paper; 10 pt. CS1 cover stock; illustrations; photos. Magazine publishing "fiction and poetry about *baseball* exclusively for an educated, literary segment of the baseball fan population." Quarterly. Estab. 1981. Circ. 1,000.

Needs: Confession, contemporary, experimental, historical, literary, mainstream and suspense. "Our only requirement concerning the type of fiction written is that the story be *primarily* about baseball." Receives 100 unsolicited fiction mss/year. Accepts 16-20 mss/year. Published work by Dallas Wiebe, Michael Gilmartin and W.P. Kinsella; published new writers within the last year. Length: 20 typed double-spaced pages. "The longer it is, the better it has to be."

How to Contact: Send complete ms with cover letter and SASE. Include brief bio about author. Reporting time varies. Publishes ms an average of 3 months after acceptance. Sample copy for $5.

Payment/Terms: "No monetary payment at present. We may offer nominal payment in the near future." 2 free contributor's copies per issue in which work appears. Acquires first North American serial rights.

Advice: "Our audience is mostly college educated and knowledgeable about baseball. The stories we have published so far have been very well written and displayed a firm grasp of the baseball world and its people. In short, audience response has been great because the stories are simply good as stories. Thus, mere use of baseball as subject is no guarantee of acceptance. We are always seeking submissions. Unlike many literary magazines, we have no backlog of accepted material. Fiction is a natural genre for our exclusive subject, baseball. There are great opportunities for writing in certain areas of fiction, baseball being one of them. Baseball has become the 'in' spectator sport among intellectuals, the general media and the 'yuppie' crowd. Consequently, as subject matter for adult fiction it has gained a much wider acceptance than it once enjoyed."

THE SPITTING IMAGE, (II), Tompkins Square Station, P.O. Box 20400, New York NY 10009. E-mail: seatopia@bway.net. Editor: Julia Solis. Magazine: 8½×7; 80 pages; 60 lb. paper; heavy cover stock; illustrations. Semiannually. Estab. 1994. Circ. 500.
Needs: Erotica, experimental, literary, occult, translations. Receives 200 unsolicited mss/month. Accepts 5 mss/issue. Recently published work by Henri Michaux, Unica Zurn, Bob Flanagan and Lance Olsen. Length: 1,500 words. Publishes short shorts. Also publishes poetry. Sometimes critiques or comments on rejected ms.
How to Contact: Send complete ms with a cover letter. Include bio with submission. Send SASE for reply, return of ms or send a disposable copy of ms. Simultaneous submissions OK. Sample copy for $5.50.
Payment/Terms: Pays 1 contributor's copy. Not copyrighted.
Advice: *"The Spitting Image* seeks dioramas for schizophrenic peeping toms—fiction that is explosive, absurd or strangely beautiful. Originality counts above all else. We usually have themes; please inquire."

SPOUT, (I, II), Spout Press, 28 W. Robie St., St. Paul MN 55107. (612)298-9846. E-mail: colb0018@ gold.tc.umn.edu. Editors: John Colburn and Michelle Filkins. Fiction Editor: Chris Watercott. Magazine: 8½×11; 40 pages; 70 lb. flat white paper; colored cover; illustrations. "We like the surprising, the surreal and the experimental. Our readers are well-read, often writers." Triannually. Estab. 1989. Circ. 300-500.
  • *Spout* editors submit work to the *Pushcart* anthology.
Needs: Condensed/excerpted novel, erotica, ethnic/multicultural, experimental, feminist, gay, humor/ satire, lesbian, literary, regional, translations. Publishes special fiction issues or anthologies. Receives 25-30 unsolicited mss/month. Accepts 4-5 mss/issue; 15 mss/year. Publishes ms 1-3 months after acceptance. Agented fiction 5%. Recently published work by Mario Benedetti (translation), Marie Manilla, Mary Kuryla, Michael Little and Richard Kostelanetz. Length: open. Publishes short shorts and "sudden" fiction. Also publishes poetry. Often comments on rejected mss.
How to Contact: Send complete ms with a cover letter. Include short bio and list of publications with submission. Reports in 1 month on queries; 2 months on mss. Send SASE for reply, return of ms or send a disposable copy of ms. Simultaneous and electronic submissions OK. Sample copy for $2, 8½×11 SAE and 5 first-class stamps. Fiction guidelines for SASE.
Payment/Terms: Pays 1 contributor's copy; additional copies for $2 plus postage. Acquires one-time rights.
Advice: Looks for "imagination, surprise and attention to language. We often publish writers on their third or fourth submission, so don't get discouraged. We need more weird, surreal fiction that lets the reader make his/her own meaning. Don't send moralistic, formulaic work."

‡SPRING FANTASY, (I), Women In The Arts, P.O. Box 2907, Decatur IL 62524. Contact: Vice President (newly elected each year). Magazine. "An annual anthology of short stories, juvenile fiction, poetry, essays and black & white artwork; *Spring Fantasy* aims to encourage beginners, especially women." Estab. 1994.
Needs: Adventure, children's/juvenile, fantasy, feminist, historical, horror, humor/satire, literary, mystery/suspense (amateur sleuth, cozy, police procedural, private eye/hardboiled, romantic suspense), romance, science fiction, young adult/teen (adventure, horror, mystery, romance, science fiction, western). Length: 1,500 words maximum.
How to Contact: Send complete ms without a cover letter. Reports in 4 months. Send SASE for reply, return of ms or send a disposable copy of ms. Simultaneous submissions and reprints OK. Sample copy for $6. Fiction guidelines for #10 SASE.
Payment/Terms: Pays $5-30 honorarium on publication and 1 contributor's copy; 20% discount on additional copies. Acquires first and reprint rights. Sponsors annual contest with cash prizes; send SASE for information.

SPSM&H, (II, IV), *Amelia* Magazine, 329 "E" St., Bakersfield CA 93304. (805)323-4064. Editor: Frederick A. Raborg, Jr. Magazine: 5½×8¼; 24 pages; matte cover stock; illustrations and photos. "*SPSM&H* publishes sonnets, sonnet sequences and fiction, articles and reviews related to the form (fiction may be romantic or Gothic) for a general readership and sonnet enthusiasts." Quarterly. Estab. 1985. Circ. 600.

READ THE BUSINESS OF FICTION WRITING section to learn the correct way to prepare and submit a manuscript.

• This magazine is edited by Frederick A. Raborg, Jr., who is also editor of *Amelia* and *Cicada*.

Needs: Adventure, confession, contemporary, erotica, ethnic, experimental, fantasy, feminist, gay, historical, horror, humor/satire, lesbian, literary, mainstream, mystery/suspense, regional, romance (contemporary, historical), science fiction, senior citizen/retirement, translations and western. All should have romantic element. "We look for strong fiction with romantic or Gothic content, or both. Stories need not have 'happy' endings, and we are open to the experimental and/or avant-garde. Erotica is fine; pornography, no." Receives 30 unsolicited mss/month. Accepts 1 ms/issue; 4 mss/year. Publishes ms 6 months to 1 year after acceptance. Agented fiction 5%. Published work by Brad Hooper, Mary Louise R. O'Hara and Clara Castelar Bjorlie. Length: 2,000 words average; 500 words minimum; 3,000 words maximum. Critiques rejected ms when appropriate; recommends other markets.

How to Contact: Send complete ms with cover letter. Include Social Security number. Reports in 2 weeks. SASE. Sample copy for $4.95. Fiction guidelines for #10 SASE.

Payment/Terms: Pays $10-25 and contributor's copies on publication for first North American serial rights; charge for extra copies.

Advice: "A good story line (plot) and strong characterization are vital. I want to know the writer has done his homework and is striving to become professional."

‡**THE STABLE COMPANION, the Literary Magazine for Horse Lovers, (II, IV)**, Houyhnhnm Press, P.O. Box 6485, Lafayette IN 47903. E-mail: stable@holli.com. Website: http://www.holli.com/~stable. Editor: Susanna Brandon. Magazine: 7½×9½; 64 pages; archival quality paper; 4-color cover stock; illustrations and photos. Semiannually. Estab. 1995. Circ. 1,000. Member of American Horse Publications.

Needs: Adventure, condensed/excerpted novel, ethnic/multicultural, historical, humor/satire, literary, mainstream/contemporary, science fiction (soft/sociological), translations, young adult/teen. "No romance, no erotica." Receives 30 unsolicited mss/month. Accepts 8 mss/issue; 16 mss/year. Publishes ms 3-6 months after acceptance. Recently published work by Alyson Hagy, Sandy Feinstein, Susanne R. Bowers, Kay Frydenborg, Margaret DelGuencio, Elizabeth B. Estes and Howard P. Giordano. Length: 2,500 words average; 4,000 words maximum. Publishes short shorts. Also publishes literary essays and poetry. Sometimes critiques or comments on rejected mss. Sponsors the Houyhnhnm Literary contest; send SASE for information.

How to Contact: Send complete ms with cover letter. Include estimated word count and 75-word bio. Send SASE for reply, return of ms or send a disposable copy of ms. Reprints OK. Sample copy for $6. Fiction guidelines for #10 SASE.

Payment/Terms: Pays 3 contributor's copies on publication. Acquires one-time rights.

Advice: "The most important thing for writers to understand is that, while *The Stable Companion* is a literary magazine for horse lovers, the short stories in the magazine are really about people and horses—tales of courage, adventure, passion and attachment. Writers should ask themselves: Would someone who knows nothing about horses enjoy and appreciate what I have written?"

‡**STILETTO III: THE REBELLION OF THE HANGED, (II, IV)**, Howling Dog Press, P.O. Box 27276, Denver CO 80227-0276. Editor: Michael Annis. Magazine: 5×11½; 300 pages; very high quality uncoated paper; Mirri Chrome cover; illustrations and photos. "*Stiletto's* theme changes with each issue. *Stilleto III* will be comprised of work relating to imprisonment and incarceration, i.e., physical, mental/psychological, religious, political, physiological, etc. General audience." Published "when it's ready." Estab. 1989.

• The design of Howling Dog Press books is impressive—full color, elaborate fold-outs and reflective cover.

Needs: Erotica, ethnic/multicultural, experimental, fantasy (adult), feminist, gay, historical (general), horror, literary, psychic/supernatural/occult, science fiction (cyber); special interest: prisons. Categories/styles are "open, but generally, I don't respect religious, 'corporate' yuppie, or 'perky' stuff." Receives 12 unsolicited mss/month. Agented fiction 0%, "but open to agents." Recently published work by Gregory Greyhawk. Length: Open. Publishes short shorts. Also publishes literary essays, poetry and dramatic plays.

How to Contact: Send complete ms with a cover letter. Include estimate word count. Reports in 1 month on queries; 18 months on mss. Send SASE (or IRC) for reply, return of ms or send a disposable copy of ms. Simultaneous submissions OK. Sample copy for $20 and $1.75 postage.

Payment/Terms: Negotiated with individual writer. Pays many contributor's copies to major contributors; additional copies available at 30% discount. Pays on publication for one-time rights; copyright is in contributor's name. Sends galleys to author.

Advice: Looks for "bold, intelligent, dynamic content *on theme*. I don't publish work that requires even moderate editing. I don't like braggarts, especially those who don't deliver. Learn to spell and where to use a comma, semicolon, etc. I'm suspicious of exclamation marks and italicized poetry. I want solid writing, with imagination and vision. Don't send cop-out 'experimental' writing that is artificial, pointless, dull and self-indulgent."

STONE SOUP, The Magazine By Young Writers and Artists, (I, IV), Children's Art Foundation, Box 83, Santa Cruz CA 95063. (408)426-5557. E-mail: gmandel@stonesoup.com. Editor: Gerry Mandel. Magazine: 6×8¾; 48 pages; high quality paper; Sequoia matte cover stock; illustrations; photos. Stories, poems, book reviews and art by children through age 13. Readership: children, librarians, educators. Published 5 times/year. Estab. 1973. Circ. 20,000.

● This is known as "the literary journal for children." *Stone Soup* has previously won the Edpress Golden Lamp Honor Award and the Parent's Choice Award.

Needs: Fiction by children on themes based on their own experiences, observations or special interests. Also, some fantasy, mystery, adventure. No clichés, no formulas, no writing exercises; original work only. Receives approximately 1,000 unsolicited fiction mss each month. Accepts approximately 15 mss/issue. Published new writers within the last year. Length: 150-2,500 words. Also publishes literary essays and poetry. Critiques rejected mss upon request.

How to Contact: Send complete ms with cover letter. "We like to learn a little about our young writers, why they like to write, and how they came to write the story they are submitting." SASE. No simultaneous submissions. Reports in 1 month on mss. Does not respond to mss that are not accompanied by an SASE. Publishes ms an average of 1-6 months after acceptance. Sample copy for $4. Guidelines for SASE. Reviews children's books.

Payment/Terms: Pays $10 plus 2 contributor's copies; $2 charge for extras. Buys all rights.

Advice: Mss are rejected because they are "derivatives of movies, TV, comic books; or classroom assignments or other formulas."

STORY, (II), F&W Publications, 1507 Dana Ave., Cincinnati OH 45207. (513)531-2222. Editor: Lois Rosenthal. Magazine: 6¼×9½; 128 pages; uncoated, recycled paper; uncoated index stock. "We publish the finest quality short stories. Will consider unpublished novel excerpts if they are self-inclusive." Quarterly. Estab. 1931.

● *Story* won the National Magazine Award for Fiction in 1992 and 1995, and was a finalist in 1994 and 1996. *Story* holds an annual contest for short short fiction.

Needs: Literary, experimental, humor, mainstream, translations. No genre fiction—science fiction, detective, young adult, confession, romance, etc. Accepts approximately 12 mss/issue. Agented fiction 50-60%. Published work by Joyce Carol Oates, Carol Shields, Tobias Wolff, Madison Smartt Bell, Rick DeMarinis, Antonya Nelson, Rick Bass, Charles Baxter, Tess Gallagher, Rick Moody, Ellen Gilchrist and Thom Jones; published new writers within the last year. Length: up to 8,000 words.

How to Contact: Send complete ms with or without cover letter, or submit through agent. SASE necessary for return of ms and response. "Will accept simultaneous submissions as long as it is stated in a cover letter." Sample copy for $6.95, 9×12 SAE and $2.40 postage. Fiction guidelines for #10 SASE.

Payment/Terms: Pays $1,000 for stories; $750 for short shorts plus 5 contributor's copies on acceptance for first North American serial rights. Sends galleys to author.

Advice: "We accept fiction of the highest quality, whether by established or new writers. Since we receive over 300 submissions each week, the competition for space is fierce. We look for original subject matter told through fresh voices. Read issues of *Story* before trying us."

STORYQUARTERLY, (II), Box 1416, Northbrook IL 60065. (708)564-8891. Co-editors: Anne Brashler and Diane Williams. Magazine: approximately 6×9; 130 pages; good quality paper; illustrations; photos. A magazine devoted to the short story and committed to a full range of styles and forms. Semiannually. Estab. 1975. Circ. 3,000.

Needs: Receives 200 unsolicited fiction mss/month. Accepts 12-15 mss/issue, 20-30 mss/year. Published new writers within the last year.

How to Contact: Send complete ms with SASE. Simultaneous submissions OK. Reports in 3 months on mss. Sample copy for $5.

Payment/Terms: Pays 3 contributor's copies for one-time rights. Copyright reverts to author after publication.

Advice: "Send one manuscript at a time, subscribe to the magazine, send SASE."

STREET BEAT QUARTERLY, (I, II), Wood Street Commons, 301 Third Ave., Pittsburgh PA 15222. (412)765-3302. Fax: (412)765-2646. E-mail: ah151@freenet.uchsc.edu. Editor: Jay Katz. Magazine: 8½×11; 32 pages; newsprint paper; newsprint cover; illustrations and photos. "*Street Beat Quarterly* publishes (primarily) literary works by those who have experienced homelessness or poverty. We reach those interested in literary magazines and others interested in homelessness issues." Quarterly. Estab. 1990. Circ. 2,000-3,000.

Needs: Adventure, ethnic/multicultural, experimental, fantasy, feminist, historical, humor/satire, literary, mainstream/contemporary, mystery/suspense, stories by children. "No religious." Receives 2 unsolicited mss/month. Accepts 2-5 mss/issue. Publishes ms 1-3 months after acceptance. Published work by Freddy Posco, James Burroughs and Mel Spivak. Length: 750 words average; 100 words minimum;

10,000 words maximum. Publishes short shorts. Also publishes literary essays and poetry. Sometimes critiques or comments on rejected mss.

How to Contact: Send complete ms with a cover letter including bio. Reports in 1 month on mss. Send a disposable copy of ms. Simultaneous, reprint and electronic submissions OK. Sample copy for 3 first-class stamps.

Payment/Terms: Pays $3 plus 1 contributor's copy on publication for one-time rights.

Advice: "We are pretty flexible. Our mission is to publish work by those who have experienced homelessness and poverty; we will consider a limited amount of works by others if it is on the topic (homelessness/poverty). Don't be afraid of us! We are very much a grass-roots publication. Be patient with us; as we sometimes take a short while to respond. We publish some very polished work; we also publish some very 'rough' yet energetic work. We are looking for stories that truly capture the experience of homelessness and poverty on a personal level."

STROKER MAGAZINE, (II), 124 N. Main St., #3, Shavertown PA 18708. Editor: Irving Stettner. Magazine: 5½×8½; average 48 pages; medium paper; 80 lb. good cover stock; illustrations; photos. "An *un-literary* literary review interested in sincerity, verve, anger, humor and beauty. For an intelligent audience—non-academic, non-media dazed in the US and throughout the world." Published 3-4 times/ year. Estab. 1974. Circ. 600.

Needs: Literary, contemporary. No academic material. Recently published work by Tom Brown and Bill Stobbs. Published new writers within the last year. Length: 10 pages (double-spaced) maximum. Also publishes poetry.

How to Contact: Send complete ms with SASE (disposable mss not accepted). Simultaneous submissions OK. Reports in 5 weeks. Sample copy for $5.50.

Payment/Terms: Pays 2 contributor's copies. $1 charge for extras. Acquires one-time rights.

STRUGGLE, A Magazine of Proletarian Revolutionary Literature, (I, II), Box 13261, Detroit MI 48213-0261. Editor: Tim Hall. Magazine: 5½×8½; 24-48 pages; 20 lb. white bond paper; colored cover; illustrations; occasional photographs. Publishes material related to "the struggle of the working class and all progressive people against the rule of the rich—including their war policies, racism, exploitation of the workers, oppression of women, etc." Quarterly. Estab. 1985.

Needs: Contemporary, ethnic, experimental, feminist, historical (general), humor/satire, literary, prose poem, regional, science fiction, senior citizen/retirement, translations, young adult/teen (10-18). "The theme can be approached in many ways, including plenty of categories not listed here." No romance, psychic, western, erotica, religious. Receives 10-12 unsolicited fiction mss/month. Publishes ms 6 months or less after acceptance. Recently published work by Billie Louise Jones, Tamar Diana Wilson de García, Pamela Bond and Joseph D. Barrett. Published new writers within the last year. Length: 1,000-3,000 words average; 4,000 words maximum. Publishes short shorts. Normally critiques rejected mss.

How to Contact: Send complete ms; cover letter optional but helpful. "Tries to" report in 3-4 months. SASE. Simultaneous and reprint submissions OK. Sample copy for $2.50. Make checks payable to Tim Hall-Special Account.

Payment/Terms: Pays 2 contributor's copies. No rights acquired. Publication not copyrighted.

Advice: "Write about the oppression of the working people, the poor, the minorities, women, and if possible, their rebellion against it—we are not interested in anything which accepts the status quo. We are not too worried about plot and advanced technique (fine if we get them!)—we would probably accept things others would call sketches, provided they have life and struggle. Just describe for us a situation in which some real people confront some problem of oppression, however seemingly minor. Observe and put down the real facts. We get poetry all the time. We have increased our fiction portion of our content in the last 3 years. The quality of fiction that we have published has continued to improve. I suggest ordering a sample."

❧SUB-TERRAIN, (II), P.O. Box 1575, Bentall Centre, Vancouver BC V6C 2P7 Canada. (604)876-8710. Fax: (604)879-2667. E-mail: subter@pinc.com. Fiction Editors: D.E. Bolen and Brian Kaufman. Magazine: 8½×11; 40 pages; offset printed paper; illustrations; photos. "*Sub-Terrain* provides a forum for work that pushes the boundaries in form or content." Estab. 1988.

Needs: "We are looking for work that expresses the experience of urban existence as we approach the closing of the century. Primarily a literary magazine; also interested in erotica, experimental, humor/ satire." Receives 100 unsolicited mss/month. Upcoming theme: "Alive or Dead: Canada Tales," a post-referendum poll on the state of the nation. Impressions of the Canadian Identity as expressed by our writers and visual artists. A call to all ethnic constituents. Deadline: May 30, 1997. Accepts 15-20 mss/issue. Publishes ms 1-4 months after acceptance. Recently published work by Steven Heighton, Clark Timmins, J. Jill Robinson, Derek McCormack, Billie Livingston and Willy Vlautin. Length: 200-3,000 words. Publishes short shorts. Length: 200 words. Also publishes literary essays, literary criticism, poetry. Sometimes critiques rejected mss and "at times" recommends other markets.

How to Contact: Send complete ms with cover letter. Simultaneous submissions OK, if notified when ms is accepted elsewhere. Reports in 3-4 weeks on queries; 2-3 months on mss. SASE. Sample copy for $5. Also features book review section. Send books marked "Review Copy, Managing Editor."

Payment/Terms: Pays (for solicited work) $25/page; $20/poem. Acquires one-time rights.

Advice: "We look for contemporary, modern fiction with something special in the voice or style, not simply something that is a well-written story—a new twist, a unique sense or vision of the world, the stuff that every mag is hoping to find. Write about things that are important to you: issues that *must* be talked about; issues that frighten or anger you. The world has all the cute, well-made stories it needs. Read a sample copy before submitting."

SUFFUSION MAGAZINE, (I), Brownhouse Graphic Arts, P.O. Box 57183, Lincoln NE 68505-7183. (402)465-5839. E-mail: suffusion@aol.com. Editor: Cris Trautner. Magazine: 8½ × 11; 24 pages; 70 lb. white vellum paper; 70 lb. color vellum cover; illustrations and photos. "Our goal is to be a stepping stone for new and unpublished writers as well as a fresh venue for established writers. Our audience includes anyone who has an open mind to the creative spirit." Quarterly. Estab. 1988. Circ. 400.

Needs: Ethnic/multicultural, experimental, feminist, humor/satire, literary, mainstream/contemporary, mystery/suspense (amateur sleuth, police procedural), regional, science fiction. "No erotica, religious/inspirational, romance." Receives 15-20 mss/month. Accepts 3 mss/issue; 12 mss/year. Publishes ms 6-12 months after acceptance. Recently published work by Deborah Christian, Paul Souders, William Harms and Ben Ohmart. Length: 3,500 words maximum. Publishes short shorts. Also publishes literary essays, literary criticism and poetry. Sometimes critiques or comments on rejected mss.

How to Contact: Send complete ms with a cover letter. Include 5- to 7-sentence bio, estimated word count, list of publications. Reports in 2 months on queries; 4 months on mss. Send SASE for reply, return of ms or send a disposable copy of ms. Simultaneous, reprint and electronic submissions OK. Sample copy for $4. Fiction guidelines for #10 SASE. Reviews novels or short story collections.

Payment/Terms: Pays 1 contributor's copy; additional copies for $2.50. "All rights revert back to author upon publication."

Advice: "Always include a cover letter neatly typed or laser print manuscript. Read a sample copy first. I would like to see more characters that aren't two-dimensional; please refrain from sending violent/pornographic writing that has no justification within the plot for being so."

SULPHUR RIVER LITERARY REVIEW, (II), P.O. Box 19228, Austin TX 78760-9228. (512)447-6809. Editor: James Michael Robbins. Magazine: 5½ × 8½; 130 pages; illustrations and photos. "*SRLR* publishes literature of quality—poetry and short fiction with appeal that transcends time. Audience includes a broad spectrum of readers, mostly educated, many of whom are writers, artists and educators." Semiannually. Estab. 1978. Circ. 400.

Needs: Ethnic/multicultural, experimental, feminist, humor/satire, literary, mainstream/contemporary and translations. No "religious, juvenile, teen, sports, romance or mystery." Receives 10-12 unsolicited mss/month. Accepts 2-3 mss/issue; 4-6 mss/year. Publishes ms 1-2 years after acceptance. Recently published work by Shirley Cochrane, Anye Dineja, Kevin Meaux, Jamie Brown and Gretchen Heyer. Publishes short shorts. Also publishes literary essays, literary criticism and poetry. Often critiques or comments on rejected mss.

How to Contact: Send complete ms with a cover letter. Include short bio and list of publications. Reports in 1 week on queries; 1 month on mss. Send SASE for reply, return of ms or send a disposable copy of ms. No simultaneous submissions. Sample copy for $6.

Payment/Terms: Pays 2 contributor's copies; additional copies for $4.50. Acquires first North American serial rights.

Advice: Looks for "originality, mastery of the language, imagination."

‡A SUMMER'S READING, A Journal of Fiction, Nonfiction, Poetry & Art, (I, II), 804 Oakland Ave., Mt. Vernon IL 62864. (618)242-8364. Fax: (618)244-8047. Editors: Ted Morrissey and Barbara Hess. Magazine: 5½ × 8½; 40-60 pages; 20 lb. paper; card cover stock; b&w illustrations. "There is so much excellent writing being produced and, by comparison, so few opportunities to publish—we want to provide one more well-edited, attractive outlet." Annually. Estab. 1997. Circ. 300.

Needs: Excerpted novel, literary, translations (provide copy of original). "We have absolutely no taboos in subject matter or imagery." Does not read mss September 15 through April 15. "One of our reasons for emerging in the summer is to provide a place for writers to send material when the majority of journals are not accepting submissions. We select, edit, produce and distribute during the 'academic' year." Publishes ms 6 months after acceptance. Length: 100 words minimum; 8,000 words maximum. Publishes short shorts. Also publishes poetry and narrative nonfiction (e.g., autobiography, biography). Sometimes critiques or comments on rejected mss.

How to Contact: Send complete ms with a concise cover letter. Include estimated word count, brief bio (under 100 words) and list of publications. "Do not explain the piece or what inspired it; allow it to speak for itself." Reports in 1-3 months on mss. Send SASE for reply or send a disposable copy of the ms. "No reply without SASE." Simultaneous and reprint submissions OK, "but please inform us in both cases." Sample copy for $5, available after first issue, Spring 1997. Fiction guidelines for #10 SASE.

Payment/Terms: Pays 2 contributor's copies. Acquires one-time rights. Sends galleys to the author "if schedule allows."

Advice: Looks for "excellence, which in our collective mind means a combination of practiced writing style and subject which keeps us turning the pages. The chances of your work getting published are better if it's on our desk rather than on yours. Send easy-to-read, error-free material, and we'll give it fair, unbiased consideration. As long as it's 'serious,' we want to see it, from the tightly structured traditional to the wildly experimental."

SURPRISE ME, (I, IV), Surprise Me Publications, P.O. Box 1762, Claremore OK 74018-1762. Editor: Lynda J. Nicolls. Magazine: 8½×11; 20 pages; illustrations. "*Surprise Me* is founded on the hope of providing a home for those souls who believe life's purpose is to serve Truth and Beauty. Our main interests are mysticism, the arts and nature. Prisoners, teenagers, the disabled and the elderly are especially welcomed here. Our intended audience is college students, college professors, prisoners, teenagers, the disabled, the elderly and people who do not like most of what is being published now." Biannual. Estab. 1994. Circ. 40.

● Please note that *Surprise Me* now accepts work from subscribers only.

Needs: Adventure, children's/juvenile, fantasy, literary, psychic/supernatural/occult, religious/inspirational, romance (futuristic/time travel, gothic), science fiction, senior citizen/retirement, serialized novel, young adult/teen (adventure, romance, science fiction), art, music, mysticism, nature, dance. "I am not interested in profanity, pro-violence, racism, intolerance and pornography. I'm very open to style, form and subject matter." Receives 200 unsolicited mss/month. Accepts 5 mss/issue; 20 mss/year. Publishes ms 1-2 years after acceptance. Recently published work by Thomas F. Brosnan, Paul Pekin and Alison Tinsley. Length: under 3 typed, double-spaced pages. Also publishes poetry.

How to Contact: *Accepts work from subscribers only.* Send complete ms with a cover letter. Include 5-line bio and list of publications. "Submissions without cover letters are too impersonal for me, so at least please include a note just to say, 'Hi. This is what I'm sending you.' " Send SASE for reply, return of ms or send a disposable copy of ms. Simultaneous, reprint and electronic submissions OK. "Disks are OK, but I don't have a modem yet." Sample copy for $6. Fiction guidelines for #10 SASE.

Payment/Terms: Pays 1 contributor's copies. Acquires one-time rights.

Advice: "I would suggest a beginning fiction writer examine a sample copy of our magazine before submitting to us. Writers also should not take a rejection too hard, since it is only one person's opinion. One editor may call it trash and another editor may call it a masterpiece. I would also suggest reading James Joyce, Hermann Hesse, Colin Wilson, Thomas Moore and Rollo May. I'm very open to subject matter, style and form, but I don't like a lot of what is being published now because it often lacks spirituality and has shock value as its motive. I would like to see more writing about the visual arts (i.e. Vincent van Gogh, Georgia O'Keeffe, Ansel Adams and Edward Weston), as well as more writing about philosophy and poetry (i.e. Soren Kierkegaard, William James, William Blake and W.B. Yeats). I would also like to see more children's literature (for or by children)."

SYCAMORE REVIEW, (II), Department of English, Purdue University, West Lafayette IN 47907. (317)494-3783. Fax: (317)494-3780. E-mail: sycamore@expert.cc.purdue.edu. Editor-in-Chief: Rob Davidson. Editors change every two years. Send fiction to Fiction Editor, poetry to Poetry Editor, all other correspondence to Editor-in-Chief. Magazine: 5½×8½; 150-200 pages; heavy, textured, uncoated paper; heavy laminated cover. "Journal devoted to contemporary literature. We publish both traditional and experimental fiction, personal essay, poetry, interviews, drama and graphic art. Novel excerpts welcome if they stand alone as a story." Semiannually. Estab. 1989. Circ. 1,000.

● Work published in *Sycamore Review* has been selected for inclusion in the *Pushcart Prize* anthology. The magazine was also named "The Best Magazine from Indiana" by the *Clockwatch Review.*

Needs: Contemporary, experimental, humor/satire, literary, mainstream, regional, translations. "We generally avoid genre literature, but maintain no formal restrictions on style or subject matter. No science fiction, romance, children's." Publishes ms 3 months to 1 year after acceptance. Recently published work by Susan Neville, Tess Gallagher, Wendell Mayo and C.J. Hribal. Length: 3,750 words preferred; 250 words minimum. Also publishes poetry. Sometimes critiques rejected mss and recommends other markets.

How to Contact: Send complete ms with cover letter. Cover letter should include previous publications and address changes. Does not read mss May through August. Reports in 4 months. SASE. Simultaneous submissions OK. Sample copy for $5.60. Fiction guidelines for #10 SASE.

Payment/Terms: Pays in contributor's copies; charge for extras. Acquires one-time rights.

Advice: "We publish both new and experienced authors but we're always looking for stories with strong emotional appeal, vivid characterization and a distinctive narrative voice; fiction that breaks new ground while still telling an interesting and significant story. Avoid gimmicks and trite, predictable outcomes. Write stories that have a ring of truth, the impact of felt emotion. Don't be afraid to submit, send your best."

‡TAMEME, (III, IV), New writing from North America/Nueva literatura de Norteamérica, Tameme, Inc., 199 First St., Suite 204, Los Altos CA 94022. Fax: (415)941-5338. Editor: C.M. Mayo. Magazine: 8×10; 220 pages; good quality paper; heavy cover stock; illustrations; photos. "*Tameme* is a semiannual fully bilingual magazine dedicated to publishing new writing from North America in side-by-side English-Spanish format. *Tameme*'s goals are to play an instrumental role in introducing important new writing from Canada and the United States to Mexico, and vice versa, and to provide a forum for the art of literary translation." Estab. 1996. Circ. 1,500. Member Council of Literary Magazines and Presses (CLMP).
Needs: Ethnic/multicultural, literary, translations. No genre fiction. Plans special fiction issue or anthology. Receives 10-15 unsolicited mss/month. Accepts 3-4 mss/issue; 6-8 mss/year, "but we are a new magazine so these numbers may not be indicative of a year from now." Publishes ms 6-12 months after acceptance. Agented fiction 5%. Recently published work by Fabio Morábito, Margaret Atwood, Juan Villoro, Jaime Sabines, Edwidge Danticat, A. Manette Ansay, Douglas Glover and Marianne Toussaint. Publishes short shorts. Also publishes literary essays and poetry. Sometimes critiques or comments on mss.
How to Contact: Send complete ms with a cover letter. Translators query or submit mss with cover letter, curriculum vita and samples of previous work. Include 1-paragraph bio and list of publications. Reports in 6 weeks on queries; 3 months on mss. Send SASE for reply, return of ms or send a disposable copy of ms. Simultaneous submissions OK, "if we are advised when the manuscript is submitted." Sample copy for $11.95. Fiction guidelines for SASE.
Payment/Terms: Pays 3 contributor's copies to writers; $20 per double-spaced WordPerfect page to translators. Pays on publication. Acquires one-time rights. Sends galleys to author.
Advice: "We're looking for whatever makes us want to stand up and shout YES! Read the magazine, send for guidelines (with SASE), then send only your best, with SASE."

TAMPA REVIEW, (I, II), 401 W. Kennedy Blvd., Box 19F, University of Tampa, Tampa FL 33606-1490. (813)253-3333, ext. 6266. Fax: (813)258-7593. E-mail: richardmathews@resnet.fmhi.usf.edu. Editor: Richard Mathews. Fiction Editor: Andy Solomon. Magazine: 7½×10½; approximately 70 pages; acid-free paper; visual art; photos. "Interested in fiction of distinctive literary quality." Semiannually. Estab. 1988.
Needs: Contemporary, ethnic, experimental, fantasy, historical, humor/satire, literary, mainstream, prose poem, translations. "We are far more interested in quality than in genre. Nothing sentimental as opposed to genuinely moving, nor self-conscious style at the expense of human truth." Buys 4-5 mss/ issue. Publishes ms within 7 months-1 year of acceptance. Agented fiction 60%. Recently published work by Elizabeth Spencer, Lee K. Abbott, Lorrie Moore, Tim O'Connor and Naomi Nye. Length: 250 words minimum; 10,000 words maximum. Publishes short shorts "if the story is good enough." Also publishes literary essays (must be labeled nonfiction), poetry.
How to Contact: Send complete ms with cover letter. Include brief bio. No simultaneous submissions. SASE. Reads September through December; reports January through March. Sample copy for $5 (includes postage) and 9×12 SAE. Fiction guidelines for #10 SASE.
Payment/Terms: Pays $10/printed page on publication for first North American serial rights. Sends galleys to author upon request.
Advice: "There are more good writers publishing in magazines today than there have been in many decades. Unfortunately, there are even more bad ones. In T. Gertler's *Elbowing the Seducer*, an editor advises a young writer that he wants to hear her voice completely, to tell (he means 'show') him in a story the truest thing she knows. We concur. Rather than a trendy workshop story or a minimalism that actually stems from not having much to say, we would like to see stories that make us believe they mattered to the writer and, more importantly, will matter to a reader. Trim until only the essential is left, and don't give up belief in yourself. And it might help to attend a good writers' conference, e.g. Wesleyan or Bennington."

TAPROOT LITERARY REVIEW, (I, II), Taproot Writer's Workshop, Inc., 302 Park Rd., Ambridge PA 15003. (412)266-8476. Editor: Tikvah Feinstein. Magazine: 5½×8½; 80 pages; #20 paper; card cover; attractively printed; saddle-stitched. "We select on quality, not topic. We have published excellent work other publications have rejected due to subject matter, style or other bias. Variety and quality are our appealing features." Annually. Estab. 1987. Circ. 500.
● This year, *Taproot* is celebrating the publication of their tenth edition.
Needs: Literary. The majority of mss published are received through their annual contest. Receives 20 unsolicited mss/month. Accepts 6 fiction mss/issue. Recently published work by Matthew Drummy, Anne Helen Jupiter, Sally Levin and Mike Murray. Length: 2,000 words preferred; 250 words minimum; 3,000 words maximum (no longer than 10 pages, double-spaced maximum). Publishes short

shorts. Length: 300 words preferred. Sometimes critiques or comments on rejected mss. Also publishes poetry. Sponsors annual contest. Entry fee: $10/story. Deadline: December 31. Send SASE for details.
How to Contact: Send for guidelines first. Send complete ms with a cover letter. Include estimated word count and bio. Reports in 6 months. Send SASE for return of ms or send a disposable copy of ms. No simultaneous submissions. Sample copy for $5, 6×12 SAE and 5 first-class stamps. Fiction guidelines for #10 SASE.
Payment/Terms: Awards $25 in prize money for first place fiction and poetry winners each issue; 1 contributor's copy. Acquires first rights.
Advice: "Our contest is a good way to start publishing. Send for a sample copy and read it through. Ask for a critique and follow suggestions. Don't be offended by any suggestions—just take them or leave them and keep writing."

♣**"TEAK" ROUNDUP, The International Quarterly, (I)**, West Coast Paradise Publishing, #5-9060 Tronson Rd., Vernon, British Columbia V1T 6L7 Canada. (604)545-4186. Fax: (604)545-4192. Editors: Yvonne and Robert Anstey. Magazine: 5½×8½; 60 pages; 20 lb. copy paper; card stock cover; illustrations and photos. " 'Teak' Roundup is a general interest showcase for prose and poetry. No uncouth material." Quarterly. Estab. 1994. Circ. 100.
Needs: Adventure, children's/juvenile, condensed/excerpted novel, ethnic/multicultural, historical, humor/satire, literary, mainstream/contemporary, mystery/suspense (police procedural), regional, religious/inspirational, romance (contemporary, historical), sports, westerns, young adult/teen (adventure). "No uncouth or porn." List of upcoming themes available for SASE. Receives 25 unsolicited mss/month. Accepts 20 mss/issue. Publishes ms 3-6 months after acceptance. Recently published work by Bill Lamb, Doris Rokosh, Alice Cundiff and B.A. Stuart. Length: 1,000 words maximum. Also publishes literary essays, literary criticism and poetry. Often critiques or comments on rejected ms.
How to Contact: *Accepts work from subscribers only.* Query first or send complete ms with a cover letter. Include estimated word count and brief bio. Reports in 1 week. Send SASE for reply, return of ms or send a disposable copy of ms. Simultaneous, reprint and electronic submissions OK. Sample copy for $5. Fiction guidelines for #10 SASE. Reviews novels and short story collections.
Payment/Terms: Acquires one-time rights (unreserved reprint if "Best of" edition done later.)
Advice: "Subscribe and see popular work which is enjoyed by our growing audience. Many good writers favor us with participation in subscribers-only showcase for prose and poetry. No criticism of generous contributors."

‡**TENNESSEE QUARTERLY, (II)**, Belmont University, Department of Literature and Language, 1900 Belmont Blvd., Nashville TN 37212-3757. (615)460-6412. Fax: (615)460-5720. Editors: Anthony Lombardy and J.H.E. Paine. Magazine: 6×9; 60-90 pages; quality paper; light matte cover stock. "We publish the best fiction, poetry and criticism we receive for a very sophisticated literary readership." Triannually. Estab. 1994.
Needs: Literary. "No genre fiction." Accepts 2-3 mss/issue; 7-9 mss/year. Does not read mss June 15-August 30. Publishes ms 6 months after acceptance. Recently published work by David Weisberg, Gary Fincke, Sherri Sizeman and Adrienne Sharp. Length: 5,000-10,000 words. Publishes short shorts. Also publishes literary essays, literary criticism and poetry. Sometimes critiques or comments on rejected mss.
How to Contact: Send complete ms with a cover letter. Include a brief letter of introduction. Reports in 2 months on mss. Send SASE for reply, return of ms or send a disposable copy of ms. Sample copy for $5.
Payment/Terms: Pays 2 contributor's copies on publication. Acquires first North American serial rights.
Advice: Looks for "the quality of the prose, vivid characters and coherent narrative. Read back copies."

♣**TEXTSHOP, A Collaborative Journal of Writing, (I, II)**, Dept. of English, University of Regina, Regina, Sasketchewan S4S 0A2 Canada. (306)585-4316. Editor: Andrew Stubbs. Magazine: 8½×11; 50 pages; illustrations. *Textshop* is "eclectic in form and open to fiction, poetry and mixed genres, including creative nonfiction." Annually. Estab. 1993.
Needs: Ethnic/multicultural, experimental, literary. Plans special fiction issues or anthologies. Receives 3-4 unsolicited mss/month. Accepts 3 mss/issue. Publishes ms in next issue after acceptance. Length: 500 words minimum; 1,000 words maximum. Also publishes literary essays, literary criticism and poetry. Sometimes critiques or comments on rejected mss.
How to Contact: Send complete ms with a cover letter. Include estimated word count and 25-word bio with submission. Reports in 1 month on queries; 3 months on mss. SASE. Reprint submissions OK. Sample copy for $2. Reviews material published in each issue.
Payment/Terms: Pays 1 contributor's copy; additional copies for $2. Rights remain with the writer.
Advice: Looks for "risk-taking, mixed genre, experimental fiction. Trust your own voice and idiom. Blur the distinction between life and writing."

TEXTURE, (II), Texture Press, P.O. Box 720157, Norman OK 73070. (405)366-7730. Fax: (405)364-3627. E-mail: texturepr@gnn.com. Editor: Susan Smith Nash. Magazine: 8½ × 11; 100 pages; high-quality offset, matte finish paper; perfect-bound matte cover; illustrations and photos. "*Texture* is interested in all writing, art and photography which probes end-of-the-millenium anxieties. Essays, reviews, and critical articles provide theoretical and philosophical underpinnings for new trends in experimental writing." Annually. Estab. 1989. Circ. 750.
 • *Texture* was a finalist for the Oklahoma Book Award in 1995 and work published in *Texture* was included in the *Gertrude Stein Anthology of Innovative Writing Awards* volume.
Needs: Experimental, feminist, "short-short fiction which has a playful, ironic, subversive element." Publishes special fiction issue or anthology. Receives 25-50 unsolicited mss/month. Accepts 25 mss/issue. Publishes ms 6-9 months after acceptance. Agented fiction 10%. Recently published work of Cydney Chadwick, Karl Roeseler, Robert Murray Davis and David Gilbert. Length: 200 words minimum; 5,000 words maximum. Also publishes literary essays, literary criticism and poetry.
How to Contact: Send complete ms with a cover letter. Include 1/2-page bio. Reports in 4-6 months. Send SASE for reply, return of ms or send a disposable copy of ms. No simultaneous submissions. Sample copy with fiction guidelines for $8. Reviews novels and short story collections.
Payment/Terms: Pays 1 contributor's copy; additional copies for half price. Acquires one-time rights.

A THEATER OF BLOOD, (III, IV), Pyx Press, P.O. Box 922648, Sylmar CA 91392-2648. Editor: C. Darren Butler. Associate Editor: Lisa S. Laurencot. Book: 100-180-page limited edition, annual book serial. "This will appear in a numbered run of about 500-1,000 copies." Estab. 1990.
Needs: "Horror fiction: cosmic, dark fantasy, quiet, supernatural (though not using Lovecraft's creations). It is unlikely that I will accept any purely realistic horror; an otherworldly or fantasy element should be included. I have a bias against excessive gore or anything gratuitous." Receives 400 unsolicited mss/month. Accepts 8-15 mss/book. Open to unsolicited mss from September 1 through November 30 only. Publishes ms 4-24 months after acceptance. No reprints. Length: 3,000-20,000 words. Rarely critiques or comments on rejected mss.
How to Contact: Query first with sample pages for works over 8,000 words. Send complete ms with a cover letter. Include estimated word count, 1-paragraph bio and list of publications. Reports in 2 months on queries; 3-6 months on mss. Send SASE for reply, return of ms or send a disposable copy of ms. Simultaneous submissions OK. Sample copy for $2.50 (old format). Fiction guidelines for #10 SASE.
Payment/Terms: Pays $2-10, "unless piece is very long, and 1 copy of the trade-paperback." Acquires limited-edition rights only.

THEMA, (II), Box 74109, Metairie LA 70033-4109. Editor: Virginia Howard. Magazine: 5½ × 8½; 200 pages; Grandee Strathmore cover stock; b&w illustrations. "Different specified theme for each issue—short stories, poems, b&w artwork must relate to that theme." Triannually. Estab. 1988.
 • *Thema* received a Certificate for Excellence in the Arts from the Arts Council of New Orleans.
Needs: Adventure, contemporary, experimental, humor/satire, literary, mainstream, mystery/suspense, prose poem, psychic/supernatural/occult, regional, science fiction, sports, western. "Each issue is based on a specified premise—a different unique theme for each issue. Many types of fiction acceptable, but must fit the premise. No pornographic, scatologic, erotic fiction." Upcoming themes: "Scrawled in a library book" (March 1, '97); "EUREKA!" (July 1, '97); "An unexpected guest" (November 1, '97). Publishes ms within 3-4 months of acceptance. Recently published work by Marvin Thrasher, Marlane Zamm, Madonna Dries Christensen, Becky Mushko and Steve Chamberlain. Length: fewer than 6,000 words preferred. Also publishes poetry. Sometimes critiques rejected mss and recommends other markets.
How to Contact: Send complete ms with cover letter, include "name and address, brief introduction, specifying the intended target issue for the mss." Simultaneous submissions OK. Reports on queries in 1 week; on mss in 5 months after deadline for specified issue. SASE. Sample copy for $8. Free fiction guidelines.
Payment/Terms: Pays $25; $10 for short shorts on acceptance for one-time rights.
Advice: "Do not submit a manuscript unless you have written it for a specified premise. If you don't know the upcoming themes, send for guidelines first, before sending a story. We need more stories told in the Mark Twain/O. Henry tradition in magazine fiction."

‡**THIN AIR, (II), The Right Kind of Trouble**, Graduate Creative Writing Association of Northern Arizona University, P.O. Box 23549, Flagstaff AZ 86002. Contact: Fiction Editor. Editors change each year. Magazine: 8½ × 11; 50-60 pages; illustrations; photos. Publishes "contemporary voices for a literary-minded audience." Semiannually. Estab. 1995. Circ. 500-1,000.
Needs: Condensed/excerpted novel, ethnic/multicultural, experimental, literary, mainstream/contemporary. "No children's/juvenile." Editorial calendar available for SASE. Receives 75 unsolicited mss/month. Accepts 5-8 mss/issue; 10-15 mss/year. Does not read mss May-September. Publishes ms 6-9

months after acceptance. Solicited fiction 35%. Recently published work by Stephen Dixon, Henry H. Roth, Brian Evenson, Charles Bowden, Shirheen Rahnema, Patricia Lawrence and Craig Rullman. Length: 6,000 words maximum. Publishes short shorts. Also publishes literary essays, literary criticism, creative nonfiction, poetry and interviews. Recent interviews include Thom Jones, Alan Lightman and Rick Bass

How to Contact: Send complete ms with a cover letter. Include estimated word count and list of publications. Reports in 1 month on queries; 3 months on mss. Send SASE for reply, return of ms or send a disposable copy of ms. Simultaneous submissions OK. Sample copy for $4.95. Fiction guidelines free. Reviews novels and short story collections.

Payment/Terms: Pays 2 contributor's copies; additional copies for $4. Pays on publication. Acquires first North American serial rights. Sends galleys to author. Sponsors contest; send SASE for guidelines.

Advice: Looks for "writers who know how to create tension and successfully resolve it. This is 'the right kind of trouble.' "

‡**THIRD COAST, (II)**, Dept. of English, Western Michigan University, Kalamazoo MI 49008-5092. (616)387-2675. Managing Editor: Theresa Coty O'Neil. Fiction Editors: Kellie Wells and Heidi Bell. Magazine: 6×9; 150 pages; illustrations and photos. "We will consider many different types of fiction and favor that exhibiting a freshness of vision and approach." Semiannually. Estab. 1995. Circ. 500.

• *Third Coast* has received *Pushcart Prize* nominations. The editors of this publication change with the university year.

Needs: Literary. "While we don't want to see formulaic genre fiction, we will consider material that plays with or challenges generic forms." Receives approximately 100 unsolicited mss/month. Accepts 6-8 mss/issue; 15 mss/year. Does not read mss May to September. Publishes ms 3-6 months after acceptance. Recently published work (fiction and nonfiction) by Anne Finger, David Shields, Leon Rooke and Janet Kauffman. Length: no preference. Publishes short shorts. Also publishes literary essays and poetry. Sometimes critiques or comments on rejected mss.

How to Contact: Send complete ms with a cover letter. Include list of publications. Reports in 1 month on queries; 2 months on mss. Send SASE for reply, return of ms or send a disposable copy of ms. Simultaneous submissions OK. Sample copy for $6. Fiction guidelines for #10 SASE.

Payment/Terms: Pays 2 contributor's copies as well as subscription to the publication and payment, dependent upon available funding; additional copies for $4. Acquires one-time rights. Not copyrighted.

Advice: "Of course, the writing itself must be of the highest quality. We love to see work that explores non-western contexts, as well as fiction from all walks of American (and other) experience."

‡**13TH MOON, A Feminist Magazine, (IV)**, Dept. of English, University at Albany, Albany NY 12222. (518)442-4181. Editor: Judith Johnson. Magazine: 6×9; 250 pages; 50 lb. paper; heavy cover stock; photographs. "Feminist literary magazine for feminist women and men." Annually. Estab. 1973. Circ. 2,000.

Needs: Excerpted novel, experimental, feminist, lesbian, literary, prose poem, science fiction, translations. No fiction by men. Plans two volumes on feminist poetics (one volume on narrative forms and one on poetry). Submissions should be accompanied by a statement of the author's poetics (a paragraph to a page long). Accepts 1-3 mss/issue. Does not read mss May-September. Time varies between acceptance and publication. Published work by F.R. Lewis, Jan Ramjerdi and Wilma Kahn. Length: Open. Publishes short shorts. Also publishes poetry. Sometimes critiques rejected mss.

How to Contact: Send complete ms with cover letter and SASE (or IRC); "no queries." Reports in 8 months on mss. SASE. Accepts electronic submissions via disk (WordPerfect 5.1 only). Sample copy for $10.

Payment/Terms: Pays 2 contributor's copies.

Terms: Acquires first North American serial rights.

Advice: Looks for "*unusual* fiction with feminist appeal."

♣**THIS MAGAZINE, (II)**, Red Maple Foundation, 401 Richmond St. W., Suite 396, Toronto, Ontario M5V 3A8 Canada. (416)979-8400. Editor: Clive Thompson. Magazine: 8½×11; 42 pages; bond paper; coated cover; illustrations and photographs. "Alternative general interest magazine." Bimonthly. Estab. 1966. Circ. 7,000.

Needs: Ethnic, contemporary, experimental, fantasy, feminist, gay, lesbian, literary, mainstream, prose poem, regional. No "commercial/pulp fiction." Receives 15-20 unsolicited mss/month. Accepts 1 mss/

CHECK THE CATEGORY INDEXES, located at the back of the book, for publishers interested in specific fiction subjects.

issue; 6 mss/year. Published work by Margaret Atwood and Peter McGehee. Length: 1,500 words average; 2,500 words maximum. Sometimes critiques rejected mss.

How to Contact: Query with clips of published work. Reports in 6 weeks on queries; 3-6 months on mss. SASE. No simultaneous submissions. Sample copy for $4 (plus GST). Fiction guidelines for #9 SASE with Canadian stamps or IRC.

Payment/Terms: Pays $100 (Canadian) fiction; $25/poem published for one-time rights.

Advice: "It's best if you're familiar with the magazine when submitting work; a large number of mss that come into the office are inappropriate. Style guides are available. Manuscripts and queries that are clean and personalized really make a difference. Let your work speak for itself—don't try to convince us."

‡**THE THREEPENNY REVIEW, (II)**, P.O. Box 9131, Berkeley CA 94709. (510)849-4545. Editor: Wendy Lesser. Tabloid: 10×17; 40 pages; Electrobrite paper; white book cover; illustrations. "Serious fiction." Quarterly. Estab. 1980. Circ. 9,000.
  • *The Threepenny Review* has received GE Writers Awards, CLMP Editor's Awards, NEA grants, Lila Wallace grants and inclusion of work in the *Pushcart Prize Anthology*.

Needs: Literary. "Nothing 'experimental' (ungrammatical)." Receives 300-400 mss/month. Accepts 3 mss/issue; 12 mss/year. Does *not* read mss June through August. Publishes 6-12 months after acceptance. Agented fiction 5%. Recently published Sigrid Nunez, Dagoberto Gilb, Gina Berriault and Leonard Michaels. Length: 5,000 words maximum. Publishes short shorts. Also publishes literary essays, literary criticism, poetry.

How to Contact: Send complete ms with a cover letter. Reports in 2-4 weeks on queries;1-2 months on mss. Send SASE for reply, return of ms or send a disposable copy of the ms. No simultaneous submissions. Sample copy for $6. Fiction guidelines for #10 SAE and 1 first-class stamp. Reviews novels and short story collections.

Payment/Terms: Pays $200 on acceptance plus free subscription to the magazine; additional copies at half price. Acquires first North American serial rights. Sends galleys to author.

TIMBER CREEK REVIEW, (III), 612 Front St. East, Glendora NJ 08029-1133. (609)863-0610. Editor: J.M. Freiermuth. Newsletter: 5½×8½; 60-80 pages; copy paper; some illustrations and photographs. "Fiction, satire, humorous poetry and travel for a general audience —80% of readers read above the 6th grade level." Quarterly. Circ. 120.

Needs: Adventure, contemporary, ethnic, feminist, historical, humor/satire, mainstream, mystery/suspense (cozy, private eye), regional, western (adult, frontier, traditional). No religion, children's, gay, romance. Plans fourth "All Woman Author" issue (October 1997). Receives 40-50 unsolicited mss/month. Accepts 15-20 mss/issue; 60-70 mss/year. Publishes ms 2-6 months after acceptance. Recently published work by Mark O'Hara, Jeff Talarigo, Kenneth W. Meyer, Rod Farmer, Suzanne Kamata, Darcy Cummings. Published first time writers last year. Length: 2,000-3,000 words average; 1,200 words minimum; 9,000 words maximum. Publishes short shorts. Length: "Long enough to develop a good bite." Sometimes critiques rejected mss and recommends other markets.

How to Contact: Send complete ms and/or DOS disk (uses MS Word) with cover letter including "name, address, SASE." Reports in 3-6 weeks on mss. SASE. Simultaneous and reprint submissions OK. Accepts electronic submissions. Sample copy for $4 postpaid. Reviews short story collections.

Payment/Terms: Pays subscription to magazine for first publication and contributor's copies for subsequent publications. Acquires one-time rights. Publication not copyrighted.

Advice: "If your story has a spark of life or a degree of humor that brings a smile to my face, you have a chance here. Most stories lack these two ingredients. Don't send something you wrote ten years ago."

TOMORROW Speculative Fiction, (I), Unifont Co., P.O. Box 6038, Evanston IL 60204. (708)864-3668. Editor and Publisher: Algis Budrys. Magazine: 8¼×10¾; 88 pages; newsprint; slick cover; illustrations. "Any good science fiction, fantasy and horror, for an audience of fiction readers." Bimonthly. Estab. 1992.
  • *Tomorrow* has twice been nominated for the Hugo and twice has appeared in the *Writer's Digest* Top 50 Markets. A collection of articles on writing, originally published in *Tomorrow*, is now available.

Needs: Fantasy, horror, science fiction—any kind. Receives 300 mss/month. Accepts 10-12 mss/issue; 60-82 mss/year. Publishes within 18 months of acceptance. Agented fiction 2%. Recently published works by Robert Reed, Michael Shea, Nina Kiriki Hoffman, Robert Frazier, Yves Meynard and Elisabeth Vonarburg. Length: 4,000 words average. Publishes short shorts. Always critiques rejected mss.

How to Contact: Send complete ms. Include estimated word count and Social Security number. No covering letters. "Creased manuscripts and/or single spaced manuscripts will not be read." Reports in 2 weeks. Send SASE for reply, return of ms if desired. No simultaneous submissions, no poetry, no cartoons. Sample copy for $5 plus 9×12 SASE.

Payment/Terms: Pays $75 minimum; 7¢/word maximum plus 3 contributor's copies between acceptance and publication. Acquires first North American serial rights. Sends galleys to author.
Advice: "Read my book, *Writing to the Point*, $10.50 from Unifont Co."

‡**TORRE DE PAPEL, (I, II, IV)**, 111 Phillips Hall, Iowa City IA 52242. (319)335-2245. Fax: (319)335-2270. E-mail: lrolon@blue.weeg.uiowa.edu. Editor: Lissette Rolón. Fiction Editor: María A. Saldías. Magazine: 8½ × 5½; 120-150 pages; recycled paper; illustrations and photos. "*Torre de Papel* is a critical and creative writing journal dedicated to Hispanic and Luso-Brazilian cultures, especially poetry and short stories. The audience is mostly academic." Triannually. Estab. 1991. Circ. 300.
Needs: Adventure, erotica, ethnic/multicultural, experimental, fantasy, feminist, gay, historical (general), horror, humor/satire, lesbian, literary, mainstream/contemporary, mystery/suspense, regional, romance, science fiction, translations. No psychic/supernatural/occult, novels, children's/juvenile. Upcoming theme: Modernity and Post Modernity: Issues in Latin American Literary Studies. Receives 5-10 unsolicited mss/month. Accepts 5-7 mss/issue; 15-21 mss/year. Publishes ms 3-5 months after acceptance. Recently published work by Oscar Hahn, Alberto Fuguet and David Toscana. Length: 1,000 words average; 800 words minimum; 3,000 words maximum. Publishes short shorts. Also publishes literary essays, literary criticism and poetry. Often critiques or comments on rejected mss.
How to Contact: Send 3 copies of ms, cv, 3.5 disk (Mac or IBM). Include bio (2-3 paragraphs) and list of publications. Send SASE for reply and SASE for return of ms and/or disk. Simultaneous and electronic submissions OK. Reports in 1 month on queries; 3 months on mss. Sample copy for $10. Fiction guidelines free. Reviews novels and short story collections. Send books to editor.
Payment/Terms: Pays 2 contributor's copies; additional copies for $10. Acquires one-time rights.
Advice: "Submit all the materials required."

TOUCHSTONE LITERARY JOURNAL, (II), P.O. Box 8308, Spring TX 77387-8308. Editor/Publisher: William Laufer. Managing Editor: Guida Jackson. Fiction Editor: Julia Gomez-Rivas. Magazine: 5½ × 8½; 40-104 pages; linen paper; kramkote cover; perfect bound; b&w illustrations; occasional photographs. "Literary and mainstream fiction, but enjoy experimental work and multicultural. Audience middle-class, heavily academic. We are eclectic and given to whims—i.e., two years ago we devoted a 104-page issue to West African women writers." Annually (with occasional special supplements). Estab. 1976. Circ. 1,000.
● Touchstone Press also publishes a chapbook series. Send a SASE for guidelines.
Needs: Humor/satire, literary, mainstream/contemporary, translations. No erotica, religious, juvenile, "stories written in creative writing programs that all sound alike." List of upcoming themes available for SASE. Publishes special fiction issue or anthology. Receives 20-30 mss/month. Accepts 2-10 mss/issue. Does not read mss in December. Publishes ms within the year after acceptance. Published work by Ann Alejandro, Lynn Bradley, Roy Fish and Julia Mercedes Castilla. Length: 2,500 words preferred; 250 words minimum; 5,000 words maximum. Publishes short shorts. Length: 300 words. Also publishes literary essays, literary criticism and poetry. Sometimes critiques or comments on rejected mss.
How to Contact: Send complete ms with a cover letter. Include estimated word count and 3-sentence bio. Reports in 3 months. Send SASE for return of ms. Simultaneous and electronic submissions OK. Sample copy for $3 or 10 first-class stamps. Fiction guidelines for #10 SASE.
Payment/Terms: Pays 2 contributor's copies; additional copies at 40% discount. Acquires one-time rights. Sends galleys to author (unless submitted on disk).
Advice: "We like to see fiction that doesn't read as if it had been composed in a creative writing class. If you can entertain, edify, or touch the reader, polish your story and send it in. Don't worry if it doesn't read like our other fiction."

TRIQUARTERLY, (II), Northwestern University, 2020 Ridge Ave., Evanston IL 60208-4302. (847)491-7614. Assistant Editor: Gwenan Wilbur. Editor: Reginald Gibbons. Magazine: 6 × 9¼; 240-272 pages; 60 lb. paper; heavy cover stock; illustration; photos. "A general literary quarterly especially devoted to fiction. We publish short stories, novellas or excerpts from novels, by American and foreign writers. Genre or style is not a primary consideration. We aim for the general but serious and sophisticated reader. Many of our readers are also writers." Triannual. Estab. 1964. Circ. 5,000.
Needs: Literary, contemporary and translations. "No prejudices or preconceptions against anything *except* genre fiction (romance, science fiction, etc.)." Accepts 10 mss/issue, 30 mss/year. Receives approximately 500 unsolicited fiction mss each month. Does not read April 1 through September 30. Agented fiction 10%. Recently published work by Adrian C. Louis, Maura Stanton, Stephen Dixon, Jianying Zha, Autonya Nelson and Angela Jackson. Published new writers within the last year. Length: no requirement. Publishes short shorts.
How to Contact: Send complete ms with SASE. No simultaneous submissions. Reports in 4 months on mss. Publishes ms an average of 6-12 months after acceptance. Sample copy for $5.
Payment/Terms: Pays $20/page (fiction) plus 2 contributor's copies on publication for first North American serial rights. Cover price less 40% discount for extras. Sends galleys to author.

TUCUMCARI LITERARY REVIEW, (I, II), 3108 W. Bellevue Ave., Los Angeles CA 90026. Editor: Troxey Kemper. Magazine: 5½×8½; about 40 pages; 20 lb. bond paper; 67 lb. cover stock; few illustrations; photocopied photographs. "Old-fashioned fiction that can be read and reread for pleasure; no weird, strange pipe dreams and no it-was-all-a-dream endings." Bimonthly. Estab. 1988. Circ. small.

Needs: Adventure, contemporary, ethnic, historical, humor/satire, literary, mainstream, mystery/suspense, regional (southwest USA), senior citizen/retirement, western (frontier stories). No science fiction, drugs/acid rock, pornography, horror, martial arts or children's stories. Accepts 6 or 8 mss/issue; 35-40 mss/year. Publishes ms 2-6 months after acceptance. Recently published work by Roger Coleman, Dawn I. Zapletal, Curtis Nelson and James M. Phelps. Length: 400-1,200 words preferred. Also publishes rhyming poetry.

How to Contact: Send complete ms with or without cover letter. Reports in 2 weeks. SASE. Simultaneous and reprint submissions OK. Sample copy for $2. Fiction guidelines for #10 SASE.

Payment/Terms: Pays in contributor's copies. Acquires one-time rights. Publication not copyrighted.

Advice: "Don't have obscure wisps not tied together in the story. Avoid dull, overdone topics."

‡TURNSTILE, (I), 175 Fifth Ave., Suite 2348, New York NY 10010. Editors: Curt Alliaume and Kit Haines. Magazine: 6×9; 128 pages; 55 lb. paper; 10 pt. cover; illustrations; photos. "Publishing work by new writers." Biannual. Estab. 1988. Circ. 1,000.

Needs: Contemporary, experimental, humor/satire, literary, regional. No genre fiction. Receives approximately 100 unsolicited fiction mss/month. Publishes approximately 5 short story mss/issue. Recently published work by Jane W. Ellis and Lauren Sarat. Published new writers within the last year. Length: 2,000 words average; 4,000 words maximum. Also publishes poetry, nonfiction essays, and interviews with well-known writers. Sometimes comments on rejected mss.

How to Contact: Query first or send complete ms with cover letter. Reports on queries in 3-4 weeks; on mss in 10-14 weeks. SASE. Simultaneous submissions OK. Sample copy for $6.50 and 7×10 SAE; fiction guidelines for #10 SAE and 1 first-class stamp.

Payment/Terms: Pays in contributor's copies; charge for extras. Acquires one-time rights.

Advice: "More than ever we're looking for *well-crafted* stories. We're known for publishing a range of new voices, and favor stories that rely on traditional narrative techniques (e.g. characterization, plot, effective endings). Do continue to submit new stories even if previous ones were not accepted. However, do not submit more than two stories at one time."

UNMUZZLED OX, (III), Unmuzzled Ox Foundation Ltd., 105 Hudson St., New York NY 10013. Editor: Michael Andre. Tabloid. "Magazine about life for an intelligent audience." Quarterly. Estab. 1971. Circ. 20,000.

● Recent issues of this magazine have included poetry, essays and art only. You may want to check before sending submissions or expect a long response time.

Needs: Contemporary, literary, prose poem and translations. No commercial material. Receives 20-25 unsolicited mss/month. Also publishes poetry. Occasionally critiques rejected mss.

How to Contact: "Cover letter is significant." Reports in 1 month. SASE. Sample copy for $7.50.

Payment/Terms: Contributor's copies.

THE URBANITE, A Journal of City Fiction & Poetry, (II, IV), Urban Legend Press, P.O. Box 4737, Davenport IA 52808. Editor: Mark McLaughlin. Magazine: 8½×11; 80 pages; bond paper; coated cover; saddle-stitched; illustrations. "We look for quality fiction in an urban setting with a surrealistic tone. Contributors include modern masters of surrealism and talented newcomers. Our audience is urbane, culture-oriented and hard to please!" Each issue includes a featured writer and a featured poet. Published three times a year. Estab. 1991. Circ. 500-1,000.

Needs: Experimental, fantasy (dark fantasy), horror, humor/satire, literary, psychic/supernatural/occult, science fiction (soft/sociological). "We love horror, but please, no tired, gore-ridden horror plots. Horror submissions must be subtle and sly." Upcoming theme: "Strange Places" (Spring '97). List of upcoming themes available for SASE. Receives over 800 unsolicited mss/month. Accepts 15 mss/issue; 45 mss/year. Publishes ms 6 months after acceptance. Recently published work by Caitlin Kiernan, Joel Lane, Poppy Z. Brite, Hertzan Chimera, Pamela Briggs and Thomas Ligotti. Length: 2,000 words preferred; 500 words minimum; 3,000 words maximum. Publishes short shorts. Length: 350 words preferred. Also publishes poetry. Sometimes critiques or comments on rejected mss.

How to Contact: Query first; each issue has its own theme and guidelines for that theme. Include estimated word count, 4- to 5-sentence bio, Social Security number and list of publications. Reports in 1 month on queries; 3-4 months on mss. Send SASE for reply, return of ms or send a disposable copy of ms. Sample copy for $5. Fiction guidelines for #10 SASE.

Payment/Terms: Pays 2-3¢/word and 2 contributor's copies for first North American serial rights and nonexclusive rights for public readings.

Advice: "The tone of our magazine is unique, and we strongly encourage writers to read an issue to ascertain the sort of material we accept. The number one reason we reject many stories is because they are inappropriate for our publication: in these cases, it is obvious that the writer is not familiar with *The Urbanite*. We like horror, but not mindless gore. People keep sending gore-horror, and they are wasting their time and postage. 'Splatter' fiction is on the way out in publishing. We want to see more slipstream fiction and more bizarre (yet urbane and thought-provoking) humor."

URBANUS MAGAZINE, (III), Urbanus Press, P.O. Box 192921, San Francisco CA 94119-2921. Editor: Peter Drizhal. Magazine: 5½×8½; 80 pages; 60 lb. offset paper; 10 pt. coated cover; illustrations; b&w photographs. "We seek writing for an audience that is generally impatient with mainstream at the same time, not falling into the underground literary mode." Semiannually. Estab. 1987. Circ. 1,500.
Needs: Contemporary, ethnic/multicultural, experimental, fantasy, feminist, gay, horror, humor/satire, lesbian, literary, "meta-fiction," science fiction (soft/sociological). "No romance tales or 'historically-specific' themes (e.g. war, westerns . . .)—simply not our angle." Receives 5,000 mss/year. Publishes ms 6-18 months after acceptance. Published work by Pat Murphy, James Sallis, Lance Olsen, Susan Moon, Sarah Schulman and Edward Kleinschmidt. Length: 6,000 words maximum. Publishes short shorts. Also publishes poetry and nonfiction. Sometimes comments on or critiques rejected mss.
How to Contact: Send complete ms with a cover letter. Reports in 2-4 weeks on queries; 1-3 months on mss. Send SASE for reply, return of ms or send a disposable copy of the ms. No multiple or simultaneous submissions. Sample copy for $5. "Extended" writer's guidelines available for #10 SASE. "First reading window of 1997 begins in March and lasts through July. Query for late year reading."
Payment/Terms: Pays 1-2¢/word and 5 contributor's copies for first North American serial rights.
Advice: "We want the atypical eye/I, dark undercurrents; the socially slanted vision without didactic politicizing; also the normal eye/I immersed in the pseudo-normal (pseudo-mainstream). One source described us as 'contemporary macabre,' which shouldn't be misinterpreted as a genre tag. . . .'"

USI WORKSHEETS, (II), % Postings, Box 1, Ringoes NJ 08551. (908)782-6492. Editor: Rotating board. Magazine: 11½×17; 20-25 pages. Publishes poetry and fiction. Annually. Estab. 1973.
Needs: "No restrictions on subject matter or style. Good storytelling or character delineation appreciated. Audience does not include children." Recently published work by Alicia Ostriker, Joan Baranow, Lois Marie Harrod, Jean Hollander and Rod Tulloss. Publishes short shorts.
How to Contact: Query first "or send a SAE postcard for reading dates. We read only once a year." Reports on queries "as soon as possible." SASE. Sample copy for $4.
Payment/Terms: Pays in contributor's copies. Acquires one-time rights. Copyright "reverts to author."

VALLEY GRAPEVINE, (I, IV), Seven Buffaloes Press, Box 249, Big Timber MT 59011. Editor/Publisher: Art Cuelho. Theme: "poems, stories, history, folklore, photographs, ink drawings or anything native to the Great Central Valley of California, which includes the San Joaquin and Sacramento valleys. Focus is on land and people and the oil fields, farms, orchards, Okies, small town life, hobos." Readership: "rural and small town audience, the common man with a rural background, salt-of-the-earth. The working man reads *Valley Grapevine* because it's his personal history recorded." Annually. Estab. 1978. Circ. 500.
Needs: Literary, contemporary, ethnic (Arkie, Okie), regional and western. No academic, religious (unless natural to theme), or supernatural material. Receives approximately 4-5 unsolicited fiction mss each month. Length: 2,500-10,000 (prefers 5,000) words.
How to Contact: Query. SASE for query, ms. Reports in 1 week. Sample copy available to writers for $6.75.
Payment/Terms: Pays 1-2 contributor's copies. Acquires first North American serial rights. Returns rights to author after publication, but reserves the right to reprint in an anthology or any future special collection of Seven Buffaloes Press.
Advice: "Buy a copy to get a feel of the professional quality of the writing. Know the theme of a particular issue. Some contributors have 30 years experience as writers, most 15 years. Age does not matter; quality does."

VERB, Stories & Verse, (I, II), (formerly *Treasure House*), Treasure House Publishing, P.O. Box 4167, Hagerstown MD 21741-4167. Website: http://users.aol.com/thpublish. Editor-in-Chief: J.G.

---

‡   **THE DOUBLE DAGGER** before a listing indicates that the listing is new in this edition.

Wolfensberger. Fiction Editor: Owen H. Green. Magazine: 8½×11; 28-36 pages; 60 lb. white paper; heavier cover; illustrations. "Published without academic affiliations and without dependence upon grants or tax-exemptions, *Verb*, the literary unjournal, is free to pursue its own independent vision, seeking talented contributors who do not fit the typical 'literary' mold. Inspired, fully committed writers of all backgrounds are welcome to submit." Triannually. Estab. 1994. Circ. 300.

Needs: Literary. "No stories about writers or writing, and no stories about tormented artists or misunderstood new bohemians." Receives more than 60 unsolicited mss/month. Accepts 5 mss/issue; 15 mss/year. Publishes ms within a year after acceptance. Length: 3,000 words average; 6,000 words maximum. Publishes short shorts. Also publishes poetry. Sometimes critiques or comments on rejected mss.

How to Contact: Send complete ms with a cover letter. Include estimated word count and brief bio. "Cover letters should serve as personal introductions, not résumés. Reports in 2 weeks on queries; 2-12 weeks on mss. Send SASE for reply, return of ms or send a disposable copy of ms. Simultaneous submissions OK. Sample copy for $4. Fiction guidelines for #10 SASE.

Payment/Terms: Pays 2 or more contributor's copies; additional copies for $3. Acquires first rights. Sends galleys to author. "We sponsor our annual Emerging Writers Fiction Contest. The 1997 prize is $1,000. Interested writers should query with SASE for current guidelines."

Advice: "We seek stories that surprise us in some way, that make us pace the room or laugh aloud, or that possibly make us uncomfortable with our own opinions. The best work lingers in one's mind long after the reading is finished. A beginner cannot move forward without fully comprehending one essential rule of fiction: show, don't tell. Next, decide, 'Am I a writer or an aspiring artist?' If the former, do reasonable market research, then send your work out like crazy. If you are the latter, exercise greater care. Determine the handful of publications you admire, read them critically, and submit to them consistently. Follow Hemingway's rule: write deliberately. We would love to see more work which crosses and transcends genres, work exhibiting greater imagination when it comes to plotting 'ordinary' characters into extraordinary conflicts. But we're not interested in fantasy! Also, don't send us any New Age spiritual material. No religious material. No agenda-driven material."

VERVE, (I, II), P.O. Box 3205, Simi Valley CA 93093. Editor: Ron Reichick. Fiction Editor: Marilyn Hochheiser. Magazine: Digest-sized, 40 pages, 70 lb. paper, 80 lb. cover, cover illustrations or photographs. "Each issue has a theme." Quarterly. Estab. 1989. Circ. 700.

Needs: Contemporary, experimental, fantasy, humor/satire, literary, mainstream, prose poem. No pornographic material. Upcoming themes: "Awakening" (deadline: March 1, 1997); "Family Ties" (deadline: August 1, 1997). Receives 100 unsolicited fiction mss/month. Accepts 4-6 mss/issue; 8-12 mss/year. Publishes ms 2 months after acceptance. Length: 1,000 words maximum. Publishes short shorts. Also publishes literary criticism, poetry.

How to Contact: "Request guidelines before submitting manuscript." Reports 4-6 weeks after deadline. SASE. Simultaneous submissions OK. Sample copy for $3.50. Fiction guidelines for #10 SASE. Reviews short story collections.

Payment/Terms: Pays in contributor's copies. Acquires one-time rights.

VIGNETTE, (II), Vignette Press, P.O. Box 109, Hollywood CA 90078-0109. (213)871-5812. E-mail: vignet@aol.com. Editor: Dawn Baillie. Magazine: 6×9; 120 pages; 60 lb. smooth opaque, paper; 10 pt. C1S glossy; perfect bound. "*Vignette* provides imaginative short fiction based on a quarterly theme. For example, 'Home' and 'Vegetable' were our first and second themes. Audience is mostly writers and fiction enthusiasts." Estab. 1995. Circ. 1,500.

● A story from the winter 1995 "Water" issue will be included in *Pushcart XXI*.

Needs: Adventure, erotica, ethnic/multicultural, experimental, feminist, gay, historical, humor/satire, lesbian, literary, mainstream/contemporary, psychic/supernatural/occult, regional. List of upcoming themes available for SASE. Publishes special fiction issue or anthology. List of upcoming themes available for SASE. Receives 450 unsolicited mss/month. Accepts 10 mss/issue; 40 mss/year. Publishes ms 2 months after acceptance. Agented fiction 10%. Recently published work by Henry Rollins, Daniel Meltzer, Nahio Rachlin, Janset Berkok Shami, John M. Daniel, David Evanier, Barry Yourarau, Wendell Mayo, Thomas F. Kennedy and William Luvaas. Length: 4,000 words average; 5,000 words maximum. Publishes short shorts.

How to Contact: Send complete ms with a cover letter. Include estimated word count and bio. Reports in 2 months on mss. Send SASE for reply, return of ms or send a disposable copy of ms. Sample copy for $9.95 plus $3.50 postage (CA residents add 8.25% tax). Fiction guidelines for #10 SASE.

Payment/Terms: Pays $100 and 1 contributor's copy on publication for first rights. Sends galleys to author.

Advice: "Be inventive and use well-rounded characters. Looking for stories that have a unique point of view, unique voice and/or location. More fiction than personal essay."

THE VINCENT BROTHERS REVIEW, (II), Vincent Brothers Publishing, 4566 Northern Circle, Riverside OH 45424-5733. Editor: Kimberly Willardson. Magazine: 5½ × 8¼; 88-100 perfect-bound pages; 60 lb. white coated paper; 60 lb. Oxford (matte) cover; b&w illustrations and photographs. "We publish two theme issues per year. Writers must send SASE for information about upcoming theme issues. Each issue of *TVBR* contains poetry, b&w art, at least six short stories and usually one nonfiction piece. For a mainstream audience looking for an alternative to the slicks." Triannually. Estab. 1988. Circ. 400.

● *TVBR* was ranked #20 in the "1996 *Writer's Digest* Fiction 50," and, subsequently, was the subject of a front-page feature story in the Sunday, July 7th, 1996, issue of *The Dayton Daily News*. It has received grants from the Ohio Arts Council for the last six years. The magazine sponsors a fall fiction contest; deadline in October. Contact them for details.

Needs: Adventure, condensed/excerpted novel, contemporary, ethnic, experimental, feminist, historical, humor/satire, literary, mainstream, mystery/suspense (amateur sleuth, cozy, private eye), prose poem, regional, science fiction (soft/sociological), senior citizen/retirement, serialized novel, translations, western (adult, frontier, traditional). Upcoming themes: "Water" (January 1997); "Bus and Train Travel" (April 1997). "We focus on the way the story is presented rather than the genre of the story. No racist, sexist, fascist, etc. work." Receives 200-250 unsolicited mss/month. Buys 6-10 mss/issue; 18-30 mss/year. Publishes ms 2-4 months after acceptance. Recently published work by Arthur Winfield, Knight Sara Backer, Gordon C. Wilson. Length: 2,500 words average; 250 words minimum; 7,000 words maximum. Publishes short shorts. Length: 250-1,000 words. Also publishes literary essays, literary criticism, poetry. Often critiques rejected mss and sometimes recommends other markets.

How to Contact: "Send query letter *before* sending novel excerpts or condensations! *Send only one short story at a time*—unless sending short shorts." Send complete ms. Simultaneous submissions OK, but not preferred. Reports in 3-4 weeks on queries; 2-3 months on mss with SASE. Sample copy for $6.50; back issues for $4.50. Fiction guidelines for #10 SASE. Reviews novels and short story collections.

Payment/Terms: Pays $10 minimum and 2 contributor's copies for one-time rights. Charge (discounted) for extras.

Advice: "The best way to discover what *TVBR* editors are seeking in fiction is to read at least a couple issues of the magazine."

VOICES WEST, A Literary Journal, (I, II), West Los Angeles College, 4800 Freshman Dr., Culver City CA 90230. (310)287-4200. Editors: R. Weinstein and B. Goldberg. Magazine: 6 × 9, 120 pages; 20 lb. bond paper; 70 lb. cover stock; illustrations and photos. *Voices West* is "a forum for most kinds of interesting and provocative writing. An educated audience." Semiannually.

Needs: Adventure, erotica, ethnic/multicultural, experimental, humor/satire, literary, mainstream/contemporary, regional. No science fiction, children's or teen. Accepts 10 mss/issue; 20 mss/year. Does not read in summer. Publishes ms 3-6 months after acceptance. Length: no minimum; 5,000 words maximum. Publishes short shorts. Length: 1,500 words. Also publishes literary essays, literary criticism and poetry. Sometimes critiques or comments on rejected mss.

How to Contact: Send complete ms with a cover letter. Include 50-word bio with submission. Reports in 1-2 months. Send SASE for reply, return of ms or send a disposable copy of ms. Simultaneous submissions OK.

Payment/Terms: Pays $50 maximum/story, $25 minimum/poem and 2 contributor's copies on publication for first North American serial rights; additional copies for $3.

Advice: "We look for fiction that is carefully worked out and that has a satisfying solution, and for poetry that is both original and accessible. Nothing can beat an involving story told in an original way with fresh language."

‡**VOX, Pace University Literary Magazine, (I)**, Pace University, Willcox Hall, Room 43, Bedford Rd., Pleasantville NY 10553. (914)773-3962. Editor: Alfred J. Menna, Jr. Magazine: 5½ × 8½; perfect-bound; 80-120 pages; illustrations and photos. "*Vox* is made for and by college students and publishes works that, we hope, will appeal to this readership. Funny, sad, everything in between, we want it if it can keep the attention of a collegian with a full course-load. This doesn't mean just the usual beer, sex and drug stories—there's a lot more to life, and that's what *Vox* is interested in giving to our readers. Just make it real, honest, avoid cliches and stereotypes and it'll be considered." Semiannually (fall and spring). Estab. 1977. Circ. 500-1,000.

● *Vox* received the Columbia Scholastic Press Association Silver Crown Award, 1994 and 1995.

Needs: College-age interests, condensed/excerpted novel, ethnic/multicultural, feminist, humor/satire, literary, mainstream/contemporary, mystery/suspense (police procedural, private eye/hardboiled, romantic suspense), romance (contemporary), No erotica, horror, senior citizen, juvenile. Does not read mss June, July, August. Recently published work by students from Pace. Length: 1,600 words average; 750 words minimum; 4,000 words maximum. Also publishes literary essays and poetry.

How to Contact: Send complete ms with a cover letter. Include estimated word count and brief bio. Reports in 4-6 weeks. Send SASE for reply; send a disposable copy of ms. Sample copy for $6, 5½×8½ SAE and 4 first-class stamps.
Payment/Terms: Pays 2 contributor's copies; additional copies for $3 and 4 first-class stamps for each copy. Acquires one-time rights. Not copyrighted.
Advice: "Send a neat, proofread manuscript; at least spell check it and let a friend or two read it over. Send an original manuscript—things that sound 'familiar' are the quickest to be forgotten."

WEST BRANCH, (II), Bucknell Hall, Bucknell University, Lewisburg PA 17837. Editors: Karl Patten and Robert Love Taylor. Magazine: 5½×8½; 96-120 pages; quality paper; coated card cover; perfect-bound; illustrations; photos. Fiction and poetry for readers of contemporary literature. Biannually. Estab. 1977. Circ. 500.
Needs: Literary, contemporary, prose poems and translations. No science fiction. Accepts 3-6 mss/issue. Recently published work by Jay Atkinson, Pete Duval, Andy Mozina, Mary Jeselnick, Sharon Brooks and Theresa Coty O'Neil. Published new writers within the last year. No preferred length. However, "the fiction we publish usually runs between 12-25 double-spaced pages."
How to Contact: Send complete ms with cover letter, "with information about writer's background, previous publications, etc." SASE. No simultaneous submissions. Reports in 6-8 weeks on mss. Sample copy for $3.
Payment/Terms: Pays 2 contributor's copies and one-year subscription; cover price less 25% discount charge for extras. Acquires first rights.
Advice: "Narrative art fulfills a basic human need—our dreams attest to this—and storytelling is therefore a high calling in any age. Find your own voice and vision. Make a story that speaks to your own mysteries. Cultivate simplicity in form, complexity in theme. Look and listen through your characters."

❧WEST COAST LINE, A Journal of Contemporary Writing & Criticism, (II), 2027 E. Academic Annex, Simon Fraser University, Burnaby, British Columbia V5A 1S6 Canada. (604)291-4287. Fax: (604)291-5737. Managing Editor: Jacqueline Larson. Magazine: 6×9; 128-144 pages. "Poetry, fiction, criticism—modern and contemporary, North American, cross-cultural. Readers include academics, writers, students." Triannual. Estab. 1990. Circ. 600.
Needs: Experimental, ethnic/multicultural, feminist, gay, literary. "We do not publish journalistic writing or strictly representational narrative." Receives 30-40 unsolicited mss/month. Accepts 2-3 mss/issue; 3-6 mss/year. Publishes ms 2-6 months after acceptance. Length: 3,000-4,000 words. Publishes short shorts. Length: 250-400 words. Also publishes literary essays and literary criticism.
How to Contact: Send complete ms with a cover letter. "We supply an information form for contributors." Reports in 3 months. Send SAE with IRCs, not US postage, for return of ms. No simultaneous submissions. Electronic submissions OK. Sample copy for $10. Fiction guidelines free.
Payment/Terms: Pays $3-8/page (Canadian); subscription; 2 contributor copies; additional copies for $6-8/copy, depending on quantity ordered. Pays on publication for one-time rights.
Advice: "Special concern for contemporary writers who are experimenting with, or expanding the boundaries of conventional forms of poetry, fiction and criticism; also interested in criticism and scholarship on Canadian and American modernist writers who are important sources for current writing. We recommend that potential contributors send a letter of enquiry or read back issues before submitting a manuscript."

WEST WIND REVIEW, (I), English Dept., Southern Oregon State College, Ashland OR 97520. (503)552-6518. E-mail: westwind@tao.sosc.osshe.edu. Editor: Gillian Gillette (1996-1997 school year). Editors change each year. Magazine: 5¾×8½; 150-250 pages; illustrations and photos. "Literary journal publishing prose/poetry/art. Encourages new writers, accepts established writers as well, with an audience of people who like to read anthologies." Annually. Estab. 1980. Circ. 500.
Needs: Adventure, erotica, ethnic/multicultural, experimental, fantasy, feminist, gay, historical (general), horror, humor/satire, lesbian, literary, mainstream/contemporary, mystery/suspense, psychic/supernatural/occult, regional, religious/inspirational, romance, science fiction, senior citizen/retirement, sports, translations, westerns, young adult/teen—"just about anything." Receives 6-60 unsolicited mss/month. Accepts 15-20 mss/issue. Does not read mss during summer months. Publishes ms almost immediately after acceptance. Recently published work by Lawson F. Inada, Tec A. Corinne and V. Craig Wright. Length: 3,000 words maximum. Publishes short shorts. Also publishes literary essays and poetry. Sometimes critiques or comments on rejected ms.
How to Contact: Send complete ms with a cover letter. Include estimated word count and short bio. Reports in 2 weeks on queries; by May 1 on mss. Send SASE for reply, return of ms or send a disposable copy of ms. No simultaneous submissions. Electronic submissions (disk) OK. Sample copy for $5. Fiction guidelines free. Rarely reviews novels or short story collections.
Payment/Terms: Awards $25 prize for best fiction. Accepted authors receive 1 free copy. Authors retain all rights.

Advice: "Good writing stands out. Content is important but style is essential. Clearly finished pieces whose content shows subtle action, reaction and transformation for the character(s) are what we like."

WESTVIEW, A Journal of Western Oklahoma, (II), Southwestern Oklahoma State University, 100 Campus Dr., Weatherford OK 73096-3098. (405)774-3168. Editor: Fred Alsberg. Magazine: 8½×11; up to 44 pages; 24 lb. paper; slick cover; illustrations and photographs. Quarterly. Estab. 1981. Circ. 400.
Needs: Contemporary, ethnic (especially Native American), humor, literary, prose poem. No pornography, violence, or gore. No overly sentimental. "We are particularly interested in writers of the Southwest; however, we accept work of quality from elsewhere." Receives 10 unsolicited mss/month. Accepts 5 ms/issue; 20 mss/year. Publishes ms 1 month-2 years after acceptance. Recently published work by Diane Glancy, Wendell Mayo, Jack Matthews, Mark Spencer and Pamela Rodgers. Length: 2,000 words average. Also publishes literary essays, literary criticism, poetry. Occasionally critiques rejected mss.
How to Contact: Simultaneous submissions OK. Send complete ms with SASE. Reports in 1-2 months. "We welcome submissions on a 3.5 disk formatted for WordPerfect 5.0, IBM or Macintosh. Please include a hard copy printout of your submission."
Payment/Terms: Pays contributor's copy for first rights.

✦WHETSTONE, (II), English Dept., University of Lethbridge, Lethbridge, Alberta T1K 3M4 Canada. (403)329-2367. Contact: Editorial Board. Magazine: 6×9; 90-140 pages; superbond paper; photos. Magazine publishing "poetry, prose, drama, prints, photographs and occasional music compositions for a general audience." Biannually. Estab. 1971. Circ. 500.
Needs: Experimental, literary, mainstream. "Interested in works by all writers/artists. Interested in multi-media works by individuals or collaborators." Write for upcoming themes. Accepts 1-2 ms/issue, 3-4 mss/year. Recently published work by Madeline Sonik, Serenity Bee, Stephen Guppy and Ronnie R. Brown. Published new writers within the last year. Length: maximum 10 pages. Publishes short shorts. Also publishes poetry, drama and art.
How to Contact: Send 2 short fictions or 6 poems maximum with SASE. Include cover letter with author's background and experience. No simultaneous submissions. Reports in 5 months on mss. Publishes ms an average of 3-4 months after acceptance. Sample copy for $7 (Canadian) and 7½×10½ or larger SAE and 2 Canadian first-class stamps or IRCs.
Payment/Terms: Pays 1 contributor's copy. Holds copyright but allows work to revert back to writer.
Advice: "We seek most styles of quality writing. Follow all submission guidelines, including number of pieces and pages. Avoid moralizing."

‡WHETSTONE, (I, II), Barrington Area Arts Council, P.O. Box 1266, Barrington IL 60011. Editors: Sandra Berris, Juliann Fleenor, Marsha Portnoy, and Jean Tolle. Magazine: 9×6; 110 pages; heavy cover stock. "We try to publish the best quality nonfiction, fiction and poetry for the educated reader." Annually. Estab. 1984. Circ. 700. Member CLMP.
● *Whetstone* has received numerous Illinois Arts Council Awards.
Needs: Humor/satire, literary, mainstream/contemporary. "No genre or plot driven fiction." Receives 30 unsolicited mss/month. Accepts 10 mss/year. Publishes ms by December 1 of year accepted. Recently published work by Edith Pearlman, Leslie Pietrzyk, Bill Roorbach and Scott Blackwood (his first published story). Length: 3,000 words average; 6,000 words maximum. Also publishes poetry. Often critiques or comments on rejected mss "depending on the work. We often write out the readers' responses if they are helpful. A work gets a minimum of two readers and up to five or six."
How to Contact Send complete ms with a cover letter. Include a 50-word bio. Reports in 3-6 months on mss "or sooner depending on the time of the year." Send SASE for return of ms or reply only. Simultaneous submissions OK. Sample copy (including guidelines) for $5.
Payment/Terms: Pays $5/page and 2 contributor's copies on publication. Acquires first North American serial rights. Sends galleys to author. "We frequently work with writers on their pieces. All submissions are considered for the $500 Whetstone Prize and the $250 McGrath Award."
Advice: "We like strong characterization and a vivid use of language and, of course, a coherent plot. We like texture and a story which resonates. Read the journal and other small literary journals. Study good writing wherever you find it. Learn from editorial comments. Read. Read. Read, but do it as a

---

MARKET CATEGORIES: (I) Open to new writers; (II) Open to both new and established writers; (III) Interested mostly in established writers; (IV) Open to writers whose work is specialized; (V) Closed to unsolicited submissions.

writer reads. We're seeing too many childhood trauma stories. There are only so many of these we can accept."

WHISKEY ISLAND MAGAZINE, (II), Dept. of English, Cleveland State University, Cleveland OH 44115. (216)687-2056. Editor: Pat Stansberry. Editors change each year. Magazine of fiction and poetry, including experimental works, with no specific theme. Biannually. Estab. 1978. Circ. 2,500.
Needs: Receives 100 unsolicited fiction mss/month. Accepts 4-6 mss/issue. Length: 6,500 words maximum. Also publishes poetry (poetry submissions should contain no more than 10 pages).
How to Contact: Send complete ms with SASE. No simultaneous or previously published submissions. Reports in 2-4 months on mss. Sample copy for $5.
Payment/Terms: Pays 2 contributor's copies. Acquires one-time rights.
Advice: "Please include brief bio."

THE JAMES WHITE REVIEW, A Gay Men's Literary Quarterly, (II, IV), The James White Review Association, P.O. Box 3356, Butler Quarter Station, Minneapolis MN 55403. (612)339-8317. E-mail: jwrmail@aol.com. Fiction Editor: David Rohlfing. Tabloid: 17×26; 24 pages; illustrations; photos. "We publish work on any subject for primarily gay males and/or gay sensitive audience." Quarterly. Estab. 1983. Circ. 5,000.
 • Awards the $500 Joseph Brian Cowgill Memorial Prize for Fiction annually to the best short story published in *TJWR* the preceding year. There is no application process for the award; all work published in the review is eligible.
Needs: Contemporary, experimental, humor/satire, literary, prose poem, translations. No pornography. Receives 50 unsolicited fiction mss/month. Buys 4 mss/issue; 16 mss/year. Publishes ms 3 months or sooner after acceptance. Recently published work by Thomas Glave, Essex Hemphill, Norberto Luis Romero, Felice Picano and George Stambolian. Published new writers within the last year. Length: 30 pages, double-spaced. Sometimes critiques rejected mss. Recommends other markets "when we can."
How to Contact: Send complete ms with cover letter and short bio. SASE. No simultaneous submissions. Electronic submissions OK; "Microsoft RTF (rich text format) and MS-Word (but NOT version 6.0), WordPerfect, MacWrite or ASCII (plain text) on 3.5″ disks (MAC or MS-DOS). We *cannot* use 5.25n disks. A paper copy of your submission must accompany the disk." Reports in 2-3 months. Sample copy for $4. Fiction guidelines available with a SASE.
Payment/Terms: Pays 2 contributor's copies and $50. Buys one-time rights; returns rights to author.
Advice: "We're looking for stories that are written with original, imaginative language and forms of narration for stories that broaden and add depth to the representation of characters and themes in this genre of gay fiction. We hope never to publish stories oozing with the superficial sentimentality that so much gay fiction presently contains."

✸WHITE WALL REVIEW, 63 Gould St., Toronto, Ontario M5B 1E9 Canada. (416)977-9924. Editors change annually. Send mss to "Editors." Magazine: 5¾×8¾; 144-160 pages; professionally printed with glossy card cover; b&w photos and illustrations. "An annual using interesting, preferably spare art. No style is unacceptable." Annually. Estab. 1976. Circ. 500.
Needs: Nothing "boring, self-satisfied, gratuitously sexual, violent or indulgent." Accepts 10 mss/ book. Accepts mss from September to 1st week in December of a given year. Recently published work by Terry Watada, Brendan Landers and Ruth Olsen Latta. Length: 3,000 words maximum.
How to Contact: Send complete ms with cover letter, SASE and *$5 non-refundable reading fee*. Include a short bio. Reports on mss "as soon as we can (usually in April or May)." Always comments on ms. No simultaneous submissions. Sample copy for $8.
Payment/Terms: Pays 1 contributor's copy. Acquires first or one-time rights.
Advice: "Keep it *short*. We look for creativity, but not to the point of obscurity."

‡WICKED MYSTIC, (I, II, IV), 532 La Guardia Place, #371, New York NY 10012. (718)373-2651. E-mail: scheluchin@wickedmystic.com. Editor: Andre Scheluchin. Magazine: Full-sized; 76 pages; 20 lb. paper; 60 lb. 4-color cover. "Horror, gothic, gore, sex, violence, blood, death." Published 3 times/year. Estab. 1990. Circ. 10,000.
Needs: Explicit, gut-wrenching, brutally twisted, warped, sadistic, deathly, provocative, nasty horror. "No vampires." Receives 120 unsolicited mss/month. Acquires 10-15 mss/issue; 30-45 mss/year. Time between acceptance of the ms and publication varies. Recently published work by James Dorr, Tony Plank, Charlee Jacob and Donald Burleson. Length: 3,000 words preferred; 1,000 words minimum; 3,500 words maximum. Also publishes literary essays, literary criticism, art and poetry.
How to Contact: Send complete ms with cover letter. Include estimated word count, short and basic bio, list of publications. Reports in 2-12 weeks. Send SASE for reply, return of ms or send a disposable copy of the ms. No simultaneous submissions. Electronic submissions OK. Sample copy for $5.95. Free fiction guidelines.
Payment/Terms: Pays $1.25/word, 3 copies of the issue and a FREE ¼ page ad (a $50 value) for a product or service you are promoting. Acquires First North American serial rights..

Advice: "Your story must have a bizarre twist to it and involve both sex and death. No predictability and no slow-moving pieces."

‡**WILLOW REVIEW, (II)**, College of Lake County, 19351 W. Washington St., Grayslake IL 60030. (847)223-6601 ext. 2956. Fax: (847)548-3383. E-mail: com426@clc.cc.il.us. Editor: Paulette Roeske. Magazine: 6×9; 80 pages; 70 lb. paper; 80 lb. 4-color cover. "*Willow Review* is nonthematic and publishes short fiction, memoir and poetry for a general and literary adult audience." Annually. Estab. 1969. Circ. 1,000.
  • *Willow Review* is partially funded by the Illinois Arts Council. Most of the work they publish is "traditional" and realistic.
Needs: Contemporary, ethnic, experimental, feminist, literary, prose poems, regional. "There is no bias against a particular subject matter, although there is a clear editorial preference for literary fiction." No "popular genre fiction; children/young adult. Although we publish a range of styles and types of fiction, we look for stories that move us presented in a distinctive voice that is stylistically compelling. We prefer a recognizable world with recognizable characters and events that engage the reader both emotionally and intellectually." Receives 50 unsolicited mss/month. Accepts 7-8 mss/issue. Accepted mss published in April of each year. Recently published work by Garrett Hongo, Diane Ackerman, David Ray and S.L. Wisenberg. Length: 1,500 words minimum; 4,000 words maximum. Publishes short shorts. Length: 500 words. Sometimes comments on rejected mss and recommends other markets.
How to Contact: Send complete ms with cover letter. Include complete mailing address, telephone number, list of previous publications and or other recognition etc., if applicable. Reports in 1-2 months on mss. SASE (if writer would like it returned). Sample copy for $4. Fiction guidelines for #10 SAE and 1 first-class stamp.
Payment/Terms: Pays 2 contributor's copies on publication for first North American serial rights. All manuscripts are automatically considered for the annual *Willow Review* awards.
Advice: "*Willow Review*, because of its length, is forced to make word count a factor although we would publish an exceptional story which exceeds our recommended length. Beyond that, literary excellence is our sole criteria. Perhaps voice, more than any other factor, causes a manuscript to distinguish itself. Study the craft—read the best little magazines, subscribe to them, maintain contact with other writers through writer's groups or informally, attend fiction readings and ask the writers questions in the discussion periods which typically follow. Read Eudora Welty's *One Writer's Beginnings* or John Gardner's *On Becoming a Novelist* or Flannery O'Connor's *Mystery and Manners* or the articles in *Poets & Writers*. Consider writing a discipline, a field of study—it won't kill 'inspiration' or 'creativity' but will augment it to help you write the best story you can write."

WIND MAGAZINE, (II), P.O. Box 24548, Lexington KY 40524. (606)885-5342. E-mail: leafk@aol .com. Editors: Charlie G. Hughes and Leatha Kendrick. Magazine: 5½×8½; 100 pages. "Eclectic literary journal with stories, poems, book reviews from small presses, essays. Readership is students, professors, housewives, literary folk, adults." Semiannually. Estab. 1971. Circ. 450.
Needs: Literary, mainstream/contemporary, translations. Accepts 6 fiction mss/issue; 12 mss/year. Publishes mss less than 1 year after acceptance. Published work by Carolyn Osborn, Jane Stuart, David Shields, Lester Goldberg and Elisabeth Stevens. Length: 5,000 words maximum. Publishes short shorts, length: 300-400 words. Also publishes literary essays, literary criticism and poetry. Sometimes critiques or comments on rejected mss.
How to Contact: Send complete ms with a cover letter. Include estimated word count and 50-word bio. Reports in 2 weeks on queries; 2 months on mss. Send SASE for reply, return of ms or send a disposable copy of ms. No simultaneous submissions. Sample copy for $3.50. Reviews novels and short story collections from small presses.
Payment/Terms: Pays 1 contributor's copy; additional copies for $3.50. Acquires first North American serial rights and anthology reprint rights.
Advice: "The writing must have an impact on the reader; the reader must come away changed, perhaps haunted, or maybe smiling. There is nothing I like better than to be able to say 'I wish I had written that.' "

✦**WINDSOR REVIEW, A Journal of the Arts, (II)**, Dept. of English, University of Windsor, Windsor, Ontario N9B 3P4 Canada. (519)253-4232, ext. 2332. Fax: (519)973-7050. E-mail: uwrevu@u windsor.ca. Fiction Editor: Alistair MacLeod. Magazine/perfect bound book: 6×9; 110 pages; illustrations and photos. Semiannually. Estab. 1965. Circ. 250.
Needs: Literary. Publishes ms 6-9 months after acceptance. Recently published work by James Reaney and Madeline Sonik. Length: 4,450 words average. Also publishes poetry.
How to Contact: Send complete ms with a cover letter. Reports in 1 month on queries; 2 months on mss. Send SASE for reply, return of ms or send a disposable copy of ms. No simultaneous or electronic submissions. Sample copy for $5. Free fiction guidelines.
Payment/Terms: Pays $50 and 1 contributor's copy on publication for first North American serial rights; additional copies available for $5.

WISCONSIN REVIEW, (I, II), University of Wisconsin, Box 158, Radford Hall, Oshkosh WI 54901. (414)424-2267. Editor: Elisa Derickson. Editors change every year. Send submissions to "Fiction Editor." Magazine: 6×9; 60-100 pages; illustrations. Literary prose and poetry. Triannual. Estab. 1966. Circ. 2,000.
Needs: Literary and experimental. Receives 30 unsolicited fiction mss each month. Published new writers within the last year. Length: up to 5,000 words. Publishes short shorts.
How to Contact: Send complete ms with SASE and cover letter with bio notes. Simultaneous submissions OK. Reports in 2-6 months. Publishes ms an average of 1-3 months after acceptance. Sample copy for $3.
Payment/Terms: Pays in contributor's copies. Acquires first rights.
Advice: "We look for well-crafted work with carefully developed characters, plots and meaningful situations. The editors prefer work of original and fresh thought when considering a piece of experimental fiction."

THE WORCESTER REVIEW, (II), Worcester Country Poetry Association, Inc., 71 Pleasant, Worcester MA 01609. (508)797-4770. Editor: Rodger Martin. Magazine: 6×9; 100 pages; 60 lb. white offset paper; 10 pt. CS1 cover stock; illustrations and photos. "We like high quality, creative poetry, artwork and fiction. Critical articles should be connected to New England." Annually. Estab. 1972. Circ. 1,000.
Needs: Literary, prose poem. "We encourage New England writers in the hopes we will publish at least 30% New England but want the other 70% to show the best of writing from across the US." Receives 20-30 unsolicited fiction mss/month. Accepts 2-4 mss/issue. Publishes ms an average of 6 months to 1 year after acceptance. Agented fiction less than 10%. Published work by Bave Weigl and Carol Glickfeld. Length: 2,000 words average; 1,000 words minimum; 4,000 words maximum. Publishes short shorts. Also publishes literary essays, literary criticism, poetry. Sometimes critiques rejected mss and recommends other markets.
How to Contact: Send complete ms with cover letter. Reports in 5-6 months on mss. SASE. Simultaneous submissions OK if other markets are clearly identified. Sample copy for $5; fiction guidelines free.
Payment/Terms: Pays 2 contributor's copies and honorarium if possible for one-time rights.
Advice: "Send only one short story—reading editors do not like to read two by the same author at the same time. We will use only one. We generally look for creative work with a blend of craftsmanship, insight and empathy. This does not exclude humor. We won't print work that is shoddy in any of these areas."

WORDPLAY, (I, II), Wordplay Publishing, P.O. Box 2248, South Portland ME 04116-2248. (207)799-7041. Editor: Helen Peppe. Magazine: 8½×11; 28 pages; 60 lb. paper; medium to heavy cover; illustrations."*Wordplay*'s audience expectations are simply enjoyable stories—I do not accept what is considered 'sophisticated' or 'New Age.' " Quarterly. Estab. 1995. Circ. 500.
Needs: Condensed/excerpted novel, ethnic/multicultural, feminist, historical, humor/satire, literary, mainstream/contemporary, mystery/suspense. "No erotica, horror, gothic romance." Plans special fiction issue or anthology. Receives 150 unsolicited mss/month. Accepts 6-10 mss/issue; 30-50 mss/year. Publishes ms 6-12 months after acceptance. Recently published work by Ned Pastor, Willard Rusch, Thomas Carper, Madeline Wise and C.B. Follett. Length: 12-1,500 words average; 7,500 words maximum. Publishes short shorts. Also publishes literary essays, poetry, recollections, letters and cartoons. Always critiques or comments on rejected mss.
How to Contact: Send complete ms with a cover letter. Include estimated word count and bio. Reports in 2 weeks on queries; 1-2 months on mss. Send SASE for reply, return of ms or send a disposable copy of ms. Simultaneous and reprint submissions OK. Sample copy for $5; back issues $4. Fiction guidelines free.
Payment/Terms: Pays 1 contributor's copy. Acquires one-time rights. Sends galleys to author.
Advice: "Quality always makes a manuscript stand out. Even if I do not like the actual plot line, if it is well-written, I'll give it serious consideration. After numerous rejections from the same magazine, read it—research what it is publishing. Submit again and again and do not get discouraged."

WORDS OF WISDOM, (II), 612 Front St., Glendora NJ 08029-1133. (609)863-0610. Editor: J.M. Freiermuth. Newsletter: 5½×8½; 72-88 pages; copy paper; some illustrations and photographs. "Fiction, satire, humorous poetry and travel for a general audience—80% of readers can read above high school level." Estab. 1981. Circ. 150.
Needs: Adventure, contemporary, ethnic, feminist, historical, humor/satire, mainstream, mystery/suspense (cozy, private eye), regional, western (adult, frontier, traditional). No religion, children's, gay, romance. Plans "All Woman Author" issue (October 1997). Fall 1997 issue to feature travel stories in foreign lands. Receives 50-60 unsolicited mss/month. Accepts 15-20 mss/issue; 60-80 mss/year. Publishes ms 2-6 months after acceptance. Recently published work by Nancy Hoffmann, Alma Jill Dizon, Karen Lee Boren, Mark Davignon, Jay Liveson, Robert N. Feinstein and Lois Green Stone.

Published first time writers last year. Length: 2,000-3,000 words average; 1,200 words minimum; 9,000 words maximum. Publishes short shorts. Length: "Long enough to develop a good bite." Sometimes critiques rejected mss and recommends other markets.

How to Contact: Send complete manuscript copy and/or DOS floppy (uses MSWord) with cover letter including "name, address, SASE." Reports in 2-12 weeks on mss. SASE. Simultaneous and electronic (disk) submissions OK. Sample copy for $4 postpaid. Reviews short story collections.

Payment/Terms: Pays subscription to magazine for first publication of story. Acquires one-time rights. Publication not copyrighted.

Advice: "If your story has a spark of life or a degree of humor that brings a smile to my face, you have a chance here. Most stories lack these two ingredients. Don't send something you wrote ten years ago."

THE WORMWOOD REVIEW, (II, IV), P.O. Box 4698, Stockton CA 95204. (209)466-8231. Editor: Marvin Malone. Magazine: 5½×8½; 48 pages; 60 lb. matte paper; 80 lb. matte cover; illustrations. "Concentrated on the prose poem specifically for literate audience." Quarterly. Estab. 1959. Circ. 700.

Needs: Prose poem. No religious or inspirational. Receives 500-600 unsolicited mss/month. Accepts 30-40 mss/issue; 120-160 mss/year. Publishes ms 6-18 months after acceptance. Published work by Charles Bukowski and Dan Lenihan. Length: 300 words preferred; 1,000 words maximum. Critiques or comments on rejected mss.

How to Contact: Send complete ms with cover letter. Reports in 1-2 months. SASE. No simultaneous submissions. Sample copy for $4. Fiction guidelines for #10 SASE.

Payment/Terms: Pays $12-140 or equivalent in contributor's copies for all rights, but reassigns rights to author on written request.

Advice: A manuscript that stands out has "economical verbal style coupled with perception and human values. Have something to say—then say it in the most effective way. Do *not* avoid wit and humor."

WRITERS' FORUM, (II), University of Colorado at Colorado Springs, Colorado Springs CO 80933-7150. Fax: (719)262-3582. Editor: C. Kenneth Pellow. "Ten to fifteen short stories or self-contained novel excerpts published once a year along with 25-35 poems. Highest literary quality only: mainstream, avant-garde, with preference to western themes. For small press enthusiasts, teachers and students of creative writing, commercial agents/publishers, university libraries and departments interested in contemporary American literature." Estab. 1974.

Needs: Contemporary, ethnic (Chicano, Native American, not excluding others), literary and regional (West). Receives approximately 40 unsolicited fiction mss each month and will publish new as well as experienced authors. Recently published fiction by José Martinez, Martin Lopez, Sheri Szeman, Julia Nunnally Duncan and Lawrence Coates; published many new writers within the last year. Length: 1,500-8,500 words. Also publishes literary essays, literary criticism, poetry. Critiques rejected mss "when there is time and perceived merit."

How to Contact: Send complete ms and letter with relevant career information with SASE. Prefers submissions between September and February. Simultaneous submissions OK. Reports in 3-5 weeks on mss. Publishes ms an average of 6 months after acceptance. Sample back copy $8 to *NSSWM* readers. Current copy $10. Make checks payable to "Writers' Forum."

Payment/Terms: Pays 2 contributor's copies. Cover price less 50% discount for extras. Acquires one-time rights.

Advice: "Read our publication. Be prepared for constructive criticism. We especially seek submissions with a strong voice that show immersion in place (trans-Mississippi West) and development of credible characters. Probably the TV-influenced fiction with trivial dialogue and set-up plot is the most quickly rejected. Our format—a 5½×8½ professionally edited and printed paperback book—lends credibility to authors published in our imprint."

WRITER'S KEEPER, (I, II, IV), Pyx Press, P.O. Box 922648, Sylmar CA 91392-2648. Editor: C. Darren Butler. Newsletter: 8½×11; 2-4 pages, 20 lb. paper. "All works must be about writing." Quarterly. Estab. 1993. Circ. 800.

● Pyx Press is a member of the Council of Literary Magazines and Presses.

MARKET CONDITIONS are constantly changing! If you're still using this book and it is 1998 or later, buy the newest edition of *Novel & Short Story Writer's Market* at your favorite bookstore or order from Writer's Digest Books.

Needs: Writing-related: fantasy, humor/satire, literary. Receives 80 unsolicited mss/month. Accepts 0-3 mss/issue; 2-10 mss/year. Publishes ms within 1 year after acceptance. Publishes short shorts only. Length: 1,500 words maximum. Also publishes literary essays and poetry. Sometimes critiques or comments on rejected mss.

How to Contact: Send complete ms with a cover letter. Include estimated word count, 1-paragraph bio and list of publications. Reports in 4 weeks on queries; 1-3 months, occasionally longer, on mss. Send SASE for reply, return of ms or send a disposable copy of ms. Simultaneous and reprint submissions OK. Sample copy for #10 SASE. Fiction guidelines for #10 SASE. Reviews novels and short story collections.

Payment/Terms: Pays $1 and 3-issue subscription including 1 contributor's copy on publication for first North American serial rights or one-time rights.

WRITES OF PASSAGE, The Literary Journal for Teenagers, (I, II, IV), Writes of Passage USA, Inc., 817 Broadway, 6th Floor, New York NY 10003. (212)473-7564. E-mail: wpusa@aol.com. Website: http://www.writes.org. Editor: Laura Hoffman. Fiction Editor: Wendy Mass. Magazine: 5½×8½; 100 pages; 60 lb. offset paper; 10 pt. cover; illustrations/photos only on cover; no artwork within magazine. "*Writes of Passage* is designed to publish the creative writing (poems and short stories) of teenagers across the country. We review work from Senior high school and Junior high school students across the country on all topics." Now *Writes of Passage* also publishes submissions on "the largest teen website on the Internet." Semiannually. Estab. 1994. Circ. 2,000.

Needs: "We accept short stories on all topics written by preteens and teens." Adventure, children's/juvenile (10-12 years), ethnic/multicultural, experimental, fantasy, feminist, gay, historical, horror, humor/satire, lesbian, literary, mainstream/contemporary, mystery/suspense, psychic/supernatural/occult, regional, religious/inspirational, romance, science fiction, sports, westerns, young adult/teen. Receives 50 unsolicited mss/month. Accepts 50 mss/issue; 100 mss/year. "Issues are published in the fall and spring so publication of mss depend on when they are received." Length: 2,000 words average; 5,000 words maximum. Publishes short shorts. Also publishes poetry.

How to Contact: Send complete ms with a cover letter. Teachers may submit the work of their students as a group. Include bio with SASE and contact information. Send SASE for reply or send disposable copy of the ms. Simultaneous and electronic submissions OK. Sample copy for $6.

Payment/Terms: Pays 2 contributor's copies; additional copies $6 for each copy up to 10; 10 or more copies are $5 each. Rights revert back to the author.

Advice: "Write from your heart. We are looking for original work, clearly written, poignant subject matter for teen readers. We are interested in more short stories, particularly about teens."

WRITING FOR OUR LIVES, Creative Expressions in Writing by Women, (I, IV), Running Deer Press, 647 N. Santa Cruz Ave., Annex, Los Gatos CA 95032. (408)354-8604. Editor: Janet M. McEwan. Magazine: 5¼×8¼; 80 pages; 70 lb. recycled white paper; 80 lb. recycled cover. "*Writing For Our Lives* is a periodical which serves as a vessel for poems, short fiction, stories, letters, autobiographies, and journal excerpts from the life stories, experiences and spiritual journeys of women. Audience is women and friends of women." Semiannually. Estab. 1992. Circ. 700.

Needs: Ethnic/multicultural, experimental, feminist, humor/satire, lesbian, literary, translations, "autobiographical, breaking personal or historical silence on any concerns of women's lives. *Women writers only, please*. We have no preannounced themes." Receives 15-20 unsolicited mss/month. Accepts 10 mss/issue; 20 mss/year. Publishes ms 2-24 months after acceptance. Recently published work by Shirley Booker Ruh, Julie K. Trevelyan, Anjali Banerjee, Padma Susan Moyer and JoAnne Yolanda Hernandez. Length: 2,100 words maximum. Publishes short shorts. Also publishes poetry. Sometimes critiques or comments on rejected mss.

How to Contact: Send complete ms with a cover letter. "Publication dates are May and November. Closing dates for mss are 2/15 and 8/15. Initial report immediate; next report, if any, in 1-18 months." Send 2 SASE's for reply, and one of them must be sufficient for return of ms if desired. Simultaneous and reprint submissions OK. Sample copy for $6 (in California add 7.75% sales tax), $8 overseas. Fiction guidelines for #10 SASE.

Payment/Terms: Pays 2 contributor's copies; additional copies for 50% discount and 1 year subscription at 50% discount. Acquires one-time rights in case of reprints and first worldwide English language serial rights.

Advice: "I welcome your writing. I like many more pieces than I can print. If I don't select yours this time, try again!"

THE WRITING ON THE WALL, (I), P.O. Box 8, Orono ME 04473. E-mail: scottp@maine.maine.edu. Editor: Scott D. Peterson. Magazine: 8½×11; 22 pages; 70 lb. paper; 70 lb. cover; illustrations and photographs. "Our goal is to combat the negativity of the mass media, build community, and provide a voice for the 20-something generation." Semiannually. Estab. 1992. Circ. 100.

Needs: Literary, mainstream/contemporary. Will also consider novel excerpts. List of upcoming themes available for SASE. Receives 20-30 unsolicited mss/month. Accepts 3-4 mss/issue; 6-8 mss/

year. Publishes ms 2-3 months after acceptance. Recently published work by Stephen Stathis, Anne Helen Jupiter and Julie Krikorian Eshbaugh. Length: 2,000 words preferred; 500 words minimum; 3,000 words maximum. Publishes short shorts. Publishes literary essays, literary criticism and poetry. Sometimes critiques or comments on rejected mss.

How to Contact: Send complete ms with a cover letter. Include estimated word count and bio (less than 50 words). Reports in 2 weeks on queries; 3 months on mss. Send SASE for reply, return of ms or send a disposable copy of ms. Reprint and electronic submissions (disk or modem) OK. Sample copy for $3. Fiction guidelines for #10 SASE.

Payment/Terms: Pays 2 contributor's copies; additional copies for $2. Acquires one-time rights.

Advice: "We're looking for fiction that edifies as well as entertains—especially stories that send readers away with a sense of positive action. Write honestly and examine your stuff for TV sitcom or movie plot/characters."

XAVIER REVIEW, (I, II), Xavier University, 7325 Palmetto St., Box 110C, New Orleans LA 70125-1098. (504)483-7303. Fax: (504)486-2385. E-mail: rskinner@xavier.xula.edu. Editor: Thomas Bonner, Jr. Managing Editor: Robert E. Skinner. Magazine: 6×9; 75 pages; 50 lb. paper; 12 pt. CS1 cover; photographs. Magazine of "poetry/fiction/nonfiction/reviews (contemporary literature) for professional writers/libraries/colleges/universities." Semiannually. Estab. 1980. Circ. 500.

Needs: Contemporary, ethnic, experimental, historical (general), literary, Latin American, prose poem, Southern, religious, serialized/excerpted novel, translations. Receives 30 unsolicited fiction mss/month. Accepts 2 mss/issue; 4 mss/year. Does not read mss during the summer months. Recently published work by Randall Ivey, Rita Porteau, John Goldfine and Christine Wiltz. Length: 10-15 pages. Publishes literary criticism, literary essays and poetry. Occasionally critiques rejected mss.

How to Contact: Send complete ms. Include 150-word bio and brief list of publications. SASE. Reports in 8-10 weeks. Sample copy for $5.

Payment/Terms: Pays 2 contributor's copies.

XIB, (II), P.O. Box 262112, San Diego CA 92126. Editor: Tolek. Magazine: 7×8½; 68 pages; offset basis 70 paper; 12 point gloss cover; 25-30 illustrations; 15-20 b&w photos. "Audience mostly of poets, hence prefer fiction concise and compact, more like prose-poem form. Published every 9 months. Estab. 1991. Circ. 300.

Needs: Ethnic/multicultural, experimental, fantasy (science fantasy, sword and sorcery), feminist, gay, historical (general), horror, humor/satire, lesbian, literary, psychic/supernatural/occult, regional, science fiction (hard science, soft/sociological), senior citizen/retirement, translations. No childrens or romance. Receives 5-10 unsolicited mss/month. Accepts 2-4 mss/issue; 4-8 mss/year. Publishes ms 1-6 months after acceptance. Recently pubilshed work by Michael Lee Smith, John Goldfine, Keith Dawson and Albert Huffstickler. Length: 1,000 words average; 1,500 words maximum. Publishes short shorts. Also publishes poetry. Seldom critiques or comments on rejected mss.

How to Contact: Send complete ms with a cover letter. Reports in 2-3 weeks. Send SASE (or IRC) for reply, return of ms or send a disposable copy of ms. Sample copy for $5. Fiction guidelines for #10 SASE. Please make checks payable to *Tolek*.

Payment/Terms: Pays 1 contributor's copy; additional copies for $3 each plus $2 s&h. Acquires one-time rights.

XTREME, The Magazine of Extremely Short Fiction, P.O. Box 678383, Orlando FL 32867-8383. E-mail: rhowiley@aol.com. Editor: Rho Wiley. Magazine: 8½×11; 4 pages; heavy bond paper and cover. "Xtreme, the magazine of extremely short fiction, publishes fiction of EXACTLY 250 words. Fiction is considered on the basis of merit only. We feel that the 250 word format affords an opportunity for all writers to push the limits of the language." Semiannually. Estab. 1993. Circ. 500.

Needs: Humor/satire, literary, mainstream/contemporary. Receives 25-30 unsolicited mss/month. Accepts 10 mss/issue; 20 mss/year. Publishes ms 6 months after acceptance. Length: exactly 250 words. Sometimes critiques or comments on rejected mss.

How to Contact: Send complete ms with a cover letter. Reports in 6 weeks on queries; up to 6 months on mss. Send SASE for reply or return of ms. No simultaneous submissions. Sample copy for 9×12 SAE and 2 first-class stamps. Fiction guidelines included with sample copy.

Payment/Terms: Pays 3 contributor's copies for first North American serial rights.

Advice: Looks for "the ability to tell a complete story in the boundaries of the 250 word format. A succinct use of the language always stands out. Work with the form. Try to push the limits of what can happen in only 250 words."

‡THE YALOBUSHA REVIEW, The Literary Journal of the University of Mississippi, University of Mississippi, P.O. Box 186, University MS 38677-0186. (601)232-7439. E-mail: yalobush@s unset.backbone.olemiss.edu. Editors change each year. Magazine: 5½×8½; 130 pages; 60 lb. off-white; card cover stock. "We look for high-quality fiction, poetry, and creative essays; and we seek a balance of regional and national writers." Annually. Estab. 1995. Circ. 500.

Needs: Literary. "No genre or formula fiction." List of upcoming themes available for SASE. Receives 30 unsolicited mss/month. Accepts 6 mss/issue. Does not read mss April through August. Recently published work by Larry Brown, Cynthia Shearer and Eric Miles Williamson. Length: 15 pages average; 35 pages maximum. Publishes short shorts. Also publishes literary essays and poetry. Sometimes critiques or comments on rejected mss.

How to Contact: Send complete ms with a cover letter. Reports in 1 month on queries; reporting time on mss varies. Send SASE for reply, return of ms or send a disposable copy of ms. Electronic submissions OK. Fiction guidelines for #10 SASE.

Payment/Terms: Pays 2 contributor's copies and $100 to the Editor's Choice winner for each issue. Pays on publication. Acquires first North American serial rights.

Advice: "We look for writers with a strong, distinct voice and good stories to tell." Would like to see more "good endings!"

YELLOW SILK: Journal of Erotic Arts, (II), Verygraphics, Box 6374, Albany CA 94706. (510)644-4188. Editor/Publisher: Lily Pond. "We are interested in nonpornographic erotic literature: joyous, mad, musical, elegant, passionate. 'All persuasions; no brutality' is our editorial policy. Literary excellence is a priority; innovative forms are welcomed, as well as traditional ones." Quarterly. Estab. 1981.

Needs: Comics, erotica, ethnic, experimental, fantasy, feminist/lesbian, gay, humor/satire, literary, prose poem, science fiction and translations. No "blow-by-blow" descriptions; no hackneyed writing except when used for satirical purposes. Nothing containing brutality. Accepts 4-5 mss/issue; 16-20 mss/year. Published work by Angela Carter, Robert Silverberg, Louise Erdrich and Galway Kinnell. Length: no preference. Occasionally critiques rejected ms.

How to Contact: Send complete ms with SASE and include short, *personal* bio notes. No queries. No pre-published material. No simultaneous submissions. Name, address and phone number on each page. Submissions on disk OK *with* hard copy only. Reports in 3 months on mss. Publishes ms up to 3 years after acceptance. Sample copy for $7.50.

Payment/Terms: Pays 3 contributor's copies plus competitive payment on publication for all periodical and anthology rights for one year following publication, at which time rights revert back to author; and nonexclusive reprint, electronic and anthology rights for the duration of the copyright.

Advice: "Read, read, read! Including our magazine—plus Nabokov, Ntozake Shange, Rimbaud, Virginia Woolf, William Kotzwinkle, James Joyce. Then send in your story! Trust that the magazine/editor will not rip you off—they don't. As they say, 'find your own voice,' then trust it. Most manuscripts I reject appear to be written by people without great amounts of writing experience. It takes years (frequently) to develop your work to publishable quality; it can take many rewrites on each individual piece. I also see many approaches to sexuality (for my magazine) that are trite and not fresh. The use of language is not original, and the people do not seem real. However, the gems come too, and what a wonderful moment that is. Please don't send me anything with blue eye shadow."

ZERO HOUR, "Where Culture Meets Crime," (I), Box 766, Seattle WA 98111. (206)621-8829. Editor: Jim Jones. Newsprint paper; illustrations and photos. "We are interested in fringe culture. We publish fiction, poetry, essays, confessions, photos, illustrations and interviews, for young, politically left audience interested in current affairs, non-mainstream music, art, culture." Semiannually. Estab. 1988. Circ. 3,000.

Needs: Confessions, erotica, ethnic, experimental, feminist, gay, humor/satire, psychic/supernatural/occult and translations. "Each issue revolves around an issue in contemporary culture: cults and fanaticism, addiction, pornography, etc." No romance, inspirational, juvenile/young, sports. Upcoming theme: "Death and Dying" (March 1997). Receives 5 unsolicited mss/month. Accepts 3 mss/issue; 9 mss/year. Publishes ms 2-3 months after acceptance. Published work by Jesse Bernstein, Rebecca Brown, Denise Ohio and Vaginal Davis. Length: 1,200 words average; 400 words minimum; 5,000 words maximum. Publishes short shorts. Length: 400 words. Sometimes critiques rejected mss.

How to Contact: Query first. Reports in 2 weeks on queries; 1 month on mss. SASE. Simultaneous submissions OK. Sample copy for $3, 9×12 SAE and 5 first-class stamps. Fiction guidelines free. Reviews novels and short story collections.

Payment/Terms: Pays $25 per short story, $650 for novels for one-time rights. Sends galleys to author.

Advice: Looking for "straight-forward narrative prose—true-to-life experiences told about unique experiences or from an unusual perspective. Ask yourself does it fit our theme? Is it well written, from an unusual point of view or on an unexplored/underexplored topic?"

ZUZU'S PETALS QUARTERLY, (II), P.O. Box 156, Whitehall PA 18052. E-mail: zuzu@lehigh.net. Editor: T. Dunn. Internet magazine. "Arouse the senses; stimulate the mind." Estab. 1992.
● *Zuzu's Petals* is now an Internet magazine at http://www.lehigh.net/zuzu/.

Needs: Ethnic/multicultural, feminist, gay, humor/satire, lesbian, literary, regional. No "romance, sci-fi, the banal, TV style plotting." Receives 110 unsolicited mss/month. Accepts 1-3 mss/issue; 4-12 mss/year. Publishes ms 4-6 months after acceptance. Agented fiction 10%. Published work by Norah Labiner, Jean Erhardt and LuAnn Jacobs. Length: 1,000 words minimum; 6,000 words maximum. Publishes short shorts. Length: 350 words. Also publishes literary essays, literary criticism and poetry. Sometimes critiques or comments on rejected mss.

How to Contact: Send complete ms with a cover letter. Include estimated word count and list of publications. Reports in 2 weeks on queries; 2 weeks to 2 months on mss. Send SASE (or IRC) for reply, return of ms or send a disposable copy of ms. Simultaneous and electronic submissions OK. Back issue for $5. Fiction guidelines free. Reviews novels and short story collections. Send to Doug DuCap, Reviewer.

Advice: Looks for "strong plotting and a sense of vision. Original situations and true to life reactions."

ZYZZYVA, the last word: west coast writers & artists, (II, IV), 41 Sutter St., Suite 1400, San Francisco CA 94104. (415)752-4393. Fax: (415)752-4391. E-mail: zyzzyvainc@aol.com. Editor: Howard Junker. Magazine: 6×9; 160 pages; graphics; photos. "Literate" magazine. Quarterly. Estab. 1985. Circ. 3,500.

Needs: Contemporary, experimental, literary, prose poem. West Coast US writers only. Receives 400 unsolicited mss/month. Accepts 5 fiction mss/issue; 20 mss/year. Agented fiction: 10%. Recently published work by Jon Billman, Tess Gallagher and Kim R. Stafford; published new writers within the last year. Length: varies. Also publishes literary essays.

How to Contact: Send complete ms. "Cover letters are of minimal importance." Reports in 2 weeks on mss. SASE. No simultaneous or reprint submissions. Sample copy for $5. Fiction guidelines on masthead page.

Payment/Terms: Pays $50 on acceptance for first North American serial rights.

Advice: "Keep the faith."

International literary magazines

The following is a list of literary publications from countries outside the U.S. and Canada that accept or buy short fiction in English (or in the universal languages of Esperanto or Ido).

Before sending a manuscript to a publication in another country, it's a good idea to query first for information on the magazine's needs and methods of submission. Send for sample copies or try visiting the main branch of your local library, a nearby college library or bookstore to find a copy.

All correspondence to markets outside your own country must include International Reply Coupons, if you want a reply or material returned. You may find it less expensive to send copies of your manuscript for the publisher to keep and just enclose a return postcard with one IRC for a reply. Keep in mind response time is slow for many overseas publishers, but don't hesitate to send a reply postcard with IRC to check the status of your submission. You can obtain IRCs from the main branch of your local post office. The charge for one in U.S. funds is $1.05.

THE ABIKO LITERARY PRESS (ALP), 8-1-8 Namiki, Abiko-Shi, Chiba-Ken 270-11 Japan. Phone/fax: (0471)84-7904. Editor: Anna Livia Plulaurelbelle. Fiction Editor: Laurel Sycks. Published irregularly. Circ. 500. Publishes 10 stories/issue. "We are a semi-bilingual (Japanese/English) magazine for Japanese and foreigners living in Japan." Needs: artwork, photos, James Joyce's *Finnegan's Wake* criticism and stories influenced by "The Lost Generation" and Joyce. "A story submitted in both English and Japanese receives special consideration. I look for something that I can't forget after reading." Length: 3,000 words average; 5,000 words maximum. Send manuscript with SAE and IRCs. Pays 1 contributor's copy; writer pays postage. Follow proper format and submission procedures. Sponsors contest ($100,000). Write for details. Include IRC for response. 600-page sample copy for $15 plus $15 postage.

AQUARIUS, Flat 10, Room-A, 116 Sutherland Ave., Maida-Vale, London W92QP England. Editor: Eddie Linden. Semiannual. Circ. 3,000. Publishes 5 stories/issue. Interested in humor/satire, literary, prose poem and serialized/excerpted novels. "We publish prose and poetry and reviews." Length: 1,000 words minimum. Payment is by agreement. "We only suggest changes. Most stories are taken on merit." Price in UK £5 plus postage and packing; in US $18 plus $3 postage. "We like writers who buy the magazine to get an idea of what we publish."

BBR MAGAZINE, P.O. Box 625, Sheffield, S1 3GY, UK. Editor: Chris Reed. Annually. Circ. 3,000. Publishes 20,000-30,000 words/issue. "*Back Brain Recluse*, the award-winning British fiction magazine, actively seeks new fiction that ignores genre pigeonholes. We tread the thin line between experimental speculative fiction and avant-garde literary fiction. We are currently reading for issue #24, for which we will pay £10 ($15) per 1,000 words on publication. Familiarity with the magazine is strongly advised. Enclose a SASE for the return of your manuscript if it is not accepted. We are unable to reply to writers who do not send return postage. We recommend two IRCs plus disposable ms for non-UK submissions. One US$ is an acceptable (and cheaper!) alternative to IRCs. Please send all submissions to Chris Reed, BBR, P.O. Box 625, Sheffield S1 3GY, UK. We aim to reply to all submissions within 2 months, but sometimes circumstances beyond our control may cause us to take longer. Please enclose SAE if enquiring about a manuscript's status. No responsibility can be accepted for loss or damage to unsolicited material, howsoever caused." Sample copy available in US for $10 from BBR, % Anne Marsden, 31192 Paseo Amapola, San Juan Capistrano CA 92675-2227. (Checks payable to Anne Marsden).

CAMBRENSIS, 41 Heol Fach, Cornelly, Bridgend, Mid-Glamorgan, CF33 4LN Wales. Editor: Arthur Smith. Quarterly. Circ. 500. "Devoted solely to the short story form, featuring short stories by writers born or resident in Wales or with some Welsh connection; receives grants from the Welsh Arts' Council and the Welsh Writers' Trust; uses artwork—cartoons, line-drawings, sketches etc." Length: 2,500 words maximum. Writers receive 3 copies of magazine. Writer has to have some connection with Wales. SAE and IRCs or similar should be enclosed "Air mail" postage to avoid long delay. Send IRCs for a sample copy. Subscriptions via Blackwell's Periodicals, P.O. Box 40, Hythe Bridge Street, Oxford, OX1 2EU, UK or Swets & Zeitlinger B V, P.O. Box 800, 2160 S Z Lisse, Holland.

‡THE CARIBBEAN WRITER, (IV), The University of the Virgin Islands, RR 02, Box 10,000—Kingshill, St. Croix, Virgin Islands 00850. (809)778-0246. Editor: Erika Waters. Magazine: 6×9; 190 pages; 60 lb. paper; glossy cover stock; illustrations and photos. "*The Caribbean Writer* is an international magazine with a Caribbean focus. The Caribbean should be central to the work, or the work should reflect a Caribbean heritage, experience or perspective." Annually. Estab. 1987. Circ. 1,500. Receives 400 unsolicited mss/year. Accepts 10 mss/issue. Length: 300 words minimum. Publishes poetry. Send complete ms with cover letter. "Blind submissions only. Send name, address and title of manuscript on separate sheet. Title only on manuscript. Manuscripts will not be considered unless this procedure is followed." Reports "once a year." SASE (or IRC). Simultaneous submissions OK. Sample copy for $5 and $2 postage. Fiction guidelines for SASE. Pays 2 contributor's copies. Acquires one-time rights. Annual prizes for best story ($400); for best poem ($250); $100 for first publication. Looks for "fiction which reflects a Caribbean heritage, experience or perspective."

CHAPMAN, 4 Broughton Place, Edinburgh EH1 3RX Scotland. Fiction Editor: Joy Hendry. Quarterly. Circ. 2,000. Publishes 4-6 stories/issue. "Founded in 1970, *Chapman*, Scotland's quality literary magazine, is a dynamic force in Scotland, publishing poetry, fiction, criticism, reviews; articles on theatre, politics, language and the arts." Length: 1,000 words minimum; 6,000 words maximum. Include SAE and return postage (or IRC) with submissions. Pays £9-50/page. Sample copy available for £3.70 (includes postage).

‡CREATIVE FORUM, Bahri Publications, 997A Gobindpuri Kalkaj, P.O. Box 4453, New Delhi 110019 India. Telephones: 011-6445710, 011-6448606. Fax: 91.11-6416116. Fiction Editor: U.S. Bahri. Circ. 1,800. Publishes 8-12 stories annually. "We accept short stories for our journal *Creative Forum* in addition to poetry and criticism on fiction and poetry (contemporary only). Novels/novellas accepted if suitable subsidy is forthcoming from the author." Length: 2,000-3,000 words. Pays in copies. Manuscripts should be "neatly typed and not beyond 200 sheets." Subscriptions $60 US. "Short stories accompanied with $50 US towards annual subscription of the journal are given preferential treatment and priority."

FRANK, An International Journal of Contemporary Writing and Art, 32 rue Edouard Vaillant, 93100 Montreuil, France. Editor: David Applefield. "Semiannual journal edited and published in Paris in English." Circ. 3,000. Publishes 20 stories/issue. "At *Frank*, we publish fiction, poetry, literary and art interviews, and translations. We like work that falls between existing genres and has social or political consciousness." Send IRC or $3 cash. Must be previously unpublished in English (world). Pays 2 copies and $10 (US)/printed page. "Send your most daring and original work. Be prepared to wait for long periods; some publishers will not answer or return manuscripts. At *Frank*, we like work that is not too parochial or insular, however, don't try to write for a 'French' market." Sample copy $10 (US/air mail included), $38 for 4 issues; guidelines available upon request. Subscriptions, inquiries, and an online edition of *Frank* available at http://www.paris-anglo.com.

THE FROGMORE PAPERS, 6 Vernon Rd., London N8 OQD United Kingdom. Fiction Editor: Jeremy Page. Semi-annual. Circ. 200. "A little magazine which publishes poetry, reviews, short stories and novel extracts, both traditional and experimental." Length: 1,000 words minimum; 3,000 words maximum. Pays in contributor's copies. "Study a sample copy before submission." Current issue available for 5 U.S. dollars (bills only) from: The Frogmore Press, 42 Morehall Ave., Folkestone, Kent CT19 4EF UK.

GHOSTS & SCHOLARS, Flat One, 36 Hamilton St., Hoole, Chester CH2 3JQ England. Fiction Editor: Rosemary Pardoe. Semiannually. Circ. 400. Publishes 6-7 stories/year. "Publishes fiction in the M.R. James tradition, and articles/discussion of same." Length: 2,000 words minimum; 8,000 words maximum. Pays in copies. "Submissions should be of ghost stories in the M.R. James tradition only. I will not consider other types of ghost stories." Sample copy for $7 cash (US) or £4 cheque (payable to R. Pardoe). Guidelines for SASE (overseas: 2 IRCs).

HORIZON, Stationsstraat 232A, 1770 Liedekerke Belgium. Fiction Editor: Johnny Haelterman. Semiannually. Circ. 100. Publishes several stories/issue. "*Horizon* is a cultural magazine for a general public, therefore fiction should be suitable for a general public. Length: 300 words minimum; 7,500 words maximum. "A realistic treatment is preferred but a touch of fantasy is sometimes acceptable. No extreme violence or sex." Enclose money or IRCs if you want your work back. Payment in Belgian funds for original fiction in Dutch only. No payment for fiction in other languages but the writers receive two copies in that case. English fiction can be translated into Dutch without payment (two copies). Submitting outside your country is mainly the same as in your own country, except that the postage costs are higher. Puns are usually not translatable, so avoid writing stories with an essential part based on puns if you want your work to be translated." Sample copy available for $8 (US).

HRAFNHOH, 32 Strŷd Ebeneser, Pontypridd, Mid Glamorgan CF37 5PB Wales. Fiction Editor: Joseph Biddulph. Circ. 200. Published irregularly. "Now worldwide and universal in scope. Suitable: fictionalized history, local history, family history. Explicitly Christian approach. Well-written stories or general prose opposed to abortion, human embryo experimentation and euthanasia particularly welcome. No payment made, but free copies provided. Be brief, use a lot of local colour and nature description, in a controlled, resonant prose or in dialect. Suitable work accepted in esperanto, français, español, and other languages, including Creole. "US stamps are of no use to me, but US banknotes acceptable." IRC will cover a brief response, but mss however small are expensive to return, so please send copy." Sample copy free.

HU (THE HONEST ULSTERMAN), 49 Main St., Greyabbey BT22 2NF, Northern Ireland. Fiction Editor: Tom Clyde. 3 times/year. Circ. 1,000. Publishes 1-4 stories/issue. "Northern Ireland's premier literary magazine. Prime focus is poetry, but continues to publish prose (story, novel extract). 3,000 words maximum. "Must include sufficient means of return (IRCs, etc.). If we decide to publish, an IBM-type floppy disk version would be very helpful." Writers receive small payment and two contributor's copies. For 4 issues send UK £14 airmail or sample issue US $7. "Contributors are strongly advised to read the magazine before submitting anything."

IMAGO, School of Media & Journalism, QUT, GPO Box 2434, Brisbane 4001 Australia. Contact: Dr. Philip Neilsen or Helen Horton. Published 3 times/year. Circ. 750. 30-50% fiction. *Imago* is a literary magazine publishing short stories, poetry, articles, interviews and book reviews. "While content of articles and interviews should have some relevance either to Queensland or to writing, stories and poems may be on any subject. The main requirement is good writing." Length: 1,000 words minimum; 3,000 words maximum; 2,000 words preferred. Pays on publication in accordance with Australia Council rates: short stories, $A90 minimum; articles, $A90 minimum; poems $A40; reviews, $A60. Also provides contributor's copy. "Contributions should be typed double-spaced on one side of the paper, each page bearing the title, page number and author's name. Name and address of the writer should appear on a cover page of longer mss, or on the back, or bottom, of single page submissions. A SAE and IRCs with sufficient postage to cover the contents should be sent for the return of ms or for notification of acceptance or rejection. No responsibility is assumed for the loss of or damage to unsolicited manuscripts." Sample copy available for $A7. Guidelines, as above, available on request.

INDIAN LITERATURE, Sahitya Akademi, National Academy of Letters, Rabindra Bhavan, 35 Ferozeshah Rd., New Delhi 110 001 India. Editor: Professor K. Sachidanandan. Circ. 4,100. Publishes 6 issues/year; 200 pages. "Presents creative work from 22 Indian languages including Indian English." Sample copy available for $7.

IRON MAGAZINE, (II), Iron Press, 5 Marden Ter., Cullercoats, North Shields, Tyne & Wear NE30 4PD England. Editor: Peter Mortimer. Circ. 1,000. Published 3 times/year. Publishes 14 stories/year. "Literary magazine of contemporary fiction, poetry, articles and graphics." Length: 6,000 words maximum. Pays approximately £10/page. No simultaneous submissions. Five poems, two stories/submission the limit. No submissions during July and August please. Sample copy for $10 (US) (no bills-no checks). "Please see magazine before submitting and don't submit to it before you're ready! Many stories submitted are obviously only of interest to the domestic market of the writer. Always try there first! And do try to find something out about the publication, or better, see a sample copy before submitting."

‡**ISLAND**, P.O. Box 210, Sandy Bay 7005 Australia. Contact: Editor. Quarterly. Circ. 1,000. Publishes 6 stories/issue. "*Island* is a quarterly of ideas, criticism, fiction and poetry." Length: 4,000 words maximum. Pays $100 (Australian) minimum. Send double-spaced laser print copy where possible. Include a brief cover letter and SASE. Sample copy available for $7.95 (Australian).

LA KANCERKLINIKO, (IV), 162 rue Paradis, 13006 Marseille France. Phone: 91-3752-15. Fiction Editor: Laurent Septier. Circ. 300. Quarterly. Publishes 40 pages of fiction annually. "An esperanto magazine which appears 4 times annually. Each issue contains 32 pages. *La Kancerkliniko* is a political and cultural magazine. General fiction, science fiction, etc. Short stories or very short novels. The short story (or the very short novel) must be written only in esperanto, either original or translation from any other language." Length: 15,000 words maximum. Pays in contributor's copies. Sample copy on request with 3 IRCs from Universal Postal Union.

LANDFALL/OXFORD UNIVERSITY PRESS, University of Otago Press, P.O. Box 56, Dunedin New Zealand. Editor: Chris Price. Publishes fiction, poetry, commentary and criticism. Length: maximum 10,000 words. Pays NZ $11 per page for fiction. "Without wishing to be unduly nationalist, we would normally give first preference to stories which contain some kind of New Zealand connection."

‡**THE LONSDALE—The International Quarterly of the Romantic Six**, VIP Meguro 802, 4-1-16 Shimo-Meguro, Meguro-Ku, Tokyo 153 Japan. Fiction Editor: Michael L. Jabri-Pickett. Quarterly. Circ. 1,500-2,000. "*The Lonsdale* deals with six writers, exclusively—W. Blake, W. Wordsworth, S.T. Coleridge, Lord Byron, P.B. Shelley and J. Keats. Unsolicited, scholarly essays, criticisms, and the like will be considered. Poetry, fiction, book reviews and interviews may also be submitted, but must be relevant. Vignettes rather than short stories." Length: 250 words minimum; 5,000 words maximum. Pays in copies. "Be sure to understand the publication's intended audience." Sample copy available upon request.

MANUSHI, A Journal About Women and Society, C/202 Lajpat Nagar 1, New Delhi 110024 India. Editor: Madhu Kishwar. Bimonthly. Circ. up to 8,000. Publishes one fiction story/issue. "*Manushi* is a magazine devoted to human rights and women's rights issues with a focus on the Indian subcontinent and the situation of Indian communities settled overseas. It includes poetry, fiction, historical and sociological studies, analysis of contemporary politics, review of mass media and literature, biographies, profiles and histories of various movements for social change." Length: 12,000 words maximum. Duplicate mss preferred.

MATTOID, Centre for Research in Cultural Communication, Deakin University, Geelong, Victoria 3217 Australia. Fiction Editor: Prof. Brian Edwards. Published 3 times/year. Circ. 650. Publishes 5-7 stories/issue. "*Mattoid* publishes short fiction, poetry, essays, interviews, reviews and graphics. At present we are running a series of special issues ('The Body,' 'Revisions in Romanticism,' 'Crossing Cultures,' 'Masculinism') but we are interested in innovative fiction." Length: 300 words minimum; 3,000 words maximum. Pays in copies. "Our main criterion is interest value, though we are pleased to see innovative/experimental writing that is well-crafted. Take some care with the choice of destination. Research the writing. Include a brief biographical statement." Single copies available for $18 overseas. Annual subscription (3 issues) $40.

‡**NEW CONTRAST**, P.O. Box 3841, Cape Town 8000 South Africa. Contact: Fiction Editor. Quarterly. Circ. 500. Publishes 2-3 stories/issue. "We publish short fiction, film scripts (extracts), plays (extracts), reviews and occasional pieces of nonfiction. The bulk of our journal is poetry, however." Length: no limit; "subject to the editor's discretion." Pays a book voucher worth R50 (50 rands) if writer already subscribes and a year's gift subscription if writer is not already subscriber. Prefers disk submissions with hard copy and any special features or instructions clearly marked. "If you are submitting on disk, the first line of each new paragraph should have a 5mm indent (please do not use spaces or the Tab key). If you want to submit your material via e-mail, please be sure to explain any special layout features which get lost in the process." Writer's guidelines available for SAE and IRCs.

NEW HOPE INTERNATIONAL, 20 Werneth Ave., Gee Cross, Hyde SK14 5NL England. Fiction Editor: Gerald England. Circ. 750. Publishes 2-6 stories annually. Publishes "mainly poetry. Fiction used must be essentially literary but not pretentious. Only short fiction used (max 2,000 words). "Most submissions are too long and often too essentially American for an international audience. A brief covering letter should be sent. 1 IRC covers a reply if mss is disposable (please state) otherwise 1 IRC per 2 sheets. Don't send return envelope or US postage stamps." Payment: 1 complimentary copy.

Guidelines available for IRC. Sample copy £3. Payment in sterling only payable to "G. England." Send cash equivalent in any currency or International Giro (available from post offices worldwide).

‡**NEW WELSH REVIEW**, Chapter Arts Centre, Market Rd., Cardiff Wales CF5 1QE UK. Editor: Robin Reeves. "*NWR*, a literary quarterly, publishes stories, poems and critical essays." Accepts 16-20 mss/year. Pays "cheque on publication and one free copy." Length: 2,000-3,000 words.

‡**OASIS**, Oasis Books, 12 Stevenage Rd., London SW6 6ES United Kingdom. Editor: Ian Robinson. Published 6 times/year. Circ. 400. Publishes 1 story/issue. "Innovative, experimental fiction." Length: 1,800 words maximum. Pays in copies. "Have a look at a copy of the magazine before submitting." Sample copy available for $2.50 check (made payable to Robert Vas Dias) and 3 IRCs.

PARIS TRANSCONTINENTAL, A Magazine of Short Stories, Institut des Pays Anglophones, Sorbonne Nouvelle, 5, rue de l'Ecole de Médecine, 75006 Paris, France. Editor-in-Chief: Claire Larrière. Assistant Editors: Albert Russo and Devorah Goldberg. Semiannually. Circ. 500. Publishes short stories exclusively; no poetry, nonfiction or artwork. "*Paris Transcontinental*, purports to be a forum for writers of excellent stories whose link is the English language, wherever it is spoken. It purports to introduce the best among today's authors, whether they hail from Europe or the Americas, from Oceania, Africa or Asia. Average length: 2,000-4,000 words maximum. "Submitters should send us no more than 3 unpublished stories at a time, along with a few lines about themselves and their work (approx. 100 words), one IRC to let them know of our decision, and *extra* IRCs (at least 3) for the return of their manuscripts. (No stamps please!)" Pays 2 contributor's copies. "Have an authentic voice and be professional. Write with your gut and read from all quarters. Author's featured include Stephen Dixon, Herbert Liebman, Jayanta Mahapatra, Joyce Carol Oates, Albert Russo, Alan Sillitoe and Michael Wilding." Send IRC for guidelines. For a sample copy, send a check for FF75 payable on a French bank, or $11 drawn on your own local bank.

PLANET-THE WELSH INTERNATIONALIST, P.O. Box 44, Aberystwyth, Ceredigion, Cymru/Wales UK. Fiction Editor: John Barnie. Bimonthly. Circ. 1,300. Publishes 1-2 stories/issue. "A literary/cultural/political journal centered on Welsh affairs but with a strong interest in minority cultures in Europe and elsewhere." Length: 1,500-4,000 words maximum. No submissions returned unless accompanied by an SAE. Writers submitting from abroad should send at least 3 IRCs. Writers receive 1 contributor's copy. Payment is at the rate of £40 per 1,000 words (in the currency of the relevant country if the author lives outside the UK). "We do not look for fiction which necessarily has a 'Welsh' connection, which some writers assume from our title. We try to publish a broad range of fiction and our main criterion is quality. Try to read copies of any magazine you submit to. Don't write out of the blue to a magazine which might be completely inappropriate to your work. Recognize that you are likely to have a high rejection rate, as magazines tend to favor writers from their own countries." Sample copy: cost (to USA & Canada) £2.87. Writers' guidelines for SAE.

THE PLAZA, A Space for Global Human Relations, U-Kan Inc., Yoyogi 2-32-1, Shibuya-ku, Tokyo 151, Japan. Tel: (81)3-3379-3881. Fax: (81)3-3379-3882. E-mail: u-kan@u-kan.co.jp. Website: http://u-kan.co.jp/~u-kan. Editor: Leo Shunji Nishida. Fiction Editor: Roger Lakhani. Quarterly. Circ. 5,000. Publishes about 3 stories/issue. "*The Plaza* is an intercultural and bilingual magazine (English and Japanese). Our focus is the 'essence of being human.' All works are published in both Japanese and English (translations by our staff if necessary). The most important criteria is artistic level. We look for works that reflect simply 'being human.' Stories on intercultural (not international) relations are desired. *The Plaza* is devoted to offering a spiritual *Plaza* where people around the world can share their creative work. We introduce contemporary writers and artists as our generation's contribution to the continuing human heritage." Length: Less than 1,000 words, minimalist short stories are welcomed. Send complete ms with cover letter. Sample copy and guidelines free.

‡**PLURILINGUAL EUROPE/EUROPE PLURILINGUE**, % Nadine Dormoy, 44, rue Perronet, 92200 Neuilly, France. Fiction Editors: Nadine Dormoy, Albert Russo. Semiannually. Circ. 1,000. 20% of published content/issue is fiction. "Fiction in English must involve or be set in one of the 15 nations of the European Union. "Plurilingual Europe" is a pluridisciplinary journal that purports to foster understanding between the countries of the EU. All articles, essays and literary work should be written

---

SENDING TO A COUNTRY other than your own? Be sure to send International Reply Coupons instead of stamps for replies or return of your manuscript.

in any of the EU's 12 official languages. High specialization is required for the non-literary material. Excellence in every field always considered." Length: 500 words minimum; 3,000 words maximum. Pays 2 contributor's copies. "Have a good knowledge of the country's customs they describe or at least an original viewpoint of that country and its people. Recent contributors: George Steiner, Umberto Eco, Hugo Claus, Albert Russo, Jacques Darras, Renzo Titone, Eduardo Lourenço, etc." Subscription rate: US $22 (for 2 issues, postage included). U.S. check made out and sent to Liliane Lazar, 37 Hill Lane, Roslyn Heights, NY 11517, U.S.A. Sample copy for 6 IRCs; send to French address.

‡THE PRAGUE REVIEW, Bohemia's Journal of International Literature, Prague Publishers Group, V jámě 7, 110 00 Prague 1, Czech Republic. (0042)(2)90000412. Fax: (0042)(2)90000413. E-mail: revue@terminal.cz. Editor: Jason Penazzi-Russell. Fiction Editors: Max Munson and David Leslie Conhaim. Magazine: 130 pages; 80 weight paper; 180 weight cover stock with dust jacket; illustrations and photos. "*The Prague Revue* is Bohemia's English language, international quarterly of contemporary fiction, poetry, performance text and nonfiction. We will publish any genre. Editorial decisions are based solely on the quality of submissions. Our quarterly English language issue brings Central European writers together with international writers for world exposure. We also publish non-English anthologies to bring the works to greater audiences." Quarterly. Estab. 1995. Circ. 1,500. Recipient of a grant from the Czech Ministry of Culture. Member of the Prague Publishers Group. Length: 6,000 words average; 10,000 words maximum. Pays $5-150 on acceptance "for those pieces which are also selected for our foreign language issues" and 2 contributor's copies; additional copies for $3. Submit complete ms with a cover letter. Include estimated word count, 1-paragraph bio, Social Security number and list of publications. SASE for reply or send a disposable copy of the ms. Reports in 3 weeks on queries; 2 months on mss. Simultaneous submissions, reprints and electronic submissions OK. Sample copy available for $7. Fiction guidelines free. "We keep an eye out for pieces which would contribute also to our foreign language anthologies—particularly our Czech language annual. Prague themes do not contribute to the piece's chances for publication."

‡PURPLE PATCH, 8 Beaconview House, Beaconview Rd., West Bromwich B71 3PL England. Fiction Editor: Geoff Stevens. Quarterly. Publishes 1-2 stories/issue. "Prefer a literary style. Short pieces only. Bulk of publication is poetry and poetry magazine reviews." Length: 50-1,000 words maximum. Pays contributor's copies to UK writers only. "Send a short letter introducing yourself. Enclose enough postage (IRC) for reply or return of mss. Sample copy for 5 dollar bill (no checks) or £1."

QUADRANT, P.O. Box 1495, Collingwood, Victoria 3066 Australia. Fiction Editor: Mr. Les Murray. Monthly. Circ. 6,000. Publishes 1-2 stories/issue. "Magazine of current affairs, culture, politics, economics, the arts, literature, ideas; stories: general and varied." Length: 800 words minimum; 5,000 words maximum. Pays contributor's copies and a minimum of $100 (Australian). For sample copy "write to us, enclosing cheque for $8 (Australian) or equivalent."

REDOUBT, Faculty of Communication, University of Canberra, P.O. Box 1, Belconnen, ACT 2616, Australia. Contact: Managing Editor. Circ. 300. Publishes 10 stories/issue. "Literary magazine—short poems, stories, reviews, articles, b&w graphics. All types of fiction welcome—quality is the main criterion." Length: 2,000 words maximum. "For reply and/or return of manuscript, enclose SAE and IRCs; do not send original." Currently unable to pay. Overseas contributors receive complimentary copy and one-year subscription (2 issues). "Read the magazine to get a feel for the kind of thing we publish. Read the guidelines printed in the magazine or send request with SAE and IRC to the above address. Provide a short biography and your name on every page of the ms. Be prepared to wait for an answer—basically, if you're rejected you'll hear fairly quickly; if held over for consideration it can take months. We make no distinction between local and distant mss. The SAE is always a problem—international postal coupons are the answer." Current issue is available for $8.50 (Australian) (back issues for $5 Australian); "please include extra for postage and packing." Guidelines are printed in the magazine, or can be sent separately on application to the above address.

‡SCARP, New Arts & Writing, % Faculty of Creative Arts, University of Wollongong, Northfields Ave., Wollongong Australia. Editor: Ron Pretty. Circ. 1,000. Publishes 3-6 fiction ms annually. Published twice a year. "We look for fiction in a contemporary idiom, even if it uses a traditional form. Preferred length: 2,000 words. We're looking for energy, impact, quality." Payment: $80 (Australian); contributor's copies supplied. "Submit to reach us in April and/or August. Include SASE. In Australia the beginning writer faces stiff competition—the number of paying outlets is not increasing, but the number of capable writers is."

SEPIA, Poetry & Prose Magazine, Kawabata Press, Knill Cross House, Knill Cross, Millbrook, Nr Torpoint, Cornwall England. Editor-in-Chief: Colin David Webb. Published 3 times/year. "Magazine for those interested in modern un-clichéd work." Contains 32 pages/issue. Length: 200-4,000 words (for short stories). Pays 1 contributor's copy. Always include SAE with IRCs. Send $1 for sample copy and guidelines. Subscription $5; "no cheques!"

‡**SOL MAGAZINE**, 24 Fowler Close, Southchurch, Southend-On-Sea, Essex SS1 2RD United Kingdom. Fiction Editor: Malcolm E. Wright. Semiannual. Circ. 400. Publishes 6 stories/issue. "*Sol* is a poetry magazine that publishes stories of a non-generic type, but also publishes articles, reviews, letters, etc." Length: 500 words minimum; 5,000 maximum. Pays in copies. "Suggest one story at a time. Please ask for submission guidelines. Send a disposable manuscript with a small SAE for reply." Sample copy available for $5 (cash, no foreign checks). Writer's guidelines available for small SAE.

STAND MAGAZINE, 179 Wingrove Rd., Newcastle Upon Tyne, NE4 9DA England. Fiction Editor: Lorna Tracy. Circ. 4,500. Quarterly. Averages 16-20 stories/year. "*Stand* is an international quarterly publishing poetry, short stories, reviews, criticism and translations." Length: 5,000 words maximum. Payment: £25 per 1,000 words of prose on publication (or in US dollars); contributor's copies. "Read copies of the magazine before submitting. Enclose sufficient IRCs for return of mss/reply. No more than 6 poems or 2 short stories at any one time. Avoid specific genre writing—e.g. science fiction, travel, etc. Should not be under consideration elsewhere." Sponsors biennial short competition: First prize, £1,500. Send 2 IRCs for information. Sample copy: $6.50. Guidelines on receipt of 2 IRCs/SASE (U.K. stamps).

STAPLE, Tor Cottage 81, Cavendish Rd., Matlock DE4 3HD U.K.. Fiction Editor: Don Measham. Published 3 times/year. Circ. up to 600. Publishes up to 50% fiction. *Staple* is "about 90 pages, perfect-bound; beautifully designed and produced. Stories used by *Staple* have ranged from social realism (through autobiography, parody, prequel, parable) to visions and hallucinations. We don't use unmodified genre fiction, i.e. adventure, crime or westerns. We are interested in extracts from larger works—provided author does the extraction." Length: 200 words minimum; 5,000 words maximum. Adequate IRCs and large envelope for return, if return is required. Otherwise IRC for decision only. Pays complimentary copy plus subscription for US contributors. Get a specimen copy of one of the issues with strong prose representation. Send $10 for airmail dispatch, $5 for surface mail. The monograph series *Staple First Editions* is a biennial. IRC for details. Please note that *Staple* requires stories to be previously unpublished worldwide.

‡**TAKAHE**, P.O. Box 13-335, Christchurch, New Zealand. Editors: Isa Moynihan, Bernadette Hall and Cassandra Fusco. "A literary magazine which appears three or four times a year, and publishes short stories and poetry by both established and emerging writers. The publisher is the Takahe Collective Trust, a charitable trust formed by established writers to help new writers and get them into print. While insisting on correct British spelling (or recognised spellings in foreign languages), smart quotes, and at least internally-consistent punctuation, we, nonetheless, try to allow some latitude in presentation. Any use of foreign languages must be accompanied by an English translation. There is a small payment for work published."

TEARS IN THE FENCE, (II), 38 Hod View, Stourpaine, Nr. Blandford Forum, Dorset DT11 8TN England. Editor: David Caddy. Triannual. A magazine of poetry, fiction and graphics and reviews, open to a variety of contemporary voices from around the world. Publishes short and long fiction. Publishes 1-2 stories/issue. Pays £7.50 per story plus complimentary copy of the magazine. Sample copy for $5 (US).

THE THIRD ALTERNATIVE, 5 Martins Lane, Witcham, Ely, Cambs CB6 2LB England. Phone: 01353 777931. Fiction Editor: Andy Cox. Quarterly. Publishes 10 stories/issue. A5, 60 pages, lithographed, glossy. "Modern, literary fiction: no mainstream or genre clichés. Innovative, quality science fiction/fantasy/horror and slipstream material (cross-genre)." Length: No minimum; 7,000-8,000 words maximum. No simultaneous submissions. Reprints only in exceptional circumstances (will read unsolicited reprint material anyway). Standard ms format and SAE (overseas: disposable ms and 2 IRCs). "A covering letter is appreciated." Payment is negotiable. Guidelines, ad rates, etc. all available for SAE or 2 IRCs.

THE THIRD HALF MAGAZINE, "Amikeco," 16, Fane Close, Stamford, Lincolnshire PE9 1HG England. Fiction Editor: Kevin Troop. Published irregularly (when possible). "*The Third Half* literary magazine publishes mostly poetry, but editorial policy is to publish as much *short* short story writing as possible in each issue. Each issue will now have over 100 pages. Short stories especially for children, for use in the classroom, with 'questions' and 'work to do' are occasionally produced, along with poetry books, as separate editions. I wish to expand on this." Length: 1,800 words maximum. Pays in contributor's copies. Sample copy £4.95; £5.50 by post in England; £6 overseas.

VIGIL, (II), Vigil Publications, 12 Priory Mead, Bruton, Somerset BA10 0DZ England. Editor: John Howard Greaves. Estab. 1979. Circ. 250. "Simply the enjoyment of varied forms of poetry and literature with an informed view of poetic technique." Plans special fiction issue. Needs: experimental, literary, regional. Length: 500-1,500 words. Pays in contributor's copies. "Most of the stories we receive are work in progress rather than finished pieces. Well structured, vibrantly expressed work is a delight when it arrives. Freshness and originality must always find an audience." Contributor guidelines available for IRC.

‡**WASAFIRI**, Dept. of English, Queen Mary & Westfield College, University of London, Mile End Road, London EI4NS UK. Editor: Ms. Susheila Nasta. Bi-annual. Circ. 1,000. Publishes 2-3 short stories/issue. "Publishes critical articles, interviews, fiction and poetry by and about African, Asian, Caribbean, Pacific and Black British writers." Length: 500 words mimimum; 2,000 words maximum. Pays contributor's copies. "We welcome any writing for consideration which falls into our areas of interest. Work from writers outside Britain is a major part of our interest. Articles should be double-spaced and follow MLA guidelines."

WESTERLY, English Dept., University of Western Australia, Nedlands, 6907 Australia. Caroline Horobin, Administrator. Quarterly. Circ. 1,000. "A quarterly of poetry, prose, reviews and articles of a literary and cultural kind, giving special attention to Australia and Southeast Asia." Pays $50 (AUS) minimum and 1 contributor's copy. Sample copy for $8 (AUS) plus postage.

‡**WRITING WOMEN**, P.O. Box 111, Newcastle Upon Tyne NE3 1WF Great Britain. Editors: Andrea Badenoch, Debbie Taylor, Maggie Hannan, Pippa Little. "From 1998 *Writing Women* will be published by Virago Press an an annual anthology in book form. This will include 12 stories by writers who have not previously published a collection, or a novel with a mainstream publisher. We are looking for submissions that take risks and break new ground." Length: 4,000 words maximum. Pays £25 per 1,000 words. Include SAE for return of ms. Sample copies of old format magazine £2. Guidelines available for SAE.

Small Circulation Magazines

This new section of *Novel & Short Story Writer's Market* contains general interest, special interest, regional and genre magazines with circulations of under 10,000. Although these magazines vary greatly in size, theme, format and management, the editors are all looking for short stories for their respective publications. Their specific fiction needs present writers of all degrees of expertise and interests with an abundance of publishing opportunities.

These publications are not as high-paying as the large-circulation commercial periodicals, but most do pay writers 1-5¢/word or more. Also unlike the big commercial magazines, these markets are very open to new writers and relatively easy to break into. Their only criteria is that your story be well written, well presented, and suitable for their particular readership.

DIVERSITY IN OPPORTUNITY

Among the diverse publications in this section are magazines devoted to almost every topic, every level of writing and every type of writer. Paying genre magazines include *Marion Zimmer Bradley's Fantasy Magazine* (3-10¢/word); *Red Herring Mystery Magazine* ($10/story); *Worlds of Fantasy & Horror* (3¢/word minimum); and *The Western Pocket* ($50-300/story).

Some of the markets listed here publish fiction about a particular geographic area or by authors who live in that locale. A few of those regional publications are *Italian Americana*; *Keltic Fringe*; *New Frontiers, The Magazine of New Mexico*; and *Texas Young Writers' Newsletter*.

Publications with even more specialized editorial needs than genre and regional fiction include *The Healing Inn*, "geared to encouraging Christians who have been wounded by a church or religious cult"; *Housewife-Writer's Forum*, offering "support for women and house husbands who juggle writing with family life"; *Inner Voices* publishing literature by prisoners; *Mentor* wanting stories that are mentoring related; and *Rosebud, For People Who Enjoy Writing*.

SELECTING THE RIGHT MARKETS FOR YOUR WORK

Your chance for publication begins as you zero in on those markets most likely to be interested in your work. If you write a particular type of fiction, such as fantasy or mystery, check the Category Index (starting on page 597) for the appropriate subject heading. If your work is more general, or, in fact, very specialized, you may wish to browse through the listings, perhaps looking up those magazines published in your state or region. Also check the new Zine section for other specialized and genre publications.

In addition to browsing through the listings and using the Category Index, check the ranking codes at the beginning of listings to find those most likely to be receptive to your work. This is especially true for beginning writers, who should look for magazines that say they are especially open to new writers (**I**) and for those giving equal weight to both new and established writers (**II**). For more explanation about these codes, see the end of this introduction.

Once you have a list of magazines you might like to try, read their listings carefully. Much of the material within each listing carries clues that tell you more about the magazine. How to Use This Book to Publish Your Fiction starting on page 3 describes in detail the listing information common to all the markets in our book.

The physical description appearing near the beginning of the listings can give you clues about the size and financial commitment to the publication. This is not always an indication of quality, but chances are a publication with expensive paper and four-color artwork on the cover has more prestige than a photocopied publication featuring a clip art self-cover. For more information on some of the paper, binding and printing terms used in these descriptions, see Printing and Production Terms Defined on page 591.

FURTHERING YOUR SEARCH

It cannot be stressed enough that reading the listing is only the first part of developing your marketing plan. The second part, equally important, is to obtain fiction guidelines and read the actual magazine. Reading copies of a magazine helps you determine the fine points of the magazine's publishing style and philosophy. There is no substitute for this type of hands-on research.

Unlike commercial periodicals available at most newsstands and bookstores, it requires a little more effort to obtain some of the magazines listed here. You may need to send for a sample copy. We include sample copy prices in the listings whenever possible.

FOR MORE INFORMATION

See The Business of Fiction Writing for the specific mechanics of manuscript submission. Above all, editors appreciate a professional presentation. Include a brief cover letter and send a self-addressed envelope for a reply or a self-addressed envelope in a size large enough to accommodate your manuscript, if you would like it returned. Be sure to include enough stamps or International Reply Coupons (for replies from countries other than your own) to cover your manuscript's return.

North American publications are listed in the following main section of listings; it is followed by listings for other English-speaking markets around the world. To make it easier to find Canadian markets, we include a maple leaf symbol (❦) at the start of those listings.

The following is the ranking system we have used to categorize the listings in this section.

  I **Publication encourages beginning or unpublished writers to submit work for consideration and publishes new writers regularly.**

  II **Publication accepts work by established writers and by writers of exceptional talent.**

  III **Publication does not encourage beginning writers; prints mostly writers with previous publication credits; very few new writers.**

  IV **Special-interest or regional publication, open only to writers in certain genres or on certain subjects or from certain geographical areas.**

  V **Closed to unsolicited submissions.**

ABOVE THE BRIDGE, (IV), Third Stone Publishing, P.O. Box 416, Marquette MI 49855. (906)228-2964. E-mail: classen@mail.portup.com. Editor: Mikel B. Classen. Magazine: 8½×11; 56 pages; 80 lb. text paper; 80 lb. LOE cover stock; illustrations and photos. "For and about the Upper Peninsula of Michigan." Quarterly. Estab. 1985. Circ. 3,000.
Needs: Regional. "Any stories pertaining to the Upper Peninsula of Michigan." "We appreciate disk submissions, using fiction online." Receives 15-20 unsolicited mss/month. Accepts 12-13 mss/year.

Publishes ms up to 2 years after acceptance. Length: 800-1,000 words average; 300 words minimum; 2,000 words maximum. Publishes short stories and short venues. Length: 300-400 words. Also publishes literary essays and literary criticism.

How to Contact: Send complete ms with a cover letter. Should include estimated word count, bio, name, address, phone number. Reports in 6-8 months. Send SASE for reply, return of ms or send a disposable copy of ms. Simultaneous and reprint submissions OK. Sample copy for $3.50. Fiction guidelines free.

Payment/Terms: Pays 2¢/word on publication. "If your material is used online, you will be paid double (online plus in print)." Buys one-time rights.

Advice: "Make certain that the manuscript pertains to the Upper Peninsula of Michigan. If you've never been there, don't fake it."

ANTERIOR FICTION QUARTERLY, (II), Anterior Bitewing Ltd.®, 993 Allspice Ave., Fenton MO 63026-4901. (314)343-1761. E-mail address: 72247.1405@compuserve.com. Editor: Tom Bergeron. Newsletter: 8½×11; 20 pages; 20 lb. bond paper; 20 lb. bond cover; some illustrations. "Good, easy-reading stories with a point or punch-line, general interest; audience tends to be over 50." Quarterly. Estab. 1993. Circ. 50.

Needs: Adventure, historical, humor/satire, literary, mainstream/contemporary, mystery/suspense, psychic/supernatural/occult, regional, romance, sports. No "protests, causes, bigotry, sickness, fanaticism, soap." Receives 25 unsolicited mss/month. Accepts 10 mss/issue; 40 mss/year. Publishes ms 3-15 months after acceptance. Recently published work by Mildred Hechler, Marian Ford Park, Wendell Metzger, Lee Wallerstein and Sylvia Roberts. Length: 1,000 words preferred; 500 words minimum; 2,500 words maximum. Occasionally publishes short shorts. Length: 100-500 words. Always critiques or comments on rejected mss.

How to Contact: *Charges $2 reading fee per story to nonsubscribers.* Reports in 1 week on queries; 2 weeks on mss. Send SASE for reply and return of ms. Simultaneous, reprint and electronic submissions OK. Sample copy for $2. Fiction guidelines for SASE.

Payment/Terms: Pays up to $25 on publication for one-time rights; "$25 prize for best story in each issue. No other payments."

Advice: Looks for "good gimmicks; twists; imagination; departures from the everyday. Read Bernard Malamud, James Thurber, Henry James."

♣BARDIC RUNES, (I, IV), 424 Cambridge St, Ottawa, Ontario K1S 4H5 Canada. (613)231-4311. E-mail address: bn872@freenet.carleton.ca. Editor: Michael McKenny. Magazine. Estab. 1990.

Needs: Fantasy. "Traditional or high fantasy. Story should be set in pre-industrial society either historical or of author's invention." Recently published work by Cecelia Holland, D.K. Latta and D. Sandy Nielsen. Length: 3,500 words or less.

How to Contact: Electronic submissions OK. For e-mail, send ASCII or unencoded WordPerfect files. "Others may not reach me and, if they do, I may not even reply." For disk, send ASCII or WordPerfect. "No need to unencode."

Payment/Terms: Pays ½¢/word on acceptance. Reports in 2 weeks.

Advice: "Writers, pay keen attention to our stated needs or your story will probably be rejected, however good it may be. We now have more subscribers and more contributors from around the world. Read on every continent except Antarctica."

BIG SKY STORIES, (II), P.O. Box 477, Choteau MT 59422. (406)466-5300. Editor: Happy Feder. "Story-letter": 8½×11; 16 pages; heavy bond paper; illustrations and photos. "We publish fiction set in Big Sky Country (Montana, Wyoming, North and South Dakota) prior to 1950. Don't fake the history or geography. Our readers want to be entertained and educated!" Monthly. Estab. 1996. Circ. 4,000.

Needs: Adventure, historical, westerns. Publishes special fiction issues or anthologies. Accepts 2-4 mss/issue. Also publishes literary essays and "cowboy poetry only—no contemporary or ranch-life poetry." Always critiques or comments on rejected ms.

How to Contact: Send complete ms with a cover letter. Should include estimated word count and list of publications with submission. Reports in 1-2 months. Send SASE for reply, return of ms or send a disposable copy of ms. Simultaneous and reprint submissions OK. Sample copy for $3, 8½×11 SAE and 2 first-class stamps. Fiction guidelines for SASE. Reviews novels and short story collections.

THE MAPLE LEAF symbol before a listing indicates a Canadian publisher, magazine, conference or contest.

Payment/Terms: Pays minimum 1¢/word on publication for "negotiable" rights.
Advice: "Your first paragraph should introduce where, when, who and what, and the story must be set in Big Sky Country. Don't bluff or offer 'soft' history, i.e., a story that, with a few name/place changes, could take place in Ohio or Maryland or Okinawa. Know your Big Sky history."

BLACK BOOKS BULLETIN: WORDSWORK, (IV), Third World Press, P.O. Box 19730, Chicago IL 60422. (312)651-0700. Fax: (312)651-7286. Editor: Haki R. Madhubuti. Magazine: 80 pages. "*Black Books Bulletin: WordsWork* publishes progressive material related to an enlightened African-American audience." Annually.
  ● In addition to publishing fiction, *Black Books Bulletin: WordsWork* is primarily a review
  publication covering nonfiction, fiction and poetry books by African-American authors.
Needs: Condensed/excerpted novel, ethnic/multicultural, feminist, historical (general). Receives 40 unsolicited mss/month. Accepts 2 mss/issue. Does not read mss January through June. Publishes ms 1 year after acceptance. Agented fiction 20%. Published work by Amiri Baraka, Keorapetse Kgositsile. Also publishes literary essays, literary criticism, poetry. Sometimes critiques or comments on rejected mss.
How to Contact: Query first. Include estimated word count and bio. Reports in 3 weeks on queries; 3 months on mss. Simultaneous and reprint submissions OK. Reviews novels and short story collections. Send books to Assistant Editor David Kelly.
Payment/Terms: Pays on publication. Acquires all rights.

BLACK FIRE, (I, IV), BLK Publishing Co., P.O. Box 83912, Los Angeles CA 90083. (310)410-0808. Fax: (310)410-9250. E-mail: newsroom@blk.com. Editor: Alan Bell. Magazine: 8⅛×10⅞; 48 pages; book 60 lb. paper; color glossy cover; illustrations and photographs. Bimonthly. Estab. 1992.
  ● BLK is a member of COSMEP.
Needs: Ethnic/multicultural, gay. Accepts 4 mss/issue. Recently published work by Shawn Hinds, Mark Haile, Daniel Garrett, Kneji Evans and Don Densmore. Publishes short shorts. Also publishes poetry.
How to Contact: Query first, query with clips of published work or send complete ms with a cover letter. Should include bio (3 sentences). Send a disposable copy of ms. No simultaneous submissions; electronic submissions OK. Sample copy for $7. Fiction guidelines free.
Payment/Terms: Pays free subscription, 5 contributor's copies. Acquires first North American serial rights and right to anthologize.
Advice: "Avoid interracial stories or idealized pornography."

THE BLOWFISH CATALOG, (I), 2261 Market St., #284, San Francisco CA 94114. (415)864-0880. Fax: (415)864-1858. E-mail: blowfish@blowfish.com. Contact: Editorial Staff. Catalog: 8½×11; 48 pages; newsprint; 50 lb. cover; illustrations and photos. "We buy short fiction for use in our catalog. Our catalog contains erotic books, videos, safer sex products, and so forth, and we add fiction which complements it." Triannually. Estab. 1994. Circ. 5,000.
Needs: Erotica. Plans special fiction issues in the future. Receives 4-7 unsolicited mss/month. Accepts 2 mss/issue; 6 mss/year. Publishes ms 1-4 months after acceptance. Published work by Trish Thomas. Length: 200 words average; 500 words maximum. Publishes short shorts. Also publishes poetry. Sometimes critiques or comments on rejected ms.
How to Contact: Send complete ms with a cover letter. Include estimated word count and Social Security number. Reports in 1 month on queries; 2 months on mss. Send a disposable copy of ms. Simultaneous, reprints and electronic submissions OK. Sample copy for $3. Fiction guidelines for #10 SASE. Reviews novels and short story collections.
Payment/Terms: Pays $10-100 and 5 contributor's copies on acceptance for one-time rights. Additional copies available for $1.
Advice: "We look for 'high density' fiction: not just arousing, but thought-provoking or poetic as well, in a very short form. Being erotic is important, but not sufficient: the piece must have merits beyond an ability to arouse."

‡BLUE SUGAR, Sound Exposure for Authors and Artists, (I, II), 1111 N. Winchester #1F, Chicago IL 60622. (312)395-1422. E-mail: foxandco@aol.com. Fiction Editor: Mary Jane Wolski. Magazine: 8½×11, 60-80 pages; 20 lb. copy paper; illustrations and photos. "We are dedicated to giving exposure to emerging artists and authors. We consider all genres and do not censor. Our audience is 20-40-year-olds, artistic, liberal, avant-garde." Triannually. Estab. 1995. Circ. 100.
Needs: Adventure, ethnic/multicultural, experimental, feminist, gay, historical, horror, humor/satire, lesbian, literary, mainstream/contemporary, mystery/suspense, psychic/supernatural/occult, regional, romance, science fiction, westerns. No pornographic or children's lit. Receives approximately 10 unsolicited mss/month. Publishes ms 2-3 months after acceptance. Recently published work by Stephen Louden. Length: 2,000 words average; 10 words minimum; 10,000 words maximum. Publishes short

shorts. Also publishes literary essays, literary criticism and poetry. Always critiques or comments on rejected mss.

How to Contact: Send complete ms with a cover letter. Include estimated word count, bio and release contract. Reports in 2 weeks. Send SASE for reply, return of ms or send a disposable copy of ms. Simultaneous and electronic submissions (disk or modem) OK. Sample copy for $5 and 9×12 SAE with 6 first-class stamps. Fiction guidelines for #10 SASE.

Payment/Terms: No payment. "You must purchase magazine to see your submission in print." Acquires one-time rights.

BOY'S QUEST, (II), The Bluffton News Publishing & Printing Co., P.O. Box 227, Bluffton OH 45817. (419)358-4610. Fax: (419)358-5027. Editor: Marilyn Edwards. Magazine: 7×9; 50 pages; enamel paper; illustrations and photos. Bimonthly. Estab. 1994.

● *Boy's Quest* received an EDPRESS Distinguished Achievement Award for Excellence in Educational Journalism.

Needs: Adventure, children's/juvenile (5-9 years, 10-12 years), ethnic/multicultural, historical, sports. Upcoming themes: Cowboys (February/March), Cars (April/May), Music (June/July), Insects (August/September), Communication (October/November), Animals (December/January). List of upcoming themes available for SASE. Receives 300-400 unsolicited mss/month. Accepts 20-40 mss/year. Agented fiction 2%. Published work by Jean Patrick, Eve Marar and Linda Herman. Length: 300-500 words average; 500 words maximum. Publishes short shorts. Length: 250-400 words. Also publishes poetry. Always critiques or comments on rejected mss.

How to Contact: Send complete ms with a cover letter. Include estimated word count, 1 page bio, Social Security number, list of publications. Reports in 2-4 weeks on queries; 6-10 weeks on mss. Simultaneous and reprint submissions OK. Sample copy for $3. Fiction guidelines for #10 SASE. Reviews novels and short story collections.

Payment/Terms: Pays 5¢/word and 1 contributor's copy on publication for first North American serial rights; additional copies $3, $2 for 10 or more.

Advice: Looks for "wholesome material. Follow our theme list and study copies of the magazine."

MARION ZIMMER BRADLEY'S FANTASY MAGAZINE, (II, IV), Box 249, Berkeley CA 94701-0249. (510)644-9222. Editor and Publisher: Marion Zimmer Bradley. Magazine: 8½×11; 64 pages; 60 lb. text paper; 10 lb. cover stock; b&w interior and 4-color cover illustrations. "Fantasy only; strictly family oriented." Quarterly.

● This magazine is named for and edited by one of the pioneers of fantasy fiction. Bradley is perhaps best known for the multi-volume Darkover series.

Needs: Fantasy. May include adventure, contemporary, humor/satire, mystery/suspense and young adult/teen (10-18) (all with fantasy elements). "No avant-garde or romantic fantasy. No computer games!" Receives 50-200 unsolicited mss/week. Accepts 8-10 mss/issue; 36-40 mss/year. Publishes ms 3-12 months after acceptance. Agented fiction 5%. Recently published work by Jo Clayton, Cynthia McQuillin, Elisabeth Waters, Steven Piziks and Richard Purtill. Length: 3,000-4,000 words average; 5,500 words maximum. Publishes short shorts.

How to Contact: Send #10 SASE for guidelines *before* sending ms. Send complete ms. SASE. Reports in 90 days. No simultaneous submissions. Sample copy for $4.

Payment/Terms: Pays 3-10¢/word on acceptance and contributor's copies for first North American serial rights.

Advice: "If I want to finish reading it—I figure other people will too. A manuscript stands out if I care whether the characters do well, if it has a rhythm. Make sure it has characters I will know *you* care about. If you don't care about them, how do you expect me to? Read guidelines *before* sending ms."

BRILLIANT STAR, (II), National Spiritual Assembly of the Baha'is of the U.S., Baha'i, National Center, 1233 Central St., Evanston IL 60201. (847)869-9039. Managing Editor: Pepper Peterson Old-ziey. Fiction Editor: Cindy Savage. Magazine: 8½×11; 33 pages; matte paper; glossy cover; illustrations; photos. "A magazine for Baha'i children about the history, teachings and beliefs of the Baha'i faith. Manuscripts should reflect spiritual principles of the baha'i" For children approximately 5-12 years old. Bimonthly. Estab. 1969. Circ. 2,300.

Needs: Adventure, children's/juvenile, ethnic, historical, humor/satire, mystery/suspense, spiritual, young adult/teen (10-12 years). "Accepts inspirational fiction if not overtly preachy or moralistic and if not directly Christian and related directly to Christian holidays." Receives 30 unsolicited mss/month. Accepts 1-2 mss/issue; 6-12 mss/year. Publishes ms no sooner than 6 months after acceptance. Published work by Susan Pethick and John Paulits; published new writers within the last year. Length: 100 words minimum; 600 words maximum. "Length should correlate with intended audience—very short mss for young readers, longer mss must be for older readers (ages 10-12), and intended for their interests." Publishes short shorts. Also publishes poetry.

INSIDER REPORT

Writing well and following guidelines are no fantasy

A good grasp of language and the ability to be one's own editor are vital for writers submitting to *Marion Zimmer Bradley's Fantasy Magazine*. "I like to see stories which are legible, follow my guidelines, and display a good grasp of proper spelling, grammar and punctuation," says editor and publisher Marion Zimmer Bradley. "My pet peeves are writers who don't proofread their own manuscripts, who use 'like' when they mean 'as if' and 'it's' when they mean 'its'—people who try to write novels when they can't write a simple declarative sentence."

Marion Zimmer Bradley

The staff at *Marion Zimmer Bradley's Fantasy Magazine* consists of "three fulltime and two parttime workaholics," according to Bradley. "I'm the first reader because I'm the only one who is willing to read everything. I flatly refuse to give up the job—although I do permit things that clearly don't fit my guidelines to be weeded out in the mailroom." Bradley emphasizes the importance of following a magazine's guidelines when submitting a story for publication, and is frustrated by the large number of inappropriate submissions she receives. "I see hard science fiction when I've asked for fantasy, parts of novels instead of short stories, poetry, rewritten fairy tales, and many other manuscripts that make it obvious that people are not reading my guidelines. Yesterday, for example, my secretary threw out two manuscripts that came in without a SASE and two which were longer than the word limit clearly stated in my guidelines. And that's just what didn't make it out of the mailroom."

Bradley's Fantasy Magazine, which she started over eight years ago, is truly a labor of love for the prolific fantasy writer. "As a child I remember reading my first science fiction story, 'The Crimson Ray,' in *Boys' Life*. I was always dissatisfied with the emphasis on hard science fiction, which was strongly preferred by the male establishment at that time." As a result, she started writing fantasy. Starting her writing career in 1952 with the publication of her first short story in *Venture Science Fiction* magazine, she is well known for her bestselling Arthurian novel *The Mists of Avalon* and her popular Darkover series. After so many years of writing fantasy, this writer/editor knows what makes a successful fantasy story. Good plot is more important than beautiful prose, and the characters should be likable and their goals worthwhile. More simply, Bradley says, "I particularly like stories that are short and funny, and stories which evoke a sense of wonder."

INSIDER REPORT, *continued*

Throughout the years, Bradley has seen fantasy blossom from an underground fringe market into a mainstream genre. "The field of fantasy has grown much larger over the years and many more of the writers are women." The settings of the stories and nationalities of the characters are also evolving. "I am starting to see stories with backgrounds other than generic Celtic/Northern European. More writers are mining the rich veins of Native American, African, Oriental and Indian folklore." With this growth and diversity come increased opportunites for fantasy writers to get their work published.

Whether writing fantasy or any other genre of fiction, Bradley offers writers this simple, direct advice: "Learn to type, spell and punctuate. Read guidelines and, if possible, the magazine you're submitting to. These are the craft skills that professional writers must possess."

—*Cindy Laufenberg*

How to Contact: No queries. Send complete ms. Cover letter not essential. Reports in 6-10 weeks on mss. SASE. Simultaneous submissions OK "but please make a notation that it is a simultaneous sub." Sample copy for $2, 9×12 SAE and 5 oz. postage. Fiction guidelines for #10 SASE.
Payment/Terms: Pays in contributor's copies (two); charges for extras.
Terms: "Writer can retain own copyright or grant to the National Spiritual Assembly of the Baha'is of the U.S."
Advice: "We enjoy working with beginning writers and try to develop a constructive collaborative relationship with those who show promise and sensitivity to our aims and focus. We feel that the children's market is open to a wide variety of writers: fiction, nonfiction, science, photo-essays. Our needs for appealing fiction especially for pre-schoolers and young readers make us a good market for new writers. *Please*, have a story to tell! The single main reason for rejection of manuscripts we review is lack of plot to infuse the story with energy and make the reader want to come along, as well as length to age/interest level mismatch. Longer stories must be intended for older children. Only very short stories are useable for young audiences. We love stories about different cultures and ethnic groups. We also welcome submissions that offer solutions to the problems kids face today. We're looking for active, child-oriented writing, not passive, preachy prose."

BRUTARIAN, The Magazine That Dares to be Lame, (III), Odium Ent., P.O. Box 25222, Arlington VA 22202-9222. (703)308-9108. Editor: D.J. Salemi. Magazine: 8½×11; 84 pages; illustrations and photos. "Our theme is 'The World of Trash & Weirdness.'" Quarterly. Estab. 1991. Circ. 3,000.
Needs: Erotica, experimental, fantasy, feminist, gay, horror, humor/satire, lesbian, literary, mainstream/contemporary, mystery/suspense (police procedural, private eye/hardboiled), psychic/supernatural/occult. Receives 150 unsolicited mss/month. Accepts 2 mss/issue; 8 mss/year. Publishes ms 3 months after acceptance. Agented fiction 10%. Recently published work by Phillip Nutman and Jack Ketchum. Length: 2,000-3,000 words average; 500 words minimum; 5,000 words maximum. Publishes short shorts. Also publishes literary essays.
How to Contact: Send complete ms with a cover letter. Include estimated word count and list of publications. "If a novice or a beginner, we are now charging two dollars if they wish to receive something other than a form letter or rejection." Reports in 2 weeks on queries, 2 months on mss. Send SASE for reply, return of ms or send a disposable copy of ms. Simultaneous and reprint submissions OK. Sample copy for $5. Fiction guidelines for SASE. Reviews novels and short story collections.
Payment/Terms: Pays 10¢/word and 3 contributor's copies; additional copies for $2.
Terms: Pays on publication for first rights. Sends galleys to author.
Advice: "The beauty of the language, the depth of ideas make a manuscript stand out. Rewrite it several times."

BURNING LIGHT, (II), A Journal of Christian Literature, Burning Light Press, 59 Treetop Court, Bloomingdale NJ 07403-1016. (201)283-9516. Editor: Carl Simmons. Magazine: 5½×8½; 32-48 pages; 50 lb. Nekoosa paper; 80 lb. classic laid cover; illustrations. "*Burning Light* publishes fiction, essays and poetry from a Christian perspective. It's worth noting, though, that we want Christians who write and not 'Christian writing.' No one's going to mistake us for *Christianity Today* or *Guideposts*, although hopefully *Kenyon Review*, et al. will come to mind before they catch on to our drift." Quarterly. Estab. 1993.

Needs: Condensed/excerpted novel, experimental, humor/satire, literary, religious/inspirational, science fiction (soft/sociological), serialized novel. Receives 15-20 unsolicited mss/month. Accepts 2-4 mss/issue; 10-15 mss/year. Publishes ms 1-9 months (4-6 months typical) after acceptance. Recently published work by Diane Glancy, Albert Haley and T.H.S. Wallace. Length: 1,500-2,000 words average; 10,000 words maximum. Publishes short shorts. Also publishes literary essays, poetry. Sometimes critiques or comments on rejected mss.

How to Contact: Send complete ms with a cover letter. Include estimated word count, 3-4 sentence bio, list of publications. Reports in 3-4 weeks. Send SASF for reply, return of ms or send a disposable copy of ms. Simultaneous and electronic (disk: WordPerfect 5.1, PageMaker 4 or Quark 3.3 preferably) submissions OK. Sample copy for $4. Fiction guidelines free. Reviews novels and short story collections.

Payment/Terms: Pays free subscription to magazine, 5-6 contributor's copies; additional copies for $2.50. Acquires all rights (negotiable).

Advice: "Make sure the writing's coming from you; don't write something because you think it's what a publisher wants."

‡THE CHINOOK QUARTERLY, (II), Chinook Press, 1432 Yellowstone Ave., Billings MT 59102. (406)245-7704. Editor: Mary Ellen Westwood. Magazine: $7 \times 8\frac{1}{2}$; 60-80 pages; acid-free paper; card cover stock; illustrations; photos. "*The Chinook Quarterly* will be a catalyst for human change and understanding. We want forward-looking and challenging submissions that will be of use to readers in the West." Quarterly. Estab. 1996.

Needs: Adventure, children's/juvenile (10-12 years), condensed/excerpted novel, ethnic/multicultural, experimental, fantasy (science fantasy), feminist, historical, humor/satire, literary, mainstream/contemporary, mystery/suspense (all kinds), regional, romance (contemporary, futuristic/time travel), science fiction (hard science, soft/sociological), sports, translations, westerns, young adult/teen (all kinds). Especially interested in stories about the contemporary West. "No fiction that degrades or discounts human beings." Accepts 4-6 mss/issue; 16-24 mss/year. Publishes ms 1-12 months after acceptance. Length: 1,600 words average; 300 words minimum; 2,000 words maximum. Publishes short shorts. Also publishes literary essays, literary criticism and poetry. Often critiques or comments on rejected mss.

How to Contact: Send complete ms with a cover letter. Include estimated word count, 250-word bio, Social Security number, list of publications and explanation of the piece submitted (why did you write it?)." Send SASE for return of ms. Reprints OK. Sample copy for $7. Fiction guidelines for #10 SASE. Reviews novels and short story collections.

Payment/Terms: Pays $2/printed page and 4 contributor's copies on publication. Acquires one-time rights. Sends galleys to the author.

Advice: "I am looking for a fresh and daring approach and a thinking view of the world. I admire risk takers. I want writing about real people, not just academic musings. I want the true life experiences of humans, not some shallow misinterpretations. Edit, edit, edit . . . after you rewrite, of course."

✤CHRISTIAN COURIER, (II, IV), Calvinist Contact Publishing Limited, Unit 4, 261 Martindale Rd., St. Catharines, Ontario L2W 1A1 Canada. (905)682-8311. Fax: (905)682-8313. Editor: Bert Witvoet. Tabloid: $11\frac{1}{2} \times 14$; 20 pages; newsprint; illustrations and photos. Weekly. Estab. 1945. Circ. 5,000.

Needs: Adventure, children's/juvenile (10-12 years), historical, religious/inspirational, senior citizen/retirement, sports and translations. No "sentimental 'religious' stuff; superficial moralizing." Receives 5-10 unsolicited mss/month. Accepts 12 mss/year. Does not read mss from the end of July to early August. Publishes ms within a month after acceptance. Length: 1,200 words average; no minimum; 1,400 words maximum. Publishes short shorts. Length 500 words. Also publishes literary essays (if not too technical), literary criticism and poetry. Always critiques or comments on rejected mss.

How to Contact: Send complete ms with a cover letter. Include word count and bio (100 words maximum). Reports in 3 weeks on queries; 4-6 weeks on mss. Send a disposable copy of ms. Simultane-

---

‡ **THE DOUBLE DAGGER** before a listing indicates that the listing is new in this edition. New markets are often the most receptive to submissions by new writers.

ous, reprint and electronic submissions OK. Sample copy free. Fiction guidelines for SASE. Reviews novels and short story collections.

Payment/Terms: Pays $25-60 on publication and 1 contributor's copy (on request). Acquires one-time rights.

Advice: Looks for work "geared to a Christian audience but reflecting the real world, real dilemmas, without pat resolutions—written in an engaging, clear manner."

COLD-DRILL MAGAZINE, (IV), English Dept., Boise State University, 1910 University Dr., Boise ID 83725. (208)385-1999. Editor: Tom Trusky. Magazine: box format; various perfect and non-perfect bound inserts; illustrations and photos. Material submitted *must be by Idaho authors or deal with Idaho*. For adult audiences. Annually. Estab. 1970. Circ. 500.

Needs: "The 1996-97 issue will not have a theme; it will be open to all forms of writing and artwork." Length: determined by submissions.

How to Contact: Query first. SASE.

Payment/Terms: Pays in contributor's copies. Acquires first rights.

COMMUNITIES MAGAZINE, (I, IV), P.O. Box 169, Masonville CO 80541-0169. Phone/fax: (970)593-5615. Editor: Diana Christian. Guest editors change with each issue. "Articles on intentional communities—cohousing, ecovillages, urban group houses, student co-ops, rural communes, land-trust communities, and other forms of community (including non-residential)—as well as worker co-ops and workplace democracy. Written for people generally interested in intentional community and cooperative ventures, current and former community members, and people seeking to form or join an intentional community or co-op venture." Quarterly. Estab. 1973. Circ. 4,000.

Needs: "Utopian" stories, science fiction (soft/sociological). "Stories set in intentional communities or cooperatively run organizations." Accepts "1-2 mss/year (more if we got them)." Length: 750 words minimum; 3,000 words maximum.

How to Contact: Query first or send complete ms. Reports in 1 month on queries; 6-8 weeks on mss. Simultaneous and previously published submissions OK. Sample copy for $5. *Communities Magazine*, 138 Twin Oaks Rd., Louisa VA 23093.

Payment/Terms: Pays 1 year subscription (4 issues) or 4 contributor's copies. Acquires first North American rights.

Advice: "We receive too many articles and stories which are completely off topic (in which the writer assumes we are about community in the generic sense, i.e., "community spirit," a neighborhood or town); by people who have no idea what an intentional community is; and/or who have never seen the magazine. We ask that writers read a sample issue first. We like the personal touch; concrete, visual, tightly written, upbeat or offbeat message; short. No abstract, negative or loosely written, long fiction."

THE COSMIC UNICORN, (I, II, IV), Silver Creation Press, 451 Hibiscus Tree Dr., Lantana FL 33462. (407)588-0907. E-mail: t.packard@genie.geis.com. Editor: Tricia Packard. Fiction Editor: Liz Dennis. Magazine: $5\frac{1}{4} \times 8\frac{1}{2}$; 160 pages; 20 lb. white paper; white index cover stock; cover illustrations only. "*TCU* looks to open doors for both new and well-seasoned writers. We want to make available a forum that has the space for really good science fiction/fantasy works of varying lengths and styles—a forum that offers writers the opportunity to say what they want to say but haven't been able to. Our readers range from 10-70." Semiannually. Estab. 1993. Circ. 100.

Needs: Fantasy, science fiction, young adult/teen (science fiction). No horror. Receives 40-50 unsolicited mss/month. Accepts 12-15 mss/issue; 24-30 mss/year. Does not read mss September 1-April 30. Publishes ms within 1 year after acceptance. Recently published work by Devon Tavern, Edward L. McFadden, Gordon Graves. Length: 4,500 words average; 100 words minimum, 10,000 words maximum. Publishes short shorts. Length: 100-400 words. Also publishes poetry. Sometimes critiques or comments on rejected ms.

How to Contact: Send complete ms with a cover letter; query first for nonfiction or long poetry. Include estimated word count, bio (100-words maximum), Social Security number and a brief list of related publications. Reports in 1 month on queries; 2 months on mss. Send SASE for reply, return of ms or send a disposable copy of ms. No simultaneous submissions. Reprint and electronic submissions OK. Sample copy for $6.75 and 6×9 SAE with 4 first-class stamps or 2 IRCs. (Make checks payable to Tricia Packard.) Fiction guidelines for #10 SASE. Reviews novels and short story collections.

Payment/Terms: Pays $\frac{1}{4}$-$\frac{1}{2}$¢ a word for one-time rights; copies available to contributors at special rate.

Advice: "We look for a strong plot, well-defined characters, unusual story or plot; a manuscript stands out if it can make me interested in what happens to the character(s). We haven't seen enough science fiction/fantasy with romantic characters, or romance. Avoid graphic sex or gore. Our readers range from adolescents to senior citizens."

DAGGER OF THE MIND, Beyond The Realms Of Imagination, (II), K'yi-Lih Productions (a division of Breach Enterprises), 1317 Hookridge Dr., El Paso TX 79925. (915)591-0541. Executive Editor: Arthur William Lloyd Breach. Magazine. 8½×11; 62-86 pages; hibright paper; high glossy cover; from 5-12 illustrations. Quarterly. Estab. 1990. Circ. 5,000.

• Do not send this publication "slasher" horror. The editor's preferences lean toward "Twilight Zone" and similar material. He says he added mystery to his needs but has received very little quality material in this genre.

Needs: Lovecraftian. Adventure, experimental, fantasy, horror, mystery/suspense (private eye, police procedural), science fiction (hard science, soft/sociological). Nothing sick and blasphemous, vulgar, obscene, racist, sexist, profane, humorous, weak, exploited women stories and those with idiotic puns. Plans special paperback anthologies. Receives 400 unsolicited mss/month. Accepts 8-15 mss/issue; 90-100 mss/year depending upon length. Publishes ms 2 years after acceptance. Agented fiction 30%. Published work by Sidney Williams, Jessica Amanda Salmonson, Donald R. Burleson. All lengths are acceptable; from short shorts to novelette lengths. Also publishes literary essays, literary criticism, poetry. Sometimes comments on rejected mss.

How to Contact: All mail should be addressed to Arthur Breach. Send complete manuscript with cover letter. "Include a bio and list of previously published credits with tearsheets. I also expect a brief synopsis of the story." Reports in 6 months on mss. SASE. Simultaneous submissions OK "as long as I am informed that they are such." Accepts electronic submissions. Sample copy for $3.50, 9×12 SAE and 5 first-class stamps. Fiction guidelines for #10 SASE.

Payment/Terms: Pays ½-1¢/word plus 1 contributor's copy on publication for first rights (possibly anthology rights as well).

Advice: "I'm a big fan of the late H.P. Lovecraft. I love reading through Dunsanian and Cthulhu Mythos tales. I'm constantly on the lookout for this special brand of fiction. If you want to grab my attention immediately, write on the outside of the envelope 'Lovecratian submission enclosed.' There are a number of things which make submissions stand out for me. Is there any sensitivity to the tale? I like sensitive material, so long as it doesn't become mushy. Another thing that grabs my attention are characters which leap out of the pages at you. Move me, bring a tear to my eye; make me stop and think about the world and people around me. Frighten me with little spoken of truths about the human condition. In short, show me that you can move me in such a way as I have never been moved before."

DARK REGIONS, (II), P.O. Box 6301, Concord CA 94524. Editor: Joe Morey. Fiction Editors: Mike Olson and John Rosenman. Magazine: 8½×11; 100 pages; newsprint; full color cover ; illustrations and photographs. "Science fiction, fantasy, horror and all subgenres. Our philosophy is to publish the most professional, fresh, original work we can find." Triannually. Estab. 1985. Circ. 3,000.

• *Dark Regions* is a member of the Small Press Writers and Artists Organization and recently received SPWAO's Best Fiction Award for the story "Darby's Bone," by Albert J. Manachino.

Needs: Fantasy, horror, science fiction, young adult/teen (horror, science fiction). List of upcoming themes available for SASE. Receives 100 unsolicited mss/month. Accepts 8/10 mss/issue; 30-45 mss/year. Publishes ms 6-12 months after acceptance. Recently published work by Mike Resnick, Kevin J. Anderson and Joe R. Lansdale. Length: 3,500 words average; 1,000 words minimum; 5,000 words maximum. Also publishes poetry. Sometimes critiques rejected mss.

How to Contact: Send complete ms with a cover letter. Should include estimated word count, brief bio, Social Security number and list of publications. Reports in 3-8 weeks on queries; 3-12 weeks on mss. Send SASE for reply, return of ms or send a disposable copy of ms. No simultaneous submissions. Considers reprints for "The Year's Best Fantastic Fiction" (by invitation only). Sample copy for $3.95, 9×12 SAE and 2 first-class stamps. Fiction guidelines free for SASE.

Payment/Terms: Pays ½-6¢/word and 1 contributor's copy; additional copies $2.50 (plus $1.28 shipping). Pays on publication. Buys first North American serial rights.

Advice: "We want fiction with good short story elements and good short story structure—stories that move through action/description and employ elements of suspense, inventive tales which push the boundaries of weirdness. The more original, the better." Avoid "overused themes such as Friday the 13th, Conan, Invaders from Mars, werewolves and vampires (unless highly original). No racism, no hard pornography and definitely no children in sexual situations."

MARKET CATEGORIES: (I) Open to new writers; (II) Open to both new and established writers; (III) Interested mostly in established writers; (IV) Open to writers whose work is specialized; (V) Closed to unsolicited submissions.

‡**DEAD LINES MAGAZINE, Exploration of the human condition and beyond, (I, II)**, Crash-landing Press, P.O. Box 907, Tolland CT 06084-0907. (860)875-4524. Editor: Nancy Purnell. Magazine: digest size; 80-92 pages; 60 lb. offset paper; glossy coated cover stock; illustrations. "Each issue of *Dead Lines* revolves around a specific theme. Life presents many challenges. We strive to explore the human condition and beyond, looking for dark, strange and surreal. We want to see familiar subjects from a new angle, as well as present original, experimental, thought-provoking writing." Semiannually. Estab. 1995. Circ. 150-200.

Needs: Experimental, horror, literary, mainstream/contemporary, psychic/supernatural/occult, science fiction (soft/sociological). "No romance, mystery, children's, young adult, western and erotica." Receives 50 unsolicite mss/month. Accepts 8-15 mss/issue; 16-30 mss/year. Publishes mss within 6 months after acceptance. Recently published work by Charlee Jacob, Kurt Newton, Mark Rich, Rhonda Eikamp, Trey R. Barker and D.F. Lewis. Length: 2,000-2,500 words average; 150 words minimum; 3,500 words maximum. Also publishes poetry. Often critiques or comments on mss.

How to Contact: Send complete ms with a cover letter. Include estimated word count and brief bio. Reports in 2-4 weeks on queries; 1-2 months on mss. Send SASE for reply, return of ms or send a disposable copy of ms. Sample copy for $4.75. Fiction guidelines for #10 SASE.

Payment/Terms: Pays 10 32¢ stamps for fiction, 5 32¢ stamps per poem and 1 contributor's copy on publication. Acquires first North American serial rights. Sends galleys to author.

Advice: "We look for original and thought-provoking writing, something with substance and meaning. We don't want a story that's weird just for the sake of being weird. Check out an issue before submitting. Go with your own style—don't try to copy someone else. I prefer subtle—don't want to be preached at or hit over the head with an idea."

DEATHREALM, (II), 2210 Wilcox Dr., Greensboro NC 27405-2845. E-mail: s.rainey@genie.com. or markrainey@aol.com. Editor: Mark Rainey. Magazine: 8½×11; 50-60 pages; 20 lb. bond paper; 8 pt. glossy coated cover stock; pen & ink, screened illustrations; b&w photos. Publishes "fantasy/horror," for a "mature" audience. Quarterly. Estab. 1987. Circ. 3,000.

● This horror and dark fantasy magazine won the 1995 International Horror Critics Guild Award for Best Magazine.

Needs: Experimental, fantasy, horror, psychic/supernatural/occult and science fiction. "Sci-fi tales should have a horror slant. Not interested in werewolf and vampire stories. *Strongly* recommend contributor buy a sample copy of *Deathrealm* before submitting." Receives 200-300 mss/month. Accepts 6-8 mss/issue; 30 mss/year. Does not read mss January 1 to May 1. Publishes ms within 1 year of acceptance. Published work by Joe R. Lansdale, Fred Chappell, Kevin J. Anderson, Jessica Amanda Salmonson. Length: 5,000 words average; 10,000 words maximum. Publishes short shorts. Also publishes literary criticism, poetry. Sometimes critiques rejected mss.

How to Contact: Send complete ms with cover letter. Include "publishing credits, some bio info, where they heard about *Deathrealm*. Never reveal plot in cover letter." May accept simultaneous submissions, but "not recommended." Reports in 2 weeks on queries; 9-12 weeks on ms. SASE. Sample copy for $4.95. Fiction guidelines for #10 SASE. Reviews novels and short story collections.

Payment/Terms: Pays 1¢/word (higher rates for established professionals) and contributor's copies for first North American serial rights.

Advice: "Concentrate on characterization; development of ideas; strong atmosphere, with an important setting. I frown on gratuitous sex and violence unless it is a mere side effect of a more sophisticated story line. Stay away from overdone themes—foreboding dreams come true; being a frustrated writer; using lots of profanity and having a main character so detestable you don't care what happens to him."

DREAM INTERNATIONAL/QUARTERLY, (I, II, IV), U.S. Address: Charles I. Jones, #H-1, 411 14th St., Ramona CA 92065-2769. E-mail: dreamiq@wizard.com. Editor-in-Chief: Charles I. Jones. Magazine: 5×7; 80-135 pages; Xerox paper; parchment cover stock; some illustrations and photos. "Publishes fiction and nonfiction that is dream-related or clearly inspired by a dream. Also dream-related fantasy." Quarterly. Estab. 1981. Circ. 80-100.

Needs: Adventure, confession, contemporary, erotica, ethnic, experimental, fantasy, historical, horror, humor/satire, literary, mainstream, mystery/suspense, prose poem, psychic/supernatural/occult, romance, science fiction, translations, young adult/teen (10-18). Receives 20-30 unsolicited mss/month. Publishes ms 8 months to 2 years after acceptance. Length: 1,000 words minimum; 2,000 words maximum. Publishes short shorts. Recently published work by Norman T. Stephens, Carmen M. Pursifull, Cathy Sparks and Dimitri Mihalas. Also publishes literary essays, poetry (poetry submissions to Tim Scott, 2101 W. Foster Ave., #1-South, Chicago IL 60625; send SASE for poetry guidelines).

How to Contact: Submit ms. Reports in 6 weeks on queries; 3 months on mss. SASE. Simultaneous and reprint submissions OK. Electronic submissions preferred. "If you really want something to have the best chance, send an MS-DOS format IBM-compatible file on a 3.5 disk in MS-Word for Windows format (ASCII and WordPerfect also acceptable). Hardcopy must accompany disk." Sample copy for $8. Guidelines free with SAE and 2 first-class stamps. "Accepted mss will not be returned unless requested at time of submission."

Payment/Terms: Pays in contributor's copies (contributors must pay $2.95 for postage and handling). Offers magazine subscription. Acquires one-time rights.

Advice: "Use your nightly dreams to inspire you to literary flights. Keep a dream journal. Avoid stereotypes and clichés. Submissions should be clear, concise and free (as much as possible) of rambling text. When contacting editor-in-chief, make all checks, money orders, and overseas drafts payable to *Charles Jones*. When contacting senior poetry editor, make checks and money orders payable to Tim Scott."

❀DREAMS & VISIONS, New Frontiers in Christian Fiction, (II), Skysong Press, RR1, Washago, Ontario L0K 2B0 Canada. Editorial Address: 35 Peter St. S., Orillia, Ontario L3V 5AB Canada. Website: http://www.bconnex.net/~skysong. Editor: Steve Stanton. Magazine: 5½×8½; 56 pages; 20 lb. bond paper; glossy cover. "Contemporary Christian fiction in a variety of styles for adult Christians." Triannually. Estab. 1989. Circ. 200.

Needs: Contemporary, experimental, fantasy, humor/satire, literary, religious/inspirational, science fiction (soft/sociological). "All stories should portray a Christian world view or expand upon Biblical themes or ethics in an entertaining or enlightening manner." Receives 20 unsolicited mss/month. Accepts 7 mss/issue; 21 mss/year. Publishes ms 2-6 months after acceptance. Length: 2,500 words; 2,000 words minimum; 6,000 words maximum.

How to Contact: Send complete ms with cover letter. "Bio is optional: degrees held and in what specialties, publishing credits, service in the church, etc." Reports in 1 month on queries; 2-4 months on mss. SASE. Simultaneous submissions OK. Sample copy for $4.95. Fiction guidelines for SASE and online at our website.

Payment/Terms: Pays ½¢/word and contributor's copy. Acquires first North American serial rights and one-time, non-exclusive reprint rights.

Advice: "In general we look for work that has some literary value, that is in some way unique and relevant to Christian readers today. Our first priority is technical adequacy, though we will occasionally work with a beginning writer to polish a manuscript. Ultimately, we look for stories that glorify the Lord Jesus Christ, stories that build up rather than tear down, that exalt the sanctity of life, the holiness of God, and the value of the family."

EARTHSONGS, By People Who Love the Earth, (I, IV), Sweetlight Books, 16625 Heitman Rd., Cottonwood CA 96022. (916)529-5392. E-mail: swtlight@snowcrest.net. Editor: Guy Mount. Booklet: 5½×8½; 48-80 pages; 20 lb. bond; parchment cover; illustrations and occasional photos. "We publish poems, stories and illustrations that perpetuate the Earth, not an empire." Annually. Estab. 1993. Circ. 120.

Needs: Adventure, condensed/excerpted novel, erotica, ethnic/multicultural, experimental, feminist, gay, historical, lesbian, literary, mainstream/contemporary, psychic/supernatural/occult, religious/inspirational (non-Christian), Native American, "Earthpeople." Upcoming theme: "Erotic Earth Stories." Publishes special fiction issues or anthologies. Publishes ms in November after acceptance. Published work by Conger Beasley. Length: 500 words minimum; 5,000 words maximum. Publishes short shorts. Also publishes literary essays and poetry. Sometimes critiques or comments on rejected mss.

How to Contact: Send complete ms with a cover letter. Include 1-paragraph bio and list of publications with submission. Reports in 1 month. SASE for reply. Simultaneous and reprint submissions OK. Sample copy for $5, 6×9 SAE.

Payment/Terms: Pays 1 contributor's copy. Acquires non-exclusive rights. Sends galleys to author.

Advice: Looking for fiction that "reveals a love of the Earth and her people. Challenge and question the Empire."

ELDRITCH TALES, (II, IV), Yith Press, 1051 Wellington Rd., Lawrence KS 66049. (913)843-4341. Editor-in-Chief: Crispin Burnham. Magazine: 6×9; 120 pages (average); glossy cover; illustrations; "very few" photos. "The magazine concerns horror fiction in the tradition of the old *Weird Tales* magazine. We publish fiction in the tradition of H.P. Lovecraft, Robert Bloch and Stephen King, among others, for fans of this particular genre." Semiannually. Estab. 1975. Circ. 1,000.

Needs: Horror and psychic/supernatural/occult. "No mad slasher stories or similar nonsupernatural horror stories." Receives about 8 unsolicited fiction mss/month. Accepts 12 mss/issue, 24 mss/year. Published work by J.N. Williamson, William F. Wu, Ron Dee and Charles Grant. Published new writers within the last year. Length: 50-100 words minimum; 20,000 words maximum; 10,000 words average. Occasionally critiques rejected mss.

How to Contact: Send complete ms with SASE and cover letter stating past sales. Previously published submissions OK. Prefers letter-quality submissions. Reports in 4 months. Publication could take up to 5 years after acceptance. Sample copy for $7.25.

Payment/Terms: ¼¢/word; 1 contributor's copy. $1 minimum payment. Pays in royalties on publication for first rights.

Advice: "Buy a sample copy and read it thoroughly. Most rejects with my magazine are because people have not checked out what an issue is like or what type of stories I accept. Most rejected stories fall into one of two categories: non-horror fantasy (sword & sorcery, high fantasy) or non-supernatural horror (mad slasher stories, 'Halloween' clones, I call them). When I say that they should read my publication, I'm not whistling Dixie. We hope to up the magazine's frequency to a quarterly. We also plan to be putting out one or two books a year, mostly novels, but short story collections will be considered as well."

‡THE ELOQUENT UMBRELLA, (I,II,IV), Linn-Benton Community College, 6500 SW Pacific Blvd., Albany OR 97321-3779. (541)753-3335. Contact: Linda Smith. Magazine: illustrations and photos. *The Eloquent Umbrella*'s purpose is "to showcase art, photography, poetry and prose of Linn and Benton Counties in Oregon." Annually. Estab. 1990. Circ. 500.

Needs: Condensed/excerpted novel, ethnic/multicultural, experimental, fantasy, feminist, gay, historical, humor/satire, literary, mainstream/contemporary, mystery/suspense, psychic/supernatural/occult, regional, religious/inspirational, romance, science fiction, senior citizen/retirement, sports, translations, westerns, young adult/teen. "No slander, pornography or other material unsuitable for community reading." Accepts 50-100 mss/issue. Reads mss during winter term only; publishes in spring. Length: 1,500 words maximum. Publishes short shorts. Also publishes literary essays, literary criticism and poetry.

How to Contact: Send complete ms with cover letter. Include 1- to 5-line bio. Reports in 6 weeks on mss. SASE for return of ms or send a disposable copy of ms. Simultaneous submissions OK. Sample copy for $2 and 8½×11 SAE.

Payment/Terms: Rights remain with author.

Advice: "The magazine is created by a collective editorial board and production team in a literary publication class."

‡EPITAPH, Tales of Dark Fantasy & Horror, (II), Pirate Writings Publishing, P.O. Box 329, Brightwaters NY 11718. E-mail: pwpubl@aol.com. Editor: Tom Piccirilli. Managing Editor: Edward J. McFadden. Magazine: digest size; 44 pages; 20 lb. paper; CS1 cover stock; illustrations; and photos. Strives "to bring chilling, eerie horror and dark fantasy fiction to the forefront; I want alarming pieces that create an air of unreal authenticity. I will be emphasizing supernatural, occult works with something to say about the mysterious and unknown, but reality-based work is also welcome so long as it contains the flavor of the strange. *Epitaph* will also be actively seeking out new talented writers and those who are gifted, proficient, yet remain under-published in the field." Quarterly. Estab. 1996. Circ. 1,000.

Needs: Fantasy (dark), horror, psychic/supernatural/occult. Receives 150 unsolicited mss/month. Accepts 5-8 mss/issue; 20-36 mss/year. Publishes ms 1 year after acceptance. Length: 2,500 words average; 750 words minimum; 5,000 words maximum. Also publishes poetry. Always critiques or comments on rejected mss.

How to Contact: Send complete ms with a cover letter. Include estimated word count, 1-paragraph bio, Social Security number and list of publications. Reports in 2 weeks on queries; 2 months on mss. SASE. Simultaneous submissions OK. Sample copy for $3.95. Fiction guidelines for #10 SASE. Pays ½-3¢/word on publication and 1 contributor's copy; additional copies for $3.95. Acquires first North American serial rights.

Advice: "I can always appreciate a well put-together story that attempts to do something unusual and rare, a tight, emotion-packed read that shows an author's confidence and skill. Genuine chills count for much more than easy scenes of carnage. Don't try to impress me with merely gore, grue, or other slimy messes; splatter is fine in the context of an embracing read, but it can't be the sole foundation. Remember that horror is an emotion, a situation, and not simply a setting. It is a means to an end—disturbing and enticing the reader. Don't send tales of vampires, werewolves or other staples of the genre; no killer cats, evil kids who do in everyone they meet, or inspirational narratives of frustrated writers who chop, hack, slice or squash an editor for not accepting a story; no continuations of the H.P. Love craft mythos—though I like reading them, I'm not interested in publishing them. Do everything you can to make your story as unpredictable as possible. Learn how to accept constructive criticism."

EYES, (I), Apt. 301, 2715 S. Jefferson Ave., Saginaw MI 48601. (517)752-5202. Editor: Frank J. Mueller, III. Magazine: 8½×11; 36 pages; 20 lb. paper; Antiqua parchment, blue 65 lb. cover. "No specific theme. Speculative fiction and surrealism most welcome. For a general, educated, not necessarily literary audience." Estab. 1991. Circ. 30-40.

Needs: Contemporary, experimental, horror, mainstream, prose poem, romance (gothic). "Especially looking for speculative fiction and surrealism. Dark fantasy OK, but not preferred." Nothing pornographic; no preachiness; children's fiction discouraged. Accepts 4-8 mss/issue. Publishes ms up to 1 year or longer after acceptance. Length: up to 6,000 words. Sometimes critiques rejected mss.

How to Contact: Query first or send complete ms. Reports in 1 month (or less) on queries; 3 months or longer on mss. SASE. No simultaneous submissions. Sample copy for $4; extras $4. Subscriptions $14. (Checks to Frank J. Mueller III.) Fiction guidelines for #10 SASE.

Payment/Terms: Pays one contributor's copy. Acquires one-time rights.

Advice: "Pay attention to character. A strong plot alone, while important, may not be enough to get you in *Eyes*. Atmosphere and mood are also important. Please proofread. If you have a manuscript you like enough to see it in *Eyes*, send it to me. Above all, don't let rejections discourage you. I would encourage the purchase of a sample to get an idea of what I'm looking for."

FIBEROPTIC ETCHINGS, A compilation of teenagers' writing from the information super highway, (IV), Platapus Press, 6645 Windsor Court, Columbia MD 21044. (410)730-2319. E-mail: foetchings@aol.com. Editor: Stacy Cowley. Fiction Editor: Marcello Teson. Magazine: 8½ × 11; 100 pages. "*FiberOptic Etchings* publishes writing by teenagers, intended for a general audience." Annually. Estab. 1995.

Needs: Adventure, condensed/excerpted novel, ethnic/multicultural, experimental, fantasy (science fiction, sword and sorcery), feminist, historical, horror, humor/satire, literary, mainstream/contemporary, mystery/suspense, psychic/supernatural/occult, regional, romance, science fiction, sports, westerns, young adult/teen. "Nothing extraordinarily violent, vulgar, or explicit; no erotica." Receives 5 unsolicited mss/month. Accepts 10-15 mss/issue. Publishes ms 1-10 months after acceptance. Length: 700 words average. Publishes short shorts. Also publishes literary essays, poetry. Always critiques or comments on rejected ms.

How to Contact: Send complete ms with a cover letter (must send via e-mail). Should include 1-2 paragraph bio, list of publications. Reports in 2 weeks. Simultaneous, reprint, electronic submissions (required). Sample copy for $6. Fiction guidelines free.

Payment/Terms: Pays 1 contributor's copy; additional copies 50% discount. Acquires one-time rights. Not copyrighted.

Advice: "We look for manuscripts with a unique viewpoint and clear, fluid writing. Don't be afraid to submit unusual or experimental pieces, and don't be afraid to submit again and again. We're always delighted to look at anything that comes our way—we never know where a treasure will be found."

FREE FOCUS/OSTENTATIOUS MIND, Wagner Press, (I, II), Bowbridge Press, P.O. Box 7415, JAF Station, New York NY 10116-7415. Editor: Patricia Denise Coscia. Editors change each year. Magazine: 8 × 14; 10 pages; recycled paper; illustrations and photos. "*Free Focus* is a small-press magazine which focuses on the educated women of today, and *Ostentatious Mind* is designed to encourage the intense writer, the cutting reality." Bimonthly. Estab. 1985 and 1987. Circ. 100 each.

Needs: Experimental, feminist, humor/satire, literary, mainstream/contemporary, mystery/suspense (romantic), psychic/supernatural/occult, westerns (traditional), young adult/teen (adventure). "X-rated fiction is not accepted." List of upcoming themes available for SASE. Plans future special fiction issue or anthology. Receives 1,000 unsolicited mss/month. Does not read mss February to August. Publishes ms 3-6 months after acceptance. Published work by Edward Janz, A. Anne-Marie Ljung, Christine Warren. Length: 500 words average; 1,000 words maximum. Publishes short shorts. Also publishes literary essays, literary criticism and poetry. Always critiques or comments on rejected mss. Sponsors contest for work submitted to *Free Focus*.

How to Contact: Query with clips of published work or send complete ms with a cover letter. Include 100-word bio and list of publications. Reports in 3 months. Send SASE for reply. Simultaneous submissions OK. Sample copy for $3, #10 SAE and $1 postage. Fiction guidelines for #10 SAE and $1 postage. Reviews novels and short story collections.

Payment/Terms: Pays $2.50-5 and 2 contributor's copies on publication for all rights; additional copies for $2. Sends galleys to author.

Advice: "This publication is for beginning writers. Do not get discouraged; submit your writing. We look for imagination and creativity; no x-rated writing."

‡FREE SPIRIT, A Guide to Scenic Two-wheel Travelling, (I, II), A.M. Publishing, 755 NE Circle Blvd. #1, Corvallis OR 97330. (541)758-5564. Editor: Andrew E. Muench. Magazine: 8½ × 11; 30-40 pages; standard paper; glossy cover; photographs. "Our magazine is looking for accounts of beautiful motorcycle and scooter travels. Our material is intended for people who love to ride motorcycles and love to read literature inspired by motorcycling." Estab. 1996. Circ. 517.

Needs: Adventure, historical, literary, travel, real life experiences, especially motorcycle and scooter travel experiences. "We have taboos against poorly written material that is centered around the drab realism of everyday life." Receives 12 unsolicited mss/month. Accepts 3-4 mss/issue; 12-16 mss/year. Publishes ms 3-4 months after acceptance. Recently published work by Andrew Muench, Jaton Rash and Shannon Cole. Length: 1,500 words average; no minimum; 3,000 words maximum. Publishes short shorts. Also publishes poetry. Often critiques or comments on rejected mss.

How to Contact: Send complete ms with a cover letter. Include estimated word count, ½-1 page bio, list of publications. Reports in 2 weeks on queries; 3-4 weeks on mss. SASE for return of ms. Simultaneous submissions OK. Sample copy for $2.50 and #10 SASE. Fiction guidelines for #10 SASE.

Payment/Terms: Pays 1 contributor's copy on publication. Acquires one-time rights.
Advice: "We select fiction that flows well and inspires readers to ride bizarre two-wheeled vehicles. We need well-thought, creatively written accounts of charming scenic places and experiences you have encountered while riding a motorcycle or scooter. Order an issue before submitting to understand our fictional needs."

THE FUDGE CAKE, A Children's Newsletter, (IV), Francora DTP, P.O. Box 197, Citrus Heights CA 95611-0197. Fiction Editor: Jancarl Campi. Newsletter: 5×8½; 20 pages; 20 lb. bond paper; illustrations. "Our purpose is to provide a showcase for young writers age 6-17. We value the work of today's children and feel they need an outlet to express themselves." Bimonthly. Estab. 1994. Circ. 125.
Needs: Young adult/teen. No erotica. Receives 2-3 unsolicited mss/month. Accepts 3 mss/issue; 18 mss/year. Publishes ms 2 months after acceptance. Length: 400 words average; 250 words minimum; 500 words maximum. Publishes short shorts. Also publishes poetry. Often critiques or comments on rejected mss.
How to Contact: Send complete ms with a cover letter. Include estimated word count and age. Reports in 1 month. Send SASE for reply, return of ms or send a disposable copy of ms. Simultaneous and reprint submissions OK. Sample copy for $3 and 1 first-class stamp. Fiction guidelines for #10 SASE.
Payment/Terms: Pays 1 contributor's copy; additional copies for $3. Acquires one-time rights.

GAY CHICAGO MAGAZINE, (II), Gernhardt Publications, Inc., 3121 N. Broadway, Chicago IL 60657-4522. (773)327-7271. Publisher: Ralph Paul Gernhardt. Associate Publisher: Jerry Williams. Entertainment Editor: Jeff Rossen. Magazine: 8½×11; 80-144 pages; newsprint paper and cover stock; illustrations; photos. Entertainment guide, information for the gay community.
Needs: Erotica (but no explicit hard core), lesbian, gay and romance. Receives "a few" unsolicited mss/month. Acquires 10-15 mss/year. Published new writers within the last year. Length: 1,000-3,000 words.
How to Contact: Send all submissions Attn: Jeff Rossen. Send complete ms with SASE. Accepts 3.5 disk submissions and Macintosh or ASCII Format. Reports in 4-6 weeks on mss. Free sample copy for 9×12 SAE and $1.45 postage.
Payment/Terms: Minimal. 5-10 free contributor's copies; no charge for extras "if within reason." Acquires one-time rights.

GRUE MAGAZINE, (II, IV), Hell's Kitchen Productions, P.O. Box 370, New York NY 10108. E-mail: nadramia@panix.com. Editor: Peggy Nadramia. Magazine: 5½×8½; 96 pages; 60 lb. paper; 10 pt. C1S film laminate cover; illustrations; photos. "We look for quality short fiction centered on horror and dark fantasy—new traditions in the realms of the gothic and the macabre for horror fans well read in the genre, looking for something new and different, as well as horror novices looking for a good scare." Triannually. Estab. 1985.
   ● Two stories from *Grue* were chosen for *The Year's Best Fantasy and Horror Anthology*. This is "cutting-edge" horror.
Needs: Horror, psychic/supernatural/occult. Receives 250 unsolicited fiction mss/month. Accepts 10 mss/issue; 25-30 mss/year. Publishes ms 1-2 years after acceptance. Published work by Thomas Ligotti, Joe R. Lansdale, Don Webb; published new writers within the last year. Length: 4,000 words average; 6,500 words maximum. Sometimes critiques rejected ms.
How to Contact: Send complete ms with cover letter. "I like to hear where the writer heard about *Grue*, his most recent or prestigious sales, and maybe a word or two about himself." Reports in 3 weeks on queries; 6 months on mss. Send SASE for return of ms. Sample copy for $4.50. Fiction guidelines for #10 SASE.
Payment/Terms: Pays ½¢/word on publication and 2 contributor's copies for first North American serial rights.
Advice: "Remember that readers of *Grue* are mainly seasoned horror fans, and *not* interested or excited by a straight vampire, werewolf or ghost story—they'll see all the signs, and guess where you're going long before you get there. Throw a new angle on what you're doing; put it in a new light. How? Well, what scares *you*? What's *your* personal phobia or anxiety? When the writer is genuinely, emotionally involved with his subject matter, and is totally honest with himself and his reader, then we can't help being involved, too, and that's where good writing begins and ends."

READ THE BUSINESS OF FICTION WRITING section to learn the correct way to prepare and submit a manuscript.

HARDBOILED, (I, II), Gryphon Publications, P.O. Box 209, Brooklyn NY 11228-0209. Editor: Gary Lovisi. Magazine: Digest-sized; 100 pages; offset paper; color cover; illustrations. Publishes "cutting edge, hard, noir fiction with impact! Query on nonfiction and reviews." Quarterly. Estab. 1988.

- By "hardboiled" the editor does not mean rehashing of pulp detective fiction from the 1940s and 1950s but, rather, realistic, gritty material. Lovisi could be called a pulp fiction "afficionado," however. He also publishes *Paperback Parade* and holds an annual vintage paperback fiction convention each year.

Needs: Mystery/suspense (private eye, police procedural, noir). Receives 40-60 mss/month. Accepts 20-25 mss/year. Publishes ms within 6 months-2 years of acceptance. Published work by Andrew Vachss, Joe Lansdale, Bill Nolan, Richard Lupoff, Bill Pronzini and Eugene Izzi. Published many new writers within the last year. Length: 2,000 words minimum; 3,000 words maximum. Sometimes critiques rejected mss and recommends other markets.

How to Contact: Query first or send complete ms with cover letter. Query with SASE only on anything over 3,000 words. No full-length novels. Reports in 1 month on queries; 1-2 months on mss. SASE. Simultaneous submissions OK, but query first. Sample copy for $7.

Payment/Terms: Pays $5-50 on publication and 2 contributor's copies for first North American serial rights. Copyright reverts to author.

HAUNTS, Tales of Unexpected Horror and the Supernatural, (II, IV), Nightshade Publications, Box 8068, Cranston RI 02926-0068. (401)781-9438. E-mail: josephkcherkes76520.56@compuserve.com. Editor: Joseph K. Cherkes. Magazine: 6×9 digest; 80-100 pages; 50 lb. offset paper; perfect-bound; pen and ink illustrations. "We are committed to publishing only the finest fiction in the genres of horror, fantasy and the supernatural from both semi-pro and established writers. We are targeted towards the 18-35 age bracket interested in tales of horror and the unknown." Triannually. Plans special fiction issue. Estab. 1984. Circ. 3,500.

Needs: Fantasy, horror, psychic/supernatural/occult. No pure adventure, explicit sex, or blow-by-blow dismemberment. Receives 700-750 unsolicited fiction mss/month. Accepts 10-12 mss/issue; 40-50 mss/year. Published work by Mike Hurley, Kevin J. Anderson, Frank Ward. Published new writers within the last year. Length: 3,500 words average; 1,000 words minimum; 8,500 words maximum. Critiques rejected mss and recommends other markets when possible.

How to Contact: Query first. "Cover letters are a nice way to introduce oneself to a new editor." Open to submissions January 1 to June 1, inclusive. Reports in 2-3 weeks on queries; 3-4 months on mss. SASE for query. Accepts magnetic media (IBM PC-MS/DOS 2.0 or higher), and most major word processing formats. Sample copy for $4.95 plus $1 postage and handling. Fiction guidelines for #10 SASE.

Payment/Terms: Pays $5-50 (subject to change) on publication and contributor's copies; charge for additional copies. Acquires first North American serial rights.

Advice: "Follow writers' guidelines closely. They are a good outline of what your publisher looks for in fiction. If you think you've got the 'perfect' manuscript, go over it again—carefully. Check to make sure you've left no loose ends before sending it out. Keep your writing *concise*. If your story is rejected, don't give up. Try to see where the story failed. This way you can learn from your mistakes. Remember, success comes to those who persist."

‡THE HEALING INN, An Ointment of Love for the Wounded Heart, (I, IV), Christian Airline Personnel Missionary Outreach, 1813 Northwood Court NE, Tacoma WA 98422. Phone/fax: (206)952-1188. Editor: June Shafhid. Magazine: 8×10; 20 pages. "*The Healing Inn* is geared to encouraging Christians that have been wounded by a church or religious cult. The content or message is to draw people back to God and a balance of healthy Christianity, using fiction stories to encourage their hearts and testimonies to teach them to be individuals before God and man." Estab. 1995. Circ. 2,000.

Needs: Adventure, humor/satire, religious/inspirational. "All stories must have an inspirational message. No judgmental or harsh stories." Publishes ms 3-6 months after acceptance. Length: 2,000 words average; 500 words minimum; 3,000 words maximum. Publishes short shorts. Also publishes poetry.

How to Contact: Send complete ms with a cover letter. Include estimated word count, a short bio and Social Security number. Reports in 2-4 weeks on mss. Send SASE for return of ms. Simultaneous submissions and reprints OK. Sample copy free.

Payment/Terms: Pays free subscription to the magazine and contributor's copies. Acquires first North American serial rights.

Advice: "I look for well-written stories that touch the heart—whether it be humorous or drama. Heartfelt, heartwrenching, life-changing themes catch my eye. Write from your heart; be expressive and honest."

♣HECATE'S LOOM, (I, II, IV), Box 5206, Station B, Victoria, British Columbia V8R 6N4 Canada. (604)478-9287. E-mail: loom@islandnet.com. Editor: Yvonne Owens. Magazine: 8½×11; 46-52 pages; 60 lb. paper, 50% recycled; 70 lb. coated cover stock; illustrations and photos. Publishes stories about "wiccans, pagans, women's spirituality, men's spirituality, goddess consciousness, alternative politics/spirituality/healing and shamanism." Quarterly. Estab. 1986. Circ. 2,000.

• *Hecate's Loom* is a member of the Canadian Magazine Publishers Association and the Wiccan/ Pagan Press Alliance.

Needs: Condensed/excerpted novel, erotica, ethnic/multicultural, fantasy (science, sword and sorcery, historic), feminist, gay, historical, humor/satire, lesbian, literary, mainstream/contemporary, psychic/ supernatural/occult, religious/inspirational, romance (contemporary, futuristic/time travel, gothic, historical), science fiction (soft/sociological), serialized novel, "green politics," eco-feminism, shamanic. Upcoming themes: "Music, Enchantment and Fantasy Media" (Spring); "Pan-sexuality" (Summer); "Harvest Festival/Harvest Gods" (Fall). List of upcoming themes available for SASE. Receives 10-20 unsolicited mss/month. Accepts 1-2 mss/issue; 4-6 mss/year. Publishes ms 3-12 months after acceptance. Recently published work by Diana Michaelis, Yvonne Owens, Robin Skelton, John Threlfall and Anne M. Kelly. Length: 1,500 words average; 1,000 words minimum; 2,000 words maximum. Publishes short shorts. Also publishes literary essays, literary criticism and poetry.

How to Contact: Send complete ms with a cover letter. Include estimated word count, bio (75-250 words), Social Security number and list of publications with submission. Reports in 3 months. Send SASE for reply, return of ms or send a disposable copy of ms. Simultaneous and electronic submissions OK. Sample copy for $7 and SAE. Fiction guidelines for SASE ("Canadian stamps only") or SAE and IRC.

Payment/Terms: Pays 1 contributor's copy; additional copies for $3. Acquires one-time rights.

Advice: Pieces "must be well written, with strong character development and memorable imagery to reflect Wiccan/pagan values and goddess/earth spirituality. Please write clearly to *communicate*, rather than to experiment with literary technique. Lyricism is fine where it serves the imagery or plot, but writing should not be too flowery. We would like to see more of the inside of the pagan 'mind.' True pagan sensibilities offer a radically alternative perspective and subtle differences in perception. Nothing trite, shallow or sleazy."

HOPSCOTCH: THE MAGAZINE FOR GIRLS, (II), The Bluffton News Publishing & Printing Co., P.O. Box 164, Bluffton OH 45817. (419)358-4610. Fax: (419)358-5027. Editor: Marilyn Edwards. Magazine: 7×9; 50 pages; enamel paper; pen & ink illustrations; photographs. Publishes stories for and about girls ages 5-12. Bimonthly. Estab. 1989. Circ. 9,000.

• *Hopscotch* is indexed in the *Children's Magazine Guide* and *Ed Press* and has received a Parents' Choice Gold Medal Award and Ed Press Awards.

Needs: Children's/juvenile (5-9, 10-12 years): adventure, ethnic/multicultural, fantasy, historical (general), sports. Upcoming themes: "Seeing is Believing" (Feb. '97); "Birds" (Apr. '97); "The Old West" (June '97); "Sports" (Aug. '97); "Teeth" (Oct. '97); "Cooking" (Dec. '97). Receives 300-400 unsolicited mss/month. Accepts 20-40 mss/year. Agented fiction 2%. Published work by Lois Grambling, Betty Killion, Jean Patrick, VaDonna Jean Leaf. Length: 500-750 words preferred; 300 words minimum; 750 words maximum. Publishes short shorts. Length: 250-400 words. Also publishes poetry, puzzles, hidden pictures and crafts. Always comments on rejected mss.

How to Contact: Send complete ms with cover letter. Include estimated word count, 1-page bio, Social Security number and list of publications. Reports in 2-4 weeks on queries; 6-10 weeks on mss. Send SASE for reply, return of ms or send disposable copy of the ms. Simultaneous and reprint submissions OK. Sample copy for $3. Fiction guidelines for #10 SASE. Reviews novels and short story collections.

Payment/Terms: Pays 5¢/word (extra for usable photos or illustrations) before publication and 1 contributor's copy for first North American serial rights; additional copies $3; $2 for 10 or more.

Advice: "Make sure you have studied copies of our magazine to see what we like. Follow our theme list. We are looking for wholesome stories. This is what our publication is all about."

‡HOR-TASY, (II, IV), Ansuda Publications, Box 158-J, Harris IA 51345. Editor/Publisher: Daniel R. Betz. Magazine: 5½×8½; 72 pages; mimeo paper; index stock cover; illustrations on cover. "*Hor-Tasy* is bringing back actual *horror* to horror lovers tired of seeing so much science fiction and SF passed off as horror. We're also very much interested in true, poetic, pure fantasy."

Needs: Fantasy and horror. "Pure fantasy: Examples are trolls, fairies and mythology. The horror we're looking for comes from the human mind—the ultimate form of horror. It must sound real—so real that in fact it could very possibly happen at any time and place. We must be able to feel the diseased mind behind the personality. No science fiction in any way, shape or form. We don't want stories in which the main character spends half his time talking to a shrink. We don't want stories that start out with: 'You're crazy,' said so and so." Receives 15-20 unsolicited fiction mss each month. Accepts 6 mss/issue.

How to Contact: Send complete ms with SASE. Simultaneous submissions OK ("if we know about it.") "If not interested (in ms), we return immediately. If interested, we may keep it as long as 2 months." Publishes ms an average of 1 year after acceptance. Sample copy for $4.

Payment/Terms: Pays 2 contributor's copies. Extras at cover price less special discount rates. Acquires first North American serial rights.

Advice: "Most stories rejected are about spooks, monsters, haunted houses, spacemen, etc. Because *Hor-Tasy* is a unique publication, I suggest the potential writer get a sample copy. Only unpublished work will be considered."

HOUSEWIFE-WRITER'S FORUM, (I, II), P.O. Box 780, Lyman WY 82937. (307)782-7003. Editor: Emma Bluemel. Fiction Editor: Edward Wahl. Magazine: 6½ × 10; 32-48 pages; glossy cover; illustrations. Offers "support for women and house husbands of all ages who juggle writing with family life. We publish short fiction, poetry, essays, nonfiction, line drawings, humor and hints." Bimonthly. Estab. 1988. Circ. over 2,000.
  ● This magazine also includes fiction marketing tips and information.

Needs: Contemporary, experimental, historical, humor/satire, literary, mainstream, mystery/suspense, romance (contemporary, historical). No pornographic material. Receives 100-200 mss/month. Accepts 1-2 mss/issue; 6-12 mss/year. Publishes ms within 6 months-1 year after acceptance. Published work by Elaine McCormick, Carol Shenold and Carole Bellacera. Length: 1,500 words preferred; 500 words minimum; 2,000 words maximum. Publishes short shorts. Publishes critiques of accepted mss.

How to Contact: Send complete ms with cover letter. Reports in 3-4 months on mss. Send SASE "with *adequate* postage." Simultaneous and reprint submissions OK. Sample copy for $4. Fiction guidelines for #10 SASE.

Payment/Terms: Pays 1¢/word on acceptance and 1 contributor's copy; additional copies half price. Sponsors annual contest "geared to the interests of housewife-writers. First place winners are published in the magazine." Entry fee: $4. Prize: $30. Send #10 SASE for guidelines and further information.

Advice: "All mss are read and sometimes suggestions are offered on the rejections. All published materials are printed with Fiction Editor Edward Wahl's critiques. Here are a few samples of our critiques to show you what we're looking for: 'Life is made up of small details. Writing often consists of finding the right ones out of the thousands that make up even the briefest moment and using them to convey information to the reader. There's more to this than just a bunch of required items and small details, though. There is also believable dialogue, controlled pacing, and a fine ending that fits the tone and the action and the narrator just right. I look for the overall effect of the story—the product of its theme, its narrative skill, its handling of detail and pace and dialogue, its felicity of beginning, transition and ending. The degree to which all these things mesh and contribute to a whole meaning that surpasses the mere sum of the constituents is the degree to which a story succeeds.' "

HURRICANE ALICE, A Feminist Quarterly, (II), Hurricane Alice Fn., Inc., Dept. of English, Rhode Island College, Providence RI 02908. E-mail: mreddy@grog.ric.edu. Executive Editor: Maureen Reddy. Fiction is collectively edited. Tabloid: 11 × 17; 12-16 pages; newsprint stock; illustrations and photos. "We look for feminist fictions with a certain analytic snap, for serious readers, seriously interested in emerging forms of feminist art/artists." Quarterly. Estab. 1983. Circ. 600-700.

Needs: Erotica, experimental, feminist, gay, humor/satire, lesbian, science fiction, translations. No coming-out stories, defloration stories, abortion stories. Upcoming themes: "Legend(s) of Bad Women," "Young Feminists" and "Transformations." Receives 80 unsolicited mss/month. Publishes 8-10 stories annually. Publishes mss up to 1 year after acceptance. Published work by Beth Brant, Nona Caspers, Gretchen Legler, Joanna Kadi, Toni McNaron; published new writers within the last year. Length: up to 3,000 words maximum. Publishes short shorts. Occasionally critiques rejected mss.

How to Contact: Send complete ms with cover letter. "A brief biographical statement is never amiss. Writers should be sure to tell us if a piece was commissioned by one of the editors." Reports in 3-4 months. SASE for ms. Simultaneous submissions OK. Sample copy for $2.50, 11 × 14 SAE and 2 first-class stamps.

Payment/Terms: Pays 5 contributor's copies. Acquires one-time rights.

Advice: "Fiction is a craft. Just because something happened, it isn't a story; it becomes a story when you transform it through your art, your craft."

INNER VOICES, A New Journal of Prison Literature, (I, IV), Inner Voices, P.O. Box 4500, #219, Bloomington IN 47402. E-mail: cnwillia@indiana.edu. Editor: C. Nolan Williams. 8½ × 5½; 50 pages; matte paper; card stock cover; illustrations. Publishes literature written by prisoners. Semianually. Estab. 1995. Circ. 200.

Needs: Open to all fiction except children's and young adult. Receives 20 unsolicited mss/month. Accepts 20-30 mss/issue; 40-60 mss/year. Time between acceptance and publication varies. Recently published work by Paul X, Salazar, Emil P. Dill and Mitchell V. Martinez. Length: 3,000 words average; 10,000 words maximum. Publishes short shorts. Also publishes poetry. Sometimes critiques or comments on rejected mss.

How to Contact: Send complete ms with a cover letter. Include a personal statement (100-150 words) with submission. Reports in 1 month on queries; 3 months on mss. Send a disposable copy of ms. Simultaneous, reprint and electronic (Mac or modem) submissions OK. Sample copy $4; some free to prisoners. Fiction guidelines free. Reviews novels and short story collections.

Payment/Terms: Pays with free subscription to magazine or 1-2 contributor's copies. Acquires first rights and reprint rights.

Advice: "Find someone who isn't afraid to critique your work and treat that person like gold. Then, give us a try. Please, no position essays or explicit descriptions of crimes or sex. These may be banned from prison libraries. We want to show the range of talent in prisons. I try for a good balance of styles and themes, so do not try to imitate past publications. We get way more religious pieces and midnight meditations than we can use, so the odds are against these. Plenty of love poetry, too. But just give it a try, whatever your best work is." Sometimes enters writers' work in other organizations' contests.

INTUITIVE EXPLORATIONS, A Journal of Intuitive Processes, (I, II, IV), Intuitive Explorations, P.O. Box 561, Quincy IL 62306-0561. (217)222-9082. Editor: Gloria Reiser. Magazine: 8½ × 11; 28 pages. "*Intuitive Explorations* publishes mind explorations for an audience very interested in exploring the unknown and inner worlds." Bimonthly. Estab. 1987. Circ. 1,000.

Needs: Ethnic/multicultural, psychic/supernatural/occult, religious/inspirational (futuristic/time travel), ancient worlds, future worlds, other realms. Accepts 1 mss/issue; 6 mss/year. Publishes ms 1-2 issues after acceptance. Published work by Father John Groff. Length 700-1,000 words average; 300 words minimum; 2,000 words maximum. Publishes short shorts. Also publishes literary essays, poetry. Sometimes critiques or comments on rejected ms.

How to Contact: Send complete ms with a cover letter. Should include estimated word count and short bio. Reports in 2 months on queries; 2-3 months on mss. Send SASE for reply, return of ms or send a disposable copy of ms. Simultaneous and reprint submissions OK. Sample copy for $1, 9 × 12 SAE and 4 first-class stamps. Reviews novels and short story collections.

Payment/Terms: Pays up to 6 contributor's copies; additional copies 75¢ each. Acquires one-time rights.

Advice: "I'd like to see more fiction in which tarot is woven into the story line as well as stories honoring intuition and/or the earth."

ITALIAN AMERICANA, (I, II, IV), URI/CCE 80 Washington St., Providence RI 02903-1803. (401)277-5306. Editor: Carol Bonomo Albright. Poetry Editor: Dana Gioia. Magazine: 6 × 9; approximately 200 pages; varnished cover; perfect-bound; photographs. "*Italian Americana* contains historical articles, fiction, poetry and memoirs, all concerning the Italian experience in the Americas." Semiannually. Estab. 1974. Circ. 1,000.

Needs: Italian American: literary. Receives 10 mss/month. Accepts 3 mss/issue; 6-7 mss/year. Publishes up to 1 year after acceptance. Agented fiction 5%. Recently published work by Paola Corso, Kenny Marotta and Albert DiBartolomeo. Length: 20 double-spaced pages. Publishes short shorts. Also publishes literary essays, literary criticism, poetry. Sometimes critiques rejected mss. Sponsors $500-1,000 literature prize annually.

How to Contact: Send complete ms (in triplicate) with a cover letter. Include 3-5 line bio, list of publications. Reports in 1 month on queries; 2-4 months on mss. Send SASE for reply, return of ms or send a disposable copy of ms. No simultaneous submissions. Sample copy for $6. Fiction guidelines for SASE. Reviews novels and short story collections. Send books to Professor John Paul Russo, English Dept., Univ. of Miami, Coral Gables, FL 33124.

Payment/Terms: Awards $250 to best fiction of year and 1 contributor's copy; additional copies $7. Acquires first North American serial rights.

Advice: "Please individualize characters, instead of presenting types (i.e., lovable uncle, aunt, etc.). No nostalgia."

IT'S YOUR CHOICE MAGAZINE, International Journal of Ethics and Morality, (I), Future-Wend Publications, P.O. Box 7135, Richmond VA 23221-0135. Editor: Dr. James Rogers. Newsletter: 8½ × 11; 8-20 pages; 20 lb. bond paper. "*It's Your Choice*— where science meets religion." Monthly. Estab. 1993.

Needs: Adventure, children's/juvenile (10-12 years), ethnic/multicultural, experimental, fantasy (science), feminist, gay, historical, horror, humor/satire, lesbian, mystery/suspense, psychic/supernatural/occult, religious/inspirational, science fiction (soft/sociological), young adult/teen. Special interests: ethics, morality. Publishes annual special fiction issue or anthology. Published work by Bill Lockwood, Kris Kincaid and Kris Neri. Length: 1,000 words maximum. Publishes short shorts.

How to Contact: Send complete ms with a cover letter. Include estimated word count. Reports in 1 month on mss. (Retention indicates continued interest. Mss returned on request.) Simultaneous and reprint submissions OK. Sample copy for $2 and #10 SASE. Fiction guidelines for #10 SASE.

Payment/Terms: Pays up to $1/word and 10 contributor's copies; additional copies $1. Sponsors annual contest. Send $2 for mss registration form.

Advice: "Do not overwrite. Follow guidelines precisely. No clips."

JEWISH CURRENTS MAGAZINE, (IV), 22 E. 17th St., New York NY 10003. (212)924-5740. Editor-in-Chief: Morris U. Schappes. Magazine: 5½ × 8½; 48 pages. "We are a progressive monthly, broad in our interests, printing feature articles on political and cultural aspects of Jewish life in the US and elsewhere, reviews of books and film, poetry and fiction, Yiddish translations; regular columns on Israel, US Jewish community, current events, Jewish women today, secular Jewish life. National audience, literate and politically left, well educated." Monthly. Estab. 1946. Circ. 2,600.

● This magazine may be slow to respond. They continue to be backlogged.

Needs: Contemporary, ethnic, feminist, historical, humor/satire, literary, senior citizen/retirement, translations. "We are interested in *authentic* experience and readable prose; Jewish themes; humanistic orientation. No religious, political sectarian; no porn or hard sex, no escapist stuff. Go easy on experimentation, but we're interested." Upcoming themes (submit at least 3 months in advance): "Black History Month" (February); "International Women's Day"; "Purim"; "Jewish Music Season" (March); "Holocaust and Resistance Commemoration" (April); "Israeli Independence Day" (May); "Jewish Book Month" (November). Receives 6-10 unsolicited fiction mss/month. Accepts 0-1 ms/issue; 8-10 mss/year. Recently published work by Joyce Charton, Paul Corriel, Rachel Ellner and Jack Levine. Published new writers within the last year. Length: 1,000 words minimum; 3,000 words maximum; 1,800 words average. Also publishes literary essays, literary criticism, poetry.

How to Contact: Send complete ms with cover letter. "Writers should include brief biographical information, especially their publishing histories." SAE. No simultaneous submissions. Reports in 2 months on mss. Publishes ms 2-24 months after acceptance. Sample copy for $3 with SAE and 3 first-class stamps. Reviews novels and short story collections.

Payment/Terms: Pays complimentary one-year subscription and 6 contributor's copies. "We readily give reprint permission at no charge." Sends galleys to author.

Advice: Noted for "stories with Jewish content, especially intergenerational relations, and personal Jewish experience—e.g., immigrant or Holocaust memories, assimilation dilemmas, etc. Matters of character and moral dilemma, maturing into pain and joy, dealing with Jewish conflicts OK. Space is increasingly a problem. Tell the truth, as sparely as possible."

JOURNAL OF POLYMORPHOUS PERVERSITY, (I), Wry-Bred Press, Inc., 10 Waterside Plaza, Suite 20-B, New York NY 10010. (212)689-5473. Editor: Glenn Ellenbogen. Magazine: 6¾ × 10; 24 pages; 60 lb. paper; antique india cover stock; illustrations with some articles. "*JPP* is a humorous and satirical journal of psychology, psychiatry, and the closely allied mental health disciplines." For "psychologists, psychiatrists, social workers, psychiatric nurses, *and* the psychologically sophisticated layman." Semiannually. Estab. 1984.

Needs: Humor/satire. "We only consider materials that are funny or that relate to psychology *or* behavior." Receives 50 unsolicited mss/month. Accepts 8 mss/issue; 16 mss/year. Most writers published last year were previously unpublished writers. Length: 1,500 words average; 4,000 words maximum. Comments on rejected mss.

How to Contact: Send complete ms *in triplicate*. Reports in 1-3 months on mss. SASE. Sample copy for $7. Fiction guidelines for #10 SASE.

Payment/Terms: Pays 2 contributor's copies; additional copies $7.

Advice: "We will *not* look at poetry. We only want to see intelligent spoofs of scholarly psychology and psychiatry articles written in scholarly scientific language. Take a look at *real* journals of psychology and try to lampoon their *style* as much as their content. There are few places to showcase satire of the social sciences, thus we provide one vehicle for injecting a dose of humor into this often too serious area. Occasionally, we will accept a piece of creative writing written in the first person, e.g. 'A Subjective Assessment of the Oral Doctoral Defense Process: I Don't Want to Talk About It, If You Want to Know the Truth' (the latter being a piece in which Holden Caulfield shares his experiences relating to obtaining his Ph.D. in Psychology). Other creative pieces have involved a psychodiagnostic evaluation of The Little Prince (as a psychiatric patient) and God being refused tenure (after having created the world) because of insufficient publications and teaching experience."

‡KELTIC FRINGE, (II, IV), Kittatinny Press, Box 3292, RD#3, Uniondale PA 18470. (717)679-2745. Editor: Maureen Williams. Magazine: 8½ × 11; 16 pages; offset printed on quality stock paper; card stock cover; illustrations and photos. Publishes "work by Kelts and/or matters Keltic." Quarterly. Estab. 1986. Circ. 300.

● *Keltic Fringe* is interested in the work of writers from the "six Keltic nations": Scotland, Isle of Man, Ireland, Wales, Cornwall, Brittany; Kelts around the world and anyone interested in Keltic culture.

Needs: Keltic: ethnic/multicultural, historical, myth, legend. Looks for "creative retelling of Keltic legends, history, modern Keltic tales." Receives 10-20 unsolicited mss/month. Accepts 1 ms/issue; 4 mss/year. Publishes ms 3-12 months after acceptance. Length: 1,500 words average, 200 words minimum; 3,000 words maximum. Publishes short shorts. Also publishes literary essays, literary criticism, and poetry (only as part of features and themes).

How to Contact: Send complete ms with a cover letter. Include estimated word count, bio (50-words maximum) and statement of Keltic connection. Reports in 2 weeks. Send SASE for reply, return of ms or send a disposable copy of ms. Simultaneous and disk submissions OK. Sample copy for $3.50. Fiction guidelines for #10 SASE. Reviews novels and short story collections.

Payment/Terms: Pays 2-10 contributor's copies; additional copies for $1.75. Acquires first North American serial rights. Sends galleys to author if ms is substantially edited.

Advice: "We want lively, Keltic flavor; not sentimental but poignant. We would like to see fictionalized family memoirs with Keltic setting; magic realism in the form of modern mythology. No trite or mawkish tales. Study sample issue."

LACUNAE, (I, II), Lacunae Publications/CFD Productions, P.O. Box 827, Clifton Park NY 12065. (518)877-4908. Fax: (518)877-0981. E-mail: lacunaemag@aol.com or 75221.560@compuserve.com. Editor: Pamela Hazelton. Magazine: 6⅝×10¼; 40-64 pages; 50 lb. offset paper; slick, glossy cover; illustrations and photos."*Lacunae* is for mature readers of fiction, poetry, comics, reviews, interviews and news." Bimonthly. Estab. 1994. Circ. 2,500-5,000.

Needs: Adventure, erotica, fantasy, horror, humor/satire, literary, mainstream/contemporary, mystery/suspense (amateur sleuth, cozy, police procedural, private eye/hardboiled), psychic/supernatural/occult, science fiction, comic books. "No romance." List of upcoming themes available for SASE. Receives 50-60 unsolicited mss/month. Accepts 5-15 mss/issue; 30-75 mss/year. Publishes ms 1-6 months after acceptance. Recently published work by H.W. Sierra, Joe Monks, Wayne Allen Sallee and Peter Quinones. Length: 2,000 words average; 400 words minimum; 4,000 words maximum. Publishes short shorts. Also publishes literary essays, literary criticism, poetry. Always critiques or comments on rejected mss. Sponsors contests, awards or grants for fiction writers. Charges $5/story, $2/poem; include SASE.

How to Contact: Send complete ms with a cover letter or upload via modem. Include estimated word count, short bio, Social Security number, list of publications. Reports in 1 week on queries; 3-6 weeks on mss. Send SASE for reply, return of ms or send a disposable copy of ms. Simultaneous, reprint and electronic submissions OK.Sample copy for $3.25. Fiction guidelines for SASE. Reviews novels and short story collections. Send books to Attention: Reviews.

Payment/Terms: Pays 5-50 contributor's copies; additional copies $1. Acquires one-time rights. Writer retains all rights.

Advice: "Read *Lacunae* to see if you want your work spotlighted with us. Then, read your work out loud to make sure the reader will understand it. Be clear and concise. Make sure to include name and address on the manuscript and SASE. I like to read horror that makes me squirm, mystery that makes me think, and humor that makes me laugh. I don't want to see lovey-dovey stories—aaachk!"

LEFT CURVE, (II), P.O. Box 472, Oakland CA 94604. (510)763-7193. E-mail: leftcurv@wco.com. Editor: Csaba Polony. Magazine: 8½×11; 130 pages; 60 lb. paper; 100 pt. C1S Durosheen cover; illustrations; photos. "*Left Curve* is an artist-produced journal addressing the problem(s) of cultural forms emerging from the crises of modernity that strive to be independent from the control of dominant institutions, based on the recognition of the destructiveness of commodity (capitalist) systems to all life." Published irregularly. Estab. 1974. Circ. 2,000.

Needs: Contemporary, ethnic, experimental, historical, literary, prose poem, regional, science fiction, translations, political. "We publish critical, open, social/political-conscious writing." Upcoming theme: "Cyberspace and Nature." Receives approximately 12 unsolicited fiction mss/month. Accepts approximately 1 ms/issue. Publishes ms a maximum of 12 months after acceptance. Recently published work by Pēter Lengyel and Michael Filas. Length: 1,200 words average; 500 words minimum; 2,500 words maximum. Publishes short shorts. Sometimes comments on rejected mss.

How to Contact: Send complete ms with cover letter. Include "statement of writer's intent, brief bio and reason for submitting to *Left Curve*." Electronic submissions OK; "prefer 3½ disk and hard copy, though we do accept e-mail submissions." Reports in 3-6 months. SASE. Sample copy for $8, 9×12 SAE and $1.24 postage. Fiction guidelines for 1 first-class stamp.

Payment/Terms: Pays in contributor's copies. Rights revert to author.

Advice: "Dig deep; no superficial personalisms, no corny satire. Be honest, realistic and gorge out the truth you wish to say. Understand yourself and the world. Have writing be a means to achieve or realize what is real."

LIBERTY, (II), Liberty Foundation, P.O. Box 1181, Port Townsend WA 98368. Phone/fax: (360)385-3704. E-mail: rwb@daka.com. Editor: R.W. Bradford. Fiction Editor: Stephen Cox. Magazine: 8½×11; 72 pages; non-coated paper; self-cover; illustrations; some photos. "We are a libertarian magazine that publishes mostly nonfiction with no more than one short story per issue. We are interested in intelligent, nondidactic fiction with individualistic and anti-authoritarian themes." Bimonthly. Estab. 1987. Circ. 14,000.

● *Liberty* has received the Mencken Award for Best Feature Story and several *Pushcart Prize* nominations.

Needs: Experimental, fantasy (science), feminist, gay, horror, humor/satire, lesbian, literary, mainstream/contemporary, mystery/suspense (private eye/hardboiled), science fiction. Receives 5-10 unsolicited mss/month. Accepts 0-1 mss/issue. Published work by Greg Jenkins, J. Orlin Grabbe, Karen Michalson and Richard Kostelanetz. Publishes short shorts. Also publishes literary essays, literary criticism and poetry.

How to Contact: Send complete ms with a cover letter. Include estimated word count and bio (1-2 sentences) with submission. Send SASE for reply, return of ms or send a disposable copy of ms. Electronic (ASCII disk) submissions OK. Sample copy for $4. Fiction guidelines for SASE. Reviews novels and short story collections. Send books to Jesse Walker, Books Editor.

Payment/Terms: Pays 3 contributor's copies; additional copies for $2. Acquires first serial rights, plus right to reprint, anthologize, or republish digitally.

Advice: "We prefer stories that don't wear their politics on their sleeve. Good writing is more important than a good message. Read the magazine first to see the kind of *non*fiction we publish. Don't try to imitate the fiction you see, but make yourself aware of the audience you're writing for. We like to see more subtlety, less overt moralizing. Messages are fine—but don't insert yourself into the story to announce them."

‡LININGTON LINEUP, (IV), Elizabeth Linington Society, 1223 Glen Terrace, Glassboro NJ 08028-1315. Editor: Rinehart S. Potts. Newsletter: 8½ × 11; 16 pages; bond paper and cover stock; illustrations and photographs. "For those interested in the publications of Elizabeth Linington (a/k/a Lesley Egan, Egan O'Neill, Anne Blaisdell, Dell Shannon)—historical fiction and detective mysteries—therefore material must relate in some way thereto." Bimonthly. Plans special fiction issue. Estab. 1984. Circ. 400.

● Elizabeth Linington wrote 90 books under her many pen names. Among the mysteries she wrote as Dell Shannon are *The Dispossessed, Destiny of Death* and *Chaos of Crime*. As Lesley Egan she wrote several books including *Little Boy Lost* and *The Miser*.

Needs: *Charges reading fee of $1. Requires magazine subscription of $12 before reading.* Historical (general), literary, mystery/suspense. Receives 3-4 fiction mss/month. Accepts 1 ms/issue; 6 mss/year. Publishes ms 3 months after acceptance. Recently published work by Stephen Wright and Lyn McConchie. Publishes short shorts. Also publishes literary essays, literary criticism, poetry. Sometimes comments on rejected mss.

How to Contact: Query first. Reports in 1 month. SASE. No simultaneous submissions. Reprint submissions OK. Sample copy for $3. Reviews novels, short story collections and reference books/criticism in mystery field.

Payment/Terms: Pays subscription to magazine. Acquires first rights.

Advice: "Become familiar with Miss Linington's books and continuing characters. We have been receiving material which completely disregards the information cited above."

LOST WORLDS, The Science Fiction and Fantasy Forum, (I, IV), HBD Publishing, P.O. Box 605, Concord NC 28025. (704)933-7998. Editor: Holley B. Drye. Newsletter: 8½ × 11; 48 pages; 24 lb. bond paper; full-color cover; b&w illustrations. "General interest science fiction and fantasy, as well as some specialized genre writing. For broad-spectrum age groups, anyone interested in newcomers." Monthly. Estab. 1988. Circ. 150.

Needs: Experimental, fantasy, horror, psychic/supernatural/occult, science fiction (hard science, soft/sociological), serialized novel. Publishes annual special fiction issue. Receives 35-45 unsolicited mss/month. Accepts 10-14 mss/issue; 100 and up mss/year. Publishes ms 1 year after acceptance (unless otherwise notified). Length: 3,000 words preferred; 2,000 words minimum; 5,500 words maximum. Publishes short shorts. Sometimes critiques rejected mss and recommends other markets. "Although we do not publish every type of genre fiction, I will, if asked, critique anyone who wishes to send me their work. There is no fee for reading or critiquing stories."

How to Contact: Query first. "Cover letters should include where and when to contact the author, a pen name, if one is preferred, as well as their real name, and whether or not they wish their real names to be kept confidential. Due to overwhelming response, we are currently unable to predict response time to mss or queries. Phone calls are welcome to check on manuscripts." SASE for return of ms. Simultaneous and reprint submissions OK. Accepts electronic submissions via disk or modem. Sample copy for $2. Fiction guidelines free.

FOR INFORMATION ON ENTERING the *Novel & Short Story Writer's Market* Cover Letter Contest, see page 16.

Payment/Terms: Pays contributor's copies. Acquires one-time rights.

Advice: "I look for originality of story, good characterization and dialogue, well-written descriptive passages, and over-all story quality. The presentation of the work also makes a big impression, whether it be good or bad. Neat, typed manuscripts will always have a better chance than hand-written or badly typed ones. All manuscripts are read by either three or four different people, with an eye towards development of plot and comparison to other material within the writer's field of experience. Plagiarism is not tolerated, and we do look for it while reading a manuscript under consideration. If you have any questions, feel free to call—we honestly don't mind. Never be afraid to send us anything, we really are kind people."

‡LOVING ALTERNATIVES MAGAZINE, (IV), Omnific Designs West, P.O. Box 459, San Dimas CA 91773. (909)592-5217. Fax: (818)915-4715. E-mail: lovalt@earthlink.net. Editor: Ric Alderson. Fiction Editor: Cindy Alderson. Magazine: 8½×11; 64 pages; 50 lb. book paper; 70 lb. matte cover stock; illustrations and photos. Trys "to present positive image for all alternative lifestyles through articles, news, event calendars, discussions, interviews, etc." Bimonthly. Estab. 1990. Circ. 5,000.

Needs: Erotica, fantasy (romantic/erotic), gay, lesbian. Especially interested in any material for any alternative lifestyle. Upcoming themes: "Censorship"; "Adult Entertainment Industry." List of upcoming themes available for SASE. Receives 10 unsolicited mss/month. Accepts 1 mss/issue; 6 mss/year. Publishes ms 2 months after acceptance. Length: 1,000 words average; 500 words minimum; 1,500 words maximum. "If longer, it can be continued to next issue(s)." Publishes short shorts. Also publishes literary essays and poetry.

How to Contact: Query first. Include short bio and list of publications. Reports in 2 weeks. Send SASE for reply, return of ms or send a disposable copy of ms. Simultaneous submissions, reprints and electronic submissions OK. Sample copy for 9×12 SAE and 4 first-class stamps. Fiction guidelines free

Payment/Terms: Pays 10 contributor's copies on publication. "We also provide a ¼-page ad in six issues for each article accepted." Acquires one-time rights.

Advice: Looks for "subtle humor, positive attitude and fun—informative pieces with a different angle."

MAIL CALL, Delivery Civil War Correspondence, (IV), Distant Frontier Press, P.O. Box 5031, South Hackensack NJ 07606. Phone/fax: (201)296-0419. E-mail: mailcall1@aol.com. Editor: Anna Pansini. Newsletter: 8½×11; 8 pages; 20 lb. paper; illustrations. *Mail Call* publishes pieces on the Civil War. Bimonthly. Estab. 1990. Circ. 500.

Needs: Historical (the Civil War). Receives 20 unsolicited mss/month. Accepts 1 mss/issue; 6 mss/year. Publishes ms up to 1½ years after acceptance. Length: 500 words minimum; 1,500 words maximum. Also publishes literary essays, literary criticism and poetry. Sometimes critiques or comments on rejected ms.

How to Contact: Send complete ms with a cover letter mentioning "any relations from the Civil War period." Reports in 1 year. SASE for return of ms. Simultaneous, reprint and electronic (disk) submissions OK. Sample copy and fiction guidelines are included in a writer's packet for $5.

Payment/Terms: Pays in contributor's copies. Acquires one-time rights.

Advice: Wants more "personal accounts" and no "overused themes. We want material written from the heart, not the pocketbook. Flashy is not a part of this publication."

MAJESTIC BOOKS, (I, IV), P.O. Box 19097A, Johnston RI 02919. Fiction Editor: Cindy MacDonald. Bound soft cover short story anthologies; 5½×8½; 192 pages; 60 lb. paper; C1S cover stock. "Majestic Books is a small press which was formed to give children an outlet for their work. We publish soft cover bound anthologies of fictional stories by children, for children and adults who enjoy the work of children." Triannually. Estab. 1993. Circ. 250.

● Although Majestic Books is a small publisher, they are in the market for short fiction for their anthologies. They do a book of stories by children.

Needs: Stories written on any subject by children (under 18) only. Children's/juvenile (10-12 years), young adult (13-18 years). Receives 50 unsolicited mss/month. Accepts 80 mss/year. Publishes ms 1 year maximum after acceptance. Length: 100 words minimum; 2,500 words maximum. Publishes short shorts. Also publishes literary essays. Always critiques or comments on rejected mss.

How to Contact: Send complete ms with a cover letter. Include estimated word count and author's age. Reports in 3 weeks. Send SASE for reply. Simultaneous submissions OK. Sample copy for $3. Fiction guidelines for #10 SASE.

Payment/Terms: Pays 10% royalty for all books sold due to the author's inclusion.

Advice: "We love stories that will keep a reader thinking long after they have read the last word. Be original. We have received some manuscripts of shows we have seen on television or books we have read. Write from inside you and you'll be surprised at how much better your writing will be. Use *your* imagination."

MEDICINAL PURPOSES, Literary Review, (I, II), Poet to Poet Inc., 86-37 120 St., #2D, % Catterson, Richmond Hill NY 11418. (718)776-8853, (718)847-2150. E-mail: scarptp@usa.pipeline.com. Editors: Robert Dunn and Thomas M. Catterson. Fiction Editor: Andrew Clark. Magazine: 8½×5½; 60 pages; illustrations. *"Medicinal Purposes* publishes quality work that will benefit the world, though not necessarily through obvious means." Ternate-annually (three times per year). Estab. 1995. Circ. 1,000.

Needs: Adventure, erotica, ethnic/multicultural, experimental, fantasy, feminist, gay, historical, horror, humor/satire, lesbian, literary, mainstream/contemporary, mystery/suspense, psychic/supernatural/occult, regional, romance, science fiction, senior citizen/retirement, sports, westerns, young adult/teen. "Please no pornography, or hatemongering." Receives 5 unsolicited mss/month. Accepts 2-3 mss/issue; 8 mss/year. Publishes ms up to four issues after acceptance. Recently published work by Audrey Borenstein, Barry Graham and Catherine Scherer. Length: 2,000 words average; 50 words minimum; 3,000 words maximum. "We prefer maximum of 10 double-spaced pages." Publishes short shorts. Also publishes literary essays, literary criticism, poetry. Sometimes critiques or comments on rejected mss.

How to Contact: Send complete ms with a cover letter. Include estimated word count, brief bio, Social Security number. Reports in 6 weeks on queries; 8 weeks on mss. SASE. Simultaneous and electronic submissions (modem through e-mail) OK. Sample copy for $6, 6×9 SAE and 4 first-class stamps. Fiction guidelines free for #10 SASE.

Payment/Terms: Pays 2 contributor's copies. Acquires first rights.

Advice: "One aspect of the better stories we've seen is that the writer enjoys (or, at least, believes in) the tale being told. Also, learn the language—good English can be a beautiful thing. We long for stories that only a specific writer can tell, by virtue of experience or style. Expand our horizons. Clichés equal death around here."

MEDIPHORS, A Literary Journal of the Health Professions, (I, II, IV), P.O. Box 327, Bloomsburg PA 17815. Editor: Eugene D. Radice, MD. Magazine: 8½×11; 73 pages; 20 lb. white paper; 70 lb. cover; illustrations and photos. "We publish broad work related to medicine and health including essay, short story, commentary, fiction, poetry. Our audience: general readers and health care professionals." Semiannually. Estab. 1993. Circ. 900.

Needs: "Short stories related to health." Adventure, experimental, historical, humor/satire, literary, mainstream/contemporary, science fiction (hard science, soft/sociological) and medicine. "No religious, erotica, fantasy." Receives 50 unsolicited mss/month. Accepts 14 mss/issue; 28 mss/year. Publishes ms 10 months after acceptance. Agented fiction 2%. Length: 2,500 words average; 3,500 words maximum. Publishes short shorts. Also publishes literary essays and poetry. Sometimes critiques or comments on rejected mss.

How to Contact: Send complete ms with a cover letter. Include estimated word count, bio (paragraph) and any experience/employment in the health professions. Reports in 4 months on mss. Send SASE for reply, return of ms or send a disposable copy of ms. No simultaneous submissions. Sample copy for $5.50. Fiction guidelines for #10 SASE.

Payment/Terms: Pays 2 contributor's copies; additional copies for $5.50 Acquires first North American serial rights.

Advice: Looks for "high quality writing that shows fresh perspective in the medical and health fields. Accurate knowledge of subject material. Situations that explore human understanding in adversity. Order a sample copy for examples of work. Start with basic quality writing in short story and create believable, engaging stories concerning medicine and health. Knowledge of the field is important since the audience includes professionals within the medical field. Don't be discouraged. We enjoy receiving work from beginning writers."

MENTOR, Recreating Community Through the Art and Practice of Mentoring, (I, IV), P.O. Box 4382, Overland Park KS 66204. (913)362-7889. Editor: Maureen Waters. Newsletter: 8½×11; 12 pages. Quarterly. Estab. 1989. Circ. 250.

Needs: "Submissions must be mentoring related." Receives 1 unsolicited ms/month. "I would run more fiction if I received more." Recently published work by Charles Chaim Wax and Brooklyn. Length: 1,200-3,000 words. Also publishes literary essays. Sometimes critiques or comments on rejected mss.

MARKET CONDITIONS are constantly changing! If you're still using this book and it is 1998 or later, buy the newest edition of *Novel & Short Story Writer's Market* at your favorite bookstore or order from Writer's Digest Books.

How to Contact: Query first or send complete ms with a cover letter. Include bio with submission. Reports in 1 month on queries; 2 months on mss. Send SASE for reply, return of ms or send a disposable copy of ms. Simultaneous, reprint and electronic submissions (Mac, IBM disks) OK. Sample copy for $6. Fiction guidelines for #10 SASE.

Payment/Terms: Pays 2 contributor's copies.

Advice: "The writer should understand the mentoring concept and the whole story should revolve around mentoring. Readers are professionals involved in mentoring programs, so the fiction we print has to paint a picture that is relevant to them—perhaps helps them understand a new aspect of mentoring or moves them into a new way of thinking. If it's a good or fixable story, I'll work with the writer."

MERLANA'S MAGICKAL MESSAGES, (I, II, IV), Navarro Publications/Literary Services, P.O. Box 1107, Blythe CA 92226-1107. Editor: Marjorie E. Navarro. Executive Editor: Richard Navarro. Magazine: digest-sized; 50-75 pages; "desk-top published;" soft cover; black-and-white, pen-and-ink illustrations. "*MMM* is a New-Age style pagan publication featuring short stories, articles and poetry." Published 3 times/year (March, July, October).

Needs: New Age, pagan, goddess/god related works. Short stories up to 3,500 words, "with positive uplifting material." No mystery or science fiction. Recently published work by Abigail Davis, Roger K. Doost, Charles Chiam Wax and James McGarry.

How to Contact: *Charges reading fee to nonsubscribers: $1/article, $1/6 poems, $3/short story (refundable).* Send complete ms with cover letter. "I like to know a little bit about the author, including publishing credits. (Don't worry if you have none; we enjoy discovering new talent.) Also, what prompted you to write this particular story?" Reports in 6-10 weeks. SASE. Sample copy for $6 (payable to Navarro Publications). Fiction guidelines for #10 SASE.

Payment/Terms: Pays 1 contributor's copy. Tearsheets available on request for SASE.

Advice: "Looking for fresh originality! Give me an uplifting/healing message of the spirit and together we shall create real magick in ours and others' lives. (If there is artwork to go along with the story/article/poem, I would like to see it.)"

MINDSPARKS, The Magazine of Science and Science Fiction, (I, II, IV), Molecudyne Research, P.O. Box 1302, Laurel MD 20725-1302. Editor: Catherine Asaro. Magazine: $8\frac{1}{2} \times 11$; 44 pages; 20 lb. white paper; 60 lb. cover; illustrations and photos. "We publish science fiction and science articles." Quarterly. Estab. 1993. Circ. 1,000.

Needs: Science fiction (hard science, soft/sociological), young adult (science fiction). "No pornography." Receives 50 unsolicited submissions/month. Accepts 2-4 mss/issue; 12-14 mss/year. Publishes ms 1-24 months after acceptance. Published work by Hal Clement, G. David Nordley, Lois Gresh and Paul Levinson. Length: 4,000 words average; 8,000 words maximum. Publishes short shorts. Also publishes literary essays, literary criticism and poetry. Often critiques or comments on rejected mss.

How to Contact: Send complete ms with a cover letter. Include estimated word count and list of publications. Reports in 1-2 months. Send SASE for reply, return of ms or send a disposable copy of ms. No simultaneous submissions. Sample copy for $4.50, $8\frac{1}{2} \times 11$ SAE and $1 postage or 2 IRCs. Fiction guidelines for #10 SASE. Reviews novels and short story collections.

Payment/Terms: Pays 2¢/word on publication for first North American serial rights. Sends galleys to author.

Advice: Looks for "well-written, well-researched, interesting science ideas with good characterization and good plot. Read a copy of the magazine. We receive many submissions that don't fit the intent of *Mindsparks*."

THE MIRACULOUS MEDAL, (IV), The Central Association of the Miraculous Medal, 475 E. Chelten Ave., Philadelphia PA 19144. (215)848-1010. Editor: Rev. William J. O'Brien, C.M. Magazine. Quarterly.

Needs: Religious/inspirational. Receives 25 unsolicited fiction mss/month. Accepts 2 mss/issue; 8 mss/year. Publishes ms up to two years or more after acceptance.

How to Contact: Query first with SASE. Sample copy and fiction guidelines free.

Payment/Terms: Pays 2¢/word minimum. Pays on acceptance for first rights.

MOCCASIN TELEGRAPH, (I, II, IV), Wordcraft Circle of Native Writers and Storytellers, 2951 Ellenwood Dr., Fairfax VA 22031-2038. Phone/fax: (703)280-1028. E-mail: wordcraft@ase.com. Editor: Lee Francis. Newsletter: $8\frac{1}{2} \times 11$; 20 pages; photographs. *Moccasin Telegraph* publishes work by Native American and non-Native American writers and storytellers who are members of Wordcraft Circle. Bimonthly. Estab. 1992. Circ. 1,500.

Needs: Native American. Publishes special fiction issues or anthologies. Accepts 1-2 mss/issue; 6-12 mss/year. Publishes ms 1 month after acceptance. Length: open. Publishes short shorts. Also publishes literary essays, literary criticism and poetry.

How to Contact: "Send a sample of your writing with your application to Wordcraft Circle. *We only publish work of dues-paid members of Wordcraft Circle.*" Include estimated word count and list

of publications with submission. Simultaneous and electronic submissions OK. Sample copy for $2.50. Reviews novels and short story collections.
Payment/Terms: Pays 2 contributor's copies.

MOUNTAIN LUMINARY, (I), P.O. Box 1187, Mountain View AR 72560-1187. (501)585-2260. Fax: (501)269-4110. Editor: Anne Thiel. Magazine; photos. *"Mountain Luminary* is dedicated to bringing information to people about the Aquarian Age; how to grow with its new and evolutionary energies and how to work with the resultant changes in spirituality, relationships, environment and the planet. *Mountain Luminary* provides a vehicle for people to share ideas, philosophies and experiences that deepen understanding of this evolutionary process and humankind's journey on Earth." Quarterly. Estab. 1985.
Needs: Humor/satire, metaphor/inspirational/Aquarian-Age topics. Accepts 8-10 mss/year. Publishes ms 6 months after acceptance. Recently published work by Alan Cohen, Patrick Drysdale, Marilyn Ferguson, Bill Marshall and Don Bradley.
How to Contact: Query with clips of published work. SASE for return of ms. Simultaneous and electronic submissions (Mac IIci, Quark XP) OK. Sample copy and writer's guidelines free.
Payment/Terms: Pays 1 contributor's copy. "We may offer advertising space as payment." Acquires first rights.

‡MURDEROUS INTENT, A Magazine Of Mystery And Suspense, (I, IV), Madison Publishing Company, P.O. Box 5947, Vancouver WA 98668-5947. (360)695-9004. Fax: (360)693-3354. E-mail: madison@teleport.com. Editor: Margo Power. Magazine: 8½ × 11; 64 pages; newsprint; glossy 2-color cover; illustrations; photos. Quarterly. Estab. 1995. Circ. 5,000.
Needs: Mystery/suspense (amateur sleuth, cozy, police procedural, private eye), psychic/supernatural/ occult, science fiction (with mystery) "occasionally." No cannibal stories, no stories with excessive violence, language or sex. Receives 200 unsolicited mss/month. Accepts 10-14 mss/issue; 40-48 mss/ year. Publishes ms up to 1 year after acceptance. Recently published work by Sara Paretsky, Jeremiah Healy, Richard Lupoff, Robert Randisi, Polly Whitney, Elena Santangelo and Michael Mallory. Length: 2,000-4,000 words average; 250 words minimum; 5,000 words maximum. Publishes short shorts. Length: 250-400 words. Also publishes mystery-related essays and poetry. Sometimes critiques or comments on rejected mss. Sponsors contest. SASE for contest guidelines, deadline for submissions November 30 each year.
How to Contact: Send complete ms with a cover letter. Include estimated word count, brief bio, name of story and telephone number and e-mail address "if you have one." Reports in 3 months on queries, 3-6 months on mss. Send SASE for reply. Simultaneous submissions OK. Sample copy for $5, 9 × 12 SAE and 4 first-class stamps. Guidelines for #10 SASE. "Minisynopsis Corner" for authors to submit minisynopses of their new mystery novels.
Payment/Terms: Pays $10 and 2 contributor's copies on acceptance; additional copies for $3.50 (issue their story appears in). Acquires first North American serial rights.

‡MY LEGACY, (I, II), Weems Concepts, HCR-13, Box 21AA, Artemas PA 17211-9405. (814)458-3102. Editor: Kay Weems. Magazine: digest size; 125-150 pages; white paper; 20 lb. colored paper cover; illustrations. "Work must be in good taste. No bad language. Audience is from all walks of life," adults and children. Quarterly. Estab. 1991. Circ. 200.
Needs: Adventure, children's/juvenile (10-12 years), fantasy (children's fantasy, science fantasy), historical, horror, humor/satire, mainstream/contemporary, mystery/suspense (amateur sleuth, cozy, police procedural, private eye/hardboiled, romantic suspense), regional, religious/inspirational, romance (contemporary, futuristic/time travel, gothic, historical), science fiction (hard science, soft/ sociological), senior citizen/retirement, westerns (frontier, traditional), young adult/teen (adventure, mystery, science fiction, western). No porno. List of upcoming themes available for SASE. Publishes special fiction issues or anthologies. Receives 15-30 unsolicited mss/month. Accepts 30-35 mss/issue; 120-140 mss/year. Publishes ms within 6 months after acceptance. Recently published work by Peter Gauthier, Jel D. Lewis (Jones); Brucie Jacobs, Joseph Farley, Mark Scott and Gerri George. Length: 2,500 words average. Publishes short shorts. Very seldom critiques or comments on rejected mss; "usually don't have time."
How to Contact: Send complete ms with a cover letter. Include estimated word count, bio (short paragraph) and list of publications. Reports within 6 months on mss. Send SASE for reply, return of ms or send a disposable copy of ms (preferable). Simultaneous and reprint submissions OK. Sample copy for $3.50, 9 × 6½ SAE and $1.70 postage. Fiction guidelines for #10 SASE.
Payment/Terms: Acquires one-time rights.
Advice: Looks for "a good beginning, tight writing, good conversations, believable characters and believable ending."

MYSTERY TIME, An Anthology of Short Stories, (I), P.O. Box 2907, Decatur IL 62524. Editor: Linda Hutton. Booklet: 5½ × 8½; 44 pages; bond paper; illustrations. "Biannual collection of short stories with a suspense or mystery theme for mystery buffs." Estab. 1983.

Needs: Mystery/suspense only. Features older women as protagonists. Receives 10-15 unsolicited fiction mss/month. Accepts 20-24 mss/year. Published work by Leigh Fox, Kristin Neri and Sylvia Roberts. Published new writers within the last year. Length: 1,500 words maximum. Occasionally critiques rejected mss and recommends other markets.

How to Contact: Send complete ms with SASE. "No cover letters." Simultaneous and previously published submissions OK. Reports in 1 month on mss. Publishes an average of 6-8 months after acceptance. Reprint submissions OK. Sample copy for $3.50. Fiction guidelines for #10 SASE.

Payment/Terms: Pays ¼-1¢/word and 1 contributor's copy; additional copies $2.50. Acquires one-time rights.

Advice: "Study a sample copy and the guidelines. Too many amateurs mark themselves as amateurs by submitting blindly."

NAKED KISS, (II), Scarlett Fever Press, 3160 Brady Lake Rd., Ravenna OH 44266. E-mail: mrwharo ld@aol.com. Editor: Wayne A. Harold. Magazine: 8½×11; 40-48 pages; 20 lb. paper; cardstock cover; illustrations and photos. "Hardboiled crime, mystery and suspense fiction. Some stories are intended for mature readers only. Hard-hitting, mature fiction." Triannually. Estab. 1994. Circ. 500.

Needs: Adventure, mystery/suspense (police procedural, private eye/hardboiled). No cozy mystery. Receives 25-30 unsolicited mss/month. Accepts 5-8 mss/issue; 15-25 mss/year. Publishes ms 6-24 months after acceptance. Published work by Gary Lovisi, Mike Black, J.D. Hunt, M.M. Lopiccolo. Length: 1,000 words minimum; 2,500 words maximum. Often critiques or comments on rejected mss.

How to Contact: Send complete ms with a cover letter. Include estimated word count, bio (1 paragraph) and list of publications. Reports in 1 month on queries; 2-3 months on mss. SASE for return of ms. Simultaneous, reprint and electronic submissions OK. Sample copy for $5 (make payable to Wayne A. Harold). Fiction guidelines for #10 SASE.

Payment/Terms: Pays $5-25 and 1-3 contributor's copies on publication for first North American serial rights.

Advice: "Looking for originality; interested in stories with a strong emotional content. No satires! We want hard-hitting crime and suspense. Be original, be creative, and use standard manuscript format. Enclose a cover letter (we want to know about you!) and a SASE. We will be going to a comic-book sized format and adding graphic fiction (i.e., comic-book stories). Query with comic script ideas or send 1-page plot synopsis. Will have 2-3 prose stories per issue as well. We will also soon have an online magazine."

NEW FRONTIER, (IV), P.O. Box 17397, Asheville NC 28806. (704)251-0109. Fax: (704)251-0727. Editor: Sw. Virato. Magazine: 8×10; 48-60 pages; pulp paper stock; illustrations and photos. "We seek new age writers who have imagination yet authenticity." Bimonthly. Estab. 1981. Circ. 60,000.

Needs: New age, body/mind consciousness. "A new style of writing is needed with a transformation theme." Receives 10-20 unsolicited mss/month. Accepts 1-2 mss/issue. Publishes ms 3 months after acceptance. Agented fiction "less than 5%." Published work by John White, Laura Anderson. Published work by new writers within the last year. Length: 1,000 words average; 750 words minimum; 2,000 words maximum. Publishes short shorts. Length: 150-500 words. Occasionally critiques rejected mss and recommends other markets.

How to Contact: Send complete ms with cover letter. Include author's bio and credits. Reports in 2 months on mss. SASE for ms. Simultaneous and reprint submissions OK. Sample copy for $2.95. Fiction guidelines for #10 SASE.

Payment/Terms: Acquires first North American serial rights and one-time rights.

Advice: "The new age market is ready for a special kind of fiction and we are here to serve it. Don't try to get an A on your term paper. Be sincere, aware and experimental. Old ideas that are senile don't work for us. Be fully alive and aware—tune in to our new age audience/readership."

NEW FRONTIERS, The Magazine of New Mexico, (I, II, IV), New Frontiers, P.O. Box 1299, Tijeras NM 87059. (505)281-1990. Fax: (505)281-7907. Editor: Wally Gordon. Magazine: 8¼×10¾; 32 pages; 50 lb. paper; illustrations and photos. "Elite audience, primarily in New Mexico, secondarily elsewhere in Southwest. General interests." Quarterly. Estab. 1993. Circ. 3,000.

Needs: Adventure, contemporary western issues and conflicts, excerpted novel, ethnic/multicultural, experimental, feminist, historical (general), humor/satire, literary, mainstream/contemporary, regional, translations, westerns. "Prefer fiction that highlights the kind of cultural, ethnic and environmental conflicts that concern New Mexicans today." Receives 25-50 unsolicited mss/month. Accepts 2-3 mss/issue. Publishes ms 1-4 months after acceptance. Recently published work by Joe Skinner, Charles Brushear, Phaedra Levy, Mollie Bushy, Rita Ciresi, Sharon Martin, Ann Newton Holmes, Audrey Schaimer, C.J. Hannah, Lisa Lenard and Janice Levy. Length: 1,500 words average; 3,000 words maximum. Publishes short shorts. Also publishes literary essays, literary criticism and poetry. Often critiques or comments on rejected mss.

How to Contact: Send complete ms with a cover letter. "Query if not already written. Send ms if already done." Include brief bio. Reports in 1 month on queries; 2 months on mss. Send SASE for reply, return of ms or send a disposable copy of ms. Simultaneous, reprint and electronic submissions (modem or disk) OK; if modem, call first. Sample copy for $2.95 and 8 × 11 SAE. Fiction guidelines for #10 SASE. Reviews novels and short story collections.

Payment/Terms: Pays $25-200 and 1 contributor's copy on publication for one-time rights.

Advice: "Have something to say about contemporary human dilemmas. Write tightly, don't overuse dialogue (a beginner's error) and let characters explain themselves, don't do it for them. The rarest of all gems is good humor. Put yourself in the shoes of a college-educated, middle-aged man or woman living in Albuquerque or Santa Fe and looking for role models on how to cope with the stress of a radically changing way of life. I want to see more lively fiction, with vivid characters, a sense of humor and strong social relevance."

NEW METHODS, The Journal of Animal Health Technology, (IV), P.O. Box 22605, San Francisco CA 94122-0605. (415)664-3469. Editor: Ronald S. Lippert, AHT. Newsletter ("could become magazine again"): 8½ × 11; 4-6 pages; 20 lb. paper; illustrations; "rarely" photos. Network service in the animal field educating services for mostly professionals in the animal field; e.g., animal health technicians. Monthly. Estab. 1976. Circ. 5,608.

Needs: Animals: contemporary, experimental, historical, mainstream, regional. No stories unrelated to animals. Receives 12 unsolicited fiction mss/month. Accepts one ms/issue; 12 mss/year. Length: Open. "Rarely" publishes short shorts. Occasionally critiques rejected mss. Recommends other markets.

How to Contact: Query first with theme, length, expected time of completion, photos/illustrations, if any, biographical sketch of author, all necessary credits or send complete ms. Report time varies (up to 4 months). SASE for query and ms. Simultaneous submissions OK. Sample copy and fiction guidelines for $2.90.

Payment/Terms: No payment. Acquires one-time rights.

Advice: Sponsors contests: theme changes but generally concerns the biggest topics of the year in the animal field. "Emotion, personal experience—make the person feel it. We are growing."

NEXT PHASE, (I, II), 5A Green Meadow Dr., Nantucket MA 02554. (508)325-0411. E-mail: 76603. 2224@compuserve.com. Editor: Kim Guarnaccia. 8½ × 11; 48 pages. "Features the best of fiction, poetry and illustration by up-and-coming writers and artists. We publish quality work as long as it is environmentally and humanely oriented." Triannually. Estab. 1989. Circ. 1,700.

Needs: Experimental, fantasy. Receives 15-25 unsolicited mss/month. Accepts 9 mss/issue; 25 mss/year. Publishes short shorts. Also publishes poetry (but poetry should be sent to: Holly Day, 134½ Congress Ave., Daytona Beach FL 32114). Critiques rejected mss.

How to Contact: Send complete manuscript with cover letter. SASE. Simultaneous and reprint submissions OK. Reports in 6 weeks. Sample copy for $4.95 includes postage.

Payment/Terms: Pays contributor's copies. Acquires one-time rights.

Advice: "We accept a broad range of fiction up to 4,000 words. We only accept environmentally or humanely-oriented fiction of all genres."

NIGHTMARES, (I, II), New Illiad Publishing, P.O. Box 587, Rocky Hill CT 06067. Editor: Ed Kobialka, Jr. Magazine: 8½ × 11; 64 pages; 20 lb. paper; 80 lb. cover; illustrations. "*Nightmares* publishes horror, from the modern age or gothic. We publish any writer, beginning or established, who submits good material." Published 3 times/year. Estab. 1994. Circ. 375.

Needs: Horror, supernatural/occult. Receives 50-70 unsolicited mss/month. Accepts 8 mss/issue; 35 mss/year. Does not read during December. Publishes ms 1 year after acceptance. Length: 2,500 words average; 500 words minimum; 6,000 words maximum. Usually critiques or comments on rejected mss.

How to Contact: Send complete ms with a cover letter. Include estimated word count, bio (1-2 paragraphs), Social Security number and list of publications. Reports in 1 month on queries; 2 months on mss. Send SASE for reply, return of ms or send a disposable copy of ms. Simultaneous submissions OK. Sample copy for $2.95. Fictions guidelines for #10 SASE.

Payment/Terms: Pays $10 maximum and 2 contributor's copies for first rights.

Advice: "It must be scary! Grab the reader's attention with a good opening; make your characters and places seem real; and don't make your ending predictable. Don't forget about the old, classic monsters—vampires, ghosts and demons still scare people. Graphic brutal violence and descriptive sex are unacceptable. Your goal as a writer should be to terrorize your reader without being disgusting or offensive."

THE NOCTURNAL LYRIC, (I, IV), Box 115, San Pedro CA 90733. (310)519-9220. Editor: Susan Moon. Digest: 5½ × 8½; 40 pages; illustrations. "We are a non-profit literary journal, dedicated to printing fiction by new writers for the sole purpose of getting read by people who otherwise might have never seen their work." Bimonthly. Estab. 1987. Circ. 400.

Needs: Experimental, fantasy, horror, humor/satire, psychic/supernatural/occult, science fiction, poetry. "We will give priority to unusual, creative pieces." Receives 50 unsolicited mss/month. Publishes ms 10-12 months after acceptance. Recently published work by Tom Eaton, Thomas J. Misuraca, Janice Gillett and Slashtipher J. Coleman. Length: 2,000 words maximum. Publishes short shorts. Also publishes poetry.

How to Contact: Send complete ms with cover letter. Include "something about the author, areas of fiction he/she is interested in." Reports in 2 weeks on queries; 4-6 months on mss. SASE. Simultaneous and reprint submissions OK. Sample copy for $3 (checks to Susan Moon). Fiction guidelines for #10 SASE.

Payment/Terms: Pays in gift certificates for subscription discounts. Publication not copyrighted.

Advice: "Please stop wasting your postage sending us things that are in no way bizarre. Do send us your wierdest, most unique creations. Don't pretend you've read us when you haven't! I can usually tell! We're getting more into strange, surrealistic horror and fantasy, or silly, satirical horror. If you're avant-garde, we want you! We're mainly accepting things that are bizarre all the way through, as opposed to ones that only have a surprise bizarre ending."

NON-STOP SCIENCE FICTION MAGAZINE, (I, II), Non-Stop Magazine, P.O. Box 981, Peck Slip Station, New York NY 10272-0981. Editor: K.J. Cypret. Magazine: 8½×11; 52 pages; glossy 4-color cover, illustrations and photos. Quarterly. Estab. 1993.

Needs: Fantasy (modern), science fiction, translations. Science fiction with strong literary/idea content. Planning special issue on alternative history science fiction. Also planning future special all-fiction issue or anthology. Receives 300-450 unsolicited mss/month. Accepts 3-5 mss/issue; 18 mss/year. Does not read mss July, August or December. Publishes ms 3-18 months after acceptance. Published work by Don Webb, Barry N. Malzberg and Paul Di Filippo. Length: 4,000 words average; 1,000 words minimum; 9,000 words maximum. Publishes literary essays, science articles and literary criticism. Sometimes critiques or comments on mss.

How to Contact: Send complete ms with a cover letter. Include estimated word count, 1- or 2-page bio and list of publications. Reports in 2-3 weeks on queries; 3 months on mss. SASE for reply. Prefers a disposable copy of ms. No simultaneous submissions. Reprint submissions OK from outside North America. Sample copy for $4.95. Reviews novels and short story collections.

Payment/Terms: Pays 3-6¢/word and 2 contributor's copies for first North American serial rights. Sends galleys to author.

Advice: Looks for "strong writing with believable characters and new science extrapolation. Read *Non-Stop* to see what we're publishing. We're seeing too many science fiction ideas coming from watching movies or TV shows. We will reject these instantly. We like to see science and technology used as a springboard for a story."

THE OAK, (I, II), 1530 Seventh St., Rock Island IL 61201. (309)788-3980. Editor: Betty Mowery. 8½×11; 8-14 pages. "Anything of help to writers." Bimonthly. Estab. 1991. Circ. 385.

Needs: Adventure, contemporary, experimental, humor/satire, mainstream, prose poem. No erotica. Receives about 25 mss/month. Accepts up to 12 mss/issue. Publishes ms within 3 months of acceptance. Published new writers within the last year. Length: 500 words maximum. Publishes short shorts. Length: 200 words.

How to Contact: Send complete ms. Reports in 1 week. SASE. Simultaneous and reprint submissions OK. Sample copy for $2. Subscription $10 for 4 issues.

Payment/Terms: None, but not necessary to buy a copy in order to be published. Acquires first rights.

Advice: "I do not want erotica, extreme violence or killing of humans or animals for killing's sake. Just be yourself when you write. Please include SASE or manuscripts will be destroyed. Be sure name and address are on the manuscript."

♣ON SPEC, The Canadian Magazine of Speculative Writing, (II), The Copper Pig Writers' Society, Box 4727, Edmonton, Alberta T6E 5G6 Canada. (403)413-0215. Fax: (403)413-0215. E-mail: onspec@freenet.edmonton.ab.ca. Magazine: 5×8; 96 pages; illustrations. "Provides a venue for Canadian speculative writing—science fiction, fantasy, horror, magic realism." Quarterly. Estab. 1989. Circ. 2,000.

Needs: Fantasy and science fiction. Receives 50 mss/month. Buys 8 mss/issue; 32 mss/year. "We read manuscripts during the month after each deadline: February 28/May 31/August 31/November 30. Please note that we want manuscripts in competition format." Publishes ms 6 months after acceptance. Published work by Peter Watts, M.A.C. Farrant, Leslie Gadallah and Dave Duncan. Length: 4,000 words average; 1,000 words minimum; 6,000 words maximum. Also publishes poetry. Sometimes critiques or comments on rejected mss.

How to Contact: Send complete ms with a cover letter. "No queries!" Include estimated word count, 2-sentence bio and phone number. Reports in 5 months on mss. SASE for return of ms or send a disposable copy of ms plus #10 SASE for response. No simultaneous submissions. Sample copy for $6. Fiction guidelines for #10 SASE.

Payment/Terms: Pays $25-150 and 2 contributor's copies; additional copies for $4. Pays on acceptance for first North American serial rights. Sends galleys to author.

Advice: "Please note we only accept work by Canadian writers. Tend to prefer character-driven stories."

OTHER WORLDS, The Paperback Magazine of Science Fiction-Science Fantasy, (II), Gryphon Publications, Box 209, Brooklyn NY 11228. Editor: Gary Lovisi. Magazine: 5×8; 100+ pages; offset paper; card cover; perfect-bound; illustrations and photographs. "Adventure—or action-oriented SF—stories that are fun to read." Annually. Estab. 1988. Circ. 300.

Needs: Science fiction (hard science) "with impact." No fantasy, supernatural or sword and sorcery. Receives 24 unsolicited mss/month. Accepts 4-6 mss/issue. Publishes ms 1-2 years (usually) after acceptance. Length: 3,000 words maximum. Publishes short shorts. Length: 500 words. Sometimes critiques rejected mss and recommends other markets.

How to Contact: Send complete ms with cover letter. Simultaneous submissions OK. Reports in 2 weeks on queries; 1 month on mss. SASE. Sample copy for $9.95 (100 pages perfect bound).

Payment/Terms: Pays 2 contributor's copies. Acquires first North American serial rights. Copyright reverts to author.

Advice: Looks for "harder science fiction stories, with *impact!*"

‡**PAPYRUS MAGAZINE, (I, II)**, Papyrus Literary Enterprises, P.O. Box 270797, West Hartford CT 06127-0797. (860)951-8331. E-mail: gwhitaker@imagine.com. Editor-in-Chief: Ginger Whitaker. Magazine: 8½×11; 20 pages. "*Papyrus* is a quarterly periodical for the cultivation of creative works by black writers. We seek, in particular, work from the unknown, underpublished or unpublished talented writer." Quarterly. Estab. 1994.

Needs: Ethnic/multicultural. Recently published work by Nina Sommers, Elizabeth Gibbs, Sonia Caulton and Michael Beres. Length: 1,500 words minimum; 3,500 words maximum. Also publishes literary essays and poetry.

How to Contact: Send complete ms on 3.5 disk along with a printed copy. Macintosh users should submit files in ClarisWorks, Microsoft Word, WordPerfect or MacWrite II format. IBM users should submit files saved in ASCII or RTF format. SASE. No simultaneous submissions. Electronic submissions OK, "but they must be pasted within the body of the note." Sample copy for $1.75 (back copy) or $2.20 (current issue). Fiction guidelines for #10 SASE.

Payment/Terms: Pays contributor's copies. Acquires first rights.

Advice: "Make sure it is literate, easily accessible (on disk), and of interest to African-Americans."

PARADOX MAGAZINE, (II), Paradox Communications, 184 Main St., Apt. 46, Northampton MA 01060. (413)567-6721. E-mail: zbodah@oberlin.edu. Editor: Dan Bodah. Magazine: size varies; 30 pages; 20 lb. paper; illustrations and photos. "*Paradox* is moving toward urgent cultural commentary and a focus on ideas over format. New issues will include more thematic focus—consider querying for themes. You should look at a sample issue to know what you're getting into." Publication varies from semiannually to annually. Estab. 1991. Circ. 300.

Needs: Condensed/excerpted novel, erotica, experimental, humor/satire, literary. Upcoming theme: "Connection between insanity and inspiration;" (deadline: May 25, 1997). Receives 30-60 unsolicited mss/month. Publishes ms 1-11 months after acceptance. Recently published work by Jake Berry and Terry Chuba. Publishes short shorts. Also publishes literary essays, articles, news reports, literary criticism and poetry. Sometimes critiques or comments on rejected mss.

How to Contact: "Send any work you feel is appropriately representative." Include SASE. Reports in 2 months. Send SASE for reply, return of ms or send a disposable copy of ms. Simultaneous, reprint and electronic submissions (disk or e-mail, generic text format) OK. Sample copy for $5.

Payment/Terms: Pays 1-2 contributor's copies. Acquires first rights.

Advice: "I prefer work that gets right into it, without a lot of superfluous or patience-demanding setup."

THE PARADOXIST LITERARY MOVEMENT, Anti-literary Journal, (IV), Xiquan Publishing House, 2456 S. Rose Peak Dr., Tucson AZ 85710. Editor: Florentin Smarandache. Magazine:

CHECK THE CATEGORY INDEXES, located at the back of the book, for publishers interested in specific fiction subjects.

8½×11; 100 pages; illustrations. "The paradoxist literary movement is an avant-garde movement set up by the editor in the 1980s in Romania. It tries to generalize the art, to make the unliterary become literary." Annually. Estab. 1993. Circ. 500.

Needs: "Crazy, uncommon, experimental, avant-garde"; also ethnic/multicultural. Plans specific themes in the next year. Publishes annual special fiction issue or anthology. Receives 3-4 unsolicited mss/month. Accepts 10 mss/issue. Published work by Arnold Skemer, Marian Barbu and Constantin Urucu. Length: 500 words minimum; 1,000 words maximum. Publishes short shorts. Also publishes literary essays, literary criticism and poetry.

How to Contact: Query with clips of unpublished work. Reports in 2 months on mss. Send a disposable copy of ms. Sample copy for $19.95 and 8½×11 SASE.

Payment/Terms: Pays 1 contributor's copy. Not copyrighted.

PERCEPTIONS, The Journal of Imaginative Sensuality, (I, II, IV), Sensuous SIG, Inc., P.O. Box 2210, Livermore CA 94550. Editor: Alexandra Lloyd. Magazine: 5½×8½; 52 pages; 70 lb. book paper; 80 lb. cover; illustrations; photographs. "*Perceptions* is a journal celebrating the nature of sensuality. We celebrate a realization that virtually everything sexual is sensual, but that sensuality's diversity far exceeds only a sexual purview." Quarterly. Estab. 1988. Circ. 250.

Needs: Erotica, gay, humor/satire, lesbian, psychic/supernatural/occult. "Any fiction with a sensual slant. We do not accept pornography or graphically obscene fiction." Receives 10 unsolicited mss/month. Acquires 4-5 mss/issue; 20 mss/year. Publishes ms 2-6 months after acceptance. Recently published work by Christy Rich, R.L. Sandiford and Timothy Hodor. Length: 1,500 words preferred; 400 words minimum; 4,000 words maximum. Publishes short shorts. Length: 400-800 words. Usually publishes literary essays, literary criticism and poetry. Usually critiques or comments on rejected mss.

How to Contact: US writers send $5 for sample issue and submission guidelines (cost is $7 to Canada and Mexico, and $9 overseas). Include 3-4 sentence bio. Reports in 2 weeks on queries; 2 months on mss. SASE required for reply. Simultaneous, reprint and electronic (3.5 disk) submissions OK.

Payment/Terms: Pays 1 contributor's copy; additional copies $3. Acquires one-time rights.

Advice: "We prefer fiction that has an original or unusual story or angle. We attempt to publish fiction from a variety of viewpoints. Steer away from the temptation to depict sexuality or erotic issues in a graphic or obscene way. We prefer more sensual or 'intellectual' stories. Spelling counts."

PHANTASM, (I, II), 1530 Seventh St., Rock Island IL 61201. (309)788-3980. Editor: Betty Mowery. 5½×8½; 10 pages; illustrations. "To provide, especially the beginner, a market. Soft horror, fantasy and mystery. No gore or violence." Quarterly. Estab. 1993. Circ. 50. *Phantasm* appears as a separate section of the publication *The Oak*.

Needs: Fantasy, soft horror. Receives 20 unsolicited mss/month. Accepts 4 mss/issue; 16 mss/year. Publishes ms next issue after acceptance. Length: 500 words average; 200 words minimum; 500 words maximum. Publishes short shorts. Also publishes poetry.

How to Contact: Send complete ms. Reports in 1 week on queries. SASE for return of ms or send a disposable copy of ms. Simultaneous and reprint submissions OK. Sample copy for $2. Fiction guidelines for #10 SASE. Subscriptions: $10/4 issues.

Payment/Terms: No payment ("but purchase isn't necessary to be published"). Acquires first rights.

Advice: "Either send for a sample and see what has been published—or just go ahead and submit. Always enclose SASE, for there is no response without one."

THE PIPE SMOKER'S EPHEMERIS, (I, II, IV), The Universal Coterie of Pipe Smokers, 20-37 120 St., College Point NY 11356. Editor: Tom Dunn. Magazine: 8½×11; 84-94 pages; offset paper and cover; illustrations; photos. Pipe smoking and tobacco theme for general and professional audience. Irregular quarterly. Estab. 1964.

Needs: Pipe smoking related: historical, humor/satire, literary. Publishes ms up to 1 year after acceptance. Length: 2,500 words average; 5,000 words maximum. Also publishes short shorts. Occasionally critiques rejected mss.

How to Contact: Send complete ms with cover letter. Reports in 2 weeks on mss. Simultaneous and reprints OK. Sample copy for 8½×11 SAE and 6 first-class stamps.

Payment/Terms: Acquires one-time rights.

PIRATE WRITINGS, Tales of Fantasy, Mystery & Science Fiction, (II), Pirate Writings Publishing, P.O. Box 329, Brightwaters NY 11718-0329. E-mail: pwpubl@aol.com. Editor: Edward J. McFadden. Assistant Editor: Tom Piccirilli. Magazine: full size, saddle stapled. "We are looking for poetry and short stories that entertain." Quarterly. Estab. 1992. Circ. 6,000.

Needs: Fantasy (dark fantasy, science fantasy, sword and sorcery), mystery/suspense, science fiction (all types). Receives 300-400 unsolicited mss/month. Accepts 8 mss/issue; 30-40 mss/year. Publishes ms 1-2 years after acceptance. Length: 3,000 words average; 750 words minimum; 8,000 words maximum. Also publishes poetry. Sometimes critiques or comments on rejected mss.

How to Contact: Send complete ms with cover letter. Include estimated word count, 1 paragraph bio, Social Security number, list of publications with submission. Reports in 1 week on queries; 2 months on mss. Send SASE for reply or return of ms or disposable copy of ms. Will consider simultaneous submissions. Sample copy for $5 (make check payable to Pirate Writings Publishing). Fiction guidelines for #10 SAE.

Payment/Terms: Pays 1-5¢/word for first North American serial rights.

Advice: "My goal is to provide a diverse, entertaining and thought provoking magazine featuring all the above stated genres in every issue. Hints: I love a good ending. Move me, make me laugh, surprise me, and you're in. Read *PW* and you'll see what I mean."

POSKISNOLT PRESS, Yesterday's Press, (I, II, IV), Yesterday's Press, JAF Station, Box 7415, New York NY 10116-4630. Editor: Patricia D. Coscia. Magazine: 7×8½; 20 pages; regular typing paper. Estab. 1989. Circ. 100.

Needs: Contemporary, erotica, ethnic, experimental, fantasy, feminist, gay, humor/satire, lesbian, literary, mainstream, prose poem, psychic/supernatural/occult, romance, senior citizen/retirement, western, young adult/teen (10-18 years). "X-rated material is not accepted!" Plans to publish a special fiction issue or anthology in the future. Receives 50 unsolicited mss/month. Accepts 30 mss/issue; 100 mss/year. Publishes ms 6 months after acceptance. Length: 200 words average; 100 words minimum; 500 words maximum. Publishes short shorts. Length: 100-500 words. Sometimes critiques rejected mss and recommends other markets.

How to Contact: Query first with clips of published work or send complete ms with cover letter. Reports in 1 week on queries; 6 months on mss. SASE. Accepts simultaneous submissions. Sample copy for $5 with #10 SAE and $2 postage. Fiction guidelines for #10 SAE and $2 postage.

Payment/Terms: Pays with subscription to magazine or contributor's copies; charges for extras. Acquires all rights, first rights or one-time rights.

THE POST, (II), Publishers Syndication International, 1422 K St. NW, Suite 856, Washington DC 20005. Editor: A.P. Samuels. Magazine: 8½×11; 32 pages. Monthly. Estab. 1988.

Needs: Adventure, mystery/suspense (private eye), romance (romantic suspense), western (traditional). "No explicit sex, gore, extreme violence or bad language." Receives 75 unsolicited mss/month. Accepts 1 ms/issue; 12 mss/year. Time between acceptance and publication varies. Agented fiction 10%. Length: 10,000 words average.

How to Contact: Send complete ms with cover letter. Reports on mss in 5 weeks. No simultaneous submissions. Fiction guidelines for #10 SASE.

Payment/Terms: Pays ½¢ to 4¢/word on acceptance for all rights.

‡PRAYERWORKS, Encouraging, God's People to Do the Real Work of Ministry—Intercessory Prayer, (I), The Master's Work, P.O. Box 301363, Portland OR 97294-9363. (503)761-2072. Fax: (503)760-1184. E-mail: jayforpryr@aol.com. Editor: V. Ann Mandeville. Newsletter: 5½×8; 4 pages; bond paper. "Our intended audience is 70% retired Christians and 30% families. We publish 300-500 word devotional material—fiction, nonfiction, biographical, poetry, clean quips and quotes. Our philosophy is evangelical Christian serving the body of Christ in the area of prayer." Weekly. Estab. 1988. Circ. 650.

Needs: Religious/inspirational. "Subject matter may include anything which will build relationship with the Lord—prayer, ways to prayer, stories of answered prayer, teaching on a Scripture portion, articles that will build faith, or poems will all work. We even use a series occasionally." Publishes 2-6 months after acceptance. Recently published work by Barb Marshal, Mary Hickey and V. Ann Mandeville. Length: 350-500 words average; 350 words minimum; 500 words maximum. Publishes short shorts. Also publishes poetry. Often critiques or comments on rejected mss.

How to Contact: Send complete ms with a cover letter. Include estimated word count and a very short bio. Reports in 1 month. Send SASE for reply, return of ms or send a disposable copy of ms. Simultaneous submissions and reprints OK. Sample copy and fiction guidelines for #10 SASE.

Payment/Terms: Pays subscription to the magazine and contributor's copies on publication. Writer retains all rights. Not copyrighted.

Advice: Stories "must have a great take-away value—no preaching; teach through action. Be thrifty with words—make them count."

PRISONERS OF THE NIGHT, An Adult Anthology of Erotica, Fright, Allure and ... Vampirism, (II, IV), MKASHEF Enterprises, P.O. Box 688, Yucca Valley CA 92286-0688. Editor: Alayne Gelfand. Magazine: 8½×11; 50-80 pages; 20 lb. paper; slick cover; perfect-bound; illustrations. "An adult, erotic vampire anthology of original character stories and poetry. Heterosexual and homosexual situations." Annually. Estab. 1987. Circ. 5,000.

Needs: "All stories must be erotic vampire stories, with unique characters, unusual situations." Adventure, contemporary, erotica, fantasy, feminist, gay, lesbian, literary, mystery/suspense, prose poem, psychic/supernatural/occult, science fiction (soft/sociological). No fiction that deals with anyone else's creations, i.e., no "Dracula" stories. Receives 80-100 unsolicited fiction mss/month. Buys 5-12 mss/issue. Publishes ms 1-11 months after acceptance. Published work by A.R. Morlan, Jacqueline Carey, Della Van Hise and Wendy Rathbone. Published new writers within the last year. Length: under 10,000 words. Publishes short shorts. Sometimes critiques rejected mss.

How to Contact: Send complete ms with short cover letter. "A brief introduction of author to the editor; name, address, *some* past credits if available." Reports in 1-3 weeks on queries; 2-4 months on mss. Reads *only* September-March. SASE. No simultaneous submissions. Accepts electronic submissions via IBM Word Perfect (4.2 or 5.1) disk. Sample copy #1-4, $15; #5, $12; #6-#10, $9.95. Fiction guidelines for #10 SASE.

Payment/Terms: Pays 1¢/word for fiction on acceptance for first North American serial rights.

Advice: "They say there's nothing new under the sun. Well, maybe . . . but *POTN* is looking for what's new under the *moon*! Although *POTN* is limited in its topic to vampires, there is no limitation within its pages on imagination. *POTN* is looking for new twists on the old theme; new perspectives, unique angles, alien visions and newborn music. *POTN* is *not* looking for re-hashes of old plots and characterizations; no 'counts' or 'countesses,' please. The pick-up in a singles bar has been beaten into the ground. The hitchhiker-turned-vampire/victim gives new meaning to the word 'boring.' *POTN* wants material that breaks all molds, that severs ties to old concepts of the vampire and creates utterly new images. *POTN* wants to read your story and be delighted, intrigued, startled in fresh, imaginatively new ways. *POTN* does *not* want to be put off by pornography or obscenity. Please do not add sex to an existing story just to fit POTN's definition of itself as 'an erotic vampire anthology'; sex must be an integral part of the tale. Explicitness is not necessary, but it is acceptable. *POTN* stresses the romantic (but not 'gothic') aspects of the vampire as opposed to the bloody, gory, horrific aspects; no 'slasher' stories, please. And, although it is an important, contemporary subject, *POTN* prefers not to address the issue of AIDS as it relates to vampires at this time. Please be sure to SASE for guidelines before submitting; *POTN*'s needs are extremely specific."

PSI, (I, II), 1422 K Street NW, Suite 856, Washington DC 20005. Editor: A.P. Samuels. Magazine: 8½×11; 32 pages; bond paper; self cover. "Mystery and romance." Bimonthly. Estab. 1987.

Needs: Romance (contemporary, historical, young adult), mystery/suspense (private eye), western (traditional). Receives 35 unsolicited mss/month. Accepts 1-2 mss/issue. Length: 10,000 words average. Critiques rejected mss "only on a rare occasion."

How to Contact: Send complete ms with cover letter. Reports in 2 weeks on queries; 4-6 weeks on mss. SASE. No simultaneous submissions. Accepts electronic submissions via disk.

Payment/Terms: Pays 1-4¢/word plus royalty on acceptance for first North American serial rights.

Advice: "Manuscripts must be for a general audience. Just good plain story telling (make it compelling). No explicit sex or ghoulish violence."

QUEEN OF ALL HEARTS, (II), Queen Magazine, Montfort Missionaries, 26 S. Saxon Ave., Bay Shore NY 11706. (516)665-0726. Managing Editor: Roger M. Charest, S.M.M. Magazine: 7¾×10¾; 48 pages; self cover stock; illustrations; photos. Magazine of "stories, articles and features on the Mother of God by explaining the Scriptural basis and traditional teaching of the Catholic Church concerning the Mother of Jesus, her influence in fields of history, literature, art, music, poetry, etc." Bimonthly. Estab. 1950. Circ. 4,000.

Needs: Religious/inspirational. "No mss not about Our Lady, the Mother of God, the Mother of Jesus." Length: 1,500-2,000 words. Sometimes recommends other markets.

How to Contact: Send complete ms with SASE. No simultaneous submissions. Reports in 1 month on mss. Publishes ms 6-12 months after acceptance. Sample copy for $2.50 with 9×12 SAE.

Payment/Terms: Varies. Pays 6 contributor's copies.

Advice: "We are publishing stories with a Marian theme."

✢QUEEN'S QUARTERLY, A Canadian Review, (I, IV), Queen's University, Kingston, Ontario K7L 3N6 Canada. Phone/fax: (613)545-2667. E-mail: qquarterly@qucdn.queensu.ca. Website: http://info.queensu.ca./quarterly. Editor: Boris Castel. Magazine: 6×9; 800 pages/year; illustrations. "A general interest intellectual review, featuring articles on science, politics, humanities, arts and letters. Book reviews, poetry and fiction." Quarterly. Estab. 1893. Circ. 3,000.

Needs: Adventure, contemporary, experimental, fantasy, historical, humor/satire, literary, mainstream, science fiction and women's. "*Special emphasis on work by Canadian writers.*" Accepts 2 mss/issue; 8 mss/year. Recently published work by Gail Anderson-Dargatz, Mark Jarman, Rick Bowers and Dennis Bock; published new writers within the last year. Length: 2,000-3,000 words. Also publishes literary essays, literary criticism, poetry.

How to Contact: "Send complete ms with SASE." No simultaneous or multiple submissions. Reports within 3 months. Sample copy for $6.50. Reviews novels and short story collections. Electronic submissions OK.

Payment/Terms: Pays $100-300 for fiction, 2 contributor's copies and 1-year subscription; $5 charge for extras. Pays on publication for first North American serial rights. Sends galleys to author.

RED HERRING MYSTERY MAGAZINE, (II), Potpourri Publications Co., P.O. Box 8278, Prairie Village KS 66208. (913)642-1503. Fax: (913)642-3128. E-mail: rhmmag@aol.com. Editors: Juliet Kinkaid, Kitty Mendenhall and Donna Trombla. Magazine: 7½×10; 70 pages; newsprint; 70 lb. gloss cover. "Our goal is to expand the genre to include more diverse suspense and mystery." Quarterly. Estab. 1994. Circ. 1,200.

Needs: Mystery/suspense. "No true crime. No gratuitous sex or violence." Receives 90 unsolicited mss/month. Accepts 15 mss/issue. Publishes mss 6-12 months after acceptance. Recently published work by Seymour Shubin, Russ Hall and Teresa Keene. Length: 6,000 words maximum. Publishes short shorts. Always critiques or comments on rejected mss.

How to Contact: Send complete ms with a cover letter. Include estimated word count, brief bio and list of publications. "When accepted, we require a copy on Macintosh or IBM 3.5 disk in Word, WordPerfect, QuarkExpress or PageMaker." Reports in 1 month on queries; 2-3 months on mss. Send SASE for reply, return of ms or send a disposable copy of ms. Simultaneous and electronic submissions OK. Sample copy for $5 including shipping and handling. Fiction guidelines for #10 SASE.

Payment/Terms: Pays $10 plus 1 contributor's copy on publication for first rights.

Advice: Looks for "intricate, unique plots in which clues are well-placed and which have well-developed characters and suspense. Read the magazine. Send for guidelines. Work on tone and structure while developing your own particular ability to tell a story."

RESPONSE, A Contemporary Jewish Review, (II, IV), 27 W. 20th St., 9th Floor, New York NY 10011. (212)620-0350. Fax: (212)929-3459. E-mail: response@panix.com. Editors: David R. Atler and Yigal Schleifer. Magazine: 6×9; 120 pages; 70 lb. paper; 10 pt. CS1 cover; illustrations; photos. "Fiction, poetry and essays with a Jewish theme, for Jewish students and young adults." Quarterly. Estab. 1967. Circ. 2,000.

● *Response* received an award from *Jewish Currents Magazine* for outstanding Jewish journalism in 1995.

Needs: Contemporary, ethnic, experimental, feminist, historical (general), humor/satire, literary, prose poem, regional, religious, spirituals, translations. "Stories in which the Holocaust plays a major role must be exceptional in quality. The shrill and the morbid will not be accepted." Receives 10-20 unsolicited mss/month. Accepts 5-10 mss/issue; 10-15 mss/year. Publishes ms 2-4 months after acceptance. Length: 15-20 pages (double spaced). Publishes short shorts. Sometimes recommends other markets.

How to Contact: Send complete ms with cover letter; include brief biography of author. "Do not summarize story in cover letter." Reports in 2-3 months on mss. SASE. No simultaneous submissions. Sample copy for $6; free guidelines.

Payment/Terms: Pays in contributor's copies. Acquires all rights.

Advice: "In the best pieces, every word will show the author's conscious attention to the craft. Subtle ambiguities, quiet ironies and other such carefully handled tropes are not lost on *Response*'s readers. Pieces that also show passion that is not marred by either shrillness or pathos are respected and often welcomed. Writers who write from the gut or the muse are few in number. *Response* personally prefers the writer who thinks about what he or she is doing, rather than the writer who intuits his or her stories."

RFD, A Country Journal for Gay Men Everywhere, (I, II, IV), Short Mountain Collective, P.O. Box 68, Liberty TN 37095. (615)536-5176. Contact: The Collective. Magazine: 8½×11; 64-80 pages. "Focus on radical faeries, gay men's spirituality—country living." Quarterly. Estab. 1974. Circ. 3,600.

Needs: Gay: Erotica, ethnic/multicultural, experimental, fantasy, feminist, humor/satire, literary, mainstream/contemporary, mystery/suspense, psychic/supernatural/occult, regional, romance. Receives 10 unsolicited mss/month. Accepts 3 mss/issue; 12 mss/year. Length: open. Publishes short shorts. Also publishes literary essays, literary criticism and poetry.

How to Contact: Send complete ms with cover letter and estimated word count. Usually reports in 6-9 months. Send SASE for reply, return of ms or send disposable copy of ms. Sample copy for $6. Free fiction guidelines.

Payment/Terms: Pays 1 or 2 contributor's copies. Not copyrighted.

RIVERSIDE QUARTERLY, (II, IV), P.O. Box 12085, San Antonio TX 78212. (210)734-5424. Editor: Leland Sapiro. Magazine: 5½×8½; 64 pages; illustrations. Quarterly. Estab. 1964. Circ. 1,100.

Needs: Fantasy and science fiction. Accepts 1 ms/issue; 4 mss/year. Publishes ms 9 months after acceptance. Length: 3,500 words maximum; 3,000 words average. Publishes short shorts. Also publishes essays, literary criticism, poetry. Critiques rejected mss.

How to Contact: Send complete ms with a cover letter. Reports in 2 weeks. SASE. Simultaneous submissions OK. Sample copy for $2.50. Reviews novels and short story collections.

Payment/Terms: Pays in contributor's copies. Acquires one-time rights. Sends galleys to author.

Advice: "We print only science fiction and fantasy, with the first requiring no specific 'approach.' However, a fantasy story is deemed relevant only if it expresses some aspect of human behavior that can't be expressed otherwise. See, for example, Kris Neville's 'The Outcasts' in our second issue or Algis Budrys': 'Balloon, Oh, Balloon' in the third."

ROSEBUD™, **For People Who Enjoy Writing, (I, II)**, P.O. Box 459, Cambridge WI 53523. Phone/fax: (608)423-9609. Editor: Roderick Clark. Magazine: 7×10; 136 pages; 60 lb. matte; 100 lb. cover; illustrations. Quarterly. Estab. 1993. Circ. 8,500.
• *Rosebud* was selected for inclusion in the *Writer's Digest* "Fiction 50" list of top fiction markets.
Needs: Adventure, condensed/excerpted novel, ethnic/multicultural, experimental, historical (general), humor/satire, literary, mainstream/contemporary, psychic/supernatural/occult, regional, romance (contemporary), science fiction (soft/sociological sf), serialized novel, translations. Each submission must fit loosely into one of the following categories to qualify: City and Shadow (urban settings), Songs of Suburbia (suburban themes), These Green Hills (nature and nostalgia), En Route (any type of travel), Mothers, Daughters, Wives (relationships), Ulysses' Bow (manhood), Paper, Scissors, Rock (childhood, middle age, old age), The Jeweled Prize (concerning love), Lost and Found (loss and discovery), Voices in Other Rooms (historic or of other culture), Overtime (involving work), Anything Goes (humor), I Hear Music (music), Season to Taste (food), Word Jazz (wordplay), Apples to Oranges (miscellaneous, excerpts, profiles). Publishes annual special fiction issue or anthology. Receives 1,200 unsolicited mss/month. Accepts 16 mss/issue; 64 mss/year. Publishes ms 1-3 months after acceptance. Published work by Florence Parry Heide, Christi Killien, Judith Beth Cohen and Russell King. Length: 1,200-1,800 words average. Occasionally uses longer pieces and novel excerpts (prepublished). Publishes short shorts. Also publishes literary essays. Often critiques or comments on rejected mss.
How to Contact: Send complete ms with a cover letter. Include estimated word count and list of publications. Reports in 3 months on mss. SASE for return of ms. Simultaneous and reprints submissions OK. Sample copy for $5.95. Fiction guidelines for legal SASE.
Payment/Terms: Pays $45 and 2 contributor's copies on publication for one-time rights; additional copies for $4.40.
Advice: "Each issue will have six or seven flexible departments (selected from a total of sixteen departments that will rotate). We are seeking stories, articles, profiles, and poems of: love, alienation, travel, humor, nostalgia, and unexpected revelation. Something has to 'happen' in the pieces we choose, but what happens inside characters is much more interesting to us than plot manipulation. We like good storytelling, real emotion and authentic voice."

RUBY'S PEARLS, (II), 9832-1 Sandler Rd., Jacksonville FL 32222. E-mail: ruby@gate.net or del.freeman@rubysbbs.gate.net (for Freeman) and mrhahn@net.com (for Hahn). Editor: Del Freeman. Assistant Editor: Michael Hahn. Electronic magazine; page number varies. "All fiction, no porn, no poetry, general interest." Monthly. Estab. 1991. "Uploaded electronically to BBSs nationwide and internationally, via satellite. Also on the World Wide Web at http://www.gate.net/~ruby/.
• *Ruby's Pearls* has received three Digital Quill Awards (sponsored by the Desktop Publishing Association). By using other bulletin boards and "echoing" across the country the magazine is accessible to the 50 states; available all over the world via Genie, Compuserve and the Internet.
Needs: Contemporary, experimental, humor/satire, mainstream, mystery/suspense. "Stories can be submitted on either size disk, ASCII, IBM format only. Will return if mailer (pre-paid) is enclosed." No porn, erotica. Accepts 1-2 mss/issue; 24-30 mss/year. Publishes ms 1-2 months after acceptance. Publishes short shorts. Length: 250 up (unless it's really killer). Sometimes comments on rejected ms.
How to Contact: Submissions are by 5.25 or 3.5 disk; stories in IBM-ASCII format only or they can be made by modem by calling "Ruby's Joint BBS," 1-904-777-6799 and uploading. Contact by mail or by disk with complete story. Reports in 1-2 months. "Prepaid disk mailer is required." Simultaneous submissions OK. Accepts electronic submissions via disk or modem. For sample copy, access at above website.
Payment/Terms: No payment. Only the privilege to reproduce electronically once. All rights remain with author.
Advice: "Any writer can be seen and judged by the public, sans agent filtering, in the electronic age. Don't worry about who turns you down, but rather who accepts your work."

‡THE SALT & THE LIGHT, A Journal for Christian Writers, (I, II), J. Jireh Desktop Publishing, 27013 Pacific Hwy. S., #157, Kent WA 98032. (206)927-4738. E-mail: johnodz@aol.com. Editor: Geoff M. Pope. Magazine: 5½×8½ (folded); 32 pages; Neenah white linen paper; Mead 80 lb. gloss enamel cover; illustrations and photos. "We publish Biblically passionate, compassionate and concise material." Quarterly. Estab. 1995. Circ. 150.
Needs: Religious/inspirational. No historical romance, juvenile. Plans specific themes. Accepts 1-2 mss/issue; 4-8 mss/year. Publishes ms 3-6 months after acceptance. Recently published work by Chuck Dean, Christopher Wise and Denella Kimura. Length: 1,500 words average; 250 words minimum;

2,500 words maximum. Publishes short shorts. Also publishes literary essays, literary criticism and poetry. Sometimes critiques or comments on rejected mss.

How to Contact: Send complete ms with a cover letter. Include estimated word count, 3-sentence bio and list of publications. Reports in 6 weeks. SASE for return of ms. Simultaneous and reprint submissions OK. Sample copy for $5. Fiction guidelines for 8½×11 SASE.

Payment/Terms: Pays 3 contributor's copies; additional copies for $4.

Advice: "We are seeking work that displays unpredictable use of language, fresh images, concise style, Biblically sound theme(s) with characters that are both spiritually and emotionally mature. We welcome dark irony, but it is hard to emulate Flannery O'Connor. We are especially open to stories pulsing with hope for the hurting and humor for the holy."

‡SCIFANT, (I, II), Box 398, Suisun CA 94585. Editor: Paul Doerr. Magazine: 8½×11; 98 pages (microfiche only); illustrations and photos. "We publish science fiction, fantasy, horror, space fiction and space high technology." Monthly.

• Paul Doerr edits a variety of periodicals and books on microfiche and paper. His company is called Luna Ventures.

Needs: Adventure, experimental, fantasy, historical (general), horror, humor/satire, romance, science fiction, serialized/excerpted novel, suspense/mystery. Receives 50 unsolicited mss/month. Accepts 30 mss/issue. Publishes ms 2 months to 2 years after acceptance. Publishes short shorts of a half page and up. Occasionally critiques rejected mss and recommends other markets.

How to Contact: Send complete ms with cover letter. Ms must be single spaced with margins no greater than a half inch and proofread (camera ready). Reports in 1 month. SASE (or IRC). Simultaneous, electronic (disk, ASCII or WordPerfect) and reprint submissions OK. Fiction guidelines for $1 and #10 SASE. Sample copy for $3. (Copy in microfiche.)

Payment/Terms: Payment schedule on spec sheet. Pays percentage of sales profit.

Advice: "Send me something! Would like to see more fiction on topics of WW II and space colonization."

‡SINISTER, (II, IV), Night Grins Publications, 816 Elm St. #227, Manchester NH 03101-2101. (603)644-3604. E-mail: hgwells@grolen.com. Editor: Primordial Sin. Magazine: 8½×11; 72-80 pages; newsprint paper; illustrations; photos. Quarterly. Estab. 1997.

Needs: Horror. Publishes special fiction issues or anthologies. Receives 100 unsolicited mss/month. Accepts 13 mss/issue; 52 mss/year. Publishes ms 18 months to 2 years after acceptance. Recently published work by Nancy Kilpatrick, Edward Lee, Tom Piccirilli, Gerard Daniel Hovaraer, Charles Eckert and Larry Tritten. Length: 3,500 words average; 100 words minimum; 15,000 words maximum. Publishes short shorts. Also publishes literary essays and literary criticism.

How to Contact: Send complete ms with cover letter. Include estimated word count and Social Security number. Reports in 1 month on mss. Send SASE for reply, return of ms or send a disposable copy of ms. Sample copy for $5.95. Fiction guidelines for #10 SASE.

Payment/Terms: Pays 2-4¢/word and 2 contributor's copies on publication; additional copies $4.50. Acquires first North American serial rights. Sends galleys to author.

Advice: "What it usually comes down to is characters: we don't have to fall in love with your characters, but we do have to feel as if we know them. The most horrible thing in the world is still less scary when it's happening to a stranger. The only things I want you to tell me in your cover letter regarding your story are: title, word count, rights you're offering and whether it's available on disk. Don't write your own blurb; don't try to sell it to me. Let the story speak for itself."

SKIPPING STONES: A Multicultural Children's Magazine, (I, II), P.O. Box 3939, Eugene OR 97403. (541)342-4956. Editor: Arun N. Toké. Magazine: 8½×11; 36 pages; recycled 50 lb. halopaque paper; 80 lb. text cover; illustrations and photos. "*Skipping Stones* is a multicultural, international, nature awareness magazine for children 8-16, and their parents and teachers." Published 5 times a year. Estab. 1988. Circ. 3,000.

Needs: Children's/juvenile (8-16 years): ethnic/multicultural, feminist, religious/inspirational, young adult/teen, international, nature. List of upcoming themes available for SASE. Receives 20 mss/month. Accepts 3-5 mss/issue; 15-25 mss/year. Publishes ms 3-6 months after acceptance. Recently published work by Victoria Collett, Charles Curatalo, Anjali Amit, Lily Hartmann and Peter Chase. Length: 750 words average; 250 words minimum; 1,000 words maximum. Publishes short shorts. Also publishes literary essays and poetry. Often critiques or comments on rejected mss. Sponsors contests, awards or grants for fiction writers under 16 years of age.

How to Contact: Send complete ms with a cover letter. Include 50- to 100-word bio with background, international or intercultural experiences. Reports in 1 month on queries; 3 months on mss. Send SASE for reply, return of ms or send a disposable copy of ms. Simultaneous submissions OK. Sample copy for $5, 9×12 SAE and 4 first-class stamps. Fiction guidelines for #10 SASE.

Payment/Terms: Pays 1-3 contributor's copies; additional copies for $3. Acquires first North American serial rights and nonexclusive reprint rights.

Advice: Looking for stories with "multicultural/multiethnic theme, use of other languages when appropriate. Realistic and suitable for 8 to 16 year olds. Promoting social and nature awareness."

SLATE AND STYLE, Magazine of the National Federation of the Blind Writers Division, (I, IV), NFB Writer's Division, 2704 Beach Dr., Merrick NY 11566. (516)868-8718. Fax: (516)868-9076. Fiction Editor: Loraine Stayer. Newsletter: 8 × 10; 32 print/40 Braille pages; cassette and large print. "Articles of interest to writers, and resources for blind writers." Quarterly. Estab. 1982. Circ. 200.

• The magazine runs an annual contest for fiction, limit 2,000 words. There is a $5 entry fee and the contest runs from September 1 to May 1. Write for details.

Needs: Adventure, contemporary, fantasy, humor/satire, blindness. No erotica. "Avoid theme of death." Does not read mss in June or July. Recently published work by Stephanie Pieck and William Pearson. Length: 1,000-3,000 words. Publishes short shorts. Also publishes literary criticism and poetry. Critiques rejected mss only if requested.

How to Contact: Reports in 3-6 weeks. Large print sample copy for $2.50. "Sent Free Matter For The Blind. If not blind, send 2 stamps."

Payment/Terms: Pays in contributor's copies. Acquires one-time rights. Publication not copyrighted. Sponsors contests for fiction writers.

Advice: "Keep a copy. Editors can lose your work. Consider each first draft as just that and review your work before you send it. SASE a must."

SLIPPERY WHEN WET, A Magazine of Sex & Fun, (IV), More! Productions, P.O. Box 3101, Berkeley CA 94703. Website: http://www.best.com/~slippery/18.html. Editor: Sunah Cherwin. Electronic magazine: illustrations and photos. "Sex is fun; the scene is fun. Here's how to publish; open to erotica, humor, observations and how-tos." Estab. 1991. Daily. Circ. 100,000

Needs: Erotica. Receives 5-10 unsolicited mss/month. Acquires 3 mss/issue; 12 mss/year. Publishes ms 3 months after acceptance. Published work by Carol Queen, Mark Pritchard and Kris Kovick. Length: 750 words minimum; 5,000 words maximum. Publishes short shorts. Often critiques or comments on rejected mss.

How to Contact: Send complete ms with a cover letter and diskette for Mac. Include estimated word count and bio (1 paragraph). Reports in 1 month on queries; 2 months on mss. Send SASE (or IRC) for reply, return of ms or send a disposable copy of ms. Simultaneous, reprint and electronic (Mac diskette preferred with/hard copy) submissions OK. World Wide Web address: http://www.best.com./~slippery/18.html. Fiction guidelines free.

Payment/Terms: Payments are arranged. Acquires one-time rights.

Advice: Looks for "hot, funny, new ideas. Ask yourself, 'what does the reader discover?' "

‡SPACE AND TIME, (I, II), 138 W. 70th St. (4B), New York NY 10023-4468. (212)595-0894. Editor: Gordon Linzner. Fiction Editor: Tom Piccirilli. Magazine: 8½ × 11; 64 pages; 50 lb. paper; index card cover stock; illustrations; photos. "We publish science fiction, fantasy, horror and our favorite, that-which-defies-categorization." Biannually. Estab. 1966. Circ. 2,000. Member of the Small Press Center and the Small Press Genre Organization.

Needs: Fantasy (science, sword and sorcery, undefinable), horror, science fiction (hard science, soft/ sociological, undefinable). Receives 100 unsolicited mss/month. Accepts 12 mss/issue; 24 mss/year. Publishes ms 6 months after acceptance. Recently published work by Patricia Russo, Mario Milosevic, Paul Di Filippo and Jessica Amanda Salmonson. Length: 5,000 words average; 10,000 words maximum. Publishes short shorts. Also publishes literary essays, literary criticism and poetry. Send poems to Lawrence Greenberg. Often critiques or comments on rejected mss.

How to Contact: Send complete ms. Include estimated word count. Reports in 1 week on queries; 2 months on mss. Send SASE for reply, return of ms or send a disposable copy of ms. Sample copy for $5 and 9 × 12 SAE with $1.25 postage or 3 IRCs. Fiction guidelines for #10 SASE or SAE and 1 IRC.

Payment/Terms: Pays 1¢/word, $5 minimum and 2 contributor's copies on acceptance; additional copies $3. Acquires first North American serial rights and option to reprint in context of magazine.

Advice: Looks for "good writing, strong characterization and unusual plot or premise."

SQUARE ONE, A Magazine of Dark Fiction, (I, II), Tarkus Press (in conjunction with Ozark Triangle Press), Box 11921, Milwaukee WI 53211-0921. Editor: William D. Gagliani. Magazine: 7 × 8½; 75-90 pages; 20 lb. white bond paper; 80 lb. colored linen cover; illustrations; pen and ink drawings or any black on white. "There is no specific theme at *Square One*, but we publish only fiction and illustrations. Aimed at a general literate audience—people who *enjoy* reading fiction." Annually. Estab. 1984. Circ. 250.

Needs: Open to all categories including mainstream, mystery, science fiction, horror (all subgenres), fantasy, magic realism, suspense, etc. "We like exciting stories in which things happen and characters *exist*. Although we still like variety, we have moved into a darker, more 'disturbing' direction—horror, dark fantasy, new noir and, as always, genre blends." Receives 40-50 unsolicited fiction mss/month. Accepts 6-12 mss/issue, depending on length. Does not read mss between May and September. Publishes ms generally 1-14 months after acceptance. Length: 3,000 words average; 7,500 words maximum. Occasionally publishes short shorts but not vignettes. "It is editorial policy to comment on at least 75% of submissions rejected, but *please* be patient—we have a very small staff. Due to financial hiatus and editor's move, a backlog has occurred . . . it will take a while to read all manuscripts. I've been using checklist rejections to save time."

How to Contact: Send complete ms with cover letter. "Too many letters explain or describe the story. Let the fiction stand on its own. If it doesn't, the letter won't help. We like a brief bio and a few credits, but some writers get carried away. Use restraint and plain language—don't try to impress (it usually backfires)." Reports in 1-14 months on mss. SASE for ms. Simultaneous (if so labeled) and reprint submissions OK. Can accept electronic submissions via disk, HD or DS/DD 3.5″ disks (using Microsoft Word 5.0, Works, or WordPerfect 2.0 + for Macintosh). "Hard copy should always accompany any electronic submissions." Sample copies of older issues for $2.50, 9×12 SAE and 7 first-class stamps. Fiction guidelines for #10 SASE. Please make checks payable to William D. Gagliani.

Payment/Terms: Pays 2 contributor's copies. Acquires one-time rights.

Advice: "*Square One* is not a journal for beginners, despite what the name may imply. Rather, the name refers to the back-to-basics approach that we take—fiction must first and foremost be compelling. We want to see stories that elicit a response from the reader. We are currently seeking more horror/dark fantasy (all subgenres welcome), as well as genre blends, but still like to see variety—strong fiction in any genre remains an overall theme. We must stress that, since we are an irregular publication, contributors should expect long response lags. Our staff is small and *Square One* is still a part-time endeavor. Patience is the best advice we can offer. Financial difficulties have delayed our new issue several times, but it is in production and we are reading for future issues. Our new partnership with Ozark Triangle Press may lead to an anthology (rather than magazine) format, as well as future anthology and/or chapbook projects. Also, we oppose the absurdity of asking that writers subscribe to every magazine they would like to write for, especially given most writers' financial state. Check local public and college libraries and bookstores to see what's going on in the small press and literary markets, and—as a matter of dignity—consider carefully before submitting to magazines that routinely charge reading fees."

‡STORY RULES, The Little Magazine of Good Storytelling, (II), P.O. Box 134, Andover KS 67002. Editor: Robert Collins. Magazine: $8\frac{1}{2} \times 5\frac{1}{2}$; 20-30 pages; plain paper. "*Story Rules* publishes science fiction and fantasy stories that are interesting, original and fun to read." Quarterly. Estab. 1996. Circ. 40-60 "and growing."

Needs: Fantasy (science, sword and sorcery), humor/satire, science fiction (hard science, soft/sociological), cross-genre stories. No horror, experimental or mainstream. Receives 20-40 unsolicited mss/month. Accepts 4-7 mss/issue; 16-25 mss/year. Publishes ms 2-3 months after acceptance. Length: 500 words minimum; 5,000 words maximum. Sometimes critiques or comments on rejected mss.

How to Contact: Send complete ms with cover letter. Include estimated word count and 1-paragraph bio. Reports in 2 weeks to 1 month on mss. Send SASE and a disposable copy of ms. Reprints OK. Sample copy for $3. Fiction guidelines for #10 SASE.

Payment/Terms: Pays 2 contributor's copies; additional copies $2.50. Acquires one-time rights.

Advice: Looks for "original ideas, crisp writing and clear storytelling. Invest in a sample copy. If you like *Story Rules*, subscribe. The small press needs readers as well as writers."

‡THE STORYTELLER, For Amateur Writers, (I), 2441 Washington Rd., Maynard AR 72444. (501)647-2137. Editor: Regina Cook. Tabloid: $8\frac{1}{2} \times 11$; 50-60 pages; typing paper; illustrations. "This magazine is open to all new writers regardless of age. I will accept short stories in any genre and poetry in any type. Please keep in mind, this is a family publication." Quarterly. Estab. 1996.

Needs: Adventure, historical, humor/satire, literary, mainstream/contemporary, mystery/suspense, regional, religious/inspirational, romance, science fiction (soft/sociological), senior citizen/retirement, sports, westerns, young adult/teen. "I will not accept pornography, erotica, foul language, horror or graphic violence." Publishes ms 3-9 months after acceptance. Recently published work by W.C. Jameson. Length: 1,500 words average; 200 words minimum. Publishes short shorts. Also publishes literary essays and poetry. Sometimes critiques or comments on rejected mss.

How to Contact: Send complete ms with a cover letter. Include estimated word count and 5-line bio. Reports 2-4 weeks on queries; 1-2 months on mss. Send SASE for reply, return of ms or send a disposable copy of ms. Simultaneous and reprint submissions OK. Sample copy for $4. Fiction guidelines for #10 SASE.

Payment/Terms: "Readers vote quarterly for their favorites in all categories. Winning authors receive certificate of merit and free copy of issue in which their story or poem appeared."

Advice: Looks for "professionalism, good plots and unique characters. Purchase a sample copy so you know the kind of material we look for. Even though this is for amateur writers, don't send us something you would not send to paying markets." Would like more "well-plotted mysteries and suspense and a few traditional westerns. Avoid sending anything that children or young adults would not (or could not) read, such as really bad language."

‡**STYGIAN VORTEX PUBLICATIONS**, 1085 NE 179th Terrace, Miami Beach FL 33162-1256. Editor-in-Chief: Glenda Woodrum. Fantasy magazines "geared to a mature adult audience." Various publications include *In Darkness Eternal* (vampires as either protagonist or antagonist); *Laughter the Best Magic of All* (humorous fantasy for adults); *Lords of the Abyss* (supernatural horror); *Neuronet: Stories, Poetry and Art from the Cyberland*; *Shadow Sword* (heroic fantasy, sword and sorcery); and *Tales from the Vortex* (dark, modern fantasy).
Needs: Fantasy, horror. "I am especially looking for action-oriented themes and prefer active works to passive ones. Violence, sex and strong language have a place in the genre of each of our publications, but these themes should not be the entire focus of any submission. If your characters would realistically react or communicate in a certain way, let them do so. I am not easily offended. This does not mean that I want to see gross-out material written for shock value alone; make certain that there is a solid reason for 'shocking' content. No Stygian Vortex Publications title accepts mainstream, literary, romance, juvenile or experimental submissions of any type." Receives 30-110 unsolicited mss/month. Accepts 8-12 mss/issue; 32-40 mss/year. Publishes ms 8 months-2 years after acceptance. Length: 5,000 words preferred; 1,800 words minimum; 10,000 words maximum. Also publishes literary essays, literary criticism and poetry chapbooks under the Shadow Five Press imprint. Always critiques or comments on rejected mss.
How to Contact: Send complete ms with a cover letter. Include 150-word personal bio. "I especially want to know if you are an unpublished or beginning writer or artist. Do not explain your submission in your cover letter; let the work speak for itself." Reports in 1-2 weeks on queries; 1-4 months on mss. Send SASE for reply, return of ms or send a disposable copy of ms. Simultaneous and reprint submissions OK. Sample copy for $5.25 (payable to Glenda Woodrum). Fiction guidelines for SASE. Reviews novels and short story collections.
Payment/Terms: Pays $10 maximum plus 1 contributor's copy; additional copies for $2.50 and $1.25 postage. Acquires one-time rights.
Advice: "Read the guidelines carefully. All our publications are very tough markets, but I encourage you to submit your work. Never be afraid to send a submission to me, even if you aren't certain that it is appropriate to my needs. I'll try to help you in any way I can. As occasionally happens, I may simply request a revision in order to accept your work. Our standards are very high because we try to create the most professional quality publications that we possibly can, while giving the writers and artists the best showcases we can create for their work."

‡**TALEBONES, Fiction on the Dark Edge, (II)**, Fairwood Press, 10531 SE 250th Place, #104, Kent WA 98031. E-mail: talebones@aol.com. Website: http://members.aol.com/talebones. Editors: Patrick and Honna Swenson. Magazine: digest size; 60 pages; standard paper; glossy cover stock; illustrations and photos. "We like stories that have punch, but still entertain. We like dark science fiction and dark fantasy, humor, psychological and experimental works." Quarterly. Estab. 1995. Circ. 250.
 • *Talebones* received the 1995 Genre Writers Association Award for Best New Magazine/Editor.
Needs: Fantasy (dark), humor/satire, science fiction (hard science, soft/sociological, dark). "No straight slash and hack horror." Receives 200 mss/month. Accepts 6-7 mss/issue; 24-28 mss/year. Publishes ms 3-4 months after acceptance. Recently published work by Nina Kiriki Hoffman, Bruce Boston, Tom Piccirilli, Leslie What, James C. Glass and Don D'Ammassa. Length: 3,000-4,000 words average; 500 words minimum; 5,000 words maximum. Publishes short shorts. Length: 1,000 words. Also publishes poetry. Often critiques or comments on rejected mss.
How to Contact: Send complete ms with a cover letter. Include estimated word count, 1-paragraph bio and list of publications. Reports in 1 week on queries; 1-3 weeks on mss. Send SASE for reply, return of ms or send a disposable copy of ms. No simultaneous submissions. Electronic submissions (e-mail and website) OK. Sample copy for $4.50. Fiction guidelines for 9½ × 9½ SAE. Reviews novels and short story collections.
Payment/Terms: Pays $10-80 on acceptance and 1 contributor's copy; additional copies for $3. Acquires first North American serial rights. Sends galleys to author.
Advice: "The story must be entertaining, but should blur the boundary between science fiction and horror. All our stories have a dark edge to them, but often are humorous or psychological. Be polite and know how to properly present a manuscript. Include a cover letter, but keep it short and to the point."

TERMINAL FRIGHT, The Journal of Traditional Haunts and Horrors, (I), P.O. Box 100, Black River NY 13612. Editor: Kenneth E. Abner Jr. Magazine: 8½ × 11; 76 pages; 60 lb. white paper; 80 lb. cover stock. "Traditional gothic and modern occult horror." Quarterly. Estab. 1993.
 • The editor says he is *not* interested in experimental, splatter punk horror.

Needs: Horror, supernatural/occult. Publishes ms 1 year after acceptance. Length: 1,500 words minimum; 10,000 words maximum.

How to Contact: Send complete ms with a cover letter. Include estimated word count and 1-2 page bio; if available, on IBM compatible floppy disk (after acceptance). Reports in 6-8 weeks. Send SASE for return of ms or send a disposable copy of ms. Simultaneous submissions OK. Sample copy for $5. Fiction guidelines for #10 SASE.

Payment/Terms: Pays ½-2¢/word; 1 contributor copy on publication for first North American serial rights.

Advice: "The most important thing is to truly scare me. Stories should be unique, well-thought out and well-written. I highly discourage excessive vulgarity, explicit sex and graphic gore. All have their place in horror but only if used sparingly and with purpose, not as a crutch to an otherwise weak story."

‡TERRA INCOGNITA, A New Generation of Science Fiction, (II), 52 Windermere Ave. 3rd Floor, Lansdowne PA 19050-1812. E-mail: incognit@netaxs.com. Editor: Jan Berrien Berends. Magazine: 64 pages; e-brite paper; full-color glossy cover; illustrations; photos. *"Terra Incognita* is devoted to earth-based science fiction stories and relevant nonfiction articles. Readers of quality fiction—even those who are not science fiction fans—enjoy *TI*. Audience ranges from ages 18 and upward. We encourage feminist and socially conscious submissions." Quarterly. Estab. 1996.

Needs: Science fiction (hard science, soft/sociological). "No sexism and gratuitous sex and violence, racism or bias; avoid prose poems and vignettes. We prefer character-driven stories with protagonists and plots." Receives 200-300 unsolicited mss/month. Accepts 6-10 mss/issue; 25-35 mss/year. Publishes ms 3 months to 1 year after acceptance. Recently published work by L. Timmel Duchamp, Sue Storm, Timons Esais, W. Gregory Stewart, Nicola Griffith, Brian Stableford, Kandis Elliot and Darrell Schweitzer. Length: 5,000 words average; 100 words minimum; 15,000 words maximum. Publishes short shorts. Also publishes literary essays, literary criticism and poetry.

How to Contact: Send complete ms with cover letter. Include estimated word count and anything you think might be interesting in a cover letter. Reports in 1-2 weeks on queries; 1-3 weeks on mss. Send SASE for reply, return of ms or send a disposable copy of ms. "A cover letter is optional; a SASE is not." Sample copy for $5; $6 overseas. Fiction guidelines for #10 SASE. Reviews novels and short story collections.

Payment/Terms: Pays $20-300 and 2 contributor's copies; additional copies $5. Pays on acceptance. Acquires first North American serial rights.

Advice: Looks for "good writing and literary merit; a story that grabs our interest and holds it straight through to the end. Write as well as you can (which means—don't overwrite, but do use the words themselves to advance your story), and tell us a story—preferably one we haven't heard before. Don't get your great idea rejected on account of lousy grammar or poor manuscript format. We take all submissions seriously."

TEXAS YOUNG WRITERS' NEWSLETTER, (I, II, IV), Texas Young Writers' Association, P.O. Box 942, Adkins TX 78101-0942. E-mail: tywn1@aol.com. Editor: Susan Currie. Newsletter: 8½×11; 8 pages; 20 lb. white paper; illustrations. *"TYWN* teaches young writers about the art and business of writing, and also gives them a place to publish their best work. We publish articles by adults with experience in publishing, and poetry and short stories by young writers 12-19." Monthly during summer, bimonthly during school year (August-May). Estab. 1994. Circ. 300.

Needs: Open to authors ages 12-19 only. Adventure, ethnic/multicultural, fantasy (children's fantasy, science fantasy), historical, humor/satire, literary, mainstream/contemporary, mystery/suspense, romance, science fiction, young adult/teen. "Anything by young writers, 12-19. No erotica, horror, gay/lesbian, or occult." List of upcoming themes available for SASE. Receives 6 unsolicited mss/month. Accepts 1 ms/issue; 9 mss/year. Publishes ms 6 months after acceptance. Published work by Sarah Elezian, Lillette Hill, Caroline Beever and Anthony Twistt. Length: 900 words average; 500 words minimum; 1,100 words maximum. Publishes short shorts. Also publishes poetry. Sometimes critiques or comments on rejected ms.

How to Contact: Send complete ms with a cover letter. Include estimated word count and 50-100 word bio. Reports in 6 weeks. Send SASE for reply, return of ms or send a disposable copy of ms. Electronic submissions (disk, files in text format) OK. Sample copy for $1. Guidelines for #10 SASE, "please specify adult or young writer's guidelines."

---

‡ THE DOUBLE DAGGER before a listing indicates that the listing is new in this edition.

Payment/Terms: Pays 2 contributor's copies for poetry, 5 for articles and short stories. Acquires first North American serial rights. Not copyrighted.

Advice: "Please read back issues and study the sort of fiction we publish, and make sure it fits our newsletter. Since *TYWN* is sent to schools and young people, we prefer upbeat, nonviolent stories. I look for work that is highly original, creative, and appropriate for our audience. Manuscripts that are professional and striking stand out. I haven't seen enough stories with strong characters and involving plots. I don't want to see dull stories with dull characters. We want to show our young writers terrific examples of stories that they can learn from."

THRESHOLDS QUARTERLY, School of Metaphysics Associates Journal, (I, II, IV), SOM Publishing, School of Metaphysics National Headquarters, HCR1, Box 15, Windyville MO 65783. (417)345-8411. Editor: Dr. Barbara Condron. Senior Editor: Dr. Laurel Fuller Clark. Magazine: 7×10; 32 pages; line drawings and b&w photos. "The School of Metaphysics is a nonprofit educational and service organization invested in education and research in the expansion of human consciousness and spiritual evolution of humanity. For all ages and backgrounds. Themes: dreams, healing, science fiction, personal insight, morality tales, fables, humor, spiritual insight, mystic experiences, religious articles, creative writing with universal themes." Quarterly. Estab. 1975. Circ. 5,000.

● *Thresholds Quarterly* has doubled its circulation.

Needs: Adventure, fantasy, humor/satire, psychic/supernatural/occult, religious/inspirational and science fiction. Upcoming themes: "Dreams, Visions, and Creative Imagination" (February); "Health and Wholeness" (May); "Intuitive Arts" (August); "Man's Spiritual Consciousness" (November). Receives 5 unsolicited mss/month. Length: 4-10 double-spaced typed pages. Publishes short shorts. Also publishes literary essays and poetry. Often critiques or comments on rejected mss.

How to Contact: Query with outline; will accept unsolicited ms with cover letter; no guarantee on time length to respond. Include bio (1-2 paragraphs). Send SASE for reply, return of ms or send a disposable copy of ms. Sample copy for 9×12 SAE and $1.50 postage. Fiction guidelines for #10 SASE.

Payment/Terms: Pays up to 5 contributor's copies. Acquires all rights.

Advice: "We encourage works that have one or more of the following attributes: uplifting, educational, inspirational, entertaining, informative and innovative."

2 AM MAGAZINE, (I, II, IV), Box 6754, Rockford IL 61125-1754. Editor: Gretta M. Anderson. Magazine: $8\frac{1}{2} \times 11$; 60 or more pages; 60 lb. offset paper; 70 lb. offset cover; illustrations; photos occasionally. "Horror, science fiction, fantasy stories, poetry, articles and art for a sophisticated adult audience." Quarterly. Summer fiction issue planned. Estab. 1986. Circ. 2,000.

Needs: Experimental, fantasy, horror, humor/satire, mystery/suspense (police procedurals, romantic suspense), prose poem, psychic/supernatural/occult, romance (gothic), science fiction (hard science, soft/sociological). No juvenile. Receives 400 unsolicited mss/month. Accepts 12-14 mss/issue; 50 mss/year. Publishes ms an average of 6-9 months after acceptance. Published work by Darrel Schweitzer, Avram Davidson, John Coyne and Larry Tritten. Published new writers within the last year. Length: 3,000 words average; 500 words minimum; 5,000 words maximum. Publishes short shorts. Sometimes critiques rejected mss.

How to Contact: Send complete ms with cover letter (cover letter optional). Simultaneous submissions OK. Reports in 1 month on queries; 10-12 weeks on mss. SASE. Sample copy for $4.95 and $1 postage. Fiction guidelines for #10 SASE.

Payment/Terms: Pays $\frac{1}{2}$¢/word minimum, negotiable maximum on acceptance for one-time rights with nonexclusive anthology option; 1 contributor's copy; 40% discount on additional copies. Sends prepublication galleys to author.

Advice: "Publishing more pages of fiction, more science fiction, and mystery, as well as horror. Put name and address on manuscript, double-space, use standard manuscript format. Pseudonym should appear under title on first manuscript page. True name and address should appear on upper left on first manuscript page."

VIRGINIA QUARTERLY REVIEW, (I, II), One West Range, Charlottesville VA 22903. (804)924-3124. Fax: (804)924-1397. Editor: Fax: (804)924-1397. E-mail: jco7e@virginia.edu. Editor: Staige Blackford. "A national magazine of literature and discussion. A lay, intellectual audience; people who are not out-and-out scholars but who are interested in ideas and literature." Quarterly. Estab. 1925. Circ. 4,500.

Needs: Adventure, contemporary, ethnic, feminist, humor, literary, romance, serialized novels (excerpts) and translations. "No pornography." Buys 3 mss/issue, 20 mss/year. Recently published William Hoffman, Mary Gray Hughes, Kim R. Stafford and Kelly Cherry. Length: 3,000-7,000 words.

How to Contact: Query or send complete ms. SASE. No simultaneous submissions. Reports in 2 weeks on queries, 2 months on mss. Sample copy for $5.

Payment/Terms: Pays $10/printed page on publication for all rights. "Will transfer upon request." Offers Emily Clark Balch Award for best published short story of the year.

Advice: Looks for "stories with a somewhat Southern dialect and/or setting. Humor is welcome; stories involving cancer and geriatrics are not."

‡VOLCANO QUARTERLY, The Village Square of Volcanodom, (I, II, IV), P.O. Box 405, Issaquah WA 98027. (206)392-7858. E-mail: vqjantan@aol.com. Website: http://memberes.aol.com/vqyantan/vq.html. New address after June 1, 1997: 420 SE Evans Lane. Editor: Janet Tanaka. Magazine: 8½×11, 16-24 pages; matte paper; illustrations; photos. "After February, 1997, an on-line publication (e-zine), with print copies only for the cyber disadvantaged. Our audience is volcano-people—both professional and amateur volcanologists, geologists, science teachers, students and volcano buffs." Quarterly. Estab. 1992. Circ. 500.

Needs: Adventure, fantasy (science), horror, humor/satire, mystery/suspense, natural disaster, regional, religious/inspirational, romance (contemporary), science fiction (hard science, soft/sociological), serialized novel. "Stories must deal with volcanoes: past, present or future; earthly or extraterrestrial, and/or volcano scientists, etc. No erotica. Must be in English." Publishes ms 3-6 months after acceptance. Length: open. Publishes short shorts. Also publishes literary criticism and poetry. Always critiques or comments on rejected ms, but "we rarely reject anything that meets our guidelines."

How to Contact: Send complete ms with cover letter. Include brief bio. Reports in 1-2 weeks on queries; 4-6 weeks on mss. Send SASE for reply, return of ms or send a disposable copy of ms. Simultaneous, reprint and electronic submissions OK. Sample copy for $5 and 8½×11 SAE. Fiction guidelines for #10 SASE.

Payment/Terms: Pays 3 contributor's copies. Not copyrighted.

Advice: "All volcanoes and volcanic activity must be scientifically accurate. Non-terrestrial volcanoes can be, of course, purely made up, but with some scientific logic."

WEIRDBOOK, (II), Box 149, Amherst Branch, Buffalo NY 14226. (716)839-2415. Editor: W. Paul Ganley. Magazine: 8½×11; 64 pages; self cover; illustrations. "Latter day 'pulp magazine' along the lines of the old pulp magazine *Weird Tales*. We tend to use established writers. We look for an audience of fairly literate people who like good writing and good characterization in their fantasy and horror fiction, but are tired of the clichés in the field." Semiannually. Estab. 1968. Circ. 1,000.

Needs: *Presently overstocked. Inquire first.* Fantasy, gothic (not modern) horror and psychic/supernatural. "No psychological horror; mystery fiction; physical horror (blood); traditional ghost stories (unless original theme); science fiction; swords and sorcery without a supernatural element; or reincarnation stories that conclude with 'And the doctor patted him on . . . THE END!' " Accepts 8-12 mss/issue. Length: 15,000 words maximum. Also publishes poetry. Sometimes recommends other markets.

How to Contact: Send complete ms with SASE. Reports in 3 months on mss. Sample copy for $6.80. Guidelines for #10 SASE.

Payment/Terms: Pays 1¢/word minimum and 1 contributor's copy on publication ("part on acceptance only for solicited mss") for first North American serial rights plus right to reprint the entire issue.

Advice: "Read a copy and then some of the best anthologies in the field (such as DAW's *Best Horror of the Year*, Arkham House anthologies, etc.) Occasionally we keep manuscripts longer than planned. When sending a SASE marked 'book rate' (or anything not first class) the writer should add 'Forwarding Postage Guaranteed.' "

‡✤WESTERN DIGEST, Crossbow Publications, 400 Whiteland Dr. NE, Calgary, Alberta T1Y 3M7 Canada. (403)280-3424. Editor: Douglas Sharp. Newsletter: 8½×11; 20 pages; illustrations. Estab. 1995. Circ. 100.

Needs: Westerns (frontier, traditional). "Do not combine westerns with science fiction." Receives 4 unsolicited mss/month. Accepts 5-8 mss/issue; 50 mss/year. Publishes ms 8-12 months after acceptance. Recently published work by Emery Mehok, S.M. Cain, A.J. Arnold and C.K. Eckhardt. Length: 3,000 words average; 1,000 words minimum; 5,000 words maximum. Publishes short shorts. Length: 1,000 words. Also publishes literary criticism and poetry. Always critiques or comments on rejected mss.

How to Contact: Send complete ms with a cover letter. Include 10- to 30-word bio. Reports in 1 week on queries; 2 weeks on mss. Send SAE and 2 IRCs for return of ms. Simultaneous submissions, reprints and electronic (Macintosh disk, WordPerfect 5.1) submissions OK. Sample copy for $4. Fiction guidelines free. Reviews novels or short story collections.

Payment/Terms: Pays $10-60 (Canadian funds) and free subscription to the magazine on publication. Acquires one-time rights.

Advice: "I enjoy stories with humorous, ironic or surprise endings. I would like to read more humorous stories. Avoid shoot-'em-ups. One gets tired of reading stories where the fastest gun wins in the end. There are other stories to be told of the pioneers. Rewrite your story until it is perfect. Do not use contractions in narration unless the story is written in first person. Do not send three consecutive pages of dialogue. Be sure to identify the speaker after three or four paragraphs. A reader should not have to reread a passage to understand it. Please, no sex or heavy duty swearing."

THE WESTERN POCKET, (I, IV), The 21st Communications Corp., P.O. Box 200308, Denver CO 80220-0308. (303)399-9985. Fax: (303)399-5575. E-mail: xxlcomm@aol.com. Editor: Glenn Meyers. Fiction Editor: Carson Reed. Magazine: 4×7; 64 pages; 60 lb. paper; 90 lb. coated cover; perfect-bound; illustrations and photos. Quarterly. Estab. 1995. Circ. 5,782.

Needs: Ethnic/multicultural, experimental (western based), historical, humor/satire, literary, regional, westerns. "No psychic, romance, science fiction, children's." Publishes special fiction issue or anthology. Receives 20-30 unsolicited mss/month. Accepts 3 mss/issue; 12 mss/year. Publishes ms 3-6 months after acceptance. Recently published work by Buck Ramsey, Baxter Black, Carson Reed and Jess Quinlan. Length: 1,200 words average; 700 words minimum; 2,200 words maximum. Publishes short shorts. Also publishes literary essays and poetry. Sometimes critiques or comments on rejected ms.

How to Contact: Send complete ms with a cover letter. Phone calls or faxes acceptable. Include estimated word count, short bio, Social Security number and list of publications. Reports in 4-6 weeks on queries; 2-3 months on mss. Send SASE for reply, return of ms or send a disposable copy of ms. Simultaneous, reprint and electronic (Mac or PC) submissions OK. Sample copy for $3.95, 5×7 or 6×9 SAE and 78¢ postage. Fiction guidelines for #10 SASE. Reviews novels and short story collections. Send books to Mark Stevens.

Payment/Terms: Pays $50-300 and 2 contributor's copies on publication for first North American serial rights; additional copies for $2.35.

Advice: "Quality and imagination are good starting points. I want to have something stick with me when I've finished reading a story, some image or sentence that I can remember."

WESTERN TALES MAGAZINE, (I), P.O. Box 33842, Granada Hills CA 91394. Editor: Dorman Nelson. Magazine: 8½×11; 100 pages; 60 lb. cover stock; b&w illustrations. Looks for "western stories and poetry for a family audience of all ages." Quarterly. Estab. 1993.

Needs: Westerns (frontier, traditional, young adult western). No porn or hard core violence. Publishes special fiction issue or anthology. Receives 150-200 mss/month. Accepts 26 mss/issue; 100 mss/year. Publishes ms 6 months after acceptance. Agented fiction 10%. Length: 4,000-5,000 words preferred. Publishes short shorts. Length: 1,000 words. Also publishes poetry.

How to Contact: Send complete ms with a cover letter or submit through an agent. Include short bio and Social Security number. Reports in 6 weeks. Send SASE for reply, return of ms or send a disposable copy of ms. Simultaneous and reprint submissions OK. Sample copy for $6. Fiction guidelines for #10 SAE.

Payment/Terms: Pays $100 (story); $25 (poetry); 1 contributor's copy on acceptance for first North American serial rights.

Advice: "*Western Tales* is a story, a fib, a trail-riding yarn, a boast or an embellishment of what really happened. Write a good tale using your own voice, and use facets of life (i.e., emotions, trauma, adventure). How do we humans interact and deal with life?"

‡WHISPERING WILLOW'S MYSTERY MAGAZINE, (IV), Whispering Willow's LTD., Co., 2517 South Central, P.O. Box 890294, Oklahoma City OK 73189-0294. (405)239-2531. Fax: (405)232-0392. Editor: Peggy D. Farris. Fiction Editor: Trula Johnson. Magazine: 5½×8½; 112 pages; offset paper; 60 lb. gloss enamel cover stock; illustrations and photos. Publishes "mystery stories for mystery readers, all ages." Quarterly. Estab. 1996.

Needs: Mystery/suspense (amateur sleuth, cozy, police procedural, private eye/hardboiled), psychic/supernatural/occult. "No romance." List of upcoming themes available for SASE. Publishes special fiction issue or anthology. Receives 25 unsolicited mss/month "however, we're a new magazine." Accepts 5-6 mss/issue; 20-24 mss/year. Publishes ms 3-6 months after acceptance. Deadlines: September 1 for January 10 publication; January 10 for April 1 publication; March 1 for July 1 publication; June 1 for October 1 publication. "We're a new magazine, however I've purchased three stories so far": "Hide and Seek," by Tim Myers; "Picture Perfect," by Lisa Lepovetsky; and "Sip A Cup of Murder," by Edie Hanes. Length: 1,800 words average; 500 words minimum; 2,500 words maximum. Also publishes poetry.

How to Contact: Send complete ms with cover letter. Include estimated word count, 1-2 paragraph bio and list of publications. Reports in 1 month on mss. Send SASE for reply, return of ms or send a disposable copy of ms. Simultaneous submissions OK. Sample copy for $6. Fiction guidelines for #10 SASE.

Payment/Terms: Pays 4¢/word on publication and 1 contributor's copy; additional copies for $2.97. Acquires first North American serial rights. Sends galleys to author. Sponsors 3 contests annually; send SASE for information.

Advice: Looks for "mystery, with suspense that is believable, holds the reader's interest, moves along and doesn't drag. An unusual approach or a successful twist makes the manuscript stand out. Check facts for accuracy."

‡THE WHITE CROW, (I, II), Osric Publishing, P.O. Box 4501, Ann Arbor MI 48106. E-mail: cherdt@umich.edu. Editor: Christopher™ Herdt. Zine: 5½×8; 32 pages; 20 lb. white paper; 60 lb.

INSIDER REPORT

Forget "Slim" and "Trigger" when writing today's westerns

A self-taught writer with lots of life experience, California editor Dorman Nelson of *Western Tales* magazine advocates common sense and perseverance when seeking publication in an unpredictable, but slowly growing field. "I'm not a literary genius. I'm more of a voracious reader of books," he says in his straight-forward manner. As such, he contends that practice makes perfect and believes above all in the power of the well-crafted story— especially if it's a western.

Dorman Nelson

As sole editor of one of the few western fiction magazines being published today, Nelson is a modern-day pioneer in his marketing of this uniquely American genre. His mission in creating *Western Tales* is simple: "I'm trying to get the western market back on its feet." Since the glory days of pulp westerns during the 1930s through the 1950s, western writers have endured a long struggle for recognition. Nelson intends to give them every opportunity to publish their "trail-riding yarns." Even though he asserts that the entertainment industry is saturated with action and who-done-it films, and the fiction market seems to have followed suit, he says, "I think the public is going to get tired of this slam, bam, shoot-'em-up stuff."

Nelson's timing appears to be right on target, despite complaints from writers that publishers sometimes embrace this genre and at other times ignore it. Amongst all the recent hoopla of other regional writings, namely "Southern" and "New England" fiction, a slow resurgence of traditional western writing has taken place, with authors such as Zane Grey and Larry McMurtry leading the way. Most recently, more contemporary western writers, Cormac McCarthy at the forefront, are inching their way into a realm historically reserved for creators of traditional western fiction.

Nelson's admiration for all facets of the western genre began during a childhood spent devouring the writings of James Fenimore Cooper, Robert Louis Stevenson and the like. Later, Nelson spent his young adulthood traveling across the country "doing a little of everything," from farming to maintenance, often ending the day with a pen in his hand, crafting stories (mostly westerns and romance) or writing letters. "Eventually, I ended up in Nebraska and got into the fur trade. I began reading and discovered that stories about 'local people' were still around." And never considering himself a writer by trade, he was surprised to discover that he'd been writing all along, "and didn't realize it. That's when I

INSIDER REPORT, *continued*

began to look for a venue for western fiction."

Nelson marketed his idea for a western magazine the old-fashioned way. "I made fliers and went cross-country, drove down dirt roads to farms and left 'em wherever people might be interested in western work." He received 4,500 submissions for the first edition, which he published in the summer of 1995.

Being a connoisseur of western writing, Nelson's requirements for publishable work are amazingly uncomplicated. "I look for a smooth flowing story" devoid of all the customary western clichés. "For example, a horse named Smoke or Trigger and a guy named Slim show a lack of imagination." Rather than conform to stereotypes, he encourages novice writers to "tell a story in your own voice."

In addition, Nelson recommends that writers experiment with western writing. "Take events that are happening now and place them back in time to write a modern-day western tale. Human beings don't change, only the time frame." One technique Nelson suggests is taking a true story and altering something that really happened—the location, for instance—to give it a western flavor. "But if your piece is historical, stick to the facts," he says. Most important, "write what you know about and are interested in. If it's fiction, the sky's the limit."

Once you've found your style and are actively seeking publication, Nelson tells writers to "get a big box and label it 'REJECTS' in big letters. Be prepared to fill it with your own stuff. You might sell one out of 50 stories, but that's just fine." He recommends Western Writers of America (listed in the Organizations and Resources section of this book) as a source of information for novice writers. Also, "get a market book such as *Novel & Short Story Writer's Market* and pick out a publisher you're interested in. Then get a copy of the magazine you'd like to submit to and read it to learn about that market."

Nelson's final pieces of advice are simple: "If you're a writer, then write— the more you bat, the better you get. Then, don't be afraid. Send 'em [your stories] in."

—Jennifer Hogan-Redmond

cover stock; illustrations and photos. "We seek solid literary works which will appeal to an intelligent but not necessarily literary audience. We ain't 'highfalutin.' " Quarterly. Estab. 1994. Circ. 100 (approximate).

Needs: Ethnic/multicultural, experimental, humor/satire, literary, translations. "No erotic fiction, no occult." Receives 3 mss/month. Accepts 1-2 mss/issue; 6 mss/year. Publishes ms up to 4 months after acceptance. Length: 2,500 words average; 300 words minimum; 4,000 words maximum. Publishes short shorts. Also publishes literary essays and poetry. Always critiques or comments on rejected mss.

How to Contact: Send complete ms with cover letter. Include estimated word count and a 30-word bio. Reports in 4 months. Send SASE for return of ms. Simultaneous submissions and reprints OK. Sample copy for $1.

Payment/Terms: Pays 1 contributor's copy; additional copies for $1. Acquires one-time rights. Not copyrighted.

Advice: "Is the story focused? Is it driven by a coherent, meaningful idea that can be grasped by an intelligent (but not literary) reader? We aren't picky, but please spell everything correctly!"

WISCONSIN ACADEMY REVIEW, (IV), Wisconsin Academy of Sciences, Arts & Letters, 1922 University Ave., Madison WI 53705. (608)263-1692. Editor-in-Chief: Faith B. Miracle. Magazine: 8½×11; 48-52 pages; 75 lb. coated paper; coated cover stock; illustrations; photos. "The *Review* reflects the focus of the sponsoring institution with its editorial emphasis on Wisconsin's intellectual, cultural, social and physical environment. It features short fiction, poetry, essays, nonfiction articles

and Wisconsin-related art and book reviews for people interested in furthering regional arts and literature and disseminating information about sciences." Quarterly. Estab. 1954. Circ. approximately 1,800.
Needs: Experimental, historical, humor/satire, literary, mainstream, prose poem. "Author must have
a Wisconsin connection or fiction must be set in Wisconsin." Receives 5-6 unsolicited fiction mss/
month. Accepts 1-2 mss/issue; 6-8 mss/year. Published new writers within the last year. Length: 1,000
words minimum; 3,500 words maximum. Also publishes poetry; "will consider" literary essays, literary criticism.
How to Contact: Send complete ms with SAE and state author's connection to Wisconsin, the
prerequisite. Sample copy for $2. Fiction guidelines for SASE. Reviews books on Wisconsin themes.
Payment/Terms: Pays 3-5 contributor's copies. Acquires first rights on publication.
Advice: "Manuscript publication is at the discretion of the editor based on space, content, and balance.
We prefer previously unpublished poetry and fiction. We publish emerging as well as established
authors; fiction and poetry, without names attached, are sent to reviewers for evaluation."

‡WOMAN, (I), 799 Water St., Meadville PA 16335. (814)336-4132. Fax: (814)333-0431. E-mail:
bwalton@gremlan.org. Editor: Babs Walton. Magazine: 8½×7; 12 or more pages; 20 lb. bond paper;
illustrations. "We are a journal, by women and for women, with articles, essays, poetry and fiction on
topics of interest to today's modern woman." Monthly. Estab. 1996. Circ. 300.
Needs: Ethnic/multicultural, experimental, feminist, humor/satire, lesbian, literary, mainstream/con-
temporary, mystery/suspense, psychic/supernatural/occult, religious/inspirational, romance, science
fiction. Receives 5-10 unsolicited mss/month. Accepts 1-2 mss/issue. Publishes ms 2-3 months after
acceptance. Recently published work by Diana Stoneberg and Barbara Locke. Length: 1,000 words
average; 100 words minimum; 1,500 words maximum. Publishes short shorts. Also publishes poetry.
Often critiques or comments on rejected mss.
How to Contact: Query first or send complete ms with cover letter. Include estimated word count
and 1-paragraph bio. "If you have a book you want to advertise, add it to your bio." Reports in 2
weeks on queries; 1 month on mss. Send SASE for reply, return of ms or send a disposable copy of
ms. Reprints and electronic submissions OK. Sample copy for $1 and #10 SAE with 2 first-class
stamps. Fiction guidelines for #10 SASE. Reviews novels and short story collections.
Payment/Terms: Pays 1-year subscription to magazine ($10 value) on acceptance. Acquires first
North American serial rights.
Advice: "We look for something different, a special use of language or striking imagery. It can be
personal, but should also reach out to our whole readership. Be brief!"

WORLDS OF FANTASY & HORROR, (II), Terminus Publishing Co., Inc., 123 Crooked Lane,
King of Prussia PA 19406-2570. Editor: Darrell Schweitzer. Magazine: 8½×11; 164 pages; white,
non-glossy paper; glossy 4-color cover; illustrations. "We publish fantastic fiction, supernatural horror
for an adult audience." Quarterly. Estab. 1923 (*Weird Tales*); 1994 (*Worlds of Fantasy & Horror*).
Circ. 8,000.
Needs: Fantasy (science, sword and sorcery), horror, psychic/supernatural/occult, translations. "We
want to see a wide range of fantasy, from sword and sorcery to supernatural horror. We can use some
unclassifiables." Receives 400 unsolicited mss/month. Accepts 8 mss/issue; 32 mss/year. Publishes
ms 6-18 months after acceptance. Agented fiction 10%. Published work by Joyce Carol Oates, Ian
Watson and Ramsey Campbell. Length: 4,000 words average; 10,000 words maximum (very few over
8,000). "No effective minimum. Shortest we ever published was about 100 words." Publishes short
shorts. Also publishes poetry. Always critiques or comments on rejected mss.
How to Contact: Send complete ms with a cover letter. Include estimated word count and list of
publications (if relevant). Reports in 2-3 weeks on mss. Send SASE for reply, return of ms or send a
disposable copy of ms. No simultaneous submissions. No reprint submissions, "but will buy first
North American rights to stories published overseas." Sample copy for $4.95. Fiction guidelines for
#10 SASE. Reviews novels and short story collections relevant to the horror/fantasy field. Send books
to S.T. Joshi, 10 W. 15th St., #312, New York NY 10011 or Douglas Winter, 506 Crown View Dr.,
Alexandria VA 22314.
Payment/Terms: Pays 3¢/word minimum and 2 contributor's copies for first North American serial
rights plus anthology option. Sends galleys to author.
Advice: "We look for imagination and vivid writing. Read the magazine. Get a good grounding in
the contemporary horror and fantasy field through the various 'best of the year' anthologies. Avoid

---

● **A BULLET INTRODUCES COMMENTS** by the editor of *Novel &
Short Story Writer's Market* indicating special information about the listing.

the obvious cliches of technicalities of the hereafter, the mechanics of vampirism, generic Tolkien-clone fantasy. In general, it is better to be honest and emotionally moving rather than clever. Avoid stories which have nothing of interest save for the allegedly 'surprise' ending."

YARNS AND SUCH, (I, IV), Creative With Words Publications, Box 223226, Carmel CA 93922. Fax: (408)655-8627. Editors: Brigitta Geltrich and Bert Howes. Editors rotate. Booklet: 5½×8½; 60-90 pages; bond paper; illustrations. Folklore. Annually. Estab. 1975. Circ. varies.
Needs: Ethnic, humor/satire, mystery/suspense (amateur sleuth, private eye), regional, folklore. "Once a year we publish an anthology of the writings of young writers, titled: *We are Writers Too!*" No violence or erotica, religious fiction. List of upcoming themes available for SASE. Receives 200-300 unsolicited fiction mss/month. Does not read mss July through December. Publishes ms 2-6 months after acceptance. Publishes after set deadlines. Recently published work by Emma Blanch, Desoree Thompson and Patricia Cranolall; published new writers within the last year. Length: 1,200 words average. Critiques rejected mss "when requested, *then we charge $20/prose, up to 1,000 words.*"
How to Contact: Query first or send complete ms with cover letter and SASE. "Reference has to be made to which project the manuscript is being submitted. Unsolicited mss without SASE will be destroyed after holding them 1 month." Reports in 2 weeks on queries; 2 months on mss; longer on specific seasonal anthologies. No simultaneous submissions. Accepts electronic (disk) submissions via Macintosh and IBM/PC. Sample copy for $6. Fiction guidelines for #10 SASE.
Payment/Terms: No payment. Acquires one-time rights. 20% reduction on each copy ordered.
Advice: "We have increased the number of anthologies we are publishing to 10 per year and offer a greater variety of themes. We look for clean family-type fiction. Also, look at the world from a different perspective, research your topic thoroughly, be creative, apply brevity, tell the story from a character's viewpoint, tighten dialogue, be less descriptive, proofread before submitting and be patient."

YOUNG JUDAEAN, (IV), Hadassah Zionist Youth Commission, 50 W. 58th St., New York NY 10019. (212)303-4575. Editor: Jonathan Mayo. National Education Supervisor: Sharon Schoenfeld. Magazine: 8½×11; 16 pages; illustrations. "*Young Judaean* is for members of the Young Judaea Zionist youth movement, ages 8-13." Quarterly. Estab. 1910. Circ. 4,000.
Needs: Children's fiction including adventure, ethnic, fantasy, historical, humor/satire, juvenile, prose poem, religious, science fiction, suspense/mystery and translations. "All stories must have Jewish relevance." Receives 10-15 unsolicited fiction mss/month. Publishes ms up to 2 years after acceptance. Accepts 1-2 mss/issue; 10-20 mss/year. Length: 750 words minimum; 1,000 words maximum.
How to Contact: Send complete ms with SASE. Reports in 3 months on mss. Sample copy for 75¢. Free fiction guidelines.
Payment/Terms: Pays five contributor's copies.
Advice: "Stories must be of Jewish interest—lively and accessible to children without being condescending."

‡**YOUNG VOICES MAGAZINE, The Magazine of Young People's Creative Work, (I, II, IV)**, P.O. Box 2321, Olympia WA 98507. (360)357-4683. Editors: Gwen Anderson and Mark Shetterly. Magazine: 8½×11; 32 pages. "All materials are by elementary through high school students for children and adults interested in children's work." Bimonthly. Estab. 1988. Circ. 5,000.
Needs: "Everything must be written by elementary, middle or high school students. (12th grade is the limit.)" Adventure, ethnic/multicultural, fantasy, feminist, humor/satire, literary, mainstream, mystery/suspense (young adult), prose poem, regional, science fiction, sports and westerns. No work by adults, excessive violence or sexual content. Plans a special fiction issue or anthology in the future. Receives 200 unsolicited mss/month. Accepts 20 mss/issue; 120 mss/year. Publishes ms 3-4 months after acceptance. Length: 600 words average; 3,000 words maximum. Publishes short shorts. Also publishes poetry. Often critiques rejected mss and recommends other markets.
How to Contact: Query first. "Make sure age, grade and school are in the letter." Reports in 6 weeks on queries; 3-4 months on mss. Simultaneous submissions OK. Sample copy for $4. Fiction guidelines for SASE.
Payment/Terms: Pays $5 and contributor's copies.
Terms: Pays on acceptance for first or one-time rights.
Advice: "Query, explaining story idea. Do not submit unsolicited manuscripts. Suggestion: Read the magazine. Look at what we publish."

International small circulation magazines

The following is a list of small circulation publications from countries outside the U.S. and Canada that accept or buy short fiction in English (or in the universal languages of Esperanto or Ido).

Before sending a manuscript to a publication in another country, it's a good idea to query first for information on the magazine's needs and methods of submission. Send for sample copies or try visiting the main branch of your local library, a nearby college library or bookstore to find a copy.

All correspondence to markets outside your own country must include International Reply Coupons, if you want a reply or material returned. You may find it less expensive to send copies of your manuscript for the publisher to keep and just enclose a return postcard with one IRC for a reply. Keep in mind response time is slow for many overseas publishers, but don't hesitate to send a reply postcard with IRC to check the status of your submission. You can obtain IRCs from the main branch of your local post office. The charge for one in U.S. funds is $1.05.

AMMONITE, 12 Priory Mead, Bruton Somerset BA100DZ (UK). Fiction Editor: John Howard-Greaves. Occasionally. Circ. 200. Publishes 3-7 stories/issue. "Myth, legend, science fiction to do with the current passage of evolution towards the possibilities of the Aquarian Age." Length: no minimum; 2,500 words maximum. Pays 2 contributor's copies.

AUGURIES, Morton Publishing, P.O. Box 23, Gosport, Hants P012 2XD England. Editor: Nik Morton. Circ. 300. Averages 15 stories/year. "Science fiction and fantasy, maximum length 4,000 words." Pays £2 per 1,000 words plus complimentary copy. "Buy back issues, then try me!" Sample copy for $10. Subscription (2 issues) $30 to 'Morton Publishing.' Member of the New SF Alliance.

AUREALIS, Australian Fantasy and Science Fiction, P.O. Box 2164, Mt. Waverley, Victoria 3149 Australia. Fiction Editors: Dirk Strasser and Stephen Higgins. Semiannually. Circ. 2,500. Publishes 6 stories/issue: science fiction, fantasy and horror short stories. Length: 1,500 words minimum; 6,000 words maximum. "No reprints; no stories accepted elsewhere. Send one story at a time." Pays 2-6¢ (Australian)/word and contributor's copy. "Read the magazine. It is available in the UK and North America." Sample copy for $8 (Australian). Writer's guidelines available for SAE with IRC.

‡DARK HORIZONS, 46 Oxford Rd., Acocks Green, Birmingham B27 6DT England. Editors: Peter Coleborn, Mike Chinn and Phil Williams. Published 2-3 times/year. Circ. 500-700. Publishes 5-8 stories (and articles)/issue. "We are a small press fantasy magazine. Our definition of fantasy knows no bounds, covering science, heroic, dark and light fantasy and horror fiction. We also use occasional poetry." Length: 8,000-10,000 words maximum. Pays contributor's copies. Send ms with brief cover letter and IRCs for return of ms or acknowledgement. Sample copy, "if stock remains," for large SAE and 5 IRCs.

‡EDDIE (the magazine), P.O. Box 199, Newtown, New South Wales 2042 Australia. Fiction Editor: Eddie Greenaway. Published 3 times/year. Circ. 5,000. Publishes 10-12 stories/issue. "*Eddie* is a theme-based magazine dealing with a range of contemporary concerns primarily focused on Australian content but with selected overseas pieces." Length: 300 words minimum; 2,000 maximum. Pays in copies. "Find out the theme in advance as we only publish three times per year and the material would sit in our files even if excellent. Don't be scared, be a little witty. It can be a fun way of making contacts. Ideas do not always translate seamlessly from one culture to another, but give it a go." Sample copy available for $6 (US). Money order or check should be made out to Eddie Magazine Publishing.

FORESIGHT, (IV), 44 Brockhurst Rd., Hodge Hill, Birmingham B36 8JB England. Editor: John Barklam. Fiction Editor: Judy Barklam. Quarterly. Magazine including "new age material, world peace, psychic phenomena, research, occultism, spiritualism, mysticism, UFOs, philosophy, etc. Shorter articles required on a specific theme related to the subject matter of *Foresight* magazine." Length: 300-1,000 words. Pays in contributor's copies. Send SAE with IRC for return of ms. Sample copy for 30p and 50p postage.

‡GLOBAL TAPESTRY JOURNAL, (II), BB Books, 1 Spring Bank, Longsight Rd., Copster Green, Blackburn, Lancashire BB1 9EU England. Editor: Dave Cunliffe. "Post-underground with avant-garde, experimental, alternative, counterculture, psychedelic, mystical, anarchist etc. fiction for a bohemian and counterculture audience." Recently published fiction by Arthur Moyse, Tina Morris and Jay Lee Findlay. Published work by new writers within the last year. Sample copy for $4 (Sterling Cheque, British Money Order or dollar currency).

HECATE, Box 99, St. Lucia Q4067 Australia. Fiction Editor: Carole Ferrier. Circ. 2,000. Publishes 6-14 stories annually. "Socialist feminist with a strong interest in issues of race and ethnicity. We like political stories (broadly defined)." Length: 10 words minimum; 1,000 words maximum. Writers receive $60 (Australian) and 5 copies. "We only rarely publish non-Australian writers of fiction." Sample copy available for a $10 note.

JEWISH QUARTERLY, P.O. Box 2078, London W1A1JR England. Editor: Elena Lappin. Quarterly. Publishes 1 contribution of fiction/issue. "It deals in the broadest sense with all issues of Jewish interest." Length: 1,500 words minimum; 7,000 words maximum. Payment for accepted items £50. Work should have either a Jewish theme in the widest interpretation of that phrase or a theme which would interest our readership. The question which contributors should ask is 'Why should it appear in the *Jewish Quarterly* and not in another periodical?' "

KRAX MAGAZINE, 63 Dixon Lane, Leeds LS12 4RR, Yorkshire, Britain, U.K. Fiction Editor: Andy Robson. Appears 9 times/year. Publishes 1 story/issue. "We publish mostly poetry of a light-hearted nature, but use comic or spoof fiction, witty and humorous essays." Length: 2,000 words maximum. Pays contributor's copies. "Don't spend too long on scene-setting or character construction as this inevitably produces an anti-climax in a short piece. Send IRCs or currency notes for return postal costs." Sample copy for $1 direct from editor. No specific guidelines.

‡MAELSTROM, 24 Fowler Close, Southchurch, Southend-On-Sea, Essex SS1 2RD United Kingdom. Fiction Editor: Malcolm E. Wright. Semiannual. Circ. 400. Publishes 10 stories/issue. "*Maelstrom* publishes all types of genre fiction, but chiefly science fiction, fantasy, horror and mystery stories." Length: 1,000 words minimum; 10,000 words maximum. Pays in copies. "Suggest one story at a time. Please ask for submission guidelines. Send a disposable manuscript with a small SAE for reply." Sample copy available for $5 (cash, no foreign checks). Writer's guidelines available for small SAE.

‡NIGHT DREAMS, 47 Stephens Rd., Walmley, Sutton Coldfield, West Midlands B76 2TS England. Fiction Editor: Kirk S. King. Quarterly. Circ. 300. Publishes 10-15 stories/issue. "The majority of stories and poems have a '50s pulp style with a '90s viewpoint. Not hot on ghost stories, but the weird and lurid and plain unexplained with twists in the end go down well." Length: 100 words minimum; 3,000 words maximum. Pays "residents of England only" for published fiction and all others receive contributor's copies. "Send one mss at a time with a decent plot which is not bled to death with verbosity. It is important to send the right story to the right magazine. Don't waste your time or the editors. Know your market." Sample copy $6; 4 issues $24.

PREMONITIONS, Pigasus Press, 13 Hazely Combe, Arreton, Isle of Wight PO30 3AJ England. Fiction Editor: Tony Lee. Annually. Publishes 12 stories/issue. "Digest-sized magazine-anthology of science fictional horror stories and genre poetry." (Also publishes *The Zone* listed in this section.) Length: 1,000 words minimum; 5,000 words maximum. Pays contributor's copies. "Send SAE/IRC for free contributor's guidelines. Study recent issues of the magazine. Unsolicited submissions are always welcome but writers must enclose SAE/IRC for reply, plus adequate postage to return 'ms' if unsuitable." Sample copies available for $7 (cash, US Dollars) or 7 IRCs. For UK and EC countries: £2.50 cheques/eurocheques, International Money Order, etc. should be made payable to: Tony Lee.

STUDIO: A JOURNAL OF CHRISTIANS WRITING, (II), 727 Peel St., Albury 2640 Australia. Managing Editor: Paul Grover. Circ. 300. Quarterly. Averages 20-30 stories/year. "*Studio* publishes prose and poetry of literary merit, offers a venue for new and aspiring writers, and seeks to create a sense of community among Christians writing." Length: 500-5,000 words. Pays in copies. Sample copy available for $8 (Australian). Subscription $40 (Australian) for 4 issues (1 year). International draft in Australian dollars and IRC required.

‡TOGETHER WITH CHILDREN, Christian Resources and Inspiration for Leaders, The National Society, Church House, Great Smith St., London SW1P 3NZ England. Editor: Mrs. P. Macnaughton. Magazine of forward-looking Christian education for children. Short stories, plays, services, projects, etc. Also songs, carols, occasional poems. Readers are church children's group leaders, primary school and Sunday school teachers, clergy.

WORKS, 12 Blakestones Rd., Slaithwaite, Huddersfield HD7 5UQ England. Fiction Editor: D. W. Hughes. Circ. 2,000. 70% of content is fiction. "A4, 40 pages speculative and imaginative fiction (science fiction) with poetry, illustrated." Quarterly. Price: £5 *cash only or cheque in sterling* for 1 issue, £10 *cash or cheque in sterling* for 2 issues; £20 *cash* or check in pounds sterling for 4 issues; enclose IRC. Member of the New Science Fiction Alliance. Pays in copies. "All manuscripts should be accompanied by a SASE (in the UK). USA send 2 IRC's with ms, if disposable or 4 IRCs, if not. Usual maximum is 4,500-5,000 words."

THE ZONE, Pigasus Press, 13 Hazely Combe, Arreton, Isle of Wight, PO30 3AJ England. Fiction Editor: Tony Lee. Published 5 times a year. Publishes 6 stories/issue. "*The Zone*: A4-size magazine of quality science fiction plus articles and reviews." (Also publishes *Premonitions* listed in this section.) Length: 1,000 words minimum; 5,000 words maximum. Pays in copies. "Token payment for stories and articles of 2,000 words and over. Send SAE/IRC for free contributor's guidelines. Study recent issues of the magazine. Unsolicited submissions are always welcome but writers must enclose SAE/IRC for reply, plus adequate postage to return ms if unsuitable." Sample copies available for $9 (cash, US dollars) or 9 IRCs; for UK, £2.75; EC countries, £3 (cheques/eurocheques, International Money Order, etc. should be made payable to: Tony Lee).

Zines

This market section, appearing for the first time in *Novel & Short Story Writer's Market*, features zines. In the Insider Report with Seth Friedman, publisher of *Factsheet Five*, Friedman defines a zine as "a small, handmade amateur publication done purely out of passion, rarely making a profit or breaking even." Likewise, in the introduction to *The World of Zines: a Guide to the Independent Magazine Revolution*, Mike Gunderloy and Cari Goldberg Janice define zines as "small publications which are produced primarily for love rather than money."

SELF-EXPRESSION AND ARTISTIC FREEDOM

Vastly different from one another in appearance and content, the common source of zines seems to be a need for self-expression. In the Insider Report with Ariel Gore, editor of *hip Mama*, Gore says that starting her zine in 1993 "was a chance to talk about all the stuff I was dealing with" as a college student, teen mom and welfare mom. Although this need to voice opinions has always been around, it was not until the 70s, and possibly beginning with the social upheaval of the 60s, that the availability of photocopiers and computers provided an easy, cheap way to produce the self-published and usually self-written "zines." It follows, then, that many zines, called "e-zines," are now springing up in an electronic format.

Although the editorial content of zines runs the gamut from traditional and genre fiction to personal rants to highly experimental work, artistic freedom is a characteristic of all zines. *Black Dog*, established in 1995 and new to *Novel & Short Story Writer's Market*, is defined by founder Lisa Hake as "a magazine for the culturally deprived, a source of information and ideas, of expression with an edge." Bryan Westbrook, "curator" of *Graffiti off the Asylum Walls, An Illiterary Journal*, says his zine contains "the stuff you would be afraid to show your mother, priest and/or psychiatrist." *Art:Mag*'s editor, Peter Magliocco, looks for "irreverent, literary-minded work by committed writers. . . ." And Soror Chen, editor of *Bahlasti Papers*, wants "occult, mythological, artistic, alternative and political material for the lunatic fringe."

Although some of the zines listed here have been published since the early 80s, many are relatively new and some were just starting publication as they filled out the questionnaire to be included in this edition of *Novel & Short Story Writer's Market*. Unfortunately, due to the waning energy and shrinking funds of their publishers (and often a lack of material), few last for more than several issues. Fortunately, though, some have been around since the late 70s and early 80s, and hundreds of new ones are launched every day.

While zines represent the most volatile group of publications in *Novel & Short Story Writer's Market*, they are also the most open to submissions by beginning writers. As mentioned above, the editors of zines are often writers themselves and welcome the opportunity to give others a chance at publication.

SELECTING THE RIGHT ZINE FOR YOUR WORK

Your chance for publication begins as you zero in on the zines most likely to be interested in your work. Begin by browsing through the listings. This is especially important since zines are the most diverse and specialized markets listed in this book.

Then check the Category Index (starting on page 597) for the appropriate subject heading, such as experimental, fantasy or mystery.

In addition to browsing through the listings and using the Category Index, check the ranking codes at the beginning of listings to find those most likely to be receptive to your work. Most all zines are open to new writers (I) or to both new and established writers (II). For more explanation about these codes, see the end of this introduction.

Once you have a list of zines you might like to try, read their listings carefully. Zines vary greatly in appearance as well as content. Some are photocopies published whenever the editor has material and money, while others feature offset printing and regular distribution schedules. And a few have evolved into four-color, commercial looking, very slick publications. The physical description appearing near the beginning of the listings gives you clues about the size and financial commitment to the publication. This is not always an indication of quality, but chances are a publication with expensive paper and four-color artwork on the cover has more prestige than a photocopied publication featuring a clip art self-cover. If you're a new writer or your work is considered avant garde, however, you may be more interested in the photocopied zine. For more information on some of the paper, binding and printing terms used in these descriptions, see Printing and Production Terms Defined on page 591. Also, How to Use This Book to Publish Your Fiction, starting on page 3, describes in detail the listing information common to all markets in our book.

FURTHERING YOUR SEARCH

It cannot be stressed enough that reading the listings is only the first part of developing your marketing plan. The second part, equally important, is to obtain fiction guidelines and a copy of the actual zine. Reading copies of the publication helps you determine the fine points of the zines' publishing style and philosophy. Especially since zines tend to be highly specialized, there is no substitute for this hands-on, eyes-on research.

Unlike commercial periodicals available at most newsstands and bookstores, it requires a little more effort to obtain most of the zines listed here. You will probably need to send for a sample copy. We include sample copy prices in the listings whenever possible.

For a comprehensive listing of zines in a number of categories and reviews of each, check out Seth Friedman's *Factsheet Five* (P.O. Box 170099, San Francisco CA 94117-0099) published twice every year. *Scavenger's Newsletter* (519 Ellinwood, Osage City KS 66523) also lists markets for science fiction, fantasy, horror and mystery. More zines and information on starting your own zine can be found in *The World of Zines: A Guide to the Independent Magazine Revolution*, by Mike Gunderloy and Cari Goldberg Janice (Penguin Books, 375 Hudson St., New York NY 10014).

The following is the ranking system we have used to categorize the listings in this section:

I **Publication encourages beginning or unpublished writers to submit work for consideration and publishes new writers regularly.**

II **Publication accepts outstanding work by beginning and established writers.**

III **Hard to break into; publishes mostly previously published writers.**

IV **Special-interest or regional publication, open only to writers in certain genres or on certain subjects or from certain geographical areas.**

ABSOLUTE MAGNITUDE, Science Fiction Adventures, (I, II, IV), DNA Publications, P.O. Box 13, Greenfield MA 01302. (413)772-0725. Editor: Warren Lapine. Zine: 8½×11; 96 pages; newsprint; color cover; illustrations. "We publish technical science fiction that is adventurous and character driven." Quarterly. Estab. 1993. Circ. 9,000.

Needs: Science fiction: adventure, hard science. No fantasy, horror, funny science fiction. Receives 300-500 unsolicited mss/month. Accepts 7-10 mss/issue; 28-40 mss/year. Publishes ms 3-6 months after acceptance. Agented fiction 5%. Recently published work by Hal Clement, Chris Bunch, C.J. Cherryh, Barry B. Longyear and Harlan Ellison. Length: 5,000-12,000 words average; 1,000 words minimum; 25,000 words maximum. Publishes very little poetry. Often critiques or comments on rejected ms.

How to Contact: Do NOT query. Send complete ms with a cover letter. Should include estimated word count and list of publications. Send SASE for reply, return of ms or send a disposable copy of ms. Simultaneous and reprint submissions OK. Sample copy for $5. Reviews novels and short story collections.

Payment/Terms: Pays 3-5¢/word on publication for first North American serial rights; 1¢/word for first reprint rights. Sometimes sends galleys to author.

Advice: "We want good writing with solid characterization, also character growth, story development, and plot resolution. We would like to see more character-driven stories."

ABYSS MAGAZINE, "Games and the Imagination," (II, IV), Ragnarok Enterprises, P.O. Box 140333, Austin TX 78714-0333. (512)472-6535. Fax: (512)472-6220. E-mail: ragnarok@aol.com. Website: http://www.ccsi.com/~garball/abyss. Editor: David F. Nalle. Fiction Editor: Patricia Fitch. Zine: 8×10; 48 pages; bond paper; glossy cover; illustrations; photos. "Heroic fantasy fiction: some fantasy, horror, SF and adventure fiction, for college-age game players." Quarterly. Plans special fiction issue. Estab. 1979. Circ. 1,500.

● *Abyss Magazine* can be contacted through Internet online service as well as their own electronic bulletin board.

Needs: Adventure, fantasy, horror, psychic/supernatural/occult, cyberpunk, science fiction, heroic fantasy, sword and sorcery. "Game-based stories are not specifically desired." Upcoming themes: "Horror Issue" (spring); "Review Issue" (summer). Receives 20-30 unsolicited mss/month. Buys 1 ms/issue; 7 mss/year. Publishes ms 1-12 months after acceptance. Published work by Antoine Sadel, Kevin Anderson, Alan Blount; published new writers within the last year. Length: 2,000 words average; 1,000 words minimum; 4,000 words maximum. Publishes short shorts occasionally. Also publishes literary essays and literary criticism. Sometimes critiques rejected mss or recommends other markets.

How to Contact: Send for sample copy first. Reports in 6 weeks on queries; 3 months on mss. "Do send a cover letter, preferably entertaining. Include some biographical info and a precis of lengthy stories." SASE. Simultaneous submissions OK. Prefers electronic submissions by modem or network. Sample copy and fiction guidelines $5. Reviews novels and short story collections (especially fantasy novels).

Payment/Terms: Pays 1-3¢/word or by arrangement, plus contributor's copies. Pays on publication for first North American serial rights.

Advice: "We are particularly interested in new writers with mature and original style. Don't send us fiction which everyone else has sent back to you unless you think it has qualities which make it too strange for everyone else but which don't ruin the significance of the story. Make sure what you submit is appropriate to the magazine you send it to. More than half of what we get is completely inappropriate. We plan to include more and longer stories."

ART:MAG, (II), P.O. Box 70896, Las Vegas NV 89170. Editor: Peter Magliocco. Zine: 5½×8½, some 8½×11; 70-90 pages; 20 lb. bond paper; b&w pen and ink illustrations and photographs. Publishes "irreverent, literary-minded work by committed writers," for "small press, 'quasi-art-oriented' " audience. Annually. Estab. 1984. Circ. under 500.

Needs: Condensed/excerpted novel, confession, contemporary, erotica, ethnic, experimental, fantasy, feminist, gay, historical (general), horror, humor/satire, lesbian, literary, mainstream, mystery/suspense, prose poem, psychic/supernatural/occult, regional, science fiction, translations and arts. No "slick-oriented stuff published by major magazines." Receives 1 plus ms/month. Accepts 1-2 mss/year. Does not read mss July-October. Publishes ms within 3-6 months of acceptance. Recently published work by James Vance Elliott, Olaf Pollmann (Elgin Barrett), Stephen D. Guiterrez, Lidia Yuknavitch, Frank Holland, Catherine Scherer featured in special fiction issue, 1996-1997. Length: 2,000 words preferred; 250 words minimum; 3,000 words maximum. Also publishes literary essays "if relevant to aesthetic preferences," literary criticism "occasionally," poetry. Sometimes critiques rejected mss.

How to Contact: Send complete ms with cover letter. Reports in 3 months. SASE for ms. Simultaneous submissions OK. Sample copy for $5, 6×9 SAE and 79¢ postage. Fiction guidelines for #10 SASE.

Payment/Terms: Pays contributor's copies. Acquires one-time rights.
Advice: "Seeking more novel and quality-oriented work, usually from solicited authors. Magazine fiction today needs to be concerned with the issues of fiction writing itself—not just with a desire to publish or please the largest audience. Think about things in the fine art world as well as the literary one and keep the hard core of life in between."

ATROCITY, Publication of the Absurd Sig of Mensa, (II), 2419 Greensburg Pike, Pittsburgh PA 15221. Editor: Hank Roll. Zine: 5½×8½; 30 pages; offset 20 lb. paper and cover; illustrations. Humor and satire for "high IQ-Mensa" members. Monthly. Estab. 1976. Circ. 250.
Needs: Humor/satire: Liar's Club, parody, jokes, funny stories, comments on the absurdity of today's world. Receives 30 unsolicited mss/month. Accepts 2 mss/issue. Publishes ms 6-12 months after acceptance. Recently published work by John Smethers, Sheryll Watt, Dolph Wave and Ellen Warts. Published new writers within the last year. Length: 50-150 words preferred; 650 words maximum.
How to Contact: Send complete ms. "No cover letter necessary if ms states what rights (e.g. first North American serial/reprint, etc.) are offered." Reports in 1 month. SASE. Simultaneous and reprint submissions OK. Sample copy for $1.
Payment/Terms: Pays contributor's copies. Acquires one-time rights.
Advice: Do not submit mss exceeding 650 words. Manuscript should be single-spaced and copy ready in a horizontal format to fit on one 5½×8½ sheet. "If you don't read the specs, you get it back. Don't waste our time."

BABYSUE, (II), P.O. Box 8989, Atlanta GA 30306-8989. (404)875-8951. E-mail: babysue@mindspring.com. Website: http://www.babysue.com. Editor: Don W. Seven. Zine: 8½×11; 32 pages; illustrations and photos. "*babysue* is a collection of music reviews, poetry, short fiction and cartoons for anyone who can think and is not easily offended." Biannually. Plans special fiction issue. Estab. 1983. Circ. 2,500.
  ● Sometimes funny, very often perverse, this 'zine featuring mostly cartoons and "comix" definitely is not for the easily offended.
Needs: Erotica, experimental and humor/satire. Receives 5-10 mss/month. Accepts 3-4 mss/year. Publishes ms within 3 months of acceptance. Recently published work by Bill Tomey, Randy Wilson, Tammy Phayron and David Willis. Publishes short shorts. Length: 1-2 single-spaced pages.
How to Contact: Query with clips of published work. SASE. Simultaneous submissions OK. No submissions via e-mail.
Payment/Terms: Pays 1 contributor's copy.
Advice: "Create out of the love of creating, not to see your work in print! Trends do not affect us here in babysueland."

BACKSPACE, A Collection of Queer Poetry & Fiction (I, II), Lock the Target Media, 33 Maplewood Ave., Suite 201, Gloucester MA 01930-6201. (508)283-3813. E-mail: charkim@tiac.net-oraol:backsp. Website: http://www.tiac.net/users/charkim. Editor: Kimberley Smith. Fiction Editor: Charlotte Stratton. Zine: 5½×8½; 48 pages; copy paper; glossy cover; illustrations and photos. "*Backspace* is a literary zine for the gay, lesbian, bisexual and transgender community." Triannually. Estab. 1991. Circ. 400-600.
Needs: Experimental, gay, humor/satire, lesbian, literary. "No sexually explicit or violent material." Plans to publish special fiction issues or anthologies. Receives 8-10 unsolicited mss/month. Accepts 4-8 mss/issue; 16-20 mss/year. Publishes ms 6 months after acceptance. Agented fiction 85%. Recently published work by B.Z. Niditch, Beth Brant, Monika Arnett, Robert Klein Engler and Leah Erickson. Length: 3,000 words average; 1,500-2,000 words minimum; 3,000 words maximum. Also publishes literary essays, poetry.
How to Contact: Send complete ms with a cover letter. Include estimated word count, 30-word bio, list of publications. Reports in 2 weeks on queries; 3-6 weeks on mss. Send SASE for reply, return of ms or send a disposable copy of ms. Simultaneous, reprint, electronic submissions (3.5 diskette, Word, QuarkXPress, Pagemaker, ASCII; or e-mail) OK. Sample copy for $1, 6×9 SAE, 2 first-class stamps. Fiction guidelines for #10 SASE. Reviews novels and short story collections. Send books to Charlotte Stratton.
Payment/Terms: Pays 1 contributor's copy; additional copies $4. Acquires one-time rights. Not copyrighted.
Advice: "Fully formed characters are important; topical allusions are distracting."

BAHLASTI PAPERS, The Newsletter of the Kali Lodge, O.T.O., (I), P.O. Box 3096, New Orleans LA 70177-3096. (504)949-2037. Editor: Soror Chén. Zine: 8½×11; 12 pages; 20 lb. paper; 20 lb. cover; 2 illustrations; occasional photographs. "Occult, mythological, artistic, alternative and political material for the lunatic fringe." Monthly. Estab. 1986. Circ. 200.
Needs: Condensed/excerpted novel, erotica, ethnic, experimental, fantasy, feminist, gay, horror, humor/satire, lesbian, literary, psychic/supernatural/occult, science fiction, serialized novel, "however

our emphasis is on the occult. We do not publish poetry." Plans special compilation issues. Receives 10 unsolicited mss/month. Accepts 2 mss/issue; 24 mss/year. Publishes mss approximately 12-18 months after acceptance. Recently published work by Darius James, Nemo, Hugo L'Estrange, Nancy Collins. Publishes short shorts. Also publishes literary essays, literary criticism.

How to Contact: Send complete ms with cover letter telling "why author is interested in being published in *Bahlasti Papers*." Reports in 1 month on queries and mss. SASE. Simultaneous, reprint and electronic (disk-Microsoft Publisher program) submissions OK. Sample copy for $2.25 with 6×9 SAE and 2 first-class stamps. Occasionally reviews novels and short story collections.

Payment/Terms: Pays subscription to magazine. Publication not copyrighted.

Advice: "We do not wish to read hackneyed, Hollywood treatments of voodoo or the occult. Our readers are interested in the odd point-of-view that creates new, empowering, and healing archetypes for the lunatic fringe. Our writers are willing to make an initial descent into shadow regions in order to sing for the gods. And please watch your grammar!"

‡**BLACK DOG, (I, II)**, 224 Adelaide Place, Munster IN 46321. (219)836-5738. E-mail: blackdogm@aol.com. Editor: Lisa Hake. Zine: 8½×10½; 48 pages; newsprint; illustrations; and photographs. "We are a magazine for the culturally deprived, a source of information and ideas, of expression with an edge." Estab. 1995. Circ. 3,000.

Needs: Adventure, erotica, ethnic/multicultural, experimental, fantasy (science, sword and sorcery), feminist, gay, historical, horror, humor/satire, lesbian, literary, mainstream/contemporary, mystery/suspense (amateur sleuth, cozy, police procedural, private eye/hardboiled, romantic suspense), psychic/supernatural/occult, regional, science fiction (hard science, soft/sociological), senior citizen/retirement, sports. Upcoming themes: Halloween (horror, supernatural, etc.). Receives 50 unsolicited mss/month. Accepts 2-3 mss/issue; 12-21 mss/year. Publishes ms 2-3 months after acceptance. Recently published work by Ben Ohmart. Publishes short shorts. Also publishes literary essays and poetry. Often critiques or comments on rejected mss.

How to Contact: Send complete ms with a cover letter. Include estimated word count, short bio and Social Security number with submission. Reports in 1 month on queries; 2 months on mss. Send SASE for reply, return of ms or send a disposable copy of ms. Simultaneous, reprint, electronic submissions OK. Sample copy for $3. Fiction guidelines for #10 SASE. Reviews novels and short story collections.

Payment/Terms: Pays ½¢/word, sometimes more, and 2 contributor's copies. Pays on publication. Acquires first North American serial rights.

Advice: Looks for "something that moves, that engages a reader and has strong characters and plot. Read our guidelines before submitting. We would like to see more supernatural horror stories—no gore though."

BLACK SHEETS, (II), % Black Books, P.O. Box 31155-NS2, San Francisco CA 94131-0155. (415)431-0171. Fax: (415)431-0172. E-mail: blackb@ios.com. Editor: Bill Brent. Zine: 8½×11; 52 pages; illustrations and photos. "We are a humorous zine of sex and popular culture for a polysexual audience. Our motto is 'kinky/queer/intelligent/irreverent.' We are bisexual owned and operated." Triannually. Estab. 1993.

● Fiction published in *Black Sheets* was included in 1995 and 1996 volumes of *Best American Erotica 1995* (Simon & Schuster).

Needs: Bi/polysexual, popular culture-based: erotica, ethnic/multicultural, experimental, feminist, gay, humor/satire, lesbian, psychic/supernatural/occult. List of upcoming themes available for SASE. Receives 20 mss/month. Accepts 2-4 mss/issue; 6-12 mss/year. Publishes ms 3 months to 1 year after acceptance. Recently published work by Paul Reed, Thomas Roche, M. Christian, Carol Queen and Lawrence Livermore. Length: 1,000 words average; 3,000 words maximum (longer can be serialized). Publishes short shorts. Also publishes essays, literary criticism and poetry. Occasionally critiques or comments on rejected mss.

How to Contact: "You must purchase at least 1 copy of *Black Sheets* before sending us your work." Send complete ms with a cover letter. Include estimated word count and a brief bio. Reports in 1 month on queries; 2-3 months on mss. Send a disposable copy of ms. Simultaneous, reprint and electronic (IBM or MAC diskette OK) submissions OK. Sample copy for $6 with age statement. Fiction guidelines free. Requests for guidelines may be made via e-mail, but submissions are *not* accepted through e-mail. Reviews novels and short story collections.

---

‡ **THE DOUBLE DAGGER** before a listing indicates that the listing is new in this edition. New markets are often the most receptive to submissions by new writers.

Payment/Terms: Pays $10-50 and 1 contributor's copy on publication for one-time rights; additional copies for $3.
Advice: "Read our magazine. *Black Sheets* has a very specific attitude and a growing stable of regular writers. If your piece matches our style and you have read at least one issue (We know who you are!), then we can talk. We love e-mail for that, but *not* for submissions."

‡**BLOODREAMS MAGAZINE, (II, IV)**, 1312 W. 43rd St., North Little Rock AR 72118. Editor-in-Chief: Kelly Gunter Atlas. Managing Editor: Jeffrey A. Stadt. Zine: Digest sized; 40-60 pages; 20 lb. paper; card stock cover; b&w drawings. "*Bloodreams* is dedicated to the preservation, continuance, and enhancement of the vampire and the werewolf legends, as well as other supernatural legends, for adult fans of the genre." Annually. Estab. 1991. Circ. 75-100.
Needs: Vampires, werewolves, supernatural horror. "We do not want to see excessive gore or pornography." Receives 20-25 unsolicited mss/month. Accepts 12-20 mss/issue. Does not read mss October through January. Publishes ms in May and October only. Recently published work by Steve Eller, Dale Patricia Hochstein and Jeffrey A. Stadt. Length: 1,500 words average; 250 words minimum; 3,500 words maximum. Publishes short shorts. Length: 250-500 words. Also publishes poetry. Sometimes critiques rejected mss and recommends other markets.
How to Contact: Send complete ms with cover letter. Include a brief introduction and past credits if any. Reports in 1-4 weeks on queries; 6-12 weeks on mss. SASE. Simultaneous submissions OK. Sample copy for $4.50 (payable to Kelly Atlas). Fiction guidelines for #10 SASE.
Payment/Terms: Pays in contributor's copies. Charges for extras.
Terms: Acquires one-time rights.
Advice: "We look for well-written, concise short stories which are complete within themselves. We like writers who have their own sense of style and imagination who write with their own 'voice' and do not try to copy others' work. We are open to a variety of interpretations of supernatural legends. For example, we like anything ranging from Stephen King to Anne Rice to Robert R. McCammon to Brian Lumley."

‡**THE BLUE LADY, A Magazine Of Dark Fiction, (I, II)**, Blue Lady Publications, 630 Bell Rd., #292, Antioch TN 37013. (615)731-6336. Editor Donna T. Burgess. Zine: digest size; 60-80 pages; illustrations. Publishes "dark fiction of all genres. Explicit material okay, if tasteful. Enjoys the surreal and bizarre—think Clive Barker, Poppy Brite, Stephen King, Anne Rice and Joe Lansdale." Estab. 1995. Circ. varies.
Needs: Experimental, fantasy (science fiction, fantasy), horror, psychic/supernatural/occult, science fiction (cyberpunk). "We do not want to see fiction that is not dark in tone or 'quiet' horror." Publishes special fiction issue or anthology. Receives 35 unsolicited mss/month. Accepts 10-12 mss/issue; 60 mss/year. Publishes ms 3-12 months after acceptance. Recently published work by James S. Dorr, Charlee Jacob, John Grey, D.F. Lewis, Deidra Cox and Scott Urban. Length: 3,000 words average; 8,000 words maximum. Publishes short shorts. Also publishes poetry.
How to Contact: Send complete ms with a cover letter. Include estimated word count and list of publications. Reports in 2 weeks on queries; 3 months on mss. Send SASE for reply, return of ms or send a disposable copy of ms. Simultaneous submissions and reprints OK. Sample copy for $5. Fiction guidelines for SASE. Reviews other zines.
Payment/Terms: Pays 1 contributor's copy on publication; additional copies for $4. Acquires one-time rights.
Advice: Looks for "good use of language and interesting characters and settings. Try experimenting with different time periods. Try me—especially if your idea is universal. I might like it. Unlike many horror publications around lately, I do want to see strong material. Don't follow trends."

‡**BOTH SIDES NOW, Journal of Spiritual Alternatives, (I, II, IV)**, Free People Press, 10547 State Highway 110 N., Tyler TX 75704-3731. (903)592-4263. Editor: Elihu Edelson. Zine: 8½×11; 10 pages; bond paper and cover; b&w line illustrations. "*Both Sides Now* explores the Aquarian frontier as the world witnesses the end of an old order and enters a New Age. Its contents include opinion, commentary, philosophy and creative writing for all who are interested in New Age matters." Published irregularly. Estab. 1969. Circ. 200.
Needs: Material with New Age slant, including fables, fantasy, humor/satire, myths, parables, psychic/supernatural, religious/inspirational, romance (futuristic/time travel), science fiction (utopian). Length: "about 2 magazine pages, more or less." Also publishes literary essays, book reviews and poetry. Often comments on rejected mss with "brief note."
How to Contact: Send complete ms with SASE. Include brief bio and list of publications. Simultaneous submissions and previously published work OK. Reports in 3 months on mss. Send SASE for reply, return of ms or send a disposable copy of ms. Sample copy for $1. Reviews "New Age fiction."
Payment/Terms: Pays 5 contributor's copies. "Authors retain rights."
Advice: Looks for "tight, lucid writing that leaves the reader with a feeling of delight and/or enlightenment. Heed our editorial interests."

A COMPANION IN ZEOR, (I, II, IV), 307 Ashland Ave., Egg Harbor Township NJ 08234. E-mail: karenlit@juno.com. Editor: Karen Litman. Fanzine: 8½×11; 60 pages; "letter" paper; heavy blue cover; b&w line illustrations; occasional b&w photographs. Publishes science fiction based on the various Universe creations of Jacqueline Lichtenberg. Occasional features on Star Trek, and other interests, convention reports, reviews of movies and books, recordings, etc. Published irregularly. Estab. 1978. Circ. 300.

• *Companion in Zeor* is one of two fanzines devoted to the work and characters of Jacqueline Lichtenberg. Lichtenberg's work includes several future world, alien and group culture novels and series including the Sime/Gen Series and The Dushau trilogy. She's also penned two books on her own vampire character and she co-authored *Star Trek Lives*.

Needs: Fantasy, humor/satire, prose poem, science fiction. "No vicious satire. Nothing X-rated. Homosexuality prohibited unless *essential* in story. We run a clean publication that anyone should be able to read without fear." Occasionally receives one manuscript a month. Accepts "as much as can afford to print." Publication of an accepted ms "can take years, due to limit of finances available for publication." Occasionally critiques rejected mss and recommends other markets.

How to Contact: Query first or send complete ms with cover letter. "Prefer cover letters about any writing experience prior, or related interests toward writing aims." Reports in 1 month. SASE. Simultaneous submissions OK. Sample copy price depends on individual circumstances. Fiction guidelines for #10 SASE. "I write individual letters to all queries. No form letter at present." SASE for guidelines required. Reviews science fiction/fantasy collections or titles.

Payment/Terms: Pays in contributor's copies. Acquires first rights.

Advice: "We take fiction based on any and all of Jacqueline Lichtenberg's published novels. The contributor should be familiar with these works before contributing material to my fanzine. May be going online in near future. Also accepts manuscripts on cassette from visually handicapped if submitted. 'Zines also on tape for those individuals."

COSMIC LANDSCAPES, An Alternative Science Fiction Magazine, (I, IV), % Dan Petitpas, D & S Associates, 19 Carroll Ave., Westwood MA 02090. (617)329-1344. E-mail: dsassoc@neponset.com. Website: http://www.neponset.com. Editor: Dan Petitpas. Zine: 7×8½; 32-56 pages; white bond paper and cover stock; illustrations; photos occasionally. "A magazine which publishes science fiction for science-fiction readers; also articles and news of interest to writers and science fiction fans. Occasionally prints works of horror and fantasy." Annually. Estab. 1983. Circ. 150.

• Submissions will automatically be considered for *Cosmic Landscapes Online*, which accepts "science fiction (all kinds), fantasy and horror stories, as well as articles and discussion about science fiction, fantasy and horror stories, writers, etc. The Web is now our primary concern."

Needs: Science fiction (hard science, soft/sociological). "We would like to see more hard science fiction." Receives 15-20 unsolicited mss/month. Accepts 8 mss/issue. Recently published work by Alex Raikhel, Fran Polito, DeAnne Timmons and Janet Glatz. Published new writers in the last year. Length: 2,500 words average; 25 words minimum. Will consider all lengths. "Every manuscript receives a personal evaluation by the editor." Sometimes recommends other markets.

How to Contact: Send complete ms with bio. Reports usually in 1 month. SASE. Simultaneous and electronic submissions OK. Sample copy for $3.50. Fiction guidelines for SASE.

Payment/Terms: Pays 2 contributor's copies; $2 for extras. Acquires one-time rights.

Advice: "We're interested in all kinds of science fiction stories. We particularly like stories with ideas we've not seen before. Don't be influenced by TV or movie plots. Be original. Take an imaginative idea and craft a story from it. Be wild. Ask yourself 'what if?' and then follow through with the idea. Tell the story through the actions of a character or characters to give the readers someone to identify with. Be careful of creating scientific theories if you don't know much science. Let your imagination go!"

CROSSROADS . . . Where Evil Dwells, (I, II), 478 Waters Rd., Jacksonville NC 28546-9756. (910)455-7047. Editor: Pat Nielsen. Zine: digest-sized; approximately 68 pages; 20 lb. paper; 64 lb. index cover. "All stories must be about people at a *Crossroad* in their lives, or set at the crossroads themselves—or both. I strongly encourage writers to do research about the crossroad legends. This is an *adult* horror magazine." Triannually. (Published February, June and October.) Estab. 1992. Circ. 100.

• Work appearing in *Crossroads* received three Honorable Mentions in *The Year's Best Horror and Fantasy*.

Needs: Horror, psychic/supernatural/occult for adults. "No futuristic or fiction set in the past. Every October issue is the Halloween issue—all material must have a Halloween theme," deadline: October 15, 1997. Receives 20 unsolicited mss/month. Accepts 10-15 mss/issue; 30 mss/year. Publishes ms 1-6 months after acceptance. Recently published work by Sue Storm, Chad Hensley, Charlee Jacob, Wayne Edwards, David Shtogryn and Mark Leslie. Length: 1,500 words average; 500 words minimum; 3,500 words maximum. Also publishes literary criticism and poetry. Often critiques or comments on rejected mss.

How to Contact: Send complete ms with a cover letter. Include estimated word count. Reports in 2 weeks on queries; 2-4 weeks on mss. Send SASE for reply, return of ms or send a disposable copy of ms. "I don't like IRCs—please use US stamps whenever possible." No simultaneous submissions. Reprints OK. Sample copy for $4.50. Fiction guidelines for #10 SASE.

Payment/Terms: Pays 1 contributor's copy; additional copies for $3.50 plus postage for multiple copies. Acquires first North American serial rights. Sends galleys to author (time permitting).

Advice: "I publish many kinds of horror, from the mild to the hard core horror. Don't copy well-known or any other writers. Find your own voice and style and go with it to the best of your ability. I don't go by any trends. I know what I like and I publish as I see fit. Do not send science fiction or fantasy in any form."

‡**CURRICULUM VITAE, (I)**, Simpson Publications, Grove City Factory Stores, P.O. Box 1309, Grove City PA 16127. (814)671-1361. E-mail: proof114@aol.com. Editor: Michael Dittman. Zine: digest-sized; 75-100 pages; standard paper; card cover stock; illustrations. "We are dedicated to new, exciting writers. We like essays, travelogues and short stories filled with wonderful, tense, funny work by writers who just happen to be underpublished or beginners. Our audience is young and overeducated." Quarterly. Estab. 1995. Circ. 2,000.

Needs: Condensed/excerpted novel, erotica, ethnic/multicultural, experimental, humor/satire, literary, mainstream/contemporary, serialized novel, sports, translations. "No sentimental 'weepers' or Bukowski-esque material." List of upcoming themes available for SASE. Publishes special fiction issues or anthologies. Receives 10 unsolicited mss/month. Accepts 2 mss/issue; 8 mss/year. Publishes mss 2-3 months after acceptance. Recently published work by Peter Greene, Jay Ponteri and Mark McClusky. Publishes short shorts. Also publishes literary essays, literary criticism, poetry. Often critiques or comments on rejected mss.

How to Contact: Send complete ms with cover letter. Reports in 1 month on queries and mss. Send SASE for reply, return of ms or send a disposable copy of ms. Simultaneous, reprint and electronic submissions OK. Sample copy for $1.50. Fiction guidelines for #10 SAE and 2 first-class stamps. Reviews novels and short story collections. Send books to Amy Kleinfelder.

Payment/Terms: Pays minimum 2 contributor's copies to $125 maximum on publication. Acquires one-time rights. Sends galleys to author.

Advice: "Looks for quality of writing, a knowledge of past works of literature and a willingness to work with our editors. Submit often and take criticism with a grain of salt."

‡**DARK TOME, (I, IV)**, P.O. Box 705, Salem OR 97308. Editor: Michelle Marr. E-mail: dktome@cyb erhighway.net. Website: http://wwide.com/darktome.htm/. Zine: 5½ × 8½; 30-80 pages; 20 lb. paper; 60 lb. cover; illustrations. "We publish horror fiction for mature readers who are not easily offended." Bimonthly. Estab. 1990. Circ. 150.

Needs: Horror, psychic/supernatural/occult. "I want original nightmares, not classic ghost stories." Receives 50 unsolicited mss/month. Accepts 6-10 mss/issue; 30-60 mss/year. Publishes manuscript 2-4 months after acceptance. Length: 1,500 words average; 4,000 words maximum. Especially looking for short shorts (to 1,000 words).

How to Contact: Send complete manuscript with cover letter. Reports in 2-5 weeks. SASE. Electronic submissions OK. Sample copy for $2.75 payable to Michelle Marr. Fiction guidelines for #10 SASE.

Payment/Terms: Pays in contributor's copies and small cash payment. Acquires first North American serial rights.

Advice: "I am looking for stories with vivid images that will remain in the mind of the reader, and horrors that affect only a small number of people."

DEAD OF NIGHT™ MAGAZINE, (II), 916 Shaker Rd., Suite 228, Longmeadow MA 01106-2416. (413)567-9524. Editor: Lin Stein. Zine: 8½ × 11; 64-96 pages; newsprint paper; slick 2-color cover stock; illustrations, and occasionally photographs. "*Dead of Night Magazine* publishes horror, fantasy, mystery, science fiction and vampire-related fiction. If we had a 'motto' it might be 'horror/fantasy/mystery/science fiction in a different vein.' " Annual. Estab. 1989. Circ. 2,500.

● Not accepting material until 1998. *Dead of Night Magazine* has suspended publication through 1997, and will resume sending guidelines in late 1997. Writers may query with SASE for the most current status of the magazine.

Needs: Condensed novel, fantasy (science fantasy, sword and sorcery), horror, mystery/suspense (mysteries need supernatural element), psychic/supernatural/occult, science fiction (soft/sociological). "We don't care for fantasy with an overabundance of elves, wizards, etc." Receives 90 unsolicited mss/month. Accepts 8-12 mss/issue. Does not read mss during June, July, August. Publishes ms 6-18 months after acceptance. Published work by Janet Fox, J.N. Williamson, Mort Castle, Gary Braunbeck. Length: 2,500-2,800 words preferred; 500 words minimum; 4,000 words maximum. Publishes literary essays, literary criticism and poetry. Often critiques or comments on rejected mss.

Payment/Terms: Pays 3-7¢/word and 1 contributor's copy (2 to cover artists) on publication for first North American serial rights; additional copies for 10% discount off cover price.

Advice: "We think our magazine takes a somewhat 'literary' approach to the dark genres; that is, we avoid unnecessary gore and splatter. Instead, we aim for moody, atmospheric tales that are genuinely frightening and that will give the reader a lasting jolt rather than a momentary gross-out type of reaction. We look for truly frightening horror, believable fantasy, mysteries with some 'mysteriousness,' and character-oriented science fiction. Vampire tales should add some fresh or unique slant to the legend. We'd like to see stories that are not so 'media-influenced'; that is, tales that don't re-hash the latest horror movie/thriller the writer has seen at the box office or on television. Horror, fantasy, mystery and science fiction in our magazine are not the same as that in films. Also, we see too many vampire stories in which the writer tries to take the gothic atmosphere too far; for example, making vampire characters speak in 'Olde English'—annoying, and often poorly done."

DIVERSIONS, Erotic Fiction for the Mainstream, (I), A'n'D Enterprises, 200 Coolwell Rd., Madison Heights VA 24572. Phone/fax: (804)929-7601. E-mail: dmason@freenet.vcu.edu. Editor: Dan Mason. Zine: 8½×5½; 64 pages; white laser paper; illustrations and photos. "We publish erotic stories, illustrations and photos intended to arouse/interest straight men and women 18 to 68 years old." Quarterly. Estab. 1995. Circ. 250.

Needs: Erotica. "No ultra violence or children." Plans to publish special fiction issues or anthologies. Receives 10-15 unsolicited mss/month. Accepts 8-12 mss/issue; 30-50 mss/year. Publishes ms 3 months after acceptance. Recently published work by Melanie Newman, Ken Seegler, James Simpson and Brandy Ayers. Length: 1,500 words average; no minimum or maximum. Also publishes literary essays and poetry. Sometimes critiques or comments on rejected mss (with SASE).

How to Contact: Send complete ms with a cover letter. Include estimated word count, 35-word bio and Social Security number with submission. Reports in 4-6 weeks. Send SASE for reply, return of ms or send a disposable copy of ms. Simultaneous, reprint and electronic (e-mail or ASCII) submissions OK. Sample copy for $3, 6×9 SAE and 2 first-class stamps. Fiction guidelines for #10 SASE.

Payment/Terms: Pays ¼-5¢/word on publication and 2 contributor's copies; additional copies half price. Acquires one-time rights.

Advice: "Looks for real characters in new situations. Must be *mainstream* erotica. Revise and edit at least three times. Spell check. Grammar check. Show, don't tell. We would like to see more interesting locations and circumstances. We've seen too many 'boy cutting grass gets seduced' stories."

DREAMS & NIGHTMARES, The Magazine of Fantastic Poetry, (IV), 1300 Kicker Rd., Tusca-loosa AL 35404. (205)553-2284. E-mail: dkmialageo@genie.com. Editor: David C. Kopaska-Merkel. Zine: 5½×8½; 24 pages; ink drawing illustrations. "*DN* is mainly a poetry magazine, but I *am* looking for short-short stories. They should be either fantasy or science fiction." Estab. 1986. Circ. 250.

Needs: Experimental, fantasy, humor/satire, science fiction. "Try me with anything *except*: senseless violence, misogyny or hatred (unreasoning) of any kind of people, sappiness." Plans 1-word poem issue; deadline September 1997. Receives 4-8 unsolicited fiction mss/month. Accepts 1-2 mss/issue; 1-5 mss/year. Publishes ms 1-9 months after acceptance. Recently published work by Charlee Jacob and D.F. Lewis. Length: 500 words average; 1,000 words maximum. Publishes short shorts. Length: 500 or fewer words. Sometimes critiques rejected mss. Also publishes poetry.

How to Contact: Send complete ms. Reports in 1-3 weeks on queries; 1-6 weeks on mss. SASE. No simultaneous submissions. Electronic submissions (ASCII or Mac WordPerfect 5.1) OK. Sample copy for $2. Fiction guidelines for #10 SASE.

Payment/Terms: Pays $3 on acceptance and 2 contributor's copies for one-time rights.

Advice: "I don't want pointless violence or meandering vignettes. I do want extremely short science fiction or fantasy fiction that engages the reader's interest from word one. I want to be *involved*. Start with a good first line, lead the reader where you want him/her to go and end with something that causes a reaction or provokes thought."

‡DREAMS OF DECADENCE, Vampire Poetry and Fiction, (I, II, IV), DNA Publications, Inc., P.O. Box 13, Greenfield MA 01302-0013. (413)772-0725. E-mail: dreams@shaysnet.com. Editor: Angela G. Kessler. Zine: digest size; 80 pages; illustrations. Specializes in "vampire fiction and poetry for vampire fans." Quarterly. Estab. 1995. Circ. 1,000.

Needs: Vampires. "I am not interested in seeing the clichés redone." Receives 50 unsolicited mss/month. Accepts 4 mss/issue; 12 mss/year. Publishes ms 1-6 months after acceptance. Length: 4,000 words average; 1,000 words minimum; 5,000 maximum. Also publishes poetry. Always critiques or comments on rejected mss.

How to Contact: Send complete ms with cover letter. Include estimated word count, 1-paragraph bio and list of publications. Reports in 1 month on queries; 2 months on mss. Send SASE for reply, return of ms or send a disposable copy of ms. Simultaneous submissions OK. Sample copy for $5. Fiction guidelines for #10 SASE. Reviews novels and short story collections.

Payment/Terms: Pays 1-5¢/word on publication and 1 contributor's copy; additional copies for $2.50. Acquires first North American serial rights.
Advice: "I like stories that take the traditional concept of the vampire into new territory, or look at it (from within or without) with a fresh perspective. Don't forget to include a SASE for reply or return of manuscript. Also, to see what an editor wants, *read an issue.*"

THE DRINKIN' BUDDY MAGAZINE: A Magazine for Art and Words, (I), Pimperial Productions, P.O. Box 7615, Laguna Niguel CA 92677. (714)452-8720. E-mail: kc@kaiwan.com. Editor: KC Bradshaw. Zine: 5½×8½; 40 pages; 20 lb. paper and cover; illustrations and photos. Quarterly. Estab. 1994. Circ. 1,000.
Needs: Adventure, condensed/excerpted novel, erotica, ethnic/multicultural, fantasy, gay, historical, horror, humor, lesbian, literary, mainstream, mystery/suspense, psychic/supernatural, regional, romance, science fiction, serialized novel, sports, translations, westerns, young adult/teen. Receives 30-40 unsolicited mss/month. Recently published work by Groundhog and C. Darner. Publishes short shorts. Also publishes poetry.
How to Contact: Sometimes critiques or comments on rejected ms. Send complete ms with a cover letter. Send SASE for reply or a disposable copy of the ms. Simultaneous, electronic submissions OK. Sample copy for 5½×8½ SAE and 3 first-class stamps. Reviews novels and short story collections.
Payment/Terms: Pays free subscription to the magazine. Acquires one-time rights.
Advice: "A manuscript stands out when its subject and writing style are unique. Shorter stories have a greater chance of being published. If I enjoy the story, it goes in."

‡ECLIPSE, (I, II, IV), Glasya Vectra Productions, 131 S. Jefferson St., Frederick MD 21701. (301)682-9168. E-mail: kiirenza@aol.com. Website: http://members.aol.com/kiirenza/Eclipse/eclipse. htm. Editor: Kiirenza Lockhorn. Zine: 8½×11; 52-56 pages; 20 lb. white paper; cardstock glossy cover; illustrations and photos. Specializes in fantasy, science fiction and horror. "*Eclipse* was created to give unpublished writers editorial advice—not form letters or checklists. If *Eclipse* can't publish it, a writer can expect advice on how to make improvements to the work." Quarterly. Estab. 1993. Circ. 200.
Needs: Experimental, fantasy (science fiction, sword and sorcery), horror, psychic/supernatural/occult, science fiction (hard science, soft/sociological). "No erotic fiction, romance, or anything that is racist or bigoted in nature." Receives 100 unsolicited mss/month. Accepts 5-6 mss/issue; 25 mss/year. Publishes ms within 6 months after acceptance. Recently published work by James Rada Jr., Deborah Hunt, Ryan G. Van Cleave, Wayne Edwards, Robert Collins, John Coffren, David Rogers and Janice Knapp. Length: 3,000 words average; 5,000 words maximum. Publishes short shorts. Also publishes literary essays, literary criticism and poetry. Always critiques or comments on rejected mss.
How to Contact: Send complete ms with a cover letter. Include estimated word count. Reports 3 months on queries and mss. Send SASE for reply, return of ms or send a disposable copy of ms. Sample copy for $5. Fiction guidelines for #10 SASE. Reviews novels and short story collections.
Payment/Terms: Pays 1 contributor's copy; additional copies for $2. Pays on publication. Acquires one-time rights. Sponsors contest; send SASE for information.
Advice: "I look for stories that make sense—they don't state one thing and contradict themselves later on. Manuscripts stand out when they have strong characters, a believable (though fantasy or other) story, and follow *type* guidelines. *Double space* and *spell/grammar check* the story. Don't forget a cover letter and a SASE. I don't necessarily care about publishing credits (or lack thereof), and just want you to say 'hi' and be friendly!"

EIDOS: Sexual Freedom and Erotic Entertainment for Women, Men & Couples, (IV), P.O. Box 96, Boston MA 02137-0096. (617)262-0096. Fax: (617)364-0096. E-mail: eidos4sex@pipeli ne.com. Toll Free: 1-800-4U-EIDOS. Editor: Brenda Loew Tatelbaum. Zine: 10×14; 96 pages; web offset printing; illustrations; photos. Zine specializing in erotica for women, men and couples of all sexual orientations, preferences and lifestyles. "Explicit material regarding language and behavior formed in relationships, intimacy, moment of satisfaction—sensual, sexy, honest. For an energetic, well informed, international erotica readership." Quarterly. Estab. 1984. Circ. 7,000.
● *Eidos* was nominated for Erotic Publication of the Year in the 1996 Erotic Oscars competition in London, England.
Needs: Erotica. Upbeat erotic fiction is especially wanted. Publishes at least 10-12 pieces of fiction/ year. Recently published work by Mark Black, Charisse Vanderlyn, Christopher Hennessey Derose and Ulla Jensen. Published new writers within the last year. Length: 1,000 words average; 500 words minimum; 2,000 words maximum. Also publishes literary criticism, poetry. Occasionally critiques rejected mss.
How to Contact: Send complete ms with SASE. "Cover letter with history of publication or short bio is welcome." Reports in 1 month on queries; 1 month on mss. Simultaneous submissions OK. Sample copy for $5. Fiction guidelines for #10 SASE. Reviews novels and short story collections, "if related to subject of erotica (sex, politics, religion, etc.)."

Payment/Terms: Pays in contributor's copies. Acquires first North American serial rights.
Advice: "We receive more erotic fiction manuscripts now than in the past. Most likely because both men and women are more comfortable with the notion of submitting these manuscripts for publication as well as the desire to see alternative sexually explicit fiction in print. Therefore we can publish more erotic fiction because we have more material to choose from. There is still a lot of debate as to what erotic fiction consists of. This is a tough market to break into. Manuscripts must fit our editorial needs and it is best to order a sample issue prior to writing or submitting material. Honest, explicitly pro-sex, mutually consensual erotica lacks unwanted power, control and degradation—no unwanted coercion of any kind."

‡**EMPTY, (II, III)**, Conception Design, 185 S. Whitney St., 3rd Floor, Hartford CT 06105. (860)236-2892. E-mail: roman_chr@ccsu.ctstateu.edu. Editor: Christopher Roman. Zine: 5×8; 40 pages; handmade covers (signed and numbered); illustrations and photos. Specializes in "ground-breaking philosophies in fiction, poetry, criticism, art and visual/literary media." Quarterly. Estab. 1995. Circ. 500.
   • *Empty* trys to stay away from the mass-produced look and instead uses a more artistic approach.
Needs: Condensed/excerpted novel. erotica, ethnic/multicultural, experimental, fantasy (science fantasy), feminist, literary, "anything that's trying to expand the boundaries of fiction." List of upcoming themes available for SASE. Publishes ms 1-2 months after acceptance. Recently published work by Amy Hart, Jean Kearns, Tim Shea and John Ensuto. Length: no preference. Publishes short shorts. Also publishes literary essays, literary criticism and poetry. Sometimes critiques or comments on rejected mss.
How to Contact: Query with or without clips of published work or send complete ms with a cover letter. Include estimated word count, short bio and list of publications. Reports in 1 month. Send SASE for reply, return of ms or send a disposable copy of ms. Simultaneous and electronic (disk or modem) submissions OK. Sample copy for $3, 8×11 SAE and 3 first-class stamps. Fiction guidelines for #10 SASE. Reviews novels and short story collections.
Payment/Terms: Pays free subscription to zine; additional copies for $2. Acquires one-time rights. Not copyrighted.
Advice: "We look for experimental, intelligent, new, inspiring, spiritual fiction."

‡**FAYRDAW, (I)**, P.O. Box 100, Shartlesville PA 19554. (610)488-6894. Editors: Loring D. Emery, Mary M. Towne and Dorotéo M. Estrago. Zine: 5½×8½; about 40 pages; 20 lb. paper; saddle-stitched; illustrations. Bimonthly. Estab. 1994. Circ. 50.
Needs: Adventure, experimental, historical, humor/satire, literary and mainstream/contemporary. "Nothing derivative or overly cute." Receives 10-20 unsolicited mss/month. Accepts 0-3 mss/issue; 20-25 mss/year. Publishes ms 3-4 months after acceptance. Recently published work by Anthony Mercury, Kiel Stuart, Judith Bergen and Larry Garrett. Length: 1,500 words maximum. Publishes short shorts. Also publishes literary essays, literary criticism. Often critiques or comments on rejected mss.
How to Contact: Send complete ms with a cover letter. Include estimated word count, bio (3-5 lines) and list of publications. "Anything chatty." Reports in 1 month. SASE for reply or send a disposable copy of ms. Simultaneous, reprint and electronic (3.5 or 5.25 disk) submissions OK. Sample copy for $2. Fiction guidelines for #10 SASE. Reviews novels and short story collections.
Payment/Terms: Pays $5 (fiction only). Pays on acceptance for one-time rights. Not copyrighted.
Advice: "Look at a sample. Read our guidelines."

‡**THE FIFTH DI/THE SIXTH SENSE/STARFLITE, (II)**, Promart Writing Lab's Small Press Family, P.O. Box 1094, Carmichael CA 95609. (916)973-1020. Editor: James B. Baker. Three zines: 5½×8½; 48 pages; 20 lb. paper; 24 lb. cover stock. Specializes in science fiction. "My intended audience is made up of those desiring to see man going to the stars. *The Fifth Di* is adult; *The Sixth Sense* is family (no excessive sex or bad language); and *Starflite* is our feature zine." Bimonthly. Estab. 1995. Circ. 192. Member of The Writers' Alliance and The National Writer's Association.
Needs: Science fiction, serialized novel. "No horror and only minimal fantasy." Receives 15-20 unsolicited mss/month. Accepts 10 mss/issue; 180 mss/year. Publishes ms 6-12 months after acceptance. Recently published work by James S. Dorr, Alexander W. Andrews and Lida Quillen. Length: 3,500 words average. Publishes short shorts. Also publishes literary essays and poetry. Always critiques or comments on rejected mss. Sponsors "Novette" contest (25,000 words or more). Entry fee: $19. Send SASE for information.
How to Contact: Send complete ms with cover letter. Include estimated word count and bio. Reports in days on queries; weeks on mss. SASE or SAE and IRCs if out of U.S. No simultaneous submissions. Sample copy for $1 and 5×9 SASE.
Payment/Terms: Pays $5-40 (.0115/word) on publication and contributor's copy; additional copies for $1.50. Acquires first rights.
Advice: "Do your own thing—ignore the trends."

‡FORTRESS, Adventures of yesterday and tomorrow, (II), (formerly *Symphonie's Gift*), SG Print, P.O. Box 22, Fairview PA 16415. (814)835-3083. E-mail: symgift@aol.com. Fiction Editors: Bryan Lindenberger and Jennifer Lynn. Zine: 8½×11; 50 pages; 20 lb. white paper; 50-60 lb. cover stock; illustrations. "I try to use fiction of various styles and not attempt to emulate the fiction of yesteryear. *Fortress* has a good mix of pro, semi-pro and new writers. The audience consists of lovers of the genre, mostly in their 20s through 40s."Triannually. Estab. 1994. Circ. 500. Member SPGA.

Needs: Adventure, fantasy (science, sword and sorcery, historical), science fiction (hard science, soft/sociological, military). "Avoid fantasy in mythical of medieval European settings. We use stories set in the wide range of other historical pasts." Publishes 1 theme issue/year. Upcoming theme: chess-inspired stories; deadline June 1997. Receives 100 unsolicited mss/month. Accepts 8 mss/issue; 24 mss/year. Publishes ms 1-12 months after acceptance. Recently published work by Charles M. Saplak, Ken Rand, Jim Lee and A.R. Morlan. Length: 4,000 words average; 100 words minimum; 10,000 words maximum. Publishes short shorts. Also publishes literary essays. Often critiques or comments on rejected mss.

How to Contact: Send complete ms with cover letter. Include estimated word count, 50-word bio, Social Security number, list of publications and "one or two sentences introducing the story." Reports in 1 week on queries; 1 week-3 months on mss. Send SASE for reply, return of ms or send a disposable copy of ms. Sample copy for $4.50. Fiction guidelines for #10 SASE.

Payment/Terms: Pays $10 minimum, $100 maximum and 1 contributor's copy on publication for one-time rights; additional copies for $3.

Advice: "I like fiction that moves from page one, but that does not mean I need explosions and a body count. I see a lot of heroes and villains, but not enough real, fallible people. Send your story! If we can't use it, don't get discouraged. Read a sample copy and send us your next story."

FUEL MAGAZINE, (II), Anaconda Press, P.O. Box 477699, Chicago IL 60647. E-mail: aolwry@tez cat.com. Editor: Andy Lowry. Zine: 5½×8½; 40 pages; 60 lb. offset paper; 110 lb. cover stock; illustrations. "*Fuel* is a very eccentric, eclectic magazine. We do not consider ourselves an academic publication; rather, we prefer to publish underground lesser-known writers." Quarterly. Estab. 1992. Circ. 2,000.

● *Fuel's* fiction needs have gone from 50% of the magazine to 75-80%. The magazine is best known for dark, realistic fiction.

Needs: Ethnic/multicultural, experimental, feminist, literary. No science fiction, romance, horror, humor/satire. List of upcoming themes available for SASE. Receives 50 unsolicited mss/month. Accepts 5 mss/issue; 20-25 mss/year. Publishes ms 3-5 months after acceptance. Recently published work by Nicole Panter, Gerald Locklin, Alan Catlin and Sesshu Foster. Length: 2,500 words preferred; 500 words minimum; 3,000 words maximum. Publishes short shorts. Length: 250 words. Also publishes poetry.

How to Contact: Query first. Include estimated word count and list of publications. Reports in 4 weeks on queries; 6 weeks on mss. SASE. No simultaneous submissions. Reprint and electronic submissions OK. Sample copy for $3. Fiction guidelines for #10 SASE.

Payment/Terms: Pays contributor's copies; additional copies at cost. Rights revert to authors.

Advice: "We are not your normal publication—we want intelligent, cutting edge, strongly written works. Persistence pays off—keep trying."

FULL-TIME DADS, The Magazine For Caring Fathers, (I, II), Big Daddy Publications, P.O. Box 577, Cumberland ME 04021. (207)829-5260. E-mail: fulltdad@usa.pipeline.com. Website: http://www.parentsplace.com/readroom/fulltdad. Editor: Stephen Harris. An e-zine published on the Internet. "*Full-Time Dads* publishes anything relating to fathers/fatherhood with a positive point of view." Estab. 1991.

Needs: Children's/juvenile, fantasy (children's), humor/satire, literary, mainstream/contemporary, religious/inspirational, young adult/teen. "No violence, sex, abuse, etc." Plans themed issues next year; list available for SASE. Plans special fiction issue or anthology. Accepts 12 mss/year. Publishes ms 2-6 months after acceptance. Length: 600-1,200 words average. Publishes short shorts. Also publishes literary essays, literary criticism, poetry. Often critiques or comments on rejected mss.

How to Contact: Query first. Send complete ms with a cover letter. Include estimated word count and 3-4 sentence bio. Reports in 4-6 weeks on queries. Send SASE for reply, return of ms or send a

MARKET CONDITIONS are constantly changing! If you're still using this book and it is 1998 or later, buy the newest edition of *Novel & Short Story Writer's Market* at your favorite bookstore or order from Writer's Digest Books.

disposable copy of ms. "No SASE, no reply." Simultaneous, reprint and electronic (Microsoft Word/Mac on disk or e-mail) submissions OK. Fiction guidelines for #10 SASE. Reviews novels and short story collections.

Payment/Terms: Pays 1 contributor's copy. Acquires one-time rights, possibly anthology rights.

Advice: "Take your time. Reread, reread, reread. Make sure what you send is exactly what you want me to read."

‡GENERATOR, Local Literary & Arts Magazine, (I), P.O. Box 980363, Ypsilanti MI 48197. (313)482-2895. Editors: Kimberly Baker and Michelle McGrath. Zine specializing in local arts and literature: 8 × 14; 52 pages; 20 lb. paper; glossy cover; illustrations and photos. "*Generator* is a literary magazine aimed at exposing new literary talents, as well as local artists from the Ypsilanti area. We have an eclectic format with material ranging from comics, poetry, short stories to memoirs and travel journals." Quarterly. Estab. 1995. Circ. 500.

● *Generator* combines the 'zine revolution with the structural format of a literary arts magazine.

Needs: Condensed/excerpted novel, ethnic/multicultural, experimental, feminist, gay, humor/satire, lesbian, literary, mainstream/contemporary, regional, science fiction (hard science, soft/sociological), translations. No children's/juvenile, fantasy, religious. Receives 15-20 unsolicited mss/month. Accepts 4-5 mss/issue; 16-20 mss/year. Publishes ms 2 months after acceptance. Recently published work by Brenda Flanagan, David Quinn, Paul McGlynn and Ken Cormier. Length: 500-1,000 words average; 1,500 words maximum. Publishes short shorts. Also publishes literary essays, literary criticism and poetry. Often critiques or comments on rejected mss. Sponsors short fiction contest. Send SASE for information.

How To Contact: Send complete ms with a cover letter. Include bio (a few sentences). Reports in 2 months on queries; 3 months on mss. Send SASE for reply, return of ms or send a disposable copy of ms. "Material returned only upon request." Simultaneous, reprint and electronic (disk) submissions OK. Sample copy for $3. Fiction guidelines for #10 SASE. Reviews novels and short story collections.

Payment/Terms: Pays 1 contributor's copy; additional copies for $3. Acquires one-time rights. Not copyrighted.

Advice: "We generally choose work which is well-written, interesting and experimental or that which strays from the conventional norms. We are receptive to many different styles and encourage new writers to submit for publication."

GRAFFITI OFF THE ASYLUM WALLS, An Illiterary Journal, (III), P.O. Box 1653, Hot Springs AR 71902-1653. Curator: Bryan Westbrook. Zine: Digest-sized; 20 pages; colored paper cover; illustrations. "The stuff you would be afraid to show your mother, priest and/or psychiatrist. Humor encouraged." Publishes "whenever enough material and funds are available." Estab. 1992. Circ. varies.

Needs: Erotica, feminist, humor/satire, fetishism, perversion, political (anti-Republican). "Nothing pro-religious, pro-animal rights, anything high fallutin.'" Published work by Robert W. Howington, Allen Renfro, Marc Swan. Length: 1,000 words maximum. Submit only 1 story at a time. Also publishes literary essays and poetry. Often critiques or comments on rejected mss.

How to Contact: Send complete ms with cover letter. Include bio (personal bio, not publication list). Reports within 6 months. Send SASE for reply, return of ms or send a disposable copy of ms. Simultaneous and reprint submissions OK. Sample copy for $3. Reviews novels and short story collections.

Payment/Terms: No payment; contributor's copies available for discounted price of $2. Acquires one-time rights.

Advice: "If it can make me laugh (not an easy task) or shock me (also a challenge) it will make it. Non-narrative stories have a harder time here. Forget everything you've ever read in school or been told in writing classes. I want to hear from the real you."

‡HAZEL GROVE MUSINGS, (I, II, IV), Black Wing Publications, 1225 E. Sunset Dr., Bellingham WA 98226. E-mail: maeschilde@aol.com. Editor: Shirley Dawson-Myers. Zine: 5 × 8½ chap style; 20-30 pages; recycled 20 lb. paper and cover stock; illustrations and photos. Specializes in "paganism, nature-based religion, earth spirituality, witchcraft and women's spirituality." Triannually. Estab. 1993. Circ. 100. Member of the Wiccan/Pagan Press Alliance (WPPA).

Needs: Ethnic/multicultural, experimental, fantasy (science, sword and sorcery), feminist, gay, humor/satire, lesbian, psychic/supernatural/occult, religious/inspirational. Receives 1-2 unsolicited mss/month. Accepts 1-2 mss/issue; 5-10 mss/year. Publishes ms usually in next issue after acceptance. Recently published work by Zella Bardsley, Maeschilde and DDK. Length: 3,000 words average; 10,000 words maximum. Publishes short shorts. Also publishes literary essays; literary criticism and poetry.

How to Contact: Query first. Include bio. Reports in 2-3 weeks on queries; 3 months on mss. SASE for reply. Reprints and electronic submissions OK. Sample copy for $3. Fiction guidelines for #10 SASE. Reviews novels and short story collections.

INSIDER REPORT

Zines offer writers artistic freedom and niche audiences

Getting published in a zine is the perfect way to start your writing career, says Ariel Gore, editor of *hip Mama*. Gore credits the continuing zine revolution with the fact that "people are understanding that, to get their 'stuff' out there, they have to publish it themselves." For a writer starting out, new at the business of exposing her work, the zine offers an audience that is almost like a community. "You don't have to bend what you're saying as much as you would in the mainstream," says Gore. That gives writers the freedom they need, especially those just finding their voice.

Ariel Gore

Because of their specific editorial content, zines serve their particular niche audiences better than mainstream publications. *hip Mama* does not serve all mothers interested in alternative parenting. They do not focus on purity, cloth diapers, minimalism and the like, says Gore. "Our trip is more survival-oriented—both financially and emotionally." The publication is reader-written and reflects what the readers are going through. The core audience of *hip Mama*, that began as younger moms and single moms, has now widened to include dads and others.

The zine market is the only place people can find publications like *hip Mama*. "There is no other market for the stuff we run," says Gore. "There are all these smaller interest groups that aren't served by the mainstream, even though some mainstream publications are getting more specialized. *Bi-Racial Child*, for instance, is pretty specialized for a parenting magazine. And *hip Mama* doesn't cover everything alternative either, so there is still room for more on parenting in the alternative market."

Gore started *hip Mama* as her senior project in college in September, 1993, and the first issue came out in December. "I had a kid the whole time I was in college so I had been a teen mom and a welfare mom, and parenting magazines didn't address any of that. So I started it as something for me and my friends and it doubled as a senior project. It was a chance to talk about all the stuff I was dealing with." Work published in *hip Mama* continues to be experimental and deals with issues of interest to young, low income parents.

Unlike some of the self-indulgent, off-the-wall zines with haphazard publication schedules just starting out, *hip Mama* is a 36-page, offset printed quarterly that includes poetry, fiction, nonfiction and columns. The one-shot, photocopied zines have more flexibility than *hip Mama*, says Gore. "They can just paste something down at the last minute and make copies." At the high end of the zine spectrum, however, are some four-color, commercial-looking, very slick publications.

One thing you don't usually get from a zine editor, according to Gore, is editing. Not only are the editors not paid, they often pay the costs of publishing their zines. To support themselves and their publications, they have other jobs and so don't have a lot of time to edit stories. Sometimes they aren't even able to send rejections. "If you don't hear from a zine, it doesn't necessarily mean your stuff wasn't good," says Gore. "It may have not made it in for some other reason, but you probably won't get personal feedback."

Gore advises beginners to learn all they can about the zines they want to write for. Even more important, she says, writers must know what they want to write. "You'll have plenty of time later in your career to worry about pleasing a particular editor. When you're starting out, you should write what you really need to say." This can be very freeing for a fiction writer. Once you've written a story, Gore says, "learn a lot about a few publications that are in line with your writing and send to those." In many cases, writers may already have favorite zines that they read and can submit their fiction to.

Emotionally-pure writing is what Gore looks for when selecting stories for *hip Mama*. "I also like stuff that sheds a new light on an issue that we think of as being somebody else's problem. We ran an experimental piece on a mom with AIDS whose baby was born drug addicted. It wasn't a political story—it didn't make it seem like she was a great mom, but it presented a whole new perspective on the subject."

A great advantage to publishing in a zine is that the competition isn't as fierce as with more mainstream publications; you have a better chance of building up a list of publishing credits. "I think no matter where you've been published, editors are going to take notice of it," says Gore. "When I get a cover letter from someone who's been published five places, even if I've never heard of any of the publications, that's still impressive to me." But always include a cover letter. "I hate to say it, but if I get a submission that has no cover letter and I've never talked to the person, that goes to the bottom of the pile. And it doesn't really matter how fabulous your work is if editors don't read it. When I first started writing, I thought my stuff should speak for itself. Unfortunately zine editors don't have that kind of time."

But the ultimate beauty of writing for a zine, according to Gore, remains the artistic freedom it provides. It means not having to follow conventions or write on particular topics. It also means, says Gore, "You don't have to worry about your grandmother reading it." Unless, of course, you want to send her a copy.

—*Donna Collingwood*

Payment/Terms: Pays 1 contributor's copy on publication. Acquires one-time rights.
Advice: Looks for "non-entry level information on subject matter; alternate, unique to author, viewpoints; typed or word processed manuscripts. Know the subject matter and write from the heart."

HELIOCENTRIC NET ANTHOLOGY, (V), Three-Stones Publications Ltd., P.O. Box 68817, Seattle WA 98168-0817. Editor: Lisa Jean Bothell. Zine: 8½×11; 80 pages; 20 lb. offset white paper; glossy 2-color cover; illustrations. "We look for dark supernatural horror for eclectic readers." Annually. Estab. 1992.
• In addition to the zine, Three Stones Publications also publishes a bimonthly newsletter, *The Network*. Work included in *Heliocentric Net* tends to be more character-driven than idea-based.
Needs: "No science fiction, fantasy, romance, suspense, mystery, young adult or serials. No nihilistic horror; no erotica, pornography or anything intentionally discriminatory." Recently published work by Edward Lee, Jessica Amanda Salmonson, Charlee Jacob, Bruce Taylor, Sue Storm and Mark McLaughlin. Length: 3,500 words maximum. Publishes short shorts. Always comments on rejected mss.
How to Contact: Query with clips of published work. Include estimated word count and 2-paragraph bio. Reports in 4-6 weeks on queries. Send SASE for reply. Sample copy for $9.95 plus book rate postage for your country. Fiction guidelines for SASE.
Advice: "We will be closed for most of 1997. Send queries only."

HEROIC TIMES, (I), Millenium, 3681 Offutt Rd., #203, Randallstown MD 21133. Editor: Gary Abraham. Zine: 8½×11; 24 pages; HQ laser paper. Illustrations. *Heroic Times* covers "comics, entertainment and pop culture." Bimonthly. Estab. 1994. Circ. 200.
Needs: Adventure, erotica, ethnic/multicultural, experimental, fantasy, horror, mystery/suspense, science fiction. Receives 4 mss/month. Accepts 8 mss/year. Publishes ms 2-3 months after acceptance. Publishes short shorts. Also publishes literary essays, literary criticism, poetry. Critiques or comments on rejected ms.
How to Contact: Query with a cover letter. Should include estimated word count. Reports in 2-3 weeks on queries; 1-2 months on mss. Send SASE for reply, return of ms or send a disposable copy of ms. Simultaneous submissions OK. Sample copy for $5. Fiction guidelines available with sample copy. Reviews novels and short story collections.
Payment/Terms: Pays 2-3 contributor's copies on publication. Acquires first rights.

hip MAMA, The parenting zine, (I, II, IV), P.O. Box 9097, Oakland CA 94613. (510)658-4508. E-mail: hipmama@aol.com. Editor: Ariel Gore. Zine: 8½×11, 32 pages; uncoated paper; glossy cover; illustrations and photos. "'Zine for progressive/liberal/feminist parents." Quarterly. Estab. 1993. Circ. 5,000.
• *hip Mama* was a finalist in the 1995 Annual Alternative Press Awards
Needs: Condensed/excerpted novel, erotica, ethnic/multicultural, experimental, feminist, gay, humor/satire, lesbian, literary, mainstream/contemporary. Nothing "anti-mother." Receives 20 unsolicited fiction mss/month. Accepts 1 ms/issue; 4 mss/year. Publishes ms up to 6 months after acceptance. Recently published work by Susan Ito and Opal Palmer Adisa. Length: 1,000 words average; 200 words minimum; 2,000 words maximum. Publishes short shorts. Length: 300-500 words. Also publishes literary essays and poetry. Sometimes critiques or comments on rejected mss.
How to Contact: Send complete ms with a cover letter. Include estimated word count and 20-word bio with submission. Reports in 1-6 months on mss. Send SASE for reply, return of ms or send a disposable copy of ms. Simultaneous, reprint and electronic submissions OK. Sample copy for $4. Reviews novels and short story collections.
Payment/Terms: Pays $100 maximum, free subscription to magazine and 3 contributor's copies on publication for one-time rights.
Advice: Wants "concise, evocative stories about some aspect of mothering in these times. We don't see enough stories about unusual but positive mothering experiences. We're tired of stories about bad mothers. Read the zine, be yourself."

HOBSON'S CHOICE, (I, II), Starwind Press, Box 98, Ripley OH 45167. (513)392-4549. Editor: Susannah West. Zine: 8½×11; 16 pages; 60 lb. offset paper and cover; b&w illustrations; line shot photos. "We publish science fiction and fantasy for young adults and adults with interest in science, technology, science fiction and fantasy." Bimonthly. Estab. 1974. Circ. 2,000.
Needs: Fantasy, science fiction (hard science, soft/sociological). "We like science fiction that shows hope for the future and protagonists who interact with their environment rather than let themselves be manipulated by it." No horror, pastiches of other authors, stories featuring characters created by others (i.e. Captain Kirk and crew, Dr. Who, etc.). Receives 50 unsolicited mss/month. Accepts 2-4 mss/issue; 16-24 mss/year. Publishes ms 4-24 months after acceptance. Recently published work by Paul Haspel, Barb Rosen and Barb Myers. Published new writers within the last year. Length: 2,000-10,000 words. Also publishes literary criticism and some literary essays. Occasionally critiques rejected mss.

How to Contact: Send complete ms. Reports in 2-3 months. "If an author hasn't heard from us by 4 months, he/she should feel free to withdraw." Send SASE for return of ms. No simultaneous submissions. Accepts electronic submissions via disk for the IBM PC or PC compatible in ASCII format and Macintosh. Sample copy for $2.50. Fiction guidelines for #10 SASE. Tipsheet packet (all guidelines plus tips on writing science fiction) for $1.50 and SASE. Checks should be payable in U.S. funds only.
Payment/Terms: Pays 1-4¢/word (25% on acceptance, 75% 30 days after publication) and contributor's copies. "We pay 25% kill fee if we decide not to publish story." Rights negotiable. Sends galleys to the author.
Advice: "I certainly think a beginning writer can be successful if he/she studies the publication *before* submitting, and matches the submission with the magazine's needs. With regards to writing, get your story going right away; lengthy introductions will lose your reader's interest. Tell your story through action and conversation, not static description."

HOME GIRL PRESS, (I, II), ZEB Publications, P.O. Box 651, New York NY 10035. Editor: Ms. Zulma E. Brooks. Zine specializing in women's literature: 8½ × 11; 12-25 pages; recycled 20 lb. bond, colored paper; illustrations and photos. "The theme of *Home Girl Press* is urban American women. Material focuses on the lifestyle of 'big city' women. Our audience is women 18-30, career-oriented and housewives." Quarterly. Estab. 1997.
• This new zine is debuting Spring 1997.
Needs: Adventure, ethnic/multicultural, humor/satire, literary, mainstream/contemporary, regional, romance (contemporary). "No lesbian, feminist, male bashing or excessive profanity." Accepts 6-8 mss/issue; 24-32 mss/year. Publishes ms 3-6 months after acceptance. Length: 2,500 words average; 500 words minimum; 3,000 words maximum. Also publishes literary criticism, poetry. Sometimes critiques or comments on rejected mss.
How to Contact: Send complete ms. Include estimated word count and 200-word bio. Reports in 2 weeks on mss. SASE. Fiction guidelines for #10 SAE and 2 first-class stamps.
Payment/Terms: Pays with HGP logo t-shirt and 3 contributor's copies on acceptance for one-time rights; additional copies $3.
Advice: "Go over your story with a fine tooth comb and work out the bugs because I definitely will! Avoid clichés, formulative writing, predictable plots and ends. I would like to see more dramatic writing and more imaginative fiction for the urban woman."

‡IDIOT WIND, (I, IV), P.O. Box 87, Occoquan VA 22125-0087. (703)494-1897. E-mail: idiotwind @radix.net. Website: http://www.radix.net/~idiotwind. Editor: Douglas Carroll (a.k.a. Ed Lynn). Zine specializing in humor: 5½ × 8½; 16-20 pages; 20 lb. paper; illustrations and photos (sometimes). "We want to provide cheap laughs at an affordable price. We grew up on the great comic magazines of the seventies, like *National Lampoon*, and strive to recapture some of that spirit. We publish humor fiction, short filler-type material, and Letterman-style Top 10 Lists (in what we call our 'crawl space.' Our intended audience doesn't offend easily." Quarterly. Estab. 1984. Circ. 100-200.
Needs: Humor/satire. Recent themes: "Science and Technology"; "Love & Litigation." List of upcoming themes available for SASE. Receives 5-10 unsolicited mss/month. Accepts 2-3 mss/issue; 8-12 mss/year. Publishes ms 3-4 months after acceptance, "sometimes longer if we're saving it for a particular theme issue." Recently published work by Mead Stone, H. Turnip Smith, Eugene Flinn and Bernie Libster. Length: 1,500 words average; no minimum; 3,000 words maximum. Publishes short shorts. Also publishes poetry. Sometimes critiques or comments on rejected mss.
How to Contact: Send complete ms with a cover letter. Include estimated word count and bio (maximum 75 words). Reports in 3-4 months on queries and mss. Send SASE for reply, return of ms or send a disposable copy of ms. Simultaneous and electronic submissions OK. Sample copy and fiction guidelines for 6 × 9 SAE and 2 first-class stamps.
Payment/Terms: Pays 3 contributor's copies on publication; additional copies for SASE. Acquires one-time rights.
Advice: "It has to be drop-to-the-floor-grasping-your-sides-laughing-so-hard-you-pee-in-your-pants-kind of funny. Okay. That's a little strict. Funny, though, is the key word. We are a humor magazine. We aren't after long missives on the mating habits of the Tse-Tse fly, unless said Tse-Tse fly's habits include truly kinky stuff like dressing up as a priest for the female and shaving its little Tse-Tse fly legs. Take what you know and exaggerate it, parody it, poke fun at it. Read up on current events and exaggerate it, parody it, poke fun at it."

JACK MACKEREL MAGAZINE, (I, II), Rowhouse Press, P.O. Box 23134, Seattle WA 98102-0434. Editor: Greg Bachar. Zine: 5½ × 8½; 40-60 pages; Xerox bond paper; glossy card cover stock; b&w illustrations and photos. "We publish unconventional art, poetry and fiction." Quarterly. Estab. 1993. Circ. 1,000.
Needs: Condensed/excerpted novel, erotica, experimental, literary, surreal, translations. "No realism." List of upcoming themes available for SASE. Publishes special fiction issues or anthologies. Receives 20-100 unsolicited mss/month. Accepts 2-10 mss/issue; 8-40 mss/year. Publishes ms 2-3

months after acceptance. Length: 250 words minimum; 5,000 words maximum. Publishes short shorts. Also publishes literary essays, literary criticism and poetry. Sometimes critiques or comments on rejected mss.

How to Contact: Send complete ms with a cover letter. Include bio with submission. Send SASE for reply, return of ms or send a disposable copy of ms. Sample copy for $4. Reviews novels and short story collections.

Payment/Terms: Pays 2 contributor's copies.

Advice: "Avoid sending conventional fiction that obeys the rules."

KARMA LAPEL, P.O. Box 441915, Somerville MA 02144. E-mail: kalel@well.com. Editor: Heath Row. Zine: size and paper vary. "*Karma Lapel* is a little magazine of personal writing and commentary on sustainable media." Published occasionally. Estab. 1992. Circ. 150.

Needs: Translations, journal entries, personal essays, new journalism. Accepts 2-3 mss/issue. Recently published work by Phil Campbell and Enrique Ramirez. Publishes short shorts. Also publishes literary essays, literary criticism. Always critiques or comments on rejected mss.

How to Contact: Send complete ms with a cover letter. Include estimated word count, bio and list of publications. Reports in 3-4 months. SASE. No simultaneous submissions. Reprints and electronic (e-mail, Mac disk) submissions OK. Sample copy for $2. Reviews novels or short story collections.

Payment/Terms: Pays contributor's copies. Not copyrighted.

Advice: A manuscript stands out "if the story is true, or surprises me. Be as honest with yourself and the reader as possible."

‡KEEN SCIENCE FICTION!, Classic Science Fiction, Written by Writers Who Love It, (I, II, IV), Keen Press, P.O. Box 9067, Spokane WA 99209-0067. (509)744-0987. Fax: (509)744-0986. E-mail: zlsk20a@prodigy.com. Website: http://pages.prodigy.com/KeenSciFi. Editor: Teresa Keene. Zine: 8½×5½; 46-66 pages; heavy laser paper; lasercast cover; illustrations. "I've found that real science fiction lovers never get tired of reading the tried and true formats of time-travel, spacefaring, terraforming, parallel universe, and any other trusty old science fiction device. The purpose of this magazine is to bring those formats back to those of us who love and miss them!" Monthly. Estab. 1996. Circ. 200.

Needs: Science fiction (hard science, soft/sociological) and "some gentle fantasy of the 'Twilight Zone'-ish nature. No sword and sorcery." Receives 300 unsolicited mss/month. Accepts 6-9 mss/issue; 100-120 mss/year. Publishes mss 1-6 months after acceptance. Agented fiction 1%. Recently published work by Don D'Ammassa, Timons Esaias, Janet Ford, Arthur Zirul, Michael Ambrose, John B. Rosenman, Terry McGarry, Jonny Duffy, Art Cosing and Gail Hayden. Length: 2,500 words average; 50 words minimum; 4,000 words maximum. Publishes short shorts. Length: 400 words. Publishes literary essays, book reviews and poetry. Always critiques or comments on rejected mss.

How to Contact: Send complete ms with cover letter or send story on IBM-compatible disk. Include estimated word count, bio, Social Security number and list of publications. "Chatty cover letters welcome!" Reports in 1 week on queries; 1 month on mss. Send SASE for reply, return of ms or send a disposable copy of ms. Simultaneous, reprint and electronic submissions (disk only) OK. "No e-mail submissions!" Sample copy for $4. Fiction guidelines for #10 SASE. Reviews novels and short story collections. Send books to: Steven Sawicki, 186 Woodruff Ave., Watertown CT 06795.

Payment/Terms: Pays 1½¢/word, minimum $5, maximum $60 and 2 contributor's copies on publication for one-time rights.

Advice: "I look for stories of clarity, with no 'head-scratching.' Stories should have a beginning, middle, a twist or surprise at the end and be fun to read. Please include information about yourself. Be excited about your work, and let it show! Submit the tidiest manuscript you can."

‡✱KICK IT OVER, (I, II, IV), Kick It Over Collective, P.O. Box 5811, Station A, Toronto, Ontario M5W 1P2 Canada. Editor: Bob Melcombe. Zine: 8½×11; 48-76 pages; newsprint; gloss cover; illustrations; photographs. "Anarchist, ecology, feminist publication; we want short stories on or informed by political/social themes."Quarterly. Estab. 1983. Circ. 1,600. Member Anarchist Media Network and Canadian Magazine Publishers Association.

Needs: Condensed/excerpted novel, experimental, feminist, gay, lesbian, science fiction (soft/sociological), translations. Receives 4-5 mss/year. Recently published work by Bob Slaymaker. Length: 500-3,000 words. Publishes short shorts. Also publishes poetry.

How to Contact: Query first or send complete ms with a cover letter. Include estimated word count. Reports in 2 months on queries and mss. Send SASE for reply, return of ms or send a disposable copy of ms. Simultaneous and reprint submissions OK. Sample copy for $3. Fiction guidelines free.

Payment/Terms: Pays 3 contributor's copies on publication. Not copyrighted.

KIDS' WORLD, The Magazine That's All Kids!, (I), Stone Lightning Press, 1300 Kicker Rd., Tuscaloosa AL 35404. (205)553-2284. Editor: Morgan Kopaska-Merkel. Zine: digest size; 16-24 pages; standard white Xerox paper; card stock cover; illustrations. Publishes stories written by children under 17: "fantasy and 'kid stuff'—themes by kids, about kids and for kids." Quarterly. Estab. 1992. Circ. 60-80.

Needs: Children's/juvenile (4-12 years): adventure, fantasy (children's), mystery/suspense (amateur sleuth), science fiction (hard science, soft/sociological); young adult/teen (adventure, mystery, science fiction). No horror or romance. Receives 18-24 unsolicited mss/month. Accepts 30 mss/issue; 70-100 mss/year. Publishes ms from 1-24 months after acceptance. Recently published work by Adam Gish, Cassandra Zistl, Bethany, Murphy and Amanda Howell. Length: 300 words average, 75 words minimum; 500 words maximum. Publishes short shorts. Length: 150-200 words. Also publishes poetry.

How to Contact: Send complete ms with a cover letter including your age. Reports in 2-12 weeks on mss. Send SASE for reply, return of ms or send a disposable copy of ms. Simultaneous and reprint submissions OK. Sample copy for $1.50 and SAE. Fiction guidelines for SASE.

Payment/Terms: Pays 1 contributor's copy. Acquires first North American serial rights.

Advice: "Stories must be appropriate for kids. Have an adult check spelling, grammar and punctuation."

THE LETTER PARADE, (I), Bonnie Jo Enterprises, P.O. Box 52, Comstock MI 49041. Editor: Bonnie Jo. Zine: legal/letter-sized; 6 pages. Quarterly. Estab. 1985. Circ. 113.

Needs: "Anything short. We print very little fiction, actually. We print more essays. But we're open to the fun little story." Receives 25-30 unsolicited mss/month. Accepts 1-2 mss/issue. Publishes ms up to a year after acceptance. Recently published work by Allison Linden. Length: 250-750 words preferred; 2,000 words maximum. Publishes short shorts. Also publishes any kind of essays.

How to Contact: Send complete ms with a cover letter. "Please single space so I can publish pieces in the form I receive them." Send disposable copy of ms. Reports in 2 months. Simultaneous and reprint submissions OK. Sample copy for $1. Reviews novels or short story collections. Send review copies to Christopher Magson.

Payment/Terms: Pays subscription to magazine. Not copyrighted.

Advice: "We're predisposed to stories about animals so long as the stories aren't sentimental. No stories ending in suicide. We like humor that's not too light, not too dark. What ridiculous thing happened on the way to the hardware store? What did you do when your cows got loose? What makes you think your husband is in love with Maggie Thatcher?"

LIME GREEN BULLDOZERS, (I), Oyster Publications, P.O. Box 4333, Austin TX 78765. E-mail: oystapress@tab.com. Editor: Alaina Duro. Zine: 8½ × 11; 50 pages; regular white paper; illustrations and photos. Zine specializing in literature and artwork. "*LGB* looks for honest works of short fiction. Anything with a degree of integrity is sought." Annually. Estab. 1986. Circ. 250.

Needs: Condensed/excerpted novel, feminist, gay, historical, horror, humor/satire, lesbian, literary, mainstream/contemporary, mystery/suspense, psychic/supernatural/occult, serialized novel. "Nothing religious." Publishes annual special fiction issue or anthology. Recently published work by Judson Crews, Sigmund Weiss, Allyson Shaw and Harland Ristau. Receives 2-3 unsolicited mss/month. Accepts 2-3 mss/issue; 2-3 mss/year. Publishes ms 1 year after acceptance. Publishes short shorts. Also publishes literary essays, poetry. Sometimes critiques or comments on rejected mss.

How to Contact: Query first. Should include a "nice, personal letter." Reports in 1 month. Send SASE for reply, return of ms or send a disposable copy of ms. Simultaneous, reprint and electronic submissions (modem) OK. Sample copy for $5. Reviews novels and short story collections. Send books to Drucilla B. Blood.

Payment/Terms: Pays 1 contributor's copy.

Advice: "I'm tired of boring, one-dimensional stories with mundane plots. I like true stories and interesting twists."

‡MEDUSA'S HAIRDO MAGAZINE, the magazine of modern mythology, (I), Byrd White Press, 15734 State Route 3, Catlettsburg KY 41129. (606)928-4631. E-mail: bymoor0@sac.uky.edu. Editor: Beverly Moore. Fiction Editor: Jason Chapmen. Zine: full-sized; 45 pages; plain white paper; illustrations. "We publish modern mythology—not remakes of classical myth but rather stories that seem to characterize or tell a story about your generation. To put it another way, we want quality literature that might, two centuries from now, be considered the mythology of the twentieth century." Triannually. Estab. 1995. Circ. 50.

Needs: Fantasy, horror, literary, mainstream/contemporary, mystery/suspense, regional, romance, science fiction, westerns. "No stories having to do with classical mythology, or any story containing sex, violence or profanity." Receives 50-75 unsolicited mss/month. Accepts 4-6 mss/issue; 12-20 mss/year. Publishes ms 4 months after acceptance. Recently published work by Steve Eller, Deidra Cox and Gary Every. Length: 2,500 words average; 4,000 words maximum. Publishes short shorts. Also publishes poetry. Always critiques or comments on rejected mss. Sponsors contest; send SASE for information.

How to Contact: Send complete ms with a "personal, informal cover letter—we want to get to know our writers!" Include 1-paragraph bio. Reports in 2 weeks on queries; 1 month on mss. SASE for reply or send a disposable copy of ms. Simultaneous submissions, reprints and electronic submissions OK. "E-mail submissions strongly encouraged!" Sample copy for $4.50. Fiction guidelines for #10 SASE.

Payment/Terms: Pays $2-5 on publication and 1 contributor's copy; additional copies for $4.50. Acquires first North American serial rights or one-time rights (if reprint).

Advice: Looks for "good characterization, readability and depth. Let us know you're a beginner! It's no detriment to you—we want to help."

THE MONTHLY INDEPENDENT TRIBUNE TIMES JOURNAL POST GAZETTE NEWS CHRONICLE BULLETIN, The Magazine to Which No Superlatives Apply, (I), 80 Fairlawn Dr., Berkeley CA 94708-2106. Editor: T.S. Child. Fiction Editor: Denver Tucson. Zine: 5½×8; 8 pages; 60 lb. paper; 60 lb. cover; illustrations and photographs. "In the past, we have published short stories, short short stories, the world's shortest story, plays, game show transcriptions, pictures made of words, teeny-weeny novelinis." Published irregularly. Estab. 1983. Circ. 500.

Needs: Adventure, experimental, humor/satire, mystery/suspense (amateur sleuth, private eye), psychic/supernatural/occult. "If it's serious, literary, perfect, well-done or elegant, we don't want it. If it's bizarre, unclassifiable, funny, cryptic or original, we might." Nothing "pretentious; important; meaningful; honest." Receives 20 unsolicited mss/month. Accepts 3-4 mss/issue. Accepted manuscripts published in next issue. Length: 400 words preferred; 1,200 words maximum. Publishes short shorts. Length: 400 words. Sometimes critiques rejected mss.

How to Contact: Send complete ms with cover letter. Reports in 1 month. SASE. "May" accept simultaneous submissions. Sample copy for 50¢, and SASE.

Payment/Terms: Pays subscription (2 issues); 3 contributor's copies. Not copyrighted.

Advice: "First of all, work must be *short*—1,200 words maximum, but the shorter the better. It must make me either laugh or scream or scratch my head, or all three. Things that are slightly humorous, or written with any kind of audience in mind are returned. We want writing that is spontaneous, unconscious, boundary-free. If you can think of another magazine that might publish your story, send it to them, not us. Send us your worst, weirdest stories, the ones you're too embarrassed to send anywhere else."

NOCTURNAL ECSTASY, Vampire Coven, (I, II, IV), Nocturnal Productions, P.O. Box 147, Palos Heights IL 60463-0147. E-mail: vampyr4@aol.com. Editor: Darlene Daniels. Zine: 8½×11; 75 pages; 20 lb. white paper; glossy cover; illustrations and photos. "We publish material on vampires, music, movies, gothic esoteria, erotica, horror, sado-masochism." Triannually. Estab. 1990. Circ. 10,000.

Needs: Vampire related: adventure, erotica, experimental, gay, horror, humor/satire, lesbian, mystery/suspense (romantic suspense), psychic/supernatural/occult; romance (gothic), science fiction (hard science). Plans to publish special fiction issue or anthology. Receives 100 unsolicited mss/month. Accepts 6 mss/issue; 40 mss/year. Published work by PJ Roberts, Jeffrey Stadt and Dale Hochstein. Length: 2,000 words average; 500 words minimum; 4,000 words maximum. Publishes short shorts. Also publishes literary essays, literary criticism and poetry. Sometimes critiques or comments on rejected mss.

How to Contact: Send complete ms with a cover letter. Include estimated word count and ¼-page bio. Reports in 1 month on queries; 2 months on mss. Send SASE for reply, return of ms or send a disposable copy of ms. Simultaneous, reprint and electronic submissions OK. Sample copy for $6. Fiction guidelines for $1 or 4 first-class stamps. Reviews novels and short story collections. Send books to NEVC Reviews.

Payment/Terms: No payment. Acquires one-time rights. Not copyrighted.

Advice: Looks for "originality, ability to hold reader's interest." Would like to see "more erotica, originality; no previously established characters of other authors."

‡THE #11, (I, II), P.O. Box 1064, Tallahassee FL 32302. Editor: D.F. Barrow. Zine specializing in art, writing, cartoons, poetry. Size, number of pages vary; illustrations and photos. "No themes. Anything goes: comics, art, poetry, short stories, historical essays. Philosophy: Believes in the First Amendment." Triannually. Estab. 1995. Circ. 300.

Needs: Condensed/excerpted novel, erotica, experimental, historical (general), humor/satire, mystery/suspense (police procedural). Receives 1-2 unsolicited mss/month. Publishes ms within 2 months after acceptance. Recently published work by D.F. Barrow, Lonnie Cormican, Frances Barrow, Paul Centra and Joe Flynn. Length: approximately 500 words. Publishes short shorts. Also publishes poetry.

How to Contact: Send complete ms with a cover letter. Include bio. Reports in 1 month on queries; 2 months on mss. Send SASE for reply, return of ms or send a disposable copy of ms. Simultaneous and reprint sumissions OK. Sample copy for $2 and 5½×8½ SAE.

Payment/Terms: Pays 5 contributor's copies; additional copies for $2. Acquires one-time rights.

Advice: "Manuscripts should be typed and photocopiable. Go for it, baby!"

NUTHOUSE, Essays, Stories and Other Amusements, (II), Twin Rivers Press, P.O. Box 119, Ellenton FL 34222. E-mail: nuthous499@aol.com. Editor: D.A. White. Zine: digest-sized; 12-16 pages; bond paper; illustrations and photos. "Humor of all genres for an adult readership that is not easily offended." Published every 6 weeks. Estab. 1993. Circ. 100.

Needs: Humor/satire: erotica, experimental, fantasy, feminist, historical (general), horror, literary, mainstream/contemporary, mystery/suspense, psychic/supernatural/occult, romance, science fiction and westerns. Plans annual "Halloween Party" issue featuring humorous verse and fiction with a horror theme. Receives 12-30 unsolicited mss/month. Accepts 3-5 mss/issue; 30 mss/year. Publishes ms 6-12 months after acceptance. Recently published work by Ken Rand, Mark McLaughlin, Gerard Daniel Houarner, Thomas J. Misuraca, A.W. DeAnnuntis, James V. Burchill, Mike Stanley, Mel Tharp, Mike Brotherton and Don Hornbostel. Length: 500 words average; 100 words minimum; 1,000 words maximum. Publishes short shorts. Length: 100-250 words. Also publishes literary essays, literary criticism and poetry. Often critiques or comments on rejected mss.

How to Contact: Send complete ms with a cover letter. Include estimated word count, bio (paragraph) and list of publications. Reports in 2-4 weeks on mss. SASE for return of ms or send disposable copy of ms. Simultaneous and reprint submissions OK. Sample copy for $1 (payable to Twin Rivers Press). Fiction guidelines for #10 SASE.

Payment/Terms: Pays 1 contributor's copy. Acquires one-time rights. Not copyrighted.

Advice: Looks for "laugh-out-loud prose. Strive for original ideas; read the great humorists—Saki, Woody Allen, Robert Benchley, Garrison Keillor, John Irving—and learn from them. We are turned off by sophomoric attempts at humor built on a single, tired, overworked gag or pun; give us a story with a beginning, middle and end."

‡OF UNICORNS AND SPACE STATIONS, (I, II, IV), %Gene Davis, P.O. Box 97, Bountiful UT 84011-0097. Editor: Gene Davis. Zine: 5½×8½; 60 pages; 20 lb. white paper; card cover stock; illustrations. "Positive SF&F is sought. It should be for adults, though graphic sex, violence and offensive language are not considered." Quarterly. Estab. 1994. Circ. 100.

Needs: Fantasy (science fantasy, sword and sorcery), science fiction (hard science, soft/sociological, utopian). Wants "clear writing that is easy to follow." Receives 20 unsolicited mss/month. Accepts 6-9 mss/issue; approximtely 32 mss/year. Publishes ms 6-12 months after acceptance. Recently published work by Laura J. Underwood, Vaseleos Garson and John Grey. Length: 3,000 words average. Publishes short shorts. Also publishes poetry. Sometimes critiques or comments on rejected mss.

How to Contact: Send complete ms with a cover letter. Include estimated word count, bio (75 words or less) and writer's classification of the piece (science fiction, fiction, poetry). Reports in 3 months. Send SASE for reply, return of ms or send a disposable copy of ms. Simultaneous, reprint and electronic (disk only) submissions OK. Sample copy for $3.50. Fiction guidelines for #10 SASE.

Payment/Terms: Pays 1 contributor's copy; additional copies for $3.50. Acquires one-time rights.

Advice: "Keep trying. It may take several tries to get published."

OFFICE NUMBER ONE, (I, II), 2111 Quarry Rd., Austin TX 78703. E-mail: onocdingus@aol.com. Editor: Carlos B. Dingus. Zine: 8½×11; 12 pages; 60 lb. standard paper; b&w illustrations and photos. "I look for short stories, imaginary news stories or essays (under 400 words) that can put a reader on edge—but *not* because of profanity or obscenity, rather because the story serves to jolt the reader away from a consensus view of the world." Quarterly zine specializing in satire, humor and views from alternate realities. Estab. 1989. Circ. 1,000.

Needs: Fictional news articles, experimental, fantasy, horror, humor/satire, literary, psychic/supernatural/occult, also fictional reviews. Limericks about fishing and fish, harvests & dogs. Receives 6 unsolicited mss/month. Buys 1-3 mss/issue; 6 mss/year. Publishes ms 6-12 months after acceptance. Length: 400 words maximum, 150 best. Also publishes literary essays and poetry. Sometimes critiques or comments on rejected mss if requested.

How to Contact: Send complete ms with optional cover letter. Should include estimated word count and summary of article and intent ("How does this reach who?") with submission. Reports in 4-6 weeks on mss. Send SASE for reply, return of ms or send disposable copy of ms. Will consider simultaneous submissions, reprints. Sample copy for $2 with SAE and 3 first-class stamps. Fiction guidelines for SASE.

Payment/Terms: Pays 1 contributor's copy. Additional copies for $1 plus postage. Acquires one-time rights.

CHECK THE CATEGORY INDEXES, located at the back of the book, for publishers interested in specific fiction subjects.

Advice: "Clean writing, no unnecessary words, perfect word choice, clear presentation. Express *one* good idea. Write for an audience that you can identify. Be able to say why you write what you write. I'm planning to publish more *shorter* fiction. I plan to be more up-beat and to focus on a journalistic style—but I will broaden what can be accomplished within this style."

ONCE UPON A WORLD, (IV), 646 W. Fleming Dr., Nineveh IN 46164. Editor: Emily Alward. Zine: 8½×11; 80-100 pages; white paper; card stock cover; pen & ink illustrations. "A science fiction and fantasy zine with emphasis on alternate-world cultures and stories of idea, character and interaction. Also publishes book reviews and poems for an adult audience, primarily readers of science fiction and fantasy. We're known for science fiction and fantasy stories with excellent wordbuilding and a humanistic emphasis." Annually. Estab. 1988. Circ. 100.
- The science fiction and fantasy published in *Once Upon a World* tends to be "centered on the human element" and explores the individual in society.
Needs: Fantasy, science fiction. No realistic "stories in contemporary settings"; horror; stories using Star Trek or other media characters; stories with completely negative endings." Upcoming theme: "Love Stories Set in Science Fiction or Fantasy Worlds" (Spring 1997). List of upcoming themes available for SASE. Receives 20 unsolicited mss/month. Accepts 8-12 mss/issue; per year "varies, depending on backlog." Publishes ms from 2 months to 1½ years after acceptance. Recently published work by Patricia Mathews, Victor Gombos, Bruce Olsen and Robyn McGrew. Length: 3,000 words average; 400 words minimum; 10,000 words maximum. Publishes short shorts. Also publishes poetry. Sometimes critiques rejected mss and recommends other markets.
How to Contact: Send complete manuscript. Reports in 2-4 weeks on queries; 2-16 weeks on mss. SASE. "Reluctantly" accepts simultaneous submissions, if noted. Sample copy for $8.50. Make checks payable to Emily Alward. Fiction guidelines for #10 SASE. Reviews novels and short story collections.
Payment/Terms: Pays contributor's copies. Acquires first rights. "Stories copyrighted in author's name; copyrights not registered."
Advice: "Create your own unique universe, and then show its texture and how it 'works' in the story. This is a good way to try out a world that you're building for a novel. But, don't forget to also give us interesting characters with believable problems."

OTISIAN DIRECTORY, (II), IGHF, P.O. Box 390783, Cambridge MA 02139-0783. (617)441-0904. E-mail: ighf@tiac.net. Editor: Jeff Stevens. Zine: 8½×11; 40 pages; 20 lb. bond paper; 50 lb. bond cover; illustrations and photos. "*Otisian Directory* is an alternative publication—mostly reviews but with the occasional piece of art/fiction/articles. Anything outside the mainstream will be considered." Quarterly. Estab. 1988. Circ. 500.
Needs: Condensed/excerpted novel, ethnic/multicultural, experimental, fantasy, feminist, gay, historical, humor/satire, lesbian, literary, psychic/supernatural/occult, regional, religious/inspirational, romance (gothic), science fiction, serialized novel, translations. List of upcoming themes available for SASE. Plans special fiction issue or anthology. Receives 5 unsolicited mss/month. Accepts 1 ms/issue; 6 mss/year. Publishes ms 3 months after acceptance. Publishes short shorts. Also publishes literary essays, literary criticism and poetry. Always critiques or comments on rejected ms.
How to Contact: Send complete ms with a cover letter. Should include 1 paragraph bio and list of publications. Reports in 2 months. Send SASE for reply, return of ms or send a disposable copy of ms. Simultaneous, reprint and electronic submissions OK. Sample copy for $5. Reviews novels and short story collections.
Payment/Terms: Pays 2 contributor's copies. Acquires one-time rights.
Advice: "Beginning writers should feel unfettered by the wishes of editors. Try me."

‡**OUTER DARKNESS, Where Nightmares Roam Unleashed, (I, II)**, Rising Star, 1312 N. Delaware Place, Tulsa OK 74110. (918)832-1246. Editors: Dennis Kirk and Keith Stayer. Zine: 8½×5½; 60-80 pages; 20 lb. paper; 60 lb. card stock cover; illustrations. Specializes in imaginative literature. "Variety is something we strive for in *Outer Darkness*. In each issue we present readers with great tales of science and horror along with poetry, artwork, an ongoing column by Illinois author L.P. Van Ness, humorous editorials and cartoons. We seek to provide readers with a magazine which, overall, is fun to read." Quarterly. Estab. 1994. Circ. 500.
Needs: Fantasy (science), horror, mystery/suspense (with horror slant), psychic/supernatural/occult, romance (gothic), science fiction (hard science, soft/sociological). "We do not publish works with children in sexual situations and graphic language should be kept to a minimum." Upcoming themes: "Darker Side of Outer Darkness"; "Fallen Angels"; "Mythical Creatures." Receives 50-75 unsolicited mss/month. Accepts 7-9 mss/issue; 20-50 mss/year. Recently published work by Gene Kokayo, Sherrie Brown, D.F. Lewis, Deborah Hunt and John Rosenman. Length: 3,000 words average; 1,000 words minimum; 5,000 words maximum. Also publishes literary essays and poetry. Always critiques or comments on rejected mss.
How to Contact: Send complete ms with a cover letter. Include estimated word count, 50- to 75-word bio, list of publications and "any awards, honors you have received." Reports in 1 week on

queries; 4-6 weeks on mss. Send SASE for reply, return of ms or send a disposable copy of ms. Simultaneous submissions and reprints OK. Sample copy for $4.50. Fiction guidelines for #10 SASE. **Payment/Terms:** Pays 2 contributor's copies for fiction, 1 for poetry and art; additional copies $2.75. Pays on publication. Acquires one-time rights.
Advice: "We want stories which keep the reader literally glued to his chair. Strong characterization, well-developed plots and twist/surprise endings are also what we seek in manuscripts. Read the works of Robert Bloch, Richard Matheson, Ray Bradbury and other authors from the 'Golden Era' of horror and science fiction. But *don't* try to mimic their styles. Write the way you write best. We publish a lot of work similar to those found in *Weird Tales* and *The Twilight Zone*. So, while we obviously seek a certain degree of originality, we also enjoy reading solid, traditional works. If possible, study a sample copy. If the price of current issues is beyond your budget, back issues may be available for less."

PABLO LENNIS, The Magazine of Science Fiction, Fantasy and Fact, (I, II, IV), Etaoin Shrolu Press, Fandom House, 30 N. 19th St., Lafayette IN 47904. Editor: John Thiel. Zine: 8½×11; 26 pages; standard stock; illustrations and "occasional" photos. "Science fiction, fantasy, science, research and mystic for scientists and science fiction and fantasy appreciators." Monthly.
Needs: Fantasy, science fiction. Receives 50 unsolicited mss/year. Accepts 4 mss/issue; 48 mss/year. Publishes ms 4 months after acceptance. Recently published work by George McCarty, Frances Taira and Adam Selzer. Published new writers within the last year. Length: 1,500 words average; 3,000 words maximum. Also publishes literary criticism, poetry. Occasionally critiques rejected mss and recommends other markets.
How to Contact: "Method of submission is author's choice but he might prefer to query. No self-statement is necessary." No simultaneous submissions. Reports in 2 weeks. Does not accept computer printouts.
Payment/Terms: Pays 1 contributor's copy. Publication not copyrighted.
Advice: "I have taboos against unpleasant and offensive language and want material which is morally or otherwise elevating to the reader. I prefer an optimistic approach, and favor fine writing. With a good structure dealt with intelligently underlying this, you have the kind of story I like. I prefer stories that have something to say to those which have something to report."

‡PANOPTICON, (I, II), Panopticon Press, 774 Forest Ave., #3, Portland ME 04101. (207)879-7032. E-mail: jmoser41@portland.maine.edu. Editor: J. Moser. Zine specializing in "rants, fiction and poetry": 5×7; 20-30 pages; illustrations and photos. "The major philosophy of *Panopticon*, named after Jeremy Bentham's prison model, is that all art and all creation of art is affected by the possibility of being seen. *Panopticon* strives for defective wakefulness through the destructive arrangement of words and images. Any material, so long as intelligent thought has gone into it, will be considered for publication." Quarterly. Estab. 1995. Circ. 500.
Needs: Erotica, experimental, fantasy (science fantasy), feminist, gay, horror, humor/satire, lesbian, literary, psychic/supernatural/occult, science fiction (soft/sociological). Receives 15-20 unsolicited mss/month. Accepts 1 mss/issue; 4-5 mss/year. Publishes ms in next issue after acceptance. Recently published work by Mike Conlon, J. Moser and Olga St. Vincent. Length: 500-1000 words average; 1 word minimum; 2,500 words maximum. Publishes short shorts. Also publishes literary essays, literary criticism and poetry. Always critiques or comments on rejected mss.
How to Contact: Send complete ms with a cover letter. Writers should include "a friendly inquiry that lets me know why they write." Reports in 2 weeks on queries; 1 month on mss. SASE. Simultaneous, reprint and electronic (disk or modem) submissions OK. Sample copy for $1; 5×7 SAE and 2 first-class stamps. Reviews novels and short story collections. "There is a special review section. Indicate it is for review rather than a submission."
Payment/Terms: Pays free subscription to magazine and 2 contributor's copies; additional copies for $1. All rights revert back to the author.
Advice: "Tight, unique and mind-reeling writing is best. Avoid cliches. Write about 'things' in a new way. Avoid falling into the traps of genre writing. Mix and match genres and literary styles to create new ones. Make your language do things for you—don't do things for your language."

PBW, (I, II), 130 W. Limestone, Yellow Springs OH 45387. (513)767-7416. E-mail: rianca@aol.com. Editor: Richard Freeman. Electronic disk zine: 700 pages; illustrations. "*PBW* is an experimental floppy disk and B.B. publication that 'prints' strange and 'unpublishable' in an above-ground-sense writing." Quarterly electronic zine. Featuring avant-garde fiction and poetry. Estab. 1988.
  ● *PBW* is an electronic zine which can be read using MacWrite (Mac disk) or available over modem on BBS. Write for details.
Needs: Erotica, experimental, gay, lesbian, literary. No "conventional fiction of any kind." Receives 3 unsolicited mss/month. Accepts 40 mss/issue; 160 mss/year. Publishes ms within 3 months after acceptance. Recently published work by Vern Frazer, Arthur Knight and Dirk Van Nouhuys. Length: open. Publishes short shorts and novels in chapters. Publishes literary essays, literary criticisms and poetry. Always critiques or comments on rejected mss.

INSIDER REPORT

Zines: a great way to "get your words out there"

Seth Friedman, publisher of *Factsheet Five* which has become known as the "bible" of the zine community, defines a zine as "a small, handmade, amateur publication done purely out of passion, rarely making a profit or breaking even. Generally people don't get paid for the work they send to zines. Many times even the publisher is losing money."

Seth Friedman

Simply put, people who publish and send submissions to zines are more interested in sharing their writing or their views than in making money. "Zines are a good place for beginning writers to hone their chops," says Friedman. "They offer writers the chance to explore their own writing." And, he says, if they are so inclined, "writers can start their own zine and see what is really involved in publishing and get a feel for what happens when they submit their work to other magazines.

"I started my own zine, *Food for Thought*, to share my writing with my friends without the restrictions involved when you submit to other publications." Like most zines, Friedman's publication is a direct reflection of his interests. He describes it as a "political, personal, food zine."

It was *Factsheet Five*, started by Mike Gunderloy in the early 1980s and acquired by Friedman in 1992, that inspired Friedman to try his hand at publishing. When *Factsheet Five* was launched, many zines were typed and reproduced on ditto machines or photocopiers and handed out to a few select friends of the publisher. Once computers became more accessible, there was an explosion of zines. It was then that *Factsheet Five* became and remains one of the few sources of information on zines and the primary resource for the growing community of writers and publishers involved with them.

Published four to five times a year, *Factsheet Five* contains hundreds of short reviews of zines divided into more than 20 categories. It also includes columns on a wide variety of topics as well as reviews of self-published books, independently-produced music and spoken-word recordings, catalogs and other items the editors find interesting. The bulk of the reviews are done by Friedman and associate Chris Becker, but the magazine has four other editors and a staff of ten regular reviewers. Sometimes Friedman includes reviews by 20 different people.

Most of the zines reviewed in *Factsheet Five* are specialized and cover everything from UFO sightings to professional dishwashing to beer brewing. In fact, anything can be a subject for a zine. In addition to science fiction, food and

INSIDER REPORT, *continued*

politics, Friedman groups zines into categories titled "quirky," "medley," "fringe" and "editor's choice." Most of the zines interested in fiction submissions can be found in the "art and letters" section, a grouping of around 50 small literary journals. Some take only poetry or artwork, but most also include short fiction.

When looking for publication in a zine, it's good to establish a relationship with the editors first. Although *Factsheet Five* does a good job of describing the publications they review, it's best to obtain copies of those that interest you. It's an unwritten rule in the zine community that writers and editors support each other. Most publications are available for a very small fee and some publishers are open to trading zines.

Since space in most zines is at a premium, Friedman says, "Write short in the zine world. There are some areas for longer stories, but you are more apt to get published with a concise, short piece than a long one."

About one-third of all print zines are now also available in electronic format. Friedman calls these "e-zines." Some publishers have also ventured onto the Internet and World Wide Web and have developed their own web pages.

"I think web pages are an outgrowth of the same character and style found in zines," says Friedman. "Many print zines began with an e-mail address and later found it easy to transport their zines into electronic format. People who had been considering publishing a zine for a long time have found it easier to establish a web page. In one way this is a good thing—a lot more people are exploring publishing, but it's also bad because the quality of what's out there may go down."

If you're interested in starting your own zine, Friedman says, "you should become familiar with what is being published. Pick up *Factsheet Five* to see what subjects and interests have been put into the zine format. There are books out there on zines, but I don't recommend them. If people follow a formula, they tend to create a formula zine. Most of the really good zines were created by trial and error."

For writers interested in contributing to zines, Friedman says, "Start small and don't expect to be paid up front. But if you want to make your writing accessible to people, zines are a great way to get your words out there."

—*Robin Gee*

How to Contact: Send complete ms with a cover letter. Reports in 2 weeks. Send SASE for reply, return of ms or send a disposable copy of ms. Simultaneous, reprint and electronic (Mac or modem) submissions OK. Sample copy for $2. Reviews novels and short story collections.
Payment/Terms: Pays 1 contributor's copy. All rights revert back to author. Not copyrighted.

PEACE MAGAZINE, (I, II, IV), 2753 E. Broadway, #101-1969, Mesa AZ 85204-1570. (602)817-0124. Editor: Linda James. Zine: 8½×11; 30 pages; recycled paper; illustrations and photos. Publishes material of "the 1960s—written by and for the people who were there and those who wish they were." Quarterly. Estab. 1994.
   ● The work published in *Peace Magazine* tends to be written in first-person. The editor would like to see more stories about the women's movement, civil rights and music.
Needs: 1960s oriented: condensed/excerpted novel, feminist; all issues dealing with the 1960s. Receives 3-10 unsolicited mss/month. Accepts 5-10 mss/issue; 40-50 mss/year. Publishes ms 6-12 months after acceptance. Recently published work by Eric Lief Davin, George Fallon, B. Merrill Wilder and

Sonya Susan. Length: 2,000 words average; 3,500 words maximum. Publishes short shorts. Sometimes critiques or comments on rejected mss.

How to Contact: Send complete ms with a cover letter. Include estimated word count and 50-word bio. Reports in 2 months on queries, 3-6 months on mss. Send SASE for reply, return of ms or send a disposable copy of ms. Simultaneous submissions, reprint and electronic submissions (Macintosh format) OK. Sample copy for $4 and 9 × 12 SASE. Fiction guidelines for SASE.

Payment/Terms: Pays 1-year subscription and additional copies (as available) of issue in which author appears. Acquires one-time rights. Sends galleys to author time permitting.

Advice: "We look for style and voice that says, 'I was there, I saw and I did.' We want to feel your passion, anger, commitment or indignation. You probably should be over 40 and lived through the '60s—or be a history buff. We are wide open to all styles, voices and opinions of the 1960s and what they meant to you."

PEOPLENET DISABILITY DATENET HOME PAGE, "Where People Meet People," (IV), Box 897, Levittown NY 11756. (516)579-4043. E-mail: mauro@chelsea.ios.com. Editor: Robert Mauro. Online zine at http://chelsea.IOS.com/~Mauro. "Romance stories featuring disabled characters." Estab. 1995.

Needs: Romance, contemporary and disabled. Main character must be disabled. Upcoming theme: "Marriage between disabled and non-disabled." Accepts 3 mss/year. Publishes immediately after acceptance. Length: 750 words. Publishes short shorts. Length: 500 words. Also publishes poetry. Especially looking for book reviews on books dealing with disabled persons and sexuality.

How to Contact: Send complete ms by e-mail. No simultaneous submissions. Fiction guidelines online.

Payment/Terms: Acquires first rights.

Advice: "We are looking for romance stories of under 1,000 words on romance with a disabled man or woman as the main character. No sob stories or 'super crip' stories. Just realistic romance. No porn. Love, respect, trust, understanding and acceptance are what I want."

PICA, (I, II), 165 N. Ashbury Ave., Bolingbrook IL 60440. E-mail: greenli@aol.com. Editor: Lisa Green. Zine: 5½ × 8½; 30-60 pages; 24 lb. paper; 30-38 lb. cover stock. "*Pica* attempts to publish the best of avant-garde fiction, essays and poetry. Our audience is generally academic: passionate about the language." Triannually. Estab. 1995. Circ. 100.

Needs: Condensed/excerpted novel, experimental, feminist, gay, humor/satire, lesbian, literary. "No pornography, nothing 'fluffy,' and nothing you would see published in any magazine you'd find in the checkout aisle at the grocery store." Receives 30 unsolicited mss/month. Accepts 5 mss/issue; 30 mss/ year. Publishes ms 6-8 months after acceptance. Recently published work by Michael David Martin, David Moses Fruchter and Robyn Parnell. Length: 10,000 words maximum. Publishes short shorts. Also publishes literary essays, literary criticism and poetry. Often critiques or comments on rejected mss.

How to Contact: Send complete ms. "Only include a cover letter if there is something you *really* need to tell us." Reports in 2 months on mss. Send SASE for return of ms. Simultaneous, reprint and electronic (Word 7.0 compatible disk) submissions OK. Sample copy for $3. Fiction guidelines for SASE.

Payment/Terms: Pays 3 contributor's copies; additional copies for $1. Acquires one-time rights.

Advice: "We are looking for writers with a broad base of knowledge. We love variety and wit, passion and opinion. We adore works that seek out ambiguity and exploit detail. And please read the magazine." The most common reason for rejections: inappropriate style. Needs more "good fiction by women!"

‡PULP: A FICTION MAGAZINE, Lurid Tales of Adventure, (I), Ramrod Productions, P.O. Box 548, Hermosa Beach CA 90254. (310)376-5959. Editor: Clancy O'Hara. Zine: digest size; 50 pages; standard 20 lb. paper; illustrations. Specializes in "genre fiction (mainly crime/horror) with an unusual spin—work that transcends the genre's humble origins." Bimonthly. Estab. 1995. Circ. 100.

• *Pulp* received an honorable mention in the *Year's Best Fantasy and Horror* and the most Human Editor Award from Green Country Ruffriters.

Needs: Fantasy (sword and sorcery), horror, mystery/suspense (private eye/hardboiled), science fiction (hard science, soft/sociological). Receives 20-50 unsolicited mss/month. Accepts 3 mss/issue; 18 mss/ year. Publishes ms within 2 months after acceptance. Recently published work by Don D'Ammassa, Kathy Watts, Rondi Springer, Aaron Larson, Walter Rhoades and R.T. Lawton. Length: 2,000 words average; 100 words minimum; 3,000 words maximum. Publishes short shorts. Also publishes literary criticism. Sometimes critiques or comments on rejected mss.

How to Contact: Send complete ms with cover letter. Include estimated word count, 1-paragraph bio, Social Security number and list of publications. Reports in 3 months on queries; 6 months on mss. SASE for reply or send a disposable copy of ms. Simultaneous submissions OK. Sample copy for $5. Reviews novels and short story collections.

Payment/Terms: Pays ½¢-1¢/word on publication and 2 contributor's copies; additional copies for $5. Acquires first North American serial rights.
Advice: "Original dialogue and real-sounding, quirky characters. I show as much interest in writers' stories as they show in my magazine. i.e., send for guidelines and read a sample copy. Shorter work has a better chance of publication."

RALPH'S REVIEW, (I), RC Publications, 97 Delaware Ave., Albany NY 12202-1333. (518)434-0512. Editor: Ralph Cornell. Zine: 8½×11; 20-35 pages; 20 lb. bond paper and cover. "To let as many writers as possible get a chance to publish their works, fantasy, sci-fi, horror, poetry." Monthly. Estab. 1988. Circ. 100.
Needs: Adventure, fantasy (children's fantasy, science fantasy), horror, humor/satire, literary, psychic/supernatural/occult, romance (futuristic/time travel), science fiction, young adult/teen (adventure, horror, science fiction), stamp collecting, dinosaurs, environmental, fishing. No extreme violence, racial, gay/lesbian/x-rated. Publishes annual special fiction issue or anthology. Receives 10-15 unsolicited mss/month. Accepts 1-2 mss/issue; 12-15 mss/year. Publishes ms 1-2 months after acceptance. Recently published work by Dr. Ralph Pray, Ralph Cornell Kim Laico, John Binns (England) and John Charles Galvin. Length: 500-1,000 words average; 50 words minimum; 2,000 words maximum. Publishes short shorts. Also publishes poetry. Sometimes critiques or comments on rejected mss.
How to Contact: Send complete ms with a cover letter. Include 1-paragraph bio and list of publications. Reports in 1-2 weeks on queries; 1-2 months on mss. Send SASE for reply, return of ms or send a disposable copy of ms. Simultaneous and reprint submissions OK. Sample copy for $2, 9×12 SAE and 5 first-class stamps. Fiction guidelines for #10 SASE. Reviews novels or short story collections.
Payment/Terms: Pays 2 contributor's copies; additional copies for $1. Acquires first North American serial rights.
Advice: Looks for manuscripts "that start out active and continue to grow until you go 'Ahh!' at the end. Something I've never read before. Make sure spelling is correct. Content is crisp and active. Characters are believable."

S.L.U.G.FEST, LTD., A Magazine of Free Expression, (I), SF, Ltd., P.O. Box 1238, Simponville SC 29681-1238. (864)297-4009. Fax: (864)297-0578. Editor: M.T. Nowak. Fiction Editor: M. Tatlow. Zine: 8½×11; 70 pages; 20 lb. paper; 30 lb. cover stock; illustrations. "We are dedicated to publishing the best poetry and fiction we can find from writers who have yet to be discovered." Quarterly. Estab. 1991. Circ. 1,000.
Needs: Adventure, ethnic/multicultural, experimental, feminist, historical, horror, humor/satire, literary, mainstream/contemporary, regional, science fiction (hard science/soft sociological), serialized novel. "No poor writing." Receives 30 unsolicited mss/month. Accepts 5-10 mss/issue; 20-40 mss/year. Publishes mss 3 months after acceptance. Length: 7,000-10,000 words preferred. Publishes short shorts. Also publishes literary essays, literary criticism and poetry. Often critiques and comments on rejected mss.
How to Contact: Send complete ms with a cover letter. Include estimated word count. Reports in 5 weeks on queries; 5 weeks on mss. Send SASE for reply, return of ms or send a disposable copy of ms. Simultaneous, reprint and electronic submissions OK. Sample copy for $5. Fiction guidelines free. Reviews novels and short story collections.
Payment/Terms: Pays 1 contributor's copy. Rights revert to author upon publication.
Advice: "We look for humor, quality of imagery. Get our interest."

‡SATELLITE FICTION, (I), Box 107, Truth or Consequences NM 87901. Editor: Willie Ettinger. Zine: 8½×11; 35 pages; white bond paper; 30 lb. cover stock; illustrations; photos. Theme is "overthrow and upheaval in American society." Quarterly. Estab. 1995. Circ. 20.
Needs: Erotica, science fiction (psychological). Receives 1-2 unsolicited mss/month. Publishes mss in next issue after acceptance. Agented fiction 10%. "Each issue is devoted to Philip K. Dick and J.G. Ballard, my two favorite *satellite fiction* writers." Length: 20,000 words average. Publishes short shorts.
How to Contact: Send complete ms with a cover letter. Include "a nice note!" Reports in 1 week on queries and mss. Send SASE for reply, return of ms or send a disposable copy of ms. Simultaneous submissions OK. Sample copy for $3. Reviews novels and short story collections.
Payment/Terms: Pays free subscription to the magazine on acceptance. Not copyrighted.
Advice: Looks for "sincere, 'felt' writing. Write and write, then send! I prefer the Dick-Ballard scheme of things—atmosphere and industrial psychology."

✦SIDETREKKED, (I, IV), Science Fiction London, Unit 78, 320 Westminster, London, Ontario Canada. (519)434-9588. E-mail: bnw@ftn.net. Editor: James Jarvis. Editors change by election. Zine: 7×8½; 36-40 pages; bond paper; b&w drawings, halftone photographs. "Science fiction for science fiction readers, mostly adults." Quarterly. Estab. 1980. Circ. 200.

Needs: Fantasy, science fiction (hard science, soft/sociological). "We will consider any story with a science fictional slant. Because science fiction tends to be all-embracing, that could include horror, humor/satire, romance, suspense, feminist, gay, ethnic, etc.—yes, even western—but the science fiction classification must be met, usually by setting the story in a plausible, futuristic universe." Receives 3-5 unsolicited fiction mss/month. Accepts 3-8 mss/issue. Time between acceptance and publication varies. Published work by Joe Beliveau and Dave Seburn. Length: 1,000-5,000 words preferred. "No hard-and-fast rules, but we can't accommodate novelettes or novellas." Publishes short shorts. Critiques or comments on rejected mss, if requested by the author. Recommends other markets on occasion.

How to Contact: Send complete ms with cover letter. No simultaneous submissions. Electronic submissions OK. Reports in 3 weeks on queries; in 1 month on mss. SASE. Sample copy for $2 (Canadian) and 9×10 SAE.

Payment/Terms: Pays in contributor's copies. Acquires first North American serial rights.

Advice: "We are more forgiving than most fiction markets and we try to work with new writers. What makes us want to work with a writer is some suggestion that he or she understands what makes a good story. What makes a manuscript stand out? Tell a good story. The secondary things are fixable if the story is there, but if it is not, no amount of tinkering can fix it."

‡**SINK FULL OF DISHES, (I, II),** P.O. Box 39500, St. Louis MO 63139-8500. Editor: Ditch Cat. Zine: 8½×11; 28 pages; 20 lb. bond paper; 40 lb. bond cover stock; illustrations; occasional photos. "*Sink Full of Dishes* seeks to offer a conglomeration of artistic and literary styles for the liberally-minded reader, thus the name. There are no taboo subjects, styles or language restraints, except for outright pornography. Honest and earthy writing gains favor. Quarterly. Estab. 1994. Circ. 200.

Needs: Adventure, erotica, ethnic/multicultural, experimental, fantasy (science), feminist, gay, historical, horror, humor/satire, lesbian, literary, mainstream/contemporary, mystery/suspense (amateur sleuth, cozy, private eye/hardboiled), psychic/supernatural/occult, regional, romance (contemporary, futuristic/time travel), science fiction (hard science, soft/sociological), westerns (frontier, traditional), young adult/teen (adventure, horror, mystery, romance, science fiction, western), confessional. Receives 10 unsolicited mss/month. Accepts 4-8 mss/issue; 16-32 mss/year. Publishes ms 3-9 months after acceptance. Recently published work by David Castleman, Alan Catlin, Ben Ohmart, Errol Miller and Angie McGregor. Length: 1,000 words average; 200 words minimum; 5,000 words maximum. Publishes short shorts. Also publishes poetry. Often critiques or comments on rejected mss.

How to Contact: Send complete ms with cover letter. Reports in 3 weeks on queries; 2 months on mss. Send a disposable copy of ms. Simultaneous, reprints and electronic (disk) submissions OK. Sample copy for $2.

Payment/Terms: Pays 1 contributor's copy; additional copies $2 for first, $1.50 for more. Acquires one-time rights.

Advice: "Writing that comes from personal experience or observation stands out, though experimental forms and imaginative writing is also favorable. Non-literary styles are encouraged, i.e. 'tell it like it is.' For beginning writers looking to be published in *Sink Full of Dishes*, forget everything you've learned in writing workshops or English classes. Let yourself go and say what's on your mind or in your heart. Avoid pretentiousness at all costs, and don't worry about form, language, or style."

‡**SORCEROUS MAGAZINE, Sword & Sorcery, Epic Fantasy, (I, IV),** Sorcerous Publications, 7325 Palmer House Dr., Sacramento CA 95828-4026. (916)399-1272. Editor: Rebecca Treadway. Zine: digest size; 60-70 pages; 20 lb. bond paper; color-laser cover stock; illustrations. Specializes in sword & sorcery and medieval renaissance-based fantasy, heroic fantasy, gritty fantasy, adventure, epic fantasy and dark fantasy. "Please note that I *do not* consider dark fantasy to be synonymous with vampires or Gothic themes; rather, I view it as fantasy with sinister, brutally realistic backgrounds and plots." Triannually. Estab. 1994. Circ. 200.

Needs: Fantasy (sword and sorcery, epic). "No parody, short shorts, romance, science fiction or hybrid genres such as fantasy westerns and urban fantasy." Receives 20-30 unsolicited mss/month. Accepts 7-8 mss/issue; 24-30 mss/year. Publishes 3-6 months after acceptance. Recently published work by L.P. Van Ness, Jim Lee, Richard Dahlstrom, Richard Novak, Bobbi Sinha, Rosemary Sullivan, Robert Collins and Timothy Elspeth. Length: 7,000 words average; 2,500 words minimum; 10,000 words maximum. Also publishes literary essays and literary criticism. Often critiques or comments on rejected mss.

How to Contact: Send complete ms with a cover letter. Include estimated word count and 1-paragraph bio. Reports in 2 weeks on queries; 1 month on mss. Send SASE for reply, return of ms or send a disposable copy of ms. Simultaneous submissions and reprints OK. Sample copy for $4. Fiction guidelines for #10 SASE. Reviews novels and short story collections.

Payment/Terms: Pays $2.50-10 on acceptance and 1-2 contributor's copies; additional copies $3. Acquires one-time rights.

Advice: "When magic is the primary focus of the tale, I notice a manuscript more than the typical 'Barbarian Adventure.' Realism, details in background and well-developed characters stand out. Read the guidelines thoroughly. This publication is very specific on this matter. If not purchasing a sample copy, be familiar with styles of authors I prefer—Tolkien, Howard, Eddings, etc."

‡STYGIAN ARTICLES, (II), 3201 Sun Lake Dr., St. Charles MO 63301-3012. (314)947-0577. E-mail: charon@i1.net. Website: http://www.i1.net/~charon/. Editor: Jeremy E. Johnson. Zine: digest-size; 60 pages; 20 lb. paper; card cover stock; illustrations and photos. "We're dedicated to publishing creative and well-executed genre works for the reader of horror, fantasy and science fiction. Contributors are treated with the respect and honesty they deserve." Quarterly. Estab. 1995. Circ. "small subscriber base."
Needs: Experimental, fantasy, horror, literary, psychic/supernatural/occult, science fiction. Receives 75 unsolicited mss/month. Accepts 7-10 mss/issue; 28-40 mss/year. Publishes ms 3 months after acceptance. Recently published work by Charlee Jacob, D.F. Lewis, A.J. Barlow and Tim Emswiler. Length: 4,000 words average; 1,000 words minimum; 8,000 words maximum. Publishes short shorts. Also publishes literary essays, literary criticism and poetry. Always critiques or comments on rejected mss.
How to Contact: Send complete ms with cover letter. Include estimated word count and 100-word bio. Send SASE for return of ms. Electronic submissions OK (query first). Sample copy for $5. Fiction guidelines for #10 SASE.
Payment/Terms: Pays ¼¢/word and 1 contributor's copy on publication. Acquires first North American serial rights.
Advice: "Fiction must be well-written and free of the many clichés which permeate most genre material. Beginning writers should work on writing well, with a dictionary, thesaurus and style manual close at hand when editing. Send out a highly polished story in standard manuscript format."

‡SYCAMORE ROOTS: THE REGIONALIST PAPERS, (II, IV), Ice Cube Press, 205 N. Front St., North Liberty IA 52317-9302. Editor: S.H. Semken. Zine: 8½×11; 8-12 pages; 60 lb. paper; illustrations and photos. "*Sycamore Roots* publishes attentive, perceptive ideas regarding regional, natural and environmental issues." Quarterly. Estab. 1994. Circ. 500.
Needs: Regional, outdoor. Receives 4 unsolicited mss/month. Accepts 1 ms/issue; 4 mss/year. Publishes ms 1-6 months after acceptance. Publishes short shorts. Also publishes essays and poetry. Usually critiques or comments on rejected ms "if it's within the ballpark of what we're looking for."
How to Contact: Query or send complete ms with SASE. Include brief bio. Reports in 3-4 weeks. Send SASE for reply, return of ms or send a disposable copy of ms. Simultaneous submissions OK. Sample copy for $1, 6×9 SAE and 2 first-class stamps. Reviews novel and short story collections.
Payment/Terms: Pays 5 contributor's copies. Acquires one-time rights.
Advice: "It is obvious, but really, you should see a copy of *Sycamore Roots* first so we both know what's going on. We may not be as big a deal as you think, and your writing may not even be close to what we mean when we say natural or environmental."

‡T.R.'S ZINE, P.O. Box 489, Milltown NJ 08850-0489. Editor: T.R. Miller. Zine: 5×8; 18 pages; bond paper; illustrations. Quarterly. Estab. 1996. Circ. 50.
Needs: Ethnic/multicultural, gay, humor/satire, lesbian, literary, mainstream/contemporary, mystery/suspense (romantic), religious/inspirational, senior citizen/retirement, sports, westerns (frontier, traditional). Upcoming themes: "Christmas," "Winter" (seasonal), "St. Patrick's Day," "Easter," "Senior Citizens." Accepts 1 ms/issue. Publishes ms in next issue after acceptance. Length: 250 words average; 50 words minimum; 500 words maximum. Also publishes literary essays, literary criticism and poetry.
How to Contact: Send complete ms with a cover letter. Include 1-page bio. Send SASE for reply or send disposable copy of ms. Simultaneous submissions and reprints OK. Sample copy for $1.
Payment/Terms: Pays 1 contributor's copy on publication. Acquires one-time rights.
Advice: Looks for "anything well written—fine use of words and descriptive writing. Each writer is looked upon by his own writing merit and not compared to others. I'd like to see more imaginative writing."

‡THE TALE SPINNER, Glasgow Publishing, (I), P.O. Box 336, Bedford IN 47421. (812)279-8863. E-mail: 103273.134.compuserve.com. Editor: Joe Glasgow. Zine: 8½×11; 32 pages; illustrations. "As a multi-genre magazine we try to give our readers a variety of their favorite genre styles." Bimonthly. Estab. 1995. Circ. 200.
Needs: Adventure, erotica, ethnic/multicultural, fantasy (science, sword and sorcery), historical, humor/satire, mystery/suspense (amateur sleuth, cozy, police procedural, private eye/hardboiled, romantic suspense), romance (contemporary, futuristic/time travel, gothic, historical), science fiction (hard science, soft/sociological), sports, westerns (frontier, traditional), young adult/teen (science fiction). Receives 60 unsolicited mss/month. Accepts 10 mss/issue; 60 mss/year. Publishes ms 6 months after acceptance. Recently published work by John B. Rosenman, Larry Tritten, Ardath Mayhar, Tom Piccirilli, Lyn McConchie, O'Neil DeNoux and Lee Paul. Length: 800 words average; 4,000 words maximum. Publishes short shorts. Length: 250-500 words. Also publishes poetry. Often critiques or comments on rejected mss.

How to Contact: Send complete ms with cover letter. Include estimated word count and 1- to 2-paragraph bio. Reports in 3 weeks on queries; 1 month on mss. Send SASE for reply, return of ms or send a disposable copy of ms. Simultaneous and reprint submissions OK. Sample copy for $3.95 and 9×12 SASE. Fiction guidelines for #10 SASE.

Payment/Terms: Pays ½¢/word minimum; 3¢/word maximum and 1 contributor's copy; additional copies $2.50. Pays on publication. Acquires first North American serial rights or one-time rights.

Advice: "The writer must give me a reason for turning the page. I like a story that gets my attention from the opening paragraphs. Read a sample issue. Write! Write! Write!"

‡THISTLE, (I, II, IV), P.O. Box 50094, Minneapolis MN 55405-0094. (612)871-3111. E-mail: thistle @iceworld.org. Editor #1: Chelsea. Editor #2: Thaylor. Zine specializing in gothic literature/art: ¼ size, 4¼×5½; 100 pages; standard photocopy paper; colored paper cover; illustrations and photos. "Our aim is to produce a zine of high literary and artistic quality, for the gothic community, and anyone who has a fascination with the darker, bleaker or romantic side of life." Semiannual to annual. Estab. 1993. Circ. 500.

Needs: Fantasy (sword and sorcery), horror, mystery/suspense (romantic suspense), psychic/supernatural/occult, romance (gothic, historical). "No poorly written cheese-goth." Receives very few mss/month. Recently published work by E. Katie Holm and Julie LaBomascus. Length: 20,000 words maximum. Publishes short shorts. Also publishes literary essays, literary criticism and poetry.

How to Contact: Send complete ms with SASE for reply, return of ms or send a disposable copy of ms. Simultaneous, reprint and electronic (IBM disk or modem) submissions OK. Sample copy for $1.50 or 5 first-class stamps. Fiction guidelines for #10 SASE. Reviews novels and short story collections. "Very biased reviews—if we like it, we review it."

Payment/Terms: Pays 1 contributor's copy; inquire about additional copies. Rights belong to author. Not copyrighted.

Advice: "Don't write about vampires, dead roses or bleeding hearts. It's trite! No graphic sex."

‡TRANSCENDENT VISIONS, (II), Toxic Evolution Press, 251 S. Olds Blvd., 84-E, Fairless Hills PA 19030-3426. (215)547-7159. Editor: David Kime. Zine: letter size; 24 pages; xerox paper; illustrations. "*Transcendent Visions* is a literary zine by and for people who have been labeled mentally ill. Our purpose is to illustrate how creative and articulate mental patients are." Quarterly. Estab. 1992. Circ. 200.

● *Transcendent Visions* has received excellent reviews in many underground publications.

Needs: Experimental, feminist, gay, humor/satire, lesbian. Especially interested in material dealing with mental illness. "I do not like stuff one would find in a mainstream publication. No porn." Receives 5 unsolicited mss/month. Accepts 7 mss/issue; 20 mss/year. Publishes ms 3-4 months after acceptance. Recently published work by Beth Greenspan, Jonathan Wayne Koerner, Peter Cogne, Steven Elroy and Paul Weihman. Length: under 10 pages typed, double-spaced. Publishes short shorts. Also publishes poetry.

How to Contact: Send complete ms with cover letter. Include half-page bio. Reports in 2 weeks on queries; 1 month on mss. Send disposable copy of ms. Simultaneous submissions and reprints OK. Sample copy for $1 and 2 first class stamps.

Payment/Terms: Pays 2 contributor's copies on publication. Acquires one-time rights.

Advice: "We like unusual stories that are quirky. Please do not go on and on about what zines you have been published in or awards you have won, etc. We just want to read your material, not know your life story."

‡THE UNKNOWN WRITER, (I, II), 5 Pothat St., Sloatsburg NY 10974. (201)666-5605. Fax: (201)666-1540. E-mail: rsidor@ix.netcom.com. Editor: D.S. Davis. Zine specializing in fiction, poetry, environmental issues: digest size; 40 pages; 24 lb. fiber paper; 80 lb. fiber cover stock; illustrations and photos. "*The Unknown Writer* is a forum for new writers and artists. Any subject matter and style goes as long as it's interesting." Triannually. Estab. 1995. Circ. 500.

Needs: Adventure, erotica, ethnic/multicultural, experimental, fantasy (science fantasy), feminist, gay, historical (general), horror, humor/satire, lesbian, literary, mainstream/contemporary, mystery/suspense, psychic/supernatural/occult, regional, sports, environmental issues. "Our zine is not really appropriate for children or young adults. We have little interest in science fiction, religious and little room for condensed or serialized novels." Receives 5 unsolicited mss/month. Accepts 3 mss/issue; 9

● **A BULLET INTRODUCES COMMENTS** by the editor of *Novel & Short Story Writer's Market* indicating special information about the listing.

mss/year. Publishes ms 3-5 months after acceptance. Recently published work by Satig Mesropian and Ben Ohmart. Length: 2,500 words average; 5,000 words maximum. Publishes short shorts. Also publishes literary essays, literary criticism and poetry.

How to Contact: Send complete ms with a cover letter. Include 100-word bio and list of publications. Reports in 2 months. Send a disposable copy of ms. Simultaneous and electronic (disk or modem) submissions OK. Sample copy for $2, #10 SAE and 3 first-class stamps. Reviews novels and short story collections.

Payment/Terms: Pays 2 contributor's copies; additional copies for $2. Acquires one-time rights. Not copyrighted.

Advice: "Almost anything goes but we prefer tightly written stories with good dialogue that are not impossible to follow."

UNO MAS MAGAZINE, (I, II), P.O. Box 1832, Silver Spring MD 20915. Fax: (301)770-6699. E-mail: unomasmag@aol.com. Editor: Jim Saah. Fiction Editor: Ron Saah. Zine: 8½×11; 50 pages; 60 lb. offset paper; glossy cover; illustrations and photos. "*Uno Mas Magazine* specializes in popular culture. Bringing new and established artists of all dimensions (music, literature, photography, poetry, etc.) together in one magazine." Quarterly. Estab. 1990. Circ. 3,500.
- *Uno Mas* has received excellent reviews in *factsheet 5*, *The Washington Post* and *Pulse Magazine*.

Needs: Condensed/excerpted novel, erotica, ethnic/multicultural, experimental, feminist, gay, historical, humor/satire, lesbian, literary, mystery/suspense (private eye/hardboiled, romantic suspense). Plans special fiction issue or anthology. Receives 4 unsolicited mss/month. Buys 2 mss/issue; 8 mss/year. Publishes ms 1-3 months after acceptance. Agented fiction 20%. Recently published work by George Logothetis and P.J. Jason. Length: 1,500-3,000 words average; 500 words minimum; 3,500 words maximum. Publishes short shorts. Also publishes literary essays, literary criticism and poetry. Sometimes critiques or comments on rejected ms.

How to Contact: Send complete ms with a cover letter. Include estimated word count, short bio and SASE. Reports in 2 weeks on queries; 1-3 months on mss. Send SASE for reply, return of ms or send a disposable copy of ms. Simultaneous, reprint and electronic submissions OK. Sample copy for $3, 9×11 SAE and 5 first-class stamps. Fiction guidelines free for #10 SASE. Reviews novels or short story collections.

Payment/Terms: Pays 3 contributor's copies; additional copies for $1.50. Acquires one-time rights. Sends galleys to author, "if requested."

Advice: "Short, tight pieces have the best chance of being published. Include word count and address on manuscript. Read *Uno Mas* before submitting anything."

VIRGIN MEAT, (I), 2325 W.K 15, Lancaster CA 93536. (805)722-1758. E-mail: virginmeat@aol.com. Editor: Steve Blum. Gothic interactive computer e-zine. Published irregularly. Estab. 1987. Circ. 5,000.

Needs: Horror. Receives 3-4 mss/day. Length: 2,000 words maximum. Also publishes poetry, art, sound and QTM's.

How to Contact: Request writers' guidelines before your first submission. Submit mss via e-mail address above. Sample copy for $5.

Payment/Terms: Pays in contributor's copies. Acquires one-time rights. Publication not copyrighted.

Advice: "Horror fiction should be horrific all the way through, not just at the end. Avoid common settings, senseless violence and humor."

VOX, Because reaction is a sound, (I, II), Cleave Press, 2118 Central SE, Suite 6, Albuquerque NM 87106. Fax: (505)243-3492. E-mail: cleavepres@aol.com. Editor: Robbyn Sanger. Zine: 8½×11; 40 pages; newsprint paper; glossy cover; illustrations and photos. "Say it like it is. (Enough said.)" Quarterly. Estab. 1994. Circ. 2,000.

Needs: Condensed/excerpted novel, erotica, ethnic/multicultural, experimental, feminist, gay, humor/satire, lesbian, literary, psychic/supernatural/occult, translations. "No formula fiction." Receives 50 mss/month. Buys 35 mss/issue; 105 mss/year. Publishes ms 1-4 months after acceptance. Published work by Hal Sirowitz, Ron Kolm, Alfred Vitale and Joe Maynard. Length: 500 words average; 5 words minimum; 1,200 words maximum. Publishes short shorts. Length: 25 plus words. Sometimes critiques or comments on rejected ms.

How to Contact: Send complete ms with a cover letter. Send first 20 pages only for longer works. Include estimated word count and brief bio. Reports in 2-4 weeks on queries; 1-2 months on mss. Send SASE for reply, return of ms or send a disposable copy of ms. Simultaneous, reprint and electronic submissions OK. Sample copy for $2. Fiction guidelines free for legal SASE.

Payment/Terms: Pays free subscription to magazine and 5 contributor's copies. Acquires one-time rights. Sends galleys to author (if requested). Not copyrighted.

Advice: "Get a sample copy before submitting! I love short shorts, novellas, too. Avoid long dull, overdone stuff. I do not want to see any plot-driven stories. At all. Ever. Have a clearly defined writing voice. Interesting characters, too."

THE W!DOW OF THE ORCH!D, (I, II, IV), Maudit Publications, 2101 Hazel Ave., Virginia MN 55792-3730. (218)749-8645. Editor: Emella Loran. Zine: 7½×8; 60 pages; 20 lb. white paper; b&w illustrations, when available. Bimonthly. Estab. 1994. Circ. 100.
Needs: Dark sykotic and experimental tales or poetry of erotica, fantasy, horror and psychic/supernatural/occult with no happy endings . . . . without a price, that is. "All tales must include one of the following: angels, demons, devils, ghouls, gods, monsters, shapeshifters, sykoz (psychos), vampires, wizardry, and whatever your devious mind in an utter state of severe sykosis can devise! None need to be of the supernatural." List of upcoming themes available for SASE. "Themes have no set deadlines and a theme issue will happen only if there are enough manuscripts." Publishes annual fiction issue. Publishes ms 1-5 issues after acceptance. Recently published work by Donna Taylor Burgess, Louis Dragon, Steve Eller, T.M. Jacobs, Eric Largo, Christopher DeRose, Bob Schmalfeldt and T.R. Tompkins. Length: 3,000 words average; 100 minimum; 5,000 words maximum. Publishes short shorts. Also publishes poetry. "We are not looking for serialized novels and novellas." Often critiques or comments on rejected mss.
How to Contact: Send complete ms with a cover letter or mail disk. "All tales longer than 5 pages send on disk. Can accept: ASCII and Microsoft Works 3.1 or better. Must include estimated word count, bio (more than a list of publications!!) of about 30 words, and words that will blow us off our duffs." Reports in 3 weeks on queries; 1-6 months on mss; 2-4 weeks on poetry; 1-2 months on artwork. Send SASE for reply, return of ms or send a disposable copy of ms. No simultaneous submissions. Reprints OK. Sample copy $5 postpaid (make checks payable to Raquel Bober). Fiction/novel guidelines for #10 SASE.
Payment/Terms: Pays 1 contributor's copy; charges for additional copies. Acquires first North American serial rights or one-time rights.
Advice: "Don't worry about offending us. We want tales that are unique, highly imaginative, and well written. Manuscripts are rejected here because they didn't stop our hearts, fry our minds, or claw at our souls. Don't bother sending us tales without structure or tales blatantly stolen from that great TV show you saw that night!"

WOMEN'S WORK, The Sound Alternative to Good Housekeeping, (II), 606 Avenue A, Snohomish WA 98290. (360)568-5914. Fax: (360)568-1620. E-mail: dammit@eskimo.com. Editor: Andrea Damm. Zine: 8×10½; 48 pages, bookstock paper; illustrations and photos. "A forum for dialogue among women of diverse cultural, economic, and generational backgrounds, celebrating women's creative expressions." Quarterly. Estab. 1991. Circ. 3,000.
Needs: Feminist, lesbian, women's issues. "No religious proselytizing." List of upcoming themes available for SASE. Receives 20 unsolicited mss/month. Accepts 1-2 mss/issue; 6-12 mss/year. Publishes ms 2-6 months after acceptance. Recently published work by Sibyl James and Kim Antieau. Length: 3,000 words average; 5,000 words maximum. Publishes short shorts. Also publishes literary essays, literary criticism and poetry.
How to Contact: Send complete ms with cover letter. Include estimated word count and 3-4 sentence bio. Reports in 2-3 months on queries; 3-4 months on mss. Send SASE for return of ms. Simultaneous, reprint and electronic submissions OK. Sample copy for $4. Fiction guidelines for #10 SASE. Reviews novels or short story collections. Send books to Attn: Kathleen Waterbury, Book Editor.
Payment/Terms: Pays free subscription to the magazine and 2 contributor's copies; additional copies for $1. Acquires first North American serial rights.
Advice: Looking for "work that obviously 'touches a nerve'; both revealing the risks the writer is taking (revealing herself in her work) and challenging the audience to openly react to the work. Many of our writers are just beginning and many have gone on from being first published with us to publishing their first novel! We wish to nurture the creative process; even if we cannot publish their work, we encourage them to continue trying—other publishers, other manuscripts. Don't despair!"

WRITERS' INTERNATIONAL FORUM, (I, II), Bristol Services International, P.O. Box 516, Tracyton WA 98393. Editor: Sandra E. Haven. Zine: 7½×8½; 40 pages; slick cover; illustrations. "*Writers' International Forum* is the only international magazine specifically designed to help new writers improve their marketability and writing skills through our unique peer critique process. We offer detailed information on writing, market listings plus print several stories per issue. Some critiques on our printed stories are published; all are mailed on to originating author." Bimonthly. Estab. 1990.
Needs: Adventure, childrens/juvenile (8-12 years), fantasy, historical, humor/satire, mainstream/contemporary, mystery/suspense, psychic/supernatural/occult, regional, romance (contemporary, young adult), science fiction, senior citizen/retirement, sports, westerns, young adult/teen. "No graphic sex, violence, vignettes or experimental formats." Prints special Juniors Edition issue. Accepts 7-12 mss/issue; 42-72 mss/year. Publishes ms 4 months after acceptance. Recently published work by Elizabeth

Klungness and Andrew Seddon. Length: 100 words minimum; 2,000 words maximum. Publishes short shorts. Includes personal response on rejected mss "that have followed our guidelines" and critiques on subscribers' mss.

How to Contact: Send complete ms with a cover letter. Include brief bio. Reports in 2 months on mss. Send SASE for reply. Sample copy for $3.50; $5 for sample of a special Juniors Edition issue. Fiction guidelines for #10 SASE.

Payment/Terms: Pays $5 minimum plus 2 contributor's copies on acceptance; additional copies for authors at discounted rates. Acquires first rights.

Advice: "We emphasize the classic storyline: a protagonist who faces an immediate challenge, confronts obstacles, and finally resolves the situation."

Commercial Periodicals

In this section of *Novel & Short Story Writer's Market* are commercial magazines with circulations of more than 10,000. Many of them, in fact, have circulations in the hundreds of thousands or millions. Among the oldest magazines listed here are ones not only familiar to us, but also to our parents, grandparents and even great-grandparents: *The Atlantic Monthly* (1857); *Christian Century* (1900); *Redbook* (1903); *The New Yorker* (1925); *Analog Science Fiction & Fact* (1930); *Esquire* (1933); and *Jack and Jill* (1938).

Commercial periodicals make excellent markets for fiction in terms of exposure, prestige and payment. Because these magazines are well-known, however, competition is great. Even the largest commercial publications buy only one or two stories an issue, yet thousands of writers submit to these popular magazines.

Despite the odds, it is possible for talented new writers to break into print in the magazines listed here. Editors at *Redbook*, a top fiction market which receives up to 600 unsolicited submissions a month, say, "We are interested in new voices and buy up to a quarter of our stories from unsolicited submissions." The fact that *Redbook* and other well-respected publications such as *The Atlantic Monthly* and *The New Yorker* continue to list their fiction needs in *Novel & Short Story Writer's Market* year to year indicates that they are open to both new and established writers. Your keys to breaking into these markets are careful research, professional presentation and, of course, top-quality prose.

Featured in this section are interviews with the editors of two of today's highest-paying commercial magazine markets. Brooke Comer, editor of *Woman's World*, says she is always eager to discover new writers, especially those who can write a 1,800-word romantic short story for which *WW* pays $1,000. C. Michael Curtis, editor of *The Atlantic Monthly*, 1996 winner of the coveted National Magazine Award for Fiction, says that one third to one half of *Atlantic* stories are the work of previously unpublished authors.

TYPES OF MAGAZINES

In this section you will find a number of popular publications, some for a broad-based, general-interest readership and others for large but select groups of readers—children, teenagers, women, men and seniors. Just a few of these publications include *Boys' Life, American Girl, Seventeen, Esquire, Harper's, Ladies' Home Journal, Lady's Circle* and *Mature Years*. You'll also find regional publications such as *Aloha, The Magazine of Hawaii and the Pacific, Florida Wildlife, Georgia Journal, Yankee Magazine* and *Portland Magazine*.

Religious and church-affiliated magazines include *The Friend Magazine*, Home Life and *Guideposts for Kids*. Other magazines are devoted to the interests of particular cultures and outlooks such as *African Voices*, publishing "enlightening and entertaining literature on the varied lifestyles of people of color," and *India Currents*, specializing in the "arts and culture of India as seen in America for Indians and non-Indians with a common interest in India."

Top markets for genre fiction include *Ellery Queen's Mystery Magazine, Alfred Hitchcock Mystery Magazine, Analog Science Fiction & Fact* and *Asimov's Science*

Fiction. These magazines are known to book publishers as fertile ground for budding genre novelists.

Special interest magazines are another possible market for fiction, but only if your story involves a particular magazine's theme. Some of the highly specialized magazines in this section are *Balloon Life* (hot air ballooning); *Beckett Baseball Card Monthly*; *Easyriders Magazine* (biker-oriented); and *Juggler's World*.

CHOOSING YOUR MARKET

Unlike smaller journals and publications, most of the magazines listed are available at newsstands and bookstores. Many can also be found in the library, and guidelines and sample copies are almost always available by mail. Start your search, then, by familiarizing yourself with the fiction included in the magazines that interest you.

Don't make the mistake of thinking, just because you are familiar with a magazine, that their fiction isn't any different today than when you first saw it. Nothing could be further from the truth—commercial magazines, no matter how well established, are constantly revising their fiction needs as they strive to reach new readers and expand their audience base.

In a magazine that uses only one or two stories an issue, take a look at the nonfiction articles and features as well. These can give you a better idea of the audience for the publication and clues to the type of fiction that might appeal to them.

If you write a particular type of fiction, such as children's stories or mysteries, you may want to look that subject up in the Category Index at the back of this book. There you will find a list of markets that say they are looking for a particular subject. Check also the subcategories given within each listing. For example, a magazine may be in the Category Index as needing mystery fiction, but check the listing to find out if only a particular subcategory interests them such as hard-boiled detective stories or police procedurals or English-style cozies.

You may want to use our ranking codes as a guide, especially if you are a new writer. At the end of this introduction is a list of the Roman numeral codes we use and what they mean.

ABOUT THE LISTINGS

See How to Use This Book to Publish Your Fiction (page 3) for information about the material common to all listings in this book. In this section in particular, pay close attention to the number of submissions a magazine receives in a given period and how many they publish in the same period. This will give you a clear picture of how stiff your competition can be.

While many of the magazines listed here publish one or two pieces of fiction in each issue, some also publish special fiction issues once or twice a year. We have indicated this in the listing information. We also note if the magazine is open to novel excerpts as well as short fiction and we advise novelists to query first before submitting long work.

The Business of Fiction Writing, beginning on page 9, covers the basics of submitting your work. Professional presentation is a must for all markets listed. Editors at commercial magazines are especially busy, and anything you can do to make your manuscript easy to read and accessible will help your chances of being published. Most magazines want to see complete manuscripts, but watch for publications in this section that require a query first.

MORE ABOUT THE LISTINGS

As in the previous section, we've included our own comments in many of the listings, set off by a bullet (●). Whenever possible, we list the publication's recent awards and honors. We've also included any special information we feel will help you in determining whether a particular publication interests you.

The maple leaf symbol (🍁) identifies our Canadian listings. All North American listings are grouped together first, and you'll find a list of commercial publications from other countries following the main section. Remember to use International Reply Coupons rather than stamps when you want a reply from a country other than your own.

FOR MORE INFORMATION

For more on trends in commercial fiction, see our Fiction Report starting on page 34. For more on commercial magazines in general, see issues of *Writer's Digest* and industry trade publications such as *Folio*, available in larger libraries.

For news about some of the genre publications listed here and information about a particular field, there are a number of magazines devoted to genre topics, including *Mystery Scene*, *Locus* (for science fiction) and *Science Fiction Chronicle*. Addresses for these and other industry magazines can be found in the section Publications of Interest to Fiction Writers.

Membership in the national groups devoted to specific genre fields is not restricted to novelists and can be valuable to writers of short fiction in these fields. Many include awards for "Best Short Story" in their annual contests. For information on groups such as the Mystery Writers of America, the Romance Writers of America and the Science fiction and Fantasy Writers of America see the Organizations and Resources section.

The following is the ranking system we have used to categorize the periodicals in this section:

I Periodical encourages beginning or unpublished writers to submit work for consideration and publishes new writers regularly.

II Periodical accepts outstanding work by beginning and established writers.

III Hard to break into; periodical publishes mostly previously published writers.

IV Special-interest or regional magazine, open only to writers in certain genres or on certain subjects or from certain geographic areas.

V Periodical closed to unsolicited submissions.

ADVENTURE CYCLIST, (I, IV), The Adventure Cycling Assn., Box 8308, Missoula MT 59807. (406)721-1776. Editor: Daniel D'Ambrosio. Magazine on bicycle touring: 8⅜ × 10⅞; 32 pages; coated paper; self cover; illustrations and b&w photos. Published 9 times annually. Estab. 1974. Circ. 30,000.
Needs: Adventure, fantasy, historical (general), humor/satire and regional and with a bicycling theme. Buys variable number of mss/year. Published new writers within the last year. Length: 2,000 words average; 1,000 words minimum; 2,500 words maximum. Publishes short shorts. Occasionally comments on rejected mss.
How to Contact: Send complete ms with SASE. Reports in 6 weeks. Simultaneous and previously published submissions OK. Accepts electronic submissions; prefers hard copy with disk submission. Sample copy for $1, 9 × 12 SAE and 60¢ postage. Fiction guidelines for #10 SASE.
Payment/Terms: Pays $25-65/published page on publication for first North American serial rights.

AFRICAN VOICES, The Art and Literary Publication With Class & Soul, (I, II), African Voices Communications, Inc., 270 W. 96th St., New York NY 10025. (212)865-2982. Editor: Carolyn A. Butts. Fiction Editor: Gail Sharbaan. Magazine: 32 pages; illustrations and photos. "*AV* publishes enlightening and entertaining literature on the varied lifestyles of people of color." Quarterly. Estab. 1993. Circ. 20,000.

Needs: African-American: children's/juvenile (10-12 years), condensed/excerpted novel, erotica, ethnic/multicultural, gay, historical (general), horror, humor/satire, literary, mystery/suspense, psychic/supernatural/occult, religious/inspirational, science fiction, young adult/teen (adventure, romance). List of upcoming themes available for SASE. Publishes special fiction issue. Receives 20-50 unsolicited mss/month. Accepts 20 mss/issue. Publishes ms 3-6 months after acceptance. Agented fiction 5%. Published work by Junot Diaz, Michel Marriott and Carol Dixon. Length: 2,000 words average; 500 words minimum; 3,000 words maximum. Occasionally publishes short shorts. Also publishes literary essays and poetry.

How to Contact: Query with clips of published work. Include short bio. Reports in 6-8 weeks on queries; 2-3 months on mss. Send SASE for return of ms. Simultaneous, reprint and electonic submissions OK. Sample copy for $3 and 9 × 12 SAE. Free fiction guidelines. Reviews novels and short story collections. Send books to Book Editor.

Payment/Terms: Pays $25 maximum on publication for first North American serial rights, free subscription and 5 contributor's copies.

Advice: "A manuscript stands out if it is neatly typed with a well-written and interesting story line or plot. Originality encouraged. We are interested in more horror, erotic and drama pieces. *AV* wants to highlight the diversity in our culture. Stories must go beyond being 'black' and touch the humanity in us all."

AIM MAGAZINE, (I, II), 7308 S. Eberhart Ave., Chicago IL 60619. (312)874-6184. Editor: Myron Apilado, EdD. Fiction Editor: Mark Boone. Newspaper: 8½ × 11; 48 pages; slick paper; photos and illustrations. "Material of social significance: down-to-earth gut. Personal experience, inspirational." For "high school, college and general public." Quarterly. Estab. 1973. Circ. 10,000.

● *Aim* sponsors an annual short story contest.

Needs: Open. No "religious" mss. Published special fiction issue last year; plans another. Receives 25 unsolicited mss/month. Buys 15 mss/issue; 60 mss/year. Recently published work by Clayton Davis, Kenneth Nunn, Charles J. Wheelan, Estelle Lurie and Jesus Diaz. Published new writers within the last year. Length: 800-1,000 words average. Publishes short shorts. Sometimes comments on rejected mss.

How to Contact: Send complete ms. Include SASE with cover letter and author's photograph. Simultaneous submissions OK. Reports in 1 month. Sample copy for $4 with SAE (9 × 12) and $1.80 postage. Fiction guidelines for #10 SASE.

Payment/Terms: Pays $15-25 on publication for first rights.

Advice: "Search for those who are making unselfish contributions to their community and write about them. Our objective is to purge racism from the human bloodstream. Write about your own experiences. Be familiar with the background of your characters." Known for "stories with social significance, proving that people from different ethnic, racial backgrounds are more alike than they are different."

ALOHA, The Magazine of Hawaii and the Pacific, (IV), Davick Publications, P.O. Box 3260, Honolulu HI 96801. (808)593-1191. Fax: (808)593-1327. Editorial Director: Cheryl Tsutsumi. Magazine about the 50th state. Upscale demographics. Bimonthly. Estab. 1977. Circ. 75,000.

● The publisher of *ALOHA* has published a coffee table book, *The Best of ALOHA*. Note *ALOHA* has a new address.

Needs: "Only fiction that illuminates the true Hawaiian experience. No stories about tourists in Waikiki or contrived pidgin dialogue." Receives 6 unsolicited mss/month. Publishes ms up to 1 year after acceptance. Length: 1,000-2,000 words average.

How to Contact: Send complete ms. No simultaneous submissions. Reports in 2 months. SASE. Electronic submissions (disk-Microsoft Word format) OK. Sample copy for $2.95—include SASE (postage is $2.90).

Payment/Terms: Pays between $200-400 on publication for first rights.

Advice: "Submit only fiction that is truly local in character. Do not try to write anything about Hawaii if you have not experienced this culturally different part of America."

AMERICAN GIRL, (III), Pleasant Company Publications, 8400 Fairway Place, Middleton WI 53562. (608)836-4848. Editor: Judith Woodburn. Magazine: 8½ × 11; 52 pages; illustrations and photos. "Four-color bimonthly magazine for girls age 8-12." Estab. 1991.

● Pleasant Company is known for its series of books featuring girls from different periods of American history.

Needs: Children's/juvenile (girls 8-12 years): "contemporary, realistic fiction, adventure, historical, problem stories." Receives 100 unsolicited mss/month. Accepts 1 ms/issue; 6 mss/year. Length: 2,500 words average. Publishes short shorts. Also publishes literary essays and poetry (if age appropriate).

How to Contact: Send complete ms with a cover letter. Include bio (1 paragraph). Send SASE for reply, return of ms or send a disposable copy of ms. Simultaneous submissions OK. Sample copy for $3.95 plus $1.93 postage.
Payment/Terms: Pays in cash; amount negotiable. Pays on acceptance for first North American serial rights. Sends galleys to author.

ANALOG SCIENCE FICTION & FACT, (II), Dell Magazines, 1270 Avenue of the Americas, New York NY 10020. (212)698-1381. E-mail: 71154.662@compuserve.com. Editor: Stanley Schmidt. Magazine: 5³⁄₁₆ × 7⅜; 160 pages; illustrations (drawings); photos. "Well-written science fiction based on speculative ideas and fact articles on topics on the present and future frontiers of research. Our readership includes intelligent laymen and/or those professionally active in science and technology." Published 11 times yearly. Estab. 1930. Circ. 60,000.
 • *Analog* is considered one of the leading science fiction publications. The magazine has won a number of Hugos, Chesleys and Nebula Awards.
Needs: Science fiction (hard science, soft sociological) and serialized novels. "No stories which are not truly science fiction in the sense of having a plausible speculative idea *integral to the story*. We would like to see good humor that is also good, solid science fiction. We do one double-size issue per year (July)." Receives 300-500 unsolicited fiction mss/month. Accepts 4-8 mss/issue. Agented fiction 20%. Recently published work by Spider Robinson, Ben Bova, Robert J. Sawyer and Lois McMaster Bujold; published new writers within the last year. Length: 2,000-80,000 words. Publishes short shorts. Critiques rejected mss "when there is time." Sometimes recommends other markets.
How to Contact: Send complete ms with SASE. Include cover letter with "anything that I need to know before reading the story, e.g. that it's a rewrite I suggested or that it incorporates copyrighted material. Otherwise, no cover letter is needed." Query with SASE only on serials. Reports in 1 month on both query and ms. No simultaneous submissions. Fiction guidelines for SASE. Sample copy for $4. Reviews novels and short story collections. Send books to Tom Easton.
Payment/Terms: Pays 5-8¢/word on acceptance for first North American serial rights and nonexclusive foreign rights. Sends galleys to author.
Advice: Mss are rejected because of "inaccurate science; poor plotting, characterization or writing in general. We literally only have room for 1-2% of what we get. Many stories are rejected not because of anything conspicuously *wrong*, but because they lack anything sufficiently *special*. What we buy must stand out from the crowd. Fresh, thought-provoking ideas are important. Familiarize yourself with the magazine—but don't try to imitate what we've already published."

✦THE ANNALS OF ST. ANNE DE BEAUPRÉ, (II), Redemptorist Fathers, P.O. Box 1000, St. Anne de Beaupré, Quebec G0A 3C0 Canada. (418)827-4538. Fax: (418)827-4530. Editor: Father Roch Achard, C.Ss.R. Magazine: 8 × 11; 32 pages; glossy paper; photos. "Our aim is to promote devotion to St. Anne and Catholic family values." Monthly. Estab. 1878. Circ. 50,000.
Needs: Religious/inspirational. "We only wish to see something inspirational, educational, objective, uplifting. Reporting rather than analysis is simply not remarkable." Receives 50-60 unsolicited mss/month. Published work by Beverly Sheresh, Eugene Miller and Aubrey Haines. Publishes short stories. Length: 1,500 maximum. Always critiques or comments on rejected ms.
How to Contact: Send complete ms with a cover letter. Include estimated word count. Reports in 3 weeks. Send SASE for reply or return of ms. No simultaneous submissions. Free sample copy and guidelines.
Payment/Terms: Pays 3-4¢/word on acceptance and 3 contributor's copies on publication for first North American serial rights.

‡APPALACHIA JOURNAL, (II, IV), Appalachian Mountain Club, 5 Joy St., Boston MA 02108. (617)523-0636. Editor: Sandy Stott. Magazine: 6 × 9; 160 pages; 50 lb. recycled paper; 10 pt. CS1 cover; 5-10 illustrations; 20-30 photographs. "*Appalachia* is the oldest mountaineering and conservation journal in the country. It specializes in backcountry recreation and conservation topics (hiking, canoeing, cross-country skiing, etc.) for outdoor (including armchair) enthusiasts." Semiannually (June and December). Estab. 1876. Circ. 13,000.
Needs: Prose, poem, sports. Receives 5-10 unsolicited mss/month. Accepts 1-4 mss/issue; 2-8 mss/year. Publishes ms 6-12 months after acceptance. Length: 500-4,000 words average. Publishes short shorts.
How to Contact: Send complete ms with cover letter. No simultaneous submissions. Reports in 1 month on queries; 2 months on mss. SASE (or IRC) for query. Sample copy for $5. Fiction guidelines for #10 SAE.
Payment/Terms: Pays contributor's copies. Occasionally pays $100-300 for a feature—usually assigned.
Advice: "All submissions should be related to conservation, mountaineering, and/or backcountry recreation both in the Northeast and throughout the world. Most of our journal is nonfiction. The

fiction we publish is mountain-related and often off-beat. Send us material that says, I went to the wilderness and *thought* this; not I went there and did this."

ART TIMES, A Literary Journal and Resource for All the Arts, (II), P.O. Box 730, Mt. Marion NY 12456. Phone/fax: (914)246-6944. Editor: Raymond J. Steiner. Magazine: 12 × 15; 20 pages; Jet paper and cover; illustrations; photos. "Arts magazine covering the disciplines for an over 40, affluent, arts-conscious and literate audience." Monthly. Estab. 1984. Circ. 15,000.
Needs: Adventure, contemporary, ethnic, fantasy, feminist, gay, historical, humor/satire, lesbian, literary, mainstream and science fiction. "We seek quality literary pieces. Nothing violent, sexist, erotic, juvenile, racist, romantic, political, etc." Receives 30-50 mss/month. Accepts 1 ms/issue; 11 mss/year. Publishes ms within 18-24 months of acceptance. Length: 1,500 words maximum. Publishes short shorts.
How to Contact: Send complete ms with cover letter. Simultaneous submissions OK. Reports in 6 months. SASE. Sample copy for $1.75, 9 × 12 SAE and 3 first-class stamps. Fiction guidelines for #10 SASE.
Payment/Terms: Pays $25, free one-year subscription to magazine and 6 contributor's copies on publication for first North American serial rights.
Advice: "Competition is greater (more submissions received), but keep trying. We print new as well as published writers."

ASIMOV'S SCIENCE FICTION, (II), 1270 Avenue of the Americas, New York NY 10020. (212)698-1313. Editor: Gardner Dozois. Executive Editor: Sheila Williams. Magazine: 5³/₁₆ × 7⅜ (trim size); 160 pages; 29 lb. newspaper; 70 lb. to 8 pt. C1S cover stock; illustrations; rarely photos. Magazine consists of science fiction and fantasy stories for adults and young adults. Publishes 11 issues/year (with one double issue). Estab. 1977. Circ. 120,000.
  ● Named for a science fiction "legend," *Asimov's* regularly receives Hugo and Nebula Awards. Editor Gardner Dozois has received several awards for editing including Hugos and those from *Locus* and *Science Fiction Chronicle* magazines.
Needs: Science fiction (hard science, soft sociological) and fantasy. No horror or psychic/supernatural. Receives approximately 800 unsolicited fiction mss each month. Accepts 10 mss/issue. Publishes ms 6-12 months after acceptance. Agented fiction 10%. Published work by George Alec Effinger, Connie Willis, Walter Jon Williams, Gregory Benford and Judith Moffett; published new writers in the last year. Length: up to 20,000 words. Publishes short shorts. Critiques rejected mss "when there is time."
How to Contact: Send complete ms with SASE. No simultaneous submissions. Reports in 2-3 months. Fiction guidelines for #10 SASE. Sample copy for $3.50 and 9 × 12 SASE. Reviews novels and short story collections. Send books to Book Reviewer.
Payment/Terms: Pays 6-8¢/word for stories up to 7,500 words; 5¢/word for stories over 12,500; $450 for stories between those limits. Pays on acceptance for first North American serial rights plus specified foreign rights, as explained in contract. Very rarely buys reprints. Sends galleys to author.
Advice: "We are looking for character stories rather than those emphasizing technology or science. New writers will do best with a story under 10,000 words. Every new science fiction or fantasy film seems to 'inspire' writers—and this is not a desirable trend. Be sure to be familiar with our magazine and the type of story we like; workshops and lots of practice help. Try to stay away from trite, cliched themes. Start in the middle of the action, starting as close to the end of the story as you possibly can."

THE ASSOCIATE REFORMED PRESBYTERIAN, (II, IV), The Associate Reformed Presbyterian, Inc., 1 Cleveland St., Greenville SC 29601. (803)232-8297. Editor: Ben Johnston. Magazine: 8½ × 11; 32-48 pages; 50 lb. offset paper; illustrations; photos. "We are the official magazine of our denomination. Articles generally relate to activities within the denomination—conferences, department work, etc., with a few special articles that would be of general interest to readers." Monthly. Estab. 1976. Circ. 6,200.
Needs: Contemporary, juvenile, religious/inspirational, spiritual and young adult/teen. "Stories should portray Christian values. No retelling of Bible stories or 'talking animal' stories. Stories for youth should deal with resolving real issues for young people." Receives 30-40 unsolicited fiction mss/month. Accepts 1 ms/some months; 10-12 mss/year. Publishes ms within 1 year after acceptance. Published work by Lawrence Dorr, Jan Johnson and Deborah Christensen. Length: 300-750 words

---

‡ **THE DOUBLE DAGGER** before a listing indicates that the listing is new in this edition. New markets are often the most receptive to submissions by new writers.

(children); 1,250 words maximum (youth). Sometimes critiques rejected mss.
How to Contact: Include cover letter. Reports in 6 weeks on queries and mss. Simultaneous submissions OK. Sample copy for $1.50; fiction guidelines for #10 SASE.
Payment/Terms: Pays $20-75 for first rights and contributor's copies.
Advice: "Currently we are seeking stories aimed at the 10 to 15 age group. We have an oversupply of stories for younger children."

THE ATLANTIC MONTHLY, (I, II), 77 N. Washington St., Boston MA 02114. (617)854-7700. Editor: William Whitworth. Senior Editors: Michael Curtis and Jack Beatty. Managing Editor: Cullen Murphy. General magazine for the college educated with broad cultural interests. Monthly. Estab. 1857. Circ. 500,000.
- Work published in *The Atlantic Monthly* has been selected for inclusion in *Best American Short Stories* and *O. Henry Prize* anthologies for 1995. The magazine was also a winner of the 1996 National Magazine Award for Fiction.
Needs: Literary and contemporary. "Seeks fiction that is clear, tightly written with strong sense of 'story' and well-defined characters." Accepts 15-18 stories/year. Receives 1,000 unsolicited fiction mss each month. Published work by Alice Munro, E.S. Goldman, Charles Baxter and T.C. Boyle; published new writers within the last year. Preferred length: 2,000-6,000 words.
How to Contact: Send cover letter and complete ms with SASE. Reports in 2 months on mss.
Payment/Terms: Pays $2,500/story on acceptance for first North American serial rights.
Advice: When making first contact, "cover letters are sometimes helpful, particularly if they cite prior publications or involvement in writing programs. Common mistakes: melodrama, inconclusiveness, lack of development, unpersuasive characters and/or dialogue."

BALLOON LIFE, The Magazine for Hot Air Ballooning, (II, IV), 2145 Dale Ave., Sacramento CA 95815-3632. (916)922-9648. E-mail: blnlife@scn.org. Editor: Tom Hamilton. Magazine: 8½ × 11; 48 pages; color, b&w photos. "Sport of hot air ballooning. Readers participate in hot air ballooning as pilots, crew, official observers at events and spectators."
Needs: Humor/satire, related to hot air ballooning. "Manuscripts should involve the sport of hot air ballooning in any aspect. Prefer humor based on actual events; fiction seldom published." Accepts 4-6 mss/year. Publishes ms within 3-4 months after acceptance. Length: 800 words minimum; 1,500 words maximum; 1,200 words average. Publishes short shorts. Length: 400-500 words. Sometimes critiques rejected mss and recommends other markets.
How to Contact: Send complete ms with cover letter that includes Social Security number. Reports in 3 weeks on queries; 2 weeks on mss. SASE. Simultaneous and reprint submissions OK. Sample copy for 9 × 12 SAE and $1.90 postage. Guidelines for #10 SASE.
Payment/Terms: Pays $25-75 and contributor's copies on publication for first North American serial, one-time or other rights.
Advice: "Generally the magazine looks for humor pieces that can provide a light-hearted change of pace from the technical and current event articles. An example of a work we used was titled 'Balloon Astrology' and dealt with the character of a hot air balloon based on what sign it was born (made) under."

THE BEAR ESSENTIAL, (I, II), ORLO, 2516 NW 29th, P.O. Box 10342, Portland OR 97210. (503)242-2330. Fax: (503)243-2645. E-mail: orlo@teleport.com. Editor: Thomas L. Webb. Magazine: 11 × 14; 72 pages; newsprint paper; Kraft paper cover; illustrations and photos. "*The Bear Essential* has an environmental focus, combining all forms and styles. Fiction should have environmental theme or thread to it, and should be engaging to a cross-section of audiences. The more street-level, the better." Semiannually. Estab. 1993. Circ. 15,000.
- *The Bear Essential* was a finalist in the 1995 *Utne Reader*'s Alternative Media Awards.
Needs: Environmentally focused: humor/satire, literary, science fiction. "We would like to see more adventure, intrigue, mystery, nontraditional forms." List of upcoming themes available for SASE. Receives 10-20 unsolicited mss/month. Accepts 2-3 mss/issue; 4-6 mss/year. Publishes ms 2 months after acceptance. Recently published work by David James Duncan, Gerald Vizenor, Janet Goldberg and Sharon Doubiago. Length: 2,500 words average; 900 words minimum; 4,500 words maximum. Publishes short shorts. Also publishes literary essays, literary criticism, poetry, reviews, opinion, investigative journalism, interviews and creative nonfiction. Sometimes critiques or comments on rejected mss.
How to Contact: Send complete ms with a cover letter, or call and discuss with editor. Include estimated word count, 10- to 15-word bio, list of publications, copy on disk, if possible. Reports in 1 month on queries; 3 months on mss. Send a disposable copy of mss. Simultaneous and electronic (disk is best, then e-mail) submissions OK. Sample copy for $3, 7½ × 11 SAE and 5 first-class stamps. Fiction guidelines for #10 SASE. Reviews novels and short story collections.

INSIDER REPORT

Precise language, flawless mechanics and a story: vital elements for *Atlantic* fiction

"Clear, direct language," says C. Michael Curtis, one of four senior editors at *The Atlantic Monthly*, "is the sign of an intelligent mind carefully at work. Someone who appreciates the language and can control it has mastered the first important step in creating excellent fiction." It is this precision of language that Curtis requires of the fiction he chooses to publish in *The Atlantic*.

C. Michael Curtis

Photo by Martin Cornel

Curtis also demands careful attention to basic writing mechanics. Unfortunately, he receives many manuscripts in which the author has overlooked such typical cosmetic mistakes as misspellings, faulty punctuation or sloppy grammar. "The best way to attract my attention is to begin a story with a compound, complex sentence in which a semi-colon is used correctly," Curtis says only half-jokingly. "So few writers seem to know how to use a semi-colon properly that it flags our attention." Upon reflection, Curtis continues, "The more truthful answer is that a controlled, complicated sentence in which the writer makes proper use of punctuation, and has a sense of how to connect modifiers with the elements they modify, will help a manuscript stand out among the daily crush of submissions."

Other shortcomings Curtis finds in the work of many writers are contrived dialogue that doesn't sound like people talking and unnecessary or inappropriate emphasis through the constant use of adverbs and adjectives with every noun and verb.

Precise language and skillful presentation, however, do not assure publication of a story in *The Atlantic*. What Curtis especially looks for are stories that indeed tell a story, stories in which the reader can see that a conclusion is reached or resolution occurs. "As opposed to a story that is static, a portrait of a character or a sketch; a glimpse into a life as it is lived by a certain kind of person or in a certain milieu. And, in the long run, a story succeeds if the reader takes pleasure in it; finds it exciting or illuminating—striking in some way."

Although Curtis's standards for fiction are high, the beginning writer of contemporary literary fiction will be heartened to know *The Atlantic Monthly* is hardly a closed market. It is not unusual for one third to one half of the stories published each year to be the work of unpublished or undiscovered authors. In fact, many of today's well-known and distinguished authors had their debuts in

INSIDER REPORT, *Curtis*

its pages. Ethan Canin, James Allen McPherson and John Sayles are but a few *Atlantic* discoveries who have gone on to greater fame.

The Atlantic receives 300 to 400 hundred submissions each week and publishes one story per issue. Approximately one-half come to Curtis personally with the remainder addressed to "The Editor" or simply to *The Atlantic Monthly.* "Of those that come to me"—and Curtis is careful to make this distinction perfectly clear—"probably half are unsolicited in the sense that they weren't invited and we don't know the author. The other half are often from people we do know or with whom we've had some contact. While we haven't specifically asked the authors to send them, they aren't the same as completely unsolicited work."

When asked about simultaneous submissions, Curtis's succint reply is, "We hate them. We will consider manuscripts sent on a simultaneous submission basis, but would rather not. We explain, if given the chance, that we act quickly on manuscripts in return for not having to consider them at the same time they're being looked at in other magazines."

Only a few from the *Atlantic* staff of nearly 50 actually see the manuscripts that arrive daily. First in a chain of events is the decision whether to return a submission or pass it on to the senior editors. Curtis, a senior editor, routinely determines whether a manuscript will be passed on to the editor-in-chief for final consideration or returned with either a friendly letter or form rejection.

With more than 12,000 submissions a year, Curtis has little need to beat the bushes for new talent. "Because the flood of manuscripts is so substantial, we don't have to look very far for good work. We have more than we can possibly accommodate as it is. So, we may fool ourselves, but we imagine that most of the people who are writing well are sending their work here at one point or another. I do read some other magazines, but not as many as I'd like or, no doubt, as I ought to." *The New Yorker, Harper's, Georgia Review, Ploughshares* and *Epic* top the list of periodicals he does make it a point to keep up with.

Curtis feels the market for literary fiction has broadened in the past ten to fifteen years due to the many M.F.A. programs and writers' conferences springing up across the country. With more than 150 schools granting graduate degrees in creative writing, Curtis says there's a greater need for anthologies and collections of stories in the classrooms. "These institutional settings need short work to teach, to use as exercises and to think and write about. This, in effect, creates a larger than usual market for short fiction as well as a greater number of fiction writers. Consequently, many more collections of stories are now published successfully. This has also led to an increased awareness of short story writers as literary celebrities, something that was not true a decade ago. Today, writers can develop a reputation on the strength of their short story collections alone."

For beginning writers of literary fiction, Curtis offers this advice: "Write steadily and carefully. Take the time to develop the editorial skills necessary to see what's going wrong in your own work and correct it. Be steadfast. Keep writing and submitting and strengthening your skills. Do not be impatient—wait to find your own voice."

—*Glenn L. Marcum*

Payment/Terms: Pays free subscription to the magazine, 20 contributor's copies; additional copies for postage. Acquires first or one-time rights. Sends galleys to author. Not copyrighted. Sponsors contests, awards or grants for fiction writers.

Advice: "Keep sending work. Write actively and focus on the connections of man, animals, nature, etc., not just flowery descriptions. Urban and suburban environments are grist for the mill as well. Have not seen enough quality humor and irony writing. Juxtaposition of place welcome. Action and hands-on great. Not all that interested in environmental ranting and simple 'walks through the park.' Make it powerful, yet accessible to a wide audience."

BECKETT BASEBALL CARD MONTHLY, (IV), Statabase, 15850 Dallas Parkway, Dallas TX 75244. (214)991-6657. Managing Editor: Mike Payne. Magazine: 8½ × 11; 128 pages; 48 pages coated glossy paper, 80 pages newspaper; 8 pt. Sterling cover; 12 illustrations; 100 photographs. "Collecting baseball cards is a leisure-time avocation. It's wholesome and something the entire family can do together. We emphasize its positive aspects. For card collectors and sports enthusiasts, 6-60." Monthly. Estab. 1984. Circ. 500,000 paid.

Needs: Humor/satire, sports, young adult/teen (10-18 years). "Sports hero worship; historical fiction involving real baseball figures; fictionalizing specific franchises of national interest such as the Yankees, Dodgers or Mets." No fiction that is "unrealistic sportswise." Publishes ms 4-6 months after acceptance. Length: 1,200 words average; 2,500 words maximum. Publishes short shorts. Comments on rejected mss or recommends other markets "if we feel we can help the reader close the gap between rejection and acceptance."

How to Contact: Send complete ms with cover letter. Include Social Security number. Reports in 6 weeks. SASE. Will consider reprints "if prior publication is in a very obscure or very prestigious publication." Sample copy for $3. Fiction guidelines free. Queries are encouraged.

Payment/Terms: Pays $150-400 on acceptance for first rights.

Advice: "Fiction must be baseball oriented and accessible to both pre-teenagers and adults; fiction must stress redeeming social values; fictionalization must involve the heroes of the game (past or present) or a major-league baseball franchise with significant national following. The writer must have a healthy regard for standard English usage. A prospective writer must examine several issues of our publication prior to submission. Our publication is extremely successful in our genre, and our writers must respect the sensitivities of our readers. We are different from other sports publications, and a prospective writer must understand our distinctiveness to make a sale here. Especially desirable at this time are action-fiction narratives that can be adapted to comic book treatments. These pieces should be directed to the attention of Fred Reed, Vice President Publishing."

BEPUZZLED, (II, IV), Lombard Marketing, Inc., 22 E. Newberry Rd., Bloomfield CT 06002. (203)769-5700. Editor: Sue Tyska. "Mystery jigsaw puzzles . . . includes short mystery story with clues contained in puzzle picture to solve the mystery for preschool, 8-12 year olds, adults." Estab. 1987.

• Most of the large bookstore chains and specialty shops carry *bePuzzled* and other mystery puzzles.

Needs: Mystery: Adventure, juvenile, mainstream, preschool, suspense, young adult—all with mystery theme. Receives 3 unsolicited fiction mss/month. Accepts 20 mss/year. Publishes ms 6-18 months after acceptance. Published work by John Lutz, Matt Christopher, Alan Robbins, Henry Slesar, Katherine Hall Page. Length: 4,000 words preferred; 3,000 words minimum; 4,000 words maximum. Sometimes recommends other markets.

How to Contact: Query for submission guidelines. Reports in 2 months. SASE. Simultaneous submissions OK. Fiction guidelines free.

Payment/Terms: Pays $200 minimum on delivery of final ms. Buys all rights.

Advice: "Thoughtful, challenging mysteries that can be concluded with the visual element of a puzzle. Many times we select certain subject matter and then send out these specifics to our pool of writers . . . List clues and red herrings. Then write the story containing supporting information. Play one of our mystery thrillers so you understand the relationship between the story and the picture."

BOMB MAGAZINE, (II), New Art Publications, 594 Broadway, Suite 1002A, New York NY 10012. (212)431-3943. Editor: Betsy Sussler. Magazine: 11 × 14; 100 pages; 70 lb. glossy cover; illustrations and photographs. "Artist-and-writer-edited magazine." Quarterly. Estab. 1981.

Needs: Contemporary, experimental, serialized novel. Publishes "Summer Reading" issue. Receives 40 unsolicited mss/week. Accepts 6 mss/issue; 24 mss/year. Publishes ms 3-6 months after acceptance. Agented fiction 80%. Published work by Jim Lewis, AM Homes, Sandra Cisneros and Leslie Dick. Length: 10-12 pages average. Publishes interviews.

How to Contact: Send complete ms with cover letter. Reports in 4 months on mss. SASE. Sample copy for $4 with $1.67 postage.

Payment/Terms: Pays $100 and contributor's copies on publication for first or one-time rights. Sends galleys to author.

Advice: "We are committed to publishing new work that commercial publishers often deem too dangerous or difficult. The problem is, a lot of young writers confuse difficult with dreadful. Read the magazine before you even think of submitting something."

BOWHUNTER MAGAZINE, The Number One Bowhunting Magazine, (IV), Cowles Magazines, Inc., Box 8200, Harrisburg PA 17105. (717)657-9555. Fax: (717)657-9526. Editor: M.R. James. Publisher: Dave Canfield. Editorial Director: Richard Cochran. Magazine: 8 × 10½; 150 pages; 75 lb. glossy paper; 150 lb. glossy cover stock; illustrations and photographs. "We are a special interest publication for people who hunt with the bow and arrow. We publish hunting adventure and how-to stories. Our audience is predominantly male, 30-50, middle income." Bimonthly. Circ. 200,000.
   ● Themes included in most fiction considered for *Bowhunter* are pro-conservation as well as pro-hunting.
Needs: Bowhunting, outdoor adventure. "Writers must expect a very limited market. We buy only one or two fiction pieces a year. Writers must know the market—bowhunting—and let that be the theme of their work. No 'me and my dog' types of stories; no stories by people who have obviously never held a bow in their hands." Receives 1-2 unsolicited fiction mss/month. Accepts 1-2 mss/year. Publishes ms 3 months to 2 years after acceptance. Length: 1,500 words average; 500 words minimum; 2,000 words maximum. Publishes short shorts. Length: 500 words. Sometimes critiques rejected mss and recommends other markets.
How to Contact: Query first or send complete ms with cover letter. Reports in 2 weeks on queries; 4 weeks on mss. Sample copy for $2 and 8½ × 11 SAE with appropriate postage. Fiction guidelines for #10 SASE.
Payment/Terms: Pays $100-350 on acceptance for first worldwide serial rights.
Advice: "We have a resident humorist who supplies us with most of the 'fiction' we need. But if a story comes through the door which captures the essence of bowhunting and we feel it will reach out to our readers, we will buy it. Despite our macho outdoor magazine status, we are a bunch of English majors who love to read. You can't bull your way around real outdoor people—they can spot a phony at 20 paces. If you've never camped out under the stars and listened to an elk bugle and try to relate that experience without really experiencing it, someone's going to know. We are very specialized; we don't want stories about shooting apples off people's heads or of Cupid's arrow finding its mark. James Dickey's *Deliverance* used bowhunting metaphorically, very effectively . . . while we don't expect that type of writing from everyone, that's the kind of feeling that characterizes a good piece of outdoor fiction."

BOYS' LIFE, For All Boys, (II), Boy Scouts of America, Magazine Division, Box 152079, 1325 W. Walnut Hill Lane, Irving TX 75015-2079. (214)580-2366. Fiction Editor: Shannon Lowry. Magazine: 8 × 11; 68 pages; slick cover stock; illustrations; photos. "*Boys' Life* covers Boy Scout activities and general interest subjects for ages 8 to 18, Boy Scouts, Cub Scouts and others of that age group." Monthly. Estab. 1911. Circ. 1,300,000.
Needs: Adventure, humor/satire, mystery/suspense (young adult), science fiction, sports and western (young adult). "We publish short stories aimed at a young adult audience and frequently written from the viewpoint of a 10- to 16-year-old boy protagonist." Receives approximately 250 unsolicited mss/month. Accepts 12-18 mss/year. Length: 500 words minimum; 1,500 words maximum; 1,200 words average. "Very rarely" critiques rejected ms.
How to Contact: Send complete ms with SASE. "We'd much rather see manuscripts than queries." Reports in 6-8 weeks. Simultaneous submissions OK. For sample copy "check your local library." Writer's guidelines available; send SASE.
Payment/Terms: Pays $300 and up ("depending on length and writer's experience with us") on acceptance for one-time rights.
Advice: "*Boys' Life* writers understand the readers. They treat them as intelligent human beings with a thirst for knowledge and entertainment. We tend to use some of the same authors repeatedly because their characters, themes, etc., develop a following among our readers. Read at least a year's worth of the magazine. You will get a feeling for what our readers are interested in and what kind of fiction we buy."

BUFFALO SPREE MAGAZINE, (II, IV), Spree Publishing Co., Inc., 4511 Harlem Rd., Buffalo NY 14226. (716)839-3405. Editor: Johanna Van De Mark. "City magazine for professional, educated and above-average income people." Quarterly. Estab. 1967. Circ. 21,000.
Needs: Literary, contemporary, adventure, humor and ethnic. No pornographic. Accepts about 15 mss/issue; 60 mss/year. Length: 2,500 words maximum.
How to Contact: Send complete ms with SASE. Reports within 3-6 months. Sample copy for $2, 9 × 12 SASE and $2.40 postage.
Payment/Terms: Pays $80-150 and 1 contributor's copy on publication for first rights.

BUGLE, Journal of Elk and the Hunt, (II, IV), Rocky Mountain Elk Foundation, P.O. Box 8249, Missoula MT 59807-8249. (406)523-4568. Fax: (406)523-4550. Editor: Dan Crockett. Magazine: 8½×11; 114-172 pages; 55 lb. Escanaba paper; 80 lb. sterling cover; b&w, 4-color illustrations and photographs. "The Rocky Mountain Elk Foundation is a nonprofit conservation organization established in 1984 to help conserve critical habitat for elk and other wildlife. *BUGLE*, the Foundation's quarterly magazine specializes in research, stories (fiction and nonfiction), art and photography pertaining to the world of elk and elk hunting." Quarterly. Estab. 1984.

Needs: Elk-related adventure, children's/juvenile (5-9 years, 10-12 years), historical, human interest, natural history, scientific. "We would like to see more humor." Upcoming themes; "Bowhunting" and "Women in the Outdoors."Receives 10-15 unsolicited mss/month. Accepts 5 mss/issue; 18-20 mss/year. Publishes ms 6 months after acceptance. Published work by Don Burgess and Mike Logan. Length: 2,500 words preferred; 1,500 words minimum; 5,000 words maximum. Publishes short shorts. Also publishes literary essays and poetry.

How to Contact: Query first or send complete ms with a cover letter. Include estimated word count and bio (100 words). Reports in 2-4 weeks on queries; 4-6 weeks on ms. Send SASE for reply, return of ms or send a disposable copy of ms. Sample copy for $5. Writers guidelines free.

Payment/Terms: Pays 25¢/word maximum on acceptance for one-time rights.

Advice: "We accept fiction and nonfiction stories about elk that show originality, and respect for the animal and its habitat. No 'formula' outdoor writing. No how-to writing."

BUZZ, The Talk of Los Angeles, (II, IV), Buzz Inc., 11845 W. Olympic, #800, Los Angeles CA 90064. (310)473-2721. Fax: (310)473-2876. E-mail: queries@buzzmag.com. Editor: Allan Mayer. Fiction Editor: Renée Vogel. Magazine: 9×10⅞; 120-160 pages; coated paper. Published 10 times/year. Estab. 1990. Circ. 125,000.

● *Buzz* was a 1996 National Magazine Award for Fiction finalist.

Needs: Literary, mainstream/contemporary, regional. *Only interested in fiction by L.A. writers or about L.A.* Receives 75-100 unsolicited mss/month. Accepts 1 ms/issue; 10 mss/year. Recently published work by Bart Kosko, Donald Rawley, Yxta Maya Murray and Greg Jones. Length: 2,000 words minimum; 5,000 words maximum. Sometimes critiques or comments on rejected mss.

How to Contact: Send complete ms with a cover letter. Reports on mss in 2 months. SASE for return of ms. Simultaneous and electronic submissions(disk) OK. Sample copy for $3, 11×14 SAE and $3 postage. Fiction guidelines for SASE. Send books to Renée Vogel.

Payment/Terms: Pays $1,000-2,500 and contributor's copies for first North American serial rights. Sends galleys to author.

CAMPUS LIFE MAGAZINE, (II), Christianity Today, Inc., 465 Gundersen Dr., Carol Stream IL 60188. (630)260-6200. Fax: (630)260-0114. Managing Editor: Christopher Lutes. Magazine: 8¼×11¼; 100 pages; 4-color and b&w illustrations; 4-color and b&w photos. "General interest magazine with a Christian point of view." Articles "vary from serious to humorous to current trends and issues, for high school and college age readers." Bimonthly. Estab. 1942. Circ. 100,000.

● *Campus Life* regularly receives awards from the Evangelical Press Association.

Needs: Condensed novel, humor/satire, prose poem, serialized/excerpted novel. "All submissions must be contemporary, reflecting the teen experience in the '90s. We are a Christian magazine but are *not* interested in sappy, formulaic, sentimentally religious stories. We *are* interested in well-crafted stories that portray life realistically, stories high school and college youth relate to. Nothing contradictory of Christian values. If you don't understand our market and style, don't submit." Accepts 5 mss/year. Reading and response time slower in summer. Published work by Barbara Durkin and Tracy Dalton. Published new writers within the last year. Length: 1,000-3,000 words average, "possibly longer." Publishes short shorts.

How to Contact: Query with short synopsis of work, published samples and SASE. Does not accept unsolicited mss. Reports in 4-6 weeks on queries. Sample copy for $2 and 9½×11 envelope.

Payment/Terms: Pays "generally" $250-400; 2 contributor's copies on acceptance for one-time rights.

Advice: "We print finely-crafted fiction that carries a contemporary teen (older teen) theme. First person fiction often works best. Ask us for sample copy with fiction story. Fiction communicates to

---

MARKET CATEGORIES: (I) Open to new writers; (II) Open to both new and established writers; (III) Interested mostly in established writers; (IV) Open to writers whose work is specialized; (V) Closed to unsolicited submissions.

our reader. We want experienced fiction writers who have something to say to or about young people without getting propagandistic."

CAPPER'S, (II), Stauffer Magazine Group, 1503 S.W. 42nd St., Topeka KS 66609-1265. (913)274-4300. Fax: (913)274-4305. Editor: Nancy Peavler. Magazine: 24-48 pages; newsprint paper and cover stock; photos. A "clean, uplifting and nonsensational newspaper for families from children to grandparents." Biweekly. Estab. 1879. Circ. 375,000.
  • *Capper's* is interested in longer works, 7,000 words or more.
Needs: Serialized novels suitable for young adults to seniors. "We accept novel-length stories for serialization. No fiction containing violence, sexual references or obscenity; no science fiction or mystery. We would like to see more western romance, pioneer stories." Receives 2-3 unsolicited fiction mss each month. Accepts 4-6 stories/year. Recently published work by Michael Anthony, Marci Albarghetti, Sandra Rinderer and Virginia M. McGuffey. Published new writers within the last year. Length: 7,000 words minimum; 40,000 words maximum.
How to Contact: Send complete ms with SASE. Cover letter and/or synopsis helpful. Electronic submissions (disk, Mac format only) OK. Reports in 6-8 months on ms. Sample copy for $1.50.
Payment/Terms: Pays $75-400 for one-time serialization and contributor's copies (1-2 copies as needed for copyright) on acceptance for second serial (reprint) rights and one-time rights.
Advice: "Since we publish in serialization, be sure your manuscript is suitable for that format. Each segment needs to be compelling enough so the reader remembers it and is anxious to read the next installment. Please proofread and edit carefully. We've seen major characters change names partway through the manuscript."

CATS MAGAZINE, (IV), CATS Magazine Inc., P.O. Box 290037, Port Orange FL 32129. (904)788-2770. Editor: Tracey Copeland. Magazine: 8 × 11; 76-100 pages; 40 lb. paper; 60 lb. cover; illustrations and photos. "*CATS Magazine* provides articles that appeal to average cat owners, as well as breeders, on a broad range of topics." Monthly. Estab. 1945. Circ. 150,000.
Needs: Inspirational. "No reformed cat haters or anything with cats in a bad light (occult ties, etc.)." Receives 50 unsolicited mss/month. Accepts 3-4 ms/issue; 36-48 mss/year. Publishes ms 6-18 months after acceptance. Length: 1,000 words average; 350 words minimum; 1,200 words maximum. Publishes short shorts.
How to Contact: Send complete ms with a cover letter. Include estimated word count and list of publications. Reports in 1-3 months on queries; 2-4 months on mss. SASE for return of ms. Simultaneous and electronic (with hard copy) submissions OK. Sample copy for $3 or send 9 × 12 SAE with $1.70 postage. Fiction guidelines for #10 SASE. "Please state if it is a simultaneous submission."
Payment/Terms: Pays $20-50 and 1 contributor's copy on publication for first rights or one-time rights.
Advice: "Our short story section, Tails & Tales, is subtitled 'Short stories from our readers about special cats in their lives.' Stories should be believable. No stories are accepted from the cats point of view. Know the basics. Study the cat market. To get the best idea of what a magazine's fiction needs are, read several of their back issues. Also, don't force yourself to write on a certain topic. Write what you know and are comfortable with and then submit to appropriate publications."

❈CHICKADEE, The Magazine for Young Children from OWL, (II), Owl Communications, 179 John St., Suite 500, Toronto, Ontario M5T 3G5 Canada. (416)971-5275. Fax: (416)971-5294. Managing Editor: Catherine Jane Wren. Editor-in-Chief: Nyla Ahmad. Magazine: 8½ × 11¾; 32 pages; glossy paper and cover stock; illustrations and photographs. "*Chickadee* is created to give children under nine a lively, fun-filled look at the world around them. Each issue has a mix of activities, puzzles, games and stories." Monthly except July and August. Estab. 1979. Circ. 110,000.
  • *Chickadee* has won several awards including the EDPRESS Golden Lamp Honor award and the Parents' Choice Golden Seal awards.
Needs: Juvenile. No religious or anthropomorphic material. Accepts 1 ms/issue; 10 mss/year. Publishes ms an average of 1 year after acceptance. Published new writers within the last year. Length: 900 words maximum.
How to Contact: Send complete ms and cover letter with $1 to cover postage and handling. Simultaneous submissions OK. Reports in 2 months. Sample copy for $4.50. Fiction guidelines for SASE.
Payment/Terms: Pays $25-250 (Canadian); 2 contributor's copies on acceptance for all rights. Occasionally buys reprints.
Advice: "Read back issues to see what types of fiction we publish. Common mistakes include: loose, rambling, and boring prose; stories that lack a clear beginning, middle and end; unbelievable characters; and overwriting."

CHILD LIFE, (IV), Children's Better Health Institute, Box 567, 1100 Waterway Blvd., Indianapolis IN 46206. (317)636-8881. Editor: Lise Hoffman. Juvenile magazine for kids aged 9-11. Looking for "nonfiction stories on health, sports, fitness, exercise, nutrition and safety; fiction stories using

contemporary kids and situations involving health, humor or adventure."
- The Children's Better Health Institute also publishes *Children's Digest*, *Children's Playmate*, *Humpty Dumpty*, *Jack and Jill* and *Turtle* magazines listed in this book.

Needs: Juvenile. No book manuscripts or adult or adolescent fiction. Recently published work by Eileen Spinelli, Ellen Senisi, Charles Ghigna and Pete Garvey. "Will publish new writers if they demonstrate knowledge of and ability to meed editorial needs." Length: 900 words maximum.

How to Contact: Send complete ms with SASE. No queries. Reports in 12 weeks. Sample copy for $1.25. Writer's guidelines for SASE.

Payment/Terms: Approximately 12¢/word on publication for all rights. One-time rights for photos.

Advice: "Don't guess at what kids like—hang out with them. What interests or concerns them? What do their conversations sound like? Use dialogue to elaborate on contemporary situations in fiction stories. Nonfiction stories with professional-quality, color slides and factual, current information with a sports/health angle will receive preference. Tell your readers (and your editors) something they don't already know. Avoid tired themes of underachiever turns hero, child rescues adult or pet, and animal main characters."

CHILDREN'S DIGEST, (II, IV), Children's Better Health Institute, P.O. Box 567, 1100 Waterway Blvd., Indianapolis IN 46206. Editor: Layne Cameron. Magazine: 6½×9; 48 pages; reflective and preseparated illustrations; color and b&w photos. Magazine with special emphasis on health, nutrition, exercise and safety for preteens.
- Other magazines published by Children's Better Health Institute and listed in this book are *Child Life*, *Children's Playmate*, *Humpty Dumpty*, *Jack and Jill* and *Turtle*. The magazine has become known for stories featuring contemporary situations and sports/fitness stories.

Needs: "Realistic stories, short plays, adventure and mysteries. We would like to see more stories that reflect today's society: concern for the environment, single-parent families and children from diverse backgrounds. Humorous stories are highly desirable. We especially need stories that *subtly* encourage readers to develop better health or safety habits. Stories should not exceed 1,500 words." Receives 40-50 unsolicited fiction mss each month. Published work by Judith Josephson, Pat McCarthy, Sharen Liddell; published new writers within the last year.

How to Contact: Send complete ms with SASE. "A cover letter isn't necessary unless an author wishes to include publishing credits and special knowledge of the subject matter." Reports in 10 weeks. Sample copy for $1.25. Fiction guidelines for SASE.

Payment/Terms: Pays 12¢/word minimum with up to 10 contributor's copies on publication for all rights.

Advice: "We try to present our health-related material in a positive—not a negative—light, and we try to incorporate humor and a light approach wherever possible without minimizing the seriousness of what we are saying. Fiction stories that deal with a health theme need not have health as the primary subject but should include it in some way in the course of events. Most rejected health-related manuscripts are too preachy or they lack substance. Children's magazines are not training grounds where authors learn to write 'real' material for 'real' readers. Because our readers frequently have limited attention spans, it is very important that we offer them well-written stories."

CHILDREN'S PLAYMATE, (IV), Children's Better Health Institute, P.O. Box 567, 1100 Waterway Blvd., Indianapolis IN 46206. (317)636-8881. Editor: Terry Harshman. Magazine: 6½×9; 48 pages; preseparated and reflective art; b&w and color illustrations. Juvenile magazine for children ages 6-8 years. Published 8 times/year.
- *Child Life*, *Children's Digest*, *Humpty Dumpty Jack and Jill* and *Turtle* magazines are also published by Children's Better Health Institute and listed in this book.

Needs: Juvenile with special emphasis on health, nutrition, safety and exercise. "Our present needs are for short, entertaining stories with a subtle health angle. Seasonal material is also always welcome." No adult or adolescent fiction. Receives approximately 150 unsolicited fiction mss each month. Published work by Batta Killion, Ericka Northrop, Elizabeth Murphy-Melas; published new writers within the last year. Length: 625 words or less.

How to Contact: Send complete ms with SASE. Indicate word count on material and date sent. Reports in 8-10 weeks. Sample copy for $1.25.

Payment/Terms: Pays up to 17¢/word and 10 contributor's copies on publication for *all* rights.

Advice: "Stories should be kept simple and entertaining. Study past issues of the magazine—be aware of vocabulary limitations of the readers."

THE CHRISTIAN CENTURY, An Ecumenical Weekly, (I, IV), 407 S. Dearborn St., Chicago IL 60605. (312)427-5380. Fax: (312)427-1302. Editor: James Wall. Magazine: 8¼×10⅞; 24-40 pages; illustrations and photos. "A liberal Protestant magazine interested in the public meaning of Christian faith as it applies to social issues, and in the individual appropriation of faith in modern circumstances." Weekly (sometimes biweekly). Estab. 1884. Circ. 35,000.
- *Christian Century* has received several awards each year from the Associated Church Press,

including: best critical review, best written humor, best feature article, etc.

Needs: Religious/inspirational: feminist, mainstream/contemporary. "We are interested in articles that touch on religious themes in a sophisticated way; we are not interested in simplistic pietistic pieces." Receives 80 unsolicited mss/month. Accepts 10% of unsolicited mss. Publishes ms 1-3 months after acceptance. Published work by Robert Drake and Madeleine Mysko. Length: 2,500 words average; 1,500 words minimum; 3,000 words maximum. Also publishes literary essays and poetry.

How to Contact: Send complete ms with a cover letter. Include bio (100 words). Reports in 1 week on queries; 1 month on mss. Send a disposable copy of ms. No simultaneous submissions. Sample copy for $2. Reviews novels and short story collections.

Payment/Terms: Pays $200 maximum and 1 contributor's copy (additional copies for $1) on publication for all rights. Sends galleys to author.

CHRISTIAN SINGLE, (II), Lifeway Press, 127 Ninth Ave. N., MSN 140, Nashville TN 37234. (615)251-2228. Editor-in-Chief: Stephen Felts. Magazine: 8½×11; 50 pages; illustrations; photographs. "We reflect the doctrine and beliefs of evangelical Christian single adults. We prefer positive, uplifting, encouraging fiction written from the single perspective." Monthly. Estab. 1979. Circ. 75,000.

Needs: Religious/inspirational. Receives 100 unsolicited mss/month. Accepts 1 ms/issue; 4-5 mss/year. Length: 600-1,200 words average. Publishes short shorts and poetry.

How to Contact: Send query with SASE. Include estimated word count and opening paragraph. Reports in 1-2 weeks on queries; 3-6 weeks on mss. Send SASE for reply, return of ms or send a disposable copy of the ms. No simultaneous submissions. Accepts reprint and electronic submissions. Sample copy for 9×12 SAE and 4 first-class stamps.

Payment/Terms: Payment is "negotiable." Pays on acceptance. Buys all rights, first rights, first North American serial rights or one-time rights.

Advice: Looks for "manuscripts that are not preachy and intended for a single audience. Write to evoke an emotion. No Pollyanna stories please. I want stories of 'real' life with 'real' people finding real answers using biblical principles. Take a lot of time to draft a well-written query letter that includes a paragraph or two of the actual piece. I can feel by the query letter what quality of an article I can expect to receive."

‡CLUBHOUSE, Focus on the Family, (II, III), 8605 Explorer Dr., Colorado Springs CO 80920. (719)531-3400. Editor: Lisa Brock. Assistant Editor: Annette Brashler. Magazine: 8×11; 24 pages; illustrations and photos. Publishes literature for kids ages 8-12. "Stories must have moral lesson included. *Clubhouse* readers are 8- to 12-year-old boys and girls who desire to know more about God and the Bible. Their parents (who typically pay for the membership) want wholesome, educational material with Scriptual or moral insight. The kids want excitement, adventure, action, humor or mystery. Your job as a writer is to please both the parent and child with each article." Monthly. Estab. 1989. Circ. 100,000.

Needs: Children's/juvenile (5-9 years, 10-12 years), religious/inspirational, young adult/teen (adventure, western). No science fiction. Receives 150 unsolicited mss/month. Accepts 3-4 mss/issue. Agented fiction 15%. Recently published work by Sigmund Brower and Nancy Rue. Length: 1,200 words average; 400 words minimum; 2,500 words maximum. "Sometimes we'll run two-part fiction." Publishes short shorts.

How to Contact: Send complete ms with cover letter. Include estimated word count, bio and list of publications. Reports in 6 weeks. Send SASE for reply, return of ms or send a disposable copy of ms. Simultaneous submissions and reprints OK. Sample copy for $1.50. Fiction guidelines free.

Payment/Terms: Pays $400 maximum on acceptance and 2 contributor's copies; additional copies for $1.50. Acquires all rights, first rights, first North American serial rights or one-time rights. Sends galleys to author.

Advice: Looks for "humor with a point, historical fiction featuring great Christians or Christians who lived during great times; contemporary, exotic settings; holiday material (Christmas, Thanksgiving, Easter, President's Day); parables; fantasy (avoid graphic descriptions of evil creatures and action); mystery stories; choose-your-own adventure stories and westerns. No contemporary, middle-class family settings (we already have authors who can meet these needs), poems (we rarely print poetry) or stories dealing with boy-girl relationships."

‡COBBLESTONE, The History Magazine for Young People, (I, II), 7 School St., Peterborough NH 03458. Editor: Margaret Chorlian. Magazine: "Historical accuracy and lively, original approaches to the subject are primary concerns of the editors in choosing material. For 8-14 year olds." Monthly (except July and August). Estab. 1979. Circ. 36,000.

● *Cobblestone* has received Ed Press and Parent's Choice awards.

Needs: Material must fit upcoming theme; write for theme list and deadlines. Childrens/juvenile (8-14 years). "Authentic historical and biographical fiction, adventure, retold legends, etc., relating to the theme." Upcoming themes available for SASE (or IRC). Published after theme deadline. Accepts 1-2 fiction mss/issue. Length: 800 words maximum. Publishes short shorts. Also publishes poetry.

How to Contact: Query first or query with clips of published work (if new to *Cobblestone*). Include estimated word count. "Include detailed outline explaining the information to be presented in the article and bibliography of material used." Reports in several months. If interested, responds to queries 5 months before publication date. Send SASE (or IRC) for reply or send self-addressed postcard to find out if query was received. Electronic submissions (disk, Microsoft Word or MS-DOS) OK. Sample copy for $4.25, 7½ × 10½ SAE and $1.05 postage. Fiction guidelines for #10 SAE and 1 first-class stamp.
Payment/Terms: Pays 20-25¢/word on publication for all rights.
Advice: Writers may send $8.95 plus $3 shipping for *Cobblestone*'s index for a listing of subjects covered in back issues.

✦**COMPANION MAGAZINE, (II)**, Conventual Franciscan Friars, Box 535, Postal Station F, Toronto, Ontario M4Y 2L8 Canada. (416)690-5611. Editor: Fr. Rick Riccioli, OFM. Conv. Managing Editor: Betty McCrimmon. Publishes material "emphasizing religious and human values and stressing Franciscan virtues—peace, simplicity, joy." Monthly. Estab. 1936. Circ. 5,000.
   • *Companion* received an award from the Canadian Church Press in 1996.
Needs: Adventure, humor, mainstream, religious. Canadian settings preferred. Receives 50 unsolicited fiction mss/month. Accepts 2 mss/issue. Time varies between acceptance and publication. Length: 1,200 words maximum. Publishes short shorts.
How to Contact: Send complete mss. Reports in 3 weeks to 1 month on mss. SAE with "cash to buy stamps" or IRC. Sample copy and fiction guidelines free.
Payment/Terms: Pays 6¢/word (Canadian funds) on publication for first North American serial rights.

COMPUTOREDGE, San Diego's Free Weekly Computer Magazine, (I, IV), The Byte Buyer, Inc., Box 83086, San Diego CA 92138. (619)573-0315. Website: http:/www.computoredge.com. Editor: John San Filippo. Magazine: 8½ × 11; 60-80 pages; newsprint; 50 lb. bookwrap cover; illustrations. Publishes material relating to "personal computers from a human point of view. For new users/shoppers." Weekly. Estab. 1983. Circ. 90,000.
Needs: Fiction that includes computers. "Keep it short! Can be science fiction including computers or 'future' stories. Would like to see stories with a more positive tone." Each issue has a theme; calendar included with guidelines and also available on website. Receives up to 3 unsolicited fiction mss/month. Accepts 10 fiction mss/year. Publishes ms 1-4 months after acceptance. Length: 800 words minimum; 1,200 words maximum.
How to Contact: Send complete ms with cover letter. Include Social Security number, phone number and e-mail address. Reports in 2 months. SASE. Electronic submission of *accepted* mss *only*. Sample copy for 9 × 12 SAE and $1.50 postage; writer's guidelines for #10 SASE.
Payment/Terms: Pays 8-10¢/word on publication for first rights or first North American serial rights. Offers $15 kill fee.
Advice: "We get too many 'my computer came to life and tried to take over the world' stories. The same, old idea, no matter how well told, is still the same, old idea. We're looking for stories that are very fresh *and* excellently written."

CONTACT ADVERTISING, (IV), Box 3431, Ft. Pierce FL 34948. (407)464-5447. Editor: Herman Nietzche. Magazines and newspapers. Publications vary in size, 56-80 pages. "Group of 26 erotica, soft core publications for swingers, single males, married males, gay males, transgendered and bisexual persons." Bimonthly, quarterly and monthly. Estab. 1975. Circ. combined is 2,000,000.
   • This is a group of regional publications with *very* explicit sexual content, graphic personal ads, etc. Not for the easily offended.
Needs: Erotica, fantasy, feminist, fetish, gay and lesbian. Receives 8-10 unsolicited mss/month. Accepts 1-2 mss/issue; 40-50 mss/year. Publishes ms 1-3 months after acceptance. Length: 2,000 words minimum; 3,500 words maximum. Sometimes critiques rejected mss.
How to Contact: Query first with clips of published work or send complete ms with cover letter. Reports in 1-2 weeks on queries; 3-4 weeks on mss. SASE. Simultaneous and reprint submissions OK. Sample copy for $6. Fiction guidelines with SASE.
Payment/Terms: First submission, free subscription to magazine; subsequent submissions $25-75 on publication for all rights or first rights; all receive 3 contributor's copies.
Advice: "Know your grammar! Content must be of an adult nature but well within guidelines of the law. Fantasy, unusual sexual encounters, swinging stories or editorials of a sexual bend are acceptable. Read Henry Miller!"

CORNERSTONE MAGAZINE, (I, II), Cornerstone Communications, Inc., 939 W. Wilson Ave., Chicago IL 60640. (312)561-2450 ext. 2394. Fax (312)989-2076. Editor: Dawn Mortimer. Fiction Editor: Misty Files. Magazine: 8½ × 11; 64 pages; 35 lb. coated matie paper; self cover; illustrations and photos. "For young adults, 18-35. We publish nonfiction (essays, personal experience, religious), music interviews, current events, film and book reviews, fiction, poetry. *Cornerstone* challenges readers to look through the window of biblical reality. Known as avant-garde, yet attempts to express orthodox belief in the language of the nineties." Approx. quarterly. Estab. 1972. Circ. 35,000.

● *Cornerstone Magazine* has won numerous awards from the Evangelical Press Association.

Needs: Ethnic/multicultural, fantasy (science fantasy), humor/satire, literary, mainstream/contemporary, religious/inspirational. Special interest in "issues pertinent to contemporary society, seen with a biblical worldview." No "pornography, cheap shots at non-Christians, unrealistic or syrupy articles." Receives 60 unsolicited mss/month. Accepts 1 mss/issue; 3-4 mss/year. Does not read mss during Christmas/New Year's week and the first week of July. Published work by Dave Cheadle, C.S. Lewis and J.B. Simmonds. Length: 1,200 words average; 250 words minimum; 2,500 words maximum. Publishes short shorts. Length: 250-450 words. Also publishes literary essays, literary criticism and poetry.

How to Contact: Send complete ms. Include estimated word count, bio (50-100 words), list of publications, and name, address, phone and fax number on every item submitted. Send disposable copy of the ms. Will consider simultaneous submissions, reprints and electronic (disk or modem) submissions. Reports in up to 3 months. Sample copy for 8½×11 SAE and 6 first-class stamps. Reviews novels and short story collections.

Payment/Terms: Pays 8-10¢/word maximum; also 6 contributor's copies on publication. Purchases first serial rights.

Advice: "Articles may express Christian world view but shouldn't be unrealistic or syrupy. We're looking for high-quality fiction with skillful characterization and plot development and imaginative symbolism." Looks for "mature Christian short stories, as opposed to those more fit for church bulletins. We want fiction with bite and an edge but with a Christian worldview."

COSMOPOLITAN MAGAZINE, (III), The Hearst Corp., 224 W. 57th St., New York NY 10019. (212)649-2000. Editor: Helen Gurley Brown. Fiction Editor: Betty Kelly. Most stories include male-female relationships, traditional plots, characterizations. Single career women (ages 18-34). Monthly. Circ. just under 3 million.

Needs: Adventure, contemporary, mystery and romance. "Stories should include a romantic relationship and usually a female protagonist. The characters should be in their 20s or 30s (i.e., same ages as our readers). No highly experimental pieces. Upbeat endings." Buys novel or book excerpts occasionally; but "only if the novel or book has been published." Agented fiction 98%. Published excerpts by Danielle Steel, Pat Booth and Belva Plain; published new writers within the last year. Occasionally recommends other markets.

How to Contact: Send complete ms with SASE. Guidelines for #10 SASE. Reports in 8-10 weeks. "We cannot contact you unless you enclose a #10 SASE." Publishes ms 6-18 months after acceptance.

Payment/Terms: Pays $750-2,000 on acceptance for first North American serial rights. Buys reprints.

COUNTRY WOMAN, (IV), Reiman Publications, Box 643, Milwaukee WI 53201. (414)423-0100. Editor: Ann Kaiser. Managing Editor: Kathleen Pohl. Magazine: 8½×11; 68 pages; excellent quality paper; excellent cover stock; illustrations and photographs. "Articles should have a rural theme and be of specific interest to women who live on a farm or ranch, or in a small town or country home, and/or are simply interested in country-oriented topics." Bimonthly. Estab. 1971.

Needs: Fiction must be upbeat, heartwarming and focus on a country woman as central character. "Many of our stories and articles are written by our readers!" Recently published work by Edna Norrell, Millie Thomas Kearney and Rita Peterson. Published new writers within last year. Publishes 1 fiction story/issue. Length: 1,000 words.

How to Contact: Send $2 and SASE for sample copy and writer's guidelines. All manuscripts should be sent to Kathy Pohl, Managing Editor. Reports in 2-3 months. Include cover letter and SASE. Simultaneous and reprint submissions OK.

Payment/Terms: Pays $90-125 on acceptance for one-time rights.

Advice: "Read the magazine to get to know our audience. Send us country-to-the-core fiction, not yuppie-country stories—our readers know the difference! Very traditional fiction—with a definite beginning, middle and end, some kind of conflict/resolution, etc. We do not want to see contemporary avant-garde fiction—nothing dealing with divorce, drugs, etc., or general societal malaise of the '90s."

‡CREATIVE KIDS, (I, IV), Prufrock Press, P.O. Box 8813, Waco TX 76714. (800)998-2208. Fax: (800)240-0333. E-mail: creative_kids@prufrock.com. Editor: Libby Lindsey. Magazine: 7½×10; 36 pages; illustrations; photos. Material by children for children. Published 4 times/year. Estab. 1980. Circ: 45,000.

● *Creative Kids* featuring work by children has won Edpress and Parents' Choice Gold Awards.

Needs: "We publish work by children ages 8-14." Publishes short stories, essays, games, puzzles, poems, opinion pieces and letters. Accepts 3-4 mss/issue; 12-16 mss/year. Publishes ms up to 2 years after acceptance. Published new writers within the last year. No novels.

How to Contact: Send complete ms with cover letter. Include name, age, birthday, home address, school, name and address, grade, statement of originality signed by teacher or parent. Must include SASE for response. Do not query. Reports in 1 month on mss. SASE. No simultaneous submissions. Sample copy for $3. Guidelines for SASE.

Payment/Terms: Pays 1 contributor's copy. Acquires all rights.

Advice: "*Creative Kids* is designed to entertain, stimulate and challenge the creativity of children ages 8 to 14, encouraging their abilities and helping them to explore their ideas, opinions and world. We would like more opinion pieces."

CRICKET MAGAZINE, (II), Carus Corporation, P.O. Box 300, Peru IL 61354. (815)224-6656. Editor-in-Chief: Marianne Carus. Magazine: 8×10; 64 pages; illustrations; photos. Magazine for children, ages 9-14. Monthly. Estab. 1973. Circ. 83,000.

● *Cricket* has received a Parents Choice Award, a Paul A. Witty Short Story Award and awards from Edpress.

Needs: Adventure, contemporary, ethnic, fantasy, historic fiction, folk and fairytales, humorous, juvenile, mystery, science fiction and translations. No adult articles. All issues have different "mini-themes." Receives approximately 1,100 unsolicited fiction mss each month. Publishes ms 6-24 months or longer after acceptance. Accepts 180 mss/year. Agented fiction 1-2%. Published work by Peter Dickinson, Mary Stolz and Jane Yolen. Published new writers within the last year. Length: 500-2,000 words.

How to Contact: Do not query first. Send complete ms with SASE. List previous publications. Reports in 3 months on mss. Sample copy for $4; guidelines for SASE.

Payment/Terms: Pays up to 25¢/word; 2 contributor's copies; $2 charge for extras on publication for first rights. Sends edited mss for approval. Buys reprints.

Advice: "Do not write *down* to children. Write about well-researched subjects you are familiar with and interested in, or about something that concerns you deeply. Children *need* fiction and fantasy. Carefully study several issues of *Cricket* before you submit your manuscript." Sponsors contests for readers of all ages.

‡DIALOGUE, A World of Ideas for Visually Impaired People of All Ages, (I, II), Blindskills Inc., P.O. Box 5181, Salem OR 97304-0181. (800)860-4224. (503)581-4224. Fax: (503)581-0178. E-mail: blindskl@teleport.com. Editor/Publisher: Carol McCarl. Magazine: 9×11; 130 pages; matte stock. Publishes information of general interest to visually impaired. Quarterly. Estab. 1961. Circ. 15,000.

Needs: Contemporary, humor/satire, literary, mainstream and senior citizen/retirement. No erotica, religion, confessional or experimental. Receives approximately 10 unsolicited fiction mss/month. Accepts 3 mss/issue, 12 mss/year. Publishes ms an average of 6 months after acceptance. Recently published work by Kim Rush, Diana Braun and Eric Cameron. Published new writers within the last year. Length: 1,000 words average; 500 words minimum; 1,300 words maximum. Publishes short shorts. Occasionally critiques rejected mss. Sometimes recommends other markets. "We give top priority to blind or visually impaired (legally blind) authors."

How to Contact: Query first or send complete ms with SASE. Also send statement of visual handicap. Reports in 2 weeks on queries; 6 weeks on mss. Reprint submissions OK. Accepts electronic submissions on disk; IBM and compatible; Word Perfect 5.1 or 6.0 preferred. Sample copy for $6 and #10 SAE with 1 first-class stamp. Fiction guidelines free.

Payment/Terms: Pays $5-25 and contributor's copy on acceptance for first rights.

Advice: "Study the magazine. This is a very specialized field. Remember the SASE!"

‡DISCOVERIES, (II), WordAction Publishing Company, 6401 The Paseo, Kansas City MO 64131. Contact: Editor. Story paper: $8\frac{1}{2} \times 11$; 4 pages; illustrations. "Committed to reinforce the Bible concept taught in Sunday School curriculum, for ages 8-10 (grades 3-4)." Weekly.

Needs: Religious, puzzles, Bible trivia, 100-200 words. Accepts 1-2 stories and 1-2 puzzles/issue. Publishes ms 1-2 years after acceptance. Length: 500-700 words.

How to Contact: Send complete ms with cover letter and SASE. Send SASE for sample copy and guidelines.

READ THE BUSINESS OF FICTION WRITING section to learn the correct way to prepare and submit a manuscript.

Payment/Terms: Pays 5¢/word for multiple rights on acceptance or on publication.
Advice: "Stories should vividly portray definite Christian emphasis or character building values, without being preachy."

‡**DISCOVERY, (IV)**, WTLN, 400 W. Lake Brantley Rd., Altamonte Springs FL 32714-2715. (407)682-9494. Fax: (407)682-7005. Features Editor: Chris Shenk. Newspaper: 14½×11⅝; 20 pages; 34 lb. paper; web press; illustrations and photos. *Discovery* is "a well-established religious newspaper reaching the Christian market throughout central Florida." Monthly. Estab. 1981. Circ. 25,000.
Needs: Religious/inspirational, senior citizen/retirement. Length: 300-500 words. Publishes short stories. Sometimes critiques or comments on rejected mss.
How to Contact: Send complete ms with cover letter. Include estimated word count and bio. Send a disposable copy of ms. Simultaneous submissions and reprints OK. Sample copy free. Reviews novels and short story collections.
Payment/Terms: Pays free subscription to the magazine and contributor's copies. Acquires one-time rights.
Advice: Looks for "a good opening paragraph, efficiency of space and Christian appeal. Keep on trying—don't give up. We keep story files."

DRAGON® MAGAZINE, The Monthly Adventure Role-Playing Aid, (IV), TSR, Inc., 201 Sheridan Springs Rd., Lake Geneva WI 53147. (414)248-3625. Contact: Fiction Editor. Magazine: 8½×11; 120 pages; 50 penn. plus paper; 80 lb. northcote cover stock; illustrations; rarely photos. "*Dragon Magazine* contains primarily nonfiction—articles and essays on various aspects of the hobby of role-playing games. One short fantasy story is published per issue. Readers are mature teens and young adults; over half our readers are under 18 years of age. The majority are male." Monthly. Estab. 1976. Circ. 85,000.
Needs: "We are looking for all types of fantasy (not horror) stories except contemporary fantasy. We are *not* interested in fictionalized accounts of actual role-playing sessions." Upcoming themes: "fantasy humor" (April); "dragons" (June); "gothic horror" (October). Receives 50-60 unsolicited fiction mss/month. Accepts 12 mss/year. Publishes ms 3-12 months after acceptance. Recently published work by Mark Anthony, J. Robert King, Doug Niles, Jeff Grubb and Jean Rabe. Published new writers within the last year. Length: 1,500 words minimum; 8,000 words maximum; 3,000-5,000 words average. Occasionally critiques rejected mss.
How to Contact: Send complete ms, estimated word length, SASE. List only credits of professionally published materials within genre. No simultaneous submissions. Reports in 6-8 weeks. Sample copy for $6.50. Fiction guidelines for #10 SASE. Reviews fantasy and science fiction novels for their application to role-playing games.
Payment/Terms: Pays 5-8¢/word; 2 free contributor's copies on acceptance for fiction only for first worldwide English language rights; $3.50 charge for extras.
Advice: "It is *essential* that you actually see a copy (better, several copies) of the magazine to which you are submitting your work. Do not rely solely on market reports, as stories submitted to the wrong publication waste both your time and the editor's. Stories need not be set in a pseudo-medieval fantasy world, but should still have fantasy or magical elements."

DRUMMER, (II, IV), Desmodus, Inc., Box 410390, San Francisco CA 94141. (415)252-1195. Fax: (415)252-9574. Editor: Wickie Stamp. Magazine: 8½×11; 92 pages; glossy full-color cover; illustrations and photos. "Gay male erotica, fantasy and mystery with a leather, SM or other fetish twist." Monthly. Estab. 1975. Circ. 45,000.
Needs: "Fiction must have an appeal to gay men." Erotica. Receives 20-30 unsolicited fiction mss/month. Accepts 3 mss/issue. Publishes ms 6-8 months after acceptance. Published work by Simon Sheppard, D. Travers Scott, Tony deBlase and Robert Payne.
How to Contact: Send complete ms with cover letter. SASE. Simultaneous submissions OK. Reprints OK. Accepts electronic submissions (disk) compatible with IBM PC. Sample copy for $6.95. Fiction guidelines for #10 SASE. Reviews novels and short story collections. No response to unsolicited submissions.
Payment/Terms: Pays $100 and contributor's copies on publication for first North American serial rights.

EASYRIDERS MAGAZINE, (II), Entertainment for Adult Riders, Box 3000, Aurora Hills CA 91301. Fiction Editor: Keith R. Ball. Magazine: 7¾×10½; 50 lb. coated paper; 70 lb. coated cover stock; illustrations; photos. Men's magazine with bike-related material: how-to's, travel, new equipment information, and fiction for adult men who own or desire to own expensive custom motorcycles, and rugged individualists who own and enjoy their choppers and the good times derived from them. Monthly. Circ. 370,000.
Needs: Adventure. Should be bike-oriented, but doesn't have to dwell on the fact. "We are only interested in hard-hitting, rugged fiction that depicts bikers in a favorable light, and we're strongly

inclined to favor material with a humorous bent." Published work by John D. Kenworthy, Mark Petterson and J.J. Solari. Published new writers within the last year. Length: 3,500-4,500 words.

How to Contact: Send complete ms with SASE and cover letter. Reports in 6 weeks on mss. Sample copy for $4.50.

Payment/Terms: Pays 15-25¢/word on publication for first rights; payment depends on quality, length and use in magazine.

Advice: "Gut level language accepted; sex scenes OK but are not to be graphically described. As long as the material is directly aimed at our macho intelligent male audience, there should be no great problem breaking into our magazine. Before submitting material, however, we strongly recommend that the writer observe our requirements and study a sample copy."

ELLERY QUEEN'S MYSTERY MAGAZINE, (II), Dell Magazines, 1270 Avenue of the Americas, New York NY 10020. (212)698-1313. Editor: Janet Hutchings. Magazine: digest-sized; 160 pages with special 288-page combined September/October issue. Magazine for lovers of mystery fiction. Published 11 times/year. Estab. 1941. Circ. 500,000 readers.
- *EQMM* has won numerous awards and sponsors its own award for Best Stories of the Year, nominated by its readership.

Needs: "We accept only mystery, crime, suspense and detective fiction." Receives approximately 400 unsolicited fiction mss each month. Accepts 10-15 mss/issue. Publishes ms 6-12 months after acceptance. Agented fiction 50%. Recently published work by Peter Lovesey, Anne Perry, Marcia Muller and Ruth Rendell. Published new writers within the last year. Length: up to 7,000 words, occasionally longer. Publishes 1-2 short novels of up to 17,000 words/year by established authors; minute mysteries of 250 words; short, humorous mystery verse. Critiques rejected mss "only when a story might be a possibility for us if revised." Sometimes recommends other markets.

How to Contact: Send complete ms with SASE. Cover letter should include publishing credits and brief biographical sketch. Simultaneous submissions OK. Reports in 3 months or sooner on mss. Fiction guidelines with SASE. Sample copy for $2.95.

Payment/Terms: Pays 3¢/word and up on acceptance for first North American serial rights. Occasionally buys reprints.

Advice: "We have a Department of First Stories and usually publish at least one first story an issue— i.e., the author's first published fiction. We select stories that are fresh and of the kind our readers have expressed a liking for. In writing a detective story, you must play fair with the reader re clues and necessary information. Otherwise you have a better chance of publishing if you avoid writing to formula."

EMERGE MAGAZINE, Black America's News Magazine, (III), 1 Bet Plaza, 1900 W. Place St. NE, Washington DC 20018-1211. (202)608-2093. Fax: (202)608-2598. Editor-in-Chief: George E. Curry. Managing Editor: Ms. Florestine Purnell. 8⅛ × 10⅞; 84 pages; 40 lb. paper; 70 lb. cover stock; 5-6 illustrations; 45 photographs. "*Emerge* is an African-American news monthly that covers news, politics, arts and lifestyles for the college educated, middle class African American audience." Published 10 times/year. Estab. 1989. Circ. 150,000.

Needs: Ethnic, fantasy, literary. "*Emerge* is looking for humorous, tightly written fiction and nonfiction no longer than 2,000 words about African-Americans."

How to Contact: Submit complete ms. Reviews novels and short story collections.

Payment/Terms: Pays $1,000-2,000 and contributor's copies for first North American serial rights. Pays 25% kill fee.

Advice: "*Emerge* stories must accomplish with a fine economy of style what all good fiction must do: make the unusual familiar. The ability to script a compelling story is what has been missing from most of our submissions."

EMPHASIS ON FAITH AND LIVING, (IV), Missionary Church, Inc., P.O. Box 9127, Fort Wayne IN 46899-9127. (219)747-2027. Fax: (219)747-5331. Editor: Robert L. Ransom. Magazine: 8½ × 11; 16 pages; offset paper; illustrations and photos. "Religious/church oriented." Bimonthly. Estab. 1969. Circ. 14,000.

Needs: Religious/inspirational. Receives 10-15 unsolicited mss/month. Accepts 2 mss/year. Publishes ms 3-6 months after acceptance. Published work by Debra Wood and Denise George. Length: 500 words average; 200 words minimum; 1,000 words maximum. Publishes short shorts. Length: 200-250 words.

How to Contact: Send complete ms with a cover letter. Include estimated word count, bio and Social Security number. Reports in 2-3 months on mss. Send SASE for reply, return of ms or send a disposable copy of ms. Simultaneous reprint and electronic submissions OK. Sample copy for 9 × 12 SAE.

Payment/Terms: Pays $10-50 and 5 contributor's copies on publication.

ESQUIRE, The Magazine for Men, (III), Hearst Corp., 250 W. 55th St., New York NY 10019. (212)649-4020. Editor: Edward Kosner. Fiction Editors: Will Blythe and Rust Hills. Magazine. Monthly. Estab. 1933. Circ. 750,000.

- *Esquire* is well-respected for its fiction and has received several National Magazine Awards. Work published in *Esquire* has been selected for inclusion in the *Best American Short Stories* anthology.

Needs: No "pornography, science fiction or 'true romance' stories." Publishes special fiction issue in July. Receives "thousands" of unsolicited mss/year. Rarely accepts unsolicited fiction. Recently published work by Cormac McCarthy, Richard Ford, Robert Stone, Martin Amis, Don DeLillo, Mark Helprin and Will Self.

How to Contact: Send complete ms with cover letter or submit through an agent. Simultaneous submissions OK. Fiction guidelines for SASE.

Payment/Terms: Pays in cash on acceptance, amount undisclosed.

Advice: "Submit one story at a time. Worry a little less about publication, a little more about the work itself."

EVANGEL, (I, II, IV), Light & Life Press, P.O. Box 535002, Indianapolis IN 46253-5002. (317)244-3660. Editor: Julie Innes. Sunday school take-home paper for distribution to adults who attend church. Fiction involves couples and singles coping with everyday crises, making decisions that show growth. Magazine: $5\frac{1}{2} \times 8\frac{1}{2}$; 8 pages; 2-color illustrations; b&w photos. Weekly. Estab. 1897. Circ. 22,000.

Needs: Religious/inspirational. "No fiction without any semblance of Christian message or where the message clobbers the reader." Receives approximately 75 unsolicited fiction mss/month. Accepts 1 ms/issue, 52 mss/year. Published work by C. Ellen Watts, Jeanne Zornes and Betty Steele Everett. Length: 1,000-1,200 words.

How to Contact: Send complete ms with SASE. Reports in 2 months. Electronic submissions ($3\frac{1}{2}$ inch disk-WordPerfect) OK; send hard copy with disk. Sample copy and writer's guidelines with #10 SASE.

Payment/Terms: Pays 4¢/word and 2 contributor's copies on publication; charge for extras.

Advice: "Choose a contemporary situation or conflict and create a good mix for the characters (not all-good or all-bad heroes and villains). Don't spell out everything in detail; let the reader fill in some blanks in the story. Keep him guessing." Rejects mss because of "unbelievable characters and predictable events in the story."

‡FACES, The Magazine About People, (II, IV), Cobblestone Publishing, Inc., 7 School St., Peterborough NH 03458. (603)924-7209. Fax: (603)924-7380. Assistant Publisher: Carolyn P. Yoder. Magazine. *Faces* is a magazine about people for 8-14 year olds. "All manuscripts are reviewed by the American Museum of Natural History in New York before being accepted." Estab. 1984. Circ. 15,000. Monthly, except June, July and August.

Needs: All material must relate to theme; send for theme list. Children's/juvenile (8-14 years), "retold legends, folk tales, stories from around the world, etc., relating to the theme." Length: 800 words preferred. Publishes short shorts.

How to Contact: Query first or query with clips of published work (send query 6-9 months prior to theme issue publication date). Include estimated word count and bio (2-3 lines). Reports 4 months before publication date. Send SASE for reply. Sample copy for $3.95, $7\frac{1}{2} \times 10\frac{1}{2}$ SAE and 98¢ postage. Fiction guidelines for SASE.

Payment/Terms: Pays 20-25¢/word on publication for all rights.

FIRST HAND, Experiences for Loving Men, (II, IV), First Hand Ltd., Box 1314, Teaneck NJ 07666. (201)836-9177. Fax: (201)836-5055. E-mail: firsthand3@aol.com. Editor: Bob Harris. Magazine: digest size; 130 pages; illustrations. "Half of the magazine is made up of our readers' own gay sexual experiences. Rest is fiction and columns devoted to health, travel, books, etc." Published 13 times/year. Estab. 1980. Circ. 60,000.

- First Hand Ltd. also publishes *Guys* and *Manscape*, listed in this book.

Needs: Erotica, gay. "Should be written in first person." No science fiction or fantasy. Erotica should detail experiences based in reality. Receives 75-100 unsolicited mss/month. Accepts 6 mss/issue; 72 mss/year. Publishes ms 9-18 months after acceptance. Length: 3,000 words preferred; 2,000 words minimum; 3,750 words maximum. Sometimes critiques rejected mss.

How to Contact: Send complete ms with cover letter. Include name, address, telephone and Social Security number and "advise on use of pseudonym if any. Also whether selling all rights or first North American rights." No simultaneous submissions. Reports in 1-2 months. SASE. Sample copy for $5. Fiction guidelines for #10 SASE.

Payment/Terms: Pays $100-150 on publication for all rights or first North American serial rights.

Advice: "Avoid the hackneyed situations. Be original. We like strong plots."

FLORIDA WILDLIFE, (IV), Florida Game & Fresh Water Fish Commission, 620 S. Meridian St., Tallahassee FL 32399-1600. (904)488-5563. Editor: Dick Sublette. Associate Editor: Frank Adams. Magazine: 8½×11; 32 pages. "Conservation-oriented material for an 'outdoor' audience." Bimonthly. Estab. 1947. Circ. 26,000.
• *Florida Wildlife* received the Governor's Environmental Communication Award in 1994.
Needs: Adventure, sports. "Florida-related adventure or natural history only. We rarely publish fiction." Accepts 24 mss/year. Length: 1,200 words average; 500 words minimum; 1,500 words maximum.
How to Contact: Send complete ms with cover letter including Social Security number. "We prefer to review article. Response time varies with amount of material on hand." Sample copy for $2.95.
Payment/Terms: Pays minimum of $50 per published page on publication for one-time rights.
Advice: "Send your best work. It must *directly* concern Florida wildlife."

THE FRIEND MAGAZINE, (II), The Church of Jesus Christ of Latter-day Saints, 50 E. North Temple, 23rd Floor, Salt Lake City UT 84150. (801)240-2210. Editor: Vivian Paulsen. Magazine: 8½×10½; 50 pages; 40 lb. coated paper; 70 lb. coated cover stock; illustrations; photos. Publishes for 3-11 year-olds. Monthly. Estab. 1971. Circ. 275,000.
Needs: Adventure, ethnic, some historical, humor, mainstream, religious/inspirational, nature. Length: 1,000 words maximum. Publishes short shorts. Length: 250 words.
How to Contact: Send complete ms. "No query letters please." Reports in 6-8 weeks. SASE. Sample copy for $1.50 with 9½×11 SAE and $1 postage.
Payment/Terms: Pays 11-13¢/word on acceptance for all rights.
Advice: "The *Friend* is particularly interested in stories with substance for tiny tots. Stories should focus on character-building qualities and should be wholesome without moralizing or preaching. Boys and girls resolving conflicts is a theme of particular merit. Since the magazine is circulated worldwide, the *Friend* is interested in stories and articles with universal settings, conflicts, and character. Other suggestions include rebus, picture, holiday, sports, and photo stories, or manuscripts that portray various cultures. Very short pieces (up to 250 words) are desired for younger readers and preschool children. Appropriate humor is a constant need."

THE GEM, (II), Churches of God, General Conference, Box 926, Findlay OH 45839. (419)424-1961. Editor: Evelyn Sloat. Magazine: 6×9; 8 pages; 50 lb. uncoated paper; illustrations (clip art). "True-to-life stories of healed relationships and growing maturity in the Christian faith for senior high students through senior citizens who attend Churches of God, General Conference Sunday Schools." Weekly. Estab. 1865. Circ. 7,000.
Needs: Adventure, humor, mainstream, religious/inspirational, senior citizen/retirement. Nothing that denies or ridicules standard Christian values. Prefers personal testimony or nonfiction short stories. Receives 30 unsolicited fiction mss/month. Accepts 1 ms every 2-3 issues; 20-25 mss/year. Publishes ms 4-12 months after submission. Published work by Betty Steele Everett, Todd Lee and Betty Lou Mell. Length: 1,500 words average; 500 words minimum; 1,700 words maximum.
How to Contact: Send complete ms with cover letter ("letter not essential, unless there is information about author's background which enhances story's credibility or verifies details as being authentic"). Reports in 6 months. SASE. Simultaneous and reprint submissions OK. Sample copy and fiction guidelines for #10 SASE. "If more than one sample copy is desired along with the guidelines, will need 2 oz. postage."
Payment/Terms: Pays $10-15 and contributor's copies on publication for one-time rights. Charge for extras (postage for mailing more than one).
Advice: "Competition at the mediocre level is fierce. There is a dearth of well-written, relevant fiction which wrestles with real problems involving Christian values applied to the crisis times and 'passages' of life. Humor which puts the daily grind into a fresh perspective and which promises hope for survival is also in short supply. Write from your own experience. Avoid religious jargon and stereotypes. Conclusion must be believable in terms of the story—don't force a 'Christian' ending. Avoid simplistic solutions to complex problems. Listen to the storytelling art of Garrison Keillor. Feel how very particular experiences of small town life in Minnesota become universal."

GENT, (II), Dugent Publishing Corp., 14411 Commerce Way, Suite 420, Miami Lakes FL 33016. (305)557-0071. Editor: Bruce Arthur. "Men's magazine designed to have erotic appeal for the reader. Our publications are directed to a male audience, but we do have a certain percentage of female readers. For the most part, our audience is interested in erotically stimulating material, but not exclusively." Monthly. Estab. 1959. Circ. 175,000.
Needs: Erotica: contemporary, science fiction, horror, mystery, adventure and humor. *Gent* specializes in "D-Cup cheesecake," and fiction should be slanted accordingly. "Most of the fiction published includes several sex scenes. No fiction that concerns children, religious subjects or anything that might be libelous." Receives 30-50 unsolicited fiction mss/month. Accepts 2 mss/issue; 26 mss/year. Publishes ms an average of 3 months after acceptance. Agented fiction 10%. Published new writers

within the last year. Length: 2,000-3,500 words. Critiques rejected mss "when there is time."
How to Contact: Send complete ms with SASE. Reports in 1 month. Sample copy for $5. Fiction guidelines for #10 SASE.
Payment/Terms: Pays minimum $200 on publication and 1 contributor's copy for first North American serial rights.
Advice: "Since *Gent* magazine is the 'Home of the D-Cups,' stories and articles containing either characters or themes with a major emphasis on large breasts will have the best chance for consideration. Study a sample copy first." Mss are rejected because "there are not enough or ineffective erotic sequences, plot is not plausible, wrong length, or not slanted specifically for us."

‡GEORGIA JOURNAL, (I, IV), The Indispensable Atlanta Co. Inc., P.O. Box 1604, Decatur GA 30031-1604. (404)377-4275. Fax: (404)377-1820. E-mail: 74467.1243@compuserve.com. Editor: David R. Osier. Magazine: 8½×11; 80 pages; free sheet paper; 60 lb. cover stock; photographs. Open only to writers from Georgia. Bimonthly. Estab. 1980. Circ. 30,000.
Needs: Adventure, condensed/excerpted novel, regional. List of upcoming themes available for SASE. Receives 12 unsolicited mss/month. Accepts 3 mss/year. Publishes ms 6 months after acceptance. Recently published work by Paul Hemphill, Ferrol Sams and Terry Kay. Length: 5,000 words average; 2,500 words minimum; 6,000 words maximum. Also publishes literary essays, literary criticism, poetry. Often critiques or comments on rejected mss.
How to Contact: Query first or query with clips of published work. Include estimated word count, 1-page bio, Social Security number, list of publications. Reports on queries/mss in 2 months. Send SASE for reply, return of ms or send a disposable copy of ms. Reprint and electronic submissions OK. Sample copy for $5. Reviews novels and short story collections.
Payment/Terms: Pays $150-500 on publication. Acquires first rights, first North American serial rights and one-time rights.
Advice: Looks for "strong point of view and well-defined beginning, middle and end with well-defined characters. Avoid passive voice."

‡GOLF JOURNAL, (II), United States Golf Assoc., Golf House, Far Hills NJ 07931-0708. (908)234-2300. Fax: (908)781-1112. Editor: Brett Avery. Managing Editor: Rich Skyzinski. Magazine: 48-56 pages; self cover stock; illustrations and photos. "The magazine's subject is golf—its history, lore, rules, equipment and general information. The focus is on amateur golf and those things applying to the millions of American golfers. Our audience is generally professional, highly literate and knowledgeable; they read *Golf Journal* because of an interest in the game, its traditions, and its noncommercial aspects." Published 9 times/year. Estab. 1948. Circ. 600,000.
Needs: Humor. "Fiction is very limited. *Golf Journal* has had an occasional humorous story, topical in nature. Generally speaking, short stories are not used. Golf jokes will not be used." Accepts 20 mss/year. Published new writers within the last year. Length: 1,000-2,000 words. Recommends other markets. Critiques rejected mss "when there is time."
How to Contact: Send complete ms with SASE. Reports in 2 months on mss. Sample copy for SASE.
Payment/Terms: Pays $500-1,000 on acceptance and 1-10 contributor's copies.
Advice: "Know your subject (golf); familiarize yourself first with the publication." Rejects mss because "fiction usually does not serve the function of *Golf Journal*, which, as the official magazine of the United States Golf Association, deals chiefly with nonfiction subjects."

GOOD HOUSEKEEPING, (II), 959 Eighth Ave., New York NY 10019. Contact: Fiction Editor. "It is now our policy that all submissions of unsolicited fiction received in our offices will be read and, if found to be unsuitable for us, destroyed by recycling. If you wish to introduce your work to us, you will be submitting material that will not be critiqued or returned. The odds are long that we will contact you to inquire about publishing your submission or to invite you to correspond with us directly, so please be sure before you take the time and expense to submit it that it is our type of material."

GRAND TIMES, Exclusively for Active Retirees, (I, II), 403 Village Dr., El Cerrito CA 94530-3355. (510)527-4337. Editor: Kira Albin. Magazine: 8½×11; 40 pages; illustrations and photographs. "All items must be upbeat in tone and written on subjects of interest to an older audience, (60+), but don't necessarily have to be about older people. Clarity should be the hallmark, and a dash of humor is always welcome. Please do not submit articles that have a newspaper format where seniors are referred to as 'them' or as a statistical group." Bimonthly. Estab. 1992. Circ. 35,000.
Needs: Senior citizen/retirement: adventure, historical (general), humor/satire, mainstream/contemporary, mystery/suspense (mature adult), romance (mature adult), sports. "All pieces should be of special interest to readers aged 60+." Receives 20-40 unsolicited mss/month. Accepts 1 ms/issue; 6-8 mss/year. Publishes ms 1-12 months after acceptance. Recently published work by Marie Sadro, Mike

Lipstock and Richard Kerckhoff. Length: 800-1,200 average; 250 words minimum; 1,700 words maximum.

How to Contact: "It is recommended that manuscripts be submitted only after obtaining Writers' Guidelines." Send complete ms with a cover letter. No queries. Include estimated word count and very short bio. Reports in 2-3 months on mss. SASE for return of ms or send a disposable copy of ms. Must send SASE for editor's reply. Simultaneous and reprint submissions OK. Sample copy for $2. Writers' guidelines for #10 SASE.

Payment/Terms: Pays 1 contributor's copy. "The amount of additional payment is dependent on subject matter, quality and length. Average payment is $10-35/ms." Pays on acceptance for one-time rights.

Advice: "The characters or plot need to have some relevance to active retirees. Writing should be creative and original but not disorganized and unfocused. Please no more pat romance or mystery stories—we want something different. Beware of any condescension, ageism or stereotyping." *Please obtain Writers' Guidelines before making a submission.*

GREEN EGG A Journal of the Awakening Earth, (IV), Church of All Worlds, Box 1542, Ukiah CA 95482. (707)463-1067. Fax: (707)463-1068. E-mail: gemagazine@aol.com (general business); maerian@aol.com (to the editor). Editor: Maerian Morris. Magazine: 8½×11; 76 pages; recycled paper; 4-color glossy cover; b&w illustrations; and photographs. "Magical fantasy, ecological, historical having to do with pagan civilizations." Bimonthly. Estab. 1968. Circ. 12,000.

● *Green Egg* has won both Gold and Bronze awards from the Wiccan Pagan Press Alliance including a Gold Award in 1994 for Best Publication.

Needs: Erotica, ethnic/multicultural, experimental, fantasy (science fantasy), historical, humor/satire, psychic/supernatural/occult, religious/inspirational (pagan). "No porn, sports, western, evil and painful." Upcoming themes: "Druids" (January-February 1997), "Science Fiction" (March-April 1997), "Modern Primitives" (May-June 1997), "Native Americans" (July-August 1997), "Witchcraft" (September-October 1997). Receives 15-18 unsolicited mss/month. Accepts 30 mss/year. Recently published work by Luisah Teish, Robert Anton Wilson, Deana Metzger and Annie Sprinkle. Length: 600 words minimum; 3,000 words maximum. Publishes short shorts. Length: 500 words. Also publishes poetry. Sometimes critiques or comments on rejected mss.

How to Contact: Send complete ms with cover letter. Should include estimated word count and bio (1 paragraph—50 words). Reports in 2 months. Send SASE for reply, return of ms or send disposable copy of the ms. Include photo of author, if possible, and graphics, if available. Electronic submissions OK. Sample copy of *Green Egg* $6. Fiction guidelines for SASE. Reviews novels and short story collections.

Payment/Terms: Pays subscription to the magazine or contributor's copies. Acquires one-time rights.

Advice: "Looks for economy of prose, artistic use of language, but most important is that the subject matter be germaine to our pagan readership. Magical stories teaching ethics for survival as healthy biosphere heroines, human/animal/otherworld interface; transformative experiences; tidy plots; good grammar, spelling, punctuation; humor; classical deities and ethnic stuff. We're especially fond of science fiction and fantasy."

GUIDEPOSTS FOR KIDS, (II), P.O. Box 538A, Chesterton IN 46304. Fiction Editor: Lurlene McDaniel. Magazine: 8¼×10¾; 32 pages. "Value-centered bimonthly for kids 7-12 years old. Not preachy, concerned with contemporary issues." Bimonthly. Estab. 1990. Circ. 200,000.

● Although the main office of the magazine is in New York, submissions should go to Fiction Editor Lurlene McDaniel. McDaniel says the magazine publishes many new writers but is primarily a market for writers who have already been published. *Guideposts for Kids* received an Award of Excellence from the Ed Press Association in 1995 and 1996.

Needs: Children's/juvenile: fantasy, historical (general), humor, mystery/suspense, religious/inspirational, westerns. "No 'adult as hero' or 'I-prayed-I-got' stories." Upcoming themes: Choices, Animals, Humor, Courage. Receives 200 unsolicited mss/month. Accepts 1-2 mss/issue; 6-10 mss/year. Recently published work by Michael McWey and Pam Zollman. Length: 1,300 words preferred; 600 words minimum; 1,400 words maximum. Publishes short shorts. Also publishes small amount of poetry. Sometimes critiques rejected mss; "only what shows promise."

MARKET CONDITIONS are constantly changing! If you're still using this book and it is 1998 or later, buy the newest edition of *Novel & Short Story Writer's Market* at your favorite bookstore or order from Writer's Digest Books.

How to Contact: Send complete ms with cover letter. Include estimated word count, Social Security number, phone number and SASE. Reports in 6-8 weeks. Send SASE for reply, return of ms or send disposable copy of ms. Simultaneous submissions OK. Sample copy for $3.25. Fiction guidelines for #10 SASE.

Payment/Terms: $250-450 on acceptance for all rights; 2 contributor's copies. Additional copies available.

GUYS, (I, II), FirstHand Ltd., Box 1314, Teaneck NJ 07666. (201)836-9177. Fax: (201)836-5055. E-mail: firsthand3@aol.com. Editor: William Spencer. Magazine: digest size; 130 pages; illustrations; photos. "Fiction and informative departments for today's gay man. Fiction is of an erotic nature, and we especially need short shorts and novella-length stories." Monthly. Estab. 1988.

Needs: Gay. "Should be written in first person. No science fiction or fantasy. No four-legged animals. All characters must be over 18. Stories including members of ethnic groups are especially welcome. Erotica should be based on reality." Accepts 6 mss/issue; 66 mss/year. Publishes ms 6-12 months after acceptance. Recently published work by Robert H. Fletcher, Daren Verne and Biff Cole. Published new writers within the last year. Length: 3,000 words average; 2,000 words minimum; 3,750 words maximum. For novellas: 7,500-8,600 words. Publishes short shorts. Length: 750-1,250 words. Sometimes critiques rejected mss and recommends other markets.

How to Contact: Send complete ms with cover letter. Include writer's name, address, telephone and Social Security number and whether selling all rights or first North American serial rights. Reports in 6-8 weeks on ms. SASE. Accepts diskette or e-mail submissions. Sample copy for $5.50. Fiction guidelines for #10 SASE. Reviews novels and short story collections.

Payment/Terms: Pays $100-150; $75 for short shorts (all rights); $250 for novellas (all rights). Acquires all rights or first North American serial rights.

Advice: "Keep it simple, keep it sexy. If it turns you on, it will turn the reader on."

HADASSAH MAGAZINE, (IV), 50 W. 58th St., New York NY 10019. E-mail: hadamag@aol.com. Executive Editor: Alan M. Tigay. Senior Editor: Zelda Shluker. Jewish general interest magazine: 8½ × 11; 48-70 pages; coated and uncoated paper; slick, medium weight coated cover; drawings and cartoons; photos. Primarily concerned with Israel, the American Jewish community, Jewish communities around the world, Jewish women's issues and American current affairs. Monthly except combined June/July and August/September issues. Circ. 300,000.

● *Hadassah* has been nominated for a National Magazine Award and has received numerous Rockower Awards for Excellence in Jewish Journalism.

Needs: Ethnic (Jewish). Receives 20-25 unsolicited fiction mss each month. Published fiction by Joanne Greenberg, Anita Desai and Lori Ubell. Published new writers within the last year. Length: 1,500-2,000 words.

How to Contact: Query first with writing samples. Reports in 3-4 months on mss. "Not interested in multiple submissions or previously published articles." Must submit appropriate size SASE.

Payment/Terms: Pays $300 minimum on acceptance for U.S. publication rights.

Advice: "Stories on a Jewish theme should be neither self-hating nor schmaltzy."

HARPER'S MAGAZINE, (II, III), 666 Broadway, 11th Floor, New York NY 10012. (212)614-6500. Editor: Lewis H. Lapham. Magazine: 8 × 10¾; 80 pages; illustrations. Magazine for well-educated, widely read and socially concerned readers, college-aged and older, those active in political and community affairs. Monthly. Circ. 218,000.

● This is considered a top but tough market for contemporary fiction.

Needs: Contemporary and humor. Stories on contemporary life and its problems. Receives 600 unsolicited fiction mss/month. Accepts 1 ms/year. Published new writers within the last year. First published David Foster Wallace. Length: 1,000-5,000 words.

How to Contact: Query to managing editor, or through agent. Reports in 6 weeks on queries.

Payment/Terms: Pays $500-1,000 on acceptance for rights, which vary on each author's material and length. Sends galleys to author.

Advice: Buys very little fiction but *Harper's* has published short stories traditionally.

HIGHLIGHTS FOR CHILDREN, 803 Church St., Honesdale PA 18431. (717)253-1080. Editor: Kent L. Brown, Jr. Address fiction to: Beth Troop, Manuscript Coordinator. Magazine: 8½ × 11; 42 pages; uncoated paper; coated cover stock; illustrations; photos. Monthly. Circ. 2.8 million.

● *Highlights* is very supportive of writers. The magazine sponsors a contest and a workshop each year at Chautauqua (New York). Several authors published in *Highlights* have received SCBWI Magazine Merit Awards.

Needs: Juvenile (ages 2-12). Unusual stories appealing to both girls and boys; stories with good characterization, strong emotional appeal, vivid, full of action. "Begin with action rather than description, have strong plot, believable setting, suspense from start to finish." Length: 400-900 words. "We also need easy stories for very young readers (100-400 words)." No war, crime or violence. Receives

600-800 unsolicited fiction mss/month. Accepts 6-7 mss/issue. Also publishes rebus (picture) stories of 125 words or under for the 3- to 7-year-old child. Published work by Virginia Kroll, Harriett Diller and Vashanti Rahaman; published new writers within the last year. Critiques rejected mss occasionally, "especially when editors see possibilities in story."

How to Contact: Send complete ms with SASE and include a rough word count and cover letter "with any previous acceptances by our magazine; any other published work anywhere." No simultaneous submissions. Reports in 1 month. Free guidelines on request.

Payment/Terms: Pays 14¢ and up/word on acceptance for all rights. Sends galleys to author.

Advice: "We accept a story on its merit whether written by an unpublished or an experienced writer. Mss are rejected because of poor writing, lack of plot, trite or worn-out plot, or poor characterization. Children *like* stories and learn about life from stories. Children learn to become lifelong fiction readers by enjoying stories. Feel passion for your subject. Create vivid images. Write a child-centered story; leave adults in the background."

ALFRED HITCHCOCK MYSTERY MAGAZINE, (I, II), Dell Magazines, 1270 Avenue of the Americas, 10th Floor, New York NY 10020. (212)698-1313. Editor: Cathleen Jordan. Mystery fiction magazine: 5¹⁄₁₆×7⅜; 160 pages; 28 lb. newsprint paper; 60 lb. machine-/coated cover stock; illustrations; photos. Published 13 times/year, including 1 double issue. Estab. 1956. Circ. 215,000; 615,000 readers.

• Stories published in *Alfred Hitchcock Mystery Magazine* have won Edgar Awards for "Best Mystery Story of the Year," Shamus Awards for "Best Private Eye Story of the Year" and Robert L. Fish Awards for "Best First Mystery Short Story of the Year."

Needs: Mystery and detection (amateur sleuth, private eye, police procedural, suspense, etc.). No sensationalism. Number of mss/issue varies with length of mss. Length: up to 14,000 words. Also publishes short shorts.

How to Contact: Send complete ms and SASE. Reports in 2 months. Guideline sheet for SASE.

Payment/Terms: Pays 8¢/word on acceptance.

HOME LIFE, (I, IV), A magazine for today's Christian family, Sunday School Board of Southern Baptist Convention, 127 Ninth Ave. N., Nashville TN 37234-0140. Fax: (615)251-5508. Magazine: 8×10¾; 66 pages; illustrations and photos. "Ours is a Christian family magazine." Monthly. Estab. 1947. Circ. 560,000.

• *Home Life* has received awards for its design and contents including a First Place Award from the Baptist Public Relations Association. The magazine is noted for fiction about family relationships.

Needs: Religious/inspirational. No fictionized Bible stories. Receives 10-15 mss/month. Accepts 1 ms/issue; 12 mss/year. Recently published work by Amy Adams, Jan Hamilton, Powell and Susan Sawyer. Length: 1,600 words minimum; 2,000 words maximum.

How to Contact: Query first. Include estimated word count and short bio. Reports in 1 month on queries; 3 months on mss. Send SASE for reply, return of ms or send a disposable copy of ms. Simultaneous and disk (with hard copy) submissions OK. Sample copy for $1, 9×12 SAE and 2 first-class stamps. Fiction guidelines for #10 SASE.

Payment/Terms: Pays $100-275 and 3 contributor's copies on acceptance for first rights or first North American serial rights.

Advice: "Stories related to marriage, parenting and family situations fit our mag best."

HOME TIMES, (I, II, IV), Neighbor News, Inc., P.O. Box 16096, West Palm Beach FL 33416. (407)439-3509. Editor: Dennis Lombard. Newspaper: tabloid; 20-32 pages; newsprint; illustrations and photographs. "Conservative news, views, fiction, poetry, sold to general public." Weekly. Estab. 1980. Circ. 5,000.

• The publisher offers "101 Reasons Why I Reject Your Manuscript," a 120-page report for a cost of $15.

Needs: Adventure, historical (general), humor/satire, literary, mainstream, religious/inspirational, romance, sports. "All fiction needs to be related to the publication's focus on current events and conservative perspective—we feel you must examine a sample issue because *Home Times* is *different*." Nothing "preachy or doctrinal, but Biblical worldview needed." Receives 50 unsolicited mss/month. Accepts 20 mss/issue. Publishes ms 1-9 months after acceptance. Recently published work by Cal Thomas, Chuck Colsen and Don Feder. Length: 700 words average; 500 words minimum; 900 words maximum.

How to Contact: Send complete manuscript with cover letter including Social Security number and word count. "Absolutely no queries." Include in cover letter "One to two sentences on what the piece is and who you are." Reports on mss in 1 month. SASE. Simultaneous and reprint submissions OK. Sample current issue for $1 ($3 for 3 issues). Guidelines for #10 SASE.

Payment/Terms: Pays $5-35 for one-time rights.

Advice: "We are very open to new writers, but read our newspaper—get the drift of our rather unusual conservative, pro-Christian, pro-Jewish but non-religious content. Looks for "historical, issues, or family orientation; also like creative nonfiction on historical and issues subjects." Send $9 for a writer's 1-year subscription (12 current issues).

‡HORIZONS, The Magazine of Presbyterian Women, (II, IV), 100 Witherspoon St., Louisville KY 40202-1396. (502)569-5366. Fax: (502)569-8085. Editor: Barbara Roche. Fiction Editor: Anna Bedford. Magazine: 8×11; 40 pages; illustrations and photos. Magazine owned and operated by Presbyterian Women with material on women's issues—religious perspective. Bimonthly. Estab. 1988. Circ. 30,000.
Needs: Children's/juvenile (5-9 years, 10-12 years), ethnic/multicultural, feminist, gay, historical, humor/satire, lesbian, literary, mainstream/contemporary, religious/inspirational, senior citizen/retirement, translations. "No sex/violence." List of upcoming themes available for SASE. Receives 3 unsolicited mss/month. Accepts 1 ms/issue. Publishes ms 4 months after acceptance. Length: 1,500-2,000 words maximum. Publishes short shorts. Length: 500 words. Also publishes literary essays, literary criticism and poetry. Sometimes critiques or comments on rejected mss.
How to Contact: Send complete ms with cover letter. Include estimated word count and Social Security number. Reports in 1 week on queries; 2 weeks on mss. SASE or send a disposable copy of ms. Simultaneous submissions OK. Sample copy for 9×12 SAE. Fiction guidelines for #10 SASE. Reviews novels and short story collections. Send books to Anna Bedford.
Payment/Terms: Pays $50/page and 2 contributor's copies on publication for all rights; additional copies for $2.50.
Advice: "Stories related to marriage, parenting and family situations fit our mag best."

HUMPTY DUMPTY'S MAGAZINE, (II), Children's Better Health Institute, Box 567, 1100 Waterway Blvd., Indianapolis IN 46206. Editor: Sandy Grieshop. Magazine: 7⅝×10⅛; 36 pages; 35 lb. paper; coated cover; illustrations; some photos. Children's magazine stressing health, nutrition, hygiene, exercise and safety for children ages 4-6. Publishes 8 issues/year.
Needs: Juvenile health-related material and material of a more general nature. No inanimate talking objects. Rhyming stories should flow easily with no contrived rhymes. Receives 250-300 unsolicited mss/month. Accepts 3-5 mss/issue. Length: 500 words maximum.
How to Contact: Send complete ms with SASE. No queries. Reports in 3 months. Sample copy for $1.25. Editorial guidelines for SASE.
Payment/Terms: Pays up to 22¢/word for stories plus 10 contributor's copies on publication for all rights. (One-time book rights returned when requested for specific publication.)
Advice: "In contemporary stories, characters should be up-to-date, with realistic dialogue. We're looking for health-related stories with unusual twists or surprise endings. We want to avoid stories and poems that 'preach.' We try to present the health material in a positive way, utilizing a light humorous approach wherever possible." Most rejected mss "are too wordy. Need short, short nonfiction."

HUSTLER BUSTY BEAUTIES, (I, IV), HG Publications, Inc., 8484 Wilshire Blvd., Suite 900, Beverly Hills CA 90211. (213)651-5400. Editor: N. Morgen Hagen. Magazine: 8×11; 100 pages; 60 lb. paper; 80 lb. cover; illustrations and photographs. "Adult entertainment and reading centered around large-breasted women for an over-18 audience, mostly male." Published 13 times/year. Estab. 1988. Circ. 150,000.
Needs: Adventure, erotica, fantasy, mystery/suspense. All must have erotic theme. Receives 25 unsolicited fiction mss/month. Accepts 1 ms/issue; 6-12 mss/year. Publishes mss 3-6 months after acceptance. Published work by Mike Dillon and H.H. Morris. Length: 1,600 words preferred; 1,000 words minimum; 2,000 words maximum.
How to Contact: Query first. Then send complete ms with cover letter. Reports in 2 weeks on queries; in 2-4 weeks on mss. SASE. Sample copy for $5. Fiction guidelines free.
Payment/Terms: Pays $350-500 (fiction) and $50 (erotic letters) on publication for all rights.
Advice: Looks for "1. plausible plot, well-defined characters, literary ingenuity; 2. hot sex scenes; 3. readable, coherent, grammatically sound prose."

IN TOUCH FOR MEN, (I, IV), 13122 Saticoy St., North Hollywood CA 91605. (818)764-2288. Fax: (818)764-2307. E-mail: glentouch@aol.com. Editor: Alan W. Mills. Magazine: 8×10¾; 100 pages; glossy paper; coated cover; illustrations and photographs. "*In Touch* is a magazine for gay men. It features five to six nude male centerfolds in each issue, but is erotic rather than pornographic. We include fiction." Monthly. Estab. 1973. Circ. 70,000.
Needs: Confession, gay, erotica, romance (contemporary, historical). All characters must be over 18 years old. Stories must have an explicit erotic content. No heterosexual or internalized homophobic fiction. Accepts 3 mss/month; 36 mss/year. Publishes ms 3 months after acceptance. Length: 2,500 words average; up to 3,500 words maximum. Sometimes critiques rejected mss and recommends other markets.
How to Contact: Send complete ms with cover letter, name, address and Social Security number. Reports in 2 weeks on queries; 2 months on mss. SASE. Simultaneous and reprint submissions, if

from local publication, OK. Disk submissions OK (call before sending by modem). Sample copy for $5.95. Fiction guidelines free. Reviews novels and short story collections.

Payment/Terms: Pays $25-75 (except on rare occasions for a longer piece) on publication for one-time rights.

Advice: Publishes "primarily erotic material geared toward gay men. Periodically (but very seldom) we will run fiction of a non-erotic nature (but still gay-related), but that's not the norm. I personally prefer (and accept) manuscripts that are not only erotic/hardcore, but show a developed story, plot and concise ending (as opposed to just sexual vignettes that basically lead nowhere). If it's got a little romance, too, that's even better. Emphasis still on erotic, though. We now only use 'safe sex' depictions in fiction, hoping that it becomes the standard for male erotica. Hopefully portraying responsible activity will prompt people to act responsibly, as well."

INDIA CURRENTS, (II,IV), The Complete Indian American Magazine, Box 21285, San Jose CA 95151. (408)274-6966. Fax: (408)274-2733. Editor: Arvind Kumar. E-mail: editor@indiacur.com. Magazine: 8½×11; 104 pages; newsprint paper; illustrations and photographs. "The arts and culture of India as seen in America for Indians and non-Indians with a common interest in India." Monthly. Estab. 1987. Circ. 25,000.

● Editor Arvind Kumar was honored by KQED Channel 9, the local PBS affiliate, as an "Unsung Hero" during Lesbian and Gay Pride Month of June 1995.

Needs: All Indian content: contemporary, ethnic, feminist, historical (general), humor/satire, literary, mainstream, prose poem, regional, religious/inspirational, romance, translations (from Indian languages). "We seek material with insight into Indian culture, American culture and the crossing from one to another." Receives 12 unsolicited mss/month. Accepts 1 ms/issue; 12 mss/year. Publishes ms 2-6 months after acceptance. Published work by Chitra Divakaruni, Jyotsna Sreenivasan and Rajini Srikanth. Published new writers within the last year. Length: 1,800 words.

How to Contact: Send complete ms with cover letter and clips of published work. Reports in 2-3 months on mss. SASE. Simultaneous and reprint submissions OK. Accepts electronic submissions. Sample copy for $3.

Payment/Terms: Pays in subscriptions on publication for one-time rights.

Advice: "Story must be related to India and subcontinent in some meaningful way. The best stories are those which document some deep transformation as a result of an Indian experience, or those which show the humanity of Indians."

JACK AND JILL, (II, IV), The Children's Better Health Institute, P.O. Box 567, 1100 Waterway Blvd., Indianapolis IN 46206. (317)636-8881. Editor: Daniel Lee. Children's magazine of articles, stories and activities, many with a health, safety, exercise or nutritional-oriented theme, ages 7-10 years. Monthly except January/February, April/May, July/August, October/November. Estab. 1938.

Needs: Science fiction, mystery, sports, adventure, historical fiction and humor. Health-related stories with a subtle lesson. Published work by Peter Fernandez, Adriana Devoy and Myra Schomberg. Published new writers within the last year. Length: 500-800 words.

How to Contact: Send complete ms with SASE. Reports in 3 months on mss. Sample copy for $1.25. Fiction guidelines for SASE.

Payment/Terms: Pays up to 20¢/word on publication for all rights.

Advice: "Try to present health material in a positive—not a negative—light. Use humor and a light approach wherever possible without minimizing the seriousness of the subject. We need more humor and adventure stories."

JIVE, BLACK CONFESSIONS, BLACK ROMANCE, BRONZE THRILLS, BLACK SECRETS, (I, II), Sterling/Mcfadden, 233 Park Ave. S., 5th Floor, New York NY 10003. (212)780-3500. Editor: Marcia Mahan. Magazine: 8½×11; 72 pages; newsprint paper; glossy cover; 8×10 photographs. "We publish stories that are romantic and have romantic lovemaking scenes in them. Our audience is basically young. However, we have a significant audience base of housewives. The age range is from 18-49." Bimonthly (*Jive* and *Black Romance* in odd-numbered months; *Black Confessions* and *Bronze Thrills* in even-numbered months). 6 issues per year. Estab. 1962. Circ. 100,000.

Needs: Confession, romance (contemporary, young adult). No "stories that are stereotypical to black people, ones that do not follow the basic rules of writing, or ones that are too graphic in content and lack a romantic element." Receives 20 or more unsolicited fiction mss/month. Accepts 6 mss/issue (2 issues/month); 144 mss/year. Publishes ms an average of 2-3 months after acceptance. Published work by Linda Smith; published new writers within the last year. Length: 18-24 pages.

How to Contact: Query with clips of published work or send complete ms with cover letter. "A cover letter should include an author's bio and what he or she proposes to do. Of course, address and phone number." Reports in 3 months. SASE. Simultaneous submissions OK. "Please contact me if simultaneously submitted work has been accepted elsewhere." Sample copy for 9×12 SAE and 5 first-class stamps; fiction guidelines for #10 SAE and 2 first-class stamps.

Payment/Terms: Pays $75-100 on publication for all rights.

Advice: "Our five magazines are a great starting point for new writers. We accept work from beginners as well as established writers. Please study and research black culture and lifestyles if you are not a black writer. Stereotypical stories are not acceptable. Set the stories all over the world and all over the USA—not just down south. We are not looking for 'the runaway who gets turned out by a sweet-talking pimp' stories. We are looking for stories about all types of female characters. Any writer should not be afraid to communicate with us if he or she is having some difficulty with writing a story. We are available to help at any stage of the submission process. Also, writers should practice patience. If we do not contact the writer, that means that the story is being read or is being held on file for future publication. If we get in touch with the writer, it usually means a request for revision and resubmission. Do the best work possible and don't let rejection slips send you off 'the deep end.' Don't take everything that is said about your work so personally. We are buying all of our work from freelance writers."

JUGGLER'S WORLD, (I, II, IV), International Juggler's Association, Box 443, Davidson NC 28036. (704)892-1296. Fax: (704)892-2499. E-mail: bigiduz@davidson.edu. Editor: Bill Giduz. Fiction Editor: Ken Letko. Magazine: 8½×11; 40 pages; 70 lb. paper and cover stock; illustrations and photos. For and about jugglers and juggling. Quarterly.

Needs: Historical (general), humor/satire, science fiction. No stories "that don't include juggling as a central theme." Receives "very few" unsolicited mss/month. Accepts 8 mss/year. Publishes ms an average of 6-12 months to 1 year after acceptance. Recently published work by Ram Prasad. Length: 2,000 words average; 1,000 words minimum; 2,500 words maximum. Sometimes critiques rejected mss.

How to Contact: Query first. Reports in 1 week. Simultaneous submissions OK. Prefers electronic submissions via IBM or Macintosh compatible disk. Sample copy for $2.50.

Payment/Terms: Pays $25-50, free subscription to magazine and 3 contributor's copies on acceptance for first rights.

Advice: "Submit a brief story outline to the editor before writing the whole piece."

JUNIOR TRAILS, (I, II), Gospel Publishing House, 1445 Boonville Ave., Springfield MO 65802. (417)862-2781. Elementary Editor: Sinda S. Zinn. Magazine: 5¼×8; 8 pages; 36 lb. coated offset paper; art illustrations; photos. "A Sunday school take-home paper of nature articles and fictional stories that apply Christian principles to everyday living for 10-to 12-year-old children." Weekly. Estab. 1954. Circ. 70,000.

Needs: Contemporary, juvenile, religious/inspirational, spiritual and sports. Adventure stories are welcome. No Biblical fiction or science fiction. Accepts 2 mss/issue. Published work by Betty Lou Mell, Mason M. Smith and Nanette L. Dunford. Published new writers within the last year. Length: 1,200-1,500 words. Publishes short shorts.

How to Contact: Send complete ms with SASE. Reports in 4-6 weeks. Free sample copy and guidelines with SASE.

Payment/Terms: Pays 5¢/word and 3 contributor's copies on acceptance for first rights.

Advice: "Know the age level and direct stories relevant to that age group. Since junior-age children (grades 5 and 6) enjoy action, fiction provides a vehicle for communicating moral/spiritual principles in a dramatic framework. Fiction, if well done, can be a powerful tool for relating Christian principles. It must, however, be realistic and believable in its development. Make your children be children, not overly mature for their age. We would like more stories with a *city* setting. Write for contemporary children, using setting and background that includes various ethnic groups."

LADIES' HOME JOURNAL, (III), Published by Meredith Corporation, 125 Park Ave., New York NY 10017. (212)557-6600. Editor-in-Chief: Myrna Blyth. Fiction/Articles Editor: Pamela Guthrie-O'Brien. Managing Editor: Carolyn Noyes. Magazine: 190 pages; 34-38 lb. coated paper; 65 lb. coated cover; illustrations and photos.

● *Ladies' Home Journal* has won several awards for journalism.

Needs: Book mss and short stories, *accepted only through an agent*. Return of unsolicited material cannot be guaranteed. Published work by Fay Weldon, Anita Shreve, Jane Shapiro, Anne Rivers Siddons. Length: approximately 2,000-2,500 words.

How to Contact: Send complete ms with cover letter (credits). Simultaneous submissions OK. Publishes ms 4-12 months after acceptance.

Payment/Terms: Acquires First North American rights.

Advice: "Our readers like stories, especially those that have emotional impact. Stories about relationships between people—husband/wife—mother/son—seem to be subjects that can be explored effectively in short stories. Our reader's mail and surveys attest to this fact: Readers enjoy our fiction, and are most keenly tuned to stories dealing with children. Fiction today is stronger than ever. Beginners can be optimistic; if they have talent, I do believe that talent will be discovered. It is best to read the magazine before submitting."

LADYBUG, (II, IV), The Cricket Magazine Group, P.O. Box 300, Peru IL 61354. (815)224-6656. Editor-in-Chief: Marianne Carus. Editor: Paula Morrow. Magazine: 8 × 10; 36 pages plus 4-page pull-out section; illustrations. "*Ladybug* publishes original stories and poems and reprints written by the world's best children's authors. For young children, ages 2-6." Monthly. Estab. 1990. Circ. 130,000.
  • *Ladybug* has received the Parents Choice Award; the Golden Lamp Honor Award and the Golden Lamp Award from the Educational Press Association, and Magazine Merit awards from the Society of Children's Book Writers and Illustrators.
Needs: Fairy tales, fantasy (children's), folk tales, juvenile, picture stories, preschool, read-out-loud stories. Length: 300-750 words preferred. Publishes short shorts.
How to Contact: Send complete ms with cover letter. Include word count on ms (do not count title). Reports in 3 months. SASE. Reprints are OK. Fiction guidelines for SASE. Sample copy for $4. For guidelines *and* sample send 9 × 12 SAE (no stamps required) and $4.
Payment/Terms: Pays up to 25¢/word (less for reprints) on publication for first publication rights or second serial (reprint) rights. For recurring features, pays flat fee and copyright becomes property of The Cricket Magazine Group.
Advice: Looks for "well-written stories for preschoolers: age-appropriate, not condescending. We look for rich, evocative language and sense of joy or wonder."

LADY'S CIRCLE, (II), GCR Publishing, 1700 Broadway, 34th Floor, New York NY 10019. (212)541-7100. Managing Editor: Sandra Kosherick. Magazine. "A lot of our readers are in Midwestern states." Bimonthly. Estab. 1963. Circ. 100,000.
Needs: Historical, humor/satire, mainstream, religious/inspirational, senior citizen/retirement. Receives 100 unsolicited fiction mss/month. Accepts about 3-4 fiction mss/year. Time between acceptance and publication "varies, usually works 6 months ahead." Length: 1,000 words minimum; 1,200 words maximum. Accepts short shorts "for fillers." Sometimes critiques rejected ms.
How to Contact: Query first. Reports in 3 months on queries. SASE. Simultaneous and reprint submissions OK. Accepts electronic submissions via disk or modem. Sample copy for $3.95; fiction guidelines for SAE.
Payment/Terms: Pay varies, depending on ms.
Terms: Pays on publication for first North American serial rights.

LIGUORIAN, (I, IV), "A Leading Catholic Magazine," Liguori Publications, 1 Liguori Dr., Liguori MO 63057. (314)464-2500. Fax: (314)464-8449. Editor-in-Chief: Allan Weinert, CSS.R. Magazine: 5 × 8½; 72 pages; b&w illustrations and photographs. "*Liguorian* is a Catholic magazine aimed at helping our readers to live a full Christian life. We publish articles for families, young people, children, religious and singles—all with the same aim." Monthly. Estab. 1913. Circ. 330,000.
  • *Liguorian* received Catholic Press Association awards for 1995 including third place for General Excellence and first place for Best Special Issue.
Needs: Religious/inspirational, young adult and senior citizen/retirement (with moral Christian thrust), spiritual. "Stories submitted to *Liguorian* must have as their goal the lifting up of the reader to a higher Christian view of values and goals. We are not interested in contemporary works that lack purpose or are of questionable moral value." Receives approximately 25 unsolicited fiction mss/month. Accepts 12 mss/year. Recently published work by Kathleen Doheny, Cindy McCabe and Beverly Sheresh. Published new writers within the last year. Length: 1,500-2,000 words preferred. Also publishes short shorts. Occasionally critiques rejected mss "if we feel the author is capable of giving us something we need even though this story did not suit us."
How to Contact: Send complete ms with SASE. Accepts disk submissions compatible with IBM, using a WordPerfect 5.1 program; prefers hard copy with disk submission. Reports in 10-12 weeks on mss. Sample copy and fiction guidelines for #10 SASE.
Payment/Terms: Pays 10-12¢/word and 5 contributor's copies on acceptance for all rights. Offers 50% kill fee for assigned mss not published.
Advice: "First read several issues containing short stories. We look for originality and creative input in each story we read. Since most editors must wade through mounds of manuscripts each month, consideration for the editor requires that the market be studied, the manuscript be carefully presented and polished before submitting. Our publication uses only one story a month. Compare this with the 25 or more we receive over the transom each month. Also, many fiction mss are written without a specific goal or thrust, i.e., an interesting incident that goes nowhere is *not a story*. We believe fiction

---

CHECK THE CATEGORY INDEXES, located at the back of the book, for publishers interested in specific fiction subjects.

is a highly effective mode for transmitting the Christian message and also provides a good balance in an unusually heavy issue."

LIVE, (II, IV), Assemblies of God, 1445 Boonville, Springfield MO 65802-1894. (417)862-2781. Editor: Paul W. Smith. "A take-home story paper distributed weekly in young adult/adult Sunday school classes. *Live* is a story paper primarily. Stories in both fiction and narrative style are welcome. Poems, first-person anecdotes and humor are used as fillers. The purpose of *Live* is to present in short story form realistic characters who utilize biblical principles. We hope to challenge readers to take risks for God and to resolve their problems scripturally." Weekly. Circ. 130,000.
Needs: Religious/inspirational, prose poem and spiritual. "Inner city, ethnic, racial settings." No controversial stories about such subjects as feminism, war or capital punishment. Accepts 2 mss/issue. Recently published work by Marlo Schalesky, Alan Cliburn and Linda Hutton. Published new writers within the last year. Length: 500-1,700 words.
How to Contact: Send complete ms. Social Security number and word count must be included. Simultaneous submissions OK. Reports in 6-8 weeks. Sample copy and guidelines for SASE.
Payment/Terms: Pays 5¢/word (first rights); 3¢/word (second rights) on acceptance.
Advice: "Study our publication and write good, inspirational true to life or fiction stories that will encourage people to become all they can be as Christians. Stories should go somewhere! Action, not just thought—life; interaction, not just insights. Heroes and heroines, suspense and conflict. Avoid simplistic, pietistic conclusions, preachy, critical or moralizing. We don't accept science or Bible fiction. Stories should be encouraging, challenging, humorous. Even problem-centered stories should be upbeat." Reserves the right to change titles, abbreviate length and clarify flashbacks for publication.

THE LOOKOUT, (II), Standard Publishing, 8121 Hamilton Ave., Cincinnati OH 45231. (513)931-4050. Fax: (513)931-0904. Editor: David Faust. Magazine: 8½×11; 16 pages; newsprint paper; newsprint cover stock; illustrations; photos. "Conservative Christian magazine for adults." Weekly. Estab. 1894. Circ. 120,000.
• *The Lookout* has won awards from the Evangelical Press Association. The magazine is using less fiction—they've cut their needs in half.
Needs: Religious/inspirational. No predictable, preachy material. Taboos are blatant sex and swear words. Receives 60 unsolicited mss/month. Accepts 15-20 mss/year. Publishes ms 2-12 months after acceptance. Write for 1997 theme list. Published new writers within the last year. Length: 1,200-2,000 words.
How to Contact: Send complete ms with SASE. Reports in 3-4 months on ms. Simultaneous and reprint submissions OK. Sample copy for 75¢. Guidelines for #10 SASE.
Payment/Terms: Pays 6-9¢/word on acceptance for first rights; 5-6¢/word for other rights and contributor's copies. Buys reprints.
Advice: "We would like to see a better balance between stories that focus on external struggles (our usual fare in the past) and those that focus on internal (spiritual, emotional, psychological) struggles. Send us good stories—not good sermons dressed up as stories. Keep stories in a contemporary setting with an adult's point of view. Many writers with a Christian viewpoint try to 'preach' in their stories. That is as deadly for our purposes as for anyone. Tell the story, and let the 'message' take care of itself."

MANSCAPE, (I, IV), First Hand Ltd., Box 1314, Teaneck NJ 07666. (201)836-9177. Fax: (201)836-5055. E-mail: firsthand3@aol.com. Editor: Bill Jaeger. Magazine: digest sized; 130 pages; illustrations. "Magazine is devoted to gay male sexual fetishes; publishes fiction and readers' letters devoted to this theme." Monthly. Estab. 1985. Circ. 60,000.
Needs: Erotica, gay. Should be written in first person. No science fiction or fantasy. Erotica must be based on real life. Receives 25 unsolicited fiction mss/month. Accepts 5 mss/issue; 60 mss/year. Publishes ms an average of 12-18 months after acceptance. Published new writers within the last year. Length: 3,000 words average; 2,000 words minimum; 3,750 words maximum. Sometimes critiques rejected ms.
How to Contact: Send complete ms with cover letter. SASE. Sample copy for $5; guidelines for #10 SASE.
Payment/Terms: Pays $100-150 on publication for all rights or first North American serial rights.
Advice: "Keep story interesting by exhibiting believability and sexual tension."

MASSAGE, Keeping You—In Touch, (IV), Noah Publishing Inc., 1315 W. Mallon Ave., Spokane WA 99201. (509)324-8117. Fax: (509)324-8606. Managing Editor: Karen Menehan. Magazine: 8¼×11; 130 pages; 70 lb. gloss paper; 80 lb. gloss cover; illustrations and photographs. "The philosophy is to spread the good word about massage therapy and other healing arts. Material published includes pieces on technique, business advice, experiential pieces and interviews/profiles on pioneers/leaders in the field. Intended audience is those who practice massage and other allied healing arts." Bimonthly. Estab. 1985. Circ. 20,000.

Needs: "We only accept fiction that places massage or bodywork in a positive light." Receives 10 unsolicited ms/month. Accepts 1 ms/issue; 6 mss/year. Publishes ms within 1 year after acceptance. Published work by Erik Lee and Mary Bond. Length: 2,000 words preferred; 1,500 words minimum; 3,000 words maximum. Always critiques or comments on rejected mss.

How to Contact: Query first. Include bio (2-3 sentences). Reports in 2 months. Send SASE for reply or send a disposable copy of ms. Writer's guidelines and sample copy free.

Payment/Terms: Pays $250 maximum and 2 contributor's copies 30 days after publication for first rights; additional copies for $3.

Advice: "Looking for stories that will touch the reader emotionally by showing the importance of human contact—which doesn't mean they have to be melodramatic. Humor is appreciated, as are descriptive detail and vibrant characterizations."

MATURE YEARS, (II, IV), United Methodist Publishing House, 201 Eighth Ave. S., Nashville TN 37202. (615)749-6292. Fax: (615)749-6512. Editor: Marvin W. Cropsey. Magazine: 8½×11; 112 pages; illustrations and photos. Magazine "helps persons in and nearing retirement to appropriate the resources of the Christian faith as they seek to face the problems and opportunities related to aging." Quarterly. Estab. 1953.

Needs: Humor, intergenerational relationships, nostalgia, older adult issues, religious/inspirational, spiritual (for older adults). "We don't want anything poking fun at old age, saccharine stories or anything not for older adults. Must show older adults (age 55 plus) in a positive manner." Accepts 1 ms/issue, 4 mss/year. Publishes ms 1 year after acceptance. Recently published work by Ann S. Gray, Betty Z. Walker and Vickie Elaine Legg. Published new writers within the last year. Length: 1,000-1,800 words.

How to Contact: Send complete ms with SASE and Social Security number. No simultaneous submissions. Reports in 2 months. Sample copy for 10½×11 SAE and $3.95 postage.

Payment/Terms: Pays 5¢/word on acceptance.

Advice: "Practice writing dialogue! Listen to people talk; take notes; master dialogue writing! Not easy, but well worth it! Most inquiry letters are far too long. If you can't sell me an idea in a brief paragraph, you're not going to sell the reader on reading your finished article or story."

‡MESSAGE MAGAZINE, (I, II), Review and Herald Publishing Association, 55 W. Oak Ridge Dr., Hagerstown MD 21740. (301)791-7000, ext. 2565. Fax: (301)714-1753. Editor: Stephen P. Ruff. Magazine: 8½×11; 31 pages; illustrations and photos. *MESSAGE* is a "Christian outreach magazine that deals with a variety of topics. Our primary audience is African-American." Bimonthly. Estab. 1798. Circ. 70,000.

● *MESSAGE* is the recipient of numerous awards from the Evangelical Press Association.

Needs: Religious/inspirational, young adult/teen. Upcoming themes: "He Said/She Said" (relationship issues) and "Educational Issue" (importance of education). Receives 5 mss/month. Accepts 1 ms/issue; 7 mss/year. Length: 500 words average.

How to Contact: Send complete ms with cover letter. Include maximum 40-word bio, Social Security number, address and telephone number. Reports in 6-10 months on mss. Send a disposable copy of ms. Simultaneous submissions, reprints and electronic submissions OK. "We prefer not to reprint articles." Sample copy and fiction guidelines free.

Payment/Terms: Pays $50-300 and 3 contributor's copies on acceptance. Acquires first North American serial rights.

Advice: "*MESSAGE* does not accept a lot of fiction. The one department we might accept fiction for is our MESSAGE Jr. section. This department is for elementary-aged children and usually teaches some sort of biblical or moral lesson. However, the lessons are sometimes taught via fictitious stories."

✦MESSENGER OF THE SACRED HEART, (II), Apostleship of Prayer, 661 Greenwood Ave., Toronto, Ontario M4J 4B3 Canada. (416)466-1195. Editors: Rev. F.J. Power, S.J. and Alfred DeManche. Magazine: 7×10; 32 pages; coated paper; self-cover; illustrations; photos. Magazine for "Canadian and U.S. Catholics interested in developing a life of prayer and spirituality; stresses the great value of our ordinary actions and lives." Monthly. Estab. 1891. Circ. 16,000.

Needs: Religious/inspirational. Stories about people, adventure, heroism, humor, drama. No poetry. Accepts 1 ms/issue. Length: 750-1,500 words. Recommends other markets.

How to Contact: Send complete ms with SAE. No simultaneous submissions. Reports in 1 month. Sample copy for $1.50 (Canadian).

Payment/Terms: Pays 4¢/word, 3 contributor's copies on acceptance for first North American serial rights. Rarely buys reprints.

Advice: "Develop a story that sustains interest to the end. Do not preach, but use plot and characters to convey the message or theme. Aim to move the heart as well as the mind. If you can, add a light touch or a sense of humor to the story. Your ending should have impact, leaving a moral or faith message for the reader."

METRO SINGLES LIFESTYLES, (I), Metro Publications, Box 28203, Kansas City MO 64118. (913)641-9291. Editor: Robert L. Huffstutter. Fiction Editor: Earl R. Stonebridge. Tabloid: 36 pages; 30. lb newspaper stock; 30 lb. cover; illustrations; photos. "Positive, uplifting, original, semi-literary material for all singles: widowed, divorced, never-married, of all ages 18 and over." Bimonthly. Estab. 1984. Circ. 25,000.
Needs: Humor/satire, literary, prose poem, religious/inspirational, romance (contemporary), special interest, spiritual, single parents. Would like to see more fiction accompanied by illustrations and stock photos. Receives 20-30 unsolicited mss/month. Accepts 5-6 mss/issue; 12-18 mss/year. Publishes ms 2 months after acceptance. Length: 1,500 words average; 1,200 words minimum; 4,000 words maximum. Publishes short shorts. Recently published work by Moby Clifton, Linn Eairheart, Noriko Shinkai, Edgar Seacliff, Betty Jean Pozinsky, Bill McDaniel, Dan Waxman and Marisha Califia. Published new writers within the last year. Length: 1,200. Occasionally critiques rejected mss. Recommends other markets. All America Singles Writers Romance Cruise contest (must be 21 or over) for best story about cruise romance; deadline: May 2, 1997.
How to Contact: Send complete ms with cover letter. Include short paragraph/bio listing credits (if any), current profession or job. Reports in 2 months on queries. SASE. Sample copy for $3.
Payment/Terms: Pays $25-50 on publication, free subscription to magazine and contributor's copies.
Advice: Looks for "singular way of life, problems and blessings of single parent families, the eternal search for the right mate—or the right date. Use a personal experience, add some imagination and create believable characters in a positive or negative relationship."

MS, 230 Park Ave., 7th Floor, New York NY 10169-0799. No unsolicited fiction.

MY FRIEND, The Catholic Magazine for Kids, (II), Pauline Books & Media, 50 St. Paul's Ave., Boston MA 02130. (617)522-8911. Editor: Sister Anne Joan. Magazine: 8½×11; 32 pages; smooth, glossy paper and cover stock; illustrations; photos. Magazine of "religious truths and positive values for children in a format which is enjoyable and attractive. Each issue contains Bible stories, lives of saints and famous people, short stories, science corner, contests, projects, etc." Monthly during school year (September-June). Estab. 1979. Circ. 12,000.
● *My Friend* was honored by Catholic Press Association for General Excellence, Best Short Story and Best Illustration in 1994; General Excellence in 1995; General Excellence and Best Short Story (Honorable Mention) in 1996.
Needs: Juvenile, religious/inspirational, spiritual (children), sports (children). Receives 60 unsolicited fiction mss/month. Accepts 3-4 mss/issue; 30-40 mss/year. Published work by Eileen Spinelli, Bob Hartman and M. Donaleen Howitt. Published new writers within the past year. Length: 200 words minimum; 900 words maximum; 600 words average.
How to Contact: Send complete ms with SASE. Reports in 1-2 months on mss. Publishes ms an average of 1 year after acceptance. Sample copy for $2 and 9×12 SAE ($1.24 postage).
Payment/Terms: Pays $20-150 (stories, articles).
Advice: "We prefer child-centered stories in a real-world setting. We are particularly interested in media-related articles and stories that involve healthy choices regarding media use. Try to write visually—be 'graphics-friendly.' "

‡NA'AMAT WOMAN, Magazine of NA'AMAT USA, The Women's Labor Zionist Organization of America, (IV), 200 Madison Ave., New York NY 10016. (212)725-8010. Editor: Judith A. Sokoloff. "Magazine covering a wide variety of subjects of interest to the Jewish community—including political and social issues, arts, profiles; many articles about Israel; and women's issues. Fiction must have a Jewish theme. Readers are the American Jewish community." Published 5 times/year. Estab. 1926. Circ. 30,000.
Needs: Contemporary, literary. Receives 10 unsolicited fiction mss/month. Accepts 3-5 fiction mss/year. Length: 1,500 words minimum; 3,000 words maximum. Also buys nonfiction.
How to Contact: Query first or send complete ms with SASE. Reports in 3 months on mss. Free sample copy for 9×11½ SAE and $1 postage.
Payment/Terms: Pays 10¢/word and 2 contributor's copies on publication for first North American serial rights; assignments on work-for-hire basis.
Advice: "No maudlin nostalgia or romance; no hackneyed Jewish humor and no poetry."

A BULLET INTRODUCES COMMENTS by the editor of *Novel & Short Story Writer's Market* indicating special information about the listing.

NEW ERA MAGAZINE, (I, II, IV), The Church of Jesus Christ of Latter-day Saints, 50 E. North Temple St., Salt Lake City UT 84150. (801)532-2951. Fax: (801)240-5997. Editor: Richard M. Romney. Magazine: 8×10½; 51 pages; 40 lb. coated paper; illustrations and photos. "We will publish fiction on any theme that strengthens and builds the standards and convictions of teenage Latter-day Saints ('Mormons')." Monthly. Estab. 1971. Circ. 200,000.

● *New Era* is a recipient of the Focus on Excellence Award from Brigham Young University. The magazine also sponsors a writing contest.

Needs: Stories on family relationships, self-esteem, dealing with loneliness, resisting peer pressure and all aspects of maintaining Christian values in the modern world. "All material must be written from a Latter-day Saint ('Mormon') point of view—or at least from a generally Christian point of view, reflecting LDS life and values." Receives 30-35 unsolicited mss/month. Accepts 1 ms/issue; 12 mss/year. Publishes ms 3 months to 3 years after acceptance. Recently published work by Jack Weyland and Alma Yates. Length: 1,500 words average; 250 words minimum; 2,000 words maximum.

How to Contact: Query letter preferred; send complete ms. Reports in 6-8 weeks. SASE. Disk submissions (WordPerfect, MacIntosh) OK. Sample copy for $1 and 9×12 SAE with 2 first-class stamps. Fiction guidelines for #10 SASE.

Payment/Terms: Pays $50-375 and contributor's copies on acceptance for all rights (reassign to author on request).

Advice: "Each magazine has its own personality—you wouldn't write the same style of fiction for *Seventeen* that you would write for *Omni*. Very few writers who are not of our faith have been able to write for us successfully, and the reason usually is that they don't know what it's like to be a member of our church. You must study and research and know those you are writing about. We love to work with beginning authors, and we're a great place to break in if you can understand us." Sponsors contests and awards for LDS fiction writers. "We have an annual contest; entry forms are in each September issue. Deadline is January; winners published in August."

THE NEW YORKER, (III), The New Yorker, Inc., 20 W. 43rd St., New York NY 10036. (212)536-5972. Fiction Department. A quality magazine of interesting, well-written stories, articles, essays and poems for a literate audience. Weekly. Estab. 1925. Circ. 750,000.

How to Contact: Send complete ms with SASE. Reports in 10-12 weeks on mss. Publishes 1 ms/issue.

Payment/Terms: Varies. Pays on acceptance.

Advice: "Be lively, original, not overly literary. Write what you want to write, not what you think the editor would like. Send poetry to Poetry Department."

NUGGET, (II), Dugent Publishing Corp., 14411 Commerce Way, Suite 420, Miami Lakes FL 33016. (305)557-0071. Editor-in-Chief: Christopher James. A newsstand magazine designed to have erotic appeal for a fetish-oriented audience. Published 12 times a year. Estab. 1956. Circ. 100,000.

Needs: Offbeat, fetish-oriented material encompassing a variety of subjects (B&D, TV, TS, spanking, amputeeism, golden showers, infantalism, catfighting, etc.). Most of fiction includes several sex scenes. No fiction that concerns children or religious subjects. Accepts 2 mss/issue. Agented fiction 5%. Length: 2,000-3,500 words.

How to Contact: Send complete ms with SASE. Reports in 1 month. Sample copy for $3.50. Guidelines for legal-sized SASE.

Payment/Terms: Pays minimum $200 and 1 contributor's copy on publication for first rights.

Advice: "Keep in mind the nature of the publication, which is fetish erotica. Subject matter can vary, but we prefer fetish themes."

NU*REAL, The Electronic Magazine of Art & Technology, (I), Mindset, P.O. Box 7000-822, Redondo Beach CA 90277. (310)435-5702. E-mail: lairdsimm@aol.com. Editor: Christopher Simmons. Digital Magazine: 28-36 pages; illustrations and photos. "*Nu*Real* publishes new technology, art and fiction." Estab. 1995. Circ. 20,000.

● *Nu*Real* is produced in digital paper format which can be read on any computer. It's distributed on disk, online and the Internet at http://members.aol.com/mindsetx/NuReal. Check with them for details.

Needs: Adventure, fantasy (science fantasy), horror, mystery/suspense (romantic suspense), psychic/supernatural/occult, romance (futuristic/time travel), science fiction. Publishes annual special fiction issue or anthology. Receives 20-30 mss/month. Accepts 4 mss/issue; 30-50 mss/year. Does not read mss between Christmas and mid-January. Publishes ms 30-60 days after acceptance. Length: 9,500 words average; 5,000 words minimum; 25,000 words maximum. Also publishes literary essays, literary criticism, poetry. Sometimes critiques or comments on rejected ms.

How to Contact: Send complete ms with a cover letter or via electronic mail. Include estimated word count, 100 word bio, list of publications. Reports in 3 weeks. Send a disposable copy of mss. Fiction guidelines for #10 SASE. Reviews novels and short story collections.

Payment/Terms: Pays $10-25 and contributor's copies on publication for one-time rights.
Advice: "Read as many of the masters of science fiction as possible. They are the best of all possible teachers."

ODYSSEY, Science That's Out of this World, Cobblestone Publishing, Inc., 7 School St., Peterborough NH 03458. (603)924-7209. Editor: Elizabeth E. Lindstrom. Magazine. "Scientific accuracy, original approaches to the subject are primary concerns of the editors in choosing material. For 8-14 year olds." Monthly (except July and August). Estab. 1991. Circ. 30,000.
Needs: Material must match theme; send for theme list and deadlines. Children's/juvenile (8-14 years), "authentic historical and biographical fiction, science fiction, retold legends, etc., relating to theme." List of upcoming themes available for SASE. Length: 750 words maximum.
How to Contact: Query first or query with clips of published work (if new to *Odyssey*). "Include estimated word count and a detailed 1-page outline explaining the information to be presented; an extensive bibliography of materials authors plan to use." Reports in several months. Send SASE for reply or send stamped postcard to find out if ms has been received. Sample copy for $3.95, 7½×10½ SAE and $1.05 postage. Fiction guidelines for SASE.
Payment/Terms: Pays 10-17¢/word on publication for all rights.
Advice: "We also include in-depth nonfiction, plays and biographies."

OMNI, (II), General Media, 277 Park Ave. 4th Floor, New York NY 10172-0003. Website: http://www.omnimag.com. Fiction Editor: Ellen Datlow. Magazine: online exclusively; illustrations; photos. "Magazine of science and science fiction with an interest in near future; stories of what science holds, what life and lifestyles will be like in areas affected by science for a young, bright and well-educated audience between ages 18-45."
● Ellen Datlow has won numerous awards (see "Advice" below). She also edits *The Year's Best Fantasy and Horror* (a reprint anthology).
Needs: Science fiction and contemporary fantasy. No sword and sorcery, horror (technological horror) or space opera. Receives approximately 400 unsolicited fiction mss/month. Accepts 20 mss/year. Agented fiction 5%. Recently published work by John Silverberg, Harlan Ellison and Pat Cadigan. Length: 2,000 words minimum, 10,000 words maximum. Critiques rejected mss that interest me "when there is time." Sometimes recommends other markets.
How to Contact: Send complete ms with SASE. No simultaneous or online submissions. Reports within 2 months. Publishes ms 3 months to 1 year after acceptance.
Payment/Terms: Pays $1,250-2,500. Acquires first electronic rights exclusive for 6 months then can resell to print.
Advice: "Beginning writers should read a lot of the best science fiction short stories today to get a feeling for what is being done. Also, they should read outside the field and nonfiction for inspiration. We are looking for strong, well-written stories dealing with the next 100 years. When submitting your stories, don't be cute, don't be negative. Keep it simple. If you have credentials (writing or workshopping or whatever may be relevant), mention them in your cover letter. Never tell the plot of your story in a cover letter. Send the full story. I don't know any editor of short fiction who wants a query letter. Rewrite and learn to be your own editor. Don't ever call an editor on the phone and ask why he/she rejected a story. You'll either find out in a personal rejection letter (which means the editor liked it or thought enough of your writing to comment) or you won't find out at all (most likely the editor won't remember a form-rejected story)." Ellen Datlow has been nominated in Best Professional editor category of the Hugos 6 years running and she has won 5 World Fantasy Awards.

ON THE LINE, (II), Mennonite Publishing House, 616 Walnut Ave., Scottdale PA 15683-1999. (412)887-8500. Editor: Mary Meyer. Magazine: 7×10; 28 pages; illustrations; b&w photos. "A religious take-home paper with the goal of helping children grow in their understanding and appreciation of God, the created world, themselves and other people." For children ages 9-14. Weekly. Estab. 1970. Circ. 6,500.
Needs: Adventure and problem-solving stories with Christian values for older children and young teens (9-14 years). Receives 50-100 unsolicited mss/month. Accepts 52 mss/year. Published work by O.B. Comer, Eileen Spinelli and Russell Lewis. Published new writers within the last year. Length: 800-1,500 words.
How to Contact: Send complete ms noting whether author is offering first-time or reprint rights. Reports in 1 month. SASE. Simultaneous and previously published work OK. Free sample copy and fiction guidelines.
Payment/Terms: Pays on acceptance for one-time rights.
Advice: "We believe in the power of story to entertain, inspire and challenge the reader to new growth. Know children and their thoughts, feelings and interests. Be realistic with characters and events in the fiction. Stories do not need to be true, but need to *feel* true."

OPTIONS, The *Bi*-Monthly, (I, IV), AJA Publishing, Box 470, Port Chester NY 10573. E-mail: dianaeditr@aol.com. Associate Editor: Diana Sheridan. Magazine: digest-sized; 114 pages; newsprint paper; glossy cover stock; illustrations and photos. Sexually explicit magazine for and about bisexuals. "Please read our Advice subhead." 10 issues/year. Estab. 1982. Circ. 100,000.

Needs: Erotica, bisexual, gay, lesbian. "First person as-if-true experiences." Accepts 6 unsolicited fiction mss/issue. "Very little" of fiction is agented. Published new writers within the last year. Length: 2,000-3,000 words. Sometimes critiques rejected mss.

How to Contact: Send complete ms with or without cover letter. No simultaneous submissions. Reports in approximately 3 weeks. SASE. Electronic submissions (disk or e-mail as textfiles) OK. "Submissions on Macintosh disk welcome and can often use IBM submissions, but please include hard copy too." Sample copy for $2.95 and 6×9 SAE with 5 first-class stamps. Fiction guidelines for SASE.

Payment/Terms: Pays $100 on publication for all rights. Will reassign book rights on request.

Advice: "Read a copy of *Options* carefully and look at our spec sheet before writing anything for us. That's not new advice, but to judge from some of what we get in the mail, it's necessary to repeat. We only buy two bi/lesbian pieces per issue; need is greater for bi/gay male mss. Though we're a bi rather than gay magazine, the emphasis is on same-sex relationships. If the readers want to read about a male/female couple, they'll buy another magazine. Gay male stories sent to *Options* will also be considered for publication in *Beau*, our gay male magazine. *Most important:* We *only* publish male/male stories that feature 'safe sex' practices unless the story is clearly something that took place pre-AIDS."

ORANGE COAST MAGAZINE, The Magazine of Orange County, (IV), 245-D Fischer Ave., Suite 8, Costa Mesa CA 92626. (714)545-1900. Fax: (714)545-1932. E-mail: ocmag@aol.com. Editor: Martin V. Smith. Managing Editor: Allison Joyce. Magazine: 8½×11; 175 pages; 50 lb. Sonoma gloss paper; Warrenflo cover; illustrations and photographs. *Orange Coast* publishes articles offering insight into the community for its affluent, well-educated Orange County readers. Monthly. Estab. 1974. Circ. 38,000.

Needs: Fiction rarely published. Fiction submissions must have Orange County setting or characters or be relevant to local sensibilities. Receives 30 unsolicited mss/month. Accepts 2 mss/year. Publishes ms 4-6 months after acceptance. Length: 2,500 words average; 1,500 words minimum; 3,000 words maximum.

How to Contact: Send complete ms with cover letter that includes Social Security number. Electronic submissions OK. Reports in 3 months. SASE. Simultaneous submissions OK. Sample copy for 9×12 SASE.

Payment/Terms: Pays $250 on acceptance for first North American serial rights.

Advice: "Read the magazine. Tell us why a specific piece of fiction belongs there. Convince us to make an exception."

‡OUTLAW BIKER, (II, IV), Outlaw Biker Enterprises, Box 447, Voorhees NJ 08003. Editor: Casey Exton. Magazine: 8½×11; 96 pages; 50 lb. color paper; 80 lb. cover stock; illustrations; photos. "Motorcycle/biker lifestyle magazine." Published 10 times/year. Estab. 1984. Circ. 120,000.

Needs: Biker fiction and humor. Upcoming theme: "Outlaw Legends." Receives 20 unsolicited mss/month. Accepts 1 fiction ms/issue. Publishes ms 2-8 months after acceptance. Length: 1,000-2,500 words.

How to Contact: Send complete ms with cover letter and SASE. Reports in 2-4 weeks. Sample copy for $5.

Payment/Terms: Payment varies according to length and quality of work. Acquires all rights.

Advice: Known for "raunchy, real-life, sexy and funny; geared much more to the biker's lifestyle—sex for humor (not even semi porn)."

‡PILLOW TALK, (I, II), 801 Second Ave., New York NY 10017. Editor: Asia Fraser. Magazine: digest-sized; 98 pages; photos. Bimonthly erotic letters magazine.

Needs: Erotica, in letter form. "We use approximately 20 short letters of no more than six manuscript pages per issue, and five long letters of between seven and ten manuscript pages. We look for well-written, graphic erotica meant to sexually titillate by being sensual, not vulgar." Published new writers within the last year. Recommends other markets.

How to Contact: "We encourage unsolicited manuscripts. Writers who have proven reliable will receive assignments."

Payment/Terms: Pays $5/page for short letters and a $75 flat rate for long letters on acceptance.

Advice: "Keep it short and sensual. We buy many more short letters than long ones. This is a 'couples-oriented' book; the sex should be a natural outgrowth of a relationship, the characters should be believable, and both male and female characters should be treated with respect. No S&M, bondage, male homosexuality, incest, underage characters or anal sex—not even in dialogue, not even in implication. No language that even implies sexual violence—not even in metaphor. No ejaculation on any part of a person's body. Romance is a big plus. Before sending in any material, request 'Submission Guidelines for Writers' to get a clear picture of what we're looking for, and how to present submissions."

PLAYBOY MAGAZINE, 680 N. Lake Shore Dr., Chicago IL 60611. (312)751-8000. Prefers not to share information.

POCKETS, Devotional Magazine for Children, (II), The Upper Room, 1908 Grand Ave., Box 189, Nashville TN 37202. (615)340-7333. Editor-in-Chief: Janet R. Knight. Magazine: 7×9; 48 pages; 50 lb. white econowrite paper; 80 lb. white coated, heavy cover stock; color and 2-color illustrations; some photos. Magazine for children ages 6-12, with articles specifically geared for ages 8 to 11. "The magazine offers stories, activities, prayers, poems—all geared to giving children a better understanding of themselves as children of God." Published monthly except for January. Estab. 1981. Estimated circ. 99,000.
- *Pockets* has received honors from the Educational Press Association of America. The magazine's fiction tends to feature children dealing with real-life situations "from a faith perspective."

Needs: Adventure, contemporary, ethnic, historical (general), juvenile, religious/inspirational and suspense/mystery. "All submissions should address the broad theme of the magazine. Each issue will be built around one theme with material which can be used by children in a variety of ways. Scripture stories, fiction, poetry, prayers, art, graphics, puzzles and activities will all be included. Submissions do not need to be overtly religious. They should help children experience a Christian lifestyle that is not always a neatly wrapped moral package, but is open to the continuing revelation of God's will. Seasonal material, both secular and liturgical, is desired. No violence, horror, sexual and racial stereotyping or fiction containing heavy moralizing." No talking animal stories. Receives approximately 200 unsolicited fiction mss/month. Accepts 4-5 mss/issue; 44-60 mss/year. Publishes short shorts. A peace-with-justice theme will run throughout the magazine. Published work by Peggy King Anderson, Angela Gibson and John Steptoe. Published new writers last year. Length: 600 words minimum; 1,600 words maximum; 1,200 words average. Sponsors annual fiction writing contest. Deadline: Aug. 15. Send for guidelines. $1,000 award and publication.
How to Contact: Send complete ms with SASE. Previously published submissions OK, but no simultaneous or faxed submissions. Reports in 1 month on mss. Publishes ms 1 year to 18 months after acceptance. Sample copy free with SAE and 4 first-class stamps. Fiction guidelines and themes with SASE. "Strongly advise sending for themes before submitting."
Payment/Terms: Pays 12¢/word and up and 2-5 contributor's copies on acceptance for first North American serial rights. $1.95 charge for extras; $1 each for 10 or more.
Advice: "Listen to children as they talk with each other. Please send for a sample copy as well as guidelines and themes. Many manuscripts we receive are simply inappropriate. Each issue is theme-related. Please send for list of themes. New themes published in December of each year. Include SASE."

PORTLAND MAGAZINE, Maine's City Magazine, (I, II), 578 Congress St., Portland ME 04101. (207)775-4339. Editor: Colin Sargent. Magazine: 48 pages; 60 lb. paper; 80 lb. cover stock; illustrations and photographs. "City lifestyle magazine—style, business, real estate, controversy, fashion, cuisine, interviews and art relating to the Maine area." Monthly. Estab. 1986. Circ. 100,000.
Needs: Contemporary, historical, literary. Receives 20 unsolicited fiction mss/month. Accepts 1 mss/issue; 10 mss/year. Publishes short shorts. Published work by Janwillem Vande Wetering, Sanford Phippen and Mamene Medwood. Length: 3 double-spaced typed pages.
How to Contact: Query first. "Fiction below 700 words, please." Send complete ms with cover letter. Reports in 6 months. SASE. Accepts electronic submissions.
Payment/Terms: Pays on publication for first North American serial rights.
Advice: "We publish ambitious short fiction featuring everyone from Frederick Barthelme to newly discovered fiction by Edna St. Vincent Millay."

POWER AND LIGHT, (I, II), Word Action Publishing Company, 6401 The Paseo, Kansas City MO 64131. (816)333-7000. Fax: (816)333-4439. E-mail: mhammer@nazarene.org. Editor: Beula J. Postlewait. Associate Editor: Melissa Hammer. Story paper: 5×8; 8 pages; storypaper and newsprint; illustrations and photos. "Relates Sunday School learning to preteens' lives. Must reflect theology of the Church of the Nazarene." Weekly. Estab. 1993. Circ. 30,000.
- *Power and Light* would like to see fiction with more natural, contemporary, positive situations.

Needs: Children's/juvenile (10-12 years): adventure, fantasy (children's fantasy), religious/inspirational. List of upcoming themes available for SASE. Receives 10-15 mss/month. Accepts 1 ms/month. Publishes ms 1 year after acceptance. Recently published work by Bob Hostetler, Betty Lou Mell and Laura Strickland. Length: 700 words average; 500 words minimum; 800 words maximum. Always critiques or comments on rejected mss.

How to Contact: Query first ("E-mail response is much quicker and more convenient for queries.") Include estimated word count and Social Security number. Reports in 1 month on queries; 3 months on mss. SASE for reply or return or ms. Simultaneous, reprint and electronic (IBM disk or e-mail) submissions OK. Sample copy for #10 SASE. Fiction guidelines for #10 SASE.
Payment/Terms: Pays 5¢/word and 4 contributor's copies on publication for multi-use rights.
Advice: Looks for "creativity—situations relating to preteens that are not trite such as shoplifting, etc."

POWERPLAY MAGAZINE, (II, IV), Brush Creek Media, Inc., 2215R Market St., #148, San Francisco CA 94114. (415)552-1506. Fax: (415)552-3244. E-mail: jwbean@brushcreek.com. Editor: Alec Wagner. Magazine: 8 ½×11; 64 pages; white husky paper; gloss cover; b&w photos. "Geared toward gay men. *Powerplay* is kink-oriented. All of our fiction is sexual and frank; quite raw and confrontational." Quarterly. Estab. 1992. Circ. 38,000.
• This publisher also publishes *Bear*.
Needs: Gay: erotica, humor/satire. Looking for "unapologetic, bold sexual experiences, real or imagined." Recently published Tim Brough and Cord Odebolt. Receives 5-10 unsolicited mss/month. Buys 2-3 mss/issue; 15-20 mss/year. Length: Open. Sometimes critiques or comments on reject mss.
How To Contact: Send complete ms with cover letter. Accepts electronically transmitted submissions (disks for PC; "e-mail accepted in emergencies.") Accepts unsolicited queries and correspondence by e-mail. Include bio and Social Security number with submission. Send SASE for return or send disposable copy of the ms. Will consider simultaneous submissions. Sample copy for $6.50. Fiction guidelines free.
Payment/Terms: Pays $75 minimum; $125 maximum on publication. Purchases first North American serial rights. Also pays 2-3 contributor's copies.

‡PRIVATE LETTERS, (I, II), 801 Second Ave., New York NY 10017. Editor: Asia Fraser. Magazine: digest-sized; 98 pages; illustrations; photographs. "Adult erotica that is well-written, using graphic terms that excite the sexual nature of the reader in a pleasant, positive manner." Bimonthly letters magazine.
Needs: Erotica, written in letter form. No S&M, incest, homosexuality, anal sex or sex-crazed women and macho, women-conquering studs. "We use approximately 20 short letters per issue of no more than six double-spaced manuscript pages and five long letters of about 10 double-spaced manuscript pages." Published work by Diana Shamblin, Frank Lee and Shirley LeRoy. Published new writers within the last year. Recommends other markets.
How to Contact: Send complete ms (only after requesting guidelines). "The majority of the material is assigned to people whose writing has proven consistently top-notch. They usually reach this level by sending us unsolicited material which impresses us. We invite them to send us some more on spec, and we're impressed again. Then a long and fruitful relationship is hopefully established. We greatly encourage unsolicited submissions. We are now printing two additional issues each year, so naturally the demand for stories is higher."
Payment/Terms: Pays $5 per page for short letters; $75 for long (7-10 page) letters. Pays on acceptance.
Advice: "If you base your writing on erotic magazines other than our own, then we'll probably find your material too gross. We want good characterization, believable plots, a little romance, with sex being a natural outgrowth of a relationship. (Yes, it can be done. Read our magazine.) Portray sex as an emotionally-charged, romantic experience—not an animalistic ritual. *Never* give up, except if you die. In which case, if you haven't succeeded as a writer yet, you probably never will. (Though there have been exceptions.) Potential writers should be advised that each issue has certain themes and topics we try to adhere to. Also, while the longer stories of more than seven pages pay more, there are only about five of them accepted for each issue. We buy far more 4-6 page manuscripts. Request with SASE our 'Submission Guidelines for Writers' to get a clear picture of what we're looking for, and how to present submissions."

PURPOSE, (I, II), Mennonite Publishing House, 616 Walnut Ave., Scottdale PA 15683-1999. (412)887-8500. Fax: (412)887-3111. Editor: James E. Horsch. Magazine: 5⅜×8⅜; 8 pages; illustrations; photos. "Magazine focuses on Christian discipleship—how to be a faithful Christian in the midst of tough everyday life complexities. Uses story form to present models and examples to encourage Christians in living a life of faithful discipleship." Weekly. Estab. 1968. Circ. 15,000.
Needs: Historical, religious/inspirational. No militaristic/narrow patriotism or racism. Receives 100 unsolicited mss/month. Accepts 3 mss/issue; 140 mss/year. Recently published work by Kayleen Reusser, Crane Delbert Bennett and Margaret Hook. Length: 600 words average; 900 words maximum. Occasionally comments on rejected mss.
How to Contact: Send complete ms only. Reports in 2 months. Simultaneous and previously published work OK. Sample copy for 6×9 SAE and 2 first-class stamps. Writer's guidelines free with sample copy only.

Payment/Terms: Pays up to 5¢/word for stories and 2 contributor's copies on acceptance for one-time rights.

Advice: Many stories are "situational—how to respond to dilemmas. Write crisp, action moving, personal style, focused upon an individual, a group of people, or an organization. The story form is an excellent literary device to use in exploring discipleship issues. There are many issues to explore. Each writer brings a unique solution. Let's hear them. The first two paragraphs are crucial in establishing the mood/issue to be resolved in the story. Work hard on developing these."

Q MAGAZINE, (II, IV), 1350-E4 Mahan Dr., #201, Tallahassee FL 32308-5101. (904)681-8917. E-mail: qmagazine@aol.com. Publisher: Melanie Annis. Editor: A.E. Ardley. Magazine. "Covers arts, leisure and entertainment in and around Tallahassee, North Florida and South Georgia." Monthly. Estab. 1992. Circ. 12,000-15,000.

Needs: Adventure, historical, slice-of-life vignettes. "Submit seasonal/holiday material six months in advance." Publishes ms 2 months after acceptance. Reports in 1 month. Simultaneous and reprint submissions OK. Sample copy for 9 × 12 SASE.

Payment/Terms: Acquires one-time rights.

Advice: "*Q Magazine* seeks to provoke, arouse and encourage readers to take part in local activities and personal expression. Our emphasis is on the written word and bringing arts, leisure and entertainment to a more mainstream audience. If it's tasty or interesting reading we'll like it."

R-A-D-A-R, (I, II), Standard Publishing, 8121 Hamilton Ave., Cincinnati OH 45231. (513)931-4050. Editor: Elaina Meyers. Magazine: 12 pages; newsprint; illustrations; a few photos. "*R-A-D-A-R* is a take-home paper, distributed in Sunday school classes for children in grades 3-6. The stories and other features reinforce the Bible lesson taught in class. Boys and girls who attend Sunday school make up the audience. The fiction stories, Bible picture stories and other special features appeal to their interests." Weekly. Estab. 1978.

Needs: Fiction—The hero of the story should be an 11- or 12-year-old in a situation involving one or more of the following: history, mystery, animals, sports, adventure, school, travel, relationships with parents, friends and others. Stories should have believable plots and be wholesome, Christian character-building, but not "preachy." No science fiction. Published new writers within the last year. Length: 900-1,000 words average.

How to Contact: Send complete ms. Prefers for authors to send business-size SASE and request theme sheet. "Writing for a specific topic on theme sheet is much better than submitting unsolicited." Reports in 6-8 weeks on mss. SASE for ms. Simultaneous submissions permitted but not desired; reprint submissions OK. Sample copy and guidelines with SASE.

Payment/Terms: Pays 3-7¢/word on acceptance for first rights, reprints, etc.; 2 contributor's copies sent on publication.

Advice: "Send SASE for sample copy, guidelines and theme list. Follow the specifics of guidelines. Keep your writing current with the times and happenings of our world. Our needs change as the needs of middlers (3rd-4th graders) and juniors (5th and 6th graders) change. Writers must keep current."

RADIANCE, The Magazine for Large Women, (II), Box 30246, Oakland CA 94604. (510)482-0680. Editor: Alice Ansfield. Fiction Editors: Alice Ansfield and Catherine Taylor. Magazine: 8½ × 11; 56 pages; glossy/coated paper; 70 lb. cover stock; illustrations; photos. "Theme is to encourage women to live fully now, whatever their body size. To stop waiting to live or feel good about themselves until they lose weight." Quarterly. Estab. 1984. Circ. 8,000. Readership: 30,000.

Needs: Adventure, contemporary, erotica, ethnic, fantasy, feminist, historical, humor/satire, mainstream, mystery/suspense, prose poem, science fiction, spiritual, sports, young adult/teen. "Want fiction to have a larger-bodied character; living in a positive, upbeat way. Our goal is to empower women." Receives 150 mss/month. Accepts 40 mss/year. Publishes ms within 1 year of acceptance. Published work by Marla Zarrow, Sallie Tisdale and Mary Kay Blakely. Length: 2,000 words average; 800 words minimum; 3,500 words maximum. Publishes short shorts. Sometimes critiques rejected mss.

How to Contact: Query with clips of published work and send complete ms with cover letter. Reports in 3-4 months. SASE. Reprint submissions OK. Sample copy for $3.50. Guidelines for #10 SASE. Reviews novels and short story collections ("with at least one large-size heroine.")

Payment/Terms: Pays $35-100 and contributor's copies on publication for one-time rights. Sends galleys to the author if requested.

Advice: "Read our magazine before sending anything to us. Know what our philosophy and points of view are before sending a manuscript. Look around within your community for inspiring, successful and unique large women doing things worth writing about. At this time, prefer fiction having to do with a larger woman (man, child). *Radiance* is one of the leading resources in the size-acceptance movement. Each issue profiles dynamic large women from all walks of life, along with articles on health, media, fashion and politics. Our audience is the 30 million American women who wear a size 16 or over. Feminist, emotionally-supportive, quarterly magazine."

RANGER RICK MAGAZINE, (II), National Wildlife Federation, 8925 Leesburg Pike, Vienna VA 22184. (703)790-4274. Editor: Gerald Bishop. Fiction Editor: Deborah Churchman. Magazine: 8 × 10; 48 pages; glossy paper; 60 lb. cover stock; illustrations; photos. "*Ranger Rick* emphasizes conservation and the enjoyment of nature through full-color photos and art, fiction and nonfiction articles, games and puzzles, and special columns. Our audience ranges in ages from 6-12, with the greatest number in the 7 to 10 group. We aim for a fourth grade reading level. They read for fun and information." Monthly. Estab. 1967. Circ. 850,000.

● *Ranger Rick* has won several EdPress awards. The editors say the magazine has had a backlog of stories recently, yet they would like to see more *good* mystery and science fiction stories (with nature themes).

Needs: Adventure, fantasy, humor, mystery (amateur sleuth), science fiction and sports. "Interesting stories for kids focusing directly on nature or related subjects. Fiction that carries a conservation message is always needed, as are adventure stories involving kids with nature or the outdoors. Moralistic 'lessons' taught children by parents or teachers are not accepted. Human qualities are attributed to animals only in our regular feature, 'Adventures of Ranger Rick.' " Receives about 150-200 unsolicited fiction mss each month. Accepts about 6 mss/year. Published fiction by Leslie Dendy. Length: 900 words maximum. Critiques rejected mss "when there is time."

How to Contact: Query with sample lead and any clips of published work with SASE. May consider simultaneous submissions. Reports in 3 months on queries and mss. Publishes ms 8 months to 1 year after acceptance, but sometimes longer. Sample copy for $2. Guidelines for legal-sized SASE.

Payment/Terms: Pays $550 maximum/full-length ms on acceptance for all rights. Very rarely buys reprints. Sends galleys to author.

Advice: "For our magazine, the writer needs to understand kids and that aspect of nature he or she is writing about—a difficult combination! Manuscripts are rejected because they are contrived and/or condescending—often overwritten. Some manuscripts are anthropomorphic, others are above our readers' level. We find that fiction stories help children understand the natural world and the environmental problems it faces. Beginning writers have a chance equal to that of established authors *provided* the quality is there. Would love to see more science fiction and fantasy, as well as mysteries."

REDBOOK, (II), The Hearst Corporation, 224 W. 57th St., New York NY 10019. (212)649-2000. Fiction Editor: Dawn Raffel. Magazine: 8 × 10¾; 150-250 pages; 34 lb. paper; 70 lb. cover; illustrations; photos. "*Redbook*'s readership consists of American women, ages 25-44. Most are well-educated, married, have children and also work outside the home." Monthly. Estab. 1903. Circ. 3,200,000.

Needs: "*Redbook* generally publishes one or two short stories per issue. Stories need not be about women exclusively; but must appeal to a female audience. We are interested in new voices and buy up to a quarter of our stories from unsolicited submissions. Standards are high: Stories must be fresh, felt and intelligent; no formula fiction." Receives up to 600 unsolicited fiction mss each month. Published new writers within the last year. Length: up to 22 ms pages.

How to Contact: Send complete ms with SASE. No queries, please. Simultaneous submissions OK. Reports in 8-12 weeks.

Payment/Terms: Pays on acceptance for first North American serial rights.

Advice: "Superior craftsmanship is of paramount importance: We look for emotional complexity, dramatic tension, precision of language. Note that we don't run stories that look back on the experiences of childhood or adolescence. Please read a few issues to get a sense of what we're looking for."

ST. ANTHONY MESSENGER, (I, II), 1615 Republic St., Cincinnati OH 45210-1298. Editor: Norman Perry, O.F.M. Magazine: 8 × 10¾; 56 pages; illustrations; photos. "*St. Anthony Messenger* is a Catholic family magazine which aims to help its readers lead more fully human and Christian lives. We publish articles which report on a changing church and world, opinion pieces written from the perspective of Christian faith and values, personality profiles, and fiction which entertains and informs." Monthly. Estab. 1893. Circ. 325,000.

● This is a leading Catholic magazine, but has won awards for both religious and secular journalism and writing from the Catholic Press Association, the International Association of Business Communicators and the Cincinnati Editors Association.

Needs: Contemporary, religious/inspirational, romance, senior citizen/retirement and spiritual. "We do not want mawkishly sentimental or preachy fiction. Stories are most often rejected for poor plotting and characterization; bad dialogue—listen to how people talk; inadequate motivation. Many stories

---

say nothing, are 'happenings' rather than stories." No fetal journals, no rewritten Bible stories. Receives 70-80 unsolicited fiction mss/month. Accepts 1 ms/issue; 12 mss/year. Publishes ms up to 1 year after acceptance. Recently published work by Arthur Powers, Joseph Pici, Marilyn A. Gardener and Kari Sharrhill. Length: 2,000-3,000 words. Critiques rejected mss "when there is time." Sometimes recommends other markets.

How to Contact: Send complete ms with SASE. No simultaneous submissions. Reports in 6-8 weeks. Sample copy and guidelines for #10 SASE. Reviews novels and short story collections. Send books to Barbara Beckwith, book review editor.

Payment/Terms: Pays 14¢/word maximum and 2 contributor's copies on acceptance for first North American serial rights; $1 charge for extras.

Advice: "We publish one story a month and we get up to 1,000 a year. Too many offer simplistic 'solutions' or answers. Pay attention to endings. Easy, simplistic, deus ex machina endings don't work. People have to feel characters in the stories are real and have a reason to care about them and what happens to them. Fiction entertains but can also convey a point in a very telling way just as the Bible uses stories to teach."

ST. JOSEPH'S MESSENGER AND ADVOCATE OF THE BLIND, (II), Sisters of St. Joseph of Peace, 541 Pavonia Ave., Jersey City NJ 07306. (201)798-4141. Magazine: 8½×11; 16 pages; illustrations; photos. For Catholics generally but not exclusively. Theme is "religious—relevant—real." Quarterly. Estab. 1903. Circ. 20,000.

Needs: Contemporary, humor/satire, mainstream, religious/inspirational, romance and senior citizen/retirement. Receives 30-40 unsolicited fiction mss/month. Accepts 3 mss/issue; 20 mss/year. Publishes ms an average of 1 year after acceptance. Published work by Eileen W. Strauch. Published new writers within the last year. Length: 800 words minimum; 1,800 words maximum; 1,500 words average. Occasionally critiques rejected mss.

How to Contact: Send complete ms with SASE. Simultaneous and previously published submissions OK. Sample copy for #10 SASE. Fiction guidelines for SASE.

Payment/Terms: Pays $15-40 and 2 contributor's copies on acceptance for one-time rights.

Advice: Rejects mss because of "vague focus or theme. Write to be read—keep material current and of interest. *Do not preach*—the story will tell the message. Keep the ending from being too obvious. Fiction is the greatest area of interest to our particular reading public."

SEEK, (II), Standard Publishing, 8121 Hamilton Ave., Cincinnati OH 45231. Editor: Eileen H. Wilmoth. Magazine: 5½×8½; 8 pages; newsprint paper; art and photos in each issue. "Inspirational stories of faith-in-action for Christian young adults; a Sunday School take-home paper." Weekly. Estab. 1970. Circ. 40,000.

Needs: Religious/inspirational. Accepts 150 mss/year. Publishes ms an average of 1 year after acceptance. Published new writers within the last year. Length: 500-1,200 words.

How to Contact: Send complete ms with SASE. No simultaneous submissions. Reports in 2-3 months. Free sample copy and guidelines.

Payment/Terms: Pays 5-7¢/word on acceptance. Buys reprints.

Advice: "Write a credible story with Christian slant—no preachments; avoid overworked themes such as joy in suffering, generation gaps, etc. Most manuscripts are rejected by us because of irrelevant topic or message, unrealistic story, or poor character and/or plot development. We use fiction stories that are believable."

SEVENTEEN, (I, II), III Magazine Corp., 850 Third Ave., New York NY 10022. (212)407-9700. Fiction Editor: Ben Schrank. Magazine: 8½×11; 125-400 pages; 40 lb. coated paper; 80 lb. coated cover stock; illustrations; photos. A general interest magazine with fashion; beauty care; pertinent topics such as current issues, attitudes, experiences and concerns of teenagers. Monthly. Estab. 1944. Circ. 2.2 million.

● *Seventeen* sponsors an annual fiction contest for writers age 13-21.

Needs: High-quality literary fiction. Receives 500 unsolicited fiction mss/month. Accepts 1 mss/issue. Agented fiction 50%. Published work by Margaret Atwood, Joyce Carol Oates and Ellen Gilchrist. Published new writers within the last year. Length: approximately 750-3,500 words.

How to Contact: Send complete ms with SASE and cover letter with relevant credits. Reports in 3 months on mss. Guidelines for submissions with SASE.

Payment/Terms: Pays $700-2,500 on acceptance for one-time rights.

Advice: "Respect the intelligence and sophistication of teenagers. *Seventeen* remains open to the surprise of new voices. Our commitment to publishing the work of new writers remains strong; we continue to read every submission we receive. We believe that good fiction can move the reader toward thoughtful examination of her own life as well as the lives of others—providing her ultimately with a fuller appreciation of what it means to be human. While stories that focus on female teenage experience continue to be of interest, the less obvious possibilities are equally welcome. We encourage writers to submit literary short stories concerning subjects that may not be immediately identifiable as 'teenage,' with narrative styles that are experimental and challenging. Too often, unsolicited submissions possess voices and themes condescending and unsophisticated. Also, writers hesitate to send stories to *Seventeen* which they think too violent or risqué. Good writing holds the imaginable and then some, and if it doesn't find its home here, we're always grateful for the introduction to a writer's work. We're more inclined to publish cutting edge fiction than simple, young adult fiction."

SHOFAR, For Jewish Kids On The Move, (II, IV), 43 Northcote Dr., Melville NY 11747. (516)643-4598. Fax: (516)643-4598. Editor: Gerald H. Grayson, Ph.D. Magazine: 8½×11; 32 pages; 60 lb. paper; 80 lb. cover; illustration; photos. Audience: Jewish children in fourth through eighth grades. Monthly (October-May). Estab. 1984. Circ. 10,000.
Needs: Children's/juvenile (middle reader): cartoons, contemporary, humorous, poetry, puzzles, religious, sports. "All material must be on a Jewish theme." Receives 12-24 unsolicited mss/month. Accepts 3-5 mss/issue; 24-40 mss/year. Published work by Caryn Huberman, Diane Claerbout and Rabbi Sheldon Lewis. Length: 500-700 words. Occasionally critiques rejected mss. Recommends other markets.
How to Contact: Send complete ms with cover letter. Reports in 6-8 weeks. SASE. Simultaneous and reprint submissions OK. Sample copy for 9×12 SAE and $1.04 first-class postage. Fiction guidelines for 3½×6½ SASE.
Payment/Terms: Pays 10¢/word and 5 contributor's copies on publication for first North American serial rights.
Advice: "Know the magazine and the religious-education needs of Jewish elementary-school-age children. If you are a Jewish educator, what has worked for you in the classroom? Write it out; send it on to me; I'll help you develop the idea into a short piece of fiction. A beginning fiction writer eager to break into *Shofar* will find an eager editor willing to help."

‡SKIN ART, (I, II, IV), Outlaw Biker Enterprises, Inc., Box 447, Voorhees NJ 08043. Editor: J. Chris Miller. Magazine: 8½×11; 96 pages; 50 lb. coated paper; 80 lb. cover stock; illustrations; photos. "Art magazine devoted to showcasing the very best of modern tattooing." Published 9 times/year. Estab. 1988. Circ. 100,000.
Needs: Fiction pertaining to subject matter (tattooing). Receives 20 unsolicited mss/month. Publishes 1 fiction ms/issue. Publishes mss 2-8 months after acceptance. Length: 1,000-2,500 words. "Very open to freelance writers and unpublished writers. Freelance photographers also needed send SASE for guidelines and needs."
How to Contact: Send complete ms with cover letter and SASE. Responds to queries within 6 weeks. Sample copy for $5 and 8½×11 SAE with 2 first-class stamps.
Payment/Terms: Payment on publication varies according to quality of work. Buys all rights.
Advice: "Very targeted market, strongly suggest you read magazine before submitting work."

SOJOURNER, A Women's Forum, (I, IV), 42 Seaverns, Jamaica Plain MA 02130. (617)524-0415. Editor: Karen Kahn. Magazine: 11×17; 48 pages; newsprint; illustrations; photos. "Feminist journal publishing interviews, nonfiction features, news, viewpoints, poetry, reviews (music, cinema, books) and fiction for women." Published monthly. Estab. 1975. Circ. 40,000.
Needs: Contemporary, ethnic, experimental, fantasy, feminist, lesbian, humor/satire, literary, prose poem and women's. Upcoming themes: "Fiction/Arts Issue" (February); "Annual Health Supplement" (March); Pride (June); Sports (May). Receives 20 unsolicited fiction mss/month. Accepts 10 mss/year. Agented fiction 10%. Recently published work by Ruth Ann Lonardelli and Janie Adams. Published new writers within the last year. Length: 1,000 words minimum; 4,000 words maximum; 2,500 words average.
How to Contact: Send complete ms with SASE and cover letter with description of previous publications; current works. Simultaneous submissions OK. Reports in 6-8 months. Publishes ms an average of 6 months after acceptance. Sample copy for $3 with 10×13 SASE. Fiction guidelines for SASE.
Payment/Terms: Pays subscription to magazine and 2 contributor's copies, $15 for first rights. No extra charge up to 5 contributor's copies; $1 charge each thereafter.
Advice: "Pay attention to appearance of manuscript! Very difficult to wade through sloppily presented fiction, however good. Do write a cover letter. If not cute, it can't hurt and may help. Mention previous publication(s)."

SPIDER, The Magazine for Children, (II), Carus Publishing Co./The Cricket Magazine Group, P.O. Box 300, Peru IL 61354. Editor-in-Chief: Marianne Carus. Associate Editor: Christine Walske. Magazine: 8×10; 33 pages; illustrations and photos. "*Spider* publishes high-quality literature for beginning readers, mostly children ages 6 to 9." Monthly. Estab. 1994. Circ. 85,000.
Needs: Children's/juvenile (6-9 years), fantasy (children's fantasy). "No religious, didactic, or violent stories, or anything that talks down to children." Accepts 4 mss/issue. Publishes ms 1-2 years after acceptance. Agented fiction 2%. Published work by Lissa Rovetch, Ursula K. LeGuin and Eric Kimmel.

Length: 775 words average; 300 words minimum; 1,000 words maximum. Publishes short shorts. Also publishes poetry. Often critiques or comments on rejected ms.

How to Contact: Send complete ms with a cover letter. Include exact word count. Reports in 3 months. Send SASE for return of ms. Simultaneous and reprint submissions OK. Sample copy for $4. Fiction guidelines for #10 SASE.

Payment/Terms: Pays 25¢/word and 2 contributor's copies on publication for first rights or one-time rights; additional copies for $2.

Advice: "Read back issues of *Spider*." Looks for "quality writing, good characterization, lively style, humor. We would like to see more multicultural fiction."

‡**SPIRIT,(I)**, Good Ground Press, 1884 Randolph Ave., St. Paul MN 55105. (612)690-7012. Fax: (612)690-7039. Editor: Joan Mitchell. Magazine: 8½×11; 4 pages; 50 lb. paper; photographs. Religious education magazine for Roman Catholic teens. "Stories must be realistic, not moralistic or pietistic. They are used as catalysts to promote teens' discussion of their conflicts." Biweekly (28 issues). Estab. 1988. Circ. 25,000.

Needs: Feminist, religious/inspirational, young adult/teen. Upcoming themes: Christmas and Easter. List of upcoming themes available for SASE. Receives 20 unsolicited mss/month. Accepts 1 mss/issue; 12 mss/year. Publishes ms 6-12 months after acceptance. Recently published work by Margaret McCarthy, Kathleen Y Choi, Heather Klassen, Kathleen Cleberg, Bob Bartlett and Ron LaGro. Length: 1,000 words minimum; 1,200 words maximum. Sometimes critiques or comments on rejected mss.

How to Contact: Send complete ms with a cover letter. Include estimated word count. Reports in 6 months on mss. SASE for return of ms or send a disposable copy of ms. Simultaneous submissions and reprints OK. Sample copy and fiction guidelines free.

Payment/Terms: Pays $150 minimum on publication and 5 contributor's copies. Acquires first North American serial rights.

Advice: Looks for "believable conflicts for teens. Just because we're religious, don't send pious, moralistic work."

STANDARD, (I, II, IV), Nazarene International Headquarters, 6401 The Paseo, Kansas City MO 64131. (816)333-7000. Editor: Everett Leadingham. Magazine: 8½×11; 8 pages; illustrations; photos. Inspirational reading for adults. Weekly. Estab. 1936. Circ. 165,000.

Needs: "Looking for fiction-type stories that show Christianity in action." Receives 350 unsolicited mss/month. Accepts 240 mss/year. Publishes ms 14-18 months after acceptance. Published new writers within the last year. Length: 1,200-1,500 words average; 300 words minimum; 1,700 words maximum. Also publishes short shorts of 300-350 words.

How to Contact: Send complete ms with name, address and phone number. Reports in 2-3 months on mss. SASE. Simultaneous submissions OK but will pay only reprint rates. Sample copy and guidelines for SAE and 2 first-class stamps.

Payment/Terms: Pays 3½¢/word; 2¢/word (reprint) on acceptance; contributor's copies on publication.

STRAIGHT, (II), Standard Publishing Co., 8121 Hamilton Ave., Cincinnati OH 45231. (513)931-4050. Editor: Heather Wallace. "Publication helping and encouraging teens to live a victorious, fulfilling Christian life. Distributed through churches and some private subscriptions." Magazine: 6½×7½; 12 pages; newsprint paper and cover; illustrations (color); photos. Quarterly in weekly parts. Estab. 1951. Circ. 40,000.

Needs: Contemporary, religious/inspirational, romance, spiritual, mystery, adventure and humor—all with Christian emphasis. "Stories dealing with teens and teen life, with a positive message or theme. Topics that interest teenagers include school, family life, recreation, friends, church, part-time jobs, dating and music. Main character should be a Christian teenager and regular churchgoer, who faces situations using Bible principles." Themes available on a quarterly basis for SASE. Receives approximately 100 unsolicited fiction mss/month. Accepts 1-2 mss/issue; 75-100 mss/year. Publishes ms an average of 1 year after acceptance. Less than 1% of fiction is agented. Published work by Alan Cliburn, Betty Steele Everett and Teresa Cleary. Published new writers within the last year. Length: 900-1,500 words. Recommends other markets.

How to Contact: Send complete ms with SASE and cover letter (experience with teens especially preferred from new writers). Reports in 1-2 months. Sample copy and guidelines for SASE.

Payment/Terms: Pays 5-7¢/word on acceptance for first and one-time rights. Buys reprints.

Advice: "Get to know us before submitting, through guidelines and sample issues (SASE). And get to know teenagers. A writer must know what today's teens are like, and what kinds of conflicts they experience. In writing a short fiction piece for the teen reader, don't try to accomplish too much. If your character is dealing with the problem of prejudice, don't also deal with his/her fights with sister, desire for a bicycle, or anything else that is not absolutely essential to the reader's understanding of the major conflict."

THE SUN, (II), The Sun Publishing Company, Inc., 107 N. Roberson St., Chapel Hill NC 27516. (919)942-5282. Editor: Sy Safransky. Magazine: 8½×11; 40 pages; offset paper; glossy cover stock; illustrations; photos. "*The Sun* is a magazine of ideas. While we tend to favor personal writing, we're open to just about anything—even experimental writing, if it doesn't make us feel stupid. Surprise us; we often don't know what we'll like until we read it." Monthly. Estab. 1974. Circ. 30,000.
Needs: Open to all fiction. Receives approximately 500 unsolicited fiction mss each month. Accepts 3 ms/issue. Recently published work by Poe Ballantine, Daniela Kuper and Heather Sellers. Published new writers within the last year. Length: 7,000 words maximum. Also publishes poetry.
How to Contact: Send complete ms with SASE. Reports in 3 months. Publishes ms an average of 6-12 months after acceptance. Sample copy for $3.50
Payment/Terms: Pays up to $500 on publication, plus 2 contributor's copies and a complimentary one-year subscription for one-time rights. Publishes reprints.

SWANK MAGAZINE, (II, IV), Swank Publication, 210 Route 4 East, Suite 401, Paramus NJ 07652. Fax: (201)843-8636. Editor: Paul Gambino. Magazine: 8½×11; 116 pages; 20 lb. paper; 60 lb. coated stock; illustrations; photos. "Men's sophisticated format. Sexually-oriented material. Our readers are after erotic material." Published 13 times a year. Estab. 1952. Circ. 350,000.
Needs: High-caliber erotica. "Fiction always has an erotic or other male-oriented theme; also eligible would be mystery or suspense with a very erotic scene. Also would like to see more humor. Writers should try to avoid the clichés of the genre." Receives approximately 80 unsolicited fiction mss each month. Accepts 1 ms/issue, 18 mss/year. Published new writers within the last year. Length: 1,500-2,750 words.
How to Contact: Send complete ms with SASE and cover letter. List previous publishing credits. Electronic submissions OK. Reports in 3 weeks on mss. Sample copy for $5.95 with SASE.
Payment/Terms: Pays $300-500. Buys first North American serial rights. Offers 25% kill fee for assigned ms not published.
Advice: "Research the men's magazine market." Mss are rejected because of "typical, overly simple storylines and poor execution. We're looking for interesting stories—whether erotic in theme or not—that break the mold of the usual men's magazine fiction. We're not only just considering strict erotica. Mystery, adventure, etc. with erotica passages will be considered."

TATTOO REVUE, (I, IV), Outlaw Biker Enterprises, Inc., Box 447, Voorhees NJ 08043. Editorial Director: J.C. Miller. Magazine: 8½×11, 96 pages; 50 lb. coated paper; 80 lb. cover stock; illustrations and photos. "Art magazine devoted to showcasing the very best of modern tattooing." Published 10 times/year. Estab. 1988. Circ. 180,000.
Needs: Fiction pertaining to subject matter (tattooing). Receives 20 unsolicited mss/month. Publishes 1 fiction ms/issue. Publishes ms 2-8 months after acceptance. Length: 1,000-2,500 words. "Very open to freelance writers and unpublished writers. Freelance photographers also needed."
How to Contact: Send complete ms with cover letter and SASE. Sample copy for $5 and 8½×11 SAE with 2 first-class stamps.
Payment/Terms: Payment varies according to length and quality of work; pays on publication. Acquires all rights.
Advice: "Very targeted market, strongly suggest you read magazine before submitting work."

TEEN LIFE, (II), Gospel Publishing House, 1445 Boonville Ave., Springfield MO 65802-1894. (417)862-2781. Fax: (417)862-6059. E-mail: tbicket@ag.publish.org. Editor: Tammy Bicket. Take-home Sunday school paper for teenagers (ages 12-19). Weekly. Estab. 1936. Circ. 60,000.
Needs: Religious/inspirational, mystery/suspense, adventure, humor, spiritual and young adult, "with a strong but not preachy Biblical emphasis. We would like to see more humor." Upcoming themes: "Family," "Discipleship," "Ministry," "Dating." Receives 100 unsolicited fiction mss/month. Recently published work by Joey O'Connor, Betty Lou Mell, Mark Matlock and Teresa Cleary. Published new writers within the last year. Length: up to 1,500 words.
How to Contact: Send complete ms with SASE. "We want manuscripts that reflect our upcoming themes. Please send for guidelines before sending manuscript." Reports in 1-3 months. Simultaneous, reprint and electronic (disk, Mac) submissions OK. Free sample copy and guidelines.
Payment/Terms: Varies. Pays on acceptance for one-time rights.
Advice: "Most manuscripts are rejected because of shallow characters, shallow or predictable plots, and/or a lack of spiritual emphasis. Send seasonal material approximately 18 months in advance."

THE TREKKER NEWS & VIEWS, (I), 8033 Sunset Blvd., Suite 42, Hollywood CA 90046. (213)871-6891. E-mail: rrjm78a@prodigy.com. Publisher: Kathy Krantz. Editor: Colin Stewart. Magazine: 8½×11; 40 pages; glossy paper; glossy cover; b&w illustrations and photos. Bimonthly. Estab. 1988. Circ. 10,000-20,000.
Needs: Children's/juvenile, experimental, fantasy (science fantasy), horror, literary, mainstream/contemporary, psychic/supernatural/occult, romance (futuristic/time travel), science fiction, young adult/teen. "Our publication is for all ages." List of upcoming themes available for SASE. Publishes ms 2-

3 months after acceptance. Recently published work by Phil Farrand, Jeri Taylor, Don Barrett, Colin Stewart, Chris Carter and Brannon Biaga. Also publishes literary essays, literary criticism and poetry. Sometimes critiques or comments on rejected ms.

How to Contact: Send comlete ms with a cover letter. Should include estimated word count, 3-4 line bio, list of publications with any experience or published works, knowledge of subject. Reports in 6-8 weeks on queries. Send SASE for reply, return of ms or send a disposable copy of ms. Simultaneous and electronic submissions OK. Send 3.5 disk and hard copy. Sample copy for $4.99. Reviews novels and short story collections.

Payment/Terms: Pays 1 contributor's copy; additional copies for $2.

Advice: "Send pieces that cover science fiction series and films. We cover reviews of film, TV and features, videos, sci-fi, NASA, SETI, UFO's, space, books, interviews with actors, poetry and environmental themed pieces. We love to inspire and discover new and talented writers. We have professional contributors and only print terrific pieces. We're always looking for a new column idea. *The Trekker* is sent to the producers and writers of these series. Send positive views, we don't like to insult the producers/writers/directors of these films and series. Our magazine is a great way for a writer to connect with Hollywood and the entertainment writing field. Our look is like *The Hollywood Reporter*, our content is like *Starlog* magazine." Worldwide-distributed.

TROIKA MAGAZINE, Wit, Wisdom, and Wherewithal, (I, II), Lone Tout Publications, Inc., P.O. Box 1006, Weston CT 06883. (203)227-5377. Fax: (203)222-9332. E-mail: troikamag@aol.com. Editor: Celia Meadow. Magazine: 8⅛×10⅝; 100 pages; 45 lb. Expression paper; 100 lb. Warren cover; illustrations and photographs. "Our magazine is geared toward an audience aged 30-50 looking to balance a lifestyle of family, community and personal success." Quarterly. Estab. 1994. Circ. 100,000.

• *Troika* received a 1995 *Print Magazine* Awards for Excellence (design) and two Ozzie Silver Awards for Excellence (design).

Needs: Adventure, condensed/excerpted novel, ethnic/multicultural, experimental, feminist, gay, historical, humor/satire, lesbian, literary, mainstream/contemporary, mystery/suspense, regional, religious/inspirational. List of upcoming themes available for SASE. Receives 50 unsolicited mss/month. Accepts 2-5 mss/issue; 8-20 mss/year. Publishes ms 3-6 months after acceptance. Recently published work by Elizabeth Edelglass and Susan Kleinman. Length: 2,000-3,000 words. Also publishes literary essays and literary criticism. Sometimes critiques or comments on rejected ms.

How to Contact: Send complete ms with a cover letter giving address, phone/fax number and e-mail address. Include estimated word count, brief bio and list of publications with submission. Reports in 1 month. Send SASE for reply to query. Send a disposable copy of ms. Simultaneous and electronic submissions OK. Sample copy for $5. Guidelines for #10 SASE.

Payment/Terms: Pays $250 maximum on publication for first North American serial rights.

TURTLE MAGAZINE FOR PRESCHOOL KIDS, (II), Children's Better Health Institute, Benjamin Franklin Literary & Medical Society, Inc., Box 567, 1100 Waterway Blvd., Indianapolis IN 46206. (317)636-8881. Editor: Nancy S. Axelrad. Magazine of picture stories and articles for preschool children 2-5 years old.

Needs: Juvenile (preschool). Special emphasis on health, nutrition, exercise and safety. Also has need for "action rhymes to foster creative movement, very simple science experiments, and simple food activities." Upcoming themes: "New Year Nutrition" (January/February); "What's In, What's Out" (March); "Spring Into Action" (April/May); "Safe Play" (June); "Young Champions" (July/August). Receives approximately 100 unsolicited fiction mss/month. Published new writers within the last year. Length: 300 words for bedtime or naptime stories.

How to Contact: Send complete ms with SASE. No queries. Reports in 8-10 weeks. Send SASE for Editorial Guidelines. Sample copy for $1.25.

Payment/Terms: Pays up to 22¢/word (approximate); varies for poetry and activities; includes 10 complimentary copies of issue in which work appears. Pays on publication for all rights.

Advice: "Become familiar with recent issues of the magazine and have a thorough understanding of the preschool child. You'll find we are catering more to our youngest readers, so think simply. Also, avoid being too heavy-handed with health-related material. First and foremost, health features should be fun! Because we have developed our own turtle character ('PokeyToes'), we are not interested in fiction stories featuring other turtles."

‡ **THE DOUBLE DAGGER** before a listing indicates that the listing is new in this edition. New markets are often the most receptive to submissions by new writers.

‡**TWN, South Florida's Weekly Gay Alternative, (IV)**, The Weekly News, Inc., 901 NE 79th St., Miami FL 33138. (305)757-6333 ext. 8910. Fax: (305)756-6488. Editor: Michael Bolden. Tabloid: 52 pages; newsprint paper; color cover stock; b&w illustrations and photographs. "TWN is a gay newspaper with 92% male readership. No sex stories. We're interested in issue-oriented writing, particularly with South Florida in mind." Weekly. Estab. 1977. Circ. 34,000.
Needs: Experimental, feminist, gay, historical (general), humor/satire, lesbian, literary. Upcoming themes: "National Coming Out Day" (October), "Valentine's Day, Multiculturalism" (February). Receives 3-5 unsolicited mss/month. Accepts 1 ms/issue; 8-12 mss/year. Publishes ms 2-3 months after acceptance. Agented fiction 50%. Length: 1,200 words preferred; 1,000 words minimum; 2,000 words maximum. Publishes short shorts. Length: 400-600 words. Also publishes literary essays and literary criticisms. Always critiques or comments on rejected mss.
How to Contact: Query with clips of published work. Include estimated word count, bio (1 paragraph), Social Security number. Reports in 1 month on queries; 2 months on ms. Send SASE for reply, return of ms or send a disposable copy of ms. Simultaneous, reprint (must not have appeared in a local competitor's product), and electronic submissions are OK. Sample copy for $1.50. Reviews novels or short story collections.
Payment/Terms: Pays $17.50-150 on publication for one-time rights.
Advice: "We choose work that is timely and fits within a product that is mostly news and cultural analysis. Write tight. Word/page length not as important as conciseness, impact and timeliness."

‡**VIRTUE, The Christian Magazine for Women, (II)**, D.C. Cook Foundation, 4050 Lee Vance View, Colorado Springs CO 80918-7102. (719)531-7776. Contact: Fiction Editor. Magazine: 8⅛×10⅞; 80 pages; illustrations; photos. Christian women's magazine featuring food, fashion, family, etc.—"real women with everyday problems, etc." Published 6 times/year. Estab. 1978. Circ. 135,000.
Needs: Contemporary, humor, religious/inspirational and romance. "Must have Christian slant." Accepts 1 ms/issue; 6 mss/year (maximum). Length: 1,000 words minimum; 1,500 words maximum; 1,200 words average.
How to Contact: Send mss to Debbie Colclough, associate editor. Reports in 6-8 weeks on ms. Sample copy for 9×13 SAE and $3 postage. Writer's guidelines for SASE.
Payment/Terms: Pays 15-25¢/published word on publication for first rights or reprint rights.
Advice: "Read the magazine! Get to know our style. *Please* don't submit blindly. Send us descriptive, colorful writing with good style. *Please*—no simplistic, unrealistic pat endings or dialogue. We like the story's message to be implicit as opposed to explicit. Show us, inspire us—don't spell it out or preach it to us. No romance considered."

WITH: The Magazine for Radical Christian Youth (II, IV), Faith & Life Press, Box 347, Newton KS 67114. (316)283-5100. Editors: Corel Duerksen and Eddy Hall. Editorial Assistant: Delia Graber. Magazine: 8½×11; 32 pages; 60 lb. coated paper and cover; illustrations and photos. "Our purpose is to help teenagers understand the issues that impact them and to help them make choices that reflect Mennonite-Anabaptist understandings of living by the Spirit of Christ. We publish all types of material—fiction, nonfiction, poetry, teen personal experience, etc." Published 8 times/year. Estab. 1968. Circ. 6,100.
   ● *With* won several awards from the Associated Church Press and the Evangelical Press Association.
Needs: Contemporary, ethnic, humor/satire, mainstream, religious, young adult/teen (15-18 years). "We accept issue-oriented pieces as well as religious pieces. No religious fiction that gives 'pat' answers to serious situations." Upcoming themes: "Pain and Praise/Easter" (March); "Trust" (April/May); "Covenant/Community/Baptism" (June). Receives about 50 unsolicited mss/month. Accepts 1-2 mss/issue; 10-12 mss/year. Publishes ms up to 1 year after acceptance. Recently published work by Nancy Rue, Mary Perham and Heather Klassen. Published new writers within the last year. Length: 1,500 words preferred; 400 words minimum; 2,000 words maximum. Rarely critiques rejected mss.
How to Contact: Send complete ms with cover letter. Include short summary of author's credits and what rights they are selling. Reports in 1-2 months on mss. SASE. Simultaneous and reprint submissions OK. Sample copy for 9×12 SAE and $1.21 postage. Fiction guidelines for #10 SASE.
Payment/Terms: Pays 3¢/word for reprints; 5¢/word for simultaneous rights (one-time rights to an unpublished story); 5¢ to 7¢/word for assigned stories (first rights). Supplies contributor's copies; charge for extras.
Advice: "Except for humorous fiction (which can be just for laughs) each story should make a single point that our readers will find helpful through applying it in their own lives. Request our theme list and detailed fiction guidelines (enclose SASE). All our stories are theme-related, so writing to our themes greatly improves your odds."

WOMAN'S WORLD MAGAZINE, The Woman's Weekly, (I), 270 Sylvan Ave., Englewood Cliffs NJ 07632. E-mail: wwweekly@aol.com. Fiction Editor: Brooke Comer. Magazine; 9½×11; 54

INSIDER REPORT

Women's magazines: a golden market for skillful writers

The short stories that entertain the readers of *Woman's World* and other popular women's magazines are easy reads. Their purpose may be no more noble than to pass that interminable five minutes waiting out the spin cycle at the local laundry, or to cheer a housewife (or househusband) snatching a well-deserved break while the baby sleeps. Reading the light, enjoyable stories in *Woman's World* might be akin to eating a piece of cake, but, according to Brooke Comer, *WW* fiction editor, *writing* one is a different story. Writers who can craft them are worth every penny of the $500 to $1,000 her magazine pays for one 1,200-word mystery and one 1,800-word romance, respectively.

Brooke Comer

Even though on a typical day, 100 to 150 submissions from hopeful writers arrive on Comer's desk, the great news about this market is that Comer is eager to discover new writers, especially those who can craft a good romantic story. Though 70% of the mysteries she buys come from new writers, Comer depends on the same authors again and again to pen 80% of the romances. "*WW* romances are trickier to write," says Comer. "Fay Thompson, Carin Ford, Tima Smith, Sarah Haffey and a handful of others just make it look easy." The rest who submit are busy trying to grasp the formula.

What's so hard about concocting an 1,800-word boy-meets-girl tale with a happy ending? Just try it sometime, says Comer, who sold stories to *WW* before she was hired as fiction editor. Though these days Comer writes a more literary brand of fiction on her off hours (she's currently working on a novella), crafting *WW* stories helped her hone her skills. The limited word count makes writing for *Woman's World* a great exercise in precision, she says. "It's like performing laser surgery. You have to get in there and cut out every unneccessary word without disturbing the rest." What normally takes paragraphs, even chapters, to describe must be reduced to tiny, strategically placed kernels of information. The best writers have a knack for inserting a word or phrase that will resonate with readers and make them smile in recognition at a lovable character trait, identify with a character's frustration or feel the poignancy of an everyday moment.

"Poignancy" is a word that crops up often as Comer discusses the effect writers should strive for when writing a *WW* story. It's part of the formula, she says. And although some writers cringe at formulaic fiction, it's a fact of publishing life. Many commercial magazines have analyzed their readers through focus groups and surveys to determine just what kind of story they like best. (See

Comer's Key to a $1,000 Market on page 29.)

Read five or six issues of *Woman's World*, and you'll notice certain elements are always present in the romances and mysteries it publishes. "Romantic stories take place in the environment where our readers live," says Comer. Stories should be set in suburban and rural middle America. Whether in a midwestern beauty parlour or a New England cottage, the story must take place in a wholesome American location. The main character can be either single, divorced, married or widowed. A widowed character must have lost his or her mate at least a year before the story takes place, so the character has had time to grieve and is now ready to love again. If the character is married, there should be a crisis in the relationship. But no extra-marital affairs can even be suggested.

Every story should contain a crisis followed by insight. "There is a section in every story, a 'golden moment' where the main character has a turnaround—a little light goes off in her head and she sees something she was blinded to before," says Comer. She suddenly notices the richness and beauty in an otherwise ordinary life, or realizes the hardworking guy next door is as exciting as the handsome millionaire of her dreams. *WW* romances always end with a movement toward romance—whether through a glance, a gesture, a kiss or a smile.

WW mysteries follow another formula. The crime is solved by a likable protagonist. There is always a twist ending where the villain comes to justice through a boomerang effect, says Comer. His cunning and cruelty backfire and he brings about his downfall through his own greed or mislaid plans.

Other women's magazines offer the writer a bit more leeway, says Comer. "I recently read a wonderful story in another woman's magazine about a grandmother and grandchild. Although it was beautifully written, I wouldn't choose one like it for *WW* because it didn't follow the specific formula our romantic fiction requires." You've got to read many issues of a magazine to get a handle on just how strictly its "formula" is adhered to. Be sure to send for guidelines to get even more specifics about each magazine's preferences.

WW's guidelines give lots of do's and don'ts: "Stories must be light and upbeat. No death or disease! Our stories are set in Hometown, USA. No foreign locales or big cities. Our protagonists are not upscale country clubbers. They are housewives, PTA members, and car pool drivers." Stories are set in the present day—no New Age or historical romances, please.

When breaking into the market, you might want to steer clear of any seasonal references in your story. Including them is tricky and could spoil your chances of acceptance, says Comer. Since issues are prepared months in advance, you have to think ahead and consider how appropriate your story will be in three or four months. A story set in the fall should be submitted in April or May. Stories set in the summertime should be submitted in December or January because that's when Comer thinks ahead to her summer issues.

You'll have a better chance of acceptance if your story does not revolve around a particular holiday, says Comer. "For some reason, writers always send us Christmas stories. Just stop and think—our magazine is published weekly; it's obvious we only publish a Christmas story once a year, so writing one lowers your chances of acceptance. And besides, we always pre-assign our Christmas issue story to a writer who has written for us before."

INSIDER REPORT, *Comer*

A lot of stories get rejected because they don't include dialogue—perhaps the most crucial element in women's magazine stories. Strive to get some colorful dialogue right up front that moves your story along. "I like to compare it to filming a movie or a TV show," says Comer. "Dialogue gives you two cameras instead of one. But don't make the mistake of just adding characters so you can add dialogue. Don't bring in your character's mother unless she has a purpose within the story." You don't even need another character to add dialogue. You can create an inner dialogue, with the character talking to herself.

Children add a lot of opportunities for dialogue, says Comer. "They can lighten up a story and add poignancy at the same time." However, don't give in to the urge to sound out a child's dialogue phonetically in an attempt to recreate babytalk. According to Comer, that's just as bad as attempting to capture a Southern twang syllable by syllable. Too often writers will have a character say things like 'Ah thank ahm gwawnnna lak it hee-ah,' or some such phonetic spelling, says Comer. Better to just say the character has a Southern accent or *suggest* it here and there in your dialogue by sprinkling in a few colorful words or expressions.

There is a way people speak in real life and then there is the way people *think* they speak, says Comer. Read your dialogue out loud with a friend to make sure it rings true. Analyze the ways in which your favorite authors use dialogue to carry a story forward. Listen to your favorite TV shows. As you listen, you will develop an ear for dialogue. But don't emulate soap operas, warns Comer. Too often characters just rehash what happened on yesterday's episode!

Dialogue is an efficient way to get more across with few words. It can carry your story forward and reveal something about the character at the same time. The *way* a character speaks can enhance what she is saying. Show how your characters feel as they speak, says Comer. Do they speak softly, angrily, wearily? Simple words, like "yes" or "always," if whispered or accompanied by a soft sigh, a shy smile or a silly grin can underline a moment and convey more feeling than the fanciest speech. Those sighs and smiles can give your dialogue an extra boost, says Comer.

WW stories must come full circle in a very satisfying way. "Our hero or heroine must start out with some kind of plight that is not too devastating. The plight can be heartache or loneliness, but primarily what she needs is the love of a mate. This crisis becomes exacerbated through a subcrisis which brings the character to a golden moment when she realizes something that will change her life for the better and bring her a new understanding."

Make sure all the pieces of the *WW* formula are in your story before you send your submission, says Comer. Then keep in mind that it's common for even the best, most experienced writers to go through several rewrites before their story is ready for publication. If an editor asks you to rework part of your story, consider it a compliment. Most writers don't get that far. Comer's ideal writer is one who is willing to take criticism and work with her to make sure the story does its job—that while the laundry is spinning and the baby is napping, a hardworking homebound reader gets to indulge in a few "golden moments."

—Mary Cox

pages. "The magazine for 'Mrs. Middle America.' We publish short romances and mini-mysteries for all women, ages 18-68." Weekly. Estab. 1980. Circ. 1.5 million.

Needs: Romance (contemporary), suspense/mystery. No humor, erotica or period pieces. "Romance stories must be light and upbeat. No death or disease. Let your characters tell the story through detail and dialogue. Avoid prolonged descriptive passages in third person. The trick to selling a mystery is to weave a clever plot full of clues that don't stand out as such until the end. If we can guess what's going to happen, we probably won't buy it." Receives 2,500 unsolicited mss/month. Accepts 2 mss/issue; 104 mss/year. Publishes mss 3-6 months after acceptance. Agented fiction 2%. Published work by Carin Ford, Randa Jarrell, Delmora Schwartz and Fay Thompson. Length: romances—1,800 words; mysteries—1,200 words. Sometimes critiques rejected mss and recommends other markets.

How to Contact: *No queries.* Send complete ms, "double spaced and typed in number 12 font." Cover letter not necessary. Include name, address and phone number on first page of mss. Reports in 6-8 weeks. SASE. E-mail submissions OK. Sample copy for $1. Fiction guidelines free.

Payment/Terms: Romances—$1,000, mysteries—$500. Pays on acceptance for first North American serial rights only.

WONDER TIME, (II), WordAction Publications, 6401 The Paseo, Kansas City MO 64131. (816)333-7000. Editor: Lois Perrigo. Magazine: 8¼ × 11; 4 pages; self cover; color illustrations. Hand-out story paper published through WordAction Publications; stories follow outline of Sunday School lessons for 6-8 year-olds. Weekly. Circ. 45,000.

Needs: Religious/inspirational and juvenile. Stories must have first- to second-grade readability. No fairy tales or science fiction. Receives 50-75 unsolicited fiction mss/month. Accepts 1 ms/issue. Recently published work by Ruth Blount and Shirley Smith. Length: 200-350 words.

How to Contact: Send complete ms with SASE. Reports in 6 weeks. Sample copy and curriculum guide with SASE.

Payment/Terms: Pays $25 minimum on production (about 1 year before publication) for multi-use rights.

Advice: "We are looking for shorter stories (200-350 words) with a 1-2 grade readability. The stories need to apply to the weekly Sunday School lesson truths. Write for guidelines and theme list first."

WRITER'S WORLD, (I, II), Mar-Jon Publishing Co., 204 E. 19th St., Big Stone Gap VA 24219. (540)523-0830. Fax: (540)523-5757. Editor: Gainelle Murray. Poetry submissions: Diane L. Krueger, 17 Oswega Ave., Rockaway NJ 07866. Magazine: 8½ × 11; 32 pages; 60 lb. paper; 80 lb. glossy cover; illustrations and photos. Publishes "writing-related material: technical and personal aspect of writing well." Bimonthly. Estab. 1990. Circ. 10,000.

Needs: Adventure, children's/juvenile (10-12 years), condensed/excerpted novel, ethnic/multicultural/ historical (general), humor/satire, literary, mainstream/contemporary, mystery/suspense (romantic suspense), religious/inspirational, romance (contemporary, futuristic/time travel, historical), senior citizen/ retirement, westerns, young adult/teen (adventure, mystery, romance). "No stories dealing with drugs, sex and violence." Receives 10-15 unsolicited mss/month. Accepts 1-3 mss/issue; 12-15 mss/year. Publishes ms 6-9 months afer acceptance. Recently published work by Glenda Baker, N.E. Chapman, Jean L. Werner and Bud Bartlett. Length: 1,950 words average; 1,500 words minimum; 2,000 words maximum. Also publishes literary essays, literary criticism and poetry. Often critiques or comments on rejected ms.

How to Contact: Send complete ms with a cover letter. Include estimated word count, 1-page bio, Social Security number and list of publication; publication history on reprints. Reports in 1 month. Send SASE for reply, return of ms or send a disposable copy of ms. Simultaneous and reprint submissions OK. Sample copy for $6.50. Fiction guidelines for #10 SASE.

Payment/Terms: Pays 2 contributor's copies; additional copies for $4.25. Acquires one-time rights.

Advice: "We want stories that the entire family can enjoy, a polished manuscript that doesn't rely on profanity to get the story told." Looks for "a neat well-crafted, professional looking manuscript that has been fine tuned to the best of the writer's ability. Send for a sample copy to familiarize yourself with our publication. We would like to see more nostalgia/historical fiction. No anti-religious, pornographic, distasteful or offensive material."

‡YANKEE MAGAZINE, (II, III), Yankee, Inc., Dublin NH 03444. Editor: Judson D. Hale. Fiction Editor: Edie Clark. Magazine: 6 × 9; 176 pages; glossy paper; 4-color glossy cover stock; illustrations; color photos. "Entertaining and informative New England regional on current issues, people, history, antiques and crafts for general reading audience." Monthly. Estab. 1935. Circ. 700,000.

Needs: Literary. Fiction is to be set in New England or compatible with the area. No religious/ inspirational, formula fiction or stereotypical dialect, novels or novellas. Accepts 6 mss/year. Published work by Andre Dubus, H. L. Mountzoures and Fred Bonnie. Published new writers within the last year. Length: 2,500 words.

How to Contact: Send complete ms with SASE and previous publications. "Cover letters are important if they provide relevant information: previous publications or awards; special courses taken; special references (e.g. 'William Shakespeare suggested I send this to you . . . .')" Simultaneous submissions OK, "within reason." Reports in 6-8 weeks.

Payment/Terms: Pays $1,000 on acceptance; rights negotiable. Makes "no changes without author consent."

Advice: "Read previous ten stories in *Yankee* for style and content. Fiction must be realistic and reflect life as it is—complexities and ambiguities inherent. Our fiction adds to the 'complete menu'—the magazine includes many categories—humor, profiles, straight journalism, essays, etc. Listen to the advice of any editor who takes the time to write a personal letter. Go to workshops; get advice and other readings before sending story out cold."

International commercial periodicals

The following commercial magazines, all located outside the United States and Canada, also accept work in English from fiction writers. As with other publications, try to read sample copies. While some of these may be available at large newsstands, most can be obtained directly from the publishers. Write for guidelines as well. Whereas one editor may want fiction with some connection to his or her own country, another may seek more universal settings and themes. Watch, too, for payment policies. Many publications pay only in their own currencies.

In all correspondence, use self-addressed envelopes (SAEs) with International Reply Coupons (IRCs) for magazines outside your own country. IRCs may be purchased at the main branch of your local post office. In general, send IRCs in amounts roughly equivalent to return postage. When submitting work to these international publications, you may find it easier to include a disposable copy of your manuscript and only one IRC with a self-addressed postcard for a reply. This is preferred by many editors, and it saves you the added cost of having your work returned.

‡**BEST MAGAZINE**, Portland House, Stag Place, London SWIE 5AU England. Fiction Editor: Pat Richardson. Weekly. Circ. 570,000. Publishes 52 stories/issue; plus 15 commissioned stories in summer and autumn fiction specials. Weekly mainstream women's magazine combining features and practicals. Looks for "twist in the tale, pacy, strong fiction." Length: 900 words minimum; 1,500 words maximum. Pays £100 sterling plus contributor's copies. "Write for guidelines first. Type and double space your story, be sure your name is on it, and keep a copy. Send a SAE, but above all read a copy of *Best* first to get the feel of it."

CHAT, King's Reach Tower, Stamford St., London SE1 9LS England. Fiction Editor: Shelley Silas. Weekly. Circ. 550,000. Publishes 1 story/issue; 2/Christmas issue; 4-8/Summer special. "We look for a twist in the tale, a surprise ending, quick pace, and relationship-based pieces. Humor welcome!" Length: 700 words minimum; 1,000 words maximum. Payment "negotiated with the fiction editor and made by cheque. I accept and buy fiction from anyone, anywhere. Send material with reply coupons if you want your story returned." Call or write editor for sample copy. Writer's guidelines available for SAE and IRCs.

‡**COMMANDO, (IV)**, D. C. Thomson Co., Ltd., Albert Square, Dundee DD1 9QJ Scotland. Publishes 96 stories/year. "War stories in pictures—mostly WWII but other modern wars considered. Scripts wanted—send synopsis first." Pays for published fiction and provides contributor's copies. "Write to us for information sheet."

FORUM, Northern and Shell Tower, Box 381, City Harbour, London E14 9GL England. Fiction Editor: Elizabeth Coldwell. Circ. 30,000. Publishes 26 stories/year. "*Forum* is the international magazine of human relations, dealing with all aspects of relationships, sexuality and sexual health. We are looking for erotic stories in which the plot and characterization are as important as the erotic content." Length: 2,000-3,000 words. Pays contributor's copy. "Try not to ask for the manuscript to be returned, just a letter of acceptance/rejection as this saves on your return postage. Anything which is very 'American' in language or content might not be as interesting to readers outside America. Writers can obtain a sample copy by saying they saw our listing."

INTERZONE: Science Fiction and Fantasy, (IV), 217 Preston Drove, Brighton BN1 6FL England. Editor: David Pringle. Monthly. Circ. 10,000. Publishes 5-6 stories/issue. "We're looking for intelligent science fiction in the 2,000-7,000 word range. Send two IRCs with 'overseas' submissions and a *disposable* ms." Pays £30 per 1,000 words on publication and 2 contributor's copies. "Please *read the magazine*—available through specialist science-fiction dealers or direct by subscription." Sample copies to USA: $5. Write for guidelines.

NOVA SF, (IV), Perseo Libri srl, Box 1240, I-40100 Bologna Italy. Fiction Editor: Ugo Malaguti. Bimonthly. Circ. 5,000. "Science fiction and fantasy short stories and short novels." Pays $100-600, depending on length, and 2 contributor's copies on publication. "No formalities required, we read all submissions and give an answer in about 20 weeks. Buys first Italian serial rights on stories."

PEOPLE'S FRIEND, 80 Kingsway East, Dundee DD4 8SL Scotland. Fiction Editor: W. Balnave. Weekly. Circ. 470,000. Publishes 5 stories/issue. Length: 1,000-3,000 words. Pays $75-85 and contributor's copies. "British backgrounds preferred (but not essential) by our readership." Sample copy and guidelines available on application.

WOMAN'S DAY, G.P.O. Box 5245, Sydney NSW 2001 Australia. *"Woman's Day* looks for two types of short stories: first for Five Minute Fiction page at the back of the magazine, around 1,000 words long; longer short stories, between 1,500 and 4,000 words in length, are used less frequently. Manuscripts should be typed with double spacing and sufficient margins on either side of the text for notes and editing. They should be sent to the Fiction Editor with SAE and IRC." Payment is usually about $250 (Australian) for the Five Minute Fiction, from $350 for longer stories. *Woman's Day* purchases the first Australian and New Zealand rights. After publication, these revert to the author. "We accept unsolicited manuscripts, but must point out that we receive around 100 of these in the fiction department each week, and obviously, are limited in the number we can accept."

WOMAN'S WEEKLY, IPC Magazines, King's Reach, Stamford St., London SE1 9LS England. Fiction Editor: Gaynor Davies. Circ. 800,000. Publishes 1 serial and at least 2 short stories/week. "Short stories can be on any theme, but must have love as the central core of the plot, whether in a specific romantic context, within the family or mankind in general. Serials need not be written in installments. They are submitted as complete manuscripts and we split them up. Send first installment of serial (7,000 words) and synopsis of the rest." Length: 1,000-3,500 words for short stories; 14,000-42,000 words for serials. Short story payment starts at £230 and rises as writer becomes a more regular contributor. Serial payments start at around £500/installment. Writers also receive contributor's copies. "Read the magazine concerned and try to understand who the publication is aimed at." Writers' guidelines available. Write to "Fiction Department."

THE WORLD OF ENGLISH, P.O. Box 1504, Beijing China. Chief Editor: Chen Yu-lun. Monthly. Circ. 300,000. "We welcome contributions of short and pithy articles that would cater to the interest of our reading public, new and knowledgeable writings on technological finds, especially interesting stories and novels, etc. As our currency is regrettably inconvertible, we send copies of our magazines as the compensation for contributions. Aside from literary works, we put our emphasis on the provision of articles that cover various fields in order to help readers expand their vocabulary rapidly and enhance their reading level effectively, and concurrently to raise their level in writing. Another motive is to render assistance to those who, while learning English, are able also to enrich their knowledge and enlarge their field of vision."

SENDING TO A COUNTRY other than your own? Be sure to send International Reply Coupons instead of stamps for replies or return of your manuscript.

Small Press

In this section we use the term "small press" in the broadest sense. Under this heading are more than 200 presses including one- and two-person operations, small or mid-size independent presses, university presses and other nonprofit publishers. Although most publish only a handful of books each year, a few publish 25 or more titles annually.

Introducing new writers to the reading public has become the most important role played by the small press today. Increasingly, too, small press publishers have devoted themselves to keeping accessible the work of talented fiction writers who are not currently in the limelight or whose work has had limited exposure. Many of the more successful small presses listed in this section, including Coffee House, Four Walls Eight Windows and Zoland Books, have built their reputations and their businesses in this way and have become known for publishing prize-winning literary fiction.

Today, small press publishers have better technology, distribution, marketing and business savvy than ever before. Despite their size, they've become big competition for their larger counterparts. More and more readers looking for good literary or experimental fiction and new, talented writers are turning to the small press to find them.

THE BENEFITS OF WORKING WITH THE SMALL PRESS

Despite the growth and success of several small presses, even the most successful are unable to afford the six-figure advances, lavish promotional budgets and huge press runs possible in the large, commercial houses. Yet, there are some very tangible benefits to working with the small press.

For one thing, small presses tend to keep books in print a lot longer than larger houses. And, since small presses publish a small number of books, each one is equally important to the publisher and each one is promoted in much the same way and with the same commitment.

Small presses also offer a much closer and more personal relationship between author and editor. In the Insider Report with Daniel Simon on page 434, Simon identifies the most important function of the independent press as that of finding new voices: "The more the big publishers shy away from developing writers, the more room there is for independent publishers to find those voices." Emilie Buchwald, publisher/editor and CEO of Milkweed Editions, says in the Insider Report featured on page 419 that the goal of her press is to publish books which "make a humane impact on society." And Simon and Buchwald both value the close relationship between authors and editors that small presses provide.

Another advantage of small presses is that many are owned by one or just a few people. Editors stay longer because they have more of a stake in the business—often they own the business. Many small press publishers are writers themselves and know first-hand the importance of this type of editor-author or publisher-author relationship.

TYPES OF SMALL PRESSES

The very small presses are sometimes called micropresses and are owned or operated by one to three people, usually friends or family members. Some are cooperatives of writers and most of these presses started out publishing their staff members' books or books by their friends. These presses can easily be swamped with submissions, but writers published by them are usually treated as "one of the family."

Nonprofit presses depend on grants and donations to help meet operating costs. Keep in mind, too, some of these presses are funded by private organizations such as churches or clubs, and books that reflect the backer's views or beliefs are most likely to be considered for publication.

Funding for university presses is often tied to government or private grants as well. Traditionally, universities tend to publish writers who are either affiliated with the university or whose work is representative of the region in which the school is located. Recently, however, university presses are trying their hand at publishing books without university connections aimed at the same readership as other publishers. This is mostly happening in nonfiction, but chances are university presses may start to publish more general fiction as well.

Many publishers in this section are independent literary and regional presses. Several have become highly sophisticated about competing in the marketplace and in carving out their own niche.

SELECTING A SMALL PRESS

As with magazines, reading the listing should be just your first step in finding markets that interest you. It's best to familiarize yourself with a press' focus and line. Most produce catalogs or at least fliers advertising their books. Whenever possible, obtain these and writers' guidelines.

If possible, read some of the books published by a press that interests you. It is sometimes difficult to locate books published by a small press (especially by micropress publishers). Some very small presses sell only through the mail. Literary and larger independent press books can be found at most independent bookstores, and the number of books from these presses that make it into the large chain super stores is growing. Also try university bookstores and libraries.

In How to Use This Book to Publish Your Fiction we discuss how to use the Category Index located near the end of this book. If you've written a particular type of novel, look in the Small Press section of the Category Index under the appropriate heading to find presses interested in your specific subject.

We've also included Roman numeral ranking codes placed at the start of each listing to help you determine how open the press is to new writers. The explanations of these codes appear at the end of this introduction.

In addition to the double dagger (‡) indicating new listings, we include other symbols to help you in narrowing your search. The maple leaf symbol (❦) identifies Canadian presses. If you are not a Canadian writer, but are interested in a Canadian press, check the listing carefully. Many small presses in Canada receive grants and other funds from their provincial or national government and are, therefore, restricted to publishing Canadian authors.

This year, there are no subsidy book publishers listed in *Novel & Short Story Writer's Market*. By subsidy, we mean any arrangement in which the writer is expected to pay all or part of the cost of producing, distributing and marketing his book. We feel a writer should not be asked to share in any cost of turning his manuscript into a book. All the book publishers listed here told us that they *do not charge writers* for publishing their work. If any of the publishers listed here ask you to pay any part of publishing or marketing your manuscript, please let us know.

IN THE LISTINGS

Again, How to Use This Book to Publish Your Fiction outlines the material common to all listings and how it will help you determine the right market for your work. Keep in mind many small presses do fewer than ten books a year and have very small staffs. We asked them to give themselves a generous amount of response time in their listing, but note it is not unusual for a small press to get behind. Add three or four weeks to the reporting time listed before checking on the status of your submission.

As with commercial book publishers, we ask small presses to give us a list of recent titles each year. If they did not change their title list from last year, it may be that, because they do so few fiction titles, they have not published any or they may be particularly proud of certain titles published earlier. If the recent titles are unchanged, we've altered the sentence to read "Published" rather than "Recently published."

The Business of Fiction Writing gives the fundamentals of approaching book publishers. The listings include information on what the publisher wishes to see in a submission package: sample chapters, an entire manuscript or other material.

Our editorial comments are set off by a bullet (●) within the listing. We use this feature to include additional information on the type of work published by the press, the awards and honors received by presses and other information we feel will help you make an informed marketing decision.

There are a number of publishing awards open to small presses or to their books. Many books published by the small press have received the Abby, a special award given by the American Booksellers Association to books they most enjoyed selling over the last year and the Pen/Faulkner Award given "to award the most distinguished book-length work of fiction published by an American writer." (An interview with David Guterson, winner of both the Pen/Faulkner and the 1996 Abby for *Snow Falling on Cedars* begins on page 60 of this book.) The Lambda Literary Awards, given to books published by gay and lesbian presses, is another award often given to small press books. The Beyond Columbus Foundation awards the American Book Awards, given to books by American authors that reflect cultural diversity in American Writing, and the National Book Foundation honors one fiction book by an American author each year. Although most of these awards are open to all book publishers, books published by the small press have received several.

In addition to grants by states and national agencies, a few private and nonprofit organizations have stepped in to help fledgling small presses by providing funding and even guidance with the business side of their operations. We asked presses to give us this information and it sometimes appears in the editorial comments. One organization frequently mentioned was the Council of Literary Magazines and Presses (CLMP) with its Lila Wallace-Readers Digest Literary Publishers Marketing Development Program. Also mentioned is COSMEP, the International Association of Independent Publishers, one of the oldest organizations devoted to supporting the small press.

FOR MORE INFORMATION

For more small presses see the *International Directory of Little Magazines and Small Presses* published by Dustbooks (P.O. Box 100, Paradise CA 95967). To keep up with changes in the industry throughout the year, check issues of two small press trade publications: *Small Press Review* (also published by Dustbooks) and *Small Press* (Jenkins Group, Inc., 121 E. Front St., 4th Floor, Traverse City MI 49684).

The ranking codes used in this section are as follows:

   I Publisher encourages beginning or unpublished writers to submit work for consideration and publishes new writers frequently.

   II Publisher accepts outstanding work by beginning and established writers.

   III Hard to break into; publishes mostly writers with extensive previous

publication credits or agented writers.

IV **Special-interest or regional publisher, open only to writers in certain genres or on certain subjects or from certain geographic areas.**

V   **Closed to unsolicited submissions.**

ACADIA PRESS, (IV), Acadia Publishing Co., P.O. Box 170, Bar Harbor ME 04609. (207)288-9025. Assistant to the President: Julie Savage. Estab. 1982. Small regional publisher. Publishes hardcover and paperback originals. Average print order: 3,000. Published new writers within the last year. Plans 1 first novel this year. Averages 2-3 total titles each year. Sometimes comments on rejected mss.
Needs: "We only publish books dealing directly with Acadia National Park and Mt. Desert Island (Maine)." Published *Parasols of Fern*, by Jack Perkins.
How to Contact: Does not accept unsolicited mss. Query first. Include bio and list of publishing credits. SASE for reply or send disposable copy of ms. Reports in 2 weeks on queries; 3 months on mss. Simultaneous submissions OK.
Terms: Pays royalties of 8% minimum; 15% maximum. Sends galleys to author. Publishes ms 18 months after acceptance. Writer's guidelines for #10 SASE. Book catalog for #10 SASE.

ACME PRESS, (I, II), P.O. Box 1702, Westminster MD 21158. (410)848-7577. Managing Editor: Ms. E.G. Johnston. Estab. 1991. "We operate on a part-time basis and publish 1-2 novels/year." Publishes hardcover and paperback originals. Published new writers within the last year. Averages 1-2 novels/year. Always comments on rejected mss.
Needs: Humor/satire. "We publish only humor novels, so we don't want to see anything that's not funny." Recently published *She-Crab Soup*, by Dawn Langley Simmons (fictional memoir/humor); *Biting the Wall*, by J. M. Johnston (humor/mystery); and *Hearts of Gold*, by James Magorian (humor/mystery).
How to Contact: Accepts unsolicited mss. Query first, submit outline/synopsis and first 50 pages or submit complete ms with cover letter. Include estimated word count with submission. SASE for reply, return of ms or send a disposable copy of ms. Agented fiction 25%. Reports in 1-2 weeks on queries; 4-6 weeks on mss. Simultaneous submissions OK.
Terms: Provides 25 author's copies; pays 50% of profits. Sends galleys to author. Publishes ms 1 year after acceptance. Writer's guidelines and book catalog for #10 SASE.

ADVOCACY PRESS, (IV), Box 236, Santa Barbara CA 93102. Executive Director: Barbara Fierro Lang. Estab. 1983. Small publisher with 3-5 titles/year. Hardcover and paperback originals. Books: perfect or Smyth-sewn binding; illustrations; average print order: 5,000-10,000 copies; first novel print order: 5,000-10,000. Averages 2 children's fiction (32-48 pg.) titles per year.
   ● Advocacy Press books have won the Ben Franklin Award and the Friends of American Writers Award. The press also received the Eleanor Roosevelt Research and Development Award from the American Association of University Women for its significant contribution to equitable education.
Needs: Juvenile. Wants only feminist/nontraditional messages to boys or girls—picture books; self-esteem issues. Published *Minou*, by Mindy Bingham (picture book); *Kylie's Song*, by Patty Sheehan (picture book); *Nature's Wonderful World in Rhyme*, by William Sheehan. Publishes the World of Work Series (real life stories about work).
How to Contact: Submit complete manuscript with SASE for return. Reports in 10 weeks on queries. Simultaneous submissions OK.
Terms: Pays in royalties of 5-10%. Book catalog for SASE.
Advice: Wants "only fictional stories for children 4-12-years-old that give messages of self-sufficiency for little girls; little boys can nurture and little girls can be anything they want to be, etc. Please review some of our publications *before* you submit to us. *Because of our limited focus, most of our titles have been written inhouse*."

AGELESS PRESS, (II, IV), P.O. Box 5915, Sarasota FL 34277-5915. Phone/fax: (941)952-0576. E-mail: irishope@juno.com. Editor: Iris Forrest. Estab. 1992. Independent publisher. Publishes paperback originals. Books: acid-free paper; notched perfect binding; no illustrations; average print order: 5,000;

● **A BULLET INTRODUCES COMMENTS** by the editor of *Novel & Short Story Writer's Market* indicating special information about the listing.

first novel print order: 5,000. Published new writers within the last year. Averages 1 title each year. Sometimes comments on rejected mss.

Needs: Experimental, fantasy, humor/satire, literary, mainstream/contemporary, mystery/suspense, New Age/mystic/spiritual, science fiction, short story collections and thriller/espionage. Looking for material "based on personal computer experiences." Stories selected by editor. Published *Computer Legends, Lies & Lore*, by various (anthology); and *Computer Tales of Fact & Fantasy*, by various (anthology).

How to Contact: Does not accept unsolicited mss. Query first. Send SASE for reply, return of ms or send a disposable copy of ms. Reports in 1 week. Simultaneous and electronic (disk, 5¼ or 3.5 IBM) submissions OK.

Terms: Offers negotiable advance. Publishes ms 6-12 months after acceptance.

ALASKA NATIVE LANGUAGE CENTER, (IV), University of Alaska, P.O. Box 757680, Fairbanks AK 99775-7680. (907)474-7874. Editor: Tom Alton. Estab. 1972. Small education publisher limited to books in and about Alaska native languages. Generally nonfiction. Publishes hardcover and paperback originals. Books: 60 lb. book paper; offset printing; perfect binding; photos, line art illustrations; average print order: 500-1,000 copies. Averages 6-8 total titles each year.

Needs: Ethnic. Publishes original fiction only in native language and English by Alaska native writers. Published *A Practical Grammar of the Central Alaskan Yup'ik Eskimo Language*, by Steven A. Jacobson; *One Must Arrive With a Story to Tell*, by the Elders of Tununak, Alaska.

How to Contact: Does not accept unsolicited mss. Electronic submissions via ASCII for modem transmissions or Macintosh compatible files on 3.5 disk.

Terms: Does not pay. Sends galleys to author.

ALYSON PUBLICATIONS, INC., (II), 6922 Hollywood Blvd., Suite 1000, Los Angeles CA 90028. (213)871-1788. Fax: (213)467-6805. Fiction Editor: Julie K. Trevelyan. Estab. 1977. Medium-sized publisher specializing in lesbian- and gay-related material. Publishes paperback originals and reprints. Books: paper and printing varies; trade paper, perfect-bound; average print order: 8,000; first novel print order: 6,000. Published new writers within the last year. Plans 4 first novels this year. Plans 40 total titles, 10 fiction titles each year.

● In addition to adult titles, Alyson Publications has been known for its line of young adult and children's books.

Needs: "We are interested in all categories; *all* materials must be geared toward lesbian and/or gay readers. No poetry." Recently published *3 Plays by Mart Crowley*; *Swords of the Rainbow*, edited by Eric Garber and Jewelle Gomez; and *Daddy's Wedding*, by Michael Willhoite. Publishes anthologies. Authors may submit to them directly.

How to Contact: Query first with SASE. Reports in 3-12 weeks.

Terms: "We prefer to discuss terms with the author. Gay and/or lesbian nonfiction and excellent fiction are our focal points." Sends galleys to author. Book catalog for SAE and 3 first-class stamps.

‡AMHERST PRESS, (I, II), 3380 Sheridan Dr., Suite 365, Amherst NY 14226. (716)633-5434. E-mail: am12press@aol.com. Contact: Dan McQueen. Estab. 1995. Small, independent publisher. Publishes 3 mss/year. Publishes hardcover and paperback originals. Books: 50-60 lb. paper; soft binding; line screen illustrations. Average print order: 5,000. First novel print order: 5,000. Plans 1 first novel this year. Averages 3 total titles maximum, 2 fiction titles maximum each year.

Needs: Adventure, family saga, fantasy (space, sword and sorcery), feminist, gay, historical, horror (psychological, supernatural), lesbian, literary, mainstream/contemporary, military/war, mystery/suspense (amateur sleuth, cozy, private eye/hardboiled), romance (contemporary, futuristic/time travel, gothic, historical, romantic suspense), science fiction (hard science/technological, soft/sociological), short story collections, thriller/espionage, western, young adult/teen (adventure, easy-to-read, fantasy/science fiction, historical, horror, mystery/suspense, problem novels, romance, series, sports, western). Especially looking for "horror, mystery and romance." Recently published *The Patron Saints of North Beach*, by Linda S. Malm (horror); and *Wizards and Witches*, by Tyrone W. Anderson (fantasy).

How to Contact: Accepts unsolicited mss. Submit complete ms with cover letter. Accepts electronically transmitted queries by e-mail. Include estimated word count, Social Security number, list of publishing credits and synopsis. Send SASE for reply, return of ms or send disposable copy of ms. Agented fiction 30%. Reports in 3 weeks on queries; 1-2 months on mss. Simultaneous submissions OK.

Terms: Pays royalties of 10% minimum; 12½% maximum. Advance negotiable. Sends galleys to author. Publishes ms 15 months after acceptance. Writer's guidelines for #10 SASE.

Advice: "We prefer professionally edited mss ready to go to galleys. Send your best; proofread; have it professionally edited (if not, it isn't crucial), and be sure it's in standard form."

✲ANNICK PRESS LTD., (IV), 15 Patricia Ave., Willowdale, Ontario M2M 1H9 Canada. (416)221-4802. Publisher of children's books. Publishes hardcover and paperback originals. Books: offset paper;

full-color offset printing; perfect and library bound; full-color illustrations. Average print order: 9,000. First novel print order: 7,000. Plans 18 first picture books this year. Averages approximately 20 titles each year, all fiction. Average first picture book print order 2,000 cloth, 12,000 paper copies. Occasionally critiques rejected mss.

Needs: Children's books only.

How to Contact: "Annick Press publishes only work by Canadian citizens or residents." Does not accept unsolicited mss. Query with SASE. Free book catalog.

Terms: No terms disclosed.

✦ANVIL PRESS, (I, II), Bentall Centre, P.O. Box 1575, Vancouver, British Columbia V6C 2P7 Canada; or Lee Building, #204-A, 175 E. Broadway, Vancouver, British Columbia V5T 1W2 Canada. (604)876-8710. Managing Editor: Brian Kaufman. Fiction Editors: Brian Kaufman and Dennis E. Bolen. Estab. 1988. "1½ person operation with volunteer editorial board." Publishes paperback originals. Books: offset or web printing; perfect-bound. Average print order: 1,000-1,500. First novel print order: 1,000. Plans 2 first novels this year. Averages 2-3 fiction titles each year. Often comments on rejected mss. Also offers a critique service for a fee.

Needs: Experimental, contemporary/modern, literary, short story collections. Published *Stupid Crimes*, by Dennis E. Bolen (literary novel); *A Circle of Birds*, by Hayden Trenholm (literary novella); and *Stolen Voices/Vacant Rooms*, by Steve Lundin and Mitch Parry (2 novellas in one volume). Published new wrtiers within the last year. Publishes the Anvil Pamphlet series: shorter works (essays, political tracts, polemics, treatises and works of fiction that are shorter than novel or novella form).

How to Contact: Canadian writers only. Accepts unsolicited mss. Query first or submit outline/synopsis and 1-2 sample chapters. Include estimated word count and bio with submission. Send SASE for reply, return of ms or a disposable copy of ms. Reports in 1 month on queries; 2-4 months on mss. Simultaneous submissions OK (please note in query letter that manuscript is a simultaneous submission).

Terms: Pays royalties of 15% (of final sales). Average advance: $200-400. Sends galleys to author. Publishes ms within contract year. Book catalog for 9 × 12 SASE and 2 first-class stamps.

Advice: "We are only interested in writing that is progressive in some way—form, content. We want contemporary fiction from serious writers who intend to be around for awhile and be a name people will know in years to come."

ARIADNE PRESS, (I), 4817 Tallahassee Ave., Rockville MD 20853. (301)949-2514. President: Carol Hoover. Estab. 1976. Shoestring operation—corporation with 4 directors who also act as editors. Publishes hardcover and paperback originals. Books: 50 lb. alkaline paper; offset printing; Smyth-sewn binding. Average print order 1,000. First novel print order 1,000. Plans 1 first novel this year. Averages 1 total title each year; only fiction. Sometimes critiques rejected mss. "We comment on selected mss of superior writing quality, even when rejected."

Needs: Adventure, contemporary, feminist, historical, humor/satire, literary, mainstream, psychological, family relations and marital, war. Looking for "literary-mainstream" fiction. No short stories or fictionalized biographies; no science fiction, horror or mystery. Published *The Greener Grass*, by Paul Bourguignon; *A Rumor of Distant Tribes*, by Eugene Jeffers; and *Cross a Dark Bridge*, by Deborah Churchman (psychological suspense).

How to Contact: *Query first.* SASE. Agented fiction 5%. Reports in 1 month on queries; 2 months on mss. Simultaneous submissions OK.

Terms: Pays royalties of 10%. No advance. Sends galleys to author. Writer's guidelines and list of books in stock for #10 SASE.

Advice: "We exist primarily for nonestablished writers. Try large, commercial presses first. Characters and story must fit together so well that it is hard to tell which grew out of the other. Send query letter with SASE in advance! Never send an unsolicited manuscript without advance clearance."

ARJUNA LIBRARY PRESS, (II), Subsidiaries include: The Journal of Regional Criticism, 1025 Garner St., D, Space 18, Colorado Springs CO 80905-1774. Director: Count Prof. Joseph A. Uphoff, Jr.. Estab. 1979. "The Arjuna Library is an artist's prototype press." Publishes paperback originals. Books: 20 lb. paper; photocopied printing; perfect-bound; b&w illustrations. Average print order: 20. Averages 6 total titles, 3 fiction titles each year. Sometimes comments on rejected mss.

● Arjuna Press has had exhibits at the Colorado Springs Fine Arts Center, KTSC Public Television (academic), University of Southern Colorado and The Poets House, New York. The press is known for its surrealist and science fiction titles.

Needs: Adventure, childrens/juvenile (fantasy), erotica, experimental, fantasy (surrealist), horror (supernatural), lesbian, romance (futuristic/time travel), science fiction (hard science/technological, soft/sociological poetry), young adult/teen (fantasy/science fiction). Nothing obscene or profane. Recently published *This Sort of Scribble*, by Gregory Moore (short story); *High*, by Michael K. White; and *The March Hare*, by Marosa Di Giorgio, translated by Kathryn A. Kopple.

How to Contact: Accepts unsolicited mss. Submit complete ms with cover letter, resume. Include list of publishing credits, a disposable copy of the ms to be filed; will return samples in envelopes. Simultaneous and electronic submissions OK.

Terms: Pays 1 author's copy, plus potential for royalties. Writer's guidelines for SASE.

Advice: "Many new writers are impatient to gain acceptance and an income. These people often send letters that are rude or even threatening. It is important to realize that in our civilization everybody has been taught to read and write. Many people think it is an occupation of last resort when a job cannot be obtained elsewhere! It has never been easy to make a living as a writer. All of us should remember that civility is a key to success where hostility obliges the recipient to redress. We should all be patient in each new encounter, but the initiative to decency arises from the pretext of the correspondence."

✤**ARSENAL PULP PRESS, (II)**, 103-1014 Homer St., Vancouver, British Columbia V6B 2W9 Canada. (604)687-4233. Fax: (604)669-8250. E-mail: arsenal@pinc.com. Editor: Linda Field. Literary press. Publishes paperback originals. Average print order: 1,500-3,000. First novel print order: 1,500. Published new writers within the last year. Plans 1 first novel this year. Averages 12-15 total titles, 2 fiction titles each year. Sometimes comments on rejected mss.

Needs: Ethnic/multicultural (general), feminist, gay, lesbian, literary and short story collections. No genre fiction, i.e. westerns, romance, horror, mystery, etc. Recently published *Hard Core Logo*, by Michael Turner (novel); *Everything but the Truth*, by Christopher McPherson (short fiction); and *Hunting with Diana*, by David Watmough (short fiction).

How to Contact: Accepts unsolicited mss. Query with outline/synopsis and 2 sample chapters. Include list of publishing credits. Send SASE for reply, return of ms or send a disposable copy of ms. Agented fiction 10%. Reports in 1 month on queries; 3-4 months on mss. Simultaneous submissions OK.

Terms: Pays royalties of 10% minimum; 10% maximum. Negotiable advance. Sends galleys to author. Publishes ms 1 year after acceptance. Writer's guidelines and book catalog free.

Advice: "We very rarely publish American writers."

ARTE PUBLICO PRESS, (II, IV), University of Houston, Houston TX 77204-2090. (713)743-2841. Imprint: Piñata Books featuring children's and young adult literature by U.S.-Hispanic authors. Publisher: Dr. Nicolas Kanellos. Estab. 1979. "Small press devoted to the publication of contemporary U.S.-Hispanic literature. Mostly trade paper; publishes 4-6 clothbound books/year. Publishes fiction and belles lettres." Publishes paperback originals and occasionally reprints. Average print order 2,000-5,000. First novel print order 2,500-5,000. Sometimes critiques rejected mss.

● Arte Publico Press received the 1994 American Book Award for *In Search of Bernabé*, by Graciela Limón; the Thorpe Menn Award for Literary Achievement; the Southwest Book Award and others.

Needs: Contemporary, ethnic, feminist, literary, short story collections written by US-Hispanic authors. Published *Rain of Gold*, by Victor Villaseñor (autobiography); *Happy Birthday Jesús*, by Ronald Ruiz; *To a Widow with Children*, by Lionel Garcia; and *The Candy Vendor's Boy and Other Stories*, by Beatriz de la Garza.

How to Contact: Accepts unsolicited mss. Submit outline/synopsis and sample chapters or complete ms with cover letter and SASE. Agented fiction 1%.

Terms: Average advance: $1,000. Provides 20 author's copies; 40% discount on subsequent copies. Sends galleys to author. Book catalog free on request.

Advice: "Include cover letter in which you 'sell' your book—why should we publish the book, who will want to read it, why does it matter, etc."

‡**ATOMIC WESTERNS, (II)**, Atomic Publishing, 111 E. Drake Rd., Suite 7106, Ft. Collins CO 80525. E-mail: edwood@fortnet.org. Fiction Editor: Kirk Whitham. Chapbooks: 5½×3¾; 24-32 pages; copier stock paper; astroparch cover stock. "We publish chapbooks of weird westerns, stories with themes not generally found in traditional westerns— ghosts, vampires, UFOs, werewolves, etc. Our audience is anyone interested in the strange Old West." Estab. 1996. First print order: 1,000 copies. Plans 6-8 chapbooks this year. Sometimes critiques or comments on rejected mss.

Needs: Adventure, horror, humor/satire, psychic/supernatural/occult, science fiction, serialized novel, westerns. Receives 50 mss/month. Accepts 6-8 mss/year. Publishes ms 2-6 months after acceptance. Agented fiction 20%. Recently published work by Jeffrey W. Roberts, Louise Marley and Russ Carpenter. Length: 5,500 words average; 4,000 words minimum; 6,000 words maximum.

How to Contact: Send complete ms with a cover letter. Include estimated word count, 100-word bio and list of publications. Reports in 1 month on queries; 2 months on mss. Send SASE for reply, return of ms or send a disposable copy of ms. Reprints and electronic (e-mail) submissions OK.

Terms: Pays $100-250 and 5 contributor's copies; additional copies $2.99. Acquires all rights. Writer's guidelines for #10 SASE.

Advice: "We look for a real grabber opening. Since our stories are so short you have to hook the reader right off the bat. A well-written story is also a plus. Try to be original. Don't telegraph your ending. We see many stories that give themselves away by the third page."

BAMBOO RIDGE PRESS, (IV), P.O. Box 61781, Honolulu HI 96839-1781. (808)599-4823. Editors: Darrell Lum and Eric Chock. Estab. 1978. "Bamboo Ridge Press publishes *Bamboo Ridge: The Hawaii Writers' Journal*, a journal of fiction and poetry with special issues devoted to the work of one writer—fiction or poetry." Publishes paperback originals and reprints. Books: 60 lb. natural; perfect-bound; illustrations. Average print order: 2,000. Published new writers within the last year. Averages 2 total titles.

• Bamboo Ridge Press received an Excellence in Literature award from the Hawaii Book Publishers Association for its anthology, *The Best of Bamboo Ridge* and Book of the Year from the National Asian American Studies Association for a book of poetry.

Needs: Ethnic, literary and short story collections. "Interested in writing that reflects Hawaii's multi-cultural ethnic mix. No psuedo-Hawaiiana myths or Hawaii-Five-O type of mentality—stereotypical portrayals of Hawaii and its people." Published *The Watcher of Waipuna*, by Gary Pak.

How to Contact: Accepts unsolicited mss. Query first. SASE. Reports in 4-6 weeks on queries; 3-6 months on mss. Simultaneous submissions OK.

Terms: Payment depends on grant/award money. Sends galleys to author. Publishes ms 6 months-1 year after acceptance. Book catalog for #10 SAE and 52¢ postage.

Advice: Ask yourself these questions before submitting: "Does the writing have a unique perspective? What does it contribute to the developing tradition of literature by and about Hawaii's people?"

BASKERVILLE PUBLISHERS, INC., (III), 7616 LBJ Freeway, Suite 510, Dallas TX 75251. (214)934-3451. Fax: (214)239-4023. Imprint: Basset Books. Acquisitions Editor: Sam Chase. Publishes hardcover and paperback originals. Books: offset printing. Average print order: 3,000-10,000. First novel print order: 3,000. Published new writers within the last year. Plans 3 first novels this year. Averages 14 titles (fiction and biography of opera singers). Sometimes comments on rejected ms.

Needs: Literary, humor/satire. Published *Fata Morgana*, by Lynn Stegner; *Playing The Game*, by Alan Lelchuk; and *The Stolen Child*, by Paul Cody.

How to Contact: Query with outline/synopsis and 2 sample chapters. Include estimated word count, bio and list of publishing credits. SASE. Agented fiction 50%. Simultaneous submissions OK.

Terms: Pays royalties of 10% minimum; 15% maximum. Average advance: $3,000. Sends galleys to author. Publishes ms 6-12 months after acceptance. Writer's guidelines for SASE. Book catalog for 6×9 SASE and 80¢ postage.

‡BEGGAR'S PRESS, (II), 8110 N. 38th St., Omaha NE 68112-2018. (402)455-2615. Imprints are Lamplight, Raskolnikov's Cellar, Beggar's Review. Publisher: Richard R. Carey. Estab. 1952. Small independent publisher. "We are noted for publishing books and periodicals in the styles of the great masters of the past. We publish three periodicals (literary), novels, poetry chapbooks and collections of short stories." Publishes paperback originals. Books: 20 lb. paper; offset; perfect binding; some illustrations. Average print order: 500-700. First novel print order: 500. Published new writers within the last year. Plans 2 first novels this year. Averages 3-5 total titles, 4 fiction titles/year. *Charges "reasonable rate" for complete ms critique.* Member of International Association of Independent Publishers and Federation of Literary Publishers.

Needs: Adventure, historical (general, 1800's), horror (psychological), humor/satire, literary, mystery/suspense, romance (gothic, historical), short story collection. Recently published *An Evening Studying the Anatomy of Jena Kruger*, by Richard Carey; *My Doorknob Is Female*, by Diane Jensen; and *Seduction of an Olive*, by Debra Knight. Plans series.

How to Contact: Accepts unsolicited mss. Query with outline/synopsis and 1 sample chapter. Include estimated word count, short bio; cover letter a must. Send SASE for reply, return of ms or send a disposable copy of ms. Agented fiction 2%. Reports in 1 month on queries; 10 weeks on mss. Simultaneous submissions OK.

Terms: Pays royalties of 10% minimum; 15% maximum; provides 2 author's copies

FREDERIC C. BEIL, PUBLISHER, INC., (II), 609 Whitaker St., Savannah GA 31401. E-mail: beilbook@beil.com. Website: http://www.beil.com. Imprints include The Sandstone Press. President: Frederic C. Beil III. Estab. 1983. General trade publisher. Publishes hardcover originals and reprints. Books: acid-free paper; letterpress and offset printing; Smyth-sewn; hardcover binding; illustrations. Average print order: 3,000. First novel print order: 3,000. Plans 2 first novels this year. Averages 14 total titles, 4 fiction titles each year.

Needs: Historical, literary, regional, short story collections, translations. Published *A Woman of Means*, by Peter Taylor; *An Exile*, by Madison Jones; and *A Master of the Century Past*, by Robert Metzger.

How to Contact: Does not accept unsolicited mss. Query first. Reports in 1 week on queries.

Terms: Payment "all negotiable." Sends galleys to author. Book catalog free on request.

BETHEL PUBLISHING, (IV), 1819 S. Main, Elkhart IN 46516.(219)293-8585. Contact: Senior Editor. Estab. 1903. Mid-size Christian book publisher. Publishes paperback originals and reprints. Averages 3-5 total titles per year. Occasionally critiques or comments on rejected mss.
Needs: Religious/inspirational, young adult/teen. No "workbooks, cookbooks, coloring books, theological studies, pre-school or elementary-age stories."
How to Contact: Accepts unsolicited complete mss. 30,000-50,000 words maximum. Query first. Enclose 8½×11 SAE and 3 first-class stamps. Reports in 2 weeks on queries; 3 months on mss. Accepts simultaneous submissions. Publishes mss 8-16 months after acceptance.
Terms: Pays royalties of 5-10% and 12 author's copies. Writer's guidelines and book catalog on request.

BILINGUAL PRESS/EDITORIAL BILINGÜE, (II, IV), Hispanic Research Center, Arizona State University, Tempe AZ 85287-2702. (602)965-3867. Editor: Gary Keller. Estab. 1973. "University affiliated." Publishes hardcover and paperback originals, and reprints. Books: 60 lb. acid-free paper; single sheet or web press printing; case-bound and perfect-bound; illustrations sometimes; average print order: 4,000 copies (1,000 case-bound, 3,000 soft cover). Published new writers within the last year. Plans 2 first novels this year. Averages 12 total titles, 6 fiction each year. Sometimes comments on rejected ms.
• A book published by Bilingual Press received the 1995 PEN Oakland Josephine Miles Award.
Needs: Ethnic, literary, short story collections, translations. "We are always on the lookout for Chicano, Puerto Rican, Cuban-American or other U.S.-Hispanic themes with strong and serious literary qualities and distinctive and intellectually important themes. We have been receiving a lot of fiction set in Latin America (usually Mexico or Central America) where the main character is either an ingenue to the culture or a spy, adventurer or mercenary. We don't publish this sort of 'Look, I'm in an exotic land' type of thing. Also, novels about the Aztecs or other pre-Columbians are very iffy." Published *MotherTongue*, by Demetria Martinez (novel); *Rita and Los Angeles*, by Leo Romero (short stories); and *Sanctuary Stories*, by Michael Smith (stories and essays).
How to Contact: Query first. SASE. Reports in 3 weeks on queries; 2 months on mss. Simultaneous submissions OK.
Terms: Pays royalties of 10%. Average advance $500. Provides 10 author's copies. Sends galleys to author. Publishes ms 1 year after acceptance. Writer's guidelines available. Book catalog free.
Advice: "Writers should take the utmost care in assuring that their manuscripts are clean, grammatically impeccable, and have perfect spelling. This is true not only of the English but the Spanish as well. All accent marks need to be in place as well as other diacritical marks. When these are missing it's an immediate first indication that the author does not really know Hispanic culture and is not equipped to write about it. We are interested in publishing creative literature that treats the U.S.-Hispanic experience in a distinctive, creative, revealing way. The kinds of books that we publish we keep in print for a very long time irrespective of sales. We are busy establishing and preserving a U.S.-Hispanic canon of creative literature."

BIRCH BROOK PRESS, (IV), P.O. Box 81, Delhi NY 13753. (212)353-3326. Publisher: Tom Tolnay. Estab. 1982. Small publisher of popular culture and literary titles in handcrafted letterpress editions. Plans 1 first novel this year. Averages 4 total titles, 2 fiction titles each year. Sometimes critiques or comments on rejected mss.
Needs: "We make specific calls for fiction when we are doing an anthology." Plans to publish anthology in the future. Will call for submissions at that time. Published *El Dorado: Lament for the Gold Double Eagle*, by William Oppenheimer and *Fiction, Flyfishing & The Search for Innocence*, by Lyons/McGuane/Enger, et al.
How to Contact: Does not seek unsolicited mss. Query first. SASE.
Terms: Modest flat fee as advance against royalties.
Advice: "We mostly generate our own anthologies and print notices to request submissions."

‡BkMk PRESS, (II), UMKC, University House, 5100 Rockhill Rd., Kansas City MO 64110-2499. (816)235-2558. Fax: (816)235-2611. E-mail: freemark@smtpgate.umkc.edu. Director: James McKinley. Estab. 1971. Small independent press. Publishes hardback and paperback originals. Books: standard paper; offset printing; perfect- and case-bound; average print order: 600; Averages 6 total titles, 1 fiction title each year.
Needs: Contemporary, ethnic, experimental, historical, literary, translations. "Fiction publishing limited to short stories and novellas. Ordinarily, prints anthologies or collections by one writer. BkMk Press does not publish commercial novels." Recently published *Urbane Tales*, by Raymond Johnson (short story collection); and *Artificial Horizon*, by Laurence Gonzalez.
How to Contact: Query first with SASE. Reports in 2-3 months on queries.
Terms: Pays in royalties (approximately 10%, in copies). Sends galleys to author. Free book catalog.
Advice: "We value the exceptional, rare, well-crafted and daring." Especially interested in Midwestern regional writers.

BLACK HERON PRESS, (I, II), P.O. Box 95676, Seattle WA 98145. Publisher: Jerry Gold. Estab. 1984. One-person operation; no immediate plans to expand. Publishes paperback and hardback originals. Average print order: 2,000; first novel print order: 1,500. Averages 4 fiction titles each year.
 • Three books published by Black Heron Press have won awards from King County Arts Commission.
Needs: Adventure, contemporary, experimental, humor/satire, literary, science fiction. Vietnam war novel—literary. "We don't want to see fiction written for the mass market. If it sells to the mass market, fine, but we don't see ourselves as a commercial press." Recently published *Renderings*, by James Sallis; *The Rat and the Rose*, by Arnold Rabin (humor); and *The Prisoner's Son*, by Jerome Gold (speculative fiction).
How to Contact: Query and sample chapters only. Reports in 3 months on queries. Simultaneous submissions OK.
Terms: Pays standard royalty rates. No advance.
Advice: "A query letter should tell me: 1) number of words; 2) number of pages; 3) if ms is available on floppy disk; 4) if parts of novel been published; 5) if so, where?"

BOOKS FOR ALL TIMES, INC., (III), Box 2, Alexandria VA 22313. Website: http://www.bfat.com. Publisher/Editor: Joe David. Estab. 1981. One-man operation. Publishes hardcover and paperback originals. Books: 60 lb. paper; offset printing; perfect binding. Average print order: 1,000. "No plans for new writers at present." Has published 1 fiction title to date. Occasionally critiques rejected mss.
Needs: Contemporary, literary, short story collections. "No novels at the moment; hopeful, though, of someday soon publishing a collection of quality short stories. No popular fiction or material easily published by the major or minor houses specializing in mindless entertainment. Only interested in stories of the Victor Hugo or Sinclair Lewis quality."
How to Contact: Query first with SASE. Simultaneous submissions OK. Reports in 1 month on queries.
Terms: Pays negotiable advance. "Publishing/payment arrangement will depend on plans for the book." Book catalog free with SASE.
Advice: Interested in "controversial, honest books which satisfy the reader's curiosity to know. Read Victor Hugo, Fyodor Dostoyevsky and Sinclair Lewis, for example. I am actively looking for short articles (up to 3,000 words) on contemporary education. I prefer material critical of the public schools when documented and convincing."

✦BOREALIS PRESS, (I, IV), 9 Ashburn Dr., Nepean, Ontario K2E 6N4 Canada. Imprint includes *Journal of Canadian Poetry*. Editor: Frank Tierney. Fiction Editor: Glenn Clever. Estab. 1970. Publishes hardcover and paperback originals and reprints. Books: standard book-quality paper; offset printing; perfect and cloth binding. Average print order: 1,000. Buys juvenile mss with b&w illustrations. Average number of titles: 4.
 • Borealis Press has a "New Canadian Drama series" with six books in print. The series won Ontario Arts Council and Canada Council grants.
Needs: Contemporary, literary, juvenile, young adult. "Must have a Canadian content or author; query first." Recently published *Josie's Song*, by Kerry Rauch; *Menominee. The Wild River People*, by Donella Knobel; *Ice Fire*, by Yvette Edmonds.
How to Contact: Submit query with SASE (Canadian postage). No simultaneous submissions. Reports in 2 weeks on queries, 3-4 months on mss. Publishes ms 1-2 years after acceptance.
Terms: Pays 10% royalties and 3 free author's copies; no advance. Sends galleys to author. Free book catalog with SASE.
Advice: " Have your work professionally edited. Our greatest challenge is finding good authors, i.e., those who do not fit the popular mode."

‡BRIDGE WORKS PUBLISHING CO., (I,II), 221 Bridge Lane, Box 1798, Bridgehampton NY 11932. (516)537-3418. Editorial Director: Barbara Phillips. Estab. 1992. "We are very small (three full-time employees) doing only 4-6 books a year. We publish quality fiction and nonfiction. Our books are routinely reviewed in such papers as *The New York Times*, *Newsday*, *The Washington Post* and *The Boston Globe*." Publishes hardcover originals. Average print order: 5,000. Published new writers within the last year. Plans 3 novels and 1 collection of short stories this year. Averages 4-6 total titles (75% fiction) each year. Sometimes critiques or comments on rejected mss.
 • *The Prince of West End Avenue*, published by Bridge Works, was a finalist for the 1995 National Book Critics Award.
Needs Experimental, feminist, gay, historical, humor/satire, literary, mainstream/contemporary, mystery/suspense, romance (historical), short story collections, translations. Recently published *Kraven Images*, by Alan Isler; *The Bride Wore Red*, by Robbie Clipper Sethi; *Zip Six*, by Jack Gantos.
How to Contact: Accepts unsolicited mss, but "must send query letter first." Query with outline/synopsis and 4 sample chapters. Include estimated word count and list of publishing credits. Send

SASE for reply, return of ms or send a disposable copy of ms. Agented fiction 50%. Reports in 2 weeks on queries; 2 months on mss.

Terms: Pays royalties of 10% maximum "based on cover price with a reserve against returns." Average advance: $1,000. Sends galleys to author. Publishes ms 1 year after acceptance. Writer's guidelines for SASE.

Advice: "We prefer literary novels; we're currently oversupplied with short story collections. It is preferable that an author have published somewhere else (short story collections, journalism, other genres) before trying us."

BUTTERNUT PUBLICATIONS, (II, IV), P.O. Box 1851, Martinsburg WV 25401. (304)267-0540. Publisher: Easther A. Watson. Estab. 1991. Midsize independent publisher. Publishes hardcover and paperback originals. Average print order: 5,000. First novel print order: 2,500. Published new writers within the last year. Plans 3 first novels this year. Averages 15 total titles, 7 fiction titles each year. Always critiques or comments on rejected mss.

Needs: Accepts work by West Virginians or about West Virginia only: children's/juvenile (historical, mystery), historical, mystery/suspense (cozy), new age/mystic/spiritual, psychic/supernatural/occult, regional (West Virginia themes), young adult/teen (historical). Especially looking for "young adult/ teen and historical/Civil War. Do not want to see anything that is suitable for family reading. No excessive violence, profanity, etc." Recently published *Civil War in the Lower Shenandoah Valley*, by Susan Crites; and *Where the Dead Live*, by Helen Cogswell.

How to Contact: Accepts unsolicited mss. Query with outline/synopsis and 3 sample chapters. Include estimated word count with submission. "We want the author's perspective on who will want the book." Send SASE for reply and disposable copy of ms. Reports in 2 weeks on queries; 1 month on mss. Simultaneous submissions OK. "We do not want entire manuscript and will not return it."

Terms: Pays royalties, offers advance. "Specifics are proprietary information." Sends galleys to author. Publishes ms 6-12 months after acceptance. Writer's guidelines for SAE and 2 first-class stamps. Book catalog for 5½ × 8½ SAE and 3 first-class stamps.

Advice: "There seems to be a growing market for family reading. Large-print requests are skyrocketing; easy-to-read has become highly lucrative. We aren't interested in boring, high-brow, literary magazine writing. We want a delightful 'story.' We would like to see more manuscripts with family values, solid entertainment, less blood and guts (a good mystery doesn't need it)."

CADMUS EDITIONS, (III), Box 126, Tiburon CA 94920. (707)431-8527. Editor: Jeffrey Miller. Estab. 1979. Emphasis on quality literature. Publishes hardcover and paperback originals. Books: Approximately 25% letterpress; 75% offset printing; perfect and case binding. Average print order: 2,000. First novel print order: 2,000. Averages 1-3 total titles.

Needs: Literary. Published *The Wandering Fool*, by Yunus Emre, translated by Edouard Roditi and Guzin Dino; *The Hungry Girls*, by Patricia Eakins; *Zig-Zag*, by Richard Thornley.

How to Contact: No unsolicited mss. Agent representative material only. SASE.

CALYX BOOKS, (I, II), P.O. Box B, Corvallis OR 97339. (503)753-9384. Fax: (541)753-0515. E-mail: calyx@proaxis.com. Editor: M. Donnelly. Fiction Editor: Micki Reaman. Estab. 1986. "We are a small feminist press, publishing fine literature and art by women." Publishes hardcover and paperback originals. Books: offset printing; paper and cloth binding. Average print order: 5,000-10,000 copies. First novel print order: 5,000. Published new writers within the last year. Averages 3 total titles each year.

- Calyx is not currently accepting fiction submissions. It will read queries for anthologies and nonfiction from Oct. 1-Nov. 15.

Needs: Contemporary, ethnic, experimental, feminist, lesbian, literary, short story collections, translations. Published *Into the Forest*, by Jean Hegland; *Four Figures in Time*, by Patricia Groosman; and *The Adventures of Mona Pinsky*, by Harriet Ziskin. Published new writers within the last year.

How to Contact: Query first. Send SASE for reply. Reports in 4 months on queries.

Terms: Pays royalties of 10% minimum, author's copies, (depends on grant/award money). Sends galleys to author. Publishes ms 2 years after acceptance. Writer's guidelines for #10 SASE. Book catalog free on request.

Advice: "Read our book catalog and journal. Be familiar with our publications. Follow our guidelines (which can be requested with a SASE) and be patient. Our process is lengthy."

MARKET CATEGORIES: (I) Open to new writers; (II) Open to both new and established writers; (III) Interested mostly in established writers; (IV) Open to writers whose work is specialized; (V) Closed to unsolicited submissions.

CATBIRD PRESS, (II), 16 Windsor Rd., North Haven CT 06473. Publisher: Robert Wechsler. Estab. 1987. Small independent trade publisher. Publishes cloth and paperback originals. Books: acid-free paper; offset printing; paper binding; illustrations (where relevant). Average print order: 4,000. First novel print order: 3,000. Averages 4 total titles, 1-2 fiction titles each year.

Needs: Humor (specialty); literary, translations (specialty Czech, French and German read in-house). No thriller, historical, science fiction, or other genre writing; only writing with a fresh style and approach. Published *Human Resources*, by Floyd Kemske (novel); *Diplomatic Pursuits*, by Joseph von Westphalen (German novel); and *Tales from Two Pockets*, by Karel Čapek (Czech stories).

How to Contact: Accepts unsolicited mss but no queries. Submit outline/synopsis with sample chapter. SASE. Reports in 2-4 weeks on mss. Simultaneous submissions OK, "but let us know if simultaneous."

Terms: Pays royalties of 7½-10%. Average advance: $2,000; offers negotiable advance. Sends galleys to author. Publishes ms approximately 1 year after acceptance. Terms depend on particular book. Writer's guidelines for #10 SASE.

Advice: "Book publishing is a business. If you're not willing to learn the business and research the publishers, as well as learn the craft, you should not expect much from publishers. They simply will have no respect for you. If you send genre or other derivative writing to a quality literary press, they won't even bother to look at it. If you can't write a decent cover letter, keep your fiction in your drawer. We are interested in unpublished novelists who combine a sense of humor with a true knowledge of and love for language, a lack of ideology, care for craft and self-criticism."

CAVE BOOKS, (IV), Subsidiary of Cave Research Foundation, 756 Harvard Ave., St. Louis MO 63130. (314)862-7646. Editor: Richard A. Watson. Estab. 1957. Small press. Publishes hardcover and paperback originals and reprints. Books: acid-free paper; various printing methods; binding sewn in signatures; illustrations. Average print order: 1,500. First novel print order: 1,500. Averages 4 total titles each year. number of fiction titles varies. Critiques or comments on rejected mss.

● For years now Cave Books has been looking for realistic adventure novels involving caves. A writer with a *quality* novel along these lines would have an excellent chance for publication.

Needs: Adventure (cave exploration). Needs any realistic novel with caves as central theme. "No gothic, romance, fantasy or science fiction. Mystery and detective OK if the action in the cave is central and realistic. (What I mean by 'realistic' is that the author must know what he or she is talking about.)"

How to Contact: Accepts unsolicited mss. Submit complete ms with cover letter. Reports in 1 week on queries; 1 month on mss. Simultaneous submissions OK.

Terms: Pays in royalties of 10%. Sends galleys to author. Book catalog free on request.

Advice: Encourages first novelists. "We would like to publish more fiction, but we get very few submissions. Why doesn't someone write a historical novel about Mammoth Cave or Carlsbad Caverns?"

‡CEDAR BAY PRESS LLC, (II), P.O. Box 751, Beaverton OR 97075-0751. (503)627-9106. E-mail: editor@cedarbay.com. Website: http://www.teleport.com/~cedarbay/index.html. Fiction Editor: Willow Bay. Estab. 1980. "Multimedia international publisher." Publishes paperback originals and reprints. Books: format varies. Published new writers within the last year. Plans 8 first novels this year. Averages 12 titles each year. Charges for ms critiques.

Needs: Adventure, children's/juvenile, fantasy, horror, mystery/suspense, new age/mystic/spiritual, romance, science fiction, short story collections, young adult/teen. Looking for "serious fiction in all main genres for all age markets." Publishes *Literary Fragments*, a quarterly short story anthology. Recently published *In a Heart Beat*, by Paul Christian (horror); *Final Statement*, by Bobbie Clark (suspense); and *100 Seconds to Charon*, by Burt Rice (fantasy). Publishes the Harrison Lloyd, Private Investigator, mystery series.

How to Contact: Accepts unsolicited mss. Accepts only electronic submissions. Query with outline/synopsis and complete ms. Accepts electronically transmitted queries by e-mail. Include estimated word count, 100-word bio and "background as related to writing the manuscript." Send SASE for reply. Reports in 2-4 months.

Terms: Pays royalties of up to 25%. Sends galleys to author. Publishes ms 6 months-1 year after acceptance. Guidelines and catalog available for $5 (refundable).

Advice: "Read our latest guidelines for the very latest opportunities, look through our latest catalog and send your work to fill in the titles/genres we're in need of. Visit our website."

CENTER PRESS, (III), P.O. Box 16452, Encino CA 91416-6452. (818)377-4301. Managing Editor: Gabriella Stone. Estab. 1979. "Small three-person publisher with expansion goals." Publishes hardcover and paperback originals, especially poetry collections. Plans 1-2 novels this year. Averages 6 total titles. Occasionally critiques or comments on rejected mss; fee varies.

Needs: Erotica, historical, humor/satire, literary, short story collections. *List for novels filled for next year or two.*

How to Contact: Does not accept unsolicited mss. Query through agent only. SASE. Agented fiction 90%. Reports in 2 months on queries. Simultaneous submissions OK.

Terms: Payment rate is "very variable." Sends galleys to author.

Advice: "Be competent, be solvent. Know who you are. Target your market."

‡**CHINOOK PRESS, (II)**, 1432 Yellowstone Ave., Billings MT 59102. (406)245-7704. Editor/Publisher: Mary Ellen Westwood. Estab. 1996. "One-person operation on a part-time basis just starting out. I hope to have a catalog of equal parts fiction, nonfiction and poetry." Publishes paperback originals. Books: acid-free paper; printing and binding suitable to product; illustrations. Average print order: 2,000-5,000. First novel print order: 2,000-5,000. Plans 1 first novel this year. Averages 4 total titles, 2 fiction titles each year. Sometimes critiques or comments on rejected mss.

Needs: Adventure, childrens/juvenile (all types), ethnic/multicultural, experimental, family saga, fantasy (all types), feminist, historical, humor/satire, literary, mainstream/contemporary, mystery/suspense (all types), regional (the West), science fiction (all types), short story collections, translations, young adult/teen (all types). "I want fiction that educates and uplifts, that shows real human beings in real or imagined situations that aid in human advancement. I do not want fiction that titillates for the sole purpose of titillation. I want fiction with a definite message and purpose."

How to Contact: Accepts unsolicited mss. Submit complete ms with cover letter. Include estimated word count, 1-page bio, Social Security number, list of publishing credits and "brief explanation of why you wrote what you wrote." Send SASE for return of ms. Reports in 2 months on queries and mss. Simultaneous submissions OK "if identified as such."

Terms: "We make individual arrangements with each author depending on book, but author must provide promotion time." Sends galleys to author. Publishes ms 2 months to 2 years after acceptance. Writer's guidelines for #10 SASE.

Advice: "I am a well-trained and well-practiced editor with 29 years experience in both journalism and law. Bad spelling, incorrect grammar and muddy thinking will not sell your work to me. But your best effort will receive attentive and enthusiastic handling here. I want more new and creative solutions to the human condition. I want fewer 'Oh, woe is me! I just can't do anything with my life.' stories."

‡**CHRISTMAS, An Annual Treasury, (I,II,IV)**, Augsburg Fortress Publishers, 426 S. Fifth St., Minneapolis MN 55440. (612)330-3300. Fax: (612)330-3215. Editor: Bob Klausmeier. Estab. 1931. An annual Christmas giftbook containing "poetry, fiction and personal essays related to Christmas and incorporating Christian heritage of the holidays. Also includes Christmas crafts and cooking features." Book: 8⅞ × 11¾; 64 pages; cloth cover with jacket; illustrations and photos. Print order: 30,000.

Needs: Children's/juvenile (Christmas, Christian), religious/inspirational. "No sentimental or maudlin stories, or ones that are not rooted in the Christian heritage of Christmas. No Santa stories." List of upcoming themes for SASE.

How to Contact: Send complete ms with a cover letter. Include estimated word count, 100-word bio and list of publications. Send SASE for reply, return of ms or send a disposable copy of ms. Reports in 3 months. Simultaneous submissions OK.

Terms: Pays $150-400 on acceptance and 1 contributor's copy; additional copies 40% off. Acquires one-time rights. Sends galleys to author. Fiction guidelines for SASE.

Advice: Looks for "engaging writing, humorous or serious, incorporating Christian heritage of Christmas."

CIRCLET PRESS, (IV), 1770 Massachusetts Ave., #278, Cambridge MA 02140. (617)864-0492 (noon-6p.m. EST). Fax: (617)864-0663, call before faxing. E-mail: circlet~info@circlet.com. Publisher: Cecilia Tan. Estab. 1992. Small, independent specialty book publisher. Publishes paperback originals. Books: perfect binding; illustrations sometimes; average print order: 2,000. Published new writers within the last year. Averages 6-8 anthologies each year. Always critiques or comments on rejected mss.

● Stories from Circlet Press appear in *Best American Erotica* 1994, 1995 and 1996.

Needs: "We publish only short stories of erotic science fiction/fantasy, of all persuasions (gay, straight, bi, feminist, lesbian, etc.). No horror! No exploitative sex, murder or rape. No degradation." No novels. All books are anthologies of short stories. Recently published *Earthly Pleasures*, by Reed Manning (short story collection); and *The New Worlds of Women* and *Of Princes & Beauties*, edited by Cecilia Tan (anthologies).

How to Contact: Accepts unsolicited mss between April 15 and August 31. "Any manuscript sent other than this time period will be held." Submit complete short story with cover letter. Include estimated word count, 50-100 word bio, list of publishing credits. Send SASE for reply, return of ms or send a disposable copy of ms. Agented fiction 10%. Reports in 2-6 weeks on queries; 3-7 months on mss. Simultaneous submissions OK.

Terms: Pays ½¢/word for 1-time anthology rights only, plus 2 copies; author is free to sell other rights. Sends galleys to author. Publishes ms 6-18 months after acceptance. Writer's guidelines for #10 SASE. Book catalog for #10 SAE and 2 first-class stamps.
Advice: "Read what we publish, learn to use lyrical but concise language to portray sex positively. Make sex and erotic interaction integral to your plot. Stay away from genre stereotypes. Use depth of character, internal monologue and psychological introspection to draw me in." Note: "We do not publish novels."

‡CLEIS PRESS, (II), P.O. Box 14684, San Francisco CA 94114. E-mail: sfcleis@aol. Acquisitions Editor: Frederique Delacoste. Estab. 1980. Midsize independent publisher. Publishes paperback originals. Published new writers within the last year. Plans 1 first novel every other year. Averages 15 total titles, 5 fiction titles/year (3 are anthologies).
  ● Cleis Press has received several Lambda Award nominations.
Needs: Comics/graphic novels, erotica, ethnic/multicultural (gay/lesbian), feminist, gay, historical (gay/lesbian), horror (vampire), humor/satire, lesbian, short story collections, thriller/espionage, translations. Recently published *Memory Mambo*, by Achy Obejas (novel); *Switch Hitters*, by Carol Queen (anthology); and *Seeing Dell*, by Carol Guess (novel).
How to Contact: Accepts unsolicited mss with SASE. Accepts unsolicited queries by e-mail. Submit complete ms with a cover letter. Include 1- or 2-page bio, list of publishing credits. Send SASE for reply or send a disposable copy of ms. Agented fiction 25%. Reports in 6 weeks. No simultaneous submissions.
Terms: Pays royalty of 7%. Advance is negotiable. Sends galleys to author. Publishes ms 12-18 months after acceptance. Writer's guidelines for SAE and 2 first-class stamps.

COFFEE HOUSE PRESS, (II), 27 N. Fourth St., Minneapolis MN 55401. (612)338-0125. Editors: Allan Kornblum and Chris Fischbach. Estab. 1984. "Nonprofit publisher with a small staff. We publish literary titles: fiction and poetry." Publishes paperback originals. Books: acid-free paper; Smyth-sewn binding; cover illustrations; average print order: 2,500. First novel print order: 3,000-4,000. Published new writers within the last year. Plans 2 first novels this year. Averages 12 total titles, 5-6 fiction titles each year. Sometimes critiques rejected mss.
  ● This successful nonprofit small press has received numerous grants from various organizations including NEA, the Mellon Foundation and Lila Wallace/Readers Digest.
Needs: Contemporary, ethnic, experimental, satire, literary. Looking for "non-genre, contemporary, high quality, unique material." No westerns, romance, erotica, mainstream, science fiction, mystery. Publishes anthologies, but they are closed to unsolicited submissions. Also publishes a series of short-short collections called "Coffee-to-Go." Published *Ex Utero*, by Laurie Foos (first novel); *Gunga Din Highway*, by Frank Chin (novel); and *A .38 Special & a Broken Heart*, by Jonis Agee (short short stories).
How to Contact: Accepts unsolicited mss. Submit samples with cover letter. SASE. Agented fiction 10%. Reports in 3 months on queries; 9 months on mss.
Terms: Pays royalties of 8%. Average advance: $1,000. Provides 15 author's copies. Writer's guidelines for #10 SASE with 55¢ postage.

CONFLUENCE PRESS INC., (II), 500 Eighth Ave., Lewis-Clark State College, Lewiston ID 83501. (208)799-2336. Imprints: James R. Hepworth Books and Blue Moon Press. Fiction Editor: James R. Hepworth. Estab. 1976. Small trade publisher. Publishes hardcover and paperback originals and reprints. Books: 60 lb. paper; photo offset printing; Smyth-sewn binding. Average print order: 1,500-5,000 copies. Published new writers within the last year. Averages 3-5 total titles each year. *Critiques rejected mss for $25/hour.*
  ● Books published by Confluence Press have received Western States Book Awards and awards from the Pacific Northwest Booksellers Association.
Needs: Contemporary, literary, mainstream, short story collections, translations. "Our needs favor serious fiction, 1 novel and 1 short fiction collection a year, with preference going to work set in the contemporary western United States." Published *Cheerleaders From Gomorrah*, by John Rember; and *Gifts and Other Stories*, by Charlotte Holmes.
How to Contact: Query first. SASE for query and ms. Agented fiction 50%. Reports in 6-8 weeks on queries and mss. Simultaneous submissions OK.
Terms: Pays royalties of 10%. Advance is negotiable. Provides 10 author's copies; payment depends on grant/award money. Sends galleys to author. Book catalog for 6×9 SASE.
Advice: "We are very interested in seeing first novels from promising writers who wish to break into serious print. We are also particularly keen to publish the best short story writers we can find. We are also interested in finding volume editors for our American authors series. Prospective editors should send proposals."

COOL HAND COMMUNICATIONS, INC., (II), 1050 N.W. First Ave., Box 28, Boca Raton FL 33432. (407)750-9826. Fax: (407)750-9869. Editor: Joella Cain. Estab. 1992. Imprint: Cool Kids Press. Estab. 1995. "Mid-size independent publisher." Publishes hardcover and trade paperback originals. Averages 15 total titles, 6 children's titles each year. Sometimes comments on rejected mss.
Needs: Mainstream/contemporary, how-to, children's. No science fiction, fantasy, religious or romance fiction. Published *Bobby Joe: In the Mind of a Monster*, by Bernie Ward.
How to Contact: Accepts unsolicited mss. Query by phone first, then query with outline/synopsis and 3 sample chapters. Include estimated word count, bio (1 page), Social Security number, and list of publishing credits. Send SASE for reply, return of ms or send a disposable copy of ms. Reports in 3 months. Simultaneous submissions OK.
Terms: Pays royalties of 3% minimum; 10% maximum. Offers negotiable advance. Sends galleys to author. Publishes ms 6-18 months after acceptance. Writer's guidelines for #10 SASE and 1 first-class stamp.
Advice: Looks for "quality writing, with professional workmanship. Neatness counts. Will consider first-time authors. Children's book illustrators must be highest quality."

✸COTEAU BOOKS, (IV), Thunder Creek Publishing Co-operative Ltd., 401-2206 Dewdney Ave., Regina, Saskatchewan S4R 1H3 Canada. (306)777-0170. Publisher: Geoffrey Ursell. Estab. 1975. Small, independent publisher. Publishes hardcover and paperback originals. Books: #2 offset or 60 lb. hi-bulk paper; offset printing; perfect and Smyth-sewn binding; 4-color illustrations. Average print order: 1,500-3,000; first novel print order: approx. 1,500. Published new writers within the last year. Publishes 14 total titles, 6-8 fiction titles each year. Sometimes comments on rejected mss.
● Books published by Coteau Books have received awards including 1995 Fiction Award for *Crosswinds*, 1995 City of Regina Award for *Club Chernobyl* and 1995 Sasketchewan Book of the Year for *Z:A Meditation on Oppression, Desire and Freedom*. The publisher does anthologies and these are announced when open to submissions.
Needs: Middle years and young adult fiction. No science fiction. No children's picture books. Recently published *Due West: 30 Great Stories From Alberta, Saskatchewan and Manitoba*, edited by Wayne Tefs, et al (anthology); *Inspection of a Small Village*, by Connie Gault (short stories); and *Crosswinds*, by Byrna Barclay.
How to Contact: *Canadian writers only.* Send submissions with query letter and résumé to Acquisitions Editor: Barbara Sapergia. SASE. No simultaneous or multiple submissions. Fiction 12.5%. Reports on queries in 2-3 months; 2-3 months on mss.
Terms: "We're a co-operative and receive subsidies from the Canadian, provincial and local governments. We do not accept payments from authors to publish their works." Sends galleys to author. Publishes ms 1-2 years after acceptance. Book catalog for 8½ × 11 SASE.
Advice: "We publish short-story collections, novels, drama, nonfiction and poetry collections, as well as literary interviews and children's books. This is part of our mandate. The work speaks for itself! Be bold. Be creative. Be persistent!"

CREATIVE ARTS BOOK CO., (II), 833 Bancroft Way, Berkeley CA 94710. (415)848-4777. Fax: (510)848-4844. Imprints: Creative Arts Communications Books, Creative Arts Life and Health Books and Saturday Night Specials. Publisher: Donald S. Ellis. Editor-in-Chief: George Samsa. Estab. 1975. Small independent trade publisher. Publishes hardcover originals and paperback originals and reprints. Average print order: 2,500-10,000. Average first novel print order: 2,500-10,000. Published new writers within the last year. Plans 3 first novels this year. Averages 10-20 titles each year.
● Books published by Creative Arts have been finalists for the American Book Award. Creative Arts is planning a new edition of *California Childhood*, an anthology of stories about growing up in California. Deadline for submissions is December 1997.
Needs: Contemporary, erotica (literary), feminist, historical, literary, mystery/suspense (Saturday night specials), regional, short story collections, translations, music, western. Publishes anthologies, *Black Lizard Crime Fiction* (Vols. I & II) and *Stolen Moments*, a collection of love stories. Recently published *Stolen Moments*, edited by M. Nagler (short stories); and *Crossing the Line*, by Joseph Moore (novel). Publishes the Childhood (growing up) series.
How to Contact: Accepts unsolicited mss. Submit outline/synopsis and 3 sample chapters (approximately 50 pages). SASE. Agented fiction 50%. Reports in 1 month on queries; 6 weeks on mss. Simultaneous submissions OK.
Terms: Pays royalties of 7½-15%; average advance of $1,000-10,000; 10 author's copies. Sends galleys to author. Writers guidelines and book catalog for SASE.
Advice: "Keep writing. Keep trying."

CREATIVE WITH WORDS PUBLICATIONS, (I), Box 223226, Carmel CA 93922. Fax: (408)655-8627. Editor-in-Chief: Brigitta Geltrich. Estab. 1975. One-woman operation on part-time basis "with guest editors, artists and readers from throughout the U.S." Books: bond and stock paper; mimeographed printing; saddle-stitched binding; illustrations. Average print order varies. Publishes paperback anthologies of new and established writers. Averages 10-12 anthologies each year. *Critiques rejected mss; $10 for short stories (less than 1,000 words); $20 for longer stories, folklore items; $5 for poetry.*

Needs: Humor/satire, juvenile (animal, easy-to-read, fantasy), nature. "Editorial needs center on folkloristic items (according to themes): tall tales and such for annual anthologies." Needs seasonal short stories appealing to general public; "tales" of folklore nature, appealing to all ages, poetry and prose written by children. Recently published anthologies, *On the Love of Animals*; *Relationships*; and *Dinosaurs, Dragons, Reptiles.*"

How to Contact: Accepts unsolicited mss. Query first; submit complete ms (prose no more than 1,200 words) with SASE and cover letter. Electronic submissions (3.5 diskette) OK. Reports in 1 month on queries; 2 months on mss. Publishes ms 1-2 months after deadline. Writer's guidelines and theme list (1 oz.) for SASE. No simultaneous submissions.

Terms: Pays in 20% reduced author copies.

Advice: "Our fiction appeals to general public: children-senior citizens. Follow guidelines and rules of Creative With Words Publications and not those the writer feels CWW should have. We only consider fiction along the lines of folklore, seasonal genres and themes set by CWW. We set our themes twice a year: July 1 and January 1. Be brief, sincere, well-informed, patient and proficient! Look at the world from a different perspective, research your topic thoroughly, apply brevity."

CROSS-CULTURAL COMMUNICATIONS, (I, IV), 239 Wynsum Ave., Merrick NY 11566-4725. (516)868-5635. Fax: (516)379-1901. Editorial Director: Stanley H. Barkan. Estab. 1971. "Small/alternative literary arts publisher focusing on the traditionally neglected languages and cultures in bilingual and multimedia format." Publishes chapbooks, magazines, anthologies, novels, audio cassettes (talking books) and video cassettes (video books, video mags); hardcover and paperback originals. Publishes new women writers series, Holocaust series, Israeli writers series, Dutch writers series, Asian-, African- and Italian-American heritage writers series, Native American writers series, Latin American writers series.

• Authors published by this press have received international awards including Nat Scammacca who won the National Poetry Prize of Italy and Gabriel Preil who won the Bialik Prize of Israel.

Needs: Contemporary, literary, experimental, ethnic, humor/satire, juvenile and young adult folktales, and translations. "Main interests: bilingual short stories and children's folktales, parts of novels of authors of other cultures, translations; some American fiction. No fiction that is not directed toward other cultures. For an annual anthology of authors writing in other languages (primarily), we will be seeking very short stories with original-language copy (other than Latin script should be print quality 10/12) on good paper. Title: *Cross-Cultural Review Anthology: International Fiction 1*. We expect to extend our *CCR* series to include 10 fiction issues: *Five Contemporary* (Dutch, Swedish, Yiddish, Norwegian, Danish, Sicilian, Greek, Israeli, etc.) *Fiction Writers.*" Published *Sicilian Origin of the Odyssey*, by L.G. Pocock (bilingual English-Italian translation by Nat Scammacca); *Sikano L'Americano!—Bye Bye America*, by Nat Scammacca; and *Milkrun*, by Robert J. Gress.

How to Contact: Accepts unsolicited mss. Query with SAE with $1 postage to include book catalog. "Note: Original language ms should accompany translations." Simultaneous and photocopied submissions OK. Reports in 1 month.

Terms: Pays "sometimes" 10-25% in royalties and "occasionally" by outright purchase, in author's copies—"10% of run for chapbook series," and "by arrangement for other publications." No advance.

Advice: "Write because you want to or you must; satisfy yourself. If you've done the best you can, then you've succeeded. You will find a publisher and an audience eventually. Generally, we have a greater interest in nonfiction novels and translations. Short stories and excerpts from novels written in one of the traditional neglected languages are preferred—with the original version (i.e., bilingual). Our kinderbook series will soon be in production with a similar bilingual emphasis, especially for folktales, fairy tales, and fables."

JOHN DANIEL AND COMPANY, PUBLISHERS, (I, II), Division of Daniel & Daniel, Publishers, Inc., Box 21922, Santa Barbara CA 93121. (805)962-1780. Fiction Editor: John Daniel. Estab. 1980; reestablished 1985. Small independent publisher with plans to expand. Publishes paperback originals. Books: 55-65 lb. book text paper; offset printing; perfect-bound paperbacks; illustrations sometimes. Average print order: 2,000. First novel print order: 2,000. Published new writers within

---

✝ THE DOUBLE DAGGER before a listing indicates that the listing is new in this edition. New markets are often the most receptive to submissions by new writers.

the last year. Plans 2 short story collections this year. Averages 5 total titles, 2-3 fiction titles each year. Sometimes critiques rejected mss.

• This press has become known for belles lettres and literary fiction, and work that addresses social issues.

Needs: "I'm open to all subjects (including nonfiction)." Literary, mainstream, short story collections. No pornographic, exploitive, illegal or badly written fiction. Recently published *Home is the Hunter*, by Meg Files (stories); *Sunset at Rosalie*, by Ann L. McLaughlin (novel); and *Nine Sisters Dancing*, by Ed Moses (novel).

How to Contact: Accepts unsolicited mss. Query first. SASE. Submit outline/synopsis and 2 sample chapters. Reports in 3 weeks on queries; 2 months on mss. Simultaneous submissions OK.

Terms: Pays in royalties of 10% of net minimum. Sends galleys to author.

Advice: "There are practical and learnable reasons why good fiction is better (and more publishable) than bad fiction. Give me an SASE and I'll send you twelve such reasons. In the meantime, remember that the real reward of being a writer is the writing itself. Anything else you get out of it (money, love, fame. . .) is gravy."

DELPHINIUM BOOKS, (II, III), 127 W. 24th St., New York NY 10011. Phone/fax: (212)255-6098. Editor-in-Chief: William G. Thompson. Executive Editor: Noah T. Lukeman. Estab. 1989/1995. Midsize independent publisher. Publishes hardcover originals. Books: 60 lb. heavy stock; offset printing; sewn binding. Average print order: 5,000. First novel print order: 5,000. Plans 3 first novels this year. Averages 6 total titles, 5-6 fiction titles each year. Sometimes comments on rejected mss.

• *Absent Without Leave*, written by Jessica Treadway, won a *Ploughshares* First Book Award; and numerous Delphinium titles have won Society of Illustrators Certificates of Merit.

Needs: Literary. Publishes anthologies. Writers may submit directly to Noah T. Lukeman, editor. "We also solicit submissions from select authors." Published *Absent Without Leave*, by Jessica Treadway (literary short story collection); *Christopher Park*, by Rosemary Clement (literary); and *Delphinium Blossoms* (literary anthology).

How to Contact: Does not accept unsolicited mss. Query first or submit through agent. Include 1-paragraph bio and list of publishing credits. Send a disposable copy of ms. Agented fiction 90%. Reports in 2-3 weeks on queries; 2-3 months on mss. Simultaneous submissions OK.

Terms: Pays royalties of 6% minimum; 15% maximum. Offers negotiable advance. Sends galleys to author. Publishes ms 6-12 months after acceptance. Book catalog for 9 × 12 SAE and 8 first-class stamps.

‡**DOWN THERE PRESS, (I, II, IV)**, Subsidiary of Open Enterprises Cooperative, Inc., 938 Howard St., #101, San Francisco CA 94103. (415)974-8985 ext 105. Fax: (415)974-8989. E-mail: goodvibe@well.com. Imprints are Yes Press and Red Alder Books. Managing Editor: Leigh Davidson. Estab. 1975. Small independent press with part-time staff; part of a large worker-owned cooperative. Publishes paperback originals. Books: Web offset printing; perfect binding; some illustrations. Average print order: 5,000. First novel print order: 3,000-5,000. Published new writers within the last year. Averages 1-2 total titles, 1 fiction title each year. Sometimes critiques or comments on rejected mss. Member of Publishers Marketing Association and Northern California Book Publicity and Marketing Association.

Needs: Erotica, feminist, lesbian. Recently published *Herotica 4*, edited by Marcy Sheiner (anthology); and *Erotic Reading Circle Stories*, edited by Carol Queen and Jack Davis (anthology).

How to Contact: Accepts unsolicited mss. Submit complete ms with cover letter (short stories for anthologies only). Include estimated word count. Accepts queries and correspondence by fax. Send SASE for reply, return of ms or send disposable copy of ms. Reports in 6-9 months on mss. Simultaneous submissions OK.

Terms: Pays royalties and 2 author's copies. Sends galleys to author. Publishes ms 18 months after acceptance. Writer's guidelines and book catalog for #10 SASE.

✤**DUNDURN PRESS, (II)**, 2181 Queen St. E., #301, Toronto, Ontario M4E 1E5 Canada. (416)698-0454. E-mail: editorial@dundurn.com. Editorial Contact Person: Kirk Howard. Estab. 1972. Subsidiaries include Hounslow Press, Simon & Pierre, Boardwalk Books and Umbrella Press. Midsize independent publisher with plans to expand. Publishes hardcover and paperback originals.

Needs: Contemporary, literary. Recently published *Love Minus One*, by Norma Harrs; *Grave Deeds*, by Betsy Struthers; and *Sherlock Holmes: Travels in the Canadian West*, by Ronald Weyman.

How to Contact: Accepts unsolicited mss. Submit outline/synopsis and sample chapters. SASE for ms. Simultaneous submissions OK. Accepts electronic submissions. Unsolicited mss *not* accepted by e-mail.

Terms: Pays royalties of 10%; 10 author's copies. Sends galleys to author. Publishes ms 6-9 months after acceptance. Book catalog free on request for SASE.

E.M. PRESS, INC., (I, IV), P.O. Box 4057, Manassas VA 20108. (540)439-0304. Editor: Beth Miller. Estab. 1991. "Expanding small press." Publishes paperback and hardcover originals. Books: 50 lb.

text paper; offset printing; perfect binding; illustrations. Average print order: 1,200-5,000. Averages 8 total titles, fiction, poetry and nonfiction, each year.

Needs: "We are focusing more on Virginia/Maryland/DC authors and subject matter. We're emphasizing nonfiction and we're launching a new children's line, though we still consider 'marketable' fiction. Recently published *The Relationship*, by John Hyman (young adult); *Santa's New Reindeer*, by Julie Shrecker; *Seagrapes*, by Roy King (literary); and *I, Anna Kerry*, by William Giannini (literary).

How to Contact: Accepts unsolicited mss. Submit outline/synopsis and sample chapters or complete ms with cover letter. Include estimated word count. Send a SASE for reply, return of ms or send a disposable copy of the ms. Agented fiction 10%. Reports in 2 months on queries; 2 months on mss. Simultaneous submissions OK.

Terms: Amount of royalties and advances varies. Sends galleys to author. Publishes ms 1 year after acceptance. Writer's guidelines for SASE.

Advice: Publishing "less fiction, more regional work, though we look for fiction that will do well in secondary rights sales."

EARTH-LOVE PUBLISHING HOUSE LTD., (IV), 3440 Youngfield St., Suite 353, Wheatridge CO 80033. (303)233-9660. Fax: (303)233-9354. Director: Laodeciae Augustine. Estab. 1989. Small publisher. Publishes paperback originals and reprints. Books: 60 lb. paper; offset printing; sew and wrap binding; halftone illustrations. Average print order: 5,000. First novel print order: 5,000. Averages 2 total titles, 1 fiction title each year. Often comments on rejected mss.

Needs: Metiphysical adventure, mystery/suspense (English amateur sleuth), new age/mystic/spiritual.

How to Contact: Does not accept unsolicited mss. Query first. Include estimated word count and list of publishing credits with submission. SASE. Reports in 3 weeks on queries; 5 weeks on mss. Simultaneous submissions OK. Accepts electronic (disk) submissions.

Terms: Pays royalties of 8% minimum; 12% maximum or 10% of run for author's copies. Publishes ms 6-10 months after acceptance.

THE ECCO PRESS, (II), 100 W. Broad St., Hopewell NJ 08525. (609)466-4748. Editor-in-Chief: Daniel Halpern. Estab. 1970. Small publisher. Publishes hardcover and paperback originals and reprints. Books: acid-free paper; offset printing; Smythe-sewn binding; occasional illustrations. Averages 50 total titles, 10 fiction titles each year. Average first novel print order: 3,000 copies.

Needs: Literary and short story collections. "We can publish possibly one or two original novels a year." No science fiction, romantic novels, western (cowboy). Published *Where Is Here*, by Joyce Carol Oates; *Have You Seen Me*, by Elizabeth Graver; *Coming Up Down Home*, by Cecil Brown.

How to Contact: Accepts unsolicited mss. Query first, especially on novels, with SASE. Reports in 3-6 months, depending on the season.

Terms: Pays in royalties. Advance is negotiable. Writer's guidelines for SASE. Book catalog free on request.

Advice: "We are always interested in first novels and feel it's important they be brought to the attention of the reading public."

ECOPRESS, (IV), 1029 N.E. Kirsten Place, Corvallis OR 97330. (503)758-7545. Fax: (541)758-5380. E-mail: ecopress@compuserve.com. Editor/Art Director: Chris Beatty. Estab. 1993. Publishes "books and art that enhance environmental awareness." Publishes hardcover and paperback originals. Books: recycled paper; offset printing; perfect binding; illustrations. Average print order 3,000. First novel print order: 2,000. Averages 2 total titles, 1 fiction title each year. Often comments on rejected mss.

Needs: Adventure, literary, mainstream/contemporary, mystery/suspense, science fiction, thriller/espionage. Fiction "must have an environmental aspect." Published *Journey of the Tern* and *Sapo*, by Robert Beatty.

How to Contact: Accepts unsolicited mss. Query with outline/synopsis and 3 sample chapters. Include estimated word count, half-page bio and list of publishing credits with submission. Send SASE for reply, return of ms or send a disposable copy of ms. Agented fiction 10%. Reports in 1 month on queries; 4 months on mss. Simultaneous, disk (ASCII text) and electronic submissions OK.

Terms: Pays royalties; offers negotiable advance. Sends galleys to author. Publishes ms 1 year after acceptance. Writer's guidelines for SASE.

Advice: "I have to be *very* excited about a book's chances to compete to consider publishing it."

THE EIGHTH MT. PRESS, (II, IV), 624 SE 29th Ave., Portland OR 97214. (503)233-3936. Publisher: Ruth Gundle. Estab. 1984. One-person operation on full-time basis. Publishes paperback originals. Books: acid-free paper; perfect-bound; average print order: 5,000. Averages 2 total titles, 1 fiction title every few years.

Needs: Books written only by women. Feminist, lesbian, literary, short story collections. Published *Cows and Horses*, by Barbara Wilson (feminist/literary); and *Minimax*, by Anna Livia.

How to Contact: Accepts unsolicited mss. Query first. SASE. Reports in 1 month.
Terms: Pays royalties of 8-10%. Sends galleys to author. Publishes ms within 1 year of acceptance.
Advice: "Query first! And present a clear and concise description of the project along with your publication credits, if any."

❦EKSTASIS EDITIONS, (IV), Box 8474, Main P.O., Victoria, British Columbia V8W 3S1 Canada. Phone/fax: (604)385-3378. Publisher: Richard Olafson. Estab. 1982. Independent publisher. Publishes paperback originals. Books: acid free paper; offset printing; perfect/Smyth binding. Average print order: 1,000-3,000. First novel print order: 1,000-2,000. Published new writers within the last year. Plans 3 first novels this year. Averages 14 total titles, 5 fiction titles each year.
Needs: Erotica, experimental, literary, mainstream/contemporary, New Age/mystic/spiritual, short story collections, translations. Published *Bread of the Birds*, by André Carpentier.
How to Contact: Accepts unsolicited mss. Submit complete ms with cover letter. Include estimated word count, bio, list of publishing credits. SASE for reply. Reports in 5 months on queries; 4 months on mss.
Terms: Pays royalties of 6%. Pays 75 author's copies. Sends galleys to author. Book catalog available for $2.

FABER AND FABER, INC., (II), 53 Shore Rd., Winchester MA 01890. Small trade house which publishes literary fiction and collections. Averages 4-6 fiction titles each year.
Needs: Literary. "No romances, juvenile, please." Allow 2 months for response. Published *Coconuts for the Saint*, by Debra Sparks; *The Legend of the Barefoot Mailman*, by John Henry Fleming.
How to Contact: Send query and 1 or 2 sample chapters with SASE for reply. Requires synopsis/description—cannot consider ms without this. Address to Publishing Assistant.

FASA CORPORATION, (II, IV), 1100 W. Cermak, B305, Chicago IL 60608. Editor: Donna Ippolito. "Company responsible for science fiction, adventure games, fantasy, to include adventures, scenarios, game designs and novels, for an audience high school age and up." Published new writers within the last year. Publishes 12 novels/year and 30 game products/year.
Needs: Novels set in our three game universes: Battle Tech® (military SF), Shadowrun® (technofantasy), Earthdawn® (high fantasy). Publishes ms an average of 12-18 months after acceptance. Recently published *Dead Aire*, by Jak Kooke; *Black Dragon*, by Victor Milan; and *Praying for Keeps*, by Mel Odom.
How to Contact: Query first. Send SASE for guidelines before submitting. Reports in 6-12 weeks. Simultaneous submissions OK.
Terms: Pays on publication for all rights. Sends galleys to author.
Advice: "Must be familiar with our product and always ask about suitability before plunging into a big piece of work that I may not be able to use. Writers *must* write to spec. Interested in writers for line of fiction and in writing for game products."

FC2/BLACK ICE BOOKS, (I), Unit for Contemporary Literature, Illinois State University, Normal IL 61790-4241. (309)438-3582. Fax: (309)438-3523. E-mail: ckwhite@rs6000.cmp.ilstu.edu. Co-director: Curtis White. Estab. 1974. "Publisher of innovative fiction." Publishes hardcover and paperback originals. Books: perfect/Smyth binding; illustrations. Average print order: 2,200. First novel print order: 2,200. Published new writers within the last year. Plans 2 first novels this year. Averages 10 total titles, 10 fiction titles each year. Often critiques or comments on rejected mss.
Needs: Feminist, gay, literary, science fiction (cyberpunk), short story collections. Plans future anthologies written by women and selected by editors. Published *Cares of the Day*, by Ivan Webster (minority); *Angry Nights*, by Larry Fondation (literary); and *Little Sisters of the Apocalypse*, by Kit Reed (science fiction).
How to Contact: Accepts unsolicited mss. Query with outline/synopsis. Include 1-page bio, list of publishing credits. SASE. Agented fiction 5%. Reports on queries in 3 weeks. Simultaneous submissions OK.
Terms: Pays royalties of 8-10%; offers $100 advance. Sends galleys to author. Publishes ms 1 year after acceptance. Writer's guidelines for SASE.
Advice: "Be familiar with our list."

SENDING TO A COUNTRY other than your own? Be sure to send International Reply Coupons instead of stamps for replies or return of your manuscript.

THE FEMINIST PRESS AT THE CITY UNIVERSITY OF NEW YORK, 311 E. 94th St., New York NY 10128. (212)360-5790. Publisher: Florence Howe. Assistant Editor: Sara Clough. Estab. 1970. "Nonprofit, tax-exempt, education and publishing organization interested in changing the curriculum, the classroom and consciousness." Publishes hardcover and paperback reprints. "We use an acid-free paper, perfect-bind our books, four color covers; and some cloth for library sales if the book has been out of print for some time; we shoot from the original text when possible. We always include a scholarly and literary afterword, since we are introducing a text to a new audience. Average print run: 4,000." Publishes no original fiction; exceptions are anthologies and international works. Averages 10-15 total titles/year; 4-8 fiction titles/year (reprints of feminist classics only).
Needs: Children's, contemporary, ethnic, feminist, gay, lesbian, literary, regional, science fiction, translations, women's. Published *Songs My Mother Taught Me: Stories, Plays, and Memoir*, by Wakako Yamauchi; *Folly*, by Maureen Brady; and *Changes*, by Ama Ata Aidoo.
How to Contact: Accepts unsolicited mss. Query first. Submit outline/synopsis and 1 sample chapter. SASE. Reports in 1 month on queries; 3 months on mss. Simultaneous submissions OK.
Terms: Pays royalties of 10% of net sales; $100 advance; 10 author's copies. Sends galleys to author. Book catalog free on request.

FIREBRAND BOOKS, (II), 141 The Commons, Ithaca NY 14850. (607)272-0000. Contact: Nancy K. Bereano. Estab. 1985. Independent feminist and lesbian press. Publishes quality trade paperback originals. Averages 8-10 total titles each year.
 • Firebrand has won the Lambda Literary Award Organization's Publisher's Service Award.
Needs: Feminist, lesbian. Published *The Gilda Stories*, by Jewelle Gomez (novel); and *Stone Butch Blues*, by Leslie Feinberg (novel).
How to Contact: Accepts unsolicited mss. Submit outline/synopsis and sample chapters or send complete ms with cover letter. SASE. Reports in 2 weeks on queries; 2 months on mss. Simultaneous submissions OK with notification.
Terms: Pays royalties.

FOUR WALLS EIGHT WINDOWS, (II), 39 W. 14th St., #503, New York NY 10011. (212)206-8965. Publisher: John Oakes. Estab. 1986. "We are a small independent publisher." Publishes hardcover and paperback originals and paperback reprints. Books: quality paper; paper or cloth binding; illustrations sometimes. Average print order: 3,000-7,000. First novel print order: 3,000-5,000. Averages 18 total titles/year; approximately 5-6 fiction titles/year.
 • Four Walls Eight Windows' books have received mention from the *New York Times* as "Notable Books of the Year" and have been nominated for *L.A. Times* fiction prizes.
Needs: Literary.
How to Contact: Does not accept unsolicited submissions. "Query letter accompanied by sample chapter and SASE is best. Useful to know if writer has published elsewhere, and if so, where." Agented fiction 70%. Reports in 2 months. Simultaneous submissions OK.
Terms: Pays standard royalties; advance varies. Sends galleys to author. Book catalog free on request.
Advice: "We get 2,000 or so submissions a year: 1. Learn what our taste is, first; 2. Be patient."

‡**FRIENDS UNITED PRESS, (I)**, 101 Quaker Hill Dr., Richmond IN 47374. (317)962-7573. Fax: (317)966-1293. Editor: Ardith Talbot. Estab. 1973. Publishes paperback originals. Books: 60 lb. paper; perfect bound. Average print order: 1,000. Plans 1 first novel this year. Averages 7 total titles, 1-2 fiction titles each year. Sometimes critiques or comments on rejected mss. Member of Protestant Church Publishers Association.
Needs: Historical (Friends' history), religious (children's, inspirational). Recently published *For The Gift of A Friend*, by Susan McCracken.
How to Contact: Accepts unsolicited mss. Submit complete ms with cover letter. Send SASE for reply, return of ms or send disposable copy of ms. Simultaneous submissions OK.
Terms: Pays royalties of 7½% maximum. Sends galleys to author. Publishes ms 1 year after acceptance. Writer's guidelines for #10 SASE.

GAY SUNSHINE PRESS AND LEYLAND PUBLICATIONS, (IV), P.O. Box 410690, San Francisco CA 94141. Fax: (415)626-1802. Editor: Winston Leyland. Estab. 1970. Midsize independent press. Publishes hardcover and paperback originals. Books: natural paper; perfect-bound; illustrations. Average print order: 5,000-10,000.
 • Gay Sunshine Press has received a Lambda Book Award for *Gay Roots* (volume 1), named "Best Book by a Gay or Lesbian Press."
Needs: Literary, experimental, translations—all gay male material only. "We desire fiction on gay themes of *high* literary quality and prefer writers who have already had work published in literary magazines. We also publish erotica—short stories and novels." Published *Partings at Dawn: An Anthology of Japanese Gay Literature from the 12th to the 20th Centuries*; and *Out of the Blue: Russia's Hidden Gay Literature—An Anthology*.

How to Contact: "Do not send an unsolicited manuscript." Query with SASE. Reports in 3 weeks on queries; 2 months on mss. Send $1 for catalog.

Terms: Negotiates terms with author. Sends galleys to author. Pays royalties or by outright purchase.

Advice: "We continue to be interested in receiving queries from authors who have book-length manuscripts of high literary quality. We feel it is important that an author know exactly what to expect from our press (promotion, distribution, etc.) before a contract is signed. Before submitting a query or manuscript to a particular press, obtain critical feedback on your manuscript from knowledgeable people. If you alienate a publisher by submitting a manuscript shoddily prepared/typed, or one needing very extensive rewriting, or one which is not in the area of the publisher's specialty, you will surely not get a second chance with that press."

‡**GIBBS SMITH, PUBLISHER/PEREGRINE SMITH, (II, IV)**, P.O. Box 667, Layton UT 84041. (801)544-9800. Fax: (801)544-5582. Editor: Gail Yngve. Children's Editor: Theresa Desmond. Estab. 1971. Small independent press. Publishes hardcover and paperback originals and reprints. Published new writers within the last year. Averages 40-60 total titles, 1-2 fiction titles each year. Sometimes critiques or comments on rejected mss.

● Gibbs Smith is the recipient of a Western Writers Association Fiction Award.

Needs: Children's (preschool/picture books), comics/graphic novels, ethnic/multicultural, feminist, humor/satire, literary, mainstream/contemporary, new age/mystic/spiritual, science fiction (hard science/technological, soft/sociological), short story collections. Publishes *The Peregrine Reader*, a series of anthologies based upon a variety of themes. Recently published *The White Rooster and Other Stories*, by Robert Bausch (literary); and *Last Buckaroo*, by Mackey Hedges (western).

How to Contact: Accepts unsolicited mss. Query with outline/synopsis and 2 sample chapters. Include estimated word count, 1-paragraph bio and list of publishing credits. SASE for reply. Reports in 3-4 weeks on queries; 2-4 months on mss. Simultaneous submissions OK.

Terms: Pays royalties; amount depends on author and author's publishing history. Provides 10 author's copies. Sends galleys to author. Publishes ms 1-2 years after acceptance. Writer's guidelines and book catalog for #10 SASE.

Advice: "The fiction editor also holds several other positions within the company. Please be patient about response time."

❀**GOOSE LANE EDITIONS, (II, IV)**, 469 King St., Fredericton, New Brunswick E3B 1E5 Canada. (506)450-4251. Acquisitions Editor: Laurel Boone. Estab. 1957. Publishes hardcover and paperback originals and occasional reprints. Books: some illustrations. Average print run: 2,000. First novel print order: 1,500. Averages 14 total titles, 4-5 fiction titles each year.

● Goose Lane has won the Atlantic Booksellers' Association Booksellers' Choice Award.

Needs: Contemporary, historical, literary, short story collections. "Not suitable for mainstream or mass-market submissions." Recently published *Looks Perfect*, by Kim Moritsugu; *Season of Apples*, by Ann Copeland; and *English Lessons*, by Shauna Singh Baldwin.

How to Contact: Considers unsolicited mss; outline or synopsis and 30-50 page sample. Query first. SASE "with Canadian stamps, International Reply Coupons, cash, check or money order. No U.S. stamps please." Reports in 6 months. Simultaneous submissions OK.

Terms: Pays royalties of 8% minimum; 12% maximum. Average advance: $100-200, negotiable. Sends galleys to author. Writers guidelines for 9 × 12 SAE and IRC.

Advice: "We consider submissions from outside Canada only when they have a strong Canadian connection and exhibit outstanding literary skill."

‡❀**GRADE SCHOOL PRESS, (I, IV)**, 3266 Yonge St., #1829, Toronto, Ontario M4N 3P6 Canada. (416)487-2883. Administrative Assistant: Shelley. Estab. 1990. "Part-time/small press." Publishes paperback originals. Averages 1-3 total titles, 0-1 fiction title/year. Sometimes critiques or comments on rejected mss. Member CANSCAP.

Needs: Children's/juvenile (historical, series, sports, hi/lo), family saga, feminist, historical (children's only), religious (Jewish only, children's), young adult/teen (easy-to-read, historical, problem novels, series), education (special needs, testing/advocacy).

How to Contact: Accepts unsolicited mss. Query with outline/synopsis and several sample chapters. Include estimated word count, bio, list of publishing credits and general author goals. Send a disposable copy of ms.

Terms: Payment depends on grants/awards. Provides author's copies. Sends galleys to author. Publishes ms 6-12 months after acceptance.

Advice: "Be interesting, original, polished, practical."

GRAYWOLF PRESS, (III), 2402 University Ave., St. Paul MN 55114. (612)641-0077. Publisher: Fiona McCrae. Estab. 1974. Growing small literary press, nonprofit corporation. Publishes hardcover and paperback originals and paperback reprints. Books: acid-free quality paper; offset printing; hardcover and soft binding; illustrations occasionally. Average print order: 3,000-10,000. First novel print order: 2,000-6,000. Averages 18-20 total titles, 6-8 fiction titles each year. Occasionally critiques rejected mss.

● Graywolf Press books have won numerous awards. Most recently, Josip Novakovich won the Richard J. Margolis Award (1995), and David Treuer won the 1996 Minnesota Book Award for Novels and Short Stories.

Needs: Literary, and short story collections. Literary fiction; no genre books (romance, western, science fiction, suspense). Recently published *The Apprentice*, by Lewis Libby (novel); *Watershed*, by Percival Everett (novel); and *Rainy Lake*, by Mary François Rockcastle (novel).

How to Contact: Query with SASE. Reports in 3 weeks. Simultaneous submissions OK.

Terms: Pays in royalties of 7½-10%; negotiates advance and number of author's copies. Sends galleys to author. Free book catalog.

GRIFFON HOUSE PUBLICATIONS, Box 81, Whitestone NY 11357. (718)767-8380. President: Frank D. Grande. Estab. 1976. Small press. Publishes paperback originals and reprints.

Needs: Contemporary, drama, ethnic (open), experimental, literary, multinational theory, poetry, reprints, theory and translations.

How to Contact: Query with SASE. No simultaneous submissions. Reports in 1 month.

Terms: Pays in 6 free author's copies. No advance.

GRYPHON PUBLICATIONS, (I, II), Imprints include Gryphon Books, Gryphon Doubles, P.O. Box 209, Brooklyn NY 11228. (718)646-6126 (after 6 pm EST). Owner/Editor: Gary Lovisi. Estab. 1983. Publishes hardcover and paperback originals and trade paperback reprints. Books: bond paper; offset printing; perfect binding. Average print order: 500-1,000. Published new writers within the last year. Plans 2 first novels this year. Averages 5-10 total titles, 4 fiction titles each year. Often critiques or comments on rejected mss.

Needs: Mystery/suspense (private eye/hardboiled, crime and true crime), science fiction (hard science/technological, soft/sociological). No horror, romance or westerns. Published *The Dreaming Detective*, by Ralph Vaughn (mystery-fantasy-horror); *The Woman in the Dugout*, by Gary Lovisi and T. Arnone (baseball novel); and *A Mate for Murder*, by Bruno Fischer (hardboiled pulp). Publishes Gryphon Double novel series.

How to Contact: "I am not looking for novels now but will see a *1-page synopsis* with SASE." Include estimated word count, 50-word bio, short list of publishing credits, "how you heard about us." Send SASE. Do not send ms. Agented fiction 5-10%. Reports in 2-4 weeks on queries; 1-2 months on mss. Simultaneous and electronic submissions OK (with hard copy—disk in ASCII).

Terms: For magazines, $5-45 on publication plus 2 contributor's copies; for novels/collections payment varies and is much more. Sends galleys to author. Publishes ms 1-3 years after acceptance. Writers guidelines and book catalog for SASE.

Advice: "I am looking for better and better writing, more cutting-edge material with *impact*! Keep it lean and focused."

✿GUERNICA EDITIONS, (III, IV), P.O. Box 117, Toronto, Ontario M5S 2S6 Canada. E-mail: 102026.1331@compuserve.com. Editor: Antonio D'Alfonso. Fiction Editor: Umberto Claudio. Estab. 1978. Publishes paperback originals. Books: offset printing; perfect/sewn binding. Average print order: 1,000. Average first novel print order: 1,000. Plans to publish 1 first novel this year. Publishes 16-20 total titles each year.

● The press has recently won the American Booksellers Association Award for *Astoria*, by Robert Viscusi.

Needs: Contemporary, ethnic, literary, translations of foreign novels. Looking for novels about women and ethnic subjects. No unsolicited works. Recently published *Valentino and the Great Italians*, by Anthony Valerio; *A Rage of Love*, by Alda Merini; and *Vinnie and Me*, by Fiorella DeLuca Calce (novel).

How to Contact: Does not accept or return unsolicited mss. Query first. IRCs. 100% of fiction is agented. Reports in 6 months. Electronic submissions via IBM WordPerfect disks.

Terms: Pays royalties of 7-10% and 10 author's copies. Book catalog for SAE and $2 postage. (Canadian stamps only).

Advice: Publishing "more pocket books."

‡HELICON NINE EDITIONS, (I, II), Subsidiary of Midwest Center for the Literary Arts, Inc., P.O. Box 22412, Kansas City MO 64113. (816)753-1095. Publisher/Editor: Gloria Vando Hickok. Estab. 1990. Small press publishing poetry, fiction, creative nonfiction and anthologies. Publishes paperback originals. Books: 60 lb. paper; offset printing; perfect-bound; 4-color cover. Average print order: 1,000-5,000. Plans 8 total titles, 2-4 fiction titles this year. Also publishes one-story chapbooks called *feuillets*, which come with envelope, 250 print run.

Needs: Contemporary, ethnic, experimental, literary, short story collections, translations. "We're only interested in fine literature." Nothing "commercial." Recently published *Knucklebones*, by Annabel

Thomas; and *Return to Sender*, by Ann Slegman. Published new writers within the last year.
How to Contact: Does not accept unsolicited mss. Query first. SASE. Reports in 1 week on queries.
Terms: Pays royalties, author's copies or honorarium. "Individual arrangement with author." Sends galleys to author. Publishes ms 1-6 months after acceptance. Writer's guidelines for SASE.
Advice: "Check spelling and grammar before submitting. Be proud of your work. Submit a clean, readable copy in a folder or box—paginated with title and name on each page. Also, do not pre-design book, i.e., no illustrations. We'd like to see books that will be read 50-100 years from now. New classics."

HOLLOW EARTH PUBLISHING, (II), P.O. Box 1355, Boston MA 02205-1355. Phone/fax: (603)433-8735. Publisher: Helian Grimes. Estab. 1983. "Small independent publisher." Publishes hardcover and paperback originals and reprints. Books: acid-free paper; offset printing; Smythe binding.
Needs: Comics/graphic novels, fantasy (sword and sorcery), feminist, gay, lesbian, literary, New Age/mystic/spiritual, translations. Looking for "computers, Internet, Norse mythology, magic." Publishes various computer application series.
How to Contact: Does not accept unsolicited mss. Query letter only first. Include estimated word count, 1-2 page bio, list of publishing credits. Send SASE for reply, return of ms or send disposable copy of ms. Agented fiction 90%. Reports in 2 months. Accepts disk submissions.
Terms: Pays in royalties. Sends galleys to author. Publishes ms as soon as possible after acceptance.
Advice: Looking for "less fiction, more computer information."

‡❋**HOUSE OF ANANSI PRESS, (II)**, Subsidiary of General Publishing, 1800 Steeles Ave. W., Concord, Ontario L4K 2P3 Canada. (905)660-0611. Fax: (905)660-0676. Imprints are Stoddart Publishing, Boston Mills Press, Macfarlane Walter and Ross. Publisher: Michael Byron Davis. Editor: Martha Sharpe. Estab. 1967. Small literary press; publishes Canadian literary fiction, poetry and nonfiction. Publishes hardcover and paperback originals and paperback reprints. Average print order: 1,000. Published new writers within the last year. Plans 1 first novel this year. Averages 10-15 total titles, 3-5 fiction titles each year. Sometimes critiques or comments on rejected mss. Member of Literary Press Group and Association of Canadian Publishers.
Needs: Erotica, ethnic/multicultural, gay, lesbian, literary, short story collections, translations (from French-Canada only). Publishes anthologies of works by previously published Anansi authors. Recently published *Burden of Dreams*, by Anne Hébert (literary, translated from French); *Like This*, by Leo McKay Jr. (short stories); and *Dead Men's Watches*, by Hugh Hood (literary fiction). Publishes the Spider Line series for new, experimental writing.
How to Contact: Submit outline/synopsis and 2 sample chapters. Include 1-page bio and list of publishing credits. Send SASE for reply, return of ms or send disposable copy of ms. Agented fiction 1%. Reports in 3 months on queries; 6 months on mss. Simultaneous submissions OK.
Terms: Pays royalties of 8% minimum; 10% maximum. Average advance: $700, negotiable. Sends galleys to author. Publishes ms 9 months after acceptance.
Advice: "We are hoping to expand and improve our fiction list. We will publish mainly in trade paperback with flaps, as this seems to be the market preference. Renewed interest in new Canadian writers (especially fiction) is bolstering our longstanding commitment to publishing excellent new fiction, as well as our previously published authors. It's best for newer writers to build up a publishing record by placing stories and/or poems in good literary journals or magazines before attempting to place a book with a publisher."

‡**ICE CUBE PRESS, (III, IV)**, 205 N. Front St., North Liberty IA 52317. (319)626-2055. Publisher/Editor: S. H. Semken. Estab. 1994. "One-person operation. Uses nature-oriented fiction and creative nonfiction." Publishes paperback originals. Books: natural, acid-free paper; offset and letterpress printing; perfect binding; illustrations, possibly. Average print order: 1,500. First novel print order: 1,500. Plans 1 first novel this year. Always critiques or comments on rejected mss.
Needs: Regional (regionalism themes), nature and environmental.
How to Contact: Accepts unsolicited mss. Query with outline/synopsis and first chapter. Include short bio. Send SASE for reply, return of ms or send a disposable copy of ms. Agented fiction 5%. Reports in 3-4 weeks. Simultaneous submissions OK.
Terms: Individual arrangements with author depending on the book. Sends galleys to author. Publishes ms approximately 1 year after acceptance. Writer's guidelines for #10 SASE.
Advice: "Stories of restoration and sense-of-place are always welcome for consideration."

‡**ILLUMINATION PUBLISHING CO., (II, IV)**, P.O. Box 1865, Bellevue WA 98009. (206)646-3670. Fax: (206)646-4144. E-mail: illumin.com. Editorial Director: Ruth Thompson. Estab. 1987. "Illumination Arts is a small company publishing high quality children's picture books with spiritual and/or inspirational values." Publishes hardcover originals. Publishes 1 children's picture book/year. Often critiques or comments on rejected mss. Member of Book Publishers of the Northwest.

● Illumination Arts received 1996 Awards of Excellence from Body Mind Spirit for two books.
Needs: Children's/juvenile (adventure, preschool/picture books).
How to Contact: Accepts unsolicited mss. Query first or submit complete ms with cover letter. Accepts electronically transmitted queries by e-mail and fax. Include estimated word count, Social Security number and list of publishing credits. Send SASE for reply or return of ms. Reports in 1 week on queries; 1 month on mss. Simultaneous submissions OK.
Terms: Pays royalties. Sends galleys to author. Publishes ms 18 months-2 years after acceptance. Writer's guidelines for SASE.
Advice: "Submit full manuscripts, neatly typed without grammatical or spelling errors. Expect to be edited many times. Be patient. We are very *painstaking*."

‡✻INSOMNIAC PRESS, (II), 378 Delaware Ave., Toronto, Ontario M6H 2T8 Canada. (416)536-4308. Fax: (416)588-4198. E-mail: insomna@pathcom.com. Publisher: Mike O'Connor. Estab. 1992. "Small press which publishes new and experimental fiction." Publishes paperback originals. Books: 60 lb. paper; offset printing; perfect binding; illustrations. Average print order: 1,500. First novel print order: 1,500. Published new writers within the last year. Plans 3 first novels this year. Averages 8 total titles, 6 fiction titles each year.
Needs: Experimental, gay, literary, new age/mystic/spiritual, short story collections. Plans anthology of gay stories. Recently published *What Passes for Love*, by Stan Rogal (short stories); *Beneath the Beauty*, by Philip Arima (poetry); and *Bootlegging Apples*, by Mary Elizabeth Grace (poetry).
How to Contact: Accepts unsolicited mss. Query with outline/synopsis. Accepts electronically transmitted queries by e-mail. Include estimated word count, bio and list of publishing credits. SASE for reply. Reports in 6 months. Simultaneous and electronic submissions OK.
Terms: Pays royalties. Sends galleys to author.

‡INTRIGUE PRESS, (II, IV), Subsidiary of Columbine Publishing Group, Inc., P.O. Box 456, Angel Fire NM 87710. (505)377-3474. Fax: (505)377-3526. E-mail: mystery302@aol.com. Imprints are Intrigue Press (fiction) and Columbine Books (nonfiction). Editor: Lee Ellison. Estab. 1994. "Small independent publisher specializing in mystery, suspense, and adventure fiction. Publishes hardcover and paperback originals and paperback reprints. Books: 50 lb. booktext paper; offset lithography printing; adhesive case or perfect-bound binding. Average print order: 3,000. First novel print order: 3,000. Published new writers within the last year. Plans 2 first novels this year. Averages 4 total titles, 3-4 fiction titles each year. Sometimes critiques or comments on rejected mss. Member of Publishers Marketing Association and Small Publishers of North America.
Needs: Adventure, mystery/suspense (amateur sleuth, police procedural, private eye/hardboiled), thriller/espionage. "Our list is fairly well filled for the next year. Generally, our fiction needs are very specific. We do not publish anything outside those categories." Recently published *Vacations Can Be Murder*, by Connie Shelton (mystery series); *Secret's Shadow*, by Alex Matthews (mystery series); and *Assault on the Venture*, by Dan Shelton (action/adventure). Publishes The Charlie Parker mysteries, by Connie Shelton and the Cassidy McCabe mysteries by Alex Matthews.
How to Contact: Accepts unsolicited mss. Query with outline/synopsis and 3-4 sample chapters. Include estimated word count, 1-page bio, list of publishing credits and "how you might contribute to marketing the book." Send SASE for reply, return of ms or send disposable copy of ms. Reports in 4-6 weeks. Simultaneous submissions OK.
Terms: Pays royalties of 10% minimum, 15% maximum of net sales price. Offers negotiable advance. Sends galleys to author. Publishes ms 6-18 months after acceptance. Writer's guidelines and book catalog for #10 SASE.
Advice: "We already receive approximately 20 times more submissions than we can buy, so it behooves writers to be sure their work is absolutely top notch before sending it. Having a freelance editor or book doctor look at the manuscript before submitting it is a good idea. Also, we like authors who want to be involved in promotion and publicity. Belonging to writing organizations like Mystery Writers of America or Sisters in Crime is a definite plus because they give members lots of creative promotion tips. Along with your query letter, tell me your marketing plans."

‡IRONWEED PRESS, (II), 77 Puritan Ave., Forest Hills NY 11375. Phone/fax: (718)268-2394. Publisher: Jin Soo Kang. Estab. 1996. Small independent publisher. Publishes hardcover and paperback originals. Plans 2 first novels this year. Averages 4 total titles, 4 fiction titles/year. Sometimes critiques or comments on rejected mss.
Needs: Ethnic/multicultural (Asian-American), experimental, humor/satire, literary.
How to Contact: Accepts unsolicited mss. Submit complete ms with a cover letter. Include list of publishing credits. SASE for return of ms. Reports in 1 month on queries; 2-3 months on mss. Simultaneous submissions OK.
Terms: Pays royalties of 8% minimum; offers advance; provides author's copies. Sends galleys to author. Publishes ms 6-12 months after acceptance.

‡**ITALICA PRESS, (II, IV)**, 595 Main St., #605, New York NY 10044. (212)935-4230. Fax: (212)838-7812. E-mail: italica@aol.com. Publishers: Eileen Gardiner and Ronald G. Musto. Estab. 1985. Small independent publisher. Publishes paperback originals. Books: 50-60 lb. natural paper; offset printing; Smythe-sewn binding; illustrations. Average print order: 1,500. "First time translators published. We would like to see translations of Italian writers well-known in Italy who are not yet translated for an American audience." Publishes 6 total titles each year; 2 fiction titles. Sometimes critiques rejected mss.

Needs: Translations of 20th Century Italian fiction. Published *Last Act in Urbino*, by Paolo Volponi; *Otronto*, by Maria Corti; and *Bakunin's Son*, by Sergio Atzeni.

How to Contact: Accepts unsolicited mss. Query first. Reports in 3 weeks on queries; 2 months on mss. Simultaneous submissions OK. Electronic submissions via Macintosh disk.

Terms: Pays in royalties of 5-15% and 10 author's copies. Sends pre-publication galleys to author. Book catalog free on request.

Advice: "A *brief* call saves a lot of postage. 90% of the proposals we receive are completely off base—but we are very interested in things that are right on target. Please send return postage if you want your manuscript back."

‡**IVY LEAGUE PRESS, INC., (II)**, P.O. Box 3326, San Ramon CA 94583-8326. (510)736-0601 or 800-IVY-PRESS. Fax: (510)736-0602. Editor: Maria Thomas. Estab. 1992. Publishes hardcover and paperback originals. Specializes in medical suspense. Books: perfect binding. First novel print order: 5,000. Plans 1 novel this year. Averages 2 total titles, 1-2 fiction titles/year. Always critiques or comments on rejected mss.

Needs: Mystery/suspense(medical). Recently published *Allergy Shots*, by Litman.

How to Contact: Accepts unsolicited mss. Query with outline/synopsis. Include estimated word count, bio and list of publishing credits. Send SASE or a disposable copy of the ms. Reports in 2 months on queries.

Terms: Royalties vary. Sends galleys to author.

Advice: "If you tell a terrific story of medical suspense, one which is hard to put down, we may publish it."

✷**JESPERSON PRESS LTD., (I)**, 39 James Lane, St. John's, Newfoundland A1E 3H3 Canada. (709)753-0633. Trade Editor: John Symonds. Midsize independent publisher. Publishes hardcover and paperback originals. Averages 7-10 total titles, 1-2 fiction titles each year. Sometimes comments on rejected mss.

Needs: Adventure, fantasy, humor/satire, juvenile (5-9 yrs. including: animal, contemporary, easy-to-read, fantasy, historical, sports, spy/adventure). Published *Daddy's Back*, by Barbara Ann Lane; *Fables, Fairies & Folklore of Newfoundland*, by Miké McCarthy and Alice Lannon; and *Justice for Julie*, by Barbara Ann Lane. Published new writers within the last year.

How to Contact: Accepts unsolicited mss. Submit complete ms with cover letter. SASE. Reports in 3 months on mss.

Terms: Pays negotiable royalties. Sends galleys to author. Book catalog free.

BOB JONES UNIVERSITY PRESS, (I, II), Greenville SC 29614. (864)242-5100, ext. 4316. E-mail: uunet!wpo.bju.edu!grepp. Website: http://www.bju.edu/press/freelnce.html. Acquisitions Editor: Mrs. Gloria Repp. Estab. 1974. "Small independent publisher." Publishes paperback originals and reprints. Books: 50 lb. white paper; Webb lithography printing; perfect-bound binding. Average print order: 5,000. First novel print order: 5,000. Published new writers within the last year. Plans 3 first novels this year. Averages 12 total titles, 10 fiction titles each year. Sometimes comments on rejected mss.

Needs: Children's/juvenile (adventure, animal, easy-to-read, historical, mystery, series, sports), young adults (adventure, historical, mystery/suspense, series, sports, western). Recently published *The Rivers of Judah*, by Catherine Farnes (contemporary teen fiction); *Arby Jenkins*, by Sharon Hambric (contemporary ages 9-12); *The Treasure Keeper*, by Anita Williams, (adventure ages 6-10).

How to Contact: Accepts unsolicited mss. Query with outline and 5 sample chapters. Submit complete ms with cover letter. Include estimated word count, short bio, Social Security number and list of publishing credits. Send SASE for reply, return of ms or send a disposable copy of ms. Reports in 3 weeks on queries; 6 weeks on mss. Simultaneous and disk submissions (IBM compatible preferred) OK. "Check our webpage for guidelines."

Terms: "Pay flat fee for first-time authors; royalties for established authors." Sends galleys to author. Publishes ms 12-18 months after acceptance. Writer's guidelines and book catalog free.

Advice: Needs "more upper-elementary adventure/mystery or a good series. Fewer picture books. Fewer didactic stories. Read guidelines carefully. Send SASE if you wish to have ms returned. Give us original, well-developed characters in a suspenseful plot with good moral tone."

KAR-BEN COPIES INC., (IV), 6800 Tildenwood Lane, Rockville MD 20852. (800)452-7236. Executive Editor: Madeline Wikler. Estab. 1975. "Publisher of books and tapes on Jewish themes for young children." Publishes hardcover and paperback originals. Books: 100 lb. coated paper; offset printing; Smythe/perfect binding; full color illustrations. Average print order: 10,000. Published new writers within the last year. Plans 1-2 first novels this year. Averages 5-6 total titles, 4-5 fiction titles each year.

• Kar-Ben Copies, Inc. has received honors from the National Jewish Book Awards.

Needs: Childrens/juvenile (easy-to-read, preschool/picture book), ethnic/multicultural (Jewish). Published *Sammy Spider's First Passover*, by Sylvia Russ (holiday fiction); and *Northern Lights—A Hanukkah Story*, by Diana Conway (holiday fiction).

How to Contact: Accepts unsolicited mss with SASE only. Submit complete ms with cover letter. SASE for reply. Reports in 4-6 weeks. Simultaneous submissions OK.

Terms: Pays royalties of 5-8%; offers negotiable advance. Sends galleys to author. Publishes ms 6-12 months after acceptance. Writer's guidelines for 9×12 SAE and 2 first-class stamps. Book catalog for 9×12 SAE and 2 first-class stamps.

‡KITCHEN TABLE: WOMEN OF COLOR PRESS (II, IV), P.O. Box 40-4920, Brooklyn NY 11240-4920. Fax: (718)935-1107. Publisher: Andrea Lockett. Estab. 1981. "Independent press with several paid employees, very good distribution." Publishes paperback originals. Books: 50 lb stock paper; offset/web press printing; perfect binding; some b&w graphic elements/designs. Average print order: 5,000. First novel print order: 3,000. "All of our books are trade paperbacks, a few of which are bound for libraries." Averages 2 total titles each year; 1 fiction title every two years. Occasionally critiques rejected mss.

Needs: Ethnic, feminist, lesbian, literary, short story collections. "We do publish anthologies that are thematic. Writers may submit work in response to our specific calls for submissions for each title. Often because of the specialized nature of the subject matter, writers in the field are identified and contacted by the anthology editors." Needs for novels include novels by women of color—authors that reflect in some way the experiences of women of color. "We are looking for high quality, politically conscious writing and would particularly like to hear from Native American women fiction writers." Has published *Cuentos: Stories by Latinas*, edited by Alma Gómez, Cherríe Moraga and Mariana Romo-Carmona (short story anthology with selections in both English and Spanish); and *Seventeen Syllables and Other Stories*, by Hisaye Yamamoto.

How to Contact: Query first with SASE. Submit outline/synopsis and 3 sample chapters. SASE. Reports in 1 month on queries; 6 months on mss. Simultaneous submissions OK. "Manuscripts and queries received without adequate return postage will be destroyed."

Terms: Pays in royalties of 7% minimum; 10% maximum and 10 author's copies. Sends galleys to author. Book catalog for 2 first-class stamps.

Advice: "One of the most common mistakes that our press tries to address is the notion that the first work a writer publishes should be a book as opposed to a submission to a periodical. Periodicals serve as a very valuable apprenticeship for a beginning writer. They should submit work to appropriate literary and other kinds of journals that publish fiction. By appropriate I mean appropriate for the kind of writing they do. Getting published in periodicals gives the writer experience and also creates a 'track record' that may interest the prospective book publisher."

LEE & LOW BOOKS, (I, II), 95 Madison Ave., New York NY 10016. (212)779-4400. Fax: (212)683-1894. Editor-in-Chief: Elizabeth Szabla. Estab. 1991. "Independent multicultural children's book publisher." Publishes hardcover originals. Averages 8-10 total titles each year. Sometimes critiques or comments on rejected mss.

Needs: Children's/juvenile (historical, multicultural, preschool/picture book for children ages 4-10). Recently published *Dear Ms. Parks: A Dialogue With Today's Youth*, by Rosa Parks (collection of correspondence); *Giving Thanks: A Native American Good Morning Message*, by Chief Jake Swamp (picture book); and *Sam and the Lucky Money*, by Karen Chinn (picture book).

How to Contact: Accepts unsolicited mss. Send complete ms with cover letter or through an agent. Send SASE for reply, return of ms or send a disposable ms. Agented fiction 30%. Reports in 1-3 months. Simultaneous submissions OK.

Terms: Pays royalties. Offers advance. Sends galleys to author. Publishes ms 18 months after acceptance. Writer's guidelines for #10 SASE. Book catalog for SASE with $1.01 postage.

Advice: "Writers should familiarize themselves with the styles and formats of recently published children's books. Lee & Low Books is a multicultural children's book publisher. We would like to see more contemporary stories set in the U.S. Animal stories and folktales are not considered at this time."

♣LEMEAC EDITEUR INC., (I, II), 1124 Marie Anne Est, Montreal, Québec H2J 2B7 Canada. (514)524-5558. Fax: (514)524-3145. Directeur Littéraire: Pierre Filion. Estab. 1957. Publishes paperback originals. Books: offset #2 paper; offset printing; allemand binding; color/cover illustration. Average print order: 1,000. First novel print order: 1,000. Published new writers within the last year.

Plans 1 first novel this year. Averages 25 total titles, 20 fiction titles each year. Often critiques or comments on rejected mss.

Needs: Literary, romance (contemporary, futuristic/time travel, historical), short story collections, translations. Writers submit to editor. Recently published *Un Ange Cornu . . .*, by Michel Tremblay (novel); *Rendez-moi Ma Mère*, by Daniel Gagnon (novel); and *La Vievolte*, by Nancy Huston (novel). Publishes *L'Oiseau de feu*, novels by Jorgus Brossard.

How to Contact: Accepts unsolicited mss. Submit complete ms with cover letter. Send a disposable copy of ms. Agented fiction 10%. Reports in 3 months on queries; 6 months on mss. No simultaneous submissions.

Terms: Pays royalties of 10%. Sends galleys to author. Publishes ms 1-2 years after acceptance.

LINCOLN SPRINGS PRESS, (II), 32 Oak Place, Hawthorne NJ 07506. Editor: M. Gabrielle. Estab. 1987. Small, independent press. Publishes poetry, fiction, photography, high quality. Publishes paperback originals. Books: 65 lb paper; offset printing; perfect binding. Average print order: 1,000. "Prefers short stories, but will publish first novels if quality high enough." Averages 4 total titles, 2 fiction titles each year.

Needs: Contemporary, ethnic, experimental, feminist, historical, literary, short story collections. No "romance, Janet Dailey variety." Published *Maybe It's My Heart*, by Abigail Stone (novel); and *Subway Home*, by Justin Vitiello.

How to Contact: Accepts unsolicited mss. Query first with 1 sample chapter. SASE. Reports in 2 weeks to 3 months. Simultaneous submissions OK.

Terms: Authors receive royalties of 5% minimum; 15% maximum "after all costs are met." Provides 10 author's copies. Sends galleys to author.

‡LINTEL, (II), P.O. Box 8609, Roanoke VA 24014. Editorial Director: Walter James Miller. Estab. 1977. Two-person organization on part-time basis. Books: 90% opaque paper; photo offset printing; perfect binding; illustrations. Average print order: 1,000. First novel print order: 1,200. Publishes hardcover and paperback originals. Occasionally comments on rejected mss.

Needs: Experimental, feminist, gay, lesbian, regional short fiction. Published second edition (fourth printing) of *Klytaimnestra Who Stayed at Home*, mythopoeic novel by Nancy Bogen; and *The Mountain*, by Rebecca Rass.

How to Contact: Accepts unsolicited mss. Query with SASE. Simultaneous and photocopied submissions OK. Reports in 2 months on queries; 3 months on mss. Publishes ms 6-8 months after acceptance.

Terms: Negotiated. No advance. Sends galleys to author. Free book catalog.

Advice: "Lintel is devoted to the kinds of literary art that will never make The Literary Guild or even the Book-of-the-Month Club: that is, literature concerned with the advancement of literary art. We still look for the innovative work ignored by the commercial presses. We consider any ms on its merits alone. We encourage first novelists. Be innovative, advance the *art* of fiction, but still keep in mind the need to reach reader's aspirations as well as your own. Originality is the greatest suspense-building factor. Consistent misspelling errors, errors in grammar and syntax can mean only rejection."

LIVINGSTON PRESS, (II), Station 22, University of Alabama, Livingston AL 35470. Imprint: Swallows Tale Press. Director: Joe Taylor. Estab. 1982. "Literary press." Publishes hardcover and paperback originals. Books: acid-free paper; offset printing; perfect binding. Average print order: 1,500. First novel print order: 1,500. Published new writers within the last year. Plans 2 first novels this year. Averages 4-6 total titles, 5 fiction titles each year. Sometimes critiques or comments on rejected mss.

Needs: Literary, short story collections. No genre. Published *Sideshows*, by B.K. Smith; *A Bad Piece of Luck*, by Tom Abrams; and *Alabama Bound*, by Colquitt.

How to Contact: Does not accept unsolicited mss. Query first. Include bio, list of publishing credits. Send SASE for reply, return of ms or send a disposable copy of ms. Agented fiction 10%. Reports in 3 weeks on queries; 6 months on mss. Simultaneous submissions OK.

Terms: Pays royalties of 6% minimum; 7½% maximum. Provides 12 author's copies. Sends galleys to author. Publishes ms 1-2 years after acceptance. Book catalog free.

LOLLIPOP POWER BOOKS, (II), 120 Morris St., Durham NC 27701. (919)560-2738. Editor: Ruth A. Smullin. Estab. 1970. "Children's imprint of the Carolina Wren Press, a small, nonprofit press which publishes non-sexist, multi-racial picture books." Publishes paperback originals. Averages 1 title (fiction) each year. Average first book run 3,000 copies.

Needs: Not currently reviewing mss. Recently published *Maria Teresa*, by Mary Atkinson (bilingual); *In Christina's Toolbox*, by Diane Homan; and *Grownups Cry Too*, by Nancy Hazen (bilingual).

Terms: Pays royalties of 10%.

Advice: "Lollipop Power Books must be well-written stories that will appeal to children. We are not interested in preachy tales where 'message' overpowers plot and character. We look for good stories told from a child's point of view. Our books present a child's perspective and feelings honestly and without condescension."

HENDRICK LONG PUBLISHING CO., (II, IV), P.O. Box 25123, Dallas TX 75225. (214)358-4677. Vice President: Joann Long. Estab. 1969. Independent publisher focusing on Texas and Southwest material geared primarily to a young audience. (K through high school). Publishes hardcover and paperback originals and hardcover reprints. Average print order: 3,000. Published new writers within the last year. Averages 8 total titles, 4 fiction titles each year. Sometimes comments on rejected mss.
Needs: Texas themes: historical, regional, for juvenile, young adult, teen. "No material not suitable for junior high/high school audience." Published *Baxter Badgen's Home*, by Doris McClellan; *I Love You, Daisy Phew*, by Ruby C. Tolliver; and *New Medicine*, by Jeanne Williams (reprint).
How to Contact: Query first or submit outline/synopsis and sample chapters (at least 2—no more than 3). SASE. Reports in 2 weeks on queries; 2 months on ms.
Terms: Offers advance. Sends galleys to author. Publishes ms 18 months after acceptance. Writer's guidelines for SASE. Book catalog for $1.

‡LOVEPRINTS NOVELETTES, (I,II,IV), Handmaiden Publishing Co., 2593 North 140 W., Sunset UT 84015. (801)774-6693. Editor: Donna Clark. Estab. 1996. "LovePrints Novelettes seeks to publish true love stories which are realistic, easy to read and emotionally satisfying. All genres are welcome excluding horror. We do not publish soft core pornography. Our intended audience is 80% women, ages teens through 55. Stories should have absolute commitments to marriage." Books: digest size; 45-90 pages; illustrations. Plans 9 total titles, all fiction, this year. Always critiques or comments on rejected mss.
Needs: Adventure, ethnic/multicultural, fantasy (science), historical, mystery/suspense (romantic), religious/inspirational, romance (contemporary, futuristic/time travel, historical), science fiction (soft/sociological), senior citizen/retirement, westerns, young adult/teen (adventure, mystery, romance, science fiction, western). Special interests include the Ancient World (2,000 B.C.-1,000 A.D.). "No horror/supernatural or romances featuring witchcraft, psychics, past lives or sorcery. Also, no up-in-the-air endings including couples living together as a resolution to their commitment." Recently published *Darling Phantom*, by Jan McDaniels (mystery); *Rosewood*, by Donna Getzinger (fantasy); *Stolen Hearts*, by Robynn Clairday (mystery thriller); *The Color of Love*, by Kathleen Babcock (historical); and *Back Home*, by Evelyn Seranne (teen romance). Length: 10,000 words average; 8,000 words minimum; 25,000 words maximum.
How to Contact: Send complete ms with a cover letter. Include estimated word count and 200-word or less bio. "In your bio, talk about your inspiration for the romance and tell readers something about you—we want romance bios to be personal and lead into the story, not résumé style." Reports in 6-8 weeks on mss. Send SASE for reply, return of ms or send a disposable copy of ms. No simultaneous submissions.
Terms: Pays $50 flat fee on publication. Acquires first North American serial rights. Sample copy of a novelette $6. Writer's guidelines free for #10 SASE.
Advice "Overall presentation and cover letter enthusiasm make a manuscript stand out. We can tell when the authors are simply trying to add more credit to their list of publications or if they have something tailored to a true romance mini-novel. The age or sex of the author does not matter to us. We first look at the length, whether they've studied our guidelines, and if they've ever read a Harlequin romance. We read the last paragraph first. If it doesn't end with a satisfying bang, we don't go to the beginning. We favor a romance that starts with dialogue and tension. We do not want very long short stories. We want compact novels with well-plotted scenes and description. We want heroines and heroes who are so real we feel as if we know them. Lastly, too many writers make the mistake of sending stories about love but not the development and resolution of a romance between a specific man and woman."

LUCKY HEART BOOKS, (II), Subsidiary of Salt Lick Press, Salt Lick Foundation, Inc., B205, 1900 West Hwy. 6, Waco TX 76712. Editor/Publisher: James Haining. Estab. 1969. Small press with significant work reviews in several national publications. Publishes paperback originals and reprints. Books: offset/bond paper; offset printing; hand-sewn or perfect-bound; illustrations. Average print order: 500. First novel print order: 500. Sometimes critiques or comments on rejected mss.
Needs: Open to all fiction categories. Published *Catch My Breath*, by Michael Lally.
How to Contact: Accepts unsolicited mss. SASE. Agented fiction 1%. Reports in 2 weeks to 4 months on mss.
Terms: Pays 10 author's copies. Sends galleys to author.
Advice: "Follow your heart. Use the head, but follow the heart."

MACMURRAY & BECK, INC., (II), 1649 Downing St., Denver CO 80218. (303)832-2152. Fax: (303)832-2158. Executive Editor: Frederick Ramey. Fiction Editor: Greg Michalson. Estab. 1990. Publishes hardcover and paperback originals. Books: average print order: 6,000; first novel print order:

6,000. Published new writers within the last year. Plans 3-4 novels this year. Averages 8 total titles, 2-3 fiction titles each year. Sometimes critiques or comments on rejected mss.

Needs: Contemporary, literary. Looking for "reflective fiction with high literary quality and commercial potential. No plot-driven, traditional, frontier western or mainstream." Published *St. Burl's Obituary*, by Daniel Akst; *Rocket City*, by Cathryn Alpert (literary); and *Stygo*, by Laura Hendrie (literary).

How to Contact: Query with outline/synopsis and 3 sample chapters. Include 1-page bio, list of publishing credits, any writing awards or grants. SASE for reply. Agented fiction 75%. Reports in 2 months on queries; 3 months on mss. Simultaneous submissions OK.

Terms: Pays royalties; offers negotiable advance. Sends galleys to author (usually at author's request). Book catalog free.

Advice: "We publish a very limited number of novels each year and base our selection on literary quality first. Submit a concise, saleable proposal. Tell us why we should publish the book, not just what it is about."

MADWOMAN PRESS, (I, II, IV), P.O. Box 690, Northboro MA 01532. (508)393-3447. Editor/Publisher: Diane Benison. Estab. 1991. "Lesbian/feminist press; one-person operation running on a part-time basis." Publishes paperback originals. Books: perfect binding. Average print order: 4,000-6,000. Averages 2-4 total titles, 2 fiction titles each year. Sometimes comments on rejected mss.

● Madwoman Press published *Thin Fire* and *Lesbians in the Military Speak Out*, which were nominated for American Library Association Gay and Lesbian Book awards. This press is becoming known for its lesbian mysteries.

Needs: "All must have lesbian themes: adventure, erotica, ethnic, feminist, mystery/suspense (amateur sleuth, police procedure, private eye), romance, science fiction (hard science, soft sociological), thriller/espionage, western. Especially looking for lesbian detective stories." No horror. No gratuitous violence. Published *Fertile Betrayal*, by Becky Bohan (mystery); and *The Grass Widow*, by Nanci Little (novel).

How to Contact: Query first. Include brief statement of name, address, phone, previous publication and a 1-2 page precis of the plot. SASE. Reports in 2 months on queries; 3 months on solicited mss. Simultaneous submissions OK.

Terms: Pays royalties of 8-15% "after recovery of publications costs." Provides 20 author's copies. Sends galleys to author. Publishes ms 1-2 years after acceptance. Writer's guidelines for #10 SASE.

Advice: "Your query letter will often cause your manuscript to be rejected before it's even read. Write clearly, succinctly, tell the publisher how the book ends and save the hype for the jacket copy. We're looking to form long-term relationships with writers, so talented first novelists are ideal for us. We want to publish an author regularly over the years, build an audience for her and keep her in print. We publish books by, for and about lesbians, books that are affirming for lesbian readers and authors."

MAGE PUBLISHERS, (IV), 1032 29th St. NW, Washington DC 20007. (202)342-1642. E-mail: mage1@access.digex.net. Editorial Contact: Amin Sepehri. Estab. 1985. "Small independent publisher." Publishes hardcover originals. Averages 4 total titles, 1 fiction title each year.

Needs: "We publish *only* books on Iran and Persia and translations of Iranian fiction writers." Ethnic (Iran) fiction. Recently published *Sutra & Other Stories*, by Simin Daneshvar; and *My Uncle Napoleon*, by Iraj Pezeshkzad.

How to Contact: Query first. SASE. Reports in 3 months on queries. Simultaneous and electronic submissions OK.

Terms: Pays royalties. Publishes ms 6-9 months after acceptance. Writer's guidelines for SASE. Book catalog free.

Advice: "If it isn't related to Persia/Iran, forget it!"

✲THE MERCURY PRESS, (III, IV), 137 Birmingham St., Stratford, Ontario N5A 2T1 Canada. Editor: Beverley Daurio. Estab. 1978. "Literary publisher." Publishes paperback originals. Books: offset printing; perfect binding. Average print order: 1,500. First novel print order: 1,000. Published new writers within the last year. Averages 12 total titles, 5 fiction titles each year.

● Books published by The Mercury Press have received awards for design, and have been shortlisted for many content awards, including the Governor General's Award, the Arthur Ellis Award from the Crime Writers of Canada and the Commonwealth Writers Prize.

MARKET CONDITIONS are constantly changing! If you're still using this book and it is 1998 or later, buy the newest edition of *Novel & Short Story Writer's Market* at your favorite bookstore or order from Writer's Digest Books.

Needs: *Canadian writers only.* Looking for "excellent literary novels under 60,000 words, and for murder mysteries set in Canada." Publishes Midnight Originals (murder mysteries). Recently published *The Anastasia Connection*, by Veronica Ross (mystery); *The Mad Game*, by Gary Barwin and Stuart Ross (literary novel); and *This Dark Embrace*, by Paul Stuewe (mystery).

How to Contact: Accepts unsolicited mss if SASE is included. Submit complete ms with cover letter. Include estimated word count, bio (1 page) and list of publishing credits. SASE for return of ms. Agented fiction 1%. Reports in 2-4 months on mss. No simultaneous submissions.

Terms: Pays royalties of 10%. Sends galleys to author. Publishes ms 1 year after acceptance. Book catalog for SASE.

Advice: "Rewrite, rewrite, rewrite. Please have a look at our books or a catalog before submitting. Please note we only publish work by Canadians."

MID-LIST PRESS, (I, II), Jackson, Hart & Leslie, Inc., 4324-12th Ave. S., Minneapolis MN 55407-3218. (612)822-3733. Associate Publisher: Marianne Nora. Senior Editor: Lane Stiles. Estab. 1989. Nonprofit literary small press. Publishes hardcover originals and paperback originals and hardcover reprints. Books: acid-free paper; offset printing; perfect or Smyth-sewn binding. Average print order: 2,000. Plans 1 first novel this year. Averages 3 fiction titles each year. Rarely comments on rejected mss.

- The publisher's philosophy is to nurture "mid-list" titles—books of literary merit that may not fit "promotional pigeonholes"—especially by writers who were previously unpublished.

Needs: General fiction. No children's/juvenile, romance, young adult, religious. Recently published *Part of His Story*, by Alfred Corn (novel); *The Sincere Cafe: Stories*, by Leslee Becker (short fiction collection); and *The Latest Epistle of Jim*, by Roy Shepard (novel). Publishes First Series Award for the Novel and First Series Award for Short Fiction.

How to Contact: Accepts unsolicited mss. Query first for guidelines. Include #10 SASE. Send SASE for reply, return of ms or send a disposable copy of the ms. Agented fiction less than 10%. Reports in 1-3 weeks on queries; 1-3 months on mss. Simultaneous submissions OK.

Terms: Pays royalty of 40% minimum; 50% maximum of profits. Average advance: $1,000. Sends galleys to author. Publishes ms 6-12 months after acceptance. Writer's guidelines for #10 SASE.

Advice: "Take the time to read some of the books the publisher you're submitting to has put out. And remember that first impressions are very important. If a query, cover letter, or first page is sloppily or ineptly written, an editor has little hope for the manuscript as a whole."

MILKWEED EDITIONS, 430 First Ave. N., Suite 400, Minneapolis MN 55401. (612)332-3192. Publisher: Emilie Buchwald. Estab. 1984. Nonprofit publisher with the intention of transforming society through literature. Publishes hardcover and paperback originals. Books: book text quality—acid-free paper; offset printing; perfect or hardcover binding. Average print order: 4,000. First novel print order depends on book. Averages 14 total titles/year. Number of fiction titles "depends on manuscripts."

- Milkweed Editions books have received numerous awards, including Finalist, *LMP* Individual Achievement Award for Editor Emilie Buchwald, awards from the American Library Association, and several Pushcarts.

Needs: For adult readers: literary fiction, nonfiction, poetry, essays; for children (ages 8-12): fiction and biographies. Translations welcome for both audiences. No legends or folktales for children. No romance, mysteries, science fiction.

How to Contact: Send for guidelines first, then submit complete ms. Reports in 1 month on queries; 6 months on mss. Simultaneous submissions OK. "Send for guidelines. Must enclose SASE."

Terms: Authors are paid in royalties of 7%; offers negotiable advance; 10 author's copies. Sends galleys to author. Book catalog for $1.50 postage.

Advice: "Read good contemporary literary fiction, find your own voice, and persist. Familiarize yourself with our list before submitting."

‡MOUNTAIN STATE PRESS, (IV), 2300 MacCorkle Ave. SE, Charleston WV 25304. (304)357-4767. Fax: (304)357-4715. Contact: Kitty Lamb. Estab. 1978. "A small nonprofit press run by a Board of 13 members who volunteer their time. We specialize in books about West Virginia or by authors from West Virginia." Publishes paperback originals and reprints. Published new writers within the last year. Averages 3 total titles, 1-2 fiction titles each year. Often critiques or comments on rejected mss.

Needs: Family saga, historical (West Virginia), military/war, new age/mystic/spiritual, religious. Currently compiling an anthology. Recently published *Scribbling and More*, by Shirley Young Campbell (collection of columns); *Behold the Man*, by Jean Battlo (religious); and *Nadine and Vinson*, by Pat Call.

How to Contact: Accepts unsolicited mss. Query with outline/synopsis and 3 sample chapters or submit complete ms with cover letter. Include estimated word count and bio. Send SASE for reply, return of ms or send disposable copy of ms. Reports in 6 months on mss. Electronic submissions OK.

INSIDER REPORT

Milkweed Editions: looking for literature that can change the world

Milkweed Editions is idealistic. "Highly so," agrees publisher/editor and CEO Emilie Buchwald. After all, Milkweed is a nonprofit press whose mission is to make "a humane impact on society in the belief that literature is a transformative art uniquely able to convey the essential experiences of the human heart and spirit." It's a challenge, but one to which Buchwald enthusiastically rises. "When acquiring books, thinking about the relation a manuscript has to our mission statement helps in making a decision. For us, that impulse to use literature to make a humane impact on the world has very actively helped us in formulating the kind of books that we acquire and in creating a list of books that is the embodiment of that mission."

Emilie Buchwald

Buchwald believes writers themselves are idealistic and up to the task at hand. "There's so much that needs to be written about, brought to light, in order to make positive change. The fact that literary nonprofit presses like Milkweed exist is probably cause for hope." But Buchwald doesn't believe a writer need slavishly adhere to Milkweed's mission statement to be published by them. Milkweed's mission includes finding the very best writing by writers who "have something to say and the wherewithal to say it really well." Milkweed's books run the gamut from Moroccan stories to turn-of-the-century children's stories to books about teaching in China.

However, the competition is stiff at Milkweed, where several thousand good, if not great, manuscripts are received each year. The challenge is making your manuscript stick out. Buchwald suggests a great one-page letter of introduction about the work. The letter should explain your work succinctly, talk about the themes of the work rather than the plot, and talk about why your work is an important or vital or unusual contribution to literature. The letter should be just as carefully plotted as the manuscript. But don't send her plot summaries; she won't read them. "I'm so interested in the caliber of the writing, I want to see a complete manuscript," she says.

When assessing a manuscript, Buchwald looks for a character-driven plot with layering and some complexity. She also stresses the importance of capturing her attention in the first few pages of the manuscript. "The author can't wait until page 20 to write in a way that captivates a reader. If the first few pages don't

INSIDER REPORT, *continued*

intrigue me, I do tend to look further into the manuscript. But it strikes me as a poor policy to save the best for later on."

Before submitting to Milkweed, Buchwald advises writers to do some research. First, she says, send for Milkweed's guidelines to better understand "that rare fusion of style and substance we look for. Then, look at a few of our books at the library. Get a sense of what we publish. Understanding what we're looking for is the essential key to success in determining if yours is a 'Milkweed book.' "

If the writing is good, it will find its way into Buchwald's hands. Her first reader is instructed to pass on to Buchwald *any* good writing, no matter what the subject matter. The important thing to remember here is that Milkweed isn't looking for romance, mysteries or science fiction. If an agent who has worked with Milkweed in the past submits something and knows what Milkweed is looking for, that is always helpful. However, the lack of an agent has never prevented Buchwald from looking at or acquiring and publishing a good manuscript regardless of whether the writer has been published before.

Among the benefits of working with a small nonprofit press is the close relationship authors enjoy with the editors, says Buchwald. Milkweed views its authors as invaluable and both editor and author are intimately involved in every step of the editing process. "You will also work with a marketing person from the time the book is accepted, and every effort will be made to launch your book in the best possible way with ingenuity and imagination.

"One of the worst things a writer can do is pay attention to market trends. The writing should be true to what you, the writer, want to say. Don't examine fiction trends; by the time you figure out what the trend is and write something for it, it's already gone."

Buchwald admits that these are turbulent times for literary nonprofit publishers, a fact she attributes to the demise of small independent bookstores and to fewer distribution channels for small press books. However, book lovers are optimistic about the future. "We are hungry for good stories. The stories that we leave behind define us as a culture. There will always be a future for fiction writers."

Although Buchwald says, "talent, as in every field, plays a huge role," she points to purpose and perseverance as important keys in becoming a published author. "If you're writing because you can't help it, because you have a story to tell and you have the drive to pursue your work, if you are serious about the refining and rewriting process, the likelihood is that you will achieve some measure of success. Continue to trust in your ability. Don't keep that manuscript in your drawer. Send it out and be active in pursuing your goal."

—Erika Taylor

Terms: Pays royalties.
Advice: "Send your manuscript in and it will get read and answered."

MOYER BELL LIMITED, Kymbolde Way, Wakefield RI 02879. (401)789-0074. President/Fiction Editor: Jennifer Moyer. Estab. 1984. "Small publisher established to publish literature, poetry, reference and art books." Publishes hardcover and paperback originals and reprints. Books: Average print order 3,000. First novel print order: 3,000. Averages 18 total titles, 6 fiction titles each year. Sometimes comments on rejected mss.

Needs: Serious literary fiction. No genre fiction. Recently published *The Orchard on Fire*, by Shena Mackay.

How to Contact: Accepts unsolicited mss. Submit outline/synopsis and 2 sample chapters. SASE. Reports in 2 weeks on queries; 2 months on mss. Simultaneous and electronic submissions OK.

Terms: Pays royalties of 10% minimum. Average advance $2,500. Sends galleys to author. Publishes ms 9-18 months after acceptance. Book catalog free.

THE NAIAD PRESS, INC., (I, II, IV), P.O. Box 10543, Tallahassee FL 32302. (904)539-5965. Fax: (904)539-9731. Editorial Director: Barbara Grier. Estab. 1973. Books: 50 lb. offset paper; sheet-fed offset; perfect-bound. Average print order: 12,000. First novel print order: 12,000. Publishes 28 total titles each year.

● The Naiad Press is one of the most successful and well-known lesbian publishers. They have also produced eight of their books on audio cassette.

Needs: Lesbian fiction, all genres. Recently published *Love's Harvest*, by Peggy Herring; *Northern Blue*, by Tracey Richardson; *First Impressions*, by Kate Calloway; and *Out of the Night*, by Kris Bruyer.

How to Contact: Query first only. SASE. Reports in 3 weeks on queries; 3 months on mss. No simultaneous submissions.

Terms: Pays 15% royalties using a standard recovery contract. Occasionally pays 7½% royalties against cover price. "Seldom gives advances and has never seen a first novel worthy of one. Believes authors are investments in their own and the company's future—that the best author is the author who produces a book every 12-18 months forever and knows that there is a *home* for that book." Publishes ms 1-2 years after acceptance. Book catalog for legal-sized SASE.

Advice: "We publish lesbian fiction primarily and prefer honest work (i.e., positive, upbeat lesbian characters). Lesbian content must be accurate . . . a lot of earlier lesbian novels were less than honest. No breast beating or complaining. Our fiction titles are becoming increasingly *genre* fiction, which we encourage. Original fiction in paperback is our main field, and its popularity increases. We publish books BY, FOR AND ABOUT lesbians. We are not interested in books that are unrealistic. You know and we know what the real world of lesbian interest is like. Don't even try to fool us. Short, well-written books do best. Authors who want to succeed and will work to do so have the best shot."

THE NAUTICAL & AVIATION PUBLISHING CO. OF AMERICA INC., (IV), 8 W. Madison St., Baltimore MD 21201. (410)659-0220. E-mail: lkeddie@aol.com or 73244@compuserve.com or ssjb86a@prodigy.com. President: Jan Snouck-Hurgronje. Estab. 1979. Small publisher interested in quality military history and literature. Publishes hardcover originals and reprints. Averages 10 total titles, 1-4 fiction titles each year. Sometimes comments on rejected mss.

Needs: Military/war (especially military history and Civil War). Looks for "novels with a strong military history orientation." Recently published *Normandy*, by VADM William P. Mack (military fiction); *Straits of Messina*, by VADM William P. Mack (military fiction); and *The Captain*, by Jan De Hartog (military fiction).

How to Contact: Accepts unsolicited mss. Query first or submit complete mss with cover letter. SASE necessary for return of mss. Agented fiction "miniscule." Reports on queries in 2-3 weeks; on mss in 3 weeks. Simultaneous submissions OK.

Terms: Pays royalties of 14%. Advance negotiable. After acceptance publishes ms "as quickly as possible—next season." Book catalog free on request.

Advice: Publishing more fiction. Encourages first novelists. "We're interested in good writing—first novel or last novel. Keep it historical, put characters in a historical context. Professionalism counts. Know your subject. *Convince us.*"

NEW RIVERS PRESS, 420 N. Fifth St., Suite 910, Minneapolis MN 55401. Publisher: C.W. Trues-dale. Estab. 1968.

Needs: Contemporary, literary, experimental, translations. "No popular fantasy/romance. Nothing pious, polemical (unless other very good redeeming qualities). We are interested in only quality litera-ture and always have been (though our concentration in the past has been poetry)." Recently published *Heathens*, by David Haynes; and *American Fiction Volume 7*, by Ellan Davis and Michael White.

How to Contact: Query. SASE. Reports in 6 months on queries; within 6 months of query approval on mss. "No multiple submissions, please."

Terms: Minnesota Voices Series pays authors $500. Free book catalog.

Advice: "We read for quality, which experience has taught can be very eclectic and can come some-times from out of nowhere. We are interested in publishing short fiction (as well as poetry and transla-tions) because it is and has been a great indigenous American form and is almost completely ignored by the commercial houses. Find a *real* subject, something that belongs to you and not what you think or surmise that you should be doing by current standards and fads."

NEW VICTORIA PUBLISHERS, (II, IV), Box 27, Norwich VT 05055. (802)649-5297. E-mail: newvic@aol.com. Editor: Claudia Lamperti. Small, four-person operation. Publishes trade paperback originals. Averages 8-10 titles/year.
- Books published by New Victoria Publishers have been nominated for Lambda Literary Awards and the Vermont Book Publishers Special Merit Award. The anthology *Visions of a Feminist Future* is planned for July 1997.
Needs: Lesbian/feminist: adventure, fantasy, historical, humor, mystery (amateur sleuth), romance, science fiction (soft sociological), thriller, western. Looking for "strong feminist characters, also strong plot and action. We will consider most anything if it is well written and appeals to a lesbian/feminist audience; mostly mysteries." Publishes anthologies or special editions. Query for guidelines. Published *Bad Company* (6th Stoner McTavish Mystery), by Sarah Dreher; *Tales from the Dyke Side*, by Jorjet Harper (humor); and *Windswept*, by Magdalena Zschokke (novel).
How to Contact: Submit outline/synopsis and sample chapters. SASE. Reports in 2 weeks on queries; 1 month on mss.
Terms: Pays royalties of 10%.
Advice: "Read guidelines carefully. Pay attention to plot and character development."

✦NEWEST PUBLISHERS LTD., (IV), 10359 Whyte Ave., #310, Edmonton, Alberta T6E 1Z9 Canada. General Manager: Liz Grieve. Editorial Coordinator: Eva Radford. Estab. 1977. Publishes trade paperback originals. Published new writers within the last year. Averages 8 total titles, fiction and nonfiction. Rarely offers comments on rejected mss.
- NeWest received the Commonwealth Writers Prize for Best First Book in the Caribbean and Canada Region for *Icefields* by Thomas Wharton (1996) and for *Chorus of Mushrooms* by Hiromi Goto (1995).
Needs: Literary. "Our press is interested in western Canadian writing." Recently published *Diamond Grill*, by Fred Wah (bio fiction); *Icefields*, by Thomas Wharton (novel); and *Moon Honey*, by Suzette Mayr (novel). Publishes the Nunatak New Fiction Series.
How to Contact: Accepts unsolicited mss. Query first or submit outline/synopsis and 3 sample chapters. SASE necessary for return of ms. Reports in 2 months on queries; 4 months on mss.
Terms: Pays royalties of 10% minimum. Sends galleys to author. Publishes ms at least 1 year after acceptance. Book catalog for 9×12 SASE.
Advice: "*We publish western Canadian writers only or books about western Canada.* We are looking for excellent quality and originality."

‡NICETOWN, (II, III), 1460 N. 52nd St., Philadelphia PA 19131. (215)477-1435. Fax: (215)473-7575. E-mail: tedcam@aol.com. Imprints are Nicetown Audio Tapes. Editor: Theodore W. Wing. Estab. 1986. Publishes hardcover and paperback originals and paperback reprints. Averages 4 total titles each year. Often critiques or comments on rejected mss.
Needs: Horror, romance, science fiction, short story collections, thriller/espionage.
How to Contact: Accepts unsolicited mss. Query with outline/synopsis and 2 sample chapters. Include estimated word count, 1-page bio, Social Security number and list of publishing credits. Reports in 3 weeks on queries; 2 months on mss. Simultaneous and electronic submissions OK.
Terms: Offers negotiable advance; provides author's copies.

NIGHTSHADE PRESS, (II), Ward Hill, Troy ME 04987. (207)948-3427. Fax: (207)948-5088. E-mail: potatoeyes@uninet.net. Contact: Carolyn Page or Roy Zarucchi. Estab. 1988. "Fulltime small press publishing literary magazine, poetry chapbooks, 1 or 2 short story collections, plus 1 or 2 nonfiction projects per year. Short stories *only, no novels please.*" Publishes paperback originals. Books: 60 lb. paper; offset printing; saddle-stitched or perfect-bound; illustrations. Average print order: 400. Published new writers within the last year. Averages 6 total titles, 1 or more fiction titles each year, plus 19th century history collection. Sometimes comments on rejected mss.
Needs: Contemporary, feminist, humor/satire, literary, mainstream, regional. No religious, romance, preschool, juvenile, young adult, psychic/occult. Published *Two If By Sea*, by Edward M. Holmes; *Grass Creek Chronicles*, by Pat Carr; and *Nightshade Nightstand Short Story Reader*, foreward by Fred Chappell.
How to Contact: Accepts unsolicited mss—short stories only. "Willing to read agented material." Reports in 1 month on queries; 3-4 months on mss.
Terms: Pays 2 author's copies. Publishes ms about 1 year after acceptance. Writer's guidelines and book catalog for SASE. Individual contracts negotiated with authors.
Advice: "Would like to see more real humor; less gratuitous violence—the opposite of TV. We have overdosed on heavily dialected southern stories which treat country people with a mixture of ridicule and exaggeration. We prefer treatment of characterization which offers dignity and respect for folks who make do with little and who respect their environment. We are also interested in social criticism, in writers who take chances and who color outside the lines. We also invite experimental forms. Read us first. An investment of $5 may save the writer twice that in postage."

‡NRG ASSOCIATES, (II), Electronic Publishing Division, P.O. Box 6023, San Diego CA 92166. (619)658-0600. Fax: (619)642-7485. E-mail: n@adnc.com. Editor: Norman Rudenberg. Fiction Editor: Barbara Harris. Electronic publication. "We publish quality fiction worldwide." Estab. 1996.
Needs: Adventure, mainstream/contemporary, mystery/suspense, science fiction. "No horror or erotica." Publishes ms within 2 weeks after acceptance. Recently published work by J. Norman and Barbara Harris. Length: 60,000 words average; 45,000 words minimum; 100,000 words maximum.
How to Contact: Query first by e-mail or fax. Include 400-word bio and list of publications. Reports in 3 weeks on queries; 1 month on mss. Send SASE for reply, return of ms or send a disposable copy of ms. Simultaneous and electronic submissions OK.
Terms: Sends galleys to author. Not copyrighted.
Advice: "Looks for originality, quality writing and good plot. Internet exposure, which we offer, will highlight work to 50,000,000 users. Also, author may get feedback from readers. Avoid submitting unedited work."

OBELESK BOOKS, (I, II, IV), P.O. Box 1118, Elkton MD 21922-1118. E-mail: obelesk@netgsi.com. Publisher: S.G. Johnson. Editor: Gary Bowen. Estab. 1993. "Small but professional press." Publishes paperback originals and reprints. Books: 70 lb. paper; perfect binding. Published new writers within the last year. Averages 3 total titles, all fiction, each year. Sometimes comments on rejected mss.

  • Gary Bowen was nominated for Best Independent Press Editor for the World Fantasy Convention Awards.

Needs: Science fiction, fantasy, horror: adventure, erotica, ethnic/multicultural, feminist, gay, historical, humor/satire, lesbian, military/war and romance. "We are especially interested in historical, ethnic, and alternative science fiction/fantasy, horror for mature readers." Published *Green Echo: Ecological Science Fiction*, edited by Gary Bowen (anthology); *Winter of the Soul: Gay Vampire*, by Gary Bowen; and *Cyber Magick: Lesbian SF*, edited by G.R. Bowen.
How to Contact: Accepts unsolicited mss. Submit complete ms with cover letter. Include estimated word count, bio (50 words) and list of publishing credits. Always send SASE for reply; prefer disposable copy of ms. Reports in 1 month on queries; 2 weeks on mss. Reprint submissions OK.
Terms: Pays $10 flat fee plus author's copy. Sends galleys to author. Publishes ms 2-12 months after acceptance. Writer's guidelines for #10 SASE. Book catalog for #10 SASE. Sample copy for $6.
Advice: "We publish short fiction only, 5,000 words maximum. No novels or poetry. Know your subject thoroughly; our readers are educated and sophisticated. Immature, underdeveloped, and ignorant fiction will not fly here. Always review samples first, we have a unique editorial perspective. Do not submit blind. Fiction must feature women and/or sexual and ethnic, and differently-abled people. We are an alternative press, traditional anything is not what we publish. Push the envelope."

‡OHIO STATE UNIVERSITY PRESS, (II), Sandstone Books, 180 Pressey Hall, 1070 Carmack Rd., Columbus OH 43210-1002. (614)292-6930. Fax: (614)292-2065. Imprint: Sandstone Books. Editor-in-Chief and Assistant Director: Charlotte Dihoff. Estab. 1957. "Small-sized university press." Publishes hardcover, paperback originals and paperback reprints. Averages 25-30 total titles, 1-2 fiction titles/year. Member of Association of American University Presses (AAUP), International Association of Scholarly Publishers (IASP) and Association of American Publishers (AAP).
Needs: Ethnic/multicultural (general), feminist, historical (general), literary, short story collections. Recently published *Love Is the Crooked Thing*, by Lee K. Abbott; *Strangers in Paradise*, by Lee K. Abbott; and *Hamlet's Planets*, by Lynda Sexson; all short stories. Publishes *The Ohio Prize in Short Fiction*.
How to Contact: Accepts unsolicited mss. Query with outline/synopsis. Include bio and list of publishing credits. Send a disposable copy of ms. Reports in 3 weeks on queries; 3 months on mss. Electronic submissions (disk or modem) OK.
Terms: Pays royalties; individual arrangment with author. Sends galleys to author. Publishes ms 9 months after acceptance. Writer's guidelines for short fiction prize and book catalog free.

ONTARIO REVIEW PRESS, (III), 9 Honeybrook Dr., Princeton NJ 08540. Generally does not accept unsolicited ms. Query first. Send SASE with query.

♣ORCA BOOK PUBLISHERS LTD., (I, IV), P.O. Box 5626, Station B, Victoria, British Columbia V8R 6S4 Canada. (604)380-1229. Publisher: R.J. Tyrrell. Estab. 1984. "Regional publisher of West Coast-oriented titles." Publishes hardcover and paperback originals. Books: quality 60 lb. book stock paper; illustrations. Average print order: 3,000-5,000. First novel print order: 2,000-3,000. Plans 1-2 first novels this year. Averages 20-25 total titles, 1-2 fiction titles each year. Sometimes comments on rejected mss.
Needs: Contemporary, juvenile (5-9 years), literary, mainstream, young adult/teen (10-18 years). Looking for "contemporary fiction." No "romance, science fiction."

How to Contact: Query first, then submit outline/synopsis and 1 or 2 sample chapters. SASE. Agented fiction 20%. Reports in 2 weeks on queries; 1-2 months on mss. Publishes Canadian authors only.
Terms: Pays royalties of 10%; $500 average advance. Sends galleys to author. Publishes ms 6 months-1 year after acceptance. Writer's guidelines for SASE. Book catalog for 8½ × 11 SASE.
Advice: "We are looking to promote and publish Canadians."

OUR CHILD PRESS, 800 Maple Glen Lane, Wayne PA 19087. (610)964-0606. CEO: Carol Hallenbeck. Estab. 1984. Publishes hardcover and paperback originals and reprints. Plans 2 first novels this year. Plans 2 titles this year. Sometimes comments on rejected mss.
Needs: Adventure, contemporary, fantasy, juvenile (5-9 yrs.), preschool/picture book and young adult/teen (10-18 years). Especially interested in books on adoption or learning disabilities. Published *Don't Call Me Marda*, by Sheila Welch (juvenile); *Oliver—An Adoption Story*, by Lois Wickstrom; and *Blue Ridge*, by Jon Patrick Harper.
How to Contact: Does not accept unsolicited mss. Query first. Reports in 2 weeks on queries; 2 months on mss. Simultaneous submissions OK.
Terms: Pays royalties of 5% minimum. Publishes ms up to 6 months after acceptance. Book catalog free.

OUTRIDER PRESS, (I, II), 1004 E. Steger Rd., Suite C-3, Crete IL 60417. (708)672-6630. Fax: (708)672-6630. President: Phyllis Nelson. Fiction Editor: Whitney Scott. Estab. 1988. "Small operation." Publishes trade paper originals. Books: offset printing; perfect binding; average print order: under 5,000. Averages 2 total titles, 1 fiction title each year. Sometimes comments on rejected mss; *charges $2 double-spaced pages with 10-page minimum, prepaid and SASE for return*.
Needs: Feminist, gay, lesbian, literary, new age/mystic/spiritual, short story collection. No Christian/religious work. Publishes anthologies. "Our anthologies are contests with cash prizes in addition to publication. Therefore, we charge a $15 reading fee for poetry and fiction." Guidelines for SASE. Scheduled for 1997 publication: *Alternatives—An Anthology on Roads Not Taken, Other Highways, Other Lives*. Published *Dancing to the End of the Shining Bar*, by Whitney Scott; and *Prairie Hearts—Women View the Midwest*.
How to Contact: Accepts unsolicited mss with SASE. Submit complete ms with cover letter (with short stories). Include estimated word count and list of publishing credits. SASE for return of ms. Reports in 1 month on queries; 2 months on mss. Simultaneous submissions OK. Accepts electronic submissions (3.5 IBM compatible—WordPerfect 5.0, 5.1, 5.2 or 6.0 for DOS).
Terms: Payment depends on award money. Sends galleys to author.
Advice: "We have a need for short and super-short fiction with pace and flair and poetry with a sense of place. Give me fresh, honest writing that reflects craft, focus and sense of place; character-driven writing exploring the terrain of human hearts exploring the non-traditional. Follow our guidelines."

THE OVERLOOK PRESS, (II), 149 Wooster St., New York NY 10012. (212)477-7162. Estab. 1972. Small-staffed, fulltime operation. Publishes hardcover and paperback originals and reprints. Averages 30 total titles, 7 fiction titles each year. Occasionally critiques rejected mss.
Needs: Fantasy, juvenile (contemporary, fantasy, historical), literary, psychic/supernatural/occult, regional (Hudson Valley), science fiction, translations. No romance or horror. No short story collections. Recently published *The Gods Are Thirsty*, by Tanith Lee (historical novel); *Footsucker*, by Geoff Nicholson (dark satire); *The Photographer's Sweethearts*, by Diana Hartog (literary).
How to Contact: Query first or submit outline/synopsis. SASE. Allow up to 6 months for reports on queries. Simultaneous submissions OK.
Terms: Vary.

‡P&K STARK PRODUCTIONS, INC., (II), 17125C W. Bluemound Rd., Suite 171, Brookfield WI 53005-0949. Fax: (414)821-1414. President: Paul Stamas. Estab 1994. "Small press in fiction." Publishes paperback originals. Books: bond paper; perfect binding; illustrations. Average print order 1,000. First novel print order: 1,000. Plans 1-2 first novels this year. Averages 1-2 fiction titles/year.
Needs: Comics/graphic novels, fantasy, mystery/suspense, romance (futuristic/time travel, gothic, historical, romantic suspense), science fiction, thriller/espionage.
How to Contact: Does not accept or return unsolicited mss. Query first. Include bio. SASE for reply.

PAPIER-MACHE PRESS, (II), 135 Aviation Way, #14, Watsonville CA 95076. (408)763-1420. Editor/Publisher: Sandra Martz. Acquisitions Editor: Shirley Coe. Estab. 1984. "Small women's press." Publishes anthologies, novels, short story. Books: 60-70 lb. offset paper; perfect-bound or case-bound. Average print order: 6,000-10,000. Publishes 6-10 total titles/year.
● Papier-Mache Press publishes a number of well-received themed anthologies. Their anthology, *I Am Becoming the Woman I've Wanted*, received a 1995 American Book Award. *Late Summer Break*, by Ann Knox was a PMA Benjamin Franklin Award Finalist.

Needs: Contemporary, feminist, short story collections, women's. Published *Late Summer Break*, by Ann Knox; and *Creek Walk and Other Stories*, by Molly Giles. Published new writers within the last year.

How to Contact: Query first. SASE. Reports in 2 months on queries; 6 months on mss. Simultaneous and photocopied submissions OK. Accepts computer printouts.

Terms: Standard royalty agreements and complimentary copy.

Advice: "Absolutely essential to query first with only sample chapters. Send complete manuscript upon request only. Please note on the query whether it's a simultaneous submission."

PAPYRUS PUBLISHERS & LETTERBOX LITERARY SERVICE, (II), P.O. Box 27383, Las Vegas NV 89126. (702)256-3838. Editor-in-Chief: Geoffrey Hutchison-Cleaves. Fiction Editor: Jessie Rosé. Estab. London 1946; USA 1982. Mid-size independent press. Publishes hardcover originals. Audio books; average print order 2,500. Averages 3 total titles each year.

Needs: "No erotica, gay, feminist, children's, spiritual, lesbian, political. Published *Is Forever Too Long?*, by Heather Latimer (romantic fiction); *Violet*, by Joan Griffith; and *Louis Wain—King of the Cat Artists 1860-1939*, by Heather Latimer (dramatized biography).

How to Contact: "Not accepting right now." Fully stocked.

Terms: Pays royalties of 10% minimum. Advance varies. Publishes ms 1 year after acceptance.

PATH PRESS, INC., (II), 53 W. Jackson, Suite 724, Chicago IL 60604. (312)663-0167. Fax: (312)663-5318. Editorial Director: Herman C. Gilbert. "Small independent publisher which specializes in books by, for and about African-Americans and Third World Peoples." Published new writers within the last year. Averages 6 total titles, 3 fiction titles each year. Occasionally critiques rejected mss.

Needs: Ethnic, historical, sports, and short story collections. Needs for novels include "black or minority-oriented novels of any genre, style or subject." Published *The Negotiations*, by Herman C. Gilbert (political thriller); and *Monroe Pinckney, My Father*, by Claudette Pinckney-Harris.

How to Contact: Accepts unsolicited mss. Query first or submit synopsis and 5 sample chapters with SASE. Reports in 2 months on queries; 4 months on mss. Simultaneous submissions OK.

Terms: Pays in royalties.

Advice: "Deal honestly with your subject matter and with your characters. Dig deeply into the motivations of your characters, regardless how painful it might be to you personally."

PEACHTREE PUBLISHERS, LTD., (IV), 494 Armour Circle NE, Atlanta GA 30324. (404)876-8761. President: Margaret Quinlin. Estab. 1977. Small, independent publisher specializing in general interest publications, particularly of Southern origin. Publishes hardcover and paperback originals and hardcover reprints. Averages 12-15 total titles, 1-2 fiction titles each year. Average first novel print run 5,000-8,000.

● Peachtree recently put a stronger emphasis on books for children and young adults.

Needs: Contemporary, literary, mainstream, regional. "We are primarily seeking Southern fiction: Southern themes, characters, and/or locales, and children's books." No science fiction/fantasy, horror, religious, romance, historical or mystery/suspense. Recently published *Over What Hill?* and *Out to Pasture*, by Effie Wilder.

How to Contact: Accepts unsolicited mss. Query, submit outline/synopsis and 50 pages, or submit complete ms with SASE. Reports in 1 month on queries; 3 months on mss. Simultaneous submissions OK.

Terms: Pays in royalties. Sends galleys to author. Free writer's guidelines. Book catalog for 2 first-class stamps.

Advice: "We encourage original efforts in first novels."

✦PEMMICAN PUBLICATIONS, (II, IV), 1635 Burrows Ave., Unit 2, Winnipeg, Manitoba R2X 0T1 Canada. (204)589-6346. Fax: (204)589-2063. Managing Editor: Sue Maclean. Estab. 1980. Metis and Aboriginal children's books, some adult. Publishes paperback originals. Books: stapled binding and perfect-bound; 4-color illustrations. Average print order: 2,500. First novel print order: 1,000. Published new writers within the last year. Averages 9 total titles each year.

Needs: Children's/juvenile (American Indian, easy-to-read, preschool/picture book); ethnic/multicultural (Native American). Publishes the Builders of Canada series.

How to Contact: Accepts unsolicited mss. Submit complete ms with cover letter. Send SASE (or IRC) for reply, return of ms or send a disposable copy of ms. Reports in 1 year. Simultaneous and disk submissions OK.

Terms: Pays royalties of 5% minimum; 10% maximum. Average advance: $350. Provides 10 author's copies.

‡THE PERMANENT PRESS/SECOND CHANCE PRESS, (I,II), Second Chance Press, 4170 Noyac Rd., Sag Harbor NY 11963. (516)725-1101. Editor: Judith Shepard. Estab. 1978. "The Permanent Press is a small press specializing in new literary fiction. Books that are at least 20 years old may be submitted for reprint by Second Chance Press." Publishes hardcover originals and reprints. First novel print order; 1,000-2,000. Published new writers within the last year. Plans 10 first novels this year. Averages 12-20 total titles, all fiction, each year.

Needs: Erotica, literary, mainstream/contemporary. Recently published *Fat Lightning*, by Howard Owen; *Lead Us Not Into Penn Station*, by Bruce Ducker; and *Homebodies*, by Joan Schweighardt.

How to Contact: Does not accept unsolicited mss. Query with outline/synopsis and first chapter. Include list of publishing credits. SASE. Agented fiction 50%. Reports in 6 weeks on queries; 3 months on mss. Simultaneous submissions OK.

Terms: Pays royalties of 10% minimum; 20% maximum. Average advance: $1,000. Sends galleys to author. Publishes ms 1-2 years after acceptance. Writers guidelines for #10 SASE. Book catalog for 7 first-class stamps.

Advice: "We are looking for material of high literary quality; material that is original and stimulating with an authentic point of view and a unique voice. Send the first 20-30 pages. Forget lengthy outlines and sales pitches. Let the writing speak for itself."

PERMEABLE PRESS, (II), 47 Noe St., #4, San Francisco CA 94114-1017. (415)648-2175. E-mail: bcclark@igc.apc.org. Imprints: Puck; Pocket Rockets™. Editor: Brian Clark. Estab. 1984. "Small literary press." Publishes hardcover and paperback originals and paperback reprints. Books: 60 lb. paper; offset printing; perfect-bound; illustrations. Average print order: 3,500. Published new writers within the last year. Plans 1 first novel this year. Averages 3 total titles, all fiction, each year. Sometimes comments on rejected mss.

- Permeable Press has been a Finalist for the Philip K. Dick award for *Tonguing the Zeitgeist*, by Lance Olsen, and a Finalist for the Lambda Literary Award for *Three-Hand Jax*, by Staszek. Permeable plans two anthologies for 1997: *Shock Waves: New Fiction* and *Puck: The Irrepressible Reader.*

Needs: Erotica, experimental, feminist, gay, lesbian, literary, psychic/supernatural/occult, science fiction (hard science, soft sociological), short story collections. Looking for "cyberpunk; conspiracy; dangerous or edgy fiction. Should be challenging to read." No romance. Recently published *Time Famine*, by Lance Olsen (science fiction novel); *Toxic Shock Syndrom*, by Carolina Starr (conspiracy thriller); *Flyscraper*, by Mark Romyn (horror).

How to Contact: Query first by letter or e-mail or submit outline/synopsis and 3 sample chapters. SASE. Reports in 4-6 weeks on queries; 3 months on mss.

Terms: Pays royalties of 5-20%. Author's copies vary. Honorarium depends on grant/award money. Sends galleys to author. Writer's guidelines and book catalog for 9 × 12 SAE and 2 first-class stamps.

Advice: "You should be familiar with the Press—our novels and our magazine—before submitting. Keep in mind that we want fiction that bites the reader in the neocortex and sends an illuminating shock down the spine. Permeable is not a genre publisher. We are extremely picky and are only interested in seeing manuscripts of very high quality."

PIEPER PUBLISHING, (I, II), P.O. Box 9136, Virginia Beach VA 23450-9136. Publisher/Editor: Ron Pieper. Estab. 1995. "We are a small company offering a personal touch on an international basis." Publishes hardcover and paperback originals and reprints. Plans to publish 2-5 books/year, including several anthologies. Often comments on rejected mss.

Needs: Adventure, children's/juvenile, erotica, ethnic/multicultural, family saga, fantasy, feminist, gay, historical, horror, humor/satire, lesbian, literary, mainstream/contemporary, military/war, mystery/suspense, psychic/supernatural, regional, romance, science fiction, short story collections, thriller/espionage, translations, western, young adult/teen. "We warmly entertain all submissions. During the next year, we are preparing anthologies of short stories and poems among other publishing efforts."

How to Contact: Query with outline/synopsis and available sample chapters or submit complete ms with cover letter. "In the cover letter, discuss your manuscript's potential and other issues pertinent to yourself." Reports in 1 week on queries; 1-2 months on novel mss; 1-2 weeks on short stories and poems. Simultaneous submissions OK. Accepts disk submissions (Microsoft Works or WordPerfect).

Terms: Pays royalties of 7% minimum; 12% maximum. "If your manuscript becomes part of an anthology, payment is prorated on the size of the publication." Sends galleys to author. "We encourage author involvement in finalizing the product to ensure author satisfaction." Publishes ms 6 months after acceptance. Writer's guidelines for SASE.

Advice: "Fiction manuscripts should present a situation or environment which is imaginative, yet so enticing it's believable. Go beyond that which is already on the book shelf; otherwise you do nothing more than offer readers what they already have."

CHECK THE CATEGORY INDEXES, located at the back of the book, for publishers interested in specific fiction subjects.

PINEAPPLE PRESS, (II, IV), P.O. Box 3899, Sarasota FL 34230-3899. (941)952-1085. Executive Editor: June Cussen. Estab. 1982. Small independent trade publisher. Publishes hardcover and paperback originals and paperback reprints. Books: quality paper; offset printing; Smyth-sewn or perfect-bound; illustrations occasionally. Average print order: 5,000. First novel print order: 2,000-5,000. Published new writers within the last year. Averages 20 total titles each year.
Needs: "In 1997 we prefer to see only Florida-related novels." Published two "Cracker Westerns" *Death in Bloodhound Red*, by Virginia Lanier; and *Guns of the Palmetto Plains*, by Rick Tonyan.
How to Contact: Prefers query, outline or one-page synopsis with sample chapters (including the first) and SASE. Then if requested, submit complete ms with SASE. Reports in 2 months. Simultaneous submissions OK.
Terms: Pays royalties of 7½-15%. Advance is not usually offered. "Basically, it is an individual agreement with each author depending on the book." Sends galleys to author. Book catalog sent if label and $1.01 postage enclosed.
Advice: "Quality first novels will be published, though we usually only do one or two novels per year. We regard the author/editor relationship as a trusting relationship with communication open both ways. Learn all you can about the publishing process and about how to promote your book once it is published."

PIPPIN PRESS, 229 E. 85th Street, Gracie Station Box 1347, New York NY 10028. (212)288-4920. Publisher: Barbara Francis. Estab. 1987. "Small, independent children's book company, formed by the former editor-in-chief of Prentice Hall's juvenile book division." Publishes hardcover originals. Books: 135-150 GSM offset-semi-matte paper (for picture books); offset, sheet-fed printing; Smythe-sewn binding; full color, black and white line illustrations and half tone, b&w and full color photographs. Averages 5-6 titles each year. Sometimes comments on rejected mss.
Needs: Juvenile only (5-9 yrs. including animal, easy-to-read, fantasy, science, humorous, spy/adventure). "I am interested in humorous novels for children of about 7-12 and in picture books with the focus on humor. Also interested in autobiographical novels for 8-12 year olds and selected historical fiction for the same age group."
How to Contact: No unsolicited mss. Query first. SASE. Reports in 2-3 weeks on queries. Simultaneous submissions OK.
Terms: Pays royalties. Sends galleys to author. Publication time after ms is accepted "depends on the amount of revision required, type of illustration, etc."

THE POST-APOLLO PRESS, (I, II), 35 Marie St., Sausalito CA 94965. (415)332-1458. Fax: (415)332-8045. E-mail: tpapress@dnai.com. Publisher: Simone Fattal. Estab. 1982. Publishes paperback originals. Book: acid-free paper; lithography printing; perfect-bound. Average print order: 2,000. First novel print order: 2,000. Published new writers within the last year. Averages 2 total titles, 1 fiction title each year. Sometimes comments on rejected mss.
Needs: Feminist, lesbian, literary, spiritual and translations. No juvenile, horror, sports or romance. "Many of our books are first translations into English." Recently published *Josef Is Dying*, by Ulla Berkéwicz (novel); and *Sitt Marie Rose*, by Etel Adnan (novel).
How to Contact: Send query or sample chapters with SASE. Reports in 3 months.
Terms: Pays royalties of 6½% minimum or by individual arrangement. Sends galleys to author. Publishes ms 1½ years after acceptance. Book catalog free.

✦**PRAIRIE JOURNAL PRESS, (I, IV)**, Prairie Journal Trust, P.O. Box 61203, Brentwood Postal Services, Calgary, Alberta T2L 2K6 Canada. Estab. 1983. Small-press, noncommercial literary publisher. Publishes paperback originals. Books: bond paper; offset printing; stapled binding; b&w line drawings. Averages 2 total titles or anthologies each year. Occasionally critiques or comments on rejected mss if requested.
Needs: Literary, short stories. No romance, horror, pulp, erotica, magazine type, children's, adventure, formula, western. Published *Prairie Journal Fiction*, *Prairie Journal Fiction II* (anthologies of short stories); *Solstice* (short fiction on the theme of aging); and *Prairie Journal Prose*.
How to Contact: Accepts unsolicited mss. Query first and send Canadian postage or IRCs and $6 for sample copy, then submit 1-2 stories with SAE and IRCs. Reports in 6 months or sooner.
Terms: Pays 1 author's copy; honorarium depends on grant/award provided by the government or private/corporate donations. Sends galleys to author. Book catalog free on request to institutions; SAE with IRC for individuals. "No U.S. stamps!"
Advice: "We wish we had the means to promote more new writers. We often are seeking theme-related stories. We look for something different each time and try not to repeat types of stories if possible."

✦**THE PRAIRIE PUBLISHING COMPANY**, Box 2997, Winnipeg, Manitoba R3C 4B5 Canada. (204)885-6496. Publisher: Ralph Watkins. Estab. 1969. Buys juvenile mss with illustrations. Books: 60 lb. high-bulk paper; offset printing; perfect-bound; line-drawings. Average print order: 2,000. First novel print order: 2,000.

Needs: Open. Published: *The Homeplace*, (historical novel); *My Name is Marie Anne Gaboury*, (first French-Canadian woman in the Northwest); and *The Tale of Jonathan Thimblemouse*. Published work by previously unpublished writers within the last year.

How to Contact: Query with SASE or IRC. No simultaneous submissions. Reports in 1 month on queries, 6 weeks on mss. Publishes ms 4-6 months after acceptance. Free book catalog.

Terms: Pays 10% in royalties. No advance.

Advice: "We work on a manuscript with the intensity of a Max Perkins. A clean, well-prepared manuscript can go a long way toward making an editor's job easier. On the other hand, the author should not attempt to anticipate the format of the book, which is a decision for the publisher to make. In order to succeed in today's market, the story must be tight, well written and to the point. Do not be discouraged by rejections."

PREP PUBLISHING, (I, II), PREP Inc., 1110½ Hay St., Fayetteville NC 28305. (910)483-6611. Editor: Anne McKinney. Estab. 1994. Publishing division affiliated with a 14-year-old company. Publishes hardcover and paperback originals. Books: acid free paper; offset printing; perfect binding; illustrations. Average print order: 5,000. First novel print order: 5,000. Averages up to 15 total titles, 10 fiction titles each year. Often comments on rejected mss.

Needs: Children's/juvenile (adventure, mystery), religious/inspirational, romance (contemporary, romantic suspense), thriller/espionage, young adult (adventure, mystery/suspense, romance, sports). "Spiritual/inspirational novels are most welcome." Published *Second Time Around* and *Back in Time*, by Patty Sleem (mysteries); and *About Martha*, by C.B. Guforth (romance).

How to Contact: Send SASE for author's guidelines and current catalog.

Terms: Pays negotiable royalties. Advance is negotiable. Individual arrangement with author depending on the book. Sends galleys to author. Publishes ms 1-2 years after acceptance.

Advice: "Rewrite and edit carefully before sending manuscript. We look for quality fiction that will appeal to future generations."

✦PRESS GANG PUBLISHERS, (II, IV), 225 E. 17 Ave., Suite 101, Vancouver, British Columbia V5V 1A6 Canada. (604)876-7787. Fax: (604)876-7892. Estab. 1974. Feminist press, 3 full-time staff. Publishes paperback originals and reprints. Books: paperback; offset printing; perfect-bound. Average print order: 3,500. First novel print order: 2,000.

● Press Gang Publishers received the 1995 Small Press Award from the Lambda Literary Awards for *Her Tongue on My Theory*, by Kiss & Tell.

Needs: Looking for "feminist, mystery/suspense, short stories." Also accepts contemporary, erotica, ethnic (native women especially), humor/satire, lesbian, literary. No children's/young adult/teen. Priority given to Canadian writers. Published *Choral*, by Karen McLaughlin (novel); *Bellydancer*, by SKY Lee; and *Her Head a Village*, by Makeda Silvera (stories).

How to Contact: Accepts unsolicited mss. Query first. SASE. Reports in 2 months on queries; 3-4 months on mss. Simultaneous submissions OK.

Terms: Pays 8-10% royalties. Sends galleys to author. Book catalog free on request.

PUCKERBRUSH PRESS, (I,II), 76 Main St., Orono ME 04473. (207)581-3832. Publisher/Editor: Constance Hunting. Estab. 1971. Small, independent press. Publishes paperback originals. Books: laser printing; perfect-bound; sometimes illustrations. Average print order: 1,000. Published new writers within the last year. Averages 3 total titles each year. Sometimes comments on rejected mss. *If detailed comment, $500.*

Needs: Contemporary, experimental, literary, high-quality work. Published *An Old Pub Near the Angel*, by James Kelman (short stories); *A Stranger Here, Myself*, by Tema Nason (female stories); and *Dorando*, by James Boswell (novel).

How to Contact: Accepts unsolicited mss. Submit complete ms with cover letter. SASE. Reports in 2 weeks on queries; 2 months on mss.

Terms: Pays royalties of 10%; 20 author's copies. Sends galleys to author. Publishes ms usually 1 year after acceptance. Writer's guidelines for #10 SASE. "I have a book list and flyers."

Advice: "Write for yourself."

PURPLE FINCH PRESS, (V), P.O. Box 758, Dewitt NY 13214. (315)445-8087. Publisher: Mrs. Nancy Benson. Estab. 1992. One-person operation. Publishes hardcover and paperback originals. Books: 60-70 lb. paper; from laser printer to commercial printer; perfect or hardcover bound; illustrations. Average print order: 250-500. First novel print order: 500. Plans 1 first novel this year. Averages 1 total fiction title each year.

Needs: Children's/juvenile (adventure, mystery), literary, short story collections. "No erotica, violence."

How to Contact: *Does not accept unsolicited mss.* Query first. Include estimated word count and list of publishing credits. Send SASE for reply.

Terms: Pays royalties of 6% minimum; 10% maximum. Provides 20 author's copies. Sends galleys to author. Publishes ms 1-2 years after acceptance ("could be less"). Writer's guidelines for #10 SASE. Book catalog for #10 SASE.

Advice: "We would like to see more literary poetry, stories—less vulgar language, curse words, erotica and violence."

♣QUARRY PRESS, (I,II), Box 1061, Kingston, Ontario, K7L 4Y5 Canada. (613)548-8429. Estab. 1965. Small independent publisher with plans to expand. Publishes paperback originals. Books: 1 lb. paper offset sheet; perfect-bound; illustrations. Average print order: 1,200. First novel print order: 1,200. Published new writers within the past year. Plans 1 first novel this year. Averages 20 total titles, 4 fiction titles each year. Sometimes comments on rejected mss.

Needs: Children's folklore and poetry, experimental, feminist, historical, literary, short story collections. Published *Ritual Slaughter,* by Sharon Drache; *Engaged Elsewhere,* edited by Kent Thompson (includes work by Mavis Gallant, Margaret Laurence, Dougles Glover, Ray Smitz, Keath Fraser and others); published fiction by previously unpublished writers within the last year.

How to Contact: Query first. SASE for query and ms. Reports in 4 months. Simultaneous submissions OK.

Terms: Pays royalties of 7-10%. Advance: negotiable. Provides 5-10 author's copies. Sends galleys to author. Publishes ms 6-8 months after acceptance. Book catalog free on request.

Advice: "Publishing more fiction than in the past. Encourages first novelists. Canadian authors only."

♣RAGWEED PRESS INC./gynergy books, (I), P.O. Box 2023, Charlottetown, Prince Edward Island C1A 7N7 Canada. (902)566-5750. Fax: (902)566-4473. E-mail: editor@ragweed.com. Contact: Managing Editor. Estab. 1980. "Independent Canadian-owned feminist press." Publishes paperback originals. Books: 60 lb. paper; perfect binding. Average print order: 3,000. Averages 12 total titles, 3 fiction titles each year.

• Plans *Thin Lines of Communication*, an anthology of experiences with anorexia or bulimia; writers submit to Anthology Editor; editor selects stories. "We do accept submissions to anthologies from U.S. writers."

Needs: *Canadian-authors only.* Children's/juvenile (adventure, picture book, girl-positive), feminist, lesbian, young adult. Recently published *Last Resort*, by Jackie Manthorne (lesbian mystery); *The Chinese Puzzle*, by Chrystine Brouillet (young adult); *The Secret Under the Whirlpool*, by Elaine Breault Hammond (young adult). Published new writers within the last year.

How to Contact: Accepts unsolicited mss with cover letter, brief bio, list of publishing credits. SASE for reply. Reports in 4 months. Simultaneous submissions OK.

Terms: Pays royalties of 10%; offers negotiable advance. Provides 5 author's copies. Sends galleys to author. Publishes ms 1-2 years after acceptance. Writer's guidelines for #10 SASE. Book catalog for large SAE and 2 first-class stamps.

Advice: "Specialized market—lesbian novels especially. Be brief, give résumé."

♣RED DEER COLLEGE PRESS, (II, IV), Box 5005, Red Deer, Alberta T4N 5H5 Canada. (403)342-3321. Managing Editor: Dennis Johnson. Estab. 1975. Publishes adult and young adult hardcover and paperback originals. Books: offset paper; offset printing; hardcover/perfect-bound. Average print order: 1,000-4,000. First novel print order: 2,500. Averages 14-16 total titles, 2 fiction titles each year. Sometimes critiques or comments on rejected mss.

• Red Deer College Press has received honors and awards from the Alberta Book Publishers Association, Canadian Children's Book Centre and the Writers Guild of Alberta.

Needs: Contemporary, experimental, literary, short story collections, young adult. No romance, science fiction. Published anthologies under Roundup Books imprint focusing on stories/poetry of the Canadian and American West. Published *100 Years of Cowboy Stories*, by Ted Stone; *Beneath the Faceless Mountain*, by Roberta Rees; and *Yellow Pages*, by Nicole Markotic.

How to Contact: *Canadian authors only.* Does not accept unsolicited mss. Query first or submit outline/synopsis and 2 sample chapters. SASE. Agented fiction 10%. Reports in 3 months on queries; in 6 months on mss. Simultaneous submissions OK. Final mss must be submitted on Mac disk in MS Word.

Terms: Pays royalties of 8-10%. Advance is negotiable. Sends galleys to author. Publishes ms 1 year after acceptance. Book catalog for 9×12 SASE.

⬥ **THE MAPLE LEAF** symbol before a listing indicates a Canadian publisher, magazine, conference or contest.

Advice: "We tend to look for authors with a proven track record (either published books or widely published in established magazines or journals) and for manuscripts with regional themes and/or a distinctive voice. We publish Canadian authors almost exclusively."

RIO GRANDE PRESS, (I), P.O. Box 71745, Las Vegas NV 89170. Imprints include *Se La Vie Writer's Journal*. Publisher: Rosalie Avara. Estab. 1989. "One-person operation on a half-time basis." Publishes paperback originals. Books: offset printing; saddle-stitched binding. Average print order: 100. Published new writers within the last year. Averages 10 total titles, 2 fiction titles each year. Sometimes comments on rejected mss.
  • The publisher also sponsors a short short story contest quarterly.
Needs: Adventure, contemporary, ethnic, family saga, fantasy, humor/satire, literary, mystery/suspense (amateur sleuth, private eye, romantic suspense), regional. Looking for "general interest, slice of life stories; good, clean, wholesome stories about everyday people. No sex, nor porn, no science fiction (although I may consider flights of fantasy, daydreams, etc.), no religious. Any subject within the 'wholesome' limits. No experimental styles, just good conventional plot, characters, dialogue." Published *The Story Shop* I-V (short story anthologies; 13 stories by individual authors).
How to Contact: Submit story after August 1. SASE. Reports in 2 weeks on queries or acceptance.
Terms: Pays, if contest is involved, up to $15 plus $5 on honorable mentions.
Advice: "I enjoy working with writers new to fiction, especially when I see that they have really worked hard on their craft, i.e., cutting out all unnecessary words, using action dialogue, interesting descriptive scenes, thought-out plots and well-rounded characters that are believable. Please read listing carefully noting what type and subject of fiction is desired."

RISING TIDE PRESS, (II), 5 Kivy St., Huntington Station NY 11746. (516)427-1289. E-mail: rtpress@aol.com. Editor: Lee Boojamra. Estab. 1988. "Independent women's press, publishing lesbian nonfiction and fiction—novels only—no short stories." Publishes paperback trade originals. Books: 60 lb. vellum paper; sheet fed and/or web printing; perfect-bound. Average print order: 5,000. First novel print order: 4,000-6,000. Plans 10 first novels this year. Averages 12 total titles. Comments on rejected mss.
  • Rising Tide plans two anthologies: *Women Cruising Women* (short stories) and *How I Met My True Love* (lesbian romance). Deadline is June 1, 1997. SASE for guidelines.
Needs: Lesbian adventure, contemporary, erotica, fantasy, feminist, romance, science fiction, suspense/mystery, western. Looking for romance and mystery. "Minimal heterosexual content." Recently published *Emerald City Blues*, by Joan Stewart (literary); *Rough Justice*, by Clairé Youmans (mystery); and *Playing for Keeps*, by Stevie Rios (romance). Developing a dark fantasy and erotica line.
How to Contact: Accepts unsolicited mss with SASE. Reports in 1 week on queries; 2-3 months on mss.
Terms: Pays 10-15% royalties. "*We will assist writers who wish to self-publish for a nominal fee.*" Sends galleys to author. Publishes ms 6-18 months after acceptance. Writer's guidelines for #10 SASE.
Advice: "Our greatest challenge is finding quality manuscripts that are well plotted and not predictable, with well-developed, memorable characters. Read your novel before you send it to any publisher."

✿RONSDALE PRESS/CACANADADADA, (II, IV), 3350 W. 21 Ave., Vancouver, British Columbia V6S 1G7 Canada. (604)738-1195. President: Ronald B. Hatch. Estab. 1988. Publishes paperback originals. Books: 60 lb. paper; photo offset printing; perfect binding. Average print order: 1,000. First novel print order: 1,000. Plans 2 first novels this year. Averages 3 fiction titles each year. Sometimes comments on rejected mss.
Needs: Experimental and literary. Recently published *The Seventh Circle*, by Benet Davetian (short stories); *Home from the Party*, by Robert Maclean (mystery); *Long Long Ago*, by Robin Skelton (children's).
How to Contact: *Canadian authors only.* Accepts unsolicited mss. Submit outline/synopsis and 2 sample chapters (60-100 pgs.). SASE. Short story collections must have some magazine publication. Reports in 2 weeks on queries; 2 months on mss.
Terms: Pays royalties of 10%. Provides author's copies. Sends galleys to author. Publishes ms 6 months after acceptance.
Advice: "We publish both fiction and poetry. Authors *must* be Canadian."

SENDING TO A COUNTRY other than your own? Be sure to send International Reply Coupons instead of stamps for replies or return of your manuscript.

‡RUBENESQUE ROMANCES, (I, IV), P.O. Box 534, Tarrytown NY 10591-0534. (914)345-7485. Publisher: Joanne K. Morse. Estab. 1995. "Small, independent publisher." Publishes paperback originals. Books: copy paper; perfect-bound. Published new writers within the last year. Plans 10 novels this year. Averages 12 total titles, all fiction, each year. Always critiques or comments on rejected mss.
Needs: Romance (contemporary, futuristic/time travel, gothic, historical, regency/period, romantic suspense, western). "All light romance for and about large-sized heroines. No alternative lifestyles or pornography." Plans anthology. Recently published *Love in the Pyramid*, by Abigail Sommers; *Moon Love*, by Cynthia MacGregor; and *So Much for Illusion*, by Deborah McClatchey (all light romances).
How to Contact: Accepts unsolicited mss. Send SASE for guidelines first, then query. Include estimated word count and 100-word bio with submissions. "No manuscripts over 50,000 words." Send SASE for reply to query or return of ms. Reports in 1 month on queries; 2 months on mss. Disk submissions OK (prefers MAC, DOS-based OK).
Terms: Pays royalties of 15% maximum. Publishes ms 2-3 months after acceptance. Writer's guidelines and book catalog for #10 SASE.
Advice: "Order our guidelines and follow them. We work closely with new authors, offering a unique opportunity to the novice writer. If your idea is good but your writing is poor, we'll help you redo your manuscript."

‡♣ST. AUGUSTINE SOCIETY PRESS, (I, IV), 68 Kingsway Crescent, Etobicoke, Ontario M8X 2R6 Canada. (416)239-1670. Editor: Frances Breckenridge. Estab. 1994. "We are a small press, independent of any church. We seek manuscripts which can expand the circle of light detailed by St. Augustine, either fiction or nonfiction." Publishes paperback originals. Average print order: 500 (depends on the type of final product). Averages 1 total title, variable number of fiction titles each year. Member of Toronto Small Press Group.
Needs: Literary, mainstream/contemporary. Recently published *Maledetti (The Forsaken)*, by Michael Gualtieri (novel).
How to Contact: Accepts unsolicited mss. Query with outline/synopsis and 2 sample chapters. Send SASE for reply, return of ms or send a disposable copy of ms. Reports in 3 weeks on queries. Simultaneous submissions OK.
Terms: Negotiable. Sends galleys to author. Publishes ms 6 months after acceptance. Free writer's guidelines.
Advice: "We welcome works by writers who have, through years of study, gained insights into the human condition. A book that is just a 'good read' is of no interest to us."

SAND RIVER PRESS, (I), 1319 14th St., Los Osos CA 93402. (805)543-3591. Fax: (805)543-7432. Editor: Bruce Miller. Estab. 1987. "Small press." Publishes paperback originals. Books: offset printing; b&w or color illustrations. Average print order: 3,000. First novel print order: 2,000. Averages 2-3 total titles, 1 fiction title each year. Sometimes comments on rejected mss.
Needs: Native American, lesbian, literary, regional (west).
How to Contact: Accepts unsolicited mss. Submit outline/synopsis and 3 sample chapters. Include list of publishing credits. SASE for return of ms or a disposable copy of the ms. Reports in 3 weeks on queries; 6 weeks on mss. Simultaneous submissions OK.
Terms: Pays royalties of 8% minimum; 15% maximum. Average advance: $500-1,000. Provides 10 author's copies. Sends galleys to author. Publishes ms 1 year after acceptance. Book catalog for SASE.

SANDPIPER PRESS, (V), Box 286, Brookings OR 97415. (503)469-5588. Owner: Marilyn Reed Riddle. Estab. 1979. One-person operation specializing in low-cost large-print 18 pt. books. Publishes paperback originals. Books: 70 lb. paper; saddle-stitched binding, perfect-bound; 84 pgs. maximum; leatherette cover; b&w sketches or photos. Average print order 2,000; no novels. Averages 1 title every 2 years. Occasionally comments on rejected mss.
Needs: Unusual quotations, sayings.
How to Contact: *Does not accept unsolicited mss.* Query first or submit outline/synopsis. SASE. Reports in 1 month on queries; 1 month on mss. Simultaneous submissions OK.
Terms: Author may buy any number of copies at 40% discount and postage. Book catalog for #10 SASE.
Advice: Send SASE for more information.

SARABANDE BOOKS, INC., (II), 2234 Dundee Rd., Suite 200, Louisville KY 40205. Editor-in-Chief: Sarah Gorham. Estab. 1994. "Small literary press." Publishes hardcover and paperback originals. Averages 6 total titles, 2-3 fiction titles each year.
Needs: Short story collections, 300 pages maximum (or collections of novellas, or single novellas of 150 pages). "Short fiction *only*. We do not publish full-length novels."

How to Contact: Submit (in September only). Query with outline/synopsis and 1 sample story or ten-page sample. Include 1 page bio, listing of publishing credits. SASE for reply. Reports in 3 months on queries; 6 months on mss. Simultaneous submissions OK.

Terms: Pays in royalties, author's copies. Sends galleys to author. Writer's guidelines available for contest only. Send #10 SASE. Book catalog available.

THE SAVANT GARDE WORKSHOP, (II, IV), a privately-owned affiliate of The Savant Garde Institute, Ltd., P.O. Box 1650, Sag Harbor NY 11963. (516)725-1414. Publisher: Vilna Jorgen II. Estab. 1953. "Midsize multiple-media publisher." Publishes hardcover and paperback originals and reprints. Averages 2 total titles. Sometimes comments on rejected mss.

• Be sure to look at this publishers' guidelines first. Works could best be described as avant-garde/post modern, experimental.

Needs: Contemporary, futuristic, humanist, literary, philosophical. "We are open to the best, whatever it is." No "mediocrity or pot boilers." Published *01 or a Machine Called SKEETS*, by Artemis Smith (avant-garde); and *Bottomfeeder*, by Mark Spitzer. Series include "On-Demand Desktop Collectors' Editions," "Artists' Limited Editions," "Monographs of The Savant Garde Institute."

How to Contact: Do not send unsolicited mss. Query first with SASE and biographical statement. Agented fiction 1%. Reports in 6 weeks on queries ("during academic year"); 2 months on mss.

Terms: Average advance: $500, provides author's copies, honorarium (depends on grant/award money). Terms set by individual arrangement with author depending on the book and previous professional experience. Sends galleys to author. Publishes ms 18 months after acceptance. Writer's guidelines free.

Advice: "Most of the time we recommend authors to literary agents who can get better deals for them with other publishers, since we are looking for extremely rare offerings. We are not interested in the usual commercial submissions. Convince us you are a real artist, not a hacker." Would like to see more "thinking for the 21st Century of Nobel Prize calibre. We're expanding into multimedia CD-ROM co-publishing and seek multitalented authors who can produce and perform their own multimedia work for CD-ROM release. We are overbought and underfunded—don't expect a quick reply or fast publication date."

SERENDIPITY SYSTEMS, (I, II, IV), P.O. Box 140, San Simeon CA 93452. (805)927-5259. E-mail: j.galuszka@genie.geis.com. Imprints include Books on Disks™ and Bookware™. Publisher: John Galuszka. Estab. 1985. "Electronic publishing for IBM-PC compatible systems." Publishes "electronic editions originals and reprints." Books on disk. Published new writers within the last year. Averages 36 total titles, 15 fiction titles each year (either publish or distribute). Often comments on rejected mss.

Needs: "Works of fiction which use, or have the potential to use, hypertext, multimedia or other computer-enhanced features. We cannot use on-paper manuscripts." No romance, religion, New Age, children's, young adult, occult. Published *Costa Azul*, by C.J. Newton (humor); *Sideshow*, by Marian Allan (science fiction); and *Silicon Karma*, by Tom Easton (science fiction).

How to Contact: Query by e-mail. Submit complete ms with cover letter and SASE. *IBM-PC compatible disk required.* ASCII files saved under system 7 or higher required unless the work is hypertext or multimedia. Send SASE for reply, return of ms or send disposable copy of ms. Reports in 2 weeks on queries; 1 month on mss.

Terms: Pays royalties of 25%. "We distribute the works of self-published authors and have a cooperative program for authors who don't have the skills to electronically self-publish. We also distribute shareware electronic editions." Publishes ms 1 month after acceptance. Writer's guidelines for SASE. Book catalog for $1 (on IBM-PC 360K or 720K disk).

Advice: "A number of new tools have recently become available, Hypertext publishing programs DART and ORPHEUS, for example, and we look forward to seeing works which can take advantage of the features of these and other programs. Would like to see: more works of serious literature—novels, short stories, plays, etc. Would like to not see: right wing adventure fantasies from 'Tom Clancy' wanna-be's."

SEVEN BUFFALOES PRESS, (II), Box 249, Big Timber MT 59011. Editor/Publisher: Art Cuelho. Estab. 1975. Publishes paperback originals. Averages 4-5 total titles each year.

Needs: Contemporary, short story collections, "rural, American Hobo, Okies, Native-American, Southern Appalachia, Arkansas and the Ozarks. Wants farm- and ranch-based stories." Published *Rig Nine*, by William Rintoul (collection of oilfield short stories).

How to Contact: Query first with SASE. Reports in 1 week on queries; 2 weeks on mss. Sample copy $6.75.

Terms: Pays royalties of 10% minimum; 15% on second edition or in author's copies (10% of edition). No advance. Writer's guidelines and book catalog for SASE.

Advice: "There's too much influence from TV and Hollywood, media writing I call it. We need to get back to the people, to those who built and are still building this nation with sweat, blood and brains. More people are into it for the money, instead of for the good writing that is still to be cranked out by isolated writers. Remember, I was a writer for ten years before I became a publisher.''

‡**SEVEN STORIES PRESS, (II)**, 632 Broadway, 7th Floor, New York NY 10012. (212)995-0908. Fax: (212)995-0720. Contact: Editor. Estab. 1995. "Publishers of a distinguished list of authors in fine literature, journalism, contemporary culture and alternative health." Publishes hardcover and paperback originals and paperback reprints. Average print order: 5,000. Published new writer within the last year. Plans 2 first novels this year. Averages 20 total titles, 10 fiction titles/year. Sometimes critiques or comments on rejected mss.
  • Seven Stories Press received the Firecracker Alternative Book Award (nonfiction), 1996; N.Y. Public Library Best Book of the Year, 1994; Nebula Award Finalist, 1995; and *New York Times* Notable Book of the Year, 1995; *L.A. Times* Book Prize Finalist.
Needs: Literary. Plans anthologies. Ongoing series of short story collections from other cultures (e.g., *Contemporary Fiction from Central America*; from Vietnam, etc.) Recently published *The House of Moses All-Stars*, by Charley Rosen (novel); . . . *And Dreams Are Dreams*, by Vassilis Vassilikos (novel); and *Exteriors*, by Annie Ernaux (novel).
How to Contact: *No unsolicited mss.* "Both fiction and nonfiction submissions must be in the form of a query letter. We will respond only if interested, however a self-addressed, stamped postcard may be enclosed if confirmation of receipt is desired."
Terms: Pays standard royalty; offers advance. Sends galleys to author. Publishes ms 1-2 years after acceptance. Free book catalog.
Advice: "Writers should only send us their work after they have read some of the books we publish and find our editorial vision in sync with theirs."

HAROLD SHAW PUBLISHERS, (II, IV), Box 567, 388 Gundersen Dr., Wheaton IL 60189. (708)665-6700. Managing Editor: Joan Guest. Literary Editor: Lil Copan. Estab. 1968. "Small, independent religious publisher with expanding fiction line." Publishes paperback originals and reprints. Average print order: 5,000. Averages 40 total titles, 1-2 fiction titles each year. Sometimes critiques rejected mss.
Needs: Literary, religious/inspirational. Looking for religious literary novels for adults. No short stories, romances, children's fiction. Recently published *The Other Side of the Sun* and *Love Letters*, by Madeleine L'Engle; and *Mask: A Psychological Thriller*, by Betty Smartt Carter (mystery). Published new writers within the last year.
How to Contact: Accepts unsolicited mss. Query first. Submit outline/synopsis and 2-3 sample chapters. SASE. Reports in 4-6 weeks on queries; 3-4 months on mss. No simultaneous submissions.
Terms: Pays royalties of 10%. Provides 10 author's copies. Sends pages to author. Publishes ms 12-18 months after acceptance. Free writer's guidelines. Book catalog for 9×12 SAE and $1.32 postage.
Advice: "Character and plot development are important to us. We look for quality writing in word and in thought. 'Sappiness' and 'pop-writing' don't go over well at all with our editorial department."

SHIELDS PUBLISHING/NEO PRESS, (V), 301 E. Liberty, Suite 120, Ann Arbor MI 48104. (313)996-9229. Fax: (313)996-4544. Editor: Ms. Joanna Henning. "Small, independent press." Publishes hardcover and paperback originals. Plans 1 first novel this year. Averages 1 fiction title each year.
  • Shields is known for works focusing on minorities and women.
Needs: Ethnic/multicultural, experimental, feminist, gay, humor/satire, lesbian, literary, religious/inspirational, romance, short story collections. Recently published *Protégé*, by C.C. Arram (novel); and *Shades of Grey*, by Barrington Watson (art, short stories).
How to Contact: *Does not accept unsolicited mss.* Query with outline/synopsis and 2 sample chapters. Include list of publishing credits with submission. Send SASE for reply, return of ms or send a disposable copy of ms.
Terms: Pays "variable" royalties. Offers negotiable advance.
Advice: "Proofread and edit your work! There's nothing worse than error-ridden manuscripts. We focus on more select audiences rather than the mainstream. 'Formula' writing has no place with us."

♣**SIMON & PIERRE PUBLISHING CO. LTD., (IV)**, A member of the Dundurn Group, 2181 Queen St. E., Suite 301, Toronto, Ontario M4E 1E5 Canada. (416)698-0454. Fax: (416)698-1102. Publisher: Jean Paton. Estab. 1972. "Small literary press." Publishes paperback originals. Books: Hi Bulk paper; book printer printing; perfect binding; b&w illustrations. Average print order: 2,000. First novel print order: 1,000. Averages 10 total titles, 2 fiction titles each year.
Needs: Literary, mainstream/contemporary, mystery/suspense (amateur sleuth, cozy). Plans Canadian mystery anthologies. Published *Grave Deeds*, by B. Struthers (mystery-cozy); and *Crime in a Cold Climate*, by D. Shene-Melvin (mystery-anthology).
How to Contact: Accepts unsolicited mss. Query first or query with outline/synopsis. Include estimated word count; 1 page bio; list of publishing credits. Send SASE for reply, return of ms or send a

INSIDER REPORT

Seven Stories Press: a home for new voices

Daniel Simon, founder of Four Walls Eight Windows Press and, more recently, Seven Stories Press, notes proudly that he "started at the bottom." Simon's first publishing job was entry-level permissions assistant for Harper and Row. Several publishing jobs later, while editing for Writers and Readers Publishing Cooperative, Simon happened upon an out-of-print volume of Nelson Algren short stories that inspired him to begin his own independent press.

Photo by Miriam Berkley

"Nelson Algren was the most wonderful user of the language I'd ever come across," says Simon. "Then I did a little research and found out that all his books were out of print." In 1984, after a year **Daniel Simon** of waiting to get permission from Algren's estate, Simon published Algren's *The Neon Wilderness* as the first title under his Four Walls Eight Windows imprint. In 1986, he formed a partnership with John Oakes and for the next ten years the two built Four Walls into "something which was still small but made a name for doing some interesting things."

In 1995, Simon left Four Walls to form Seven Stories Press which he describes as "a continuation of what I was doing at Four Walls." With a fulltime staff of two other editors and one part-time person, Seven Stories will release 15 titles this year. Among those will be books by Octavia Butler, Annie Ernaux and health and nutrition author Gary Null. Simon will also continue publishing works from the estate of Nelson Algren and the annual *Censored: The News That Didn't Make the News—And Why*, edited by Carl Jensen. Newly signed writers to Seven Stories include Cynthia Voigt, novelist Charley Rosen, and Greek author Vassilis Vassilikos.

Simon sees his job as that of shaping the books he publishes. "If all of the books came to us with anything approaching the quality we expect them to have when they go to the printer, many wouldn't be available to us. They would be going to bigger houses for more money than we could afford to pay. So, because we're independent, our method of operation has to be a rigorous, opinionated and powerful editorial shaping process. Typically, a manuscript will come into us and we will say this has problems but there's a fire, there's an excitement to it—this writer is saying something important that needs to be said because there's nothing else out there like it; this is an important voice that needs to be heard."

Simon stresses, however, that ultimately the writer makes a manuscript publishable. "It's almost impossible to take an unpublishable book and make it better

INSIDER REPORT, *Simon*

inhouse. Editing can do important things, but it's not the same as what a writer can do. We hold up a certain standard, put some demands on the writer. If what we're saying makes sense, the writer will, with some specific context and some specific input and direction, bring the book along in a second or third draft."

The close, ongoing, multibook working relationship between writers and editors is something Simon values. "The quality of relationships is the most important asset in my publishing company. To do my job well I need a writer I can help build over time, one who will keep an ongoing body of work coming to me. That way, I can really develop a look for the books, and can over time help create a readership for that writer."

Simon also emphasizes the importance of the relationship between writers and their work. "The biggest problem for a writer is not how to get a publisher to read your work or how to get the right agent. The problem is finding your subject and getting to the point where you're listening to yourself and listening to the world around you. Annie Ernaux and Octavia Butler are very clear about what their subjects are. They're committed to their work; they listen to their own voices and rhythms; and they listen to what's going on in the world. With writers like these, marvelous things happen. Instead of having to knock down doors that won't open, the booksellers get very excited and people buy the books and the media people are figuring out ways to feature that author—it's wonderful."

Finding new voices, says Simon, is perhaps the most important function of today's independent press. "The more the big publishers shy away from developing writers and become more concerned with the commercial side of publishing, the more room there is for independent publishers to find those voices. There is a trend among larger publishers to think of the writer as playing a smaller part in the production of a successful book. The big publishers are becoming more driven by marketing, by sales, by bottom-line businessmen, and so the gulf between those people and the people actually writing the books keeps getting larger."

Referring to the need for independent presses to remain strong in the current publishing climate, Simon says, "this is a time of strategic alliances. The trick is to make these alliances, but also hold onto our independence." Although Simon points out that some independent presses are surviving by simply cutting back on the number of titles they publish, he sees great advantage in sublicensing paperback editions of original hardback titles to big presses. "We benefit substantially from sublicensing, and the author has the best of both worlds—the special handling we provide when the hardcover edition is being created and the larger reach of the big press for mass market editions."

Simon's advice for writers wishing to survive in today's publishing world is to "not be distracted by the difficulties in getting published. Instead, keep your primary objective of writing in mind, which is to be searching for your subject and for your voice. Editors and publishers are looking for strong writers whose voices are clear, who are saying things that are exciting, who are speaking to the moment. When we see that work, we want it. It's important for writers to remember that."

—Barbara Kuroff

disposable copy of ms. Reports in 2 months on queries; 3 months on mss. Simultaneous submissions OK.

Terms: Pays royalties of 10%. Average advance $750. Provides 10 author's copies. Sends galleys to author. Publishes ms 8-12 months after acceptance. Writer's guidelines free. Book catalog for 9×12 SASE and $1 postage.

‡**SLOUGH PRESS, (II)**, %English, Texas A&M University, College Station TX 77843-4227. Fiction Editor: Chuck Taylor. Estab. 1973. Publishes hardcover and paperback originals. Books: acid-free paper; offset printing; glue binding. Average print order: 500-1,000. Averages 1-5 total titles, 0-2 fiction titles each year. Sometimes comments on rejected mss.

Needs: Erotica, ethnic, experimental, literary, mainstream and short story collections.

How to Contact: Accepts unsolicited mss. Submit outline/synopsis and sample chapters. SASE. Reports in 2 months on mss. Simultaneous submissions OK.

Terms: Pays royalties of 15% maximum. Sometimes sends pre-publication galleys to author. Publishes ms one year after acceptance.

Advice: "We never encourage anyone in the creative writing field. It's a religious calling, not a career or profession, with little monetary reward for most. We like fiction with extra-literary appeal. I'd like to see some suggestions in the author cover letter that are concrete and specific on how the book could find readers and sell."

THE SMITH, (I, II), 69 Joralemon St., Brooklyn NY 11201. Editor: Harry Smith. Estab. 1964. Books: 70 lb. vellum paper for offset and 80 lb. vellum for letterpress printing; perfect binding; often uses illustrations. Average print order: 1,000. First novel print order: 1,000. Plans 2 fiction titles this year.

● The Poor Richard Award was presented to publisher Harry Smith for his "three decades of independent literary publishing activities."

Needs: *Extremely limited* book publishing market—currently doing only 3-5 books annually, and these are of a literary nature, usually fiction or poetry. Published *The Cleveland Indian* (novel) and *Blue Eden* (connected long stories), both by Luke Salisbury; and *Bodo*, by John Bennett (novel).

Advice: "We find most synopses are stupid. Send one or two chapters, or one to three stories, depending on length. Complete manuscripts may not be read. Our list is our only guide and our motto is: Anything goes as long as it's good. Remember that we publish outside the mainstream, and do not publish any self-help, recovery or inspirational books. And SASE, please! Because of unusual working hours, we are unable to accept registered or certified mail or bulky packages which will not fit through our mail slot. The post office is not conveniently located for us to pick up mail."

‡❀**SNOWAPPLE PRESS, (I, II)**, P.O. Box 66024, Heritage Postal Outlet, Edmonton, Alberta T6J 6T4 Canada. (403)437-0191. Editor: Vanna Tessier. Estab. 1991. Small independent press. Publishes hardcover and paperback originals. Books: non-acid paper; offset printing; perfect binding; illustrations. Average print order: 500. First novel print order: 500. Plans 1 first novel this year. Averages 3-4 total titles, 1-2 fiction titles each year.

Needs: Adventure, children's/juvenile (adventure, fantasy, mystery), experimental, historical, literary, mainstream/contemporary, short story collections, translations, young adult/teen (adventure, mystery/suspense). Recently published *Gypsy Drums*, by Vanna Tessier (short stories).

How to Contact: Accepts unsolicited mss. Query first. Include estimated word count, 300-word bio and list of publishing credits. SASE. Reports in 3-4 weeks on queries; 3 months on mss. Simultaneous submissions OK.

Terms: Pays honorarium; provides 10-25 author's copies. Sends galleys to author. Publishes ms 12-18 months after acceptance.

SOHO PRESS, (I, II), 853 Broadway, New York NY 10003. (212)260-1900. Publisher: Juris Jurjevics. Publishes hardcover originals and trade paperback reprints. Published new writers within the last year. Averages 25 titles/year.

Needs: Ethnic, literary, mainstream, mystery/espionage, suspense. "We do novels that are the very best of their kind." Published *The Sixteen Pleasures*, by Robert R. Hellenga; *Kirk? Kark!*, by Edwidge Danticat; and *Adrian Mole: The Lost Years*, by Sue Townsend. Also publishes the Hera series (serious historical fiction reprints with strong female leads).

How to Contact: Submit query with SASE. Reports in 1 month on queries; 6 weeks on mss. Simultaneous submissions OK.

Terms: Pays royalties of 10-15% on retail price. For trade paperbacks pays 7½%. Offers advance. Book catalog plus $1 for SASE.

Advice: Greatest challenge is "introducing brand new, untested writers. We do not care if they are agented or not. Half the books we publish come directly from authors. We look for a distinctive writing style, strong writing skills and compelling plots. We are not interested in trite expression of mass market formulae."

SOUTHERN METHODIST UNIVERSITY PRESS, (I, II), P.O. Box 415, Dallas TX 75275. (214)768-1433. Senior Editor: Kathryn M. Lang. Estab. 1936. "Small university press publishing in areas of film/theater, Southwest life and letters, religion/medical ethics and contemporary fiction." Publishes hardcover and paperback originals and reprints. Books: acid-free paper; perfect-bound; some illustrations. Average print order 2,000. Published new writers within the last year. Plans 2 first novels this year. Averages 10-12 total titles; 3-4 fiction titles each year. Sometimes comments on rejected mss.
Needs: Contemporary, ethnic, literary, regional, short story collections. "We are always willing to look at 'serious' or 'literary' fiction." No "mass market, science fiction, formula, thriller, romance." Recently published *Children of the World*, by Martha Stephens (literary); and *Go the Distance*, by W.P. Kinsella (stories).
How to Contact: Accepts unsolicited mss. Query first. Submit outline/synopsis and 3 sample chapters. SASE. Reports in 3 weeks on queries; 6 months on mss. No simultaneous submissions.
Terms: Pays royalties of 10% net, negotiable advance, 10 author's copies. Publishes ms 1 year after acceptance. Book catalog free.
Advice: "We view encouraging first time authors as part of the mission of a university press. Send query describing the project and your own background. Research the press before you submit—don't send us the kinds of things we don't publish." Looks for "quality fiction from new or established writers."

THE SPEECH BIN, INC., (IV), 1965 25th Ave., Vero Beach FL 32960. (407)770-0007. Fax: (407)770-0006. Senior Editor: Jan J. Binney. Estab. 1984. Small independent publisher and major national and international distributor of books and material for speech-language pathologists, audiologists, special educators and caregivers. Publishes hardcover and paperback originals. Averages 15-20 total titles/year. "No fiction at present time, but we are very interested in publishing fiction relevant to our specialties."
Needs: "We are most interested in seeing fiction, including books for children, dealing with individuals experiencing communication disorders, other handicaps, and their families and caregivers, particularly their parents, or family members dealing with individuals who have strokes, physical disability, hearing loss, Alzheimer's and so forth."
How to Contact: Accepts unsolicited mss. Query first. SASE. Agented fiction 10%. Reports in 4-6 weeks on queries; 1-3 months on mss. Simultaneous submissions OK, but only if notified by author.
Terms: Pays royalties. Sends galleys to author. Writer's guidelines for #10 SASE. Book catalog for 9×12 SAE with 4 first-class stamps.
Advice: "We are most interested in publishing fiction about individuals who have speech, hearing and other handicaps."

SPINSTERS INK, (II, IV), 32 E. First St., #330, Duluth MN 55802. Fax: (218)727-3119. E-mail: spinsters@aol.com. Contact: Acquisitions. Estab. 1978. Moderate-size women's publishing company growing steadily. Publishes paperback originals and reprints. Books: 55 lb. acid-free natural paper; photo offset printing; perfect-bound; illustrations when appropriate. Average print order: 5,000. Published new writers within the last year. Plans 3 first novels this year. Averages 6 total titles, 3-5 fiction titles each year. Occasionally critiques rejected mss.
  ● Spinsters Ink published *Mother Journeys*, by M. Reddy, M. Roth and A. Sheldon, which received the 1995 Minnesota Book Award and also the 1995 Susan Koppelman Award; and *Martha Moody*, by Susan Stinson, a 1996 PMA Benjamin Franklin Award Winner. Spinsters plans an anthology called *Women of Color in the Midwest.*
Needs: Feminist, lesbian. Wants "full-length quality fiction—thoroughly revised novels which display deep characterization, theme and style. We *only* consider books by women. No books by men, or books with sexist, racist or ageist content." Recently published *Martha Moody*, by Susan Stinson (feminist western); *Goodness*, by Martha Roth (fiction); and *Silent Woods*, by Joan Drury (mystery). Publishes anthologies. Writers may submit directly. Series include: "Coming of Age Series" and "Forgotten Women's Series."
How to Contact: Query or submit outline/synopsis and 2-5 sample chapters not to exceed 50 pages with SASE. Reports in 1 month on queries; 2 months on mss. Simultaneous submissions discouraged. Disk submissions OK (DOS or Macintosh format—MS Word 4.0). Prefers hard copy with disk submission.
Terms: Pays royalties of 7-10%, plus 10 author's copies; unlimited extra copies at 40% discount. Free book catalog.
Advice: "In the past, lesbian fiction has been largely 'escape fiction' with sex and romance as the only required ingredients; however, we encourage more complex work that treats the lesbian lifestyle with the honesty it deserves. Look at our catalog and mission statement. Does your book fit our criteria?"

‡**THE SPIRIT THAT MOVES US PRESS, (II)**, P.O. Box 720820-N, Jackson Heights NY 11372-0820. (718)426-8788. Editor/Publisher: Morty Sklar. Estab. 1974. Small independent literary publisher. Publishes hardcover and paperback originals. "We do, for the most part, simultaneous clothbound and trade paperbacks for the same title." Books: 60 lb. natural acid-free paper; mostly photo-offset, some letterpress; cloth and perfect binding; illustrations. Average print order: 3,000. Averages 2 fiction titles, mostly multi-author. Comments on rejected mss "when author requests that or when we are compelled to by the writing (good or bad)."

Needs: Literary. "Our choice of 'literary' does not exclude almost any other category—as long as the writing communicates on an emotional level, and is involved with people more than things. Nothing sensational or academic." Published *Patchwork of Dreams: Voices from the Heart of the New America*, a multiethnic collection of fiction and other genres; and *Editor's Choice: Fiction, Poetry & Art from the U.S. Small Press*, biennially, edited by Morty Sklar (work nominated by other publishers). Published new writers within the last year.

How to Contact: Accepts unsolicited mss. "We are undergoing major changes. Please query before sending work." Query letter only first "unless he/she sees an announcement that calls for manuscripts and gives a deadline." Include estimated word count, bio and whether or not ms is a simultaneous submission. SASE for reply or return of ms. Reports on mss "if rejected, soon; if under consideration, from 1-3 months."

Terms: Pays royalties of 10% net, $1,000 advance for first novel, and authors copies, also honorarium, depends on grant/award money. Sends galleys to author. Publishes up to 1 year after acceptance. Plans and time-frames for #10 SASE "but the guidelines are only for certain books, like novels. We don't use general guidelines." Catalog for 6×9 SAE and 2 first-class stamps.

Advice: "We are interested in work that is not only well written, but that gets the reader involved on an emotional level. No matter how skilled the writing is, or how interesting or exciting the story, if we don't care about the people in it, we won't consider it. Also, we are open to a great variety of styles, so just be yourself and don't try to second-guess the editor. You may have our newest collection *Patchwork of Dreams* as a sample, for $10 (cover price and postage is $14.50)."

STARBURST PUBLISHERS, (II), P.O. Box 4123, Lancaster PA 17604. (717)293-0939. Editorial Director: Ellen Hake. Estab. 1982. Midsize independent press. Publishes trade paperback and hardcover originals and trade paperback reprints. Receives 1,000 submission/year. 60% of books by first-time authors. Averages 10-15 total titles each year.

Needs: Religious/inspirational: Adventure, contemporary, fantasy, historical, horror, military/war, psychic/supernatural/occult (with Judeo-Christian solution), romance (contemporary, historical), spiritual, suspense/mystery, western. Wants "inspirational material." Recently published *Beyond the River*, by Gilbert Morris.

How to Contact: Submit outline/synopsis, 3 sample chapters, bio, photo and SASE. Agented fiction less than 25%. Reports in 6-8 weeks on manuscripts; 1 month on queries. Accepts electronic submissions via disk and modem, "but also wants clean double-spaced typewritten or computer printout manuscript."

Terms: Pays royalties of 6% minimum; 16% maximum. "Individual arrangement with writer depending on the manuscript as well as writer's experience as a published author." Publishes ms up to one year after acceptance. Writer's guidelines for #10 SASE. Book catalog for 9×12 SAE and 4 first-class stamps.

Advice: "50% of our line goes into the Christian marketplace; 50% into the general marketplace. We are one of the few publishers that has direct sales representation into both the Christian and general marketplace."

STORMLINE PRESS, (I, II), P.O. Box 593, Urbana IL 61801. Publisher: Raymond Bial. Estab. 1985. "Small independent literary press operated by one person on a part-time basis, publishing one or two books annually." Publishes hardcover and paperback originals. Books: acid-free paper; paper and cloth binding; b&w illustrations. Average print order: 1,000-2,000. First novel print order: 1,000-2,000. Published new writers within the last year. Averages 1-2 total titles, all fiction each year.

● Stormline's title, *First Frost*, was selected for a Best of the Small Presses Award.

Needs: Literary. Looks for "serious literary works, especially those which accurately and sensitively reflect rural and small town life." Published *Silent Friends: A Quaker Quilt*, by Margaret Lacey (short story collection).

How to Contact: Accepts unsolicited mss. Query (with SASE), preferably during November or December. Include estimated word count, bio, list of publishing credits. SASE for reply or return of ms. Reports in 2 weeks on queries; 1 month on mss. Simultaneous submissions OK.

Terms: Pays royalties of 10% maximum. Provides author's copies. Sends galleys to author. Publishes ms 6-12 months after acceptance. Writer's guidelines for SASE. Book catalog free.

Advice: "We look for a distinctive voice and writing style. We are always interested in looking at manuscripts of exceptional literary merit. We are not interested in popular fiction or experimental writing. Please review other titles published by the press, notably *Silent Friends: A Quaker Quilt*, to get an idea of the type of books published by our press."

STORY LINE PRESS, (II), Three Oaks Farm, Brownsville OR 97327-9718. (541)466-5352. Fax: (541)466-3200. Editor: Robert McDowell. Estab. 1985. "Nonprofit literary press." Publishes hardcover and paperback originals and hardcover and paperback reprints. Published new writers within the last year. Plans 1 first novel this year. Averages 10 total titles, 3 fiction titles each year.
● Story Line Press books have received awards including the Oregon Book Award.

Needs: Adventure, ethnic/multicultural, literary, mystery/suspense, regional, short story collections and translations. Published *Among the Immortals*, by Paul Lake (vampire mystery); *Second Story Theatre*, by James Brown (literary); and *The Raquet*, by George Hitchcock (picaresque). Publishes Stuart Mallory Mystery series.

How to Contact: Accepts unsolicited mss. Returns mss "if postage is included." Query with outline. Include bio and list of publishing credits. Send SASE for reply, return of ms or send a disposable copy of ms. Agented fiction 2.7%. Reports in 9-12 weeks on queries; 6-9 months on mss. Simultaneous submissions OK.

Terms: Provides author's copies; payment depends on grant/award money. Sends galleys to author. Publishes ms 1-3 years after acceptance. Book catalog for 7×10 SASE.

Advice: "Patience . . . understanding of a nonprofit literary press' limitations."

SUNSTONE PRESS, (IV), P.O. Box 2321, Santa Fe NM 87504-2321. (505)988-4418. Contact: James C. Smith, Jr. Estab. 1971. Midsize publisher. Publishes hardcover and paperback originals. Average first novel print order: 2,000. Published new writers within the last year. Plans 2 first novels this year. Averages 16 total titles, 2-3 fiction titles, each year.
● Sunstone Press published *Ninez*, by Virginia Nylander Ebinger which received the Southwest Book Award from the Border Regional Library Association.

Needs: Western. "We have a Southwestern theme emphasis. Sometimes buys juvenile mss with illustrations." No science fiction, romance or occult. Published *Apache: The Long Ride Home*, by Grant Gall (Indian/Western); *Sorrel*, by Rita Cleary; and *To Die in Dinetah*, by John Truitt.

How to Contact: Accepts unsolicited mss. Query first or submit outline/synopsis and 2 sample chapters with SASE. Reports in 2 weeks. Simultaneous submissions OK. Publishes ms 9-12 months after acceptance.

Terms: Pays royalties, 10% maximum, and 10 author's copies.

THIRD SIDE PRESS, INC., (II), 2250 W. Farragut, Chicago IL 60625-1802. (312)271-3029. Fax: (312)271-0459. E-mail: 102171.771@compuserve.com. Publisher: Midge Stocker. Estab. 1991. "Small, independent press, feminist." Publishes paperback originals. "experimental and contemporary lesbian novels." Books: 50 lb. recycled, acid-free paper; offset-web or sheet printing; perfect binding. Average print order: 3,000. First novel print order: 3,000. Published new writers within the last year. Averages 4 total titles, 2 fiction titles each year. Sometimes comments on rejected mss.

Needs: Lesbian: erotica (lesbian only), feminist, literary, mainstream/contemporary. No "collections of stories; horror; homophobic" material. Recently published *Not So Much the Fall*, by Kerry Hart (first novel); *Speaking in Whispers*, by Kathleen Morris (erotica); and *Entwined*, by Beatrice Stone (novel). Series include Royce Madison mysteries; Women/Cancer/Fear/Power series.

How to Contact: Query first. Include bio (1-2 paragraphs) and synopsis. Send SASE for reply, return of ms or send a disposable copy of ms. Reports in 2-3 weeks on queries; 3-6 months on mss. Simultaneous submissions OK with notice.

Terms: Pays royalties (varies). Provides 10 author's copies. Publishes ms 6-18 months after acceptance. Writer's guidelines for 9×12 SAE and 2 first-class stamps. Book catalog for 2 first-class stamps.

Advice: "Look at our catalog and read one or two of our other books to get a feel for how your work will fit with what we've been publishing. Plan to book readings and other appearances to help sell your book. And don't quit your day job."

THIRD WORLD PRESS, P.O. Box 19730, Chicago IL 60619. (312)651-0700. Publisher/Editor: Haki Madhubuti. Estab. 1967. Black-owned and operated independent publisher of fiction and nonfiction books about the black experience throughout the Diaspora. Publishes paperback originals. Plans 1 first novel this year, as well as short story collections. Averages 10 total titles, 3 fiction titles each year. Average first novel print order 15,000 copies.

Needs: Ethnic, historical, juvenile (animal, easy-to-read, fantasy, historical, contemporary), preschool/picture book, short story collections, and young adult/teen (easy-to-read/teen, folktales, historical). "We primarily publish nonfiction, but will consider fiction by and about blacks."

How to Contact: Accepts unsolicited mss October-May each year. Query or submit outline/synopsis and 1 sample chapter with SASE. Reports in 6 weeks on queries; 5 months on mss. Simultaneous submissions OK. Accepts computer printout submissions.

Terms: Individual arrangement with author depending on the book, etc.

✦THISTLEDOWN PRESS, (II, IV), 633 Main St., Saskatoon, Saskatchewan S7H 0J8 Canada. (306)244-1722. Editor-in-Chief: Patrick O'Rourke. Estab. 1975. Publishes paperback originals. Books: Quality stock paper; offset printing; perfect-bound; occasional illustrations. Average print order 1,500-2,000. First novel print order: 1,000-1,500. Publishes 12 titles, 6 or 7 fiction, each year.

• A story included in the press' *The Blue Jean Collection* received a Vicky Metcalf Award, and books published by Thistledown have been selected as "Our Choice" by the Canadian Children's Book Centre and the Arthur Ellis Crime Writers Award (Best Juvenile Story).

Needs: Literary, experimental, short story collections, novels.

How to Contact: "We *only* want to see Canadian-authored submissions. We will *not* consider multiple submissions." No unsolicited mss. Query first with SASE. Photocopied submissions OK. Reports in 2 months on queries. Publishes anthologies. "Stories are nominated." Published *It's A Hard Cow*, by Terry Jordan (short stories); *Soldier Boys*, by David Richards; *The Woman on the Bridge*, by Mel Dagg (short stories); and *The Blue Camaro*, by R.P. MacIntyre. Also publishes The Mayer Mystery Series (mystery novels for young adults) and The New Leaf Series (first books for poetry and fiction).

Advice: "We are primarily looking for quality writing that is original and innovative in its perspective and/or use of language. Thistledown would like to receive queries first before submission—perhaps with novel outline, some indication of previous publications, periodicals your work has appeared in. *We publish Canadian authors only.* We are continuing to publish more fiction and are looking for new fiction writers to add to our list. New Leaf Editions line is first books of poetry or fiction by emerging Western Canadian authors. Familiarize yourself with some of our books before submitting a query or manuscript to the press."

THREE CONTINENTS PRESS, (III, IV), P.O. Box 38009, Colorado Springs CO 80937-8009. Fiction Editor: Donald Herdeck. Estab. 1973. Small independent publisher with expanding list. Publishes hardcover and paperback originals and reprints. Books: library binding; illustrations. Average print order: 1,000-1,500. First novel print order: 1,000. Averages 15 total titles, 6-8 fiction titles each year. Occasionally critiques ("a few sentences") rejected mss.

Needs: "We publish original fiction only by writers from Africa, the Caribbean, the Middle East, Asia and the Pacific. No fiction by writers from North America or Western Europe." Published *Lina: Portrait of a Damascene Girl*, by Samar Altar; *The Native Informant*, by Ramzi Salti (stories); and *Repudiation*, by Rachid Boudjedra.

How to Contact: Query with outline/synopsis and sample pages with SASE. State "origins (non-Western), education and previous publications." Reports in 1 month on queries; 2 months on mss. Simultaneous submissions OK.

Terms: "Send inquiry letter first and ms only if so requested by us. We are not a subsidy publisher, but do a few specialized titles a year with grants. In those cases we accept institutional subventions. Foundation or institution receives 20-30 copies of book and at times royalty on first printing. We pay royalties twice yearly (against advance) as a percentage of net paid receipts." Royalties of 5% minimum; 10% maximum. Offers negotiable advance, $300 average. Provides 10 author's copies. Sends galleys to author. Free book catalog available; inquiry letter first and ms only if so requested by us.

Advice: "Submit professional work (within our parameters of interest) with well worked-over language and clean manuscripts prepared to exacting standards."

THRESHOLD BOOKS, RD 4, Box 600, Dusty Ridge Rd., Putney VT 05346. (802)254-8300. Director: Edmund Helminski. Estab. 1981. Small independent publisher with plans for gradual expansion. Books: 60 lb. natural paper; offset litho printing; sew-wrap binding; average print order: 2,500. Averages 2-3 total titles each year.

Needs: Spiritual literature and translations of sacred texts. Published *Awakened Dreams*, by Ahmet Hilmi, translated by Camille Helminski and Refik Algan.

How to Contact: Accepts unsolicited mss. Query first, submit outline/synopsis and sample chapters or complete ms with SASE. Reports in 2 months. Simultaneous submissions OK. Publishes ms an average of 18 months after acceptance.

Terms: Pays in royalties of 7% of gross. Sometimes sends galleys to author. Book catalog free on request.

Advice: "We are still small and publishing little fiction." Publishing "less fiction, more paperbacks due to our particular area of concentration and our size."

TURTLE POINT PRESS, (II), 103 Hog Hill, Chappaqua NY 10514. (800)453-2992. President: J.D. Rabinowitz. Estab. 1990. "Small press publishing mostly lost literary fiction in quality paperback editions. Beginning in 1994 doing contemporary fiction as well." Publishes paperback originals and reprints. Books: recycled 60 lb. stock paper; sewn binding; occasional illustrations. Average print order: 1,500. First novel print order 800-1,500. Plans 2 first novels this year. Averages 4-5 fiction titles each year. Sometimes comments on rejected mss.
Needs: Literary, novels, translations. "Literary fiction, *tranlations* particularly from French, Spanish and Italian." Published *The Toys of Princes*, by Ghislain de Diesbach (Richard Howard, translator) (short stories); *Clovis*, by Michael Ferrier (social-satire fiction); and *The Diary of a Forty-Niner*, edited by Jackson/Carfield (journal).
How to Contact: Submit outline/synopsis and sample chapters. Include estimated word count, short bio, list of publishing credits. Send SASE for reply, return of ms or send a disposable copy of ms. Reports in 1 month.
Terms: Pays royalty (varies), negotiable advance or honorarium. Publishes ms 4-12 months after acceptance. Book catalogs are free.
Advice: "We are publishers of lost fiction with a keen interest in doing contemporary writing and contemporary translation."

ULTRAMARINE PUBLISHING CO., INC., (V), Box 303, Hastings-on-the-Hudson NY 10706. (914)478-1339. Fax: (914)478-1365. Publisher: Christopher P. Stephens. Estab. 1973. Small publisher. "We have 200 titles in print. We also distribute for authors where a major publisher has dropped a title." Averages 15 total titles, 12 fiction titles each year. Buys 90% agented fiction. Occasionally critiques rejected mss.
Needs: Experimental, fantasy, mainstream, science fiction, short story collections. No romance, westerns, mysteries.
How to Contact: *Does not accept unsolicited mss.*
Terms: Pays royalties of 10% minimum; advance is negotiable. Publishes ms an average of 8 months after acceptance. Free book catalog.

THE UNIVERSITY OF ARKANSAS PRESS, (II), Fayetteville AR 72701. (501)575-3246. Fax: (501)575-6044. E-mail: kbrock@comp.uark.edu. Director: Miller Williams. Acquisitions Editor: Kevin Brock. Estab. 1980. Small university press. Publishes hardcover and paperback originals. Average print order: 750 cloth and 2,000 paper copies. Averages 36 total titles, 2 short fiction titles (a novel only in translation or reprint) each year.
● This press has won the Spur Award for best western nonfiction.
Needs: Literary, mainstream, short story collections and translations. Publishes anthologies or special editions. Stories are usually selected by the editor. Published *Augustus*, by John Williams (novel); *Horses into the Night*, by Baltasar Porcel, translated by John Gatman (novel); and *Overgrown with Love*, by Scott Ely (short story collection).
How to Contact: Accepts unsolicited mss. Query first with SASE. Reports in 2 weeks. Simultaneous and electronic (disk) submissions OK.
Terms: Pays royalties of 10% on hardback, 6% on paperback; 10 author's copies. Publishes ms an average of 1 year after acceptance. Writer's guidelines and book catalog for 9 × 12 SASE.
Advice: "We are looking for fiction—primarily short fiction—written with energy, clarity and economy. Apart from this, we have no predisposition concerning style or subject matter. The University of Arkansas Press does not respond to queries or proposals not accompanied by SASE. Be prepared to submit on disk plus hard copy."

UNIVERSITY OF MISSOURI PRESS, (II), 2910 LeMone Blvd., Columbia MO 65201. (573)882-7641. Fax: (573)884-4498. Acquisitions Editor: Clair Willcox. Estab. 1958. "Mid-size university press." Publishes paperback originals and reprints (short story collections only). Published new writers within the last year. Averages 52 total titles, 4 short story collections each year. Sometimes comments on rejected mss.

---

‡ **THE DOUBLE DAGGER** before a listing indicates that the listing is new in this edition. New markets are often the most receptive to submissions by new writers.

• The University of Missouri Press is a member of the Association of American University Presses.

Needs: Short story collections. No children's fiction. Recently published *The Other Floor*, by Heuler (stories); *In the Funny Papers*, by Miller (stories); and *A Visit to Strangers*, by Swan (stories).

How to Contact: Accepts unsolicited mss. Query first. Submit cover letter and sample story or two. Include bio/publishing credits. SASE for reply. Reports in 2 weeks on queries; 3 months on mss. Simultaneous submissions OK.

Terms: Pays royalties of 6%. Sends galleys to author. Publishes ms 1-1½ years after acceptance. Book catalogs are free.

‡UNIVERSITY OF NEVADA PRESS,(II, IV), MS 166, Reno NV 89557-0076. (702)784-6573. Fax: (702)784-6200. E-mail: dalrympl@scs.unr.edu. Editor-in-Chief: Margaret Dalrymple. Estab. 1961. "Small university press. Publishes fiction that focuses primarily on the American West." Publishes hardcover and paperback originals and paperback reprints. Books: acid-free paper. Publishes approximately 25 total titles, 4 fiction titles/year. Sometimes critiques or comments on rejected mss. Member AAUP.

Needs: Ethnic/multicultural (general), family saga, historical (American West), humor/satire, mystery/suspense (U.S. West), regional (U.S. West). Recently published *Wild Indians & Other Creatures*, by Adrian Louis (short stories); *Bad Boys and Black Sheep*, by Robert Franklin Gish (short stories); and *The Measurable World*, by Katharine Coles (novel). "We have series in Basque studies, gambling studies, history and humanities, ethnonationalism, western literature."

How to Contact: Accepts unsolicited mss. Query with outline/synopsis and 2-4 sample chapters. E-mail and fax queries OK. Include estimated word count, 1-2 page bio and list of publishing credits. Send SASE for reply, return of ms or send a disposable copy of ms. Agented fiction 20%. Reports in 3-4 weeks on queries; 2-4 months on mss.

Terms: Pays royalties; negotiated on a book-by-book basis. Sends galleys to author. Publishes ms 9-24 months after acceptance. Writer's guidelines for #10 SASE.

Advice: "We are not interested in genre fiction."

‡UNIVERSITY PRESS OF COLORADO, (IV), P.O. Box 849, Niwot CO 80544. (303)530-5337. Fax: (303)530-5306. Director: Luther Wilson. Estab. 1965. "Small, independent, scholarly publisher, nonprofit." Publishes hardcover and paperback originals and reprints. Books: acid-free paper; offset printing; case bound. Average print order: 1,000. First novel print order: 1,500. Averages 30 total titles, 2 fiction titles each year. Sometimes critiques or comments on rejected mss. Member of The Association of American University Presses. "Generally, our authors are responsible for proofreading and indexing their own manuscripts. If they do not wish to do so, we will hire proofreaders and/or indexers at the author's expense."

Needs: Regional (western), western (modern). "All of our fiction projects will be part of our Women's West series." Recently published *Fire in the Hole*, by Sybil Downing (historical western); and *The Eagle Catcher*, by Margaret Coel (historical Native American).

How to Contact: Query with outline/synopsis and 3 sample chapters. Include estimated word count, bio and list of publishing credits. Send SASE for reply, return of ms or send disposable copy of ms. Agented fiction 90%. Reports in 3 weeks on queries; 4 months on mss.

Terms: Pays royalties of 12% maximum. Provides 10 author's copies. Sends galleys to author. Publishes ms within 2 years after acceptance. Writer's guidelines and book catalog free.

Advice: "We look for high quality fiction that might not appeal to the larger trade houses. We are interested in publishing fiction that fits into our series *Women's West*."

‡VAN NESTE BOOKS, (I, II), 12836 Ashtree Rd., Midlothian VA 23113. Phone/fax: (804)897-3568. Publisher: Karen Van Neste Owen. Estab. 1996. "We are a small independent publisher interested in publishing serious fiction." Publishes hardcover originals. Books: 55 lb. acid-free paper; cloth binding; illustrations (cover only). Average print order: 1,500. Plans 2-4 first novels for 1998. Averages 2-4 total titles, 2-4 fiction titles each year. Sometimes critiques or comments on rejected mss.

Needs: Feminist, historical, humor/satire, literary, mainstream/contemporary, mystery/suspense, regional (southern), thriller/espionage. "We are accepting manuscripts now for 1998."

How to Contact: Accepts unsolicited mss. Query with 3 sample chapters. Include estimated word count, 2-paragraph bio, Social Security number and list of publishing credits. Send SASE for reply, return of ms or send disposable copy of ms. Reports in 2 months on queries; 6 months on mss.

Terms: Pays royalties of 10-15% minimum on print runs of more than 2,500 copies; half that on print runs under 2,500 copies. Average advance: $500 for finished disk. Sends galleys to author. Publishes ms 12-18 months after acceptance.

Advice: "Write well! And make the copy as clean as possible."

VANDAMERE PRESS, (II), P.O. Box 5243, Arlington VA 22205. Editor: Jerry Frank. Estab. press 1984; firm 1976. "Small press, independent publisher of quality hard and softcover books." Publishes hardcover and paperback originals. Published new writers within the last year. Averages 6 total titles, 1 fiction title each year. Sometimes comments on rejected mss.

Needs: Adventure, erotica, humor/satire, military/war. No children's/juvenile/young adult. Published *Hegemon*, by Alexander M. Grace; and *Ancestral Voices*, by Hugh Fitzgerald Ryan.

How to Contact: Accepts unsolicited mss. Submit outline/synopsis and 3-4 sample chapters or complete ms with cover letter. Include bio (1-2 pages), list of publishing credits. Send SASE for reply, return of ms or send a disposable copy of the ms. Reporting time varies with work load. Simultaneous submissions OK.

Terms: Pays royalties; negotiable small advance. Sends galleys to author. Publishes ms 3 months-2 years after acceptance.

Advice: "Submissions must be neat, clean and double spaced. Author should include a résumé. Manuscript package should not take ten minutes to unwrap. And do not send registered or certified."

✦VÉHICULE PRESS, (IV), Box 125, Place du Parc Station, Montreal, Quebec H2W 2M9 Canada. Imprint: Signal Editions for poetry. Publisher/Editor: Simon Dardick. Estab. 1973. Small publisher of scholarly, literary and cultural books. Publishes hardcover and paperback originals. Books: good quality paper; offset printing; perfect and cloth binding; illustrations. Average print order: 1,000-3,000. Averages 13 total titles each year.

• A Véhicule Press book, *Friends & Marriages*, by George Szanto received the QSPELL Prize for Fiction.

Needs: Feminist, literary, regional, short story collections, translations—"*by Canadian residents only.*" No romance or formula writing. Published *Evil Eye*, by Ann Diamond; *Snow Over Judaea*, by Kenneth Radu; *Friends & Marriages*, by George Szanto; and *True Romance with a Sailor*, by Yeshim Ternar.

How to Contact: Query first or send sample chapters. SASE ("no U.S. stamps, please"). Reports in 3 months on mss.

Terms: Pays in royalties of 10% minimum; 12% maximum. "Depends on press run and sales." Sends galleys to author. "Translators of fiction can receive Canada Council funding, which publisher applies for." Book catalog for 9 × 12 SASE.

Advice: "Quality in almost any style is acceptable. We believe in the editing process."

‡VISTA PUBLISHING, INC., (I, IV), 473 Broadway, Long Branch NJ 07740. (908)229-6500. Fax: (908)229-9647. President: Carolyn Zagury. Estab. 1991. "Small, independent press, owned by women and specializing in nurse authors." Publishes paperback originals. Plans 4 first novels this year. Averages 12 total titles, 6 fiction titles each year. Comments on rejected mss.

Needs: Adventure, humor/satire, mystery/suspense, romance, short story collections. Recently published *Medicine Bow*, by Beth Roberts Kotarski (novel); *Green Angels*, by Brenda Burkhart Schnoor (romance); and *Of Lovers and Madmen*, by Anita Bush (mystery).

How to Contact: Accepts unsolicited mss. Query with complete ms. Fax query OK. Include bio. Send SASE for reply, return of ms or send disposable copy of ms. Reports in 2 months on mss. Simultaneous submissions OK.

Terms: Pays royalties. Sends galleys to author. Publishes ms 2 years after acceptance. Writer's guidelines and book catalog for SASE.

Advice: "We prefer to read full manuscripts. Authors should be nurses or allied health professionals."

W.W. PUBLICATIONS, (IV), Subsidiary of A.T.S., Box 373, Highland MI 48357-0373. (813)585-0985. Also publishes *Minas Tirith Evening Star*. Editor: Philip Helms. Estab. 1967. One-man operation on part-time basis. Publishes paperback originals and reprints. Books: typing paper; offset printing; staple-bound; black ink illustrations. Average print order: 500. First novel print order: 500. Averages 1 title (fiction) each year. Occasionally critiques rejected mss.

• The publisher is an arm of the American Tolkien Society.

Needs: Fantasy, science fiction, and young adult/teen (fantasy/science fiction). "Specializes in Tolkien-related or middle-earth fiction." Published *The Adventures of Fungo Hafwirse*, by Philip W. Helms and David L. Dettman.

How to Contact: Accepts unsolicited mss. Submit complete ms with SASE. Reports in 1 month. Simultaneous submissions OK.

Terms: Individual arrangement with author depending on book, etc.; provides 5 author's copies. Free book catalog.

Advice: "We are publishing more fiction and more paperbacks. The author/editor relationship: a friend and helper."

WHITE PINE PRESS, (II), 10 Village Square, Fredonia NY 14063. (716)672-5743. Fax: (716)672-4724. Director: Dennis Maloney. Fiction Editor: Elaine La Mattina. Estab. 1973. Small literary publisher. Publishes paperback originals and reprints. Books: 60 lb. natural paper; offset; perfect binding.

Average print order: 2,000-3,000. First novel print order: 2,000. Averages 8-10 total titles, 6-7 fiction titles each year.

Needs: Ethnic/multicultural, literary, short story collections, translations. Looking for "strong novels." No romance, science fiction. Publishes anthologies. Editors select stories. Recently published *The Voice of Manush*, by Victor Waltor (literary novel); *Goldsmith's Return*, by T.R. Bazes (literary novel); and *I Saw A Man Hit His Wife*, by M. Greenside (short stories). Publishes Dispatches series (international fiction), a Human Rights series, and Secret Weavers series (writing by Latin American Women).

How to Contact: Accepts unsolicited mss. Query letter with outline/synopsis and 2 sample chapters. Include estimated word count and list of publishing credits. SASE for reply or return of ms. Agented fiction 10%. Reports in 2 weeks on queries; 3 months on mss. Simultaneous submissions OK.

Terms: Pays royalties of 5% minimum; 10% maximum. Offers negotiable advance. Pays in author's copies; payment depends on grant/award money. Sends galleys to author. Publishes 1-2 years after acceptance. Book catalog free.

Advice: "Follow our guidelines."

WILLOWISP PRESS, (I, II), Division of PAGES, Inc., 801 94th Ave. N., St. Petersburg FL 33702-2426. (813)578-7600. Imprints include Worthington Press, Hamburger Press, Riverbank Press. Address material to Acquisitions Editor. Estab. 1984. "Children's mid-size press." Publishes paperback originals for children. Published new writers within the last year.

● Ruth E. Kelley's *Boomer's Journal* was nominated for the 1996 Arizona State Award Book. Willowisp is planning anthologies of romance short stories and original horror stories for grades 5-8.

Needs: "Children's fiction and nonfiction, K-8." Adventure, contemporary and romance, for grades 5-8; preschool/picture book. No "violence, sex; romance must be very lightly treated." Riverbank Press is specifically for professional storytellers." Recently published *Dangerous Dan*, by Jef Mallett (picture book); and *Boomer's Journal*, by Ruth E. Kelley (fiction, grades 5-8).

How to Contact: Accepts unsolicited mss. Query (except picture books) with outline/synopsis and 3 sample chapters. Must send SASE. Reporting time on queries varies; 2 months on mss. Simultaneous submissions OK. "Prefer hard copy for original submissions; prefer disk for publication."

Terms: Pay "varies." Publishes ms 6-12 months after acceptance. Writer's guidelines for #10 SASE.

Advice: "We need *fresh* ideas that speak to children. Our consumer is *the child*, so the story must appeal to him or her at a kid's level. 'Fun' and 'engaging' are the watchwords."

WOMAN IN THE MOON PUBLICATIONS, (I, IV), 1409 The Alameda, San Jose CA 95126. (408)279-WOMAN. E-mail: sb02701@mercury.fhda.edu. Publisher: Dr. SDiane A. Bogus. Editor-in-Chief: Phillip Lynch. Estab. 1979. "We are a small press with a primary publishing agenda for poetry, New Age and reference books of no more than 1,000 words biannually. For our news magazine *The Spirit* we accept short story manuscripts." Averages 2-4 total titles each year. Comments on rejected mss.

Needs: Contemporary, ethnic, fantasy, gay, lesbian, psychic/supernatural/occult, prisoner's stories, short story collections.

How to Contact: Accepts unsolicited mss between January 1-April 30 only up to 100 mss. Query first or submit outline/synopsis and sample chapters. Query by letter, phone, fax or e-mail. SASE for query. Acknowledges in 1 week; reports during or at end of season. Simultaneous submissions OK.

Terms: *$45 reading fee required.* Pays royalties of 5% minimum; 10% maximum. Pays $25 plus 2 copies for short stories in quarterly newsletter. Publishes ms within 2 years after acceptance. Writer's guidelines for #10 SASE. Book sample for 6×9 SAE and $4 postage. Book catalog for $5.

Advice: "To the short story writer, write us a real life lesbian gay set of stories. Tell us how life is for an African American person in an enlightened world. Create a possibility, an ideal that humanity can live toward. Write a set of stories that will free, redeem and instruct humanity. The trends in fiction by women have to do with the heroine as physical and capable and not necessarily defended by or romantically linked to a male." Sponsors fiction and nonfiction prose contest in the name of Audre Lorde. Awards two $250 prizes. Contest runs from September 1 to November 30. Winners announced in February.

WOODLEY MEMORIAL PRESS, (IV), English Dept., Washburn University, Topeka KS 66621. (913)234-1032. E-mail: zzlaws@acc.wuacc.edu.Editor: Robert N. Lawson. Estab. 1980. "Woodley Memorial Press is a small, nonprofit press which publishes book-length poetry and fiction collections by Kansas writers only; by 'Kansas writers' we mean writers who reside in Kansas or have a Kansas connection." Publishes paperback originals. Averages 2 titles each year. Sometimes comments on rejected ms.

● Check for next short story collection contest. Work must be by a Kansas resident only. Most of the fiction the press publishes comes from its short story competition.

Needs: Contemporary, experimental, literary, mainstream, short story coll... see genre fiction, juvenile, or young adult." Recently published *Gathering*... man (short stories).

How to Contact: *Charges $5 reading fee.* Accepts unsolicited mss. Acce... correspondence by e-mail. Send complete ms. SASE. Reports in 2 weeks... mss.

Terms: "Terms are individually arranged with author after acceptance of ... one year after acceptance. Writer's guidelines for #10 SASE.

Advice: "We only publish one work of fiction a year, on average, and de... Kansas author. We are more likely to do a collection of short stories by a si... ...

WRITE WAY PUBLISHING, (I, II), Suite 210, 10555 E. Dartmouth, Aurora CO 80014. (303)695-0001. Fax: (303)368-8004. E-mail: writewy@aol.com Owner/Editor: Dorrie O'Brien. Estab. 1993. Small press. Publishes hardcover originals. Average print order: 2,500. First novel print order: 1,000. Published new writers within the last year. Averages 10-12 total titles, all fiction, each year. Often comments on rejected mss.

Needs: Adventure, fantasy/fairy tale, horror (soft), mystery/suspense (amateur sleuth, cozy, police procedural, private eye/hardboiled), psychic/supernatural, science fiction (soft/sociological, space trilogy/series), thriller/espionage. Recently published *Show Control*, by Keith Snyder; *Shards*, by Tom Piccirilli; and *Frogskin & Muttonfat*, by Carol Caverly (mysteries).

How to Contact: Query with short outline/synopsis and 1-2 sample chapters. Include estimated word count, bio (reasonably short) and list of publishing credits. Send SASE for reply, return of ms or send a disposable copy of ms. Agented fiction 10%. Reports in 2-4 weeks on queries; 6-8 months on mss. Simultaneous submissions OK.

Terms: Pays royalties of 8% minimum; 10% maximum. Does not pay advances. Sends galleys to author. Writer's guidelines for SASE.

Advice: "Always have the query letter, synopsis and the first chapters edited by an unbiased party prior to submitting them to us. Remember: first impressions are just as important to a publisher as they might be to a prospective employer."

ZEPHYR PRESS, (III), 13 Robinson St., Somerville MA 02145. Fax: (617)776-8246. Subsidiary of Aspect, Inc. Editorial Directors: Ed Hogan and Leora Zeitlin. Estab. 1980. Small nonprofit publisher of Russian/Slavic literary and travel books. Publishes hardcover and paperback originals. Books: acid-free paper; offset printing; Smyth-sewn binding; some illustrations. Average print order: 1,500-2,000. First novel print order: 1,000-1,500. Averages 3-4 total titles, 1 fiction title each year.

Needs: Contemporary, ethnic, feminist/lesbian, literary, mainstream, short story collections, translations (Russian, Eastern European fiction). Published *The Shoemaker's Tale*, by Mark Ari; and *Sleeper at Harvest Time*, by Leonid Latynin.

How to Contact: "We no longer read unsolicited manuscripts outside of our specialty of Russian/Slavic writing. Our focus in fiction is now on contemporary Russian writers in translation. We accept queries from agents, and from authors whose previous publications and professional credits (you must include a summary of these) evince work of exceptional talent and vision. Queries should include vita, list of publications, and up to 10 sample pages, photocopies only. If we are interested, we will request the full manuscript. Otherwise, we will probably not respond."

Terms: Pays royalties of approximately 12% of publisher's net for first edition. Occasional flexibility of terms." Sends galleys to author. Book catalog for SASE.

Advice: "Seek well qualified feedback from literary magazine editors or agents and/or professionally established writers before submitting manuscripts to publishers. We regard the author/editor relationship as one of close cooperation, from editing through promotion."

ZOLAND BOOKS, INC., (II, III), 384 Huron Ave., Cambridge MA 02138. (617)864-6252. Publisher: Roland Pease. Managing Editor: Michael Lindgren. Marketing Director: Stephen Hull. Estab. 1987. "We are a literary press, publishing poetry, fiction, nonfiction, photography, and other titles of literary interest." Publishes hardcover and paperback originals. Books: acid-free paper; sewn binding; some with illustrations. Average print order: 2,000-5,000. Averages 10 total titles each year.

● *An Altogether Different Language*, by Ann Porter and published by Zoland Books, was a finalist for the 1995 National Book Award.

Needs: Contemporary, feminist, literary, short story collections. Recently published *Rosalind*, by Myra Goldberg; *Among the Ginzburgs*, by Ellen Pall; and *Ocean of Words*, by Ita Jin.

How to Contact: Accepts unsolicited mss. Query first, then send complete ms with cover letter. SASE. Reports in 4-6 weeks on queries; 3-6 months on mss.

Terms: Pays royalties of 5-8%. Average advance: $1,500; negotiable (also pays author's copies). Sends galleys to author. Publishes ms 1-2 years after acceptance. Book catalog for 6×9 SAE and 2 first-class stamps.

national small press

The following small presses from countries outside the U.S. and Canada will consider novels or short stories in English. Many of these markets do not pay in cash, but may provide author copies. Always include a self-addressed envelope with International Reply Coupons to ensure a response or the return of your manuscript. International Reply Coupons are available at the main branch of your local post office. To save the cost of return postage on your manuscript, you may want to send a copy of your manuscript for the publisher to keep or throw away and enclose a self-addressed postcard with one IRC for a reply.

ADAEX EDUCATIONAL PUBLICATIONS, P.O. Box AK188, Kumasi, Ghana. Publisher/Fiction Editor: Asare Konadu Yamoah. Average 5-10 fiction titles/year. "Publication development organization for Ghanaian, African and world literature: novels, workbooks, language development, etc." Length: 8-250 typed pages. Send brief summary and first and last chapter. Pays advance and royalties. Looks for cultural development, romance, literary translators and copyright brokers.

ATTIC PRESS, (IV), 29 Upper Mount St., Dublin 2, Ireland. Contact: Managing Editor. E-mail: atticirl@iol.ie. Website: http://www.iol.ie/~atticirl/. Averages 6-8 fiction titles/year. "Attic Press is an independent, export-oriented, Irish-owned publishing house with a strong international profile. The press specializes in the publication of fiction and nonfiction books for and about women by Irish and international authors." Publishes a series of teenage fiction, Bright Sparks. Send cover letter, synopsis, brief summary, sample chapters. Pays advance on signing contract and royalties. Write for catalog.

BASEMENT PRESS, 29 Upper Mount St., Dublin 2, Ireland. E-mail: atticirl@iol.ie. Website: http://www.iol.ie. Contact: Managing Editor. "Basement Press is the general division of Attic Press, publishing fiction and nonfiction by both men and women, specializing in biography, business and political writing. Basement Press aims to be fresh, irreverent, controversial and entertaining, and publishes a series of Gay and Lesbian fiction and nonfiction entitled Queer Views." Send cover letter, synopsis, brief summary and sample chapters. Pays advance on signing contract and royalties.

BIBLIOTECA DI NOVA SF, FUTURO, GREAT WORKS OF SF, (IV), Perseo Libri srl, Box 1240, I-40100 Bologna, Italy. Fiction Editor: Ugo Malaguti. "Science fiction and fantasy; novels and/or collections of stories." Pays 7% royalties on cover price; advance: $800-1,000 on signing contract. Buys Italian book rights; other rights remain with author. "While preferring published writers, we also consider new writers."

CHRISTCHURCH PUBLISHERS LTD., 2 Caversham St., London S.W.3, 4AH UK. Fiction Editor: James Hughes. Averages 25 fiction titles/year. "Miscellaneous fiction, also poetry. More 'literary' style of fiction, but also thrillers, crime fiction etc." Length: 30,000 words minimum. Send a cover letter, synopsis, brief summary. "Preliminary letter and *brief* synopsis favored." Pays advance and royalties. "We have contacts and agents worldwide."

AIDAN ELLIS PUBLISHING, Cobb House, Nuffield, Henley-on-Thames, Oxon RG9 5RT England. Fiction Editor: Aidan Ellis. Averages 12 fiction titles/year. "Founded in 1971, we are a small publishing house publishing fiction and general trade books." Send a cover letter, synopsis, brief summary, sample chapter/s. Pays advance on publication, royalties twice yearly. Write for catalog.

‡GMP PUBLISHERS LTD., Box 247, Swaffham PE37 8PA England. Editor: David Fernbach. Publishes 12-13 novels yearly and the occasional short story collection. "Principally publishing works of gay interest—both popular and literary." Pays royalties. Send synopsis and/or sample chapters first.

HANDSHAKE EDITIONS, Atelier A2, 83 rue de la Tombe Issoire, 75014 Paris France. Editor: Jim Haynes. Publishes 4 story collections or novels/year. "Only face-to-face submissions accepted.

---

‡   **THE DOUBLE DAGGER** before a listing indicates that the listing is new in this edition. New markets are often the most receptive to submissions by new writers.

More interested in 'faction' and autobiographical writing." Pays in copies. Writers interested in submitting a manscript should "have lunch or dinner with me in Paris."

HEMKUNT, Publishers A-78 Naraina Industrial Area Ph.I, New Delhi India 110028. Managing Director: G.P. Singh. Export Directors: Deepinder Singh/Arvinder Singh. "We would be interested in novels, preferably by authors with a published work. Would like to have distribution rights for US, Canada and UK beside India." Send a cover letter, brief summary, 3 sample chapters (first, last and one other chapter). "Writer should have at least 1-2 published novels to his/her credit." Catalog on request.

KAWABATA PRESS, (II), Knill Cross House, Knill Cross, Millbrook, Torpoint, Cornwall PL10 1DX England. Fiction Editor: C. Webb. "Mostly poetry—but prose should be realistic, free of genre writing and clichés and above all original in ideas and content." Length: 200-4,000 words (for stories). "Don't forget return postage (or IRC)." Writers receive half of profits after print costs are covered. Write for guidelines and book list.

THE LITERATURE BUREAU, P.O. Box CY749 Causeway, Harare Zimbabwe. Fiction Editor: B.C. Chitsike. Averages 12 fiction titles/year. "All types of fiction from the old world novels to the modern ones with current issues. We publish these books in association with commercial publishers but we also publish in our own right. We specialize in Shona and Ndebele, our local languages in Zimbabwe. Manuscripts in English are not our priority." Length: 7,000-30,000 words. Send entire manuscript. Pays royalties. "Send the complete manuscript for assessment. If it is a good one it is either published by the Bureau or sponsored for publication. If it needs any correction, a full report will be sent to the author." Obtain guidelines by writing to the Bureau. "We have 'Hints to New Authors,' a pamphlet for aspiring authors. These can be obtained on request."

THE LUTTERWORTH PRESS, P.O. Box 60, Cambridge CB1 2NT England. Managing Director: Adrian Brink. "Almost 200-year-old small press publishing wide range of adult nonfiction, religious and children's books. The only fiction we publish is for children: picture books (with text from 0-10,000 words), educational, young novels, story collections. Also nonfiction as well as religious children's books." Send synopsis and sample chapter. Pays royalty. "Send IRCs. English language is universal, i.e., mid-Atlantic English."

DAVID PHILIP PUBLISHERS, P.O. Box 23408, Claremont 7735 Cape Province South Africa. "Fiction with Southern African concern or focus. Progressive, often suitable for school or university prescription, literary, serious." Send synopsis and 1 sample chapter. Pays royalties. "Familiarize yourself with list of publisher to which you wish to submit work." Write for guidelines.

‡RENDITIONS, (IV), Chinese University of Hong Kong. Editor: Dr. Eva Hung. Averages 2-3 fiction titles annually. "Academic specialist publisher. Will only consider English translations of Chinese fiction. Fiction published either in semiannual journal (*Renditions*) or in the Renditions Paperback series." For fiction over 5,000 words in translation, sample is required. Sample length: 1,000-2,000 words. Send sample chapter. Pays honorarium for publication in *Renditions*; royalties for paperback series. "Submit only works in our specialized area. One copy of translation accompanied by one copy of original Chinese text." Fax requests for information and guidelines to Mrs. Cecila Yip, (852)6035149.

‡SERPENT'S TAIL, 4 Blackstock Mews, London N4 2BT UK. Fiction Editor: Peter Ayrton. Averages 30 fiction titles/year. "We are an up-market literary house whose tastes are well out of the mainstream. We see our audience as young and urban-based. Translations, literary fiction and cultural studies are our forte." Length: 30,000 words minimum; 100,000 words maximum. Send cover letter; enclose IRC or postage. Pays advance plus royalties. "Send query letter first, and only after you have looked at the books we publish. For us, writers need not give extra background to their work, its context, etc. regarding the fact that they are not British. We are a cosmopolitan bunch." Write office for catalog.

SINCLAIR-STEVENSON, Reed Trade Books, Michelin House, 81 Fulham Rd., London SW3 England. Publisher: Penelope Hoare. Averages 10 fiction titles/year. "Trade hardbacks of quality fiction from new and established authors: Rose Tremain, Susan Hill, Lionel Davidson, Peter Ackroyd." Length: open. Send cover letter. Pays advance and royalties. Contact Sales Manager for catalog. No guidelines available.

Commercial Book Publishers

In this section, you will find many of the "big-name" book publishers—Avon, The Berkley Publishing Group, Harcourt Brace & Company, Harlequin, Alfred A. Knopf and Little Brown and Company, to name a few. Many of the publishers listed here remain tough markets for new writers or for those whose work might be considered literary or experimental. Indeed, some of the publishers listed here only accept work from established authors, and then often only through an author's agent.

Although breaking into the commercial publishing market is difficult, it is not impossible. The trade magazine *Publishers Weekly* regularly features interviews with writers whose first novels are being released by top publishers. David Guterson's first novel *Snow Falling on Cedars* has enjoyed phenomenal success. (See the interview with Guterson on page 60 of this book.) And Robert Redford paid an unprecedented three million dollars for the movie rights to *The Horse Whisperer*, a first novel written by Nicholas Evans.

Many editors find great satisfaction in publishing a writer's first novel. In the Insider Report on page 453 with Marcia Markland, vice president and publisher of Avalon Books, Markland says, "I'm always, always, always looking for good writing. There are a lot of good writers out there who simply don't know how to get a literary agent. We'd like to work with them." Sara Ann Freed, executive editor at Mysterious Press, says in the Insider Report interview with her on page 475 that a new writer with a good manuscript and no track record can often be viewed more favorably than a published writer with a bad sales history.

TYPES OF COMMERCIAL PUBLISHERS

The publishers in this section publish books "for the trade." That is, unlike textbook, technical or scholarly publishers, trade publishers publish books to be sold to the general consumer through bookstores, chain stores or other retail outlets. Within the trade book field, however, there are a number of different types of books.

The easiest way to categorize books is by their physical appearance and the way they are marketed. Hardcover books are the more expensive editions of a book, sold through bookstores and carrying a price tag of around $20 and up. Trade paperbacks are soft-bound books, also sold mostly in bookstores, but they carry a more modest price tag of usually around $10 to $20. Today a lot of fiction is published in this form because it means a lower financial risk than hardcover.

Mass market paperbacks are another animal altogether. These are the smaller "pocket-size" books available at bookstores, grocery stores, drug stores, chain retail outlets, etc. Much genre or category fiction is published in this format. This area of the publishing industry is very open to the work of talented new writers who write in specific genres such as science fiction, romance and mystery.

At one time publishers could be easily identified and grouped by the type of books they do. Today, however, the lines between hardcover and paperback books are blurred. Many publishers known for publishing hardcover books also publish trade paperbacks and have paperback imprints. This enables them to offer established authors (and a very few lucky newcomers) hard-soft deals in which their book comes out in both versions. Thanks to the mergers of the past decade, too, the same company may own several hardcover and paperback subsidiaries and imprints, even though their editorial focuses may remain separate.

CHOOSING A COMMERCIAL PUBLISHER

In addition to checking the bookstores and libraries for books by publishers that interest you, you may want to refer to the Commercial Publisher section of the Category Index to find publishers divided by specific subject categories. The subjects listed in the Index are general. Read the individual listings to find which subcategories interest a publisher. For example, you will find several romance publishers listed under that heading in the Category Index, but read the listings to find which type of romance is considered—gothic, contemporary, Regency or futuristic. See How to Use This Book to Publish Your Fiction for more on how to refine your list of potential markets.

The Roman numeral ranking codes appearing after the names of the publishers will also help you in selecting a publisher. These codes are especially important in this section, because many of the publishing houses listed here require writers to submit through an agent. A numeral **III** identifies those that mostly publish established and agented authors, while a numeral **I** points to publishers most open to new writers. See the end of this introduction for a complete list of ranking codes.

IN THE LISTINGS

As with other sections in this book, we identify new listings with a double-dagger symbol (‡). In this section, many of these are not new publishers, but instead are established publishers who decided to list this year in the hope of finding promising new writers.

We use a maple leaf symbol (❋) to identify the Canadian publishers. North American commercial publishers are grouped together and are followed by a group of publishers from around the world. Remember, self-addressed envelopes for replies from countries other than your own should include International Reply Coupons rather than stamps.

We're continuing to include editorial comments this year, set off by a bullet symbol (●) within the listing. This is where we can tell you of any honors or awards received by publishers or their books. We include information about any special requirements or circumstances that will help you know even more about the publisher's needs and policies.

Jay Schaefer, fiction editor at Chronicle Books, asked us to emphasize the importance of paying close attention to the Needs and How to Contact subheads of listings for book publishers. Unlike magazine editors who want to see complete manuscripts of short stories, most of the book publishers listed here ask that writers send a query letter with an outline and/or synopsis and several chapters of their novel. Leonard Goss, vice president and editor-in-chief of Crossway Books, says in the Insider Report with him on page 458 that the best way to catch his attention is with a well-written book proposal. For information on preparing the query letter and novel outline and synopsis, see Approaching Agents and Editors: Tools and Tactics beginning on page 24. For more inside tips on what today's book publishers expect from writers, see the Book Publishers' Roundtable beginning on page 17.

This year, there are no subsidy book publishers listed in *Novel & Short Story Writer's Market*. By subsidy, we mean any arrangement in which the writer is expected to pay all or part of the cost of producing, distributing and marketing his book. We feel a writer should not be asked to share in any cost of turning his manuscript into a book. All the book publishers listed here told us that they *do not charge writers* for publishing their work. If any of the publishers listed here ask you to pay any part of publishing or marketing your manuscript, please let us know.

A NOTE ABOUT AGENTS

The Business of Fiction Writing outlines how to prepare work to submit directly to a publisher. Many publishers are willing to look at unsolicited submissions, but most feel having an agent is to the writer's best advantage. In this section more than any other, you'll find a number of publishers who prefer submissions from agents.

Because the commercial fiction field has become so competitive, and publishers have so little time, more and more are relying on agents. For publishers, agents act as "first readers," wading through the deluge of submissions from writers to find the very best. For writers, a good agent can be a foot in the door—someone willing to do the necessary work to put your manuscript in the right editor's hands.

Because it is almost as hard to find a good agent as it is to find a publisher, many writers see agents as just one more roadblock to publication. Yet those who have agents say they are invaluable. Not only can a good agent help you make your work more marketable, an agent acts as your business manager and adviser, keeping your interests up front during contract negotiations.

Still, finding an agent can be very difficult for a new writer. Those already published in magazines or other periodicals have a better chance than someone with no publishing credits. Although many agents will read queries, packages and manuscripts from unpublished authors without introduction, referrals from other clients can be a big help. If you don't know any published authors, you may want to try to meet an agent at a conference before approaching them with your manuscript. Some agents even set aside time at conferences to meet new writers.

For listings of agents and more information on how to approach and deal with them, see the 1997 *Guide to Literary Agents*, published by Writer's Digest Books. The book separates nonfee- and fee-charging agents. While many agents do not charge any fees up front, a few charge writers to cover the costs of using outside readers. Be wary of those who charge large sums of money for reading a manuscript. Reading fees do not guarantee representation. Think of an agent as a potential business partner and feel free to ask tough questions about his or her credentials, experience and business practices.

FOR MORE . . .

Several of the mystery, romance and science fiction publishers included in this section are also included in *Mystery Writer's Sourcebook*, *Romance Writer's Sourcebook* or *Science Fiction and Fantasy Writer's Sourcebook* (all published by Writer's Digest Books). These books include in-depth interviews with editors and publishers. Also check issues of *Publishers Weekly* for publishing industry trade news in the U.S. and around the world or *Quill & Quire* for book publishing news in the Canadian book industry.

The ranking system we've used for listings in this section is as follows:

I **Publisher encourages beginning or unpublished writers to submit work for consideration and publishes new writers frequently.**

II **Publisher accepts outstanding work by beginning and established writers.**

III **Hard to break into; publishes mostly writers with extensive previous publication credits or agented writers.**

IV **Special-interest or regional publisher, open only to writers in certain genres or on certain subjects or from certain geographic areas.**

V **Closed to unsolicited submissions.**

ACADEMY CHICAGO PUBLISHERS, (II), 363 W. Erie St., Chicago IL 60610. (312)751-7302. Senior Editor: Anita Miller. Estab. 1975. Midsize independent publisher. Publishes hardcover and paperback originals and paperback reprints.

Needs: Biography, history, feminist, academic and anthologies. Only the most unusual mysteries, no private-eyes or thrillers. No explicit sex or violence. Serious fiction, not romance/adventure. "We will consider historical fiction that is well researched. No science fiction/fantasy, no religious/inspirational, no how-to, no cookbooks. In general, we are very conscious of women's roles. We publish very few children's books." Recently published *Hiwassee*, by Charles F. Price; *Murder at the Movies*, by A.E. Eddenden; and *Threshold of Fire*, by Hella Haasse.

How to Contact: Accepts unsolicited mss. Query and submit first three chapters, triple spaced, with SASE and a cover letter briefly describing the content of your work. No simultaneous submissions. "Manuscripts without envelopes will be discarded. *Mailers* are a *must*."

Terms: Pays 5-10% on net in royalties; no advance. Sends galleys to author.

Advice: "At the moment we are swamped with manuscripts and anything under consideration can be under consideration for months."

ACE SCIENCE FICTION, Berkley Publishing Group, 200 Madison Ave., New York NY 10016. (212)951-8800. Estab. 1977. Publishes paperback originals and reprints. See Berkley/Ace Science Fiction.

ALGONQUIN BOOKS OF CHAPEL HILL, 708 Broadway, New York NY 10003. Prefers not to share information at this time.

ARCHWAY PAPERBACKS/MINSTREL BOOKS, (II), 1230 Avenue of the Americas, New York NY 10020. (212)698-7268. Vice President/Editorial Director: Patricia MacDonald. Published by Pocket Books. Imprints: Minstrel Books (ages 7-11); and Archway (ages 11 and up). Publishes paperback originals and reprints.

Needs: Young adult: mystery, suspense/adventure, thrillers. Young readers (80 pages and up): adventure, animals, humor, family, fantasy, friends, mystery, school, etc. No picture books. Published *Fear Street: The New Boy*, by R.L. Stine; and *Aliens Ate My Homework*, by Bruce Coville. Published new writers this year.

How to Contact: Submit query first with outline; SASE "mandatory. If SASE not attached, query letter will not be answered."

ASPECT, (V), Imprint of Warner Books, 1271 Avenue of the Americas, New York NY 10020. (212)522-5320. Fax: (212)522-7990. E-mail: 72662.2617@compuserve.com. Editor-in-Chief: Betsy Mitchell. Estab. 1994. Science fiction/fantasy imprint of Warner Books. Publishes hardcover and paperback originals and hardcover reprints. Published new writers within the last year. Plans 2 first novels this year. Averages 32 total fiction titles this year. Often critiques or comments on rejected ms.

Needs: Epic fantasy, science fiction. "No humorous fantasy or short story collections." Recently published *Luthien's Gample*, by R.A. Salvatore (fantasy hardcover); *Encounter with Tiber*, by Buzz Aldrin and John Barnes (science fiction hardcover); and *Voices of Hope*, by David Feintuch (science fiction paperback). Plans to publish ongoing series in the future.

How to Contact: No unsolicited mss. Submit through agent. Include estimated word count, ½-page bio and list of publishing credits with submission. Send SASE for reply, return of ms or send a disposable copy of ms. Agented fiction 98%. Reports in 3 weeks on queries; 2 months on mss.

Terms: Offers negotiable advance. Sends galleys to author. Publishes ms approximately 1 year after acceptance.

Advice: "We have launched several bestselling authors in both science fiction and fantasy because they brought us writing that was truly new and different. Being a beginner isn't necessarily a negative with us—as long as you find an agent who will bring you to us, we'll be happy to consider first-timers."

ATHENEUM BOOKS FOR YOUNG READERS, (II), Imprint of the Simon & Schuster Children's Publishing Division, 1230 Avenue of the Americas, New York NY 10022. (212)698-2721. Vice President/Editorial Director: Jonathan J. Lanman. Fiction Editors: Marcia Marshall, Ana Cerro, Anne Schwartz. Second largest imprint of large publisher/corporation. Publishes hardcover originals. Books: Illustrations for picture books, some illustrated short novels; average print order: 6,000-7,500; first novel print order: 5,000. Averages 60 total titles, 30 middle grade and YA fiction titles each year. Very rarely critiques rejected mss.

● Books published by Atheneum Books for Children have received the Newbery Medal (*Shiloh*, by Phyllis Reynolds Naylor) and the Christopher Award (*The Gold Coin*, by Alma Flor Ada, illustrated by Neal Waldman). Because of the merger of Macmillan and Simon & Schuster, Atheneum Books has absorbed the Scribners imprint of Macmillan.

Needs: Juvenile (adventure, animal, contemporary, fantasy, historical, sports), preschool/picture book, young adult/teen (fantasy/science fiction, historical, mystery, problem novels, sports, spy/adventure). No "paperback romance type" fiction. Published *Albert's Thanksgiving*, by Lesle Tryon (3-6, picture book); *Downriver*, by Will Hobbs (3-6, picture book); *Alice the Brave*, by Phyllis Reynolds Naylor (8-12, middle grade novel); and *Uncle Vampire*, by Cynthia Grant (12 & up young adult novel).
How to Contact: Accepts queries only. SASE. Agented fiction 40%. Reports in 4-6 weeks on queries. Simultaneous submissions OK "if we are so informed and author is unpublished."
Terms: Pays in royalties of 10%. Average advance: $3,000 "along with advance and royalties, authors standardly receive ten free copies of their book and can purchase more at a special discount." Sends galleys to author. Writer's guidelines for #10 SASE.
Advice: "We publish all hardcover originals, occasionally an American edition of a British publication. Our fiction needs have not varied in terms of quantity—of the 60-70 titles we do each year, 30 are fiction in different age levels. We are less interested in specific topics or subject matter than in overall quality of craftsmanship. First, know your market thoroughly. We publish only children's books, so caring for and *respecting* children is of utmost importance. Also, fad topics are dangerous, as are works you haven't polished to the best of your ability. (Why should we choose a 'jewel in the rough' when we can get a manuscript a professional has polished to be ready for publication?) The juvenile market is not one in which a writer can 'practice' to become an adult writer. In general, be professional. We appreciate the writers who take the time to find out what type of books we publish by visiting the libraries and reading the books. Neatness is a pleasure, too."

AVALON BOOKS, (I, II, IV), 401 Lafayette St., New York NY 10003. (212)598-0222. Vice President/Publisher: Marcia Markland. Imprint of Thomas Bouregy Company, Inc. Publishes hardcover originals. Averages 60 titles/year.
Needs: "Avalon Books publishes wholesome romances, mysteries, westerns. Intended for family reading, our books are read by adults as well as teenagers, and their characters are all adults. There is no graphic sex in any of our novels. Currently, we publish five books a month: two romances, one mystery, one career romance and one western. All the romances are contemporary; all the westerns are historical." Recently published *Ride the Rainbow Home*, by Susan Aylworth (career romance); *Bachelor for Rent*, by Karen Morrell (career romance); *The Curious Cape Cod Skull*, by Marie Lee (mystery); and *Frontier Justice*, by Dan Hepler (western). Books range in length from a minimum of 40,000 words to a maximum of 50,000 words.
How to Contact: Submit the first three chapters. "We'll contact you if we're interested." Publishes many first novels. Enclose ms-size SASE. Reports in about 3 months. "Send SASE for a copy of our tip sheet."
Terms: The first half of the advance is paid upon signing of the contract; the second within 30 days after publication. Usually publishes within 6 to 8 months after acceptance.

AVON BOOKS, (II), The Hearst Corporation, 1350 Avenue of the Americas, New York NY 10019. (212)261-6800. Imprints include Avon, Camelot and Flare. Senior Vice President/Publisher: Lou Aronica. Estab. 1941. Large hardcover and paperback publisher. Publishes hardcover and paperback originals and reprints. Averages 300 titles a year.
Needs: Fantasy, historical romance, mainstream, science fiction, medical thrillers, intrigue, war, western and young adult/teen. No poetry, short story collections, religious, limited literary or esoteric nonfiction. Published *Butterfly*, by Kathryn Harvey; *So Worthy My Love*, by Kathleen Woodiwiss. Sponsors Flare Novel competition.
How to Contact: Query letters only. SASE to insure response.
Terms: Vary.

BAEN BOOKS, (II), P.O. Box 1403, Riverdale NY 10471. (718)548-3100. Imprints are Baen Science Fiction and Baen Fantasy. Publisher and Editor: Jim Baen. Executive Editor: Toni Weisskopf. Estab. 1983. Independent publisher; books are distributed by Simon & Schuster. Publishes hardcover and paperback originals and paperback reprints. Published new writers within the last year. Plans 6-10 first novels this year. Averages 60 fiction titles each year. Occasionally critiques rejected mss.
Needs: Fantasy and science fiction. Interested in science fiction novels (generally "hard" science fiction) and fantasy novels "that at least strive for originality." Recently published *Paths to Otherwhere*, by James P. Hogan (science fiction); *Glenraven*, by Marion Zimmer Bradley and Holly Lisle (fantasy); and *Cetasanda*, by Lois McMaster Bujold. Published new writers within the last year.
How to Contact: Accepts unsolicited mss. Submit ms or outline/synopsis and 3 consecutive sample chapters with SASE (or IRC). Reports in 4-6 months. Will consider simultaneous submissions, "but grudgingly and not as seriously as exclusives."
Terms: Pays in royalties; offers advance. Sends galleys to author. Writer's guidelines for SASE.
Advice: "Keep an eye and a firm hand on the overall story you are telling. Style is important but less important than plot. Good style, like good breeding, never calls attention to itself. Read *Writing to the Point*, by Algis Budrys. We like to maintain long-term relationships with authors."

INSIDER REPORT

Avalon Books: always looking for good writing

"Very often publishing decisions have nothing to do with the quality of your work," says Marcia Markland, vice president and publisher of Avalon Books. "More often they have to do with a marketing decision of some sort."

The key to getting published, says Markland, is simply to keep submitting your work. "Don't keep it in a drawer. Send it to somebody. Every once in a while I'll get something that isn't right for us, but I'll know somebody in the industry who should take a look at it. I can also give writers suggestions."

Markland says she often gets submissions with drug references or stories with a lot of four-letter words or graphic sex—things that she just can't

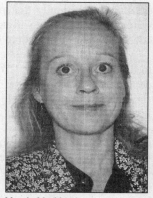

Marcia Markland

publish. "They may be perfectly splendid for another publisher, but we try to keep excessive sex and violence out of our books." Avalon steers clear of such subjects because the majority of their books are exclusively for the library market. "Our books are shipped to libraries automatically. In exchange, we promise not to send them anything that their patrons will find offensive."

Markland has been working in the publishing industry since the early '70s with stints at Penguin, St. Martin's, Prentice Hall, Bantam and the Mystery Guild. In 1992, she began at Avalon, a press that specializes in career romances, westerns and mysteries (all 192 pages, about 50,000 words).

"The market has gotten much more difficult than it was," says Markland. "There are fewer and fewer publishing companies, and fewer and fewer slots for books in those companies. What has happened in response, is that special markets with special categories have sprung up. There are all sorts of different approaches. Writers are very ingenious and so are publishers, so both just keep testing the market."

Avalon has had success with several series, such as a western collection called *Frontier Justice*, by Don Hepler. They've also gotten into the realm of regional publishing with a mystery series set in Cape Cod and another in Milwaukee. The Cape Cod mystery series, written by Marie Lee, has gotten a great reception from critics. "These mysteries have been compared to Agatha Christie and *Murder She Wrote*." The main character "is very interesting and will be a good series character for us."

Avalon gives regional series larger print runs and does a great deal of local promotion. Mystery series titles are being sold in local bookstores, an expansion

INSIDER REPORT, *continued*

for Avalon beyond the library market. "Given that we're a small company, we can't promise that authors will get nationwide distribution, but we can promise that we can do a limited area distribution. We see to it that we've saturated all the local media and bookstores, and we do a lot of special sales."

Avalon hadn't published series before Markland joined their team. "Although big conglomerates have made massive bestsellers possible," she says, "there are a lot of readers out there who don't want to read big, massive bestsellers, but they are looking for interesting things to read. I think they're looking for an extensive community that perhaps they don't have in their real lives, so they watch television. They watch the same series over and over again. I'm very conscious that these people like to *read* series, too."

Markland is not necessarily seeking out series books, but is certainly open to doing more of them. "When I'm making publishing decisions, I'm entirely dependent on finding good books first. Then we figure out how to sell them," she says. "I'm always looking for good regional mysteries and good romances. I love fiction."

Since Avalon is a small company, Markland does most of the manuscript reading herself. "When I'm trying to decide whether to buy something, I first look for the characters to see if I like them and want to read more about them. I'm always, always, always looking for good writing. Our house is a very good place for beginning writers. There aren't that many other publishers left that will look at unsolicited manuscripts. I believe that there are a lot of excellent writers out there who simply don't know how to get a literary agent. We'd like to work with them."

—*Alice P. Buening*

BAKER BOOKS, (II, IV), a division of Baker Book House, (formerly Baker Book House), P.O. Box 6287, Grand Rapids MI 49516. (616)676-9185. Assistant Editor, Trade Books: Jane Schrier. Estab. 1939. "Midsize Evangelical publisher." Publishes hardcover and paperback originals. Books: web offset print; average print order: 5,000-10,000; first novel print order: 5,000. Averages 130 total titles. Sometimes comments on rejected ms.

Needs: "We are mainly seeking Christian fiction of two genres: Contemporary women's fiction and mystery." No fiction that is not written from a Christian perspective or of a genre not specified. Recently published *I Read It In the Wordless Book*, by Betty Smartt Carter; *A Multitude of Sins*, by Virginia Stem Owens; and *In The Silence There Are Ghosts*, by James Schaap.

How to Contact: Does not accept unsolicited mss. Submit query letter, outline/synopsis and 3 sample chapters. SASE. Agented fiction 80% (so far). Reports in 3-4 weeks on queries. Simultaneous submissions OK.

Terms: Pays royalties of 14% (of net). Sometimes offers advance. Sends galleys to author. Publishes ms 1 year after acceptance. Writer's guidelines for #10 SASE. Book catalog for 9½ × 12½ SAE and 3 first-class stamps.

Advice: "We are not interested in historical fiction, romances, science fiction, Biblical narratives, or spiritual warfare novels. Please write for further information regarding our fiction lines. Send a cover letter describing your novel and your credentials as an author. Do not call to 'pass by' your idea. Do not send complete manuscripts."

BALLANTINE BOOKS, 201 E. 50th St., New York NY 10022. Subsidiary of Random House. Assistant Editor: Betsy Flagler. Publishes originals (general fiction, mass-market, trade paperback and hardcover). Published new writers this year. Averages over 120 total titles each year.

Needs: Major historical fiction, women's mainstream and general fiction.
How to Contact: Submit query letter or brief synopsis and first 100 pages of ms. SASE required. Reports in 2 months on queries; 4-5 months on mss.
Terms: Pays in royalties and advance.

‡**BANTAM BOOKS, (II)**, Division of Bantam Dell Doubleday Publishing Group, Inc. 1540 Broadway, New York NY 10036. (212)354-6500. Fax: (212)782-9523. Imprints include Crime Line, Domain, Fanfare, Loveswept, Spectra. Editor: Shauna Summers. Estab. 1945. Complete publishing: hard-cover, trade, mass market.
Needs: Contemporary, literary, mystery, historical, western, romance, science fiction, fantasy.
How to Contact: Query letter only first. No unsolicited mss. Include estimated word count and list of publishing credits. Simultaneous submissions OK. Reports on queries in 2-3 months.
Terms: Individually negotiated. Writer's guidelines (for romance only) free for SASE.

BANTAM/DOUBLEDAY/DELL BOOKS FOR YOUNG READERS DIVISION, (III), Bantam/Doubleday/Dell, 1540 Broadway, New York NY 10036. Imprints include Delacort Hardcover, Doubleday Picture Books; Paperback line: Dell Yearling, Laurel-Leaf, Skylark, Star Fire, Little Rooster, Sweet Dreams, Sweet Valley High. Editor-in-Chief to the Young Readers Division: Beverly Horowitz. Estab. 1945. Complete publishing: hardcover, trade, mass market.
● The Young Readers Division offers two contests, the Delacorte Press Annual Prize for a First Young Adult Novel and the Marguerite DeAngeli Prize.
Needs: Childrens/juvenile, young adult/teen. Published *Baby*, by Patricia MacLachlan; *Whatever Happened to Janie*, by Caroline Cooney; *Nate the Great and the Pillowcase*, by Marjorie Sharmat.
How to Contact: Does not accept unsolicited mss. Submit through agent. Agented fiction 100%. Reports on queries "as soon as possible." Simultaneous submissions OK.
Terms: Individually negotiated; offers advance.

THE BERKLEY PUBLISHING GROUP, (III), Subsidiary of G.P. Putnam's Sons, 200 Madison Ave., New York NY 10016. (212)951-8800. Imprints are Berkley, Jove, Boulevard, Ace Science Fiction. Editor-in-Chief: Leslie Gelbman. Fiction Editors: Natalee Rosenstein, Judith Stern, John Talbot, Gail Fortune, Susan Allison, Ginjer Buchanan, Laura Anne Gilman, Gary Goldstein and Hillary Cige. Nonfiction: Elizabeth Beier, Denise Silvestro and Hillary Cige. Large commercial category line. Publishes paperback originals, trade paperbacks and hardcover and paperback reprints. Books: Paperbound printing; perfect binding; average print order: "depends on position in list." Plans approx. 10 first novels this year. Averages 1,180 total titles, 1,000 fiction titles each year. Sometimes critiques rejected mss.
Needs: Fantasy, mainstream, mystery/suspense, romance (contemporary, historical), science fiction.
How to Contact: Accepts no unsolicited mss. Submit through agent only. Agented fiction 98%. Reports in 6-8 weeks on mss. Simultaneous submissions OK.
Terms: Pays royalties of 4-10%. Provides 25 author's copies. Writer's guidelines and book catalog not available.
Advice: "Aspiring novelists should keep abreast of the current trends in publishing by reading *The New York Times* Bestseller Lists, trade magazines for their desired genre and *Publishers Weekly*."

BERKLEY/ACE SCIENCE FICTION, (II), Berkley Publishing Group, 200 Madison Ave., New York NY 10016. (212)951-8800. Editor-in-Chief: Susan Allison. Estab. 1948. Publishes paperback originals and reprints and 6-10 hardcovers per year. Number of titles: 8/month. Buys 85-95% agented fiction.
Needs: Science fiction and fantasy. No other genre accepted. No short stories. Published *The Cat Who Walks Through Walls*, by Robert Heinlein; and *Neuromancer*, by William Gibson.
How to Contact: Submit outline/synopsis and 3 sample chapters with SASE. No simultaneous submissions. Reports in 2 months minimum on mss. "Queries answered immediately if SASE enclosed." Publishes ms an average of 18 months after acceptance.
Terms: Standard for the field. Sends galleys to author.
Advice: "Good science fiction and fantasy are almost always written by people who have read and loved a lot of it. We are looking for knowledgeable science or magic, as well as sympathetic characters

---

MARKET CATEGORIES: (I) Open to new writers; (II) Open to both new and established writers; (III) Interested mostly in established writers; (IV) Open to writers whose work is specialized; (V) Closed to unsolicited submissions.

with recognizable motivation. We are looking for solid, well-plotted science fiction: good action adventure, well-researched hard science with good characterization and books that emphasize characterization without sacrificing plot. In fantasy we are looking for all types of work, from high fantasy to sword and sorcery." Submit fantasy and science fiction to Susan Allison and Ginjer Buchanan.

JOHN F. BLAIR, PUBLISHER, (II, IV), 1406 Plaza Dr., Winston-Salem NC 27103. (910)768-1374. President: Carolyn Sakowski. Estab. 1954. Small independent publisher. Publishes hardcover and paperback originals. Books: Acid-free paper; offset printing; illustrations; average print order: 5,000. Number of titles: 17 in 1996, 20 in 1997. "Among our 17-20 books, we do one novel a year."
Needs: Prefers regional material dealing with southeastern U.S. No confessions or erotica. "Our editorial focus concentrates mostly on nonfiction." Recently published works include *The Big Ear*, by Robin Hemley (short story collection); *How to Get Home*, by Bret Lott; and *Cape Fear Rising*, by Philip Gerard.
How to Contact: Query or submit with SASE. Simultaneous submissions OK. Reports in 1 month. Publishes ms 1-2 years after acceptance. Free book catalog.
Terms: Negotiable.
Advice: "We are primarily interested in nonfiction titles. Most of our titles have a tie-in with North Carolina or the southeastern United States. Please enclose a cover letter and outline with the manuscript. We prefer to review queries before we are sent complete manuscripts. Queries should include an approximate word count."

BOOKS IN MOTION, (II), 9212 E. Montgomery, Suite #501, Spokane WA 99206. (509)922-1646. President: Gary Challender. Estab. 1980. "Audiobook company, national marketer. Publishes novels in audiobook form *only*." Published new writers within the last year. Plans 12 first novels this year. Averages 70 total titles, 65 fiction titles each year.
● Books in Motion is known for its audio westerns and mysteries. The publisher has received favorable reviews from *Library Journal*, *Kliatt Magazine* and *Audio-File* magazine.
Needs: Action/adventure, westerns, mystery, science fiction (non-technical), some romance. Recently published *Kiahawk*, by Craig Fraley; *The Isle of Venus Mystery*, by Tom Neet; and *Name Withheld*, by J.A. Jance. Have published over 140 new authors in last 3 years.
How to Contact: Accepts unsolicited mss. Submit synopsis and sample chapters (first and middle). SASE for ms. Reports within 3 weeks to 3 months. Simultaneous submissions OK.
Terms: Pays royalties of 10%. "We pay royalties every 6 months. Royalties that are received are based on the gross sales that any given title generates during the 6-month interval. Authors must be patient since it usually takes a minimum of one year before new titles will have significant sales." Publishes ms 6-12 months after acceptance. Book catalog free on request.
Advice: "We prefer a minimum of profanity and no gratuitous sex. We want novels with a strong plot. The fewer the characters, the better it will work on tape. Six-tape audiobooks sell and rent better than any other size in the unabridged format. One hour of tape is equal to 40 pages of double-spaced, 12 pitch, normal margin, typed pages. Manuscript should be between 200 and 400 pages."

THOMAS BOUREGY & COMPANY, INC., 401 Lafayette St., New York NY 10003. Small category line. See Avalon Books.

BOYDS MILLS PRESS, (II), Subsidiary of Highlights for Children, 815 Church St., Honesdale PA 18431. (800)490-5111. Manuscript Coordinator: Beth Troop. Estab. 1990. "Independent publisher of quality books for children of all ages." Publishes hardcover. Books: Coated paper; offset printing; case binding; 4-color illustrations; average print order varies. Plans 4 fiction titles (novels).
Needs: Juvenile, young adult (adventure, animal, contemporary, ethnic, historical, sports). Recently published *Imitate the Tiger*, by Jan Cheripko; *Nellie Bishop*, by Clara Gillow Clarke; and *The Fall of the Red Star*, by Helen M. Szablya and Peggy King Anderson.
How to Contact: Accepts unsolicited mss. Send first three chapters and synopsis. Reports in 1 month. Simultaneous submissions OK.
Terms: Pays standard rates. Sends pre-publication galleys to author. Time between acceptance and publication depends on "what season it is scheduled for." Writer's guidelines for #10 SASE.
Advice: "We're interested in young adult novels of real literary quality as well as middle grade fiction that's imaginative with fresh ideas. Getting into the mode of thinking like a child is important. We publish very few novels each year, so make sure your story is as strong and as polished as possible before submitting to us. We do not deal with romance, science fiction or fantasy novels, so please do not submit those genres."

BRANDEN PUBLISHING CO., (I, II), Subsidiary of Branden Press, Box 843, 17 Station St., Brookline Village MA 02147. Imprint: I.P.L. Estab. 1967. Publishes hardcover and paperback originals and reprints. Books: 55-60 lb. acid-free paper; case- or perfect-bound; illustrations; average print order: 5,000. Plans 5 first novels this year. Averages 15 total titles, 5 fiction titles each year.

Needs: Ethnic, historical, literary, military/war, short story collections and translations. Looking for "contemporary, fast pace, modern society." No porno, experimental or horror. Published *I, Morgan*, by Harry Robin; *The Bell Keeper*, by Marilyn Seguin; and *The Straw Obelisk*, by Adolph Caso.

How to Contact: Does not accept unsolicited mss. Query *only* with SASE. Reports in 1 week on queries.

Terms: Pays royalties of 5-10% minimum. Advance negotiable. Provides 10 author's copies. Sends galleys to author. Publishes ms "several months" after acceptance.

Advice: "Publishing more fiction because of demand. *Do not make phone inquiries.* Do not oversubmit; single submissions only; do not procrastinate if contract is offered."

CARROLL & GRAF PUBLISHERS, INC., (III), 260 Fifth Ave., New York NY 10001. (212)889-8772. Editor: Kent Carroll. Estab. 1983. Publishes hardcover and paperback originals and paperback reprints. Plans 5 first novels this year. Averages 120 total titles, 75 fiction titles each year. Average first novel print order 7,500 copies. Occasionally critiques rejected mss.

Needs: Contemporary, erotica, fantasy, science fiction, literary, mainstream and mystery/suspense. No romance.

How to Contact: Does not accept unsolicited mss. Query first or submit outline/synopsis and sample chapters. SASE. Reports in 2 weeks.

Terms: Pays in royalties of 6% minimum; 15% maximum; advance negotiable. Sends galleys to author. Free book catalog on request.

CHARIOT VICTOR PUBLISHING, (formerly Cook Communications Ministry), 4050 Lee Vance View, Colorado Springs CO 80918. (719)536-3280. Imprints: Chariot Books, Victor Books, Lion Publishing. Editorial Director: Karl Schaller. Editorial Assistant: Kathy Davis (children). Acquisitions Editor: Dave Horton (adult). Estab. 1875. Publishes hardcover and paperback originals. Number of fiction titles: 35-40 juvenile, 4-6 adult. Encourages new writers.

Needs: Religious/inspirational, juvenile, young adult and adult; sports, animal, spy/adventure, historical, Biblical, fantasy/science fiction, picture book and easy-to-read. Recently published *California Pioneer* series, by Elaine Schulte; *The Patriots*, by Jack Cavanaugh. Published new writers within the last year.

How to Contact: All unsolicited mss are returned unopened. Send query with SASE to Kathy Davis. Simultaneous submissions OK.

Terms: Royalties vary ("depending on whether it is trade, mass market or cloth" and whether picture book or novel). Offers advance. Writer's guidelines with SASE.

Advice: "Focus on Christians, not Christianity. Chariot Victor Publishing publishes books for toddlers through adults which help people better understand their relationship with God, and/or the message of God's book, the Bible. Interested in seeing contemporary novels (*not* Harlequin-type) adventure, romance, suspense with Christian perspective."

CHRONICLE BOOKS, (II), 85 Second St., San Francisco CA 94103. (415)777-7240. Fiction Editor: Jay Schaefer. Estab. 1966. "Full-line publisher of 150 books per year." Publishes hardcover and paperback originals. Averages 150 total titles, 10 fiction this year. Sometimes comments on rejected ms.

Needs: Open. Looking for novellas, collections and novels. No romances, science fiction, or any genre fiction: no category fiction. Publishes anthologies. Recently published *Griffin & Sabine*, by Bantock; *Loving Wanda Beaver*, by Baker; *Lies of the Saints*, by McGraw; *Spirits of the Ordinary*, by Alcalá.

How to Contact: Accepts unsolicited mss. Submit complete ms with cover letter. "No queries, please." Send SASE for reply and return of ms. Agented fiction 50%. Prefers no simultaneous submissions.

Terms: Standard rates. Sends galleys to author. Publishes ms 9-12 months after acceptance. No writer's guidelines available.

CROSSWAY BOOKS, (II, IV), Division of Good News Publishers, 1300 Crescent, Wheaton IL 60187. Vice President/Editorial Director: Leonard G. Goss. Estab. 1938. Midsize independent religious publisher with plans to expand. Publishes paperback originals. Average print order 5,000-10,000 copies. Averages 50 total titles, 15-20 fiction titles each year.

FOR INFORMATION ON ENTERING the *Novel & Short Story Writer's Market* Cover Letter Contest, see page 16.

INSIDER REPORT

Religious fiction: growing up with "salt and light"

"Religious fiction is 'growing up,' " says Leonard Goss, vice president and editor-in-chief of Crossway books. "It's becoming more sophisticated and we'll be looking for better storytellers."

With a mission to "make a difference in people's lives for Christ," Crossway is committed to publishing books that introduce readers to Christianity and help them grow stronger in the Christian faith. Crossway publishes the works of bestselling authors Frank Peretti, Tony Evans, Joni Eareckson Tada and Max Lucado. Their stories relate Christian experiences to contemporary life and ideas and examine crucial issues through a Christian worldview. According to Goss, Crossway editors "want the books themselves to be 'salt and light' in society, to have some real reason for being." Authors' viewpoints should not conflict with orthodox Christianity in any way that would cause the reader to question the genuine faith and integrity of that author.

Leonard Goss

Photo by Motophoto

Religious publishers today are looking for well-crafted adult contemporary stories of "real people, in the here and now, going through real problems," says Goss. The Christian novelist needs to weave a spellbinding story, a work of art that captures the imagination and the heart of the reader. But, while presenting the Christian viewpoint, Goss advises writers not to preach to their readers. "If you want to preach, become a preacher. If you want to write novels, become a storyteller."

Writers wanting to publish with Crossway, however, should *not* be looking to become crossover authors. Many writers wanting to create a work that will cross over into the secular market try to hold onto the religious thread, but are rarely able to weave it into the fabric of their storyline. True, the spiritual techno-thrillers of celebrated Crossway Books author Frank Peretti have been enormously popular in both Christian and secular markets. But Peretti's style has not successfully been emulated by others. That's why, as the Book of Joshua suggests, it would be better for writers to "choose for yourselves whom you will serve" (Joshua 24:15).

Goss points to the "New Age" movement as something today's religious publishers and writers must deal with. His concern is that, "We have thrown the baby out with the bath water. We need to throw the bath water out, but keep the baby." By this, Goss means that religious publishers should be more positive, understanding that those drawn to the New Age movement are genuinely inter-

INSIDER REPORT, *Goss*

ested in spiritual things. Christian writers and publishers should "appreciate where people in the New Age movement are and, rather than attacking their ideas, provide a better way for New Age 'seekers' to find truth and grace."

As for the future of religious fiction, Goss says, "The Christian fiction market is declining." But the reason for the decline, in his view, is a good thing. "There's too much fiction already on the shelves, and much of it is not what publishers would go for today." The market has become more sophisticated and publishers have a better vision and understanding of what will serve the needs of the readers. "This shakedown has caused some publishers to trim back or abandon religious fiction altogether." But Crossway, in the Christian fiction market for the long haul, remains true to its calling to publish fiction in the categories of fantasy, Christian realism, supernatural fiction, historical fiction, mystery, intrigue, western and children's literature. Crossway also plans expansion into the areas of young adult fiction and nonfiction and possibly humor.

Crossway remains open to unsolicited manuscripts and is committed to evaluating any material that comes in. The best way to catch their attention, however, is not with a manuscript, but with a "red hot" book proposal. Goss says a well-written book proposal tells the publisher that you, as a writer, have seriously thought a book through and have done all the legwork. An accurate book description, complete table of contents and several sample chapters will give a pretty solid idea of whether the finished manuscript will fit into a publisher's editorial model and vision.

So what are the chances of a newcomer getting published in today's religious fiction field? As an authority on what is accepted at Crossway and as facilitator of writing talent through his new book, *The Christian Writer's Book: A Practical Guide to Writing* (Bridge-Logos), Goss encourages writers: "It's still possible for new authors to get published." The key is "to be good at what you do—and persevere." And, if your "author's passion meets the publisher's vision," your book could be on the shelves in the near future.

—Karen Moore Artl

• Crossway Books is known as a leader in Christian fiction. Several of their books have received "Gold Medallion" awards from the Evangelical Christian Publishers Association.

Needs: Contemporary, adventure, historical, literary, religious/inspirational and young adult. "All fiction published by Crossway Books must be written from the perspective of evangelical Christianity. It must understand and view the world through a Christian worldview." No sentimental, didactic, "inspirational" religious fiction; heavy-handed allegorical or derivative fantasy. Recently published *The Lost Manuscript of Martin Taylor Harrison*, by Stephen Bly; *Fated Genes*, by Harry Kraus; and *Veiled Threats*, by Frank Simon.

How to Contact: Does not accept unsolicited mss. Send query with synopsis and sample chapters only. Reports in 6-8 weeks on queries. Publishes ms 1-2 years after acceptance.

Terms: Pays in royalties and negotiates advance. Writer's guidelines for SASE. Book catalog for 9 × 12 SAE and 6 first-class stamps.

Advice: "We feel called to publish fiction in the following categories: Supernatural fiction, fantasy, Christian realism, historical fiction, mystery fiction, intrigue, western fiction and children's fiction. All fiction should include explicit Christian content, artfully woven into the plot, and must be consistent with our statements of vision, purpose and commitment. Crossway can successfully publish and market *quality* Christian novelists. Also read John Gardner's *On Moral Fiction*. We require a minimum word count of 25,000 words."

‡**THE CROWN PUBLISHING GROUP, (II)**, 201 E. 50th St., New York NY 10022. (212)572-6190. Imprints include Crown, Harmony Books, Clarkson N. Potter, Inc. Executive Vice Pres., Editor-in-Chief: Betty A. Prashker. Executive Editor, Crown: Steven Ross. Editorial Director, Harmony Books: Lauren Shakeley. President and Publisher, Clarkson N. Potter: Chip Gibson. Executive Editor: Lauren Shakely.
Needs: Adventure, contemporary, historical, horror, humor/satire, literary, mainstream, science, war.
How to Contact: Does not accept unsolicited mss. "Query letters only addressed to the Editorial Department. Complete mss are returned unread . . ." SASE. Reports in 3-4 months.
Terms: Pays advance against royalty; terms vary and are negotiated per book.

DARK HORSE COMICS, INC., (I, IV), 10956 SE Main St., Milwaukie OR 97222. (503)652-8815. Website: http://www.dhorse.com. Contact: Submissions Editor. Estab. 1986. "Dark Horse publishes all kinds of comics material, and we try not to limit ourselves to any one genre or any one philosophy. Most of our comics are intended for readers 15-40, though we also publish material that is accessible to younger readers." Comic books: newsprint or glossy paper, each title 24-28 pages. Averages 10-30 total titles each year.
• Dark Horse Press' comics have won several awards including the Eisner, Harvey and Parent's Choice awards.
Needs: Comics: adventure, childrens/juvenile, fantasy (space fantasy, super hero, sword and sorcery), horror, humor/satire, mystery/suspense (private eye/hardboiled), psychic/supernatural, romance (contemporary), science fiction (hard science, soft/sociological), western (traditional). Proposals or scripts for comic books only. Plans anthology. Recently published comics by Andrew Vachss, Frank Miller, Mark Hamill, Steven Grant, Eric Luke and Harlan Ellison. Published short story comic anthologies: *Dark Horse Presents*.
How to Contact: Does not accept unsolicited mss. Query letter first. Include one-page bio, list of publishing credits. Send SASE or disposable copy of ms. Reports in 1-2 months. Simultaneous submissions OK.
Terms: Pays $25-100/page and 5-25 author's copies. "We usually buy first and second rights, other rights on publication." Writer's guidelines free for #10 SASE.
Advice: "Read comics. Know comics. Understand comics. Have a reason to want to publish your story as a comic, beyond it not working as a novel or screenplay. Obtain copies of our Writer's Guidelines before making a submission."

DAW BOOKS, INC., (I), 375 Hudson St., New York NY 10014. Fax: (212)366-2090. Publishers: Elizabeth R. Wollheim and Sheila E. Gilbert. Submissions Editor: Peter Stampfel. Estab. 1971. Publishes paperback originals and hardcover originals. Books: Illustrations sometimes; average print and number of first novels published per year vary widely. Averages 40 new titles plus 40 or more reissues, all fiction, each year. Occasionally critiques rejected mss.
Needs: Science fiction (hard science, soft sociological), fantasy and mainstream thrillers only. Recently published *The Golden Key*, by Melanie Rawn, Jennifer Roberson and Kate Elliott (novel); *Otherland: City of Golden Shadows*, by Tad Williams (novel); *Storm Breaking*, by Mercedes Lackey (novel); *Inheritor*, by C.J. Cherryh; *Killjoy*, by Elizabeth Forrest. Publishes many original anthologies including *Sword & Sorceress* (edited by Marion Zimmer Bradley); *Cat Fantastic* (edited by Andre Norton and Martin H. Greenberg). "You may write to the editors (after looking at the anthology) for guidelines ℅ DAW."
How to Contact: Submit complete ms with return postage and SASE. Usually reports in 3-5 months on mss, but in special cases may take longer. "No agent required."
Terms: Pays an advance against royalties. Sends galleys to author.
Advice: "We strongly encourage new writers. Research your publishers and submit only appropriate work."

DELACORTE/DELL BOOKS FOR YOUNG READERS/DOUBLEDAY, (II, III, IV), Division of Bantam Doubleday Dell Publishing Group, Inc., 1540 Broadway, New York NY 10036. See listing for Bantam/Doubleday/Dell Books for Young Readers.

✴ **DELL PUBLISHING**, 1540 Broadway, New York NY 10036. (212)354-6500. Imprints include Delacorte Press, Delta, Dell, Dial Press, Laurel. Estab. 1922. Publishes hardcover and paperback originals and paperback reprints.
Needs: See below for individual imprint requirements.
How to Contact: Reports in 4-5 months. Simultaneous submissions OK. "Submit entire manuscript with a cover letter and narrative synopsis. Limit synopsis to 10 pages. Dell is composed of several imprints, each with its own editorial department. Please review carefully the following information

and direct your submissions to the appropriate department. Your envelope must be marked: Attention: (One of the following names of imprints), Dell Editorial Department—Book Proposal. Enclose SASE."
DELACORTE: Publishes in hardcover; looks for top-notch commercial fiction and nonfiction; 35 titles/year.
DELTA: Publishes trade paperbacks including original fiction and nonfiction; 20 titles/year.
DELL: Publishes mass-market and trade paperbacks; looks for family sagas, historical romances, sexy modern romances, adventure and suspense thrillers, mysteries, psychic/supernatural, horror, war novels, fiction and nonfiction. 200 titles/year.
DIAL PRESS: Publishes literary fiction and high-end nonfiction 2 titles/year.
Terms: Pays 6-15% in royalties; offers advance. Sends galleys to author.
Advice: Not presently publishing any fantasy books. "Don't get your hopes up. Query first only with 4-page synopsis plus SASE. Study the paperback racks in your local drugstore. We encourage first novelists. We also encourage all authors to seek agents."

DIAL BOOKS FOR YOUNG READERS, (V), Division of Penguin Books U.S.A. Inc., 375 Hudson St., New York NY 10014. (212)366-2000. Imprints include Pied Piper Books, Easy-to-Read Books. Editor-in-Chief/Pres./Publisher: Phyllis Fogelman. Estab. 1961. Trade children's book publisher, "looking for agented picture book mss and novels." Publishes hardcover originals. Plans 1 first novel this year. Averages 100 titles, mainly fiction. Occasionally critiques or comments on rejected ms.
Needs: Juvenile (1-9 yrs.) including: animal, fantasy, spy/adventure, contemporary and easy-to-read; young adult/teen (10-16 years) including: fantasy/science fiction, literary and commercial mystery and fiction. Recently published *Sam and the Tigers*, by Julius Lester and Jerry Pinckney; *Language of Dores*, by Rosemary Wells; and *Great Interactive Dream Machine*, by Richard Peck.
How to Contact: Does not accept unsolicited mss; no queries.
Terms: Pays advance against royalties.
Advice: "To agents: We are publishing more fiction books than in the past, and we publish only hardcover originals, most of which are fiction. At this time we are particularly interested in both fiction and nonfiction for the middle grades, and innovative picture book manuscripts. We also are looking for easy-to-reads for first and second graders. Plays, collections of games and riddles, and counting and alphabet books are generally discouraged. Before submitting a manuscript to a publisher, it is a good idea to request a catalog to see what the publisher is currently publishing. We will send a catalog to anyone who sends four first-class stamps with a self-addressed, 9×12 envelope."

✦**DOUBLEDAY CANADA LIMITED**, 105 Bond St., Toronto, Ontario M5B 1Y3 Canada. No unsolicited submissions. Prefers not to share information.

DUTTON SIGNET, (III), A division of Penguin USA, Inc., 375 Hudson St., New York NY 10014. (212)366-2000. Imprints include Dutton, Onyx, Signet, Topaz, Mentor, Signet Classic, Plume, Plume Fiction, Meridian, Roc. Contact: Michaela Hamilton, vice president/publisher, Signet and Onyx; Arnold Dolin, associate publisher, Dutton, publisher, Plume; Laura Gilman, editorial director, Roc. Estab. 1948. Publishes hardcover and paperback originals and paperback reprints. Published new writers within the last year.
Needs: "All kinds of commercial and literary fiction, including mainstream, historical, Regency, New Age, western, thriller, science fiction, fantasy, gay. Full length novels and collections." Published *Trial by Fire*, by Nancy Taylor Rosenberg; *Black Cross*, by Greg Iles; and *The Takeover*, by Stephen Frey.
How to Contact: Agented mss only. Queries accepted with SASE. "State type of book and past publishing projects." Simultaneous submissions OK. Reports in 3 months.
Terms: Pays in royalties and author's copies; offers advance. Sends galleys to author. Book catalog for SASE.
Advice: "Write the complete manuscript and submit it to an agent or agents. We publish The Trailsman, Battletech and other western and science fiction series—all by ongoing authors. Would be receptive to ideas for new series in commercial fiction."

EAKIN PRESS, (II, IV), P.O. Box 90159, Austin TX 78709-0159. (512)288-1771. Imprint: Nortex. Editor: Edwin M. Eakin. Estab. 1978. Publishes hardcover originals. Books: Old style (acid-free); offset printing; case binding; illustrations. Average print order 2,000. First novel print order 5,000.

READ THE BUSINESS OF FICTION WRITING section to learn the correct way to prepare and submit a manuscript.

Published new writers within the last year. Plans 2 first novels this year. Averages 80 total titles each year.

Needs: Juvenile. Specifically needs historical fiction for school market, juveniles set in Southwest for Southwest grade schoolers. Published *Wall Street Wives*, by Ande Ellen Winkler; *Jericho Day*, by Warren Murphy; and *Blood Red Sun*, by Stephen Mertz.

How to Contact: Prefers queries, but accepts unsolicited mss. Send SASE for guidelines. Agented fiction 5%. Simultaneous submissions OK. Reports in 3 months on queries.

Terms: Pays royalties; average advance: $1,000. Sends galleys to author. Publishes ms 1-1½ years after acceptance. Writers guidelines for #10 SASE. Book catalog for 75¢.

Advice: "Juvenile fiction only with strong Southwest theme. We receive around 600 queries or unsolicited mss a year."

‡WM. B. EERDMANS PUBLISHING CO., (II), 255 Jefferson Ave. SE, Grand Rapids MI 49503-4570. (800)253-7521. Fax: (616)459-6540. Imprint: Eerdmans Books for Young Readers. Editor-in-Chief: Jon Pott. Estab. 1911. "We are a midsize independent publisher. Although Eerdmans publishes some regional books and other nonreligious titles, it is essentially a religious publisher, whose titles range from the academic to the semi-popular. Our children's fiction is meant to help a child explore life in God's world and to foster a child's exploration of her or his faith. We publish a few adult novels a year, and these tend to address spiritual issues from a Christian perspective." Publishes hardcover and paperback originals and reprints. Published new writers within the last year. Plans 2-3 first novels this year. Averages 140 total titles, 10-15 fiction titles (mostly for children) each year. Sometimes critiques or comments on rejected mss.

Needs: Religious (children's, general, fantasy, mystery/suspense, thriller). Recently published *Deadly Waters*, by Chris Meehan (mystery); *Flight to Hollow Mountain*, by Mark Sebanc (fantasy); and *The Gifts of the Child Christ*, by George MacDonald (stories and fairy tales).

How to Contact: Accepts unsolicited mss. Query with outline/synopsis and 2 sample chapters. Accepts unsolicited queries and correspondence by fax. Include 150- to 200-word bio and list of publishing credits. SASE for reply or send a disposable copy of ms. Agented fiction 25%. Reports in 3-4 weeks on queries; 2-3 months on mss. Simultaneous submissions OK.

Terms: Pays royalties of 7% minimum; 10% maximum. Offers negotiable advance. Sends galleys to author. Publishes ms 12-18 months after acceptance. Writer's guidelines and book catalog free.

Advice: "Our readers are educated and fairly sophisticated, and we are looking for novels with literary merit."

PAUL S. ERIKSSON, PUBLISHER, (II), P.O. Box 62, Forest Dale VT 05745. (802)247-4210. Editor: Paul S. Eriksson. Estab. 1960. Publishes hardcover and paperback originals.

Needs: Mainstream. Published *The Headmaster's Papers*, by Richard A. Hawley; and *Hand in Hand*, by Tauno Yliruusi.

How to Contact: Query first. Publishes ms an average of 6 months after acceptance.

Terms: Pays 10-15% in royalties; advance offered if necessary. Free book catalog.

Advice: "Our taste runs to serious fiction."

M. EVANS & CO., INC., (II), 216 E. 49th St., New York NY 10017. (212)688-2810. Fax: (212)486-4544. E-mail: mevans@spiynet.com. Editor: Betty Ann Crawford. Publishes hardcover and trade paper nonfiction and a small fiction list. Publishes 30-40 titles each year.

Needs: "Small general trade publisher specializing in nonfiction titles on health, nutrition, diet, cookbooks, parenting, popular psychology." Recently published *A Fine Italian Hand*, by William Murray; and *Presumption*, by Julia Barnett.

How to Contact: Query first with outline/synopsis and 3 sample chapters. SASE. Agented fiction: 100%. Simultaneous submissions OK.

Terms: Pays in royalties and offers advance; amounts vary. Sends galleys to author. Publishes ms 6-12 months after acceptance.

FANTAGRAPHICS BOOKS, (II, IV), 7563 Lake City Way NE, Seattle WA 98115. (206)524-1967. Publisher: Gary Groth. Estab. 1976. Publishes comic books, comics series and graphic novels. Books: offset printing; saddle-stitched periodicals and Smythe-sewn books; heavily illustrated. Publishes originals and reprints. Publishes 25 titles each month.

Needs: Comic books and graphic novels (adventure, fantasy, horror, mystery, romance, science, social parodies). "We look for subject matter that is more or less the same as you would find in mainstream fiction." Published *Blood of Palomar*, by Gilbert Hernandez; *The Dragon Bellows Saga*, by Stan Sakai; *Death of Speedy*; *Housebound with Rick Geary*; *Little Nemo in Slumberland*.

How to Contact: Send a plot summary, pages of completed art (photocopies only) and character sketches. May send completed script if the author is willing to work with an artist of the publisher's choosing. Include cover letter and SASE. Reports in 1 month.

Terms: Pays in royalties of 8% (but must be split with artist) and advance.

FARRAR, STRAUS & GIROUX, (III), 19 Union Square W., New York NY 10003. (212)741-6900. Imprints include Hill & Wang, The Noonday Press and North Point Press. Editor-in-Chief: Jonathan Galassi. Midsized, independent publisher of fiction, nonfiction, poetry. Publishes hardcover originals. Published new writers within the last year. Plans 2 first novels this year. Averages 100 total hardcover titles, 30 fiction titles each year.
Needs: Open. No genre material. Recently published *The Autobiography of My Mother*, by Jamaica Kincaid; *Smilla's Sense of Snow*, by Peter Hoeg; and *The Laws of Our Fathers*, by Scott Turow.
How to Contact: Does not accept unsolicited mss. Query first. "Vast majority of fiction is agented." Reports in 2 months. Simultaneous submissions OK.
Terms: Pays royalties (standard, subject to negotiation). Advance. Sends galleys to author. Publishes ms one year after acceptance. Writer's guidelines for #10 SASE.

FARRAR, STRAUS & GIROUX/CHILDREN'S BOOKS, (I), 19 Union Square W., New York NY 10003. Children's Books Editorial Director: Margaret Ferguson. Number of titles: 40. Published new writers within the last year. Buys juvenile mss with illustrations. Buys 25% agented fiction.
Needs: Children's picture books, juvenile novels, nonfiction. Recently published *Sheep in Wolves' Clothing*, by Satoshi Kitamura; *Remembering Mog*, by Colby Rodowsky; and *Starry Messenger*, by Peter Sis.
How to Contact: Submit outline/synopsis and 3 sample chapters, summary of ms and any pertinent information about author, author's writing, etc. Reports in 2 months on queries, 3 months on mss. Publishes ms 18-24 months after acceptance.
Terms: Pays in royalties; offers advance. Book catalog with 9 × 12 SASE and 96¢ postage.
Advice: "Study our list before sending something inappropriate. Send query letters for long manuscripts; don't ask for editorial advice (just not possible, unfortunately); and send SASEs!"

FAWCETT, (I, II, III), Division of Random House/Ballantine, 201 E. 50th St., New York NY 10022. (212)751-2600. Imprints include Ivy, Crest, Gold Medal, Columbine and Juniper. Editor-in-Chief: Leona Nevler. Estab. 1955. Major publisher of mass market and trade paperbacks. Publishes paperback originals and reprints. Prints 160 titles annually. Encourages new writers. "Always looking for *great* first novels."
Needs: Mysteries. Published *Noelle*, by Diana Palmer; *Writing for the Moon*, by Kristin Hannah.
How to Contact: Query with SASE. Send outline and sample chapters for adult mass market. If ms is requested, simultaneous submissions OK. Prefers letter-quality. Reports in 2-4 months.
Terms: Pays usual advance and royalties.
Advice: "Gold Medal list consists of four paperbacks per month—usually three are originals."

DONALD I. FINE, INC., (III), 375 Hudson St., New York NY 10014. (212)727-3270. Fax: (212)727-3277. Imprint of Penguin USA. President/Publisher: Don Fine. Associate Editor: Thomas Burke. Estab. 1983. "Mini-major book publisher." Publishes hardcover originals. Published new writers within the last year. Plans 6 first novels this year. Averages 20 total titles, 12 fiction titles each year.
Needs: Adventure, historical, horror (dark fantasy, psychological), literary, military/war, mystery/ suspense, thriller/espionage. Upcoming anthology themes include mystery, sports/literary. Published *A Certain Justice*, by John T. Lescroart (trial novel/mystery); *Collected Short Fiction of Bruce Jay Friedman* (literary fiction); and *Grand Jury*, by Philip Friedman (novel).
How to Contact: No unsolicited mss. Submit through agent only. Agented fiction 100%. Simultaneous submissions OK.
Terms: Pays royalties; offers negotiable advance.

FLARE BOOKS, (II), Imprint of Avon Books, Div. of the Hearst Corp., 1350 Avenue of the Americas, New York NY 10019. (212)261-6800. Executive Editor: Elise Howard. Estab. 1981. Small, young adult line. Publishes paperback originals and reprints. Plans 2-3 first novels this year. Averages 24 titles, all fiction each year.
Needs: Young adult (easy-to-read [hi-lo], problem novels, historical romance, spy/adventure), "very selective." Looking for contemporary fiction. No science fiction/fantasy, heavy problem novels, poetry. Published *Nothing But the Truth, A Documentary Novel*, by Avi; *Night Cries*, by Barbara Steiner; and *The Weirdo*, by Theodore Taylor.
How to Contact: Accepts unsolicited mss. Submit complete ms with cover letter (preferred) or outline/synopsis and 3 sample chapters. Agented fiction 75%. Reports in 3-4 weeks on queries; 3-4 months on mss. Simultaneous submissions OK.

Terms: Royalties and advance negotiable. Sends galleys to author. Writer's guidelines for #10 SASE. Book catalog for 9×12 SAE with 98¢ postage. "We run a young adult novel competition each year."

‡FORGE BOOKS, (I), Tom Doherty Associates, 175 Fifth Ave., New York NY 10010. Assistant Editor: Stephen de las Heras. Estab. 1993. "Midsize company that specializes in genre fiction, mainly thrillers, historicals and mysteries." Publishes hardcover and paperback originals. Published new writers within the last year. Plans 2-3 first novels this year. Averages 130 total titles, 129 fiction titles each year. Sometimes critiques or comments on rejected mss.
● Forge Books won the Golden Spur Award for Best Publisher.
Needs: Erotica, historical, horror, mainstream/contemporary, mystery/suspense (amateur sleuth, cozy, police procedural, private eye/hardboiled), thriller/espionage, western (frontier saga, traditional). Plans anthology. Recently published *Relic*, by Douglas Preston and Lincoln Child (thriller); *Mirage*, by Soheir Khashoggi (contemporary fiction); *1812*, by David Nevin (historical).
How to Contact: Accepts unsolicited mss. Query with outline/synopsis and 5 sample chapters. Include estimated word count, bio and list of publishing credits. SASE for reply. Agented fiction 90%. Reports in 5 weeks. Simultaneous submissions OK.
Terms: Pays royalties. Average advance $30,000, negotiable. Sends galleys to author. Publishes ms 9 months after acceptance.
Advice: "The writing mechanics must be outstanding for a new author to break in to today's market."

GESSLER PUBLISHING COMPANY, (IV), 10 E. Church Ave., Roanoke VA 24011. (703)345-1429. Fax: (540)342-7172. E-mail: gesslerco@aol.com. Contact: Richard Kurshan. Estab. 1932. "Publisher/distributor of foreign language educational materials (primary/secondary schools)." Publishes paperback originals and reprints, videos and software. Averages 75 total titles each year. Sometimes comments on rejected ms.
Needs: "Foreign language or English as a Second Language." Needs juvenile, literary, preschool/picture book, short story collections, translations. Published *Don Quixote de la Mancha* (cartoon version of classic, in Spanish); *El Cid* (prose and poetry version of the classic, In Spanish); and *Les Miserables* (simplified version of Victor Hugo classic, in French).
How to Contact: Query first, then send outline/synopsis and 2-3 sample chapters; complete ms with cover letter. Agented fiction 40%. Reports on queries in 1 month; on mss in 6 weeks. Simultaneous submissions OK.
Terms: Pay varies with each author and contract. Sends galleys to author. "Varies on time of submission and acceptance relating to our catalog publication date." Writer's guidelines not available. Book catalog free on request.
Advice: "We specialize in the foreign language market directed to teachers and schools. A book that would interest us has to be attractive to the market. A teacher would be most likely to create a book for us."

GLOBE FEARON, (II), Subsidiary of Simon & Schuster, Secondary Education Group, 1 Lake St., Upper Saddle River NJ 07458. (201)236-5810. Estab. 1954. Publisher of multicultural, remedial and special education products. Publishes paperback originals and reprints. Books: 3 lb. book set paper; offset printing; perfect or saddle-wired binding; line art illustrations; average print order: 5,000.
Needs: "All materials are written to specification. It's a hard market to crack without some experience writing at low reading levels. Manuscripts for specific series of fiction are solicited from time to time, and unsolicited manuscripts are accepted occasionally." Published *A Question of Freedom*, by Lucy Jane Bledsoe (adventure novella—one of series of eight); *Just for Today*, by Tana Reiff (one novella of series of seven life-issues stories); and *The Everett Eyes*, by Bernard Jackson & Susie Quintanilla (one of 20 in a series of extra-short thrillers).
How to Contact: Submit outline/synopsis and sample chapters. SASE. Reports in 3 months. Simultaneous submissions OK.
Terms: Authors usually receive a predetermined project fee. Book catalog for 9×12 SAE with 4 first-class stamps.

DAVID R. GODINE, PUBLISHER, INC., (V), P.O. Box 9103, 9 Lewis St., Lincoln MA 01773. Imprints: Nonpareil Books (trade paperbacks), Verba Mundi (literature in translation), Imago Mundi (photography). President: David R. Godine. Editorial Director: Mark Polizzotti. Estab. 1970. Average print order: 4,000-5,000; first novel print order: 3,500-5,000. Small independent publisher (5-person staff). Publishes hardcover and paperback originals and reprints.
Needs: Literary, mystery, historical, children's. Recently published *Little Jordan*, by Marly Youmans.
How to Contact: Does not accept unsolicited mss.
Terms: Standard royalties; offers advance.

GOLDEN BOOKS FAMILY ENTERTAINMENT INC., (formerly Western Publishing Company, Inc.), 850 Third Ave., New York NY 10022. (212)583-6700. Imprint: Golden Books. Editorial

INSIDER REPORT

Gary Jennings: writing "the other half" of history

History may be the thread of historical novels, but it's imagination and lots of research that embroider a good historical yarn. At least that's the case for the stories Gary Jennings spins into novels. Jennings's first success with historical fiction came in 1980 with *Aztec*, an eventual worldwide bestseller that explores the life of the pre-conquest Indians. In 1984, he traced the path of Marco Polo in *Journeyer. Spangle*, published in 1987, has readers wandering with a 19th century circus troupe; and *Raptor*, a memoir of a Goth, was published in 1992. *Aztec Autumn*, a sequel to *Aztec*, is scheduled for release in August 1997 by Forge Books.

Gary Jennings

Writing has been an important part of Jennings's personal history. At 12, he worked alongside his father, Glen Jennings, as a printer's apprentice. He was an army correspondent during the Korean War after which he worked as an advertising copywriter until leaving to concentrate on his first novel. That book, *Sow the Seeds of Hemp*, set in Mississippi in the 1830s, was rejected by 25 publishers before Norton published it 16 years after it was written. Jennings has also written innumerable short stories and articles, plus nonfiction and juvenile books.

Each of Jennings's novels starts with a scrap from history. "The angle for *Journeyer* was the epigraph in the front of a book that I'd come across somewhere," Jennings says. "When urged by a priest to tell the truth before he died, Marco Polo responded, 'I have not told the half of what I saw and did.' So that was my clue. I was going to tell the other half of Marco Polo's story. If you read *Journeyer*, and if you've read Marco Polo's original book, you will find that I incorporated every single thing he actually did, then 'embroidered' to tell the other half."

The task Jennings sets for himself is to "tell a good story without warping history too much." He stays true to characters and history, but makes logical leaps when necessary. *Aztec*'s narrator Mixtli, for example, was handicapped nearly all of his life by nearsightedness. But, while traveling in the Maya region, Jennings was shown a square piece of granite, augmented at the corners with ground, convex quartz lenses used to light ceremonial candles. "From that I extrapolated; I figured if they could sculpt a beveled double convex lens to use as a burning glass, then they could make just about any kind of lens. And so, in the novel, I have a Maya craftsman sculpt a plano-concave lens out of topaz. From then on Mixtli is able to see perfectly, using the lens as a monocle. Although

INSIDER REPORT, *continued*

I had my hero outfitted with a fictional prosthesis, it was based firmly on fact."

Jennings tells his stories from the perspective of a narrator, someone who can roam from historical character to character, adventure to adventure. "In all of my books there are historical characters; you can easily spot them. They actually existed—I do not warp their behavior in any way. But if I took a definite, known historical character as a narrator, I would be constrained to the adventures that he actually had or could have had. I couldn't wander farther afield than he did. So I invent a character who has reason and opportunity and motive to be in all sorts of places, and see the subject from all angles, different sides." And those narrators themselves are not always purely fictitious, says Jennings. Mixtli, the narrator in *Aztec*, "is based on me; just like me, he's nearsighted and incurably curious."

The books Jennings writes are rich with historical detail and adventure. But those details don't come easily. Getting there takes some legwork, beginning most often with the library. "You dig," says Jennings. "If you want to set a novel in the Franco-Prussian War, for instance, first get a standard history of France and Prussia. From that, you'll learn basic things. Then go to the footnotes and to the bibliography of that history, and check out as many of those books as you can. You'll find what was covered in the book you started with, but you'll also discover extra details that weren't in the first book. Then check out the books in the bibliography of each of those books and keep going. Eventually you may be reading a doctoral dissertation on the Franco-Prussian War that was published in Nuremberg back in the 19th century."

Jennings averages two years researching each of his novels—one year with books and another in the field. But, when completed, his novels contain only about one-sixth of the material his hard work unearths. "I spent ten years researching *Aztec*. Not through choice. I didn't have any grants or funds or anything like that, so I was doing a lot of other work for subsistence in the meantime. So far as I could afford it, I haunted every archaeological dig I could find and get into. I would save up my money to go and live in the jungle or on the coast, or in the desert or up in the mountains for as long as I could. And, of course, I haunted museums and read everything that was written on the subject."

Jennings makes readers feel as if they are actually beside his characters, sharing their adventures. This comes from seeing for himself what his historical characters might have seen. For *Journeyer*, Jennings's travels included every locale between Venice and Djakarta. While writing *Aztec*, he lived in Mexico. To make his travels even more worthwhile, Jennings learns enough of the native language to authenticate his books—or to eavesdrop on interpreters. "You learn those little tricks. What often passes between the interpreter and the interviewee is far more interesting than what gets passed on to me."

On-site research is something Jennings highly recommends for writers. "There's no substitute for going to the actual scene of a story. In *Journeyer*, there's a scene where Marco Polo is drinking green tea, and thinking to himself, 'Here I am in the one place on earth that's farthest from any ocean whatsoever, so why does this tea taste like fish?' Since I was actually there, I know what the tea tastes like. Not one reader in one hundred million is ever going to notice that little line. But somewhere in the shires of England there's a retired old Asia hand,

---

INSIDER REPORT, *Jennings*

an old Colonel Blimp or someone, who is going to come across that scene and say, 'This writer was really there; I know because I've been there, too, and that tea does taste like fish.' " It is this possibility of validation from even one reader who has had the same experience, says Jennings, that makes all his painstaking research worthwhile.

To endure the arduous process of researching and writing historical novels, Jennings says writers must be motivated by things other than pleasing readers and selling books. "I write to please myself." Fortunately, the novels Jennings writes also please many people who may never travel the route of Marco Polo or drink the fishy-tasting green tea of a distant land.

—Mary Jennings

Director: Marilyn Salomon. Estab. 1907. High-volume mass market and trade publisher. Publishes hardcover and paperback originals. Number of titles: Averages 160/year. Buys 20-30% agented fiction.
Needs: Juvenile: Adventure, mystery, humor, sports, animal, easy-to-read picture books, and "a few" nonfiction titles. Published *Little Critter's Bedtime Story*, by Mercer Mayer; *Cyndy Szekeres' Mother Goose Rhymes*; and *Spaghetti Manners*, by Stephanie Calmenson, illustrated by Lisa MaCue Karsten.
How to Contact: Unsolicited mss are returned unread. Publishes ms an average of 1 year after acceptance.
Terms: Pays by outright purchase or royalty.
Advice: "Read our books to see what we do. If you do illustrations, call for appointment to show your work. Do not send illustrations; can send color copies. Illustrations are not necessary; if your book is what we are looking for, we can use one of our artists."

HARCOURT BRACE & CO., (III), 525 B St., Suite 1900, San Diego CA 92101. (619)231-6616. Fax: (619)699-6777. Imprints include Harcourt Brace Children's Books, Gulliver Books, Jane Yolen Books, Browndeer Press, Red Wagon Book and Silver Whistle. Publisher: Louise Pelan. Executive Editor: Diane D'Andrade. Editorial Director: Allyn Johnston. Editor: Karen Grove. Editorial Director of Browndeer Press: Linda Zuckerman. Editorial Director of Gulliver Books: Elizabeth Van Doren. Editorial Director of Silver Whistle: Paula Wiseman. Publishes hardcover originals and paperback reprints. Averages 150 titles/year. Published new writers within the last year.
  ● Books published by Harcourt Brace & Co. have received numerous awards including the Caldecott and Newbery medals and selections as the American Library Association's "Best Books for Young Adults." Note that the publisher now only accepts manuscripts through an agent. Unagented writers may query only.
Needs: Nonfiction for all ages, picture books for very young children, historical, mystery. Published *Coyote*, by Gerald McDermott; *Stellaluna*, by Janell Cannon; *The Car*, by Gary Paulsen; and *Mole's Hill*, by Lois Ehlert.
How to Contact: No unsolicited mss. Query first. Submit through agent only.
Terms: Terms vary according to individual books; pays on royalty basis. Catalog for 9 × 12 SASE.
Advice: "Read as much current fiction as you can; familiarize yourself with the type of fiction published by a particular house; interact with young people to obtain a realistic picture of their concerns, interests and speech patterns."

✦HARLEQUIN ENTERPRISES, LTD., (II, IV), 225 Duncan Mill Rd., Don Mills, Ontario M3B 3K9 Canada. (416)445-5860. Imprints include Harlequin Romances, Harlequin Presents, Harlequin American Romances, Superromances, Temptation, Intrigue and Regency, Silhouette, Worldwide Mysteries, Gold Eagle. Editorial Director Harlequin: Randall Toye; Silhouette: Isabel Swift; Gold Eagle: Randall Toye. Estab. 1949. Publishes paperback originals and reprints. Books: Newsprint paper; web printing; perfect-bound. Published new writers within the last year. Number of titles: Averages 700/year. Buys agented and unagented fiction.
  ● Harlequin introduced a new imprint, Mira, for single-title women's fiction. Query for more information/guidelines.

Needs: Romance, heroic adventure, mystery/suspense (romantic suspense *only*). Will accept nothing that is not related to the desired categories.

How to Contact: Send query letter or send outline and first 50 pages (2 or 3 chapters) or submit through agent with SASE (Canadian). Absolutely no simultaneous submissions. Reports in 1 month on queries; 2 months on mss.

Terms: Offers royalties, advance. Must return advance if book is not completed or is unacceptable. Sends galleys to author. Guidelines available.

Advice: "The quickest route to success is to follow directions for submissions: Query first. We encourage first novelists. Before sending a manuscript, read as many current Harlequin titles as you can. It's very important to know the genre and the series most appropriate for your submission." Submissions for Harlequin Romance and Harlequin Presents should go to: Mills & Boon Limited Eton House, 18-24 Paradise Road, Richmond, Surrey TW9 1SR United Kingdom, Attn: Karin Stoecker; Superromances: Paula Eykelhof, senior editor; Temptation: Birgit Davis-Todd, senior editor. American Romances and Intrigue: Debra Matteucci, senior editor and editorial coordinator, Harlequin Books, 6th Floor, 300 E. 42 Street, New York, NY 10017. Silhouette submissions should also be sent to the New York office, attention Isabel Swift. "The relationship between the novelist and editor is regarded highly and treated with professionalism."

HARMONY BOOKS, (V), Subsidiary of Crown Publishers, 201 E. 50th St., New York NY 10022. (212)572-6179. Contact: General Editorial Department. Publishes hardcover and paperback originals.
Needs: Literary fiction. Also publishes serious nonfiction, history, personal growth, media and music fields.
How to Contact: Does not accept unsolicited mss.

HARPER, 10 E. 53rd St., New York NY 10022. See listing for HarperPaperbacks.

HARPERCOLLINS CHILDREN'S BOOKS, (II), 10 E. 53rd St., New York NY 10022. (212)207-7044. Senior Vice President/Publisher: Susan Katz. Vice President/Associate Publisher/Editor-in-Chief: Kate Jackson. Vice President/Editorial Director, Joanna Cotler Books: Joanna Cotler. Vice President/Publisher, Michael di Capua Books: Michael di Capua. Vice President/Editorial Director, Laura Geringer Books: Laura Geringer. Vice President/Editorial Director, Harper Trophy: Stephanie Spinner. Editorial Director, HarperFestival: Mary Alice Moore. Executive Editors: Sally Doherty, Kate M. Jackson, Ginee Seo, Katherine B. Tegen, and Robert O. Warren. Publishes hardcover trade titles and paperbacks.
Needs: Picture books, easy-to-read, middle-grade, teenage and young adult novels; fiction, fantasy, animal, sports, spy/adventure, historical, science fiction, problem novels and contemporary. Published Harper: *Walk Two Moons*, by Sharon Creech (ages 8-12); *The Best School Year Ever*, by Barbara Robinson (ages 8 up); Harper Trophy (paperbacks): *Catherine, Called Birdy*, by Karen Cushman (ages 12 and up). Also publishes The Danger Guys series by Tony Abbott (ages 7-10).
How to Contact: Query; submit complete ms; submit outline/synopsis and sample chapters; submit through agent. SASE for query, ms. Please identify simultaneous submissions. Reports in 2-3 months.
Terms: Average 10% in royalties. Royalties on picture books shared with illustrators. Offers advance. Writer's guidelines and book catalog for SASE.
Advice: "Write from your own experience and the child you once were. Read widely in the field of adult and children's literature. Realize that writing for children is a difficult challenge. Read other young adult novelists as well as adult novelists. Pay attention to styles, approaches, topics. Be willing to rewrite, perhaps many times. We have no rules for subject matter, length or vocabulary but look instead for ideas that are fresh and imaginative. Good writing that involves the reader in a story or subject that has appeal for young readers is also essential. One submission is considered by all imprints."

HARPERPAPERBACKS, (V), 10 E. 53rd St., New York NY 10022. (212)207-7000. Fax: (212)207-7759. Imprints include HarperPaperbacks, Spotlight, Prism. Editorial Director: Carolyn Marino. Independent publisher. Publishes paperback originals and reprints. Published new writers within the last year.
Needs: Children's/young adult, fantasy, historical (romance), horror, mainstream/contemporary, mystery/suspense, romance (contemporary, historical, romantic suspense), thriller/espionage, western, young adult/teen.
How to Contact: Query by letter or agent. No unsolicited mss accepted.
Terms: Pays advance and royalties.

HARPERPRISM, imprint of HarperPaperbacks, 10 E. 53rd St., New York NY 10022. New HarperPaperbacks imprint for science fiction and fantasy. Query for more information. Contact: John Silbersack.

HARVEST HOUSE PUBLISHERS, (II, IV), 1075 Arrowsmith, Eugene OR 97402. (541)343-0123. Editorial Manager: LaRae Weikert. Editorial Director: Carolyn McCready. Estab. 1974. Midsize independent publisher with plans to expand. Publishes hardcover and paperback originals and reprints. Books: 40 lb. ground wood paper; offset printing; perfect binding; average print order: 10,000; first novel print order: 10,000-15,000. Averages 80 total titles, 6 fiction titles each year.

Needs: Christian living, contemporary issues, family saga, humor, Christian mystery (romantic suspense), religious/inspirational and Christian romance (historical). Especially seeks inspirational, romance/historical and mystery. Recently published *Where the Wild Rose Blooms*, by Lori Wick; *Conquered Heart*, by Lisa Samson; and *Israel, My Beloved*, by Kay Arthur.

How to Contact: Accepts unsolicited mss. Query first or submit outline/synopsis and 2 sample chapters with SASE. Submit all work to Manuscript Coordinator. Reports on queries in 2-8 weeks; on mss in 6-8 weeks. Simultaneous submissions OK.

Terms: Pays in royalties of 14-18%; 10 author's copies. Sends galleys to author. Writer's guidelines for SASE. Book catalog for 8½×11 SASE.

Advice: "Contact us to get a copy of our guidelines. We seek exceptional manuscripts which are original, relevant, well-written, and grounded in the teachings of scripture."

HOLIDAY HOUSE, INC., (I, II), 425 Madison, New York NY 10017. (212)688-0085. Editor-in-Chief: Regina Griffin. Estab. 1935. Independent publisher of children's books, picture books, nonfiction and novels for young readers. Books: high quality printing. Publishes hardcover originals and paperback reprints. Published new writers within the last year. Number of titles: Approximately 50 hardcovers and 15 paperbacks each year.

● *The Wright Brothers: How They Invented the Airplane* by Russell Freedman and published by Holiday House is a Newbery Honor Book.

Needs: Children's books only: literary, contemporary, Judaica and holiday, adventure, humor and animal stories for young readers. Recently published *I Am an Artichoke*, by Lucy Frank; *Maizie*, by Linda Oatman High; and *Tarantula Shoes*, by Tom Birdseye. "We're not in a position to be too encouraging, as our list is tight, but we're always open to good writing."

How to Contact: "We prefer query letters and three sample chapters for novels; complete manuscripts for shorter books and picture books." Simultaneous submissions OK as long as a cover letter mentions that other publishers are looking at the same material. Reports in 1 month on queries, 10-12 weeks on mss. "No phone calls, please."

Terms: Advance and royalties are flexible, depending upon whether the book is illustrated.

Advice: "Please submit only one project at a time."

HENRY HOLT & COMPANY, (II), 115 W. 18th St., 6th Floor, New York NY 10011. (212)886-9200. Imprint includes Owl (paper). Publishes hardcover and paperback originals and reprints. Averages 80-100 total original titles, 35% of total is fiction each year.

● Henry Holt is publishing more titles and more fiction.

How to Contact: Accepts queries; no unsolicited mss. Agented fiction 95%.

Terms: Pays in royalties of 10% minimum; 15% maximum; advance. Sends galleys to author.

General titles are marketed nationwide." Looking for "good quality writing in salable subject areas. Will also consider well-written books on social problems and issues." Published *The Couchman and the Bells*, by Ted C. Hindmarsh.

How to Contact: Accepts unsolicited mss. Query first. SASE. Include Social Security number with submission. Reports in 2-4 weeks on queries; 12-16 weeks on mss. Simultaneous submissions OK if identified as such.

Terms: Pays royalties of 6% minimum; 12% maximum. Provides 10 author's copies. Sends page proofs to author. Publishes ms 3-9 months after acceptance. "We are not a subsidy publisher but we do job printing, book production for private authors and book packaging." Writer's guidelines for #10 SAE and 1 first-class stamp.

Advice: Encourages "only those first novelists who write very well, with saleable subjects. Please avoid the trite themes which are plaguing LDS fiction such as crossing the plains, conversion stories, and struggling courtships that always end in temple marriage. While these themes are important, they have been used so often that they are now frequently perceived as trite and are often ignored by those shopping for new books. In religious fiction we hope to see a process of moral, spiritual, or emotional growth presented. Some type of conflict is definitely essential for good plot development. Watch your vocabulary too—use appropriate words for the age group for which you are writing. We don't accept children's mss for elementary grades."

HOUGHTON MIFFLIN COMPANY, (III), 222 Berkeley St., Boston MA 02116. (617)351-5000. Managing Editor: Christina Coffin. Publishes hardcover and paperback originals and paperback reprints. Averages 100 total titles, 50 fiction titles each year.

Needs: None at present. Published *The Translator*, by Ward Just.

How to Contact: Does not accept unsolicited mss. Buys virtually 100% agented fiction.

HYPERION, (III), Walt Disney Co., 114 Fifth Ave., New York NY 10011. (212)633-4400. Fax: (212)633-4811. Editorial Contact: Brian DeFiore. Estab. 1990. "Mainstream commercial publisher." Publishes hardcover and paperback originals. Published new writers within the last year. Averages 110 total titles, 20 fiction titles each year.
Needs: Ethnic/multicultural, gay, literary, mainstream/contemporary, mystery/suspense, religious/inspirational, thriller/espionage. Recently published *Cadillac Jukebox*, by James Lee Burke; *Bone*, by Fae Mynne Ng (literary); and *No Witnesses*, by Ridley Pearson (suspense).
How to Contact: Does not accepted unsolicited mss. Query first. Include bio (1 page) and list of publishing credits. Send SASE for reply, return of ms or send a disposable copy of ms. Agented fiction 100%. Reports in 2 weeks on queries; 1 month on mss. Simultaneous submissions OK.
Terms: Pays royalties; offers negotiable advance. Sends galleys to author. Publishes ms 6 months after acceptance.

INTERLINK PUBLISHING GROUP, INC., (V), 46 Crosby St., Northampton MA 01060. (413)582-7054. Fax: (413)582-7057. E-mail: interpg@aol.com. Imprints include: Interlink Books, Olive Branch Press and Crocodile Books USA. Contemporary fiction in translation published under Emerging Voices: New International Fiction. Publisher: Michel Moushabeck. Fiction Editor: Phyllis Bennis. Estab. 1987. "Midsize independent publisher." Publishes hardcover and paperback originals. Books: 55 lb. Warren Sebago Cream white paper; web offset printing; perfect binding; average print order: 5,000; first novel print order: 5,000. Published new writers within the last year. Plans 5-8 first novels this year. Averages 30 total titles, 5-8 fiction titles each year.
Needs: "Adult fiction from around the world." Published *A Woman of Nazareth*, by Hala Deeb Jabbour; *The Children Who Sleep by the River*, by Debbie Taylor; *Prairies of Fever*, by Ibrahim Nasrallah; and *The Silencer*, by Simon Louvish. Publishes the International Folk Tales series.
How to Contact: *Does not accept unsolicited mss.* Submit outline/synopsis only. SASE. Reports in 2 weeks on queries.
Terms: Pays royalties of 5% minimum; 8% maximum. Sends galleys to author. Publishes ms 1-1½ years after acceptance.
Advice: "Our Emerging Voices Series is designed to bring to North American readers the once-unheard voices of writers who have achieved wide acclaim at home, but were not recognized beyond the borders of their native lands. We are also looking for folktale collections (for adults) from around the world that fit in our International Folk Tale Series."

JAMESON BOOKS, (I, II, IV), Jameson Books, Inc., The Frontier Library, 722 Columbus St., Ottawa IL 61350. (815)434-7905. Editor: Jameson G. Campaigne, Jr. Estab. 1986. Publishes hardcover and paperback originals and reprints. Books: free sheet paper; offset printing; average print order: 10,000; first novel print order: 5,000. Plans 6-8 novels this year. Averages 12-16 total titles, 4-8 fiction titles each year. Occasionally critiques or comments on rejected mss.
Needs: Very well-researched western (frontier pre-1850). No cowboys, no science fiction, mystery, poetry, et al. Published *Yellowstone Kelly*, by Peter Bowen; *Wister Trace*, by Loren Estelman; and *One-Eyed Dream*, by Terry Johnston.
How to Contact: Does not accepted unsolicited mss. Submit outline/synopsis and 3 consecutive sample chapters. SASE. Agented fiction 50%. Reports in 2 weeks on queries; 2-5 months on mss. Simultaneous submissions OK.
Terms: Pays royalties of 5% minimum; 15% maximum. Average advance: $1,500. Sends galleys to author. Book catalog for 6×9 SASE.

KENSINGTON PUBLISHING CORP., (II), 850 Third Ave., New York NY 10022. (212)407-1500. Editor, Arabesque: Monica Harris. Executive Editor, Kensington Trade Paperbacks: Tracy Bernstein. Executive Editor, Pinnacle Books: Paul Dinas. Executive Editor, Zebra Books and Kensington Mass Market: Ann La Farge. Estab. 1975. Publishes hardcover originals, trade paperbacks and mass market originals and reprints. Averages 400 total titles/year.
Needs: Contemporary, adventure, mysteries, romance (contemporary, historical, regency, multicultural), true crime, nonfiction, women's, erotica and thrillers. No science fiction. Published *Destiny Mine*, by Janelle Taylor; *The Fall Line*, by Mark T. Sullivan; and *Cemetary of Angels*, by Noel Hynd. Ms length ranges from 100,000 to 125,000 words.
How to Contact: Contact with agent. Reports in 3-5 months.
Terms: Pays royalties and advances. Free book catalog.
Advice: "We want fiction that will appeal to the mass market and we want writers who want to make a career."

ALFRED A. KNOPF, (II), Division of Random House, 201 E. 50th St., New York NY 10022. Contact: The Editors. Estab. 1915. Publishes hardcover originals. Number of titles: approximately 46 each year. Buys 75% agented fiction. Published new writers in the last year.

Needs: Contemporary, literary, suspense and spy. No western, gothic, romance, erotica, religious or science fiction. Published *Mystery Ride*, by Robert Boswell; *The Night Manager*, by John Le Carre; *Lasher*, by Anne Rice. Published new writers within the last year.
How to Contact: Submit outline or synopsis with SASE. Reports within 1 month on mss. Publishes ms an average of 1 year after acceptance.
Terms: Pays 10-15% in royalties; offers advance. Must return advance if book is not completed or is unacceptable.
Advice: Publishes book-length fiction of literary merit by known and unknown writers.

KNOPF BOOKS FOR YOUNG READERS, (II), Division of Random House, 201 E. 50th St., New York NY 10022. Editor-in-Chief: Arthur Levine. Publishes hardcover and paperback originals and reprints. New paperback imprint includes Dragonfly Books (picture books). Averages 30 total titles, approximately 7 fiction titles each year.
Needs: "High-quality contemporary, humor, picture books, middle grade novels." Recently published *The Ballot Box Battle*, by Emily McCully; *Crash*, by Jerry Spinelli; and *The Golden Compass*, by Philip Pullman.
How to Contact: Query with outline/synopsis and 2 sample chapters with SASE. Simultaneous submissions OK. Reports in 6-8 weeks on queries.
Terms: Sends galleys to author.

LEISURE BOOKS, (I, II), Division of Dorchester Publishing Co., Inc., 276 Fifth Ave., Suite 1008, New York NY 10001. (212)725-8811. Address submissions to Don D'Auna, editorial assistant. Mass-market paperback publisher—originals and reprints. Books: Newsprint paper; offset printing; perfect-bound; average print order: variable; first novel print order: variable. Plans 25 first novels this year. Averages 150 total titles, 145 fiction titles each year. Comments on rejected ms "only if requested ms requires it."
Needs: Historical romance, horror, techno-thriller, western. Looking for "historical romance (90,000-115,000 words)." Recently published *Pure Temptation*, by Connie Mason (historical romance); and *Frankly My Dear*, by Sandra Hill (time-travel romance).
How to Contact: Accepts unsolicited mss. Query first. SASE. Agented fiction 70%. Reports in 1 month on queries; 2 months on mss. "All mss must be typed, double-spaced on one side and left unbound."
Terms: Offers negotiable advance. Payment depends "on category and track record of author." Sends galleys to author. Publishes ms within 2 years after acceptance. Romance guidelines for #10 SASE.
Advice: Encourages first novelists "if they are talented and willing to take direction, *and* write the kind of category fiction we publish. Please include a brief synopsis if sample chapters are requested."

LERNER PUBLICATIONS COMPANY, (II), 241 First Ave. N., Minneapolis MN 55401. Imprints include First Avenue Editions. Editor: Jennifer Martin. (612)332-3344. Estab. 1959. "Midsize independent *children's* publisher." Publishes hardcover originals and paperback reprints. Books: Offset printing; reinforced library binding; perfect binding; average print order: 5,000-7,500; first novel print order: 5,000. Averages 70 total titles, 1-2 fiction titles each year.
● Lerner Publications' joke book series is recommended by "Reading Rainbow" (associated with the popular television show of the same name).
Needs: Young adult: general, problem novels, sports, adventure, mystery (young adult). Looking for "well-written middle grade and young adult. No *adult fiction* or single short stories." Recently published *Dancing Pink Flamigos and Other Stories*, by Maria Testa.
How to Contact: Accepts unsolicited mss. Query first or submit outline/synopsis and 2 sample chapters. Reports in 1 month on queries; 2 months on mss. Simultaneous submissions OK.
Terms: Pays royalties. Offers advance. Provides author's copies. Sends galleys to author. Publishes ms 12-18 months after acceptance. Writer's guidelines for #10 SASE. Book catalog for 9×12 SAE with $1.90 postage.
Advice: Would like to see "less gender and racial stereotyping; protagonists from many cultures."

LITTLE, BROWN AND COMPANY, (II, III), 1271 Avenue of the Americas, New York NY 10020 and 34 Beacon St., Boston MA 02108. (212)522-8700 and (617)227-0730. Imprints include

MARKET CONDITIONS are constantly changing! If you're still using this book and it is 1998 or later, buy the newest edition of *Novel & Short Story Writer's Market* at your favorite bookstore or order from Writer's Digest Books.

Little, Brown; Back Bay; Bulfinch Press. Medium-size house. Publishes adult and juvenile hardcover and paperback originals. Averages 200-225 total adult titles/year. Number of fiction titles varies.
- Send children's submissions to Submissions Editor, Children's Books, at Boston address. Include SASE.

Needs: Open. No science fiction. Published *Along Came a Spider*, by James Patterson; *The Poet*, by Michael Connelly; *The Pugilist at Rest: Stories*, by Thom Jones. Published new writers within the last year.

How to Contact: Does not accept unsolicited adult mss. "We accept submissions from authors who have published before, in book form, magazines, newspapers or journals. No submissions from unpublished writers." Reports in 4-6 months on queries. Simultaneous and photocopied submissions OK.

Terms: "We publish on a royalty basis, with advance."

LITTLE, BROWN AND COMPANY CHILDREN'S BOOKS, (III), Trade Division; Children's Books, 34 Beacon St., Boston MA 02108. (617)227-0730. Fax: (617)227-8344. Editorial Department. Contact: Maria Modugno, editor-in-chief. Books: 70 lb. paper; sheet-fed printing; illustrations. Sometimes buys juvenile mss with illustrations "if by professional artist." Published new writers within the last year.
- *Maniac Magee*, by Jerry Spinelli and published by Little, Brown and Company Children's Books, received a Newbery Award.

Needs: Middle grade fiction and young adult. Recently published *A Time for Dancing*, by Davida Hurwin; *How Do You Spell Geek?*, by Julie Anne Peters; and *The Son of Summer Stars*, by Meredith Ann Pierce.

How to Contact: Submit through agent; authors with previous credits in children's book or magazine publishing may submit directly (include list of writing credits).

Terms: Pays on royalty basis. Sends galleys to author. Publishes ms 1-2 years after acceptance.

Advice: "We are looking for trade books with bookstore appeal. We are especially looking for young children's (ages 3-5) picture books. New authors should be aware of what is currently being published. We recommend they spend time at the local library and bookstore familiarizing themselves with new publications." Known for "humorous middle grade fiction with lots of kid appeal. Literary, multi-layered young adult fiction with distinctive characters and complex plots."

LITTLE SIMON, Imprint of Simon & Schuster Children's Publishing Division, 866 Third Ave., New York NY 10022. This imprint publishes novelty books only (pop-ups, lift-the-flaps board books, etc). Query for more information.

LODESTAR BOOKS, (II, V), An affiliate of Dutton Children's Books; A division of Penguin Books USA, Inc., 375 Hudson St., New York NY 10014. (212)366-2627. Editorial Director: Virginia Buckley. Executive Editor: Rosemary Brosnan. Books: 50 or 55 lb. antique cream paper; offset printing; printing from SyQuest disk; hardcover binding; illustrations sometimes; average print order: 5,000-6,500; first novel print order 5,000. Published new writers within the last year. Averages 20 total titles, 12-15 fiction titles each year.
- Books published by Lodestar have won numerous awards including the American Library Association's "Notable Children's Books" and "Best Books for Young Adults," the New England Book Award for Children's Books and the Scott O'Dell Award for Historical Fiction.

Needs: Contemporary, family saga, humorous, sports, mystery, adventure, for middle-grade and young adult. Recently published *Like Sisters on the Homefront*, by Rita Williams-Garcia; *Wiley and the Hairy Man*, by Judy Sierra; and *Who Killed Mr. Chippendale?*, by Mel Glenn.

How to Contact: Does not accept unsolicited mss. Send query letter plus first three chapters. SASE. Simultaneous submissions OK. Agented fiction 50%. Reports in 2-4 months. Publishes ms an average of 18 months after acceptance.

Terms: Pays 8-10% in royalties; offers negotiable advance. Sends galleys to author. Free book catalog.

Advice: "A strong individual is important. It is also important to know the needs of each publisher. We are still looking for more books about contemporary African-American, Hispanic, Native American, and Asian children, but the market has become tighter and excellent writing is more important than ever."

LOTHROP, LEE & SHEPARD BOOKS, (III), William Morrow & Co., 1350 Sixth Ave., New York NY 10019. (212)261-6641. Fax: (212)261-6648. Imprints: Morrow Junior Books (Contact: Diana Capriotti), and Greenwillow Books (Contact: Barbara Trueson). Vice President/Editor-in-Chief: Susan Pearson. Senior Editor: Melanie Donovan. Estab. mid 19th century. "We publish children's books for all ages—about 25 books a year—primarily picture books." Publishes hardcover originals. Published new writers within the last year. Averages 25 total titles, 2-3 fiction titles each year. Sometimes comments on rejected mss.
- The press received the Coretta Scott King Award for Illustration for *Meet Danitra Brown*,

Mildred L. Batchelder Honor Award for Translation for *Sister Shako & Kolo the Goat*, and the Archer/Eckblad Children's Picture Book Award for *Circus of the Wolves*.

Needs: "Our needs are not by category but by quality—we are interested only in fiction of a superlative quality." Recently published *Sister Shako & Kolo the Goat*, by Vedat Dalokay; *What Kind of Love?*, by Shelia Cole; and *Dreamtime*, by Oodgeroo (anthology of Aboriginal stories).

How to Contact: Does not accept unsolicited mss. Submit through agent only. SASE for return of ms. Agented fiction 100%. Reports in 3-6 months on mss.

Terms: Pays royalties of 10% minimum; negotiable advance. Sends galleys to author.

Advice: "I'd like to see more quality. More mss that move me to out-loud laughter or real tears—i.e. mss that touch my heart. Find an agent. Work on the craft. We are less able to work with beginners with an eye to the future; mss must be of a higher quality than ever before in order to be accepted."

LOVE SPELL, (I, II), Division of Dorchester Publishing Co., Inc., 276 Fifth Ave., Suite 1008, New York NY 10001. (212)725-8811. Assistant Editor: Christopher Reeslar. Mass market paperback publisher—originals and reprints. Books: newsprint paper; offset printing; perfect-bound; average print order: varies; first novel print order: varies. Plans 15 first novels this year. Comments "only if requested ms requires it."

Needs: Romance (futuristic, time travel, paranormal, historical). Looking for romances of 90,000-115,000 words. Recently published *Hidden Heart*, by Anne Avery (futuristic romance).

How to Contact: Accepts unsolicited mss. Query first. "All mss must be typed, double-spaced on one side and left unbound." SASE for return of ms. Agented fiction 70%. Reports in 1 month on queries; 2 months on mss.

Terms: Offers negotiable advance. "Payment depends on category and track record of author." Sends galleys to author. Publishes ms within 2 years after acceptance. Writer's guidelines for #10 SASE.

Advice: "The best way to learn to write a Love Spell Romance is by reading several of our recent releases. The best written stories are usually ones writers feel passionate about—so write from your heart! Also, the market is very tight these days so more than ever we are looking for refreshing, standout original fiction."

LOVESWEPT, (I, II), Bantam Books, 1540 Broadway, New York NY 10036. (212)354-6500. Associate Publisher: Nita Taublib. Senior Editors: Wendy McCurdy and Beth de Guzman. Imprint estab. 1982. Publishes paperback originals. Plans several first novels this year. Averages 72 total titles each year.

Needs: "Contemporary romance, highly sensual, believable primary characters, fresh and vibrant approaches to plot. No gothics, regencies or suspense."

How to Contact: Query with SASE; no unsolicited mss or partial mss. "Query letters should be no more than two to three pages. Content should be a brief description of the plot and the two main characters."

Terms: Pays in royalties of 6%; negotiates advance.

Advice: "Read extensively in the genre. Rewrite, polish and edit your own work until it is the best it can be—before submitting."

‡MARGARET K. McELDERRY BOOKS, (V), Imprint of the Simon & Schuster Children's Publishing Division, 1230 Sixth Ave., New York NY 10020. (212)698-2761. Publisher: Margaret K. McElderry. Publishes hardcover originals. Books: High quality paper; offset printing; cloth and three-piece bindings; illustrations; average print order: 10,000; first novel print order: 6,000. Published new writers within the last year. Number of titles: 25/year. Buys juvenile and young adult mss, agented or nonagented.

● Books published by Margaret K. McElderry Books have received numerous awards including the Newbery and the Caldecott Awards, and a *Boston Globe/Horn Book* honor award. Because of the merger between Macmillan and Simon & Schuster this imprint (still intact) is under a new division (see above).

Needs: All categories (fiction and nonfiction) for juvenile and young adult: adventure, contemporary, early chapter books, fantasy, literary, mystery and picture books. "We will consider any category. Results depend on the quality of the imagination, the artwork and the writing." Recently published *Flowers on the Wall*, written and illustrated by Miriam Nerlove; *Dog Friday*, by Hilary McKay; and *The Moorchild*, by Eloise McGraw.

Terms: Pays in royalties; offers advance.

Advice: "Imaginative writing of high quality is always in demand; also picture books that are original and unusual. Picture book manuscripts written in prose are totally acceptable. Keep in mind that McElderry Books is a very small imprint which only publishes 12 or 13 books per season, so we are very selective about the books we will undertake for publication. The YA market is tough right now, so we're being very picky. We try not to publish any 'trend' books. Be familiar with our list and with what is being published this year by all publishing houses."

WILLIAM MORROW AND COMPANY, INC., (II), 1350 Avenue of the Americas, New York NY 10019. (212)261-6500. Imprints include Greenwillow Books; Hearst Books; Hearst Marine Books; Lothrop, Lee & Shepard; Morrow; Morrow Junior Books; Mulberry Books; Quill Trade Paperbacks; Tambourine Books; Tupelo Books and Rob Weisbach Books. Estab. 1926. Approximately one fourth of books published are fiction.
Needs: "Morrow accepts only the highest quality submissions" in contemporary, literary, experimental, adventure, mystery/suspense, spy, historical, war, feminist, gay/lesbian, science fiction, horror, humor/satire and translations. Juvenile and young adult divisions are separate.
How to Contact: Submit through agent. All unsolicited mss are returned unopened. "We will accept queries, proposals or mss only when submitted through a literary agent." Simultaneous submissions OK.
Terms: Pays in royalties; offers advance. Sends galleys to author. Free book catalog.
Advice: "The Morrow divisions of Greenwillow Books; Lothrop, Lee & Shepard; Mulberry Books and Morrow Junior Books handle juvenile books. We do five to ten first novels every year and about one-fourth of the titles are fiction. Having an agent helps to find a publisher."

MORROW JUNIOR BOOKS, (III), 1350 Avenue of the Americas, New York NY 10019. (212)261-6691. Editor-In-Chief: David L. Reuther. Plans 1 first novel this year. Averages 55 total titles each year.
Needs: Juvenile (5-9 years) including animal, easy-to-read, fantasy (little), spy/adventure (very little), preschool/picture book, young adult/teen (10-18 years) including historical, sports. Published *Birthday Surprises*, edited by Johanna Horwitz; *My Own Two Feet*, by Beverly Cleary; and *The White Deer*, by John Bierhoust.
How to Contact: Does not accept unsolicited mss.
Terms: Authors paid in royalties. Books published 12-18 months after acceptance. Book catalog free on request.
Advice: "Our list is very full at this time. No unsolicited manuscripts."

MULTNOMAH BOOKS, (II), Questar Publishers, Inc. P.O. Box 1720, Sisters OR 97759. (541)549-1144. Fax: (541)549-2044. Contact: Editorial Dept. Estab. 1987. Midsize independent publisher of evangelical fiction and nonfiction. Publishes paperback originals. Books: perfect binding; average print order: 12,000. Averages 75 total titles, 10-12 fiction titles each year.
  • Multnomah Books has received several Gold Medallion Book Awards from the Evangelical Christian Publishers Association.
Needs: Literary, religious/inspirational issue or thesis fiction. Recently published *Dominion*, by Randy Alcorn (contemporary); *Virtually Eliminated*, by Jefferson Scott (technothriller); and *Love to Water My Soul*, by Jane Kirkpatrick (historical novel). Publishes "Battles of Destiny" (Civil War series).
How to Contact: Submit outline/synopsis and 2 sample chapters. "Include a cover letter with any additional information that might help us in our review." Send SASE for reply, return of ms or send a disposable copy of ms. Reports in 10 weeks. Simultaneous submissions OK.
Terms: Pays royalties. Provides 100 author's copies. Sends galleys to author. Publishes ms 1-2 years after acceptance. Writer's guidelines for SASE.
Advice: "Looking for clean, moral, uplifting fiction. We're particularly interested in contemporary women's fiction, historical fiction, superior romance, and thesis fiction."

THE MYSTERIOUS PRESS, (III), 1271 Avenue of the Americas, New York NY 10120. (212)522-7200. Crime and mystery fiction imprint for Warner Books. Editor-in-Chief: William Malloy. Editor: Sara Ann Freed. Estab. 1976. Publishes hardcover originals and paperback reprints. Books: Hardcover (some Smythe-sewn) and paperback binding; illustrations rarely. Average first novel print order: 5,000 copies. Published new writers within the last year. Critiques "only those rejected writers we wish particularly to encourage."
Needs: Mystery/suspense. Published *The Yellow Room Conspiracy*, by Peter Dickinson; *A Wild and Lonely Place*, by Marcia Muller; and *Ah, Treachery*, by Ross Thomas.

CHECK THE CATEGORY INDEXES, located at the back of the book, for publishers interested in specific fiction subjects.

INSIDER REPORT

Mysterious Press: looking for "something new" from mystery writers

Sara Ann Freed doesn't mind taking her work home with her. As executive editor of Mysterious Press, she's doing what she likes best. "I love reading mystery novels," she says, "so this is a dream job for me."

Freed's dream job began while she was working in the rights department of Walker & Company, where she got a "crash course" in editing mysteries from Ruth Cavin. Freed took over editing Walker's mystery line until 1985, when she joined Mysterious Press. "My colleague, William Malloy, who was the other editor at Mysterious Press, is now the editor-in-chief. We've been working together for over ten years."

Sara Ann Freed

In that time, Freed has seen substantial growth, both in Mysterious Press and in the mystery industry in general. "The days of the three-martini lunches are over," Freed says. "The average editor's load is 20 or more books per year." Freed and Malloy are no exceptions; with only one assistant to help them, the pair is responsible for editing 24 hardcover and 24 or more paperback releases each year. This load, plus other books they edit for Warner Books (the parent company of Mysterious Press), is the reason they will only look at manuscripts that come from agents.

Even with that limitation, the business of producing those books often forces Freed and other editors to take their work home. "We never seem to get any editing done in the office," she says. "There are so many other things you have to do to get everyone else in the company excited about the books we're editing. We're always on the phone or in meetings, selling the books in-house. We do just about everything in the office but edit."

Freed has noticed a slight dip in mystery sales in the past few years and says that many houses are trimming down their lines. "The genre is still strong, but publishers are keeping their lists lean and being a bit more ruthless if a series isn't selling. The accountants are getting into the act much earlier these days." What this means for writers is that they can't rely on past success. But it also is somewhat good news for new writers, Freed says, since the climate is kinder to people with no sales history; there are no poor sales figures to count against them.

So what are editors seeking? Basically, something new. "I want to read a *good* novel," Freed says. "I want to be transformed, moved, absorbed. What really

INSIDER REPORT, *continued*

catches my eye is a novel with intriguing characters, an interesting setting, a fresh plot and an engaging voice. New writers often slavishly copy successful mystery writers and neglect their own voice. They see Patricia Cornwell on the bestseller list and then try to write a book about a pathologist doing a lot of autopsies. What they end up with is a manuscript that copies Patricia Cornwell but lacks the voice and the special quality that make her books bestsellers. They don't respond to mysteries as readers, so they don't know how to write them."

Freed's best advice for new writers is to go to bookshops specializing in mysteries and research the market. "Those store owners are often tied into the mystery community and may even know what editors are buying. They are a great source of help and one might even become your greatest friend." Conventions and conferences where writers have the opportunity to meet with agents, editors and established writers are also good places to gather market information.

As for trends, Freed feels the mystery field in general is tired of bandwagon approaches to mystery. "I think many editors have had their fill of serial killer plots," she says. "It seems like every solution writers are coming up with has something to do with a serial killer, or it involves drugs or the mafia or some kind of epic disaster. And we're especially tired of sexual sadists. They're all unoriginal plots; we want something new."

Historical mysteries and mysteries with exotic locales are two areas which Freed feels still offer much territory to be explored. Exotic locales are popular, she says, because they combine an element of armchair travel with mystery. In a similar way, historicals also inform as well as entertain. Freed names Lindsey Davis, Laurie King, Anne Perry, Ellis Peters and Sharon Newman as examples of writers who create good historical mysteries.

But the key to selling your novel, Freed says, is to write it well. "Write the best novel you can possibly write. Keep shaping and polishing, and never send an editor or an agent anything that might be considered a first draft. That may sound obvious, but it's something that happens very often. We get many manuscripts that simply are not polished, that are nowhere near a publishable state. It makes it very hard for the writer to get an agent or an editor to read beyond the first 30 pages." She adds that other manuscripts may get rejected because they are good, but not great. "We'll work with the writer to a certain extent. That happens quite often; I can't remember ever buying a perfect first novel. What we're really responding to is the writing. If there's something about the writing that really stands out, other problems can be fixed."

—David Borcherding

How to Contact: Agented material only.
Terms: Pays in royalties of 10% minimum; offers negotiable advance. Sends galleys to author. Buys hard and softcover rights. Book catalog for SASE.
Advice: "Write a strong and memorable novel, and with the help of a good literary agent, you'll find the right publishing house. Don't despair if your manuscript is rejected by several houses. All publishing houses are looking for new and exciting crime novels, but it may not be at the time your novel is submitted. Hang in there, keep the faith—and good luck."

‡**THOMAS NELSON PUBLISHERS, (IV)**, Nelson Place at Elm Hill Pike, P.O. Box 141000, Nashville TN 37214-1000. (615)889-9000. Imprints: Janet Thoma Books, Oliver-Nelson Books, Thomas Nelson Trade Book Division, Nelson Biblical Reference Publishing. Estab. 1798. "Largest Christian book publishers." Publishes hardcover and paperback originals. Averages 150-200 total titles each year.

Needs: Adventure, children's/juvenile (adventure), mystery/suspense, religious/inspirational (general), western (frontier saga, traditional). "All work must be Christian in focus." No short stories. Published *A Skeleton in God's Closet*, by Paul Maier (suspense/mystery); *The Twilight of Courage*, by Brock and Bodie Thoene (historical suspense); and *The Secrets of the Roses*, by Lila Peiffer (romance).

How to Contact: Corporate office does not accept unsolicited mss. "No phone queries." Send brief prosaic résumé, 1 page synopsis, an SASE and one sample chapter to acquisitions editors at the following locations: Janet Thoma, Janet Thoma Books, 1157 Molokai, Tega Cay SC 29715, fax: (803)548-2684; Vic Oliver, Oliver-Nelson Books, 1360 Center Dr., Suite 102-B, Atlanta GA 30338, fax: (770)391-9784; Rick Nash, Thomas Nelson Trade Book Division, P.O. Box 141000, Nashville TN 37214-1000, fax: (615)391-5225; for biblical reference books contact: Phil Stoner, Nelson Biblical Reference Publishing, P.O. Box 141000, Nashville TN 37214. Fax: (615)391-5225. Reports in 3 to 12 months.

Terms: Offers negotiable advance. Sends galleys to author. Publishes ms 1-2 years after acceptance. Writer's guidelines for #10 SASE. Simultaneous submissions OK if so stated in cover letter.

Advice: "We are a conservative publishing house and want material which is conservative in morals and in nature."

W.W. NORTON & COMPANY, INC., (II), 500 Fifth Ave., New York NY 10110. (212)354-5500. For unsolicited mss contact: Liz Malcolm. Estab. 1924. Midsize independent publisher of trade books and college textbooks. Publishes hardcover originals. Occasionally comments on rejected mss.

Needs: High-quality fiction (preferably literary). No occult, science fiction, religious, gothic, romances, experimental, confession, erotica, psychic/supernatural, fantasy, horror, juvenile or young adult. Published *Seduction Theory*, by Thomas Beller; *Come and Go, Molly Snow*, by Mary Ann Taylor-Hall; and *The Book of Knowledge*, by Doris Grumbach.

How to Contact: Submit outline/synopsis and first 50 pages. SASE. Simultaneous submissions OK. Reports in 8-10 weeks. Packaging and postage must be enclosed to ensure safe return of materials.

Terms: Graduated royalty scale starting at 7½% or 10% of list price, in addition to 15 author's copies; offers advance. Free book catalog.

Advice: "We will occasionally encourage writers of promise whom we do not immediately publish. We are principally interested in the literary quality of fiction manuscripts. A familiarity with our current list of titles will give you an idea of what we're looking for. Chances are, if your book is good and you have no agent you will eventually succeed; but the road to success will be easier and shorter if you have an agent backing the book. We encourage the submission of first novels."

PANTHEON BOOKS, (III), Subsidiary of Random House, 201 E. 50th St., New York NY 10022. (212)572-2854. Estab. 1942. "Small but well-established imprint of well-known large house." Publishes hardcover and trade paperback originals and trade paperback reprints. Averages 75 total titles, about one-third fiction, each year.

Needs: Quality fiction and nonfiction.

How to Contact: Query letter and sample material. SASE. Attention: Editorial Department.

PELICAN PUBLISHING COMPANY, (IV), Box 3110, Gretna LA 70054. Editor-in-Chief: Nina Kooij. Estab. 1926. Publishes paperback reprints and hardcover originals. Books: Hardcover and paperback binding; illustrations sometimes. Buys juvenile mss with illustrations. Comments on rejected mss "infrequently."

Needs: Juvenile fiction, especially with a regional and/or historical focus. No young adult contemporary fiction or fiction containing graphic language, violence or sex. Also no "psychological" novels. Recently published *That Printer of Udell's*, by Harold Bell Wright (reprint).

How to Contact: Prefers query. May submit outline/synopsis and 2 sample chapters with SASE. No simultaneous submissions. "Not responsible if writer's only copy is sent." Reports in 1 month on queries; 3 months on mss. Publishes ms 12-18 months after acceptance.

Terms: Pays 10% in royalties; 10 contributor's copies; advance considered. Sends galleys to author. Catalog of titles and writer's guidelines for SASE.

Advice: "Research the market carefully. Order and look through publishing catalogs to see if your work is consistent with our list. For ages 8 and up, story must be planned in chapters that will fill at least 90 double-spaced manuscript pages. Topic should be historical and, preferably, linked to a particular region or culture. We look for stories that illuminate a particular place and time in history and that are clean entertainment. The only original adult work we might consider is historical fiction, preferably Civil War (not romance). For middle readers, regional historical or regional adventure could be considered. Please don't send three or more chapters unless solicited. Follow our guidelines listed under 'How to Contact.' "

PENGUIN USA, 375 Hudson St., New York NY 10014. See the listing for Dutton Signet.

PHILOMEL BOOKS, (II), The Putnam & Grosset Book Group, 200 Madison Ave., New York NY 10016. (212)951-8700. Editorial Director: Patricia Gauch. Editor: Michael Green. "A high-quality oriented imprint focused on stimulating picture books, middle-grade novels, and young adult novels." Publishes hardcover originals and paperback reprints. Averages 25 total titles, 5-7 novels/year. Sometimes comments on rejected ms.
  ● Books published by Philomel have won numerous awards. Their book, *The War of Jenkin's Ear*, by Michael Morpurgo, was selected as the "Top of the List" in the Youth Fiction category by *Booklist*.
Needs: Adventure, ethnic, family saga, fantasy, historical, juvenile (5-9 years), literary, preschool/ picture book, regional, short story collections, translations, western (young adult), young adult/teen (10-18 years). Looking for "story-driven novels with a strong cultural voice but which speak universally." No "generic, mass-market oriented fiction." Recently published *The Outcast of Redwall*, by Brian Jacques; *The Merlin Effect*, by T.A. Barron; *Moon of Two Dark Horses*, by Sally Keehn.
How to Contact: Accepts unsolicited mss. Query first or submit outline/synopsis and first 3 chapters. SASE. Agented fiction 40%. Reports in 6-8 weeks on queries; 8-10 weeks on mss. Simultaneous submissions OK.
Terms: Pays royalties, negotiable advance and author's copies. Sends galleys to author. Publishes ms anywhere from 1-3 years after acceptance. Writer's guidelines for #10 SASE. Book catalog for 9 × 12 SASE.
Advice: "We are not a mass-market publisher and do not publish short stories independently. In addition, we do just a few novels a year."

PINNACLE BOOKS, 850 Third Ave., New York NY 10022. See Kensington Publishing Corp.

‡PRESIDIO PRESS, (IV), 505B San Marin Dr., Suite 300, Novato CA 94945. (415)898-1081. Editor-in-Chief: E.J. McCarthy. Estab. 1976. Small independent general trade—specialist in military. Publishes hardcover originals. Publishes an average of 2 works of fiction per list under its Lyford Books imprint. Averages 24 new titles each year. Critiques or comments on rejected ms.
Needs: Historical with military background, war. Also mystery/suspense (police procedural, private eye), thriller/espionage. Recently published *Synbat*, by Bob Mayer; *In a Heartbeat*, by Eric Stone; and *A Murder of Crows*, by Steve Shepard. Regularly publishes new writers.
How to Contact: Accepts unsolicited mss. Query first. SASE. Reports in 2 weeks on queries; 2-3 months on mss. Simultaneous submissions OK.
Terms: Pays in royalties of 15% of net minimum; advance: $1,000 average. Sends edited manuscripts and page proofs to author. Book catalog and guidelines free on request. Send 9 × 12 SASE with $1.30 postage.
Advice: "Think twice before entering any highly competitive genre; don't imitate; do your best. Have faith in your writing and don't let the market disappoint or discourage you."

G.P. PUTNAM'S SONS, (III), The Putnam Publishing Group, 200 Madison Ave., New York NY 10016. (212)951-8400. Imprints include Perigee, Philomel and Grosset. Publishes hardcover originals.
Needs: Published fiction by Stephen King, Lawrence Sanders, Alice Hoffman; published new writers within the last year.
How to Contact: Does not accept unsolicited mss.

‡QUESTAR PUBLISHERS, (II), P.O. Box 1720, Sisters OR 97759. (541)549-1144. Fax: (541)549-2044. Imprints are Multnomah Books and Palisades Romances. Estab. 1987. "Mid-size Christian publisher of innovative, high-quality fiction." Publishes hardcover and paperback originals. Published new writers within the last year. Plans 1-4 first novels this year. Averages 100-200 total titles, 40-50 fiction titles each year. Sometimes comments on rejected ms.
Needs: Adventure, children's/juvenile (adventure, mystery, series), historical, literary, mystery/suspense, religious, romance (contemporary, historical), western, young adult/teen (adventure, mystery/suspense, romance, series). Recently published *A Sweetness to the Soul*, by Jane Kirkpatrick (literary/ historical); *The President*, by Parker Hudson (suspense/political); and *Angel of Mercy Series*, by Al Lacy (historical).
How to Contact: Accepts unsolicited mss. Query with outline/synopsis and 3 sample chapters. Fax OK. Include estimated word count, Social Security number, list of publishing credits and "genre/age group." Send SASE for reply, return of ms or send disposable copy of ms. Reports in 2 months. Simultaneous submissions OK.

Terms: Pays royalties and advance. Sends galleys to author. Publishes ms 6-12 months after acceptance. Writer's guidelines for free #10 SASE or 1 IRC.
Advice: "Please send clear and concise queries and tell us why we should consider your proposal—how is it different? Whose needs will it meet?"

RANDOM HOUSE, INC., 201 E. 50th St., New York NY 10022. (212)751-2600. Imprints include Pantheon Books, Panache Press at Random House, Vintage Books, Times Books, Villard Books and Knopf. Contact: Adult Trade Division. Publishes hardcover and paperback originals. Encourages new writers. Rarely comments on rejected mss.
Needs: Adventure, contemporary, historical, literary, mainstream, short story collections, mystery/suspense. "We publish fiction of the highest standards." Authors include James Michener, Robert Ludlum, Mary Gordon.
How to Contact: Query with SASE. Simultaneous submissions OK. Reports in 4-6 weeks on queries, 2 months on mss.
Terms: Payment as per standard minimum book contracts. Free writer's guidelines.
Advice: "Please try to get an agent because of the large volume of manuscripts received, agented work is looked at first."

✤RANDOM HOUSE OF CANADA, (III), Division of Random House, Inc., 33 Yonge St., Suite 210, Toronto, Ontario M5E 1G4 Canada. Prefers not to share information.

RESOURCE PUBLICATIONS, INC., (I, IV), 160 E. Virginia St., Suite 290, San Jose CA 95112. (408)286-8505. Book Editor: Kenneth Guentert. Estab. 1973. "Independent book and magazine publisher focusing on imaginative resources for professionals in ministry, education and counseling." Publishes paperback originals. Averages 12-14 total titles, 2-3 fiction titles each year.
Needs: Story collections for storytellers, "not short stories in the usual literary sense." Published *Morgan's Baby Sister: A Read-Aloud Book For Families Who Have Experienced the Death of a Newborn*, by Patricia Polin Johnson and Donna Reilly Williams; and *Dream Catcher: Lectionary-based stories for Preaching and Teaching*, by James Henderschedt. Occasionally publishes book-length stories that meet some need (*The Cure: The Hero's Journey with Cancer*). No novels in the literary sense.
How to Contact: Query first or submit outline/synopsis and 1 sample chapter with SASE. Reports in 2 weeks on queries; 6 weeks on mss. No simultaneous submissions. Accepts disk submissions compatible with CP/M, IBM system. Prefers hard copy with disk submissions.
Terms: Pays in royalties of 8% minimum, 10% maximum; 10 author's copies. "We do not subsidy publish under the Resource Publications imprint. However, our graphics department will help author's self-publish for a fee."

REVELL PUBLISHING, (III), Subsidiary of Baker Book House, P.O. Box 6287, Grand Rapids MI 49516-6287. (616)676-9185. Fax: (616)676-9573. Imprints include Spire Books. Editorial Director: Wm. J. Petersen. Estab. 1870. "Midsize evangelical book publishers." Publishes paperback originals. Average print order: 7,500. Published new writers within the last year. Plans 1 first novel this year. Averages 60 total titles, 8 fiction titles each year. Sometimes comments on rejected mss.
Needs: Religious/inspirational (general). Published *Ordeal at Iron Mountain*, by Linda Rae Rao (historical); *A Time to Weep*, by Gilbert Morris (historical); and *The End of the Age*, by David Dolan (suspense).
How to Contact: Query with outline/synopsis. Include estimated word count, bio and list of publishing credits. Send SASE for reply, return of ms or send a disposable copy of ms. Agented fiction 20%. Reports in 3 weeks on queries; 2 weeks on mss. Simultaneous submissions OK.
Terms: Pays royalties. Sends galleys to author. Publishes ms 1 year after acceptance. Writer's guidelines for SASE.

ROC, (II, III), Imprint of Dutton Signet, a division of Penguin USA, Inc., 375 Hudson St., New York NY 10014. (212)366-2000. Fax: (212)366-2888. Executive Editor: Laura Anne Gilman. Associate Editor: Jennifer Smith. Publishes hardcover, trade paperback and mass market originals and hardcover, trade paperback (and mass market) reprints. Published new writers within the last year. Averages 40 (all fiction) titles each year. Sometimes comments on rejected mss.
● A Roc book, *The Innkeeper's Song*, by Peter S. Beagle won a Locus Award and was nominated for a World Fantasy Award.
Needs: Fantasy, horror (dark fantasy) and science fiction. Publishes science fiction, horror and fantasy anthologies. Anthologies by invitation only. Recently published *The Knights of the Black Earth*, by Margaret Weis and Don Perrin (science fiction); *No One Noticed the Cat*; by Anne McCaffrey (fantasy); and *The Immortals*, by Tracy Hickman (science fiction). Publishes the Battletech® and Shadowrun® series.

How to Contact: Accepts unsolicited mss. Query with outline/synopsis and 3 sample chapters. Include list of publishing credits. Not responsible for return of submission if no SASE is included. Agented fiction 99%. Reports in 2 weeks on queries; 3-4 months on mss. Simultaneous submissions OK.
Terms: Offers negotiable advance. Sends galleys to author. Publishes ms 1-2 years after acceptance.

‡ROYAL FIREWORKS PRESS, (I), (formerly Trillium Press), First Avenue, Unionville NY 10988. (914)726-4444. E-mail: rfpress@nyfrontiercomm. Website: rfpress@ny.frontiercomm.net. Vice President: Thomas Holland. Fiction Editor: Charles Morgan and William Neumann. Science Fiction Editor: Myrna Kemnitz. Estab. 1978. Independent publisher. Publishes hardcover and paperback originals and paperback reprints. Plans 60 first novels this year. Averages 150 total titles, 100 fiction titles each year.
Needs: Young adult/teen (10-18 years), fantasy/science fiction, historical, romance (ya), sports and mystery/adventure, middle school/young adult (10-18) series. Published the following young adult series: Mystery & Adventure (including historical novels); Growing Up Right (values, relationships, adult development); Science Fiction. Recently published *Dragon Charmer*, by Ruth Siburt (science fiction); *Invisible Alex*, by Kristi Holl (Growing Up); *Cherokee Windsong*, by Evelin Sanders (historical fiction); *Mosquito Point*, by Chris Barry (mystery/adventure); and *Uphill & Into the Wind*, by Willard Helmuth (special needs).
How to Contact: Accepts unsolicited mss. SASE. Reports in 6 weeks on mss. No simultaneous submissions.
Terms: Negotiated "as appropriate." Sends galleys to author. Writer's guidelines for #10 SAE and 1 first-class stamp (or IRC). Book catalog for 9×12 SAE and 3 first-class stamps.

ST. MARTIN'S PRESS, 175 Fifth Ave., New York NY 10010. (212)674-5151. Imprint: Thomas Dunne. Chairman and CEO: Thomas J. McCormack. President: Roy Gainsburg. Publishes hardcover and paperback reprints and originals.
Needs: Contemporary, literary, experimental, adventure, mystery/suspense, spy, historical, war, gothic, romance, confession, feminist, gay, lesbian, ethnic, erotica, psychic/supernatural, religious/inspirational, science fiction, fantasy, horror and humor/satire. No plays, children's literature or short fiction. Published *The Silence of the Lambs*, by Thomas Harris; *The Shell Seekers* and *September* by Rosamunde Pilcher.
How to Contact: Query or submit complete ms with SASE. Simultaneous submissions OK (if declared as such). Reports in 2-3 weeks on queries, 4-6 weeks on mss.
Terms: Pays standard advance and royalties.

ST. PAUL BOOKS AND MEDIA, (I), Subsidiary of Daughters of St. Paul, 50 St. Paul's Ave., Jamaica Plain, Boston MA 02130. (617)522-8911. Children's Editor: Sister Patricia Edward Jablonski, fsp. Estab. 1934. Roman Catholic publishing house. Publishes hardcover and paperback originals. Averages 20 total titles, 5 fiction titles each year.
Needs: Juvenile (easy-to-read, historical, religion, contemporary), preschool/picture book. All fiction must communicate high moral and family values. "Our fiction needs are entirely in the area of children's literature. We are looking for bedtime stories for children. Would like to see characters who manifest faith and trust in God." Does not want "characters whose lifestyles are not in conformity with Catholic teachings."
How to Contact: Does not accept unsolicited mss. Query first. SASE. Reports in 2-3 months.
Terms: Pays royalties of 8% minimum; 12% maximum. Provides negotiable number of author's copies. Publishes ms 2 or 3 years after acceptance. Writer's guidelines for #10 SASE.
Advice: "There is a dearth of juvenile fiction appropriate for Catholics and other Christians."

SCRIBNER'S, 1230 Avenue of the Americas, New York NY 10020. Prefers not to share information.

SIGNAL HILL PUBLICATIONS, (IV), (Imprint New Readers Press), Publishing imprint of Laubach Literacy International, Box 131, Syracuse NY 13210. (315)422-9121. Estab. 1959. Publishes paperback originals. Books: offset printing; paper binding; 6-12 illustrations per fiction book; average print order: 7,500; first novel print order: 5,000. Fiction titles may be published both in book form and as read-along audio tapes. Averages 30 total titles, 8-12 fiction titles each year.
Needs: High-interest, low-reading-level materials for adults with limited reading skills. Romance novels of 7,500 words, written on 3rd-5th grade level. "Characters are well-developed, situations realistic, and plot developments believable." All material must be suitable for classroom use in public education, i.e., little violence and no explicit sex. "We will not accept anything at all for readers under 16 years of age." Published *The Orange Grove & Other Stories*, by Rosanne Keller; *The Kite Flyer & Other Stories* by Rosanne Keller.
How to Contact: Accepts unsolicited mss. Query first or submit outline/synopsis and 3 sample chapters. SASE. Reports in 1 month on queries; 3 months on mss.

Terms: Pays royalties of 5% minimum, 7.5% maximum on net sales. Average advance: $200. "We may offer authors a choice of a royalty or flat fee. The fee would vary depending on the type of work." Book catalog free.

Advice: "Many of our fiction authors are being published for the first time. It is necessary to have a sympathetic attitude toward adults with limited reading skills and an understanding of their life situation. Direct experience with them is helpful."

SILHOUETTE BOOKS, (I, II, IV), 300 E. 42nd St., 6th Floor, New York NY 10017. (212)682-6080. Imprints include Silhouette Romance, Silhouette Special Edition, Silhouette Desire, Silhouette Intimate Moments, Silhouette Yours Truly, Harlequin Historicals; also Silhouette and Harlequin Historicals' short story collections. Editorial Director: Isabel Swift. Senior Editor and Editorial Coordinator (SIM): Leslie J. Wainger. Seniors Editors: (SE) Tara Hughes Gavin, (SD) Lucia Macro, (SR) Anne Canadeo. Editors (SYT): Melissa Senate, Gail Chasan, Marcia Adirim. Historicals: Senior Editor: Tracy Farrell. Estab. 1979. Publishes paperback originals. Published 10-20 new writers within the last year. Buys agented and unagented adult romances. Averages 360 total titles each year. Occasionally comments on rejected mss.

● Books published by Silhouette Books have received numerous awards including Romance Writers of America's Rita Award, awards from *Romantic Times* and bestselling awards from Walden and B. Dalton bookstores.

Needs: Contemporary romances, historical romances. Published *Sheik Daddy*, by Barbara McMahon (SR); *Saddle Up*, by Mary Lynn Baxter (SD); *New Year's Daddy*, by Lora Jackson (SE); *Nighthawk*, by Rachel Lee (IM); *Blackguard*, by Evelyn Vaughn (SS); *Wanted: Perfect Partner*, by Debbie Macumben (SYT); and *The Wedding Promise*, by Cheryl Reams (HH).

How to Contact: Submit query letter with brief synopsis and SASE. No unsolicited or simultaneous submissions. Publishes ms 9-24 months after acceptance.

Terms: Pays in royalties; offers advance (negotiated on an individual basis). Must return advance if book is not completed or is unacceptable.

Advice: "You are competing with writers that love the genre and know what our readers want—because many of them started as readers. Please note that the fact that our novels are fun to read doesn't make them easy to write. Storytelling ability, clean compelling writing and love of the genre are necessary."

SIMON & SCHUSTER, 1230 Avenue of the Americas, New York NY 10020. (212)698-7000. Imprints include Pocket Books, Poseidon Press.

Needs: General adult fiction, mostly commercial fiction.

How to Contact: Agented material 100%.

SIMON & SCHUSTER BOOKS FOR YOUNG READERS, (V), Subsidiary of Simon & Schuster Children's Publishing Division, 1230 Avenue of the Americas, New York NY 10020. (212)698-2851. Fax: (212)698-2796. Vice President/Editorial Director: Stephanie Owens Lurie. "Flagship children's imprint of large children's publishing division." Publishes hardcover originals. Published new writers within the last year. Plans 4 first novels this year. Averages 100 total titles, 25 fiction titles each year.

● Books from Simon & Schuster have been the recipients in 1996 of two Caldecott honor awards, one Coretta Scott King Honor Award, seven ALA Notable books for children, eight ALA Best Books for Young Adults and six ALA Quick Picks for Reluctant Readers.

Needs: Children's/juvenile, young adult/teen (adventure, historical, mystery, picture book, contemporary fiction). No chapter books. No problem novels. No anthropomorphic characters. Publishes anthologies; editor solicits from established writers. Recently published *Rats Saw God*, by Rob Thomas (young adult novel); *Running Out of Time*, by Margaret Peterson Haddix (middle school novel); and *Zin! Zin! Zin! A Violin*, by Lloyd Moss/Marjorie Priceman (picture book).

How to Contact: *Does not accept unsolicited mss.* Submit query letter and SASE. Agented fiction 90%. Reports in 2 months on queries. Simultaneous submissions OK.

Terms: Pays royalties. Offers negotiable advance. Sends galleys to author. Publishes ms within 2 years of acceptance. Writer's guidelines for #10 SASE. Book catalog available in libraries.

THE MAPLE LEAF symbol before a listing indicates a Canadian publisher, magazine, conference or contest.

SINGER MEDIA CORP., (III, IV), Unit 106, Seaview Business Park, 1030 Calle Cordillera, San Clemente CA 92673. (714)498-7227. Fax: (714)498-2162. "Book packagers based on our newspaper/syndicates production. License books to foreign publishers; co-production, co-financing."

• This is a book packager that licenses books to foreign publishers (usually books *already* published in North America). They will work with agents or directly with authors.

Needs: Very little fiction. Will do fiction and biography.

How to Contact: Query first. Include list of publishing credits. Send SASE for reply. Agented fiction 15% US, 20% foreign. Reports on queries in 3 weeks; 1 month on mss.

Terms: Pays royalties plus advance (varies from country to country and book). Guidelines for SASE. "Please, no phone calls."

✦STODDART, 34 Lesmill Rd., Toronto, Ontario M3B 2T6 Canada. No American authors. Prefers not to share information.

THORNDIKE PRESS, (IV), Division of McMillan Library U.S.A., Box 159, Thorndike ME 04986. (800)223-6121. Contact: Jamie Knobloch. Estab. 1979. Midsize publisher of hardcover and paperback large print *reprints*. Books: alkaline paper; offset printing; Smythe-sewn library binding; average print order: 2,000. Publishes 500 total titles each year.

Needs: *No fiction that has not been previously published.*

How to Contact: Does not accept unsolicited mss. Query.

Terms: Pays 10% in royalties.

Advice: "We do not accept unpublished works."

TOR BOOKS, (II), 175 Fifth Ave., New York NY 10010. (212)388-0100. Imprint: Forge Books. Manager of Science Fiction: Patrick Nielsen Hayden. Estab. 1980. Publishes hardcover and paperback originals, plus some paperback reprints. Books: 5 point Dombook paper; offset printing; Bursel and perfect binding; few illustrations. Averages 200 total titles, mostly fiction, each year. Some nonfiction titles.

Needs: Fantasy, mainstream, science fiction and horror. Published *Moving Mars*, by Greg Bear; *Alvin Journeyman*, by Orson Scott Card; *A Crown of Swords*, by Robert Jordan; and *The Two Georges*, by Richard Dreyfuss and Harry Turtledove.

How to Contact: Agented mss preferred. Buys 90% agented fiction. No simultaneous submissions. Address manuscripts to "Editorial," *not* to the Managing Editor's office.

Terms: Pays in royalties and advance. Writer must return advance if book is not completed or is unacceptable. Sends galleys to author. Free book catalog on request.

TROLL ASSOCIATES, (II), Watermill Press, 100 Corporate Dr., Mahwah NJ 07430. (201)529-4000. Editorial Contact Person: M. Frances. Estab. 1968. Midsize independent publisher. Publishes hardcover originals, paperback originals and reprints. Averages 100-300 total titles each year.

Needs: Adventure, historical, juvenile (5-9 yrs. including: animal, easy-to-read, fantasy), preschool/picture book, young adult/teen (10-18 years) including: easy-to-read, fantasy/science fiction, historical, romance (young adult), sports, spy/adventure. Published new writers within the last year.

How to Contact: Accepts and returns unsolicited mss. Query first. SASE. Submit outline/synopsis and sample chapters. Reports in 2-3 weeks on queries.

Terms: Pays royalties. Sometimes sends galleys to author. Publishes ms 6-18 months after acceptance.

TYNDALE HOUSE PUBLISHERS, (II, IV), P.O. Box 80, 351 Executive Drive, Wheaton IL 60189. (630)668-8300. Vice President of Editorial: Ron Beers. Acquisition Director: Ken Petersen. Estab. 1962. Privately owned religious press. Publishes hardcover and trade paperback originals and paperback reprints. Averages 100 total titles, 10-15 fiction titles each year. Average first novel print order: 5,000-15,000 copies.

• Three books published by Tyndale House have received the Gold Medallion Book Award. They include *An Echo in the Darkness*, by Francine Rivers; *The Sword of Truth*, by Gilbert Morris; and *A Rose Remembered*, by Michael Phillips.

How to Contact: Does not accept unsolicited mss. Queries only. Reports in 6-10 weeks. Publishes ms an average of 1-2 years after acceptance.

Terms: Writer's guidelines and book catalog for 9×12 SAE and $2.40 for postage.

Advice: "We are a religious publishing house with a primarily evangelical Christian market. We are looking for spiritual themes and content within established genres."

WALKER AND COMPANY, (I), 435 Hudson St., New York NY 10014. Editors: Michael Seidman (mystery), Jacqueline Johnson (western), Emily Easton (young adult). Midsize independent publisher with plans to expand. Publishes hardcover and trade paperback originals. Average first novel print order: 2,500-3,500. Number of titles: 120/year. Published many new writers within the last year. Occasionally comments on rejected mss.

• Books published by Walker and Company have received numerous awards including the Spur Award (for westerns) and the Shamus Awards for Best First Private Eye Novel and Best Novel.

Needs: Nonfiction, sophisticated, quality mystery (amateur sleuth, cozy, private eye, police procedural), traditional western and children's and young adult nonfiction. Published *The Killing of Monday Brown*, by Sandra West Prowell; *Murder in the Place of Anubis*, by Lynda S. Robinson; and *Who In Hell Is Wanda Fuca*, by G.M. Ford.

How to Contact: Submit outline and chapters as preliminary. Query letter should include "a concise description of the story line, including its outcome, word length of story (we prefer 70,000 words), writing experience, publishing credits, particular expertise on this subject and in this genre. Common mistakes: Sounding unprofessional (i.e. too chatty, too braggardly). Forgetting SASE." Agented fiction 50%. Notify if multiple or simultaneous submissions. Reports in 3-5 months. Publishes ms an average of 1 year after acceptance.

Terms: Negotiable (usually advance against royalty). Must return advance if book is not completed or is unacceptable.

Advice: "As for mysteries, we are open to all types, including suspense novels and offbeat books that maintain a 'play fair' puzzle. We are always looking for well-written western novels that are offbeat and strong on characterization. Character development is most important in all Walker fiction. We expect the author to be expert in the categories, to know the background and foundations of the genre. To realize that just because some subgenre is hot it doesn't mean that that is the area to mine—after all, if everyone is doing female p.i.s, doesn't it make more sense to do something that isn't crowded, something that might serve to balance a list, rather than make it top heavy? Finally, don't tell us why your book is going to be a success; instead, show me that you can write and write well. It is your writing, and not your hype that interests us."

WARNER BOOKS, 1271 Avenue of the Americas, New York NY 10020. Prefers not to share information. See also the listing for Mysterious Press and Aspect.

WASHINGTON SQUARE PRESS, (III), Subsidiary of Pocket Books/Simon & Schuster, 1230 Avenue of the Americas, New York NY 10020. Fiction Editor: Amy Einhorn. Estab. 1959. Quality imprint of mass-market publisher. Publishes very few paperback originals, mostly reprints. Averages 15 titles, mostly fiction, each year.

Needs: Literary, high quality novels; serious nonfiction. Published *Pizza Face*, by Ken Siman; *Montana 1948*, by Larry Watson; and novels by Susan Minot and Stephen McCauley.

How to Contact: Query first. Publishes mostly agented fiction. Simultaneous submissions OK. "We cannot promise an individual response to unsolicited mss."

DANIEL WEISS ASSOCIATES, INC., (II), 33 W. 17th St., New York NY 10011. (212)645-3865. Fax: (212)633-1236. Estab. 1987. "Book packager of 140 titles a year including juvenile and young adult fiction as well as nonfiction titles. We package for a range of publishers within their specifications." Publishes paperback originals. All titles by first-time writers are commissioned for established series.

Needs: Juvenile (ballet, friendship, horse, mystery), mainstream, preschool/picture book, young adult (continuity series, romance, romantic suspense, thriller). Publishes Sweet Valley Kids, Sweet Valley Twins, Sweet Valley High and Sweet Valley University series. "We cannot acquire single-title manuscripts that are not part of a series the author is proposing or submitted specifically according to our guidelines for an established series." Published *Sweet Valley High*, by Francine Pascal (young adult series); *Thoroughbred*, by Joanna Campbell (juvenile horse series); and *Boyfriends & Girlfriends*, by Katherine Applegate (young adult continuity series).

How to Contact: Accepts unsolicited mss. Query first with synopsis/outline and 2 sample chapters. SASE. Agented fiction 60%. Reports in 2 months. Simultaneous submissions OK.

Terms: Pays flat fee plus royalty. Advance is negotiable. Publishes ms 1 year after acceptance. Writer's guidelines for #10 SASE.

Advice: "We are always happy to work with and encourage first-time novelists. Being packagers, we often create and outline books by committee. This system is quite beneficial to writers who may be less experienced. Usually we are contacted by the agent rather than the writer directly. Occasionally, however, we do work with writers who send in unsolicited material. I think that a professionally presented manuscript is of great importance."

✤**WORLDWIDE LIBRARY, (II)**, Division of Harlequin Books, 225 Duncan Mill Rd., Don Mills, Ontario M3B 3K9 Canada. (416)445-5860. Imprints are Worldwide Mystery; Gold Eagle Books. Senior Editor/Editorial Coordinator: Feroze Mohammed. Estab. 1979. Large commercial category line. Publishes paperback originals and reprints. Averages 72 titles, all fiction, each year. Sometimes critiques rejected ms. "Mystery program is reprint; no originals please."

Needs: "We publish action-adventure series; future fiction." Published *Black Ops* and *Destroyer*. "We are launching a new series in June 1997."

How to Contact: Query first or submit outline/synopsis/series concept or overview and sample chapters. SAE. U.S. stamps do not work in Canada; use International Reply Coupons or money order. Agented fiction 95%. Reports in 10 weeks on queries. Simultaneous submissions OK.

Terms: Advance and sometimes royalties; copyright buyout. Publishes ms 1-2 years after acceptance.

Advice: "Publishing fiction in very selective areas. As a genre publisher we are always on the lookout for innovative series ideas, especially in the men's adventure area."

ZONDERVAN, (III, IV), 5300 Patterson SE, Grand Rapids MI 49530. (616)698-6900. Website: http://www.zondervan.com. Contact: Manuscript Submissions. Large evangelical Christian publishing house. Publishes hardcover and paperback originals and reprints, though fiction is generally in paper only. Published new writers in the last year. Averages 150 total titles, 5-10 fiction titles each year. Average first novel: 5,000 copies.

  ● At the 1996 Christian Booksellers Association convention, Zondervan was named CBA Supplier of the Year and won the CBA Telemarketer of the Year award and the CBA Editor's Choice award for best advertiser, among other honors.

Needs: Adult fiction, (mainstream, biblical, historical, adventure, sci-fi, fantasy, mystery), "Inklings-style" fiction of high literary quality and juvenile fiction (primarily mystery/adventure novels for 8-12-year-olds). Christian relevance necessary in all cases. Will *not* consider collections of short stories or inspirational romances. Recently published *The Campaign*, by Marilyn Quayle and Nancy Northcutt (mystery); *Byzantium*, by Steven Lawhead (fantasy); and *Blood of Heaven*, by Bill Myers (suspense).

How to Contact: Accepts unsolicited mss. Write for writer's guidelines first. Include #10 SASE. Query or submit outline/synopsis and 2 sample chapters. Reports in 4-6 weeks on queries; 3-4 months on mss.

Terms: "Standard contract provides for a percentage of the net price received by publisher for each copy sold, usually 14-17% of net."

Advice: "Almost no unsolicited fiction is published. Send plot outline and one or two sample chapters. Most editors will *not* read entire mss. Your proposal and opening chapter will make or break you."

International commercial book publishers

The following commercial publishers, all located outside the United States and Canada, also accept work from fiction writers. The majority are from England, a few are from Scotland and even India. As with other publishers, obtain catalogs and writer's guidelines from those that interest you to determine the types of fiction published and how well your work might fit alongside other offerings.

  Remember to use self-addressed envelopes (SAEs) with International Reply Coupons (IRCs) in all correspondence with publishers outside your own country. IRCs may be purchased at the main branch of your local post office. In general, send IRCs in amounts roughly equivalent to return postage. When submitting work to international publishers, you may want to send a disposable copy of your manuscript and only one IRC along with a self-addressed postcard for a reply.

MARION BOYARS PUBLISHERS INC., 237 E. 39th St., New York NY 10016. Editorial Office (all submissions): 24 Lacy Road, London SW15 1NL England. Fiction Editor: Marion Boyars. Publishes 15 novels or story collections/year. "A lot of American fiction. Authors include Ken Kesey, Eudora Welty, Stephen Koch, Samuel Charters, Page Edwards, Viatia Spiegelman, Kenneth Gangemi, Tim O'Brien, Julian Green. British and Irish fiction. Translations from the French, German, Turkish, Arabic, Italian, Spanish." Send cover letter and entire manuscript "always with sufficient return postage by check." Pays advance against royalties. "Most fiction working *well* in one country does well in another. We usually have world rights, i.e. world English plus translation rights." Enclose return postage by check, minimum $3, for catalog. "No manuscripts to New York office."

‡CONSTABLE AND COMPANY, (IV), 3 The Lanchesters, 162 Fulham Palace Rd., London W6 9ER England. Editorial Director: Carol O'Brien. Averages 40 fiction titles/year. Publishes "literary fiction and crime fiction (mysteries)." Length: 30,000 words minimum; 100,000 words maximum. Send brief summary and 3 sample chapters. Pays advance and royalties. Write to publishers for catalog.

GHANA PUBLISHING CORPORATION, PUBLISHING DIVISION, Private Post Bag, Tema, Accra, 1001 Ghana. Fiction Editor: Muhammed, Amuda Iddi. Ghana Publishing "is the largest publishing house in Ghana; owned by the government, but run independently in the main. We publish all types of fiction but are biased towards classics, the sort that the Ministry of Education may prescribe to students. In general, the merit of a book lends itself to publication however." Length: 40,000-80,000 words. Send cover letter, synopsis, brief summary, 3 sample chapters or entire manuscript. Pays royalties of 10%. "Research the area of concern and market. Material should be contemporary and relevent. Technique must be clear and accessible to target readership. We prefer novels to short stories, which must be around 40 to 80,000 words. Novella's should be about 40,000. Materials must deal with relations affecting Ghanaian (African) culture under transition—clash of cultures, clash of old and new, personalities, young and aged, socio-economic conventions and morals. Treatment could have humorous bent. Ghanaians love to be relaxed and entertained; and they admire adventure and success worn through hard work—against corruption and indirection." Write for guidelines. "Ghana Publishing Corporation shall not be held answerable to lost or misplaced full-length manuscript sent for consideration."

ROBERT HALE LIMITED, (II), Clerkenwell House, 45/47 Clerkenwell Green, London EC1R 0HT England. Publishes hardcover and trade paperback originals and hardcover reprints. Historical, mainstream and western. Length: 40,000-150,000 words. Send cover letter, synopsis or brief summary and 2 sample chapters.

‡HAMISH HAMILTON LTD., (IV), 27 Wrights Lane, London W8 5TZ England. Fiction Editors: Clare Alexander, Kate Jones and Charles Drazin. General trade hardback and paperback publisher of quality fiction—literary plus some crime and thrillers. Advance on delivery of accepted book or on accepted commission. Send first chapter with synopsis before submitting whole manuscript. SAE essential.

HARPERCOLLINS PUBLISHERS (NEW ZEALAND) LIMITED, (IV), P.O. Box 1, Auckland, New Zealand. Publisher: Ian Watt. Averages 15-20 fiction titles/year (15-20 nonfiction). Adult fiction: Flamingo imprint; Teen fiction: 12 years plus: Tui imprint; Junior fiction: 8-11 years: Tui Junior imprint. Length: Flamingo: 40,000 + words; Tui: 20-35,000 words; Tui Junior: 15-17,000 words. Full ms preferred. Pays royalties. "It helps if the author and story have New Zealand connections/content. Write and ask for guidelines."

‡HEADLINE BOOK PUBLISHING LTD., 338 Euston Road, London NW1 3BH England. Publishing Director (Fiction): Jane Morpeth. Publishing Director (nonfiction): Alan Brooke. Averages approximately 600 titles/year. Mainstream publisher of popular fiction and nonfiction in hardcover and mass-market paperback. Length: 95,000-150,000 words. "Study UK publishers' catalogs to see what is published in both the US and the UK. Read the UK trade press: *The Bookseller* and *Publishing News* to get a feel for our market. *The Writers' & Artists' Yearbook* is useful." Pays advance against royalties. "Send a synopsis/5 consecutive chapters and *curriculum vitae* first, and return postage." Catalog available.

MILLENNIUM, Orion Publishing Group, Orion House, 5 Upper St. Martin's Lane, London WC2H 9EA England. Editorial Director: Caroline Oakley. Averages 12-15 fiction titles/year. "Midsize commercial genre imprint. Hardcover and paperback originals and paperback reprints. Science fiction, fantasy and horror." Novel-length material only. Accepts 90% agented submissions. Send cover letter (including estimated word count and list of publishing credits), synopsis and first 50 sample pages. Pays advance plus royalties.

MY WEEKLY STORY LIBRARY, (IV), D.C. Thomson and Co., Ltd., 22 Meadowside, Dundee DD19QJ, Scotland. Fiction Editor: Mrs. D. Hunter. Publishes 48, 30,000-word romantic novels/year. "Cheap paperback story library with full-colour cover. Material should not be violent, controversial or sexually explicit." Length: approximately 30,000 words. Writers are paid on acceptance. "Send the opening 3 chapters and a synopsis. Avoid too many colloquialisms/Americanisms. Stories can be set anywhere but local colour not too 'local' as to be alien." Both contemporary and historical novels considered. Guidelines available on request.

ORIENT PAPERBACKS, A division of Vision Books Pvt Ltd., Madarsa Rd., Kashmere Gate, Delhi 110 006 India. Editor: Sudhir Malhotra. Publishes 10-15 novels or story collections/year. "We are one

---

SENDING TO A COUNTRY other than your own? Be sure to send International Reply Coupons instead of stamps for replies or return of your manuscript.

of the largest paperback publishers in S.E. Asia and publish English fiction by authors from this part of the world." Length: 40,000 words minimum. Pays royalty on copies sold. Send cover letter, brief summary, 1 sample chapter and author's bio data. "We send writers' guidelines on accepting a proposal."

‡**PICADOR, (IV)**, MacMillan General Books, 25 Eccleseon, London SW1W 9NF England. Publishing Director: Jonathan Riley. Publishes hardbound and paperback titles. "Picador is a literary imprint specializing in the best international fiction and nonfiction in recent years. Its authors include Cormac McCarthy, Bruce Chatwin, Clive James, Julian Barnes, Graham Swift, John Banville, John Lanchester, Toni Morrison, Tom Wolfe." Length: 50,000-150,000 words. Send cover letter, synopsis, brief summary and 2 sample chapters. For catalog, send large addressed envelope and IRC.

‡**QUARTET BOOKS LIMITED, (IV)**, 27 Goodge Street, London W1P1FD England. Publishing Director: Stella Kane. Publishes 30 novels/year. Contemporary literary fiction including translations, popular culture, biographies, music, history and politics. Payment is: advance—half on signature, half on delivery or publication. "Send brief synopsis and sample chapters. *No* romantic fiction, science fiction or poetry."

VISION BOOKS PVT LTD., Madarsa Rd., Kashmere Gate, Delhi 110006 India. Fiction Editor: Sudhir Malhotra. Publishes 25 titles/year. "We are a large multilingual publishing house publishing fiction and other trade books." Pays royalties. "A brief synopsis should be submitted initially. Subsequently, upon hearing from the editor, a typescript may be sent."

THE WOMEN'S PRESS, (IV), 34 Great Sutton St., London EC1V 0DX England. Publishes approximately 50 titles/year. "Women's fiction, written by women. Centered on women. Theme can be anything—all themes may be women's concern—but we look for political/feminist awareness, originality, wit, fiction of ideas. Includes literary fiction, crime, and teenage list *Livewire*." Writers receive royalty, including advance. Writers should ask themselves, "Is this a manuscript which would interest a feminist/political press?"

Contests and Awards

In addition to honors and, quite often, cash awards, contests and awards programs offer writers the opportunity to be judged on the basis of quality alone without the outside factors that sometimes influence publishing decisions. New writers who win contests may be published for the first time, while more experienced writers may gain public recognition of an entire body of work.

The contest listings in this section include literary magazines and small presses that have developed award programs to garner attention and to promote writers. Grant programs that lost funding in the past are starting to bounce back with renewed commitment. All this represents increased opportunities for writers.

There are contests for almost every type of fiction writing. Some focus on form, such as *Story*'s Short Short Fiction Contest, for stories up to 1,500 words. Others feature writing on particular themes or topics including The Isaac Asimov Award for science fiction, the ASF Translation Prize and the Arthur Ellis Awards for crime fiction. Still others are prestigious prizes or awards for work that must be nominated such as the Pulitzer Prize in Fiction and the Whiting Writers' Awards. Chances are no matter what type of fiction you write, there is a contest or award program that may interest you.

SELECTING AND SUBMITTING TO A CONTEST

Use the same care in submitting to contests as you would sending your manuscript to a publication or book publisher. Deadlines are very important and where possible we've included this information. At times contest deadlines were only approximate at our press deadline, so be sure to write or call for complete information.

Follow the rules to the letter. If, for instance, contest rules require your name on a cover sheet only, you will be disqualified if you ignore this and put your name on every page. Find out how many copies to send. If you don't send the correct amount, by the time you are contacted to send more it may be past the submission deadline.

One note of caution: Beware of contests that charge entry fees that are disproportionate to the amount of the prize. Contests offering a $10 prize, but charging $7 in entry fees, are a waste of your time and money.

If you are interested in a contest or award that requires your publisher to nominate your work, it's acceptable to make your interest known. Be sure to leave them plenty of time, however, to make the nomination deadline.

The Roman numeral coding we use to rank listings in this section is different than that used in previous sections. The following is our ranking system:

I **Contest for unpublished fiction, usually open to both new and experienced writers.**

II **Contest for published (usually including self-published) fiction, which may be entered by the author.**

III **Contest for fiction, which must be nominated by an editor, publisher or other nominating body.**

IV **Contest limited to residents of a certain region, of a certain age or to writing on certain themes or subjects.**

ABIKO QUARTERLY INTERNATIONAL FICTION CONTEST/TSUJINAKA AWARD (I), 8-1-8 Namiki, Abiko-shi, Chiba-ken 270-11 Japan. Editor: Laurel Sicks. Award to "best short story in English of up to 5,000 words." Award: 100,000 yen. Entry fee $10. Open September 1-December 31 each year. Previously unpublished submissions. Word length: up to 5,000 words. "Include SAE with 2 IRCs for notification. No American postage."

AIM MAGAZINE SHORT STORY CONTEST, (I), P.O. Box 20554, Chicago IL 60620. (312)874-6184. Contact: Ruth Apilado and Mark Boone, publisher and fiction editor. Estab. 1984. "To encourage and reward good writing in the short story form. The contest is particularly for new writers." Contest offered annually if money available. Award: $100 plus publication in fall issue. "Judged by *Aim*'s editorial staff." Sample copy for $4. Contest rules for SASE. Unpublished submissions. "We're looking for compelling, well-written stories with lasting social significance."

✤AIR CANADA AWARD, (IV), Canadian Authors Association and Air Canada, 27 Doxsee Ave. N., Campbellford Ontario K0L 1L0 Canada. (705)653-0323. Fax: (705)653-0593. Contact: Awards Chairperson. "It takes many years for a Canadian writer to achieve national (and, increasingly, international) recognition, but Air Canada believes the signs of greatness can usually be detected before the writer reaches 30. That is why the airline offers a trip for two to the winner of the annual Canadian Author Association competition. The Air Canada Award goes to the writer under age 30 deemed to show the most promise in the field of literary creation." Annual competition for "body of work." Award: 2 tickets to any destination on Air Canada route. Judges: the Awards chairperson/Canadian Authors Association. Guidelines for SASE. Deadline April 30. Writers must be Canadian and 30 years old or under by the deadline. The nomination can be in any form but the recommended approach is to submit a 1-page outline of why the writer shows promise and attach samples of the writer's work or reviews of that work. Full-length works need not be sent; copies of a few pages are sufficient. Note date of birth of writer on submitted samples. Nominations are made through CAA branches or other writing organizations to the Canadian Authors Association. The nominee need not be a CAA member.

AKC GAZETTE, 51 Madison Ave., New York NY 10010. (212)696-8350. Managing Editor: Mary Witherell. Annual contest for short stories under 2,000 words. Award: Prizes of $350, $250 and $150 for top three entries. Top entry published in magazine. Judges: Panel. Contest requirements available for SASE. "The *Gazette* sponsors an annual fiction contest for short short stories on some subject relating to purebred dogs. Fiction for our magazine needs a slant toward the serious fancier with real insight into the human/dog bond and breed-specific purebred behavior."

AKRON MANUSCRIPT CLUB ANNUAL FICTION CONTEST (I), Akron Manuscript Club and A.U., Falls Writer's Workshop, and Taylor Memorial Library, P.O. Box 1101, Cuyahoga Falls OH 44223-0101. (216)923-2094. Contest Director: M.M. LoPiccolo. Award to "encourage writers with cash prizes and certificates and to provide in-depth critique that most writers have never had the benefit of seeing." Annual competition for short stories. Award: $50 (first prize in three fiction categories); certificates for second and third prizes. Competition receives approx. 20-50 submissions per category. Judge: M.M. LoPiccolo. Guidelines will be sent *only* with SASE. Deadline March-April. Unpublished submissions. Word length: 2,500 words (12-13 pages). "Send *no* manuscript without obtaining current guidelines. *Nothing* will be returned without SASE."

‡ALASKA STATE COUNCIL ON THE ARTS CAREER OPPORTUNITY GRANT AWARD, IV, Alaska State Council on the Arts, Suite 1E, 411 West 4th Ave., Anchorage AK 99501-2343. (907)269-6610. Grants help artists take advantage of impending, concrete opportunities that will significantly advance their work or careers. Professional artists working in the literary arts who are requesting support for unique, short-term opportunities are eligible. Awards up to $1,000. Deadline: applications must be received in the office 30 days prior to dates of career opportunity. Alaskan residents only.

THE NELSON ALGREN AWARD FOR SHORT FICTION, (I), *Chicago Tribune*, 435 N. Michigan Ave., Chicago IL 60611. Annual award to recognize an outstanding, unpublished short story, minimum 2,500 words, maximum 10,000 words. Awards: $5,000 first prize; 3 runners-up receive

---

MARKET CATEGORIES: (I) Unpublished entries; (II) Published entries nominated by the author; (III) Published entries nominated by the editor, publisher or nominating body; (IV) Specialized entries.

$1,000 awards. Publication of 4 winning stories in the *Chicago Tribune*. No entry fee. Entries must be typed, double spaced. For guidelines, send business-size SASE. Guidelines mailed in the fall. Deadline: Entries are accepted only from November 1-February 1.

‡AMATEUR SLEUTH, (I, IV), *Whispering Willow's Mystery Magazine*, 2517 S. Central, P.O. Box 890294, Oklahoma City OK 73189-0294. (405)239-2531. Fax: (405)232-3848. Editor-in-Chief: Peggy D. Farris. Annual competition for short stories. Award: $200 (1st place), $125 (2nd place), $100 (3rd place), plus publication. Competition receives approximately 30 submissions. Judge: Trula Johnson. Entry fee $10. Guidelines for SASE. Deadline December 31. Unpublished submissions. Mystery or mystery/suspense stories only. Length: 500-2,500 words. "Your main character is an amateur sleuth involved in a mystery. No explicit sex, gore, or extreme violence. You have freedom in creating exciting mysteries weaving your readers down winding roads of clues."

AMELIA MAGAZINE AWARDS, (I), 329 "E" St., Bakersfield CA 93304. (805)323-4064. Contact: Frederick A. Raborg, Jr., editor. The Reed Smith Fiction Prize; The Willie Lee Martin Short Story Award; The Cassie Wade Short Fiction Award; The Patrick T. T. Bradshaw Fiction Award; and four annual genre awards in science fiction, romance, western and fantasy/horror. Estab. 1984. Annual. "To publish the finest fiction possible and reward the writer; to allow good writers to earn some money in small press publication. *Amelia* strives to fill that gap between major circulation magazines and quality university journals." Unpublished submissions. Length: The Reed Smith—3,000 words maximum; The Willie Lee Martin—3,500-5,000 words; The Cassie Wade—4,500 words maximum; The Patrick T. T. Bradshaw—25,000 words; the genre awards—science fiction, 5,000 words; romance, 3,000 words; western, 5,000 words; fantasy/horror, 5,000 words. Award: "Each prize consists of $200 plus publication and two copies of issue containing winner's work." The Reed Smith Fiction Prize offers two additional awards when quality merits of $100 and $50, and publication; Bradshaw Book Award: $250, 2 copies. Deadlines: The Reed Smith Prize—September 1; The Willie Lee Martin—March 1; The Cassie Wade—June 1; The Patrick T. T. Bradshaw—February 15; *Amelia* fantasy/horror—February 1; *Amelia* western—April 1; *Amelia* romance—October 1; *Amelia* science fiction—December 15. Entry fee: $5. Bradshaw Award fee: $10. Contest rules for SASE. Looking for "high quality work equal to finest fiction being published today."

AMERICAN FICTION AWARDS, (I), New Rivers Press, Moorhead State University, P.O. Box 229, Moorhead MN 56563. (218)236-4681. Editor: Alan Davis. "To find and publish short fiction by emerging writers." Annual award for short stories. Award: $1,000 (1st prize), $500 (2nd prize), $250 (3rd prize). Competition receives approx. 1,000 submissions. Editor chooses finalists: guest judge chooses winners; past judges have included Tim O'Brien and Wallace Stegner. Entry fee $7.50. Guidelines for SASE. Deadline May 1. Unpublished submissions. Word length: up to 10,000 words. "We are looking for quality literary or mainstream fiction—all subjects and styles. No genre fiction. For a sample copy, contact your bookstore or New Rivers Press, 420 N. Fifth St., Suite 910, Minneapolis MN 55401. Send ms and cover letter with bio "after reading our ads in *AWP* and *Poets and Writers* each spring." (Previous editions published by Birch Lane Press/Carol Publishing Groups.)

AMERICAN SHORT FICTION CONTEST, (I), English Dept., Parlin 108, University of Texas at Austin, Austin TX 78712. (512)471-1772. Contact: Joseph Kruppa, editor. Annual competition for short stories. Award: $1,000 and publication (1st prize); $500 (2nd place); $300 (3rd prize). Entry fee: $20 (includes subscription to *ASF*). Guidelines and entry form in *ASF*. Deadline May 15. Unpublished submissions.

ANALECTA COLLEGE FICTION CONTEST, (I, IV), The Liberal Arts Council, FAC 17, Austin TX 78712. (512)471-6563. Awards Coordinator: Marc Saletti. Award to "give student writers, at the University of Texas and universities across the country, a forum for publication. We believe that publication in a magazine with the quality and reputation of *Analecta* will benefit student writers." Annual competition for short stories. Award: $100. Competition receives approximately 80 submissions. Judges: Student editiorial board of approximately 25 people. No entry fee. Guidelines for SASE. Deadline: mid-October. Unpublished submissions. Limited to college students. Length: 15 pages or less. "We also accept poetry, drama and art submissions."

SHERWOOD ANDERSON SHORT FICTION PRIZE, (I), *Mid-American Review*, Dept. of English, Bowling Green State University, Bowling Green OH 43403. (419)372-2725. Contact: Rebecca Meacham, fiction editor. "Winners are selected from stories published by the magazine, so submission for publication is the first step." Award frequency is subject to availability of funds. "To encourage the writer of quality short fiction." No entry fee. No deadline. Unpublished material.

ANDREAS-GRYPHIUS-PREIS (LITERATURPREIS DER KÜNSTLERGILDE), (II, IV), Die Kunstlergilde e.V., Hafenmarkt 2, D-73728 Esslingen a.N., Germany. 0711/39 69 01-0. "The prize is awarded for the best piece of writing or for complete literary works." Annual competition for short stories, novels, story collections, translations. Award: 1 prize of DM 15,000; 3 prizes of DM 7,000. Competition receives 30-50 entries. Judges: Jury members (8 persons). Fiction should be published in the last 5 years. "The prize is awarded to writers who are dealing with the particular problems of the German culture in eastern Europe."

ANTIETAM REVIEW LITERARY AWARD, (I, IV), *Antietam Review*, 7 W. Franklin St., Hagerstown MD 21740-4804. (301)791-3132. Executive Editor: Susanne Kass. Annual award to encourage and give recognition to excellence in short fiction. Open to writers from Maryland, Pennsylvania, Virginia, West Virginia, Washington DC and Delaware. "We consider only previously unpublished work. We read manuscripts between April 1 and September 1." Award: $100 for the story; the story is printed as lead in the magazine. "We consider all fiction mss sent to *Antietam Review* as entries for the prize. We look for well-crafted, serious literary prose fiction under 5,000 words." Award dependent on funding situation. Send #10 SASE for guidelines.

❀**ANVIL PRESS 3-DAY NOVEL WRITING CONTEST, (I)**, Anvil Press, Box 1575, Bentall Centre, Vancouver, British Columbia V6C 2P7 Canada. (604)876-8710. Fax: (604)879-2667. E-mail: subter@pinc.com. Editor: Brian Kaufman. Annual prize for best novel written in 3 days, held every Labor Day weekend. "Prize is publication plus 15% royalties on sales." Receives approx. 500 entries for each award. Judges: Anvil Press editorial board. Entry fee $25. Guidelines for SASE. Deadline Friday before Labor Day weekend. "Entrants must register with Anvil Press. Winner is announced November 30."

ARIZONA AUTHORS' ASSOCIATION NATIONAL LITERARY CONTEST, (I), 3509 E. Shea Blvd., Suite 117, Phoenix AZ 85028. (602)867-9001. Contact: Iva Martin. Estab. 1981. Annual award "to encourage AAA members and all other writers in the country to write regularly for competition and publication." Award: "Cash prizes totalling $1,000 for winners and honorable mentions in short stories, essays and poetry. Winning entries are published in the *Arizona Literary Magazine*." Entry fee: $5 for poetry, $7 for essays and short stories. Contest rules for #10 SASE. Deadline July 29. Unpublished submissions. Looking for "strong concept; good, effective writing, with emphasis on the subject/story."

ARTIST TRUST ARTIST FELLOWSHIPS; GAP GRANTS, (I, II, IV), Artist Trust, 1402 Third Ave., Suite 404, Seattle WA 98101-2118. (206)467-8734. Associate Director: Olivia Taguinod. Artist Trust has 2 grant programs for generative artists in Washington State; the GAP and Fellowships. The GAP (Grants for Artist's Projects) is an annual award of up to $1,000 for a project proposal. The program is open to artists in all disciplines. The Fellowship grant is an award of $5,000 in unrestricted funding. Fellowships for Craft, Media, Literature and Music will be awarded in 1997, and Fellowships for Dance, Design, Theater and Visual Art will be awarded in 1998. Competition receives approximately 200-300 submissions. Judges: Fellowship—Peer panel of 3 professional artists and arts professionals in each discipline; GAP—Interdisciplinary peer panel of 6-8 artists and arts professionals. Deadlines: Fellowship—summer; GAP—late winter. Call or write for more information with SASE.

ASF TRANSLATION PRIZE, (II, IV), American-Scandinavian Foundation, 725 Park Ave., New York NY 10021. (212)879-9779. Contact: Publishing office. Estab. 1980. "To encourage the translation and publication of the best of contemporary Scandinavian poetry and fiction and to make it available to a wider American audience." Annual competition for poetry, drama, literary prose and fiction translations. Award: $2,000, a bronze medallion and publication in *Scandinavian Review*. Competition rules and entry forms available with SASE. Deadline June 2, 1997. Submissions must have been previously published in the original Scandinavian language. No previously translated material. Original authors should have been born within past 200 years.

THE ISAAC ASIMOV AWARD, (I, IV), International Association for the Fantastic in the Arts and *Asimov*'s magazine, School of Mass Communications, U. of South Florida, 4202 E. Fowler, Tampa FL 33620. (813)974-6792. Awards Administrator: Rick Wilber. "The award honors the legacy of one of science fiction's most distinguished authors through an award aimed at undergraduate writers." Annual award for short stories. Award: $500 and consideration for publication in *Asimov's*. Judges: *Asimov*'s editors. Entry fee $5. Guidelines available for SASE. Deadline December 15. Unpublished submissions. Full-time college undergraduates only.

❀**ASTED/GRAND PRIX DE LITTERATURE JEUNESSE DU QUEBEC-ALVINE-BE-LISLE, (III, IV)**, Association pour l'avancement des sciences et des techniques de la documentation, 3414 Avenue du Parc, Bureau 202, Montreal, Quebec H2X 2H5 Canada. (514)281-5012. Fax: (514)281-8219. President: Vesna Dell'Olio. "Prize granted for the best work in youth literature edited in French in the Quebec Province. Authors and editors can participate in the contest." Annual competition for fiction and nonfiction for children and young adults. Award: $500. Deadline June 1. Contest entry limited to editors of books published during the preceding year. French translations of other languages are not accepted.

THE ATHENAEUM LITERARY AWARD, (II, IV), The Athenaeum of Philadelphia, 219 S. Sixth St., Philadelphia PA 19106. (215)925-2688. Contact: Literary Award Committee. Annual award to recognize and encourage outstanding literary achievement in Philadelphia and its vicinity. Award: A bronze medal bearing the name of the award, the seal of the Athenaeum, the title of the book, the name of the author and the year. Judged by committee appointed by Board of Directors. Deadline December. Submissions must have been published during the preceding year. Nominations shall be made in writing to the Literary Award Committee by the author, the publisher or a member of the Athenaeum, accompanied by a copy of the book. The Athenaeum Literary Award is granted for a work of general literature, not exclusively for fiction. Juvenile fiction is not included.

AUTHORS IN THE PARK/FINE PRINT CONTEST, (I), P.O. Box 85, Winter Park FL 32790-0085. (407)658-4520. Fax: (407)275-8688. Contact: David Foley. Annual competition. Award: $500 (1st prize), $250 (2nd prize), $125 (3rd prize). Competition receives approx. 200 submissions. Entry fee $8 (includes copy of *Fine Print*). Guidelines for SASE. Deadline March 31. Word length: 5,000 words maximum.

AWP AWARD SERIES IN THE NOVEL AND SHORT FICTION, (I), The Associated Writing Programs, Tallwood House, Mail Stop 1E3, George Mason University, Fairfax VA 22030. Annual award. The AWP Award Series was established in cooperation with several university presses in order to publish and make fine fiction available to a wide audience. Awards: $2,000 honorarium and publication with a university press. In addition, AWP tries to place mss of finalists with participating presses. Judges: Distinguished writers in each genre. Entry fee $15 nonmembers, $10 AWP members. Contest/award rules and guidelines for SASE. No phone calls please. Mss must be postmarked between January 1-February 28. Only book-length mss in the novel and short story collections are eligible. Manuscripts previously published in their entirety, including self-publishing, are not eligible. No mss returned.

EMILY CLARK BALCH AWARDS, (I), *The Virginia Quarterly Review*, One West Range, Charlottesville VA 22903. Editor: Staige D. Blackford. Annual award "to recognize distinguished short fiction by American writers." For stories published in *The Virginia Quarterly Review* during the calendar year. Award: $500.

MILDRED L. BATCHELDER AWARD, (II), Association for Library Service to Children/American Library Association, 50 E. Huron St., Chicago IL 60611. (312)944-6780, ext. 2164. To encourage international exchange of quality children's books by recognizing US publishers of such books in translation. Annual competition for translations. Award: Citation. Judge: Mildred L. Batchelder award committee. Guidelines for SASE. Deadline: December. Books should be US trade publications for which children, up to and including age 14, are potential audience.

BAUHINIA LITERARY AWARDS, (I, IV), *Idiom 23 Literary Magazine*, Regional Centre of the Arts, Central Queensland University, Rockhampton, Queensland 4702 Australia. (079)309665. Contact: Contest Director. "To promote the work of students under age 25 and writers from Central Queensland." Annual competition for short stories. Open Award: $500 (Australian); Student Award: $250 (Australian); Regional Award: $250 (Australian). Poetry open award: $100; student award $50. Judges: the editors. Guidelines for SASE. Deadline June 30. Unpublished submissions. Student Award is open to full-time students, under age 25. Regional Award open to writers living in Central Queensland. Word length: 2,000 words; 3 story limit. "Outstanding entries will be published in *The Morning Bulletin* and *Idiom 23*."

BELLETRIST REVIEW ANNUAL FICTION CONTEST, (I), Belletrist Review, P.O. Box 596, Plainville CT 06062-0596. Editor: Marlene Dube. "To provide an incentive for writers to submit quality fiction for consideration and recognition." Annual competition for short stories. Award: $200. Competition receives approximately 150-250 submissions. Judges: Editorial panel of *Belletrist Review*. Entry fee $5. Guidelines for SASE. Deadline July 15. Unpublished submissions. Word length: 2,500-5,000 words. "An interview with the winning author will also be published with the winning story in the September issue."

GEORGE BENNETT FELLOWSHIP, (I), Phillips Exeter Academy, Exeter NH 03833. Coordinator, Selection Committee: Charles Pratt. "To provide time and freedom from monetary concerns to a person contemplating or pursuing a career as a professional writer." Annual award of writing residency. Award: A stipend ($6,000 at present), plus room and board for academic year. Competition receives approximately 150 submissions. Judges are a committee of the English department. Entry fee $5. SASE for application form and guidelines. Deadline December 1.

BEST FIRST NEW MYSTERY AWARD, (I, IV), *New Mystery Magazine*, 175 Fifth Ave., Suite 2001, New York NY 10010. (212)353-1582. Awards coordinator: Miss Linda Wong. Award to "find the best new mystery, crime or suspense writer, and promote high standards in the short story form. For writers who have never been paid for their writing." Annual award for short stories. Award: publication in *New Mystery Magazine*. Competition receives approximately 800 submissions. Judges: editorial panel of veteran mystery writers. No entry fee. No guidelines available. Deadline July 4. Unpublished submissions. Word length: 1,000-5,000 words. "Please mark ms 'First Mystery Award.' Study back issues of *New Mystery* for style. Sample copy: $7 plus 9 × 12 SAE with $1.24 postage.

BEST FIRST PRIVATE EYE NOVEL CONTEST, (I, IV), Private Eye Writers of America, Thomas Dunne Books, St. Martin's Press, 175 Fifth Ave., New York NY 10010. Annual award. To publish a writer's first "private eye" novel. Award: Publication of novel by St. Martin's Press. Advance: $10,000 against royalties (standard contract). Judges are selected by sponsors. Guidelines for #10 SASE. Deadline August 1. Unpublished submissions. "Open to any professional or nonprofessional writer who has never published a 'private eye' novel and who is not under contract with a publisher for the publication of a 'private eye' novel. As used in the rules, 'private eye' novel means: a novel in which the main character is an independent investigator who is not a member of any law enforcement or government agency."

‡**"BEST OF OHIO WRITERS" CONTEST, (I, IV)**, *Ohio Writer Magazine*, P.O. Box 91801, Cleveland OH 44101. (216)932-8444. Executive Director: Darlene Montonaro. Award "to encourage and promote the work of writers in Ohio." Annual competition for short stories. Awards: $100 (1st prize), $50 (2nd prize), $25 (3rd prize). Competition receives 250 submissions. Judges: "a selected panel of prominent Ohio writers." Entry fee $10; includes subscription to *Ohio Writer*. Guidelines for SASE. Deadline June 30. Unpublished submissions. Ohio writers only. Length: 2,500 words.

BEST OF SOFT SCIENCE FICTION CONTEST, (II, IV), Soft SF Writers Assoc., 1277 Joan Dr., Merritt Island FL 32952. (407)454-2424. Contest Director: Lela E. Buis. Award to "encourage the publication of science fiction styles in which values, emotional content and artistic effect are emphasized rather than plot and deterministic science. Adult issues are encouraged, but gratuitous violence and graphic sex are not the emotional impacts we want." Annual award for short stories. Awards: $100 (1st prize), $50 (2nd prize), $25 (3rd prize). Judges: members of the Soft SF Writers Association. No entry fee. Guidelines for SASE. Entries accepted October 1 through December 15. Entries must have been submitted for publication or published between January 1 and December 15. Word length: 7,000 words. Story must have elements of science fiction, though cross-genre stories are acceptable. Judging criteria: emotional impact, artistic style, clarity, originality, characterization, theme weight, imagery, sensuality; violence or sex added for shock value are discouraged. Format: Send disposable manuscript in standard format. Securely attach name and address.

✿**THE GEOFFREY BILSON AWARD FOR HISTORICAL FICTION FOR YOUNG PEOPLE, (II, IV)**, The Canadian Children's Book Centre, 35 Spadina Rd., Toronto, Ontario M5R 2S9 Canada. (416)975-0010. Fax: (416)975-1839. E-mail: ccbc@lglobal.com. Website: http://www.lglobal.com/~ccbc. Program Coordinator: Jeffrey Canton. "Award given for best piece of historical fiction for young people." Annual competition for novels. Award: $1,000 (Canadian). Competition receives approximately 8-12 submissions. Judged by a jury of five people from the children's literature community. Previously published submissions. Canadian authors only. "Publishers of Canadian children's books regularly submit copies of their books to the Centre for our library collection. From those books, selections are made for inclusion in the Our Choice list of recommended Canadian children's books each year. The shortlist for the Bilson Award is created after the selections have been made for Our Choice, as the book must first be selected for Our Choice to be part of the Bilson shortlist."

IRMA S. AND JAMES H. BLACK CHILDREN'S BOOK AWARD, (II), Bank Street College, 610 W. 112th St., New York NY 10025. (212)875-4452. E-mail: lindag@bnk1.bnkst.edu. Children's Librarian: Linda Greengrass. Annual award "to honor the young children's book published in the preceding year judged the most outstanding in text as well as in art. Book must be published the year preceding the May award." Award: Press function at Harvard Club, a scroll and seals by Maurice Sendak for attaching to award book's run. No entry fee. Deadline January 4. "Write to address above. Usually publishers submit books they want considered, but individuals can too. No entries are returned."

‡**JAMES TAIT BLACK MEMORIAL PRIZES, (III, IV)**, Department of English Literature, University of Edinburgh, Edinburgh EH8 9JX Scotland. Contact: Professor R.D.S. Jack. "Two prizes are

awarded: one for the best work of fiction, one for the best biography or work of that nature, published during the calendar year: October 1st to September 30th." Annual competition. Award: £3,000 each. Competition receives approximately 300 submissions. Judge: Professor R.D.S. Jack, Dept. of English Literature. Guidelines for SASE or SAE and IRC. Deadline: September 30. Previously published submissions. "Eligible works are those written in English, originating with a British publisher, and first published in Britain in the year of the award. Works should be submitted by publishers."

THE BLACK WARRIOR REVIEW LITERARY AWARD, (II, III), P.O. Box 862936, Tuscaloosa AL 35496-0277. (205)348-4518. Editor: Mindy Wilson. "Award is to recognize the best fiction published in *BWR* in a volume year. Only fiction accepted for publication is considered for the award." Competition is for short stories and novel chapters. Award: $500. Competition receives approximately 3,000 submissions. Prize awarded by an outside judge.

BOARDMAN TASKER PRIZE, (III, IV), 14 Pine Lodge, Dairyground Rd., Bramhall, Stockport, Cheshire SK7 2HS United Kingdom. Contact: Mrs. D. Boardman. "To reward a book which has made an outstanding contribution to mountain literature. A memorial to Peter Boardman and Joe Tasker, who disappeared on Everest in 1982." Award: £2,000. Competition receives approx. 15 submissions. Judges: A panel of 3 judges elected by trustees. Guidelines for SASE. Deadline August 1. Limited to works published or distributed in the UK for the first time between November 1 and October 31. Publisher's entry only. "May be fiction, nonfiction, poetry or drama. Not an anthology. Subject must be concerned with a mountain environment. Previous winners have been books on expeditions, climbing experiences; a biography of a mountaineer; novels."

BOOK PUBLISHERS OF TEXAS AWARD, (II, IV), The Texas Institute of Letters, TCU Press, TCU Box 298300, Fort Worth TX 76129. (817)921-7822. Secretary: Judy Alter. "Award to honor the best book written for children or young people that was published the year prior to that in which the award is given." Annual competition for children's literature. Award: $250. Competition receives approximately 15 submissions. Judges: Committee selected by TIL. Guidelines for SASE. Deadline January 2. Previously published submissions from January 1 through December 31 of the year prior to the award. "To be eligible, the writer must have been born in Texas or have lived in the state for two years at some time, or the subject matter of the work must be associated with Texas."

BOSTON GLOBE-HORN BOOK AWARDS, (II), *Horn Book Magazine, Inc.*, 11 Beacon St., Suite 1000, Boston MA 02108. Annual award. "To honor most outstanding children's fiction or poetry, picture and nonfiction books published within the US." Award: $500 and engraved silver bowl first prize in each category; engraved silver plate for the 2 honor books in each category. No entry fee. Entry forms or rules for SASE. Deadline May 15. Previously published material from July 1-June 30 of previous year. Books must be submitted by publisher, not individuals.

BRAZOS BOOKSTORE (HOUSTON) AWARD (SINGLE SHORT STORY), (II, IV), The Texas Institute of Letters, % TCU Press, TCU Box 298300, Ft. Worth TX 76129. (817)921-7822. Awards Coordinator: Judy Alter. Award to "honor the writer of the best short story published for the first time during the calendar year before the award is given." Annual competition for short stories. Award: $1,000. Competition receives approximately 40-50 submissions. Judges: Panel selected by TIL Council. Guidelines for SASE. Deadline: January 2. Previously published submissions. Entries must have appeared in print between January 1 and December 31 of the year prior to the award. "Award available to writers who, at some time, have lived in Texas at least two years consecutively or whose work has a significant Texas theme. Entries must be sent directly to the three judges. Their names and addresses are available from the TIL office. Include SASE."

BREVILOQUENCE, (I, IV), Media Weavers, P.O. Box 86190, Portland OR 97286-0190. (503)771-5166. Contact: J. Colombo. "To create—with 99 words or less—a story with all the important elements of the form. Only open to writers in the Northwest—Oregon, Washington, Alaska, Idaho, Montana, Alberta and British Columbia." Annual competition for short stories. Award: Books—usually reference. Judges: Editors of newspaper. Entry fee $5. Deadline May 1. Unpublished submissions.

BRONX RECOGNIZES ITS OWN (B.R.I.O.), (I, IV), Bronx Council on the Arts, 1738 Hone Ave., New York NY 10461. (718)931-9500. Fax: (718)409-6445. Arts Services Associate: Evelyn Collazo. Award "To recognize local artistic talent in Bronx County." Annual competition for novels. Award: $1,500 fellowship (awards 15/year in visual, performing and literary arts). Competition receives approximately 125 submissions. Judges: A collective of non-Bronx based artists to avoid conflict. Guidelines for SASE. Deadline March. Unpublished submissions. Only Bronx-based individual artists may apply. Proof of Bronx residency required. Word length: 20 typed pages of ms.

♣GEORGES BUGNET AWARD FOR THE NOVEL, (II, IV), Writers Guild of Alberta, 3rd Floor, Percy Page Centre, 11759 Groat Rd., Edmonton, Alberta T5M 3K6 Canada. (403)422-8174.

Fax: (403)422-2663. Assistant Director: Darlene Diver. "To recognize outstanding books published by Alberta authors each year." Annual competition for novels. Award: $500 (Canadian) and leather-bound book. Competition receives 20-30 submissions. Judges: selected published writers across Canada. Guidelines for SASE. Deadline December 31. Previously published submissions. Must have appeared in print between January 1 and December 31. Open to Alberta authors only.

♦BURNABY WRITERS' SOCIETY ANNUAL COMPETITION, (I, IV), 6584 Deer Lake Ave., British Columbia V5G 2J3 Canada. (604)435-6500. Annual competition to encourage creative writing in British Columbia. "Category varies from year to year." Award: $200, $100 and $50 (Canadian) prizes. Receives 400-600 entries for each award. Judge: "independent recognized professional in the field." Entry fee $5. Contest requirements for SASE. Deadline: May 31. Open to British Columbia authors only.

BUSH ARTIST FELLOWSHIPS, (I, IV), The Bush Foundation, E-900 First Nat'l Bank Building, 332 Minnesota St., St. Paul MN 55101. (612)227-5222. Contact: Sally Dixon, Program Director. "To provide support for artists to work in their chosen art forms." Annual grant. Award: $36,000 for 12-18 months. Competition receives approximately 500 submissions. Judges are writers, critics and editors from outside Minnesota, South Dakota, North Dakota or Wisconsin. Applicants must be at least 25 years old, and Minnesota, South Dakota, North Dakota or Western Wisconsin residents. Students not eligible.

BYLINE MAGAZINE LITERARY AWARDS, (I, IV), P.O. Box 130596, Edmond OK 73013. (405)348-5591. Executive editor/publisher: Marcia Preston. "To encourage our subscribers in striving for high quality writing." Annual awards for short stories and poetry. Award: $250 in each category. Judges are published writers not on the *Byline* staff. Entry fee $5 for stories; $3 for poems. Postmark deadline: November 1. "Entries should be unpublished and not have won money in any previous contest. Winners announced in February issue and published in February or March issue with photo and short bio. Open to subscribers only."

CACHH GRANTS/CREATIVE ARTIST PROGRAM, (I, II, IV), Cultural Arts Council of Houston/Harris County, P.O. Box 131027, Houston TX 77219-1027. (713)527-9330. Fax: (713)630-5210. E-mail: cachh@neosoft.com. Grants Director: Amy Weaver Hollister. "To recognize the significant accomplishments of local artists and their contributions to the community." Annual competition for creative nonfiction, fiction, poetry, playwriting. Award: $5,000 unrestricted grant. Competition receives approximately 100-130 submissions. Judges: jury panel of literary professionals. Guidelines with SASE. Deadline fall of every year. "Applicants must reside within the city limits of Houston and must be a resident for the past two years prior to the application deadline."

CALIFORNIA WRITERS' ROUNDTABLE ANNUAL WRITING CONTESTS, (I), The Los Angeles Chapter, Women's National Book Association, 11684 Ventura Blvd., Suite 807, Studio City CA 91604-2613. Contact: Lou Carter Keay. Annual competition for short stories. Award: $150 first prize; $75 second prize; $25 third prize. Entry fee $5 to nonmembers of Women's National Book Association. Guidelines for SASE. Deadline September 30. Previously unpublished submissions. 3,000 word limit. "Manuscripts must be typed, on standard paper, 8½x11 inches. Margins of one inch on all sides. The title of short story must appear on each page, all pages numbered. Send 3 copies of the short story. Include in a small envelope a card containing the author's name, address and phone number, along with the title of short story. Do not put the name of author on the manuscript itself. If you wish one copy of your manuscript returned, include a SASE."

JOHN W. CAMPBELL MEMORIAL AWARD FOR THE BEST SCIENCE-FICTION NOVEL OF THE YEAR; THEODORE STURGEON MEMORIAL AWARD FOR THE BEST SF SHORT FICTION, (II, III), Center for the Study of Science Fiction, English Dept., University of Kansas, Lawrence KS 66045. (913)864-3380. Professor and Director: James Gunn. "To honor the best novel and short science fiction of the year." Annual competition for short stories and novels. Award: Certificate. "Winners' names are engraved on a trophy." Campbell Award receives approximately 50-100 submissions. Judges: 2 separate juries. Deadline: May 1. For previously published submissions. "Ordinarily publishers should submit work, but authors have done so when publishers would not. Send for list of jurors." Entrants for the Sturgeon Award are selected by nomination only.

♦ THE MAPLE LEAF symbol before a listing indicates a Canadian publisher, magazine, conference or contest.

❀**CANADA COUNCIL AWARDS, (III, IV)**, Canada Council, P.O. Box 1047, 350 Albert St., Ottawa, Ontario K1P 5V8 Canada. (613)566-4376. The Canada Council sponsors the following awards, for which no applications are accepted. *Canada-French Community of Belgium Literary Prize*: 1 prize of $5,000 (Canadian), awarded in alternate years to a Canadian or Belgian writer on the basis of the complete works of the writer; *Canada-Switzerland Literary Prize*: 1 prize of $2,500 (Canadian), awarded in alternate years to a Canadian or Swiss writer for a work published in French during the preceding 8 years.

❀**CANADA COUNCIL GOVERNOR GENERAL'S LITERARY AWARDS, (III, IV)**, Canada Council, 350 Albert St., P.O. Box 1047, Ottawa, Ontario K1P 5V8 Canada. (613)566-4376. E-mail: josiane.polidori@canadacouncil.ca. Contact: Writing and Publishing Section. "Awards of $10,000 each are given annually to the best English-language and best French-language Canadian work in each of seven categories: children's literature (text) and children's literature (illustration), drama, fiction, poetry, nonfiction and translation." All literary works published by Canadians between October 1 and September 30 the following year are considered. Canadian authors, illustrators and translators only. Books must be submitted by publishers (4 copies must be sent to the Canada Council) and accompanied by a Publisher's Submissions Form, available from the Writing and Publishing Section. All entries (books only) must be received by August 15. Self-published books are not eligible.

❀**CANADIAN AUTHORS ASSOCIATION LITERARY AWARDS, (FICTION), (II, IV)**, Canadian Authors Association, 27 Doxsee Ave. N., Campbellford, Ontario K0L 1L0 Canada. (705)653-0323. Fax: (705)653-0593. President: Cora Taylor. Annual award "to honor writing that achieves literary excellence without sacrificing popular appeal." For novels published during the previous calendar year. Award: $5,000 plus silver medal. No entry fee. Entry forms or rules for SASE. Deadline December 15. Restricted to *full-length* English language novels. Author must be Canadian or Canadian landed immigrant. CAA also sponsors the Air Canada Award, literary awards in poetry, nonfiction and drama, and the Vicky Metcalf Awards for children's literature.

❀**CANADIAN AUTHORS ASSOCIATION STUDENTS' CREATIVE WRITING CONTEST, (I, IV)**, 27 Doxsee Ave. N., Campbellford, Ontario K0l 1L0 Canada. (705)653-0323. Fax: (705)653-0593. Contact: Bernice Lever-Farrar. Annual competition for short stories, articles and poems. Awards $500 for best short story, $500 for best article, $500 for best poem, 4 honorable mentions in each category. All 15 winners will receive *Canadian Author* magazine for 1 year; first-place winners will be published in *Canadian Author*. "Entry form in winter and spring issues of *Canadian Author*." Entry fees $5/short story of 2,000 words or less; $5/article of 2,000 words of less; $5/2 to 3 poems of not more than 30 lines each. Deadline March. Unpublished submissions except in a student class anthology, newspaper or yearbook. Writers must be enrolled in secondary schools, colleges or universities and must be Canadian residents or citizens.

THE CAPRICORN AWARD, (I), The Writer's Voice, 5 W. 63rd St., New York NY 10023. (212)875-4124. Fax: (212)875-4177. E-mail: wtrsvoice@aol.com. Annual competition for novels or story collections. Award: $1,000, plus featured reading. Entry fee $15. Deadline December 31. Applicants may submit excerpts of work that have been previously published, however complete work cannot have been previously published elsewhere. Submit first 150 pgs. of novel/story collection. Guidelines/entry form for SASE.

RAYMOND CARVER SHORT STORY CONTEST, (I, IV), Dept. of English, Humboldt State University, Arcata CA 95521-4957. Contact: Coordinator. Annual award for previously unpublished short stories. First prize: $1,000 and publication in *Toyon*. Second Prize: $300 and honorable mention in *Toyon*. Third Prize: $100 and honorable mention in *Toyon*. Entry fee $10/story. SASE for rules. Deadline November 1. For U.S. citizens only. Send 2 copies of story; author's name, address, phone number and title of story on separate cover page only. Story must be no more than 6,000 words. Title must appear on first page. For notification of receipt of ms, include self-addressed, stamped postcard. For Winners List include SASE. For a copy of the *Toyon*, send $2.

WILLA CATHER FICTION PRIZE, (I, IV), Helicon Nine Editions, 3607 Pennsylvania, Kansas City MO 64111. (816)753-1095. Contact: Gloria Vando Hickok. Annual competition for novels, story collections and novellas. Award: $1,000. Winners chosen by nationally recognized writers. Entry fee $15. Guidelines for SASE. Deadline May 1. Unpublished submissions. Open to all writers residing in the US and its territories. Mss will not be returned. Past judges include Robley Wilson, Daniel Stern, Leonard Michaels, Carolyn Doty.

THE CHELSEA AWARDS, (II), P.O. Box 773, Cooper Station, New York NY 10276. *Mail entries to*: Richard Foerster, Editor, P.O. Box 1040, York Beach ME 03910. Annual competition for short stories. Prize: $750 and publication in *Chelsea* (all entries are considered for publication). Judges: the editors. Entry fee $10 (for which entrants also receive a subscription). Guidelines available for SASE. Deadline June 15. Unpublished submissions. Manuscripts may not exceed 30 typed pages or about 7,500 words. The stories must not be under consideration elsewhere or scheduled for book publication within 6 months of the competition deadline. Include separate cover sheet; no name on ms. Mss will not be returned; include SASE for notification of results.

CHEVRON AWARD AND WRITERS UNLIMITED AWARD, Writers Unlimited, 910 Grant Ave., Pascagoula MS 39567-7222. (601)762-4230. Contest Chairman: Nina Mason. "Part of an annual contest to encourage first-class writing of poetry and prose." Annual competition for short stories. Prize amounts vary with $50 being the maximum. Deadline September 1. Send SASE for guidelines.

CHICANO/LATINO LITERARY CONTEST, (I, IV), Dept. of Spanish & Portuguese, University of California-Irvine, Irvine CA 92714. (714)824-5702. Fax: (714)824-2803. Coordinator: Ruth M. Gratzer. Annual award for novels, short stories, poetry and drama (different genre every year). Award: Usually $1,000. Guidelines for SASE. Deadline April 1997. Unpublished submissions.

‡THE CHILDREN'S BOOK AWARD, (II), Federation of Children's Book Groups, 30 Senneleys Park Rd., Northfield, Birmingham B31 1AL England. Award "to promote good quality books for children." Annual award for short stories, novels, story collections and translations. Award: "Portfolio of children's writing and drawings and a magnificent trophy of silver and oak." Judges: thousands of children from all over the United Kingdom. Guidelines for SASE or SAE and IRC. Deadline: December 31. Published and previously unpublished submissions (first publication in UK). "The book should be suitable for children."

THE CHRISTOPHER AWARD, (II), The Christophers, 12 E. 48th St., New York NY 10017. (212)759-4050. Contact: Ms. Peggy Flanagan, awards coordinator. Annual award "to encourage creative people to continue to produce works which affirm the highest values of the human spirit in adult and children's books." Published submissions only. Award: Bronze medallion. "Award judged by a grassroots panel and a final panel of experts. Juvenile works are 'children tested.' " Examples of books awarded: *Dear Mr. Henshaw*, by Beverly Cleary (ages 8-10); *Sarah, Plain and Tall*, by Patricia MacLachlan (ages 10-12).

COMMONWEALTH CLUB OF CALIFORNIA, (II, IV), California Book Awards, 595 Market St., San Francisco CA 94105. (415)597-6700. Director of Member Services: James L. Coplan. Main contest established in 1931. Annual. "To encourage California writers and honor literary merit." Awards: Gold and silver medals. Judges: Jury of literary experts. For books published during the year preceding the particular contest. Three copies of book and a completed entry form required. "Write or phone asking for the forms. Either an author or publisher may enter a book. "We usually receive over 300 entries."

CONNECTICUT COMMISSION ON THE ARTS ARTIST FELLOWSHIPS, (I, II, IV), One Financial Plaza, Hartford CT 06103. (203)566-4770. Program Manager: Linda Dente. "To support the creation of new work by creative artists *living in Connecticut*." Biennial competition for the creation or completion of new works in literature, i.e. short stories, novels, story collections, poetry and playwriting. Awards: $5,000 and $2,500. Judges: Peer professionals (writers, editors). Guidelines available in August. Deadline January 1998. Writers may send either previously published or unpublished submissions—up to 20 pages of material. Connecticut residents only.

‡✽CONSEIL DE LA VIE FRANCAISE EN AMÉRIQUE/PRIX CHAMPLAIN, (II, IV), Conseil de la vie Française en Amérique, 56 rue St-Pierre 1ᵉʳ étage, Quebec G1K 4A1 Canada. Prix Champlain estab. 1957. Annual award to encourage literary work in novel or short story in French by Francophiles living outside Quebec and in the US or Canada. "There is no restriction as to the subject matter. If the author lives in Quebec, the subject matter must be related to French-speaking people living outside of Quebec." Award: $1,500 in Canadian currency. The prize will be given alternately; one year for fiction, the next for nonfiction. Next fiction award in 1997. 3 different judges each year. Guidelines for SASE or IRC. Deadline: December 31. For previously published or contracted submissions, published no more than 3 years prior to award. Author must furnish 4 examples of work, curriculum vitae, address and phone number.

THE CRUCIBLE POETRY AND FICTION COMPETITION, (I), *Crucible*, Barton College, College Station, Wilson NC 27893. Annual competition for short stories. Award: $150 (1st prize); $100 (2nd prize) and publication in *Crucible*. Judges: The editors. Guidelines for SASE. Deadline April. Unpublished submissions. Fiction should be 8,000 words or less.

‡DAGGER MYSTERY CONTEST, (I, IV), *Whispering Willow's Mystery Magazine*, 2517 S. Central, P.O. Box 890294, Oklahoma City OK 73189-0294. (405)239-2531. Fax: (405)232-3848. Editor-in-Chief: Peggy D. Farris. Annual competition for short stories. Award: $200 plus publication. Competition receives approximately 30 submissions. Judge: Trula Johnson. Entry fee $10. Guidelines for SASE. Deadline March 10. Unpublished submissions. Mystery or mystery/suspense stories only. Length: 500-2,500 words. "No explicit sex, gore, or extreme violence."

DALY CITY POETRY AND SHORT STORY CONTEST, (I), Daly City History, Arts, and Science Commission, % Serramonte Library, 40 Wembley Dr., Daly City CA 94015. (415)991-8025. Contest coordinator: Ruth Hoppin. "To encourage poets and writers and to recognize and reward excellence." Annual competition for short stories. Awards: $40, $25, $10 and $5. Competition receives approximately 50 submissions. Judges are usually teachers of creative writing. Entry fee: $2/story. Guidelines for SASE. Deadline: January 18. Unpublished submissions. Length: 3,000 words maximum. "No profanity."

‡THE JACK DANIEL'S FAUX FAULKNER CONTEST, (I), Jack Daniel Distillery, *Faulkner Newsletter of Yoknapatawpha Press* and University of Mississippi, P.O. Box 248, Oxford MS 38655. (601)234-0909. E-mail: boozernhb@aol.com. "To honor William Faulkner by imitating his style, themes and subject matter in a short parody." Annual competition for a 500-word (2-pages) parody. Award: 2 round-trip tickets to Memphis, plus complimentary registration and lodging for the annual Faulkner and Yoknapatawpha Conference at the University of Mississippi. Competition receives approximately 750-1,000 submissions. Judges: George Plimpton, Tom Wicker, John Berendt and Arthur Schlesinger, Jr. (judges rotate every year or so—well-known authors). Guidelines for SASE. Deadline: February 1. Previously unpublished submissions. Winner will be notified April 1—announcement made August 1, at Faulkner's home in Oxford MS. Contestants grant publication rights and the right to release entries to other media—to the sponsors."

MARGUERITE DE ANGELI PRIZE, (I), Bantam Doubleday Dell Books for Young Readers, 1540 Broadway, New York NY 10036. "To encourage the writing of fiction that examines the diversity of the American experience (either contemporary or historical) in the same spirit as the works of Marguerite de Angeli." Open to US and Candian writers. Annual competition for first novels for middle-grade readers (ages 7-10). Award: One BDD hardcover and paperback book contract, with $1,500 cash prize and $3,500 advance against royalties. Judges: Editors of BDD Books for Young Readers. Guidelines for SASE. Deadline: Submissions must be postmarked between April 1 and June 30. Previously unpublished (middle-grade) fiction.

DELACORTE PRESS ANNUAL PRIZE FOR A FIRST YOUNG ADULT NOVEL, (I), Delacorte Press, Department BFYR, 1540 Broadway, New York NY 10036. (212)354-6500. Estab. 1983. Annual award "to encourage the writing of contemporary young adult fiction." Award: Contract for publication of book; $1,500 cash prize and a $6,000 advance against royalties. Judges are the editors of Delacorte Press Books for Young Readers. Contest rules for SASE. Unpublished submissions; fiction with a contemporary setting that will be suitable for ages 12-18. Deadline: December 30 (no submissions accepted prior to October 1). Writers may be previously published, but cannot have published a young adult novel before.

DELAWARE DIVISION OF THE ARTS, (I, IV), 820 N. French St., Wilmington DE 19801. (302)577-3540. Coordinator: Barbara R. King. "To help further careers of emerging and established professional artists." Annual awards for Delaware residents only. Awards: $5,000 for established professionals; $2,000 for emerging professionals. Judges are out-of-state professionals in each division. Entry forms or rules for SASE. Deadline March 1.

JOHN DOS PASSOS PRIZE FOR LITERATURE, (III, IV), Longwood College, Farmville VA 23909. (804)395-2155. "The John Dos Passos Prize for Literature annually commemorates one of the greatest of 20th-century American authors by honoring other writers in his name." Award: A medal and $1,000. "The winner, announced each fall in ceremonies at the college, is chosen by an independent jury charged especially to seek out American creative writers in the middle stages of their careers—men and women who have established a substantial body of significant publication, and particularly those whose work demonstrates one or more of the following qualities: all characteristics of the art of the man for whom the prize is named; an intense and original exploration of specifically American themes; an experimental tone; and/or writing in a wide range of literature forms." Application for prize is by nomination only.

• This competition is celebrating its 16th anniversary.

EATON LITERARY ASSOCIATES' LITERARY AWARDS PROGRAM, (I), Eaton Literary Associates, P.O. Box 49795, Sarasota FL 34230. (941)366-6589. Fax: (941)365-4679. Vice President: Richard Lawrence. Biannual award for short stories and novels. Award: $2,500 for best book-length ms, $500 for best short story. Competition receives approx. 2,000 submissions annually. Judges are 2 staff members in conjunction with an independent agency. Entry forms or rules for SASE. Deadline March 31 for short stories; August 31 for book-length mss.

♣ARTHUR ELLIS AWARDS, (II, IV), Crime Writers of Canada, Box 113, 3007 Kingston Rd., Scarborough, Ontario M1M 1P1 Canada. E-mail: ap113@torfree.net. Contact: Secretary-Treasurer. "To recognize excellence in all aspects of crime-writing." Annual competition for short stories and novels. Award: statuette (plus *maybe* cash or goods). Judges: panels of members and experts. Guidelines for SASE. Deadline December 31 for published submissions that appeared in print between January 1 and December 31 of that year. Open to Canadian residents (any citizenship) or Canadian citizens living abroad. Four complete copies of each work must be submitted. Every entry must state category entered. Categories include Best Novel, Best First Novel, Best Short Story, Best Nonfiction, Best Play and Best Juvenile.

EMERGING LESBIAN WRITERS FUND AWARDS, (II), Astraea National Lesbian Action Foundation, 116 E. 16th St., 7th Floor, New York NY 10003. (212)529-8021. Fax: (212)982-3321. Executive Director: Katherine Acey. Award to "recognize and encourage new/emerging writers and poets." Annual competition for fiction and poetry. Award: $10,000 (one time only grantees). Competition receives 600-700 submissions. Judges: Established writers/poets (2 each category). Entry fee $5. Guidelines for SASE (application form required). Deadline March 8. Previously published submissions. U.S. residents only. Write for guidelines. "Must have at least one published work. No submissions accepted without application form."

EYSTER PRIZES, (II), *The New Delta Review*, LSU/Dept. of English, Baton Rouge LA 70803. (504)388-4079. Contact: Editors. "To honor author and teacher Warren Eyster, who served as advisor to *New Delta Review* predecessors *Manchac* and *Delta*." Semiannual awards for best short story and best poem in each issue. Award: $50 and 2 free copies of publication. Competition receives approximately 400 submissions/issue. Judges are published authors. Deadlines: September 15 for fall, February 15 for spring.

JOAN FASSLER MEMORIAL BOOK AWARD, (II, IV), Association for the Care of Children's Health, 7910 Woodmont Ave., #300, Bethesda MD 20814. (301)654-6549. Fax: (301)986-4553. Website: http://www.wsd.com/acch.org. "Recognizes outstanding literature that makes a distinguished contribution to a child's or young person's understanding of hospitalization, illness, disabling conditions, dying and death, and preventive care." Annual competition for short stories and novels. Award: $1,000 honorarium and plaque. Competition receives approximately 50-70 submissions. Judges: multidisciplinary committee of 8 ACCH members. Deadline December 31. Previously published submissions must have appeared in print within previous year.

VIRGINIA FAULKNER AWARD FOR EXCELLENCE IN WRITING, (II), Prairie Schooner, 201 Andrews Hall, University of Nebraska, Lincoln NE 68588-0334. (402)472-0911. Editor: Hilda Raz. "An award for writing published in *Prairie Schooner* in the previous year." Annual competition for short stories, novel excerpts and translations. Award: $1,000. Judges: Editorial Board. Guidelines for SASE. "We only read mss from September through May." Work must have been published in *Prairie Schooner* in the previous year.

WILLIAM FAULKNER COMPETITION IN FICTION, (I), The Pirate's Alley Faulkner Society Inc., 632 Pirate's Alley, New Orleans LA 70116-3254. (504)586-1609. Fax: (504)522-9725. Contest Director: Joseph J. DeSalvo, Jr. "To encourage publisher interest in writers with potential." Annual competition for short stories, novels and novellas. Award: $7,500 for novel, $2,500 for novella, $1,500 for short story and gold medals, plus trip to New Orleans for presentation. Competition receives approximately 200-300 submissions. Judges: professional writers, academics. Entry fee $25 for short story; $30 for novella; $35 for novel. Guidelines for SASE. Deadline April 1. Unpublished submissions. Word length: for novels, over 50,000; for novellas, under 20,000; for short stories, under 20,000. All entries must be accompanied by official entry form which is provided with guidelines.

FC2/ILLINOIS STATE UNIVERSITY NATIONAL FICTION COMPETITION (I), Illinois State University, Unit for Contemporary Literature, Normal IL 61790-4241. (309)438-3582. Fax: (309)438-3523. Director: Curtis White. Annual competition for novels, story collections. Award: Publication, standard royalties. Competition receives approximately 300 submissions. Judges: Fiction writers of national note. Entry fee $15. Guidelines for SASE. Unpublished submissions. Word length: 400 pages. "Contest winners include: Gerald Vizenor, Richard Grossman, Eurudice and Don Webb. Contest judges include: Robert Coover, Toby Olsen, William Vollmann, Paul Auster." Deadline November 15.

FELLOWSHIPS/WRITER-IN-RESIDENCE, (IV), Idaho Commission on the Arts, Box 83720, Boise ID 83720-0008. (208)334-2119 or (800)ART-FUND. "Fellowships awarded to Idaho writers for artistic excellence. Writer-in-Residence awarded to one Idaho writer for distinguished work and artistic excellence." Biennial competition for fiction, creative nonfiction and poetry. Award: $3,500 fellowship, $8,000 writer-in-residence. Competition receives approximately 85 submissions. Judges: nationally-known panel of poets and writers from outside Idaho. Guidelines for SASE. All work must have been completed within the last 5 years. Idaho authors only.

FEMINIST WRITER'S CONTEST, Des Plaines/Park Ridge NOW Chapter, P.O. Box 2440, Des Plaines IL 60018. (847)696-1817. "To encourage and reward feminist writers, to give them an opportunity to be read by competent judges, and to be published in our chapter newsletter." Annual competition for short stories and essays. Award: $100 (1st place), $50 (2nd place). Competition receives approximately 75 submissions. Judges are feminist professors, teachers, writers, political activists, social workers and entrepeneurs. Entry fee $10. Guidelines for SASE. Deadline August 31. May be either published or unpublished. "We accept both foreign or domestic entries. Stories/essays may be on any subject, but should reflect feminist awareness." Word length: 5,000 words or less.

ROBERT L. FISH MEMORIAL AWARD, (II, IV), Mystery Writers of America, Inc., 17 E. 47th St., 6th Floor, New York NY 10017. Estab. 1984. Annual award "to encourage new writers in the mystery/detective/suspense short story—and, subsequently, larger work in the genre." Award: $500 and plaque. Judges: The MWA committee for best short story of the year in the mystery genre. Deadline December 1. Previously published submissions published the year prior to the award. Looking for "a story with a crime that is central to the plot that is well written and distinctive."

DOROTHY CANFIELD FISHER AWARD, (III), Vermont Dept. of Libraries, 109 State St., Pavilion Office Bldg., Montpelier VT 05609-0601. (802)828-3261. E-mail: ggreene@dol.state.vt.us. Contact: Grace Greene, Children's Services Consultant. Estab. 1957. Annual award. "To encourage Vermont schoolchildren to become enthusiastic and discriminating readers and to honor the memory of one of Vermont's most distinguished and beloved literary figures." Award: Illuminated scroll. Publishers send the committee review copies of books to consider. Only books of the current publishing year can be considered for next year's award. Master list of titles is drawn up in March each year. Children vote each year in the spring and the award is given before the school year ends. Submissions must be "written by living American authors, be suitable for children in grades 4-8, and have literary merit. Can be nonfiction also."

FLORIDA ARTS COUNCIL/LITERATURE FELLOWSHIPS, (I, IV), Division of Cultural Affairs, Florida, Dept. of State, The Capitol, Tallahassee FL 32399-0250. (904)487-2980. Director: Ms. Peyton C. Fearington. "To allow Florida artists time to develop their artistic skills and enhance their careers." Annual awards for fiction, poetry or children's literature. Award: $5,000; approximately 7 fellowships awarded/year. Competition receives approximately 150 submissions/year. Judges are review panels made up of individuals knowledgeable in the arts. Deadline January. Entry restricted to practicing, professional writers who are legal residents of Florida and have been living in the state for a minimum of 12 consecutive months at the time of the deadline. Graduate or undergraduate students enrolled in any degree-seeking programs are not eligible.

FLORIDA FIRST COAST WRITERS' FESTIVAL NOVEL, SHORT FICTION & POETRY AWARDS, Writers' Festival & Florida Community College at Jacksonville, FCCJ North Campus, 4501 Capper Rd., Jacksonville FL 32218. (904)766-6559. Fax: (904)766-6654. E-mail: hdenson@fccj. cc.fl.us. Website: http://jax.jaxnet.com/~media-pr/festival.html. Festival Coordinator/Contest Director: Howard Denson. Conference and contest "to create a healthy writing environment, honor writers of merit, select some stories for *The State Street Review* (a literary magazine) and find a novel manuscript to recommend to St. Martin's Press for 'serious consideration.' " Annual competition for short stories and novels. Competition receives 60 novel, 150-200 short fiction and 300-600 poetry submissions. Judges: university faculty and freelance and professional writers. Entry fees $30 (novels), $10 (short fiction), $5 (poetry). Deadlines: October 1 all categories. Winners announced at the Florida First Coast Writers' Festival held in April. Unpublished submissions. Word length: none for novel; short fiction, 6,000 words.

FLORIDA STATE WRITING COMPETITION, (I), Florida Freelance Writers Association, P.O. Box A, North Stratford NH 03590. (603)922-8338. "To offer additional opportunities for writers to earn income and recognition from their writing efforts." Annual competition for short stories and novels. Award: varies from $75-125. Competition receives approximately 100 short stories; 50 novels. Judges: authors, editors and teachers. Entry fee from $5-20. Guidelines for SASE. Deadline: March 15. Unpublished submissions. Categories include literary, genre, short short and novel chapter. "Guidelines are revised each year and subject to change. New guidelines are available in fall of each year."

❦**FOUNDATION FOR THE ADVANCEMENT OF CANADIAN LETTERS CANADIAN LETTERS AWARD, (II, IV)**, (formerly the Foundation for the Advancement of Canadian Letters

Author's Awards), In conjunction with Periodical Marketers of Canada (PMC), South Tower, 175 Bloor St., E., Suite 1007, Toronto, Ontario M4W 3R8 Canada. (416)968-7218. Award Coordinator: Janette Hatcher. "To recognize a Canadian individual who has made an outstanding contribution to writing, publishing, teaching or literary administration." Award: a statuette and a $5,000 donation to the charitable literary organization or educational institution of the winner's choice.

H.E. FRANCIS SHORT STORY AWARD, (I), Ruth Hindman Foundation, 2007 Gallatin St., Huntsville AL 35801. (205)539-3320. Fax: (205)533-6893. Chairperson: Patricia Sammon. Annual short story competition to honor H.E. Francis, retired professor of English at the University of Alabama in Huntsville. Award: $1,000. Competition receives approximately 1,000 submissions. Judges: distinguished writers. Entry fee. Guidelines for SASE. Unpublished submissions.

MILES FRANKLIN LITERARY AWARD, (II, IV), Arts Management Pty. Ltd., 180 Goulburn St., Darlinghurst NSW 2010 Australia. Associate Director Projects & Artists: Hanne Larsen. "For the advancement, improvement and betterment of Australian literature." Annual award for novels. Award: AUS $25,000, to the author. Competition receives approx. 60 submissions. Guidelines for SASE. Deadline January 31. Previously published submissions. "The novel must have been published in the year of competition entry, and must present Australian life in any of its phases."

SOUERETTE DIEHL FRASER AWARD, (II, IV), The Texas Institute of Letters, TCU Box 298300, Fort Worth TX 76129. (817)921-7822. Secretary: Judy Alter. "To recognize the best literary translation of a book into English, the translation published between January 1 and December 30 of the year prior to the award's announcement in the spring." Annual competition for translations. Award: $1,000. Judges: committee of three. Guidelines for SASE. Deadline: January 4. "Award available to translators who were born in Texas, or who have lived in the state at some time for two consecutive years."

‡FRENCH BREAD AWARDS, (I), *Pacific Coast Journal*, P.O. Box 355, Campbell CA 95009. Editor: Stillson Graham. Award with the goal of "finding the best fiction and poetry out there." Annual competition for short stories and poetry. Award: $50 (1st prize), $25 (2nd prize). Competition receives approximately 50 submissions. Judges: editorial staff of the *Pacific Coast Journal*. Entry fee $6. Guidelines for SASE. Deadline August 1. Unpublished submissions. Length: 4,000 words. "Manuscripts will not be returned. Send SASE for winners' list. all entrants will receive issue in which first place winners are published."

GLIMMER TRAIN'S SHORT-STORY AWARD FOR NEW WRITERS, (I), Glimmer Train Press, Inc., 710 SW Madison St., Suite 504, Portland OR 97205. (503)221-0836. Fax: (503)221-0837. Contest Director: Linda Davies. Contest offered 2 times/year for any writer whose fiction hasn't appeared in a nationally distributed publication with a circulation over 5,000. "Send original, unpublished short (1,200-8,000 words) story with $11 reading fee (covers up to two stories sent together in same envelope) during the months of February/March and August/September. Title page must include name, address, phone and Short Story Award for New Writers must be written on outside of envelope. No need for SASE as materials will not be returned. Notification on July 1 (for February/March entrants) and January 1 (for August/September entrants). Winner receives $1,200 and publication in *Glimmer Train Stories*. First/second runners-up receive $500/$300, respectively, and consideration for publication. All applicants receive a copy of the issue in which winning entry is published and runners-up announced."

JEANNE CHARPIOT GOODHEART PRIZE FOR FICTION, (I), Shenandoah, 2nd Floor, Troubadour Theater, Washington & Lee University, Lexington VA 24450. (203)463-8765. Editor: R.T. Smith. Award to "recognize the best story from a calendar year of *Shenandoah*." Award: $1,000. Competition receives approx. 800 submissions. Judge: previous winner. Guidelines for SASE. Deadline on-going. Unpublished submissions.

GREAT LAKES COLLEGES ASSOCIATION NEW WRITERS AWARD, Great Lakes Colleges Association, 2929 Plymouth Rd., Suite 207, Ann Arbor MI 48105-3206. Director of New Writers Award: Mark Andrew Clark. Annual award. Winners are invited to tour the GLCA colleges. An honorarium of at least $300 will be guaranteed the author by each of the GLCA colleges they visit. Receives 30-40 entries in each category annually. Judges: Professors from member colleges. No entry fee. Deadline February 28. Unpublished submissions. First publication in fiction or poetry. Writer must be nominated by publisher. Four copies of the book should be sent to: Mark Andrew Clark, Director, New Writers Award, GLCA Philadelphia Center, North American Bldg., 121 South Broad St., Seventh Floor, Philadelphia PA 19107.

GREAT PLAINS STORYTELLING & POETRY READING CONTEST, (I,II), P.O. Box 438, Walnut IA 51577. (712)784-3001. Director: Robert Everhart. Estab. 1976. Annual award "to provide an outlet for writers to present not only their works, but also to provide a large audience for their presentation *live* by the writer. Attendance at the event, which takes place annually in Avoca, Iowa, is *required*." Award: 1st prize $75; 2nd prize $50; 3rd prize $25; 4th prize $15; and 5th prize $10. Entry fee: $5. Entry forms available at contest only. Deadline is day of contest, which takes place over Labor Day Weekend. Previously published or unpublished submissions.

GREEN RIVER WRITERS CONTEST, (I, II), Green River Writer, 1043 Thornfield, Cincinnati OH 45224. (513)522-2493. Contact: Linda Frisa. Annual competition for short stories and novels. Award: for short stories up to 2,000 words, $150; 2,000-3,000 words $150, first chapter of novel, $50. Competition receives approx. 30-75 submissions. Judges are appointed by sponsors. Entry fee $5 each, $25 total. Guidelines for SASE. Deadline October 31. Unpublished submissions. Word length: up to 3,000 words, depends on category.

THE GREENSBORO REVIEW LITERARY AWARDS, (I), Dept. of English, UNC-Greensboro, Greensboro NC 27412. (910)334-5459. E-mail: clarkj@fagan.uncg.edu. Editor: Jim Clark. Annual award. Award: $250. Contest rules for SASE. Deadline September 15. Unpublished submissions.

HACKNEY LITERARY AWARDS, (I), Box 549003, Birmingham Southern College, Birmingham AL 35254. (205)226-4921. Fax: (205)226-4931. Director of Special Events: Martha Andrews. Annual award for previously unpublished short stories, poetry and novels. Award: $2,000 (novel); $2,000 (poetry and short stories; 6 prizes). Competition receives approx. 700 submissions. Entry fee: $25 novel; $10 poetry and short story. Rules/entry form for SASE. Novel submissions must be postmarked on or before September 30. Short stories and poetry submissions must be postmarked on or before December 31.

HAMMETT PRIZE (NORTH AMERICAN), (II, IV), International Association of Crime Writers, North American Branch, JAF Box 1500, New York NY 10116. (212)757-3915. E-mail: mfrisque@igc.a pc.org. Award to promote "excellence in the field of crime writing as reflected in a book published in the English language in the US and/or Canada." Annual competition for novels or nonfiction. Award: trophy. Competition receives approximately 150 submissions. Judges: Nominations committee made up of IACW members screens titles and selects 3-5 nominated books. These go to three outside judges, who choose the winner. Guidelines for SASE. Deadline December 1. Previously published submissions. Published entries must have appeared in print between January 1 and December 31 (of contest year). "Writers must be US or Canadian citizens or permanent residents working in the field of crime writing (either fiction or nonfiction). No word-length requirement."

THE HEARTLAND PRIZES, (III), *The Chicago Tribune*, 435 N. Michigan Ave., Chicago IL 60611-4041. "The Heartland Prizes are for nonfiction and the novel. To honor a novel and a book of nonfiction embodying the spirit of the nation's Heartland." Annual award for novels. Award: $5,000. Winners are notified in August. Submission by publishers.

DRUE HEINZ LITERATURE PRIZE, (II), University of Pittsburgh Press, 127 N. Bellefield Ave., Pittsburgh PA 15260. Annual award "to support the writer of short fiction at a time when the economics of commercial publishing make it more and more difficult for the serious literary artist working in the short story and novella to find publication." Award: $10,000 and publication by the University of Pittsburgh Press. Request complete rules of the competition before submitting a manuscript. Submissions will be received only during the months of July and August. Deadline August 31. Manuscripts must be unpublished in book form. The award is open to writers who have published a book-length collection of fiction or a minimum of three short stories or novellas in commercial magazines or literary journals of national distribution.

HEMINGWAY DAYS SHORT STORY COMPETITION, (I), Hemingway Days Festival, P.O. Box 4045, Key West FL 33041. (305)294-4440. "To honor Nobel laureate Ernest Hemingway, who was often pursued during his lifetime by young writers hoping to learn the secrets of his success." Annual competition for short stories. Awards: $1,000—1st; $500—2nd; $500—3rd. Competition receives approximately 900 submissions. Judges: Panel lead by Lorian Hemingway, granddaughter of Ernest Hemingway and novelist based out of Seattle, WA. Entry fee $10/story. Deadline postmarked June 1. "Open to writers who have not been published in national magazines with circulations over 5,000. No longer than 3,000 words." Send SASE for guidelines.

ERNEST HEMINGWAY FOUNDATION/PEN AWARD FOR FIRST FICTION, (II), PEN American Center, 568 Broadway, New York NY 10012. Awards Coordinator: John Morrone. Annual award "to give beginning writers recognition and encouragement and to stimulate interest in first novels among publishers and readers." Award: $7,500. Novels or short story collections must have been published during calendar year under consideration. Entry form or rules for SASE. Deadline

December 15. "The Ernest Hemingway Foundation/PEN Award For First Fiction is given to an American author of the best first-published book-length work of fiction published by an established publishing house in the U.S. each calendar year."

HIGHLIGHTS FOR CHILDREN, (I, IV), 803 Church St., Honesdale PA 18431. Editor: Kent L. Brown, Jr. "To honor quality stories (previously unpublished) for young readers." Three $1,000 awards. Stories: up to 500 words for beginning readers (to age 8) and 900 words for more advanced readers (ages 9 to 12). No minimum word length. No entry form necessary. To be submitted between January 1 and February 28 to "Fiction Contest" at address above. "No violence, crime or derogatory humor." Nonwinning entries returned in June if SASE is included with ms. "This year's category is mystery stories for children." Send SASE for information.

THE ALFRED HODDER FELLOWSHIP, (II), The Council of the Humanities, Princeton University, 122 E. Pyne, Princeton NJ 08544. Executive Director: Carol Rigolot. "This fellowship is awarded for the pursuit of independent work in the humanities. The recipient is usually a writer or scholar in the early stages of his or her career, a person 'with more than ordinary learning' and with 'much more than ordinary intellectual and literary gifts.' " Traditionally, the Hodder Fellow has been a humanist outside of academia. Candidates for the Ph.D. are not eligible. Award: $43,000. The Hodder Fellow spends an academic year in residence at Princeton working independently. Judges: Princeton Committee on Humanistic Studies. Deadline November 15. Applicants must submit a résumé, a sample of previous work (10 page maximum, not returnable), and a project proposal of 2 to 3 pages. Letters of recommendation are not required.

THEODORE CHRISTIAN HOEPFNER AWARD, (I), *Southern Humanities Review*, 9088 Haley Center, Auburn University AL 36849. Contact: Dan R. Latimer or Virginia M. Kouidis, co-editors. Annual. "To award the authors of the best essay, the best short story and the best poem published in *SHR* each year." Award: $100 for the best short story. Judges: Editorial staff. Only published work in the current volume (4 issues) will be judged.

PEARL HOGREFE FELLOWSHIP, (I, II, IV), The Pearl Hogrefe Fund and Department of English, 203 Ross Hall, Iowa State University, Ames IA 50011. (515)294-8753. Contact: Graduate Studies Coordinator. "To provide new M.A. students with writing time." Annual competition for manuscript sample of 25 pages, any genre. Award: $900/month for 9 months and full payment of tuition and fees. Competition receives approximately 60 submissions. Judges: the creative writing staff at Iowa State University. Guidelines upon request. Deadline January 31. Either published or unpublished submissions. "No restrictions, except the applicant cannot hold or expect to receive a masters in English or creative writing during the current year."

HONOLULU MAGAZINE/BORDERS BOOKS & MUSIC FICTION CONTEST, (I, IV), *Honolulu* Magazine, 36 Merchant St., Honolulu HI 96813. (808)524-7400. Editor: John Heckathorn. "We do not accept fiction except during our annual contest, at which time we welcome it." Annual award for short stories. Award: $1,000 and publication in the April issue of *Honolulu* Magazine. Competition receives approximately 400 submissions. Judges: Panel of well-known Hawaii-based writers. Rules for SASE. Deadline early December. "Stories must have a Hawaii theme, setting and/or characters. Author should enclose name and address in separate small envelope. Do not put name on story."

HOUSEWIFE WRITER'S FORUM SHORT STORY CONTEST, (I), *Housewife Writer's Forum*, P.O. Box 780, Lyman WY 82937. (307)782-7003. "To give new fiction writers a chance to have their work recognized." Annual contest for short stories. Awards: $30, $20, $10. Competition receives approximately 75 submissions. Judges: Fiction Editor Edward Wahl and Editor Emma Bluemel. Entry fee $4. Guidelines for SASE. Unpublished submissions. Any genre except risqué; 2,000 words maximum.

L. RON HUBBARD'S WRITERS OF THE FUTURE CONTEST, (I, IV), P.O. Box 1630N, Los Angeles CA 90078. Website: http://www.authorservicesinc.com/wof_home.htm. Contest Administrator: Edith Shields. Estab. 1984. Quarterly. "Foremost contest for new writers of science fiction, fantasy and horror. Awards $2,250 in quarterly prizes, annual $4,000 Grand Prize, five-day Writer's Workshop with major authors, publication in leading international anthology. Outstanding professional judges panel. No entry fee. Entrants retain all rights. For explicit instructions on how to enter send SASE to the above address."

ZORA NEALE HURSTON/RICHARD WRIGHT AWARD, (I, IV), Zora Neale Hurston/Richard Wright Foundation, English Dept., Virginia Commonwealth University, Richmond VA 23284-2005. (804)828-1331. President: Marita Golden. "Awards best fiction written by African-American college students enrolled full- or part-time in a U.S. college or university." Annual award for short stories and novels. Award: $1,000 first prize and publication in *Catalyst Magazine*; $500 second prize. Competition receives 50-75 submissions. Judges: published writers. Guidelines for SASE. Deadline: December 7. Unpublished submissions. Word length: 25 pages maximum.

ILLINOIS ARTS COUNCIL ARTISTS FELLOWSHIPS, (I, IV), Illinois Arts Council, #10-500, James R. Thompson Center, 100 W. Randolph, Chicago IL 60601. (312)814-4990. Contact: Richard Gage. Award "to enable Illinois artists of exceptional talent to pursue their artistic goals." Biannual for short stories, novels, story collections and creative nonfiction (essays, memoirs) completed within four years prior to the deadline. Awards: $500, $5,000 and $10,000. Competition receives approximately 200 prose submissions and 140 poetry submissions. Judges: non-Illinois writers/editors of exceptional talent. Deadline September 1 in odd years (next deadline September 1, 1997). Applicants must have been Illinois residents for at least 1 year prior to deadline and cannot be degree-seeking students. Prose applicants limited to 30 pages; poetry limited to 15 pages.

INTERNATIONAL JANUSZ KORCZAK LITERARY COMPETITION, (II, IV), Joseph H. and Belle R. Braun Center for Holocaust Studies Anti-Defamation League of B'nai B'rith, 823 United Nations Plaza, New York NY 10017. (212)490-2525. Contact: Mark A. Edelman. Biennial award for published novels, novellas, translations, short story collections. "Books for or about children which best reflect the humanitarianism and leadership of Janusz Korczak, a Jewish and Polish physician, educator and author." Inquire for details and deadline.

INTERNATIONAL READING ASSOCIATION CHILDREN'S BOOK AWARDS, (II), Sponsored by IRA, P.O. Box 8139, 800 Barksdale Rd., Newark DE 19714-8139. (302)731-1600. Annual awards given for a first or second book in three categories (younger readers: ages 4-10; older readers: ages 10-16 and up; informational book ages 4-16 and up) to authors who show unusual promise in the children's book field. Books from any country and in any language copyrighted during the previous calendar year will be considered. Entries in a language other than English must include a one-page abstract in English and a translation into English of one chapter or similar selection that in the submitter's estimation is representative of the book. The awards each carry a US $500 stipend. Entries must be received by December 1. To submit a book for consideration by the selection committee, send 10 copies to Judith A. Maegher, School of Education, University of Connecticut, 249 Glenbrook Rd., Storrs CT 06268-2064, USA.

IOWA SCHOOL OF LETTERS AWARD FOR SHORT FICTION, THE JOHN SIMMONS SHORT FICTION AWARD, (I), Iowa Writers' Workshop, 436 English-Philosophy Building, The University of Iowa, Iowa City IA 52242. Annual awards for short story collections. To encourage writers of short fiction. Award: publication of winning collections by University of Iowa Press the following fall. Entries must be at least 150 pages, typewritten, and submitted between August 1 and September 30. Stamped, self-addressed return packaging must accompany manuscript. Rules for SASE. Iowa Writer's Workshop does initial screening of entries; finalists (about 6) sent to outside judge for final selection. "A different well-known writer is chosen each year as judge. Any writer who has not previously published a volume of prose fiction is eligible to enter the competition for these prizes. Revised manuscripts which have been previously entered may be resubmitted."

IOWA WOMAN CONTEST, INTERNATIONAL WRITING CONTEST, (I, IV), P.O. Box 680, Iowa City IA 52244-0680. Annual award for short fiction, poetry, and essays. Awards first place of $500; second place $250, in each category. Judges: anonymous, women writers who have published work in the category. Entry fee $15 for one story, essay, or up to 3 poems; $5 for each additional story, essay, or group of 3 poems. Guidelines available for SASE. Entries accepted between November 15 and December 31 only. Previously unpublished submissions only. Entries may not be simultaneously under consideration elsewhere in any form. Limited to women writers, with a 6,500 word limit on fiction and essays. "Submit typed or computer-printed manuscripts with a cover sheet listing category, title, name, address, and phone number. A single cover sheet per category is sufficient. Identify actual

---

MARKET CATEGORIES: (I) Unpublished entries; (II) Published entries nominated by the author; (III) Published entries nominated by the editor, publisher or nominating body; (IV) Specialized entries.

entry by title only. Do not identify author on the manuscript. Manuscripts cannot be returned; do not send SASE for return."

JOSEPH HENRY JACKSON AWARD, (I, IV), Intersection for the Arts/The San Francisco Foundation, 446 Valencia St., San Francisco CA 94103. (415)626-2787. E-mail: intrsect@thecity.sfsu.edu. Literary Program Director: Charles Wilmoth. Award "to encourage young, unpublished writers." Annual award for short stories, novels and story collections. Award: $2,000. Competition receives approximately 200 submissions. Entry form and rules available for SASE. Deadline January 31. Unpublished submissions only. Applicant must be resident of northern California or Nevada for 3 consecutive years immediately prior to the deadline date. Age of applicant must be 20 through 35. Work cannot exceed 100 double-spaced, typed pages.

JAMES FELLOWSHIP FOR THE NOVEL IN PROGRESS, (I), The Heekin Group Foundation, P.O. Box 1534, Sisters OR 97759. (503)548-4147. Fiction Director: Sarah Heekin Redfield. Award to "support unpublished writers in their writing projects." Two annual awards for novels in progress. Awards: $3,000. Receives approximately 500 applications. Judges: Invitation of publisher: past judges, Graywolf Press, SOHO Press, Dalkey Archive Press, The Ecco Press. Application fee $25. Guidelines for SASE. Deadline December 1. Unpublished submissions. Word length: Submit first 50-75 pages only.

JAPAN FOUNDATION ARTISTS FELLOWSHIP PROGRAM, (IV), 152 W. 57th St., 39th Floor, New York NY 10019. (212)489-0299. Fax: (212)489-0409. Program Assistant: Maki Uchiyama. "This program provides artists and specialists in the arts with the opportunity to pursue creative projects in Japan and to meet and consult with their Japanese counterparts." Annual competition. Several artists fellowships from two to six months' duration during the 1997 Japanese fiscal year (April 1-March 31) are available to artists, such as writers, musicians, painters, sculptors, stage artists, movie directors, etc.; and specialists in the arts, such as scenario writers, curators, etc. Benefits include transportation to and from Japan; settling-in, research, activities and other allowances and a monthly stipend. See brochure for more details. Competition receives approximately 30-40 submissions. Judges: foundation staff in Japan. Deadline December 1. "Work should be related substantially to Japan. Applicants must be accredited artists or specialists. Affiliation with a Japanese artist or institution is required. Three letters of reference, including one from the Japanese affiliate must accompany all applications.

JAPANOPHILE SHORT STORY CONTEST, (I, II, IV), *Japanophile*, P.O. Box 223, Okemos MI 48864. (517)669-2109. Editor: Earl R. Snodgrass. Estab. 1974. Annual award "to encourage quality writing on Japan-America understanding." Award: $100 plus possible publication. Entry fee: $5. Send $4 for sample copy of magazine. Contest rules for SASE. Deadline December 31. Prefers unpublished submissions. Stories should involve Japanese and non-Japanese characters.

JESSE JONES AWARD FOR FICTION (BOOK), (II, IV), The Texas Institute of Letters, % TCU Press, TCU Box 298300, Fort Worth TX 76129. (817)921-7822. Awards Coordinator: Judy Alter. "To honor the writer of the best novel or collection of short fiction published during the calendar year before the award is given." Annual award for novels or story collections. Award: $6,000. Competition receives 30-40 entries per year. Judges: Panel selected by TIL Council. Guidelines for SASE. Deadline: January 4. Previously published fiction, which must have appeared in print between January 1 and December 31 of the prior year. "Award available to writers who, at some time, have lived in Texas at least two years consecutively or whose work has a significant Texas theme."

JAMES JONES FIRST NOVEL FELLOWSHIP, (I), James Jones Society, Wilkes University, Wilkes-Barre PA 18766. (717)831-4520. E-mail: shaffer@wilkesl.wilkes.edu. Chair, English Department: Patricia B. Heaman. Award to "honor the spirit of unblinking honesty, determination, and insight into modern culture exemplified by the late James Jones by encouraging the work of an American writer who has not published a book-length work of fiction." Annual award for unpublished novel, novella, or collection of related short stories in progress. Award: $2,500. Receives approximately 500 applications. Judges: Kaylie Jones, J. Michael Lennon, Patricia Heaman, Kevin Heisler, Jon Shirota. Application fee: $10. Guidelines for SASE. Deadline: March 1. Unpublished submissions. "Award is open to American writers." Word length: 50 opening pages and a two-page thematic outline.

THE JANET HEIDINGER KAFKA PRIZE FOR FICTION BY AN AMERICAN WOMAN, (III, IV), University of Rochester, Susan B. Anthony Institute for Women's Studies, 538 Lattimore Hall, Rochester NY 14627. Award for fiction by a "woman who is a US citizen, and who has written the best, recently published, book-length work of prose fiction, whether novel, short stories, or experimental writing." Annual competition for short stories, story collections and novels. Award: Cash prizes

INSIDER REPORT

The Heekin Group Foundation: three sisters supporting writers

While vacationing with her sisters in Italy in 1992, Sarah Heekin Redfield experienced "a moment of inspiration, a sort of crossroads in my life where I realized that I wanted to combine doing something with my sisters and doing something for the literary arts community." Redfield, a journalist turned fiction writer, had no problem enlisting the support of her sisters Deirdre Heekin who was applying to graduate school for creative writing and Anne Heekin-Canedy, a screenplay writer and essayist.

Sarah Heekin Redfield

Once back to their respective homes—Sarah in Oregon, Deirdre in Vermont and Anne in Connecticut—the sisters had The Heekin Group Foundation Writing Fellowship Program up and running in three weeks. "We had our judge lined up for the '92-'93 writing fellowships program and we had our ads made up and that was that," says Redfield. The role they defined for themselves was "to help new and emerging writers launch their careers by providing financial support that would enable them to finish their projects and make their writing the best it can be."

For the first three years, the foundation was self-financed and awards included the $10,000 James Fellowship for the Novel in Progress and the $5,000 Tara Fellowship for Short Fiction. In 1996 the program was restructured to offer more fellowships with lower cash awards. "We didn't make this change just by a decision from our board," explains Redfield. "It was the applicants who felt they would rather have more, smaller awards so their chances of winning would be greater." The Heekin Group Foundation now offers two $3,000 James Fellowships and two $1,500 Tara Fellowships. Both fiction categories are directed by Sarah. In addition, they have added the $2,000 Mary Molloy Fellowship in Children's Working Fiction, directed by Deirdre, and the $2,000 Siobhan Fellowship for Nonfiction Essay, directed by Anne. There also is a new fundraising program with plans to launch an anthology of the works of fellowship recipients, and goals to get involved with elementary educational programs.

The sisters' writing backgrounds help them understand and work with applicants. "We're not high profile writers. We're in the trenches ourselves and in that respect feel compassion toward our applicants. We really do try to give writers as much as we possibly can through our grants but also through feedback and in the way we deal with them. We treat our applicants with respect."

The Heekin Group Foundation receives 1,200-1,300 applications annually in the fiction division, 200 in the children's division, and 100 in the nonfiction

INSIDER REPORT, *continued*

division. The selection process begins with three disqualifying rounds judged by a team of readers, "everybody from booksellers to writers to teachers—people connected to the literary arts," says Redfield. The preliminary elimination rounds are followed by the semifinalist, finalist and publishers' finalist rounds. Those selected from the publishers' finalists are forwarded to a judge in the respective categories. For instance, the publisher of a literary journal judges short fiction and a book publisher judges the novel in progress.

The only application criterion is writers must be unpublished in the genre to which they are applying. Redfield says most who submit "are very close to having everything open up for them. We're seeing that the fellowships really give them a big push in the right direction and that's very exciting for us." Max Garland's story "Chiromancy," winner of the first Tara Fellowship in 1993, was subsequently published in *The New England Review* and *The Best American Short Stories 1995*. Winning the 1995 James Fellowship enabled novelist Adria Bernardi to travel to Italy where she conducted research. Barbara Branscomb, 1994 James Fellow for her novel *Father and Daughter*—then in progress, now completed—is quoted as saying, "I don't know that I would be pursuing my writing . . . if not for the acknowledgement by HGF." And *Past Perfect*, written by 1996 James Fellow Joshua Henkin, was published by Putnam in spring 1997.

As director of the fiction division awards, Redfield sees first-hand what works and does not. "These manuscripts that surround me in my office are like living and breathing organisms. I live with them for six months. They go out to readers and they come back. I feel like I'm part of them and they're part of me. Maybe that's good and maybe it's not, but I can become passionate about what I feel is good in them or what is a problem."

Redfield advises applicants that presentation, creativity and excellent language and writing skills push a manuscript through the various selection stages. "Writers should be as professional as they can in their presentations. A clean manuscript that is well formatted with a cover page and a letter always stands out. This shows that the writers respect their work and that they are serious and committed about what they are doing." When reading novels in progress, Redfield says judges are not looking for "a slick, finished piece of work" but are judging the work for its essence. "By essence," says Redfield, "I mean creativity, the skillful use of language and the writer's understanding of fiction." For short fiction, judges look for "short stories that are in fact stories." Redfield notes that, although a good deal of the work they receive can be called "experimental," winning stories are "traditional in the sense that they do have a beginning, a middle and an end."

In discussing the concept of the story, Redfield says too many writers unsuccessfully try to turn real experiences into fiction. "Certainly we take nuggets of our lives and put them into our fiction. But our experience is not a whole story within itself." Redfield also finds recurring mistakes with language and grammar. "I see problems with tense, sentence structure, with failing to use the word that truly defines what the writer wants to say, and with the repetition of the same word too many times, even in the same sentence or paragraph."

Redfield suggests a two-year self-help regime to strengthen weaknesses and become a better writer. "For one year, read everything you can get your hands on: nonfiction, B-grade fiction and excellent fiction. The second year, reread

INSIDER REPORT, *Redfield*

some of those books, but this time analyze them—take them apart to see how the writers put stories together, how they use language and point of view and how they manage their time lines." Redfield also advises writers to read books on the craft of writing, including those with differing opinions.

To become more disciplined, Redfield encourages writers to apply to contests and awards programs for the experience that meeting deadlines provides. "By giving yourself these deadlines, you get used to writing every day." And, insists Redfield, it is writing that makes writers. "People who are really writers will not worry that they need a fresh head of lettuce for dinner because they would rather write for an extra 45 minutes. To them, it is the act of writing that is important. And, chances are, with that commitment and with that obsession, a writer is going to get somewhere."

—Barbara Kuroff

---

to be announced. Guidelines for SASE. Deadline March 15, 1997. Recently published submissions. American women only. Writer must be nominated by publisher.

‡KATHA: INDIAN AMERICAN FICTION CONTEST, *India Currents* Magazine, P.O. Box 21285, San Jose CA 95151. (408)274-6966. Fax: (408)274-2733. Editor: Arvind Kumar. Award "to encourage creative writing which has as its focus India, Indian culture, Indian-Americans and America's views of India." Annual competition for short stories. Awards: $100 (1st prize), $75 (2nd prize), 2 honorable mentions. All entrants receive a 1-year subscription to *India Currents*. Competition received 60 submissions last year. Judges: "A distinguished panel of Indian-American authors. Reading fee $10. Guidelines for SASE. Deadline December 31. Unpublished submissions. Length: 2,000 words maximum.

‡EZRA JACK KEATS/KERLAN COLLECTION MEMORIAL FELLOWSHIP, (I, II), University of Minnesota, 109 Walter Library, 117 Pleasant St. SE, Minneapolis MN 55455. (612)624-4576. Fax: (612)625-5525. Contact: Carrie Tahtamouni. Award to provide "travel expenses to a talented writer and/or illustrator of children's books who wishes to use the Kerlan Collection for the furtherance of his or her artistic development." Annual competition for books of children's literature. Award: $1,500. Competition receives approximately 10 submissions. Judges: panel of non-Kerlan Collection staff; area professionals, educators, etc. Guidelines for SASE or SAE and IRC. Deadline early May. Accepts unpublished and previously published submissions.

ROBERT F. KENNEDY BOOK AWARDS, (II, IV), 1206 30th St. NW, Washington DC 20007. (202)333-1880. Endowed by Arthur Schlesinger, Jr., from proceeds of his biography, *Robert Kennedy and His Times*. Annual. "To award the author of a book which most faithfully and forcefully reflects Robert Kennedy's purposes." For books published during the calendar year. Award: $2,500 cash prize awarded in the spring. Deadline: January 2. Looking for "a work of literary merit in fact or fiction that shows compassion for the poor or powerless or those suffering from injustice." Four copies of each book submitted should be sent, along with a $25 entry fee.

KENTUCKY ARTS COUNCIL, KENTUCKY ARTISTS FELLOWSHIPS, (I, IV), 31 Fountain Place, Frankfort KY 40601. (502)564-3757. "To encourage and assist the professional development of Kentucky artists." 10-15 writing fellowships offered every other (or even-numbered) year in fiction, poetry, playwriting. Award: $5,000. Judges are out-of-state panelists (writers, editors, playwrights, etc.) of distinction. Open only to Kentucky residents (minimum one year). Entry forms available for *Kentucky residents in July 1997*." Deadline September 1997.

AGA KHAN PRIZE FOR FICTION, *The Paris Review*, 541 E. 72nd St., New York NY 10021. (212)861-0016. Editor: George Plimpton. Best previously unpublished short story. Annual competition for short stories. Award: $1,000. Competition receives approximately 1,000 submissions/month. Guidelines with SASE. Unpublished submissions. Word length: approximately 1,000-10,000 words.

KILLER FROG CONTEST, (I, II, IV), *Scavenger's Newsletter*, 519 Ellinwood, Osage City KS 66523. (913)528-3538. Contact: Janet Fox. Competition "to see who can write the funniest/most overdone horror story, or poem, or produce the most outrageous artwork on a horror theme." Annual award for short stories, poems and art. Award: $25 for each of 4 categories and "coveted froggie statuette." Winners also receive complimentary copies of *The Killer Frog* Anthology. Judge: Editor of *Scavenger*, Janet Fox. Guidelines available for SASE. Submissions must be postmarked between April 1 and July 1. Published or previously unpublished submissions. Limited to horror/humor. Length: up to 4,000 words.

LATINO LITERATURE PRIZE, (II, IV), Latin American Writers Institute, % Hostos Community College, 500 Grand Concourse, Bronx NY 10451. (718)518-4195. Fax: (718)518-4294. Director: Isaac Goldemberg. "To recognize the work of Latino writers in the U.S. The competition is for books published in English or Spanish." Annual competition for novels and poetry. Award: $1,000 in each category (fiction and poetry). Competition receives approximately 125 submissions. Judges: recognized critics and writers. Guidelines for SASE. Deadline February 28, 1997. Previously published submissions published between January 1995 and December 1996. Open only to Latino writers who live in the United States. Publishers may also submit books for competition. "A special issue of our bilingual literary journal, *Brújula/Compass*, is devoted to the winning authors."

LAWRENCE FOUNDATION PRIZE, (I), *Michigan Quarterly Review*, 3032 Rackham Bldg., Ann Arbor MI 48109-1070. (313)764-9265. Editor: Laurence Goldstein. "An annual cash prize awarded to the author of the best short story published in *Michigan Quarterly Review* each year—chosen from both solicited and unsolicited submissions. Approximately eight short stories are published each year." Annual competition for short stories. Award: $1,000. The Review receives approximately 2,000 mss/year. Judges: Editorial Board.

✹STEPHEN LEACOCK MEDAL FOR HUMOUR, (II, IV), Stephen Leacock Associates, P.O. Box 854, Orillia, Ontario L3V 6K8 Canada. (705)325-6546. Award "to encourage writing of humour by Canadians." Annual competition for short stories, novels and story collections. Award: Stephen Leacock (silver) medal for humour and Manulife Bank of Canada cash award of $5,000 (Canadian). Receives 25-40 entries. Five judges selected across Canada. Entry fee $25 (Canadian). Guidelines for SASE. Deadline December 30. Submissions should have been published in the previous year. Open to Canadian citizens or landed immigrants only.

LINES IN THE SAND SHORT FICTION CONTEST, Le Sand Publications, 1252 Terra Nova Blvd., Pacifica CA 94044-4340. (415)355-9069. Associate Editor: Barbara J. Less. "To encourage the writing of good short fiction, any genre." Annual competition for short stories. Award: $50, $25, or $10 and publication in *Lines in the Sand*. January/February awards edition. Honorable mentions will be published as space allows. Competition receives approximately 80 submissions. Judges: the editors. Entry fee $5. Guidelines for SASE. Deadline October 31. Previously published or unpublished submissions. Word length: 2,000 words maximum.

LOFT-MCKNIGHT WRITERS AWARDS, (I, IV), The Loft, Pratt Community Center, 66 Malcolm Ave. SE, Minneapolis MN 55414. (612)379-8999. Program Coordinator: Deidre Pope. "To give Minnesota writers of demonstrated ability an opportunity to work for a concentrated period of time on their writing." Annual awards of $10,000; 2 in poetry and 3 in creative prose; 2 awards of distinction of $20,000. Competition receives approximately 525 submissions/year. Judges are from out-of-state. Entry forms or rules for SASE. Deadline November. "Applicants *must* be Minnesota residents and must send for and observe guidelines."

LONG FICTION CONTEST, (I), White Eagle Coffee Store Press, P.O. Box 383, Fox River Grove IL 60021-0383. (847)639-9200. Contact: Publisher. To promote and support the long fiction form. Annual award for short stories. Winning story receives A.E. Coppard Award—publication as chapbook plus $200, 25 contributor's copies; 40 additional copies sent to book publishers/agents and 10 press kits. Entry fee $10. SASE for results. Deadline December 15. Accepts previously unpublished submissions, but previous publication of small parts with acknowledgements is okay. Simultaneous submissions okay. No limits on style or subject matter. Length: 8,000-14,000 words (30-50 pages double spaced) single story; may have multiparts or be a self-contained novel segment. Send cover with title, name, address, phone; second title page with title only. Submissions are not returned; they are recycled.

LOUISIANA LITERARY AWARD, (II, IV), Louisiana Library Association (LLA), PO Box 3058, Baton Rouge LA 70821. (504)342-4928. Contact: Chair, Louisiana Literary Award Committee. Annual award "to promote interest in books related to Louisiana and to encourage their production." Submissions must have been published during the calendar year prior to presentation of the award (the award is presented in March or April). Award: Bronze medallion and $250. No entry fee. Books must be published by December 31 to be eligible. "All Louisiana-related books which committee members can locate are considered, whether submitted or not. Interested parties may correspond with the committee chair at the address above. All books considered *must* be on subject(s) related to Louisiana or be written by a Louisiana author. Each year, there may be a fiction *and/or* nonfiction award. Most often, however, there is only one award recipient."

MARY MCCARTHY PRIZE IN SHORT FICTION, (I, IV), Sarabande Books, Inc., P.O. Box 4999, Louisville KY 40204. Editor-in-Chief: Sarah Gorham. "To award publication and $2,000 to an outstanding collection of short stories or novellas or single novella of 150-300 pages." Competition receives approximately 700 submissions. Judge: A.M. Homes. Entry fee $15. Guidelines for SASE. Unpublished submissions. US citizens. Word length: 150-300 pages. "Writers must submit a required entry form and follow contest guildelines for ms submission. Writers must include a #10 SASE with their inquiries."

THE JOHN H. MCGINNIS MEMORIAL AWARD, (I), *Southwest Review*, Box 374, 307 Fondren Library West, Southern Methodist University, Dallas TX 75275. (214)768-1037. Contact: Elizabeth Mills, senior editor. Annual awards (fiction and nonfiction). Stories or essays must have been published in the *Southwest Review* prior to the announcement of the award. Awards: $1,000. Pieces are not submitted directly for the award, but simply for publication in the magazine.

JENNY MCKEAN MOORE WRITER IN WASHINGTON, (II), Jenny McKean Moore Fund & The George Washington University, Dept. of English, George Washington University, Washington DC 20052. (202)994-6180. Fax: (202)994-7915. Associate Professor of English: Faye Moskowitz. Annual award "of a teaching residency for a different genre each year." Award: $40,000 and an "attractive benefits package." Receives approximately 100 applications. Judges: George Washington University English faculty and members of the J.M. Moore Fund. Guidelines for SASE. Deadline November 15. Previously published submissions.

THE ENID MCLEOD LITERARY PRIZE, (II, IV), Franco-British Society, Room 623, Linen Hall, 162-168 Regent St., London W1R 5TB England. Executive Secretary: Mrs. Marian Clarke. "To recognize the work of the author published in the UK which in the opinion of the judges has contributed most to Franco-British understanding." Annual competition for short stories, novels and story collections. Award: Monetary sum. Competition receives approximately 6-12 submissions. Judges: The Marquis of Lansdowne (FBS President), Martyn Goff and Professor Douglas Johnson. Guidelines for SASE. Deadline December 31. Previously published submissions. "Writers, or their publishers, may submit 4 copies to the London Office. No nominations are necessary."

MAGGIE AWARD, (I, IV), %Lillian Richey, 4605 Settles Point Rd., Suwanee GA 30174-1988. (770)945-2184. "To encourage and instruct unpublished writers in the romance genre." Annual competition for novels. Award: Silver pendant (1st place), certificates (2nd-4th). 5 categories—short contemporary romance, long contemporary romance, historical romance, mainstream, paranormal. Judges: Published romance authors. Entry fee $25. Guidelines for SASE. Deadline is on or about June 15 (deadline not yet final). Unpublished submissions. Writers must be members of Romance Writers of America. Entries consist of 60 pages including synopsis.

MAGIC-REALISM MAGAZINE SHORT-FICTION AWARD, (II), Magic Realism/Pyx Press, P.O. Box 922648, Sylmar CA 91392-2648. Editor and Publisher: C. Darren Butler. Annual short story competition "to honor original works of magic realism in English published in the previous year." Author receives $50 and chapbook publication; publisher also receives $50. Judges: the editors of *Magic Realism*. Guidelines for SASE. Deadline: February 15. Previously published submissions. Published entries must have appeared in print between January and December of previous year. Reprint rights must be available. Length: 20,000 words maximum.

MARKET CONDITIONS are constantly changing! If you're still using this book and it is 1998 or later, buy the newest edition of *Novel & Short Story Writer's Market* at your favorite bookstore or order from Writer's Digest Books.

MALICE DOMESTIC GRANT, (I, IV), % Bookstore, 27 W. Washington St., Hagerstown MD 21740. (301)797-8896. Fax (301)797-9453. Grants Chair: Pam Reed. Given "to encourage unpublished writers in their pursuit—grant may be used to offset registration, travel or other expenses relating to attending writers' conferences, etc., within one year of award." Annual competition for novels and nonfiction. Award: $500. Competition receives 8-25 submissions. Judges: the Malice Domestic Board. Guidelines for SASE. Unpublished submissions. "Our genre is loosely translated as mystery stories of the Agatha Christie type, that is 'mysteries of manners.' These works usually feature amateur detective characters who know each other. No excessive gore or violence." Submit plot synopsis and 3 chapters of work in progress. Include resume, a letter of reference from someone familiar with your work, a typed letter of application explaining qualifications for the grant, and the workshop/conference to be attended or the research to be funded.

✤MANITOBA ARTS COUNCIL SUPPORT TO INDIVIDUAL ARTISTS, (II, IV), Manitoba Arts Council, 525-93 Lombard Ave., Winnipeg, Manitoba R3B 3B1 Canada. (204)945-2237. Grants "to encourage and support Manitoba writers." Awards: Major Arts Grant ($25,000 Canadian) for writers of national or international reputation. Writers Grants "A" ($10,000 Canadian) for writers who have published 2 books or had a full-length script produced. Writers Grants "B" for writers who have published a book. Writers Grants "C" for writers with modest publication history, research and travel. Deadlines: April 15 and September 15. Open only to Manitoba writers.

WALTER RUMSEY MARVIN GRANT, (I, IV), Ohioana Library Association, 65 S. Front St., Room 1105, Columbus OH 43215. (614)466-3831. Contact: Linda Hengst. "To encourage young unpublished (meaning not having a book published) writers (under age 30)." Biennial competition for short stories. Award: $1,000. Guidelines for SASE. Deadline January 31, 1998. Open to unpublished authors born in Ohio or who have lived in Ohio for a minimum of five years. Must be under 30 years of age. Up to six pieces of prose may be submitted; maximum 60 pages, minimum 10 pages.

MASTERS LITERARY AWARD, (I), Center Press, P.O. Box 16452, Encino CA 91416-6452. "One yearly Grand Prize of $1,000, and four quarterly awards of "Honorable Mention" each in either 1) fiction; 2) poetry and song lyrics; 3) nonfiction." Judges: Three anonymous literary professionals. Entry fee $10. Awards are given on March 15, June 15, September 15 and December 15. Any submission received prior to an award date is eligible for the subsequent award. Submissions accepted throughout the year. Fiction and nonfiction must be no more than 20 pages (5,000 words); poetry no more than 150 lines. All entries must be in the English language. #10 SASE required for guidelines.

THE MENTOR AWARD, (IV), *Mentor Newsletter*, P.O. Box 4382, Overland Park KS 66204. (913)362-7889. Editor: Maureen Waters. "The Mentor Award is given for supporting and promoting the art and practice of mentoring through the written word, and thereby helping to create a new sense of community." Quarterly and annually: Grand Prize ($100) will be awarded each January to the 1 best submission from all quarterly first-prize winners in all categories from the previous year. Competition for short stories (1,000-3,000 words); essay (700-1,500 words); feature article (1,500-3,000 words); interview (1,000-3,000 words); book review (500-1,000 words); and movie review (500-1,000 words). "The Athena Award is for published (after January 1, 1993) material. Entry fee varies by category (book, article, academic dissertation, videos, etc.). All material must be mentoring related. Plaque awarded, no monetary reward." Guidelines for SASE. Deadlines for quarterly competitions: March 31, June 30, September 30, December 31. Previously published (prior to January 1, 1993) and unpublished submissions. Submissions must be about "a mentor or a mentoring relationship."

✤THE VICKY METCALF BODY OF WORK AWARD, (II, IV), Canadian Authors Association, 27 Doxsee Ave. N., Campbellford, Ontario K0L 1L0 Canada. (705)653-0323. Fax: (705)653-0593. President: Murphy Schewchuk. Annual award. "The prize is given solely to stimulate writing for children, written by Canadians, for a *number* of strictly children's books—fiction, nonfiction or even picture books. No set formula." To be considered, a writer must have published at least 4 books. Award: $10,000 for a body of work inspirational to Canadian youth. Deadline December 31. No entry fee. "Nominations may be made by any individual or association by letter *in triplicate* listing the published works of the nominee and providing biographical information. The books are usually considered in regard to their inspirational value for children. Entry forms or rules for SASE."

✤VICKY METCALF SHORT STORY AWARD, (II, IV), Canadian Authors Association, 27 Doxsee Ave. N., Campbellford, Ontario K0L 1L0 Canada. (705)653-0323. Fax: (705)653-0593. President: Murphy Schewchuk. "To encourage Canadian writing for children (open only to Canadian citizens)." Submissions must have been published during previous calendar year in Canadian children's magazine or anthology. Award: $3,000 (Canadian). Award of $1,000 to editor of winning story if published in a Canadian journal or anthology. No entry fee. Entry forms or rules for #10 SASE. Deadline December 31. Looking for "stories with originality, literary quality for ages 7-17."

MICHIGAN AUTHOR AWARD, (II, IV), Michigan Library Association/Michigan Center for the Book, 6810 S. Cedar, Suite 6, Lansing MI 48911. (517)694-6615. Fax: (517)694-4330. Executive Director: Marianne Hartzell. "Award to recognize an outstanding published body of fiction, nonfiction, poetry and/or playscript, by a Michigan author." Annual competition for short stories, novels, story collections. Award: $1,000. Competition receives approximately 30 submissions. Judges: Panel members represent a broad spectrum of expertise in writing, publishing and book collecting. Guidelines for SASE. Previously published submissions. Michigan authors only. "Nominee must have three published works."

MIDLAND AUTHORS' AWARD, (II, IV), Society of Midland Authors, P.O. Box 10419, Fort Dearborn Station, Chicago IL 60610. "To honor outstanding books published during the previous year by Midwestern authors and professionally produced plays." Award: Monetary sum and plaque. Competition receives approximately 400-500 book and play submissions. Judges are librarians, book reviewers radio, network program reviewers, bookstore executives and university faculty members. Entry forms or rules for SASE. Authors must be residents of Illinois, Indiana, Iowa, Kansas, Michigan, Minnesota, Missouri, Nebraska, Ohio, South Dakota, North Dakota or Wisconsin. Send for entry form.

MID-LIST PRESS FIRST SERIES AWARD FOR SHORT FICTION, (I, II), Mid-List Press, 4324-12th Ave. South, Minneapolis MN 55407-3218. (612)822-3733. Senior Editor: Lane Stiles. To encourage and nurture short fiction writers who have never published a collection of fiction. Annual competition for fiction collections. Award: $1,000 advance and publication. Judges: manuscript readers and the editors of Mid-List Press. Entry fee $15. Deadline July 1. Previously published or unpublished submissions. Word length: 50,000 words minimum. "Application forms and guidelines are available for a #10 SASE."

MID-LIST PRESS FIRST SERIES AWARD FOR THE NOVEL , (I), Mid-List Press, 4324-12th Ave. South, Minneapolis MN 55407-3218. (612)822-3733. Senior Editor: Lane Stiles. To encourage and nurture first-time novelists. Annual competition for novels. Award: $1,000 advance and publication. Competition receives approximately 500 submissions. Judges: manuscript readers and the editors of Mid-List Press. Entry fee $15. Deadline February 1. Unpublished submissions. Word length: minimum 50,000 words. "Application forms and guidelines are available for a #10 SASE."

MILKWEED EDITIONS NATIONAL FICTION PRIZE, (II), Milkweed Editions, 430 First Ave. N., Suite 400, Minneapolis MN 55401. (612)332-3192. Publisher: Emilie Buchwald. Annual award for a novel, a short story collection, one or more novellas, or a combination of short stories and novellas. The Prize will be awarded to the best work of fiction that Milkweed accepts for publication during each calendar year by a writer not previously published by Milkweed Editions. The winner will receive $2,000 cash over and above any payment agreed upon at the time of acceptance. Must request guidelines; send SASE. There is no deadline. Judged by Milkweed Editions. "Please look at previous winners: *The Empress of One*, by Faith Sullivan; *Confidence of the Heart*, by David Schweidel; *Montana 1948*, by Larry Watson; and *Aquaboogie*, by Susan Straight—this is the caliber of fiction we are searching for. Catalog available for $1.50 postage, if people need a sense of our list."

MILKWEED EDITIONS PRIZE FOR CHILDREN'S LITERATURE, (II), Milkweed Editions, 430 First Ave. N., Suite 400, Minneapolis MN 55401. (612)332-3192. Publisher: Emilie Buchwald. "Our goal is to encourage writers to create books for the important age range of middle readers." Annual award for novels and biographies for children ages 8 to 12. The prize will be awarded to the best work for children ages 8 to 12 that Milkweed accepts for publication during each calendar year by a writer not previously published by Milkweed. The winner will receive $2,000 cash over and above any advances, royalties, or other payment agreed upon at the time of acceptance. There is no deadline. Judges: Milkweed Editions. Guidelines for SASE. Unpublished in book form. Page length: 110-350 pages.

‡MINNESOTA STATE ARTS BOARD/ARTIST ASSISTANCE FELLOWSHIP, (I, II, IV), Park Square Court, 400 Sibley St., Suite 200, St. Paul MN 55101-1928. (612)215-1600. Fax: (612)215-1602. Artist Assistance Program Associate: Karen Mueller. "To provide support and recognition to Minnesota's outstanding literary artists." Annual award for fiction writers, creative nonfiction writers and poets. Award: Up to $6,000. Competition receives approximately 150 submissions/year. Deadline: October. Previously published or unpublished submissions. Send request or call the above number for application guidelines. *Minnesota residents only.*

MINNESOTA VOICES PROJECT, (IV), New Rivers Press, 420 N. Fifth St., #910, Minneapolis MN 55401. (612)339-7114. Contact: C.W. Truesdale, editor/publisher. Annual award "to foster and encourage new and emerging regional writers of short fiction, novellas, personal essays and poetry." Requires entry form. Awards: $500 to each author published in the series plus "a generous royalty agreement if book goes into second printing." No entry fee. Send request with SASE for guidelines in October. Deadline: April 1. Restricted to new and emerging writers from Minnesota, Wisconsin, North and South Dakota and Iowa.

MISSISSIPPI ARTS COMMISSION ARTIST FELLOWSHIP GRANT, (I, IV), 239 N. Lamar St., Suite 207, Jackson MS 39201. (601)359-6030. Contact: Program Director . "To support the creation of new work and recognize the contributions made by artists of exceptional talent to Mississippi's culture. Awards are based on mastery of artistic discipline and originality of prior art work; and evidence that new work of significant value and originality be produced during the grant period." Award granted every 2 years on a rotating basis. Award for writers of short stories, novels and story collections and screenwriters. Grant: $5,000. Judges: Peer panel. Guidelines for SASE. "The next available grants for creative writing, including fiction, nonfiction and poetry will be in 1997-98." Deadline: March 1. Applicants must be Mississippi residents. The Mississippi Arts Commission's Art in Education Program contains a creative writing component. For more information, contact the AIE Coordinator. The Mississippi Touring Arts program offers writers the opportunity to give readings and workshops. For more information, contact the Program Director.

THE MISSOURI REVIEW EDITORS' PRIZE CONTEST, 1507 Hillcrest Hall, Columbia MO 65211. (573)882-4474. Annual competition for short stories, poetry and essays. Award: Cash and publication in *The Missouri Review*. Competition receives approximately 1,200 submissions. Judges: *The Missouri Review* staff. Page restrictions: 25 typed, double-spaced, for fiction and essays, 10 for poetry. Entry fee $15 for each entry (checks payable to The Missouri Review). Each fee entitles entrant to a one-year subscription to MR, an extension of a current subscription, or a gift. Outside of envelope should be marked "Fiction," "Essay," or "Poetry." Enclose an index card with author's name, address, and telephone number in the left corner and, for fiction and essay entries only, the work's title in the center. Entries must be previously unpublished and will not be returned. Enclose SASE for notification of winners. No further guidelines necessary.

✤**MR. CHRISTIE'S BOOK AWARD, (II, IV)**, Christie Brown & Co., 2150 Lakeshore Blvd. W., Toronto, Ontario M8V 1A3 Canada. (416)503-6050. Fax: (416)503-6010. Program Coordinator: Marlene Yustin. Award to "honor excellence in the writing and illustration of Canadian children's literature and to encourage the development and publishing of high quality children's books." Annual competition for short stories and novels. Award: Six awards of $7,500 (Canadian) each given in 3 categories to works published in English and French. Competition receives approximately 300 submissions. Judges: Two judging panels, one English and one French. Guidelines for SASE. Submissions must be published within the year prior to the award ceremony. The author/illustrator must be a Canadian resident. A Canadian is defined as a person having Canadian citizenship or having landed immigrant status at the time of his/her book's publication. Books will be judged based on their ability to: inspire the imagination of the reader; recognize the importance of play; represent the highest standard of integrity; bring delight and edification; help children understand the world both intellectually and emotionally.

MOBIL PEGASUS PRIZE, (III), (formerly Pegasus Prize), Mobil Corporation, (Room 3C906), 3225 Gallows Rd., Fairfax VA 22037-0001. (703)846-1005. E-mail: slmoore@ffx.mobil.com. Contact: Director. To recognize distinguished works of literature from around the globe. Award for novels. "Prize is given on a country-by-country basis and does not involve submissions unless requested by national juries."

"MY FAVORITE HOLIDAY STORY" COMPETITION, (I), Fortney Publishing, P.O. Box 1564, Centreville VA 22020. (703)612-5501. Contact: Daniel R. Fortney. "Fortney Publishing's mission is to generate profitable markets for writers." Third annual competition for short stories. Awards: $500, $250, $125, $75, $50. "In addition, the authors of the top 40 stories will be offered a royalty contract for publication in the book, *My Favorite Holiday Stories II.*" Entry fee $10. Guidelines for SASE. Deadline November 15. Unpublished submissions. Word length: 500-5,000 words. "Holidays can be real or fictitious. All entries will be judged on originality and creativity demonstrating the true spirit of holiday celebrations."

MYSTERY MAYHEM CONTEST, (I), *Mystery Time*/Hutton Publications, P.O. Box 2907, Decatur IL 62524. Editor: Linda Hutton. Award "to encourage writers to have fun writing a mystery spoof." Annual competition for short stories. Award: $10 cash and publication in *Mystery Time*. Competition receives approximately 100 submissions. Judge: Linda Hutton, Editor of *Mystery Time*. Guidelines for SASE. Deadline September 15 annually. Unpublished submissions. Word length: Must be one sentence of any length. "One entry per person, of one sentence which can be any length, which is the opening of a mystery spoof. Must include SASE. Entry form not required."

NATIONAL BOOK FOUNDATION, INC., (III), 260 Fifth Ave., Room 904, New York NY 10001. (212)685-0261. E-mail: natbkfdn@interramp.com. Executive Director: Neil Baldwin. Assistant Director: Meg Kearney. Program Officer: Kevin LaFollette. Program Associate: Sherrie Young. Annual award to honor distinguished literary achievement in 4 categories: nonfiction, fiction, poetry and Young People's Literature. Books published December 1 through November 30 are eligible. Award: $10,000 to each winner; $1,000 to 4 runners-up in each category. Awards judged by panels of critics and writers. Entry fee $100 per title. Deadline July 15. November ceremony. Selections are submitted by publishers only, or may be called in by judges. Read *Publishers Weekly* for additional information.

NATIONAL ENDOWMENT FOR THE ARTS CREATIVE WRITING FELLOWSHIP, (I), Room 720, 1100 Pennsylvania Ave. NW, Washington DC 20506. (202)682-5428. "The mission of the NEA is to foster the excellence, diversity and vitality of the arts in the United States, and to help broaden public access to the arts." The purpose of the fellowship is to enable creative writers "to set aside time for writing, research or travel and generally to advance their careers." Competition open to fiction writers who have published a novel or novella, a collection of stories or at least five stories in two or more magazines since January 1, 1992. Award: $20,000. The Endowment now alternates years between fiction and poetry; fiction applications will be accepted in 1997. All mss are judged anonymously. Application and guidelines available upon request.

NATIONAL FEDERATION OF THE BLIND WRITER'S DIVISION FICTION CONTEST, (I), National Federation of the Blind Writer's Division, 2704 Beach Dr., Merrick NY 11566. (516)868-8718. Fax: (516)868-9076. First Vice President, Writer's Division: Lori Stayer. "To promote good writing for blind writers and Division members, blind or sighted." Annual competition for short stories. Award: $40, $25, $15. Entry fee $5/story. Guidelines for SASE. Deadline May 1, 1997 (contest opens 9/1/96). Unpublished submissions. "You don't have to be blind, but it helps. Story must be in English, and typed. SASE necessary." Critique on request, $5. Word length: 2,000 max.

NATIONAL FICTION COMPETITION, (I), FC2, Illinois State University, Campus Box 4241, Normal IL 61790-4241. (309)438-3025. Director: Curtis White. Award to "publish new authors in the experimental, avant-garde, post-modern genre." Annual competition for novels and short story collections. Awards publication to winning ms. Competition receives 350 submissions. "Final judging done by a prose writer of national prominence." Entry fee $15. Guidelines available for SASE. Deadline: November 15. (Fliers are sent in August/September.) Unpublished submissions. Word length: 400 double-spaced, typewritten pages maximum.

NATIONAL WRITERS ASSOCIATION ANNUAL NOVEL WRITING CONTEST, (I), National Writers Association, 1450 S. Havana, Suite 424, Aurora CO 80012. (303)751-7844. Contact: Sandy Whelchel, director. Annual award to "recognize and reward outstanding ability and to increase the opportunity for publication." Award: $500 first prize; $300 second prize; $100 third prize. Award judged by successful writers. Charges $35 entry fee. Judges' evaluation sheets sent to each entry. Contest rules and entry forms available with SASE. Opens December 1. Deadline: April 1. Unpublished submissions, any genre or category. Length: 20,000-100,000 words.

NATIONAL WRITERS ASSOCIATION ANNUAL SHORT STORY CONTEST, (I), National Writers Association, 1450 S. Havana, Suite 424, Aurora CO 80012. (303)751-7844. Contact: Sandy Whelchel, executive director. Annual award to encourage and recognize writing by freelancers in the short story field. Award: $200 first prize; $100 second prize; $50 third prize. Opens April 1. Charges $15 entry fee. Write for entry form and rule sheet. All entries must be postmarked by July 1. Evaluation sheets sent to each entrant if SASE provided. Unpublished submissions. Length: No more than 5,000 words.

THE NATIONAL WRITTEN & ILLUSTRATED BY . . . AWARDS CONTEST FOR STUDENTS, (I, IV), Landmark Editions, Inc., P.O. Box 270169, Kansas City MO 64127. (816)241-4919. Contact: Nan Thatch. "Contest initiated to encourage students to write and illustrate original books and to inspire them to become published authors and illustrators." Annual competition. "Each student whose book is selected for publication will be offered a complete publishing contract. To ensure that students benefit from the proceeds, royalties from the sale of their books will be placed in an individual trust fund, set up for each student by his or her parents or legal guardians, at a bank of their choice. Funds may be withdrawn when a student becomes of age, or withdrawn earlier (either in whole or in part) for educational purposes or in case of proof of specific needs due to unusual hardship. Reports of book sales and royalties will be sent to the student and the parents or guardians annually." Winners also receive an all-expense-paid trip to Kansas City to oversee final reproduction phases of their books. Books by students may be entered in one of three age categories: A—6 to 9 years old; B—10 to 13 years old; C—14 to 19 years old. Each book submitted must be both written and illustrated by the same student. "Any books that are written by one student and illustrated by another will be automatically disqualified." Book entries must be submitted by a teacher or librarian. Entry fee $1. For rules and guidelines, send a #10 SAE with 64¢ postage. Deadline May 1 of each year.

NEGATIVE CAPABILITY SHORT FICTION COMPETITION, (I, IV), *Negative Capability*, 62 Ridgelawn Dr. E., Mobile AL 36608. (334)343-6163. E-mail: negcap@aol.com. Contact: Sue Walker. "To promote and publish excellent fiction and to promote the ideals of human rights and dignity." Annual award for short stories. Award: $1,000 best story. Judge: Eugene Walter. Reading fee $10, "includes copy of journal publishing the award." Deadline January 15. Length: 1,500-4,500 words. Send one copy without name and a card with name and address. Include SASE for results.

NEUSTADT INTERNATIONAL PRIZE FOR LITERATURE, (III), *World Literature Today*, 110 Monnet Hall, University of Oklahoma, Norman OK 73019-0375. Contact: Djelal Kadir, director. Biennial award to recognize distinguished and continuing achievement in fiction, poetry or drama. Awards: $40,000, an eagle feather cast in silver, an award certificate and a special issue of *WLT* devoted to the laureate. "We are looking for outstanding accomplishment in world literature. The Neustadt Prize is not open to application. Nominations are made only by members of the international jury, which changes for each award. Jury meetings are held in March of even-numbered years. Unsolicited manuscripts, whether published or unpublished, cannot be considered."

NEVADA STATE COUNCIL ON THE ARTS ARTISTS' FELLOWSHIPS, (I, IV), 602 N. Curry St., Carson City NV 89710. (702)687-6680. Fax: (702)687-6688. Director of Artists' Services: Sharon Rosse. Award "to honor individual artists and their artistic achievements to support artists' efforts in advancing their careers." Annual competition for fiction, nonfiction, poetry, playwriting. Award: $5,000 ($4,500 immediately, $500 after public service component completed). Judges: Peer panels of professional artists. Guidelines available, no SASE required. Deadline August 15. "Only available to Nevada writers." Word length: 25 pages.

THE NEW ERA WRITING, ART, PHOTOGRAPHY AND MUSIC CONTEST, (I, IV), *New Era Magazine* (LDS Church), 50 E. North Temple, Salt Lake City UT 84150. (801)240-2951. Managing Editor: Richard M. Romney. "To encourage young Mormon writers and artists." Annual competition for short stories. Award: partial scholarship to Brigham Young University or Ricks College or cash awards. Competition receives approximately 300 submissions. Judges: *New Era* editors. Guidelines for SASE. Deadline December 31. Unpublished submissions. Contest open only to 12-23-year-old members of the Church of Jesus Christ of Latter-Day Saints.

NEW HAMPSHIRE STATE COUNCIL ON THE ARTS INDIVIDUAL ARTIST FELLOW-SHIP, (I, II, IV), 40 N. Main St., Concord NH 03301-4974. (603)271-2789. Artist Services Coordinator: Audrey V. Sylvester. Fellowship "for career development to professional artists who are legal/permanent residents of the state of New Hampshire." Award: Up to $3,000. Competition gives 8 awards in disciplines such as crafts, literature, music, dance, etc. Judges: Panels of in-state and out-of-state experts review work samples. Guidelines for SASE. Postmark deadline July 1 (1997, 1999). Submissions may be either previously published or unpublished. Applicants must be over 18 years of age; not enrolled as fulltime students; permanent, legal residents of New Hampshire 1 year prior to application. Application form required.

NEW LETTERS LITERARY AWARD, (I), UMKC, 5101 Rockhill Rd., Kansas City MO 64110-2499. (816)235-1168. Awards Coordinator: Glenda McCrary. Award to "discover and reward unpublished work by new and established writers." Annual competition for short stories. Award: $750 and publication. Competition receives 600 entries/year. Entry fee $10. Guidelines for SASE. Deadline May 15. Submissions must be unpublished. Length requirement: 5,000 words or less.

‡NEW MILLENNIUM WRITINGS, (I), Room 101, P.O. Box 40987, Nashville TN 37204. (423)428-0389. Editor: Don Williams. Award "to promote literary excellence in contemporary fiction." Semiannual competition for short stories, poetry and essays. Award: $1,000 (short story), $500 (poetry and essay) plus publication in *New Millennium Writings*. Competition receives approximately 1,000 submissions. Judges: novelists and short story writers. Entry fee: $10. Guidelines for SASE. Deadlines December 1 and June 1. Unpublished submissions. No required word length.

‡NEW WRITING AWARD, (I), *New Writing Magazine*, PO Box 1812, Amherst NY 14226-7812. E-mail: newwriting@aol.com. "We wish to reward *new* writing. Looking for originality in form and content." New and beginning writers encouraged. Annual open competition for prose (novel, novel excerpt, scripts, short story, essay, humor, other) and poetry. Deadline: December 31. Award: up to $3,000 for best entry. Additional awards for finalists. Possible publication. Judges: Panel of editors. Entry fee $10, $5 for each additional plus 15¢/page after 20 pages. Guidelines for SASE. No application form required—simply send submission with reading fee, SASE for manuscript return or notification, and 3×5 card for each entry, including: story name, author and address.

NEW YORK FOUNDATION FOR THE ARTS FELLOWSHIP, (I, II, IV), New York Foundation for the Arts, 14th Floor, 155 Avenue of the Americas, New York NY 10013. Contact: Penelope Dannenberg. Biennial competition for poetry, short stories, plays, screenplays, nonfiction literature and novels. Approximately 15 awards of $7,000 each. Competition receives approximately 700 submissions per category. Judges: Writers from New York State. Call for guidelines or send SASE. Manuscript sample (20 pp maximum) may be drawn from published or unpublished work. Applicants must be over 18; must have lived in New York state at least 2 years immediately prior to application deadline; and may not be currently enrolled in any degree program. Deadline: early October. "All submissions must be in manuscript form; copies of published work will not be accepted."

NEW YORK STATE EDITH WHARTON CITATION OF MERIT, (State Author), (III, IV), NYS Writers Institute, Humanities 355, University at Albany, Albany NY 12222. (518)442-5620. Associate Director: Donald Faulkner. Awarded biennially to honor a New York State fiction writer for a lifetime of works of distinction. Fiction writers living in New York State are nominated by an advisory panel. Recipients receive an honorarium of $10,000 and must give two public readings a year.

JOHN NEWBERY AWARD, (III, IV), American Library Association (ALA) Awards and Citations Program, Association for Library Service to Children, 50 E. Huron St., Chicago IL 60611. Executive Director: S. Roman. Annual award. Only books for children published in the US during the preceding year are eligible. Award: Medal. Entry restricted to US citizens-residents.

NFB WRITERS' FICTION CONTEST, (I), The Writers' Division of the National Federation of the Blind, 1203 S. Fairview Rd., Columbia MO 65203-0809. (Send submission to: Loraine Stayer, 2704 Beach Dr., Merrick NY 11566.) (573)445-6091. President: Tom Stevens. Award to "encourage members and other blind writers to write fiction." Annual competition for short stories. Three prizes of $40, $25, $15, plus two honorable mentions and possible publication in *Slate & Style*. Competition receives approximately 20 submissions. Entry fee $5 per story. For guidelines send SASE to Loraine Stayer at above address. Deadline May 1, 1997. Unpublished submissions. Word length: 2,000 words (maximum). "Send a 150-word bio with each entry. Please, no erotica."

‡CHARLES H. AND N. MILDRED NILON EXCELLENCE IN MINORITY FICTION AWARD, (I, IV), University of Colorado at Boulder and the Fiction Collective Two, English Dept. Publications Center, Campus Box 494, University of Colorado, Boulder CO 80309-0494. "We recognize excellence in new minority fiction." Annual competition for novels, story collections and novellas. Award: $1,000 cash prize; joint publications of mss by CU-Boulder and Fiction Collective Two. Competition receives approximately 60 submissions. Judges: Well-known minority writers. Guidelines for SASE. Deadline: November 30. Unpublished submissions. "Only specific recognized US racial and ethnic minorities are eligible. The definitions are in the submission guidelines. The ms must be book length (a minimum of 250 pages)."

NORTH AMERICAN NATIVE AUTHORS FIRST BOOK AWARD, (I, II, IV), *The Greenfield Review* Literary Center, P.O. Box 308, Greenfield Center NY 12833. (518)584-1728. Fax: (518)583-9741. Editor: Joe Bruchac. "To recognize and encourage writing by Native American authors (American Indian)." Annual award for fiction. Award: $500 and publication by the Greenfield Review Press. Competition receives 50-100 submissions. Judges: Anonymous. Guidelines for SASE. Deadline April 1. Published or unpublished (as a book) submissions. Native American authors only. Word length: prose mss no longer than 240 typed double-spaced pages.

NORTH CAROLINA ARTS COUNCIL FELLOWSHIP, (IV), 221 E. Lane St., Raleigh NC 27611. (919)733-2111. Literature Director: Deborah McGill. Grants program "to encourage the continued achievements of North Carolina's writers of fiction, poetry, literary nonfiction and literary translation." Biannual awards: Up to $8,000 each. Council receives approximately 200 submissions. Judges are a panel of editors and published writers from outside the state. Writers must be over 18 years old,

---

FOR INFORMATION ON ENTERING the *Novel & Short Story Writer's Market* Cover Letter Contest, see page 16.

not currently enrolled in degree-granting program, and must have been a resident of North Carolina for 1 full year prior to applying. Deadline November 1.

NORTH CAROLINA ARTS COUNCIL RESIDENCIES, (IV), 407 N. Person St., Raleigh NC 27601-2807. (919)733-7897. E-mail: dmcgill@ncacmail.dcr.state.nc.us. Literature Director: Deborah McGill. "To recognize and encourage North Carolina's finest creative writers." "We offer two- to three-month residencies for two writers at the LaNapoule Foundation in southern France every two years, an annual two- to three-month residency for one writer at Headlands Center for the Arts (California), and an annual one-month master class/residency for one writer at Vermont Studio Center." Judges: Editors and published writers from outside the state. Deadline for France, November 1, 1996; for US residencies, early June, 1997. Writers must be over 18 years old, not currently enrolled in degree-granting program on undergraduate or graduate level and *must have been a resident of North Carolina for 1 full year prior to applying*.

NORTH CAROLINA WRITERS' NETWORK SCHOLARSHIPS, (IV), P.O. Box 954, Carrboro NC 27510. Executive Director: Linda W. Hobson. "To provide North Carolina writers of fiction, poetry, and literary nonfiction (including children's literature) with opportunities for research or enrichment. Available on a minimum of three weeks' notice throughout the year." Award up to $500 (with $4,500 budgeted for the category). "To be eligible writers *must have lived in the state for at least a year*." Send SASE for application.

NORWEGIAN LITERATURE ABROAD GRANT (NORLA), (I), Bygdoy Allè 21, 0262 Oslo Norway. (47)22 43 48 70. Fax: (47) 22 44 52 42. E-mail: norla@nbr.no. Manager: Kristin Brudevoll. Award to "help Norwegian fiction to be published outside Scandinavia and ensure that the translator will be paid for his/her work." Annual compensation for translations, 50-60% of the translation's cost. Receives approx. 40-50 submissions. Judges: an advisory (literary) board of 5 persons. Guidelines for SASE. Deadline December 15. Previously published submissions. "Application form can be obtained from NORLA. Foreign (non-Scandanavian) publishers may apply for the award."

‡NTPWA ANNUAL POETRY & FICTION CONTEST, North Texas Professional Writer's Association, P.O. Box 563, Bedford TX 76095-0563. (817)428-2822. Fax: (817)428-2181. E-mail: justel@cris.com. Secretary: Elaine Lanmon. Award "to recognize and encourage previously unpublished writers." Annual competition for short stories, novels and poetry. Fiction awards: $50 (1st prize), $25 (2nd prize). Poetry awards: $25 (1st prize), $10 (2nd prize). Judges: published writers. Entry fee: $5 fiction, $3/2 poems. Guidelines for SASE. Deadline May 31, 1997. Unpublished submissions. Length: 25 pages (fiction); 25 lines (poetry). Winners announced July 15, 1997.

THE FLANNERY O'CONNOR AWARD FOR SHORT FICTION, (I), The University of Georgia Press, 330 Research Dr., Athens GA 30602. (706)369-6140. Fax: (708)369-6131. Contact: Award coordinator. Annual award "to recognize outstanding collections of short fiction. Published and unpublished authors are welcome." Award: $1,000 and publication by the University of Georgia Press. Deadline June 1-July 31. "Manuscripts cannot be accepted at any other time." Entry fee $10. Contest rules for SASE. Ms will not be returned.

FRANK O'CONNOR FICTION AWARD, (I), *descant*, Dept. of English, Texas Christian University, Fort Worth TX 76129. (817)921-7240. Business Manager: Claudia Knott. Estab. 1979 with *descant*; earlier awarded through *Quartet*. Annual award to honor the best published fiction in *descant* for its current volume. Award: $500 prize. No entry fee. "About 12 to 15 stories are published annually in *descant*. Winning story is selected from this group."

✦HOWARD O'HAGAN AWARD FOR SHORT FICTION, (II, IV), Writers Guild of Alberta, 3rd Floor, Percy Page Centre, 11759 Groat Rd., Edmonton, Alberta T5M 3K6. (403)422-8174. Fax: (403)422-2663. Assistant Director: Darlene Diver. "To recognize outstanding books published by Alberta authors each year." Annual competition for short stories. Award: $500 (Canadian) cash and leather bound book. Competition receives 20-30 submissions. Judges: selected published writers across Canada. Guidelines for SASE. Deadline December 31. Previously published submissions published between January and December 31. Open to Alberta authors only.

OHIOANA AWARD FOR CHILDREN'S LITERATURE, ALICE WOOD MEMORIAL, (IV), Ohioana Library Association, 65 S. Front St., Room 1105, Columbus OH 43215. (614)466-3831. Director: Linda Hengst. Competition "to honor an individual whose body of work has made, and continues to make, a significant contribution to literature for children or young adults." Annual award for body of work. Amount of award varies (approximately $500-1,000). Guidelines for SASE. Deadline December 31 prior to year award is given. "Open to authors born in Ohio or who have lived in Ohio for a minimum of five years."

OHIOANA BOOK AWARDS, (II, IV), Ohioana Library Association, 65 S. Front St., Room 1105, Columbus OH 43215. Contact: Linda R. Hengst, director. Annual awards granted (only if the judges believe a book of sufficiently high quality has been submitted) to bring recognition to outstanding books by Ohioans or about Ohio. Five categories: Fiction, Nonfiction, Juvenile, Poetry and About Ohio or an Ohioan. Criteria: Books written or edited by a native Ohioan or resident of the state for at least 5 years; two copies of the book MUST be received by the Ohioana Library by December 31 prior to the year the award is given; literary quality of the book must be outstanding. Awards: Certificate and glass sculpture (up to 6 awards given annually). Each spring a jury considers all books received since the previous jury. Award judged by a jury selected from librarians, book reviewers, writers and other knowledgeable people. No entry forms are needed, but they are available. "We will be glad to answer letters asking specific questions."

✸THE OKANAGAN SHORT FICTION AWARD, (I, IV), *Canadian Author*, 27 Doxsee Ave. N., Campbellford, Ontario K0L 1L0 Canada. (705)653-0323. Fax: (705)653-0593. Contact: Bill Valgardson, fiction editor. Award offered 4 times a year. To present good fiction "in which the writing surpasses all else" to an appreciative literary readership, and in turn help Canadian writers retain an interest in good fiction. Award: $125 to each author whose story is accepted for publication. Entries are invited in each issue of the quarterly *CA*. Sample copy for $5.50. "Our award regulations stipulate that writers must be Canadian, stories must not have been previously published, and be under 3,000 words. Mss should be typed double-spaced on 8½×11 bond. SASE with Canadian postage or mss will not be returned. Looking for superior writing ability, stories with good plot, movement, dialogue and characterization. A selection of winning stories has been anthologized as *Pure Fiction: The Okanagan Award Winners*, and is essential reading for prospective contributors."

OOPS AWARD, (I, IV), Oops Foundation, P.O. Box 1723, Costa Mesa, CA 92628. (619)598-7315. Contact: Dr. Oops. Award to "motivate people to write science fiction and science fiction satire." Annual competition for short stories. Award: first prize: $25; second prize: $10. Competition receives approx. 100 submissions. Guidelines available for SASE. Deadline June 13. Unpublished submissions. Open to amateur writers with less than 3 published short stories and no published books. Word length: 600 words minimum; 3,000 words maximum. "All submissions must be science fiction satire or science fiction. Please, no dungeons and dragons, fantasy, horror, sword and sorcery, vampire or werewolf stories. They won't be accepted."

OPEN VOICE AWARDS, (I), Westside YMCA—Writer's Voice, 5 W. 63rd St., New York NY 10023. (212)875-4124. E-mail: wtrsvoice@aol.com. Competition for fiction or poetry. Award: $500 honorarium and featured reading. Deadline December 31. "Submit 10 double-spaced pages in a single genre. Enclose $10 entry fee." Guidelines for SASE.

OPUS MAGNUM DISCOVERY AWARDS, (I), C.C.S. Entertainment Group, 433 N. Camden Dr., #600, Beverly Hills CA 90210. (310)288-1881. Fax: (310)288-0257. E-mail: awards@screenwriters.com. President: Carlos Abreu. Award "to discover new unpublished manuscripts." Annual competition for novels. Award: Film rights options up to $10,000. Judges: Industry professionals. Entry fee $75. Deadline December 1 of each year. Unpublished submissions.

ORANGE BLOSSOM FICTION CONTEST, (I), *The Oak*, 1530 Seventh St., Rock Island IL 61201. (309)788-3980. Editor: Betty Mowery. "To build up circulation of publication and give new authors a chance for competition and publication along with seasoned writers." Award given every 6 months for short stories. Award: $10 (first prize); $5 (second prize); 1-year subscription to *The Oak* (third prize). Competition receives approximately 75 submissions. Judges: various editors from other publications, some published authors and previous contest winners. Entry fee six 32¢ stamps. Guidelines for SASE. Deadline October 1. Word length: 500 words maximum. "May be on any subject, but avoid gore and killing of humans or animals."

‡OREGON INDIVIDUAL ARTIST FELLOWSHIP, (I, IV), Oregon Arts Commission, 775 Summer St. N.E., Salem OR 97310. (503)986-0082. Assistant Director: Vincent Dunn. "Award enables professional artists to undertake projects to assist their professional development." Biennial competition for short stories, novels, poetry and story collections. Award: $3,000. (Please note: ten $3,000 awards are spread over 5 disciplines—literature, music/opera, media arts, dance and theatre awarded in even-numbered years.) Competition receives approximately 140 entries/year. Judges: Professional advisors from outside the state. Guidelines and application for SASE. Deadline: September 1. Competition limited to Oregon residents.

DOBIE PAISANO FELLOWSHIPS, (IV), Office of Graduate Studies, University of Texas at Austin, Austin TX 78712. (512)471-7213. Coordinator: Audrey N. Slate. Annual fellowships for creative writing (includes short stories, novels and story collections). Award: 6 months residence at ranch;

$7,200 stipend. Competition receives approximately 100 submissions. Judges: faculty of University of Texas and members of Texas Institute of Letters. Entry fee: $10. Application and guidelines on request. "Open to writers with a Texas connection—native Texans, people who have lived in Texas at least two years, or writers with published work on Texas and Southwest." Deadline is the third week in January.

KENNETH PATCHEN COMPETITION, (I, II), Pig Iron Press, P.O. Box 237, Youngstown OH 44501. (330)747-6932. Contact: Jim Villani. Awards works of fiction and poetry in alternating years. Award: publication; $500. Judge with national visibility selected annually. Entry fee $10. Guidelines available for SASE. Reading period: January 1 to December 31. Award for fiction: 1998, 2000; fiction award for novel or short story collection, either form eligible. Previous publication of individual stories, poems or parts of novel OK. Ms should not exceed 500 typed pages.

PEARL SHORT STORY CONTEST, (I), *Pearl* Magazine, 3030 E. Second St., Long Beach CA 90803. (310)434-4523. Editor: Marilyn Johnson. Award to "provide a larger forum and help widen publishing opportunities for fiction writers in the small press; and to help support the continuing publication of *Pearl*." Annual competition for short stories. Award: $50, publication in *Pearl* and 10 copies. Competition receives approximately 100 submissions. Judges: Editors of *Pearl* (Marilyn Johnson, Joan Jobe Smith, Barbara Hauk). Entry fee $7 per story. Guidelines for SASE. Deadline December 1-March 15. Unpublished submissions. Length: 4,000 words maximum. Include a brief biographical note and SASE for reply or return of manuscript. Accepts simultaneous submissions, but asks to be notified if story is accepted elsewhere. All submissions are considered for publication in *Pearl*. "Although we are open to all types of fiction, we look most favorably upon coherent, well-crafted narratives, containing interesting, believable characters and meaningful situations."

JUDITH SIEGEL PEARSON AWARD, (I, IV), Wayne State University, Detroit MI 48202. Contact: Chair, English Dept. Competition "to honor writing about women." Annual award. Short stories up to 20 pages considered every third year (poetry and drama/nonfiction in alternate years). Fiction: 1997. Deadline: March 3, 1997. Award: Up to $400. Competition receives up to 100 submissions/year. Submissions are internally screened; then a noted writer does final reading. Entry forms for SASE.

WILLIAM PEDEN PRIZE IN FICTION, (I), *The Missouri Review*, 1507 Hillcrest Hall, University of Missouri, Columbia MO 65211. (573)882-4474. Contact: Speer Morgan, Greg Michalson, editors. Annual award "to honor the best short story published in *The Missouri Review* each year." Submissions are to be previously published in the volume year for which the prize is awarded. Award: $1,000. No entry deadline or fee. No rules; all fiction published in *MR* is automatically entered.

PEN CENTER USA WEST LITERARY AWARD IN FICTION, (II, IV), PEN Center USA West, 672 S. LaFayette Park Place, #41, Los Angeles CA 90057. (213)365-8500. Fax: (213)365-9616. Program Coordinator: Rachel Hall. To recognize fiction writers who live in the western United States. Annual competition for novels and story collections. Award: $500, plaque, and honored at a ceremony in Los Angeles. Competition receives approximately 100-125 submissions. Judges: panel of writers, booksellers, editors. Guidelines for SASE. Previously published submissions published between January 1, 1996 and December 31, 1996. Open only to writers living west of the Mississippi.

PEN/BOOK-OF-THE-MONTH CLUB TRANSLATION PRIZE, (II, IV), PEN American Center, 568 Broadway, New York NY 10012. (212)334-1660. Awards Coordinator: John Morrone. Award "to recognize the art of the literary translator." Annual competition for translations. Award: $3,000. Deadline December 15. Previously published submissions within the calendar year. "Translators may be of any nationality, but book must have been published in the US and must be a book-length literary translation." Books may be submitted by publishers, agents or translators. No application form. Send three copies. "Early submissions are strongly recommended."

THE PEN/FAULKNER AWARD FOR FICTION, (II, III, IV), c/o The Folger Shakespeare Library, 201 E. Capitol St. SE, Washington DC 20003. (202)675-0345. Fax: (202)608-1719. E-mail: delaney@folger.edu. Website: http://www.folger.edu. Attention: Janice Delaney, PEN/Faulkner Foundation Executive Director. Annual award. "To award the most distinguished book-length work of fiction published by an American writer." Award: $15,000 for winner; $5,000 for nominees. Judges: Three writers chosen by the Trustees of the Award. Deadline December 31. Published submissions only. Writers and publishers submit four copies of eligible titles published the current year. No juvenile. Authors must be American citizens.

PEN/NORMA KLEIN AWARD, (III), PEN American Center, 568 Broadway, New York NY 10012. (212)334-1660. Award Director: John Morrone. "Established in 1990 in memory of the late PEN member and distinguished children's book author, the biennial prize recognizes an emerging voice of literary merit among American writers of children's fiction. Candidates for the award are new authors whose books (for elementary school to young adult readers) demonstrate the adventuresome and innovative spirit that characterizes the best children's literature and Norma Klein's own work (but need not resemble her novels stylistically)." Award: $3,000. Judges: a panel of three distinguished children's authors. Guidelines for SASE. Previously published submissions. Writer must be nominated by other authors or editors of children's books. Next award: 1997.

JAMES D. PHELAN AWARD, (I, IV), Intersection for the Arts/The San Francisco Foundation, 446 Valencia St., San Francisco CA 94103. (415)626-2787. E-mail: intrsect@thecity.sfsu.edu. Literary Program Director: Charles Wilmoth. Annual award "to author of an unpublished work-in-progress of fiction (novel or short story), nonfictional prose, poetry or drama." Award: $2,000 and certificate. Rules and entry forms available after November 1 for SASE. Deadline January 31. Unpublished submissions. Applicant must have been born in the state of California, but need not be a current resident, and be 20-35 years old.

PLAYBOY COLLEGE FICTION CONTEST, (I, IV), *Playboy* Magazine, 680 N. Lake Shore Dr., Chicago IL 60611. (312)751-8000. Fiction Editor: Alice K. Turner. Award "to foster young writing talent." Annual competition for short stories. Award: $3,000 plus publication in the magazine. Judges: Staff. Guidelines available for SASE. Deadline: January 1. Submissions should be unpublished. No age limit; college affiliation required. Stories should be 25 pages or fewer. "Manuscripts are not returned. Results of the contest will be sent via SASE."

‡THE PLUM REVIEW FICTION CONTEST, (I), P.O. Box 1347, Philadelphia PA 19105-1347. (215)413-3158. Fiction Editor: Karen Faul. Annual competition for stories, all lengths, styles and subject matters. Award: $500 and publication in *The Plum Review*. Entry fee $10. Guidelines for SASE. Deadline November. Unpublished submissions. Word length: open.

POCKETS FICTION WRITING CONTEST, (I), *Pockets Magazine*, Upper Room Publications, P.O. Box 189, Nashville TN 37202-0189. (615)340-7333. Fax: (615)340-7006. (Do not send submissions via fax.) Associate Editor: Lynn Gilliam. To "find new freelance writers for the magazine." Annual competition for short stories. Award: $1,000 and publication. Competition receives approximately 600 submissions. Judged by *Pockets* editors and editors of other Upper Room publications. Guidelines for SASE. Deadline August 15. Former winners may not enter. Unpublished submissions. Word length: 1,000-1,600 words. "No historical fiction or fantasy."

EDGAR ALLAN POE AWARDS, (II, IV), Mystery Writers of America, Inc., 17 E. 47th St., Sixth Floor, New York NY 10017. Executive Director: Priscilla Ridgway. Annual awards to enhance the prestige of the mystery. For mystery works published or produced during the calendar year. Award: Ceramic bust of Poe. Awards for best mystery novel, best first novel by an American author, best softcover original novel, best short story, best critical/biographical work, best fact crime, best young adult, best juvenile novel, best screenplay, best television feature and best episode in a series. Contact above address for specifics. Deadline December 1.

KATHERINE ANNE PORTER PRIZE FOR FICTION, (I), *Nimrod International Journal of Prose and Poetry*, University of Tulsa, 600 S. College, Tulsa OK 74104. (918)584-3333. Editor: Francine Ringold. "To award promising young writers and to increase the quality of manuscripts submitted to *Nimrod*." Annual award for short stories. Award: $2,000 first prize, $1,000 second prize plus publication, two contributors copies and $5/page up to $5 total. Receives approx. 700 entries/ year. Judge varies each year. Past judges: Ron Carlson, Rosellen Brown, Alison Lurie, Gordon Lish, George Garrett, Toby Olson, John Leonard and Gladys Swan. Entry fee: $20. Guidelines for #10 SASE. Deadline for submissions April 15. Previously unpublished manuscripts. Length: 7,500 words maximum. "Must be typed, double-spaced. Our contest is judged anonymously, so we ask that writers take their names off of their manuscripts (need 2 copies total). Include a cover sheet containing your name, full address, phone and the title of your work. Include a SASE for notification of the results. We encourage writers to read *Nimrod* before submission to discern whether or not their work is compatible with the style of our journal. Back awards issues are $6 (book rate postage included), current issue is $8."

PRAIRIE SCHOONER THE LAWRENCE FOUNDATION AWARD, (II), 201 Andrews Hall, University of Nebraska, Lincoln NE 68588-0334. (402)472-0911. Contact: Hilda Raz, editor. Annual award "given to the author of the best short story published in *Prairie Schooner* during the preceding year." Award: $1,000. "Only short fiction published in *Prairie Schooner* is eligible for consideration. Manuscripts are read September-May."

THE PRESIDIO LA BAHIA AWARD, (II, IV), The Sons of the Republic of Texas, 1717 8th St., Bay City TX 77414. (409)245-6644. "To promote suitable preservation of relics, appropriate dissemination of data, and research into our Texas heritage, with particular attention to the Spanish Colonial period." Annual competition for novels. Award: "A total of $2,000 is available annually for winning participants, with a minimum first place prize of $1,200 for the best published book. At its discretion, the SRT may award a second place book prize or a prize for the best published paper, article published in a periodical or project of a nonliterary nature." Judges: recognized authorities on Texas history. Entries will be accepted from June 1 to September 30. Previously published submissions and completed projects. Competition is open to any person interested in the Spanish Colonial influence on Texas culture.

✤PRISM INTERNATIONAL SHORT FICTION CONTEST, (I), *Prism International*, Dept. of Creative Writing, University of British Columbia, E462-1866 Main Mall, Vancouver, British Columbia V6T 1Z1 Canada. (604)822-2514. E-mail address: prism@unixg.ubc.ca. Contact: Publicity Manager. Award: $2,000 first prize and five $200 consolation prizes. Deadline December 1 of each year. Entry fee $15 plus $5 reading fee for each story (includes a 1 year subscription). SASE for rules/entry forms.

✤PRIX LITTÉRAIRE CHAMPLAIN, (IV), Conseil De La Vie Francaise En Amérique, 56, Rue Saint-Pierre, 1, Le Étage, Quebec G1K 4A1 Canada. (418)692-1150. Fax: (418)692-4578. Director: Esther Taillon. Annual competition. Judges: jury. Guidelines for SASE. Deadline December 31. Previously published submissions. French-speaking Americans only.

PULITZER PRIZE IN FICTION, (III, IV), Columbia University, 702 Journalism Bldg., Mail Code 3865, New York NY 10027. (212)854-3841. Annual award for distinguished short stories, novels and story collections *first* published in America in book form during the year by an American author, preferably dealing with American life. Award: $5,000 and certificate. Guidelines available for SASE. Deadline: Books published between January 1 and June 30 must be submitted by July 1. Books published between July 1 and December 31 must be submitted by November 1; books published between November 1 and December 31 must be submitted in galleys or page proofs by November 1. Submit 4 copies of the book, entry form, biography and photo of author and $50 handling fee. Open to American authors.

PUSHCART PRIZE, (III), Pushcart Press, P.O. Box 380, Wainscott NY 11975. (516)324-9300. President: Bill Henderson. Annual award "to publish and recognize the best of small press literary work." Previously published submissions, short stories, poetry or essays on any subject. Must have been published during the current calendar year. Award: Publication in *Pushcart Prize: Best of the Small Presses*. Deadline: December 1. Nomination by small press publishers/editors only.

✤QSPELL BOOK AWARDS/HUGH MCLENNAN FICTION AWARD, (II, IV), Quebec Society for the Promotion of English Language Literature, 1200 Atwater, Montreal, Quebec H3Z 1X4 Canada. Phone/fax: (514)933-0878. Secretary: Carle Steele. "To honor excellence in writing in English in Quebec." Annual competition for short stories, novels, poetry and nonfiction. Award: $2,000 (Canadian) in each category. Competition receives approximately 50 submissions. Judges: panel of 3 jurors, different each year. Entry fee $10 (Canadian) per title. Guidelines for SASE. Previously published submissions published in previous year from May 15 to May 15. "Writer must have resided in Quebec for three of the past five years." Books may be published anywhere. Page length: more than 48 pages.

QUARTERLY WEST NOVELLA COMPETITION, (I), University of Utah, 317 Olpin Union, Salt Lake City UT 84112. (801)581-3938. Biennial award for novellas. Award: 2 prizes of $500 and publication in *Quarterly West*. Send SASE for contest rules. Deadline: postmarked by December 31.

QUINCY WRITERS GUILD ANNUAL CREATIVE WRITING CONTEST, (I), P.O. Box 433, Quincy IL 62306-0433. (217)222-2898. Contest Chairperson: Michael Barrett. "Award to promote writing." Annual competition for short stories, nonfiction, poetry. Awards: cash for first, second, third place entries; certificates for honorable mention. Competition receives approximately 40 submissions. Judges: Independent panel of writing professionals not affiliated with Quincy Writers Guild. Entry fee: $4 (Fiction and nonfiction, each entry); $2 (poetry each entry). Guidelines for SASE. Deadline April 15, 1997. Unpublished submissions. Word length: Fiction: 3,500 words; Nonfiction: 2,000 words. Poetry: any length, any style. "Guidelines are very important and available for SASE. No entry form is required. Entries accepted after January 1."

SIR WALTER RALEIGH AWARD, (II, IV), North Carolina Literary and Historical Association, 109 E. Jones St., Raleigh NC 27601-2807. (919)733-7305. Secretary-Treasurer: Jeffrey J. Crow. "To promote among the people of North Carolina an interest in their own literature." Annual award for novels. Award: Statue of Sir Walter Raleigh. Judges: University English and history professors. Guide-

"WE WANT TO PUBLISH YOUR WORK."

You would give anything to hear an editor speak those 6 magic words. So you work hard for weeks, months, even years to make that happen. You create a brilliant piece of work and a knock-out presentation, but there's still one vital step to ensure publication. You still need to submit your work to the right buyers. With rapid changes in the publishing industry it's not always easy to know who those buyers are. That's why each year thousands of writers, just like you, turn to the most current edition of this indispensable market guide.

Totally Updated Each Year

Keep ahead of the changes by ordering *1998 Novel & Short Story Writer's Market* today! You'll save the frustration of getting manuscripts returned in the mail stamped MOVED: ADDRESS UNKNOWN. And of NOT submitting your work to new listings because you don't know they exist. All you have to do to order the upcoming 1998 edition is complete the attached order card and return it with your payment. Order now and you'll get the 1998 edition at the 1997 price—just $22.99—no matter how much the regular price may increase! *1998 Novel & Short Story Writer's Market* will be published and ready for shipment in January 1998.

Keep on top of the ever-changing industry and get a jump on selling your work with help from the *1998 Novel & Short Story Writer's Market*. Order today—you deserve it!

Turn Over for More Great Books to Help Get Your Fiction Published! ➡

☐ **Yes!** I want the most current edition of *Novel & Short Story Writer's Market*. Please send me the 1998 edition at the 1997 price – $22.99. (NOTE: *1998 Novel & Short Story Writer's Market* will be ready for shipment in January 1998.) #10525

I also want more great books to help me sell my work!

Book # _____ Price $ _____

Book # _____ Price $ _____

Book # _____ Price $ _____

Book # _____ Price $ _____

Subtotal $_____

Add $3.50 postage and handling for one book; $1.00 for each additional book.

Postage and handling $_____

Payment must accompany order. Ohioans add 6% sales tax. Canadians add 7% GST.

Total $ _____

> **30-Day Money Back Guarantee on every book you buy!**

VISA/MasterCard orders call
TOLL-FREE 1-800-289-0963
8:30 to 5:00 Mon.-Fri. Eastern Time

☐ Payment enclosed $ _____ (or)

Charge my: ☐ Visa ☐ MasterCard Exp._____

Account #_____

Signature _____

Name _____

Address_____

City _____ State _____ Zip_____

Phone Number _____
(will be used only if we must contact you regarding this order.)

Mail to:

Writer's Digest Books
1507 Dana Avenue
Cincinnati, OH 45207

6941

Get Your Fiction Published with help from these Writer's Digest Books!

lines for SASE. Book must be an original work published during the 12 months ending June 30 of the year for which the award is given. Writer must be a legal or physical resident of North Carolina for the three years preceding the close of the contest period. Authors or publishers may submit 3 copies of their book to the above address.

READ WRITING & ART AWARDS, (I, IV), *Read* Magazine & Weekly Reader Corp., 245 Long Hill Rd., Middletown CT 06457. (203)638-2406. Fax: (203)346-5826. Associate Editor: Kate Davis. "To recognize and publish outstanding writing and art by students in grades 6-12." Annual awards for short story, essay and art. Award: $100 (first prize), $75 (second prize), $50 (third prize); publication of first-prize winner, certificates of excellence. Competition receives approximately 2,000 submissions. Judges: editors of Weekly Reader Corp. Guidelines for SASE or phone (860)638-2400. Guideline coupon must accompany each submission. Submissions should not be previously published. Word length: 5-6 pages typed double-space. "Fiction category may include short stories or play formats."

REGINA MEDAL AWARD, (III), Catholic Library Association, St. Joseph Central High School Library, 22 Maplewood Ave., Pittsfield MA 01201. Contact: Jean R. Bostley, SSJ Chair, CLA Awards Committee. Annual award. To honor a continued distinguished contribution to children's literature. Award: silver medal. Award given during Easter week. Selection by a special committee; nominees are suggested by the Catholic Library Association Membership.

RHODE ISLAND STATE COUNCIL ON THE ARTS, (I, IV), Individual Artist's Fellowship in Literature, 95 Cedar St., Suite 103, Providence RI 02903-1062. (401)277-3880. Contact: Individual Artist Program. Biennial fellowship. Award: $5,000. Competition receives approximately 50 submissions. In-state panel makes recommendations to an out-of-state judge, who recommends finalist to the council. Entry forms for SASE. Deadline: April 1, 1997. Artists must be Rhode Island residents and not undergraduate or graduate students. "Program guidelines may change. Prospective applicants should contact RISCA prior to deadline."

HAROLD U. RIBALOW PRIZE, (II, IV), *Hadassah Magazine*, 50 W. 58th St., New York NY 10019. (212)688-0227. Fax: (212)446-9521. E-mail: hadamag@aol.com. Contact: Alan M. Tigay, Executive Editor. Estab. 1983. Annual award "for a book of fiction on a Jewish theme. Harold U. Ribalow was a noted writer and editor who devoted his time to the discovery and encouragement of young Jewish writers." Book should have been published the year preceding the award. Award: $1,000 and excerpt of book in *Hadassah Magazine*. Deadline is April of the year following publication.

RITE OF SPRING FICTION CONTEST, (I), *Phantasm*, 1530 Seventh St., Rock Island IL 61201. (309)788-3980. Editor: Betty Mowery. "To build up circulation of publication and provide new authors a home for work along with seasoned authors." Award given every 6 months from March 31 to September 30. Competition for short stories. Awards: $10 (first place), $5 (second place), 1-year subscription to *Phantasm* (third place). Entry fee six 32¢ stamps. Guidelines for SASE. Deadline September 30. "Writers must submit their own fiction of no more than 500 words. We are looking for fiction of quiet horror or fantasy."

SUMMERFIELD G. ROBERTS AWARD, (I, II, IV), The Sons of the Republic of Texas, 1717 8th St., Bay City TX 77414. Executive Secretary: Melinda Williams. "Given for the best book or manuscript of biography, essay, fiction, nonfiction, novel, poetry or short story that describes or represents the Republic of Texas, 1836-1846." Annual award of $2,500. Deadline January 15. "The manuscripts must be written or published during the calendar year for which the award is given. Entries are to be submitted in quintuplicate and will not be returned."

‡ROMANTIC NOVELISTS' ASSOCIATION ROMANTIC NOVEL OF THE YEAR AWARD, (II, IV), 3 Arnesby Lane, Peatling Magna, Leicester LE8 5UN England. Tel: 0116/2478330. Contact: Major Award Organiser, Romantic Novelists' Association. "To publish good romantic fiction and therefore raise the prestige of the genre." Annual competition for novels. Award: under consideration. Competition receives approximately 150 submissions. Submissions period: September 1-December 1. For novels "published in the U.K. A modern or historical romantic novel. Three copies of each entry are required. They may be hardback or paperback. Only novels written in English and published in the U.K. during the previous 12 months (December 1-November 30) are eligible. Authors must be domiciled in U.K. or temporarily living abroad whilst in possession of British passport."

BRUCE P. ROSSLEY LITERARY AWARDS, (I, II, III, IV), 96 Inc., P.O. Box 15559, Boston MA 02215. (617)267-0543. Fax: (617)267-6725. Associate Director: Nancy Mehegan. "To increase the attention for writers of merit who have received little recognition." Annual award for short stories, novels and story collections. Award: $1,000 for the literary award and $100 for Bruce P. Rossley New Voice Award. Competition receives approximately 75 submissions. Judges: professionals in the fields of writing, journalism and publishing. Entry fee $10. Guidelines for SASE. Deadline September 30. Published or unpublished submissions. "In addition to writing, the writer's accomplishments in the fields of teaching and community service will also be considered." Open to writers from New England. Work must be nominated by "someone familiar with the writer's work."

CARL SANDBURG AWARDS, (I, IV), Friends of the Chicago Public Library, Harold Washington Library Center, 400 S. State St., Chicago IL 60605. (312)747-4905. Annual. To honor excellence in Chicago or Chicago area authors (including 6 counties). Books published between June 1 and May 31 of the following year. $1,000 honorarium for fiction, nonfiction, poetry and children's literature. Medal awarded also. Deadline August 1. All entries become the property of the Friends.

‡SATIRE WRITING CONTEST, (I), P.O. Box 340, Hancock MO 21750-0340. (301)678-6999. E-mail: satire@intrepid.net. Editor: Larry Logan. Award: "to promote the classic literary form/genre that is satire. We tried our first competition in 1996. If we decide it was successful, we plan to do it annually." For short stories, poems and essays. Award: "The total of the $5 entry fees will be split evenly among the three winners." Entry fee $5. Guidelines for SASE. Unpublished submissions. Length: 1,000 words.

THE SCHOLASTIC WRITING AWARDS, (I, IV), 555 Broadway, New York NY 10012. Program Coordinator: Evelyn Guzman. To provide opportunity for recognition of young writers. Annual award for short stories and other categories. Award: Cash awards and grants. Competition receives 25,000 submissions/year. Judges vary each year. Deadline: varies. "Please request entry form between September and December." Unpublished submissions. Contest limited to junior high and senior high students; grades 7-12. Entry blank must be signed by teacher. "Program is run through school and is only open to students in grades 7 through 12, regularly and currently enrolled in public and non-public schools in the United States and its territories, U.S.-sponsored schools abroad or any schools in Canada."

SCIENCE FICTION WRITERS OF EARTH (SFWoE) SHORT STORY CONTEST, (I, IV), Science Fiction Writers of Earth, P.O. Box 121293, Fort Worth TX 76121. (817)451-8674. SFWoE Administrator: Gilbert Gordon Reis. Purpose "to promote the art of science fiction/fantasy short story writing." Annual award for short stories. Award: $200 (first prize); $100 (second prize); $50 (third prize). Competition receives approximately 75 submissions/year. Judge: Author Edward Bryant. Entry fee $5 for 1st entry; $2 for additional entries. Guidelines for SASE. Deadline October 30. Submissions must be unpublished. Stories should be science fiction or fantasy, 2,000-7,500 words. "Although many of our past winners are now published authors, there is still room for improvement. The odds are good for a well-written story. Contestants enjoy international competition."

SE LA VIE WRITER'S JOURNAL CONTEST, (I, IV), Rio Grande Press, P.O. Box 71745, Las Vegas NV 89170. Contact: Rosalie Avara, editor. Competition offered quarterly for short stories. Award: Publication in the *Se La Vie Writer's Journal* plus up to $10 and contributor's copy. Judge: Editor. Entry fee $4 for each or $7 for two. Guidelines for SASE. Deadlines: March 31, June 30, September 30, December 31. Unpublished submissions. Themes: slice-of-life, mystery, adventure, social. Length: 500 words maximum.

SEATTLE ARTISTS PROGRAM, (IV), Seattle Arts Commission, 312 First Ave. N., Suite 200, Seattle WA 98109. (206)684-7171. Fax: (206)684-7172. "Award to support development of new works by Seattle's independent, generative writers." Biannual competition for short stories, novels. Award: $2,000 or $7,500. Competition receives approx. 150 submissions. Judges: peer review panels. Guidelines/application for SASE. Deadline June 28, 1997. Previously published submissions or unpublished submissions. Only Seattle residents or residents with a Seattle studio or office may apply. Word length: Word-length requirements vary; the guidelines must be read.

SEVENTEEN MAGAZINE FICTION CONTEST, (I, IV), *Seventeen Magazine*, 850 Third Ave., New York NY 10022. Contact: Ben Schrank. To honor best short fiction by a young writer. Rules published in the November issue. Contest for 13-21 year olds. Deadline April 30. Submissions judged by a panel of outside readers and *Seventeen*'s editors. Cash awarded to winners. First-place story considered for publication.

SFWA NEBULA® AWARDS, (III, IV), Science-fiction and Fantasy Writers of America, Inc., 5 Winding Brook Dr., #1B, Guilderland NY 12084. (518)869-5361. Executive Secretary: Peter Dennis Pautz. Annual awards for previously published short stories, novels, novellas, novelettes. Science fiction/fantasy only. "No submissions; nominees upon recommendation of members only." Deadline December 31. "Works are nominated throughout the year by active members of the SFWA."

SHORT AND SWEET CONTEST, (II, IV), Perry Terrell Publishing, M.A. Green Shopping Center, Inc., Metairie Bank Bldg., 7809 Airline Hwy., Suite 215-A, Metairie LA 70003. (504)737-7781. "The purpose is to inspire and encourage creativity in humor. (My personal purpose is to see who has a sense of humor and who doesn't.)" Monthly competition, 1 to 2 months after deadline, for short stories. Award: $5. Receives 15 to 47/month. Judges: Perry Terrell. Entry fee 50¢/entry. Guidelines for SASE. Send SASE for details."

✿SHORT GRAIN CONTEST, (I), Box 1154, Regina, Saskatchewan S4P 3B4 Canada. E-mail: grain.mag@sk.sympatico.ca. Website: http://www.sasknet.com/corporate/skwriter. ("E-mail entries not accepted.") Contact: J. Jill Robinson. Annual competition for postcard stories, prose poems and dramatic monologues. Awards: $500 (first prize), $300 (second prize) and $200 (third prize) in each category. "All winners and Honourable Mentions will also receive regular payment for publication in *Grain*." Competition receives approximately 1,500 submissions. Judges: Canadian writers with national and international reputations. Entry fee $20 for 2 entries in one category (includes one-year subscription); each additional entry in the same category $5. U.S. and International entries in U.S. dollars. U.S. writers add $4 U.S. postage. International writers add $6 U.S. postage. Guidelines for SASE or SAE and IRC. Deadline January 31. Unpublished submissions. Contest entries must be either an original postcard story (a work of narrative fiction written in 500 words or less) or a prose poem (a lyric poem written as a prose paragraph or paragraphs in 500 words or less), or a dramatic monologue (a self-contained speech given by a single character in 500 words or less).

SIDE SHOW ANNUAL SHORT STORY CONTEST, (II), Somersault Press, P.O. Box 1428, El Cerrito CA 94530-1428. (510)215-2207. Editors: Shelley Anderson, M.K. Jacobs and Kathe Stolz. "To attract quality writers for our 300-odd page paperback fiction annual." Awards: first: $500; second: $200; third: $100; $10/printed page paid to all accepted writers (on publication). Judges: The editors of *Side Show*. Entry fee $10 (includes subscription). Leaflet available but no guidelines or restrictions on length, subject or style. Sample copy for $10 plus $2 postage. Deadline June 30. Multiple submissions (in same mailing envelope) encouraged (only one entry fee required for each writer). Manuscripts with SASE critiqued, if requested. "A story from *Side Show* was selected for inclusion in *Pushcart Prize XVIII: Best of the Small Presses*."

BERNICE SLOTE AWARD, (II), *Prairie Schooner*, 201 Andrews Hall, University of Nebraska, Lincoln NE 68588-0334. (402)472-0911. Editor: Hilda Raz. "An award for the best work by a beginning writer published in *Prairie Schooner* during the previous year." Annual award for short stories, novel excerpts and translations. Award: $500. Judges: editorial board. Guidelines for SASE. Unpublished submissions. Must be beginning writers (not have a book published). "We only read mss September through May."

‡SNAKE NATION PRESS ANNUAL FALL CONTEST, (I), 110-#2 W. Force St., Valdosta GA 31601. (912)249-8334. Contact: Roberta George. "Because we pay only in contributor's copy, this contest allows us to give some financial compensation." Annual award for short stories. Awards: $300, $200, $100. Competition receives approximately 500 submissions. Judge: Independent ("it varies"). Entry fee $5 (includes contest issue). Guidelines for SASE. Deadline: September 1 (for annual summer issue). Unpublished submissions only. Length: 5,000 words maximum.

KAY SNOW CONTEST, (I, IV), Willamette Writers, 9045 SW Barbur Blvd., Suite 5-A, Portland OR 97219. (503)452-1592. Fax: (503)452-0372. E-mail: wilwrite@teleport.com. Contact: Contest Coordinator. Award "to create a showcase for writers of all fields of literature." Annual competition for short stories; also poetry (structured and nonstructured), nonfiction, juvenile and student writers. Award: $200 first prize in each category, second and third prizes, honorable mentions. Competition receives approximately 500 submissions. Judges: nationally recognized writers and teachers. Entry fee $15, nonmembers; $10, members; $5, students. Guidelines for #10 SASE. Deadline May 15 postmark. Unpublished submissions. Maximum 5 double-spaced pages or up to 3 poems per entry fee with maximum 5 double-spaced pages. Prize winners will be honored at the two-day August Willamette Writers Conference. Press releases will be sent to local and national media announcing the winners, and excerpts from winning entries may appear in our newsletter.

SOCIETY OF CHILDREN'S BOOK WRITERS AND ILLUSTRATORS GOLDEN KITE AWARDS, (II, IV), Society of Children's Book Writers and Illustrators, 22736 Vanowen St., Suite 106, West Hills CA 91307. (818)888-8760. Contact: Sue Alexander, chairperson. Annual award. "To recognize outstanding works of fiction, nonfiction and picture illustration for children by members of the Society of Children's Book Writers and Illustrators and published in the award year." Published submissions should be submitted from January to December of publication year. Deadline December 15. Rules for SASE. Award: Statuette and plaque. Looking for quality material for children. Individual "must be member of the SCBWI to submit books."

SOCIETY OF CHILDREN'S BOOK WRITERS AND ILLUSTRATORS WORK-IN-PROG-RESS GRANTS, (I, IV), 22736 Vanowen St., Suite 106, West Hills CA 91307. (818)888-8760. Contact: SCBWI. Annual grant for any genre or contemporary novel for young people; also nonfiction research grant and grant for work whose author has never been published. Award: First-$1,000, second-$500 (work-in-progress). Competition receives approximately 180 submissions. Judges: Members of children's book field—editors, authors, etc. Guidelines for SASE. Deadline February 1-May 1. Unpublished submissions. Applicants must be SCBWI members.

SONORA REVIEW SHORT STORY CONTEST, (I, II), Dept. of English, University of Arizona, Tucson AZ 85721. (520)626-2555. Contact: Fiction Editor. Annual contest to encourage and support quality short fiction. $500 first prize plus publication in *Sonora Review*. All entrants receive copy of the magazine. Entry fee $10. Send SASE for contest rules and deadlines.

SOUTH CAROLINA ARTS COMMISSION AND *THE POST AND COURIER* NEWSPAPER (CHARLESTON, SC) SOUTH CAROLINA FICTION PROJECT, (I, IV), 1800 Gervais St., Columbia SC 29201. (803)734-8696. Steve Lewis, director, Literary Arts Program. The purpose of the award is "to get money to fiction writers and to get their work published and read." Annual award for short stories. Award: $500 and publication in *The Post and Courier*. Competition receives between 200 and 400 submissions for 12 awards (up to 12 stories chosen). Judges are a panel of professional writers and Book Editor/Features Assistant Editor for *The Post and Courier*. Deadline: March 15. *South Carolina residents only*. Stories must not be over 2,500 words. Query for guidelines.

SOUTH CAROLINA ARTS COMMISSION LITERATURE FELLOWSHIPS AND LITERATURE GRANTS, (I, IV), 1800 Gervais St., Columbia SC 29201. (803)734-8696. Steve Lewis, director, Literary Arts Program. "The purpose of the fellowships is to give a cash award to a deserving writer (one year in poetry, one year in creative prose) whose works are of the highest caliber." Award: $7,500 fellowship. Matching project grants up to $5,000. Judges are out-of-state panel of professional writers and editors for fellowships, and panels and SCAC staff for grants. Query for entry forms or rules. Fellowship deadline September 15. Grants deadline November 15. *South Carolina residents only*. "The next deadline is for creative prose."

SOUTH DAKOTA ARTS COUNCIL, (IV), 800 Governors Dr., Pierre SD 57501-2294. (605)773-3131. "Individual artist's project grants—ranging from $500 to $3,000—are planned for the fiscal year 1998 through 2000." Guidelines for SASE. Deadline: March 1. Grants are open only to residents of South Dakota.

SOUTHERN ARTS LITERATURE PRIZE, (II, IV), 13 St. Clement St., Winchester, Hampshire S023 9DQ England. Award "to recognize good works by authors (known or unknown) in the southern region of the United Kingdom." Annual competition run on a 3-year cycle alternating fiction, poetry and nonfiction. Award £1,000 (plus winner commissions piece of work; value to £600). Competition receives 20-30 submissions. Judges: 3 people involved in literature or authors themselves; different each year. Guidelines for SASE. Southern arts region covers Hampshire, Berkshire, Wiltshire, Oxfordshire, Buckinghamshire, Isle of Wight and East Dorset. Write for information.

THE SOUTHERN PRIZE, (I), *The Southern Anthology*, 2851 Johnston St., #123, Lafayette LA 70503. Managing Editor: Dr. R. Sebastian Bennett. Award to "promote and reward outstanding writing; to encourage both traditional and avant-garde forms." Annual competition for short stories, novel excerpts and poetry. Award: $600 Grand Prize and publication; six finalists are also published. Judges: Editorial Panel. Entry fee $10. Guidelines for SASE. Postmark deadline: May 30, 1997. Unpublished submissions. "Available to all authors writing in English, regardless of citizenship. There are no form or genre restrictions. Submissions need not address 'Southern' themes. *The Southern Anthology* encourages both traditional and avant-garde writing." Word length: 7,500 words. "*The Southern Anthology* has no restrictions on style. However, we tend to prefer work which is oppositional or formally innovative in nature; which destablilizes established institutions or genres; or which portrays often-overlooked elements of society, avoiding or mimicking stereotypes. We do not subscribe to any political, aesthetic, or moral agenda; and detest conformance to 'political correctness' for its own sake. Often, we publish work which has been deemed 'too risky' for other journals. We also publish a variety of traditional forms."

THE SOUTHERN REVIEW/LOUISIANA STATE UNIVERSITY ANNUAL SHORT FICTION AWARD, (II), *The Southern Review*, 43 Allen Hall, Louisiana State University, Baton Rouge LA 70803. (504)388-5108. Contact: Editors, *The Southern Review*. Annual award "to encourage publication of good fiction." For a first collection of short stories by an American writer appearing during calendar year. Award: $500 to author. Possible campus reading. Deadline a month after close of each calendar year. The book of short stories must be released by a US publisher. Two copies to be submitted by publisher or author. Looking for "style, sense of craft, plot, in-depth characters."

WALLACE E. STEGNER FELLOWSHIP, (I, IV), Creative Writing Program, Stanford University, Stanford CA 94305-2087. (415)723-2637. Fax: (415)725-0755. Program Administrator: Gay Pierce. Annual award for short stories, novels, poetry and story collections. Five fellowships in fiction ($15,000 stipend plus required tuition of $5,000 annually). Entry fee $40. Guidelines for SASE. Deadline: the first working day following January 1st. For unpublished or previously published fiction writers. Residency required. Word length: 9,000 words or 40 pages.

STORY'S SHORT SHORT STORY COMPETITION, *Story* Magazine, 1507 Dana Ave., Cincinnati OH 45207. (513)531-2222. Editor: Lois Rosenthal. Award to "encourage the form of the short short and to find stories for possible publication in the magazine." Contest begins June 1 and closes October 31. Award: $1,000 (first prize); $500 (second prize); $250 (third prize); plus other prizes that change annually. Entry fee $10. Guidelines are published in the magazine. Word length: 1,500 words or less.

❧SUB-TERRAIN ANNUAL SHORT STORY CONTEST, (I), (formerly Penny Dreadful Annual Short Story Contest), *sub-TERRAIN Magazine*, P.O. Box 1575, Bentall Center, Vancouver, British Columbia V6C 2P7 Canada. (604)876-8710. Fax: (604)879-2667. E-mail: subter@pinc.com. Contact: Brian Kaufman. "To inspire writers to get down to it and struggle with a form that is condensed and difficult. To encourage clean, powerful writing." Annual award for short stories. Prize: $250 and publication. Runners-up also receive publication. Competition receives 300-400 submissions. Judges: An editorial collective. Entry fee $15 for one story, $5 extra for each additional story (includes 4-issue subscription). Guidelines for SASE in November. "Contest kicks off in November." Deadline May 15. Unpublished submissions. Length: 2,000 words maximum. "We are looking for fiction that has MOTION, that goes the distance in fewer words."

SUGAR MILL PRESS CONTESTS, (I, II), Perry Terrell Publishing, M.A. Green Shopping Center, Inc., Metairie Bank Bldg., 7809 Airline Hwy., Suite 215-A, Metairie LA 70003. (504)737-7781. "The purpose is to draw manuscripts from all writers, especially new writers, pay the winners first and reserve the right to print all (acceptable) material that is sent to Perry Terrell Publishing in *The Ultimate Writer, The Bracelet Charm, Amulet* or *The Veneration Quarterly*; also, to choose manuscripts of unique and outstanding quality to recommend to a small movie production company I have been invited to work with in California. (Writers will be notified before recommendation is made.)" Award is granted monthly, 4 to 6 months after contest deadlines. For short stories. Award: $100, $75, $50, $25 and 2 honorable mentions ($5). Competition receives 25 to 75/deadline. Judges: Perry Terrell, Editor; Jonathan Everett, Associate Editor; Julie D. Terrell, Features Editor. Entry fee $5. Guidelines for SASE. Deadlines are throughout each month. Previously published or unpublished submissions. "Please specify which deadline and/or contest being entered. If not specified, the editor will read, when time permits, and place the entry the next month." Send SASE for theme list.

THE JOAN G. SUGARMAN CHILDREN'S BOOK AWARD, (II, IV), Washington Independent Writers Legal and Educational Fund, Inc., 220 Woodward Bldg. 733 Fifteenth St. NW, Washington DC 20005. (202)347-4973. The Joan G. Sugarman Children's Book Award was established in 1987 to recognize excellence in children's literature. Biennial competition for novels "children's literature, both fiction and nonfiction, geared for children ages 15 and under." Award: $1,000. Competition receives approximately 100 submissions. Judges are selected by the WIW Legal and Educational Fund, Inc. They have included librarians, professors of children's literature and children's bookstore owners. Guidelines for SASE. For the 1996-1997 Award, the expected deadline is the end of January 1998. Previously published submissions. The authors must reside in Washington DC, Maryland or Virginia. There is no word-length requirement.

TARA FELLOWSHIP FOR SHORT FICTION, (I), The Heekin Group Foundation, P.O. Box 1534, Sisters OR 97759. (503)548-4147. Fiction Director: Sarah Heekin Redfield. "To support unpublished, beginning career writers in their writing projects." Two annual awards for completed short stories. Award: $1,500. Receives approximately 500 applications. Judges: Invitation of Publisher judge. Past judges: Graywolf Press, SOHO Press, Dalkey Archive Press, The Ecco Press. Application fee $25. Guidelines for SASE. Deadline December 1. Unpublished submissions. Word length: 2,500-10,000 words.

TENNESSEE ARTS COMMISSION LITERARY FELLOWSHIP, (I, II, IV), 404 James Robertson Pkwy., Suite 160, Nashville TN 37243-0780. (615)741-1701. Fax: (615)741-8559. E-mail: aswanson@mail.state.tn.us. Contact: Alice Swanson, director of literary arts. Award to "honor promising writers." Annual award for fiction. Award: at least $2,000. Competition receives approximately 30 submissions. Judges are out-of-state jurors. Previously published and unpublished submissions. Writers must be residents of Tennessee. Word length: 20 ms pages. Write for guidelines.

‡**TEXAS-WIDE WRITERS CONTEST, (I, IV)**, Byliners, P.O. Box 6218, Corpus Christi TX 78466. Contact: Contest Chairman. "Contest to fund a scholarship in journalism or creative writing." Annual contest for adult and children's short stories, novels and poems. Award: Novels—1st $75, 2nd $55, 3rd $30; short stories—1st $55, 2nd $40, 3rd $20. Competition receives approximately 30 novel, 60 short story and 45 children's story submissions. Judges: Varies each year. Entry fee $5/story, $10/ novel. Guidelines available for SASE. Deadline is February 28 (date remains same each year). Unpublished submissions. Limited to Texas residents and winter Texans. Length: Children's story limit 2,000 words; short story limit 3,000 words; novel 3-page synopsis plus chapter one. "Contest also has nostalgia, article and nonfiction book categories."

THURBER HOUSE RESIDENCIES, (II), The Thurber House, 77 Jefferson Ave., Columbus OH 43215. (614)464-1032. Literary Director: Michael J. Rosen. "Four writers/year are chosen as writers-in-residence, one for each quarter." Award for writers of novels and story collections. $5,000 stipend and housing for a quarter in the furnished third-floor apartment of James Thurber's boyhood home. Judges: Advisory panel. To apply, send letter of interest and curriculum vitae. Deadline: December 15. "The James Thurber Writer-in-Residence will teach a class in the Creative Writing Program at The Ohio State University in either fiction or poetry and will offer one public reading and a short workshop for writers in the community. Significant time outside of teaching is reserved for the writer's own work-in-progress. Candidates should have published at least one book with a major publisher, in any area of fiction, nonfiction, or poetry and should possess some experience in teaching."

✦**TICKLED BY THUNDER ANNUAL FICTION CONTEST**, Tickled By Thunder, 7385-129 St., Surrey, British Columbia V3W 7B8 Canada. Phone/fax: (604)591-6095. Editor: Larry Lindner. "To encourage new writers." Annual competition for short stories. Award: 50% of all fees, $100 minimum (Canadian), 1 year's (4-issue) subscription plus publication. Competition receives approximately 25 submissions. Judges: the editor and other writers. Entry fee $10 (Canadian) per entry (free for subscribers but more than one story requires $5 per entry.) Deadline February 15. Unpublished submissions. Word length: 2,000 words or less.

TOWSON STATE UNIVERSITY PRIZE FOR LITERATURE, (II, IV), Towson State University Foundation, Towson State University, Towson MD 21204. (410)830-2128. Contact: Dan L. Jones, Dean, College of Liberal Arts. Annual award for novels or short story collections, previously published. Award: $1,000. Requirements: Writer must not be over 40; must be a Maryland resident. SASE for rules/entry forms. Deadline May 15.

‡**TRAVEL MYSTERY CONTEST, (I, IV)**, *Whispering Willow's Mystery Magazine*, 2517 S. Central, P.O. Box 890294, Oklahoma City OK 73189-0294. (405)239-2531. Fax: (405)232-3848. Editor-in-Chief: Peggy D. Farris. Annual competition for short stories. Award: $200 (1st place), $125 (2nd place), plus publication. Competition receives approximately 30 submissions. Judge: Trula Johnson. Entry fee $10. Guidelines for SASE. Deadline July 1. Unpublished submissions. Mystery or mystery/ suspense stories only. Length: 500-2,500 words. "Write about a character in a setting away from his or her home. No explicit sex, gore, or extreme violence."

TRI-STATE FAIR LITERARY AWARDS, (I), % Cleo Smith, 8303 Broadway, Amarillo TX 79108-2206. (806)383-5772. Annual competition for prose and poetry. Offers small cash awards and Best of Show Awards in Adult and Youth (grades 1 through 12) Divisions. Judges: Different each year. Entry fee: $5 prose, $3 poetry, $1 haiku, students free. Guidelines for SASE. Deadline: August 1 (adults), August 30 (youth). Unpublished submissions. "Categories and length requirements may change a bit from year to year. Guidelines required. Open. Winners are displayed at Literary Booth at Tri-State Fair during Fair Week."

STEVEN TURNER AWARD, (II, IV), The Texas Institute of Letters, TCU Box 298300, Fort Worth TX 76129. (817)921-7822. Secretary: Judy Alter. "To honor the best first book of fiction published by a writer who was born in Texas or who has lived in the state for two years at some time,

---

MARKET CATEGORIES: (I) Unpublished entries; (II) Published entries nominated by the author; (III) Published entries nominated by the editor, publisher or nominating body; (IV) Specialized entries.

or whose work concerns the state." Annual award for novels and story collections. Award: $1,000. Judges: committee. Guidelines for SASE. Previously published submissions appearing in print between January 1 and December 31.

MARK TWAIN AWARD, (III, IV), Missouri Association of School Librarians, 8049 Highway E, Bonne Terre MO 63628-3771. Estab. 1970. Annual award to introduce children to the best of current literature for children and to stimulate reading. Award: A bronze bust of Mark Twain, created by Barbara Shanklin, a Missouri sculptor. A committee selects pre-list of the books nominated for the award; statewide reader/selectors review and rate the books, and then children throughout the state vote to choose a winner from the final list. Books must be published two years prior to nomination for the award list. Publishers may send books they wish to nominate for the list to the committee members. 1) Books should be of interest to children in grades 4 through 8; 2) written by an author living in the US; 3) of literary value which may enrich children's personal lives.

‡**VERY SHORT FICTION AWARD, Glimmer Train Stories**, 710 SW Madison St., Suite 504, Portland OR 97205. (503)221-0836. Editor: Linda Davis. Annual award offered to encourage the art of the very short story. Contest opens April 1 and ends July 31; entry must be postmarked between these dates. Awards: $1,200 and possible publication in *Glimmer Train Stories* (first place), $500 (second place), $300 (third place). Entry fee: $10 per story. Word length: 2,000 words maximum. First page of story should include name, address and phone number. "VSF AWARD" must be written on outside of envelope. No need for SASE as materials will not be returned. Results mailed to entrants in November. Editor will telephone winners by November 1.

VIOLET CROWN BOOK AWARD, (I, IV), Austin Writers' League, 1501 W. Fifth St., Suite E-2, Austin TX 78703. (512)499-8914. Fax: (512)499-0441. Executive Director: Angela Smith. Award "to recognize the best books published by Austin Writers' League members over the period September 1 to August 31 in fiction, nonfiction and literary (poetry, short story collections, etc.) categories." Annual competition for novels, story collections, translations. Award: Three $1,000 cash awards and trophies. Competition receives approximately 100 submissions. Judges: A panel of judges who are not affiliated with the Austin Writers' League. Entry fee $10. Guidelines for SASE. Deadline August 31. Previously published submissions between September 1 and August 31. "Entrants must be Austin Writers' League members. League members reside all over the U.S. and some foreign countries. Persons may join the League when they send in entries." Publisher may also submit entry in writer's name. "Awards are co-sponsored by the University Co-op Bookstore. Special citations are presented to finalists."

EDWARD LEWIS WALLANT MEMORIAL BOOK AWARD, (II, IV), 3 Brighton Rd., West Hartford CT 06117. Sponsored by Dr. and Mrs. Irving Waltman. Contact: Mrs. Irving Waltman. Annual award. Memorial to Edward Lewis Wallant offering incentive and encouragement to beginning writers, for books published the year before the award is conferred in the spring. Award: $500 plus award certificate. Books may be submitted for consideration to Dr. Sanford Pinsker, Department of English, Franklin & Marshall College, P.O. Box 3003, Lancaster PA 17604-3003. "Looking for creative work of fiction by an American which has significance for the American Jew. The novel (or collection of short stories) should preferably bear a kinship to the writing of Wallant. The award will seek out the writer who has not yet achieved literary prominence."

WELLSPRING SHORT FICTION CONTEST, *Wellspring Magazine*, The Writing Center, 4080 83rd Ave. N, Suite A, Brooklyn Park MN 55443. (612)566-6663. Award "to select well-crafted short fiction with interesting story lines." Biannual competition for short stories. Awards: $100, $75, $25 and publication. Competition receives approximately 80 submissions. Judges: writers and readers. Entry fee $10. Guidelines for SASE. Deadlines July 1, January 1. Unpublished submissions. Word length: 2,000 words maximum.

❦**WESTERN CANADIAN MAGAZINE AWARDS, (II, IV)**, 3898 Hillcrest Ave., North Vancouver, British Columbia V7R 4B6 Canada. (604)985-8991. "To honour and encourage editorial excellence." Annual competition for short stories (fiction articles in magazines). Award: $500. Entry fee: $18-24 (depending on circulation of magazine). Deadline: January. Previously published submissions (between January and December). "Must be Canadian or have earned immigrant status or be a full-time Canadian resident, and the fiction article must have appeared in a publication (magazine) that has its main editorial offices located in the 4 Western provinces, the Yukon or Northwest territories."

WESTERN HERITAGE AWARDS, (II, IV), National Cowboy Hall of Fame, 1700 NE 63rd St., Oklahoma City OK 73111. (405)478-2250. Contact: Lynda Haller, public relations director. Annual award "to honor outstanding quality in fiction, nonfiction and art literature." Submissions are to have been published during the previous calendar year. Award: The Wrangler, a replica of a C.M. Russell

Bronze. No entry fee. Entry forms and rules available October 1 for SASE. Deadline November 30. Looking for "stories that best capture the spirit of the West."

WESTERN STATES BOOK AWARDS, (III, IV), Western States Arts Federation, 236 Montezuma, Santa Fe NM 87501. (505)988-1166. Literature Coordinator: Robert Sheldon. Annual award "to recognize writers living in the West; encouragement of effective production and marketing of quality books published in the West; increase of sales and critical attention." For unpublished manuscripts submitted by publisher. Award: $5,000 for authors; $5,000 for publishers. Contest rules for SASE. Write for information on deadline.

WHITING WRITERS' AWARDS, (III), Mrs. Giles Whiting Foundation, 1133 Avenue of the Americas, New York NY 10036-6710. Director: Dr. Gerald Freund. Annual award for writers of fiction, poetry, nonfiction and plays with an emphasis on emerging writers. Award: $30,000 (10 awards). Candidates are submitted by appointed nominators and chosen for awards by an appointed selection committee. Direct applications and informal nominations not accepted by the foundation.

‡LAURA INGALLS WILDER AWARD, (III), American Library Association/Association for Library Service to Children, 50 E. Huron St., Chicago IL 60611. Executive Director: S. Roman. Award offered every 3 years; next year 1998. "To honor a significant body of work for children, for illustration, fiction or nonfiction." Award: Bronze medal.

WISCONSIN INSTITUTE FOR CREATIVE WRITING FELLOWSHIP, (I, II, IV), University of Wisconsin—Creative Writing, English Department, 600 N. Park St., Madison WI 53706. Director: Ron Wallace. Competition "to provide time, space and an intellectual community for writers working on first books." Annual award for short stories, novels and story collections. Award: $20,000/9-month appointment. Competition receives approximately 400 submissions. Judges: English Department faculty. Required guidelines available for SASE; write to Ron Kuka. Deadline is month of February. Published or unpublished submissions. Applicants must have received an M.F.A. or comparable graduate degree in creative writing. Limit one story up to 30 pages in length. Two letters of recommendation required.

PAUL A. WITTY SHORT STORY AWARD, (II), International Reading Association, P.O. Box 8139, 800 Barksdale Rd., Newark DE 19714-8139. (302)731-1600. Annual award given to the author of an original short story published for the first time in 1996 in a periodical for children. Award: $1,000. "The short story should serve as a literary standard that encourages young readers to read periodicals." For guidelines write to: Debra Gail Herrera, 111 E. Conner, Eastland, TX 76448. Deadline December 1. Published submissions.

THOMAS WOLFE FICTION PRIZE, (I), North Carolina Writers' Network, 3501 Hwy. 54 W., Studio C, Chapel Hlll NC 27516. "Our international literary prizes seek to recognize the best in today's writing." Annual award for fiction. Award: $500 and publication. Competition receives approximately 1,000 submissions. Entry fee $5. Guidelines for SASE. Deadline August 31. Unpublished submissions. Length: 12 double-spaced pages maximum.

WRITERS AT WORK FELLOWSHIP COMPETITION, Writers at Work (W@W), P.O. Box 1146, Centerville, UT 84014-5146. (801)292-9285. President: Dawn Marano. Program Administrator: Niquie Love. "Through the recognition of excellence in fiction and poetry, we hope to foster the growth of the supportive literary community which characterizes our annual conference in Park City, Utah." Annual competition for short stories, novels (novel excerpts) and poetry. Award: $1,500, a featured reading at and tuition for the afternoon sessions at 1997 conference, and publication in *Quarterly West* literary magazine (first prize); $500, tuition for the afternoon sessions at the 1997 conference and publication in the anthology (second prize). Competition receives 1,500 submissions. Judges: Faculty of Writers at Work Conference. Entry fee $12. Guidelines available for SASE. Deadline: March 15. Unpublished submissions. Open to any writer who has not yet published a book-length volume of original work. Word length: 20 double-spaced pages, one story (or excerpt) only; 6 poems, up to 10 total pages. "The 13th Annual Writers At Work Conference is scheduled for July 13-18, 1997."

THE WRITERS COMMUNITY RESIDENCY AWARDS, (II), The National Writer's Voice Project of the YMCA of the USA. 5 W. 63rd St., New York NY 10023. (212)875-4261. Program Director: Jennifer O'Grady. Offers semester-long residencies to mid-career writers at YMCAs nationwide. Biannual award for novels and story collections. Award: A semester-long residency. Residents conduct a master-level workshop and give a public reading at their host Writer's Voice center. Honoraria currently range from $6,000. Judges: A committee at each Writer's Voice center. Deadlines vary. Previously published submissions in book form. "Writers should apply directly to the Writer's Voice center, as application procedures vary. For a list of Writer's Voice center addresses, send SASE to The Writers Community, The National Writer's Voice Project, 5 W. 63rd St., New York NY 10023."

WRITER'S DIGEST ANNUAL WRITING COMPETITION, (Short Story Division), (I), *Writer's Digest*, 1507 Dana Ave., Cincinnati OH 45207. (513)531-2222. Contact: Contest Director. Grand Prize is an expenses-paid trip to New York City with arrangements to meet editors/agents in winning writer's field. Other awards include cash, reference books and certificates of recognition. Names of grand prize winner and top 100 winners are announced in the November issue of *Writer's Digest*. Top entry published in booklet ($5.75). Send SASE to *WD* Writing Competition for rules and entry form, or see January through May issues of *Writer's Digest*. Deadline: May 31. Entry fee $7 per manuscript. All entries must be original, unpublished and not previously submitted to a *Writer's Digest* contest. Length: 2,000 words maximum. No acknowledgment will be made of receipt of mss nor will mss be returned. Contest includes 2 short fiction categories: literary and genre/mainstream.

❀WRITERS GUILD OF ALBERTA LITERARY AWARD, (II, IV), Writers Guild of Alberta, 3rd Floor, Percy Page Centre, 11759 Groat Rd., Edmonton, Alberta T5M 3K6 Canada. (403)422-8174. Fax: (403)422-2663. Executive Director: Miki Andrejevic. "To recognize, reward and foster writing excellence." Annual competition for novels and story collections. Award: $500, plus leather-bound copy of winning work. Short story competition receives 5-10 submissions; novel competition receives about 20; children's literature category up to 40. Judges: 3 published writers. Guidelines for SASE. Deadline December 31. Previously published submissions (between January and December). Open to Alberta authors, resident for previous 18 months. Entries must be book-length and published within the current year.

❀WRITERS GUILD OF ALBERTA NEW FICTION COMPETITION, (I, IV), 3rd Floor, 11759 Groat Rd., Edmonton, Alberta T5M 3K6 Canada. (403)422-8174. Fax: (403)422-2663. Project Coordinator: Darlene Diver. Award "to encourage and publicize Albertan fiction writers." Biannual competition for novels. Award: $4,500 including a 12 month option for motion picture and TV rights. Competition receives approximately 50 submissions. Judges: A jury of respected writers. Entry fee $25. Guidelines for SASE. Deadline December 1, 1997. Unpublished submissions. The writer must have been a resident of the province of Alberta for 12 of the last 18 months. Word length: approx. 60,000 words. "On alternate years there is the *Write for Youth* competition. This competition is for children's literature."

WRITERS' INTERNATIONAL FORUM WRITING COMPETITION, (I), *Writers' International Forum*, P.O. Box 516, Tracyton WA 98393. Editorial Director: Sandra E. Haven. Award "to encourage strong storyline in a tight package." Two or more competitions per year for short stories. Awards: Cash prizes and certificates (amounts vary per competition). Competitions receive approx. 150 entries. Judges: *Writers' International Forum* staff. No entry fee for subscribers; entry fee for nonsubscribers for some competitions. Guidelines available for SASE. Previously unpublished submissions. "Length, theme, prizes, deadline, fee and other requirements vary for each competition. Send for guidelines. Entries are judged on creativity, technique, mechanics and appeal."

WRITERS' JOURNAL ANNUAL FICTION CONTEST, (I), Val-Tech Publishing, Inc., P.O. Box 25376, St. Paul MN 55125-0376. Publisher/Managing Editor: Valerie Hockert. Annual award for short stories. Award: first place, $50; second place, $25; third place, $15. Also gives honorable mentions. Competition receives approximately 500 submissions/year. Judges are Valerie Hockert, Glenda Olsen and others. Entry fee $5 each. Maximum of 3 entries/person. Entry forms or rules for SASE. Maximum length is 2,000 words. Two copies of each entry are required—one *without* name or address of writer.

WRITERS' JOURNAL ROMANCE CONTEST, (I), *Writers' Journal*, Val-Tech Publishing, Inc., P.O. Box 25376, St. Paul MN 55125-0376. Competition for short stories. Award: $50 (first prize), $25 (second prize), $15 (third prize), plus honorable mentions. Entry fee $5/entry. Guidelines for SASE (4 entries/person). Unpublished submissions. Word length: 2,000 words maximum. "Enclose #10 SASE for winner's list."

THE WRITERS' WORKSHOP INTERNATIONAL FICTION CONTEST, (I), The Writers' Workshop, P.O. Box 696, Asheville NC 28802. (704)254-8111. Executive Director: Karen Tager. Annual awards for fiction. Awards: $500 (1st prize), $250 (2nd prize), $100 (3rd prize). Competition receives approximately 350 submissions. Past judges have been D.M. Thomas, Mark Mathabane and Robert Creely. Entry fee $18/$15 members. Guidelines for SASE. Deadline: February 1. Unpublished submissions. Length: 20 typed, double-spaced pages per story. Multiple submissions are accepted.

WYOMING ARTS COUNCIL LITERARY FELLOWSHIPS, (I, IV), Wyoming Arts Council, 2320 Capitol Ave., Cheyenne WY 82002. (307)777-7742. Contact: Literature consultant. Annual awards to "honor the most outstanding new work of Wyoming writers—fiction, nonfiction, drama, poetry." Award: 4 awards of $2,000 each. Competition receives approx. 70-90 submissions. Judges: Panel of three writers selected each year from outside Wyoming. Guidelines for SASE. Deadline: June 15. Applicant "must be Wyoming resident for two years prior to application deadline. Must not be a full-time student." No genre exclusions; combined genres acceptable. 25 pages double-spaced maximum; 10 pages maximum for poetry. Winners may not apply for 4 years after receiving fellowships.

YOUNG READER'S CHOICE AWARD, (III), Pacific Northwest Library Association, Graduate School of Library and Information Sciences, P.O. Box 352930, FM-30, University of Washington, Seattle WA 98195. (206)543-1897. Contact: Carol A. Doll. Annual award "to promote reading as an enjoyable activity and to provide children an opportunity to endorse a book they consider an excellent story." Award: silver medal. Judges: children's librarians and teachers nominate; children in grades 4-8 vote for their favorite book on the list. Guidelines for SASE. Deadline February 1. Previously published submissions. Writers must be nominated by children's librarians and teachers.

Resources

Conferences and Workshops............ 532

Retreats and Colonies....................... 566

Organizations and Resources.......... 575

**Publications of Interest
to Fiction Writers**............................. 584

Websites of Interest........................ 588

Canadian Writers Take Note............. 590

**Printing and Production Terms
Defined**.. 591

Glossary.. 593

Category Index............................... 597

Markets Index................................. 621

Resources
Conferences and Workshops

Why are conferences so popular? Writers and conference directors alike tell us it's because writing can be such a lonely business otherwise—that at conferences writers have the opportunity to meet (and commiserate) with fellow writers, as well as meet and network with publishers, editors and agents. Conferences and workshops provide some of the best opportunities for writers to make publishing contacts and pick up valuable information on the business, as well as the craft, of writing.

The bulk of the listings in this section are for conferences. Most conferences last from one day to one week and offer a combination of workshop-type writing sessions, panel discussions, and a variety of guest speakers. Topics may include all aspects of writing from fiction to poetry to scriptwriting, or they may focus on a specific area such as those sponsored by the Romance Writers of America for writers specializing in romance or the SCBWI conferences on writing for children's books.

Workshops, however, tend to run longer—usually one to two weeks. Designed to operate like writing classes, most require writers to be prepared to work on and discuss their work-in-progress while attending. An important benefit of workshops is the opportunity they provide writers for an intensive critique of their work, often by professional writing teachers and established writers.

Each of the listings here includes information on the specific focus of an event as well as planned panels, guest speakers and workshop topics. It is important to note, however, some conference directors were still in the planning stages for 1997 when we contacted them. If it was not possible to include 1997 dates, fees or topics, we have provided information from 1996 so you can get an idea of what to expect. For the most current information, it's best to send a self-addressed, stamped envelope to the director in question about three months before the date(s) listed.

FINDING A CONFERENCE

Many writers try to make it to at least one conference a year, but cost and location count as much as subject matter or other considerations, when determining which conference to attend. There are conferences in almost every state and province and even some in Europe open to North Americans.

To make it easier for you to find a conference close to home—or to find one in an exotic locale to fit into your vacation plans—we've divided this section into geographic regions. The conferences appear in alphabetical order under the appropriate regional heading.

Note that conferences appear under the regional heading according to where they will be held, which is sometimes different than the address given as the place to register or send for information. For example, the Women's Wilderness Canoe Trips Writing Retreat is held in Mexico and is listed under the International heading, although writers are instructed to write to Sante Fe, New Mexico, for information.

The regions are as follows:

Northeast (pages 534-539): Connecticut, Maine, Massachusetts, New Hampshire, New York, Rhode Island, Vermont

Midatlantic (pages 539-542): Washington DC, Delaware, Maryland, New Jersey, Pennsylvania

Midsouth (pages 542-543): North Carolina, South Carolina, Tennessee, Virginia, West Virginia

Southeast (pages 543-546): Alabama, Arkansas, Florida, Georgia, Louisiana, Mississippi, Puerto Rico

Midwest (pages 546-550): Illinois, Indiana, Kentucky, Michigan, Ohio

North Central (pages 550-552): Iowa, Minnesota, Nebraska, North Dakota, South Dakota, Wisconsin

South Central (pages 552-556): Colorado, Kansas, Missouri, New Mexico, Oklahoma, Texas

West (pages 556-560): Arizona, California, Hawaii, Nevada, Utah

Northwest (pages 560-562): Alaska, Idaho, Montana, Oregon, Washington, Wyoming

Canada (pages 562-563)

International (pages 563-565)

LEARNING AND NETWORKING

Besides learning from workshop leaders and panelists in formal sessions, writers at conferences also benefit from conversations with other attendees. Writers on all levels enjoy sharing insights. Often, a conversation over lunch can reveal a new market for your work or let you know which editors are most receptive to the work of new writers. You can find out about recent editor changes and about specific agents. A casual chat could lead to a new contact or resource in your area.

Many editors and agents make visiting conferences a part of their regular search for new writers. A cover letter or query that starts with "I met you at the National Writers Association Conference," or "I found your talk on your company's new romance line at the Cape Cod Writers Conference most interesting . . . " may give you a small leg up on the competition.

While a few writers have been successful in selling their manuscripts at a conference, the availability of editors and agents does not usually mean these folks will have the time there to read your novel or six best short stories (unless, of course, you've scheduled an individual meeting with them ahead of time). While editors and agents are glad to meet writers and discuss work in general terms, usually they don't have the time (or energy) to give an extensive critique during a conference. In other words, use the conference as a way to make a first, brief contact.

SELECTING A CONFERENCE

Besides the obvious considerations of time, place and cost, choose your conference based on your writing goals. If, for example, your goal is to improve the quality of your writing, it will be more helpful to you to choose a hands-on craft workshop rather than a conference offering a series of panels on marketing and promotion. If, on the other hand, you are a science fiction novelist who would like to meet your fans, try one of the many science fiction conferences or "cons" held throughout the country and the world.

Look for panelists and workshop instructors whose work you admire and who seem to be writing in your general area. Check for specific panels or discussions of topics relevant to what you are writing now. Think about the size—would you feel more comfortable with a small workshop of eight people or a large group of 100 or more attendees?

If your funds are limited, start by looking for conferences close to home, but you may want to explore those that offer contests with cash prizes—and a chance to recoup your expenses. A few conferences and workshops also offer scholarships, but the competition is stiff and writers interested in these should find out the requirements early. Finally, students may want to look for conferences and workshops that offer college credit. You will find these options included in the listings here. Again, send a self-addressed, stamped envelope for the most current details.

The science fiction field in particular offers hundreds of conventions each year for writers, illustrators and fans. To find additional listings for these, see *Locus* (P.O. Box 13305, Oakland CA 94661). For more information on conferences and even more conferences from which to choose, check the May issue of *Writer's Digest*. *The Guide to Writers Conferences* (ShawGuides, 10 W. 66th St., Suite 30H, New York NY 10023) is another helpful resource now available on their website at http://www.shawguides.com.

Northeast (CT, MA, ME, NH, NY, RI, VT)

BREAD LOAF WRITERS' CONFERENCE, Middlebury College, Middlebury VT 05753. (802)388-3711 ext. 5286. E-mail: blwc@mail.middlebury.edu. Administrative Coordinator: Carol Knauss. Estab. 1926. Annual. Conference held in late August. Conference duration: 11 days. Average attendance: 230. For fiction, nonfiction and poetry. Held at the summer campus in Ripton, Vermont (belongs to Middlebury College).
Costs: $1,600 (includes room/board) (1996).
Accommodations: Accommodations are at Ripton. Onsite accommodations $560 (1996).

CAPE COD WRITERS' CONFERENCE of Cape Cod Writers Center, Inc., % Cape Cod Conservatory, Route 132, West Barnstable MA 02668. (508)375-0516. Executive Director: Arlene Joffe Pollack. Estab. 1963. Annual. Conference held: August 19-23. Conference duration: one week. Average attendance: 125. For fiction, nonfiction, poetry, juvenile writing and mystery/suspense. Held at Craigville Conference Center, a campus arrangement on shore of Cape's south side. Previous guest speakers and panelists have been Christine Tomasino, agent; Denise Little, editor; Art Buchwald; Bernard Cornwell, novelist and Sandra Goroff-Mailley, publicist.
Costs: $75 registration and $85 per course; housing and meals separate, paid to the Conference Center.
Accommodations: Information on overnight accommodations made available. On-site accommodations at Craigville Conference Center plus 3 meals, approx. $70/day.
Additional Information: Conference brochures/guidelines are available for SASE.

DOWNEAST MAINE WRITER'S WORKSHOPS, P.O. Box 446, Stockton Springs ME 04981. (207)567-4317. Fax: (207)567-3023. E-mail: 6249304@mcimail.com. Director: Janet J. Barron. Estab. 1994. Held periodically throughout the year. Writing workshops geared towards beginning writers: 1-, 2-, 3-, 5- and 7-day "modular" workshops (writers can attend complete workshops, or for the specific days during the summer and fall each year. 1997 workshops will include Writing for the Children's Market, Creative Writing (basics of Fiction & Nonfiction), How to Get Your Writing Published, and a Sampler (a half-day gourmet taste of Fiction, Nonfiction, Writing for the Children's Market, Poetry, Scriptwriting, and How to Get Published). Average attendance: 3-15. Workshops held "in the studio of a 275-year-old historic building on the beautiful coast of Maine. Our director/teacher is a 27-year publishing industry author/editor, publisher and instructor."
Costs: Tuition (includes lunch): by-the-day, $115; 3-day, $295; 5-day, $4.95; 7-day, $675 ("we accept Visa and MC"). Accommodations additional. "Accomodations and meals at area locations are extremely reasonable."
Accommodations: Attendees must make their own transportation arrangements. Discounts and a list of area B&Bs and inns are available.
Additional Information: "DEMWW has a 'Writer's Clinic' for those who seek feedback on their work. We do not require writers to submit work before or during. Our workshops are for beginning writers who want to learn practical, inside-the-industry-information on how to write for publication. Each of our workshops concentrates on only one aspect of writing and has only one professional

author/editor/publisher instructor." Conference brochures/guidelines are available for SASE.

EASTERN WRITERS' CONFERENCE, English Dept., Salem State College, Salem MA 01970. (508)741-6330. E-mail: rkessler@mecn.mass.edu. Conference Director: Rod Kessler. Estab. 1977. Annual. Conference held over a weekend in late June. Average attendance: 60. Conference to "provide a sense of community and support for area poets and prose writers. We try to present speakers and programs of interest, changing our format from time to time. Conference-goers have an opportunity to read to an audience or have manuscripts professionally critiqued. We tend to draw regionally." Previous speakers have included Nancy Mairs, Susanna Kaysen, Katha Pollitt, Bill Littlefield.
Costs: "Under $100."
Accommodations: Available on campus.
Additional Information: "Optional manuscript critiques are available for an additional fee." Conference brochures/guidelines available for SASE.

THE FIGURATIVE LANGUAGE MASTER CLASS, 441 E. 20th St., Suite 11B, New York NY 10010-7515. (212)674-1143. Director: Sheila Davis. Estab. 1993. 3 times a year. Workshop duration: 8 weeks. Average attendance: limited to 10. "A unique enrichment for all writers of: fiction, ad copy, cartoons, lyrics, editorials, press releases, newsletters and brochures. This course will expand and enhance your usual ways of thinking and expressing ideas through the practice of figurative language. You'll also acquire new skills in structuring your thoughts to make your writing more forceful and thus—more marketable." The conference is held at the New York headquarters of the Songwriters Guild of America.
Costs: $300.
Additional Information: Application form available for SASE.

FINE ARTS WORK CENTER IN PROVINCETOWN, 24 Pearl St., Provincetown MA 02657. (508)487-9960. Summer Program Coordinator: Jon Loomis. Conference "located on the grounds of the former Days Lumberyard complex. The facility has offered studio space to artists and writers since 1914." Offers 1-week open enrollment workshops in fiction, poetry and nonfiction, June 23-August 31. Faculty includes Grace Paley, Michael Cunningham, Mark Doty, Yusef Komunyazlez, Tama Janowitz and Carole Maso.
Costs: Catalog available January 1997.
Additional Information: Writers' apartments are in "several houses and a refurbished Victorian barn."

DOROTHY CANFIELD FISHER WRITERS CONFERENCE, P.O. Box 1058, Waitsfield VT 05673-1058. (802)496-3271. Fax: (802)496-7271. E-mail: kwerner@aol.com; Director: Kitty Werner. Estab. 1990. Annually, fourth weekend in June. Conference duration: 2 days. Average attendance: 100-116. For "fiction, nonfiction, marketing, journalism, occasionally screenplays. Emphasis on improving writing skills and marketing." Conference held at the Sheraton-Burlington Hotel in Burlington VT. Workshop leaders come from NY and Vermont and have included: Dawn Raffel (*Redbook*); Margaret Daly (*BH&G*); Meg Ruley (agent); Jackier Cantor (Dell), Hamilton Cain (Scribner), Sue Yuen (agent), and writers Dawn Renor, Mark T. Sullivan, Archer Mayor, William Noble, Ron Powers.
Costs: $100-160 registration includes snacks and lunch, two dinners are separate.
Accommodations: Burlington airport is 2 miles away—Sheraton has free shuttle service. "Our brochure has all the information for registration and staying at the Sheraton at special rates." Costs are from $177 quad to $324 single; includes conference registration.
Additional Information: Conference brochures/guidelines are available for SASE.

‡THE FOUNDATIONS OF CREATIVITY® WRITING WORKSHOP, The Elizabeth Ayres Center for Creative Writing, 155 E. 31st St., Suite 4-R, New York NY 10016. (212)689-4692. Founder: Elizabeth Ayres. Estab. 1990. Conference held 10 times/year. Workshops begin every 7 weeks, 1 time/ week for 6 weeks. Average attendance: 10. "The purpose of the workshop is to help fledgling writers conquer their fear of the blank page; develop imaginative tools; capitalize on the strengths of their natural voice and style; develop confidence; and interact with other writers in a stimulating, supportive atmosphere."

CAN'T FIND A CONFERENCE? Conferences are listed by region. Check the introduction to this section for a list of regional categories.

Costs: $235 (1996).
Additional Information: Workshop brochures and guidelines free.

IWWG SUMMER CONFERENCE, % International Women's Writing Guild, P.O. Box 810, Gracie Station, New York NY 10028. (212)737-7536. Executive Director: Hannelore Hahn. Estab. 1977. Annual. Average attendance: 400, including international attendees. Conference to promote writing in all genres, personal growth and professional success. Conference is held "on the tranquil campus of Skidmore College in Saratoga Springs, NY, where the serene Hudson Valley meets the North Country of the Adirondacks." Fifty different workshops are offered. Overall theme: "Writing Towards Personal and Professional Growth."
Costs: $300 for week-long program, plus room and board.
Accommodations: Transportation by air to Albany, New York, or Amtrak train available from New York City. Conference attendees stay on campus.
Additional Information: Features "lots of critiquing sessions and contacts with literary agents." Conference brochures/guidelines available for SASE.

MANHATTANVILLE COLLEGE WRITERS' WEEK, 2900 Purchase St., Purchase NY 10577. (914)694-3425. Dean of Adult and Special Programs: Ruth Dowd, R.S.C.J. Estab. 1982. Annual. Conference held last week in June. Average attendance: 90. "The Conference is designed not only for writers but for teachers of writing. Each workshop is attended by a Master teacher who works with the writers/teachers in the afternoon to help them to translate their writing skills for classroom use. Workshops include children's literature, journal writing, creative nonfiction, personal essay, poetry, fiction, travel writing and short fiction. Manhanttanville is a suburban campus 30 miles from New York City. The campus centers around Reid Castle, the administration building, the former home of Whitelaw Reid. Workshops are conducted in Reid Castle. We usually feature a major author as guest lecturer during the Conference. Past speakers have included such authors as Toni Morrison, Mary Gordon, Gail Godwin, Pete Hamill and poet Mark Doty."
Costs: Conference cost was $733 in 1996 for 2 graduate credits plus $40 fee.
Accommodations: Students may rent rooms in the college residence halls. More luxurious accommodations are available at neighboring hotels. In the summer of 1996 the cost of renting a room in the residence halls was $25 per night.
Additional Information: Conference brochures/guidelines are available for SASE.

MOHONK'S WRITERS RETREAT, Lake Mohonk, New Paltz NY 12561. (914)255-1000. Fax: (914)256-2161. Contact: Helen Dorsey. Estab. 1993. Annual. Conference held March 6-9, 1997. Conference duration: 4 nights and 3 days. Average attendance: 80. "The conference is held at Mohonk Mountain House, a 128-year-old National Historic Landmark, featuring 275 guest rooms, situated on mountaintop and lakeside resort property." Conference includes lectures, hands-on writing workshops and individual ms consultations. Retreat leaders have included Cynthia Blair, Carole Hebald, Priscilla Dunhill and William Least-Heatmoon.
Costs: "The cost of the workshop is included in the overnight room rate of $171-287/day plus $25 program fee; service charge and tax are additional."
Accommodations: "Transportation from Stewart airport and the Poughkeepsie train station can be arranged through our transporation desk."
Additional Information: Critiques mss; should be 4 pages, double-spaced, mailed at least 1 month prior to the event. A private consultation is available during the workshop. Conference brochures/ guidelines are available for SASE.

NEWPORT WRITERS CONFERENCE, % Community Writers Association, P.O. Box 12, Newport RI 02840. (401)846-9884. E-mail: comwriters@wsii.com. Executive Director: Eleyne Austen Sharp. Estab. 1992. Annual. Conference held in fall. Conference duration: 3 days. For fiction, magazine writing, screenwriting, writing for children, hypertext fiction and getting your book published. "Held at The Inn at Shadow Lawn, a beautiful Victorian home with a pleasant view of rolling lawns and gardens. Guest rooms are named for female Victorian writers; some have kitchens and working fireplaces. Writing workshops are located in the downstairs parlor and library." Previous speakers have been Robert B. Parker (*Spenser* detective series author), Marci Coyote Rose (comedy writer and

---

MARKET CONDITIONS are constantly changing! If you're still using this book and it is 1998 or later, buy the newest edition of *Novel & Short Story Writer's Market* at your favorite bookstore or order from Writer's Digest Books.

performer), John G. McDaid (science fiction author), James Gabriel Berman (author of *Uninvited*), Jennifer Moyer (editor), Britt Bell (former publisher of *Small Press Magazine*), and Cynthia Sterling (literary agent at Lee Shore Agency).
Costs: (1996) full tuition, $295.
Accommodations: Accommodations available at The Inn at Shadow Lawn (conference site). Ranges from $95 per night.
Additional Information: Offers evaluations on mss (short stories, essays and novel chapters). Sponsors the annual CWA Writing Competition. Poetry and short story submissions accepted. Entries judged by panel of qualified writing professionals. Conference brochures/guidelines are available for #10 SASE.

‡ODYSSEY, 316 Perley Rd., Francestown NH 03043. Phone/fax: (603)547-3530. Director: Jeanne Cavelos. Estab. 1995. Annual. Workshop to be held June 16 to July 25, 1997. Attendance limited to 20. "A workshop for fantasy, science fiction and horror writers. An additional workshop on romance writing may be added in 1997." Conference held at New Hampshire College in Manchester, New Hampshire. 1996 guest lecturers included: Hal Clement, Jane Yolen, Elizabeth Hand, Ellen Kushner, Craig Shaw Gardner and Leigh Grossman.
Costs: In 1996: $980 tuition, $270 housing (double room), $20 application fee, $525 food (approximate), $55 processing fee to receive college credit.
Accommodations: "Workshop students stay at a New Hampshire College dorm and eat at college."
Additional Information: Students must apply and include a writing sample. Students' works are critiqued throughout the 6 weeks. Workshop brochures and guidelines available for SASE.

‡ROBERT QUACKENBUSH'S CHILDREN'S BOOK WRITING & ILLUSTRATING WORKSHOPS, 460 E. 79th St., New York NY 10021. (212)744-3822. Instructor: Robert Quackenbush. Estab. 1982. Annual. Workshop held the second week in July. Average attendance: limited to 10. Workshops to promote writing and illustrating books for children. Held at the Manhattan studio of Robert Quackenbush, author and illustrator of over 160 books for young readers. "Focus is generally on picture books. All classes led by Robert Quackenbush."
Costs: $650 tuition covers all costs of the workshop, but does not include housing and meals. A $100 nonrefundable deposit is required with the $550 balance due two weeks prior to attendance.
Accommodations: A list of recommended hotels and restaurants is sent upon receipt of deposit.
Additional Information: Class is for beginners and professionals. Critiques during workshop. Private consultations also available at an hourly rate. "Programs suited to your needs; individualized schedules can be designed. Write or phone to discuss your goals and you will receive a prompt reply." Conference brochures are available for SASE.

‡SCBWI CONFERENCE IN CHILDREN'S LITERATURE, NYC, P.O. Box 20233, Park West Finance Station, New York NY 10025. Chairman: Kimberly Colen. Estab. 1975. Annual. Conference held 1st (or 2nd) Saturday in November. Average attendance: 350. Conference is to promote writing for children: picture books; fiction; nonfiction; middle grade and young adult; meet an editor; meet an agent; financial planning for writers; marketing your book; children's multimedia, etc. Held at Bank Street College, 610 W. 112th St., New York City.
Costs: $60, members; $65 nonmembers; $10 additional on day of conference.
Accommodations: No accommodations available. Write for information; hotel names will be supplied.
Additional Information: Conference brochures/guidelines are available for SASE. For information, call (214)363-4491 or (718)937-6810.

SCBWI/HOFSTRA CHILDREN'S LITERATURE CONFERENCE, 375 Hofstra University, University College of Continuing Education, Republic Hall, Hempstead NY 11550. (516)463-5016. Co-organizers: Connie C. Epstein, Adrienne Betz and Lewis Shena. Estab. 1985. Annual. Conference to be held April 26, 1997. Average attendance: 150. Conference to encourage good writing for children. "Purpose is to bring together various professional groups—writers, illustrators, librarians, teachers—who are interested in writing for children. Each year we organize the program around a theme. Last year it was The Path to Excellence." The conference takes place at the Student Center Building of Hofstra University, located in Hempstead, Long Island. "We have two general sessions, an editorial panel and five break-out groups held in rooms in the Center or nearby classrooms." This year's conference will feature Diane Roback of *Publishers Weekly* as one of the 2 general speakers, and 2 children's book editors will critique randomly selected first-manuscript pages submitted by registrants. Special interest groups will be offered in picture books (Kay Chorao), nonfiction (Ann McGovern) and writing mysteries (Carol Barkin and Betsy James) with others in fiction. Submission procedures to be decided.
Cost: $53 (previous year) for SCBWI members; $60 for nonmembers. Lunch included.

STATE OF MAINE WRITERS' CONFERENCE, P.O. Box 7146, Ocean Park ME 04063. (207)934-9806 June-August; (413)596-6734 September-May. Chairman: Richard F. Burns. Estab. 1941. Annual. Conference held August 19-22, 1997. Conference duration: 4 days. Average attendance: 50. "We try to present a balanced as well as eclectic conference. There is quite a bit of time and attention given to poetry but we also have children's literature, mystery writing, travel, novels/fiction and lots of items and issues of interest to writers such as speakers who are: publishers, editors, illustrators and the like. Our concentration is, by intention, a general view of writing to publish. We are located in Ocean Park, a small seashore village 14 miles south of Portland. Ours is a summer assembly center with many buildings from the Victorian Age. The conference meets in Porter Hall, one of the assembly buildings which is listed on the National Register of Historic Places. Within recent years our guest list has included Lewis Turco, Bob Anderson, David McCord, Dorothy Clarke Wilson, John N. Cole, Betsy Sholl, John Tagliabue, Christopher Keane and many others. We usually have about 10 guest presenters a year."
Costs: $85 includes the conference banquet. There is a reduced fee, $40, for students ages 21 and under. The fee does not include housing or meals which must be arranged separately by the conferees.
Accommodations: An accommodations list is available. "We are in a summer resort area and motels, guest houses and restaurants abound."
Additional Information: "We have a contest announcement which comes out in January-March and has about 15 contests on various genres. The prizes, all modest, are awarded at the end of the conference and only to those who are registered." Send SASE for program guide available in April-June.

‡STONECOAST, University of Southern Maine, P.O. Box 9300, Portland ME 04104-9300. (207)780-5617. Conference Director: Barbara Hope. Estab. 1979. Annual. Conference held in mid-July. Conference duration: 10 days. Average attendance: 90-100. "Conference concentrates on fiction, poetry, genre and creative nonfiction. Freeport, Maine, is the site of the conference. Workshops are at the University of Southern Maine Stone House Conference Center." 1996 speakers included Joyce Johnson, Manette Ansay, Michael Seidman, David Huddle, Carolyn Chute and David Bradley.
Costs: $440 includes tuition.
Accommodations: Accommodations provided in university housing.
Additional Information: Scholarships available for various groups.

WELLS WRITERS' WORKSHOPS, 69 Broadway, Concord NH 03301. (603)225-9162. Director: Victor A. Levine. Estab. 1988. Held: 2 times/year in Wells, Maine. Conferences held in May and September. Maximum attendance: 6. "Workshop concentrates on short and long fiction, especially the novel. Focus is on the rational structuring of a story, using Aristotelian and scriptwriting insights. Throughout, the workshop balances direct instruction with the actual plotting and writing of the basic scenes of a novel or short story." Workshops located in a "large, airy and light house overlooking the ocean with ample individual space for writers and group conferences. While the purpose of the workshop is to teach the process of plotting as it applies across the board—to all kinds of fiction, including novels, short stories, movies—it strives to meet the specific needs of participants, especially through individual conferences with the instructors."
Costs: "The cost of $1,050 covers tuition, room and board. Registration cost is $95 (nonrefundable). Payment may be in two or three installments."
Accommodations: Workshop supplies transportation from/to Portland International Airport—or other places, by arrangement. Workshop supplies accommodations.
Additional Information: Conference brochures/guidelines available for SASE. "Workshop has a scholarship fund which can, as it has in the past, defray part of the total expense."

WESLEYAN WRITERS CONFERENCE, Wesleyan University, Middletown CT 06459. (860)685-3604. Director: Anne Greene. Estab. 1956. Annual. Conference held the last week in June. Average attendance: 100. For fiction techniques, novel, short story, poetry, screenwriting, nonfiction, literary journalism, memoir. The conference is held on the campus of Wesleyan University, in the hills overlooking the Connecticut River. Meals and lodging are provided on campus. Features readings of new fiction and guest lectures on a range of topics including publishing.
Costs: In 1996, tuition $450; meals $185; room $105.
Accommodations: "Participants can fly to Hartford or take Amtrak to Meriden, CT. We are happy to help participants make travel arrangements." Overnight participants stay on campus.
Additional Information: Manuscript critiques are available as part of the program but are not required. Participants may attend seminars in several different genres. Scholarships and teaching fellowships are available, including the Jakobson awards for new writers and the Jon Davidoff Scholarships for journalists. Send 7½×10½ SASE for brochure/guidelines.

THE WRITERS' CENTER AT CHAUTAUQUA, P.O. Box 408, Chautauqua NY 14722. (716)357-2445 or (717)872-8337. Director: Mary Jean Irion. Estab. 1987. Annual. Workshops held late June through August "are offered in combination with a vacation at historic Chautauqua Institution, a large cultural resort in western New York for families and singles. Workshops are two hours, Monday-Friday; average attendance is 12." Past workshop leaders: Gloria Frym and Kristin Kovacic, short story; Nina da Vinci Nichols, novel; David McKain, Writing the Stories of Your Life; Susan Rowan Masters, writers 6-12 years old and 13-18 years old; Carol H. Behrman and Margery Facklam, Writing for Children.

Costs: In 1996, $70/week. Meals, housing, gate ticket (about $160 per week), parking ($20) are in addition.

Accommodations: Information is available; but no special rates have been offered.

Additional Information: Each leader specifies the kind of workshop offered. Most accept submissions in advance; information is made available in March on request. Conference brochures/guidelines are available for 55¢ SASE.

WRITERS RETREAT WORKSHOP, % Write It/Sell It, P.O. Box 139, South Lancaster MA 01561-0139. Phone/fax: (508)368-0287. Director: Gail Provost. Assistant Directors: Lance Stockwell, Carol Dougherty. Estab. 1987. May 1997 workshop held at Marydale Retreat Center in Erlanger, KY (just south of Cincinnati, OH). Workshop duration: 10 days. Average attendance: 25. Focus on fiction and narrative nonfiction books in progress. All genres. "The Writers Retreat Workshop is an intensive learning experience for small groups of serious-minded writers. Founded by the late Gary Provost, one of the country's leading writing instructors and his wife Gail, an award-winning author, the WRW is a challenging and enriching adventure. Alice Orr, nationally known author, agent and editor conducted classes in 1996 and will return in 1997. The goal of the WRW staff is for students to leave with a new understanding of the marketplace and the craft of writing. In the heart of a supportive and spirited community of fellow writers, students are able to make remarkable creative leaps over the course of the 10-day workshop."

Costs: Costs (discount for past participants) $1,595 for 10 days which includes all food and lodging. The Marydale Retreat Center is 5 miles from the Cincinnati airport and offers shuttle services.

Additional Information: Participants are selected based upon the appropriateness of this program for the applicant's specific writing project. Participants are asked to submit a brief overview and synopsis before the workshop and are given assignments and feedback during the 10-day workshop. Additional workshops in other regions of the country may be scheduled for late 1997 and 1998. Brochures/guidelines are available for SASE.

Midatlantic (DC, DE, MD, NJ, PA)

CUMBERLAND VALLEY FICTION WRITERS WORKSHOP, Dickinson College, Carlisle PA 17013-2896. (717)245-1291. Director: Judy Gill. Estab. 1990. Annual. Workshop held in late June. Average attendance: 30-40. "5-day fiction workshop. Workshop is held on the campus of Dickinson College, a small liberal arts college, in Carlisle, PA." Panel: "Writers Roundtable"—faculty responds to wide variety of questions submitted by participants.

Costs: Tuition for 5-day workshop: $325; Room (optional): $130.

Accommodations: Special accommodations made. A residence hall on campus is reserved for workshop participants. Cost is $25 per night.

Additional Information: Applicants must submit a 10-page manuscript for evaluation prior to the workshop. Conference brochures/guidelines are available for SASE.

HIGHLIGHTS FOUNDATION WRITERS WORKSHOP AT CHAUTAUQUA, Dept. NM, 814 Court St., Honesdale PA 18431. (717)253-1192. Conference Director: Jan Keen. Estab. 1985. Annual. Workshop held in July. Average attendance: 100. "Writer workshops geared toward those who write for children—beginner, intermediate, advanced levels. Small group workshops, one-to-one interaction between faculty and participants plus panel sessions, lectures and large group meetings. Workshop site is the picturesque community of Chautauqua, New York." Classes offered include Children's Interests, Writing Dialogue, Outline for the Novel, Conflict and Developing Plot. Past faculty has included Eve Bunting, James Cross Giblin, Walter Dean Myers, Laurence Pringle, Richard Peck, Jerry Spinelli and Ed Young.

Accommodations: "We coordinate ground transportation to and from airports, trains and bus stations in the Erie, PA and Jamestown/Buffalo, NY area. We also coordinate accommodations for conference attendees."

Additional Information: "We offer the opportunity for attendees to submit a manuscript for review at the conference." Workshop brochures/guidelines are available for SASE.

METROPOLITAN WRITERS CONFERENCE, Seton Hall University, South Orange NJ 07079. (201)761-9430. Fax: (201)761-9794. E-mail: degnanja@lanmail.shu.edu. Contact: Jane Degnan. Estab.

1987. Annual. Conference duration: 1-3 days (varies). Average attendance: 100. Conference to help writers get their fiction and writing for children published. Held on the campus of Seton Hall University. Workshop topics focus on helping writers improve their use of plot, characterization, setting, point of view, etc., as well as a discussion on how to get an agent. Speakers have included Belva Plain, Meredith Sue Willis, Stefanie Matteson and Mary Higgins Clark.
Costs: $55 (meals not included).
Accommodations: On-site dorm rooms available for $20/night.
Additional Information: Maximum 10-page submissions critiqued for $20. Conference brochures/guidelines are available for SASE.

MID-ATLANTIC MYSTERY BOOK FAIR & CONVENTION, Detecto Mysterioso Books at Society Hill Playhouse, 507 S. Eighth St., Philadelphia PA 19147. (215)923-0211. Fax: (923)923-1789. Contact: Deen Kogan, chairperson. Estab. 1991. Annual. Convention held 1997: October 3-5. Average attendance: 450-500. Focus is on mystery, suspense, thriller, true crime novels. "An examination of the genre from many points of view." The convention is held at the Holiday Inn-Independence Mall, located in the historic area of Philadelphia. Previous speakers included Lawrence Block, Jeremiah Healy, Neil Albert, Michael Connelly, Paul Levine, Eileen Dreyer, Earl Emerson, Wendy Hornsby.
Costs: $50 registration fee.
Accommodations: Attendees must make their own transportation arrangements. Special room rate available at convention hotel.
Additional Information: "The Bookroom is a focal point of the convention. Twenty-five specialty dealers are expected to exhibit and collectables range from hot-off-the-press bestsellers to 1930's pulp; from fine editions to reading copies."

MONTROSE CHRISTIAN WRITER'S CONFERENCE, 5 Locust St., Montrose Bible Conference, Montrose PA 18801. (717)278-1001. (800)598-5030. Bible Conference Director: Jim Fahringer. Conference Co-Director: Jill Renich-Meyers. (717)766-1100. Estab. 1990. Annual. Conference held July, 1997. Average attendance: 65. "We try to meet a cross-section of writing needs, for beginners and advanced, covering fiction, poetry and writing for children. We meet in the beautiful village of Montrose, Pennsylvania, situated in the mountains. The Bible Conference provides motel-like accommodations and good food. The main sessions are held in the chapel with rooms available for other classes. Fiction writing has been taught each year."
Costs: In 1996 registration was $80.
Accommodations: Will meet planes in Binghamton NY and Scranton PA; will meet bus in Binghamton. Information on overnight accommodations is available. On-site accommodations: room and board $204-$300/week; $34-$50/day including food.
Additional Information: "Writers can send work ahead and have it critiqued for $20." Brochures/guidelines are available for SASE. "The attendees are usually church related (interchurch). The writing has a Christian emphasis."

‡JENNY McKEAN MOORE COMMUNITY WORKSHOPS, English Dept., George Washington University, Washington DC 20052. (202)994-8223. Fax: (202)363-8628. Associate Professor: F. Moskowitz. Estab. 1976. Workshop held each semester. Next semester begins September 1997. Length: semester. Average attendance: 15. Workshop concentration varies depending on professor—usually fiction or poetry. Workshop held at university.
Costs: Free.
Additional Information: Admission is competitive and by ms.

NEW JERSEY ROMANCE WRITERS PUT YOUR HEART IN A BOOK CONFERENCE, P.O. Box 513, Plainsboro NJ 08536. (201)263-8477. E-mail: elainibonz@aol.com. President: Elaine Charton. Estab. 1984. Annual. Conference held October 3 and October 4. Average attendance: 300. Conference concentrating on romance fiction. "Workshops offered on various topics for all writers of romance, from beginner to multi-published." Held at the Holiday Inn in Jamesburg, New Jersey. Offers workshops with a panel of editors and a panel of agents. Speakers have included Diana Gabaldon, Nora Roberts, Alice Orr, Susan Elizabeth Phillips and Tami Hoag.
Costs: $120 (New Jersey Romance Writers members) and $135 (nonmembers).
Accommodations: Special hotel rate available for conference attendees.
Additional Information: Sponsors Put Your Heart in a Book Contest for unpublished writers and the Golden Leaf Contest for published members of RWA. Conference brochures, guidelines and membership information are available for SASE. "Appointments offered for conference attendees, both published and unpublished, with editors and/or agents in the genre." Mid-Atlantic Booksellers Association promotion available for published conference attendees.

OUTDOOR WRITERS ASSOCIATION OF AMERICA ANNUAL CONFERENCE, Suite 101, 2017 Cato Ave., State College PA 16801-2768. (814)234-1011. E-mail: 76711.1725@compuserve

.com. Meeting Planner: Eileen King. Estab. 1927. Annual. Conference held in June. Will be held in Florida in 1997. Average attendance: 800-950. Conference concentrates on outdoor communications (all forms of media). Featured speakers have included Don Ranley, University of Missouri, Columbia; US Forest Service Chief Jack Ward Thomas; Nina Leopold Bradley (daughter of Aldo Leopold); Secretary of the Interior, Bruce Babbitt; and Director Bureau of Land Management, Michael Dombeck.
Costs: $130 for nonmembers; "applicants must have prior approval from Executive Director." Registration fee includes cost of most meals.
Accommodations: List of accommodations available after April. Special room rate for attendees.
Additional Information: Sponsors contests, "but all is done prior to the conference and you must be a member to enter them." Conference brochures/guidelines are available for SASE.

ST. DAVIDS CHRISTIAN WRITERS CONFERENCE, 87 Pines Rd. E., Hadley PA 16130. Registrar: Audrey Stallsmith. Estab. 1957. Annual. Conference will be held June 15-20, 1997. "Second year in new location at picturesque Geneva College, Beaver Falls PA, north of Pittsburgh." Attendance: 70. Conference will train writers in religious and general writing through workshops in fiction, nonfiction, beginning and advanced writing, poetry, children's writing, devotional/inspirational writing. Optional tutorials and market consultations. Recent workshop leaders have included Colonel Henry Gariepy, Janet Hoover, and David Page.
Cost: Tuition is $225 (1996); room and board is $160. Optional programs are extra.
Accommodations: College dormitory rooms with linens provided, excellent food in college cafeteria. "We provide transportation from the Pittsburgh airport if prior arrangements are made."
Additional Information: Small informal critique groups do not require pre-conference manuscript submission. Sponsors annual contest for registered conferees. Categories are humorous poetry, serious poetry, fiction (short story), op-ed, children's lit, character sketch, personal experience, humorous prose. Judges are faculty members, editors or agents. Conference brochure available for SASE.

SANDY COVE CHRISTIAN WRITERS CONFERENCE, Sandy Cove Bible Conference, North East MD 21901. (800)287-4843. Director: Gayle Roper. Estab. 1991. Annual. Conference begins first Sunday in October. Conference duration: 4 days (Sunday dinner to Thursday breakfast). Average attendance: 100. "There are major, continuing workshops in fiction, article writing, nonfiction books and beginner's and advanced workshops. Twenty-eight one-hour classes touch many topics. While Sandy Cove has a strong emphasis on available markets in Christian publishing, all writers are more than welcome. Sandy Cove is a full-service conference center located on the Chesapeake Bay. All the facilities are first class with suites, single or double rooms available." Past faculty has included William Petersen, editor, Revell; Ken Petersen, editor, Tyndale House; Linda Tomblin, editor, *Guideposts*; Col. Henry Gariepy, editor-in-chief, The Salvation Army; and Andrew Scheer, *Moody Magazine*.
Costs: Tuition is $225.
Accommodations: "If one flies into Philadelphia International Airport, we will transport them the one-hour drive to Sandy Cove. Accommodations are available at Sandy Cove. Information available upon request." Cost is $225 double occupancy room and board, $275 single occupancy room and board for 4 nights and meals.
Additional Information: Special critiques are available—a 1-time critique for $30 and a continuing critique for $75 (1-time is 30-minute appointment and written critique; continuing is 3 30-minute appointments). Conference brochures/guidelines are available for SASE.

TRENTON STATE COLLEGE WRITERS' CONFERENCE, English Dept., Trenton State College, Hillwood Lakes CN 4700, Trenton NJ 08650-4700. (609)771-3254. Director: Jean Hollander. Estab. 1980. Annual. Conference held every spring. Conference duration: 9 a.m. to 10:30 p.m. Average attendance: 600-1,000. "Conference concentrates on fiction (the largest number of participants), poetry, children's literature, play and screenwriting, magazine and newspaper journalism, overcoming writer's block, nonfiction books. Conference is held at the student center at the college in two auditoriums and workshop rooms; also Kendall Theatre on campus." We focus on various genres: romance, detective, mystery, TV writing, etc. Topics have included "How to Get Happily Published," "How to Get an Agent" and "Earning a Living as a Writer." The conference usually presents twenty or so authors, plus two featured speakers, who have included Arthur Miller, Saul Bellow, Toni Morrison, Joyce Carol Oates, Erica Jong. Alice Walker will be a featured speaker at the 1996 conference.
Costs: General registration $45, plus $10 for each workshop. Lower rates for students.
Additional Information: Brochures/guidelines available.

TRI-STATE WRITER'S GUILD, (formerly Fairview Summit Center Writer's Workshops), 10800 Mt. Fairview Rd. SE, Cumberland MD 21502. (301)724-6842. Director: Petrina Aubol. Estab. 1992. Tri-State Writer's Guild, based in Cumberland, Maryland and an affiliate of the Allegany Arts Council, has 50 members in Eastern U.S., and holds 2 workshops a year. Retreat is scheduled for second weekend in July at various locations in the Mid-Atlantic region. Conference is held last weekend in October at, and in conjunction with, Allegany College in Cumberland. Awards dinner for annual literary contest held during conference. 1996 speakers included Bonni Goldberg, poet, author (*Room to Write*) and creative writing teacher; Joanna Scott, award-winning poet (Baltimore Artscape '96) and novelist (*Charlie and His Children*); Eli Flam, editor of literary quarterly, *Potomac Review*; Hilary Tham, poet, author and creative writing teacher; Harold Collier, editor, White Mane Press; and Isaac Olaleye renowned children's author (*Bitter Bananas*).

Midsouth (NC, SC, TN, VA, WV)

AMERICAN CHRISTIAN WRITERS CONFERENCES, P.O. Box 110390, Nashville TN 37222. (800)21-WRITE. Director: Reg Forder. Estab. 1981. Annual. Conference duration: 3 days. Average attendance: 100. To promote all forms of Christian writing. Conferences held throughout the year in cities such as Houston, Dallas, Minneapolis, St. Louis, Detroit, Atlanta, Washington DC, San Diego, Seattle, Ft. Lauderdale and Phoenix. Usually located at a major hotel chain like Holiday Inn.
Costs: Approximately $199 plus meals and accommodation.
Accommodations: Special rates available at host hotel.
Additional Information: Conference brochures/guidelines are available for SASE.

‡APPALACHIAN WRITERS CONFERENCE, Western Carolina University, Cullowhee NC 28723. (704)227-7397. E-mail: eberly@wcu.edu. Website: http://www.wcu.edu/eberly/steve/awa/awa/html. Office of Continuing Education: Sue Dietz. AWA President: Stephens (Steve) Eberly. Estab. 1980. Conference held 2nd weekend of July: July 11-13, 1997. Average attendance: 50. Fiction, nonfiction, poetry, drama, story telling, and ways to publish. Writing focuses mainly on Appalachian people and places, but members are defined as "those anywhere whose writing is identified in some way with Appalachia, and those in Appalachia who write well about anything." Western Carolina University is located off I-40 near historic Cherokee, NC, 50 miles west of Asheville. Participants may stay in an air-conditioned conference center centrally located on the small mountain campus: rates include meals. Guest speakers, writing contests, and Appalachian achievement awards. Most AWA members are themselves writers known regionally and/or nationally.
Costs: Annual dues—$15 (students $5).
Accommodations: Less than $150 single room for 3 days, 2 nights (slightly less for double occupancy), including meals.
Contests: Poetry, short story (open section and under 30), essay.
Additional Information: Conference brochure available in February for SASE. Information also available by e-mail or at Website.

HIGHLAND SUMMER CONFERENCE, Box 7014, Radford University, Radford VA 24142. (703)831-5366. Chair, Appalachian Studies Program: Dr. Grace Toney Edwards. Estab. 1978. Annual. Conference held in mid-June. Conference duration: 12 days. Average attendance: 25. "The HSC features one (two weeks) or two (one week each) guest leaders each year. As a rule, our leaders are well-known writers who have connections, either thematic, or personal, or both, to the Appalachian region. The genre(s) of emphasis depends upon the workshop leader(s). In the past we have had as our leaders Jim Wayne Miller, poet, novelist, teacher; and Wilma Dykemen, novelist, journalist, social critic, author of *Tall Woman* among others. The Highland Summer Conference is held at Radford University, a school of about 9,000 students. Radford is in the Blue Ridge Mountains of southwest Virginia about 45 miles south of Roanoke, VA."
Costs: "The cost is based on current Radford tuition for 3 credit hours plus an additional conference fee. On-campus meals and housing are available at additional cost. In 1996 conference tuition was $415 for undergraduates, $436 for graduate students."
Accommodations: "We do not have special rate arrangements with local hotels. We do offer accommodations on the Radford University Campus in a recently refurbished residence hall. (In 1996 cost was $17-27 per night.)"
Additional Information: "Conference leaders do typically critique work done during the two-week conference, but do not ask to have any writing submitted prior to the conference beginning." Conference brochures/guidelines are available for SASE.

MID SOUTH WRITERS FESTIVAL, 5858 Sweet Oak Cove, Bartlett TN 38134-5545. (901)377-8250. Festival Director: Michael Denington. Estab. 1994. Annual. Usually held the second Saturday in May. Average attendance: 80. "To support, encourage and praise writers is our reason for being. The areas of concentration are fiction, poetry, nonfiction, playwriting, and children's literature." Festival held at local hotel. Panelists have included editors, a theater director, novelists, freelance writers, a publisher, poets, an author of children's books, and an agent.

Costs: Registration fee was $7. Awards Banquet was $17.50.
Accommodations: "We try to get reduced rates if people want to stay overnight."
Additional Information: Sponsors a contest as part of conference. Fee is charged. Judges are professional writers. Conference brochures/guidelines are available around January 1 for SASE.

‡**NATIONAL LEAGUE OF AMERICAN PEN WOMEN**, Richmond Branch, P.O. Box 35935, Richmond VA 23235. (804)323-0417. Director: Sara Bird Wright. Estab. 1970. Biennial. Next conference will be held "probably in fall 1997." Conference duration: 1 day. Average attendance: 100. "The purpose of our conference is to reach out to the writing community with a conference geared to a wide range of interests except poetry. We meet in the lovely Fort Magruder Inn in Williamsburg, Virginia." Past speakers include: David Baldacci, "Writing & Publishing a First Novel"; Claudine Wirths and Mary Bowman-Kruhm, "Online for Research and Networking"; and Rebecca Greer, "Freelancing for Major Magazines."
Costs: $70 members and $80 nonmembers plus $10 contest fee.
Accommodations: Discounts available for attendees at Fort Magruder Inn for Friday through Sunday.
Additional Information: Conference brochures/guidelines are available for SASE.

NORTH CAROLINA WRITERS' NETWORK FALL CONFERENCE, P.O. Box 954, Carrboro NC 27510. (919)967-9540. Executive Director: Linda G. Mobson. Estab. 1985. Annual. "Conference will be held in Wilmington, NC, November." Average attendance: 400. "The conference is a weekend full of workshops, panels, readings and discussion groups. We try to have *all* genres represented. In the past we have had novelists, poets, journalists, editors, children's writers, young adult writers, storytellers, puppetry, screenwriters, etc. We take the conference to a different location in North Carolina each year in order to best serve our entire state. We hold the conference at a conference center with hotel rooms available."
Costs: "Conference cost is approximately $110-125 and includes three to four meals."
Accommodations: "Special conference hotel rates are obtained, but the individual makes his/her own reservations. If requested, we will help the individual find a roommate."
Additional Information: Conference brochures/guidelines are available for 2 first-class stamps.

THE WRITERS' WORKSHOP, P.O. Box 696, Asheville NC 28802. (704)254-8111. Executive Director: Karen Tager. Estab. 1984. Held throughout the year. Conference duration: varies from 1 day to 20 weeks. Average attendance: 10. "All areas, for adults and children. We do not offer workshops dealing with romance or religion, however." Sites are throughout the South, especially North Carolina. Past guest speakers include John Le Carré, Peter Matthiessen and D.M. Thomas. Retreat locations have included the Florida Keys and Nice, France.
Costs: Vary. Financial assistance available to low-income writers. Information on overnight accommodations is made available.

Southeast (AL, AR, FL, GA, LA, MS, PR [Puerto Rico])

ALABAMA WRITERS' CONCLAVE, P.O. Box 230787, Montgomery AL 36123-0787. President: Donna Tennis. Estab. 1923. Annual. Conference held for three days, the first week in August. Average attendance: 75-100. Conference to promote "all phases" of writing. Held at the Ramsay Conference Center (University of Montevallo). "We attempt to contain all workshops under this roof."
Costs: In 1996 fees for 3 days were $35 for members; $45 for nonmembers. Lower rates for 1- or 2-day attendance.
Accommodations: Accommodations available on campus (charged separately).
Additional Information: "We have had a works-in-progress group with members helping members." Sponsors a contest. Conference brochures/guidelines available for SASE. Membership dues are $15. Membership information from Harriette Dawkins, 117 Hanover Rd., Homewood AL 35209.

ARKANSAS WRITERS' CONFERENCE, 6817 Gingerbread, Little Rock AR 72204. (501)565-8889. Director: Peggy Vining. Estab. 1944. Annual. Conference held: first weekend in June. Average attendence: 225. "We have a variety of subjects related to writing—we have some general sessions, some more specific, but try to vary each year's subjects."
Costs: Registration: $10; luncheon: $11; banquet: $13.
Accommodations: "We meet at a Holiday Inn—rooms available at reasonable rate." Holiday Inn has a bus to bring anyone from airport. Rooms average $56/single.
Additional Information: "We have 36 contest categories. Some are open only to Arkansans, most are open to all writers. Our judges are not announced before conference, but are qualified, many from out of state." Conference brochures are available for SASE after February 1. "We have had 226

attending from 12 states—over 3,000 contest entries from 43 states and New Zealand, Mexico and Canada. We have a get acquainted party at my home on Thursday evening for early arrivers."

‡**FLORIDA CHRISTIAN WRITERS CONFERENCE**, 2600 Park Ave., Titusville FL 32780. (407)269-6702, ext. 202. Conference Director: Billie Wilson. Estab. 1988. Annual. Conference is held in late January. Conference duration: 5 days. Average attendance: 200. To promote "all areas of writing." Conference held at Park Avenue Retreat Center, a conference complex at a large church near Kennedy Space Center. Editors will represent over 30 publications and publishing houses.
Costs: Tuition $360, included tuition, room and board (double occupancy).
Accommodations: "We provide shuttle from the airport and from the hotel to retreat center. We make reservations at major hotel chain."
Additional Information: Critiques available. "Each writer may submit two works for critique. We have specialists in every area of writing to critique." Conference brochures/guidelines are available for SASE.

FLORIDA FIRST COAST WRITERS' FESTIVAL, 3939 Roosevelt Blvd., FCCJ Kent Campus, Box 109, Jacksonville FL 32205. (904)766-6559. Fax: (904)766-6654. E-mail: hdenson@fccj.cc.fl.us. Director: Howard Denson. Estab. 1985. Annual. 1997 Festival: April 11-12. Average attendance: 150-250. All areas: mainstream plus genre. Held on Kent Campus of Florida Community College at Jacksonville.
Costs: Maximum of $75 for 2 days, plus $25 for banquet tickets.
Accommodations: Orange Park Holiday Inn, (904)264-9513, has a special festival rate.
Additional Information: Conference brochures/guidelines are available for SASE. Sponsors a contest for short fiction, poetry and novels. Novel judges are David Poyer and Elisabeth Graves. Entry fees: $30, novels; $10, short fiction; $5, poetry. Deadline: October 1 in each year.

FLORIDA ROMANCE WRITERS' ANNUAL CONFERENCE, 9630 NW 25th St., Sunrise FL 33324. (305)749-3736. Fax: (305)749-2724. Procurement Chairman: Barry Glusky. Estab. 1986. Annual. Conference held last weekend in February. Average attendance: 200. Conference covering "all areas of writing but mainly romance. Our membership includes published authors in historical, mystery, paranormal, regency, romance, science fiction, westerns and nonfiction areas." Conference is held at the Airport Hilton Hotel, Griffin Rd., Ft. Lauderdale, FL, where there are conference and meeting rooms and adequate facilities for parking. Conference concentration is on romance writing and guest speakers include editors and agents from the romance genre.
Costs: $150 for conference includes luncheon Saturday and all workshops. There will be a cocktail party Friday night, continental breakfast Saturday morning. Sunday morning buffet breakfast with editor or agent of choice. Book signing Sunday afternoon.
Accommodations: Special conference rates available at Hilton Hotel for conference attendees.
Additional Information: Conference brochures/guidelines are available for SASE.

FLORIDA SUNCOAST WRITERS' CONFERENCE, University of South Florida, Division of Lifelong Learning, 4202 E. Fowler Ave., MGZ144, Tampa FL 33620-6610. (813)974-2403. Fax: (813)974-5732. Directors: Steve Rubin and Ed Hirshberg. Estab. 1970. Annual. Held in February. Conference duration: 3 days. Average attendance: 450. Conference covering poetry, short story, novel and nonfiction, including science fiction, detective, travel writing, drama, TV scripts, photojournalism and juvenile. "We do not focus on any one particular aspect of the writing profession. The conference is held on the picturesque university campus fronting the bay in St. Petersburg, Florida." Features panels with agents and editors. Guest speakers have included Lady P.D. James, Carolyn Forche and Marge Piercy.
Costs: Call for verification.
Accommodations: Special rates available at area motels. "All information is contained in our brochure."
Additional Information: Participants may submit work for critiquing. Extra fee charged for this service. Conference brochures/guidelines are available for SASE.

HEMINGWAY DAYS WRITER'S WORKSHOP AND CONFERENCE, P.O. Box 4045, Key West FL 33041. (305)294-4440. Director of Workshop: Dr. James Plath. Festival Director: Michael Whalton. Estab. 1987. Annual. Conference/workshop held third week in July. Average attendance: 75. "The Hemingway Days Writer's Workshop and Conference focuses on fiction, poetry and Ernest Hemingway and his work. The workshop and conference is but one event in a week-long festival which honors Ernest Hemingway."
Costs: $120. Guaranteed admission on a space-available basis includes admission to all sessions, workshop t-shirt and 2 socials.
Accommodations: "As the time draws nearer, Hemingway Days packages will be available through Ocean Key House, Pier House, Southernmost Motel and Holiday Inn LaConcha. Last year the cost

for 3 nights ranged from $60/2 in room per night plus tax; $160/3 in room per night suite, plus tax."
Additional Information: Brochures/guidelines are available for SASE. "The conference/workshop is unique in that it combines studies in craft with studies in literature, and serious literary-minded events to celebrate Hemingway the writer with a week-long festival celebrating 'papa' the myth."

KEY WEST LITERARY SEMINAR, 419 Petronia St., Key West FL 33040. (305)293-9291. E-mail: keywestlit@earthlink.net. Executive Director: Miles Frieden. Estab. 1983. Annual. Conference held second week in January. Conference duration: 3-5 days. Average attendance: 450. "Each year a different topic of literary interest is examined. Writers, scholars, editors, publishers, critics, and the public meet for panel discussions and dialogue. The agenda also includes readings, performances, question and answer sessions, book sales, a writers' workshop, social receptions, and a literary walking tour of Key West. The sessions are held at various locations in Key West, Florida, including the San Carlos Institute, 516 Duval Street and the Key West Art and Historical Society's East Martello Museum. Upcoming theme: Literature in the Age of AIDS, featuring Larry Kramer, Tony Kushner, Sarah Schulman. Past speakers include William Goldman, Elmore Leonard, Jan Morris, Octavio Paz, Russell Banks, Mary Higgins Clark, James Merrill, John Wideman, Anna Quindlen, David Halberstam, Ellen Hume.
Costs: Seminar $295 and workshop $200 plus tax.
Accommodations: Catalogs detailing the seminar schedule, guest speakers, registration, and accommodations are available. Special room rates are available at participating hotels, motels, guest houses and inns. Room rates usually begin around $100.
Additional Information: Manuscript critique is an optional component of the writers' workshop. No more than 10 typewritten, double spaced pages may be submitted with workshop registration.

SCBWI/FLORIDA ANNUAL FALL CONFERENCE, 2158 Portland Ave., Wellington FL 33414. (407)798-4824. Florida Regional Advisor: Barbara Casey. Estab. 1985. Annual. Conference duration: one-half day. Average attendance: 70. Conference to promote "all aspects of writing and illustrating for children. The facilities include the meeting rooms of the Library and Town Hall of Palm Springs FL (near West Palm Beach)."
Costs: $50 for SCBWI members, $55 for non-SCBWI members.
Accommodations: Special conference rates at Airport Hilton, West Palm Beach, Florida.
Additional Information: Conference brochures/guidelines are available for SASE.

SOUTHEASTERN WRITERS CONFERENCE, Rt. 1, Box 102, Cuthbert GA 31740. (912)679-5445. Advertising Director: Pat Laye. Estab. 1975. Annual. Conference held June 15-21, 1997. Conference duration: 1 week. Average attendance: 100 (limited to 100 participants). Concentration is on fiction, poetry and juvenile—plus nonfiction and playwriting. Site is "St. Simons Island, GA. Conference held at Epworth-by-the-Sea Conference Center—tropical setting, beaches. Each year we offer market advice, agent updates. All our instructors are professional writers presently selling in New York."
Costs: $235. Meals and lodging are separate. Senior citizen discount.
Accommodations: Information on overnight accommodations is made available. "On-site-facilities at a remarkably low cost. Facilities are motel style of excellent quality. Other hotels are available on the island."
Additional Information: "Three manuscripts of one chapter each are allowed in three different categories." Sponsors a contest, many cash prizes. Brochures are available for SASE.

SOUTHWEST FLORIDA WRITERS' CONFERENCE, P.O. Box 60210, Ft. Myers FL 33906-6210. (813)489-9226. Conference Director: Joanne Hartke. Estab. 1980. Annual. Conference held Feb. 28-March 1 (always the 4th Friday and Saturday of February). Average attendance: 150. "This year's conference will include fiction, poetry, nonfiction, an agent and others. The purpose is to serve the local writing community, whether they are novice or published writers." The conference is held on the Edison Community College campus.
Costs: "Reasonable." Call or write for conference brochures/guidelines and to be put on mailing list.
Additional Information: "We do sponsor a writing contest annually, with the prizes being gift certificates to local bookstores. Local, published writers offer volunteer critique/judging services."

WRITE FOR SUCCESS WORKSHOP: CHILDREN'S BOOKS, 3748 Harbor Heights Dr., Largo FL 34644. (813)581-2484. Speaker/Coordinator: Theo Carroll. Estab. 1995. Held 3 separate evenings the last 3 weeks in March. Conference duration: 1 day. Average attendance: 52. Concentration is writing for children. Site is the Clearwater, Florida Community Center. "Teaching assignments and classroom/personal critique sessions cover characterization, plotting, the importance of setting, dialogue and more. Assignments given on writing the picture book."
Costs: $85 includes breakfast, lunch and materials. Limo available from Tampa airport. Information on special conference attendee accommodations available.

Additional Information: Brochures for latest seminar are available for SASE.

WRITING STRATEGIES FOR THE CHRISTIAN MARKET, 2712 S. Peninsula Dr., Daytona Beach FL 32118. (904)322-1111. Instructor: Rosemary Upton. Estab. 1991. Seminars given approximately 4 times a year. Conference duration: 3 hours. Average attendance: 10-20. Seminars include Basics I, Marketing II, Business III, Building the novel. Held in a conference room: 3-4 persons seated at each table; instructor teaches from a podium. Question and answer session provided. Critique shop included once a month, except summer (July and August). Instructors include Rosemary Upton, novelist; Kistler London, editor.
Costs: $30 for each 3-hour seminar.
Additional Information: Those who have taken Writing Strategies instruction are able to attend an on-going monthly critiqueshop where their peers critique their work. Manual provided with each seminar. Conference brochures/guidelines are available for SASE. Independent study by mail also available.

WRITING TODAY—BIRMINGHAM-SOUTHERN COLLEGE, Box 549003, Birmingham AL 35254. (205)226-4921. Director of Special Events: Martha Andrews. Estab. 1978. Annual. Conference held March 14-15. Average attendance: 400-500. "This is a two-day conference with approximately 18 workshops, lectures and readings. We try to offer workshops in short fiction, novels, poetry, children's literature, magazine writing, and general information of concern to aspiring writers such as publishing, agents, markets and research. The conference is sponsored by Birmingham-Southern College and is held on the campus in classrooms and lecture halls." The 1996 conference featured novelist, historian and playwright Shelby Foote. Albert Murray, James Tate, Claudia Johnson, Madison Jones and Dara Wier were some of the workshop presenters.
Costs: $85 for both days. This includes lunches, reception and morning coffee and rolls.
Accommodations: Attendees must arrange own transporation. Local hotels and motels offer special rates, but participants must make their own reservations.
Additional Information: "We usually offer a critique for interested writers. We have had poetry and short story critiques. There is an additional charge for these critiques." Sponsors the Hackney Literary Competition Awards for poetry, short story and novels. Brochures available for SASE.

Midwest (IL, IN, KY, MI, OH)

CLARION SCIENCE FICTION & FANTASY WRITING WORKSHOP, Lyman Briggs School, E—185 Holmes Hall, Michigan State University, East Lansing MI 48825-1107. (517)355-9598. E-mail address: 22323mes@msu.edu. Administrative Assistant: Mary Sheridan. Estab. 1968. Workshop held annually for 6 weeks in the summer. Average attendance: 17-20. "Workshop concentrates on science fiction and fantasy writing. The workshop is held at Michigan State University and is sponsored by Lyman Briggs School, a residential program linking the sciences and humanities. Participants are housed in single rooms in a graduate residence hall adjoining the workshop site. Facilities are handicapped accessible." Writers in residence during the summer of 1997 will be Octavia Butler, Juan Vinge, Terry Bisson, Richard Kassey, Karen Joy Fowler and Tim Fowler.
Costs: Course fees for the 1996 Clarion workshop were $814. Students will be enrolled as Life-Long Education students and will receive 4 undergraduate semester credits and a transcript from MSU.
Accommodations: Rates for a single room and meals in a graduate residence hall on the MSU campus are being negotiated; 1996 costs were approximately $800.
Additional Information: Admission to the workshop is based on submission of a writing sample of 2 complete short stories between 10 and 25 pages long and a completed application form with a $25 application fee. A $100 enrollment fee is required upon acceptance. For brochures/guidelines, send SASE.

THE COLUMBUS WRITERS CONFERENCE, P.O. Box 20548, Columbus OH 43220. (614)451-3075. Fax: (614)451-0174. Director: Angela Palazzolo. Estab. 1993. Annual. Conference held September 27, 1997. Average attendance: 200. The conference is held in the Fawcett Center for Tomorrow, 2400 Olentangy River Road, Columbus, OH. "The conference covers a wide variety of fiction and

CAN'T FIND A CONFERENCE? Conferences are listed by region. Check the introduction to this section for a list of regional categories.

nonfiction topics. Fiction topics have included novel, short story, children's, science fiction, fantasy, humor, and mystery writing; playwriting and screenwriting. Nonfiction writing topics have included travel, humor, technical, query letter, corporate, educational, and greeting card writing. Other topics: finding and working with an agent, targeting markets, research, time management, obtaining grants, and writers colonies." Speakers have included Lee K. Abbott, Lore Segal, Mike Harden, Oscar Collier, Stephanie S. Tolan, Dennis L. McKiernan, Karen Harper, Melvin Helitzer, Susan Porter, Les Roberts, Tracey E. Dils, J. Patrick Lewis, and many other professionals in the writing field.
Costs: $78 includes morning and afternoon refreshments and lunch (cost is $78 if registration postmarked by September 14; after September 14, $92).
Additional Information: Call or write to obtain a conference brochure, available mid-summer.

EASTERN KENTUCKY UNIVERSITY CREATIVE WRITING CONFERENCE, Eastern Kentucky University, Richmond KY 40475. (606)622-5861. Conference Director: Dorothy Sutton. Estab. 1962. Annual. Conference held 3rd week in June. Average attendance: 15-20. Conference to promote poetry and fiction. Includes lectures, workshops, private individual and peer group manuscript evaluation. The conference is held on the campus of Eastern Kentucky University "in the rolling hills of Eastern Kentucky, between the horse farms of the Bluegrass and the scenic mountains of the Appalachian chain." Three distinguished visiting writers will teach at the conference. Past speakers have included Donald Justice, Maggie Anderson, Maura Stanton, Richard Marius, Gregory Orr, David Citino, Reginald Gibbons. Also helping with workshops will be EKU faculty Harry Brown, Hal Blythe, Charlie Sweet.
Costs: $75 for undergraduates ($207 if out-of-state); $109 for graduates ($302 if out-of-state). Cost includes 1 hour of credit in creative writing and is subject to change (please check brochure for changes). Auditors welcome at same price. Dining in the cafeteria is approximately $6-8/day.
Accommodations: Air-conditioned dormitory rooms are available for $39 (double) or $55 (single) per week. "Linens furnished. Bring your own blankets, pillow and telephone, if desired. Subject to change. Check brochure."
Additional Information: "Participants are asked to submit manuscript by May 15 to be approved before June 1." For conference brochure, send SASE to English Department (attn: Creative Writing Conference).

CHARLENE FARIS SEMINARS FOR BEGINNERS, 610 W. Poplar St., Zionsville IN 46077. (317)873-0738. Director: Charlene Faris. Estab. 1985. Held 2 or 3 times/year in various locations in spring, summer and fall. Conference duration: 2 days. Average attendence: 10. Concentration on all areas of publishing and writing, particularly marketing and working with editors. Locations have included Phoenix, Los Angeles, Madison WI and Indianapolis.
Costs: $150, tuition only; may attend only 1 day for $75.
Accommodations: Information on overnight accommodations available.
Additional Information: Guidelines available for SASE.

GREEN RIVER WRITERS NOVELS-IN-PROGRESS WORKSHOP, 11906 Locust Rd., Middletown KY 40243. (502)245-4902. Director: Mary E. O'Dell. Estab. 1991. Annual. Conference held March 15-21, 1997. Conference duration: 1 week. Average attendance: 40. Open to persons, college age and above, who have approximately 3 chapters (60 pages) or more of a novel. Mainstream and genre novels handled by individual instructors. Short fiction collections welcome. "Each novelist instructor works with a small group (5-7 people) for five days; then agents/editors are there for panels and appointments on the weekend." Site is The University of Louisville's Shelby Campus, suburban setting, graduate dorm housing (private rooms available w/shared bath for each 2 rooms). "Meetings and classes held in nearby classroom building. Grounds available for walking, etc. Lovely setting, restaurants and shopping available nearby. Participants carpool to restaurants, etc. This year we are covering mystery, romance, mainstream/literary, suspense."
Costs: Tuition—$350, housing $20 per night private, $16 shared. Does not include meals.
Accommodations: "We do meet participants' planes and see that participants without cars have transportation to meals, etc. If participants would rather stay in hotel, we will make that information available."
Additional Information: Participants send 60 pages/3 chapters with synopsis $25 reading fee which applies to tuition. Deadline will be in late January. Conference brochures/guidelines are available for SASE.

THE HEIGHTS WRITER'S CONFERENCE, P.O. Box 24684, Cleveland OH 44124-0684. Director: Lavern Hall. Estab. 1992. Annual. Conference held first Saturday in May. Average attendance: 100. "Fiction, nonfiction, science fiction, poetry, children's, marketing, etc." The conference is sponsored by Writer's World Press and held at the Cleveland Marriott East, Beachwood OH. Offers seminars on the craft, business, and legal aspects of writing plus 2 teaching, hands-on workshops. "No theme; published authors and experts in their field sharing their secrets and networking for success."

Additional Information: Conference brochure available in March for SASE.

IMAGINATION, Cleveland State University, Division of Continuing Education, 2344 Euclid Ave., Cleveland OH 44115. (216)687-4522. Contact: Neal Chandler. Estab. 1990. Annual. Conference lasts 5 days and is held in mid-July. Average attendance: 60. "Conference concentrates on fiction and poetry. Held at Mather Mansion, a restored 19th Century Mansion on the campus of Cleveland State University." 1996 themes included Writing Beyond Realism and Business of Writing. For more information send for brochure.

MIDLAND WRITERS CONFERENCE, Grace A. Dow Memorial Library, 1710 W. St. Andrews, Midland MI 48640. (517)835-7151. Conference Chair: Katherine Redwine. Estab. 1980. Annual. Conference held June 14. Average attendance: 100. "The Conference is composed of a well-known keynote speaker and six workshops on a variety of subjects including poetry, children's writing, freelancing, agents, etc. The attendees are both published and unpublished authors. The Conference is held at the Grace A. Dow Memorial Library in the auditorium and conference rooms. Keynoters in the past have included Dave Barry, Pat Conroy, Kurt Vonnegut, David Halberstam."
Costs: Adult - $45 before May 17, $55 after May 17; students, senior citizens and handicapped - $35 before May 17, $45 after May 17. A box lunch is available. Costs are approximate until plans for upcoming conference are finalized.
Accommodations: A list of area hotels is available.
Additional Information: Conference brochures/guidelines are available for SASE.

MIDWEST WRITERS WORKSHOP, Dept. of Journalism, Ball State University, Muncie IN 47306. (317)285-8200. Co-Director: Earl L. Conn. Estab. 1974. Annual. Workshop to be held July 30-Aug. 2, 1997. Average attendance: 130. For fiction, nonfiction, poetry. Conference held at Hotel Roberts in downtown Muncie.
Costs: In 1996, cost was $185 including opening reception, hospitality room and closing banquet.
Accommodations: Special hotel rates offered.
Additional Information: Critiques available. $20 for individual critiquing. Conference brochures/guidelines are available for SASE.

MISSISSIPPI VALLEY WRITERS CONFERENCE, 3403 45th St., Moline IL 61265. (309)762-8985. Conference Founder/Director: David R. Collins. Estab. 1973. Annual. Conference held June 8 to June 13, 1997. Average attendance: 80. "Conference for all areas of writing for publication." Conference held at Augustana College, a liberal arts school along the Mississippi River. 1997 guest speakers will be Evelyn Witter, Mel Boring, Max Collins, David McFarland, Karl Largent, Roald Tweet, Rich Johnson.
Costs: $25 for registration; $50 for 1 workshop; $90 for two; plus $40 for each additional workshops; $25 to audit.
Accommodations: On-campus facitilites available. Accommodations are available at Westerlin Hall on the Augustana College campus. Cost for 6 nights is $100; cost for 15 meals is $100.
Additional Information: Conferees may submit mss to workshop leaders for personal conferences during the week. Cash awards are given at the end of the conference week by workshop leaders based on mss submitted. Conference brochures/guidelines are available for SASE. "Conference is open to the beginner as well as the polished professional—all are welcome."

‡OAKLAND UNIVERSITY WRITERS' CONFERENCE, 265 SFH, Rochester MI 48309-4401. (810)370-3120. E-mail: ouce@oakland.edu. Program Director: Nadine Jakobowski. Estab. 1961. Annual. Conference held in October. Average attendance: 400. "All areas; all purposes." Held at Oakland University Oakland Center: meetings rooms, dining area; O'Dowd Hall: lecture rooms. "Each annual conference covers all aspects and types of writing in 36 concurrent workshops on Saturday. Major writers from various genres are speakers for the Saturday conference luncheon program. Individual critiques and hands-on writing workshops are conducted Friday. Areas: poetry, articles, fiction, short stories, playwriting, nonfiction, young adult, children's literature. Guest speaker in 1996: Sharyn Mc-Crumb, award-winning Appalachian novelist and crime fiction author.
Costs: 1996: Conference registration: $65; lunch, $8; individual ms, $48; writing workshop, $38; writing ms audit, $28.
Accommodations: List is available.
Additional Information: Conference brochure/guidelines available for SASE.

OF DARK & STORMY NIGHTS, Mystery Writers of America—Midwest Chapter, P.O. Box 1944, Muncie IN 47308-1944. (317)288-7402. Workshop Director: W.W. Spurgeon. Estab. 1982. Annual. Workshop held June. Workshop duration: 1 day. Average attendance: 200. Dedicated to "writing *mystery* fiction and crime-related nonfiction. Workshops and panels presented on techniques of mystery writing from ideas to revision, marketing, investigative techniques and more, by published

writers, law enforcement experts and publishing professionals." Site is Holiday Inn, Rolling Meadows IL (suburban Chicago).
Costs: $95 for MWA members; $120 for non-members; $40 extra for ms critique.
Accommodations: Easily accessible by car or train (from Chicago) Holiday Inn, Rolling Meadows $70 per night plus tax; free airport bus (Chicago O'Hare) and previously arranged rides from train.
Additional Information: "We accept manuscripts for critique (first 30 pages maximum); $40 cost. Writers meet with critics during workshop for one-on-one discussions." Brochures available for SASE after February 28.

OHIO WRITERS' HOLIDAY, COFW P.O. Box 292106, Columbus OH 43229. Estab. 1990. Annual. Conference held May 3, 1997. Average attendance: 120. "Womens' fiction, particularly romance fiction." Held at the Radisson, Columbus, Ohio. Guest speakers Mary Jo Putney (historical romance author) and Candy Lee (V.P. Harlequin/Silhouette). Includes a meet-the-authors bookfair.
Costs: $40 (includes lunch and seminar).
Additional Information: Conference brochures for SASE.

ROPEWALK WRITERS' RETREAT, 8600 University Blvd., Evansville IN 47712. (812)464-1863. E-mail: lcleek.ucs@smtp.usi.edu. Conference Coordinator: Linda Cleek. Estab. 1989. Annual. Conference held June 8-14, 1997. Average attendance: 42. "The week-long RopeWalk Writers' Retreat gives participants an opportunity to attend workshops and to confer privately with one of four or five prominent writers. Historic New Harmony, Indiana, site of two nineteenth century utopian experiments, provides an ideal setting for this event with its retreat-like atmosphere and its history of creative and intellectual achievement. At RopeWalk you will be encouraged to write—not simply listen to others talks about writing. Each workshop will be limited to twelve participants. The New Harmony Inn and Conference Center will be headquarters for the RopeWalk Writers' Retreat. Please note that reservations at the Inn should be confirmed by May 1." 1996 faculty were Pam Houston, Stephen Dobyns, Bob Shacochis and Ellen Bryant Voigt.
Costs: $375 (1995), includes breakfasts and lunches.
Accommodations: Information on overnight accommodations is made available. "Room-sharing assistance; some low-cost accommodations."
Additional Information: For critiques submit mss approx. 6 weeks ahead. Brochures are available after January 15.

SELF PUBLISHING YOUR OWN BOOK, 34200 Ridge Rd., #110, Willoughby OH 44094. (216)943-3047 or (800)653-4261. E-mail address: fa837@cleveland.freenet.edu. Teacher: Lea Leever Oldham. Estab. 1989. Quarterly. Conferences usually held in February, April, August and October. Conference duration: 2½ hours. Average attendance: up to 25. Conference covers copyright, marketing, pricing, ISBN number, Library of Congress catalog number, reaching the right customers and picking a printer. Held at Lakeland Community College, Kirtland, OH (east of Cleveland off I-90). Classrooms are wheelchair accessible.
Additional Information: Conference guidelines are available for SASE.

WESTERN RESERVE WRITERS & FREELANCE CONFERENCE, 34200 Ridge Rd., #110, Willoughby OH 44094. (216)943-3047 or (800)653-4261. E-mail address: fa837@cleveland.freenet.e du. Coordinator: Lea Leever Oldham. Estab. 1984. Annual. Conference held every September. Conference duration: 1 day. Average attendance: 150. "Fiction, nonfiction, inspirational, children's, poetry, humor, scifi, copyright and tax information, etc." Held "at Lakeland Community College, Kirtland, OH. Classrooms wheelchair accessible. Accessible from I-90, east of Cleveland." Panels include "no themes, simply published authors and other experts sharing their secrets."
Costs: $55 plus lunch.
Additional Information: Conference brochures/guidelines are available for SASE.

WESTERN RESERVE WRITERS MINI CONFERENCE, 34200 Ridge Rd., #110, Willoughby OH 44094. (216)943-3047 or (800)653-4261. E-mail address: fa837@cleveland.freenet.edu. Coordinator: Lea Leever Oldham. Estab. 1991. Annual. Conference held in late March. Conference duration: ½ day. Average attendance: 175. Conference to promote "fiction, nonfiction, children's, poetry, science fiction, etc." Held at Lakeland Community College, Kirtland, OH (east of Cleveland off I-90). Classrooms are wheelchair accessible. "Conference is for beginners, intermediate and advanced writers." Past speakers have included Mary Grimm, Nick Bade, James Martin and Mary Ryan.
Costs: $29.
Additional Information: Conference brochures/guidelines are available for SASE.

WRITING FOR MONEY WORKSHOP, 34200 Ridge Rd., #110, Willoughby OH 44094. (216)943-3047 or (800)653-4261. E-mail: fa837@cleveland.freenet.edu. Contact: Lea Leever Oldham. Conference held several times during the year. 1997 dates: February 22; March 8; April 19; May

17; July 26; September 27 and October 18. Conference duration: one day. "Covers query letters, characterization for fiction, editing grammar, manuscript preparation and marketing saleable manuscripts." Held at Lakeland Community College, Kirtland, OH. Right off I-90 and in Mayfield, OH, east of Cleveland.
Costs: $39/day.

North Central (IA, MN, NE, ND, SD, WI)

BLACK HILLS WRITERS GROUP WORKSHOP, P.O. Box 1539, Rapid City SD 55709-1539. (605)343-8661. Workshop Chair: R.T. Lawton. One-day conference held every odd-numbered year; next conference Spring 1997. Average attendance: 100. Conference concentrates on "elements of successful writing, leading to publication. All genres are covered." Held in a motel/hotel with individual rooms for seminars and large room for main speaking event. Themes planned for next conference include "What do editors want?": various fiction elements, article writing, beginners' tips, various poetry types and book-length fiction. "Our main speaker for the 1997 conference is Michael Seidman, editor at Walker & Co. Seminars and panels have featured published authors from several genres."
Costs: $40 includes lunch.
Accommodations: "For those traveling a long distance to attend our workshop, the host motel/hotel offers a special conference rate."
Additional Information: "In even-numbered years, we offer the Laura Bower Van Nuys Writing Contest." Conference brochures/guidelines are available for SASE.

COPYRIGHT WORKSHOP, 610 Langdon St., Madison WI 53703. (608)262-3447. Director: Christine DeSmet. Offered 2 times/year. Average attendance: 50. "Copyright law for writers, publishers, teachers, designers." Conference held at Wisconsin Center, University of Wisconsin—Madison.
Costs: $145.
Additional Information: Conference brochures/guidelines are available.

PETER DAVIDSON'S WRITER'S SEMINAR, 982 S. Emerald Hills Dr., P.O. Box 497, Arnolds Park IA 51331. (712)362-7968. Seminar Presenter: Peter Davidson. Estab. 1985. Seminars held about 30 times annually, in various sites. Offered year round. Seminars last 1 day, usually 9 a.m.-4 p.m. Average attendance: 35. "All writing areas including books of fiction and nonfiction, children's works, short stories, magazine articles, poetry, songs, scripts, religious works, personal experiences and romance fiction. All seminars are sponsored by community colleges or colleges across the U.S. Covers many topics including developing your idea, writing the manuscript, copyrighting, and marketing your work. A practical approach is taken."
Costs: Each sponsoring college sets own fees, ranging from $35-55, depending on location, etc.
Accommodations: "Participants make their own arrangements. Usually, no special arrangements are available."
Additional Information: "Participants are encouraged to bring their ideas and/or manuscripts for a short, informal evaluation by seminar presenter, Peter Davidson." Conference brochures/guidelines are available for SASE. "On even-numbered years, usually present seminars in Colorado, Wyoming, Nebraska, Kansas, Iowa, Minnesota, and South Dakota. On odd-numbered years, usually present seminars in Illinois, Iowa, Minnesota, Arkansas, Missouri, South Dakota, and Nebraska."

GREAT LAKES WRITER'S WORKSHOP, Alverno College, 3401 S. 39 St., P.O. Box 343922, Milwaukee WI 53234-3922. (414)382-6176. Director: Debra Pass. Telesis Institute. Estab. 1985. Annual. Workshop held during second week in July (Friday through Thursday). Average attendance: 250. "Workshop focuses on a variety of subjects including fiction, writing for magazines, freelance writing, writing for children, poetry, marketing, etc. Participants may select individual workshops or opt to attend the entire week-long session. Classes are held during evenings and weekends. The workshop is held in Milwaukee, WI at Alverno College."
Costs: In 1996, cost was $99 for entire workshop. "Individual classes are priced as posted in the brochure with the majority costing $20 each."
Accommodations: Attendees must make their own travel arrangments. Accommodations are available on campus; rooms are in residence halls and are not air-conditioned. Cost in 1996 was $25 for single, $20 per person for double. There are also hotels in the surrounding area. Call (414)382-6040 for information regarding overnight accommodations.
Additional Information: "Some workshop instructors may provide critiques, but this changes depending upon the workshop and speaker. This would be indicated in the workshop brochure." Brochures available for SASE.

GREEN LAKE 1997 WRITERS CONFERENCE, Green Lake Conference Center/American Baptist Assembly, Green Lake WI 54941-9300. (800)558-8898. Estab. 1948. Annual. 1997 conference date is July 5-12. Average attendance: 75. "This conference provides quality instructors who are published authors and experienced at being both friend and coach. Held annually at this 1,000 acre conference center located on a lake offering a wide range of recreational and creative craft opportunities in a hospitable accepting environment." Conference speakers have included Marion Dane Bauer, Ben Logan and many excellent workshop leaders.
Costs: Tuition is $80/person.
Accommodations: "We can provide ground transportation from Appleton and Oshkosh airports; the Amtrak station in Columbus and Greyhound Bus Stop in Fond du Lac for a modest fee. Room costs vary depending on facilities. All rooms are on the American Food Plan. Campground and cabin facilities also available."
Additional Information: Conference brochures are available upon request.

INTERNATIONAL MUSIC CAMP CREATIVE WRITING WORKSHOP, 1725 11th St. SW, Minot ND 58701. (701)838-8472. Camp Director: Joseph T. Alme. Estab. 1970. Annual. Conference usually held in July. Conference duration: 6 days. Average attendance: 20. "Conference to promote fiction, poetry, children's writing, plays and mystery stories including feedback from the professionals. The conference is held in the Frances Leach Library at the International Music Camp. The summer Arts camp is located at the International Peace Garden on the border between Manitoba and North Dakota. 3,000 acres of hand-planted flowers, fountains and natural beauty create a perfect setting for a creative writing workshop."
Costs: $190 including room, board and tuition. "The food in the new cafeteria is excellent. Housing in the spacious new dormitories provide privacy and comfort."
Accommodations: Northwest and Frontier Airlines fly to Minot, ND. AMTRAK goes to Rugby, ND. A shuttle service is available from both terminals. "Area motels vary in rates. However, the accommodations located on sight are excellent and at no additional cost."
Additional Information: No auditions are required. Critiques are given throughout the week. Conference brochures/guidelines are available for SASE. "A $50 deposit is required. It is refundable until June 1st, 1997. When an application is received, a list of materials needed for the workshop is sent to the student. A promotional video is available upon request."

IOWA SUMMER WRITING FESTIVAL, 116 International Center, University of Iowa, Iowa City IA 52242. (319)335-2534. E-mail: peggy-houston@uiowa.edu; amy-margolis@uiowa.edu. Director: Peggy Houston. Assistant Director: Amy Margolis. Estab. 1987. Annual. Festival held in June and July. Workshops are one week or a weekend. Average attendance: limited to 12/class—over 1,250 participants throughout the summer. "We offer courses in most areas of writing: novel, short story, essay, poetry, playwriting, screenwriting, nonfiction, writing for children, memoir, women's writing, romance and mystery." Site is the University of Iowa campus. Guest speakers are undetermined at this time. Readers and instructors have included Lee K. Abbott, Susan Power, W.P. Kinsella, Joy Harjo, Gish Jen, Abraham Verghese, Robert Olen Butler, Ethan Canin, Clark Blaise, Gerald Stern, Donald Justice, Michael Dennis Browne.
Costs: $375/week; $150, weekend workshop (1996 rates). Discounts available for early registration. Housing and meals are separate.
Accommodations: "We offer participants a choice of accommodations: dormitory, $25/night; Iowa House, $56/night; Holiday Inn, $58/night (rates subject to changes)."
Additional Information: Brochure/guidelines are available.

SCBWI/MINNESOTA CHAPTER CONFERENCES, 7080 Coachwood Rd., Woodbury MN 55125. (612)739-0119. "Although schedule may vary as space is available, conferences are usually held one day in spring and one day in fall. The smaller conference features local authors and editors only. The larger conference features children's book editors from New York publishing houses and well-known authors." Average attendance: 100. Recent speakers have included editors from Bantam Doubleday Dell and Hyperion Books for Children, authors Barbara Esbensen, Jane Resh Thomas and others.
Costs: Varies: around $20 for local conference or $85 for larger conference with discounts given for SCBWI members and early registration.
Accommodations: Not included in conference cost.
Additional Information: For conference brochure or list of local hotels, send SASE no more than 6 weeks in advance. Ms critiques and portfolio reviews available at larger conference for an additional fee.

SINIPEE WRITERS' WORKSHOP, P.O. Box 902, Dubuque IA 52004-0902. (319)556-0366. Director: John Tigges. Estab. 1985. Annual conference held in April. Average attendance: 50-75. To promote "primarily fiction although we do include a poet and a nonfiction writer on each program."

The two mentioned areas are treated in such a way that fiction writers can learn new ways to expand their abilities and writing techniques." The workshop is held on the campus of Loras College in Dubuque. "This campus holds a unique atmosphere and everyone seems to love the relaxed and restful mood it inspires. This in turn carries over to the workshop and friendships are made that last in addition to learning and experiencing what other writers have gone through to attain success in their chosen field." Speakers for the Twelfth Annual Workshop include: Valerie Woerdehoff, poet; John Tigges, novelist, writing coach and editor/critiquer.

Costs: $60 early registration/$65 at the door. Includes all handouts, necessary materials for the workshop, coffee/snack break, lunch, drinks and snacks at autograph party following workshop.

Accommodations: Information is available for out-of-town participants, concerning motels, etc., even though the workshop is 1-day long.

Additional Information: Sponsors fiction, nonfiction and poetry contests: limit 1,500 words (fiction), 40 lines (poetry). 1st prize in all 3 categories: $100 plus publication in an area newspaper or magazine; 2nd prize in both categories: $50; 3rd prize in both categories: $25. Written critique service available for contest entries, $15 extra.

UNIVERSITY OF WISCONSIN AT MADISON WRITERS INSTITUTE, 610 Langdon St., Madison WI 53703. (608)262-3447. Director: Christine DeSmet. Estab. 1990. Annual. Conference held in July. Average attendance: 175. "Day 1 is nonfiction—journalism freelance writing; Day 2 is fiction—genre writing." Conference held at University of Wisconsin at Madison. Themes: mystery, suspense, science fiction, romance, mainstream for fiction. Guest speakers are published authors, editors and agents.

Costs: $125/day or $175 for 2 days; critique fees.

Accommodations: Info on accommodations sent with registration confirmation. Critiques available. Conference brochures/guidelines are available for SASE.

WRITING WORKSHOP, P.O. Box 65, Ellison Bay WI 54210. (414)854-4088. E-mail: buchholz@ mail.wiscnet.net. Resident Manager: Don Buchholz. Estab. 1935. Annual. Conference held in June. Average attendance: 16. "General writing journal, poetry as well as fiction and nonfiction." Held in a "quiet, residential setting in deep woods on the shore of Green Bay." Past guest speakers include Lowell B. Komie (short story), T.V. Olsen (novelist) and Barbara Vroman (novelist).

Costs: In 1996, cost was $549 (twin bed) or $509 (dormitory).

Accommodations: "Two to a room with private bath in rustic log and stone buildings. Great hall type of classroom for the conference."

Additional Information: Catalog (8½ × 11) available upon request.

South Central (CO, KS, MO, NM, OK, TX)

AUSTIN WRITERS' LEAGUE WORKSHOPS/CONFERENCES/CLASSES, E-2, 1501 W. Fifth, Austin TX 78703. (512)499-8914. Fax: (512)499-0441. Executive Director: Angela Smith. Estab. 1982. Programs ongoing through the year. Duration: varies according to program. Average attendance from 15 to 200. To promote "all genres, fiction and nonfiction, poetry, writing for children, screenwriting, playwriting, legal and tax information for writers, also writing workshops for children and youth." Programs held at AWL Resource Center/Library, other sites in Austin and Texas. Topics include: finding and working with agents and publishers; writing and marketing short fiction; dialogue; characterization; voice; research; basic and advanced fiction writing/focus on the novel; business of writing; also workshops for genres. Past speakers have included Dwight Swain, Natalie Goldberg, David Lindsey, Shelby Hearon, Gabriele Rico, Benjamin Saenz, Rosellen Brown, Sandra Scofield, Reginald Gibbons, Anne Lamott and Sterling Lord.

Costs: Vary from free to $185, depending on program. Most classes, $20-50; workshops $35-75; conferences: $125-185.

Accommodations: Austin Writers' League will provide assistance with transportation arrangements on request. List of hotels is available for SASE. Special rates given at some hotels for program participants.

Additional Information: Critique sessions offered at some programs. Individual presenters determine critique requirements. Those requirements are then made available through Austin Writers' League office and in workshop promotion. Contests and awards programs are offered separately. Brochures/guidelines are available on request.

CRAFT OF WRITING, UTD Box 830688, CN 1.1, Richardson TX 75083. (214)883-2204. E-mail: janeth@utdallas.edu. Director: Janet Harris. Estab. 1983. Annual. Conference held September 19-20, 1997. Average attendance: 150. "To provide information to accomplished and aspiring writers on how to write and how to get published. All genres are included. Areas of writing covered include

There are seven **Writer's Digest School** courses to help you write better and sell more:

Novel Writing Workshop. A professional novelist helps you iron out your plot, develop your main characters, write the background for your novel, and complete the opening scene and a summary of your novel's complete story. You'll even identify potential publishers and write a query letter.

Marketing Your Nonfiction Book. You'll work with your mentor to create a book proposal that you can send directly to a publisher. You'll develop and refine your book idea, write a chapter-by-chapter outline of your subject, line up your sources of information, write sample chapters, and complete your query letter.

Writing & Selling Short Stories. Learn the basics of writing/selling short stories: plotting, characterization, dialogue, theme, conflict, and other elements of a marketable short story. Course includes writing assignments and one complete short story.

Writing & Selling Nonfiction Articles. Master the fundamentals of writing/selling nonfiction articles: finding article ideas, conducting interviews, writing effective query letters and attention-getting leads, targeting your articles to the right publication. Course includes writing assignments and one complete article manuscript (and its revision).

Writing Your Life Stories. With the help of a professional writer you'll chronicle your life or your family's. Learn the important steps to documenting your history including researching and organizing your material, continuity, pacing and more!

Writer's Digest Criticism Service. Have your work evaluated by a professional writer before you submit it for pay. Whether you write books, articles, short stories or poetry, you'll get an objective review plus the specific writing and marketing advice that only a professional can provide.

Secrets of Selling Your Manuscripts. Discover all the best-kept secrets for mailing out strategic, targeted manuscript submissions. Learn how to "slant" your writing so you can publish the same material over and over, which publishing houses are your best bet, and much more.   Mail this card today for **FREE** information!

characterization and dialogue to working with an agent." Workshops in 1996 included a panel of editors and agents (both national and local), "Using the Internet to Research and Market Your Writing," "The Novice Older Writer," "How and Why Editors Acquire the Books They Do," "The Power of Symbolism in Short Stories" and "Avoiding the Most Common Mistakes Writers Make."
Costs: $195; includes a lunch and a banquet.
Accommodations: A block of rooms is held at the OMNI Richardson Hotel for $59/night. Call (214)231-9600 for reservations.
Additional Information: Critiques available. "There are no requirements. Participants may have manuscripts critiqued by members of the Greater Dallas Writers Association. Two manuscript critique sessions are scheduled. A manuscript contest is held prior to the conference. The deadline for submissions is July. Judges are specialists in the areas they are critiquing. There are 11 categories with several cash prizes. Conference brochures/guidelines are available. Twenty-eight workshops are scheduled on a wide range of topics. Presenters include nationally known authors, agents, editors and publishers."

‡**FRONTIERS IN WRITING CONFERENCE**, P.O. Box 19303, Amarillo TX 79114. (806)764-3458, 379-6721 or 358-9389. Sponsored by Amarillo College and Panhandle Professional Writers. Annual conference held 2 days in August. For fiction, nonfiction and poetry. Conference held on the campus of Amarillo College.
Costs: In 1996, cost was $60 for PPW members, $75 for nonmembers.
Accommodations: Special conference rates available at hotel.
Additional Information: Conference brochure/registration form available for SASE.

GULF COAST WRITERS CONFERENCE AT THE UNIVERSITY OF HOUSTON-CLEAR LAKE, 2700 Bay Area Blvd., Box 198, Houston TX 77058. (713)283-2560. Fax: (713)283-2566. E-mail: glendenning@cl4.cl.uh.edu. Graduate Asst. of Cultural Arts: Joanie Glendenning. Coordinator, UHCL Cultural Arts: Mark Dolney. Estab. 1995. Annual. Conference held the last weekend in May, beginning Thursday evening and ending on Saturday afternoon. Conference duration: 2½ days. Average attendance: 80. "The overall purpose of the conference is to celebrate multicultural literature. By focusing annually on a specific theme, the conference questions how the divergence of cultures has enriched the way contemporary writers perceive society, and how those new and evolving perceptions speak through their literature. We welcome submissions in all genres which reflect the ever-growing topic of multiculturalism." The Gulf Coast Writers Conference is held on the University of Houston-Clear Lake campus. Most workshops and presentations take place on university grounds, although entertainment is held at nearby off-campus locations. Festivities include an opening ceremony and reception, an international banquet with a noted keynote speaker, a panel discussion specific to the annual theme, various workshops and presentations, a conference bookstore, and networking opportunities with writers and literary publishers.
Costs: General preregistration rate, $55; $60 at the door. Student/senior preregistration rate, $30; $35 at the door. International banquet fee: $10.
Accommodations: With advance notice, limited arrangements can be made for transportation to and from William P. Hobby Airport. "Two to three weeks notice is appreciated and preferred. We publicize information about the area hotel which offers the most competitive rate, but we will provide additional information on alternate area hotels upon request."
Additional Information: The Gulf Coast Writers Conference sponsors an annual prose and poetry competition. Individuals may submit original works which will go through a jury process. From that process, individuals are invited to read their works at the conference. In each category, Prose (includes fiction and nonfiction) and Poetry, $100 is awarded to the first-place winner. A jury panel of writers and faculty evaluates submissions according to craft excellence and relevance to theme. For entry guidelines and additional conference information, write or call Conference Organizer, Joanie Glendenning, (713)283-2560. "We encourage writers to examine the manner in which multiculturalism is bringing a new voice to contemporary literature. However, we do not limit writers to thematic constraints. We welcome submissions which embrace a diversity of themes in addition to culture."

HEART OF AMERICA WRITERS' CONFERENCE, Johnson County Community College, 12345 College Blvd., Overland Park KS 66210. Program Director: Judith Choice. Estab. 1984. Annual. Conference held April 11-12, 1997. Average attendance: 110-160. "The conference features a choice

---

MARKET CONDITIONS are constantly changing! If you're still using this book and it is 1998 or later, buy the newest edition of *Novel & Short Story Writer's Market* at your favorite bookstore or order from Writer's Digest Books.

of 16 plus sections focusing on nonfiction, children's market, fiction, journaling, essay, poetry and genre writing." Conference held in state-of-the-art conference center in suburban Kansas City. Individual sessions with agents and editors are available. Ms critiques are offered for $40. Past keynote speakers have included Natalie Goldberg, Ellen Gilchrist, Linda Hogan, David Ray, Stanley Elkin, David Shields, Luisa Valenzuela.
Costs: $100 includes lunch, reception, breaks.
Accommodations: "We provide lists of area hotels."

‡MAPLE WOODS COMMUNITY COLLEGE WRITER'S CONFERENCE, 2601 NE Barry Rd., Kansas City MO 64156. (816)437-3010. Coordinator Continuing Education: Paula Schumacher. Conference is held September 7. Conference duration: 1 day. Average attendance: 100-125. Nonfiction, mystery, poetry, agent. Conference site: Maple Woods Community College.
Costs: $59 for registration, lunch and entrance to conference.

NATIONAL WRITERS ASSOCIATION CONFERENCE, 1450 S. Havana, Suite 424, Aurora CO 80012. (303)751-7844. Fax: (303)751-8593. E-mail address: sandy.nwa@genie.geis.com. Executive Director: Sandy Whelchel. Estab. 1926. Annual. Conference held in June. Conference duration: 3 days. Average attendance: 200-300. General writing and marketing. 1997 conference in Denver, CO.
Costs: $300 (approx.).
Accommodations: All accommodations are included.
Additional Information: Awards for previous contests will be presented at the conference. Conference brochures/guidelines are available for SASE.

THE NEW LETTERS WEEKEND WRITERS CONFERENCE, University of Missouri-Kansas City, College of Arts and Sciences Continuing Ed. Division, 215 SSB, 5100 Rockhill Rd., Kansas City MO 64110-2499. (816)235-2736. Estab. in the mid-70s as The Longboat Key Writers Conference. Annual. Runs during June. Conference duration is 3 days. Average attendance: 75. "The New Letters Weekend Writers Conference brings together talented writers in many genres for lectures, seminars, readings, workshops and individual conferences. The emphasis is on craft and the creative process in poetry, fiction, screenwriting, playwriting and journalism; but the program also deals with matters of psychology, publications and marketing. The conference is appropriate for both advanced and beginning writers. The conference meets on the beautiful campus of The University of Missouri-Kansas City."
Costs: Several options are available. Participants may choose to attend as a non-credit student or they may attend for 1-3 hours of college credit from the University of Missouri. Conference registration includes continental breakfasts. For complete information, contact the University of Missouri-Kansas City.
Accommodations: Registrants are responsible for their own transportation, but information on area accommodations is made available. Also, special arrangements are made with the dormitory located on the University of Missouri-Kansas City campus. "On-campus rates are very reasonable."
Additional Information: Those registering for college credit are required to submit a ms in advance. Ms reading and critique is included in the credit fee. Those attending the conference for non-credit also have the option of having their ms critiqued for an additional fee. Conference brochures/guidelines are available for SASE.

NORTHWEST OKLAHOMA WORKSHOP, P.O. Box 1308, Enid OK 73702. (405)234-4562. Workshop Chairman: Earl Mabry. Estab. 1991. Annual. Conference held in March or April. Conference duration: 6 hours. Average attendance: 20-30. "Usually fiction is the concentration area. The purpose is to help writers learn more about the craft of writing and encourage writers 'to step out in faith' and submit." Held in the Community Room at Oakwood Mall. Past speakers have been Norma Jean Lutz, inspirational and magazine writing; Deborah Bouziden, fiction and magazine writing; Anna Meyers, children's writing; Sondra Soli, poetry; Marcia Preston, magazines.
Costs: $40; does not include meal.
Additional Information: Conference brochures/guidelines are available for SASE.

OKLAHOMA FALL ARTS INSTITUTES, P.O. Box 18154, Oklahoma City OK 73154. (405)842-0890. Contact: Associate Director of Programs. Estab. 1983. Annual. Conference held in late October.

CAN'T FIND A CONFERENCE? Conferences are listed by region. Check the introduction to this section for a list of regional categories.

Conference duration: 4 days. Average attendance 100. 1996 workshops included: Screenwriting (James Ragan); Poetry (E. Ethelbert Miller); Fiction (Rosa Shand); Writing for Children (Anna Grossnickle Hines); and Nonfiction (Ronald Christ). Held at "Quartz Mountain Arts and Conference Center, an Oklahoma state lodge located in southwest Oklahoma at the edge of Lake Altus/Lugert in the Quartz Mountains. Workshop participants are housed either in the lodge itself (in hotel-room accommodations) or in cabins or duplexes with kitchens. Classes are held in special pavilions built expressly for the Arts Institute. Pavilions offer a view of the lake and mountains." No featured panelists. Classes are taught by nationally recognized writers. Evenings include presentations and readings by faculty members and a Friday night chamber music concert.
Costs: $450, which includes double-occupancy lodging, meals, tuition and registration fee.
Accommodations: The Oklahoma Arts Institute leases all facilities at Quartz Mountain Arts and Conference Center for the exclusive use of the Fall Arts Institutes participants. Lodging is included in workshop cost.
Additional Information: Critique is usually done in class. Writers will need to bring completed works with them. 1996 Course Catalog is available. The Institutes are open to anyone.

‡OKLAHOMA WRITERS' WORKSHOP, *Nimrod,* University of Tulsa, 600 S. College, Tulsa OK 74104. (918)631-3080. Fax: (918)631-3033. E-mail: http://www.si.umich.edu/~jringold/nimrod.html. Editor-in-Chief: Francine Ringold, PhD. Estab. 1978. Workshop held annually in October. Workshop duration: 1 day. Average attendance: 100-150. Workshop in fiction and poetry. "Prize winners (*Nimrod/Hardman* Prizes) conduct workshops as do contest judges. 1996 winners included Alexandra Shelley and Patrick Phillips; judges were Lucille Clifton and Antonya Nelson. Past judges: Rosellen Brown, Stanley Kunitz and Toby Olson."
Costs: Not yet determined; generally nominal. Lunch provided.
Additional Information: *Nimrod International Journal* sponsors *Nimrod*/Hardman Literary Awards: The Katherine Anne Porter Prize for fiction and The Pablo Neruda Prize for poetry. Poety and fiction prizes: $2,000 each and publication (1st prize); $1,000 each and publication (2nd prize). Deadline: must be postmarked no later than April 17, 1997. Guidelines for SASE.

‡ROCKY MOUNTAIN BOOK FESTIVAL, P.O. Box 360, Denver CO 80211. (303)273-5933. Fax: (303)273-5935. E-mail: 103134.3675@compuserve.com. Program Director: Bonnie Sutherland. Estab. 1991. Annual. Festival held October, 1997. Festival duration: 2 days. Average attendance: 40,000. Festival promotes work from all genres. Held at Currigan Exhibition Hall in downtown Denver. Offers a wide variety of panels. Approximately 400 authors are scheduled to speak at the next festival including Ridley Pearson, Sherman Alexie, Rudolfo Anaya, Dixie Carter, Joann Greenberg and Will Shortz.
Costs: None.
Accommodations: Information on overnight accommodations is available.
Additional Information: Brochures/guidelines available for SASE.

SOUTHWEST WRITERS WORKSHOP CONFERENCE, 1338 Wyoming NE, Suite B, Albuquerque NM 87112-5000. (505)293-0303. Fax: (505)237-2665. Estab. 1983. Annual. Conference held in August. Average attendance: about 400. "Conference concentrates on all areas of writing." Workshops and speakers include writers and editors of all genres for all levels from beginners to advanced. 1996 theme was "The Writer's Passion, Power and Profit." Keynote speaker was Nancy Taylor Rosenberg, bestselling author of *Mitigating Circumstances.* Featured speakers: Claudia Shear, Catherine Lanigan and Tom Colgan.
Costs: $240 (members) and $295 (nonmembers); includes conference sessions, 2 luncheons, 2 banquets, and 2 breakfasts.
Accommodations: Usually have official airline and discount rates. Special conference rates are available at hotel. A list of other area hotels and motels is available.
Additional Information: Sponsors a contest judged by authors, editors and agents from New York, Los Angeles, etc., and from major publishing houses. Seventeen categories. Deadline: May 1. Entry fee is $24 (members) or $34 (nonmembers). Brochures/guidelines available for SASE. "An appointment (10 minutes, one-on-one) may be set up at the conference with editor or agent of your choice on a first-registered/first-served basis."

STEAMBOAT SPRINGS WRITERS GROUP, P.O. Box 774284, Steamboat Springs CO 80477. (970)879-9008. E-mail: 104560.2475@compuserve.com. Chairperson: Harriet Freiberger. Estab. 1982. Annual. Conference held August 9. Conference duration: 1 day. Average attendance: 30. "Our conference emphasizes instruction within the seminar format. Novices and polished professionals benefit from the individual attention and the camaraderie which can be established within small groups. A pleasurable and memorable learning experience is guaranteed by the relaxed and friendly atmosphere of the old train depot. Registration is limited." Steamboat Arts Council sponsors the group at the restored Train Depot.

Costs: $35 before June 15, $45 after. Fee covers all conference activities, including lunch. Lodging available at Steamboat Resorts; 10% discount for participants."

TAOS SCHOOL OF WRITING, P.O. Box 20496, Albuquerque NM 87154. (505)294-4601. E-mail: spletzer@swcp.com. Administrator: Suzanne Spletzer. Estab. 1993. Annual. Conference held in mid-July. Conference duration: 1 week. Average attendance: 60. "All fiction and nonfiction. No poetry or screenwriting. Purpose—to promote good writing skills. We meet at the Thunderbird Lodge in the Taos Ski Valley, NM. (We are the only ones there.) No telephones or televisions in rooms. No elevator. Slightly rustic landscape. Quiet mountain setting at 9,000 feet." Conference focuses on writing fiction and nonfiction and publishing. Previous speakers include David Morrell, Suzy McKee Charnas, Stephen R. Donaldson, Norman Zollinger, Denise Chavez and Richard S. Wheeler.
Costs: $1,200, includes tuition, room and board.
Accommodations: "Travel agent arranges rental cars or shuttle rides to Ski Valley from Albuquerque Sunport."
Additional Information: "Acceptance to school is determined by evaluation of submitted manuscript. Manuscripts are critiqued by faculty and students in the class during the sessions." Conference brochures/guidelines are available for SASE.

MARK TWAIN WRITERS CONFERENCE (12TH ANNUAL), 921 Center, Hannibal MO 63401. (800)747-0738. Contact: Cyndi Allison. Estab. 1985. Annual. "New format for 1997, four separate weeks of five days each with different topics and presenters for each week. Each week limited to 25 participants. Site is the Heartland Lodge in Pike County, Illinois, across the Mississippi River from Hannibal. Each conference will feature lectures on the craft of writing, hands-on workshops and one-on-one conferences. At the end of each week, participants should take home a good beginning on new pieces, or a more polished version of a work in progress." Each conference begins at 3 p.m. on Monday and concludes at 2 p.m. on Friday. Magazine & Short Story, Fiction & Nonfiction, June 16-20. Featured presenters: Mary Ann O'Roark, senior staff editor, *Guideposts* magazine; and Bruce Holland Rogers, award-winning author and English professor. Writing for Children & Storytelling, June 30-July 4. Featured presenters: Writing for Children (to be announced); Storytelling: Gladys Coggswell, premier midwestern storyteller and author. Travel Writing, Adventure Writing, Writing Your Autobiography, August 4-8. Featured presenters: Sharon Lloyd Spence, award-winning travel writer; James C. Hefley, award-winning author of over 90 books; Ron Snell, author, linguist, adventurer. Books and Humor, September 15-19. Featured presenters: Dusty Richards, author; James C. Hefley; and Karyn Buxman, nationally acclaimed humorist, author and presenter.
Costs: $465; includes tuition, lodging (double occupancy), meals, snacks and special evening events.
Accommodations: First-class lodging, dining and classroom facilities at Heartland Lodge, all rooms double occupancy, private baths, air-conditioned, all linens provided.
Additional Information: Brochures are available by calling or writing.

WRITERS WORKSHOP IN SCIENCE FICTION, English Department/University of Kansas, Lawrence KS 66045. (913)864-3380. Professor: James Gunn. Estab. 1985. Annual. Conference held June 30-July 13, 1997. Average attendance: 15. Conference for writing and marketing science fiction. "Housing is provided and classes meet in university housing on the University of Kansas campus. Workshop sessions operate informally in a lounge." 1996 guest writers: Frederik Pohl, SF writer and former editor and agent; John Ordover, writer and editor.
Costs: Tuition: $400. Housing and meals are additional.
Accommodations: Several airport shuttle services offer reasonable transportation from the Kansas City International Airport to Lawrence. In 1996 students were housed in a student dormitory at $12/day double, $20/day single.
Additional Information: "Admission to the workshop is by submission of an acceptable story. Two additional stories should be submitted by the end of June. These three stories are copied and distributed to other participants for critiquing and are the basis for the first week of the workshop; one story is rewritten for the second week." Brochures/guidelines are available for SASE. "The Writers Workshop in Science Fiction is intended for writers who have just started to sell their work or need that extra bit of understanding or skill to become a published writer."

West (AZ, CA, HI, NV, UT)

BE THE WRITER YOU WANT TO BE MANUSCRIPT CLINIC, 23350 Sereno Court, Villa 30, Cupertino CA 95014. (415)691-0300. Contact: Louise Purwin Zobel. Estab. 1969. Workshop held irregularly—usually semiannually at several locations. Workshop duration: 1-2 days. Average attendance: 20-30. "This manuscript clinic enables writers of any type of material to turn in their work-in-progress—at any stage of development—to receive help with structure and style, as well as marketing

advice." It is held on about 40 campuses at different times, including University of California and other university and college campuses throughout the west.
Costs: Usually $45-65/day, "depending on campus."
Additional Information: Brochures/guidelines available for SASE.

‡**COME WRITE WITH US**, Society of Southwestern Authors, P.O. Box 30355, Tucson AZ 85751. (520)296-5996. President: Darrell Beach. Estab. 1971. Annual. Conference held two days in January. Attendance: limited to 225. Conference "to assist writers in whatever ways we can. We cover many areas." Held at the Plaza Hotel Conference Center with hotel rooms available. Author Tony Hillerman, Tom Clark, editor of *Writer's Digest* magazine, Bill Brohaugh, editorial director of Writer's Digest Books, Linda Tomblin from *Guideposts*, Nina Bell Alan from *Reader's Digest* and others are speakers at the 1997 conference.
Costs: $150, includes dinner first day, and continental breakfast and lunch the second day.
Accommodations: Plaza Hotel in Tucson. Information included in brochure available for SASE.
Additional Information: Critiques given if ms sent ahead. Sponsors short story contest (2,500 words or less) separate from the conference. Deadline May 31, 1997. Awards given September 21, 1997. Brochures/guidelines available for SASE.

INLAND EMPIRE CHRISTIAN WRITERS GUILD, 10653 Ridgefield Terrace, Moreno Valley CA 92557. (909)924-0610. Founders: Bill Page and Carole Gift Page. President: Bill Page. Estab. 1990. Workshops in February and September. Conference lasts one day, Saturday, 9 a.m.-5 p.m. Average attendance: 90. "Conference to promote all areas of writing with Christian emphasis. Held in hotel conference room with extra room(s) for small groups."
Costs: Early registration, $54; $70 at door; breakfast and lunch included.
Accommodations: "One-day conference, but if overnight stay is desired, hotel gives special rate."
Additional Information: Conference brochure/guidelines are available for SASE or by phone.

I'VE ALWAYS WANTED TO WRITE BUT . . ., 23350 Sereno Court, Villa 30, Cupertino CA 95014. (415)691-0300. Contact: Louise Purwin Zobel. Estab. 1969. Workshop held irregularly, several times a year at different locations. Workshop duration: 1-2 days. Average attendance: 30-50. Workshop "encourages real beginners to get started on a lifelong dream. Focuses on the basics of writing." Workshops held at about 40 college and university campuses in the West, including University of California.
Costs: Usually $45-65/day "depending on college or university."
Additional Information: Brochures/guidelines available for SASE.

JACK LONDON WRITERS' CONFERENCE, 135 Clark Dr., San Mateo CA 94402-1002. (415)342-9123. Coordinator: Marlo Faulkner. Estab. 1987. Annual. Conference held March 8 from 8:00-4:30. Average attendance: 200. "Our purpose is to provide access to professional writers. Workshops have covered genre fiction, nonfiction, marketing, poetry and children's." Held at the San Francisco Airport Holiday Inn. Speakers scheduled for 1997 include Harriett Doerr, Naomi Epel and James N. Frey.
Costs: $75; includes continental breakfast, lunch and all sessions.
Additional Information: "Special rates on accommodations available at Holiday Inn." Sponsors a contest judged by the Peninsula branch of the California Writers Club (requirements in brochure). Brochures/guidelines available for SASE. The Jack London Conference has had over 80 professional writers speak and 800 participants. It's sponsored by the California Writers' Club.

‡**ROBERT MCKEE'S STORY STRUCTURE**, 12021 Wilshire Blvd., #868, Los Angeles CA 90025. (310)312-1002. Estab. 1983. Workshops held in March, June, September, December in Los Angeles and March and September in New York. Average attendance: 280 (LA), 215 (NY). "Primary emphasis of workshops is on screenwriting with applications for novels, playwriting and journalism." Workshops held in LA at Pacific Design Center (385 seat theatre) and in NY at Fashion Institute (305 seat lecture hall).
Costs: $450/person; group discounts available.
Accommodations: Discount hotel rates available.
Additional Information: Workshop brochures free.

‡**MILLS ANNUAL CHILDREN'S WRITER'S CONFERENCE**, Mills College, 5000 MacArthur Blvd., Oakland CA 94613. (510)430-2019. Network Programs Coordinator: Roxi Sater. Estab. 1993. Annual. Conference held November 8, 1997. Average attendance: 75-100. Conference on Writing for Children—fiction, nonfiction, multimedia. "The conference is held on the lovely grounds of Mills College. Theater seating affords a good view of the speakers for all participants. The general theme is always Writing for Children with an emphasis on getting published." Speakers include: editors, agents, illustrators, published authors and booksellers of children's literature.

Costs: $60 if paid by October 22, 1997; $75 at the door. Box lunch available for $10 including beverage and dessert.
Accommodations: Easily accessible from Hwy. 13 and I-580.
Additional Information: A flier is available for SASE. "Mills College offers a certificate program in children's literature. Courses such as Publishing and Marketing Issues, Writing and Illustrating Picture Books, How to Write a Middle Grade Novel, etc., are offered at various times during the year."

MOUNT HERMON CHRISTIAN WRITERS CONFERENCE, P.O. Box 413, Mount Hermon CA 95041. (408)335-4466. Fax: (408)335-9218. Director of Specialized Programs: David R. Talbott. Estab. 1970. Annual. Conference held Friday-Tuesday over Palm Sunday weekend, March 21-25, 1997. Average attendance: 175. "We are a broad-ranging conference for all areas of Christian writing, including fiction, children's, poetry, nonfiction, magazines, books, educational curriculum and radio and TV scriptwriting. This is a working, how-to conference, with many workshops within the conference involving on-site writing assignments. The conference is sponsored by and held at the 440-acre Mount Hermon Christian Conference Center near San Jose, California, in the heart of the coastal redwoods. Registrants stay in hotel-style accommodations, and full board is provided as part of conference fees. Meals are taken family style, with faculty joining registrants. The faculty/student ratio is about 1:6 or 7. The bulk of our faculty are editors and publisher representatives from major Christian publishing houses nationwide."
Costs: Registration fees include tuition, conference sessions, resource notebook, refreshment breaks, room and board and vary from $485 (economy) to $650 (deluxe), double occupancy.
Accommodations: Airport shuttles are available from the San Jose International Airport. Housing is not required of registrants, but about 95% of our registrants use Mount Hermon's own housing facilities (hotel style double-occupancy rooms). Meals with the conference are required, and are included in all fees.
Additional Information: Registrants may submit 2 works for critique in advance of the conference, then have personal interviews with critiquers during the conference. No advance work is required, however. Conference brochures/guidelines are available for SASE. "The residential nature of our conference makes this a unique setting for one-on-one interaction with faculty/staff. There is also a decided inspirational flavor to the conference, and general sessions with well-known speakers are a highlight."

PIMA WRITERS' WORKSHOP, Pima College, 2202 W. Anklam Rd., Tucson AZ 85709. (520)884-6974. Fax: (520)884-6975. Director: Meg Files. Estab. 1988. Annual. Conference held in May. Conference duration 3 days. Average attendance 200. "For anyone interested in writing—beginning or experienced writer. The workshop offers sessions on writing short stories, novels, nonfiction articles and books, children's and juvenile stories, poetry and screenplays." Sessions are held in the Center for the Arts on Pima Community College's West Campus. Past speakers include Michael Blake, Ron Carlson, Gregg Levoy, Nancy Mairs, Linda McCarriston, Sam Smiley, Jerome Stern, Connie Willis and literary agents Judith Riven and Fred Hill.
Costs: $65 (can include ms critique). Participants may attend for college credit, in which case fees are $68 for Arizona residents and $310 for out-of-state residents. Meals and accommodations not included.
Accommodations: Information on local accommodations is made available, and special workshop rates are available at a specified motel close to the workshop site (about $50/night).
Additional Information: Participants may have up to 20 pages critiqued by the author of their choice. Mss must be submitted 2 weeks before the workshop. Conference brochure/guidelines available for SASE. "The workshop atmosphere is casual, friendly, and supportive, and guest authors are very accessible. Readings, films and panel discussions are offered as well as talks and manuscript sessions."

SAN DIEGO STATE UNIVERSITY WRITERS' CONFERENCE, SDSU College of Extended Studies, San Diego CA 92182-1920. (619)594-2517. E-mail address: ealcaraz@mail.sdsu.edu. Website: http://rohan.sdsu.edu/dept/extstd/writers.html. Assistant to Director of Extension and Conference Facilitator: Erin Grady Alcaraz. Estab. 1984. Annual. Conference held on 3rd weekend in January. Conference duration: 2 days. Average attendance: approximately 350. "This conference is held on the San Diego State University campus at the Aztec Center. The Aztec Center is conveniently located near parking; the meeting rooms are spacious and comfortable and all sessions meet in the same general area. Each year the SDSU Writers Conference offers a variety of workshops for the beginner and the advanced writer. This conference allows the individual writer to choose which workshop best suits his/her needs. In addition to the workshop, read and critique appointments and office hours are provided so attendees may meet with speakers, editors and agents in small, personal groups to discuss specific questions. A reception is offered Saturday immediately following the workshops where attendees may socialize with the faculty in a relaxed atmosphere. Keynote speaker is to be determined."
Costs: Not to exceed $225. This includes all conference workshops and office hours, coffee and pastries in the morning, lunch and reception Saturday evening.

Accommodations: Call or write for a listing of nearby hotels and their rates. Attendees must make their own travel arrangements.

Additional Information: Read and Critique sessions are private, one-on-one opportunities to meet with editors and agents to discuss your submission. Also featured is the research emporium where experts will lecture and answer questions about various topics such as forensics, police procedures, historical clothing and customs, weapons, etc. To receive a brochure, call or send a postcard with address to: SDSU Writers Conference, College of Extended Studies, 5250 Campanile Drive, San Diego State University, San Diego CA 92182-1920 or e-mail. No SASE required.

SCBWI/NORCAL CHAPTER RETREAT AT ASILOMAR, 1316 Rebecca Dr., Suisun CA 94585-3603. (707)426-6776. Contact: Bobi Martin, Regional Advisor. Estab. 1984. Annual. Conference held during last weekend in February. Attendance limited to 65. "The retreat is designed to refresh and encourage writers and illustrators for children. Speakers are published writers, illustrators and editors. Topics vary year to year and have included writing techniques, understanding marketing, plotting, pacing, etc. The retreat is held at the Asilomar conference grounds in Monterey. There is time for walking on the beach or strolling through the woods. Rooms have private baths and 2 beds. Meals are served semi-cafeteria style and the group eats together. Vegetarian meals also available.
Costs: $200 for SCBWI members; $235 for nonmembers.
Accommodations: "All accommodations are on-site and are included in the cost. All rooms are double occupancy and disabled-accessible. Those insisting on a private room may stay off grounds." Attendees must make their own transportation arrangements.
Additional Information: Scholarships available to SCBWI members. "Applicants for scholarships should write a letter explaining their financial need and describing how attending the retreat will help further their career. All applications are kept fully confidential." Brochures available for SASE. "Registration begins in October of previous year and fills quickly, but a waiting list is always formed and late applicants frequently do get in."

SOCIETY OF SOUTHWESTERN AUTHORS WRITERS' CONFERENCE, P.O. Box 30355, Tucson AZ 85751-0355. (520)296-5299. Fax: (520)296-0409. Conference Chair: Penny Porter. Estab. 1972. Annual. Two-day conferences held in January. Average attendance: 300. Conference "covers a spectrum of practical topics for writers. Each year varies, but there is a minimum of 16 different classes during the day, plus the keynote speaker." Keynote speakers for 1997: author Tony Hillerman and Tom Clarke, *Writer's Digest* editor-in-chief. Conference held at University of Arizona.
Costs: $150 general.
Additional Information: Conference brochures/guidelines are available for SASE.

SQUAW VALLEY COMMUNITY OF WRITERS, 10626 Banner Lava Cap Rd., Nevada City CA 96146. (916)274-8551. (September-June address). P.O. Box 2352, Olympic Valley CA 96146. (916)583-5200. (June-September address). Programs Director: Brett Hall Jones. Estab. 1969. Annual. Conference held in July and August. Each program is 1 week. Average attendance approximately 120. "Squaw Valley Workshops include four separate one-week programs—Art of the Wild, Poetry, Fiction and Screenwriting. Each concentrates on its particular discipline except the Art of the Wild which includes poetry, fiction and nonfiction about nature, the environment and the ecological crisis. The workshops are conducted in the Olympic House, a large ski lodge built for the 1960 Winter Olympics. The environment includes pine trees, alpine lakes, rivers and streams; the elevation is 6,200 feet, and we have cool mornings and sunny, warm afternoons."
Costs: Tuition is $555 for the week. Scholarships are available.
Accommodations: "We have vans which will pick up participants at the Reno airport and at the Truckee Bus and train stations. The Community of Writers rents large ski houses in the Valley to house the attendees. This fosters the community atmosphere which makes our experience unique, as well as allowing us to keep the weekly rate reasonable: $160 multi, 220 double and 350 single."
Additional Information: "Acceptance is based on submitted work. Each participant's manuscript is critiqued in depth during the week of the workshop. A written critique is not available for each work submitted. Brochures/guidelines available. Each participant will have an opportunity to have an additional manuscript read by a staff member who will then meet with them for a private conference."

UCI EXTENSION ANNUAL WRITERS' CONFERENCE, Pereira & Berkeley, P.O. Box 6050, Irvine CA 92716-6050. (714)824-5990. Fax: (714)824-3651. Director, Arts & Humanities: Nancy Warzer-Brady. Estab. 1994. Conference held in July. Conference duration: 2 days. Average attendance: 100. Conference to promote nonfiction and fiction writing." Conference held in UCI Extension classroom facility equipped for conference-type meetings. "In addition to the annual summer writers' conference, we offer approximately ten short courses and workshops on fiction, nonfiction, poetry, and screenwriting on a quarterly basis. A new Screenwriting Certificate Program is being launched in Fall 1996."

Costs: Fees range from $150 to $295.
Accommodations: Accommodations available for out of town participants if requested. Special University rates at Holiday Inn, $64.80/night including breakfast.
Additional Information: Conference brochures/guidelines available for SASE.

WRITE YOUR LIFE STORY FOR PAY, 23350 Sereno Court, Villa 30, Cupertino CA 95014. (415)691-0300. Contact: Louise Purwin Zobel. Estab. 1969. Workshop held irregularly, usually semiannually at several locations. Workshop duration: 1-2 days. Average attendance: 30-50. "Because every adult has a story worth telling, this conference helps participants to write fiction and nonfiction in books and short forms, using their own life stories as a base." This workshop is held on about 40 campuses at different times, inluding University of California and other university and college campuses in the West.
Costs: Usually $45-65/day, "depending on campus."
Additional Information: Brochures/guidelines available for SASE.

WRITERS CONNECTION SELLING TO HOLLYWOOD, P.O. Box 24770, San Jose CA 95154-4770. (408)445-3600. Fax: (408)445-3609. E-mail: writerscx@aol.com. Directors: Steve and Meera Lester. Estab. 1988. Annual. Conference held in August in LA area. Conference duration: 3 days. Average attendance: 275. "Conference targets scriptwriters and fiction writers, whose short stories, books, or plays have strong cinematic potential, and who want to make valuable contacts in the film industry. Full conference registrants receive a private consultation with the film industry producer or professional of his/her choice who make up the faculty. Panels, workshops, and 'Ask a Pro' discussion groups include agents, professional film and TV scriptwriters, and independent as well as studio and TV and feature film producers."
Costs: In 1996: full conference by June, $495 members, $520 nonmembers; after June 10, $520 (members); $545 (nonmembers). Includes meals. Partial registration available.
Accommodations: $100/night (in LA) for private room; $50/shared room. Discount with designated conference airline.
Additional Information: "This is the premier screenwriting conference of its kind in the country, unique in its offering of an industry-wide perspective from pros working in all echelons of the film industry. Great for making contacts." Conference brochure/guidelines available.

WRITER'S CONSORTIUM, P.O. Box 234112, Encinitas CA 92023-4112. (619)259-5321. Director: Carol Roper. Estab. 1990. Annual. Conference held in July or August. Conference duration: 2 days. Average attendance: 50. "Emphasis is on the writer's process primarily for beginning to midlevel screenwriters. Attention is given to craft and the market place." Held in "rustic cabins and conference rooms at Camp Cedar Glen in Julian County, 50 miles east of San Diego in the mountains. Altitude 4,000 feet." Guests for 1996 included John Adams, Susan Wittering and Tim Miller.
Costs: $175, includes dormitory room, meals and workshops. Some scholarships available. Write for details.
Accommodations: "Conference includes overnight accommodations, but Julian has several hotels and B&Bs for those who prefer more luxury than the cottages. Hotels cost $68-160 per night."
Additional Information: Ten pages of a screenplay must be submitted 30 days prior to the conference and include final or full payment for conference.

Northwest (AK, ID, MT, OR, WA, WY)

CLARION WEST WRITERS' WORKSHOP, 340 15th Ave. E., Suite 350, Seattle WA 98112. (206)322-9083. Contact: Admissions Department. Estab. 1983. Annual. Workshop held June 16-July 26. Workshop duration 6 weeks. Average attendance: 20. "Conference to prepare students for professional careers in science fiction and fantasy writing. Held at Seattle Central Community College on Seattle's Capitol Hill, an urban site close to restaurants and cafes, not too far from downtown." Deadline for applications: April 1.
Costs: Workshop: $1,300 ($100 discount if application received by March 1). Dormitory housing: $750, meals not included.
Accommodations: Students are strongly encouraged to stay on-site, in dormitory housing at Seattle University. Cost: $750, meals not included, for 6-week stay.
Additional Information: "This is a critique-based workshop. Students are encouraged to write a story a week; the critique of student material produced at the workshop forms the principal activity of the workshop. Students and instructors critique manuscripts as a group." Conference guidelines available for SASE. Limited scholarships are available, based on financial need. Students must submit 20-30 pages of ms to qualify for admission. Dormitory and classrooms are handicapped accessible.

FLIGHT OF THE MIND—SUMMER WRITING WORKSHOP FOR WOMEN, 622 SE 29th Ave., Portland OR 97214. (503)236-9862. E-mail: womenwrite@aol.com. Director: Judith Barrington. Estab. 1984. Annual. Workshops held June 13-20 and June 22-29. Conference duration: each workshop lasts 1 week. Average attendance: 65. "Conference held at an old retreat center on the Mackenzie River in the foothills of the Oregon Cascades. Right on the river—hiking trails, hot springs nearby. Most students accommodated in single dorm rooms; a few private cabins available. We have our own cooks and provide spectacular food." Five classes—topics vary year to year; 1996 included "Steering the Craft" taught by Ursula K. LeGuin.
Costs: Approximately $780 for tuition, board and single dorm room. Extra for private cabin; bunk room cheaper alternative.
Accommodations: Special arrangements for transportation: "We charter a bus to pick up participants in Eugene, OR, at airport, train station and bus station." Accommodations are included in cost.
Additional Information: "Critiquing is part of most classes; no individual critiques. We require manuscript submissions for acceptance into workshop. (Receive about twice as many applications as spaces)." Workshop brochures/guidelines are available for 1 first-class stamp (no envelope). "This is a feminist-oriented workshop with a focus on work generated at the workshop."

HAYSTACK WRITING PROGRAM, PSU School of Extended Studies, P.O. Box 1491, Portland OR 97207. (503)725-8500. Contact: Maggie Herrington. Estab. 1968. Annual. Program runs from last week of June through first week of August. Workshop duration varies; one-week and weekend workshops are available throughout the six-week program. Average attendance: 10-15/workshop; total program: 325. "The program features a broad range of writing courses for writers at all skill levels. Classes are held in Cannon Beach, Oregon." Past instructors have included William Stafford, Ursula K. LeGuin, Craig Lesley, Molly Gloss, Mark Medoff, Tom Spanbauer, Sallie Tisdale.
Costs: Approximately $320/course. Does not include room and board.
Accommodations: Attendees make their own transportation arrangements. Various accommodations available including: B&B, motel, hotel, private rooms, camping, etc. A list of specific accommodations is provided.
Additional Information: Free brochure available. University credit (graduate or undergraduate) is available.

MAKING WAVES WITH WRITERS, (II), AHRRC, P.O. Box 6024, Flagstaff AZ 86011-6024. (520)523-3559. Fax: (520)523-5233. Director: Ray Newton. Estab. 1994. Biennial. Conference held in September. Conference duration: 8 days. Average attendance: 50-60. Conference concentrating on "both fiction and nonfiction for all levels of writers—beginners through established. We place lots of emphasis upon marketing and publishing." Conference held aboard the MS Ryndam cruise ship to Alaska, with stops at various ports along the Inland Passage to Alaska from Vancouver. 1996 speakers included Tom Clark, editor, *Writer's Digest*; Caroll Shreeve, editor, Gibbs-Smith Publishing; Robert Early, editor, *Arizona Highways*; Ray Newton, professor-writing; Bud Gardner, professor-writing and speaking; Nancy Elliott, award-winning novelist/writer; and Carol O'Hara, award-winning editor-publisher, Cat-Tales Press.
Costs: $995-2,515; includes shipboard accommodations, meals and workshop. Does not include airfare to Anchorage from home city.
Accommodations: Handicapped facilities are available. Rooms are also available in Vancouver and Anchorage for early or late arrivals.
Additional Information: "A special feature will be the addition of a 'Learn to Speak Publicly' workshop, taught by Bud Gardner."

SITKA SYMPOSIUM ON HUMAN VALUES & THE WRITTEN WORD, P.O. Box 2420, Sitka AK 99835. (907)747-3794. Fax: (907)747-6554. Director: Carolyn Servid. Estab. 1984. Annual. Conference held in June. Conference duration: 1 week. Average attendance: 50. Conference "to consider the relationship between writing and the ideas of a selected theme focusing on social and cultural issues." The Symposium is held in downtown Sitka. Many points of visitor interest are within walking distance. The town looks out over surrounding water and mountains. Guest speakers have included Alison Deming, Daniel Kemmis, Scott Russell Sanders, Rina Swentzell, Barry Lopez, William Kittredge, Gary Snyder, Margaret Atwood, Terry Tempest Williams and Robert Hass.
Costs: $220 before May 1; $250 after May 1.
Accommodations: Accommodation rates are listed on Symposium brochure.
Additional Information: Ms critiques (individually with faculty) are available for people submitting work before May 20. Conference brochures/guidelines are available for SASE.

‡**SWA WINTER WORKSHOP**, Seattle Writers Association, P.O. Box 33265, Seattle WA 98133. (206)860-5207. President: Claudia McCormick. Estab. 1986. Annual (February 8, 1997). Workshop 1 day, 9 a.m.-4 p.m. Average attendance: approximately 50. "A 'brown bag' intensive workshop that augments and offsets SWA's annual program, e.g., 1995-96 concentrated on fiction; 1996 workshop

presented Elizabeth Lyon on nonfiction book proposals." Site varies. 1997 themes: "What Sells and Why" and "How do editors make their selections?" Guest speakers and panelists are regional publishing representatives (editors), radio representatives and booksellers.
Costs: $20; snacks provided, bring lunch.
Additional Information: SWA sponsors Writers in Performance, a jury-selected public presentation of Seattle's best writing. Judges are published and unpublished writers, editors and consultants. Guidelines for SASE. "Workshop 1997 includes critique of Tier I of all Writers In Performance 1997 submissions and explaines the critique and the selection and sales process."

WILLAMETTE WRITERS CONFERENCE, 9045 SW Barbur, Suite 5-A, Portland OR 97219. (503)495-1592. Fax: (503)495-0372. E-mail: wilwrite@teleport.com. Contact: Conference Director. Estab. 1968. Annual. Conference held in August. Average attendance: 220. "Willamette Writers is open to all writers, and we plan our conference accordingly. We offer workshops on all aspects of fiction, nonfiction, marketing, the creative process, etc. Also we invite top notch inspirational speakers for key note addresses. Most often the conference is held on a local college campus which offers a scholarly atmosphere and allows us to keep conference prices down. Recent theme was 'Craft and Creativity.' We always include at least one agent or editor panel and offer a variety of topics of interest to both fiction and nonfiction writers." Past editors and agents in attendance have included: Marc Aronson, senior editor, Henry Holt & Co.; Tom Colgan, senior editor, Avon Books; Charles Spicer, Senior Editor, St. Martin's Press; Sheree Bykofsky, Sheree Bykofsky Associates; Laurie Harper, Sebastian Agency; F. Joseph Spieler, The Spieler Agency; Robert Tabian and Ruth Nathan.
Costs: Cost for full conference including meals is $195 members; $250 nonmembers.
Accomodations: If necessary, these can be made on an individual basis. Some years special rates are available.
Additional Information: Conference brochures/guidelines are available for catalog-size SASE.

WRITE ON THE SOUND WRITERS' CONFERENCE, 700 Main St., Edmonds WA 98020. (206)771-0228. Arts Coordinator: Christine Weed. Estab. 1986. Annual. Conference held first weekend in October. Conference duration: 2 days. Average attendance: 160. "Workshops and lectures are offered for a variety of writing interests and levels of expertise."
Costs: $75 for 2 days, $40 for 1 day; includes tuition, continental breakfast and 1 ticket to keynote lecture. Box lunches available at additional cost.
Additional Information: Brochures available in August for SASE.

WRITERS WEEKEND AT BEACH, P.O. Box 877, Ocean Park WA 98640. (360)665-6576. Co-Director: Birdie Etchison. Estab. 1992. Annual. Conference held last weekend in February. Average attendance: 60. Conference covers fiction, nonfiction, writing for children, poetry and photography. Held at a location "with a fantastic view of the Pacific Ocean. The new conference center provides all workshops, sleeping and eating on one floor." 1997 guest keynote speaker: Dennis Stovall, publisher Blue Heron Press.
Costs: $125, includes meals, lodging and workshop fees.
Additional Information: Conference brochures/guidelines are available for SASE.

Canada

✤**MARITIME WRITERS' WORKSHOP**, Extension & Summer Session, UNB Box 4400, Fredericton, New Brunswick E3B 5A3 Canada. (506)453-4646. Coordinator: Glenda Turner. Estab. 1976. Annual. Conference held in July. Conference duration: 1 week. Average attendance: 50. "Workshops in four areas: fiction, poetry, nonfiction, writing for children." Site is University of New Brunswick, Fredericton campus.
Costs: $300, tuition; $135 meals; $120/double room; $140/single room (Canadian funds).
Accommodations: On-campus accommodations and meals.
Additional Information: "Participants must submit 10-20 manuscript pages which form a focus for workshop discussions." Brochures are available. No SASE necessary.

✤**SAGE HILL WRITING EXPERIENCE**, Box 1731, Saskatoon, Saskatchewan S7K 3S1 Canada. Executive Director: Steven Smith. Annual. Workshops held in August and October. Workshop duration 7-21 days. Attendance: limited to 36-40. "Sage Hill Writing Experience offers a special working and learning opportunity to writers at different stages of development. Top quality instruction, low instructor-student ratio and the beautiful Sage Hill setting offer conditions ideal for the pursuit of excellence in the arts of fiction, poetry and playwriting." The Sage Hill location features "individual accommodation, in-room writing area, lounges, meeting rooms, healthy meals, walking woods and vistas in several directions." Seven classes are held: Introduction to Writing Fiction & Poetry; Fiction Workshop;

Writing Young Adult Fiction Workshop; Poetry Workshop, Intermediate; Poetry Colloquium; Fiction Colloquium, Advanced; Playwriting Lab. 1996 faculty included Patrick Lane, Sharon Pollock, Bonnie Burnard, Kevin Major, Janice Kulyk Keefer, Di Brandt, William Robertson and Rosemary Nixon. **Costs:** $425-495 (Canadian) includes instruction, accommodation, meals and all facilities. Fall Poetry Colloquium: $700. **Accommodations:** On-site individual accommodations located at Lumsden 45 kilometers outside Regina. Fall Colloquium is at Muenster, Saskatchewan, 150 kilometers east of Saskatchewan. **Additional Information:** For Introduction to Creative Writing: A five-page sample of your writing or a statement of your interest in creative writing; list of courses taken required. For intermediate and colloquium program: A resume of your writing career and a 12-page sample of your work plus 5 pages of published work required. Application deadline is May 1. Guidelines are available for SASE. Scholarships and bursaries are available.

❤THE VANCOUVER INTERNATIONAL WRITERS FESTIVAL, 1243 Cartwright St., Vancouver, British Columbia V6H 4B7 Canada. (604)681-6330. Estab. 1988. Annual. Held during the 3rd week of October. Average attendance: 8,000. "This is a festival for readers and writers. The program of events is diverse and includes readings, panel discussions, seminars. Lots of opportunities to interact with the writers who attend." Held on Granville Island—in the heart of Vancouver. Two professional theaters are used as well as Performance Works (an open space). "We try to avoid specific themes. Programming takes place between February and June each year and is by invitation." **Costs:** Tickets are $10-15 (Canadian). **Accommodations:** Local tourist info can be provided when necessary and requested. **Additional Information:** Brochures/guidelines are available for SASE. "A reminder—this is a festival, a celebration, not a conference or workshop."

‡❤THE VICTORIA SCHOOL OF WRITING, Write Away!, 607 Linden Ave., Victoria, British Columbia V8B 4G6 Canada. (604)385-8982. Contact: Margaret Dyment. "Five-day intensive workshop on beautiful Vancouver Island with outstanding author-instructors in fiction, poetry, children's literature and playwriting." **Cost:** $395. **Accommodations:** Special hotel rates available. **Additional Information:** Workshop brochures available.

International

THE AEGEAN CENTER FOR THE FINE ARTS WORKSHOPS, Paros 84400, Cyclades, Greece. (30)284-23287. Director: John A. Pack. Held 7 times/year. Workshop held May, June, July, September, October and November. Workshop duration: Spring—4-13 weeks; Summer sessions: 2-3 weeks; Fall—4-15 weeks. Average attendance: 15. "Creative writing in all its aspects." Spring workshop held at the Aegean Center "in a neoclassical 16th century townhouse in the village of Parikia with a gallery/lecture hall, well-equipped darkroom, modest library, rooms for studio space and classrooms." Location is on Paros, an island about 100 miles southeast of Athens. Fall workshop held in Italy starting in Pistoia in 16th century Villa Rospigliosi and includes travel to Pisa, Lucca, Prato, Siena, Venice, Florence and Rome in Italy as well as Athens and, finally, Paros. **Costs:** There is a $75 application fee. For 13-week Spring workshop, tuition is $6,000 in 1997 or $2,500/monthly session (housing included). Summer session tuition is $2,500 (includes housing). For 15-week Fall workshop, tuition is $7,500 in 1997, or $2,500 for monthly session ($3,500 Italy session only). Includes housing (villa accommodation and hotels in Italy); half board in villa accommodation; travel while in Italy; museum entrance fees. **Accommodations:** In Paros, accommodations (single occupancy apartment). All apartments have small equipped kitchen areas and private bathrooms. Italy, villa accommodation and hotels. **Additional Information:** College credit is available. Workshop brochures/guidelines are available for SASE.

‡THE ARVON FOUNDATION LTD. WORKSHOPS, Totleigh Barton Sheepwash, Beaworthy, Devon EX21 5NS United Kingdom 00 44 14 09231338. National Director: David Pease. Estab. 1968 (workshops). Workshops held April through November at 3 centers. Workshops last 4½ days. Average attendence: 16/workshop. Workshops cover all types of fiction writing. "Totleigh Barton in Devon was the first Arvon centre. Next came Lumb Bank (Hebden Bridge, West Yorkshire HX7 6DF) and now, 12 courses at Moniack Mhor (Moniack, Kirkhill, Inverness IV 5 7PQ)." Totleigh Barton is a thatched manor house. Lumb Bank is an 18th century mill owner's home and Moniack Mhor is a traditional croft house. All are in peaceful, rural settings. In the three houses there are living rooms, reading rooms, rooms for private study, dining rooms and well equipped kitchens."

Costs: In 1997 course fee will be £275 which includes food, tuition and accommodation. For those in need, a limited number of grants and bursaries are available from the Arvon Foundation.

Accommodations: There is sleeping accommodation for up to 16 course members, but only limited single room accommodation (there are 8 bedrooms at Lumb Bank, 12 bedrooms at Moniack Mhor and 9 bedrooms at Totleigh Barton). The adjacent barns at Lumb Bank and Totleigh Barton have been converted into workshop/studio space and there are writing huts in the garden.

Additional Information: Sometimes writers are required to submit work. Check for details. Conference brochure/guidelines available for SASE.

EDINBURGH UNIVERSITY CENTRE FOR CONTINUING EDUCATION CREATIVE WRITING WORKSHOPS, 11 Buccleuch Place, Edinburgh Scotland EH8 9LW. (31)650-4400. E-mail: b.stevens@ed.ac.uk. Administrative Director of International Summer Schools: Bridget M. Stevens. Estab. 1990. Introductory course July 5-11; short story course July 12-18; playwriting course July 19-August 1. Average attendance: 15. Courses cover "basic techniques of creative writing, the short story and playwriting. The University of Edinburgh Centre for Continuing Education occupies traditional 18th century premises near the George Square Campus. Located nearby are libraries, banks, recreational facilities and the university faculty club which workshop participants are invited to use."

Costs: In 1996 cost was £195 per one-week course (tuition only).

Accommodations: Information on overnight accommodations is available. Accommodations include student dormitories, self-catering apartment and local homes.

Additional Information: Participants are encouraged to submit work in advance, but this is not obligatory. Conference brochures/guidelines available for SASE.

FICTION WRITING RETREAT IN ACAPULCO, 3584 Kirkwood Place, Boulder CO 80304. (303)444-0086. Conference Director: Barbara Steiner. Estab. 1991. Annual. Conference held in November. Conference duration: 1 week. Average attendance: 10. Conference concentrates on creativity and fiction technique/any market. Oceanfront accommodations on private estate of Mexican artist Nora Beteta. Rooms in villa have bath (private) but usually dual occupancy. Swimming in pool or ocean/bay. Classes held on large porches with ocean breeze and views.

Costs: $595 for 1 week includes room, meals, classes.

Accommodations: Airfare separate. Travel agent books flights for groups from Denver. Will book from anyplace in US.

Additional Information: "Writers submit one short fiction piece in advance of workshop. Classes include writing, lecture and assignments." Brochures/guidelines available for SASE.

TŶ NEWYDD WRITER'S CENTRE, Llanystumdwy, Cricieth Gwynedd LL52 OLW, 01766-522811 United Kingdom. Administrator: Sally Baker. Estab. 1990. Regular courses held throughout the year. Every course held Monday-Saturday. Average attendance: 14. "To give people the opportunity to work side by side with professional writers." Site is Ty Newydd. Large manor house. Last home of the prime minister, David Lloyd George. Situated in North Wales, Great Britain-between mountains and sea." Past featured tutors include novelists Beryl Bainbridge and Bernice Rubens.

Costs: £255 for Monday-Saturday (includes full board, tuition).

Accommodations: Transportation from railway stations arranged. Accommodation in TyNewydd (onsite).

Additional Information: "We have had several people from U.S. on courses here in the past three years. More and more people come to us from the U.S. often combining a writing course with a tour of Wales."

WOMEN'S WILDERNESS CANOE TRIPS WRITING RETREAT, P.O. Box 9109, Santa Fe NM 87504. (505)984-2268. Owner and Guide: Beverly Antaeus. Estab. 1985. Annual. Conference held June 24-30, 1997. Conference duration: 8 days. Average attendence: 20. Writing retreat with Deena Metzger. "All genres welcome as the means to bring forth something truer and newer than ever before." Held "on the beach, Heron Lake NM, California and Mexico. Living under sun and moon; tents available for sleeping."

Costs: $1,195-$1,997; land costs, tuition and food included in fee.

Accommodations: All transportation details are provided upon enrollment. "We live outdoors throughout the workshop—all rendezvous and departure details provided in full."

FOR INFORMATION ON ENTERING the *Novel & Short Story Writer's Market* Cover Letter Contest, see page 16.

Additional Information: Brochures/guidelines available upon request.

THE WRITERS' SUMMER SCHOOL, SWANWICK, The New Vicarage, Woodford Halse, Daventry, NN11 3RE England. E-mail: courties@dial.pipex.com. Secretary: Brenda Courtie. Estab. 1949. Annual. Conference held August 10-16. Average attendance: 300 plus. "Conference concentrates on all fields of writing." In 1996 courses included Popular Contemporary Novels, Poetry, Beginners, The Novel, Short Stories, New Technology, Nonfiction, Comedy for Radio and TV. Speakers in 1996 included Deric Longden, Sue Teddern, Terry Fletcher, Julian Atlerton, Alan Sillitue.
Costs: £185 inclusive.
Accommodations: Buses from main line station to conference centre provided.
Additional Information: "Some course leaders will accept manuscripts prior to the conference. The Writers' Summer School is a nonprofit-making organization."

Retreats and Colonies

If you are looking for a quiet place to start or complete your novel or short story collection, a retreat or writers' colony may offer just what you need. Often located in tranquil settings, these are places for writers to find solitude and concentrated time to focus solely on their writing. Unlike conferences or workshop settings, communal meals may be the only scheduled activities. Also, a writer's stay at a retreat or colony is typically anywhere from one to twelve weeks (sometimes longer), while time spent at a conference or workshop is generally anywhere from one day to two weeks (perhaps a month at most).

Like conferences and workshops, however, retreats and colonies span a wide range. Some offer residencies for established writers, while most, such as Dorset Colony House for Writers, are open to writers on all levels. Other programs are restricted to writers from certain areas or who write on certain subjects such as the Camargo Foundation retreat for a writer working on a project relating to French culture. And you'll find retreats and colonies located in Pahoa, Hawaii; County Monaghan, Ireland; Cape Cod, Massachusetts; and Taos, New Mexico. Accommodations vary from a restored antebellum home in Mississippi to a castle in Scotland to wood-frame cottages on an island off the coast of Washington state.

Despite different focuses and/or locations, all retreats and colonies have one thing in common: They are places where writers may work undisturbed, usually in nature-oriented and secluded settings. A retreat or colony serves as a place for rejuvenation; a writer can find new ideas, rework old ones or put the finishing touches to works-in-progress.

Arrangements at retreats and colonies differ dramatically so it may help to determine your own work habits before you begin searching through these pages. While some retreats house writers in one main building, others provide separate cottages. In both cases, residents are generally given private work space, although they usually must bring along their own typewriters or personal computers. Some colonies offer communal, family-style meals at set times; some prepare meals for each resident individually and still others require residents to prepare meals themselves. If you tend to work straight through meals now, you might want to consider a retreat or colony that offers the last option.

A related consideration for most folks is cost. Again, the types of arrangements vary. A good number of residencies are available at no cost or only a minimal daily cost, sometimes including the cost of meals, sometimes not. The Ragdale Foundation charges a mere $15 a day and offers scholarships, for example, and the Millay Colony for the Arts charges no fees. Other residencies are "awards," resulting from competitive applications. Finally, for those residencies that are fairly expensive, scholarships or fee waivers are often available.

In general, residencies at retreats and colonies are competitive because only a handful of spots are available at each place. Writers must often apply at least six months in advance for the time period they desire. While some locations are open year-round, others are available only during certain seasons. Planning to go during the "off-season" may lessen your competition. Also, most places will want to see a writing sample with your application, so be prepared to show your best work—whether you are a beginning or established writer. In addition, it will help to have an idea of the project you'll work on while in residence, since some places request this information with their applications as well.

Each listing in this section provides information about the type of writers the retreat or colony accepts; the location, accommodations and meal plan available; the costs; and, finally, the application process. As with markets and conferences and workshops, changes in policies may be made after this edition has gone to press. Send a self-addressed, stamped envelope to the places that interest you to receive the most up-to-date details.

For other listings of retreats and colonies, you may want to see *The Guide to Writers Conferences* (ShawGuides, 10 W. 66th St., Suite 30H, New York NY 10023), which not only provides information about conferences, workshops and seminars but also residencies, retreats and organizations. It is now available on their website at http:// www.shawguides.com. An exceptional resource is *Havens for Creatives*, available from ACTS Institute, Inc. (c/o Charlotte Plotsky, P.O. Box 30854, Palm Beach Gardens FL 33420), which features almost 400 retreats, colonies, art programs and creative vacation opportunities for writers, artists, photographers and other creative types. This directory also includes a bibliography of works written about art and writing colonies and a selection of creative work written during residencies.

EDWARD F. ALBEE FOUNDATION, (THE BARN), 14 Harrison St., New York NY 10013. (212)226-2020. Foundation Secretary: David Briggs. For writers (fiction, nonfiction, playwrights, etc.) and visual artists (painters, sculptors, etc.). " 'The Barn' is located in Montauk, NY." Available for 1 month residencies from June through September. Provisions for the writer include private rooms. Accommodates 2-3 writers at one time. Residencies supported by the Edward F. Albee Foundation Fellowship.
Costs: No cost, but residents are responsible for their food, travel and supplies.
To Apply: Write or call for information and applications (accepted January 1 to April 1). Brochures or guidelines are available for SASE.

‡ATLANTIC CENTER FOR THE ARTS, 1414 Art Center Ave., New Smyrna Beach FL 32168. (904)427-6975. Program Director: Nicholas Conroy. Estab. 1977. "Residencies at Atlantic Center are open to all who meet selection requirements. Master Artists, who are selected in consultation with the National Council, set the structure of the residency, determine what will be accomplished and set criteria for selection of Associates. Associates, who are typically artists at mid-career, are selected by Master Artists through portfolio review (in this case, examples of writing, résumés, etc.). Atlantic Center is located on 67 acres of hammockland on Turnbull Bay, a tidal estuary in New Smyrna Beach, Florida. Buildings include the administration building, commons, fieldhouse, black box theater, numerous studios, library with two word processors, three Master Artists' cottages and 28 units of Associate housing. All buildings are air-conditioned and connected by raised wooden walkways. Associate units have private bath, desk and refrigerator. Writers often meet in fieldhouse, which has copy machine, kitchen, bath, tables and chairs." The Center usually offers 6 residencies each year, usually 3 weeks in length. Residencies occur throughout the year, but may not always offer opportunities to writers. Accommodates up to 28 Associates (including all disciplines).
Costs: $800, including private room/bath; $300, residency fee only, no housing. Associates provide their own meals and transportation. Scholarships are available.
To Apply: Application requirements are different for each residency. Send for information or call toll free 1-800-393-6975. Application deadlines are generally 4-5 months before start of a residency; notification usually occurs 3-4 weeks after application deadline. Brochure/guidelines available. Some college credit available.

THE MARY INGRAHAM BUNTING INSTITUTE, 34 Concord Ave., Cambridge MA 02138. (617)495-8212. E-mail: bunting_fellowships@radcliffe@harvard.edu. Fellowships Coordinator: Linda Roach. Estab. 1960. For women scholars, researchers, creative writers, and visual and performing artists. "The Institute occupies three recently renovated 19th century buildings which house staff and fellows' offices, art and music studios, a colloquium room, a common room, a library/conference room, and a small exhibition gallery." Eleven-month appointments available for the Bunting Fellowship Program: September 15, 1997-August 15, 1998. Office space, auditing privileges, and access to most other resources of Radcliffe College and Harvard University are provided. Eleven-month to six-month appointments available for the Affiliation Program: fall (September 15, 1997-January 31, 1998); spring (February 1, 1998-August 15, 1998); or 11-month (September 15, 1997-August 15, 1998). Accommodates multiple writers.

Costs: Fellowships are available. "Applications are judged on the quality and significance of the proposed project, the applicant's record of accomplishment, and the potential importance of the fellowship at this stage in the applicant's career. To be considered for a fellowship in fiction or nonfiction, applicants must have a contract for the publication of a book-length manuscript, or at least three short works published. Evidence of publication in the last five years is highly desirable."

To Apply: Call or write for information/applications.

‡**BYRDCLIFFE ARTS COLONY**, 34 Tinker St., Woodstock NY 12498. (914)679-2079. Fax: (914)679-4529. Administrator: Katherine Burger. Estab. 1990. For visual artists and writers. "The historic Byrdcliffe Arts Colony is in Woodstock, one and a half miles from the village center. Woodstock, an internationally famous arts community, is ninety miles north of New York City in the Catskill Mountains. Residents are accommodated in the Villetta Inn, a spacious turn-of-the-century mountain lodge with a large common dining room and living room." Available in 4 one-month sessions, June-September. Provisions for the writer include private room and private writing studio. Residents provide own meals (big communal kitchen). Accommodates 10 residents, artists and writers; split varies.

Costs: $400/month, June and September; $500/month, July and August.

To Apply: Send SASE for application. Submit application with work sample, recommendations, description of work plan, $5 fee. Brochure for SASE.

CAMARGO FOUNDATION, W-1050 First National Bank Bldg., 332 Minnesota St., St. Paul MN 55101-1312. Administrative Assistant: Ricardo Bloch. Estab. 1971. For 1 artist, 1 writer, 1 musician; and graduate students and scholars working on projects in the humanities and social sciences relating to French and Francophone culture. There are facilities for 12 grantees each semester. "Grantees are given a furnished apartment, rent free, on an estate on the Mediterranean about 20 miles east of Marseilles. Families may accompany grantee, but must remain the entire period of the grant." Grant period is from early September to mid-December or from mid-January to May 31. Minimum residency is 3 months. "A workroom is available and computer facilities, though it is suggested that writers bring their own equipment; space and scheduling may be tight."

Costs: None. There is no stipend.

To Apply: "There is no fee. Write to Administrative Assistant giving name and address to request application materials. Packet will be mailed upon request. All application materials requested must be received in this ofice by February 1. Applicants will be notified of selection decisions by April 1."

‡**CENTRUM ARTIST-IN-RESIDENCE**, P.O. Box 1158, Port Townsend WA 98368. (360)385-3102. Contact: Program Coordinator. Estab. 1978. Open to writers, visual artists, composers, performers. "Artists stay in private 2-3 bedroom cottages on the grounds of Fort Worden State Park, a former military fort. Located on Admiralty Inlet with beaches, woods, trails, turn-of-the century buildings." Month-long residencies, September-May. Stipend of $75 per week. Accommodates approximately 4/month. "Well suited to those who enjoy solitude."

Costs: $10 application fee.

To Apply: Call or send SASE for brochure.

CHÂTEAU DE LESVAULT, Onlay 58370 France. (33)86-84-32-91 Fax: (33)86-84-35-78. Director: Bibbi Lee. Estab. 1984. Open to writers of fiction and nonfiction, poets, playwrights, researchers. Located in "Burgundy within the National Park 'Le Morvan', the Château de Lesvault is a classic French manor with fully furnished rooms including a salon, dining room and library. The château is surrounded by a large private park and there is a lake on the property." Available in 4-week sessions from October through April. Provisions for the writer include a large private room for sleeping and working, complete use of the château facility. Accommodates 5.

Costs: Cost for a 4-week session is 4,500 French francs (approximately US $900). All lodging and meals included.

To Apply: Send a letter to the Selection Committee briefly describing the writing project, 2 references and a sample of work (maximum 3 pages). Specify the 4-week session requested. No application fee required. Brochure/guidelines available for SASE.

‡**THE CLEARING**, P.O. Box 65, Ellison Bay WI 54210. (414)854-4088. E-mail: buchholz@mail.wi scnet.net. Resident Manager: Louise or Don Buchholz. Estab. 1935. Open to "any adult over 18." Located in "historic native log and stone buildings on 128-acres of native forest on the shore of Green Bay. Hiking trails, beach, swimming, enjoyable countryside for bicycling. Housed in twin-bedded, private bath facility. Meals served family style. Classroom is large hall in wooded setting. Clearing open mid-May to mid-October for week-long sessions beginning Sunday night with supper, ending Saturday morning with breakfast—usually two or three writing weeks per year." Provisions for the

writer include options of sharing a twin bedroom or 6-bed dorm, meals furnished, workspace in bedroom, living room, school building or quiet nooks on the grounds. Accommodates 20-24 writers. **Costs:** $509-549/person per week includes board, room and tuition. (No Thursday night supper.) Scholarships are available. Brochure/guidelines available.

CURRY HILL PLANTATION WRITER'S RETREAT, 404 Cresmont Ave., Hattiesburg MS 39401. (601)264-7034. Director: Elizabeth Bowne. Estab. 1977. Open to all fiction and nonfiction writing, except poetry and technical writing. This workshop is held at an antebellum home, located on 400 acres of land. It is limited to only 8 guests who live in, all of whom receive individual help with their writing, plus a 3-hour workshop each evening when the group meets together. The location is 6 miles east of Bainbridge, Georgia. "The date of the retreat is different every year but always in the spring—March/April or May." Provisions for the writer include room and board. Accommodates 8 writers.
Costs: $500 for the week; includes room and board and individual help, 1 hour per guest each day.
To Apply: Interested persons should apply as *early* as possible. Brochure/guidelines available for SASE.

DJERASSI RESIDENT ARTISTS PROGRAM, 2325 Bear Gulch Rd., Woodside CA 94062-4405. Executive Director: Charles Amirkhanian. "The Djerassi Program appoints approximately 60 artists a year to spend one month to six weeks working on independent or collaborative projects in a setting of unusual beauty and privacy. The facility is located on a former cattle ranch one hour south of San Francisco in the Santa Cruz Mountains above Stanford University, facing the Pacific Ocean. We are seeking applications at all levels." Provisions for the writer include living/studio accommodations with balcony or garden access, as well as meals. Accommodates 10 artists of various disciplines at one time. Open April 1 through November 15.
Costs: The Djerassi Program award is strictly a residential grant. All accommodations are provided at no cost.
To Apply: Send SASE to: Djerassi Resident Artists Program at above address and request application packet. Deadline for 1998 season is February 15, 1997.

DORLAND MOUNTAIN ARTS COLONY, P.O. Box #6, Temecula CA 92593. (909)676-5039. E-mail: dorland@ez2.net. Director of Operations: Karen Parrott. Estab. 1978. Open to visual artists, composers, writers, playwrights, theater artists. Provides uninterrupted time in a natural environment. The colony is located on a 300-acre nature preserve. No electricity, rustic single wall constructed cabins; large oak grove; 2 ponds; trails. Available for 1- to 2-month residencies year round. Provisions for the writer include private cabins with living and work space. Manual (older) typewriters provided. Responsible for own meals. There are a total of 6 cabins.
Costs: $300/month.
To Apply: Application deadlines: March 1 and September 1. Brochure/guidelines available for SASE or via e-mail.

DORSET COLONY HOUSE FOR WRITERS, Box 519, Dorset VT 05251. (802)867-5777. Director: John Nassivera. Estab. 1980. Colony is open to all writers. Facility and grounds include large 19th century house in New England village setting; national historic landmark house and village. Available in spring and fall. Accommodates 8 writers.
Costs: $95/week; meals not included; fully functional kitchen in house and restaurants easy walk away.
To Apply: No fees to apply; send inquiry anytime. Brochures are available for SASE.

FAIRVIEW SUMMIT RETREAT HOUSE, 10800 Mt. Fairview Rd. SE, Cumberland MD 21502. (301)724-6842. Director: Petrina Aubol. Estab. 1991. For writers and artists. "Individuals wishing to get away to a creative environment." The retreat center is located on a dead end road on top of Irons Mountain in the middle of a 100-acre forest. Available year-round. Provisions for the writer include private room, workspace, indoor pool, hiking trails, scenic vistas, only 6½ miles from town.
Costs: $30/day includes breakfast and dinner.
To Apply: Send reservation form plus 25% deposit on full cost to hold space.

FINE ARTS WORK CENTER IN PROVINCETOWN, 24 Pearl St., Provincetown MA 02657. (508)487-9960. Contact: Writing Coordinator. Estab. 1968. Open to emerging writers and visual artists. "Located on the grounds of the former Days Lumberyard complex, the facility has offered studio space to artists and writers since 1914. Renovated coal bins provide artist studios; several houses and a refurbished Victorian barn offer apartments for writers. The complex encircles the Stanley Kunitz Common Room where fellows and visiting artists offer readings to the public." A 7-month residency offered from October 1 to May 1 each year. "Each writer is awarded his/her own apartment with kitchen and bath. All apartments are furnished and equipped with kitchen supplies. A monthly stipend of $375 is also provided." Accommodates 10 writers (five fiction, five poets).

Costs: No fees other than application fee ($35).

To Apply: Application deadline: February 1. Writing sample: Send 1 or 2 short stories. If novel, excerpt including opening section and synopsis. Limit: 35 pages. Send up to 15 pages of poetry. Send 6 copies. Check guidelines for details. Brochure/guidelines available for SASE.

THE GELL WRITERS CENTER OF THE FINGER LAKES, % Writers & Books, 740 University Ave., Rochester NY 14607. (716)473-2590. Fax: (716)729-0982. Executive Director: Joseph Flaherty. Estab. 1989. For active writers. "A two-bedroom house located on 25 acres of wooded hillside in New York's Finger Lakes area." Offered year-round for periods of time from 1-4 weeks. Provisions for the writer include private room with bathroom, shared kitchen, dining and living room areas. Accommodates 2 writers.

Costs: $35 per day. Does not include meals.

To Apply: Call or write for application. "Must send résumé showing a publication history or a writing sample." Brochure/guidelines available for SASE.

THE TYRONE GUTHRIE CENTRE AT ANNAGHMAKERRIG, Newbliss, County Monaghan, Ireland. 353-047-54003. Fax: 353-047-54380. E-mail: 101450.3652@compuserve.com. Resident Director: Bernard Loughlin. Estab. 1981. Open to writers, painters, sculptors, composers, directors, artists. There are "11 work rooms in house, generally with private bathroom. Also five new houses which are self-contained; 400 acres, large lake and gardens; sitting room, library, kitchen, dining room." Closed for 2-week period at Christmas only. Provisions for the writer include private room and meals. Accommodates 16 writers and other artists.

Costs: IR £1,200-1,600, depending on season, per month in Big House, all meals included. IR £300/week for self-contained houses—also have to pay food, heating, electricity and outgoings.

To Apply: Write for application form. Considered at bimonthly board meeting. Brochure/guidelines available for SASE.

THE HAMBIDGE CENTER, P.O. Box 339, Rabun Gap GA 30568. Estab. 1934. Open to artists from all fields. Includes "600 acres of wooded, rural property serenely set in north Georgia mountains; traversed by streams and waterfalls." 2-week to 6-week stays from May to October, with limited winter residencies also. Provisions for writers include private cottages and studios. Accommodates 8 artists.

Costs: $125/week with dinner provided Monday-Friday. Some scholarships available (very limited and reviewed individually).

To Apply: Deadline for reviews is August 31 (May to October), (November to April). Application fee is $20. Application form mailed upon request. Brochure/guidelines available for SASE.

‡HAWTHORNDEN CASTLE, Lasswade, Midlothian, Scotland EH181EG. 0131-440-2180. Contact: Administrator. Estab. 1982. "For dramatists, novelists, poets or other creative writers who have published one piece of work." Located in a "remotely situated castle amid wild romantic scenery, a 30-minute bus ride to Edinburgh." Offers 8 four-week sessions from February to July and September to December. Provisions for the writer include: study bedrooms; daytime silence rule; communal breakfast and evening meal. Accommodates 5 writers.

Costs: Residence is free.

To Apply: "Application form is available from Administrator. September 30 deadline for following year."

‡HEADLANDS CENTER FOR THE ARTS, 944 Fort Barry, Sausalito CA 94965. (415)331-2787. Fax: (415)331-3857. Public Relations Manager: Heather Peeler. Estab. 1982. For writers, visual artists, performance artists, musicians, composers, film and video artists, and arts professionals. "Headlands has a number of different residency programs, each with different eligibility requirements and application procedures. Currently, the Center is only taking applications from artists residing in California, Ohio, North Carolina, the Czech Republic, Denmark, Slovakia, Sweden and Taiwan. These eligibility requirements can change from year to year. The Center is located on 13,000 coastal acres in Marin County, north of San Francisco, just a few minutes across the Golden Gate Bridge and includes 13 studios, 2 live-work spaces for writers, others live in one of three shared 4-bedroom houses. The program begins in February of each year. The average length of residencies is 3-11 months, depending upon the specific residency program." Provisions for the writer include live/work space, meals five nights per week and a stipend. Accommodates 4 writers at one time.

Costs: No cost to artists accepted into the program.

To Apply: Application guidelines are available in April for SASE. "Application deadline is early June each year for California, North Carolina and Ohio programs. Deadlines vary for the international residencies and some countries have additional eligibility requirements. An outside panel of professionals in each category selects the residents."

HEDGEBROOK, 2197 E. Millman Rd., Langley WA 98260. (360)321-4786. Director: Linda Bowers. Estab. 1988. For "women writers, published or not, of all ages and from all cultural backgrounds." Located on "30 acres on Whidbey Island one hour north of Seattle WA. Six individual cottages, a bathhouse for showers and a farmhouse where dinner is served. The cottages are wood frame, wood heat, electricity, no TV or phone." Applicants request a stay of 1 week to 2 months (may attend only once). Two application periods a year: mid-January through May; mid-June through early December. "Writers must provide their writing equipment. Very good writing space and relaxing space in each cottage; sleeping loft, down comforters. Lunch delivered, small kitchen facility—dinner in the farmhouse." Accommodates 6 writers.
Costs: $15 application fee. No charge for food or housing. Meals are nutritious, diet conscious. There is a travel scholarship fund.
To Apply: Deadlines are October 1 and April 1. Application form—5 copies needed for committee review. Approximately 25 writers are invited each of 2 sessions a year. Limited facility for a differently abled person. Application available for SASE.

KALANI HONUA, Eco-Resort, RR2, Box 4500, Pahoa HI 96778. (808)965-7828. (800)800-6886. E-mail: kh@ilhawaii.net. Website: http://www.randm.com/kh.html. Director: Richard Koob. Estab. 1980. Open to all education interests. "Kalani Honua, the 'harmony of heaven and earth,' provides an environment where the spirit of Aloha flourishes. Located on 113 secluded acres bordered by lush jungle and rugged coastline forged by ancient lava flows, Kalani Honua offers an authentic experience of rural Hawaii. The surrounding area, including sacred sites and state and national parks, is rich with the island's history and magic." Available year-round, although greatest availability is May, June, September, October, November and December. Provisions for the writer include "comfortable, private room/workspace. Three meals offered/day, beautiful coastal surroundings and recreation facilities (pool, sauna, jacuzzi, tennis, volleyball, biking) near beaches and Volcanoes National Park. (Qualifying writers receive stipend to help with costs.)" Accommodates 60.
Costs: $60-85/night depending on choice of lodging (varying from private room with shared bath to private cottage with private bath). Professionals qualify for 50% reduction on rates. Meals are approximately $24/day or may be self-provided in lodge kitchen.
To Apply: Application fee $10. Brochure/guidelines available for SASE. College credit may be arranged through University of Hawaii.

❧**LEIGHTON STUDIOS, THE BANFF CENTRE**, P.O. Box 1020 Station 22, Banff, Alberta T0L 0C0 Canada. (403)762-6180. E-mail: arts_info@banffcentre.ab.ca. Website: http://www.banffcent re.ab.ca/. Assistant Registrar: Theresa Boychuck. Estab. 1984. "The Leighton Studios provide a year-round working retreat for professional artists. Set in a mountainside pine grove slightly apart from the Centre's main buildings and above the town of Banff, Alberta, the eight studios are part of the Banff Centre for the Arts within The Banff Centre for Continuing Education. Available for one week to three month residencies. Apply at anytime. Adjudications are ongoing. Space is limited and artists are encouraged to apply at least six months in advance of start date. Provisions include private room, studio and flexible meal. Accommodates 8 professional artists at one time.
Costs: Approximately $90/day (Canadian). Financial assistance provided in the form of a studio fee discount which varies according to need and will be indicated at the time of acceptance.
To Apply: Send completed application form, resume, press releases, reviews and a selection of published work or manuscripts in progress to The Banff Centre. Brochures or guidelines available for free.

THE MACDOWELL COLONY, 100 High St., Peterborough NH 03458. (603)924-3886 or (212)535-9690. Website: http://www.macdowellcolony.org. Admissions Coordinator: Pat Dodge. Estab. 1907. Open to writers, composers, visual artists, film/video artists, interdisciplinary artists and architects. Includes main building, library, 3 residence halls and 32 individual studios on over 450 mostly wooded acres, 1 mile from center of small town in southern New Hampshire. Available up to 8 weeks year-round. Provisions for the writer include meals, private sleeping room, individual secluded studio. Accommodates variable number of writers, 10 to 20 at a time.
Costs: Artists are asked to contribute toward the cost of their residency according to their financial resources.
To Apply: Application forms available. Application deadline: January 15 for summer, April 15 for fall/winter, September 15 for winter/spring. Writing sample required. For novel, send a chapter or section. For short stories, send 2-3. Send 6 copies. Brochure/guidelines available; SASE appreciated.

MILLAY COLONY FOR THE ARTS, P.O. Box 3, Austerlitz NY 12017-0003. (518)392-3103. Executive Director: Ann-Ellen Lesser. Assistant Director: Gail Giles. Estab. 1973. Open to professional writers, composers, visual artists. Includes "600 acres—mostly wooded, fields, old farm. Two buildings house artists—separate studios (14×20) and bedrooms." Available year round. Accommodates 5 people at a time for 1 month residencies.

Costs: No fees.

To Apply: Requires sample of work and 1 professional reference. Application deadlines: February 1 for June through September; May 1 for October through January; September 1 for February through May. Brochure/guidelines available for SASE. Applications also available via e-mail, use application-@millayecolony.org.

MY RETREAT, P.O. Box 1077, Lincoln Rd., South Fallsburg NY 12779. (914)436-7455. Owner: Cora Schwartz. Estab. 1993. For writers, poets, "artists of life." "Retreat is situated in the foothills of the Catskill Mountains, 90 miles from Albany or New York City (near Ashram); consists of main house and summer cottages." A "room of one's own" offered year-round. Provisions for the writer include private room, breakfast foods, kitchen facilities for own cooking. Accommodates 12 to 20 singles or couples.
Costs: $45/night per person; $65/night per couple. Reduced rates for longer stays.
To Apply: Brochure available for SASE.

N.A.L.L. ASSOCIATION, 232, Blvd. de Lattre, 06140 Vence France. (33)93 58 13 26. Fax: (33)93 58 09 00. Contact: N.A.L.L. founder. Estab. 1993. "The N.A.L.L. is open to artists of all vocations—painters, sculptors, writers, playwrights, musicians—regardless of race, religion or age. There are nine houses available on eight acres of grounds between Saint Paul and Vence." Available in "minimal seasonal three-month terms. Yearly sabbatical programs are also available." Provisions for the artist include housing only; meals not included. Accommodates 10 writers at a time.
Costs: Range from 1,500-6,000 FF/month, depending on type of accommodation and season.
To Apply: "The artist is to send a curriculum vitae of accomplishments and future projects. Upon being chosen for residency, artists must become members of the N.A.L.L. by paying an annual Membership Donation of 500 Francs."

NEW YORK MILLS ARTS RETREAT, P.O. Box 246, New York Mills MN 56567. (218)385-3339. Estab. 1989. For any visual, performing, or literary artist or musician. "The retreat offers both very private time and the experience of immersion in the rural culture of a tiny town in north central Minnesota. Five to eight artists are selected annually for residencies ranging from 2 to 4 weeks."
Costs: Offers stipends ($750-1,500) to each artist. "Stipends are used, partially, for the artists' meals, supplies and transportation. Lodging is at a local B&B and studio space is in the town arts center." Send SASE for application packet. Brochure/guidelines available for SASE.

‡NORCROFT: A WRITING RETREAT FOR WOMEN, 32 E. First St. #330, Duluth MN 55802. (218)727-5199. Fax: (218)727-3119. Contact: Jean Sramek. Estab. 1993. "For women writers, all genres, 21 years and older, regardless of experience." Located in a beautiful Scandinavian-designed lodge on the north shore of Lake Superior. Each resident has private room and own writing shed. Also includes common dining and living area with fireplace, books galore, modern bath and kitchen facilities. No phone, no TV, no distractions. Wheelchair accessible." Offers 1-4 week residencies from May through November. Provisions for the writer include private room, private writing shed, food, towels and linens washed. "Residents do their own cooking and bring own computers, writing supplies etc. Washer and dryer available." Accommodates 4 writers.
Costs: No cost. "Residents are responsible for transportation to and from Duluth. (We will pick up/ drop off at Greyhound or airport and drive to Norcroft.)"
To Apply: Deadline is October 1 for following year. Send SASE for application instructions.

OREGON WRITERS COLONY, P.O. Box 15200, Portland OR 97215. (503)771-0428. Contact: Marlene Howard, property manager. Estab. 1986. The Oregon Writers Colony is open to members only ($25 annual dues). The colony is located in a large log house containing 4 bedrooms and 2 baths. Available from September through May only. Accommodates a maximum of 3 writers.
Costs: $350/week; during second week of month, $100/week.
To Apply: Brochure/guidelines available for SASE.

PENDLE HILL, Box G, 338 Plush Mill Rd., Wallingford PA 19086-6099. (800)742-3150. Website: http://www.quaker.org/pendle-hill. Information Services Associate: Mary Gabel. Estab. 1930. "Grounded in the social and spiritual values of the Religious Society of Friends (Quakers), Pendle Hill welcomes people of all faiths who seek a time of spiritual strengthening through reading, writing, study, solitude, or time in community. It is an adult inter-faith center for study and contemplation, set on 23 acres of beautiful trees and gardens 12 miles southwest of Philadelphia. Its 16 buildings include a conference center, crafts studio, library, bookstore, meeting room, dining room, classrooms and dormitories." The Resident Study Program offers three 10-week terms between October and June. "People may also come to 'sojourn' or come for a short stay for a self-directed retreat. Sojourning is an ideal way to come and have time for writing." The Extension Program offers weekend conferences on topics of interest to writers. The conference center is also available for groups wishing to rent it for their own program. Provisions for the writer include private room, meals, a library, crafts studio, and bookstore. Accommodates 30 in Resident Study program; 12 sojourners; 30 conferees. The cost of sojourning is $58 per day; $53.50 per day after one week. Conferences range from $165 for a weekend to $340 for 1 week in the summer. The cost of the Resident Study Program is $3,780 per term; $11,030 for 3. All rates include room and board. Please call for rental rates. Scholarships and financial aid available for Resident Study Program.

To Apply: Call 1-800-742-3150, or write for more information. Applications for Resident Study Program are accepted throughout the year. Those interested in sojourning or conferences may call the registrar at the toll-free number to make arrangements.

RAGDALE FOUNDATION, 1260 N. Green Bay Rd., Lake Forest IL 60045. (847)234-1063. Estab. 1976. For qualified writers, artists and composers. Ragdale, located 30 miles north of Chicago near Lake Michigan, is "the grounds of acclaimed Chicago architect Howard Van Doren Shaw's historic family home." Accommodations include the Ragdale House, the Barnhouse and the new Friends Studio. Available in 2 week to 2 month sessions year-round, except for the month of May and 2 weeks in December. Provisions for the writer include room, linens laundered by Ragdale and meals. "Breakfast and lunch supplies are stocked in communal kitchens, enabling residents to work throughout the day uninterrupted by scheduled meals. The evening meal is the only exception: wholesome, well-prepared dinners are served six nights a week. The Ragdale House and Barnhouse both contain informal libraries, and the property overlooks a large nature preserve." Accommodates 12.

Costs: $15/day. Fee waivers based on financial need are available. "Fee waiver application and decision process is separate from artistic admission process."

To Apply: "Residents are chosen by a selection committee composed of professionals in their artistic discipline." Application fee: $20. Deadlines: January 15 for June through December 15; June 1 for January through April 30. Brochure/guidelines available for SASE or call.

‡SELU WRITERS RETREAT, Box 6935, Radford University, Radford VA 24142-6935. (703)831-5269 or (703)639-0812. E-mail: planier@runet.edu. Estab. 1992. "Offers unstructured time in congenial, quiet campus setting. Writers stay in a newly-renovated air-conditioned dormitory with private baths. Radford University is located off I-81 on the banks of the historic New River, 40 miles southwest of Roanoke." Available last two weeks of June. Writers may stay 1 week or 2. Accommodates 12 writers at a time.

Costs: Private room, $252; meal plan, $16/day.

To Apply: "Writers should apply six months in advance. Include a brief bio."

VERMONT STUDIO CENTER, P.O. Box 613NW, Johnson VT 05656. (802)635-2727. Fax: (802)635-2730. E-mail: vscvt@pwshift.com. Development Director: Gary Clark. Estab. 1984. For emerging and mid-career writers and artists. "The Vermont Studio Center is located in Johnson, Vermont, a traditional Vermont Village in the heart of the Green Mountains and includes 19 historic buildings on the banks of the Gihon river. These serve as studios, lecture hall, dining facilities, gallery, art supply store, lounge, offices and residences. The Center offers 2-week Writing Retreats for up to 12 writers from February through April. The retreats are led by prominent writers and focus on fiction, creative nonfiction and poetry. Independent Writing Residencies are also available year-round for 2-12 weeks. Room/private studio and excellent meals are included in all our programs."

Costs: All-inclusive fees are $1,350 per 2-week Writing Retreat and $2,600 per 4-week Writing Residency. Generous financial assistance is available based both on merit and need. Applications are accepted year-round. The application deadline for full fellowships for the Writing Retreats is October 15. Please write or call for an application.

VILLA MONTALVO ARTIST RESIDENCY PROGRAM, P.O. Box 158, Saratoga CA 95071. (408)741-3421. Artist Residency Program Director: Judy Moran. Estab. 1942. For "writers, visual artists, musicians and composers. Villa Montalvo is a 1912 Mediterranean-style villa on 176 acres. There are extensive formal gardens and miles of redwood trails. Residencies are from 1-3 months, year-round. Each writer is given a private apartment with kitchen. Apartments for writers have either 2 rooms or a unique balcony or veranda. All apartments are fully-stocked (dishes, linens, etc.), except for food. Artists provide their own food." Accommodates 2 writers (5 artists in total).

Costs: "There are no costs for residency. We require a $100 security deposit, which is returned at end of residency. There are four fellowships available each year. These are awarded on the basis of merit to the four most highly-rated applicants. One of these must be a writer, and one a woman artist or writer."

To Apply: Application form, résumé, statement of proposed project, $20 application fee. Brochure/guidelines available.

‡VIRGINIA CENTER FOR THE CREATIVE ARTS, Mt. San Angelo, Box VCCA, Sweet Briar VA 24595. (804)946-7236. Fax: (804)946-7239. E-mail: vcca@sbc.edu. Director: William Smart. Estab. 1971. For writers, visual artists and composers. "Located at Mt. San Angelo, a 450-acre estate in Amherst County, approximately 160 miles southwest of Washington, D.C. The VCCA provides residential Fellowships in a rural setting where artists may work, free from the distractions and responsibilities of day-to-day life. VCCA Fellows have private bedrooms in a modern, comfortable residential building and separate studios in the Studio Barn. There is space for 24 artists at a time year round: twelve studios for writers, nine for visual artists, and three for composers. Breakfast and dinner are served in the dining room of the residence and lunches are delivered to the studios. Facilities at the Fellows' Residence include a library, dining room, living room, game room, and laundry facilities." Available year-round for residencies from 2 weeks to 2 months.

Costs: "The standard fee is $30/day, which includes everything." Scholarships are available.

To Apply: $20 application fee. Write or call for application form. Deadlines: Jan. 15, May 15, Sept. 15. Brochure/guidelines available for SASE.

WALKER WOODS, 1397 LaVista Rd. Northeast, Atlanta GA 30324-3833. (404)634-3309. Fax: (404)728-1995. E-mail: writers@mindspring.com. Founder: Dalian Moore. Walker Woods "offers six week to eight month residencies to writers completing their first book (novels, short stories, poetry, etc.), and to foreign authors writing or translating a book into the English language. Writers yet to publish a full-length book in the English language are eligible for residency." Situated on 1½ acres of prime real estate in North Atlanta. Property features a waterfall into a pond stocked with fish, a stone-lined stream, hot tub, rose garden and easy access to public transportation. Eight writers may live here at any given time. Writers may share a room or have one of their own, and all meals are taken communally. Three private suites shared, convertible rooms, and a dormitory arrangement for five plus two full bathrooms are available. Kitchen, living room and library are shared. There are complete work stations for all writers equipped with WordPerfect software, but writers are encouraged to bring laptops and journals for portability and privacy.

Costs: Writers pay what they can ($250-600) per month depending upon accommodation and needs. Residents selected for support live at Walker Woods free, but pay for food, phone calls, etc. and are on a work exchange program to suit their tastes and abilities. Everyone in residence takes up small projects on the property. Partial or work scholarship/residencies are available on a competitive basis, and writers must submit one chapter of a novel, nonfiction book, short story collection or 20 poems for a collection in progress. Deadlines vary, and are usually two or three months in advance of desired residency. A once in a lifetime fee of $20 is required, and writers may reapply at any time throughout their lives.

To Apply: Send SASE with 96¢ postage for application package, and leave your questions on our answering service or e-mail.

HELENE WURLITZER FOUNDATION OF NEW MEXICO, Box 545, Taos NM 87571. (505)758-2413. Estab. 1953. "No restrictions. 11 separate houses, studios." Available April 1 through September 30 annually. Provisions for the writer include single house/studio dwelling. "Presently booked into 2000, for all creative (not interpretive) media."

Costs: No charge. (Must supply own food.) Rent-free and utility-free housing.

To Apply: Write to the Foundation.

Organizations and Resources

When you write, you write alone. It's just you and the typewriter or computer screen. Yet the writing life does not need to be a lonely one. Joining a writing group or organization can be an important step in your writing career. By meeting other writers, discussing your common problems and sharing ideas, you can enrich your writing and increase your understanding of this sometimes difficult, but rewarding life.

The variety of writers' organizations seems endless—encompassing every type of writing and writer—from small, informal groups that gather regularly at a local coffee house for critique sessions to regional groups that hold annual conferences to share technique and marketing tips. National organizations and unions fight for writers' rights and higher payment for freelancers, and international groups monitor the treatment of writers around the world.

In this section you will find state-, province-, regional-based groups such as the Arizona Authors Association and the Manitoba Writer's Guild. You'll also find national organizations including the National Writers Association. The Mystery Writers of America, Western Writers of America and the Genre Writer's Association are examples of groups devoted to a particular type of writing. Whatever your needs or goals, you're likely to find a group listed here to interest you.

SELECTING A WRITERS' ORGANIZATION

To help you make an informed decision, we've provided information on the scope, membership and goals of the organizations listed on these pages. We asked groups to outline the types of memberships available and the benefits members can expect. Most groups will provide additional information for a self-addressed, stamped envelope, and you may be able to get a sample copy of their newsletter for a modest fee.

Keep in mind joining a writers' organization is a two-way street. When you join an organization, you become a part of it and, in addition to membership fees, most groups need and want your help. If you want to get involved, opportunities can include everything from chairing a committee to writing for the newsletter to helping set up an annual conference. The level of your involvement is up to you and almost all organizations welcome contributions of time and effort.

Selecting a group to join depends on a number of factors. As a first step, you must determine what you want from membership in a writers' organization. Then send away for more information on the groups that seem to fit your needs. Start, however, by asking yourself:

• Would I like to meet writers in my city? Am I more interested in making contacts with other writers across the country or around the world?

• Am I interested in a group that will critique and give me feedback on work-in-progress?

• Do I want marketing information and tips on dealing with editors?

• Would I like to meet other writers who write the same type of work I do or am I interested in meeting writers from a variety of fields?

• How much time can I devote to meetings and are regular meetings important to me? How much can I afford to pay in dues?

- Would I like to get involved in running the group, working on the group's newsletters, planning a conference?
- Am I interested in a group devoted to writers' rights and treatment or would I rather concentrate on the business of writing?

FOR MORE INFORMATION

Because they do not usually have the resources or inclination to promote themselves widely, finding a local writers' group is usually a word-of-mouth process. If you think you'd like to join a local writer's group and do not know of any in your area, check notices at your library or contact a local college English department. You might also try contacting a group based in your state, province or region listed here for information on smaller groups in your area.

If you have a computer and would like to meet with writers in other areas of the country, you will find many commercial online services, such as GEnie and America Online, have writers' sections and "clubs" online. Many free online services available through Internet also have writers' "boards."

For more information on writers' organizations, check *The Writer's Essential Desk Reference: A Companion to Writer's Market*, 2nd edition (Writer's Digest Books, 1507 Dana Ave., Cincinnati OH 45207). Other directories listing organizations for writers include the *Literary Market Place* or *International Literary Market Place* (R.R. Bowker, 121 Chanlon Rd., New Providence NJ 07974). The National Writers Association also maintains a list of writers' organizations.

ARIZONA AUTHORS ASSOCIATION, 3509 E. Shea Blvd., Suite 117, Phoenix AZ 85028. (602)867-9001. President: Iva Martin. Estab. 1978. Number of Members: 500. Type of Memberships: Professional, writers with published work; associate, writers working toward publication; affiliate, professionals in the publishing industry. "Primarily an Arizona organization but open to writers nationally." Benefits include bimonthly newsletter, discount rates on seminars, workshops and newsletter ads, discounts on writing books, discounts at bookstores, copy shops, critique groups and networking events. "Sponsors workshops on a variety of topics of interest to writers (e.g., publishing, marketing, structure, genres)." Publishes *Authors Newsletter*, bimonthly ($25/yr.). Dues: Professional and associate, $40/year; affiliate: $45/year; student: $25/year. Holds monthly critique group, quarterly networking events and annual literary contest. Send SASE for information.

ASSOCIATED WRITING PROGRAMS, Tallwood House, Mail Stop 1E3, George Mason University, Fairfax VA 22030. (703)993-4301. E-mail: awp@gmu.edu. Publications Manager: Gwyn McVay. Estab. 1967. Number of Members: 5,000 individuals and 290 institutions. Types of Membership: Institutional (universities); graduate students, individual writers; and *Chronicle* subscribers. Open to any person interested in writing; most members are students or faculty of university writing programs (worldwide). Benefits include information on creative writing programs; grants and awards to writers; a job placement service for writers in academe and beyond. AWP holds an Annual Conference in a different US city every spring; also conducts an annual Award Series in poetry, short story collections, novel and creative nonfiction, in which winner receives $2,000 honorarium and publication by a participating press. AWP acts as agent for finalists in Award Series and tries to place their manuscript with publishers throughout the year. Manuscripts accepted January 1-February 28 only. Guidelines for novel competition will change in 1997. Send SASE for new guidelines. Publishes *AWP Chronicle* 6 times/year; 3 times/academic semester. Available to members for free. Nonmembers may order a subscription for $20/yr. Also publishes the *AWP Official Guide to Writing Programs* which lists about 330 creative writing programs in universities across the country and in Canada. *Guide* is updated every 2 years; cost is $19.95 plus $5 for first-class mail. Dues: $50 for individual membership and an additional $45 for our placement service. AWP keeps dossiers on file and sends them to school or organization of person's request. Holds two meetings per year for the Board of Directors. Send SASE for information.

AUSTIN WRITERS' LEAGUE RESOURCE CENTER, Austin Writers' League, 1501 W. Fifth, E-2, Austin TX 78703. (512)499-8914. Fax: (512)499-0441. Executive Director: Angela Smith. Estab. 1981. Number of Members: 1,600. Types of Memberships: Regular, student/senior citizen, family. Monthly meetings and use of resource center/library is open to the public. "Membership includes both aspiring and professional writers, all ages and all ethnic groups." Job bank is also open to the public.

Public also has access to technical assistance. Partial and full scholarships offered for some programs. Of 1,600 members, 800 reside in Austin. Remaining 800 live all over the US and in other countries. Benefits include monthly newsletter, monthly meetings, study groups, resource center/library-checkout privileges, discounts on workshops, seminars, classes, job bank, discounts on books and tapes, participation in awards programs, technical/marketing assistance, copyright forms and information, access to computers and printers. Center has 5 rooms plus 2 offices and storage area. Public space includes reception and job bank area; conference/classroom; library/computer room; and copy/mail room. Library includes 1,000 titles. Two computers and printers are available for member use. Sponsors fall and spring workshops, weekend seminars, informal classes, sponsorships for special events such as readings, production of original plays, media conferences, creative writing programs for children and youth; Violet Crown Book Awards, newsletter writing awards, Young Texas Writers awards, contests for various anthologies. Publishes *Austin Writer* (monthly newsletter), sponsors with Texas Commission on the Arts Texas Literary Touring Program. Membership/subscription: $40, $35-students, senior citizens, $60 family membership. Monthly meetings. Study groups set their own regular meeting schedules. Send SASE for information.

THE AUTHORS GUILD, 330 W. 42nd St., 29th Floor, New York NY 10036. (212)563-5904. Executive Director: Paul Aiken. Purpose of organization: membership organization of 6,700 members offers services and information materials intended to help published authors with the business and legal aspects of their work, including contract problems, copyright matters, freedom of expression and taxation. Qualifications for membership: book author published by an established American publisher within 7 years or any author who has had 3 works, fiction or nonfiction, published by a magazine or magazines of general circulation in the last 18 months. Associate membership also available. Annual dues: $90. Different levels of membership include: associate membership with all rights except voting available to an author who has a firm contract offer from an American publisher. Workshops/conferences: "The Guild and the Authors Guild Foundation conduct several symposia each year at which experts provide information, offer advice, and answer questions on subjects of interest and concern to authors. Typical subjects have been the rights of privacy and publicity, libel, wills and estates, taxation, copyright, editors and editing, the art of interviewing, standards of criticism and book reviewing. Transcripts of these symposia are published and circulated to members." "The *Author's Guild Bulletin*, a quarterly journal, contains articles on matters of interest to published writers, reports of Guild activities, contract surveys, advice on problem clauses in contracts, transcripts of Guild and League symposia, and information on a variety of professional topics. Subscription included in the cost of the annual dues."

THE BRITISH FANTASY SOCIETY, 2 Harwood St., Stockport SK4 1JJ U.K. Secretary: Robert Parkinson. Estab. 1971. Open to: "Anyone interested in fantasy. The British Fantasy Society was formed to provide coverage of the fantasy, science fiction and horror fields. To achieve this, the Society publishes its *Newsletter*, packed with information and reviews of new books and films, plus a number of other booklets of fiction and articles: *Winter Chills*, *Mystique*, *Masters of Fantasy* and *Dark Horizons*. The BFS also organizes an annual Fantasy Conference at which the British Fantasy Awards are presented for categories such as Best Novel, Best Short Story and Best Film." Dues and subscription fees are £17 (UK); $35 (US); £20 (Europe), £25 (elsewhere). Payment in sterling or US dollars only. Send SASE or IRC for information.

❧**BURNABY WRITERS' SOCIETY**, 6584 Deer Lake Ave., Burnaby, British Columbia V5G 2J3. (604)435-6500. Corresponding Secretary: Eileen Kernaghan. Estab. 1967. Number of members: 300. "Membership is regional, but open to anyone interested in writing." Benefits include monthly market newsletter; workshops/critiques; guest speakers; information on contests, events, reading venues, etc.; opportunity to participate in public reading series. Sponsors annual competition open to all British Columbia residents; monthly readings at Burnaby Art Gallery; Canada Council sponsored readings; workshops. Publishes *Burnaby Writers Newsletter* monthly (except July/August), available to anyone for $25/year subscription. Dues: $25/year (includes newsletter subscription). Meets second Thursday of each month. Send SASE for information.

❧**CANADIAN SOCIETY OF CHILDREN'S AUTHORS, ILLUSTRATORS AND PERFORMERS (CANSCAIP)**, 35 Spadina Rd., Toronto, Ontario M5R 2S9 Canada. (416)654-0903. Fax: (416)515-7022. E-mail: canscaip@interlog.com. Executive Secretary: Nancy Prasad. Estab. 1977. Number of Members: 1,100. Types of membership: Full professional member and friend (associate member). Open to professional active writers, illustrators and performers in the field of children's culture (full members); beginners and all other interested persons and institutions (friends). International scope, but emphasis on Canada. Benefits include quarterly newsletter, marketing opportunities, publicity via our membership directory and our "members available" list, jobs (school visits, readings, workshops, residencies, etc.) through our "members available" list, mutual support through monthly meetings. Sponsors annual workshop, "Packaging Your Imagination," held every October for beginners. Publishes *CANSCAIP News*, quarterly, available to all (free with membership, otherwise $25 Canadian). Dues: professional fees: $60 Canadian/year; friend fees: institutional $30/year; individual $50/year. "Professionals must have written, illustrated or performed work for children commercially, sufficient to satisfy the membership committee (more details on request)." CANSCAIP National has open meetings from September to June, monthly in Toronto. CANSCAIP West holds bimonthly meetings in Vancouver. Send SASE for information.

GARDEN STATE HORROR WRITERS, Manalapan Library, P.O. Box 178, Beverly NJ 08010. (609)778-2159. President: Dina Leacock. Estab. 1991. Number of Members: 50. Membership levels: active and associate. Open to "anyone interested in pursuing a career in fiction writing." Scope is national. Benefits include "latest market news, use of library meeting rooms, free copies of guidelines for magazine and book publishers, free in-house critique service in person and by mail." Sponsors monthly guest speakers and/or workshops, annual short fiction contest. A future conference/convention is being planned. A free sample of monthly newsletter *The Graveline* is available for SASE. Subscription is included in the cost of any membership. Dues: $30 active; $20 associate/annually. Active members must be 16 years of age. Holds regular monthly meetings. Send SASE for information.

GENRE WRITER'S ASSOCIATION (GWA), (formerly Small Press Genre Association), P.O. Box 6301, Concord CA 94524. (510)254-7053. Editor: Bobbi Sinha-Morey. The Genre Writer's Association (GWA) is an international service organization dedicated to the promotion of excellence in the fields of Science Fiction, Fantasy, Mystery, Western and Horror. Membership is open to any writer, poet, artist, editor, publisher or calligrapher who participates through his/her creative endeavors in the literary genres espoused by the organization. Members receive: 2 copies of *The Genre Writer's News*; 2 copies of *The Genre Writer's News Market Supplements*; 4 issues of *Horror: The News Magazine of the Horror & Fantasy Field*; a free membership roster (mailed in June/July); The Genre Writer's Association Plaque Awards; and 5-10% off any order to Dark Regions Press or Orinda Press products. "Members enjoy commentary/critique services, reviews, market news, grievance arbitration, promotion of member's work, how-to articles, research services, and much more." Dues for US members are $25, new and renewable. All others $30, new and renewable. Checks payable to GWA. For more information or to join, write with SASE for reply.

‡**HORROR WRITERS ASSOCIATION (HWA)**, P.O. Box 423, Oak Forest IL 60452. President: Lawrence Watt-Evans. Fax: (301)990-9395. E-mail: lawrence@clark.net or horrors@aol.com. Estab. 1983. Number of Members: 600. Type of Memberships: AC Active—professional writers who have sold work. Affiliate—people interested in the horror genre. Sponsors the "Bram Stoker Award" for excellence in horror writing. Publishes newsletter, membership directory and bimonthly market reports. Dues: $55/year (US); $65/year (overseas). Meets once a year. Send SASE for information.

INTERNATIONAL ASSOCIATION OF CRIME WRITERS (NORTH AMERICAN BRANCH), JAF Box 1500, New York NY 10116. (212)243-8966. Executive Director: Mary A. Frisque. Estab. 1987. Number of Members: 225. Open to: "Published authors of crime fiction, nonfiction, screenplays and professionals in the mystery field (agents, editors, booksellers). Our branch covers the US and Canada, there are other branches world-wide." Benefits include information about crime-writing world-wide and publishing opportunities in other countries. "We sponsor annual members' receptions during the Edgar awards week in New York in the spring and in the fall we host a reception at the Bouchercon. We also have occasional receptions for visiting authors/publishers. We give an annual award, the North American Hammett Prize, for the best work (fiction or nonfiction) of literary excellence in the crime writing field. We publish a quarterly newsletter, *Border Patrol*, available to members only." Dues: $50 year. Send SASE for information.

‡✽**MANITOBA WRITERS' GUILD**, 206-100 Arthur St., Winnipeg, Manitoba R3B, 1H3 Canada. (204)942-6134. Fax: (204)942-5754. E-mail: mbwriter@escape.ca. Number of members: approximately 500. Type of memberships: regular, student, senior and fixed income. Open to anyone: writers, emerging and established; readers, particularly those interested in Manitoba literature. "Membership is provincial generally, although we have members from across Canada, USA and international locations." Benefits include special discounts on programs, goods and services; regular mailings of program notices; and *WordWrap*, published 7 times/year, featuring articles, regular columns, information on current markets and competitions, announcements, and profiles of Manitoba writers. Programs include Mentor/Apprentice program; small resource center (3-staff, small nonlending resource library); open workshops once a month in fall and winter; annual fall conference, usually September; and Cafe Reading series. Dues: $40 regular; $20 seniors, students, fixed income. Send SASE for information.

MYSTERY WRITERS OF AMERICA (MWA), 17 E. 47th St., 6th Floor, New York NY 10017. Executive Director: Priscilla Ridgway. Estab. 1945. Number of Members: 2,600. Type of memberships: Active (professional, published writers of fiction or nonfiction crime/mystery/suspense); associate (professionals in allied fields, i.e., editor, publisher, critic, news reporter, publicist, librarian, bookseller, etc.); corresponding (writers qualified for active membership who live outside the US). Unpublished writers may petition for Affiliate member status. Benefits include promotion and protection of writers' rights and interests, including counsel and advice on contracts, MWA courses and workshops, a national office, an annual conference featuring the Edgar Allan Poe Awards, the *MWA Anthology*, a national newsletter, regional conferences, meetings and newsletters. Newsletter, *The Third Degree*, is published 10 times/year for members. Annual dues: $65 for US members; $32.50 for Corresponding members.

THE NATIONAL LEAGUE OF AMERICAN PEN WOMEN, INC., Headquarters: The Pen Arts Building, 1300 17th St., NW, Washington DC 20036. Phone/fax: (202)785-1997. Contact: National President. Estab. 1897. Number of Members: 5,000. Types of Membership: Three classifications: Art, Letters, Music. Open to: Professional women. "Professional to us means our membership is only open to women who sell their art, writings or music compositions. We have 200 branches in the continental US, Hawaii and the Republic of Panama. Some branches have as many as 100 members, some as few as 10 or 12. It is necessary to have 5 members to form a new branch." Benefits include marketing advice, use of a facility, critiques and competitions. Our facility is The Pen Arts Building. It is a 20-room Victorian mansion. It's most distinguished resident was President Abraham Lincoln's son, Robert Todd Lincoln, the former Secretary of War and Minister of Great Britain. It has a few rooms available for Pen Women visiting the D.C. area, and for Board members in session 3 times a year. Branch and State Association competitions, as well as biennial convention competitions. Offers a research library of books and histories of our organization only. Sponsors awards biennially to Pen Women in each classification: Art, Letters, Music, and $1,000 award biennially in even-numbered year to non-Pen Women in each classification for women age 35 and over who wish to pursue special work in her field. *The Pen Woman* is our membership magazine, published 6 times a year, free to members, $18 a year for nonmember subscribers. Dues: $30/year for national organization, from $5-10/year for branch membership and from $1-5 for state association dues. Branches hold regular meeting each month, September through May except in northern states which meet usually March through September (for travel convenience). Send SASE for information.

NATIONAL WRITERS ASSOCIATION, 1450 S. Havana, Suite 424, Aurora CO 80012. (303)751-7844. Executive Director: Sandy Whelchel. Estab. 1937. Number of Members: 4,000. Types of Memberships: Regular membership for those without published credits; professional membership for those with published credits. Open to: Any interested writer. National/International plus we have 16 chapters in various states. Benefits include critiques, marketing advice, editing, literary agency, complaint service, chapbook publishing service, research reports on various aspects of writing, 4 contests, National Writers Press—self-publishing operation, computer bulletin board service, regular newsletter with updates on marketing, bimonthly magazine on writing related subjects, discounts on supplies, magazines and some services. Sponsors periodic conferences and workshops: short story contest opens April, closes July 1; novel contest opens December, closes April 1. Publishes *Flash Market News* (monthly publication for professional members only); *Authorship Magazine* (bimonthly publication available by subscription $18 to nonmembers). Dues: $50 regular; $60 professional. For professional membership requirement is equivalent of 3 articles or stories in a national or regional magazine; a book published by a royalty publisher, a play, TV script, or movie produced. Send SASE for information. Chapters hold meetings on a monthly basis.

NEW HAMPSHIRE WRITERS AND PUBLISHERS PROJECT, P.O. Box 2693, Concord NH 03302-2693. (603)226-6649. Executive Director: Patricia Scholz-Cohen. Estab. 1988. Number of Members: 750. Type of Memberships: Senior/student; individual; business. Open to anyone interested in the literary arts—writers (fiction, nonfiction, journalists, poets, scriptwriters, etc.), teachers, librarians, publishers and *readers*. Statewide scope. Benefits include a bimonthly publication featuring articles about NH writers and publishers; leads for writers, new books listings; and NH literary news. Also discounts on workshops, readings, conferences. Dues: $35 for individuals; $15 for seniors, students; $50 for businesses. Send SASE for information.

NORTH CAROLINA WRITERS' NETWORK, P.O. Box 954, Carrboro NC 27510. (919)967-9540. Fax: (919)929-0535. Executive Director: Linda W. Hobson. Estab. 1985. Number of Members: 1,700. Open to: All writers, all levels of skill and friends of literature. Membership is approximately 1,500 in North Carolina and 200 in 28 other states. Benefits include bimonthly newsletter, reduced rates for competition entry fees, fall and spring conferences, workshops, etc., use of critiquing service, use of library and resource center, press release and publicity service, information database(s). Sponsors annual Fall Conference, Creative Nonfiction Competition, statewide workshops, Writers & Readers Series, Randall Jarrell Poetry Prize, Poetry Chapbook Competition, Thomas Wolfe Fiction Prize, Fiction Competition, Paul Green Playwright Prize. Publishes the 28-page bimonthly *Network News*, and *North Carolina's Literary Resource Guide*. Subscription included in dues. Dues: $35/year, $20/year (students to age 23, seniors 65+ and disabled). Events scheduled throughout the year. Send SASE for information.

‡OZARKS WRITERS LEAGUE, P.O. Box 1433, Branson MO 65616. (417)725-0444. Board Member: Suzann Ledbetter. Estab. 1983. Number of Members: 250. Open to: Anyone interested in writing, photography and art. Regional Scope: Missouri, Arkansas, Oklahoma, Kansas—"Greater Ozarks" area. Benefits include mutual inspiration and support; information exchange. Sponsors quarterly seminars/workshops, two annual writing competitions, one annual photography competition, special conferences. Publishes quarterly newsletter, the *Owls Hoot*. Dues: $10/year. Meets quarterly—February, May, August, November. Send SASE for information.

PHILADELPHIA WRITERS ORGANIZATION, P.O. Box 42497, Philadelphia PA 19101. (610)630-8670. Administrative Coordinator: Jane Brooks. Estab. 1981. Number of Members: 250. Types of Memberships: Full (voting), associate, student. Open to any writer, published or unpublished. Scope is tri-state area—Pennsylvania, Delaware, New Jersey, but mostly Philadelphia area. Benefits include medical insurance (for full members only), monthly meetings with guest panelists, spring workshop (full day) plus Editors Marketplace. Publishes a monthly newsletter for members only. Dues: $50 (full and associate); $25 (student). Proof of publication required for full members (minimum of 2,000 words). Meets monthly throughout year except July and August. Send SASE for information.

PIG IRON LITERARY & ART WORKS, INC., Pig Iron Press, 26 North Phelps St., Youngstown OH 44503. (330)747-6932. Fax: (330)747-0599. Director: Jim Villani. Estab. 1980. Number of Members: 75. Open to: Writers, readers, artists, musicians and dancers living in northeast Ohio and western Pennsylvania. Benefits include use of Independent Press research library, museum and gallery, copy center, meeting spaces and discounts on publishing services. Sponsors workshops and conferences. Publishes *Out of the Pen*, a quarterly newsletter; subscriptions are $10/year. Dues: $25/year. Send SASE for information.

‡SCIENCE FICTION AND FANTASY WORKSHOP, 1193 S. 1900 East, Salt Lake City UT 84108. (801)582-2090. E-mail: sf-woodbury@genie.com for more information. Director/Editor: Kathleen D. Woodbury. Estab. 1980. Number of members: 400. Type of memberships: "Active" is listed in the membership roster and so is accessible to all other members; "inactive" is not listed in the roster. Open to "anyone, anywhere. Our scope is international although over 96% of our members are in the US." Benefits include "several different critique groups: short stories, novels, articles, screenplays, poetry, etc. We also offer services such as copyediting, working out the numbers in planet building (give us the kind of planet you want and we'll tell you how far it is from the sun, etc.—or tell us what kind of sun you have and we'll tell you what your planet is like), brainstorming story, fragments or cultures or aliens, information on groups who write/critique science fiction and fantasy in your area, etc." Publishes *SF and Fantasy Workshop* (monthly); non-members subscribe for $15/year; samples are $1.50 and trial subscription: $8/6 issues. "We have a publication that contains outlines, synopses, proposals that authors submitted or used for novels that sold. The purpose is to show new and aspiring novelists what successful outlines, etc. look like, and to provide authors (with books coming out) advance publicity. Authors may contact Kathleen about publication. Cost is $2.50/issue or $9/4 issues. We also publish a fiction booklet on an irregular basis. It contains one short story and three critiques by professional writers. Cost to anyone is $5/5 issues or $8/10 issues." Dues: Members pay a one-time fee of $5 (to cover the cost of the roster and the new-member information packet) and the annual $15 subscription fee. To renew membership, members simply renew their subscriptions. "Our organization is strictly by mail though that is now expanding to include e-mail." Or send SASE (or IRC).

SCIENCE FICTION WRITERS OF EARTH, P.O. Box 121293, Fort Worth TX 76121. (817)451-8674. Administrator: Gilbert Gordon Reis. Estab. 1980. Number of Members: 64-100. Open to: Unpublished writers of science fiction and fantasy short stories. "We have a few writers in Europe, Canada and Australia, but the majority are from the US. Writers compete in our annual contest. This allows the writer to find out where he/she stands in writing ability. Winners often receive requests for their story from publishers. Many winners have told us that they believe that placing in the top ten of our contest gives them recognition and has assisted in getting their first story published." Dues: One must submit a science fiction or fantasy short story to our annual contest to be a member. Cost is $5 for membership and first story. $2 for each additional ms. The nominating committee meets several times a year to select the top ten stories of the annual contest. Author Edward Bryant selects the winners from the top ten stories. Contest deadline is October 30 and the awards results are mailed out on January 31 of the following year. Information about the organization is available for SASE.

SCIENCE-FICTION AND FANTASY WRITERS OF AMERICA, INC., 5 Winding Brook Drive #1B, Guilderland NY 12084. (518)869-5361. Executive Secretary: Peter Dennis Pautz. Estab.

1965. Number of Members: 1,200. Type of Memberships: Active, associate, affiliate, institutional, estate. Open to: "Professional writers, editors, anthologists, artists in the science fiction/fantasy genres and allied professional individuals and institutions. Our membership is international; we currently have members throughout Europe, Australia, Central and South America, Canada and some in Asia." We produce a variety of journals for our members, annual membership directory and provide a grievance committee, publicity committee, circulating book plan and access to medical/life/disability insurance. We award the SFWA Nebula Awards each year for outstanding achievement in the genre at novel, novella, novelet and short story lengths." Quarterly *SFWA Bulletin* to members; nonmembers may subscribe at $15/4 issues within US/Canada; $18.50 overseas. Bimonthly *SFWA Forum* for active and associate members only. Annual *SFWA Membership Directory* for members; available to professional organizations for $60. Active membership requires professional sale in the US of at least 3 short stories or 1 full-length book. Affiliate or associate membership require at least 1 professional sale in the US or other professional sale in the US or other professional involvement in the field respectively. Dues are pro-rated quarterly; info available upon request. Business meetings are held during Annual Nebula Awards weekend and usually during the annual World SF Convention. Send SASE for information.

‡**SEATTLE WRITERS ASSOCIATION**, P.O. Box 33265, Seattle WA 98133. (206)860-5207. Fax: (206)483-3519 (contact phone). President: Claudia McCormick. Estab. 1986. Number of members: approximately 130. "Open to all writers from the Pacific Northwest, published and unpublished, dedicated to writing professionally and for publication." Benefits include areawide monthly meetings, networking, market advice, critique groups/mss review. Sponsors winter workshop and Writers in Performance (contest and performance). Publishes monthly newsletter for members, available upon request. Writers in Performance anthology in progress. Dues: $30/year, includes newsletter. Meets first Thursday of month, 7-10, September through May. Send SASE for information.

SOCIETY OF SOUTHWESTERN AUTHORS, P.O. Box 30355, Tucson AZ 85751-0355. (520)296-5299. Fax:(520)296-0409. President/Chairman: Penny Porter. Estab. 1972. Number of Members: 170. Memberships: Professional, Associate and Honorary. Professional: published authors of books, articles, poetry, etc.; Associate: aspiring writers not yet published; Honorary: one whose contribution to the writing profession or to SSA warrants such regonition. Benefits include conference, short story writing contest, critiques, marketing advice. Sponsors annual conference in January and annual short story writing contest. Publishes *The Write Word* which appears 6 times/year. Dues: $20/year. Meets monthly. Send SASE for information.

WASHINGTON CHRISTIAN WRITERS FELLOWSHIP, P.O. Box 11337, Bainbridge Island WA 98110. (206)842-9103. Director: Elaine Wright Colvin. Estab. 1982. Number of Members: 300. Open to: All writers. Scope is state-wide. Benefits include meetings, speakers, how-to critiques, private consultation. Sponsors a quarterly seminar; date, time and place varies. Ask to be put on the mailing list. Publishes a bimonthly newsletter, *W.I.N.* Dues: $25. Meets quarterly in Seattle. Brochures are available for SASE.

WESTERN WRITERS OF AMERICA, Office of the Secretary Treasurer, 1012 Fair St., Franklin TN 37064. (615)791-1444. Secretary Treasurer: James A. Crutchfield. Estab. 1953. Number of Members: 600. Type of Membership: Active, associate, patron. Open to: Professional, published writers who have multiple publications of fiction or nonfiction (usually at least three) about the West. Associate membership open to those with one book, a lesser number of short stories or publications or participation in the field such as editors, agents, reviewers, librarians, television producers, directors (dealing with the West). Patron memberships open to corporations, organizations and individuals with an interest in the West. Scope is international. Benefits: "By way of publications and conventions, members are kept abreast of developments in the field of Western literature and the publishing field, marketing requirements, income tax problems, copyright law, research facilities and techniques, and new publications. At conventions members have the opportunity for one-on-one conferences with editors, publishers and agents." Sponsors an annual four-day conference during fourth week of June featuring panels, lectures and seminars on publishing, writing and research. Includes the Spur Awards to honor authors of the best Western literature of the previous year. Publishes *Roundup Magazine* (6 times/year) for members. Available to nonmembers for $30. Publishes membership directory. Dues: $60 for active membership, $60 for associate membership, $250 for patron. For information on Spur Awards, send SASE.

WILLAMETTE WRITERS, 9045 SW Barbur Blvd., Suite 5A, Portland OR 97219. (503)452-1592. Fax: (503)452-0372. E-mail: wilwrite@teleport.com. Office Manager: Paul Merchant. Estab. 1965. Number of members: 700. "Willamette Writers is a nonprofit, tax exempt corporation staffed by volunteers. Membership is open to both published and aspiring writers. WW provides support, encouragement and interaction for all genres of writers." Open to national membership, but serves primarily the Pacific Northwest. Benefits include a writers' referral service, critique groups, membership discounts, youth programs (4th-12th grades), monthly meetings with guest authors, intern program, annual writing contest, community projects, library and research services, as well as networking with other writing groups, office with writing reference and screenplay library. Sponsors annual conference held the second weekend in August; quarterly workshops; annual Kay Snow Writing Contest; and the Distinguished Northwest Writer Award. Publishes *The Willamette Writer* monthly: a 12-page newsletter for members and complimentary subscriptions. Information consists of features, how-to's, mechanics of writing, profile of featured monthly speaker, markets, workshops, conferences and benefits available to writers. Dues: $36/year; includes subscription to newsletter. Meets first Tuesday of each month; board meeting held last Tuesday of each month. Send SASE for information.

THE WRITERS ALLIANCE, 12 Skylark Lane, Stony Brook NY 11790. Executive Director: Kiel Stuart. Estab. 1979. Number of Members: 125. Open to all writers: Professional, aspiring, those who have to write business memos or brochures; those interested in desktop publishing. National scope. Benefits: Members can run one classified or display ad in each issue of membership newsletter, *Backup Street*; which also provides software and hardware reviews, how-to articles, market information and general support. Sponsors local writer's workshops. Publishes *Backup Street*, $10/year (payable to Kiel Stuart) covers both the cost of membership and newsletter. Local writer's critique group meets every two weeks. Send SASE for information.

THE WRITER'S CENTER, 4508 Walsh St., Bethesda MD 20815. (301)654-8664. Director: Jane Fox. Estab. 1977. Number of Members: 2,200. Open to: Anyone interested in writing. Scope is regional DC, Maryland, Virginia, West Virginia, Pennsylvania. Benefits include newsletter, discounts in bookstore, workshops, public events, subscriptions to *Poet Lore*, use of equipment and library, computer BBS (301)656-1638, annual small press book fair. Center offers workshops, reading series, research library, equipment, newsletter and limited workspace. Sponsors workshops, conferences, award for narrative poem. Publishes *Writer's Carousel*, bimonthly. Nonmembers can pick it up at the Center. Dues: $30/year. Fees vary with service, see publications. Brochures are available for SASE.

♣WRITERS' FEDERATION OF NEW BRUNSWICK, P.O. Box 37, Station A, Fredericton, New Brunswick E3B 4Y2 Canada. (902)423-8116. Project Coordinator: Anna Mae Snider. Estab. 1983. Number of Members: 230. Membership is open to anyone interested in writing. "This a provincial organization. Benefits include promotion of members' works through newsletter announcements and readings and launchings held at fall festival and annual general meeting. Services provided by WFNB include a Writers-in-Schools Program and manuscript reading. The WFNB sponsors a fall festival and an annual general meeting which feature workshops, readings and book launchings." There is also an annual literary competition, open to residents of New Brunswick only, which has prizes of $200, $100 and $30 in four categories: Fiction, nonfiction, children's literature and poetry; two $400 prizes for the best manuscript of poems (48 pgs.); the best short novel or collection of short stories and a category for young writers (14-18 years of age) which offers $150 (1st prize), $100 (2nd prize), $50 (3rd prize). Publishes a quarterly newsletter. Dues: $30/year. Board of Directors meets approximately 5 times a year. Annual general meeting is held in the spring of each year. Send SASE for information.

‡♣WRITERS' FEDERATION OF NOVA SCOTIA, Suite 901, 1809 Barrington St., Halifax, Nova Scotia B3J 3K8 Canada. Executive Director: Jane Buss. Estab. 1976. Number of Members: 500. Type of Memberships: General membership, student membership, Nova Scotia Writers' Council membership (professional), Honorary Life Membership. Open to anyone who writes. Provincial scope, with a few members living elsewhere in the country or the world. Benefits include advocacy of all kinds for writers, plus such regular programs as workshops and regular publications, including directories and a newsletter. Sponsors workshops, two annual conferences (one for general membership, the other for the professional wing), two book awards, one annual competition for unpublished manuscripts in seven categories; a writers in the schools program, a manuscript reading service, reduced photocopying rates. Publishes *Eastword*, 6 issues annually, available by subscription for $30 (Canadian) to nonmembers. Dues: $30/year (Canadian). Holds an annual general meeting, an annual meeting of the Nova Scotia Writers' Council, several board meetings annually. Send 5×7 SASE for information.

♣WRITERS GUILD OF ALBERTA, Percy Page Centre, 11759 Groat Rd., 3rd Floor, Edmonton, Alberta T5M 3K6 Canada. (403)422-8174. Fax: (403)422-2663. Executive Director: Miki Andrejevic. Estab. 1980. Number of Members: 700. Membership open to current and past residents of Alberta. Regional (provincial) scope. Benefits include discounts on programs offered; manuscript evaluation service available; bimonthly newsletter; contacts; info on workshops, retreats, readings, etc. Sponsors workshops 2 times/year, retreats 3 times/year, annual conference, annual book awards program (Alberta writers only). Publishes *WestWord* 6 times/year; available for $55/year (Canadian) to nonmembers. Dues: $55/year for regular membership; $20/year senior/students/limited income; $100/year donating membership—charitable receipt issued (Canadian funds). Organized monthly meetings. Send SASE for information.

WRITERS INFORMATION NETWORK, P.O. Box 11337, Bainbridge Island WA 98110. (206)842-9103. Director: Elaine Wright Colvin. Estab. 1980. Number of Members: 1,000. Open to: All interested in writing for religious publications/publishers. Scope is national and several foreign countries. Benefits include bimonthly newsletter, market news, advocacy/grievance procedures, professional advice, writers conferences, press cards, author referral, free consultation. Sponsors workshops, conferences throughout the country each year—mailing list and advertised in *W.I.N.* newsletter. Bimonthly newsletter: $25 US; $35 foreign/year. Dues: $25 US (newsletter subscription included). Holds quarterly meetings in Seattle WA. Brochures are available for SASE.

WRITERS OF KERN, P.O. Box 6694, Bakersfield CA 93386-6694. (805)871-5834. President: Barbara Gabel. Estab. 1993. Number of members: 100. Affiliated with the California Writer's Club. Types of memberships: Professional, writers with published work; writers working toward publication, students. Open to published writers and any person interested in writing. Benefits of membership: Monthly meetings on the third Saturday of every month, except September which is our conference month, with speakers who are authors, agents, etc., on topics pertaining to writing; critique groups for several fiction genres, nonfiction and screenwriting which meet weekly or biweekly; several of our members are successfully published and full-time writers; members receive a monthly newsletter with marketing tips, conferences and contests; access to club library; discount to annual conference. Annual conference held the third Saturday in September; annual writing contest with winners announced at the conference. Dues: $35/year, discount for students. Send SASE for information.

 THE WRITERS ROOM, INC., 10 Astor Place, 6th Floor, New York NY 10003. (212)254-6995. Executive Director: Donna Brodie. Estab. 1978. Number of Members: 185. Open to: Any writer who shows a serious commitment to writing. "We serve a diverse population of writers, but most of our residents live in or around the NYC area. We encourage writers from around the country (and world!) to apply for residency if they plan to visit NYC for a while." Benefits include 24-hour access to the facility. "We provide desk space, storage areas for computers, typewriters, etc., a kitchen where coffee and tea are always available, bathrooms and a lounge. We also offer in-house workshops on topics of practical importance to writers and monthly readings of work-in-progress." Dues: $175 per quarter/ year. Send SASE for application and background information.

THE WRITERS' WORKSHOP, P.O. Box 696, Asheville NC 28802. (704)254-8111. Executive Director: Karen Tager. Estab. 1984. Number of Members: 1,250. Types of Memberships: Student/ low income $25; family/organization $55; individual $30. Open to all writers. Scope is national and international. Benefits include discounts on workshops, quarterly newsletter, admission to Annual Celebration every summer, critiquing services through the mail. Center offers reading room, assistance with editing your work, contacts with NY writers and agents. Publishes a newsletter. Available to nonmembers. Offers workshops year-round in NC and the South; 6 retreats a year, 25 readings with nationally awarded authors. Contests and classes for children and teens as well. Advisory board includes Kurt Vonnegut, E.L. Doctorow, Peter Matthiessen and Eudora Welty. Also sponsors international contests in fiction, poetry and creative nonfiction. Brochures are available for SASE.

Publications of Interest to Fiction Writers

This section features listings for magazines and newsletters that focus on writing or the publishing industry. While many of these are not markets for fiction, they do offer articles, marketing advice or other information valuable to the fiction writer. Several magazines in this section offer actual market listings while others feature reviews of books in the field and news on the industry.

The timeliness factor is a primary reason most writers read periodicals. Changes in publishing happen very quickly and magazines can help you keep up with the latest news. Some magazines listed here, including *Writer's Digest* cover the entire field of writing, while others such as *The Mystery Review* and *Children's Book Insider* focus on a particular type of writing. We've also added publications which focus on a particular segment of the publishing industry, including *Locus* and *Factsheet Five*.

Information on some publications for writers can be found in the introductions to other sections in this book. In addition, many of the literary and commercial magazines for writers listed in the markets sections are helpful to the fiction writer. Keep an eye on the newsstand and the library shelves for others and let us know if you've found a publication particularly useful.

AWP CHRONICLE, Associated Writing Programs, George Mason University, Tallwood House, Mail Stop 1E3, Fairfax VA 22030. (703)993-4301. E-mail: awp@gmu.edu. Editor: D.W. Fenza. 6 times/year. Essays on contemporary literature and articles on the teaching of creative writing only. Does *not* publish fiction. Lists fiction markets (back pages for "Submit"). Sample copies available; single copy price $3.95. Subscription: $20/year; $25/year Canada; $35/year overseas.

CHILDREN'S BOOK INSIDER, P.O. Box 1030, Fairplay CO 80440-1030. E-mail: cbi@rmi.net. Editor/Publisher: Laura Backes. Monthly. "Publication is devoted solely to children's book writers and illustrators. 'At Presstime' section gives current market information each month for fiction, nonfiction and illustration submissions to publishers. Other articles include writing and illustration tips for fiction and nonfiction, interviews with published authors and illustrators, features on alternative publishing methods (self-publishing, co-op publishing, etc.), how to submit work to publishers, industry trends. Also publishes books and writing tools for both beginning and experienced children's book writers." Sample copy and catalog for SASE with 55¢ postage. Single copy price: $3.25. Subscription price: $29.95/year (US); $35/year (Canadian).

CROW QUARTERLY REVIEW, 147 Vera Marie Lane, Box 340, Rollinsville CO 80474. (303)258-0442. E-mail: kpmc@indra.com. Editor: Kevin McCarthy. Quarterly. "A review of *unpublished* and self-published work—sent to writers, editors, agents and producers. Helps writers market their work. Also serves to bridge the gap between the professions with writer's Crow Bar columns; writer's, editor's, agent's, producer's POV columns, feature articles and classified ads. Send 9×12 SASE for more info." Critiques and reviews unpublished and self-published novels, short story collections and nonfiction. Sample copies available for 9×12 SASE. Also available on the World Wide Web: http://ReadersNdex.com/crow/. "Writers should visit the website or write for info before sending anything.'

‡FACTSHEET FIVE, P.O. Box 170099, San Francisco CA 94117-0099. Editor: R. Seth Friedman. Biannually. "The definitive guide to the 'zine revolution. *Factsheet Five* reviews over 2,000 small press publications each issue. Send in your independent magazine for review." Sample copy: $6. Subscriptions: $20 for individuals and $40 for institutions.

FEMINIST BOOKSTORE NEWS, P.O. Box 882554, San Francisco CA 94188. (415)626-1556. Fax: (415)626-8970. Editor: Carol Seajay. Bimonthly. "*FBN* is a 124-page bimonthly magazine with

reviews of more than 300 new feminist and lesbian titles and articles on the world of women and books. Regular columns include a 'Writing Wanted' section featuring calls for submission from various publishers." Reviews novels and short story collections. Send review copies to Beth Morgan. Sample copies available; single copy price is $6. Subscriptions: $70/year ($9 Canadian postage/$19 international postage). *Note: As with other listings in this section, this is not a "market;" do not send mss.*

‡**GOTTA WRITE NETWORK LITMAG**, Maven Publications, 612 Cobblestone Circle, Glenview IL 60025. Fax: (847)296-7631. E-mail: netera@aol.com. Editor: Denise Fleischer. Semiannually. Zine specializing in writing techniques. "Objective is to support the beginning writer, to teach him/her how to submit work, improve writing skills and look beyond rejection. The magazine is divided into three major sections: general information, Sci-Fi-Galleria and Literary Beat. It includes articles, fiction, interviews, poetry and market news." Sample copy for $5, 9×12 SAE and $1.50 postage. Subscriptions: $12.75/year (US); $15/year overseas.

HAVENS FOR CREATIVES, ACT I Creativity Center, P.O. Box 30854, Palm Beach Gardens FL 33420. Editor: Char Plotsky. Annual directory of information on retreats and colonies for artists of all disciplines, including writers. Send SASE for information.

LAMBDA BOOK REPORT, 1625 Connecticut Ave. NW, Washington DC 20009-1013. (202)462-7924. Editor: Kanani Kauka. Monthly. "This review journal of contemporary gay and lesbian literature appeals to both readers and writers. Fiction queries published regularly." Lists fiction markets. Reviews novels and short story collections. Send review copies to Attn: Book Review Editor. Single copy price is $3.95/US. Subscriptions: $34.95/year (US); international rate: $58.95 (US $); Canada/Mexico: $46.95/year (US $).

LOCUS, The Newspaper of the Science Fiction Field, P.O. Box 13305, Oakland CA 94661. Editor: Charles N. Brown. Monthly. "Professional newsletter of science fiction, fantasy and horror; has news, interviews of authors, book reviews, column on electronic publishing, forthcoming books listings, monthly books-received listings, etc." Lists markets for fiction. Reviews novels or short story collections. Sample copies available. Single copy price: $4.50. Subscription price: $43/year, (2nd class mail) for US, $48 (US)/year, (2nd class) for Canada; $48 (US)/year (2nd class) for overseas.

❦**THE MYSTERY REVIEW, A Quarterly Publication for Mystery & Suspense Readers**, P.O. Box 233, Colborne, Ontario K0K 1S0 Canada. (613)475-4440. Editor: Barbara Davey. Quarterly. "Book reviews, information on new releases, interviews with authors and other people involved in mystery, 'real life' mysteries, out-of-print mysteries, mystery/suspense films, word games and puzzles with a mystery theme." Reviews mystery/suspense novels and short story collections. Send review copies to editor. Single copy price is $5.95 CDN in Canada/$5.95 US in the United States. Subscriptions: $21.50 (CDN, includes GST) in Canada; $20 (US) in the US and $28 (US) elsewhere.

NEW WRITER'S MAGAZINE, P.O. Box 5976, Sarasota FL 34277. E-mail: newriters@aol.com. (941)953-7903. Editor: George J. Haborak. Bimonthly. *"New Writer's Magazine* is a publication for aspiring writers. It features 'how-to' articles, news and interviews with published and recently published authors. Will use fiction that has a tie-in with the world of the writer." Lists markets for fiction. Reviews novels and short story collections. Send review copies to Editor. Send #10 SASE for guidelines. Sample copies available; single copy price is $3. Subscriptions: $15/year, $25/two years. Canadian $20 (US funds). International $35/year (US funds).

‡**OHIO WRITER**, P.O. Box 528, Willoughby OH 44094. (216)257-6410. Editor: Linda Rome. Bimonthly. "Interviews with Ohio writers of fiction and nonfiction; current fiction markets in Ohio." Lists fiction markets. Reviews novels and short story collections. Sample copies available for $2. Subscriptions: $12/year; $30/3 years; $18/institutional rate.

POETS & WRITERS, 72 Spring St., New York NY 10012. E-mail: pwsubs@pw.org. Website: http://www.pw.org. Covers primarily poetry and fiction writing. Bimonthly. "Keeps writers in touch with the news they need. Reports on grants and awards, including deadlines for applications; publishes manuscript requests from editors and publishers; covers topics such as book contracts, taxes, writers' colonies and publishing trends; features essays by and interviews with poets and fiction writers. Lists markets for fiction. Sample copies available; single copy price is $3.95. Subscriptions: $19.95/year; $38/2 years.

PROSETRY, Newsletter For, By, About Writers, P.O. Box 117727, Burlingame CA 94011-7727. Editor: P.D. Steele. Monthly. Estab. 1986. "A newsletter for writers, offering markets, conferences, exercises, information, workshops, and a monthly guest writer column with tips to the fiction and nonfiction writer." Reviews short story and poetry collections. Send review copies to P.D. Steele or E. B. Maynard. Sample copy available for 3 first-class stamps. Subscriptions: $12/year. Guidelines for #10 SASE.

THE REGENCY PLUME, 711 D. St. N.W., Ardmore OK 73401. Editor: Marilyn Clay. Bimonthly. "The newsletter focus is on providing accurate historical facts relating to the Regency period: customs, clothes, entertainment, the wars, historical figures, etc. I stay in touch with New York editors who acquire Regency romance novels. Current market info appears regularly in newsletter—see Bits & Scraps." Current Regency romances are "Previewed." Sample copy available for $3; single copy price is $3, $4 outside States. Subscriptions: $15/year for 6 issues; $18 Canada; $22 foreign. ("Check must be drawn on a US bank. Postal money order okay.") Back issues available. Send SASE for subscription information, article guidelines or list of research and writing aids available, such as audiotapes, historical maps, books on Regency period furniture, regency romance writing contest, etc.

SCAVENGER'S NEWSLETTER, 519 Ellinwood, Osage City KS 66523. (913)528-3538. Editor: Janet Fox. Monthly. "A market newsletter for SF/fantasy/horror/mystery writers with an interest in the small press. Articles about SF/fantasy/horror/mystery writing/marketing. Now using Flash fiction to 1,200 words, genres as above. No writing-related material for fiction. Payment for articles and fiction is $4 on acceptance." Lists markets for fiction. Sample copies available. Single copy price: $2. Subscription price: $15.50/year, $7.75/6 months. Canada: $18.50, $9.25 overseas $24.50, $12.25 (US funds only).

SCIENCE FICTION CHRONICLE, P.O. Box 022730, Brooklyn NY 11202-0056. (718)643-9011. Editor: Andrew I. Porter. Monthly. "Monthly newsmagazine for professional writers, editors, readers of SF, fantasy, horror." Lists markets for fiction "updated every 4 months." Reviews novels, small press publications, audiotapes, software, and short story collections. Send review copies to SFC and to Don D'Ammassa, 323 Dodge St., E. Providence RI 02914. Sample copies available with 9×12 SAE with $1.24 postage; single copy price is $3.50 (US) or £3.50 (UK). Subscriptions: $35 bulk, $42 first class US and Canada; $49 overseas. *Note: As with other listings in this section, this is not a "market"—Do not send mss or artwork.*

SMALL PRESS REVIEW/SMALL MAGAZINE REVIEW, P.O. Box 100, Paradise CA 95967. (916)877-6110. Editor: Len Fulton. Monthly. "Publishes news and reviews about small publishers, books and magazines." Lists markets for fiction and poetry. Reviews novels, short story and poetry collections. Sample copies available. Subscription price: $25/year.

THE WRITER, 120 Boylston St., Boston MA 02116-4615. Editor: Sylvia K. Burack. Monthly. Contains articles on improving writing techniques and getting published. Includes market lists of magazine and book publishers. Subscription price: $28/year, $52/2 years. Canadian and foreign at additional $8 (US) per year. Also publishes *The Writer's Handbook*, an annual book on all fields of writing plus market lists of magazine and book publishers.

WRITERS BLOC MAGAZINE, A Collection of Collaborative Literature, 1278 Morgan St., Santa Rosa CA 95401. (800)544-7033. Editor: Bernie Hamilton-Lee. Semi-annually. "We publish only collaborative writing of Writers Bloc members." Annual membership is $40 which enables members to participate in stories in the genre of their choice (mystery, science fiction, romance, etc.). Sample copies available for $2.95. Subscriptions: $10.50 for one year.

WRITER'S CAROUSEL, The Writer's Center, 4508 Walsh St., Bethesda MD 20815. (301)654-8664. Editors: Allan Lefcowitz and Jeff Minerd. Bimonthly. "*Writer's Carousel* publishes book reviews and articles about writing and the writing scene." Lists fiction markets. Reviews novels and short story collections. Sample copies available. Subscriptions: $30 Writer's Center Membership.

WRITERS CONNECTION, P.O. Box 24770, San Jose CA 95154-4770. (408)445-3600. Fax: (408)445-3609. Editor: Jan Stiles. Monthly. "How-to articles for writers, editors and self-publishers. Topics cover all types of writing, from fiction to technical writing. Columns include markets, contests and writing events and conferences for fiction, nonfiction and scriptwriting." Lists markets for fiction. Sample copies for $3. Single copy price: $3. Subscription: $25/year. "We do not publish fiction or poetry."

WRITER'S DIGEST, 1507 Dana Ave., Cincinnati OH 45207. (513)531-2690. Editor: Thomas Clark. Monthly. "*Writer's Digest* is a magazine of techniques and markets. We *inspire* the writer to write, *instruct* him or her on how to improve that work, and *direct* him or her toward appropriate markets." Lists markets for fiction, nonfiction, poetry. Single copy price: $2.99. Subscription price: $27.

WRITER'S DIGEST BOOKS–MARKET BOOKS, 1507 Dana Ave., Cincinnati OH 45207. (513)531-2222. Annual. In addition to *Novel & Short Story Writer's Market*, Writer's Digest Books also publishes *Writer's Market, Poet's Market, Children's Writer's and Illustrator's Market, Mystery Writer's Sourcebook, Science Fiction and Fantasy Writer's Sourcebook, Romance Writer's Sourcebook* and the *Guide to Literary Agents.* All include articles and listings of interest to writers. All are available at bookstores, libraries or through the publisher. (Request catalog.)

WRITERS' JOURNAL, Val-Tech Publishing, Inc., P.O. Box 25376, St. Paul MN 55125-0376. Managing Editor: Valerie Hockert. Bimonthly. "Provides a creative outlet for writers of fiction." Sample copies available. Single copy price: $3.99; $5.75 (Canadian). Subscription price: $19.97; $23.97 Canada.

WRITER'S YEARBOOK, 1507 Dana Ave., Cincinnati OH 45207. (513)531-2690. Editor: Thomas Clark. Annual. "A collection of the best writing *about* writing, with an exclusive survey of the year's 100 top markets for freelancers." Single copy price: $4.99.

ZENE, 5 Martins Lane, Witcham Ely, Cambs CB6 2LB England. Editor: Andy Cox. Quarterly (but may be monthly soon). *Zene* is a guide to independent literary markets worldwide. We list complete contributors' guidelines, including subscription details, plus updates, news and feedback from writers. Every issue contains wide-ranging articles by leading small press writers, editors, publishers, ER, plus interviews, letters, market info, etc. We are international, with correspondents and guidelines from all over the world." Lists fiction markets. Reviews novels, magazines and short story collections. Subscriptions: $16 (AIR), "US checks OK, payable to TTA Press."

Websites of Interest

BY MEGAN LANE

The Internet can be a quick, convenient and fairly cheap way to find information about many kinds of writing from genre to literary to experimental. It can also serve as a link to other writers and writers' organizations, creating a creative community in cyberspace with the ability to communicate the way writers do it best—with words. But the strength of the Internet, the massive amount of information it contains, is also its weakness. To make your travels on the information superhighway as smooth as possible, we've compiled a short (read: incomplete) list of websites for writers.

Genre writers should check out these pages:

Science Fiction and Fantasy Writers of America: http://www.greyware.com/sfwa/. This site includes organization information such as by-laws, officers' names and how to join, as well as information about the craft and business of writing and links to other sf/f sites.

The Horror Writers Association: http://www.horror.org/HWA/. This site includes general information about the organization including its history and the awards it presents, as well as links to other horror sites.

SF/F/H Markets: http://users.aol.com/marketlist. This site is a "free bimonthly resource that includes an extensive listing of science fiction, fantasy and horror short fiction markets." It also includes "Tips and Hints on Submitting Your Work," magazine reviews and a list of recently closed markets.

Resources for Romance Writers: http://www.interlog.com/~ohi/www/romance.html. This site lists and links other sites of interest to romance writers, including places to find historical information and lists of authors and workshops. The site also includes market and organization information.

Children's Literature Web Guide: http://www.ucalgary.ca/~dkbrown/index.html. This comprehensive site for children's book writers and illustrators includes links to authors, publishers, booksellers, conferences and events, as well as other sites of interest.

Kensington Publishing: http://www.kensingtonbooks.com. The site of this important genre publisher includes general information about the company and its imprints, but also lists the names, titles and backgrounds of editors, along with group pictures. Internet users also can "chat" with Kensington president Steven Zacharius in real time.

Of course, there are many, many more Internet resources for genre writers. To find more sites or to search for sites addressing other writing topics, try searching **Yahoo:** http://www.yahoo.com. This Internet index allows you to look for websites by entering keywords or by browsing. Once you sift through /Arts/Humanities/Literature, you'll find headings for /Genre, /Journals, /Organizations, /Contests, etc. Once you link to a site you can write down its address and, next time, go directly to it. Some useful and fun sites we dug up on Yahoo include:

Straycat's Writer Workshop: http://www.generation.net/~straycat/workshop.html. This site publishes short stories and poetry with writers' e-mail addresses so they can receive feedback from readers.

Inklings: http://www.interlog.com/~oh/ink/inklings.html. This is an online newsletter for writers that includes market information, Internet resources for writers, writers' tips, interviews and profiles. The site is updated biweekly and can also be accessed through an e-mail subscription. The site has 5,422 e-mail subscribers.

11 Rules of Grammar: http://www.mailzone.com/users/pub/rgiaquinta/js.htm. This site includes important rules for grammatical writing with both correct and incorrect examples, as well as links to other grammar-related sites.

Writes of Passage: http://www.writes.org. This is a site specifically for teenage writers. They can post their own work or read the writing of other teens. This is high quality, fun writing.

To search by keyword for writing sites, you can also try **The World Wide Web Worm:** http://wwww.cs.colorado.edu/wwww. This site allows you to enter words to search for other websites. It's easy to use but not nearly as much fun to look at as Yahoo. To skip right to an index of sites specifically of interest to writers try **The Writer's Edge:** http://www.nashville.net/~edge. This site includes links for contests, markets, publishers and workshops, among others. You can find an alphabetical index of publishing company websites at **Commercial Publishers:** http://www.edoc.com/jrl-bin/wilma/pco.

Finally, as you read through the Markets section, be sure to check the listings for webpage addresses. Many publications, especially literary magazines, have webpages where you can find writers' guidelines and other submission advice. Some pages also include examples of writing from past issues or even an entire issue of the magazine. Reading the examples will help you determine if your work is appropriate for a particular publication. Some of the magazines in this year's NSSWM that have a webpage include:

Byline: http://www.bylinemag.com

Dreams and Visions: http://www.bconnex.net/~skysong

Ruby's Pearls: http://www.gate.net/~ruby/

Marion Zimmer Bradley's Fantasy Magazine: http://www.well.com/user/mzbfm.

❦Canadian Writers Take Note

While much of the information contained in this section applies to all writers, here are some specifics of interest to Canadian writers:

Postage: At press time, the cost of one International Reply Coupon in Canada is $3.50 (Canadian). A 7 percent GST tax is required on postage in Canada and for mail with postage under $5 going to destinations outside the country. Since Canadian postage rates are voted on in January of each year (after we go to press), contact a Canada Post Corporation Customer Service Division, located in most cities in Canada, for the most current rates.

Copyright: For information on copyrighting your work and to obtain forms, write Copyright and Industrial Design, Phase One, Place du Portage, 50 Victoria St., 5th Floor, Hull, Quebec K1A 0C9 or call (819)997-1936.

The public lending right: The Public Lending Right Commission has established that eligible Canadian authors are entitled to payments when a book is available through a library. Payments are determined by a sampling of the holdings of a representative number of libraries. To find out more about the program and to learn if you are eligible, write to the Public Lending Right Commission at 350 Albert St., P.O. Box 1047, Ottawa, Ontario K1P 5V8 or call (613)566-4378 for information. The Commission which is part of The Canada Council, produces a helpful pamphlet, *How the PLR System Works,* on the program.

Grants available to Canadian writers: Most province art councils or departments of culture provide grants to resident writers. Some of these, as well as contests for Canadian writers, are listed in our Contests and Awards section. For national programs, contact The Canada Council, Writing and Publishing Section, P.O. Box 1047, Ottawa, Ontario K1P 5V8 or call (613)566-4334 for information. For more information on grants available to writers, contact the Arts Awards Section of the Council at the same address.

For more information: More details on much of the information listed above and additional information on writing and publishing in Canada are included in the *Writer's Essential Desk Reference: A Companion to Writer's Market*, 2nd edition, published by Writer's Digest Books. In addition to information on a wide range of topics useful to all writers, the book features a detailed chapter for Canadians, Writing and Selling in Canada, by Fred Kerner.

See the Organizations and Resources section of *Novel & Short Story Writer's Market* for listings of writers' organizations in Canada. Also contact The Writer's Union of Canada, 24 Ryerson Ave., Toronto, Ontario M5T 2P3; call them at (416)703-8982 or fax them at (416)703-0826. This organization provides a wealth of information (as well as strong support) for Canadian writers, including specialized publications on publishing contracts; contract negotiations; the author/editor relationship; author awards, competitions and grants; agents; taxes for writers, libel issues and access to archives in Canada.

Printing and Production Terms Defined

In most of the magazine listings in this book you will find a brief physical description of each publication. This material usually includes the number of pages, type of paper, type of binding and whether or not the magazine uses photographs or illustrations.

Although it is important to look at a copy of the magazine to which you are submitting, these descriptions can give you a general idea of what the publication looks like. This material can provide you with a feel for the magazine's financial resources and prestige. Do not, however, rule out small, simply produced publications as these may be the most receptive to new writers. Watch for publications that have increased their page count or improved their production from year to year. This is a sign the publication is doing well and may be accepting more fiction.

You will notice a wide variety of printing terms used within these descriptions. We explain here some of the more common terms used in our listing descriptions. We do not include explanations of terms such as Mohawk and Karma which are brand names and refer to the paper manufacturer. *Getting it Printed*, by Mark Beach (Writer's Digest Books), is an excellent publication for those interested in learning more about printing and production.

PAPER

acid-free: Paper that has a low or no acid content. This type of paper resists deterioration from exposure to the elements. More expensive than many other types of paper, publications done on acid-free paper can last a long time.

bond: Bond paper is often used for stationery and is more transparent than text paper. It can be made of either sulphite (wood) or cotton fiber. Some bonds have a mixture of both wood and cotton (such as "25 percent cotton" paper). This is the type of paper most often used in photocopying or as standard typing paper.

coated/uncoated stock: Coated and uncoated are terms usually used when referring to book or text paper. More opaque than bond, it is the paper most used for offset printing. As the name implies, uncoated paper has no coating. Coated paper is coated with a layer of clay, varnish or other chemicals. It comes in various sheens and surfaces depending on the type of coating, but the most common are dull, matte and gloss.

cover stock: Cover stock is heavier book or text paper used to cover a publication. They come in a variety of colors and textures and can be coated on one or both sides.

CS1/CS2: Most often used when referring to cover stock, CS1 means paper that is coated only on one side; CS2 is paper coated on both sides.

newsprint: Inexpensive absorbent pulp wood paper often used in newspapers and tabloids.

text: Text paper is similar to book paper (a smooth paper used in offset printing), but it has been given some texture by using rollers or other methods to apply a pattern to the paper.

vellum: Vellum is a text paper that is fairly porous and soft.

Some notes about paper weight and thickness: Often you will see paper thickness described in terms of pounds such as 80 lb. or 60 lb. paper. The weight is determined by figuring how many pounds in a ream of a particular paper (a ream is 500 sheets). This can be confusing, however, because this figure is based on a standard sheet size and standard sheet sizes vary depending on the type of paper used. This information is most helpful when comparing papers of the same type. For example, 80 lb. book paper versus 60 lb. book paper. Since the size of the paper is the same it would follow that 80 lb. paper is the thicker, heavier paper.

Some paper, especially cover stock, is described by the actual thickness of the paper. This is expressed in a system of points. Typical paper thicknesses range from 8 points to 14 points thick.

PRINTING

letterpress: Letterpress printing is printing that uses a raised surface such as type. The type is inked and then pressed against the paper. Unlike offset printing, only a limited number of impressions can be made, as the surface of the type can wear down.

offset: Offset is a printing method in which ink is transferred from an image-bearing plate to a "blanket" and from the blanket to the paper.

sheet-fed offset: Offset printing in which the paper is fed one piece at a time.

web offset: Offset printing in which a roll of paper is printed and then cut apart to make individual sheets.

There are many other printing methods but these are the ones most commonly referred to in our listings.

BINDING

case binding: In case binding, signatures (groups of pages) are stitched together with thread rather than glued together. The stitched pages are then trimmed on three sides and glued into a hardcover or board "case" or cover. Most hardcover books and thicker magazines are done this way.

comb binding: A comb is a plastic spine used to hold pages together with bent tabs that are fed through punched holes in the edge of the paper.

perfect binding: Used for paperback books and heavier magazines, perfect binding involves gathering signatures (groups of pages) into a stack, trimming off the folds so that the edge is flat and gluing a cover to that edge.

saddle stitched: Publications in which the pages are stitched together using metal staples. This fairly inexpensive type of binding is usually used with books or magazines that are under 80 pages.

Smythe-sewn: Binding in which the pages are sewn together with thread. Smythe is the name of the most common machine used for this purpose.

spiral binding: A wire spiral that is wound through holes punched in pages is a spiral bind. This is the binding used in spiral notebooks.

Glossary

Advance. Payment by a publisher to an author prior to the publication of a book, to be deducted from the author's future royalties.

All rights. The rights contracted to a publisher permitting a manuscript's use anywhere and in any form, including movie and book club sales, without additional payment to the writer.

Anthology. A collection of selected writings by various authors.

Auction. Publishers sometimes bid against each other for the acquisition of a manuscript that has excellent sales prospects.

Backlist. A publisher's books not published during the current season but still in print.

Belles lettres. A term used to describe fine or literary writing more to entertain than to inform or instruct.

Book producer/packager. An organization that may develop a book for a publisher based upon the publisher's idea or may plan all elements of a book, from its initial concept to writing and marketing strategies, and then sell the package to a book publisher and/or movie producer.

Category fiction. See Genre.

Chapbook. A booklet of 15-30 pages of fiction or poetry.

Cheese-goth. Literature that strays from the values of traditional Gothic (e.g., Bram Stoker's *Dracula*) into the campy area of *Buffy the Vampire Slayer*.

Cliffhanger. Fictional event in which the reader is left in suspense at the end of a chapter or episode, so that interest in the story's outcome will be sustained.

Clip. Sample, usually from a newspaper or magazine, of a writer's published work.

Cloak-and-dagger. A melodramatic, romantic type of fiction dealing with espionage and intrigue.

Commercial. Publishers whose concern is salability, profit and success with a large readership.

Contemporary. Material dealing with popular current trends, themes or topics.

Contributor's copy. Copy of an issue of a magazine or published book sent to an author whose work is included.

Copublishing. An arrangement in which the author and publisher share costs and profits.

Copyediting. Editing a manuscript for writing style, grammar, punctuation and factual accuracy.

Copyright. The legal right to exclusive publication, sale or distribution of a literary work.

Cover letter. A brief letter sent with a complete manuscript submitted to an editor.

"Cozy" (or "teacup") mystery. Mystery usually set in a small British town, in a bygone era, featuring a somewhat genteel, intellectual protagonist.

Cyberpunk. Type of science fiction, usually concerned with computer networks and human-computer combinations, involving young, sophisticated protagonists.

Division. An unincorporated branch of a company (e.g. Viking Penguin, a division of Penguin USA).

Elf punk. Type of fantasy involving magical creatures such as elves who behave like urban punks and live on the fringe of society in a bleak, urban setting.

E-mail. Mail that has been sent electronically using a computer and modem.

Experimental fiction. Fiction that is innovative in subject matter and style; avant-garde, non-formulaic, usually literary material.

Exposition. The portion of the storyline, usually the beginning, where background information about character and setting is related.

Fair use. A provision in the copyright law that says short passages from copyrighted material may be used without infringing on the owner's rights.

Fanzine. A noncommercial, small-circulation magazine usually dealing with fantasy, horror or science-fiction literature and art.

First North American serial rights. The right to publish material in a periodical before it appears in book form, for the first time, in the United States or Canada.

Formula. A fixed and conventional method of plot development, which varies little from one book to another in a particular genre.

Frontier novel. Novel that has all the basic elements of a traditional western but is based upon the frontier history of "unwestern" places like Florida or East Tennessee.

Galleys. The first typeset version of a manuscript that has not yet been divided into pages.

Genre. A formulaic type of fiction such as romance, western or horror.

Gothic. A genre in which the central character is usually a beautiful young woman and the setting an old mansion or castle, involving a handsome hero and real danger, either natural or supernatural.

Graphic novel. An adaptation of a novel into a long comic strip or heavily illustrated story of 40 pages or more, produced in paperback.

Hard-boiled detective novel. Mystery novel featuring a private eye or police detective as the protagonist; usually involves a murder. The emphasis is on the details of the crime.

Honorarium. A small, token payment for published work.

Horror. A genre stressing fear, death and other aspects of the macabre.

Imprint. Name applied to a publisher's specific line (e.g. Owl, an imprint of Henry Holt).

Interactive fiction. Fiction in book or computer-software format where the reader determines the path the story will take by choosing from several alternatives at the end of each chapter or episode.

International Reply Coupon (IRC). A form purchased at a post office and enclosed with a letter or manuscript to a international publisher, to cover return postage costs.

Juvenile. Fiction intended for children 2-12.

Libel. Written or printed words that defame, malign or damagingly misrepresent a living person.

Literary. The general category of serious, non-formulaic, intelligent fiction, sometimes experimental, that most frequently appears in little magazines.

Literary agent. A person who acts for an author in finding a publisher or arranging contract terms on a literary project.

Mainstream. Traditionally written fiction on subjects or trends that transcend experimental or genre fiction categories.

Malice domestic novel. A traditional mystery novel that is not hard-boiled; emphasis is on the solution. Suspects and victims know one another.

Manuscript. The author's unpublished copy of a work, usually typewritten, used as the basis for typesetting.

Mass market paperback. Softcover book on a popular subject, usually around 4×7, directed to a general audience and sold in drugstores and groceries as well as in bookstores.

Ms(s). Abbreviation for manuscript(s).

Multiple submission. Submission of more than one short story at a time to the same editor. Do not make a multiple submission unless requested.

Narration. The account of events in a story's plot as related by the speaker or the voice of the author.

Narrator. The person who tells the story, either someone involved in the action or the voice of the writer.

New Age. A term including categories such as astrology, psychic phenomena, spiritual healing, UFOs, mysticism and other aspects of the occult.

Nom de plume. French for "pen name"; a pseudonym.

Novella (also novelette). A short novel or long story, approximately 7,000-15,000 words.

#10 envelope. $4 \times 9\frac{1}{2}$ envelope, used for queries and other business letters.

Novels of the West. Novels that have elements of the western but contain more complex characters and subjects such as fur trading, cattle raising and coal mining.

Offprint. Copy of a story taken from a magazine before it is bound.

One-time rights. Permission to publish a story in periodical or book form one time only.

Outline. A summary of a book's contents, often in the form of chapter headings with a few sentences outlining the action of the story under each one; sometimes part of a book proposal.

Over the transom. Slang for the path of an unsolicited manuscript into the slush pile.

Page rate. A fixed rate paid to an author per published page of fiction.

Payment on acceptance. Payment from the magazine or publishing house as soon as the decision to print a manuscript is made.

Payment on publication. Payment from the publisher after a manuscript is printed.

Pen name. A pseudonym used to conceal a writer's real name.

Periodical. A magazine or journal published at regular intervals.

Plot. The carefully devised series of events through which the characters progress in a work of fiction.

Proofreading. Close reading and correction of a manuscript's typographical errors.

Proofs. A typeset version of a manuscript used for correcting errors and making changes, often a photocopy of the galleys.

Proposal. An offer to write a specific work, usually consisting of an outline of the work and one or two completed chapters.

Prose poem. Short piece of prose with the language and expression of poetry.

Protagonist. The principal or leading character in a literary work.

Public domain. Material that either was never copyrighted or whose copyright term has expired.

Pulp magazine. A periodical printed on inexpensive paper, usually containing lurid, sensational stories or articles.

Purple prose. Ornate writing using exaggerated and excessive literary devices.

Query. A letter written to an editor to elicit interest in a story the writer wants to submit.

Reader. A person hired by a publisher to read unsolicited manuscripts.

Reading fee. An arbitrary amount of money charged by some agents and publishers to read a submitted manuscript.

Regency romance. A genre romance, usually set in England between 1811-1820.

Remainders. Leftover copies of an out-of-print book, sold by the publisher at a reduced price.

Reporting time. The number of weeks or months it takes an editor to report back on an author's query or manuscript.

Reprint rights. Permission to print an already published work whose rights have been sold to another magazine or book publisher.

Roman à clef. French "novel with a key." A novel that represents actual living or historical characters and events in fictionalized form.

Romance. The genre relating accounts of passionate love and fictional heroic achievements.

Royalties. A percentage of the retail price paid to an author for each copy of the book that is sold.

SAE. Self-addressed envelope.

SASE. Self-addressed stamped envelope.

Science fiction. Genre in which scientific facts and hypotheses form the basis of actions and events.

Second serial (reprint) rights. Permission for the reprinting of a work in another periodical after its first publication in book or magazine form.

Self-publishing. In this arrangement, the author keeps all income derived from the book, but he pays for its manufacturing, production and marketing.

Sequel. A literary work that continues the narrative of a previous, related story or novel.

Serial rights. The rights given by an author to a publisher to print a piece in one or more periodicals.

Serialized novel. A book-length work of fiction published in sequential issues of a periodical.

Setting. The environment and time period during which the action of a story takes place.

Short short story. A condensed piece of fiction, usually under 700 words.

Simultaneous submission. The practice of sending copies of the same manuscript to several editors or publishers at the same time. Some people refuse to consider such submissions.

Slant. A story's particular approach or style, designed to appeal to the readers of a specific magazine.

Slice of life. A presentation of characters in a seemingly mundane situation which offers the reader a flash of illumination about the characters or their situation.

Slush pile. A stack of unsolicited manuscripts in the editorial offices of a publisher.

Social Fiction. Fiction written with the purpose of bringing about positive changes in society.

Speculation (or Spec). An editor's agreement to look at an author's manuscript with no promise to purchase.

Speculative Fiction (SpecFic). The all-inclusive term for science fiction, fantasy and horror.

Splatterpunk. Type of horror fiction known for its very violent and graphic content.

Subsidiary. An incorporated branch of a company or conglomerate (e.g. Alfred Knopf, Inc., a subsidiary of Random House, Inc.).

Subsidiary rights. All rights other than book publishing rights included in a book contract, such as paperback, book club and movie rights.

Subsidy publisher. A book publisher who charges the author for the cost of typesetting, printing and promoting a book. Also Vanity publisher.

Subterficial fiction. Innovative, challenging, nonconventional fiction in which what seems to be happening is the result of things not so easily perceived.

Suspense. A genre of fiction where the plot's primary function is to build a feeling of anticipation and fear in the reader over its possible outcome.

Synopsis. A brief summary of a story, novel or play. As part of a book proposal, it is a comprehensive summary condensed in a page or page and a half.

Tabloid. Publication printed on paper about half the size of a regular newspaper page (e.g. *The National Enquirer*).

Tearsheet. Page from a magazine containing a published story.

Theme. The dominant or central idea in a literary work; its message, moral or main thread.

Trade paperback. A softbound volume, usually around 5×8, published and designed for the general public, available mainly in bookstores.

Unsolicited manuscript. A story or novel manuscript that an editor did not specifically ask to see.

Vanity publisher. See Subsidy publisher.

Viewpoint. The position or attitude of the first- or third-person narrator or multiple narrators, which determines how a story's action is seen and evaluated.

Western. Genre with a setting in the West, usually between 1860-1890, with a formula plot about cowboys or other aspects of frontier life.

Whodunit. Genre dealing with murder, suspense and the detection of criminals.

Work-for-hire. Work that another party commissions you to do, generally for a flat fee. The creator does not own the copyright and therefore cannot sell any rights.

Young adult. The general classification of books written for readers 12-18.

Category Index

Our Category Index makes it easy for you to identify publishers in this edition of *Novel & Short Story Writer's Market* who are looking for a specific type of fiction. [Publishers new to this edition are identified with a double dagger (‡).] The index is divided into our six markets sections: Literary Magazines, Small Circulation Magazines, Zines, Commercial Periodicals, Small Press and Commercial Book Publishers. Under each market section is an alphabetical list of fiction types, followed by the names of publishers who accept each type of fiction. Publishers who are in this edition but not listed under a fiction category either accept all types of fiction or have not indicated specific subject preferences. Also not appearing here are listings that need very specific types of fiction, e.g., "fiction about fly fishing only."; To use this index to find a book publisher for your mystery novel, for instance, go to the Commercial Book Publishers section and look under the Mystery category. There you will find a list of commercial book publishers looking for mysteries. Then go to our Markets Index, beginning on page 621, to find page numbers for particular publishers. Finally, read the listings *carefully* to determine the mystery publishers best suited to your work.

LITERARY

Adventure: ‡Acorn, The; Aguilar Expression, The; Allegheny Review; Amelia; Arnazella; artisan; Asian Pacific American Journal; ‡Barbaric Yawp; Belletrist Review, The; Black Jack; Blackwater Review; Blue Mesa Review; Blueline; BookLovers; Bouillabaisse; Brownstone Review, The; Capers Aweigh Magazine; Chrysalis Reader; Climbing Art, The; Compenions; Dan River Anthology; Djinni; Dogwood Tales Magazine; Downstate Story; Echoes; 8; Elf: Eclectic Literary Forum; Eureka Literary Magazine; Every So Often . . . ; Expressions; Fugue; Grasslands Review; Green Mountains Review; Green's Magazine; i.e. magazine; Iconoclast, The; ‡Implosion; ‡In the Spirit of the Buffalo; Jeopardy; Just Write; Lactuca; Lines In The Sand; Lynx Eye; MacGuffin, The; Merlyn's Pen; Musing Place, The; nerve; ‡New Writing; Nimrod; Nite-Writer's International Literary Arts Journal; Northwoods Journal; ‡Oatmeal & Poetry; ‡Out of the Cradle; Palo Alto Review; Pink Chameleon, The; Place to Enter, A; ‡Poetry in Motion Magazine; Portland Review; Potpourri; Prairie Dog; Rag Mag; ‡Reader's Break; RE:AL; ‡Se La Vie Writer's Journal; Short Stuff Magazine for Grown-ups; ‡Spring Fantasy; SPSM&H; Street Beat Quarterly; Surprise Me; "Teak" Roundup; Thema; Timber Creek Review; ‡Torre De Papel; Tucumcari Literary Review; Vignette; Vincent Brothers Review, The; Voices West; West Wind Review; Words of Wisdom; Writes of Passage

Childrens/Juvenile: Echoes; Lamp-Post, The; ‡Oatmeal & Poetry; Pink Chameleon, The; ‡Spring Fantasy; Stone Soup; Street Beat Quarterly; Surprise Me; "Teak" Roundup; Writes of Passage

Comic/Graphic Novels: Corona; Fat Tuesday; Rag Mag; Yellow Silk

Condensed Novel: Antietam Review; Aphrodite Gone Berserk; Ararat Quarterly; artisan; Asian Pacific American Journal; Atom Mind; ‡Boston Literary Review (BLuR); Bouillabaisse; Burnt Aluminum; Cayo; Chaminade Literary Review; Climbing Art, The; Confluence; ‡Cripes Cripes!; Djinni; Echoes; Every So Often. . .; Excursus; ‡Flying Horse; G.W. Review, The; Georgetown Review; Glass Cherry, The; Hopewell Review, The; Just Write; ‡Kansas Quarterly/Arkansas Review; Kennesaw Review; Kenyon Review, The; Kestrel; Lactuca; Libido; ‡Lullwater Review; Lynx Eye; Magic Realism; Matriarch's Way; Journal of Female Supremacy; Missouri Review, The; ‡modern words; Musing Place, The; Oracle Story; Pangolin Papers; ‡Paperplates; Pink Chameleon, The; Place to Enter, A; ‡Porcupine Literary Arts Magazine; Puck; ‡Satire;

‡Shockwaves; Spout; ‡Summer's Reading, A; "Teak" Roundup; ‡Thin Air; Vincent Brothers Review, The; ‡Vox A; Wordplay

Erotica: Adrift; Alpha Beat Press; Amelia; Aphrodite Gone Berserk; artisan; Asian Pacific American Journal; Atom Mind; Belletrist Review, The; Bouillabaisse; Brownstone Review, The; Djinni; 8; Every So Often. . .; Fat Tuesday; Fish Drum Magazine; Gathering of the Tribes, A; Happy; Jeopardy; Lactuca; Libido; Literary Rocket; Lynx Eye; Matriarch's Way; Journal of Female Supremacy; ‡Mississippi Mud; ‡modern words; nerve; Nite-Writer's International Literary Arts Journal; Northwoods Journal; ‡Nyx Obscura Magazine; Old Crow Review; ‡Paper Radio; Paramour Magazine; ‡Pavlov Neruda/Manuslave Press; ‡Poetic Space; Portland Review; Prairie Dog; Puck; Rag Mag; Raw Fiction; ‡the review; Salt Lick Press; Sanskrit; Screaming Toad Press; Shattered Wig Review; ‡Shockwaves; Slipstream; Spitting Image, The; Spout; SPSM&H; ‡Stiletto III; Sub-Terrain; ‡Torre De Papel; Vignette; Voices West; West Wind Review; Yellow Silk; Zero Hour

Ethnic/Multicultural: ACM (Another Chicago Magazine); Acorn Whistle; Adrift; African American Review; Aguilar Expression, The; Allegheny Review; Amelia; ‡American Writing; Americas Review, The; Antietam Review; Arnazella; artisan; Asian Pacific American Journal; Atom Mind; Aura Literary/Arts Review; Azorean Express, The; Beneath the Surface; Bilingual Review; Black Hammock Review, The; Black Jack; Black Lace; ‡Black Writer Magazine; Blue Mesa Review; BookLovers; Briar Cliff Review, The; Brownstone Review, The; Brújula/Compass; Callaloo; Canadian Author; Capers Aweigh Magazine; ‡Caribbean Writer, The; Chaminade Literary Review; Chiricú; Cicada; Climbing Art, The; Collages and Bricolages; ‡Colorado Review; Compenions; Concho River Review; Confluence; Crazyquilt; Cream City Review, The; Crucible; Dan River Anthology; Djinni; Downstate Story; Echoes; Elf: Eclectic Literary Forum; Epoch Magazine; Eureka Literary Magazine; Every So Often. . .; Excursus; Expressions; Fault Lines; Feminist Studies; Fish Drum Magazine; Fish Stories; ‡Flying Horse; Flying Island, The; Footwork; ‡Fourteen Hills; Fugue; Gathering of the Tribes, A; Georgetown Review; Grasslands Review; Green Hills Literary Lantern, The; Gulf Coast; Happy; Hayden's Ferry Review; Heartlands Today, The; Hill and Holler; Home Planet News; Iconoclast, The; International Quarterly; Iowa Review, The; Japanophile; Jeopardy; Just Write; Kennesaw Review; Kenyon Review, The; Kerem; ‡Long Story, The; ‡Lullwater Review; Lynx Eye; MacGuffin, The; Mangrove; manna; Many Mountains Moving; Mark; Maryland Review; Matriarch's Way; Journal of Female Supremacy; Midland Review; ‡Mississippi Mud; Missouri Review, The; Mobius; ‡modern words; Musing Place, The; nerve; New Laurel Review; New Letters Magazine; Nimrod; North Dakota Quarterly; Northeast Arts Magazine; ‡Oatmeal & Poetry; Obsidian II: Black Literature in Review; Onionhead; Oracle Story; ‡Out of the Cradle; Oxford Magazine; Pacific Coast Journal; Painted Bride Quarterly; Palo Alto Review; ‡Paperplates; ‡Passages North; ‡Pavlov Neruda/Manuslave Press; Phoebe (New York); Pikeville Review; Pink Chameleon, The; Place to Enter, A; ‡Pleiades; Plowman, The; ‡Poetic Space; Poetry Forum Short Stories; Pointed Circle, The; ‡Porcupine Literary Arts Magazine; Portland Review; Potpourri; Prairie Dog; Puck; Puerto Del Sol; Rag Mag; ‡the review; River Styx; RiverSedge; Riverwind; ‡Rock Springs Review; Rockford Review, The; Salt Lick Press; Sanskrit; ‡Se La Vie Writer's Journal; Shattered Wig Review; ‡Shockwaves; Side Show; Sing Heavenly Muse!; Skylark; Slipstream; So To Speak; South Dakota Review; Southern California Anthology; ‡Spare Room, A; ‡spelunker flophouse; Spindrift; Spout; SPSM&H; ‡Stiletto III; Street Beat Quarterly; Struggle; Suffusion Magazine; Sulphur River Literary Review; ‡Tameme; Tampa Review; "Teak" Roundup; Textshop; ‡Thin Air; This Magazine; Timber Creek Review; ‡Torre De Papel; Tucumcari Literary Review; Urbanus Magazine; Valley Grapevine; Vignette; Vincent Brothers Review, The; Voices West; ‡Vox A; West Coast Line; West Wind Review; Westview; ‡Willow Review; Wordplay; Words of Wisdom; Writers' Forum; Writes of Passage; Writing For Our Lives; Xavier Review; Xib; Yellow Silk; Zero Hour; Zuzu's Petals Quarterly

Experimental: ACM (Another Chicago Magazine); Adrift; African American Review; Aguilar Expression, The; Alabama Literary Review; Alaska Quarterly Review; Allegheny Review; Alpha Beat Press; Amelia; ‡American Writing; Antietam Review; Antioch Review; Aphrodite Gone Berserk; Arnazella; Artful Dodge; artisan; Asian Pacific American Journal;

Athena Incognito Magazine; Atom Mind; Azorean Express, The; B&A: New Fiction; ‡Barbaric Yawp; Beneath the Surface; Berkeley Fiction Review; Black Hammock Review, The; ‡Black Ice; Black River Review; Black Warrior Review; Blackwater Review; Blue Moon Quarterly, The; Bogg; ‡Bone & Flesh; ‡Boston Literary Review (BLuR); Boulevard; Brownstone Review, The; Calliope; Canadian Author; ‡Capilano Review, The; Cayo; Chaminade Literary Review; Chariton Review, The; Chicago Review; Chiron Review; Chrysalis Reader; Climbing Art, The; Clockwatch Review; Collages and Bricolages; ‡Colorado Review; Compenions; Conduit; Context South; Corona; Cream City Review, The; ‡Cripes Cripes!; Crucible; Dan River Anthology; Denver Quarterly; Djinni; Dodobobo; Downstate Story; ‡Drop Forge; Echoes; 8; 1812; Eureka Literary Magazine; Every So Often. . .; Excursus; Explorations '97; Expressions; Fat Tuesday; Fault Lines; Fiction; Fish Drum Magazine; Fish Stories; Flipside; Florida Review, The; ‡Flying Horse; Flying Island, The; Fugue; G.W. Review, The; Gathering of the Tribes, A; Georgetown Review; Georgia Review, The; Gettysburg Review, The; Grain; Grand Street; Grasslands Review; Green Hills Literary Lantern, The; Green Mountains Review; Greensboro Review; Gulf Coast; Happy; Hayden's Ferry Review; Heaven Bone; Home Planet News; Hopewell Review, The; Hunted News, The; i.e. magazine; ‡Implosion; ‡Interim; International Quarterly; Iris (VA); Jeopardy; Just Write; Kennesaw Review; Kenyon Review, The; Kinesis; ‡Licking River Review, The; Lines In The Sand; Literal Latté; Literary Rocket; Lost and Found Times; Louisville Review, The; ‡Lullwater Review; Lynx Eye; MacGuffin, The; ‡Madison Review, The; Magic Realism; Many Mountains Moving; Matriarch's Way; Journal of Female Supremacy; Maverick Press, The; Mid-American Review; Midland Review; Mind in Motion; Minnesota Review, The; ‡Mississippi Mud; Mississippi Review; Mobius; ‡modern words; Musing Place, The; nerve; New Letters Magazine; New Press Literary Quarterly, The; ‡New Writing; Nimrod; North Dakota Quarterly; Northwest Review; Northwoods Journal; Ohio Review, The; Old Crow Review; Onionhead; Other Voices; Oxford Magazine; Pacific Coast Journal; Painted Bride Quarterly; Palo Alto Review; Pangolin Papers; ‡Paper Radio; Partisan Review; ‡Pavlov Neruda/Manuslave Press; Phoebe (New York); Pikeville Review; Pink Chameleon, The; ‡Pleiades; ‡Poetic Space; Poetry Forum Short Stories; ‡Poetry in Motion Magazine; Portland Review; Potpourri; Prairie Dog; Prairie Fire; Puck; Puckerbrush Review; Puerto Del Sol; Quarterly West; Rag Mag; Rambunctious Review; Raw Fiction; RE:AL; ‡Reed Magazine; ‡the review; River Styx; RiverSedge; Rockford Review, The; Salt Lick Press; Sanskrit; Screaming Toad Press; Shattered Wig Review; ‡Shockwaves; Sidewalks; Sierra Nevada College Review; Silver Web, The; Skylark; Slipstream; So To Speak; South Dakota Review; Southern California Anthology; ‡Spare Room, A; ‡spelunker flophouse; Spindrift; Spitting Image, The; Spout; SPSM&H; ‡Stiletto III; Story; Street Beat Quarterly; Struggle; Sub-Terrain; Suffusion Magazine; Sulphur River Literary Review; Sycamore Review; Tampa Review; Textshop; Texture; Thema; ‡Thin Air; This Magazine; ‡Torre De Papel; ‡Turnstile; Urbanite, The; Urbanus Magazine; Verve; Vignette; Vincent Brothers Review, The; Voices West; West Coast Line; West Wind Review; Whetstone (Canada); ‡Willow Review; Wisconsin Review; Writes of Passage; Writing For Our Lives; Xavier Review; Xib; Yellow Silk; Zero Hour; Zyzzyva

Fantasy: ‡Adventures of Sword & Sorcery; Allegheny Review; Amelia; Arnazella; artisan; ‡Barbaric Yawp; Beneath the Surface; Black Hammock Review, The; BookLovers; Capers Aweigh Magazine; Climbing Art, The; Compenions; Corona; Crazyquilt; Dan River Anthology; Djinni; Echoes; 8; Elf: Eclectic Literary Forum; Eureka Literary Magazine; Every So Often. . .; Expressions; Fish Drum Magazine; Flying Island, The; Fugue; Grasslands Review; Green's Magazine; Happy; Hayden's Ferry Review; Heaven Bone; i.e. magazine; ‡Implosion; ‡In the Spirit of the Buffalo; Just Write; Lamp-Post, The; Lines In The Sand; Literal Latté; Lynx Eye; MacGuffin, The; Magic Realism; Matriarch's Way; Journal of Female Supremacy; Merlyn's Pen; Minas Tirith Evening-Star; Mind in Motion; Mississippi Review; Mobius; Musing Place, The; Mythic Circle, The; Nassau Review; Northwoods Journal; ‡Nyx Obscura Magazine; ‡Oatmeal & Poetry; ‡Palace Corbie; Palo Alto Review; ‡Paper Radio; Pink Chameleon, The; Poetry Forum Short Stories; ‡Poetry in Motion Magazine; Poet's Fantasy; Portland Review; Potpourri; Prairie Dog; Primavera; Puck; Quanta; Rag Mag; ‡Reader's Break; Rockford Review, The; Screaming Toad Press; Sensations Magazine; ‡Shockwaves; Skylark; Southern Humanities Review; ‡Spring Fantasy; SPSM&H; ‡Stiletto III; Street Beat Quarterly; Surprise Me; Tampa Review; This Magazine;

Tomorrow; ‡Torre De Papel; Urbanite, The; Verve; West Wind Review; Writes of Passage; Xib; Yellow Silk

Feminist: ACM (Another Chicago Magazine); Acorn Whistle; Adrift; African American Review; Allegheny Review; Amelia; ‡American Writing; Americas Review, The; Antietam Review; Aphrodite Gone Berserk; Arnazella; artisan; Asian Pacific American Journal; Aura Literary/Arts Review; Beneath the Surface; Blackwater Review; Blue Mesa Review; Blue Moon Quarterly, The; Briar Cliff Review, The; Brownstone Review, The; Brújula/Compass; Callaloo; Calyx; Canadian Author; Capers Aweigh Magazine; Collages and Bricolages; Compenions; Confluence; Context South; Corona; Crucible; Djinni; Dodobobo; Echoes; Elf: Eclectic Literary Forum; Emrys Journal; Eureka Literary Magazine; Event; Every So Often. . .; Excursus; Expressions; Farmer's Market, The; Feminist Studies; Fish Stories; Flying Island, The; ‡Frontiers; Gathering of the Tribes, A; Georgetown Review; Green Hills Literary Lantern, The; Happy; Hayden's Ferry Review; Home Planet News; Iowa Woman; Iris (VA); Jeopardy; Just Write; Kennesaw Review; Kenyon Review, The; Kerem; Kestrel; ‡Long Story, The; ‡Lullwater Review; Lynx Eye; manna; Many Mountains Moving; Matriarch's Way; Journal of Female Supremacy; Midland Review; Minnesota Review, The; Mobius; ‡modern words; Musing Place, The; nerve; North Dakota Quarterly; Northwest Review; Obsidian II: Black Literature in Review; Onionhead; ‡Out of the Cradle; Oxford Magazine; Pacific Coast Journal; Painted Bride Quarterly; Palo Alto Review; ‡Paperplates; ‡Pavlov Neruda/Manuslave Press; Phoebe (New York); Pikeville Review; ‡Pleiades; ‡Poetic Space; Poetry Forum Short Stories; Portland Review; Potato Eyes; Primavera; Puck; Rag Mag; Rambunctious Review; RE:AL; ‡the review; River Styx; RiverSedge; Riverwind; Salt Lick Press; Sanskrit; Shattered Wig Review; ‡Shockwaves; Side Show; Sing Heavenly Muse!; Skylark; So To Speak; Southern California Anthology; Southern Humanities Review; ‡spelunker flophouse; Spout; ‡Spring Fantasy; SPSM&H; ‡Stiletto III; Street Beat Quarterly; Struggle; Suffusion Magazine; Sulphur River Literary Review; Texture; ‡13th Moon; This Magazine; Timber Creek Review; ‡Torre De Papel; Urbanus Magazine; Vignette; Vincent Brothers Review, The; ‡Vox A; West Coast Line; West Wind Review; ‡Willow Review; Wordplay; Words of Wisdom; Writes of Passage; Writing For Our Lives; Xib; Yellow Silk; Zero Hour; Zuzu's Petals Quarterly

Gay: ACM (Another Chicago Magazine); Adrift; African American Review; Allegheny Review; Amelia; ‡American Writing; Aphrodite Gone Berserk; Arnazella; Asian Pacific American Journal; Beneath the Surface; Blue Mesa Review; Blue Moon Quarterly, The; Brave New Tick, (the); Brownstone Review, The; Brújula/Compass; Crazyquilt; Crucible; Djinni; Dodobobo; Echoes; Evergreen Chronicles, The; Every So Often. . .; Expressions; Feminist Studies; Fish Drum Magazine; Fish Stories; Flying Island, The; ‡Fourteen Hills; Gathering Of The Tribes, A; Georgetown Review; Glass Cherry, The; Happy; Hayden's Ferry Review; Home Planet News; Jeopardy; Kennesaw Review; Kenyon Review, The; Libido; ‡Lullwater Review; Lynx Eye; Many Mountains Moving; Minnesota Review, The; Mobius; ‡modern words; Musing Place, The; nerve; 96 Inc.; Northeast Arts Magazine; Onionhead; ‡Out of the Cradle; Oxford Magazine; Painted Bride Quarterly; ‡Paperplates; ‡Pavlov Neruda/Manuslave Press; Phoebe (New York); ‡Pleiades; ‡Poetic Space; Portland Review; Primavera; Puck; Puckerbrush Review; ‡the review; River Styx; Salt Lick Press; Sanskrit; Sensations Magazine; Shattered Wig Review; ‡Shockwaves; Side Show; Spout; SPSM&H; ‡Stiletto III; This Magazine; ‡Torre De Papel; Urbanus Magazine; Vignette; West Coast Line; West Wind Review; White Review, The James; Writes of Passage; Xib; Yellow Silk; Zero Hour; Zuzu's Petals Quarterly

Historical: Acorn Whistle; Allegheny Review; Amelia; Appalachian Heritage; Ararat Quarterly; Arnazella; Asian Pacific American Journal; ‡Barbaric Yawp; Beneath the Surface; ‡Black Writer Magazine; Blackwater Review; Blue Mesa Review; BookLovers; Briar Cliff Review, The; Brownstone Review, The; Callaloo; Canadian Author; Capers Aweigh Magazine; ‡Caribbean Writer, The; Chrysalis Reader; Climbing Art, The; Compenions; Concho River Review; Crazyquilt; Dan River Anthology; Djinni; Dodobobo; Downstate Story; Echoes; Elf: Eclectic Literary Forum; Eureka Literary Magazine; Every So Often. . .; Expressions; Fugue; Gathering of the Tribes, A; Gettysburg Review, The; Glass Cherry, The; Hayden's Ferry Review; Home Planet News; Hunted News, The; i.e. magazine; ‡In the Spirit of the Buffalo; Iowa Woman; Jeopardy;

Just Write; Kenyon Review, The; Lamplight, The; Lynx Eye; MacGuffin, The; Many Mountains Moving; Merlyn's Pen; Midland Review; Mind Matters Review; Minnesota Review, The; Mobius; Musing Place, The; Nassau Review; nerve; 96 Inc.; Nite-Writer's International Literary Arts Journal; North Dakota Quarterly; Northeast Arts Magazine; ‡Oatmeal & Poetry; Oracle Story; ‡Out of the Cradle; Pacific Coast Journal; Palo Alto Review; Pink Chameleon, The; Poetry Forum Short Stories; Portland Review; Potpourri; Prairie Dog; Puck; RE:AL; ‡the review; RiverSedge; Riverwind; ‡Rock Springs Review; Sensations Magazine; ‡Shockwaves; Short Stuff Magazine for Grown-ups; Southern California Anthology; Spindrift; ‡Spring Fantasy; SPSM&H; ‡Stiletto III; Street Beat Quarterly; Struggle; Tampa Review; "Teak" Roundup; Timber Creek Review; ‡Torre De Papel; Tucumcari Literary Review; Vignette; Vincent Brothers Review, The; West Wind Review; ‡Willow Review; Wordplay; Words of Wisdom; Writes of Passage; Xavier Review; Xib

Horror: Aguilar Expression, The; Allegheny Review; artisan; Aura Literary/Arts Review; ‡Barbaric Yawp; Belletrist Review, The; Beneath The Surface; Blackwater Review; Briar Cliff Review, The; Brownstone Review, The; Compenions; Dan River Anthology; Djinni; Downstate Story; Echoes; 8; Every So Often. . .; Expressions; Fugue; Gathering of the Tribes, A; Glass Cherry, The; Grasslands Review; Happy; ‡Implosion; ‡In the Spirit of the Buffalo; Just Write; Lines In The Sand; Lynx Eye; Matriarch's Way; Journal of Female Supremacy; Merlyn's Pen; Mobius; Musing Place, The; ‡New Writing; Oracle Story; ‡Palace Corbie; ‡Pavlov Neruda/Manuslave Press; Phantasm (California); Puck; ‡the review; Riverwind; Screaming Toad Press; Sensations Magazine; ‡Shockwaves; Silver Web, The; ‡Spring Fantasy; SPSM&H; ‡Stiletto III; Theater of Blood, A; Tomorrow; ‡Torre De Papel; Urbanite, The; Urbanus Magazine; West Wind Review; ‡Wicked Mystic; Wordplay; Writes of Passage; Xib

Humor/Satire: Acorn Whistle; Alabama Literary Review; Allegheny Review; Amelia; Ararat Quarterly; Arnazella; artisan; Asian Pacific American Journal; Atom Mind; Azorean Express, The; B&A: New Fiction; ‡Barbaric Yawp; Belletrist Review, The; Beneath the Surface; Black Hammock Review, The; Black Jack; Black River Review; Blackwater Review; Blue Mesa Review; Blueline; BookLovers; Briar Cliff Review, The; Brownstone Review, The; Brújula/Compass; By the Wayside; Callaloo; Canadian Author; Capers Aweigh Magazine; ‡Caribbean Writer, The; Chaminade Literary Review; Chiron Review; Clockwatch Review; Collages and Bricolages; Compenions; Concho River Review; Confluence; Corona; ‡Crab Creek Review; Crazyquilt; Cream City Review, The; ‡Cripes Cripes!; Dan River Anthology; Djinni; Dodobobo; Downstate Story; Echoes; 8; 1812; Elf: Eclectic Literary Forum; Eureka Literary Magazine; Event; Every So Often. . .; Excursus; Explorations '97; Expressions; Farmer's Market, The; Fat Tuesday; Fault Lines; Fiction; Flying Island, The; ‡Fourteen Hills; Fugue; G.W. Review, The; Gathering of the Tribes, A; Georgetown Review; Gettysburg Review, The; Grasslands Review; Green Hills Literary Lantern, The; Green Mountains Review; Green's Magazine; Happy; Hayden's Ferry Review; Heartlands Today, The; High Plains Literary Review; Hill and Holler; Hopewell Review, The; i.e. magazine; Iconoclast, The; ‡Idiot, The; ‡Image; ‡In the Spirit of the Buffalo; International Quarterly; Jeopardy; Just Write; Kennesaw Review; Kenyon Review, The; Kerem; Kinesis; Lamplight, The; Light Quarterly; Lines In The Sand; Literal Latté; Literary Rocket; ‡Lullwater Review; Lynx Eye; MacGuffin, The; Many Mountains Moving; Mark; Maryland Review; Matriarch's Way; Journal of Female Supremacy; Merlyn's Pen; Mind in Motion; ‡Mississippi Mud; Mississippi Review; Missouri Review, The; Mobius; Musing Place, The; Nebraska Review, The; nerve; New Letters Magazine; New Press Literary Quarterly, The; new renaissance, the; ‡New Writing; 96 Inc.; Nite-Writer's International Literary Arts Journal; North Dakota Quarterly; ‡Oatmeal & Poetry; Onionhead; Oracle Story; Other Voices; Oxford Magazine; Pacific Coast Journal; Palo Alto Review; Pangolin Papers; ‡Pavlov Neruda/Manuslave Press; Pearl; Pegasus Review, The; Phoebe (New York); Pikeville Review; Pink Chameleon, The; Place to Enter, A; ‡Pleiades; Portland Review; Potato Eyes; Potpourri; Prairie Dog; Primavera; Puck; Rambunctious Review; ‡Reed Magazine; River Styx; Riverwind; ‡Rock Springs Review; Rockford Review, The; Sanskrit; ‡Satire; Screaming Toad Press; ‡Se La Vie Writer's Journal; Sensations Magazine; Shattered Wig Review; ‡Shockwaves; Short Stuff Magazine for Grown-ups; Side Show; Sidewalks; Skylark; Slipstream; Southern California Anthology; Southern Humanities Review; ‡spelunker flophouse; Spout; ‡Spring Fantasy; SPSM&H; Story; Street Beat Quarterly; Struggle; Sub-Terrain; Suffusion Magazine; Sulphur River Literary Review; Sycamore Review; Tampa Review; "Teak" Roundup; Thema; Timber Creek Review; ‡Torre De Papel; Touchstone Literary Journal; Tucumcari Literary Review; ‡Turnstile; Urbanite, The; Urbanus Magazine; Verve; Vignette; Vincent Brothers Review, The; Voices West; ‡Vox A; West Wind Review; ‡Whetstone (Illinois); Words of Wisdom; Writes of Passage; Writing For Our Lives; Xib; Xtreme; Yellow Silk; Zero Hour; Zuzu's Petals Quarterly

Lesbian: ACM (Another Chicago Magazine); Adrift; African American Review; Allegheny Review; Amelia; ‡American Writing; Aphrodite Gone Berserk; Arnazella; Asian Pacific American Journal; Beneath the Surface; Black Lace; Blue Mesa Review; Blue Moon Quarterly, The; Brownstone Review, The; Brújula/Compass; Crucible; Djinni; Dodobobo; Echoes; Evergreen Chronicles, The; Every So Often. . . ; Expressions; Feminist Studies; Fish Drum Magazine; Fish Stories; Flying Island, The; ‡Fourteen Hills; ‡Frontiers; Gathering of the Tribes, A; Georgetown Review; Glass Cherry, The; Happy; Home Planet News; Iris (VA); Kenyon Review, The; Libido; ‡Lullwater Review; Lynx Eye; Many Mountains Moving; Minnesota Review, The; Mobius; ‡modern words; Musing Place, The; nerve; 96 Inc.; Onionhead; ‡Out of the Cradle; Oxford Magazine; Painted Bride Quarterly; ‡Paperplates; ‡Pavlov Neruda/Manuslave Press; Phoebe (New York); ‡Pleiades; Portland Review; Primavera; Puck; ‡the review; River Styx; Salt Lick Press; Sanskrit; Sensations Magazine; Shattered Wig Review; ‡Shockwaves; Side Show; So To Speak; Spout; SPSM&H; This Magazine; ‡Torre De Papel; Urbanus Magazine; Vignette; West Wind Review; Writes of Passage; Writing For Our Lives; Xib; Yellow Silk; Zuzu's Petals Quarterly

Literary: ACM (Another Chicago Magazine); ‡Acorn, The; Acorn Whistle; Adrift; Aethlon; African American Review; Alabama Literary Review; Alaska Quarterly Review; Allegheny Review; Alpha Beat Press; Amelia; American Literary Review; American Short Fiction; ‡American Writing; Americas Review, The; ‡Amethyst Review, The; Antietam Review; Antigonish Review, The; Antioch Review; Aphrodite Gone Berserk; Appalachian Heritage; Ararat Quarterly; ARK/ Angel Review; Arnazella; Artful Dodge; artisan; ‡Ascent; Asian Pacific American Journal; Atom Mind; Aura Literary/Arts Review; Azorean Express, The; B&A: New Fiction; ‡Barbaric Yawp; Belletrist Review, The; Bellingham Review, The; Bellowing Ark; Beloit Fiction Journal; Beneath the Surface; Berkeley Fiction Review; Black Hammock Review, The; ‡Black Ice; Black Jack; Black River Review; Black Warrior Review; ‡Black Writer Magazine; Blackwater Review; Blue Mesa Review; Blue Moon Quarterly, The; Blueline; ‡Bone & Flesh; BookLovers; ‡Boston Literary Review (BLuR); Bottomfish Magazine; Bouillabaisse; Boulevard; Briar Cliff Review, The; Brownstone Review, The; Brújula/Compass; Burnt Aluminum; ‡Button; Byline; Callaloo; Calliope; Canadian Author; Capers Aweigh Magazine; ‡Capilano Review, The; ‡Caribbean Writer, The; Carolina Quarterly; Cayo; Chaminade Literary Review; Chariton Review, The; Chattahoochee Review, The; Chelsea; Chicago Review; Chiron Review; Chrysalis Reader; Cimarron Review; Climbing Art, The; Clockwatch Review; Collages and Bricolages; ‡Colorado Review; Columbia: A Journal of Literature & Art; Compenions; Concho River Review; Conduit; Confluence; Confrontation; Context South; Corona; ‡Crab Creek Review; Crazyquilt; Cream City Review, The; ‡Cripes Cripes!; Crucible; Dalhousie Review, The; Dan River Anthology; Denver Quarterly; Djinni; Dodobobo; Downstate Story; Eagle's Flight; Echoes; 8; 1812; Elf: Eclectic Literary Forum; Emrys Journal; Epoch Magazine; Eureka Literary Magazine; Event; Every So Often. . .; Excursus; Explorations '97; Explorer Magazine; Expressions; Farmer's Market, The; Fat Tuesday; Fault Lines; Feminist Studies; Fiction; Fiction International; Fish Drum Magazine; Fish Stories; Flipside; Florida Review, The; ‡Flying Horse; Flying Island, The; Folio: A Literary Journal; Footwork; ‡Fourteen Hills; Fugue; G.W. Review, The; Gathering of the Tribes, A; Georgetown Review; Georgia Review, The; Gettysburg Review, The; Glass Cherry, The; Glimmer Train Stories; Grain; Grand Street; Grasslands Review; Green Hills Literary Lantern, The; Green Mountains Review; Green's Magazine; Greensboro Review; Gulf Coast; Gulf Stream Magazine; Happy; Hayden's Ferry Review; Heartlands Today, The; Heaven Bone; High Plains Literary Review; Hill and Holler; Home Planet News; Hopewell Review, The; Hunted News, The; i.e. magazine; Iconoclast, The; ‡Image; ‡In the Spirit of the Buffalo; Indiana Review;

‡Interim; International Quarterly; Iowa Review, The; Iowa Woman; Iris (VA); Janus, A Journal of Literature; Jeopardy; Journal, The (Ohio); Just Write; Kaleidoscope; Kalliope; Kelsey Review; Kennesaw Review; Kenyon Review, The; Kerem; Kestrel; Kinesis; Kiosk; Lactuca; Lamplight, The; Lamp-Post, The; Laurel Review, The; ‡Licking River Review, The; Light Quarterly; Limestone: A Literary Journal; Lines In The Sand; Literal Latté; Literary Review, The; Literary Rocket; ‡Long Story, The; Loonfeather; Lost and Found Times; Louisiana Literature; Louisville Review, The; ‡Lullwater Review; Lynx Eye; MacGuffin, The; ‡Madison Review, The; Magic Realism; Mangrove; Manoa; Many Mountains Moving; Mark; Maryland Review; Matriarch's Way; Journal of Female Supremacy; Maverick Press, The; Merlyn's Pen; Michigan Quarterly Review; Mid-American Review; Midland Review; Mind in Motion; Mind Matters Review; Minnesota Review, The; ‡Mississippi Mud; Mississippi Review; Missouri Review, The; Mobius; ‡modern words; ‡Moody Street Review, The; Musing Place, The; Nassau Review; Nebo; Nebraska Review, The; nerve; New England Review; New Laurel Review; New Letters Magazine; New Orleans Review; new renaissance, the; ‡New Writing; 96 Inc.; Nite-Writer's International Literary Arts Journal; North American Review, The; North Dakota Quarterly; Northeast Arts Magazine; Northeast Corridor; Northwest Review; Northwoods Journal; Oasis; ‡Oatmeal & Poetry; Ohio Review, The; Old Crow Review; Old Red Kimono, The; Onionhead; Oracle Story; Other Voices; ‡Out of the Cradle; Outerbridge; Oxford Magazine; Pacific Coast Journal; Pacific Review; Painted Bride Quarterly; Palo Alto Review; Pangolin Papers; ‡Paper Radio; ‡Paperplates; Paris Review, The; Parting Gifts; Partisan Review; ‡Passages North; ‡Pavlov Neruda/Manuslave Press; Pearl; Pegasus Review, The; Pennsylvania English; Phoebe (New York); Pig Iron; Pikeville Review; Pink Chameleon, The; Place to Enter, A; ‡Pleiades; Ploughshares; ‡Poetic Space; Poetry Forum Short Stories; Poetry WLU; Pointed Circle, The; Pointed Circle, The; ‡Porcupine Literary Arts Magazine; Portland Review; Potato Eyes; Potomac Review; Potpourri; Prairie Dog; Prairie Fire; Prairie Journal of Canadian Literature, The; ‡Press; Primavera; Prism International; Puck; Puckerbrush Review; Puerto Del Sol; Quarterly, The; Quarterly West; Rag Mag; Rambunctious Review; Raw Fiction; ‡Reader's Break; Red Cedar Review; ‡Reed Magazine; Review: Latin American Literature and Arts; ‡the review; River Styx; RiverSedge; Riverwind; ‡Rock Springs Review; Rockford Review, The; Salt Lick Press; Sanskrit; Santa Barbara Review; ‡Satire; ‡Se La Vie Writer's Journal; Sensations Magazine; Shattered Wig Review; ‡Shenandoah; ‡Shockwaves; Short Stories Bimonthly; Side Show; Sidewalks; Sierra Nevada College Review; Silverfish Review; Sing Heavenly Muse!; Skylark; Slipstream; So To Speak; Soft Door, The; South Carolina Review; South Dakota Review; Southern California Anthology; Southern Review, The; Southwest Review; ‡Spare Room, A; ‡spelunker flophouse; Spitting Image, The; Spout; ‡Spring Fantasy; SPSM&H; ‡Stiletto III; Story; Street Beat Quarterly; Stroker Magazine; Struggle; Sub-Terrain; Suffusion Magazine; Sulphur River Literary Review; ‡Summer's Reading, A; Surprise Me; Sycamore Review; ‡Tameme; Tampa Review; Taproot Literary Review; "Teak" Roundup; ‡Tennessee Quarterly; Textshop; Thema; ‡Thin Air; ‡Third Coast; This Magazine; ‡Threepenny Review, The; ‡Torre De Papel; Touchstone Literary Journal; Triquarterly; Tucumcari Literary Review; ‡Turnstile; Unmuzzled Ox; Urbanite, The; Urbanus Magazine; Valley Grapevine; Verb; Verve; Vignette; Vincent Brothers Review, The; Voices West; ‡Vox A; West Branch; West Coast Line; West Wind Review; Westview; Whetstone (Canada); ‡Whetstone (Illinois); ‡Willow Review; Wind Magazine; Windsor Review; Wisconsin Review; Worcester Review, The; Wordplay; Writers' Forum; Writes of Passage; Writing For Our Lives; Writing on the Wall, The; Xavier Review; Xib; Xtreme; ‡Yalobusha Review, The; Yellow Silk; Zuzu's Petals Quarterly; Zyzzyva

Mainstream/Contemporary: ACM (Another Chicago Magazine); ‡Acorn, The; Acorn Whistle; Adrift; African American Review; Aguilar Expression, The; Alabama Literary Review; Alaska Quarterly Review; Allegheny Review; Amelia; American Literary Review; ‡American Writing; Americas Review, The; Antietam Review; Antigonish Review, The; Antioch Review; Ararat Quarterly; Arnazella; artisan; Asian Pacific American Journal; Atom Mind; Aura Literary/Arts Review; Azorean Express, The; ‡Barbaric Yawp; Belletrist Review, The; Bellowing Ark; Beloit Fiction Journal; Berkeley Fiction Review; Black Hammock Review, The; Black Jack; Black River Review; Black Warrior Review; Blue Mesa Review; Blue Moon Quarterly, The; Blueline; BookLovers; ‡Boston Literary Review (BLuR); Boulevard; Briar Cliff Review, The;

Brownstone Review, The; Brújula/Compass; Burnt Aluminum; Callaloo; Calliope; Canadian Author; Capers Aweigh Magazine; ‡Capilano Review, The; ‡Caribbean Writer, The; Chariton Review, The; Chattahoochee Review, The; Chicago Review; Chiron Review; ‡Christianity and the Arts; Chrysalis Reader; Cimarron Review; Climbing Art, The; Clockwatch Review; Collages and Bricolages; ‡Colorado Review; Compenions; Concho River Review; Confluence; Confrontation; Corona; ‡Crab Creek Review; Crazyquilt; ‡Cripes Cripes!; Crucible; Dan River Anthology; Djinni; Dogwood Tales Magazine; Downstate Story; Eagle's Flight; Echoes; 1812; Elf: Eclectic Literary Forum; Emrys Journal; Epoch Magazine; Eureka Literary Magazine; Event; Every So Often. . .; Excursus; Explorer Magazine; Expressions; Farmer's Market, The; Feminist Studies; Fiction; Fish Drum Magazine; Flipside; Florida Review, The; ‡Flying Horse; Flying Island, The; Folio: A Literary Journal; Footwork; ‡Fourteen Hills; Fugue; G.W. Review, The; Gathering of the Tribes, A; Gettysburg Review, The; Glass Cherry, The; Grain; Grasslands Review; Green Hills Literary Lantern, The; Green Mountains Review; Green's Magazine; Greensboro Review; Gulf Coast; Gulf Stream Magazine; Hayden's Ferry Review; Heartlands Today, The; High Plains Literary Review; Hill and Holler; Home Planet News; Hopewell Review, The; Hunted News, The; i.e. magazine; Iconoclast, The; ‡Interim; International Quarterly; Iris (VA); Janus, A Journal of Literature; Jeopardy; Journal, The (Pennsylvania); Just Write; ‡Kansas Quarterly/Arkansas Review; Kennesaw Review; Kenyon Review, The; Kinesis; Lactuca; Laurel Review, The; ‡Licking River Review, The; Limestone: A Literary Journal; Lines In The Sand; ‡Long Story, The; Lost and Found Times; Louisiana Literature; Louisville Review, The; ‡Lullwater Review; Lynx Eye; MacGuffin, The; Mangrove; Manoa; Many Mountains Moving; Mark; Maryland Review; Maverick Press, The; Merlyn's Pen; ‡Mississippi Mud; Mississippi Review; Missouri Review, The; Mobius; ‡Moody Street Review, The; Musing Place, The; Nassau Review; Nebo; Nebraska Review, The; nerve; New Letters Magazine; New Orleans Review; New Press Literary Quarterly, The; ‡New Writing; Nite-Writer's International Literary Arts Journal; North Dakota Quarterly; Northwest Review; Northwoods Journal; ‡Oatmeal & Poetry; Ohio Review, The; Old Crow Review; Onionhead; Oracle Story; Other Voices; ‡Out of the Cradle; Painted Bride Quarterly; Palo Alto Review; ‡Paperplates; Partisan Review; ‡Passages North; Pearl; Pennsylvania English; Pikeville Review; Pink Chameleon, The; Place to Enter, A; ‡Pleiades; Poetry Forum Short Stories; ‡Poetry in Motion Magazine; Pointed Circle, The; ‡Porcupine Literary Arts Magazine; Portland Review; Potato Eyes; Potpourri; Prairie Dog; Prairie Fire; Prairie Journal of Canadian Literature, The; Primavera; Prism International; Puerto Del Sol; Quarterly West; Rag Mag; Rambunctious Review; Raw Fiction; ‡Reader's Break; RE:AL; River Styx; RiverSedge; Riverwind; ‡Rock Springs Review; Salt Lick Press; Sanskrit; Shattered Wig Review; ‡Shockwaves; Short Stories Bimonthly; Short Stuff Magazine for Grown-ups; Side Show; Sidewalks; Sierra Nevada College Review; Skylark; Slipstream; So To Speak; Soft Door, The; South Carolina Review; South Dakota Review; Southern California Anthology; ‡Spare Room, A; Spindrift; SPSM&H; Story; Street Beat Quarterly; Stroker Magazine; Struggle; Suffusion Magazine; Sulphur River Literary Review; Sycamore Review; Tampa Review; "Teak" Roundup; Thema; ‡Thin Air; This Magazine; Timber Creek Review; ‡Torre De Papel; Touchstone Literary Journal; Triquarterly; Tucumcari Literary Review; ‡Turnstile; Unmuzzled Ox; Urbanus Magazine; Valley Grapevine; Verve; Vignette; Vincent Brothers Review, The; Voices West; ‡Vox A; West Branch; West Wind Review; Westview; Whetstone (Canada); ‡Whetstone (Illinois); ‡Willow Review; Wind Magazine; Wordplay; Words of Wisdom; Writers' Forum; Writes of Passage; Writing on the Wall, The; Xavier Review; Xtreme; Zyzzyva

Mystery/Suspense: Aguilar Expression, The; Allegheny Review; Amelia; Arnazella; artisan; Belletrist Review, The; Beneath the Surface; BookLovers; Brownstone Review, The; Capers Aweigh Magazine; Chrysalis Reader; Climbing Art, The; Compenions; Confluence; Crazyquilt; Dan River Anthology; Djinni; Dodobobo; Dogwood Tales Magazine; Downstate Story; Eagle's Flight; Echoes; 8; Elf: Eclectic Literary Forum; Eureka Literary Magazine; Every So Often. . .; Expressions; Flying Island, The; Fugue; Grasslands Review; Green's Magazine; i.e. magazine; Just Write; Lamplight, The; Lines In The Sand; Lynx Eye; Merlyn's Pen; Musing Place, The; New Press Literary Quarterly, The; Northeast Arts Magazine; Northwoods Journal; ‡Oatmeal & Poetry; Oracle Story; Palo Alto Review; ‡Pavlov Neruda/Manuslave Press; Phantasm CA; Pink Chameleon, The; Place to Enter, A; Poetry Forum Short Stories; ‡Poetry in Motion Magazine;

Portland Review; Potpourri; ‡Reader's Break; Screaming Toad Press; ‡Se La Vie Writer's Journal; Sensations Magazine; Short Stuff Magazine for Grown-ups; Skylark; ‡Spring Fantasy; SPSM&H; Street Beat Quarterly; Suffusion Magazine; "Teak" Roundup; Thema; Timber Creek Review; ‡Torre De Papel; Tucumcari Literary Review; Vincent Brothers Review, The; ‡Vox A; West Wind Review; Wordplay; Words of Wisdom; Writes of Passage

New Age/Mystic/Spiritual: Chrysalis Reader; ‡Spare Room, A

Psychic/Supernatural/Occult: Allegheny Review; artisan; ‡Barbaric Yawp; Beneath the Surface; Black Hammock Review, The; Capers Aweigh Magazine; Compenions; Dan River Anthology; Djinni; Dodobobo; Downstate Story; 8; Eureka Literary Magazine; Every So Often. . .; Expressions; Fat Tuesday; Flying Island, The; Happy; Hayden's Ferry Review; Heaven Bone; ‡Implosion; MacGuffin, The; Matriarch's Way; Journal of Female Supremacy; Northwoods Journal; ‡Nyx Obscura Magazine; ‡Oatmeal & Poetry; Old Crow Review; ‡Palace Corbie; ‡Pavlov Neruda/Manuslave Press; ‡Poetry in Motion Magazine; Puck; Quanta; ‡the review; Shattered Wig Review; ‡Shockwaves; Spitting Image, The; ‡Stiletto III; Surprise Me; Thema; Urbanite, The; Vignette; West Wind Review; Writes of Passage; Xib; Zero Hour

Regional: ‡Acorn, The; Acorn Whistle; Allegheny Review; Amelia; Antietam Review; Appalachian Heritage; Arnazella; Asian Pacific American Journal; Aura Literary/Arts Review; Azorean Express, The; ‡Barbaric Yawp; Belletrist Review, The; Black Hammock Review, The; Blackwater Review; Blue Mesa Review; Blue Moon Quarterly, The; Blueline; BookLovers; Briar Cliff Review, The; Brownstone Review, The; Callaloo; Canadian Author; Capers Aweigh Magazine; Cayo; Chaminade Literary Review; Climbing Art, The; Clockwatch Review; Compenions; Concho River Review; Confluence; Confrontation; Corona; Cream City Review, The; Crucible; Dan River Anthology; Djinni; Dodobobo; Downstate Story; Echoes; Elf: Eclectic Literary Forum; Emrys Journal; Eureka Literary Magazine; Event; Every So Often. . .; Expressions; Farmer's Market, The; Fish Drum Magazine; Fish Stories; Fugue; Gettysburg Review, The; Grasslands Review; Green Hills Literary Lantern, The; Gulf Coast; Hayden's Ferry Review; Heartlands Today, The; Heaven Bone; High Plains Literary Review; Hill and Holler; Hopewell Review, The; Hunted News, The; ‡Image; ‡In the Spirit of the Buffalo; International Quarterly; Iowa Woman; Japanophile; Jeopardy; Kennesaw Review; Kinesis; Lactuca; Loonfeather; Louisiana Literature; ‡Lullwater Review; Mangrove; Manoa; Mark; Midland Review; Musing Place, The; nerve; NeWest Review; Northwoods Journal; ‡Oatmeal & Poetry; Old Crow Review; Onionhead; Palo Alto Review; Partisan Review; ‡Passages North; Pikeville Review; ‡Pleiades; ‡Poetry in Motion Magazine; Pointed Circle, The; Portland Review; Potato Eyes; Potomac Review; Prairie Dog; Prairie Journal of Canadian Literature, The; Puck; Rag Mag; RE:AL; ‡Reed Magazine; ‡review, the ; RiverSedge; Riverwind; Rockford Review, The; Sanskrit; ‡Se La Vie Writer's Journal; Shattered Wig Review; Short Stuff Magazine for Grown-ups; Sidewalks; Sierra Nevada College Review; Skylark; So To Speak; South Dakota Review; Southern California Anthology; Southern Humanities Review; Spindrift; Spout; SPSM&H; Struggle; Suffusion Magazine; Sycamore Review; "Teak" Roundup; Thema; This Magazine; Timber Creek Review; ‡Torre De Papel; Tucumcari Literary Review; ‡Turnstile; Valley Grapevine; Vignette; Vincent Brothers Review, The; Voices West; West Wind Review; ‡Willow Review; Words of Wisdom; Writers' Forum; Writes of Passage; Xavier Review; Xib; Zuzu's Petals Quarterly; Zyzzyva

Religious Inspirational: Allegheny Review; Ararat Quarterly; ‡Barbaric Yawp; Beloit Fiction Journal; ‡Black Writer Magazine; Chaminade Literary Review; ‡Christianity and the Arts; Echoes; Every So Often. . .; Explorer Magazine; Expressions; Heaven Bone; Hunted News, The; ‡Image; Kerem; manna; Matriarch's Way; Journal of Female Supremacy; Nite-Writer's International Literary Arts Journal; ‡Oatmeal & Poetry; ‡Pavlov Neruda/Manuslave Press; Pegasus Review, The; Pink Chameleon, The; Place to Enter, A; Poetry Forum Short Stories; Puck; Riverwind; ‡Rock Springs Review; Surprise Me; "Teak" Roundup; West Wind Review; Writes of Passage; Xavier Review

Romance: Aguilar Expression, The; Aura Literary/Arts Review; BookLovers; Compenions; Dan River Anthology; Dogwood Tales Magazine; Downstate Story; Eagle's Flight; Echoes; Eureka Literary Magazine; Every So Often. . .; Explorer Magazine; Expressions; Fugue; Gathering of the Tribes, A; Hayden's Ferry Review; i.e. magazine; Jeopardy; Lamplight, The; Lynx Eye; Matriarch's Way; Journal of Female Supremacy; Merlyn's Pen; Musing Place, The; ‡New Writing; Nite-Writer's International Literary Arts Journal; Northwoods Journal; ‡Oatmeal & Poetry; Palo Alto Review; ‡Pavlov Neruda/Manuslave Press; Pink Chameleon, The; Place to Enter, A; Poetry Forum Short Stories; Potpourri; ‡Reader's Break; Short Stuff Magazine for Grown-ups; Skylark; ‡Spring Fantasy; SPSM&H; Surprise Me; "Teak" Roundup; ‡Torre De Papel; ‡Vox A; West Wind Review; Writes of Passage

Science Fiction: Alabama Literary Review; Allegheny Review; Amelia; artisan; Aura Literary/Arts Review; ‡Barbaric Yawp; Beneath the Surface; Blackwater Review; Brownstone Review, The; Callaloo; Capers Aweigh Magazine; Chrysalis Reader; Climbing Art, The; Compenions; Confluence; Crazyquilt; Dan River Anthology; Djinni; Dodobobo; Downstate Story; Echoes; Elf: Eclectic Literary Forum; Eureka Literary Magazine; Every So Often. . .; Explorer Magazine; Expressions; Fish Drum Magazine; Flying Island, The; Fugue; Gathering of the Tribes, A; Georgetown Review; Glass Cherry, The; Grasslands Review; Green's Magazine; Happy; Hayden's Ferry Review; Home Planet News; i.e. magazine; Iconoclast, The; ‡Implosion; ‡In the Spirit of the Buffalo; Jeopardy; Lamp-Post, The; Lines In The Sand; Literal Latté; Lynx Eye; MacGuffin, The; Mark; Matriarch's Way; Journal of Female Supremacy; Merlyn's Pen; Mind in Motion; Mobius; Musing Place, The; Nimrod; Northwoods Journal; ‡Oatmeal & Poetry; Pacific Coast Journal; ‡Palace Corbie; Palo Alto Review; ‡Paper Radio; ‡Pavlov Neruda/Manuslave Press; Phantasm (CA); Pink Chameleon, The; Place to Enter, A; Poetry Forum Short Stories; ‡Poetry in Motion Magazine; Portland Review; Potpourri; Prairie Dog; Primavera; Puck; Quanta; ‡Reader's Break; RE:AL; Rockford Review, The; Sensations Magazine; ‡Shockwaves; Silver Web, The; Skylark; Spindrift; ‡Spring Fantasy; SPSM&H; ‡Stiletto III; Struggle; Suffusion Magazine; Surprise Me; Thema; Tomorrow; ‡Torre De Papel; Urbanite, The; Urbanus Magazine; Vincent Brothers Review, The; West Wind Review; Writes of Passage; Xib; Yellow Silk

Senior Citizen/Retirement: ‡Acorn, The; Amelia; Brownstone Review, The; Canadian Author; Dan River Anthology; Echoes; Expressions; Gathering of the Tribes, A; Hayden's Ferry Review; Lines In The Sand; manna; Nite-Writer's International Literary Arts Journal; ‡Oatmeal & Poetry; ‡Pavlov Neruda/Manuslave Press; Pink Chameleon, The; Poetry Forum Short Stories; SPSM&H; Struggle; Surprise Me; Tucumcari Literary Review; Vincent Brothers Review, The; West Wind Review; Xib

Serialized/Excerpted Novel: Agni; Alabama Literary Review; ‡American Writing; Asian Pacific American Journal; Atom Mind; Bellowing Ark; Black Jack; BookLovers; Callaloo; Chaminade Literary Review; Crazyquilt; Dodobobo; Echoes; Farmer's Market, The; Fat Tuesday; Gettysburg Review, The; Glass Cherry, The; Green Mountains Review; Hunted News, The; Lactuca; Lynx Eye; ‡Madison Review, The; Magic Realism; Manoa; Matriarch's Way; Journal of Female Supremacy; ‡modern words; Musing Place, The; Nassau Review; New Laurel Review; Oracle Story; Other Voices; Portland Review; Potomac Review; Prairie Journal of Canadian Literature, The; Puerto Del Sol; River Styx; ‡Shockwaves; Skylark; South Dakota Review; Southern California Anthology; Spindrift; Surprise Me; Vincent Brothers Review, The; ‡Vox A; Writing on the Wall, The; Xavier Review

Short Story Collections: Ararat Quarterly; Aura Literary/Arts Review; Painted Bride Quarterly

Sports: Aethlon; Amelia; artisan; Beloit Fiction Journal; BookLovers; Brownstone Review, The; Chrysalis Reader; Climbing Art, The; Echoes; Elf: Eclectic Literary Forum; Expressions; Fugue; nerve; Nite-Writer's International Literary Arts Journal; Northwoods Journal; Pink Chameleon, The; Riverwind; Skylark; Spitball; "Teak" Roundup; Thema; West Wind Review; Writes of Passage

Translations: ACM (Another Chicago Magazine); Adrift; Agni; Alabama Literary Review; Alaska Quarterly Review; Amelia; ‡American Writing; Antigonish Review, The; Antioch Review; Aphrodite Gone Berserk; Ararat Quarterly; Artful Dodge; Asian Pacific American Journal; Atom Mind; ‡Black Ice; Blue Moon Quarterly, The; ‡Boston Literary Review (BLuR); Brújula/

Compass; Callaloo; Chaminade Literary Review; Chariton Review, The; Chelsea; ‡Colorado Review; Columbia: A Journal of Literature & Art; Compenions; Conduit; Confluence; Confrontation; ‡Crab Creek Review; Cream City Review, The; Djinni; 1812; Eureka Literary Magazine; Fault Lines; Fiction; ‡Flying Horse; Folio: A Literary Journal; ‡Fourteen Hills; G.W. Review, The; Gathering of the Tribes, A; Glass Cherry, The; Grand Street; Green Mountains Review; Gulf Coast; Hopewell Review, The; Hunted News, The; i.e. magazine; ‡Image; International Quarterly; Jeopardy; ‡Kansas Quarterly/Arkansas Review; Kenyon Review, The; Kestrel; Lynx Eye; MacGuffin, The; Magic Realism; Mangrove; Manoa; Many Mountains Moving; Mid-American Review; Midland Review; ‡Mississippi Mud; Mississippi Review; ‡modern words; New Laurel Review; New Letters Magazine; New Orleans Review; new renaissance, the; ‡New Writing; Nimrod; 96 Inc.; Northwest Review; Old Crow Review; Oxford Magazine; Oxygen; Painted Bride Quarterly; Palo Alto Review; Pangolin Papers; ‡Paperplates; Partisan Review; ‡Pavlov Neruda/Manuslave Press; Phoebe (New York); Pikeville Review; ‡Pleiades; Portland Review; Potomac Review; Prairie Dog; Prism International; Puck; Puerto Del Sol; Quarterly West; River Styx; RiverSedge; Riverwind; Sanskrit; Silverfish Review; So To Speak; ‡spelunker flophouse; Spindrift; Spitting Image, The; Spout; SPSM&H; Story; Struggle; Sulphur River Literary Review; ‡Summer's Reading, A; Sycamore Review; ‡Tameme; Tampa Review; Touchstone Literary Journal; Triquarterly; Unmuzzled Ox; Vincent Brothers Review, The; West Branch; West Wind Review; Wind Magazine; Writing For Our Lives; Xavier Review; Xib; Yellow Silk; Zero Hour

Western: Allegheny Review; Amelia; artisan; Azorean Express, The; Black Jack; Blue Mesa Review; Brownstone Review, The; Compenions; Concho River Review; Dan River Anthology; Downstate Story; Echoes; Elf: Eclectic Literary Forum; Expressions; Fugue; Grasslands Review; ‡In the Spirit of the Buffalo; Lines In The Sand; Lynx Eye; Merlyn's Pen; ‡New Writing; Northwoods Journal; ‡Oatmeal & Poetry; Palo Alto Review; ‡Pavlov Neruda/Manuslave Press; Pink Chameleon, The; ‡Poetry in Motion Magazine; Potpourri; Riverwind; Sensations Magazine; Short Stuff Magazine for Grown-ups; Skylark; SPSM&H; "Teak" Roundup; Thema; Timber Creek Review; Tucumcari Literary Review; Valley Grapevine; Vincent Brothers Review, The; West Wind Review; Words of Wisdom; Writes of Passage

Young Adult/Teen: BookLovers; Claremont Review, The; Echoes; Every So Often. . .; Lamp-Post, The; Lines In The Sand; Merlyn's Pen; Nite-Writer's International Literary Arts Journal; ‡Oatmeal & Poetry; Oracle Story; Pink Chameleon, The; Poetry Forum Short Stories; Shadow; ‡Spring Fantasy; Struggle; Surprise Me; "Teak" Roundup; West Wind Review; Writes of Passage

SMALL CIRCULATION

Adventure: Anterior Fiction Quarterly; Big Sky Stories; ‡Blue Sugar; Boy's Quest; ‡Chinook Quarterly, The; Christian Courier; Dagger of the Mind; Dream International/Quarterly; Earthsongs; FiberOptic Etchings; ‡Free Spirit; ‡Healing Inn, The; It's Your Choice Magazine; Lacunae; Medicinal Purposes; Mediphors; ‡My Legacy; Naked Kiss; New Frontiers; Oak, The; Post, The; Queen's Quarterly; Rosebud™; ‡Scifant; Slate and Style; ‡Storyteller, The; Texas Young Writers' Newsletter; Thresholds Quarterly; Virginia Quarterly Review; ‡Volcano Quarterly

Childrens/Juvenile: Boy's Quest; Brilliant Star; ‡Chinook Quarterly, The; Christian Courier; Hopscotch: The Magazine for Girls; It's Your Choice Magazine; Majestic Books; ‡My Legacy; Skipping Stones; Young Judaean; ‡Young Voices Magazine

Condensed Novel: Black Books Bulletin: WordsWork; Burning Light; ‡Chinook Quarterly, The; Earthsongs; ‡Eloquent Umbrella, The; FiberOptic Etchings; Hecate's Loom; Paradox Magazine; Rosebud™

Erotica: Blowfish Catalog, The; Brutarian; Dream International/Quarterly; Earthsongs; Gay Chicago Magazine; Green Egg; Hecate's Loom; Lacunae; ‡Loving Alternatives Magazine; Medicinal Purposes; Paradox Magazine; Perceptions; Poskisnolt Press; Slippery When Wet

Ethnic/Multicultural: Black Books Bulletin: WordsWork; Black Fire; ‡Blue Sugar; Boy's Quest; ‡Chinook Quarterly, The; Dream International/Quarterly; Earthsongs; ‡Eloquent Umbrella, The; FiberOptic Etchings; Hecate's Loom; Intuitive Explorations; Italian Americana; It's Your Choice Magazine; Jewish Currents Magazine; ‡Keltic Fringe; Left Curve; Medicinal Purposes; Moccasin Telegraph; New Frontiers; ‡Papyrus Magazine; Paradoxist Literary Movement, The; Poskisnolt Press; Response; Rosebud™; Skipping Stones; Texas Young Writers' Newsletter; Virginia Quarterly Review; Western Pocket, The; ‡White Crow, The; ‡Woman; Yarns and Such

Experimental: ‡Blue Sugar; Brutarian; Burning Light; ‡Chinook Quarterly, The; Dagger of the Mind; ‡Dead Lines Magazines; Deathrealm; Dream International/Quarterly; Dreams & Visions; Earthsongs; ‡Eloquent Umbrella, The; Eyes; FiberOptic Etchings; Free Focus/Ostentatious Mind; Housewife-Writer's Forum; It's Your Choice Magazine; Left Curve; Liberty; Lost Worlds; Medicinal Purposes; Mediphors; New Frontiers; New Methods; Next Phase; Nocturnal Lyric, The; Oak, The; Paradox Magazine; Paradoxist Literary Movement, The; Poskisnolt Press; Queen's Quarterly; Response; Rosebud™; Ruby's Pearls; ‡Scifant; 2 AM Magazine; Western Pocket, The; ‡White Crow, The; Wisconsin Academy Review; ‡Woman

Fantasy: Bardic Runes; Bradley's Fantasy Magazine, Marion Zimmer; Brutarian; ‡Chinook Quarterly, The; Cosmic Unicorn, The; Dagger of the Mind; Dark Regions; Deathrealm; Dream International/Quarterly; Dreams & Visions; ‡Eloquent Umbrella, The; ‡Epitaph; FiberOptic Etchings; Haunts; Hecate's Loom; ‡Hor-Tasy; It's Your Choice Magazine; Lacunae; Liberty; Lost Worlds; ‡Loving Alternatives Magazine; Medicinal Purposes; ‡My Legacy; Next Phase; Nocturnal Lyric, The; Non-Stop Science Fiction Magazine; On Spec; Phantasm; Pirate Writings; Poskisnolt Press; Queen's Quarterly; Riverside Quarterly; ‡Scifant; Slate and Style; ‡Space And Time; Square One; ‡Story Rules; ‡Talebones; Texas Young Writers' Newsletter; Thresholds Quarterly; 2 AM Magazine; ‡Volcano Quarterly; Weirdbook; Worlds of Fantasy & Horror

Feminist: Black Books Bulletin: WordsWork; ‡Blue Sugar; Brutarian; ‡Chinook Quarterly, The; Earthsongs; ‡Eloquent Umbrella, The; FiberOptic Etchings; Free Focus/Ostentatious Mind; Hecate's Loom; Hurricane Alice; It's Your Choice Magazine; Liberty; Medicinal Purposes; New Frontiers; Poskisnolt Press; Response; Skipping Stones; Virginia Quarterly Review; ‡Woman

Gay: Black Fire; ‡Blue Sugar; Brutarian; Earthsongs; ‡Eloquent Umbrella, The; Gay Chicago Magazine; Hecate's Loom; It's Your Choice Magazine; Liberty; ‡Loving Alternatives Magazine; Medicinal Purposes; Perceptions; Poskisnolt Press; RFD

Historical: Anterior Fiction Quarterly; Big Sky Stories; Black Books Bulletin: WordsWork; ‡Blue Sugar; Boy's Quest; ‡Chinook Quarterly, The; Christian Courier; Dream International/Quarterly; Earthsongs; ‡Eloquent Umbrella, The; FiberOptic Etchings; ‡Free Spirit; Hecate's Loom; Housewife-Writer's Forum; It's Your Choice Magazine; Left Curve; ‡Linington Lineup; Mail Call; Medicinal Purposes; Mediphors; ‡My Legacy; New Frontiers; New Methods; Pipe Smoker's Ephemeris, The; Queen's Quarterly; Response; Rosebud™; ‡Scifant; ‡Storyteller, The; Texas Young Writers' Newsletter; Western Pocket, The; Wisconsin Academy Review

Horror: ‡Blue Sugar; Brutarian; Dagger of the Mind; Dark Regions; ‡Dead Lines Magazines; Deathrealm; Dream International/Quarterly; Eldritch Tales; ‡Epitaph; Eyes; FiberOptic Etchings; Grue Magazine; Haunts; ‡Hor-Tasy; It's Your Choice Magazine; Lacunae; Liberty; Lost Worlds; Medicinal Purposes; ‡My Legacy; Nightmares; Nocturnal Lyric, The; Phantasm; ‡Scifant; ‡SInister; ‡Space And Time; Square One; Terminal Fright; 2 AM Magazine; ‡Volcano Quarterly; Weirdbook; Worlds of Fantasy & Horror

Humor/Satire: Anterior Fiction Quarterly; ‡Blue Sugar; Brutarian; Burning Light; ‡Chinook Quarterly, The; Dream International/Quarterly; Dreams & Visions; ‡Eloquent Umbrella, The; FiberOptic Etchings; Free Focus/Ostentatious Mind; ‡Healing Inn, The; Hecate's Loom; Housewife-Writer's Forum; It's Your Choice Magazine; Journal of Polymorphous Perversity; Lacunae; Liberty; Medicinal Purposes; Mediphors; Mountain Luminary; ‡My Legacy; New Frontiers; Nocturnal Lyric, The; Oak, The; Paradox Magazine; Perceptions; Pipe Smoker's Ephemeris, The; Poskisnolt Press; Queen's Quarterly; Response; Rosebud™; Ruby's Pearls; ‡Scifant; Slate and Style; ‡Story Rules; ‡Storyteller, The; ‡Talebones; Texas Young Writers' Newsletter; Thresholds Quarterly; 2 AM Magazine; Virginia Quarterly Review; ‡Volcano Quarterly; Western Pocket,

The; ‡White Crow, The; Wisconsin Academy Review; ‡Woman; Yarns and Such

Lesbian: ‡Blue Sugar; Brutarian; Earthsongs; Gay Chicago Magazine; Hecate's Loom; Hurricane Alice; It's Your Choice Magazine; Liberty; ‡Loving Alternatives Magazine; Medicinal Purposes; Perceptions; Poskisnolt Press; ‡Woman

Literary: Anterior Fiction Quarterly; ‡Blue Sugar; Brutarian; Burning Light; ‡Chinook Quarterly, The; ‡Dead Lines Magazines; Dream International/Quarterly; Dreams & Visions; Earthsongs; ‡Eloquent Umbrella, The; FiberOptic Etchings; Free Focus/Ostentatious Mind; ‡Free Spirit; Hecate's Loom; Housewife-Writer's Forum; Hurricane Alice; Italian Americana; Lacunae; Left Curve; Liberty; ‡Linington Lineup; Medicinal Purposes; Mediphors; New Frontiers; Paradox Magazine; Pipe Smoker's Ephemeris, The; Poskisnolt Press; Queen's Quarterly; Response; Rosebud™; ‡Storyteller, The; Texas Young Writers' Newsletter; Virginia Quarterly Review; Western Pocket, The; ‡White Crow, The; Wisconsin Academy Review; ‡Woman

Mainstream/Contemporary: Anterior Fiction Quarterly; ‡Blue Sugar; Brutarian; ‡Chinook Quarterly, The; ‡Dead Lines Magazines; Dream International/Quarterly; Dreams & Visions; Earthsongs; ‡Eloquent Umbrella, The; Eyes; FiberOptic Etchings; Free Focus/Ostentatious Mind; Hecate's Loom; Housewife-Writer's Forum; Lacunae; Left Curve; Liberty; Medicinal Purposes; Mediphors; ‡My Legacy; New Frontiers; New Methods; Oak, The; Poskisnolt Press; Queen's Quarterly; Response; Rosebud™; Ruby's Pearls; Slate and Style; Square One; ‡Storyteller, The; Texas Young Writers' Newsletter; Virginia Quarterly Review; ‡Whispering Willow's Mystery Magazine; Wisconsin Academy Review; ‡Woman

Mystery/Suspense: Anterior Fiction Quarterly; ‡Blue Sugar; Brutarian; ‡Chinook Quarterly, The; Dagger of the Mind; Dream International/Quarterly; ‡Eloquent Umbrella, The; FiberOptic Etchings; Free Focus/Ostentatious Mind; Hardboiled; Housewife-Writer's Forum; It's Your Choice Magazine; Lacunae; Liberty; ‡Linington Lineup; Medicinal Purposes; ‡Murderous Intent; ‡My Legacy; Mystery Time; Naked Kiss; Pirate Writings; Post, The; PSI; Red Herring Mystery Magazine; Ruby's Pearls; ‡Scifant; Square One; ‡Storyteller, The; Texas Young Writers' Newsletter; 2 AM Magazine; ‡Volcano Quarterly; Yarns and Such

New Age/Mystic/Spiritual: Merlana's Magickal Messages; Mountain Luminary; New Frontier

Psychic/Supernatural/Occult: Anterior Fiction Quarterly; ‡Blue Sugar; Brutarian; ‡Dead Lines Magazines; Deathrealm; Dream International/Quarterly; Earthsongs; Eldritch Tales; ‡Eloquent Umbrella, The; ‡Epitaph; FiberOptic Etchings; Free Focus/Ostentatious Mind; Grue Magazine; Haunts; Hecate's Loom; Intuitive Explorations; It's Your Choice Magazine; Lacunae; Lost Worlds; Medicinal Purposes; ‡Murderous Intent; Nightmares; Nocturnal Lyric, The; Perceptions; Poskisnolt Press; Rosebud™; Terminal Fright; Thresholds Quarterly; 2 AM Magazine; Weirdbook; ‡Whispering Willow's Mystery Magazine; ‡Woman; Worlds of Fantasy & Horror

Regional: Above the Bridge; Anterior Fiction Quarterly; ‡Blue Sugar; ‡Chinook Quarterly, The; ‡Eloquent Umbrella, The; FiberOptic Etchings; Left Curve; Medicinal Purposes; ‡My Legacy; New Frontiers; New Methods; Response; Rosebud™; ‡Storyteller, The; ‡Volcano Quarterly; Western Pocket, The; Wisconsin Academy Review; Yarns and Such

Religious/Inspirational: Burning Light; Christian Courier; Dreams & Visions; Earthsongs; ‡Eloquent Umbrella, The; ‡Healing Inn, The; Hecate's Loom; Intuitive Explorations; It's Your Choice Magazine; Miraculous Medal, The; ‡My Legacy; ‡Prayerworks; Queen of All Hearts; Response; ‡Salt & The Light, The; Skipping Stones; ‡Storyteller, The; Thresholds Quarterly; ‡Volcano Quarterly; ‡Woman; Young Judaean

Romance: Anterior Fiction Quarterly; ‡Blue Sugar; ‡Chinook Quarterly, The; Dream International/Quarterly; ‡Eloquent Umbrella, The; Eyes; FiberOptic Etchings; Gay Chicago Magazine; Hecate's Loom; Housewife-Writer's Forum; Medicinal Purposes; ‡My Legacy; Poskisnolt Press; Post, The; PSI; Rosebud™; ‡Scifant; ‡Storyteller, The; Texas Young Writers' Newsletter; 2 AM Magazine; Virginia Quarterly Review; ‡Volcano Quarterly; ‡Woman; Hurricane Alice; Lost Worlds; Stygian Vortex Publications

Science Fiction: ‡Blue Sugar; Burning Light; ‡Chinook Quarterly, The; Communities Magazine; Cosmic Unicorn, The; Dagger of the Mind; Dark Regions; ‡Dead Lines Magazines; Deathrealm; Dream International/Quarterly; Dreams & Visions; ‡Eloquent Umbrella, The; FiberOptic Etchings; Hecate's Loom; It's Your Choice Magazine; Lacunae; Left Curve; Liberty; Lost Worlds; Medicinal Purposes; Mediphors; Mindsparks; ‡Murderous Intent; ‡My Legacy; Nocturnal Lyric, The; Non-Stop Science Fiction Magazine; On Spec; Other Worlds; Pirate Writings; Queen's Quarterly; Riverside Quarterly; Rosebud™; ‡Scifant; ‡Space And Time; Square One; ‡Story Rules; ‡Storyteller, The; ‡Talebones; ‡Terra Incognita; Texas Young Writers' Newsletter; Thresholds Quarterly; 2 AM Magazine; ‡Volcano Quarterly; ‡Woman

Senior Citizen/Retirement: Christian Courier; ‡Eloquent Umbrella, The; Medicinal Purposes; ‡My Legacy; Poskisnolt Press; ‡Storyteller, The

Serialized/Excerpted Novel: Burning Light; Hecate's Loom; Lost Worlds; New Frontiers; Rosebud™; ‡Scifant; Virginia Quarterly Review; ‡Volcano Quarterly

Sports: Anterior Fiction Quarterly; Boy's Quest; ‡Chinook Quarterly, The; Christian Courier; ‡Eloquent Umbrella, The; FiberOptic Etchings; Medicinal Purposes; ‡Storyteller, The

Translations: ‡Chinook Quarterly, The; Christian Courier; Dream International/Quarterly; ‡Eloquent Umbrella, The; Jewish Currents Magazine; Left Curve; New Frontiers; Non-Stop Science Fiction Magazine; Response; Rosebud™; Virginia Quarterly Review; ‡White Crow, The; Worlds of Fantasy & Horror

Western: Big Sky Stories; ‡Blue Sugar; ‡Chinook Quarterly, The; ‡Eloquent Umbrella, The; FiberOptic Etchings; Free Focus/Ostentatious Mind; Medicinal Purposes; ‡My Legacy; New Frontiers; Poskisnolt Press; Post, The; PSI; ‡Storyteller, The; ‡Western Digest; Western Pocket, The; Western Tales Magazine

Young Adult/Teen: Brilliant Star; ‡Chinook Quarterly, The; Cosmic Unicorn, The; Dream International/Quarterly; ‡Eloquent Umbrella, The; FiberOptic Etchings; Free Focus/Ostentatious Mind; Fudge Cake, The; It's Your Choice Magazine; Majestic Books; Medicinal Purposes; Mindsparks; ‡My Legacy; Poskisnolt Press; Skipping Stones; ‡Storyteller, The; Texas Young Writers' Newsletter

ZINES

Adventure: Abyss Magazine; ‡Black Dog; Drinkin' Buddy Magazine, The; ‡Fayrdaw; ‡Fortress; Heroic Times; Home Girl Press; Monthly Independent Tribune Times Journal Post Gazette News Chronicle Bulletin, The; Ralph's Review; S.L.U.G.fest, Ltd.; ‡Sink Full of Dishes; ‡Tale Spinner, The; ‡Unknown Writer, The; Writers' International Forum

Childrens/Juvenile: Full-Time Dads; Kids' World; Writers' International Forum

Condensed Novel: Art:Mag; Bahlasti Papers; ‡Curriculum Vitae; Dead of Night™ Magazine; Drinkin' Buddy Magazine, The; ‡Empty; ‡Generator; hip MAMA; Jack, Mackerel Magazine; ‡Kick It Over; Lime Green Bulldozers; ‡The #11; Otisian Directory; Pica; Uno Mas Magazine; Vox

Erotica: Art:Mag; babysue; Bahlasti Papers; ‡Black Dog; Black Sheets; ‡Curriculum Vitae; Diversions; Drinkin' Buddy Magazine, The; Eidos; ‡Empty; Graffiti Off The Asylum Walls; Heroic Times; hip MAMA; Jack, Mackerel Magazine; ‡The #11; ‡Panopticon; PBW; ‡Satellite Fiction; ‡Sink Full of Dishes; ‡Tale Spinner, The; ‡Unknown Writer, The; Uno Mas Magazine; Vox; W!dow of the Orch!d, The

Ethnic/Multicultural: Art:Mag; Bahlasti Papers; ‡Black Dog; ‡Curriculum Vitae; Drinkin' Buddy Magazine, The; ‡Empty; Fuel Magazine; ‡Generator; ‡Hazel Grove Musings; Heroic Times; hip MAMA; Home Girl Press; Otisian Directory; S.L.U.G.fest, Ltd.; ‡Sink Full of Dishes; ‡T.R.'s Zine; ‡Tale Spinner, The; ‡Unknown Writer, The; Uno Mas Magazine; Vox

Experimental: Art:Mag; babysue; Bahlasti Papers; ‡Black Dog; ‡Blue Lady, The; ‡Curriculum Vitae; Dreams & Nightmares; ‡Eclipse; ‡Empty; ‡Fayrdaw; Fuel Magazine; ‡Generator; ‡Hazel Grove Musings; Heroic Times; hip MAMA; Jack, Mackerel Magazine; ‡Kick It Over; Monthly Independent Tribune Times Journal Post Gazette News Chronicle Bulletin, The; ‡The #11; Office Number One; Otisian Directory; ‡Panopticon; PBW; Pica; S.L.U.G.fest, Ltd.; ‡Sink Full of Dishes; ‡Stygian Articles; ‡Transcendent Visions; ‡Unknown Writer, The; Uno Mas Magazine; Vox; W!dow of the Orch!d, The

Fantasy: Abyss Magazine; Art:Mag; Bahlasti Papers; ‡Black Dog; ‡Blue Lady, The; Companion in Zeor, A; Dead of Night™ Magazine; Dreams & Nightmares; Drinkin' Buddy Magazine, The; ‡Eclipse; ‡Fortress; Full-Time Dads; ‡Hazel Grove Musings; Heroic Times; Hobson's Choice; Home Girl Press; ‡Keen Science Fiction!; ‡Medusa's Hairdo Magazine; ‡Of Unicorns and Space Stations; Office Number One; Once Upon A World; Otisian Directory; ‡Outer Darkness; Pablo Lennis; ‡Panopticon; ‡Pulp: A Fiction Magazine; Ralph's Review; Sidetrekked; ‡Sink Full of Dishes; ‡Sorcerous Magazine; ‡Stygian Articles; ‡Tale Spinner, The; ‡Thistle; ‡Unknown Writer, The; W!dow of the Orch!d, The; Writers' International Forum

Feminist: Art:Mag; Bahlasti Papers; ‡Black Dog; ‡Empty; Fuel Magazine; ‡Generator; Graffiti Off The Asylum Walls; ‡Hazel Grove Musings; hip MAMA; ‡Kick It Over; Lime Green Bulldozers; Otisian Directory; ‡Panopticon; Pica; ‡Sink Full of Dishes; ‡Transcendent Visions; ‡Unknown Writer, The; Uno Mas Magazine; Vox; Women's Work

Gay: Art:Mag; Backspace; Bahlasti Papers; ‡Black Dog; Drinkin' Buddy Magazine, The; ‡Generator; ‡Hazel Grove Musings; hip MAMA; ‡Kick It Over; Lime Green Bulldozers; Otisian Directory; ‡Panopticon; PBW; Pica; ‡Sink Full of Dishes; ‡T.R.'s Zine; ‡Transcendent Visions; ‡Unknown Writer, The; Uno Mas Magazine; Vox

Historical: Art:Mag; ‡Black Dog; Drinkin' Buddy Magazine, The; ‡Fayrdaw; Lime Green Bulldozers; ‡The #11; Otisian Directory; S.L.U.G.fest, Ltd.; ‡Sink Full of Dishes; ‡Tale Spinner, The; ‡Unknown Writer, The; Uno Mas Magazine; Writers' International Forum

Horror: Abyss Magazine; Art:Mag; Bahlasti Papers; ‡Black Dog; ‡Bloodreams Magazine; ‡Blue Lady, The; Crossroads; ‡Dark Tome; Dead of Night™ Magazine; Drinkin' Buddy Magazine, The; ‡Eclipse; Heliocentric Net Anthology; Heroic Times; Lime Green Bulldozers; ‡Medusa's Hairdo Magazine; Office Number One; ‡Outer Darkness; ‡Panopticon; ‡Pulp: A Fiction Magazine; Ralph's Review; S.L.U.G.fest, Ltd.; ‡Sink Full of Dishes; ‡Stygian Articles; ‡Thistle; ‡Unknown Writer, The; Virgin Meat; W!dow of the Orch!d, The

Humor/Satire: Art:Mag; Atrocity; babysue; Bahlasti Papers; ‡Black Dog; Companion in Zeor, A; ‡Curriculum Vitae; Dreams & Nightmares; Drinkin' Buddy Magazine, The; ‡Fayrdaw; Full-Time Dads; ‡Generator; Graffiti Off The Asylum Walls; ‡Hazel Grove Musings; hip MAMA; Home Girl Press; ‡idiot wind; Lime Green Bulldozers; Monthly Independent Tribune Times Journal Post Gazette News Chronicle Bulletin, The; ‡The #11; Nuthouse; Office Number One; Otisian Directory; ‡Panopticon; Pica; Ralph's Review; S.L.U.G.fest, Ltd.; ‡Sink Full of Dishes; ‡T.R.'s Zine; ‡Tale Spinner, The; ‡Transcendent Visions; ‡Unknown Writer, The; Uno Mas Magazine; Vox; Writers' International Forum

Lesbian: Art:Mag; Backspace; Bahlasti Papers; ‡Black Dog; Drinkin' Buddy Magazine, The; ‡Generator; ‡Hazel Grove Musings; hip MAMA; ‡Kick It Over; Lime Green Bulldozers; Otisian Directory; ‡Panopticon; PBW; Pica; ‡Sink Full of Dishes; ‡T.R.'s Zine; ‡Transcendent Visions; ‡Unknown Writer, The; Uno Mas Magazine; Vox; Women's Work

Literary: Art:Mag; Bahlasti Papers; ‡Black Dog; ‡Curriculum Vitae; Drinkin' Buddy Magazine, The; ‡Empty; ‡Fayrdaw; Fuel Magazine; Full-Time Dads; ‡Generator; hip MAMA; Home Girl Press; Jack, Mackerel Magazine; Karma Lapel; Lime Green Bulldozers; ‡Medusa's Hairdo Magazine; Office Number One; Otisian Directory; ‡Panopticon; PBW; Pica; Ralph's Review; S.L.U.G.fest, Ltd.; ‡Sink Full of Dishes; ‡Stygian Articles; ‡T.R.'s Zine; ‡Unknown Writer, The; Uno Mas Magazine; Vox

Mainstream/Contemporary: Art:Mag; ‡Black Dog; ‡Curriculum Vitae; Drinkin' Buddy Magazine, The; ‡Fayrdaw; Full-Time Dads; ‡Generator; hip MAMA; Home Girl Press; Lime Green Bulldozers; ‡Medusa's Hairdo Magazine; S.L.U.G.fest, Ltd.; ‡Sink Full of Dishes; ‡T.R.'s Zine; ‡Unknown Writer, The; Uno Mas Magazine; Writers' International Forum

Mystery/Suspense: Art:Mag; ‡Black Dog; Dead of Night™ Magazine; Drinkin' Buddy Magazine, The; Heroic Times; Lime Green Bulldozers; ‡Medusa's Hairdo Magazine; Monthly Independent Tribune Times Journal Post Gazette News Chronicle Bulletin, The; ‡The #11; ‡Outer Darkness; ‡Pulp: A Fiction Magazine; ‡Sink Full of Dishes; ‡T.R.'s Zine; ‡Tale Spinner, The; ‡Thistle; ‡Unknown Writer, The; Writers' International Forum

New Age/Mystic/Spiritual: ‡Both Sides Now

Psychic/Supernatural/Occult: Abyss Magazine; Art:Mag; Bahlasti Papers; ‡Black Dog; ‡Bloodreams Magazine; ‡Blue Lady, The; Crossroads; ‡Dark Tome; Dead of Night™ Magazine; Drinkin' Buddy Magazine, The; ‡Eclipse; ‡Hazel Grove Musings; Lime Green Bulldozers; Monthly Independent Tribune Times Journal Post Gazette News Chronicle Bulletin, The; Office Number One; Otisian Directory; ‡Outer Darkness; ‡Panopticon; Ralph's Review; S.L.U.G.fest, Ltd.; ‡Sink Full of Dishes; ‡Stygian Articles; ‡Thistle; ‡Unknown Writer, The; Vox; W!dow of the Orch!d, The; Writers' International Forum

Regional: Art:Mag; ‡Black Dog; Drinkin' Buddy Magazine, The; ‡Generator; Home Girl Press; ‡Medusa's Hairdo Magazine; Otisian Directory; S.L.U.G.fest, Ltd.; ‡Sink Full of Dishes; ‡Sycamore Roots: The Regionalist Papers; ‡Unknown Writer, The; Writers' International Forum

Religious/Inspirational: Full-Time Dads; ‡Hazel Grove Musings; Otisian Directory; S.L.U.G.fest, Ltd.; ‡T.R.'s Zine

Romance: Drinkin' Buddy Magazine, The; Home Girl Press; ‡Medusa's Hairdo Magazine; Otisian Directory; ‡Outer Darkness; PeopleNet, Disability DateNet Home Page; Ralph's Review; ‡Thistle; Writers' International Forum

Science Fiction: Absolute Magnitude; Abyss Magazine; Art:Mag; Bahlasti Papers; ‡Black Dog; ‡Blue Lady, The; Companion in Zeor, A; Cosmic Landscapes; Dead of Night™ Magazine; Dreams & Nightmares; Drinkin' Buddy Magazine, The; ‡Eclipse; ‡Fifth Di, The/Sixth Sense, The/Starflite; ‡Fortress; ‡Generator; Heroic Times; Hobson's Choice; Home Girl Press; ‡Keen Science Fiction!; ‡Kick It Over; ‡Medusa's Hairdo Magazine; ‡Of Unicorns and Space Stations; Once Upon A World; Otisian Directory; ‡Outer Darkness; Pablo Lennis; ‡Panopticon; ‡Pulp: A Fiction Magazine; Ralph's Review; ‡Satellite Fiction; Sidetrekked; ‡Sink Full of Dishes; ‡Stygian Articles; ‡Tale Spinner, The; Writers' International Forum

Senior Citizen/Retirement: ‡Black Dog; ‡T.R.'s Zine; Writers' International Forum

Serialized/Excerpted Novel: Art:Mag; Bahlasti Papers; ‡Curriculum Vitae; Drinkin' Buddy Magazine, The; ‡Empty; ‡Generator; Lime Green Bulldozers; ‡The #11; Otisian Directory; Vox

Sports: ‡Black Dog; ‡Curriculum Vitae; Drinkin' Buddy Magazine, The; ‡T.R.'s Zine; ‡Tale Spinner, The; ‡Unknown Writer, The; Writers' International Forum

Translations: Art:Mag; ‡Curriculum Vitae; Drinkin' Buddy Magazine, The; ‡Generator; Jack, Mackerel Magazine; Karma Lapel; ‡Kick It Over; Otisian Directory; Vox

Western: Drinkin' Buddy Magazine, The; ‡Medusa's Hairdo Magazine; ‡Sink Full of Dishes; ‡T.R.'s Zine; ‡Tale Spinner, The; Writers' International Forum

Young Adult/Teen: Drinkin' Buddy Magazine, The; Full-Time Dads; Ralph's Review; ‡Sink Full of Dishes; ‡Tale Spinner, The; Writers' International Forum

COMMERCIAL PERIODICALS

Adventure: Art Times; Bowhunter Magazine; Boys' Life; Buffalo Spree Magazine; Bugle; Companion Magazine; Cosmopolitan Magazine; Easyriders Magazine; Florida Wildlife; ‡Georgia Journal; Junior Trails; Nureal Nu*Real; Q Magazine; Troika Magazine; Writer's World

Childrens/Juvenile: American Girl; Associate Reformed Presbyterian, The; Bugle; Chickadee; Child Life; Children's Digest; Children's Playmate; ‡Clubhouse; ‡Cobblestone; ‡Creative Kids; Cricket Magazine; ‡Discoveries; ‡Faces; Friend Magazine, The; Guideposts for Kids; Highlights for Children; ‡Horizons; Humpty Dumpty's Magazine; Jack and Jill; Junior Trails; Ladybug; My Friend; Odyssey; On the Line; Pockets; Power and Light; R-A-D-A-R; Ranger Rick Magazine; Shofar; Spider; Trekker News & Views, The; Turtle Magazine for Preschool Kids; Wonder Time; Writer's World

Condensed Novel: Campus Life Magazine; ‡Georgia Journal; Writer's World

Erotica: Contact Advertising; First Hand; Gent; Guys; Hustler Busty Beauties; Manscape; Nugget; Options; ‡Pillow Talk; ‡Private Letters; Swank Magazine

Ethnic/Multicultural: African Voices; Art Times; Buffalo Spree Magazine; Emerge Magazine; Hadassah Magazine; ‡Horizons; India Currents; Jive, Black Confessions, Black Romance, Bronze Thrills, Black Secrets; Live; Shofar; Troika Magazine; Writer's World

Experimental: Bomb Magazine; Trekker News & Views, The; Troika Magazine

Fantasy: Art Times; Asimov's Science Fiction; Contact Advertising; Dragon® Magazine; Emerge Magazine; Green Egg; Nureal Nu*Real; Omni; Playboy Magazine; Trekker News & Views, The

Feminist: Art Times; Christian Century, The; Contact Advertising; ‡Horizons; Radiance; Sojourner; ‡Spirit; Troika Magazine

Gay: Art Times; Contact Advertising; Drummer; First Hand; Guys; ‡Horizons; In Touch for Men; Manscape; Options; Powerplay Magazine; Troika Magazine; ‡TWN

Historical: Art Times; Beckett Baseball Card Monthly; Bugle; ‡Cobblestone; ‡Horizons; Juggler's World; Lady's Circle; Portland Magazine; Q Magazine; Troika Magazine; Writer's World

Horror: Nu*Real; Playboy Magazine; Trekker News & Views, The

Humor/Satire: Art Times; Balloon Life; Bear Essential, The; Beckett Baseball Card Monthly; Boys' Life; Buffalo Spree Magazine; Campus Life Magazine; Companion Magazine; ‡Dialogue; Emerge Magazine; ‡Golf Journal; Harper's Magazine; ‡Horizons; Juggler's World; Lady's Circle; Metro Singles Lifestyles; ‡Outlaw Biker; Playboy Magazine; St. Joseph's Messenger and Advocate of the Blind; Troika Magazine; ‡Virtue; Writer's World

Lesbian: Art Times; Contact Advertising; ‡Horizons; Options; Troika Magazine

Literary: Art Times; Atlantic Monthly, The; Bear Essential, The; Buffalo Spree Magazine; Buzz; Emerge Magazine; Esquire; ‡Horizons; Metro Singles Lifestyles; ‡NA'AMAT Woman; New Yorker, The; Portland Magazine; Seventeen; Trekker News & Views, The; Troika Magazine; Writer's World; ‡Yankee Magazine

Mainstream/Contemporary: Art Times; Associate Reformed Presbyterian, The; Atlantic Monthly, The; Bomb Magazine; Buffalo Spree Magazine; Buzz; Christian Century, The; Companion Magazine; Cosmopolitan Magazine; ‡Dialogue; Esquire; Harper's Magazine; ‡Horizons; Junior Trails; Ladies' Home Journal; Lady's Circle; ‡NA'AMAT Woman; New Yorker, The; Portland Magazine; Redbook; St. Anthony Messenger; St. Joseph's Messenger and Advocate of the Blind; Trekker News & Views, The; Troika Magazine; ‡Virtue; Writer's World

Mystery/Suspense: bePuzzled; Boys' Life; Cosmopolitan Magazine; Ellery Queen's Mystery Magazine; Hitchcock Mystery Magazine, Alfred; Nureal Nu*Real; Troika Magazine; Woman's World Magazine; Writer's World

Psychic/Supernatural/Occult: Green Egg; Nureal Nu*Real; Trekker News & Views, The

Regional: Aloha; Buzz; ‡Georgia Journal; Lady's Circle; Troika Magazine; ‡TWN; ‡Yankee Magazine

Religious/Inspirational: Annals of St. Anne De Beaupré, The; Associate Reformed Presbyterian, The; Campus Life Magazine; Christian Century, The; Christian Single; ‡Clubhouse; Companion Magazine; Cornerstone Magazine; ‡Discoveries; ‡Discovery; Emphasis on Faith and Living; Evangel; Friend Magazine, The; Gem, The; Guideposts for Kids; Home Life; ‡Horizons; Junior Trails; Lady's Circle; Liguorian; Live; Lookout, The; Mature Years; ‡Message Magazine; Messenger of the Sacred Heart; Metro Singles Lifestyles; My Friend; New Era Magazine; On the Line; Pockets; Power and Light; Purpose; R-A-D-A-R; St. Anthony Messenger; St. Joseph's Messenger and Advocate of the Blind; Seek; Shofar; ‡Spirit; Standard; Straight; Teen Life; Troika Magazine; ‡Virtue; With; Wonder Time; Writer's World

Romance: Cosmopolitan Magazine; Jive, Black Confessions, Black Romance, Bronze Thrills, Black Secrets; Metro Singles Lifestyles; Nureal Nu*Real; St. Anthony Messenger; St. Joseph's Messenger and Advocate of the Blind; Trekker News & Views, The; ‡Virtue; Woman's World Magazine; Writer's World

Science Fiction: Analog Science Fiction & Fact; Art Times; Asimov's Science Fiction; Bear Essential, The; Boys' Life; Computoredge; Juggler's World; Nureal Nu*Real; Omni; Playboy Magazine; Trekker News & Views, The

Senior Citizen/Retirement: ‡Dialogue; ‡Discovery; Grand Times; ‡Horizons; Lady's Circle; Mature Years; St. Anthony Messenger; St. Joseph's Messenger and Advocate of the Blind; Writer's World

Serialized/Excerpted Novel: Analog Science Fiction & Fact; Bomb Magazine; Campus Life Magazine; Capper's; Troika Magazine

Sports: Adventure Cyclist; ‡Appalachia Journal; Balloon Life; Beckett Baseball Card Monthly; Bowhunter Magazine; Boys' Life; Florida Wildlife; ‡Golf Journal; Junior Trails; ‡Outlaw Biker; Playboy Magazine

Translations: ‡Horizons; India Currents

Western: Boys' Life; Playboy Magazine; Writer's World

Young Adult/Teen: Associate Reformed Presbyterian, The; Beckett Baseball Card Monthly; Boys' Life; Campus Life Magazine; ‡Clubhouse; ‡Creative Kids; ‡Message Magazine; New Era Magazine; On the Line; Seventeen; ‡Spirit; Straight; Teen Life; Trekker News & Views, The; With; Writer's World

Small Press

Adventure: ‡Amherst Press; Ariadne Press; Arjuna Library Press; ‡Atomic Westerns; ‡Beggar's Press; Black Heron Press; Cave Books; ‡Cedar Bay Press LLC; ‡Chinook Press; Earth-Love Publishing House Ltd.; Ecopress; Gryphon Publications; ‡Intrigue Press; Jesperson Press Ltd.; ‡Loveprints Novelettes; ‡NRG Associates; Our Child Press; Pieper Publishing; Rio Grande Press; ‡Snowapple Press; Story Line Press; Vandamere Press; ‡Vista Publishing, Inc.; Write Way Publishing

Childrens/Juvenile: Advocacy Press; Annick Press Ltd.; Arjuna Library Press; Borealis Press; ‡Cedar Bay Press LLC; ‡Chinook Press; ‡Christmas; Cool Hand Communications, Inc.; Creative with Words Publications; Cross-Cultural Communications; E.M. Press, Inc.; Feminist Press at the City University of New York, The; ‡Gibbs Smith, Publisher/Peregrine Smith; ‡Grade

School Press; ‡Illumination Publishing Co.; Jesperson Press Ltd.; Jones University Press, Bob; Kar-Ben Copies Inc.; Lee & Low Books; Lollipop Power Books; Long Publishing Co., Hendrick; Milkweed Editions; Orca Book Publishers Ltd.; Our Child Press; Overlook Press, The; Peachtree Publishers, Ltd.; Pemmican Publications; Pieper Publishing; Pippin Press; Prairie Publishing Company, The; Prep Publishing; Quarry Press; Ragweed Press Inc./gynergy books; ‡Snowapple Press; Third World Press; Willowisp Press

Comic/Graphic Novels: ‡Cleis Press; ‡Gibbs Smith, Publisher/Peregrine Smith; Hollow Earth Publishing; ‡P&K Stark Productions, Inc.

Erotica: Arjuna Library Press; Center Press; Circlet Press; ‡Cleis Press; Creative Arts Book Co.; ‡Down There Press; Ekstasis Editions; ‡House of Anansi Press; ‡Permanent Press/Second Chance Press; Permeable Press; Pieper Publishing; Press Gang Publishers; ‡Slough Press; Vandamere Press

Ethnic/Multicultural: Alaska Native Language Center; Arsenal Pulp Press; Arte Publico Press; Bamboo Ridge Press; Bilingual Press/Editorial Bilingüe; ‡BkMk Press; Calyx Books; ‡Chinook Press; ‡Cleis Press; Coffee House Press; Cross-Cultural Communications; Feminist Press at the City University of New York, The; ‡Gibbs Smith, Publisher/Peregrine Smith; Griffon House Publications; Guernica Editions; ‡Helicon Nine Editions; ‡House of Anansi Press; ‡Ironweed Press; Kar-Ben Copies Inc.; ‡Kitchen Table: Women of Color Press; Lincoln Springs Press; ‡Loveprints Novelettes; Mage Publishers; ‡Ohio State University Press; Path Press, Inc.; Pemmican Publications; Pieper Publishing; Press Gang Publishers; Rio Grande Press; Sand River Press; Seven Buffaloes Press; Shields Publishing/NEO Press; ‡Slough Press; Soho Press; Southern Methodist University Press; Story Line Press; Third World Press; Three Continents Press; ‡University of Neveda Press; White Pine Press; Woman in the Moon Publications; Zephyr Press

Experimental: Ageless Press; Anvil Press; Arjuna Library Press; ‡BkMk Press; Black Heron Press; ‡Bridge Works Publishing Co.; Calyx Books; ‡Chinook Press; Coffee House Press; Cross-Cultural Communications; Ekstasis Editions; Griffon House Publications; ‡Helicon Nine Editions; ‡Insomniac Press; ‡Ironweed Press; Lincoln Springs Press; ‡Lintel; New Rivers Press; Permeable Press; Puckerbrush Press; Quarry Press; Red Deer College Press; Ronsdale Press/Cacanadadada; Shields Publishing/NEO Press; ‡Slough Press; ‡Snowapple Press; Thistledown Press; Ultramarine Publishing Co., Inc.

Family Saga: ‡Amherst Press; ‡Chinook Press; ‡Grade School Press; ‡Mountain State Press; Pieper Publishing; Rio Grande Press; ‡University of Neveda Press

Fantasy: Ageless Press; ‡Amherst Press; Arjuna Library Press; ‡Cedar Bay Press LLC; ‡Chinook Press; Circlet Press; Fasa Corporation; Hollow Earth Publishing; Jesperson Press Ltd.; ‡Loveprints Novelettes; Obelesk Books; Our Child Press; Overlook Press, The; ‡P&K Stark Productions, Inc.; Pieper Publishing; Rio Grande Press; Savant Garde Workshop, The; Ultramarine Publishing Co., Inc.; W.W. Publications; Woman in the Moon Publications; Write Way Publishing

Feminist: ‡Amherst Press; Ariadne Press; Arsenal Pulp Press; ‡Bridge Works Publishing Co.; Calyx Books; ‡Chinook Press; ‡Cleis Press; Creative Arts Book Co.; ‡Down There Press; Eighth Mt. Press, The; FC2/Black Ice Books; Feminist Press at the City University of New York, The; Firebrand Books; ‡Gibbs Smith, Publisher/Peregrine Smith; Hollow Earth Publishing; ‡Kitchen Table: Women of Color Press; Lincoln Springs Press; ‡Lintel; New Victoria Publishers; Nightshade Press; ‡Ohio State University Press; Outrider Press; Papier-Mache Press; Permeable Press; Pieper Publishing; Post-Apollo Press, The; Press Gang Publishers; Quarry Press; Ragweed Press Inc./gynergy books; Shields Publishing/NEO Press; Spinsters Ink; Third Side Press, Inc.; ‡Van Neste Books; Véhicule Press; Zephyr Press; Zoland Books, Inc.

Gay: Alyson Publications, Inc.; ‡Amherst Press; Arsenal Pulp Press; ‡Bridge Works Publishing Co.; ‡Cleis Press; FC2/Black Ice Books; Feminist Press at the City University of New York, The; Gay Sunshine Press and Leyland Publications; Hollow Earth Publishing; ‡House of Anansi

Press; ‡Insomniac Press; ‡Lintel; Outrider Press; Permeable Press; Pieper Publishing; Shields Publishing/NEO Press; Woman in the Moon Publications

Historical: ‡Amherst Press; Ariadne Press; ‡Beggar's Press; Beil, Publisher, Inc., Frederic C.; ‡BkMk Press; ‡Bridge Works Publishing Co.; Center Press; ‡Chinook Press; ‡Cleis Press; Creative Arts Book Co.; ‡Friends United Press; Goose Lane Editions; ‡Grade School Press; Lincoln Springs Press; Long Publishing Co., Hendrick; ‡Loveprints Novelettes; ‡Mountain State Press; ‡Ohio State University Press; Path Press, Inc.; Pieper Publishing; Quarry Press; ‡Snowapple Press; Third World Press; ‡University of Neveda Press; ‡Van Neste Books

Horror: ‡Amherst Press; Arjuna Library Press; ‡Atomic Westerns; ‡Beggar's Press; ‡Cedar Bay Press LLC; ‡Cleis Press; ‡Nicetown; Obelesk Books; Pieper Publishing; Write Way Publishing

Humor/Satire: Acme Press; Ageless Press; Ariadne Press; ‡Atomic Westerns; Baskerville Publishers, Inc.; ‡Beggar's Press; Black Heron Press; ‡Bridge Works Publishing Co.; Catbird Press; Center Press; ‡Chinook Press; ‡Cleis Press; Coffee House Press; Creative with Words Publications; Cross-Cultural Communications; ‡Gibbs Smith, Publisher/Peregrine Smith; ‡Ironweed Press; Jesperson Press Ltd.; Nightshade Press; Pieper Publishing; Press Gang Publishers; Rio Grande Press; Shields Publishing/NEO Press; ‡University of Neveda Press; ‡Van Neste Books; Vandamere Press; ‡Vista Publishing, Inc.

Lesbian: Alyson Publications, Inc.; ‡Amherst Press; Arjuna Library Press; Arsenal Pulp Press; Calyx Books; ‡Cleis Press; ‡Down There Press; Eighth Mt. Press, The; Feminist Press at the City University of New York, The; Firebrand Books; Hollow Earth Publishing; ‡House of Anansi Press; ‡Kitchen Table: Women of Color Press; ‡Lintel; Madwoman Press; Naiad Press, Inc., The; New Victoria Publishers; Outrider Press; Permeable Press; Pieper Publishing; Post-Apollo Press, The; Press Gang Publishers; Ragweed Press Inc./gynergy books; Rising Tide Press; Sand River Press; Shields Publishing/NEO Press; Spinsters Ink; Third Side Press, Inc.; Woman in the Moon Publications

Literary: Ageless Press; ‡Amherst Press; Anvil Press; Ariadne Press; Arsenal Pulp Press; Bamboo Ridge Press; Baskerville Publishers, Inc.; ‡Beggar's Press; Beil, Publisher, Inc., Frederic C.; Bilingual Press/Editorial Bilingüe; ‡BkMk Press; Black Heron Press; Books for All Times, Inc.; Borealis Press; ‡Bridge Works Publishing Co.; Cadmus Editions; Calyx Books; Catbird Press; Center Press; ‡Chinook Press; Coffee House Press; Confluence Press Inc.; Creative Arts Book Co.; Cross-Cultural Communications; Daniel and Company, Publishers, John; Delphinium Books; Ecco Press, The; Ecopress; Eighth Mt. Press, The; Ekstasis Editions; Faber and Faber, Inc.; FC2/Black Ice Books; Feminist Press at the City University of New York, The; Four Walls Eight Windows; ‡Gibbs Smith, Publisher/Peregrine Smith; Goose Lane Editions; Graywolf Press; Griffon House Publications; Guernica Editions; ‡Helicon Nine Editions; Hollow Earth Publishing; ‡House of Anansi Press; ‡Insomniac Press; ‡Ironweed Press; ‡Kitchen Table: Women of Color Press; Lemeac Editeur Inc.; Lincoln Springs Press; Livingston Press; Macmurray & Beck, Inc.; Mercury Press, The; Milkweed Editions; Moyer Bell Limited; New Rivers Press; NeWest Publishers Ltd.; Nightshade Press; ‡Ohio State University Press; Orca Book Publishers Ltd.; Outrider Press; Overlook Press, The; Peachtree Publishers, Ltd.; ‡Permanent Press/Second Chance Press; Permeable Press; Pieper Publishing; Post-Apollo Press, The; Prairie Journal Press; Press Gang Publishers; Puckerbrush Press; Quarry Press; Red Deer College Press; Rio Grande Press; Ronsdale Press/Cacanadadada; ‡St. Augustine Society Press; Sand River Press; Savant Garde Workshop, The; ‡Seven Stories Press; Shields Publishing/NEO Press; Simon & Pierre Publishing Co. Ltd.; ‡Slough Press; Smith, The; ‡Snowapple Press; Soho Press; Southern Methodist University Press; ‡Spirit That Moves Us Press, The; Stormline Press; Story Line Press; Thistledown Press; Turtle Point Press; University of Arkansas Press, The; ‡Van Neste Books; Véhicule Press; White Pine Press; Zephyr Press; Zoland Books, Inc.

Mainstream/Contemporary: Ageless Press; ‡Amherst Press; Anvil Press; Ariadne Press; ‡BkMk Press; Black Heron Press; Books for All Times, Inc.; Borealis Press; ‡Bridge Works Publishing Co.; Calyx Books; Catbird Press; ‡Chinook Press; Coffee House Press; Confluence

Press Inc.; Cool Hand Communications, Inc.; Creative Arts Book Co.; Cross-Cultural Communications; Daniel and Company, Publishers, John; Dundurn Press; Ecopress; Ekstasis Editions; Feminist Press at the City University of New York, The; ‡Gibbs Smith, Publisher/Peregrine Smith; Goose Lane Editions; Griffon House Publications; Guernica Editions; ‡Helicon Nine Editions; Lincoln Springs Press; Macmurray & Beck, Inc.; New Rivers Press; Nightshade Press; ‡NRG Associates; Orca Book Publishers Ltd.; Our Child Press; Papier-Mache Press; Peachtree Publishers, Ltd.; ‡Permanent Press/Second Chance Press; Pieper Publishing; Press Gang Publishers; Puckerbrush Press; Red Deer College Press; Rio Grande Press; ‡St. Augustine Society Press; Savant Garde Workshop, The; Seven Buffaloes Press; Simon & Pierre Publishing Co. Ltd.; ‡Slough Press; ‡Snowapple Press; Soho Press; Southern Methodist University Press; Ultramarine Publishing Co., Inc.; University of Arkansas Press, The; ‡Van Neste Books; Woman in the Moon Publications; Zephyr Press; Zoland Books, Inc.

Military/War: ‡Amherst Press; ‡Mountain State Press; Nautical & Aviation Publishing Co. of America Inc., The; Pieper Publishing; Vandamere Press

Mystery/Suspense: Ageless Press; ‡Amherst Press; ‡Beggar's Press; ‡Cedar Bay Press LLC; ‡Chinook Press; Creative Arts Book Co.; Earth-Love Publishing House Ltd.; Ecopress; Gryphon Publications; ‡Intrigue Press; ‡Ivy League Press, Inc.; ‡Loveprints Novelettes; Mercury Press, The; ‡NRG Associates; ‡P&K Stark Productions, Inc.; Pieper Publishing; Rio Grande Press; Simon & Pierre Publishing Co. Ltd.; Soho Press; Story Line Press; ‡University of Neveda Press; ‡Van Neste Books; ‡Vista Publishing, Inc.; Write Way Publishing

New Age/Mystic/Spiritual: Ageless Press; ‡Cedar Bay Press LLC; Earth-Love Publishing House Ltd.; Ekstasis Editions; ‡Gibbs Smith, Publisher/Peregrine Smith; Hollow Earth Publishing; ‡Insomniac Press; ‡Mountain State Press; Outrider Press

Psychic/Supernatural/Occult: ‡Atomic Westerns; Overlook Press, The; Permeable Press; Pieper Publishing; Woman in the Moon Publications; Write Way Publishing

Regional: Acadia Press; Beil, Publisher, Inc., Frederic C.; Butternut Publications; ‡Chinook Press; Creative Arts Book Co.; E.M. Press, Inc.; Feminist Press at the City University of New York, The; ‡Ice Cube Press; ‡Lintel; Long Publishing Co., Hendrick; ‡Mountain State Press; NeWest Publishers Ltd.; Nightshade Press; Orca Book Publishers Ltd.; Overlook Press, The; Peachtree Publishers, Ltd.; Pieper Publishing; Pineapple Press; Red Deer College Press; Rio Grande Press; Sand River Press; Seven Buffaloes Press; Southern Methodist University Press; Story Line Press; Three Continents Press; ‡University of Neveda Press; ‡University Press of Colorado; ‡Van Neste Books; Véhicule Press; Woodley Memorial Press

Religious/Inspirational: Bethel Publishing; ‡Christmas; ‡Friends United Press; ‡Grade School Press; ‡Loveprints Novelettes; ‡Mountain State Press; Post-Apollo Press, The; Prep Publishing; Shaw Publishers, Harold; Shields Publishing/NEO Press; Starburst Publishers; Threshold Books

Romance: ‡Amherst Press; Arjuna Library Press; ‡Beggar's Press; ‡Bridge Works Publishing Co.; ‡Cedar Bay Press LLC; Lemeac Editeur Inc.; ‡Loveprints Novelettes; ‡Nicetown; ‡P&K Stark Productions, Inc.; Pieper Publishing; Prep Publishing; ‡Rubenesque Romances; Shields Publishing/NEO Press; ‡Vista Publishing, Inc.

Science Fiction: Ageless Press; ‡Amherst Press; Arjuna Library Press; ‡Atomic Westerns; Black Heron Press; ‡Cedar Bay Press LLC; ‡Chinook Press; Circlet Press; Ecopress; Fasa Corporation; FC2/Black Ice Books; Feminist Press at the City University of New York, The; ‡Gibbs Smith, Publisher/Peregrine Smith; Gryphon Publications; ‡Loveprints Novelettes; ‡Nicetown; ‡NRG Associates; Obelesk Books; Overlook Press, The; ‡P&K Stark Productions, Inc.; Permeable Press; Pieper Publishing; Savant Garde Workshop, The; Ultramarine Publishing Co., Inc.; W.W. Publications; Write Way Publishing

Senior Citizen/Retirement: ‡Loveprints Novelettes

Serialized/Excerpted Novel: ‡Atomic Westerns

Short Story Collections: Ageless Press; ‡Amherst Press; Anvil Press; Arsenal Pulp Press; Bamboo Ridge Press; ‡Beggar's Press; Beil, Publisher, Inc., Frederic C.; Bilingual Press/Editorial Bilingüe; Books for All Times, Inc.; Calyx Books; ‡Cedar Bay Press LLC; Center Press; ‡Chinook Press; ‡Cleis Press; Confluence Press Inc.; Creative Arts Book Co.; Daniel and Company, Publishers, John; Ecco Press, The; Eighth Mt. Press, The; Ekstasis Editions; FC2/Black Ice Books; ‡Gibbs Smith, Publisher/Peregrine Smith; Goose Lane Editions; Graywolf Press; Gryphon Publications; ‡Helicon Nine Editions; ‡House of Anansi Press; ‡Insomniac Press; ‡Kitchen Table: Women of Color Press; Lemeac Editeur Inc.; Lincoln Springs Press; Livingston Press; New Rivers Press; ‡Nicetown; ‡Ohio State University Press; Outrider Press; Papier-Mache Press; Path Press, Inc.; Permeable Press; Pieper Publishing; Prairie Journal Press; Press Gang Publishers; Quarry Press; Red Deer College Press; Rio Grande Press; Sarabande Books, Inc.; Seven Buffaloes Press; Shields Publishing/NEO Press; ‡Slough Press; ‡Snowapple Press; Southern Methodist University Press; Story Line Press; Third World Press; Thistledown Press; Ultramarine Publishing Co., Inc.; University of Missouri Press; University of Arkansas Press, The; Véhicule Press; ‡Vista Publishing, Inc.; White Pine Press; Woman in the Moon Publications; Zephyr Press; Zoland Books, Inc.

Sports: Path Press, Inc.

Thriller/Espionage: Ageless Press; ‡Amherst Press; ‡Cleis Press; Ecopress; Gryphon Publications; ‡Intrigue Press; ‡Nicetown; ‡P&K Stark Productions, Inc.; Pieper Publishing; Prep Publishing; ‡Van Neste Books; Write Way Publishing

Translations: Beil, Publisher, Inc., Frederic C.; Bilingual Press/Editorial Bilingüe; ‡BkMk Press; ‡Bridge Works Publishing Co.; Calyx Books; Catbird Press; ‡Chinook Press; ‡Cleis Press; Confluence Press Inc.; Creative Arts Book Co.; Cross-Cultural Communications; Ekstasis Editions; Feminist Press at the City University of New York, The; Griffon House Publications; Guernica Editions; ‡Helicon Nine Editions; Hollow Earth Publishing; ‡House of Anansi Press; ‡Italica Press; Lemeac Editeur Inc.; Mage Publishers; Milkweed Editions; New Rivers Press; Overlook Press, The; Pieper Publishing; Post-Apollo Press, The; ‡Snowapple Press; Story Line Press; Turtle Point Press; University of Arkansas Press, The; Véhicule Press; White Pine Press; Zephyr Press

Western: ‡Amherst Press; ‡Atomic Westerns; Creative Arts Book Co.; ‡Loveprints Novelettes; Pieper Publishing; Sunstone Press; ‡University Press of Colorado

Young Adult/Teen: ‡Amherst Press; Arjuna Library Press; Bethel Publishing; Borealis Press; ‡Cedar Bay Press LLC; ‡Chinook Press; Coteau Books; Cross-Cultural Communications; ‡Grade School Press; Jones University Press, Bob; Long Publishing Co., Hendrick; ‡Loveprints Novelettes; Orca Book Publishers Ltd.; Our Child Press; Peachtree Publishers, Ltd.; Pieper Publishing; Prep Publishing; Ragweed Press Inc./gynergy books; Red Deer College Press; ‡Snowapple Press; Third World Press; Thistledown Press; W.W. Publications

Commercial Book Publishers

Adventure: Books In Motion; Bouregy & Company, Inc., Thomas; Crossway Books; ‡Crown Publishing Group, The; Dell Publishing; Fine, Inc., Donald I.; Harlequin Enterprises, Ltd.; Holt & Company, Henry; Kensington Publishing Corp.; Morrow And Company, Inc., William; ‡Nelson Publishers, Thomas; Philomel Books; ‡Questar Publishers; Random House, Inc.; St. Martin's Press; Worldwide Library

Childrens/Juvenile: Atheneum Books for Young Readers; Bantam/Doubleday/Dell Books for Young Readers Division; Boyds Mills Press; Chariot Victor Publishing; Dial Books for Young Readers; Eakin Press; Farrar, Straus & Giroux/Children's Books; Godine, Publisher, Inc., David R.; Golden Books Family Entertainment Inc.; Harcourt Brace & Co.; HarperCollins Children's

Books; HarperPaperbacks; Holiday House, Inc.; Holt & Company, Henry; Knopf Books for Young Readers; Little, Brown and Company Children's Books; Little, Brown and Company; Lodestar Books; ‡McElderry Books, Margaret K.; Morrow Junior Books; ‡Nelson Publishers, Thomas; Pelican Publishing Company; Philomel Books; ‡Questar Publishers; St. Paul Books and Media; Simon & Schuster Books for Young Readers; Troll Associates; Walker and Company; Weiss Associates, Inc., Daniel; Zondervan

Comic/Graphic Novels: Dark Horse Comics, Inc.; Fantagraphics Books

Erotica: Carroll & Graf Publishers, Inc.; ‡Forge Books; Kensington Publishing Corp.; Kensington Publishing Corp.; St. Martin's Press

Ethnic/Multicultural: ‡Bantam Books; Branden Publishing Co.; Hyperion; Interlink Publishing Group, Inc.; Philomel Books; St. Martin's Press

Experimental: Morrow And Company, Inc., William; St. Martin's Press

Family Saga: ‡Bantam Books; Dell Publishing; Harvest House Publishers; Philomel Books; Philomel Books

Fantasy: Aspect; Avon Books; Baen Books; ‡Bantam Books; Berkley Publishing Group, The; Berkley/Ace Science Fiction; Carroll & Graf Publishers, Inc.; Daw Books, Inc.; Delecorte/Dell Books for Young Readers; Dutton Signet; HarperPaperbacks; Philomel Books; ROC; St. Martin's Press; Tor Books

Feminist: Academy Chicago Publishers; Holt & Company, Henry; Morrow And Company, Inc., William; St. Martin's Press

Gay: Dutton Signet; Hyperion; Morrow And Company, Inc., William; St. Martin's Press

Glitz: ‡Bantam Books; Harlequin Enterprises, Ltd.

Historical: Academy Chicago Publishers; Avon Books; Ballantine Books; ‡Bantam Books; Branden Publishing Co.; Crossway Books; ‡Crown Publishing Group, The; Dell Publishing; Dutton Signet; Fawcett; Fine, Inc., Donald I.; ‡Forge Books; Godine, Publisher, Inc., David R.; Harcourt Brace & Co.; HarperPaperbacks; Holt & Company, Henry; Kensington Publishing Corp.; Morrow And Company, Inc., William; Philomel Books; ‡Presidio Press; ‡Questar Publishers; Random House, Inc.; St. Martin's Press

Horror: Avon Books; ‡Crown Publishing Group, The; Dell Publishing; Fine, Inc., Donald I.; ‡Forge Books; HarperPaperbacks; Leisure Books; Morrow And Company, Inc., William; ROC; St. Martin's Press; Tor Books

Humor/Satire: Books In Motion; ‡Crown Publishing Group, The; Harvest House Publishers; Holt & Company, Henry; Morrow And Company, Inc., William; St. Martin's Press

Lesbian: Morrow And Company, Inc., William; St. Martin's Press

Literary: Branden Publishing Co.; Carroll & Graf Publishers, Inc.; ‡Crown Publishing Group, The; Fine, Inc., Donald I.; Godine, Publisher, Inc., David R.; Harmony Books; Holt & Company, Henry; Hyperion; Knopf, Alfred A.; Morrow And Company, Inc., William; Multnomah Books; Norton & Company, Inc., W.W.; Philomel Books; ‡Questar Publishers; Random House, Inc.; St. Martin's Press; Washington Square Press

Mainstream/Contemporary: Avon Books; Ballantine Books; Berkley Publishing Group, The; Branden Publishing Co.; Carroll & Graf Publishers, Inc.; Crossway Books; ‡Crown Publishing Group, The; Dell Publishing; Dutton Signet; Eriksson, Publisher, Paul S.; ‡Forge Books; HarperPaperbacks; Harvest House Publishers; Holt & Company, Henry; Hyperion; Kensington Publishing Corp.; Knopf, Alfred A.; Morrow And Company, Inc., William; Random House, Inc.; St. Martin's Press; Tor Books; Weiss Associates, Inc., Daniel

Military/War: Avon Books; ‡Bantam Books; Branden Publishing Co.; ‡Crown Publishing Group, The; Dell Publishing; Fine, Inc., Donald I.; Kensington Publishing Corp.; Morrow And Company, Inc., William; ‡Presidio Press; St. Martin's Press

Mystery/Suspense: Avalon Books; ‡Bantam Books; Berkley Publishing Group, The; Books In Motion; Carroll & Graf Publishers, Inc.; Dell Publishing; Fawcett; Fine, Inc., Donald I.; ‡Forge Books; Godine, Publisher, Inc., David R.; Harcourt Brace & Co.; Harlequin Enterprises, Ltd.; HarperPaperbacks; Harvest House Publishers; Holt & Company, Henry; Hyperion; Kensington Publishing Corp.; Knopf, Alfred A.; Morrow And Company, Inc., William; Mysterious Press, The; ‡Nelson Publishers, Thomas; Philomel Books; ‡Presidio Press; ‡Questar Publishers; Random House, Inc.; St. Martin's Press; Tor Books; Walker and Company

New Age/Mystic/Spiritual: Dutton Signet

Psychic/Supernatural/Occult: Avon Books; Dell Publishing; St. Martin's Press

Regional: Blair, Publisher, John F.; Philomel Books

Religious/Inspirational: Baker Books; Chariot Victor Publishing; Crossway Books; ‡Eerdmans Publishing Co., Wm., B.; Harvest House Publishers; Hyperion; Multnomah Books; ‡Nelson Publishers, Thomas; ‡Questar Publishers; Resource Publications, Inc.; Revell Publishing; St. Martin's Press; St. Paul Books and Media; Tyndale House Publishers; Zondervan

Romance: Avalon Books; ‡Bantam Books; Berkley Publishing Group, The; Books In Motion; Bouregy & Company, Inc., Thomas; Dell Publishing; Dutton Signet; Harlequin Enterprises, Ltd.; HarperPaperbacks; Harvest House Publishers; Kensington Publishing Corp.; Leisure Books; Love Spell; Loveswept; ‡Questar Publishers; St. Martin's Press; Signal Hill Publications; Silhouette Books

Science Fiction: Aspect; Avon Books; Baen Books; ‡Bantam Books; Berkley Publishing Group, The; Berkley/Ace Science Fiction; Books In Motion; Carroll & Graf Publishers, Inc.; ‡Crown Publishing Group, The; Daw Books, Inc.; Dutton Signet; Morrow And Company, Inc., William; ROC; St. Martin's Press; Tor Books

Short Story Collections: Branden Publishing Co.; Philomel Books; Random House, Inc.; Resource Publications, Inc.

Thriller/Espionage: Dutton Signet; Fine, Inc., Donald I.; ‡Forge Books; HarperPaperbacks; Hyperion; Kensington Publishing Corp.; Morrow And Company, Inc., William; ‡Presidio Press; St. Martin's Press

Translations: Branden Publishing Co.; Holt & Company, Henry; Interlink Publishing Group, Inc.; Morrow And Company, Inc., William; Philomel Books

Western: Avalon Books; Avon Books; Books In Motion; Bouregy & Company, Inc., Thomas; Dutton Signet; Evans & Co., Inc., M.; ‡Forge Books; HarperPaperbacks; Jameson Books; Leisure Books; ‡Nelson Publishers, Thomas; Philomel Books; ‡Questar Publishers; Tor Books; Walker and Company

Young Adult/Teen: Archway Paperbacks/Minstrel Books; Atheneum Books for Young Readers; Avon Books; Bantam/Doubleday/Dell Books for Young Readers Division; Boyds Mills Press; Crossway Books; Delecorte/Dell Books for Young Readers; Flare Books; Godine, Publisher, Inc., David R.; HarperCollins Children's Books; HarperPaperbacks; Holt & Company, Henry; Lerner Publications Company; Little, Brown and Company Children's Books; Lodestar Books; ‡McElderry Books, Margaret K.; Morrow Junior Books; Philomel Books; ‡Questar Publishers; ‡Royal Fireworks Press; Troll Associates; Walker and Company; Weiss Associates, Inc., Daniel

Markets Index

A double-dagger (‡) precedes listings that are new to this edition. Markets that appeared in the 1996 edition of *Novel & Short Story Writer's Market* but are not included in this edition are identified by a two-letter code explaining why the market was omitted: **(ED)**—Editorial Decision, **(NS)**—Not Accepting Submissions, **(NR)**—No (or late) Response to Listing Request, **(OB)**—Out of Business, **(RR)**—Removed by Market's Request, **(UC)**—Unable to Contact, **(UF)**—Uncertain Future.

A

A.R.T. Arbitrary Random Thought (NR)
Abiko Literary Press (ALP), The 246
Abiko Quarterly International Fiction Contest/Tsujinaka Award 488
Aboriginal Science Fiction (NR)
Above the Bridge 255
Abrupt Edge (OB)
Absolute Magnitude 306
Abyss Magazine 306
Academy Chicago Publishers 451
Acadia Press 392
Ace Science Fiction 451 (also see Berkley Publishing Group 455)
ACM (Another Chicago Magazine) 91
Acme Press 392
‡Acorn, The 92
Acorn Whistle 92
Acta Victoriana (NR)
Acumen (NR)
Adaex Educational Publications 446
Addams Children's Book Award, Jane (NR)
Adrift 92
Adventure Cyclist 339
‡Adventures of Sword & Sorcery 93
Advocacy Press 392
‡Aegean Center for the Fine Arts Workshops, The 563
Aethlon 93
Africa Christian Press (NR)
African American Review 93
African Voices 339
African Voices Short Story Contest (NR)
Ageless Press 392
Agni 94
Aguilar Expression, The 94
Aim Magazine 340
Aim Magazine Short Story Contest 488
Air Canada Award 488
AKC Gazette 488

Akron Manuscript Club 488
Alabama Literary Review 94
Alabama State Council on the Arts Individual Artist Fellowship (RR)
Alabama Writers' Conclave 543
Aladdin Paperbacks (NR)
Alaska Native Language Center 393
Alaska Quarterly Review 94
‡Alaska State Council on the Arts Career Opportunity Grant Award 488
Albee Foundation (The Barn), Edward F. 567
Aldebaran (NR)
Algonquin Books of Chapel Hill 451
Algren Award for Short Fiction, The Nelson 488
Allegheny Review 95
Aloha 340
Alpha Beat Press 95
Alyson Publications, Inc. 393
‡Amateur Sleuth 489
Amateur Writers Journal (OB)
Ambit (NR)
Amelia 95
Amelia Magazine Awards 489
American Christian Writers Conferences 542
American Citizen Italian Press, The (NR)
American Fiction Awards 489
American Girl 340
American Literary Review 96
American Newspaper Carrier, The (NR)
American Short Fiction 96
American Short Fiction Contest 489
American University in Cairo Press, The (NR)
‡American Writing 96
Americas Review, The 97
‡Amethyst Review, The 97
‡Amherst Press 393
Amherst Review, The (NR)
Ammonite 301
Analecta College Fiction Contest 489

Analog Science Fiction & Fact 341
Anarchy (NR)
Anderson Short Fiction Prize, Sherwood 489
Andreas-Gryphius-Preis 489
Annals of St. Anne De Beaupré, The 341
Annick Press Ltd. 393
Annual/Atlantic Writing Competitions, The (NR)
Another Chicago Press (UC)
Anterior Fiction Quarterly 256
Antietam Review 97
Antietam Review Literary Award 490
Antigonish Review, The 98
Antioch Review 98
Antioch Writers' Workshop (NR)
Anvil Press 394
Anvil Press 3-Day Novel Writing Contest 490
Aphrodite Gone Berserk 98
‡Appalachia Journal 341
Appalachian Heritage 98
‡Appalachian Writers Conference 542
Aquarius 246
Arabesque (see Kensington 470)
Ararat Quarterly 99
Arba Sicula (NR)
Archway Paperbacks/Minstrel Books 451
Area of Operations (NR)
Ariadne Press 394
Arizona Authors Association 576
Arizona Authors' Association National Literary Contest 490
Arizona Coast (NR)
Arizona Commission on the Arts Creative Writing Fellowships (NR)
Arjuna Library Press 394
ARK/Angel Review 99
Arkansas Writers' Conference 543
Arnazella 99
Arsenal Pulp Press 395
Art Times 342
Art Workshop International (NR)
Arte Publico Press 395
Artemis (NR)
Artful Dodge 99
Arthur's Cousin (NR)
artisan 100
Artist Trust Artist Fellowships; GAP Grants 490
Art:Mag 306
Arts at Menucha (NR)
‡Arvon Foundation Ltd. Workshops, The 563
Ascending Shadows (NR)
‡Ascent 100
ASF Translation Prize 490
Asian Pacific American Journal 100

Asimov Award, The Isaac 490
Asimov's Science Fiction 342
Aspect 451 (also see Warner Books 483)
Aspire Publishing Co (NR)
Associate Reformed Presbyterian, The 342
Associated Writing Programs 576
‡Asspants 101
Asted/Grand Prix de Litterature Jeunesse du Quebec-Alvine-Belisle 490
Athena Incognito Magazine 101
Athenaeum Literary Award, The 491
Atheneum Books for Young Readers 451 (also see Simon & Schuster 481)
Atlantean Press Review, The (OB)
‡Atlantic Center for the Arts 567
Atlantic Monthly, The 343
Atom Mind 101
‡Atomic Westerns 395
Atrocity 307
Attic Press 446
Auguries 301
Aura Literary/Arts Review 102
Aurealis 301
Austin Writers' League Resource Center 576
Austin Writers' League Workshops/Conferences/Classes 552
Authors Guild, The 577
Authors in the Park/Fine Print Contest 491
Autumn Authors' Affair (NR)
Avalon Books 452
Avon Books 452 (also see Flare 463)
Avon Nova (NR)
AWP Award Series in the Novel and Short Fiction 491
AWP Chronicle 584
AWP Intro Journals Project (NR)
Azorean Express, The 102

B

Baby Connection News Journal, The (NR)
babysue 307
Backspace 307
Baen Books 452
Bagman Press (OB)
Bahlasti Papers 307
Baker Books 454 (also see Revell 479)
Balch Awards, Emily Clark 491
Ballantine Books 454
Balloon Life 343
Baltimore Science Fiction Society Writer's Workshop (NR)
Bamboo Ridge (RR)
Bamboo Ridge Press 396
B&A: New Fiction 102

‡Bantam Books 455 (also see Loveswept 473)
Bantam Spectra Books (NR)
Bantam/Doubleday/Dell Books for Young
  Readers Division 455 (also see Delacorte/
  Dell Books for Young Readers 460)
‡Barbaric Yawp 103
Bardic Runes 256
Basement Press 446
Baskerville Publishers, Inc. 396
Batchelder Award, Mildred L. 491
Bauhinia Literary Awards 491
Bay Area Writers Workshop (NR)
BBR Magazine 246
Be the Writer You Want to Be Manuscript
  Clinic 556
Bear Essential, The 343
Beckett Baseball Card Monthly 346
Become a More Productive Writer (NR)
‡Beggar's Press 396
Beil, Publisher, Inc., Frederic C. 396
Bella Magazine (NR)
Bellagio Study and Conference Center (NR)
Belletrist Review Annual Fiction Contest 491
Belletrist Review, The 103
Bellingham Review, The 103
Bellowing Ark 104
Beloit Fiction Journal 104
Beneath the Surface 104
Bennett Fellowship, George 491
bePuzzled 346
Berkeley Fiction Review 105
Berkley Publishing Group, The 455 (also see
  Ace Science Fiction 451, G.P. Putnam's
  Sons 478)
Berkley/Ace Science Fiction 455
Best First Malice Domestic Novel (NR)
Best First New Mystery Award 492
Best First Private Eye Novel Contest 492
‡Best Magazine 387
‡"Best of Ohio Writers" Contest 492
Best of Soft Science Fiction Contest 492
Bethel Publishing 397
Biblioteca Di Nova SF, Futuro, Great Works
  of SF 446
Big Sky Stories 256
Bilingual Press/Editorial Bilingüe 397
Bilingual Review 105
Bilson Award for Historical Fiction for Young
  People, The Geoffrey 492
Birch Brook Press 397
Bizara (OB)
‡BkMk Press 397
Black Belt (NR)
Black Books Bulletin: WordsWork 257

Black Children's Book Award, Irma S. and
  James H. 492
‡Black Dog 308
Black Fire 257
Black Hammock Review, The 105
Black Heron Press 398
Black Hills Writers Group Workshop 550
Black Hole Literary Review, The 106
‡Black Ice 106
Black Jack 106
Black Lace 107
‡Black Memorial Prizes, James Tait 492
Black Moss Press (NR)
Black River Review 107
Black Sheets 308
Black Tears (NR)
Black Tie Press (RR)
Black Warrior Review 107
Black Warrior Review Literary Award, The
  493
‡Black Writer Magazine 108
Blackstaff Press, The (NR)
Blackstone Circular, The 108
Blackwater Review 108
Blair, Publisher, John F. 456
Blink (NR)
‡Bloodreams Magazine 309
Bloodsongs (NR)
Blowfish Catalog, The 257
‡Blue Lady, The 309
Blue Mesa Review 108
Blue Moon Review, The 111
Blue Mountain Center, The (NR)
‡Blue Sugar 257
Blue Water Review, The (RR)
Bluegrass Writer Workshop (NR)
Blueline 112
Boardman Tasker Prize 493
Bogg 112
Bohemian Chronicle (NR)
Bomb Magazine 346
‡Bone & Flesh 112
Book Publishers of Texas Award 493
BookLovers 113
Books for All Times, Inc. 398
Books In Motion 456
Borealis Press 398
Boston Globe-Horn Book Awards 493
‡Boston Literary Review (BLuR) 113
Boston Review (NR)
Boston Review Short Story Contest (NR)
‡Both Sides Now 309
Bottomfish Magazine 113
Bouillabaisse 113
Boulevard 114

Boulevard (see the Berkley Publishing Group 455)

Bouregy & Company, Inc., Thomas 456 (also see Avalon 452)

Bowhunter Magazine 347

Boyars Publishers Inc., Marion 484

Boyds Mills Press 456

Boys' Life 347

Boy's Quest 258

Bradley's Fantasy Magazine, Marion Zimmer 258

Branden Publishing Co. 456

Brave New Tick, (the) 114

Brazos Bookstore (Houston) Award 493

Bread Loaf Writers' Conference 534

Breviloquence 493

Briar Cliff Review, The 114

Bridge, The (RR)

‡Bridge Works Publishing Co. 398

Brilliant Star 258

British Fantasy Society, The 577

Brody Arts Fund Literary Fellowship (NR)

Bronx Recognizes Its Own (B.R.I.O.) 493

Brownbag Press (NR)

Browndeer Press (see Harcourt Brace & Co. 467)

Brownstone Review, The 115

Brújula/Compass 115

Brutarian 260

Buffalo Spree Magazine 347

Bugle 348

Bugnet Award for the Novel, Georges 493

Bunting Institute, The Mary Ingraham 567

Burnaby Writers' Society 577

Burnaby Writers' Society Annual Competition 494

Burning Gate Press (OB)

Burning Light 260

Burnt Aluminum 115

Bush Artist Fellowships 494

Butternut Publications 399

‡Button 115

Buzz 348

By the Wayside 116

Byline 116

Byline Magazine Literary Awards 494

‡Byrdcliffe Arts Colony 568

C

CACHH Grants/Creative Artist Program 494

Cadmus Editions 399

Cafe Magazine (OB)

California Writers' Club (NR)

California Writer's Club Conference (NR)

California Writers' Club Contest (NR)

California Writers' Roundtable Annual Writing Contests 494

Callaloo 116

Calliope 116

Calyx 117

Calyx Books 399

Camargo Foundation 568

Cambrensis 247

Camelot Books (see Avon Books 452)

Campbell Memorial Award, John W. 494

Campus Life Magazine 348

Canada Council Awards 495

Canada Council Governor General's Literary Awards 495

Canadian Author 117

Canadian Authors Association (NR)

Canadian Authors Association Conference (NR)

Canadian Authors Association Literary Awards 495

Canadian Authors Association Students' Creative Writing Contest 495

Canadian Children's Literature/Litterature Canadienne Pour La Jeunesse (NR)

Canadian Society of Children's Authors, Illustrators & Performers (CANSCAIP) 577

Canadian Writer's Journal (NR)

Canongate Books Ltd. (NR)

Cape Cod Writers' Conference 534

Cape Writing Workshop (NR)

Capers Aweigh Magazine 117

‡Capilano Review, The 118

Capper's 349

Capricorn Award, The 495

Career Focus (NR)

‡Caribbean Writer, The 247

Carolina Quarterly 118

Carousel Literary Arts Magazine (NR)

Carroll & Graf Publishers, Inc. 457

Carver Short Story Contest, Raymond 495

Catbird Press 400

‡Cather Fiction Prize, Willa 495

Cat's Ear (NR)

CATS Magazine 349

Cave Books 400

Cavendish Tourist Association Creative Writing Award (NR)

Cayo 118

‡Cedar Bay Press LLC 400

Cencrastus (NR)

Center Press 400

‡Centrum Artist-In-Residence 568

Century (NR)

Chaminade Literary Review 118

Changing Men (NS)
Chapman 247
Chariot Victor Publishing 457
Chariton Review, The 119
Charleston Writers' Conference, The (NR)
Chat 387
Château de Lesvault 568
Chattahoochee Review, The 119
Chelsea 119
Chelsea Awards, The 495
Chevron Award and Writers Unlimited Award 496
Chicago Review 120
Chicano/Latino Literary Contest 496
Chickadee 349
Child Life 349
Child Study Children's Book Award (NR)
‡Children's Book Award, The 496
Children's Book Insider 584
Children's Digest 350
Children's Playmate 350
Chills (OB)
‡Chinook Press 401
‡Chinook Quarterly, The 261
Chiricú 120
Chiron Review 120
Christchurch Publishers Ltd. 446
Christian Century, The 350
Christian Courier 261
Christian Single 351
Christian Writers Conference (NR)
‡Christianity and the Arts 120
‡Christmas 401
Christopher Award, The 496
Christopher Newport University Writers' Conference (NR)
Chronicle Books 457
Chrysalis Reader 121
Cicada 121
Cimarron Review 121
Cimmerian Journal Tales of the Weird and Unusual, The (RR)
Cintas Fellowship (UF)
Circlet Press 401
Claremont Review, The 121
Clarion Science Fiction & Fantasy Writing Workshop 546
Clarion West Writers' Workshop 560
‡Clearing, The 568
‡Cleis Press 402
Climbing Art, The 122
Clockwatch Review 122
Cloverdale Press Inc. (ED)
‡Clubhouse 351
‡Cobblestone 351

Cochran's Corner (NR)
Coffee House Press 402
CoffeeHouse (OB)
Cold-Drill Magazine 262
Collages and Bricolages 122
Colorado Christian Writers Conference (NR)
‡Colorado Review 123
Columbia: A Journal of Literature & Art 123
Columbine (see Fawcett 463)
Columbus Writers Conference, The 546
‡Come Write With Us 557
‡Commando 387
Common Lives/Lesbian Lives (NR)
Commonwealth Club of California 496
Communities Magazine 262
Companion in Zeor, A 310
Companion Magazine 352
Compenions 123
Computoredge 352
Concho River Review 124
Conduit 124
Confluence 124
Confluence Press Inc. 402
Confrontation 125
Conmocion (UC)
Connecticut Commission on the Arts Artist Fellowships 496
‡Conseil de la Vie Francaise en Amérique/Prix Champlain 496
‡Constable And Company 484
Contact Advertising 352
Contemporary Books (RR)
Context South 125
Cook Communications (see Chariot Victor 457)
Cool Hand Communications, Inc. 403
Copyright Workshop 550
Cornerstone Magazine 352
Corona 125
Cosmic Landscapes 310
Cosmic Unicorn, The 262
Cosmopolitan Magazine 353
Coteau Books 403
Council for Wisconsin Writers Annual Writing Contest (NR)
Country Woman 353
‡Crab Creek Review 126
Craft of Writing 552
Crazyhorse (UF)
Crazyquilt 126
Cream City Review, The 126
Creative Arts Book Co. 403
Creative Challenges Literary Writing Competitions (NR)
‡Creative Forum 247

‡Creative Kids 353
Creative with Words Publications 403
Creativity Unlimited Press (NR)
Crescent Review, The 126
Crest (see Fawcett 463)
Cricket Magazine 354
Crime Writers' Association Awards (NR)
‡Cripes! 127
Critic Biannual Short Story Contest, The (RR)
Crocodile Books USA (see Interlink 470)
Cross-Cultural Communications 404
Crossroads 310
Crossway Books 457
Crow Quarterly Review 584
Crowbar Press (OB)
‡Crown Publishing Group, The 460 (also see
    Harmony Books 468)
Crucible 127
Crucible Poetry and Fiction Competition, The
    496
Crusader Magazine (NR)
Crystal River Press (NR)
Cumberland Valley Fiction Writers Workshop
    539
‡Curriculum Vitae 311
Curry Hill Plantation Writer's Retreat 569
Cutbank (NR)
CWM (NR)

D
‡Dagger Mystery Contest 496
Dagger of the Mind 263
Dalhousie Review, The 127
Daly City Poetry and Short Story Contest 497
DAM, Disability Arts Magazine (NR)
Dan River Anthology 127
Daniel and Company, Publishers, John 404
‡Daniel's Faux Faulkner Contest, The Jack
    497
‡Dark Horizons 301
Dark Horse Comics, Inc. 460
Dark Kiss (NS)
Dark Regions 263
‡Dark Tome 311
Daughters of Nyx (OB)
Davids' Place Journal 128
Davidson's Writer's Seminar, Peter 550
Daw Books, Inc. 460
Dawnwood Press (RR)
de Angeli Prize, Marguerite 497
‡Dead Lines Magazines 264
Dead of Night™ Magazine 311
Deathrealm 264
Deep South Writers' Conference (NR)

Del Rey Books (NR)
Delacorte Press (see Dell Publishing 460)
Delacorte Press Annual Prize for a First
    Young Adult Novel 497
Delacorte/Dell Books for Young Readers 460
    (also see Bantam/Doubleday/Dell 455)
Delaware Division of the Arts 497
Dell Publishing 460
Dell Yearling (see Bantam/Doubleday/Dell
    Books for Young Readers 455)
Delphinium Books 405
Delta (see Dell Publishing 460)
Denver Quarterly 128
Depth Charge (OB)
Descant (CN) (NR)
Descant (TX) (RR)
Desert Writers Workshop/Canyonlands Field
    Institute (NR)
Dexter Review Writing Competition, The
    (UF)
Dial Books for Young Readers 461
Dial Press (see Dell Publishing 460)
‡Dialogue 354
Diliman Review (NR)
Disability Rag & Resource, The (NR)
‡Discoveries 354
‡Discovery 355
Disturbed Guillotine (NR)
Diversions 312
Djerassi Resident Artists Program 569
Djinni 128
Dodobobo 128
Dogwood Tales Magazine 129
Doherty Associates, Thomas (see Forge
    Books 464)
Dorchester Publishing (see Leisure Books
    471, Love Spell 473)
Dorland Mountain Arts Colony 569
Dorset Colony House for Writers 569
Dos Passos Prize for Literature, John 497
Doubleday (NR)
Doubleday Canada Limited 461
‡Down There Press 405
DownEast Maine Writer's Workshops 534
Downstate Story 129
Dragon® Magazine 355
Dragonfly Books (see Knopf Books for Young
    Readers 471)
Dream Forge The Electronic Magazine for
    Your Mind! (NR)
Dream International/Quarterly 264
Dreams & Nightmares 312
Dreams & Visions 265
Dreams from the Strangers' Cafe (NR)
‡Dreams of Decadence 312

Drinkin' Buddy Magazine, The 313
‡Drop Forge 129
Drummer 355
Duckworth & Co. Ltd., Gerald (NR)
Duke University Writers' Workshop (NR)
Dundurn Press 405
Dutton Signet 461 (also see Roc 479)

E

E.M. Press, Inc. 405
Eagle's Flight 130
Eakin Press 461
Earth-Love Publishing House Ltd. 406
Earthsongs 265
Eastern Kentucky University Creative Writing
     Conference 547
Eastern Writers' Conference 535
Easyriders Magazine 355
Easy-to-Read Books (see Dial Books for
     Young Readers 461)
Eaton Literary Associates' Literary Awards
     Program 497
Ecco Press, The 406
Echoes 130
‡Eclipse 313
Ecopress 406
‡Eddie 301
Edinburgh University Centre for Continuing
     Education Creative Writing Workshops
     564
‡Eerdmans Publishing Co., Wm. B. 462
Eidos 313
8 130
1812 131
Eighth Mt. Press, The 406
Ekstasis Editions 407
Eldritch Tales 265
Elephant-Ear, The (NR)
Elf: Eclectic Literary Forum 131
Ellery Queen's Mystery Magazine 356
Ellis Awards, Arthur 498
Ellis Publishing, Aidan 446
‡Eloquent Umbrella, The 266
Emerge Magazine 356
Emerging Lesbian Writers Fund Awards 498
Emphasis on Faith and Living 356
‡Empty 314
Emrys Journal 131
Entelechy the Chronicle of the New Renais-
     sance (NR)
‡Epitaph 266
Epoch Magazine 132
Eriksson, Publisher, Paul S. 462
Erotic Stories (OB)

Esquire 357
Eureka Literary Magazine 132
Evangel 357
Evans & Co., Inc., M. 462
Event 132
Evergreen Chronicles, The 132
Every So Often. . . 133
Excursus 133
Explorations '97 133
Explorer Magazine 134
Expressions 134
Extreme, A Magazine for Three Finkers, The
     (NR)
Eyes 266
Eyster Prizes 498

F

Faber and Faber, Inc. 407
‡Faces 357
‡Factsheet Five 584
Fairbanks Arts (NR)
Fairbanks Arts Association (NR)
Fairview Summit Retreat House 569
Family Circle Mystery-Suspense Short Story
     Contest (RR)
Family, The (OB)
Fantagraphics Books 462
Far Gone (NR)
Faris Seminars for Beginners, Charlene 547
Farmer's Market, The 134
Farrar, Straus & Giroux 463
Farrar, Straus & Giroux/Children's Books 463
Fasa Corporation 407
Fassler Memorial Book Award, Joan 498
Fat Tuesday 135
Fathoms a Journal of Poetry and Prose (NR)
Faulkner Award for Excellence in Writing,
     Virginia 498
Faulkner Competition in Fiction, William 498
Fault Lines 135
Fawcett 463
‡Fayrdaw 314
FC2/Black Ice Books 407
FC2/Illinois State University National Fiction
     Competition 498
Federation Standard (OB)
Felicity (NR)
Fellowships/Writer-in-Residence 498
Feminist Bookstore News 584
Feminist Press at the City University of New
     York, The 408
Feminist Studies 136
Feminist Women's Writing Workshops, Inc.
     (NR)

Feminist Writer's Contest 499
Festival of the Written Arts (NR)
FiberOptic Etchings 267
Fiction 136
Fiction Furnace (NR)
Fiction International 136
Fiction Writer's Guideline (NR)
Fiction Writing Retreat in Acapulco 564
Fiddlehead, The (NR)
‡Fifth Di, The/Sixth Sense, The/Starflite 314
Fifty Something Magazine (RR)
Figurative Language Master Class, The 535
Filling Station (NR)
Fine Arts Work Center in Provincetown 535, 569
Fine, Inc., Donald I. 463
Firebrand Books 408
First Hand 357
First Word Bulletin (NR)
Fish Drum Magazine 136
Fish Memorial Award, Robert L. 499
Fish Stories 137
Fisher Award, Dorothy Canfield 499
Fisher Writers Conference, Dorothy Canfield 535
Fishtrap Gathering: Writing in the West Winter and Summer (NR)
Flare Books 463 (also see Avon 452)
Flight of the Mind 561
Flipside 137
Florida Arts Council/Literature Fellowships 499
‡Florida Christian Writers Conference 544
Florida First Coast Writers' Festival 544
Florida First Coast Writers' Festival Novel, Short Fiction & Poetry Awards 499
Florida Review, The 137
Florida Romance Writers' Annual Conference 544
Florida State Writing Competition 499
Florida Suncoast Writers' Conference 544
Florida Wildlife 358
Flummery Press, The (NR)
‡Flying Horse 137
Flying Island, The 138
Folio: A Literary Journal 138
Foolscap (OB)
Footwork 138
Foresight 301
‡Forge Books 464
Fort Concho Museum Press Literary Festival (NR)
Fort Dearborn Press (ED)
‡Fortress 315
Forum 387

Foster City International Writers Contest (NR)
Foundation for the Advancement of Canadian Letters Canadian Letters Award 499
‡Foundations of Creativity® Writing Workshop, The 535
Four Directions, The (RR)
Four Walls Eight Windows 408
‡Fourteen Hills 139
Francis Short Story Award, H.E. 500
Frank 247
Franklin Literary Award, Miles 500
Fraser Award, Souerette Diehl 500
Frayed (NR)
Free Focus/Ostentatious Mind 267
‡Free Spirit 267
‡French Bread Awards 500
Friend Magazine, The 358
‡Friends United Press 408
Frogmore Papers, The 247
‡Frontiers 139
‡Frontiers in Writing Conference 553
Fudge Cake, The 268
Fuel Magazine 315
Fugue 139
Full Clip: A Magazine of Mystery & Suspense (OB)
Full-Time Dads 315
Funniest Women in the World Contest (NR)

G

G.W. Review, The 140
Galaxy Magazine (NR)
Gallery Magazine (NR)
Garden State Horror Writers 578
Gathering of the Tribes, A 140
Gay Chicago Magazine 268
Gay Sunshine Press and Leyland Publications 408
Gell Writers Center of the Finger Lakes, The 570
Gem, The 358
‡Generator 316
Genre Writer's Association (GWA) 578
Gent 358
Georgetown Review 140
Georgetown Review Short Story and Poetry Contest (NR)
Georgia Council for the Arts Individual Artist Grants (RR)
‡Georgia Journal 359
Georgia Review, The 140
Gessler Publishing Company 464
Gettysburg Review, The 141

Ghana Publishing Corporation, Publishing Division 484
Ghosts & Scholars 248
‡Gibbs Smith, Publisher/Peregrine Smith 409
Gila Writers' conference (NR)
Glass Cherry, The 141
Glimmer Train Stories 142
Glimmer Train's Short-Story Award for New Writers 500
‡Global Tapestry Journal 301
Globe Fearon 464
‡GMP Publishers Ltd. 446
Godine, Publisher, Inc., David R. 464
Going Down Swinging (NR)
Gold and Treasure Hunter (NR)
Gold Eagle (see Harlequin 467)
Gold Medal (see Fawcett 463)
Gold Medallion Book Awards (NR)
Golden Books Family Entertainment Inc. 464
Golden Isis Magazine (OB)
Golden Triangle Writers Guild (NR)
‡Golf Journal 359
Good Housekeeping 359
Goodheart Prize for Fiction, Jeanne Charpiot 500
Goose Lane Editions 409
Gothic Journal (NR)
‡Gotta Write Network Litmag 585
Government of Newfoundland and Labrador Arts & Letters Competition (NR)
Goyen Prize for Fiction, The William (NR)
‡Grade School Press 409
Graffiti off the Asylum Walls 316
Grain 142
Grand Street 142
Grand Times 359
Grasslands Review 142
Graywolf Press 409
Great Lakes Colleges Association New Writers Award 500
Great Lakes Writer's Workshop 550
Great Plains Storytelling & Poetry Reading Contest 500
Green Egg 360
Green Hills Literary Lantern, The 143
Green Lake 1997 Writers Conference 551
Green Mountains Review 143
Green River Writers Contest 501
Green River Writers Novels-in-Progress Workshop 547
Green's Magazine 143
Greensboro Review 144
Greensboro Review Literary Awards, The 501
Greenwillow Books (see Lothrop, Lee & Shepard 472, William Morrow 474)

Griffon House Publications 410
Grosset & Dunlap, Inc. (RR)
Grosset (see G.P. Putnam's Sons 478)
Grotesque (NR)
Grue Magazine 268
Gryphon Publications 410
Guernica Editions 410
Guide Magazine (NR)
Guideposts for Kids 360
Gulf Coast 144
Gulf Coast Writers Conference at the University of Houston-Clear Lake 553
Gulf Stream Magazine 144
Gulliver Books (see Harcourt Brace & Co. 467)
Guthrie Centre at Annaghmakerrig, The Tyrone 570
Guys 361

H

Habersham Review (RR)
Hackney Literary Awards 501
Hadassah Magazine 361
Hale Limited, Robert 485
Half Tones to Jubliee 144
Hambidge Center, The 570
‡Hamish Hamilton Ltd. 485
Hammett Prize (North American) 501
Handshake Editions 446
Happy 145
Harcourt Brace & Co. 467
Harcourt Brace Children's Books (see Harcourt Brace & Co. 467)
Hard Row to Hoe Division (NR)
Hardboiled 269
Hardcore, The (NR)
Harlequin Enterprises, Ltd. 467 (also see Worldwide Library 483)
Harlequin Historicals (see Silhouette 481)
Harmony Books 468 (also see The Crown Publishing Group 460)
Harper 468
HarperCollins Children's Books 468
HarperCollins Publishers (New Zealand) Limited 485
HarperPaperbacks 468
HarperPrism 468
Harper's Magazine 361
Harvest House Publishers 468
Hathaway Prize, Baxter (OB)
Haunts 269
Havens for Creatives 585
Hawaii Pacific Review (NR)
Hawaii Review (NR)

‡Hawthornden Castle 570
Hayden's Ferry Review 145
Haystack Writing Program 561
‡Hazel Grove Musings 316
‡Headland Center for the Arts 570
‡Headline Book Publishing Ltd. 485
‡Healing Inn, The 269
Hearst Books (see William Morrow 474)
Hearst Corporation, The (see Avon Books 452)
Heart of America Writers' Conference 553
Heartland Prizes, The 501
Heartlands Today, The 145
Heaven Bone 145
Hecate 301
Hecate's Loom 269
Hedgebrook 571
Heights Writer's Conference, The 547
Heinz Literature Prize, Drue 501
‡Helicon Nine Editions 410
Heliocentric Net Anthology 319
Hemingway Days Short Story Competition 501
Hemingway Days Writer's Workshop and Conference 544
Hemingway Foundation/Pen Award For First Fiction, Ernest 501
Hemkunt 447
Henry Awards, The O. (NR)
Herald Press (NS)
Herbooks (NS)
Heroic Times 319
High Adventure (NR)
High Plains Literary Review 146
Highland Summer Conference 542
Highlights Foundation Writers Workshop at Chautauqua 539
Highlights for Children 361, 502
Hilai Residencies (NR)
Hill and Holler 146
Hill & Wang (see Farrar, Straus & Giroux 463)
hip MAMA 319
Hitchcock Mystery Magazine, Alfred 362
Hobson's Choice 319
Hodder Fellowship, The Alfred 502
Hoepfner Award, Theodore Christian 502
Hofstra University Summer Writers' Conference (NR)
Hogrefe Fellowship, Pearl 502
Holiday House, Inc. 469
Hollow Earth Publishing 411
Holt & Company, Henry 469
Home Girl Press 320
Home Life 362

Home Office Opportunities (NR)
Home Planet News 146
Home Times 362
Honolulu Magazine/Borders Books & Music Fiction Contest 502
Hopewell Review, The 147
Hopscotch: The Magazine for Girls 270
Horizon 248
‡Horizons 363
‡Horror Writers Association 578
‡Hor-Tasy 270
Hot Shots (NR)
Houghton Mifflin Company 469
‡House of Anansi Press 411
Housewife-Writer's Forum 271
Housewife-Writer's Forum Short Story Contest 502
Hrafnhoh 248
HU (The Honest Ulsterman) 248
Hubbard's Writers of the Future Contest, L. Ron 502
"Hugo" Award (Science Fiction Achievement Award), The (NR)
Humpty Dumpty's Magazine 363
Hunted News, The 147
Hurricane Alice 271
Hurston/Richard Wright Award, Zora Neale 502
Hustler (NS)
Hustler Busty Beauties 363
Hyperion 470
‡Hyphen Magazine 147

I

i.e. magazine 148
‡Ice Cube Press 411
Iconoclast, The 148
Idiom 23 (NR)
‡Idiot, The 148
‡idiot wind 320
Illinois Arts Council Artists Fellowships 503
Illinois Review, The (OB)
‡Illumination Publishing Co. 411
‡Image 149
Imagination 548
Imago 248
‡Implosion 149
‡In the Spirit of the Buffalo 149
In Touch for Men 363
India Currents 364
India Papers, Short Stories by Middle and High School Authors, The (NR)
Indian Life Magazine (NR)
Indian Literature 248

Indian Writer (NR)
Indiana Review 150
Indiana University Writers' Conference (NR)
Inland Empire Christian Writers Guild 557
Inner Voices 271
Inside (NR)
‡Insomniac Press 412
‡Interim 150
Interlink Publishing Group, Inc. 470
International Association of Crime Writers
    (North American Branch) 578
International Film Workshops, The (NR)
International Janusz Korczak Literary Com-
    petition 503
International Music Camp Creative Writing
    Workshop 551
International Quarterly 150
International Reading Association Children's
    Book Awards 503
International Writers Contest (NR)
Interrace Magazine (NR)
Interzone 387
Into the Darkness (NR)
Intrigue (see Harlequin 467)
‡Intrigue Press 412
Intuitive Explorations 272
Inverted-A, Inc. (RR)
Iowa Review, The 153
Iowa School of Letters Award for Short Fic-
    tion, The John Simmons Short Fiction
    Award 503
Iowa Summer Writing Festival 551
Iowa Woman 153
Iowa Woman Contest, International Writing
    Contest 503
Ireland's Own (NR)
Iris (VA) 153
Iron Magazine 248
‡Ironweed Press 412
‡Island 249
Isle Royale Artist-in-Residence Program
    (NR)
Italian Americana 272
‡Italica Press 413
It's Your Choice Magazine 272
I've Always Wanted to Write But . . . 557
Ivy (see Fawcett 463)
‡Ivy League Press, Inc. 413
IWWG Early Spring in California Conference
    (NR)
IWWG New Jersey Conference (NR)
IWWG Summer Conference 536

J

Jacaranda (NR)
Jack and Jill 364
Jack, Mackerel Magazine 320
Jackson Award, Joseph Henry 504
Jambalaya Magazine (UF)
James Fellowship for the Novel in Progress
    504
Jameson Books 470
Janus, A Journal of Literature 153
Japan Foundation Artists Fellowship Program
    504
Japanophile 154
Japanophile Short Story Contest 504
Jefferson Cup (NR)
Jeopardy 154
Jesperson Press Ltd. 413
Jewish Currents Magazine 273
Jewish Quarterly 302
Jive, Black Confessions, Black Romance,
    Bronze Thrills, Black Secrets 364
Jones Award for Fiction (book), Jesse 504
Jones First Novel Fellowship, James 504
Jones University Press, Bob 413
Journal, The (Ohio) 155
Journal, The (Pennsylvania) 155
Journal of Polymorphous Perversity 273
Jove (see the Berkley Publishing Group 455)
Juggler's World 365
Junior Trails 365
Juniper (see Fawcett 463)
Just Buffalo Literary Center, Inc. (NR)
Just Write 155

K

Kafka Prize For Fiction By An American
    Woman, The Janet Heidinger 504
Kalani Honua 571
Kaleidoscope 156
Kalliope 156
‡Kansas Quarterly/Arkansas Review 156
Kar-Ben Copies Inc. 414
Karma Lapel 321
Karnak House (NR)
‡Katha: Indian American Fiction Contest 507
Kawabata Press 447
‡Keats/Kerlan Collection Memorial Fellow-
    ship, Ezra Jack 507
‡Keen Science Fiction! 321
Kelsey Review 157
‡Keltic Fringe 273
Kennedy Book Awards, Robert F. 507
Kennesaw Review 157
Kensington Publishing Corp. 470

Kentucky Arts Council, Kentucky Artists Fellowships 507
Kenyon Review, The 157
Kerem 158
Kerouac Literary Prize, Jack (NR)
Kestrel 158
Key West Literary Seminar 545
Khan Prize for Fiction, Aga 507
‡Kick It Over 321
Kids' World 321
Killer Frog Contest 508
Kinesis 158
Kiosk 158
‡Kitchen Table: Women of Color Press 414
Knopf, Alfred A. 470 (also see Random House 479)
Knopf Books for Young Readers 471
Korean Literature Translation Award (NR)
Krax Magazine 302
Kumquat Meringue (RR)

L

La Kancerkliniko 249
Lactuca 159
Lacunae 274
Ladies' Home Journal 365
Ladybug 366
Lady's Circle 366
Lakewood Community College Writers' Seminar (NR)
Lambda Book Report 585
L'Amour Western Magazine, Louis (OB)
Lamplight, The 159
Lamp-Post, The 159
Landfall/Oxford University Press 249
Latino Literature Prize 508
Laughing Times (NR)
Laurel (see Dell Publishing 460)
Laurel Review, The 160
Laurel-Leaf (see Bantam/Doubleday/Dell Books for Young Readers 455)
Lawrence Foundation Prize 508
Le Prix Molson De L'Academie Des Lettres Du Quebec (NR)
Leacock Medal for Humour, Stephen 508
Ledge Poetry and Fiction Magazine, The (RR)
Lee & Low Books 414
Left Bank (RR)
Left Curve 274
Legal Fiction (RR)
Leighton Studios, The Banff Centre 571
Leisure Books 471
Lemeac Editeur Inc. 414
Lerner Publications Company 471

Les Grands Prix Du Journal De Montreal (OB)
Lester Publishing Limited (NR)
Letras De Oro Spanish Literary Prizes (OB)
Letter Parade, The 322
Liberty 274
Libido 160
‡Licking River Review, The 160
Light Quarterly 161
Lighthouse (NR)
Ligonier Valley Writers Conference (NR)
Liguorian 366
Lilith Magazine (NR)
Lilliput Press, The (NR)
Lime Green Bulldozers 322
Limestone: A Literary Journal 161
Lincoln Springs Press 415
Lines In The Sand 161
Lines in the Sand Short Fiction Contest 508
‡Linington Lineup 275
Linq (NR)
‡Lintel 415
Lion Publishing (see Chariot Victor Publishing 457)
Liquid Ohio Voice of the Unheard (NR)
Lite (RR)
Literal Latté 162
Literary Fragments 162
Literary Review, The 162
Literary Rocket 163
Literature and Belief Writing Contest (NR)
Literature Bureau, The 447
Little, Brown and Company 471
Little, Brown and Company Children's Books 472
Little Rooster (see Bantam/Doubleday/Dell Books for Young Readers 455)
Little Simon 472
Live 367
Livingston Press 415
Locus 585
Lodestar Books 472
Loft-McKnight Writers Awards 508
Lollipop Power Books 415
London Magazine (NR)
London Review of Books (NR)
London Writers' Conference, Jack 557
Long Fiction Contest 508
Long Publishing Co., Hendrick 416
‡Long Story, The 163
Longneck, The (NR)
Longstreet Press (RR)
‡Lonsdale, The 249
Looking Ahead-NAPA, A Monthly Publication for Active Retirees (NR)

Lookout, The 367
Loonfeather 163
Loop, The (RR)
Los Angeles Times Book Prizes (NR)
Lost and Found Times 164
Lost Worlds 275
Lothrop, Lee & Shepard Books 472 (also see
    William Morrow & Company 474)
Louisiana Literary Award 508
Louisiana Literature 164
Louisville Review, The 164
Love Spell 473
‡Loveprints Novelettes 416
Loveswept 473 (also see Bantam 455)
‡Loving Alternatives Magazine 276
Loving Magazine (NR)
Lowell Pearl, The (NR)
LSU/Southern Review Short Fiction Award
    (NR)
Lucas/Evans Books, Inc. (ED)
Lucky Heart Books 416
‡Lullwater Review 164
Luna Negra 165
Lutheran Journal, The (NR)
Lutterworth Press, The 447
Lynx Eye 165

M

McCall's (RR)
McCarthy Prize in Short Fiction, Mary 509
MacDowell Colony, The 571
‡McElderry Books, Margaret K. 473
McGinnis Memorial Award, The John H. 509
MacGuffin, The 165
McKean Moore Writer in Washington, Jenny
    509
‡McKee's Story Structure, Robert 557
McLeod Literary Prize, The Enid 509
McMillan Library U.S.A. (see Thorndike
    Press 482)
Macmillan Publishing Co, Inc. (NS)
Macmurray & Beck, Inc. 416
Macrae Books, Julia (NR)
Mademoiselle Magazine (RR)
‡Madison Review, The 166
Madwoman Press 417
‡Maelstrom 302
Mage Publishers 417
Maggie Award 509
Magic Changes (NR)
Magic Realism 166
Magic-Realism Magazine Short-Fiction
    Award 509
Mail Call 276

Majestic Books 276
Making Waves With Writers 561
Malahat Review 166
Malice Domestic Grant 510
Malvern Publishing Co. Ltd., The (NR)
Mangrove 166
Manhattanville College Writers' Week 536
Manitoba Arts Council Support to Individual
    Artists 510
‡Manitoba Writers' Guild 578
manna 167
Manoa 167
Manscape 367
Manushi 249
Many Leaves One Tree, Stories of the Surviv-
    ing Spirit (NS)
Many Mountains Moving 167
‡Maple Woods Community College Writer's
    Conference 554
Marin Arts Council Individual Artist Grants
    (NR)
Marion Writers' Conference, Francis (NR)
Maritime Writers' Workshop 562
Mark 168
Maroverlag (NR)
Marten Bequest Award, The (NR)
Marvin Grant, Walter Rumsey 510
Maryland Review 168
Massachusetts Cultural Council Artist Grants
    (NR)
Massachusetts Review, The 168
Massacre (NR)
Massage 367
Masters Literary Award 510
Matriarch's Way; Journal of Female Suprem-
    acy 168
Mattoid 249
Mature Living (NR)
Mature Years 368
Maverick Press, The 169
Meanjin (NR)
Medicinal Purposes 277
Medina-Wayne Writers Conference (OB)
Mediphors 277
Medley of Pens (RR)
‡Medusa's Hairdo Magazine 322
Memories into Stories (NR)
Men as We Are (OB)
Mendocino Coast Writers Conference (NR)
Mentor (Kansas) 277
Mentor (New York) (see Dutton Signet 461)
Mentor Award, The 510
Mentors Writers' Conference in Eugene, The
    (NR)
Mercury Press, The 417

Meridian (see Dutton Signet 461)
Merlana's Magickal Messages 278
Merlyn's Pen 169
Meshuggah (OB)
‡Message Magazine 368
Messenger of the Sacred Heart 368
Metcalf Body of Work Award, The Vicky 510
Metcalf Short Story Award, Vicky 510
Metro Singles Lifestyles 369
Metropolitan Writers Conference 539
Michigan Author Award 511
Michigan Quarterly Review 169
Mid South Writers Festival 542
Mid-American Review 170
Mid-Atlantic Mystery Book Fair & Convention 540
Midland Authors' Award 511
Midland Review 170
Midland Writers Conference 548
Mid-List Press 418
Mid-List Press First Series Award for Short Fiction 511
Mid-List Press First Series Award for the Novel 511
Midnight in Hell (NR)
Midstream (NR)
Midwest Writers' Conference (NR)
Midwest Writers Workshop 548
Milkweed Editions 418
Milkweed Editions National Fiction Prize 511
Milkweed Editions Prize For Children's Literature 511
Millay Colony for the Arts 571
Millennium 485
Mills & Boon (NR)
‡Mills Annual Children's Writer's Conference 557
Milner Award, The (NR)
Mimsy Musing (OB)
Minas Tirith Evening-Star 170
Mind Book of the Year, The Allen Lane Award (NR)
Mind in Motion 171
Mind Matters Review 171
Mindsparks 278
Ministry Today (NR)
Mink Hills Journal (NR)
Minnesota Review, The 171
‡Minnesota State Arts Board/Artist Assistance Fellowship 511
Minnesota Voices Project 511
Minority Literary Expo the Journal (NR)
Miraculous Medal, The 278
Mississippi Arts Commission Artist Fellowship Grant 512

‡Mississippi Mud 171
Mississippi Review 172
Mississippi Valley Writers Conference 548
Missouri Review Editors' Prize Contest, The 512
Missouri Review, The 172
Mr. Christie's Book Award 512
Mobil Pegasus Prize 512
Mobius 172
Moccasin Telegraph 278
‡modern words 173
Mohonk's Writers Retreat 536
Money for Women (NR)
Monocacy Valley Review, The (OB)
Monolith Magazine Science Fiction Stories and Computer Games (NR)
Montana Arts Council First Book Award (NR)
Montana Arts Council Individual Artist Fellowship (OB)
Montana Book Awards (NR)
Montana Senior Citizens News (NR)
Montgomery PEI Children's Literature Award, L.M. (NR)
Monthly Independent Tribune Times Journal Post Gazette News Chronicle Bulletin, The 323
Montrose Christian Writer's Conference 540
‡Moody Street Review, The 173
Moonlight and Magnolias Writer's Conference (NR)
Moore Community Workshops, Jenny McKean 540
More Dead Trees (NR)
Morrow And Company, Inc., William 474 (also see Lothrop, Lee & Shepard 472)
Morrow Junior Books 474
Mostly Maine (OB)
Mother Courage Press (RR)
Mount Hermon Christian Writers Conference 558
Mountain Luminary 279
‡Mountain State Press 418
Mower, The (NR)
Moyer Bell Limited 420
Ms 369
Mulberry Books (see William Morrow 474)
Multnomah Books 474
‡Murderous Intent 279
Musing Place, The 173
Musk Gland Sally, 21st Century Zine for Grrrls (NR)
"My Favorite Holiday Story" Competition 512
My Friend 369
‡My Legacy 279

My Retreat 572
My Weekly Story Library 485
Mysterious Press, The 474
Mysterious Wysteria (NR)
Mystery Mayhem Contest 512
Mystery Review, The 585
Mystery Time 279
Mystery Writers of America 578
Mystic Fiction (NR)
Mythic Circle, The 173

N

N.A.L.L. Association 572
‡NA'AMAT Woman 369
Naiad Press, Inc., The 421
Naked Kiss 280
Nassau Review 174
National Book Council/Banjo Awards (NR)
National Book Foundation, Inc. 513
National Chapter of Canada IODE, Violet
  Downey Book Award, The (NR)
National Endowment for the Arts Creative
  Writing Fellowship 513
National Federation of the Blind Writer's Di-
  vision Fiction Contest 513
National Fiction Competition 513
National Foundation for Advancement in the
  Arts, Arts Recognition and Talent Search
  (ARTS) (NR)
National Jewish Book Awards (NR)
National League of American Pen Women
  543, 579
National Writers Association 579
National Writers Association Annual Novel
  Writing Contest 513
National Writers Association Annual Short
  Story Contest 513
National Writers Association Conference 554
National Writers Union (NR)
National Written & Illustrated by . . . Awards
  Contest for Students, The 513
Nautical & Aviation Publishing Co. of
  America Inc., The 421
Nebo 174
Nebraska Review, The 174
Negative Capability Short Fiction Competi-
  tion 514
Nelson Biblical Reference Publishing (see
  Thomas Nelson 477)
‡Nelson Publishers, Thomas 477
‡Neologisms 175
nerve 175
Neustadt International Prize for Literature 514

Nevada State Council on the Arts Artists' Fel-
  lowships 514
‡New Contrast 249
New Delta Review (NR)
New England Review 175
New England Writers' Workshop at Simmons
  College (NR)
New Era Magazine 370
New Era Writing, Art, Photography and Mu-
  sic Contest, The 514
New Europam (NR)
New Frontier 280
New Frontiers 280
New Hampshire State Council on the Arts In-
  dividual Artist Fellowship 514
New Hampshire Writers and Publishers Proj-
  ect 579
New Hope International 249
New Jersey Romance Writers Put Your Heart
  in a Book Conference 540
New Jersey State Council on the Arts Prose
  Fellowship (UF)
New Laurel Review 176
New Letters Literary Award 514
New Letters Magazine 176
New Letters Weekend Writers Conference,
  The 554
New Methods 281
‡New Millennium Writings 514
New Mystery (NR)
New Orleans Review 176
New Press Literary Quarterly, The 176
New Quarterly, The (RR)
New Readers Press (see Signal Hill Publica-
  tions 480)
new renaissance, the 177
New Rivers Press 421
New Victoria Publishers 422
New Voices in Poetry and Prose (NR)
New Voices in Poetry and Prose Spring and
  Fall Competition (NR)
‡New Welsh Review 250
New Writer's Magazine 585
‡New Writing 177
‡New Writing Award 514
New York Foundation for the Arts Fellowship
  515
New York Mills Arts Retreat 572
New York State Edith Wharton Citation of
  Merit 515
New Yorker, The 370
Newbery Award, John 515
NeWest Publishers Ltd. 422
NeWest Review 178
Newport Writers Conference 536

Next Phase 281
Nexus (NR)
NFB Writer's Fiction Contest 515
‡Nicetown 422
‡Night Dreams 302
Night Shadows (NR)
Nightmare Express, The (NR)
Nightmares 281
Nightshade Press 422
Nightsun 178
‡Nilon Excellence in Minority Fiction Award, Charles H. and N. Mildred 515
Nimrod 178
96 Inc. 178
Nite-Writer's International Literary Arts Journal 179
Nocturnal Ecstasy 323
Nocturnal Lyric, The 281
Noma Award for Publishing in Africa, The (NR)
Nonpareil Books (see David R. Godine 464)
Nonsense, "Hofstra Univerity's Only Intentional Humor Magazine" (NR)
Non-Stop Science Fiction Magazine 282
Noonday Press, The (see Farrar, Straus & Giroux 463)
‡Norcroft: A Writing Retreat for Women 572
North American Native Authors First Book Award 515
North American Review, The 179
North Atlantic Review (NR)
North Carolina Arts Council Fellowship 515
North Carolina Arts Council Residencies 516
North Carolina Writers' Network 579
North Carolina Writers' Network Fall Conference 543
North Carolina Writers' Network Scholarships 516
North Dakota Quarterly 179
North Point Press (see Farrar, Straus & Giroux 463)
Northeast (NR)
Northeast Arts Magazine 179
Northeast Corridor 180
Northern Contours (NR)
Northwest Christian Writers Conference (NR)
Northwest Oklahoma Workshop 554
Northwest Review 180
Northwood University Alden B. Dow Creativity Center (NR)
Northwoods Journal 180
Northwords, The Journal of Canadian Content in Speculative Literature (NR)
Norton & Company, Inc., W.W. 477
Norwegian Literature Abroad Grant 516

Nova SF 388
‡NRG Associates 423
‡NTPWA Annual Poetry & Fiction Contest 516
Nugget 370
‡#11, The 323
Nu*Real 370
Nuthouse 324
‡Nyx Obscura Magazine 181

O

Oak, The 282
‡Oakland University Writers' Conference 548
‡Oasis (England) 250
Oasis (Florida) 181
‡Oatmeal & Poetry 181
Obelesk Books 423
Obsidian II: Black Literature in Review 182
O'Connor Award for Short Fiction, The Flannery 516
O'Connor Fiction Award, Frank 516
‡Odyssey (conference) 537
Odyssey (magazine) 371
Of Dark & Stormy Nights 548
‡Of Unicorns and Space Stations 324
Office Number One 324
Ogalala Review, The (RR)
O'Hagan Award for Short Fiction, Howard 516
Ohio Review, The 182
‡Ohio State University Press 423
‡Ohio Writer 585
Ohio Writers' Holiday 549
Ohioana Award for Children's Literature, Alice Wood Memorial 516
Ohioana Book Awards 517
Okanagan Short Fiction Award, The 517
Oklahoma Fall Arts Institutes 554
‡Oklahoma Writers' Workshop 555
Old Chatham Fiction Workshop (NR)
Old Crow Review 182
Old Red Kimono, The 182
Olive Branch Press (see Interlink 470)
Oliver-Nelson Books (see Thomas Nelson 477)
Olympia Review, The (NR)
Ommation Press Book Award (NR)
Omni 371
On Spec 282
On the Line 371
Once Upon a World 325
One Hundred Suns (NR)
Onionhead 183
Ontario Review Press 423

Onyx (see Dutton Signet 461)
Oops Award 517
Open Voice Awards 517
Options 372
Opus Magnum Discovery Awards 517
Oracle Story 183
Orange Blossom Fiction Contest 517
Orange Coast Magazine 372
Orange Coast Review (NR)
Orca Book Publishers Ltd. 423
Oregon East (NR)
‡Oregon Individual Artist Fellowship 517
Oregon Writers Colony 572
Orient Paperbacks 485
Other Voices 183
Other Worlds 283
Otisian Directory 325
Our Child Press 424
Ouroboros (NR)
‡Out of the Cradle 184
Outdoor Writers Association of America Annual Conference 540
‡Outer Darkness 325
Outerbridge 184
‡Outlaw Biker 372
Outrider Press 424
Overlook Press, The 424
Overseas (NR)
Owen Publishers, Peter (NR)
Owen Wister Review (NR)
Oxford American, The (NR)
Oxford Magazine 184
Oxygen 185
Ozark Creative Writers, Inc. (NR)
‡Ozarks Writers League 580

P

Pablo Lennis 326
Pacific Coast Journal 185
Pacific Northwest Writers Summer Conference (NR)
Pacific Review 185
Pagan Review, The (NR)
Painted Bride Quarterly 186
Paisano Fellowships, Dobie 517
‡Palace Corbie 186
Palisades (see Questar 478)
Palm Springs Writers' Conference (NR)
Palo Alto Review 186
Panache Press (see Random House 479)
‡P&K Stark Productions, Inc. 424
Pangolin Papers 187
‡Panopticon 326
Pantheon Books 477

Panurge (OB)
‡Paper Radio 187
‡Paperplates 187
Papier-Mache Press 424
‡Papyrus Magazine 283
Papyrus Publishers & Letterbox Literary Service 425
Parabola (NR)
Paradox Magazine 283
Paradoxist Literary Movement, The 283
Paragraph (NR)
Paramour Magazine 188
Paris Review, The 188
Paris Transcontinental 250
Paris Writers' Workshop/WICE (NR)
Paris/Atlantic (NR)
Parting Gifts 188
Partisan Review 188
Pasadena Writers' Forum (NR)
Passager 191
‡Passages North 191
Patchen Competition, Kenneth 518
Path Press, Inc. 425
‡Pavlov Neruda/Manuslave Press 191
PBW 326
Peace Magazine 328
Peachtree Publishers, Ltd. 425
Pearl 192
Pearl Short Story Contest 518
Pearson Award, Judith Siegel 518
Peden Prize in Fiction, William 518
Pegasus Review, The 192
Pelican Publishing Company 477
Pembroke Magazine 192
Pemmican Publications 425
PEN Center USA West Literary Award in Fiction 518
PEN/Book-of-the-Month Club Translation Prize 518
Pendle Hill 572
PEN/Faulkner Award for Fiction, The 518
Penguin USA 478 (also see Dial Books for Young Readers 461, Dutton Signet 461, Lodestar 472, Roc 479)
Pen/Norma Klein Award 518
Pennsylvania Council on the Arts, Fellowship Program (NR)
Pennsylvania English 192
PeopleNet, Disability DateNet Home Page 329
People's Friend 388
Pequod a Journal of Contemporary Literature and Literary Criticism (NR)
Perception Writings (NR)
Perceptions 284

Peregrine 193
Perigree (see G.P. Putnam's Sons 478)
‡Permanent Press/Second Chance Press 425
Permeable Press 426
Phact Sheet Newsletter of the Philadelphia Association for Critical Thinking (OB)
Phantasm (CA) 193
Phantasm (IL) 284
Phelan Award, James D. 519
Philadelphia Writers Organization 580
Philip Publishers, David 447
Philomel Books 478
Phoebe (New York) 193
Phoebe (Virginia) 194
Pica 329
‡Picador 486
Pied Piper Books (see Dial Books for Young Readers 461)
Pieper Publishing 426
Pig Iron 194
Pig Iron Literary & Art Works, Inc. 580
Pikeville Review 194
‡Pillow Talk 372
Pima Writers' Workshop 558
Pineapple Press 427
Pink Chameleon, The 195
Pinnacle Books 478
Pipe Smoker's Ephemeris, The 284
Pippin Press 427
Pirate Writings 284
PKA'S Advocate (formerly The Advocate) (NR)
Place to Enter, A 195
PLANET-The Welsh Internationalist 250
Playboy College Fiction Contest 519
Playboy Magazine 373
Plaza, The 250
‡Pleiades 195
Pleiades Magazine/Philae (ED)
Ploughshares 196
Plowman, The 196
‡Plum Review Fiction Contest, The 519
Plume (see Dutton Signet 461)
‡Plurilingual Europe/Europe Plurilingue 250
Pocket Books (see Simon & Schuster 481)
Pockets 373
Pockets Fiction Writing Contest 519
Poe Awards, Edgar Allan 519
‡Poetic Space 196
Poetry Forum Short Stories 197
‡Poetry in Motion Magazine 197
Poetry WLU 197
Poets & Writers 585
Poet's Fantasy 197
Pointed Circle, The 198

Poor Katy's Almanac, Home of Pulp Fiction and More! (NR)
‡Porcupine Literary Arts Magazine 198
Port Townsend Writers' Conference (NR)
Portable Wall, The (NR)
Porter International, Bern (NR)
Porter Prize for Fiction, Katherine Anne 519
Portland Magazine 373
Portland Review 198
Portland State University Haystack Writing Program (NR)
Poseidon Books (see Simon & Schuster 481)
Poskisnolt Press 285
Possibilitiis Literary Arts Magazine (NR)
Post, The 285
Post-Apollo Press, The 427
Postmodern Culture (RR)
Potato Eyes 198
Potomac Review 199
Potpourri 199
Pottersfield Portfolio, The 200
Power and Light 373
Power Tool (NR)
Powerplay Magazine 374
‡Prague Review, The 251
Prairie Dog 200
Prairie Fire 200
Prairie Journal of Canadian Literature, The 201
Prairie Journal Press 427
Prairie Publishing Company, The 427
Prairie Schooner 201
Prairie Schooner, The Lawrence Foundation Award 519
‡Prayerworks 285
Premonitions 302
Prep Publishing 428
Presidio La Bahia Award, The 519
‡Presidio Press 478
‡Press 201
Press Gang Publishers 428
Primavera 202
Prime Time Sports and Fitness (NR)
Prism International Short Fiction Contest 520
Prism (see HarperPaperbacks 468)
Prism International 202
Prisoners of the Night 285
‡Private Letters 374
Prix Littéraire Champlain 520
Processed World (NR)
Professionalism in Writing School (OB)
Prosetry 585
Provincetown Arts 203
PSI 286
Psychotrain (NR)

Puck 203
Puckerbrush Press 428
Puckerbrush Review 203
Pudding House Writers Resource Center (NR)
Puerto Del Sol 203
Pulitzer Prize in Fiction 520
‡Pulp: A Fiction Magazine 329
Pulphouse (OB)
Purple Finch Press 428
‡Purple Patch 251
Purpose 374
Pushcart Prize 520
Putnam's Sons, G.P. 478 (also see The Berkley Publishing Group 455, Philomel 478)
Pyx Press (ED)

Q

Q Magazine 375
Qspell Book Awards/Hugh Mclennan Fiction Award 520
‡Quackenbush's Children's Book Writing & Illustrating Workshops, Robert 537
Quadrant 251
Quanta 204
Quarry (NR)
Quarry Press 429
Quarterly, The 204
Quarterly West 204
Quarterly West Novella Competition 520
‡Quartet Books Limited 486
Quartos (NR)
Queen of All Hearts 286
Queen's Quarterly 286
‡Questar Publishers 478
Quill Trade Paperbacks (see William Morrow 474)
Quincy Writers Guild Annual Creative Writing Contest 520

R

Raconteur (OB)
RACS/Rent-A-Chicken Speaks, A Little Little Magazine (NR)
R-A-D-A-R 375
Radiance 375
Rafale (NR)
Rag Mag 205
Ragdale Foundation 573
Ragweed Press Inc./gynergy books 429
Raleigh Award, Sir Walter 520
Ralph's Review 330
Rambunctious Review 205

Rambunctious Review, Annual Fiction Contest (NR)
Random House, Inc. 479 (also see Ballantine 454, Fawcett 463, Alfred A. Knopf 470, Knopf Books for Young Readers 471, Pantheon 477, Random House of Canada 479)
Random House of Canada 479
Random House PTY Ltd. (NR)
Ranger Rick Magazine 376
Rant (OB)
Rashi (NR)
Raven Chronicles, The (NR)
Raw Fiction 205
Read Writing & Art Awards 521
‡Reader's Break 205
RE:AL 206
Reality Magazine (NR)
Rebel Yell (OB)
Red Cedar Review 206
Red Deer College Press 429
Red Herring Mystery Magazine 287
Red Wagon Books (see Harcourt Brace & Co. 467)
Redbook 376
Redneck Review of Literature, The (OB)
Redoubt 251
‡Reed Magazine 206
Reed Publishing Ltd. (NR)
Reflect 207
Reform Judaism (NR)
Regency (see Harlequin 467)
Regency Plume, The 586
Regina Medal Award 521
‡Renditions 447
Renegade (NR)
Renovated Lighthouse Publications (NR)
Report to Hell (NR)
Resource Publications, Inc. 479
Response 287
Revell Publishing 479 (also see Baker 454)
Review: Latin American Literature and Arts 207
‡review, the 207
RFD 287
Rhino (NR)
Rhode Island State Council on the Arts 521
Ribalow Prize, Harold U. 521
Rice University Writer's Conference (NR)
Rinehart Fund, The Mary Roberts (NR)
Rio Grande Press 430
Rising Star (NR)
Rising Tide Press 430
Rite of Spring Fiction Contest 521
River City (NR)
River City Writing Awards in Fiction (NR)

River Styx 207
RiverSedge 208
Riverside Quarterly 287
Riverwind 208
Roanoke Review 208
Roberts Award, Summerfield G. 521
Robin's Nest (RR)
ROC 479 (also see Dutton Signet 461)
Rock Falls Review (OB)
‡Rock Springs Review 208
Rockford Review, The 209
‡Rocky Mountain Book Festival 555
Romance & More (NR)
Romance Writers of America (RWA) (NR)
Romance Writers of America National Con-
    ference (NR)
Romance Writers of America/NYC Chapter/
    From Dream to Reality Workshop (NR)
Romanian Review (NR)
Romantic Interludes (RR)
‡Romantic Novelists' Association Romantic
    Novel of the Year Award 521
Ronsdale Press/Cacanadadada 430
RopeWalk Writers' Retreat 549
Rose Creek Publishing (OB)
Rosebud™ 288
Rossley Literary Awards, Bruce P. 521
Round Table, The (NR)
‡Royal Fireworks Press 480
‡Rubenesque Romances 431
Ruby's Pearls 288

S

S.L.U.G.fest, Ltd. 330
S.U.N.Y. College Writing Arts Festivals (NR)
Sage Hill Writing Experience 562
St. Anthony Messenger 376
‡St. Augustine Society Press 431
St. David's Christian Writers Conference 541
St. Joseph's Messenger and Advocate of the
    Blind 377
St. Martin's Press 480
St. Paul Books and Media 480
‡Salome 209
‡Salt & The Light, The 288
Salt Lick Press 209
Samsara (NR)
San Diego State University Writers' Confer-
    ence 558
San Jose Studies Best Story Award (OB)
Sand River Press 431
Sandburg Awards, Carl 522
Sandpiper Press 431
Sandy Cove Christian Writers Conference 541

Sanskrit 209
Santa Barbara Review 210
Sarabande Books, Inc. 431
Saskatchewan Writers'/Artists' Colonies
    (NR)
Sassy Fiction Contest (NR)
Sassy Magazine (NR)
‡Satellite Fiction 330
‡Satire 210
‡Satire Writing Contest 522
Savant Garde Workshop, The 432
‡Scarp 251
Scavenger's Newsletter 586
‡SCBWI Conference in Children's Literature,
    NYC 537
SCBWI/Drury College Writing for Children
    Workshop (NR)
SCBWI/Florida Annual Fall Conference 545
SCBWI/Hofstra Children's Literature Confer-
    ence 537
SCBWI/Mid-Atlantic (NR)
SCBWI/Minnesota Chapter Conferences 551
SCBWI/National Conference on Writing & Il-
    lustrating for Children (NR)
SCBWI/Norcal Chapter Retreat at Asilomar
    559
SCBWI/Southern California SCBWI Writers'
    Day (NR)
SCBWI/Wisconsin Fall Retreat (NR)
Scholastic Writing Awards, The 522
School Magazine (NR)
‡Science Fiction and Fantasy Workshop 580
Science Fiction Chronicle 586
Science Fiction Convention Register (OB)
Science Fiction Writers of Earth 580
Science Fiction Writers of Earth (SFWoE)
    Short Story Contest 522
Science-Fiction and Fantasy Writers of
    America, Inc. 580
‡Scifant 289
Scorpio Moon, A Literary Magazine for the
    New Age (NR)
Scots Magazine, The (NR)
Screaming Toad Press 210
Scribner's 480
‡Se La Vie Writer's Journal 211
Se La Vie Writer's Journal Contest 522
Sea Oats Writer's Conference (NR)
Seacoast Writer's Association Spring Meeting
    and Fall Conference (NR)
Seal Press (NS)
Seattle Artists Program 522
Seattle Pacific University Christian Writers
    Conference (NR)
Seattle Review, The (NR)

‡Seattle Writers' Association 581
Secret Alameda, The (NR)
Seek 377
Seems (NR)
Self Publishing Your Own Book 549
‡Selu Writers Retreat 573
Semiotext (E) (NR)
Sensations Magazine 211
Sentner Short Story Award, Carl (NR)
Sepia 251
Sequoia (NR)
Serendipity Systems 432
‡Serpent's Tail 447
Seven Buffaloes Press 432
‡Seven Stories Press 433
Seventeen 377
Seventeen Magazine Fiction Contest 522
Sewanee Review, The (NR)
Sewanee Writers' Conference (NR)
SFWA Nebula® Awards 522
Shadow 212
Shadowdance (NR)
Shattered Wig Review 212
Shaw Publishers, Harold 433
Sheba Feminist Press (NR)
‡Shenandoah 212
Shields Publishing/NEO Press 433
Shift Magazine (NR)
Shiksha Bharati (NR)
‡Shockwaves 212
Shofar 378
Shoggoth (NR)
Short and Sweet Contest 523
Short Grain Contest 523
Short Stories Bimonthly 213
Short Stuff Magazine for Grown-ups 213
Side Show 213
Side Show Annual Short Story Contest 523
Sidetrekked 330
Sidewalks 214
Sierra Club Books (UC)
Sierra Nevada College Review 214
Sign of the Times (NR)
Signal Hill Publications 480
Signet (see Dutton Signet 461)
Signet Classic (see Dutton Signet 461)
Silence, The (NR)
Silhouette Books 481
Silhouette Desire (see Silhouette Books 481)
Silhouette Intimate Moments (see Silhouette Books 481)
Silhouette Romance (see Silhouette Books 481)
Silhouette Special Edition (see Silhouette Books 481)

Silhouette Yours Truly (see Silhouette Books 481)
Silver Mountain Press (NR)
Silver Web, The 214
Silver Whistle (see Harcourt Brace & Co. 467)
Silverfish Review 215
Simon & Pierre Publishing Co. Ltd. 433
Simon & Schuster 481 (also see Atheneum 451, Globe Fearon 464, Margaret K. McElderry 473, Simon & Schuster Books for Young Readers 481, Washington Square Press 483)
Simon & Schuster Books for Young Readers 481 (also see Little Simon 472)
Simon Book Award, Charlie May (NR)
Sinclair-Stevenson 447
Sing Heavenly Muse! 215
Singer Media Corp. 482
Sinipee Writers' Workshop 551
‡SInister 289
Sinister Wisdom (NR)
‡Sink Full of Dishes 331
Siren, The (NR)
Sitka Symposium on Human Values & the Written Word 561
Sixpack: Poems & Stories (I) (NR)
‡Skin Art 378
Skipping Stones 289
Skylark 215
Skylark (see Bantam/Doubleday/Dell Books for Young Readers 455)
Slate and Style 290
Slate, The (NR)
Slightly West (NR)
Slippery When Wet 290
Slipstream 215
Slote Award, Bernice 523
‡Slough Press 436
Small Pond Magazine, The 216
Small Press Book Review, The (NR)
Small Press Review/Small Magazine Review 586
Smith, The 436
Smithbooks/Books in Canada First Novel Award (NR)
‡Snake Nation Press Annual Fall Contest 523
Snow Contest, Kay 523
‡Snowapple Press 436
Snowy Egret 216
So To Speak 216
Society of Children's Book Writers and Illustrators Golden Kite Awards 524
Society of Children's Book Writers and Illustrators Work-In-Progress Grants 524

Society of Midland Authors (NR)
Society of Southwestern Authors 581
Society of Southwestern Authors Writers'
   Conference 559
Soft Door, The 217
Soho Press 436
Sojourner 378
‡Sol Magazine 252
Sonora Review (NR)
Sonora Review Short Story Contest 524
‡Sorcerous Magazine 331
Soundings East (NR)
South Carolina Arts Commission and The
   Post and Courier Newspaper (Charleston,
   SC) South Carolina Fiction Project 524
South Carolina Arts Commission Literature
   Fellowships and Literature Grants 524
South Carolina Review 217
South Dakota Arts Council 524
South Dakota Review 217
Southeastern Writers Association Annual
   Workshop (NR)
Southeastern Writers Conference 545
Southern Arts Literature Prize 524
Southern California Anthology 218
Southern California Writers Conference/San
   Diego (NR)
Southern Exposure (NR)
Southern Humanities Review 218
Southern Methodist University Press 437
Southern Prize, The 524
Southern Review, The 218
Southern Review/Louisiana State University
   Annual Short Fiction Award, The 524
Southwest Christian Writers Association (NR)
Southwest Florida Writers' Conference 545
Southwest Review 219
Southwest Writers Workshop Conference 555
Sou'Wester 219
‡Space And Time 290
‡Spare Room, A 219
Spectrum (CA) (NR)
Spectrum (MA) (OB)
Spectrum Press (RR)
Speech Bin, Inc., The 437
‡spelunker flophouse 219
Spider 378
Spindrift 220
Spinsters Ink 437
Spire Books (see Revell 479)
‡Spirit 379
Spirit Magazine, Exploring Alternative Ideas
   (NR)
Spirit Talk (NR)
‡Spirit That Moves Us Press, The 438

Spirit That Moves Us, The (RR)
Spitball 220
Spitting Image, The 221
Split Rock Arts Program (NR)
Spotlight (see HarperPaperbacks 468)
Spout 221
‡Spring Fantasy 221
SPSM&H 221
Square (NR)
Square One 290
Squaw Valley Community Of Writers 559
Squib, The (OB)
‡Stable Companion, The 222
Stand Magazine 252
Stand Magazine Short Story Competition
   (NR)
Standard 379
Standard Publishing (RR)
Staple 252
Star Fire (see Bantam/Doubleday/Dell Books
   for Young Readers 455)
Starblade (NR)
Starburst Publishers 438
State of Maine Writers' Conference 538
Steamboat Springs Writers Group 555
Stegner Fellowship, Wallace E. 525
Sterling House Publisher (ED)
‡Stiletto III 222
Stoddart 482
Stone Bridge Press (RR)
Stone Soup 223
‡Stonecoast 538
Stonecoast Writers' Conference (NR)
Stormline Press 438
Story 223
Story Friends (NR)
Story Line Press 439
‡Story Rules 291
Storyhead (NR)
StoryQuarterly 223
Story's Short Short Story Competition 525
‡Storyteller, The 291
Straight 379
Street Beat Quarterly 223
Stroker Magazine 224
Struggle 224
Student Leadership Journal (NR)
Studio: A Journal of Christians Writing 302
‡Stygian Articles 332
Stygian Vortex Publications 292
Sub-Terrain 224
Sub-Terrain Annual Short Story Contest 525
Suffusion Magazine 225
Sugar Mill Press Contests 525

Sugarman Children's Book Award, The Joan G. 525
Sulphur River Literary Review 225
‡Summer's Reading, A 225
Sun Dog: The Southeast Review (NR)
Sun, The 380
Sunk Island Review (NR)
Sunstone Press 439
Super Romances (see Harlequin 467)
Surfing Magazine (NR)
Surprise Me 226
Surreal (OB)
‡SWA Winter Workshop 561
Swank Magazine 380
Sweet Dreams (see Bantam/Doubleday/Dell Books for Young Readers 455)
Sweet Valley High (see Bantam/Doubleday/ Dell Books for Young Readers 455)
Sycamore Review 226
‡Sycamore Roots: The Regionalist Papers 332

T

‡T.R.'s Zine 332
‡Takahe 252
‡Tale Spinner, The 332
‡Talebones 292
Tamaqua (NR)
Tambourine Books (see William Morrow 474)
‡Tameme 227
Tampa Review 227
Taos School Of Writing 556
Taproot Literary Review 227
Tara Fellowship for Short Fiction 525
Tattoo Revue 380
"Teak" Roundup 228
Tears in the Fence 252
Teen Life 380
Teen Magazine (NR)
Teen Power (RR)
Teenagers in China & Abroad (NR)
Temptation (see Harlequin 467)
Tennessee Arts Commission Literary Fellowship 525
‡Tennessee Quarterly 228
10th Muse (NR)
Terminal Fright 292
‡Terra Incognita 293
Terrible Work (NR)
Terror Time Again (ED)
Texas Connection Magazine (NR)
Texas Review, The (NR)
Texas Young Writers' Newsletter 293
‡Texas-Wide Writers Contest 526
Textshop 228

Texture 229
Thalia: Studies in Literary Humor (NR)
Theater of Blood, A 229
Thema 229
‡Thin Air 229
Third Alternative, The 252
‡Third Coast 230
Third Half Magazine, The 252
Third Side Press, Inc. 439
Third World Press 439
‡13th Moon 230
This Magazine 230
‡Thistle 333
Thistledown Press 440
Thoma Books, Janet (see Thomas Nelson 477)
Thorndike Press 482
Three Continents Press 440
‡Threepenny Review, The 231
Threshold Books 440
Thresholds Quarterly 294
Thurber House Residencies 526
Tickled By Thunder Annual Fiction Contest 526
Tiger Moon (NR)
Tilden Canadian Literary Awards (NR)
Timber Creek Review 231
Time Pilot (NR)
Times Books (see Random House 479)
Times Eagle Books (RR)
‡Together With Children 302
Tomorrow 231
Topaz (see Dutton Signet 461)
Tor Books 482
‡Torre De Papel 232
Touch (NR)
Touchstone Literary Journal 232
Touchstone Publishing, PVT. Limited (ED)
Towson State University Prize for Literature 526
Trafika (NR)
‡Transcendent Visions 333
Transition (RR)
‡Travel Mystery Contest 526
Trekker News & Views, The 380
Trenton State College Writers' Conference 541
Tribute to Officer Dallies "The Man Behind Badge 126" (NR)
Trillium Press (see Royal Fireworks 480)
Triquarterly 232
Tri-State Fair Literary Awards 526
Tri-State Writer's Guild 541
Troika Magazine 381
Troll Associates 482
Tucumcari Literary Review 233

Tudor Publishers, Inc. (NR)
Tupelo Books (see William Morrow 474)
Turner Award, Steven 526
‡Turnstile 233
Turnstone Press (NR)
Turtle Magazine for Preschool Kids 381
Turtle Point Press 441
Twain Award, Mark 527
Twain Writers Conference (12th Annual),
    Mark 556
Twisted (NR)
‡TWN 382
2 AM Magazine 294
Tŷ Newydd Writer's Centre 564
Tyndale House Publishers 482

U

UCI Extension Annual Writers' Conference
    559
UCLA Extension Writers' Program (NR)
Ucross Foundation (NR)
Ultramarine Publishing Co., Inc. 441
Unforgettable Fire, The (NR)
University of Missouri Press 441
‡University of Neveda Press 442
University of Wisconsin at Madison School of
    the Arts at Rhinelander (NR)
University of Arkansas Press, The 441
University of Wisconsin at Madison Writers
    Institute 552
‡University Press of Colorado 442
‡Unknown Writer, The 333
Unmuzzled Ox 233
Uno Mas Magazine 334
Unreality (OB)
UPC Science Fiction Award (NR)
Upstate New Yorker Magazine (NR)
Urbanite, The 233
Urbanus Magazine 234
US1 Worksheets 234
Utah Original Writing Competition (NR)

V

Valley Grapevine 234
‡Van Neste Books 442
Vancouver International Writers Festival, The
    563
Vandamere Press 442
Vassar College Institute of Publishing and
    Writing: Children's Books in the Market-
    place (NR)
Véhicule Press 443
Venture (OB)

Venus Magazine (NR)
Verandah (NR)
Verb 234
Verba Mundi (see David R. Godine 464)
VeriTalesRG (NS)
Vermont Council on the Arts Fellowship (OB)
Vermont Studio Center 573
Verve 235
‡Very Short Fiction Award 527
Very Small Magazine, A (OB)
Victor Books (see Chariot Victor Publishing
    457)
‡Victoria School of Writing, The 563
Videomania (NR)
View for the Loft, A (NR)
Vigil 252
Vignette 235
Villa Montalvo Artist Residency Program 573
Villager, The (NR)
Villard Books (see Random House 479)
Vincent Brothers Review, The 236
Vine Books Imprint (NR)
Vintage Books (see Random House 479)
Vintage Northwest (NR)
Violet Crown Book Award 527
Virago Press Limited (NR)
Virgin Meat 334
‡Virginia Center for the Creative Arts 573
Virginia Quarterly Review 294
Virtual Press Annual Writers Contest, The
    (NR)
‡Virtue 382
Vision Books Pvt Ltd. 486
Vista (NR)
Vista Publications (NR)
‡Vista Publishing, Inc. 443
Vogelstein Foundation Grants (NR)
Voices West 236
‡Volcano Quarterly 295
Vox (NM) 334
‡Vox (NY) 236

W

W.W. Publications 443
Walden Fellowship (NR)
Walker and Company 482
Walker Woods 574
Wallant Memorial Book Award, Edward
    Lewis 527
Warner Books 483 (also see Aspect 451)
‡Wasafiri 253
Wascana Review of Contemporary Poetry and
    Short Fiction (NR)
Washingmachine, The (NR)

Washington Christian Writers Fellowship 581
Washington Independent Writers (NR)
Washington Independent Writers (WIW)
    Spring Writers Conference (NR)
Washington Prize for Fiction (OB)
Washington Square Press 483
Watermill Press (see Troll Associates 482)
Waters Southwest Writing Award for the
    Novel (NR)
Webster Review (NR)
Weekly Synthesis, The (NR)
Weirdbook 295
Weisbach Books, Rob (see William Morrow
    474)
Weiss Associates, Inc., Daniel 483
Wells Writers' Workshops 538
Wellspring Short Fiction Contest 527
Welter (NR)
Wesleyan Writers Conference 538
West Branch 237
West Coast Line 237
West Wind Review 237
Westchester Writers' Conference (NR)
Westerly 253
Western Canadian Magazine Awards 527
‡Western Digest 295
Western Heritage Awards 527
Western Humanities Review (NR)
Western Pocket, The 295
Western Publishing (see Golden Books Fam-
    ily Entertainment 464)
Western Reserve Writers & Freelance Confer-
    ence 549
Western Reserve Writers Mini Conference
    549
Western States Book Awards 528
Western Tales Magazine 296
Western Writers of America 581
Westview 238
Whetstone (Canada) 238
‡Whetstone (IL) 238
Whiskey Island Magazine 239
Whisper (NR)
Whispering Pines Quarterly (OB)
‡Whispering Willow's Mystery Magazine 296
‡White Crow, The 296
White Pine Press 443
White Review, The James 239
White Wall Review 239
Whiting Writers' Awards 528
Whitman & Company, Albert (RR)
‡Wicked Mystic 239
Widener Review (NR)
W!dow of the Orch!d, The 335
Wilde Oaks (NR)

‡Wilder Award, Laura Ingalls 528
Willamette Writers 581
Willamette Writers Conference 562
William and Mary Review, The (NR)
‡Willow Review 240
Willow Springs (NR)
Willowisp Press 444
Wind Magazine 240
Windsor Review 240
Wisconsin Academy Review 298
Wisconsin Arts Board Individual Artist Pro-
    gram (NR)
Wisconsin Institute for Creative Writing Fel-
    lowship 528
Wisconsin Review 241
With 382
Witty Short Story Award, Paul A. 528
Wolfe Fiction Prize, Thomas 528
‡Woman 299
Woman in the Moon Publications 444
Woman's Day (Australia) (RR)
Woman's Day (NY) 388
Woman's Weekly 388
Woman's World Magazine 382
Women's Harpoon (NR)
Women's Press (NR)
Women's Press, The 486
Women's Wilderness Canoe Trips Writing Re-
    treat 564
Women's Work 335
Wonder Time 386
Woodley Memorial Press 444
Woodstock Guild's Byrdcliffe Artist Resi-
    dency Program, The (NR)
Worcester Review, The 241
Wordplay 241
Words of Wisdom 241
Works 302
World of English, The 388
World's Best Short Short Story Contest (NR)
Worlds of Fantasy & Horror 299
Worldwide Library 483 (also see Harlequin
    467)
Wormwood Review, The 242
Write For Success Workshop: Children's
    Books 545
Write on the Sound Writers' Conference 562
Write to Sell Writer's Conference (NR)
Write Way Publishing 445
Write Your Life Story for Pay 560
Writer, The 586
Writers Alliance, The 582
Writers At Work Fellowship Competition 528
Writers Bloc Magazine 586
Writer's Carousel 586

Writers' Center at Chautauqua, The 538
Writer's Center, The 582
Writers Community Residency Awards, The 528
Writers' Conference at Santa Fe (NR)
Writers Connection 586
Writers Connection Selling to Hollywood 560
Writer's Consortium 560
Writer's Digest 586
Writer's Digest Annual Writing Competition (Short Story Division) 529
Writer's Digest Books—Market Books 586
Writers' Federation of New Brunswick 582
‡Writers' Federation of Nova Scotia 582
Writers' Forum 242
Writer's Guidelines (NR)
Writers Guild of Alberta 582
Writers Guild of Alberta Literary Award 529
Writers Guild of Alberta New Fiction Competition 529
Writers in Residence Programs (NR)
Writers Information Network 583
Writers' International Forum 335
Writers' International Forum Writing Competition 529
Writers' Journal 587
Writers' Journal Annual Fiction Contest 529
Writers' Journal Romance Contest 529
Writers' Journal Science Fiction Contest (NR)
Writer's Keeper 242
Writers News (NR)
Writers of Kern 583
Writers Retreat Workshop 539
Writers Room, Inc., The 583
Writers' Summer School, Swanwick, The 565
Writers Weekend at Beach 562
Writers Workshop in Science Fiction 556
Writers' Workshop International Fiction Contest, The 529
Writers' Workshop, The 543, 583
Writer's World 386
Writer's Yearbook 587
Writes of Passage 243
Writing Competition for Writers Over 50 (NR)
Writing for Money Workshop 549
Writing for Our Lives 243
Writing for Publication (UF)

Writing on the Wall, The 243
Writing Self, The (RR)
Writing Strategies for the Christian Market 546
Writing Today—Birmingham-Southern College 546
‡Writing Women 253
Writing Workshop 552
Wurlitzer Foundation of New Mexico, Helene 574
Wy'East Historical Journal (NR)
Wyoming Arts Council Literary Fellowships 529

X

Xavier Review 244
Xenos (NR)
Xib 244
Xtreme 244

Y

Yachats Literary Festival (NR)
Yaddo (NR)
‡Yalobusha Review, The 244
‡Yankee Magazine 386
Yarns and Such 300
Yellow Bay Writers' Workshop (NR)
Yellow Silk 245
Yolan Books, Jane (see Harcourt Brace & Co. 467)
Young Judaean 300
Young Reader's Choice Award 530
Young Salvationist (NR)
‡Young Voices Magazine 300

Z

Zelos (RR)
Zene 587
Zephyr (NR)
Zephyr Press 445
Zero Hour 245
Zoland Books, Inc. 445
Zondervan 484
Zone, The 302
Zuzu's Petals Quarterly 245
Zyzzyva 246

More Inside Views

Here are more tips for fiction writers from magazine editors and others inside the publishing industry.

- "Clear, direct language is the sign of an intelligent mind carefully at work. Someone who appreciates the language and can control it has mastered the first important step in creating excellent fiction."
  —**C. Michael Curtis, senior fiction editor, *The Atlantic Monthly*, page 344**

- "Smaller magazines serve as a proving ground for new writers. You get exposure, recognition. People see you; some work gets selected for prize volumes. Sometimes agents notice the work and write letters that say, 'How can we get in touch with so-and-so?' and sometimes books come from that."
  David Hamilton, editor of *The Iowa Review*, page 151

- "I would guess that if you've never read the magazine and you submit to it, you don't have a chance, because you won't have a sense of what we're about, what we're doing, the kind of stories we're interested in publishing and the level of stories we present. We're always looking for solid writing, a fresh style and a well-told story. There's nothing other than writing extremely well that's going to attract my attention."
  —**Daniel Kunitz, managing editor of *The Paris Review*, page 189**